UNITED STATES HISTORY

In the Course of Human Events

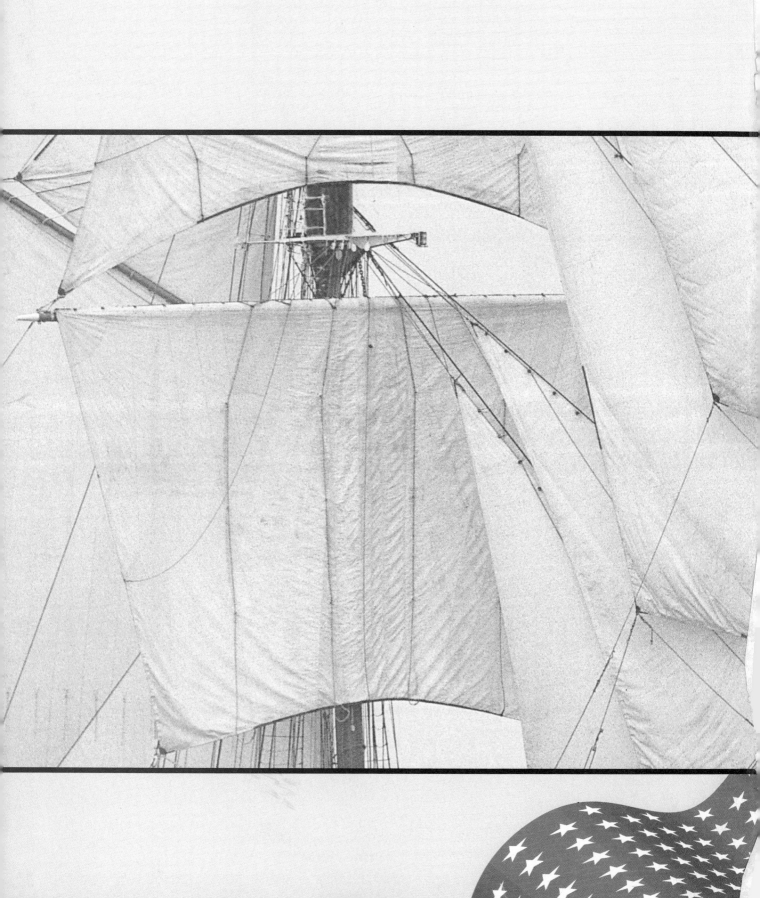

UNITED STATES HISTORY
In the Course of Human Events

Matthew T. Downey
University of California, Berkeley

James R. Giese
Social Science Education Consortium

Fay D. Metcalf

National Textbook Company
a division of NTC/CONTEMPORARY PUBLISHING GROUP
Lincolnwood, Illinois USA

Cover image: AP/ Wide World Photos

Acknowledgements begin following the Index, which is to be considered an extension of this copyright page.

ISBN: 0-314-04021-8

Published by National Textbook Company, a division of NTC/Contemporary Publishing Group, Inc.
4255 West Touhy Avenue, Lincolnwood (Chicago), Illinois 60712-1975 U.S.A.
©1997 NTC/Contemporary Publishing Group, Inc.

04 03 02 01 00   8 7 6

Contents-in-Brief

Contents

Unit 2
WORKING WITH THE ARCHIVES
Reaching a Valid Conclusion

111

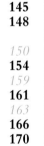

ARCHIVES
Unit 3
232

Unit 3
WORKING WITH THE ARCHIVES
Making Generalizations with Primary Source Materials
239

ARCHIVES
Unit 4
326

Unit 4
WORKING WITH THE ARCHIVES
Analyzing Persuasive Arguments in Primary Sources
333

ARCHIVES Unit 5   420

Unit 5
WORKING WITH THE ARCHIVES
Indentifying Bias in Primary Sources

427

THE JUNGLE
BY
UPTON SINCLAIR

DOUBLEDAY, PAGE & C?
NEW YORK

ARCHIVES
Unit 7
638

Unit 7
WORKING WITH THE ARCHIVES
More Practice with Supported Induction
645

Unit 10
WORKING WITH THE ARCHIVES
Comparing Perspectives Using Primary Sources

954

ARCHIVES
Unit 11
1038

Features

Enduring Constitution

Practicing Your Skills

AMERICAN SCENES

Arts and Letters

People Who Made a Difference

SCIENCE AND TECHNOLOGY

Maps

Tables, Graphs, and Diagrams

Editorial Review Board

About the Authors

 Matthew **T. Downey** is director of the Clio Project in History-Social Science Education in the Graduate School of Education at the University of California, Berkeley. He also directs the U.C. Berkeley site of the California History-Social Science Project. Downey was formerly Professor of History at the University of Colorado and at Louisiana State University. He has a Ph.D. in American History from Princeton University.

 James **R. Giese** received his Ph.D. in history and history education from the University of Colorado, Boulder. Giese has taught history at both secondary and college levels. Since 1985 he has been Director of the Social Science Education Consortium, a firm devoted to the research and development of history and social science education. Giese has developed curriculum materials and teacher resources and has conducted many institutes and training workshops for history and social studies teachers.

 Fay **D. Metcalf** taught American history and American studies for 25 years. She served as executive director of the National Commission on Social Studies in the Schools, a joint project of the American Historical Association, the Carnegie Foundation for the Advancement of Teaching, the National Council for the Social Studies, and the Organization of American Historians. She is a writer and senior editor for the Teaching with Historic Places program of the National Register of Historic Places.

Preface

A Word from the Authors

Greetings! We would like to introduce you to our book. We have written it because we think history is of great importance. History helps us better understand ourselves and the times in which we live. We must look back to the past when we want to know more about the present. We can see the present more clearly when we see how it resembles and how it differs from the past. We know ourselves better when we try to understand the ways in which we are similar to those who have lived before us and the ways in which we are different. We also know ourselves better when we understand how our culture differs from the cultures of people who lived in other times. When we attempt to understand and evaluate the full story of our past, we are able to make more informed judgments in our personal and private lives. History, in brief, is a way of knowing.

Why does history differ as a way of knowing from other school subjects? Partly because it tells a story. Historians use the narrative or story form. It helps them link events that happened over time. In a narrative something happens, which leads to something else happening, which then causes still other things to happen. Writing history as a story helps us to understand not just what happened, but why things happened as they did. The use of narrative in historical explanation is essential.

History Is Everyone's Story

This textbook is the story of the American people. By that we mean all of the people. We have tried to make this textbook as inclusive as possible. American history is not just the story of the rich and famous. It is the story of men and women, of immigrants and native born, and of farmers and factory workers. It is the history of people of different races, ethnic groups, and cultures. The history of the United States is a multicultural and multiracial history. Any other kind of American history would not only be incomplete, it would also be terribly false and misleading. American society has been an experiment in multiracial and multicultural living from the very beginning. History, in other words, is not just one story. It is a multiplicity of stories.

This textbook emphasizes what historians call social history. It does not neglect presidential elections, wars, or the building of industrial empires. But it is especially concerned with the forces and events that affected the everyday lives of ordinary people. Most of us are not presidents, generals, or captains of industry. The best way for us to put our lives into historical perspective is to know what happened in the past to people like us.

Firsthand Accounts

Each unit in this textbook includes a selection from the Archives consisting of firsthand and eyewitness accounts. You will also find many such accounts woven into the text itself. These accounts were written by people who lived at the time. These types of accounts are called primary sources. They are the evidence that historians use to create their historical narratives, which are called secondary accounts. Primary sources let people from the past tell their own stories. Often the most interesting accounts of events are those told by the people who witnessed them. These accounts are sometimes contradictory. That should not be surprising. People often have different accounts of the same event. Judging the differences gives you an opportunity to decide for yourself what you think really happened. Primary sources can help you to tell the American story in your own words.

History's Links to Other Subjects

While history is a unique way of knowing, it is not self-contained. It serves as a bridge to other areas of knowledge. For example, it is closely linked to the humanities. For each period of American history that we examine in this book, we include developments in literature, music, and the arts. History is also tied to the social sciences, especially to geography. Historical understanding depends on knowing where things happened, as well as when they took place. History is strongly linked also to sociology, political science, and economics. It is about the groups of people that make up American society, their political behavior, and their economic decisions.

Finally, we hope that you will use this textbook itself as a bridge. We would like it to take you beyond where you are now and to help you arrive at a better understanding of yourself, your society, and the times in which you live.

Matthew T. Downey   James R. Giese   Fay D. Metcalf

About This Book

Themes

You may better understand *United States History* if you view the details of the story as parts of larger ideas or patterns. The themes listed and briefly described below apply to every period of U.S. history. The stories you will read in this textbook are consistently related to these themes. Thinking about these themes will help you understand how events and people are linked across time and how they relate directly to you.

Democracy and Citizenship The growth of democracy is a central theme in American history. From the town meetings of colonial America to the political debates of the present, the United States has been a continuing experiment in self-government. Each generation has produced men and women who worked to improve the American system of constitutional government. We study history, in part, to meet such people and to learn from them what it means to be an American citizen.

Geography and the Environment History and geography are inseparable partners. They are the matrix of time and space within which human events occur. Historical knowledge depends on knowing when these events happened and where they took place. *United States History* incorporates the basic themes of geography, with particular emphasis on the interaction between the American people and their environment.

Multicultural Society From the very beginnings of its history, the United States has been a multicultural society. Diverse peoples from all over the world have become part of the United States. On the one hand, these diverse peoples have shared a commitment to certain goals such as political, economic, and religious freedom and a devotion to the civic values and government that helped maintain these freedoms. On the other hand, they have held a variety of religious, ethical, and moral beliefs which have sometimes led to disagreements and clashes.

This textbook traces the interaction of cultures from the first European-Indian contacts in North America to our multicultural society of the present time.

Everyday Life American history is not just the story of famous people and great events. The stories of ordinary people living their everyday lives—the decisions they have made, the values they have held, the problems they have faced, and the joys they have experienced—comprise the largest part of America's story. In fact, it is through the stories of ordinary people that the majority of us can relate to our nation's history, for it is their stories that have been most like ours.

Arts and Humanities American history is also the study of American contributions to the humanities including music, art, and literature, as well as forms of popular culture such as cartoons, media reports, diaries, and others. These expressions of culture provide windows through which we can better see and understand how people in the past are both similar to, and different from, us.

Economics The United States has developed a remarkably successful economy. How various economic processes have contributed to the national experience is a

major theme of the text. Concrete historical events introduce economic concepts, and students will begin to understand how the forces of economics may affect the future.

Technological Developments   An important part of the American story can be told through the history of technology. New technology has been a major engine of change throughout our history. Developments in manufacturing, transportation, and communications technology have had far-reaching consequences for each generation of Americans. In this book, these changes are treated within the chapters and in special features entitled Science and Technology.

Global Interactions   Finally, we can understand American history only in a global context. From the European colonial period to the present, America has been a global meeting place. It has also been a crossroads for the exchange of ideas.

In every period of history, American lives have been influenced by events that occur in distant places. American culture, in turn, has radiated to the most remote corners of the world. To miss either of these interactions is to fail to grasp what it means to be an American.

Primary Sources

United States History relies heavily upon primary sources to tell the nation's story. Historians have long known the importance of examining firsthand accounts, and educators know the value of students becoming familiar with primary sources when studying history.

The Archives   To help students anticipate important unit themes, an illustrated Archives section containing extensive excerpts from primary source materials has been included at the beginning of each unit. Teachers and students will appreciate the extensive use of quotations and excerpts from such firsthand accounts as diaries, letters, autobiographies, broadsides, travelers' accounts, newspaper reports, campaign speeches, pamphlets, and debates. These excerpts have been carefully selected by the authors to extend and complement themes, events, and characters in the chapter narratives.

The Narrative   Through liberally integrated primary sources within the text narrative, the authors convey the attitudes and achievements of Americans of varying occupations, ages, races, and classes in their own words. The smooth transition between text narrative and primary source quotations helps to bring history alive for the student. The text also uses artifacts, photographs, editorial cartoons, and reproductions of fine art to help students visualize important social and cultural aspects of their history.

Comprehensive Skills Program

Working with the Archives   Primary sources have been chosen to reflect the wide perspective of the American experience. Students may read about an event such as a strike from many viewpoints: from the point of view of a corporate stockholder, a plant manager, a working woman or man, and a labor leader. These primary source accounts often appear to contradict each other. The Archives for each unit contain a valuable skill exercise that will help students learn how to analyze and evaluate primary sources. Such critical thinking skills include how to determine accuracy, recognize bias, draw valid conclusions, make generalizations, and avoid stereotyping.

Practicing Your Skills   In addition to the critical thinking skills activities in the Archives, each chapter contains a *Practicing Your Skills* feature. This in-depth skills exercise is developed around an important image, chart, graph, table, or map that is an integral part of the chapter content. *Practicing Your Skills* features are organized into four broad categories: (1) those that examine images,

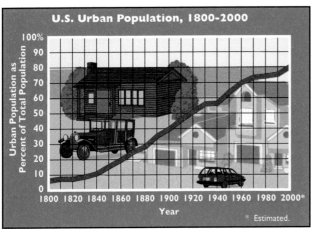

U.S. Urban Population, 1800-2000

Source: U.S. Department of Commerce, Bureau of the Census.

such as Analyzing Fine Art and Interpreting Editorial Cartoons; (2) those that analyze statistical data, such as Understanding Graphs and Analyzing Public Opinion Polls; (3) those that develop geographical skills, such as Special Purpose Maps: Looking at Movement and Comparing Information from Two Maps; and (4) those that look at speech, such as Identifying Propaganda and Interpreting Symbolic Speech. The skills exercises provide general guidelines for mastering the skills as well as practice in applying this knowledge.

Additional Skills Practice   In order to provide reinforcement for the skills described above, the text includes an *Additional Skills Practice* on every chapter review page. This activity asks the student to demonstrate mastery of the particular skill in an entirely new application.

Organization

Units   *United States History* is made up of eleven units, each covering an important period in history. At the beginning of each unit the Archives provide a variety of primary sources that give insight and richness to the time. A time line that displays events in four strands (Society and Culture, U.S. Politics and Government, Science and Technology, and Diplomacy and World Affairs) highlights events from the time period. The unit review also includes Personalizing History and Linking Past and Present activities.

Chapters   The thirty-four chapters in *United States History* comprise the well-told story of our country from its beginning until today. Each chapter opens with background information that gives the reader a sense of

the time period covered. Review material at the end of each chapter provides opportunities for reinforcing student understanding of the material, critical thinking experience, and practicing skills. The Critical Historical Thinking questions not only provide an opportunity for higher order thinking, but also guide students to think like historians and to interpret primary source materials in the Archives. The Making Connections activities link history to other disciplines.

Sections   Generally, each chapter contains five sections. The sections are introduced with an interesting narrative and questions that will help the reader focus on the main ideas. Review questions at the end of the sections provide a check for understanding.

Features

- AMERICAN LANDSCAPE features in each unit provide the necessary information for understanding geography and the important relation it has to history.

- ENDURING CONSTITUTION features focus on important Supreme Court cases that have shaped our legal system over time. These eleven features provide a brief look at the evolution of the interpretation of the Constitution.

- AMERICAN SCENES focuses on ordinary people and events that exemplify everyday life in America throughout history.

- PEOPLE WHO MADE A DIFFERENCE features give insight into famous as well as ordinary individuals who made significant contributions to the American story.

- SCIENCE AND TECHNOLOGY features help students understand the continuing effect technological development has on society.

- ARTS AND LETTERS spotlights artists and writers and their works from periods throughout history. These features focus on major developments in fine arts and literature.

Resources

A selection of additional resources is available at the end of the text for student use. These resources include important documents, maps, and data, as well as information about the presidents and the fifty states, and a Guide to Historical Writing.

UNIT 1

The Settling of America to 1750

Our nation's origins can be traced back to Asian hunters and gatherers who crossed the Bering Strait and spread slowly throughout North and South America. Although many details about the origin of the settlers are still uncertain, scholars have learned much about the lives and cultures of these early peoples. Eventually, Europeans introduced their cultures to America through exploration, conquest, and commerce. At the same time, African cultures took root in the islands of the Caribbean and on the mainlands. American history in this period is the story of diverse empires, mass enslavement, and political and religious rivalries. This period of colliding cultures is the source of the unique multiculturalism that would later characterize the United States.

| **Chapter 1** Backgrounds of Early Americans | **Chapter 2** European Settlements in the Americas | **Chapter 3** The Growth of Colonial Society |

◄ This colorful mural by famed Mexican artist Diego Rivera provides some idea of the complexity of Aztec civilization. The Spaniards were amazed at the variety of exotic foods and products that could be seen at the great marketplace in Tenochtitlán. What do you think is the significance of the figure in the chair?

Themes

- **Global Interactions** For the first time cultures from Africa and Europe collided with diverse groups in the Americas, laying the foundation for a multicultural society.
- **Technological Developments** From the development of the caravel, to the introduction of guns and iron tools to the Americas, technology affected how people lived.
- **Economics** Abundant natural resources and commerce made New England the cradle of American industrialization. The emerging cotton industry in the South fostered a growing dependency on slave labor.
- **Democracy and Citizenship** The English model of government was slowly—but sometimes dramatically—molded to fit the needs of an independent and self-reliant people.

Mohawk Creation Story

They think that a pregnant woman fell down from heaven, and that a tortoise (tortoises are plenty and large here, in this country, two, three and four feet long, some with two heads, very mischievous and addicted to biting) took this pregnant woman on its back, because every place was covered with water; and that the woman sat upon the tortoise, groped with her hands in the water, and scraped together some of the earth, whence it finally happened that the earth was raised above the water....

The Mohawk Indians are divided into three tribes ... the Bear, the Tortoise and the Wolf. Of these, the Tortoise is the greatest and most prominent; and they boast that they are the oldest descendants of the woman before mentioned.

 Johannes Megapolensis, *A Short Account of the Mohawk Indians* (1644).

Indian Societies Described by Europeans

Giovanni da Verrazzano described the Indians that he visited along the Carolina coast.

We saw their houses made in circular or round form 10 to 12 paces in compass, made with half circles of timber ... covered with mats of straw....They move the ... houses from one place to another according to the commodity of the place and season wherein they will make their abode....They observe in their [planting] the course of the moon and the rising of certain stars.... Moreover they live by hunting and fishing. They live long, and are seldom sick, and if they chance to fall sick at any time, they

▲ *Secotan village house*

heal themselves with fire without any physician, and they say that they die [from old] age.

 Lawrence C. Wroth, *The Voyages of Giovanni da Verrazzano, 1524–1528* (1970).

In 1634, a Dutch trader wrote the following description of a Mohawk village in what is now New York State.

In the morning ... we arrived at their first castle [fortified village], which is built on a high hill. There stood but 36 houses, in rows like streets, so that we could pass nicely. The houses are made and covered with bark of trees, and mostly are flat at the top. Some are 100, 90, or 80 paces long and 22 and 23 feet high.... Most of the people were out hunting deer and bear. The houses were full of corn....They make canoes and barrels of the bark of trees, and sew with bark [the inner bark of elm trees] as well. We had a good many pumpkins cooked and baked .... [The chief] gave us two bearskins to sleep upon, and presented me with three beaver skins.... We slept in this house, ate heartily of pumpkins, beans and venison, so that we were not hungry, but were treated as well as is possible in their land....

▲ *Eastern Woodland Indian harvest*

We bought some bread, that we wanted to take on our march. Some of the loaves were baked with nuts and cherries and dry blueberries and the grains of the sunflower.

 J. Franklin Jameson, ed., *Narratives of New Netherland, 1609–1664* (New York, 1909), pp. 140–141.

Francisco de Coronado reported on the Indians he saw in present-day Kansas.

And after seventeen days' march I came to a settlement of Indians who are called Querechos, who travel around with these cows [buffalo], who do not plant, and who eat the raw flesh and drink the blood of the cows they kill, and they tan the skins of the cows, with which all the people of this country dress themselves here. They have little field tents made of the hides of the cows, tanned and greased, very well made, in which they live while they travel around near the cows, moving with these. They have dogs which they load, which carry their tents and poles and belongings.

The people here are large. I had several Indians measured, and found that they were 10 palms [80 inches] in height; the women are well proportioned and their features are more like Moorish women than Indians.

G. P. Winship, "The Coronado Expedition, 1540–1542," *Smithsonian Institution, Bureau of American Ethnology, Fourteenth Report* (1896).

Traveling along the Gulf Coast in present-day Texas, the Spanish explorer Cabeza de Vaca described the Indians he encountered there.

For three months in the year they eat nothing besides [oysters], and drink very bad water. There is great want of wood: mosquitoes are in great plenty. The houses are of mats, set up on masses of oyster shells, which they sleep upon, and in skins, should they accidentally possess them. In this way we lived until April [1529], when we went to the seashore, where we ate blackberries all the month. . . .

The inhabitants of all this region go naked. The women alone have any part of their persons covered, and it is with a wool [Spanish moss] that grows on trees. The damsels dress themselves in deerskin. The people are generous to each other of what they possess. They have no chief. All that are of a lineage keep together.

Frederick W. Hodge, ed., *The Narrative of Alvar Nunez Cabeza de Vaca* (New York, 1907).

Columbus First Encounters the Indians

In his journal, Columbus described the first natives of North America.

I, that we might form great friendship, for I knew that they were a people who could be more easily freed and converted to our holy faith by love than by force, gave to some of them red caps, and glass beads to put round their necks, and many other things of little value, which gave them great pleasure, and made them so much our friends that it was a marvel to see. They afterwards come to the ship's boats where we were, swimming and bringing us parrots, cotton threads in skeins, darts, and many other things; and we exchanged them for other things that we gave them, such as glass beads and small bells. In fine, they took all, and gave what they had with good will. It appeared to me to be a race of people very poor in everything. They go as naked as when their mothers bore them, and so the women, although I did not see more than one young girl. All I saw were youths, none more than thirty years of age. They are very well made, with very handsome bodies, and very good countenances. Their hair is short and coarse, almost like the hairs of a horse's tail. They wear the hairs brought down to the eyebrows, except a few locks behind, which they wear long and never cut. . . . Some paint themselves white, others red, and others of what color they find. Some paint their faces, others the whole body, some only round the eyes, others only on the nose. They neither carry nor know anything of arms, for I showed them swords, and they took them by the blade and cut themselves through ignorance.

J. Franklin Jameson, ed., *Original Narratives of Early American History* (1909), p. 110.

Making Boats with Fire

A European visitor to the colonies in 1750 described the process that Indians there used to make canoes.

When the Indians intend to fell a thick strong tree, they cannot use their [stone] hatchets, but for want of proper instruments employ fire. They set fire to a great quantity of wood at the roots of the tree, and make it fall by that means. In order that the fire does not reach higher than they would have it, they fasten some rags to a pole, dip them into water, and keep continually washing the tree, a little above the fire. Whenever they intend to hollow out a thick tree for a canoe, they lay dry branches all along the felled trunk of the tree as far as it must be hollowed out. They then put fire to those dry branches, and as soon as they are burnt, they are replaced by others. While these branches are burning, the Indians are busy with wet rags, pouring water upon the tree to prevent the fire from spreading too far on the sides and at the ends. The tree being burnt hollow as far as they find it sufficient, or as far as it can be without damaging the canoe, they take the above described stone hatchets, or sharp pieces of flint and quartz, or sharp shells, and scrape off the burnt part of the wood, and smoothen the boats within. By this means they likewise give what shape they please. Instead of cutting with a hatchet such a piece of wood as is necessary for making a canoe, they employ fire. A canoe is commonly between thirty and forty feet long.

Peter Kalm, *Travels in North America* (1770), pp. 229–230.

Hard Times in Virginia

Captain John Smith published the following account of the Jamestown colonists' first winter (1607–1608) in Virginia.

The first we heard [upon returning from an exploration up the James River] was that 400 Indians the day before had assaulted the fort and surprised it.... In which conflict most of the Council [governing body] was hurt, a boy slain in the pinnace, and thirteen or fourteen more hurt.

With all speed, we [built a wall of poles around] our fort; each other day for six or seven days we had alarms by [ambushes], and four or five cruelly wounded by being [outside the fort].

The living were scarce able to bury the dead; our want of sufficient and good victuals [food]... being the chief cause.

Shortly after Captain Gosnold fell sick, and within three weeks died. Captain Ratcliffe being then also very sick and weak... and shortly after it

pleased God... to move the Indians to bring us corn ere it was half ripe, to refresh us, when we rather expected they would destroy us.

About the tenth of September there was about 46 of our men dead....

As yet we had no houses to cover us, our tents were rotten, and our cabins worse than nought.

The Indians, thinking us near famished.... offered us little pieces of bread and small handfuls of beans or wheat for a hatchet or a piece of copper.

Within five or six days after the arrival of the ship [January 13, 1608], by a mischance our fort was burned and the most of our apparel, lodging, and private provision. Many of our old men [became] diseased, and [many] of our new for want of lodging perished....

John Smith, *A True Relation of. . . Virginia* (1608).

The Arrival of the Pilgrims

Separatist leader, William Bradford, described how the colonists felt when they arrived.

Being thus arrived in a good harbor and brought safe to land, they fell upon their knees and blessed the God of Heaven who had brought them over the vast and furious ocean and delivered them from all the perils and miseries thereof, again to set their feet on the firm and stable earth, their proper element.

... Being thus past the vast ocean and a sea of troubles before in their preparation..., they had now no friends to welcome them, nor inns to entertain or refresh their weatherbeaten bodies, no houses or much less towns to repair to, to seek for succor. It is recorded in Scripture as a mercy to the apostle and his shipwrecked company, the barbarians showed them no small kindness in refreshing them, but these savage barbarians, when they met with them... were readier to fill their sides full of arrows than otherwise. And for the season, it was winter, and they that know the winters of that country know them to be sharp and violent and subject to cruel and fierce storms, dangerous to travel to known places, much more to search an unknown coast. Besides, what could they see but a hideous and desolate wilderness full of wild beasts and wild men? And what multitudes there might be of them they knew not.

William Bradford, *History of Plymouth Plantation* (Boston, 1899).

Penn Buys Indian Land

In a letter written to his friends in England, William Penn described a tribal council meeting at which he purchased land from the Indians of eastern Pennsylvania.

Every King hath his Council, and that consists of all the Old and Wise men of his Nation, which perhaps is two hundred People; nothing of Moment is undertaken, be it War, Peace, Selling of Land or Traffick [trade], without advising with them; and, which is more, with the young men too. . . . Having consulted and resolved their business, the King ordered one of the [council members] to speak to me; he stood up, came to me, and in the Name of his King saluted me, then took me by the hand, and told me, That he was ordered by his King to speak to me, and that now it was not he, but the King that spoke, because what he should say, was the King's mind. . . . Having thus introduced his matter, he fell to the Bounds of the Land they had agreed to dispose of, and the Price, (which now is little [the land] and dear [the cost], that which would have bought twenty Miles, not buying now two.) . . . I have never seen more natural Sagacity [shrewdness]. . . and he will deserve the Name of Wise, that Outwits them in any Treaty about a thing they understand. When the Purchase was agreed, great Promises past between us of Kindness and good Neighbourhood, and that the Indians and English must live in Love, as long as the Sun gave light.

Letter from William Penn to the Committee of the Free Society of Traders (1683).

John Smith's Narrow Escape

Captain John Smith described his narrow escape at the hands of Emperor Powhatan.

At last they brought him to Werowocomoco, where was Powhatan, their emperor. . . Having feasted him after their best barbarous manner they could, a long consultation was held, but the conclusion was, two great stones were brought before Powhatan: then as many as could laid hands on him, dragged him to them, and thereon laid his head, and being ready with their clubs to beat out his brains.

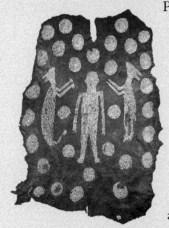

▲ *Powhatan's mantle at Ashmolean Museum, Oxford*

Pocahontas, the king's dearest daughter, when no entreaty could prevail, got his head in her arms, and laid her own upon him to save his from death: whereat the emperor was contented he should live to make him hatchets, and her bells, beads, and copper; for they thought him [capable] as well of all occupations as themselves. For the king himself will make his own robes, shoes, bows, arrows, pots; plant, hunt, or do anything so well as the rest.

Two days after, Powhatan. . . came unto him and told him now they were friends, and presently he should go to Jamestown, to send him two great guns, and a grindstone, for which he would give him the county of Capahowosick, and for ever esteem him as his son Nantaquoud.

John Smith, *The Genreall Historie of Virginia.*

The Puritans Count Their Blessings

Hoping to attract more colonists to Massachusetts, the Puritans published a pamphlet in 1643 that listed the ways God had blessed their efforts thus far.

Thus farre hath the good hand of God favored our beginnings; see whether he hath not engaged us to wait still upon his goodness for the future, by such further remarkable passages of his providence to our Plantation [colony] in such things as these:

1. In sweeping away great multitudes of the Natives by the Small Pox, a little before we went thither, that he might make room for us there.
2. In giving such merveilous safe Passage from first to last, to so many thousands that went thither,

▲ *Transportation to the colonies*

the like hath hardly been ever observed in any Sea-voyages.

3. In blessing us generally with health and strength.... That whereas diverse other Plantations have been the graves of their Inhabitants and their numbers much decreased: God hath so prospered the climate to us, that our bodies are hailer, and Children there born stronger, whereby our number is exceedingly increased.

4. In giving us such peace and freedome from enemies... (excepting that short trouble with the Pequits).... And in that Warre which we made against them, God's hand from heaven was so manifested, that a very few of our men in a short time pursued through the Wildernesse, slew and took prisoners about 1400 of them... so that the name of the Pequits... is blotted out from under heaven, there being not one that is, or (at least) dare call himself a Pequit.

5. In subduing those erroneous opinions carried over from hence by some of the Passengers, which for a time infested our Churches peace....

6. In settling and bringing civil matters to such a maturity in a short time amongst us having planted 50 Townes and Villages, built 30 or 40 Churches, and more Ministers' houses; a Castle, a Colledge, Prisons....

7. In giving such plenty of all manner of Food in a Wildernesse....

8. In prospering Hempe and Flaxe so well, that it's frequently sowen, spun, and woven into linnen Cloath....

9. In affording us many materialls... for Staple commodities to supply all other defects....

10. In giving of such Magistrates, as are all of them godly men, and members of our Churches, who countenance those that be good, and punish evill doers....

Old South Leaflet #51, Chapin, *Provincial America,* pp. 103–104.

Servants and Slaves in Virginia

In his report on Virginia society in 1705, Robert Beverly described the status of servants in that colony.

Their Servants, they distinguish by the Names of Slaves for Life, and Servants for a time.

Slaves are the Negroes, and their Posterity.... They are call'd Slaves, in respect of the time of their Servitude, because it is for Life.

Servants, are those which serve only for a few years, according to the time of their Indenture, or the Custom of the Country. The Custom of the Country takes place upon such as have no Indentures.... If such Servants be under Nineteen years of Age... they must serve until they reach four and twenty: But if they be adjudged upwards of Nineteen, they are then only to be Servants for the term of five Years.

The Male-Servants, and Slaves of both Sexes, are employed together in Tilling and Manuring the Ground, in Sowing and Planting Tobacco, Corn Etc. Some Distinction indeed is made between them in their Cloaths, and Food....

Sufficient Distinction is also made between the Female-Servants, and Slaves; for a White Woman is rarely or never put to work in the Ground, if she be good for any thing else.... Whereas on the other hand, it is a common thing to work a Woman Slave out of Doors.

Robert Beverly, *The History and Present State of Virginia,* Louis B. Wright, ed. (Chapel Hill, 1947), pp. 271–272.

Indentured Servants

Gottlieb Mittelberger described how immigrants paid for their passage to America by becoming indentured servants, that is, by selling their labor for a period of years.

When the ships have landed at Philadelphia after their long voyage, no one is permitted to leave them except those who pay for their passage or can give good security; the others, who cannot pay, must remain on board the ships till they are purchased and are released from the ships by their purchasers. The sick always fare the worst for the healthy are naturally preferred and purchased first, and so the sick and the wretched must often remain on board in front of the city for 2 or 3 weeks, and frequently die, whereas many a one, if he could pay his debt and were permitted to leave the ship immediately, might recover and remain alive.

The sale of human beings in the market on board the ship is carried on thus: Every day Englishmen, Dutchmen and High-German people come from the city of Philadelphia and other places, in part from a great distance, say 20, 30, or 40 hours away, and go on board the newly arrived ship that has brought and offers for sale passengers from Europe, and select among the healthy persons such as they deem suitable for their business, and bargain with them how long they will serve for their passage-money, which most of them are still in debt for. When they have come to an agreement, it happens that adult persons bind themselves in writing to serve 3, 4, 5 or 6 years for the amount due by them, according to their age and strength. But very young people, from 10 to 15 years, must serve till they are 21 years old.

Many parents must sell and trade away their children like so many head of cattle; fit if their children take the debt upon themselves, the parents can leave the ship free and unrestrained; but as the parents often do not know where and to what people their children are going, it often happens that [they]. . . do not see each other again for many years, perhaps no more in all their lives.. . .

It often happens that whole families, husband, wife, and children, are separated by being sold to different purchasers, especially when they have not paid any part of their passage money.

 Gottlieb Mittelberger's Journey to Pennsylvania in the Year 1750.

Runaway Servants

The following ads appeared in colonial newspapers in the mid-1700s.

Run away from his Master, *James Powner*, about 19 Years of Age, he is a stout lusty Fellow, with light coloured short Hair . . . his left Foot has been cut, so that his great Toe falls down He had on when he ran away, a striped Woollen Jacket, a striped Woollen Shirt, and a pair of old Ozenbrigs Trowsers. Whosoever shall take the said Run-away, and convey him to his Master *Nathaniel Noyes of Falmouth in New Casco*, shall have *Five Pounds*. . . Reward, and all necessary Charges paid.

 Boston Evening Post (July 11, 1748).

Run away the 25th of December last, from John Scott, of Hanover Township, Morris County, and Province of New Jersey, a Servant Man Named James Murphy, about 5 Feet 3 Inches high, much pitted with the Small-Pox, long yellow Hair tyed behind; he has been a soldier in the French Service, talks good French. Served with said Scott, as a School-Master; had on when he went away a new Bearskine Coat with Broad Hair Buttons. . . and Leather Breeches; new Worsted Stockings, and new Pumps. Whoever secures said Servant, so as his Master may have him again, shall have Forty Shillings Reward and reasonable Charges paid by me.

 New York Gazette or Weekly Post-Boy (Feb. 4, 1754).

Five Pounds Reward

Run away from on board the ship Wolfe, Richard Hunter, master, from Londonderry, a redemptioner named COLLIN MCDONALD, born in the Highlands of Scotland, and will be easily known by his accent; about 36 years of age, a taylor by trade, about six feet high with black short hair; had on a blue coat and red waistcoat; said he had a wife near Albany, and is supposed to have gone that way. Whoever apprehends the same, and brings him to the subscribers, shall have THREE POUNDS reward, if taken in this province, and if out of it, shall be entitled to the above reward, and all reasonable charges, paid by
GRAY, FLETCHER, AND CO.

 Pennsylvania Packet and General Advertiser (Nov. 16, 1772).

Handbook of Primary and Secondary Sources

Primary Sources

Primary sources exist all around us. They include letters, official documents, journals and diaries, maps, photographs, and television and radio broadcasts. Primary sources in the daily newspaper include eyewitness articles that record events for future historians, some editorials, and editorial cartoons.

▼ *In Nazi Germany, passports for all Jews were stamped with the letter "J" for* Jude *(Jew). [Simon Wiesenthal Center, Los Angeles (SWC).]*

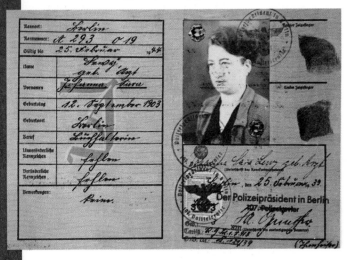

Secondary Accounts

Secondary sources are accounts written by a person who was not present at the time of the event. The person recording the event may, however, have interviewed people who did witness the historical occurrence. This textbook is also a secondary source.

For much of our very early history, we must rely largely on secondary sources. One well-known secondary source is the Greek historian Herodotus, who was born in Asia Minor (Turkey) sometime between 490 and 480 B.C. As a young man, he traveled to such places as Egypt, Palestine, Mesopotamia, the southern parts of Russia, and the coastline of northern Africa. His book *History* records, among other things, the wars between Greece and the Persian Empire of the East. Once called "the Father of Lies" because he included fables and legends in his writing, modern historians and archeologists have found his writings to be in the main, accurate and reliable. His accounts of history were based on the visible evidence of buildings and monuments and certain local chronicles written in Greek, which he probably read. He also got information on the spot from the people whom he met and talked with during his travels.

How Historians Use Primary Sources and Secondary Accounts

Historians and students of history find both primary and secondary sources invaluable for understanding and analyzing an event. An eyewitness account by a journalist covering the Persian Gulf War—while dodging missiles himself—brings the intensity and emotions of the war—to his accounts.

No less valuable in understanding history are secondary sources. Writers of history add their own perspective to an event. Provided with various options, your mind is stimulated to debate, evaluate, and form more questions. This process is essential not only to education, but to a democratic society, as well. Throughout your life, you will be bombarded with radio and television news reports, advertisements, and government reports which all have their own agendas and biases. Using the primary and secondary sources in this book will give you experience in evaluating evidence and in forming your own opinions.

◀ *This Spanish map of the Aztec city of Tenochtitlán dates back to 1524.*

The Impartial Use of Primary Sources and Secondary Accounts

The critical historian and student must be cautious using primary and secondary sources. All written history is subjective, that is, it is based on the past experiences and perceptions of the observer. Historians bring in their own biases when writing history. For example, students of the Industrial Revolution may rely heavily on primary and secondary sources which emphasize economic rather than social factors. Or, when looking at the Progressive Era, students may focus on the muckrakers, writers who exposed the corruption and evil in business and government, such as Ida Tarbell and Upton Sinclair. To be impartial, students should also read about the "captains of industry"—industrialists who through their own initiative, leadership qualities, and willingness to assume risks, have become giants in their fields. Without balancing these two perspectives, the student of history is at a disadvantage. Without examining many different perspectives, your point of view concerning historical events lacks accuracy—it is unreliable.

As you progress through the unit archives in this text, you will learn some basic techniques and methods that historians use to analyze primary sources. These skills include identifying cause and effect, making valid generalizations, recognizing bias, drawing conclusions, and developing sound arguments. The most remarkable thing about learning these skills is that they can help you achieve success in every area of your life, not only school.

▲ *An American soldier wrote this letter home during World War II.*

WORKING WITH THE ARCHIVES

Extracting and Organizing Information from Primary Sources

Read the archive selections entitled "Indian Societies Described By Europeans" in preparation for completing a graphic organizer and a diary. A graphic organizer is a chart, table, graph, outline, or any other way of arranging information that allows for easy comparing or contrasting.

1. On a separate piece of paper, draw a chart with four columns and four rows. Label the columns "Food," "Housing," "Agriculture," and "Appearance." As you read, in each row note on the chart how each American Indian group in the four regions lived, including how food was acquired, the types of homes that were built, methods of agriculture, and the physical appearance of the people.

2. The primary sources on Indian societies in the archives suggest that European attitudes toward Indians varied greatly. Describe some of the different attitudes reflected in these sources and explain how one might account for these differences.

3. The English colonies had different degrees of unfree labor. These included apprenticeships, indentured or temporary servitude, and outright slavery. To what extent did race determine how laborers were classified and the way in which they were treated?

Backgrounds of Early Americans

The American character has been shaped by diverse groups of people. The first humans to inhabit the North American continent came from Asia thousands of years before European explorers and settlers set foot on American shores.

The Europeans came in pursuit of riches and glory. Africans were brought to America—most as enslaved laborers. Each group carried age-old cultures with them and would adapt to the new land in different ways. All of them would have a profound influence on a developing American culture.

◀ *This human profile from a grave mound of the Hopewell people dates from 200 B.C. to A.D. 300. Why were artifacts put into graves?*

The Ancient Americans

There are many significant dates in American history, but one important date will never be known exactly. We will never be able to point to the hour, the day, or even the year when the first people came to American shores. But from the moment the first hunter set foot on the land we now call Alaska, the story of America began. Starting approximately 40,000 years ago and continuing to about 10,000 years ago, Asian peoples crossed the Bering Strait that today separates Alaska from Siberia. Eventually, these peoples fanned out some 15,000 miles south to the tip of South America, and some 6,000 miles east to the Atlantic coast of North America.

Why is it so difficult to determine when America was first settled?
How did the lives of the Indians change over time?
How did new ideas spread across the continents?

The First Americans

The work is both physically and mentally exhausting, the hours are long, and the conditions are hot and dusty. She is a long way from home, a long way from her family, and a long way from modern conveniences. Despite the hardships, she is pleased to be where she is and pleased to be playing her part in the quest to solve the mysteries. She works with the clues she has found and the clues discovered by others. She must rely on the facts she has available to her and on the knowledge and training she has acquired through her experiences and her education.

She has braved the conditions and followed the clues to this spot. Now, as she feels the midday sun beat down on the back of her neck, she carefully unearths another piece to the puzzle. It is the stone blade of a knife buried long ago. As she brushes the sand from the blade, she is filled with excitement and awe. With this find, she is confi-

dent that she and others like her are now one more small step closer to solving the mysteries.

The woman described above is not a detective. She is an **archeologist**. Archeologists seek to solve the mysteries that are locked in the vaults of the past. Archeologists are scientists who study the material things of past human life and activities. They seek to reconstruct, or describe, the cultures of people who no longer exist. **Anthropologists** study the physical, cultural, and social factors of human behavior. **Geologists** examine the history and physical structure of the earth. **Ethnohistorians** use data from other specialists, as well as oral histories and written records, to provide a picture of the changes that have occurred over time. It is only through the efforts of archeologists and other scientists that we know what we do of the lives of the first Americans.

Geologists tell us that for thousands of years great glaciers covered the northern regions of the world. Sheets of ice extended as far south as present-day Pennsylvania and Kansas in North America, and present-day London, Kiev, and Kraków in Europe. Asia had fewer glaciers, but ice did cover most of Siberia. Because so much of the earth's moisture was locked up in great glacial sheets, part of the floor of the Bering Strait was exposed from time to time, forming a land bridge between northeastern Asia and Alaska.

Early Migrations Many geologists believe this land bridge was open twice, first from about 40,000 to 32,000 years ago and again from about 20,000 to 10,000 years ago. This suggests that there were periods of several thousand years when human beings could simply have walked the fifty miles or so that separated Siberia from Alaska. But, as some archeologists believe, it is also possible that people walked across the ice, or crossed in boats during the summer. It is known that boats or rafts carried the first people to Australia some 40,000 to 30,000 years ago, so a short voyage from Asia to America was certainly possible. The question of whether the Asian immigrants crossed the Bering Strait by walking across dry land, by walking across ice, or by crossing the open water in boats is important. The answer

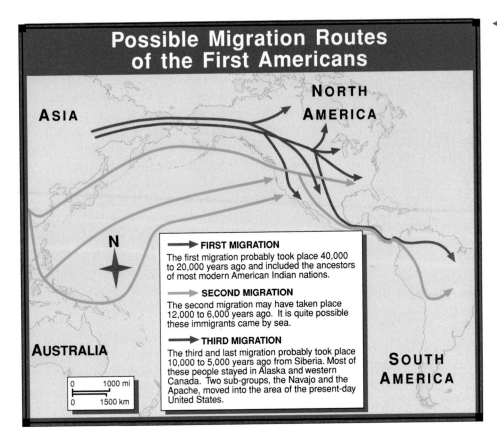

Possible Migration Routes of the First Americans

ASIA

NORTH AMERICA

N

FIRST MIGRATION
The first migration probably took place 40,000 to 20,000 years ago and included the ancestors of most modern American Indian nations.

SECOND MIGRATION
The second migration may have taken place 12,000 to 6,000 years ago. It is quite possible these immigrants came by sea.

THIRD MIGRATION
The third and last migration probably took place 10,000 to 5,000 years ago from Siberia. Most of these people stayed in Alaska and western Canada. Two sub-groups, the Navajo and the Apache, moved into the area of the present-day United States.

AUSTRALIA

SOUTH AMERICA

0   1000 mi
0   1500 km

◀ *Genetic studies suggest that there were at least two, and probably three, major migrations from Asia to America. Why do you think there were long periods of time between the major migrations?*

might help scholars to determine both when migrations occurred and how many migrations there were.

Because traces of early human life have been found in many regions of the American continents, archeologists once believed that many separate, small groups moved into the Americas over thousands of years. They thought that each of these groups had different sets of ancestors. More recent theories about the migrations of Paleo-Indians (*paleo* means "old") to America come from considering such evidence as comparisons of the languages spoken by Indians and Asians of today, and of the tooth shapes of both populations. Neither basic language structures nor tooth shape change much over time. Through study of these two traits in both American and Asian populations, many archeologists now believe that there were only three separate migrations of unrelated peoples who came to America at widely spaced time periods.

A recent theory based on genetics holds that the first migrants came across the land bridge 40,000 to 20,000 years ago. The second migration probably came by sea some 12,000 to 6,000 years ago and blended with the existing Paleo-Indian groups. The third migration, 10,000 to 5,000 years ago, included Inuits, who stayed in Alaska and Western Canada, and the Navajo and Apache, who slowly moved to the Southwest about a thousand years ago.

Archeological and anthropological studies continue. Each year brings more data, and scholars still seek to solve the mysteries surrounding the origins of the first Americans.

Ways of Life Change

There is some clear-cut evidence about the ways of life of the early Americans. Archeological

▲ *Paleo-Indians made tools such as spear points, awls, and scrapers from bone and stone. How might scrapers such as these have been used by the mammoth hunters in the picture at right?*

▲ *Mammoths were large, prehistoric elephants. They had long tusks that curved upward and a good deal of body hair. Why do you think the hunters are all men?*

digs provide data indicating that Paleo-Indians followed wild game, killing animals when they could and subsisting on wild plants when a hunt was not successful. Sites from 12,000 to about 10,000 years ago show that big-game hunters used well-crafted spear points made from flint and flint-like rocks. These large points could penetrate such huge game animals as the woolly mammoth, the mastodon, and the giant bison. Hunters set up kill sites by water holes and springs where the animals would come to drink. There the hunters could slay them at will. With an abundance of food, the people could stay in one place for long periods of time.

About 9,000 to 7,000 years ago, the Archaic Era began. The climate slowly changed, and glacial ice melted. The warmer period turned grasslands into near deserts. Huge game animals became extinct. Archaic Indians learned to hunt for other animals, such as deer, elk, and a smaller species of bison, and they became more dependent on fishing and gathering edible plants. As Archaic Indians turned to new sources of food derived from plants, some people realized that wild seeds could be planted and would grow in moist, fertile soil. This discovery, a great technological breakthrough called the **agricultural revolution**, occurred independently in widely separated parts of the world.

In the Americas, several crops were domesticated but the most important was maize, or Indian corn. It was grown in Mesoamerica, which included parts of what are now Mexico and Central America. Indian corn became a dependable food crop, and knowledge of its cultivation spread to both North and South America. Other plants first domesticated in the Americas include squash, pumpkins, tomatoes, sweet potatoes, beans, bell and chili peppers, and tobacco.

Division of Labor   People who depended on domesticated crops needed to stay near their fields to care for their crops and to set up storage facilities for surplus food. As their need to gather wild plants and chase game diminished, many groups settled in permanent villages. Because only some of the people were needed to grow crops, labor became specialized. The needs and wants of the community were divided up, and different tasks were done by different people with special skills. In most farming areas, men cleared the fields and continued to hunt while women planted, cultivated, and harvested the crops. Some people became so expert at fashioning weapons, pottery, or cloth that they no longer participated in farming. Others in a village would provide these artisans with food in exchange for their handiwork.

Religious or political leaders became the rulers in some societies because of their supposed ability to communicate with the gods or because of their military strength. They organized work groups and demanded goods and surplus crops as **tribute** (a payment made for protection). These leaders and their relatives became a hereditary nobility that ruled over the rest of the people. As their power grew, the nobility forced the ordinary people to build large temples to glorify the gods, irrigation ditches to water their crops, and roads to help them extend their power over more and more people.

No one knows definitely why the Olmec culture produced such immense sculptures. This helmeted head, known as the San Lorenzo monument, was found near Veracruz, Mexico. What do you think it might represent?

Trading Networks

Domesticated crops led to surplus food; specialized labor led to the development of goods that could be traded. Both foods and goods served as items of exchange in the trading networks that quickly spread across vast regions of the Americas. Salt for seasoning and preserving food, obsidian and flint for the projectile points of spears and arrows, bird feathers for clothing and decoration, and seashells and copper for jewelry became valued exchange goods. Everywhere that traders went, they exchanged more than goods. They also brought fresh ideas and new technologies for farming, hunting, fishing, or waging war. While not all American

Indians adopted the practice of agriculture, most were profoundly influenced by the trading networks.

The **Olmecs**, who lived on the Gulf shore of present-day Mexico, were particularly influential. Called a **mother culture** because so much of their way of life was adopted by other people, the Olmecs rose to prominence about 1000 B.C. The Olmecs lived in a society that had many classes of people. Religious leaders and merchants were the most powerful and formed the highest classes. Farmers and laborers formed the lowest class. The Olmecs built great temples on large mounds of earth. They developed a form of writing that used images and symbols to stand for ideas and words. Their calendar became the basis for a later Mayan calendar that was more accurate than any in Europe at the time. They played a game much like soccer on ball fields as large as today's football fields. Like other cultures of the time, the Olmecs may have practiced human sacrifice.

Because the Olmecs conducted trade both by land and along coastal waters, covering a vast network, their way of life spread. They had a direct influence on many societies in Mesoamerica. Through the many trading networks, the Olmecs also seem to have had an indirect influence on the peoples of the Southwest. However, the greater the distance between the cultures, the more difficult it is to trace Olmec influences.

1. **Name** three ways that the first immigrants might have reached America.
2. **Describe** how native peoples adapted to the melting of the glaciers.
3. **Define** the term *mother culture*.
4. **Analyze** the list of objects that became valued trade goods. What characteristics did these items share?
5. **Explain** how the agricultural revolution led eventually to an exchange of goods and ideas between cultures.

SECTION 2

A Diversity of Peoples and Cultures

One of the small ironies of history occurred in 1787, when the planners of Marietta, Ohio, discovered some ancient remains at the center of their new city. One feature was a carefully formed mound, 30 feet high and surrounded by a nearly circular wall. The planners did not know what the mound was for, but they preserved it in a tract set aside for the city cemetery. It was later discovered that the mound was one of those used for centuries as burial grounds by ancient people of the Hopewell culture. Without knowing what they were doing, the people of Marietta simply enclosed one cemetery within another. But they can hardly be blamed for not realizing what lay within the mound they fortunately preserved. Clues to the complexity and diversity of early American Indian societies are still being discovered.

What were the major characteristics of the Mound Builders and the southwestern peoples?

What attributes and values did American Indians have toward the land?

How were the Indian cultures of America about A.D. 1500 similar, and how were they different?

Ancient Mound Builders

The mound of earth that the people of Marietta found is only one of thousands that once spread across the lands along the Ohio and Mississippi valleys. They were built by groups of people collectively known to us as **Mound Builders**. While it is certainly possible that these different cultures decided on their own to build mounds, it is also possible that they learned of the idea from migrants from Mesoamerica or from their trading partners. These trading partners included people of Mexico and people living as far north as the Great Lakes.

The **Adena** people, who are generally held to be responsible for the Great Serpent Mound in Ohio, may have flourished between 1000 B.C. and A.D. 200. Members of this culture grew some plants—pumpkins, gourds, and sunflowers—but they were primarily hunters and gatherers. Their burial mounds were conical and dome-shaped with the corpses placed in log-lined tombs. Other distinctive mounds were sometimes shaped like animals, such as the Great Serpent Mound itself, which

▼ *People of the Adena culture built mounds in the shapes of birds, tortoises, and snakes. Seen from the air, this effigy (representation) of a snake is a quarter of a mile long, 20 feet wide, and 5 feet high. What skills would be needed to build such an effigy mound?*

◄ *The Hopewell people cut shapes, like this peregrine falcon, from sheets of copper.*

▶

Mississippian pottery often bears images of skulls, bones, human eyes, axes, and shields. How might such pottery have been used?

from these mound cities. They may have suffered a drought, they may have worn out their farm land, or they may have simply decided that they wanted to explore new territory. At any rate, some of the largest tribes of the Southeast such as the Creek, Cherokee, and Catawba seem to have been influenced by the Mississippian people, and the Choctaw and Chickasaw may even be descended from Mississippian groups. Natchez, a temple mound site in modern-day Mississippi, was still inhabited when it was visited by the French in the 1720s. It provided important evidence about the complexity of the Mound Builders' culture.

stretches a quarter mile from tail to jaw along a creek bluff near Cincinnati.

Earthen mounds from the **Hopewell** culture dating between 300 B.C. and A.D. 700 were larger than those of the Adena. Many of their huge mounds were shaped like birds, snakes, or humans. The people of the Hopewell culture were particularly artistic. Found buried along with human bodies were exquisite carvings of birds and animals, as well as jewelry made of pearls, worked copper, and grizzly bear teeth. These valuable items suggest the people believed they would have some use in an afterlife. They practiced more extensive agriculture than the Adena, and they had a stricter class system.

A third great mound-building society, known as the **Mississippian**, reached its peak about A.D. 1100. Across the Mississippi River from present-day St. Louis, the city of Cahokia (kuh-HOH-kee-uh), had a population of 20,000 to 30,000 people and over 1,000 mounds. It was the largest city in North America before the arrival of the Europeans. Monk's Mound, the largest of the mounds, spanning 15 acres, is a temple once inhabited by the Great Sun, Cahokia's god-like leader. Both the size of the structures of this Mississippian people and the superior workmanship of their artifacts indicate a highly sophisticated culture.

The region of mound cities stretched from present-day Oklahoma to the western edge of West Virginia, and from present-day Louisiana to Indiana and Ohio. Long before European explorers first entered this region most of the cities had been deserted. No one can be certain of why the people moved

Complex Societies of the Southwest

Southwestern Indians showed a very clear influence from Mesoamerica. The very foods that sustained their lives were first developed in Mesoamerica. The techniques they used for making the pottery jars in which they stored their food crops might also have been borrowed from Mesoamericans.

The southwestern Indians called corn, squash, and beans the "three sisters." These foods were fairly easy to grow in the arid climate of the Southwest, and they provided the basis for a balanced diet. One group who depended on the three sisters, the **Hohokam** (hoh-HOH-kuhm), settled in what is now central Arizona about A.D. 300. They are known as the Vanished Ones because all we know of their past is what we can learn by examining their pit houses, their ball courts, their pottery, and their 30-mile-long, hand-dug canals. Of the people there is no trace. It is possible that they were the ancestors of the modern, peaceful Pima (PEE-muh) and Papagos (PAH-pah-gohs), who now live farther to the south in Arizona.

To the north, on the Colorado Plateau, another farming society thrived. Known as the Ancient Ones, the **Anasazi** (ahn-uh-SAH-zee), like other southwestern Indians, depended on irrigation ditches to catch and hold rainwater. When they weren't farming, they engaged in long-distance

▲ *Located in southwestern Colorado, Mesa Verde contains spectacular ruins of Anasazi towns built into the sides of cliffs or in narrow river valleys. This group of apartments, known as Cliff Palace, once housed as many as 400 people. Why would kivas have been built so close to the living quarters?*

trade. They may even have traded with the Mound Builders to the east. Most of the Anasazi villages and cities were built against canyon walls or within the canyon itself. Rather than building temples on great mounds of earth, the Anasazi built **kivas** (KEE-vuhs), round structures built mostly underground and entered by a ladder through an opening in the roof. These chambers were used for religious ceremonies, for discussion of tribal affairs, and sometimes as workshops. The people lived in small cities that included several large "apartment buildings" known as **pueblos**. Pueblo Bonito in New Mexico, for example, built by A.D. 1085, had more than 600 rooms.

The Anasazi began to leave their pueblos by about A.D. 1100. They moved south across the plateaus of Arizona and New Mexico and along the Rio Grande. By about A.D. 1350 the cities were completely deserted. No one is sure why the Anasazi left their lands. There was a severe drought

about that time, and Indians from the north had begun to encroach on their territory. Perhaps this was the reason. In any event, the Anasazi carried much of their way of life with them as they moved south. Their probable descendants, the Hopi, the Zuni, and the Rio Grande Pueblo Indians, use kivas and grow corn as the Anasazi did. Some modern Pueblo pottery looks remarkably like that found by archeologists at Anasazi sites. Most scholars believe that two towns, Oraibi (oh-RY-bee) in Arizona and Acoma (AK-oh-maw) in New Mexico, were settled by the Anasazi in about A.D. 1100. They are the oldest continuously occupied urban settlements in America.

The Mound Builders and the Anasazi were not the only ancient societies in America. As scholars continue their work, we will learn more about other important centers of early American civilizations.

▶ *The Anasazi probably traded with the Mound Builders to the east.*

▼ *These kivas are part of the Pueblo Bonito structures found in Chaco Canyon in New Mexico. What does their presence suggest about the people?*

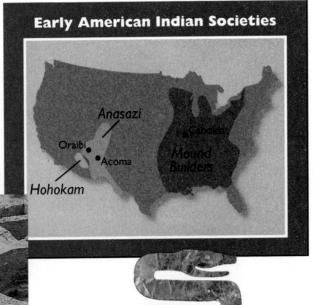

Early American Indian Societies

Anasazi

Oraibi
•Acoma

Hohokam

Cahokia

Mound Builders

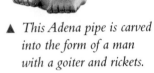

▲ *This Adena pipe is carved into the form of a man with a goiter and rickets.*

▲ *Hopewell mica snake.*

Diverse Indian Cultures

Scholars know a great deal about the American Indians of more modern times. Their studies show that by A.D. 1500 there were several million (estimates vary from 5 to 10 million) Indians living north of Mexico. These people lived in different cultural groups, had different physical characteristics, spoke a multitude of languages, and made their living in a variety of ways. Many Indian groups lived in self-governing villages with wooden houses. Others lived in easy-to-build structures that they occupied for a few days or a few weeks before they moved to a new location.

The Eastern Woodland Indian tribes included both settled villagers and migratory people. Those who lived along rivers and creeks grew corn and other plants, and they hunted and fished for other foods. Those who lived in the far northern regions around the Great Lakes used their birchbark canoes to move quickly to good fishing and hunting spots and areas rich in wild foods.

The people of the Southeast, Southwest, and some regions of the Great Plains depended on farm crops. The people of the Plateau, Great Basin, and parts of California lived in such arid lands that they had to rely on small game, such as rabbits, and on wild foods, such as seeds, acorns, and roots. In areas where these foods were plentiful and dependable, life was relatively easy. A few hours of work a day were all that was needed to feed a family. In other areas, the people spent all their waking hours searching for food.

In the Northwest, finding food was a simple task. Not only were nutritious wild plants abundant, but the ocean and rivers also provided fish, shellfish, and sea mammals. Every summer, huge numbers of salmon, weighing 15 pounds or more apiece, swam up the rivers. As an early English explorer noted, it seemed as if "you could walk across the river on their backs." Since salmon could be smoked and dried, they provided a dependable staple food.

It is clear that, wherever they lived, the American Indians managed to make a living from the land and to develop a workable society.

Native American Cultures, A.D. 1500

Inuit

Kutchin

Ingalik

Aleut

Gulf of Alaska

Dogrib

Inuit

Kaska

Slave

Chippewyan

Inuit

Hudson Bay

Naskapi

Montagnais

Beothuk

Tlingit

Blackfeet

Cree

Micmac

Penobscot

Haida

Nootka

Ojibwa

Ottawa

Huron

Massachuset

Pacific Ocean

Chinook

Yakima

Nez Perce

Flathead

Salish

Assiniboine

Mandan

Sauk

Fox

Potawatomi

Iroquois

Narraganset

Wampanoag

Crow

Hidatsa

Miami

Erie

Atlantic Ocean

Yurok

Paiute

Cheyenne

Dakota

(Sioux)

Pawnee

Illinois

Delaware

Powhatan

Klamath

Shoshone

Arapaho

Pomo

Yokut

Paiute

Querechos

Tuscarora

Chumash

Hopi

Pueblo

Kiowa

Osage

Shawnee

Cherokee

Pima

Zuni

Wichita

Chickasaw

Yamasee

Papago

Apache

Choctaw

Creek

Cochimi

Concho

Comanche

Caddo

Natchez

Calusa

Yaqui

Coahuiltec

Gulf of Mexico

Ciboney

Tropic of Cancer

Tamaulipec

Taino

Arawak

Tarascan

Toltec

AZTEC EMPIRE

Olmec

MAYAN EMPIRE

Mixtec

Zapotec

Mosquito

Lenca

Caribbean Sea

Legend:

- Arctic
- Subarctic
- Plains
- Eastern Woodlands
- Southwest
- Southeast
- Great Basin
- Northwest Coast
- Plateau
- California
- Mesoamerica
- Caribbean

0 — 1000 mi

0 — 1500 km

▲ *To help understand how different peoples live and how their societies developed, anthropologists have grouped societies into culture areas. Each culture area shares certain climates, resources, and technologies. How many culture areas are defined on this map?*

Values and Beliefs

Most American Indians believed that all things on earth were created by a supernatural being and that humans were responsible for the **stewardship**, or care, of nature's bounty. For example, the Arapaho believed that "Great Mystery Above" created the earth from bits of dirt. Then he made the sun and the moon, man and woman, vegetable and animal life, night and day, and the four seasons. The Arapaho, descendants of the first man and first woman, have been responsible for taking care of their people and their environment ever since.

Most American Indians held a religious belief known as **animism**. That is, they believed in a chief god, or creator, and a number of lesser gods

AMERICAN SCENES

Growing Up to Be a Creek Warrior

In the early morning, a barefoot warrior emerges from his bark-covered dwelling. Dressed only in a loincloth made of animal skin but with tattoos covering his torso, arms, and legs, this clan elder leads the young boys of the village to bathe. Following a plunge into the waters of the icy cold creek, the boys have their arms and legs scratched with the sharp teeth of the garfish. This accustoms them to the sight of blood, which they will see often as grown men. To be brave, to earn the right to be tattooed, and to wear the paint and feathers of a great warrior are the desires of most Creek boys.

Warfare played an important part in Creek life. Most conflicts consisted of short raids on neighboring tribes. When he planned a raid, a war chief literally "drummed up" a war party by beating on a drum as he walked around the outside of his house. Men wanting to go on the raid gathered in the center of the village and prepared themselves for battle. For four days

▲ *Tomochichi, ruler of the Creek town of Yamacraw, and his nephew Toonahowi. Why might a man accept more responsibility for his nephew than for his son?*

they fasted and danced for hours at a time. Finally, they smoked a pipe to show their commitment to the group and to the task at hand.

To win prestige, a warrior tried to capture an enemy alive. The captive might be adopted into the tribe to replace a fallen Creek warrior, or might be tortured. Both the tortured warrior and the torturer understood that ritual torture was not just a spectacle, but a means by which bereaved families compensated for the loss of loved ones. To show fortitude under ordeal was to earn for oneself both the respect of the torturers and also perhaps a favored place in the afterlife. Once a captive knew his fate, he was ready with his own death song. For warriors, facing pain and danger were accepted parts of life.

1. How were Creek boys taught to be brave?
2. In what ways did the Creeks prepare for war?

or spirits who controlled animals, rain, wind, and human fertility. This type of religious belief meant everything in nature had to be treated with care and respect. Such a belief also implied that no one could own what had been created for all. While personal possessions such as houses, tools, baskets, pottery, and clothing were owned by individuals, land belonged to the whole group. Families could be allotted fields for their crops, but the allotment was temporary. In a different year, another family might use these fields.

Families would take what they needed of their crop. Excess harvest was donated to hungry people in the community, stored in the public granary for use in bad times, or used to feed visitors to the village. The yield from a hunting or fishing expedition was likewise shared.

These caring attitudes did not mean that Indians never engaged in practices that were destructive to the environment. The early Indians may have hunted some big-game animals to extinction. Some scholars believe the Anasazi deforested broad swaths of land. They cut down the small trees and burned over the land to provide wood ashes as fertilizer for their crops.

However, communal ownership of the earth meant that everything was part of the whole, so all relationships had to be reciprocal, each party receiving something of value. When a man hunted, the animal gave up its life. The hunter then thanked the spirit of that animal species not only to show his gratitude, but also to let the spirit know he had taken the animal's life with a reverent attitude and that he wanted to be able to hunt such animals again. In much the same way, some American Indian women thanked the plants for growing, and they preserved the best seeds to be returned to the soil for the next year's crops.

Patterns of Social Organization

The sharing of the land promoted an **egalitarian**, or classless, society in which all people were considered equal. There were, however, important exceptions. For example, the cultures of some Northwest Indians included several tiers, with the ruling class at the top and slaves at the bottom.

In the majority of American Indian societies, leadership was not hereditary, and chiefs were chosen for their ability. They could always be removed from office. If an Iroquois **sachem** (SAY-chem), or head of the tribe, did not perform well, the matron, or oldest woman, of the clan would give him three warnings. If he did not improve his performance, she would "pull his horns" or take away his headdress, thus removing him from office.

Most women in Indian societies had a degree of equality with men unknown in other lands. Many societies were both **matrilineal**, meaning that descent was traced through the mother's family, and **matrilocal**, meaning that males upon marriage would move in with the wife's family. Women owned the house, tools, pottery, or baskets—everything but her husband's clothes and weapons. Divorce was usually the woman's right. Among the Pueblo, all a woman had to do to divorce her husband was to set his belongings outside the door.

With the coming of the Europeans, Indian societies would change dramatically. Some would disappear completely. Others would adapt as they could. Most retained their own worldview and their sense of connection with others in their tribe and with the land.

SECTION 2 REVIEW

1. **Name** the distinctive features that characterized the Mound Builder cultures.
2. **Identify** the "three sisters" of the southwestern Indians.
3. **Compare** the tasks of providing food in the Southwest and in the Northeast. Which would have been more of a challenge?
4. **Define** egalitarian.
5. **Explain** what advantage the Anasazi might have found in building underground kivas instead of temples or wooden structures.

Woodland Indians and the Technology of Fire

We usually think of technology as a set of methods and materials used for industrial or commercial purposes. Robotic arms that assemble automobiles and the remote control devices used to program television sets fit this definition. Archeologists use the term more broadly. They define technology as the body of knowledge available to a culture that can be used in fashioning implements, extracting and collecting materials, and practicing arts and skills. A good example is the knowledge of how to make fire and how this knowledge came to be used by Woodland Indians, such as the Iroquois or the Creeks, to improve both farming and hunting and to protect their villages.

Fire was used in a practice known as slash-and-burn agriculture. Land was first burned over to eliminate underbrush and to provide wood ash as fertilizer. Then Indians slashed the trunks of unburned trees. As the trees began to die, sunlight filtered through their withering branches, and planting could begin. Fields created using this method would produce crops for only a few years. As the wood ash in the soil leached out, fertility declined, and farmers prepared fields that were farther away. When distance from the fields to the vil-

▲ *How many examples of the importance of fire in the daily life of these Algonquin Indians can you find in this painting? What other technologies do you see being used?*

lage became too great, the whole village moved to a new region.

Fire was also used to improve hunting. Deer and other plant-eating animals were attracted to the tender new vegetation in grassy areas around well-watered sites. In burned-over areas, both grass and shrubs grew quickly. Accordingly, every fall some Woodland Indians burned small areas to ensure that wild game would come to their lands in the spring. Sometimes they would also set fires to drive game into enclosures where the animals would be easy targets for men armed with bows and arrows.

Natural fires caused by lightning were a constant threat to Woodland Indians. To protect their wooden and brush houses, they would set controlled fires to make firebreaks around their villages. The firebreaks not only prevented lightning-caused fires from destroying their villages, but also kept enemies from sneaking up too close to their homes. The controlled use of fire became an important technology, ingeniously developed and utilized by the Woodland Indians.

━━━⟢⟣⟢━━━

1. Why do archeologists consider the controlled use of fire a form of technology?
2. Describe how fire was used to improve farming and hunting methods.

Parallels on the African Continent

Just as in the Americas prior to 1492, there were also many thriving cultures and civilizations in Africa at this time. Merchants established trading networks that connected urban centers in Africa to merchants in China and Arabia. Throughout the continent, the diverse peoples of Africa lived in varying social structures with a rich variety of belief systems and traditions.

How did the majority of Africans meet their basic needs?

How were African ideas and American Indian ideas about the natural world similar?

How did slavery in Africa differ from slavery in America?

Africa Before 1492

Contrary to the opinions of the Europeans of the time, rich civilizations and cultures had flourished throughout Africa for centuries. For example, when Arab geographer **Ibn Battuta** (IB-uhn bah-TOO-tah) traveled through West Africa in the 1330s, he found a civilization at the height of its power. Mali was a civilization in which the ruling families and top government officials lived in luxury, supported by vast quantities of gold dust found along the Niger river, by ivory garnered from large herds of elephants, and by agricultural products grown by tribute-paying tribes. Within this civilization was Timbuktu, the great trading city. Timbuktu was also a center of Islamic culture and learning. (Islam is the religion founded by the prophet **Muhammad** and explained in the sacred book the Koran, or Qur'an.) The university in Timbuktu drew students from all over North Africa. A few even came from Southern Europe to study at this university. Ibn Battuta found the city, indeed the entire kingdom, well run. He wrote:

> The [blacks] are seldom unjust and have a greater abhorrence of injustice than any other people. There is complete security in their country. Neither traveler nor inhabitant... has anything to fear from robbers or men of violence. They do not confiscate the property of any white man who dies in their country... on the contrary, they give it into the charge of some trustworthy person among the whites, until the rightful heir takes possession of it.

The majority of the people in Africa, however, did not live in large cities like Timbuktu. Instead, they lived in distinct tribal groups in remote villages in the countryside. There they survived, working their small farms, hunting, raising livestock, or plying a trade, such as woodworking, metalworking, or cloth making. Women and children worked the fields along with men. Surplus crops found their way to local markets, where women took part in a robust barter economy in which goods were exchanged for other goods. Land was owned communally.

Diverse African Cultures Africans had cultures as distinct as those found in the Americas, and they lived in equally diverse environments. Rain forests and high grasslands were inhabited by some 50 million people. The deserts, though inhabited by few people, were not the impenetrable seas of sand depicted in novels and movies. For centuries these deserts had been regularly crossed by trading caravans.

Social and religious belief systems in Africa were similar to those of the American Indians of the same time period. Here, too, most groups were matrilineal and matrilocal. The West Africans also practiced animism and generally treated the things found in nature with respect.

Ancestor worship also played a role in African religions. Many Africans practiced ritual ceremonies dedicated to their ancestors. The more ancient the ancestors, the greater the power they had in pleading the cause of the person to the gods. Family ties and knowledge of past generations were extremely

◀ *This detail of an ancient Ibo sculpture from Nigeria reflects the importance ancestors played in West African belief systems. Why would ancestors be depicted in statues?*

important. The exploits of ancestors were kept alive through storytelling. The frequent repetition of the stories meant that even the young people knew how to call on an ancestor for support.

Slavery was a part of the social system of West Africa. The enslaved people were usually captives from different tribal groups, criminals who were enslaved as punishment, or people who sold themselves into slavery to pay off their debts. While these enslaved people had little opportunity to change their station in life, they could marry, have children, and were protected by law. Their enslavement was not necessarily permanent, and it did not automatically pass on to their children.

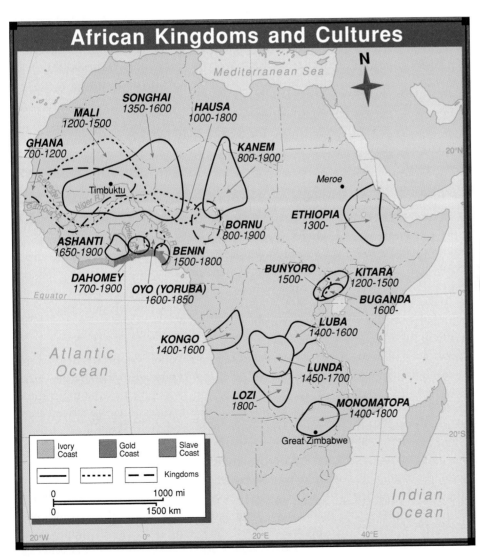

African Kingdoms and Cultures

Mediterranean Sea

N

SONGHAI
1350-1600

MALI
1200-1500

HAUSA
1000-1800

GHANA
700-1200

KANEM
800-1900

Timbuktu

Niger R.

Meroe

BORNU
800-1900

ETHIOPIA
1300-

ASHANTI
1650-1900

BENIN
1500-1800

BUNYORO
1500-

KITARA
1200-1500

DAHOMEY
1700-1900

OYO (YORUBA)
1600-1850

BUGANDA
1600-

Equator

LUBA
1400-1600

KONGO
1400-1600

Atlantic
Ocean

LUNDA
1450-1700

LOZI
1800-

MONOMATOPA
1400-1800

Great Zimbabwe

20°S

Indian
Ocean

Ivory Coast	Gold Coast	Slave Coast

Kingdoms

0   1000 mi
0   1500 km

20°W   0°   20°E   40°E

◀ *Timbuktu was at the center of many early African kingdoms. Which cultures were flourishing when Columbus made his voyages to the Americas?*

▲ *This ancient bronze head from Nigeria shows an extreme example of scarification. Marking the skin with cuts was once important in some African societies. Why might people scar their bodies in certain patterns?*

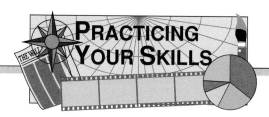

Working with the Time Line

While it is important to know when things happened, a single date or event gives the historian very little helpful information. A **chronology** is an arrangement of events in their order of happening (*chronos* comes from the Greek word for "time"). Having a sense of chronology can help us understand how events relate to each other. It can help explain cause-and-effect relationships, the duration (length) of events, and ideas of continuity and change. For example, it can help us understand how new problems grow out of old ones, and how new inventions are built on the knowledge of earlier inventions.

Having a sense of chronology can also help us understand related events. The relationship between the building of railroads and the admitting of new states to the Union, or the relationship between the defeat of the Spanish Armada in 1588 and the development of the English colonies are examples.

The time line is a visual tool that is used to show the flow of history. To be accurate, the time line should be divided into regular, or periodic, segments. Many events on time lines will relate to other events. For example, if three events on a time line are "Prince Henry explores the African coast," "Columbus's first voyage to the New World," and "Chocolate introduced to Spain from the New World," you may theorize that one event led to the other. You may not know, however, until you read the chapter whether your supposition is accurate.

Examine the time line on pages 100 and 101 to answer the following questions:

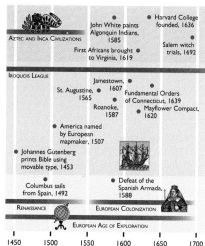

1. (a) How many years does this time line cover? (b) What is the earliest date? (c) What is the latest date?
2. What is the time span (interval) between segments in this time line?
3. Events on this time line may be classified as social/cultural, political/economic, scientific/technological, and diplomatic. What is one problem with trying to classify events by these categories?
4. Which events seem to have a cause-and-effect relationship?
5. Some events do not seem to be related to the others. Why do you think these were included?

Trade Kingdoms

From ancient times, Egypt and other areas of North Africa were part of Mediterranean civilization. For centuries North Africans traded with Europeans and with the people of the Middle East.

The people of East Africa tended to look eastward for trade, using small sailing vessels to haul goods back and forth from Arabia, India, and even China.

North Africans traded along a vast stretch of West Africa. In the eleventh century, invading North African Muslims (followers of Islam) brought chaos to the West African kingdom of Ghana, a sizable empire with its wealth based on gold production.

The empire of Ghana fell, and, when order was restored, the Islamic kingdom of Mali arose in its stead. Mali, in turn, was eventually taken over by the Songhai empire, which reached its peak in A.D. 1475. All these successive kingdoms prospered through trade, as did the lesser kingdoms of Benin and Kongo.

The rulers and traders of the West African kingdoms lived in great luxury, trading gold dust, ivory, and enslaved people for goods, particularly salt, from the Arab world. Their cities and large towns contained well-constructed buildings adorned with designs painted in brilliant colors. The sculpture, sometimes carved of wood and sometimes cast in metal, was usually ceremonial and reflected animistic beliefs.

Highest in the social order of these West African kingdoms were the ruling families and priests. The middle class was comprised of the majority of the people, including the farmers and artisans. At the bottom of the social order were the enslaved persons.

Like the people of the Americas, the Africans of that time were a diverse people. They, too, were remote from contact with European events. And as with the peoples of the Americas, their lives and social structures were to be disrupted by Europeans as the Age of Exploration dawned. This was especially true for the people of West Africa, where slave traders would soon come to uproot and enslave people to use as labor in the New World.

Europe and the Age of Exploration

In A.D. 1298, a new book captured the attention of the small proportion of Europeans who were literate. Dictated by its Italian author, *The Book of Marco Polo* described the wonders Polo claimed to have seen during his 20-year trip to the Orient, a term used to describe the lands of the Far East in Asia. China and the Spice Islands (the Moluccas) contained fabulous riches. Of the island of Java, Polo wrote, "The country abounds with rich commodities. Pepper, nutmegs, ... cloves, all other valuable spices and drugs.... The quantity of gold collected there exceeds all calculation and belief." For the next three centuries, Marco Polo's Orient remained the focus of European dreams of adventure and wealth. It became a magnet, pulling the thoughts and energies of a growing number of people to the economic possibilities that lay beyond Europe.

What economic changes were taking place in fifteenth-century Europe?

How did trade with the Orient foster these changes?

Why could Prince Henry the Navigator be described as a model of Renaissance thinking?

SECTION 3 REVIEW

1. **List** elements of the Kingdom of Mali that Ibn Battuta found admirable.
2. **Describe** how most village Africans made their living.
3. **Explain** why African religious beliefs encouraged storytelling and an oral tribal history.
4. **Name** the main economic activity common to the early African kingdoms described in this section.
5. **Identify** three ways in which early American and African cultures were similar.

European Cultures Expand

By the mid-1400s, European cultures were much different from those found in America or Africa. New forces were rapidly changing European society. Increasingly, the countries of Europe were in competition for land and wealth. Cities expanded, agricultural production rose, and the crafting of handmade articles increased. Commerce became more organized. Economic growth came with the rise in trade. European trading routes connected with networks that stretched into China, India, Southeast Asia, and along the coasts of Africa.

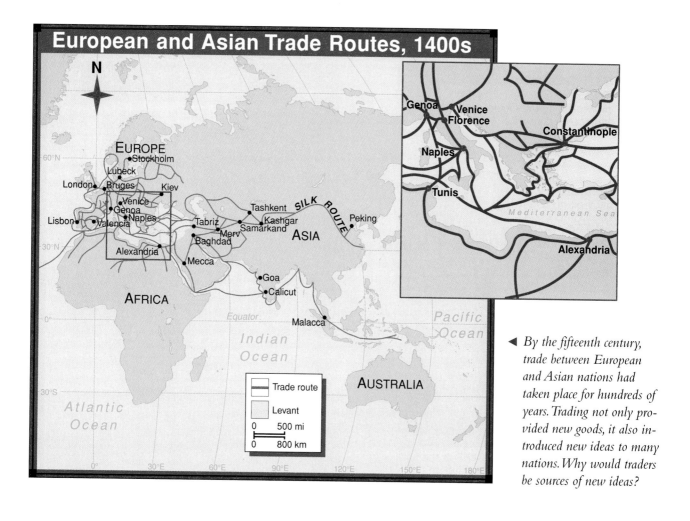

European and Asian Trade Routes, 1400s

By the fifteenth century, trade between European and Asian nations had taken place for hundreds of years. Trading not only provided new goods, it also introduced new ideas to many nations. Why would traders be sources of new ideas?

Both spices and precious metals were important. Lacking enough grain to feed their cattle during the winter, Europeans slaughtered most of their herds in the fall and used spices—salt primarily—to preserve the meat, or at least to disguise the taste of spoiled meat. Precious metals were needed to coin money for the developing cash economy.

Trade with the Orient was largely controlled by Arab traders in Egypt and the Levant (countries bordering on the Eastern Mediterranean). Sailing across the Mediterranean Sea to the Middle East, merchants from Venice, Naples, and Genoa carried woolen cloth, furs, and lumber to be exchanged for goods from the Orient. Spices and precious metals from the Orient came to the Middle East by ship across the Indian Ocean, or by camel caravan on an overland journey of some 4,000 miles. To recover the costs of such long journeys, the Middle East merchants charged high prices for their merchandise. In turn, the Italian merchants had to recover their costs in bringing the goods to Europe. By the time the goods were offered for sale in Europe, only the wealthy could afford them.

Because these goods from the Orient were so essential to the European economy, merchants from other European nations tried to figure out ways to break the Arab and Italian monopoly. They wanted their own trade routes to the East, and it would not be long before Portugal took the lead in the search.

The Renaissance

By the fifteenth century, Europeans were beginning to feel confident about their ability to conquer

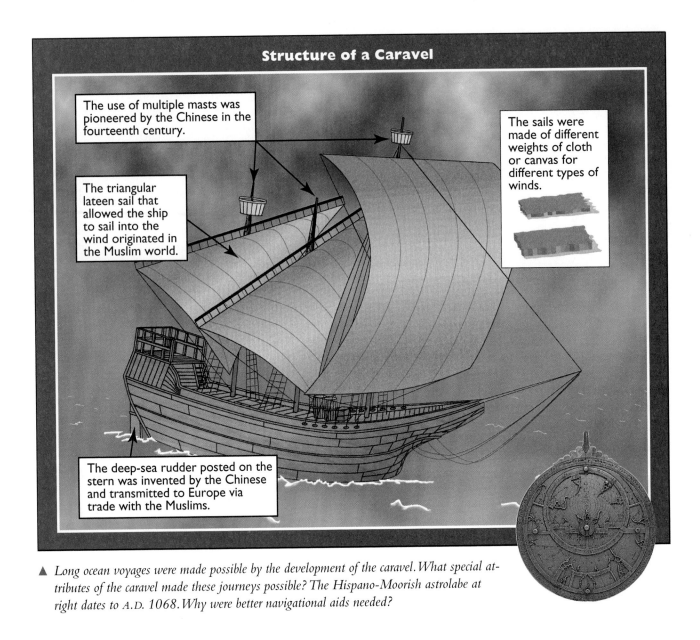

Structure of a Caravel

The use of multiple masts was pioneered by the Chinese in the fourteenth century.

The triangular lateen sail that allowed the ship to sail into the wind originated in the Muslim world.

The sails were made of different weights of cloth or canvas for different types of winds.

The deep-sea rudder posted on the stern was invented by the Chinese and transmitted to Europe via trade with the Muslims.

▲ *Long ocean voyages were made possible by the development of the caravel. What special attributes of the caravel made these journeys possible? The Hispano-Moorish astrolabe at right dates to A.D. 1068. Why were better navigational aids needed?*

the unknown. The **Renaissance**—the rebirth of classical Greek and Roman knowledge that had begun in the 1300s—was expanding knowledge in one area of life after another. New ideas were revitalizing European literature, philosophy, painting, sculpture, architecture, and science. The pace of life quickened.

One of those who exemplified the spirit of the Renaissance was **Prince Henry the Navigator**, of Portugal. Prince Henry had a consuming interest in the art of navigation. Although he never personally sailed farther than the coast of Morocco, he was

willing to sponsor the voyages of those who would chart unknown waters. To supply his sailors with the best information available, he established an academy for navigation at his seaside home on the southern tip of Portugal. From all over Europe he invited astronomers, geographers, and mathematicians to meet and put together all the known facts about the physical world.

Technology Aids Exploration The compass and the **quadrant**, in use since about 1200, showed direction; the **astrolabe** helped determine latitude.

But because sailors still had no way to figure longitude, they could not determine how far east or west they sailed, or even compute how wide the ocean might be. Sailors of the fifteenth century were also handicapped by their clumsy ships, which were at the mercy of the prevailing winds.

Members of Prince Henry's academy helped in two ways. First, they designed a new sailing vessel called the **caravel**. Smaller and easier to maneuver than other ships of the time, the caravel also had sails that could be moved to take advantage of winds from any direction. Second, the scientists of the academy produced maps and navigational charts based on information brought back by the sailors supported by Prince Henry.

The Portuguese were certain that if they could sail around Africa, they would find the Spice Islands. In 1441, Portuguese ships began transporting enslaved Africans from a region dubbed the Slave Coast and selling them to wealthy Europeans. Soon afterwards, they discovered gold along the coast in an area that became known as the Gold Coast. But Africa was a much larger continent than any of the Europeans of the time realized. Even though Prince Henry supported voyage after voyage, it was not until 1488, 30 years after his death, that explorer Bartholomeu Dias rounded the Cape of Good Hope. In 1497, Vasco da Gama followed Dias's route to the southern tip of Africa and then sailed on to the west coast of India. By then, sailors and navigators from many lands were convinced that new sea routes to the Indies could indeed be found, and everyone wanted to be first.

SECTION 4 REVIEW

1. **Contrast** the cultures of Europe and Western Africa in the mid-1400s. Discuss the cities, farming, and trade.
2. **State** how spices and precious metals were used in Western Europe.
3. **Define** Renaissance.
4. **Name** two ways in which Prince Henry helped improve the science and technology of navigation.
5. **Justify** the decision of a country such as Portugal to spend money financing risky sea voyages.

SECTION 5

The Collision of Cultures

Christopher Columbus was searching for a route to the Orient when he made his historic voyage in 1492. In spite of his conviction that he would find the East Indies, Columbus had his moments of self-doubt. On October 11, 1492, he recorded in his log: "At ten o'clock at night ... I thought I saw a light to the west. ... I am the first to admit that I was so eager to find land that I did not trust my own senses, so I called for Pedro Gutierrez ... and asked for him to watch for the light. ... Then, at two hours after midnight, the *Pinta* fired a cannon, my prearranged signal for the sighting of land."

What was the major unexpected discovery of the voyage of Columbus?

Why is it said that the Spanish exploited the Americas?

What motivated other nations to send out their own explorers?

The Voyages of Columbus

Christopher Columbus was born in 1451 in the Italian city of Genoa, where his father was a wool merchant. The manufacture and sale of woolen cloth was the most important business in Europe at that time, and the Columbus family was well off. As a youth, Columbus took up his father's trade, buying raw materials and selling finished products to countries in the Mediterranean region and the Atlantic ports of Portugal and England. After his marriage to a wealthy Portuguese woman had given him citizenship rights, he traveled to the Portuguese-controlled ports on the West African coast. Between 1485 and 1492, Columbus also did business in the port cities and commercial centers of Spain. Throughout those seven years, Columbus constantly petitioned the Spanish court for permission to establish trading posts on any islands he might discover by sailing west across the Atlantic.

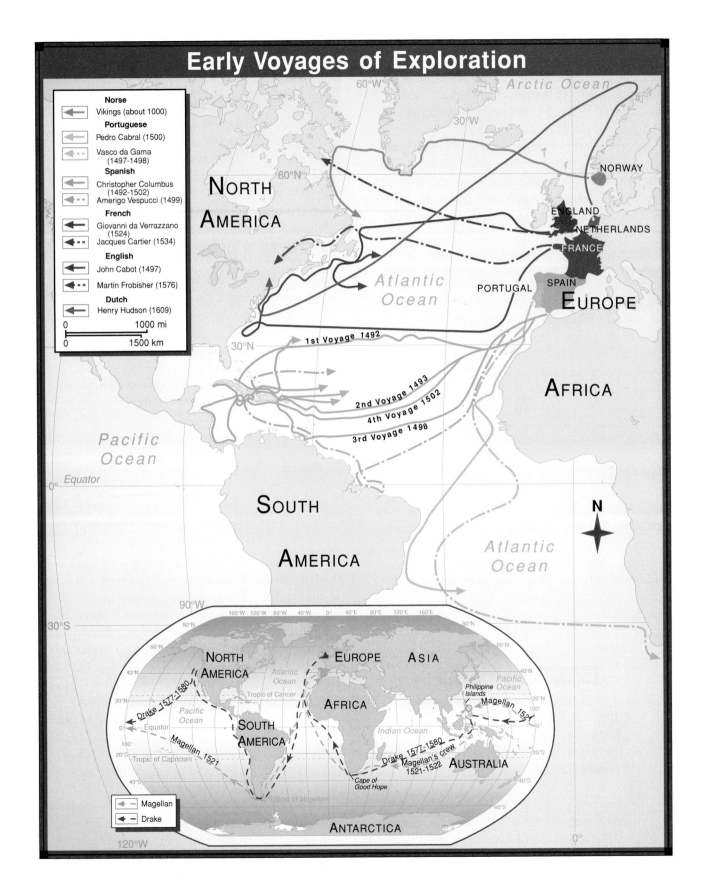

Early Voyages of Exploration

Norse
Vikings (about 1000)

Portuguese
Pedro Cabral (1500)
Vasco da Gama (1497-1498)

Spanish
Christopher Columbus (1492-1502)
Amerigo Vespucci (1499)

French
Giovanni da Verrazzano (1524)
Jacques Cartier (1534)

English
John Cabot (1497)
Martin Frobisher (1576)

Dutch
Henry Hudson (1609)

0   1000 mi
0   1500 km

1st Voyage 1492
2nd Voyage 1493
4th Voyage 1502
3rd Voyage 1498

Arctic Ocean

NORTH AMERICA

Atlantic Ocean

Pacific Ocean

Equator

SOUTH AMERICA

Atlantic Ocean

NORWAY

ENGLAND
NETHERLANDS
FRANCE
PORTUGAL   SPAIN

EUROPE

AFRICA

N

60°W
30°W
60°N
30°N
0°
30°S
90°W
120°W

Magellan
Drake

NORTH AMERICA
EUROPE   ASIA
Atlantic Ocean
Tropic of Cancer
AFRICA
Pacific Ocean
Philippine Islands
Magellan 1521
Drake 1577-1580
Pacific Ocean
Equator
SOUTH AMERICA
Indian Ocean
Magellan 1521
Tropic of Capricorn
Drake 1577-1580
Magellan's crew 1521-1522
AUSTRALIA
Cape of Good Hope
Strait of Magellan
ANTARCTICA

160°W 120°W 80°W 40°W 0° 40°E 80°E 120°E 160°E
80°N
60°N
40°N
20°N
0°
20°S
40°S
60°S
80°N
60°N
40°N
20°S
40°S
60°S
0°

He was certain that you could reach China and Japan by sailing west, and that the fabled East Indies would lie in the path. Finally, in April 1492, Queen Isabella provided him with three ships, 90 sailors, and the trading rights to any lands he might discover.

Like many sailors and merchants of his time, Columbus had studied geography and read Marco Polo's description of the East. Other sailors and navigators agreed with Columbus that by sailing west a ship could reach China and the Indies. What his critics found ridiculous was Columbus's belief that the journey would be only about 3,000 miles. The critics were certain the voyage would have to cover some 10,000 to 12,000 miles, and no ship could carry enough provisions for such a long trip. The critics were right. What Columbus and his critics did not know was that a huge uncharted land mass existed, some 3,000 miles sailing distance west between Europe and the rich East Indies of the Pacific.

On August 3, 1492, Columbus set out on his voyage. The winds were with him, and the weather was fair. Two months later, on October 12, 1492, Christopher Columbus and his crews gratefully drew near an island he named San Salvador. He must have been perplexed at his first sight of the islanders. He expected to find people dressed in the rich silks of the Orient. What he saw was something

▲ *This undated, fanciful lithograph was made to commemorate Columbus's landing on the "new" continent. What elements seem most realistic?*

◀ *From the early sixteenth century, Europeans explored vast territories in America. Identify the routes of the Portuguese explorers on this map. What result of Portuguese exploration can be observed in Brazil today?*

quite different. In his log he recorded that "at dawn we saw naked people, [but] I went to shore in the ship's boat, armed, and followed by the captain of the *Pinta* and his brother the captain of the *Niña*." Still convinced he had landed in the Indies, Columbus called the friendly people who met his ships "Indios." He was surprised to find they had no knowledge of the spices, the silks, and the precious metals Marco Polo had written about so long before. But still satisfied that he was near the Spice Islands, Columbus continued to explore. Altogether, he made four journeys searching for gold, for more developed Indian societies, and for the elusive all-water route to the Orient.

It was **Amerigo Vespucci** who, after sailing to the "Indies" in 1500 and 1501, first understood the importance of Columbus's voyages. Vespucci concluded that the lands Columbus described and the ones he himself saw were not connected to Asia. He called them a "New World," and he claimed they were part of a continent previously unknown to

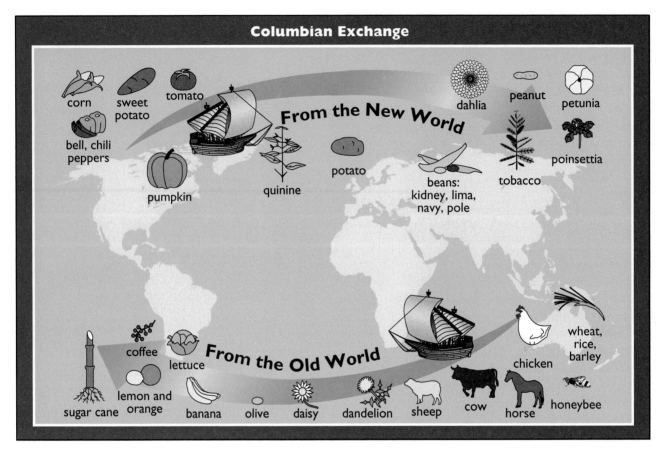

Columbian Exchange

From the New World

corn, sweet potato, tomato, bell, chili peppers, pumpkin, quinine, potato, beans: kidney, lima, navy, pole, dahlia, peanut, petunia, poinsettia, tobacco

From the Old World

coffee, lettuce, sugar cane, lemon and orange, banana, olive, daisy, dandelion, sheep, cow, horse, chicken, wheat, rice, barley, honeybee

▲ *The exchange of goods and ideas across the Atlantic Ocean has been named both the Columbian Exchange and the Atlantic Exchange. Historically, how important was this process?*

Europeans. Shortly thereafter, a European mapmaker decided to label the lands of the Western Hemisphere "America," after Vespucci.

Exploration and Exploitation

Other explorers sponsored by Spain soon exploited the lands claimed by Columbus by demanding tribute from the Indians they encountered. In 1513, Vasco Núñez de Balboa sighted the Pacific Ocean from the coast of Panama, and received a tribute of gold from a group of Indians who claimed there were vast quantities of that precious metal in lands nearby. In 1513, and again in 1521, Ponce de León visited and named the peninsula of Florida. Hernando Cortés conquered the Aztecs in Mexico in 1519, and Francisco Pizarro overwhelmed the Incas of Peru in 1531. Between 1539 and 1541, Hernando de Soto traveled east from Florida to the Mississippi River. In 1540, Francisco Vásquez de Coronado set out from Mexico to explore the vast lands to the north.

Throughout Mesoamerica the **conquistadores**, Spanish explorers and soldiers, forced the native peoples to accept Spanish rule. They enslaved some to work in the Mexican mines, forced others to work as interpreters, soldiers, and servants, and slaughtered hundreds who resisted their control.

It was easier for the Spanish to control the scattered people they found north of Mexico. Although they enslaved some groups, the method they more often used for control was to pit the Pueblos, Pimas, Papagos, Apaches, and other Indians against one another. But not all Spanish explorers and conquistadores who came to America supported this policy of conquest. For example, **Bartolomé de Las Casas**, the first priest ordained in America, fought enslavement of the Indians and spoke out against their harsh treatment.

Finding it hard to keep sufficient supplies flowing across the Atlantic Ocean to feed all of the soldiers, administrators, and priests involved in their expeditions of conquest, the Spanish started raising cattle and growing food crops in their new empire. At first they tried to make the conquered Indians work the newly established ranches and farms. But when the Indian laborers either died from diseases or rebelled, refusing to work, the Spanish turned to other sources of labor. In 1517, the Spanish monarchs authorized a request to send 15,000 African slaves to Santo Domingo to work the sugar plantations and the ranches. These slaves provided yet another kind of riches, for sugar, grown and refined with enslaved labor, had a ready market in Europe. The Spanish exploited both Indians and Africans as they established control over the immense territory they called New Spain.

Europeans Bring Deadly Diseases

Not only enslavement but also disease took a toll on the na-

▲ *This Aztec codex, or pictorial representation, shows a sacrifice to the god Tezcatlipoca, rival of Quetzalcoatl. Aztec myths tell of conflicts between these two gods. Can you identify another belief system in which gods struggle for power?*

tive peoples. The greatest number of deaths came from the ordinary contagious diseases that had once been epidemic in Europe. During an epidemic nearly everyone in a population catches the disease

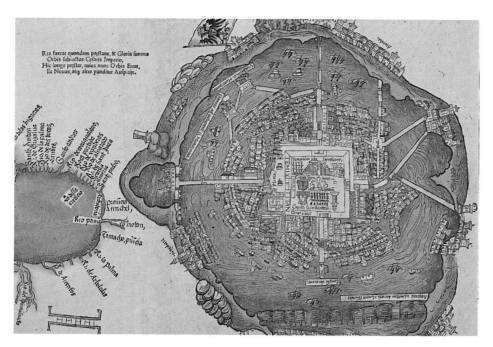

◀ *This Spanish map of the city of Tenochtitlán was published in 1524, soon after the Aztec Empire fell to the Spanish. How does this view of the city compare to Diego Rivera's rendition in the mural that opens Unit 1?*

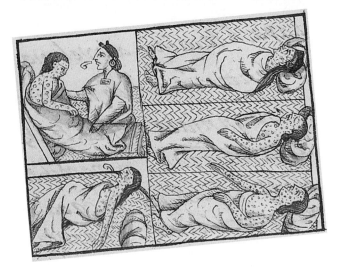

▲ *This codex shows Indians suffering from smallpox. Why was this European disease so deadly to the Indians?*

in some form. Many die, but children born after a woman recovers from the disease inherit antibodies which help them survive when they contact the disease in childhood. Chicken pox is the best example of this principle in American society today. Nearly everyone catches it, but few become seriously ill. Because American Indians had no previous exposure to such illness, epidemics struck them hard. Once exposed, they died at rapid rates.

The cruelest disease for the Indians was smallpox. Not only did it cause the most deaths, but it badly disfigured those who survived. But cholera, measles, or influenza could destroy an entire village in a few weeks' time. Among the Spanish-controlled populations in Mesoamerica, the number of deaths was staggering. From about 25 million in 1500, the population had fallen to 3 million by 1650. In the regions north of Mexico, disease was also devastating. Because the Indian groups of that region were more scattered, however, disease did not kill in such high numbers.

Other Nations in North America

The gold and silver taken from the Americas in Spanish ships excited the envy of monarchs all over Europe. Several nations began to send out their own expeditions in search of empires like those of the Incas and the Aztecs. Other expeditions continued the search for a sea route, a "Northwest Passage," to the Indies. Giovanni da Verrazzano, an Italian sailing under the French flag, touched the American coast in 1542. Englishman Henry Hudson sailed for two nations: in 1609 he claimed the Hudson River (New York) for the Dutch, and in 1610 he claimed Hudson's Bay (Canada) for England.

While the Spanish took note of all these voyages, the French explorers were the ones who worried them. Frenchman Jacques Cartier had made three trips to Canada beginning in 1535. He traveled up the St. Lawrence River to what is now Montreal. Within another century the French had reached present-day Wisconsin. Between 1659 and 1670, they explored to the west through Lake Superior. In 1672 Louis Joliet, an American-born fur trader, and Jacques Marquette, a Jesuit priest, charted hundreds of miles of the Mississippi River. A few years later Robert de La Salle led an expedition down the Mississippi to its mouth on the Gulf of Mexico. La Salle claimed for France the Mississippi **watershed**, that is, all the rivers that entered it, and the drainage area of those rivers. He named the entire area Louisiana for his king, Louis XIV. In 1718, the French built a fort and established a settlement at New Orleans. It was this last move that made the Spanish feel that the French were in America to stay. They began to worry that the French would try to claim lands west of the Mississippi that Spain had already claimed.

There were no great Indian empires on the North Atlantic coast to rival those of the Aztecs or the Incas. European explorers did, however, chart and map the lands they saw, and claim those lands for their sponsors. They also reported on the other riches of America, including the great fishing banks in the North Atlantic and the large quantities of fur-bearing animals. Especially important to the Europeans, whose own lands were becoming deforested, were the huge stands of valuable timber.

The reports of these lands excited the interest of many Europeans. They imagined that the lands they read or heard about could be theirs for the taking. This was the generation of Europeans who would come to America to stay.

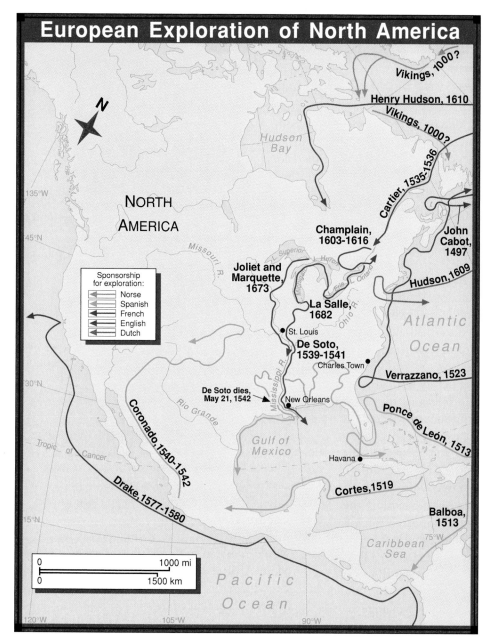

European Exploration of North America

NORTH AMERICA

Hudson Bay

Vikings, 1000?

Henry Hudson, 1610

Vikings, 1000?

Cartier, 1535-1536

Champlain, 1603-1616

John Cabot, 1497

Joliet and Marquette, 1673

La Salle, 1682

Hudson, 1609

L. Superior

L. Huron

L. Erie

L. Ontario

Missouri R.

St. Louis

De Soto, 1539-1541

Charles Town

Atlantic Ocean

Verrazzano, 1523

Sponsorship for exploration:
- Norse
- Spanish
- French
- English
- Dutch

De Soto dies, May 21, 1542

New Orleans

Mississippi R.

Ponce de León, 1513

Coronado, 1540-1542

Rio Grande

Gulf of Mexico

Havana

Cortes, 1519

Drake, 1577-1580

Tropic of Cancer

Balboa, 1513

Caribbean Sea

135°W

45°N

30°N

15°N

120°W

105°W

90°W

75°W

0 — 1000 mi
0 — 1500 km

Pacific Ocean

◄ *Many European nations sponsored exploratory voyages to the New World. Why did the French concentrate their exploration efforts in the Northeast and on the watershed of the Mississippi River?*

SECTION 5 REVIEW

1. **List** two reasons that critics of Columbus thought his journey must fail.
2. **Relate** briefly the origin of the name *America*.
3. **Explain** why so many indigenous people died from diseases that were not usually fatal to Europeans.
4. **Describe** the conditions that resulted in enslaved people from Africa being brought to Santo Domingo in 1517.
5. **Summarize** briefly, from clues in the chapter, the general attitude of Europeans regarding the resources of the Americas.

Summary

For hundreds of centuries, Indians were the sole occupants of the American continents. We cannot be certain when they first came to this land or how many migrations took place. But there is a growing understanding of how these first Americans lived during the thousands of years when they were isolated from people in other parts of the world. In A.D. 1500, American Indian societies were still dynamic and changing.

African societies possessed many characteristics similar to those of American Indians. Although great civilizations created extensive trading networks across Africa, most Africans lived in small villages, making their living through farming, hunting, and fishing. Like American Indians, they, too, had great regard for nature and had strong family ties.

By the late 1400s, several European nations were struggling to break Italy's monopoly of trade with the East. The desire to get a share of this trade and a lively interest in geography and navigation led to the search for new routes to the Orient. Columbus's voyage opened up a whole new world to the Europeans. The Spanish were the first to explore the new lands. Other Europeans began to search for a northwest passage to the East Indies as well as for riches. Although they found no easy routes to Asia and no empires to pillage, they did discover the other great resources of America.

The explorers themselves did little to change the nature of Indian societies in North America. The colonists would be the ones who would alter the traditional ways of life of the American Indians and of generations of West Africans.

Vocabulary

agricultural revolution	archeologist
ancestor worship	astrolabe
animism	caravel
anthropologist	conquistador
egalitarian	pueblo
ethnohistorian	quadrant
geologist	Renaissance
kivas	sachem
matrilineal	stewardship
matrilocal	tribute
mother culture	watershed

On a sheet of paper write the vocabulary term from the list that correctly completes each sentence. You will not use every term.

1. A(n) ||||||||| studies the physical, cultural, and social factors of human behavior.
2. A professional who uses data from other specialists, as well as oral history and written records, to study human behavior is called a(n) ||||||||| .
3. The period that describes when cultures learned to plant and harvest grain and other crops on a regular, predictable basis is called the ||||||||| .
4. Round, underground structures built by the Anasazi were called ||||||||| .
5. The concept of being responsible for something without owning it is known as ||||||||| .
6. The belief that many forces in nature were controlled by spirits is known as ||||||||| .
7. The ||||||||| was the head of the tribe in the Iroquois nation.
8. In a(n) ||||||||| culture, males, upon marriage, would move in with the wife's family.
9. Many African societies, where family ties and knowledge of past generations were extremely important, practiced ||||||||| .
10. The ||||||||| was a navigational tool that helped determine latitude.

Review Questions

1. Why is it difficult for scholars to completely explain the origins and early life of America's first people?
2. Why would the Mexican Olmecs be considered a mother culture?
3. Why did only some American Indians practice agriculture?

4. How did many early American Indian cultures regard the land?
5. How did widespread trading networks affect both American Indians and West Africans?
6. In what ways were early American Indian and African cultures and religious beliefs similar?
7. Why were European nations anxious to control trade routes to Asia?
8. What European nations were actively engaged in exploration of the New World?
9. Why were Columbus's voyages so important to Spain?
10. What actions by France in the New World caused Spain the most worry?

Critical Historical Thinking

Writing Answer each of the following questions by writing one or more complete paragraphs:

1. The first people to settle in the Americas migrated in groups from Asia. What are two possible reasons for the mass migrations?
2. Why do archeologists believe the Mound Builder cultures are of key importance to our knowledge of history?
3. How would the discovery of an all-water route between Europe and Asia have lowered prices of Eastern goods?
4. Man's exploration of his environment continues to the present day. In what ways are the motives guiding the exploration of outer space similar to or different from the motives of early European explorations?

Making Connections with Archeology

Archeologists reconstruct their societies by close examination of material left behind by various cultures. By comparing the sites of many groups of

people within a region, it is usually possible for archeologists to draw conclusions about their lives.

▪ Work with a group of four or five other students and imagine you are a team of archeologists "working a dig" of an agricultural people, such as the Anasazi or Hohokam in the American Southwest. You have uncovered items of material culture such as those illustrated in the chapter. Imagine what use these people might have made of these remains. What additional material could they have left behind to help you uncover their past? Report your findings to the class.

▪ Work with a group of four or five students to bring recyclable trash from one location (such as a home or office) over several days. Each day, visit the scene and place the trash in a large plastic bag exactly as you found it. After collecting for 3 or 4 days, spread out the contents of the plastic bags in rows, being careful to preserve the order of the material. You now have a simple "archeological dig" representing recent history. Make inferences about the activities of the people from your collection site. Present your findings to the whole class.

Additional Skills Practice

Choose ten events you think have been especially important in your life and use them to make a personal time line. Remember to select beginning and ending dates, as well as the intervals for the time line segments. Give your time line a title and illustrate it. Then answer the following questions about your time line:

1. How many years does the time line cover?
2. What interval did you use between the segments of the time line?
3. Could any of the events be classified as political, military, or economic?
4. Which events seem to have a cause-and-effect relationship?
5. Is any event clearly not related to any of the others? If so, why did you include it?

European Settlements in the Americas

By the early 1600s, the colonization of North America had begun in earnest. The monarchs of Spain, France, Holland, and England hoped that possessing colonies would make their nations more powerful and more respected. European colonists had a variety of motives for braving the dangerous ocean crossing. Some wanted to make their fortunes; others simply wanted land of their own. Many wanted to escape intolerable conditions at home. Puritans, Quakers, and other religious and social visionaries hoped to establish a new life in a place where they would be free from persecution. Whatever the reasons for European settlements in America, the first colonies displayed distinct differences in religious and economic character. Such diversity would become a hallmark of American society.

◄ *This figurine represents a European sea captain as seen by Haida Indians on the Pacific coast. What feeling is implied by the stance of the figure?*

Spanish Colonies in North America

It was inevitable that the colonizing nations of Europe would clash over control of the North American continent. The first confrontation came in 1565, between the French and the Spanish. A group of French Protestants tried to establish a foothold in Florida at Fort Caroline, near present-day Jacksonville. These settlers wanted to escape persecution in France, and the French king was anxious to get rid of them. But a French fleet bringing supplies to the colonists was threatened by a Spanish warship. The fleet moved farther out to sea, and a raging storm scattered the ships. Thus, the colonists were unprotected when the Spanish commander, Pedro Menéndez de Avilés ordered them killed. Menéndez had once boasted that he would "hang and behead all Lutherans [Protestants] whom I shall find." At Fort Caroline, he fulfilled this boast. Aided by 500 Spanish soldiers, he destroyed the fort and killed all of its occupants. The French quickly lost interest in Florida. The Spanish then accelerated their efforts to colonize Florida and the western lands they believed were theirs by right of discovery.

What were the motives for Spanish colonization?
What different kinds of Spanish settlements evolved?
Why were the Spanish more successful in the Southwest than in the Southeast?

▲ *This lithograph shows the Spanish fort at St. Augustine. Some of the city's walls and houses still stand. Why did the Spanish think they needed forts all across the northern borders of the land they claimed as Florida?*

The Spanish Missions

From the first voyage of discovery, the Spanish regarded the Americas as their own territory. They had taken vast amounts of gold and silver from Mexico and South America. It was natural that they would expect to find more riches in North America. In addition to the goal of increasing their wealth, the Spanish had two further goals for colonization.

They wanted to convert the Indians to Catholicism, and they wanted to keep other European nations out of the lands they had claimed.

When the French attempted to settle Fort Caroline, the Spanish decided they needed to protect their claim by colonizing that region. After destroying the French colony, Commander Menéndez and his men built their own stronghold, St. Augustine, in 1565. (It is now the oldest continuously inhabited city founded by Europeans in North America.) Then the Spanish established a chain of 32 missions stretching as far as the present-day southern border of South Carolina. Completed by 1665, these missions were deserted by 1690. The Indians would not accept the Spanish religion, and they frequently raided Spanish settlements in retaliation for the enslavement of some of their people. The Spanish maintained some coastal settlements in Florida to protect their Caribbean shipping, but they now turned most of their attention to the lands west of the Mississippi.

Because the French were exploring the lower reaches of the Mississippi River and had established settlements by the early 1700s, the Spanish feared they might try to colonize west of the Mississippi in

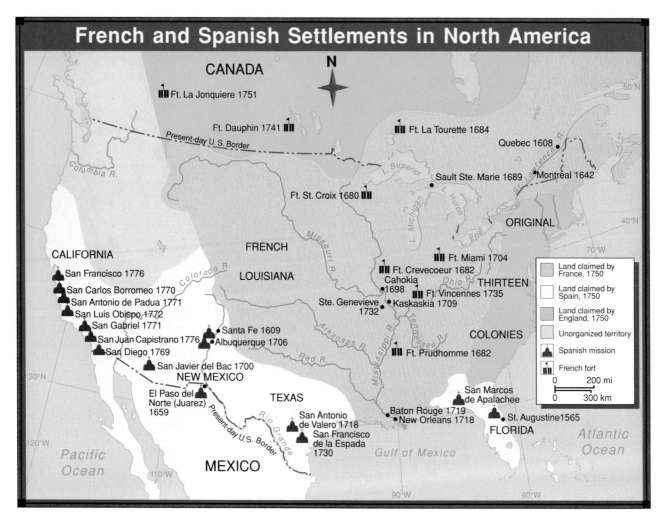

French and Spanish Settlements in North America

▲ *In North America, the French established many fur trading forts and the Spanish established many missions and presidios. Why were the Spanish more worried about French claims to the land than about British claims?*

Texas. This led the Spanish to establish a number of missions and **presidios**, or forts, from East Texas to present-day El Paso. One of the most famous missions, San Antonio de Valero, is better known to us as the Alamo. Many of these missions were short-lived because they did not receive adequate supplies from the Spanish forces in Mexico. These forces were preoccupied with events in California and New Mexico.

The Spanish moved into California because they feared that the Russians, who had successfully established fur-trading outposts in Alaska, might begin to move down the Pacific coast. Beginning in 1769, **Father Junípero Serra** set up a chain of missions that stretched from San Diego to San Francisco. Presidios supported the missions, just as they did in Texas.

The mission and the presidio were the keys to Spanish control in both California and Texas. The Indians were forced to provide labor; the priests taught them Catholicism and new methods of agriculture. The soldiers of the presidio made these Indians stay at the mission and repelled attacks by Indians living outside of the mission. Many of the

This Navajo pictograph in Arizona's Canyon del Muerto shows a black-robed friar and his party. The Indians had never seen horses before so it was important to record this startling event. Why do you think the Indians were so anxious to get horses of their own?

California Indians who lived at the missions died of epidemic disease. Many nearby Indians died of starvation because they could not find or produce sufficient food on the poor lands allotted to them by the Spanish.

New Mexico

Although there were problems between the Indians and the Spaniards in the colony of New Mexico, it would become the most successful of Spain's colonies north of Mexico. The early Spanish explorers had not found riches there, but they did note that the open land could be irrigated by the fast-flowing rivers and could become a productive area for growing crops.

As early as 1598, Juan de Oñate (ohn-YAH-tay) had led a group of colonists to the region north of the Rio Grande. These colonists set up small agricultural villages and ranches along the rivers and established the mission and town of Santa Fe in 1609. The Spanish forced the local Indians to tend the settlers' fields and livestock.

The **Pueblo Indians** resisted these settlers, killing those who ventured away from the villages and stealing livestock whenever they could. In 1680, under the leadership of **Popé** (poh-PAY), they launched a coordinated attack against Santa Fe and the outlying villages, managing to drive the Spanish out of the region. When Popé died in 1692, the rebellion collapsed and the Spanish returned. At the time of Popé's Rebellion, there were about 2,800 Spanish and 30,000 Pueblos living along the Rio Grande. By 1750, the Spanish population had increased to 5,200, while the Pueblo population had fallen to 13,500.

Eventually, through the missionary efforts of the Spanish priests and through intermarriages, the two groups developed relatively friendly relationships and were able to maintain them. The Pueblo Indians were treated just like other subjects in the Spanish empire, and they adopted many aspects of Spanish culture. They learned the language, took Spanish names, and incorporated Catholicism into their own religious practices. Even today, many Pueblo Indians hold their annual corn dance on the feast day of the village saint, chosen long ago by the village's resident Spanish priest.

▲ *Spanish explorers and settlers in the Southwest found ancient societies that depended on corn as a staple food. The Green Corn Dance ceremony was held in the fall to thank the gods for a good harvest and to ask for their continued blessings. What kinds of ceremonial costumes and headdresses were worn?*

In spite of the harshness of the early conquistadores and the abuses and inefficiencies of the early mission system, the 500,000 or so Spaniards who settled in Mexico and North America had much positive impact. By combining their traditional way of life with cultural ideas and agricultural methods they learned from the Indians, they produced a uniquely American culture. Today this culture is called either Spanish American, Mexican American, Hispanic, or Latino.

SECTION 1 REVIEW

1. **List** three goals of Spanish colonization.
2. **Describe** the Spanish plan for controlling the American Indian population.
3. **Name** the regions of the present-day United States where the Spanish concentrated their settlements.
4. **Identify** Father Junípero Serra.
5. **Summarize** briefly what lasting effect Spanish colonization efforts had on North America.

French and Dutch Colonies

....The French and the Dutch interests in establishing colonies grew slowly. Neither nation could find many people who were interested in becoming colonists. Perhaps the French were deterred by the remark made by Jacques Cartier in 1534, when he set foot on the rocky shore of Labrador in northeast Canada. He complained, "I am rather inclined to believe that this is the land God gave to Cain." The Dutch were so busy making enormous profits from trade with Africa and Asia that they didn't think much about moving across the ocean to the west. But when both the French and the Dutch began to realize how much money could be made from the fur trade in America, their interests in establishing American colonies were sharpened.

How were the French able to make huge profits from the fur trade?

What factors worked against the development of a large population in New France?

Why did New Amsterdam so quickly become an international city?

French Explorations

It was not until 65 years after Cartier's trip to Labrador that a successful French colony was established. **Samuel de Champlain** (sham-PLAYN) set up the first permanent settlements at Quebec (1608) and Montreal (1611). Both attracted some farmers, but both became more important as centers for the highly profitable fur trade.

Fur traders became central figures in New France, as the vast territory where these new settlements were located was then called. The region was covered with forests, and it supported enormous numbers of beaver, otter, mink, and lynx. Their pelts brought good money in Europe. Fur was used for cloaks, bed covers, rugs, and trim on fancy garments. Beaver pelts were used for making felt hats, which were popular from about 1500 to 1840.

Each year, French fur traders set out from Montreal to spend the winter in Indian camps to the west. Indian men did the trapping, and Indian women cleaned and pressed the skins to preserve them and make them less bulky for transport. In the spring, the traders, often accompanied by their Indian wives and friends, returned to Montreal with

◄ *These French Canadians are practicing an unusual method of obtaining furs: shooting instead of trapping the otter. The majority of furs were obtained through trapping. Why would trapping be more efficient?*

their canoes loaded with furs. The fur trade did not require a large French workforce. So, since few farmers were willing to settle so far north, the French colonies never became highly populated. By 1663, only about 3,000 French had made their homes in New France.

Through the fur trade, the French established a close relationship with many of the regional Indian tribes. They often traveled with Huron fur-trapping and raiding parties, and they explored and laid claim to the territories west and south of Montreal and Quebec. Armed with French guns and having the French as allies, the Hurons and their Algonquin allies defeated the Mohawks several times. The Mohawks were members of the **Iroquois League**, which was formed as a religious and ritual organization around 1350. By 1570, the league had also become a **diplomatic alliance**, the member tribes working together to meet political goals. Its other members acted with the Mohawks to block French movement south of the St. Lawrence River.

The French continued to explore areas west and south of their colony, and in 1682 La Salle traveled down the Mississippi River to the Gulf of Mexico and claimed its entire watershed for King Louis XIV. In 1699, the French established a colony at Biloxi. They soon set up plantations along the Mississippi River farmed by enslaved laborers imported from the West Indies.

The French also set up a few trading posts between Louisiana and Spanish Florida. Louisiana never became self-sufficient, and by the 1760s it contained fewer than 10,000 people. Included in that number were more than 5,000 enslaved Africans. Another group of Louisianan settlers were the **Cajuns**, exiles from the French colony of Acadia (present-day Nova Scotia and adjacent areas) from which the word *Cajun* is derived.

The French king and his supporters were never very interested in owning colonies in North America. Their island possessions in the West Indies seemed more valuable than the cold lands north of the St. Lawrence River or the hot and humid lands along the Mississippi. They were content to take part of the profits from the fur trade and to help support the Catholic missionaries who went out among the Indians.

New Netherland

During the 1600s, the Dutch grew to be the greatest sea power in the world, controlling the trade routes from Africa to India, Indonesia, and beyond to China and Japan. They were active in the Atlantic as well. In 1628, they seized a fleet of Spanish ships that was taking gold and silver from the Americas back to Spain. They also raided English ships loaded with expensive tobacco. To provide a land base for attacks on Spanish ships and to exploit the riches of the fur trade, the Dutch wanted to set up a North American colony to be called New Netherland. Because of their preoccupation with trade, the Dutch government placed their colonizing venture under the direction of a commercial firm, the Dutch West India Company. This company was to colonize the land and extract what riches it could from the area around present-day New York, which had been claimed in 1609 by explorer **Henry Hudson**.

The West India Company did grant a few large landed estates along the Hudson River to landowners, who were known as **patroons**, but the majority of Dutch settlers came to trade. For the Dutch, like the French, successful colonization depended on establishing a cooperative relationship with the Indians. The Dutch merchants operated trading posts, and the Indians trapped animals and delivered fur pelts. The Dutch built their first trading post, Fort Orange, in 1624 on the present site of Albany, New York. There they traded with the Iroquois and the Mahicans. They also took control of New Sweden, a colony founded in 1638 as a joint enterprise of Dutch and Swedish merchants. This colony, which would become Delaware, consisted of about 400 Swedish and Finnish settlers and a few trading posts strung out along the Delaware River.

The city of New Amsterdam, founded in 1624 on the present site of New York City, became the most important Dutch commercial center. It served as headquarters for the Dutch fur trade of the interior and became known for its good port facilities. Since the Dutch permitted religious freedom, the city acted as a haven for diverse religious groups

▲ *What characteristics of Dutch architecture can be seen in New Amsterdam's city hall?*

from several European nations, as well as for religious **dissenters**, those who did not agree with the commonly held views. A few Africans who had made their way north from the West Indies island of Barbados, or from Virginia, also settled there. By 1643, a visitor claimed that one could hear 18 different languages spoken on the streets of New Amsterdam.

The Dutch never were serious contenders in the race to colonize North America. Their main interest in the 1600s was to increase their worldwide naval power. In North America, they were content to make money from their trade with the Indians.

SECTION 2 REVIEW

1. **Describe** how French efforts differed from those of the Spanish in establishing relationships with the Indians.
2. **Define** the term *diplomatic alliance.*
3. **Explain** why the Dutch wanted to establish a colony in North America.
4. **Name** the territories claimed by the Dutch in North America.
5. **Discuss** why the French and Dutch were more interested in the fur trade than in establishing permanent settlements.

England's Southern Colonies

England's motives for attempting to establish a base in the Americas were sparked by envy of the great riches the Spanish had taken from their American empire. The English wanted the gold and silver that Europeans of the time believed could be found all over the American continent. They also wanted a source for food crops, such as sugar and rice, that could not be grown in England. Above all, they wanted to compete with the Spanish for power and prestige.

The very first English colonists must have felt, however, that the dream of growing rich had turned into a nightmare. They lived with constant hardship and misery. George Percy, a settler in Jamestown in 1607–1608, described the suffering of the colonists. "Our men," he wrote, "were destroyed by cruel diseases ... and by wars. Some departed suddenly, but for the most part they died of meer famine ... which brought our men to be most feeble wretches." Four out of five of these first settlers perished from starvation, disease, or Indian attack. Still, more colonists continued to make the dangerous journey to a new land, and eventually they carved five colonies out of the lands from Chesapeake Bay to Spanish Florida.

What motives lay behind English colonization of North America?

Why did the English colony at Jamestown come close to failing?

How were the colonies south of Virginia settled?

English and Spanish Rivalry

In 1584, **Sir Walter Raleigh**, an adventurous man of great wit and ability, obtained a charter from Queen Elizabeth I to settle a region that extended from present-day South Carolina north to about

Early Images of the Algonquin Indians

Two thoughtful scholars took part in Raleigh's 1585 attempt to colonize Roanoke Island. Thomas Hariot, a brilliant recent graduate of England's prestigious Oxford University, studied the land and its resources, and made a thorough report on Indian culture. Hariot prepared for this mission by studying the native language for a year with two Indians who had traveled to England with the Barlowe expedition Raleigh sent out in 1584.

John White, who had some reputation as an artist and mapmaker, was hired to illustrate Hariot's report. The maps the two prepared together were the most accurate ones made in the sixteenth century. White's sketches and watercolors provide the best description we have of the way of life of the Algonquin Indians at the time of first European contact. White prepared some of his many paintings while he served as governor of the ill-fated Roanoke Colony.

1. If White.'s paintings provided the only information you had about the Indians, what conclusions would you draw about their way of life?
2. What attitudes toward the Indians held by the painter are reflected in these paintings?

◄ *The plan of the Indian village of Secoton was drawn by John White. Note the multifamily lodges and the communal fields. Can you imagine the purpose of the sheltered platform in the cornfield?*

◄ *This work, also by White, shows the Secotons on a typical evening fishing expedition. White's companion, Thomas Hariot, wrote, "As they have neither steel nor iron, they fasten the sharp tail of a certain fish ... to reeds or to the end of a long rod, and with this they spear fish both by day and by night." How many different methods of fishing can you describe?*

▲ *This detail from a colored drawing shows Sir Walter Raleigh spreading his cloak so that Queen Elizabeth may protect her shoes and skirts from the damp and dirty ground. Most historians believe the story of this event is apocryphal. What does the term* apocryphal *mean?*

what is now New York City. He named the territory Virginia in honor of his sponsor, who never married and liked to be called the Virgin Queen. Raleigh felt it was imperative that the English have a presence in North America. He wanted the English to share in the immense wealth to be had from the Americas.

During the sixteenth-century Reformation, Henry VIII, the father of Elizabeth I, had declared England a Protestant nation. He established the Church of England—the Anglican church—and this church adopted a structure different from that of the Roman Catholic Church. While the Church of England retained a **hierarchy**, or ranking, made up of priests and bishops, it cut all ties with Rome. The clergy now answered to the monarch rather than to the pope. Spain, as the world's "most Catholic nation," hoped to bring the English back into the fold.

Political and religious differences between England and Spain led to Elizabeth I expelling the Spanish ambassador, and the Spanish seized all English ships in Spanish ports. A sea war erupted. The English had no real navy, so Elizabeth I issued commissions to individuals who would attack Spanish shipping. Known as **privateers**, these seamen essentially practiced state-sponsored piracy, enriching the government as well as themselves by seizing Spanish cargoes and sharing their booty with the queen and her court. As part of their efforts, Raleigh and his associates sent ships to America to explore the possibilities of setting up a base near the Spanish shipping lanes in the Caribbean. They also hoped to find a location for the first English colony.

The Roanoke Settlement

Raleigh first sent two sea captains to search out a likely spot. On their return, the two men had glowing comments to make about Roanoke Island, off the coast of present-day North Carolina. One captain, Arthur Barlowe, claimed the location would serve as a shelter for English ships, would be near enough to prey on Spanish treasure ships, and would be productive enough to support a thriving colony. Barlowe claimed that "the soile is the most plentifull, sweete, fruitfull and wholesome of all the worlde."

The first attempt at settlement (1585) ended in failure, but in 1587 Raleigh sent out another group of more than 100 men, women, and children under the leadership of **John White**. White had participated in the earlier venture. This group landed in July and got off to a good start, using the houses built by the earlier colonists and planning for gardens and field crops. On August 18, they celebrated the birth of White's granddaughter, **Virginia Dare**, the first English child to be born in the colonies. A few days later, White sailed to England to recruit more colonists and obtain more provisions.

White's return trip to the colony was delayed, however, because the Spanish chose this time to retaliate against English privateers who had been

picking off Spanish ships. They assembled the great **Spanish Armada**—130 ships, 8,000 sailors, and 19,000 soldiers—to destroy British shipping. Instead, some 54 Spanish ships were broken up by storms and by British ships, and the battle ended in a rout of the Spanish. This defeat of the Spanish Armada in 1588 would lead to England's control of the seas in the next century. But for the immediate future, conditions remained unsettled. No one was sure if the Spanish would regroup to fight the English, so it was not until 1590 that White managed to return to Roanoke Island.

The colonists were missing. Their houses remained standing, and White's personal books, drawings, and suit of armor had been carefully buried. The word *Croatoan* (kroh-ah-TOH-uhn) was carved on a post and *CRO* on a nearby tree. White and others believed the colonists had gone off with the Croatoan Indians, but before a thorough search could be made, a storm began to break up the English ships, and the party decided to return to England. The colony at Roanoke Island had been lost, and Raleigh, who had put much of his personal fortune into the efforts to found these colonies, turned to other pursuits.

Changes Under King James I

In 1603, Queen Elizabeth died, and her successor, James I, signed a treaty with Spain. Attacks on Spanish shipping became the work of pirates, rather than of privateers who had a queen's official backing. For a time, it seemed that efforts at colonization would also be curtailed. Raleigh had lost so much of his personal fortune through the failed attempts to colonize Roanoke that others were discouraged from investing. Eventually, however, interested speculators found another source of funding.

Joint-stock companies were already used to establish business enterprises, especially overseas trading companies. In a joint-stock company, many individuals invested money by purchasing stock. They shared both the profits and the risk of failure. Because so many others had also invested, the amount that each individual might lose was not too burdensome. With the Spanish no longer able to control the Atlantic trade, investors felt ready to gamble that colonies would make a profit. They believed that the colonies had precious resources that could be sent back to England and sold for a profit. In 1606, James I issued charters to two separate groups of investors. The Virginia Company of Plymouth and the Virginia Company of London obtained exclusive rights from the king to settle North America. The Virginia Company of London's charter authorized a colony in Virginia, where rumors had it that gold and silver could easily be found.

Jamestown Colony

Aboard the three small ships sent out by the London Company in 1607, 104 men and boys prepared to try their luck. Their first attempt to land

▼ *This engraving of Jamestown shows the colonists getting off to a good start by felling trees and building houses. Why did their leader write that "they never did knowe what a days work was"?*

failed. Repelled by Indians, they decided to sail into Chesapeake Bay until they found a safer location. Choosing a river with a northwest bend, some 30 miles upstream they found their site. They named both the river and the settlement after their king.

From the beginning, the **Jamestown Colony** was in trouble. The peninsula on which the settlers built their first stockade seemed as if it could be easily protected from outside attacks. But it was swampland that harbored water- and insect-borne diseases. Many settlers quickly succumbed to dysentery and typhoid. Disease was only one cause of death. Hunger was another. These colonists—and those who followed in the next few years—simply did not know how to make the wilderness fit for domestic life. One-third of the settlers in the first three groups were gentlemen adventurers who spent their time seeking gold and other precious metals. Others were unskilled servants who, according to the colony's leader, **Captain John Smith**, "never did knowe what a days work was." What the colony needed, he claimed, were carpenters, farmers, fishermen, and blacksmiths.

What is more, the colonists did not get along with the Indians. About 14,000 people representing some 30 Indian groups had formed a confederacy under the leader **Powhatan** (pow-uh-TAN). This able leader brought corn and other food supplies to the Jamestown settlers during the first fall season. Then the colonists foolishly raided Indian supplies for more corn and tried to frighten the Indians with military might. Powhatan and his allies refused further help, and they began to kill settlers who left the community in search of food. When supply ships sent by the company were delayed by storms, the colonists simply went without food. The winter of 1609–1610 became known as the

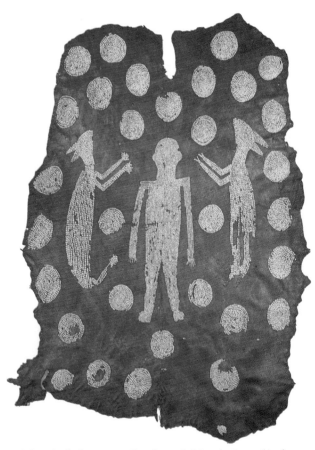

▲ *This cloak, known as Powhatan's Mantle, is made of tanned buckskin decorated with shells. It was probably used in ritual ceremonies. Taken to England by early explorers, it aroused considerable curiosity about American Indians. (Ashmolean Museum, Oxford.)*

"starving time." George Percy did not exaggerate when he described the "meer famine" and the "feeble wretches" who were soon to die.

The Virginia Company of London, however, would not give up. More supplies and more settlers, including farmers, came to the struggling colony. At first, the company promised colonists free land after seven years' settlement. When the company needed still more settlers, it began to offer 50 acres of land to anyone who would pay for transporting settlers to Virginia. With that incentive, more than 9,000 people traveled to Virginia between 1610 and 1622. Only 2,000 survived.

In spite of the horrendous death rate, some colonists carried on with their attempts to make the colony a successful venture. A number of men began profitable businesses, but it was the skill of planter **John Rolfe** that brought a more widespread prosperity to the colony. Rolfe experimented with the sweet-flavored, mild types of tobacco grown in the West Indies. By 1616, the first Virginia-grown crop reached England, and it brought huge profits. It seemed the colony could survive and make profits for the investors after all.

The next year Powhatan retired, and the leadership of the Chesapeake-area tribes passed to **Opechancanough** (oh-PEK-ahn-kahn-oh). Opechancanough began organizing for an all-out attack on the settlements. On Good Friday, 1622, Indians slaughtered cattle, burned buildings and crops, and killed more than one-fourth of Virginia's European population. The London Company could not recover from this disaster. In 1624, the king declared Virginia a royal colony to be ruled by the king through appointed officials.

A Haven for English Catholics

In spite of the difficulties experienced by the people of the Jamestown Colony, the next English colonizer in the Chesapeake region regarded the land north of Virginia as a haven. **Sir George Calvert**, Lord Baltimore, was a Roman Catholic

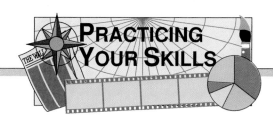

Evaluating an Engraving

One of the oldest methods of reproducing a picture is by making an engraving. An engraving is a picture that is cut or etched into wood or metal. The surface is spread with ink and then stamped on paper. Before the invention of the camera and photocopier, this was the most common method of making pictures available to a wide audience.

In the past, when many people could not read or write, using images was an important way to convey information. Today, studying pictures is an important tool for historians. Pictures show the environment, the daily tasks that occupied the people, and styles of architecture, clothing, tools, and utensils. The artist tried to convey the atmosphere of a place—peaceful, dangerous, lush, barren, etc.

Just as with written documents, however, pictures need to be analyzed and interpreted. Pictures can be misleading. Important issues must be considered when using pictures as historical sources. To analyze a picture ask yourself these questions:

- **Does the artist have a particular bias or point of view to express?** For what purpose did the artist create the picture? Was it an advertisement? A decorative piece? A political campaign?
- **Was the picture created in the same time period it depicts or at a later date?** The greater the time that has elapsed, the less reliable the picture may be in showing events as they happened.
- **What do the details of the picture tell you about its context?** Study the details of the picture. Look beyond the main subject to the background.

- **How accurate is the scene?** Read about the event and look at other pictures to help you decide.

Examine the engraving of early Jamestown on page 51 and answer the following questions:

1. What is your first impression of the scene that is shown? Describe the atmosphere of the engraving.
2. Make three columns on your paper and label them *People*, *Objects*, and *Activities*. List as many items from the picture as you can under each column. Which of these categories was most important to the artist? Why?
3. Write four questions that come to mind as you look at this picture. From text readings and class discussions, can you make educated guesses as to the answers? For example, you might wonder what is in the barrels the men are unloading. You might guess it is water, ale, or even pitch for building the houses.
4. Does the evidence in this engraving support or contradict anything you have already learned about life in early Jamestown? Has the artist left out any important information that would make the picture more accurate?
5. For what purpose might this engraving have been made?

convert and, like other English Catholics of the time, was persecuted for his faith. He persuaded his friend, King Charles I, to give him a grant of 10 million acres located on both sides of Chesapeake Bay. On that land, Calvert hoped his Catholic friends and relatives would be able to support themselves from huge grants of land while they practiced their religion freely. Calvert envisioned grand manor houses surrounded by lush fields cared for by happy peasants. These aristocratic landholders were to provide political leadership, while peasant farmers performed the labor. The colony would be called Maryland after King Charles's wife, Henrietta Maria. But before Calvert could act on this scheme, he died, leaving his 26-year-old son to carry out the project.

▲ *The two priests standing to the right of the cross indicate that this is a Roman Catholic group that has just landed in America. It appears that Lord Calvert is making a promise to God. Why would this scene be both an accurate and inaccurate depiction of the actual founding of the Maryland colony?*

Cecilius Calvert, now the second Lord Baltimore and holder of the charter, found that as lord proprietor of Maryland he had great power. Not only did he own an enormous quantity of land, he also held extensive governmental powers. He could run the colony any way he chose. For a time, he tried to carry out his father's wishes. He did give huge grants of land to aristocrats, but he soon found that few farmers wanted to work like peasants. They would not emigrate if the only reward would be to enrich others. Accordingly, Calvert offered 100 acres of land to each married couple who agreed to settle in Maryland, and he offered additional acreage if the couple had children old enough to work, or if they agreed to bring other settlers with them. He even allowed a few single women to own land.

Several thousand Puritans took up this offer, and the colony that had been founded in 1634 as a Catholic land became overwhelmingly Protestant.

To prevent religious dissension and to protect the Catholic colonists, Calvert issued the **Toleration Act of 1649**, which guaranteed freedom of religion to all Christians. The Maryland settlers followed the example of the Virginia colonists, spreading out along the riverbanks, living on isolated farms, and growing tobacco. By 1670, the colony held 13,000 people with 823 farms located on the shores of Chesapeake Bay and along the major rivers.

Carolina Emerges as Two Colonies

In 1663, King Charles II of England presented eight of his friends and supporters with territory that they named Carolina. (The Latin version of Charles is *Carolus*.) The grant included all the land extending along the Atlantic coast from Virginia to Florida and west to the Pacific Ocean. The fact that France and Spain had claimed much of this territory did not greatly disturb King Charles II.

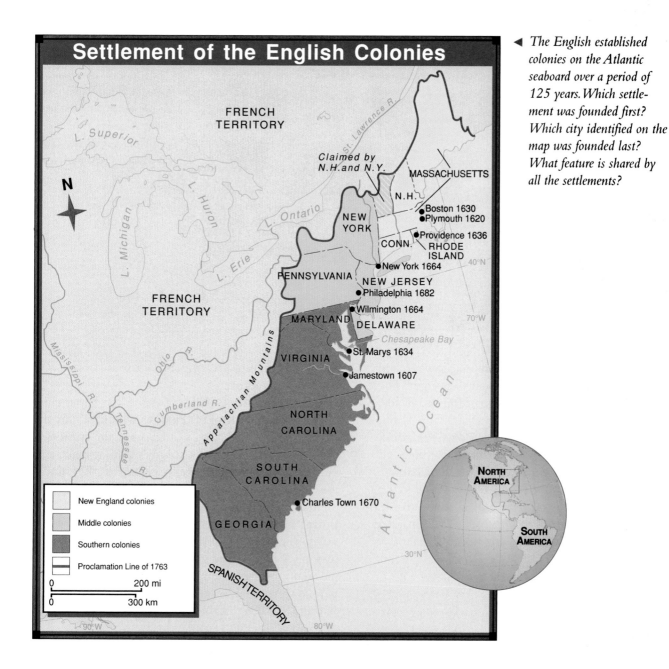

Settlement of the English Colonies

FRENCH TERRITORY

L. Superior

L. Michigan

L. Huron

St. Lawrence R.

Claimed by N.H. and N.Y.

MASSACHUSETTS

N.H.

L. Ontario

NEW YORK

● Boston 1630
● Plymouth 1620

L. Erie

CONN.

● Providence 1636

RHODE ISLAND

● New York 1664

40°N

FRENCH TERRITORY

PENNSYLVANIA

NEW JERSEY

● Philadelphia 1682

Mississippi R.

Ohio R.

Appalachian Mountains

● Wilmington 1664

MARYLAND

DELAWARE

70°W

Chesapeake Bay

Cumberland R.

VIRGINIA

● St. Marys 1634

Tennessee R.

● Jamestown 1607

NORTH CAROLINA

Atlantic Ocean

SOUTH CAROLINA

● Charles Town 1670

GEORGIA

NORTH AMERICA

SOUTH AMERICA

SPANISH TERRITORY

30°N

80°W

90°W

Legend:
- New England colonies
- Middle colonies
- Southern colonies
- Proclamation Line of 1763

0 — 200 mi
0 — 300 km

◄ *The English established colonies on the Atlantic seaboard over a period of 125 years. Which settlement was founded first? Which city identified on the map was founded last? What feature is shared by all the settlements?*

The eight **proprietors**, or legal owners, held most of the power to govern and dispose of the land. By 1670, they had encouraged the settlement of 140 English families, many of whom had migrated with their slaves from the sugar island of Barbados in the West Indies. These colonists founded what is now the city of Charleston. Although the tiny settlement became the target of raids by Indians and by Spaniards from Florida, the colonists held out. By 1700, they had established rice plantations along the numerous winding rivers. By 1720, they were successfully growing indigo, a source of blue dye. Indigo was an important **cash crop**, a product grown for sale as a source of income, in those days. Both rice and indigo required intensive hand labor. Increasingly, landowners turned to slaves to perform that work. In 1680, white settlers made up four-fifths of the population. By 1720, enslaved Africans outnumbered Europeans two to one.

This is a depiction of Oglethorpe's interview with Tomochichi in Savannah, Georgia. What impressions do you think the artist was trying to convey? What do you think might have been the purpose of the interview?

In the northern part of Carolina, however, a different kind of economy and society emerged. There was little fertile land near the coast for rice or tobacco plantations, and few rivers were large enough to allow for the shipment of crops on oceangoing vessels. Since the settlers in northern Carolina did not have an adequate market system for the few cash crops they grew, they had to become self-sufficient in food production and in government. By 1729, the two sections of the colony had separated to become North Carolina and South Carolina.

Georgia

Not founded until more than a century after Jamestown, Georgia was the last of the southern colonies established by England. Named for King George II, this colony was designed to serve two purposes. First, it would act as a buffer between the expanding South Carolina plantations and the Spanish settlements in Florida. Second, it would be a place where English debtors could be sent to give them a new start in life. In England, whole families lived in squalor and helplessness in debtors' prisons because they could not pay their bills. Since prisoners could not work to earn money, how could they ever leave their prisons? To relieve this hopeless situation, the English government sent some of the debtors to America.

Georgia, with its major settlement at Savannah, was under the control of **trustees** who acted for the crown. Unlike proprietors of colonies, the trustees could not own any of the colony's land or make any personal profit from their efforts. Instead, they acted for the king and out of their concern for England's debtors. Foremost among the trustees, **General James Oglethorpe** had been a member of a commission set up to investigate conditions in debtors' prisons. While he had great sympathy for poor people, like most rich men of his time he believed that people were poor because they had something wrong with their character. As a trustee, Oglethorpe developed rules and regulations by which the colonists had to agree to live. He believed that from such experiences the colonists would learn to be better people and would then become self-sufficient.

For the debtor colonists, being sent to America seemed little better than being in jail. They were completely regulated by the trustees, and they could not own more than 50 acres of land or plant crops of their own choosing. Later settlers, who came by choice, refused to pay attention to such rules. They purchased large tracts of land and slowly began to develop plantations run by slave labor. When the trustees' charter expired in 1752 as planned, Georgia became a royal colony. It had been a failure as a social experiment, but it did serve as a buffer against the Spanish.

SECTION 3 REVIEW

1. List three of England's motives for seeking colonies.
2. Describe some of the conditions that made settlement in Roanoke and Jamestown so difficult.
3. Analyze why Maryland was more successful as a colony than earlier attempts.
4. Explain the difference between a proprietor and a trustee.
5. Identify James Oglethorpe.

SECTION 4

Colonies in New England

While the Jamestown Colony struggled, other English people were hoping to establish religious colonies far to the north, in New England. Two groups took part: the **Puritans**, who wanted to purify and make changes within the Church of England; and the **Separatists**, who believed the English church to be so corrupt that it could not be saved. They wanted to do away with the Church of England, or at least separate from it. Both groups started their own churches in England, and both found themselves harassed by Church of England authorities. Both determined to brave the unknown dangers of the long trip across the Atlantic Ocean and settle in what they called "the wilderness of America" so they could be true to their beliefs. As William Bradford, governor of the Separatist colony at Plymouth, recorded, "They committed themselves to the will of God and resolved to proceed."

What motives brought colonists to New England?
What type of government did the Puritans establish in the Massachusetts Bay Colony?
Why did some colonists want to leave the Massachusetts Bay Colony?

The Separatists Leave England

In 1609, a group of about 125 Separatists moved from England to Holland (a part of the Netherlands) because the Dutch had a policy of religious tolerance. Although the Separatists found they could practice their religion freely in Holland, they feared that their children would forget the English language and way of life. When offered the opportunity to emigrate, about 30 of the group decided to make the journey to Virginia and start a community of their own.

The Separatists (also known as the Pilgrims) sailed from Holland in the summer of 1620. They stopped at Southampton in England to pick up more passengers, making a total of 35 Pilgrims and

▼ *Despite the fact that the* Mayflower *arrived well after Jamestown was established, the tiny ship that landed in New England has come to symbolize North America's first European colonists. Why do you think the Pilgrims remain such important representatives of our past?*

Introduction: Connecting History and Geography

A true understanding of history involves a basic knowledge of geography, the study of Earth and people's relationship to it. Studying Earth's character as a planet helps provide a deeper understanding of where things are and why they are there. Variations in such characteristics as landforms, climate, vegetation, and soils help explain the distribution of population and the development of societies.

Geographers work to understand the differences and similarities among places on Earth. To do this, they organize data into themes. Five themes of great importance in geography are location, place, region, people-environment relations, and movement. These five themes help provide a framework for understanding the world in which we live.

Location. Locations are reference points in space in the same way that dates are reference points in time. Location helps to define the distribution of climates, vegetation, natural resources, and patterns of human settlement.

Geography and City Location: The Fall Line

For 250 years, the Europeans who lived in Britain's thirteen colonies were confined to the Atlantic coastal plain, a narrow strip of land between the Atlantic Ocean and the Appalachian Mountains. Few settlers crossed the Appalachians into the continental interior until after the Revolutionary War. It was on the coastal plain and in the neighboring foothills, or piedmont, that the American nation took form.

Early on, most colonists were farmers who adapted their modes of land use to the different climates and landscapes of the New World. Other colonists were fishermen who plied the surrounding waters of the Atlantic. As the colonial economy matured, however, cities grew to serve the needs of a rapidly growing New World population and to maintain the burgeoning transatlantic trade between Britain and its New World colonies.

Geography played an important role in the sites of these cities. Some of the largest colonial cities were seaports located on deep, sheltered harbors—places like Boston and New York. Others, however, were located farther inland along the *fall line*, a natural break in terrain where streams plunged down from the old, hard rocks of the Appalachian Piedmont to the soft sands of the Atlantic coastal plain. The fall line was marked by rapids and waterfalls. It stretched from the outskirts of New York southward to Atlanta.

The fall line was a desirable site for city location for several reasons. First, its waterfalls provid-

▶ *Waterfalls such as these denote the location of the fall line, where highlands meet the coastal plain.*

Place. A place is a particular city, village, or area with physical and human characteristics that distinguish it from other places. These unique characteristics affect the unfolding of a place's history.

Region. Regions are parts of the Earth sharing one or more characteristics that distinguish them from surrounding areas. Geographers divide the world into regions to show similarities and differences among areas.

People-Environment Relations. The study of interactions between people and the environment helps us understand how people use the Earth. People modify their surroundings to suit their needs. How people change their environments and adapt to them depends on their beliefs, ideas, economy, social organization, and technology. The story of how people relate to their environment becomes an important part of their history.

Movement. Movement is the study of interactions among people and other life forms located in different places and different environments. Three types of movement are of special interest to geographers and historians. These are migration, transportation, and the spread of ideas. Movements of people have brought together a rich blend of cultures and talents that form the fabric of America's history.

---

ed a reliable source of water power for early industries. Second, the fall line was also the head of navigation. It was as far inland as possible that a city could still have access to ocean shipping. Finally, goods for export and those imported were usually loaded and unloaded at fall line cities. Bulky shipments from Europe were broken into smaller loads and goods for export were processed and assembled. Fall line cities came to operate as "break-in-bulk" points in colonial America's transatlantic trade. For these reasons, location on the fall line had substantial economic advantages in colonial America.

Among the largest cities located along the fall line are Trenton, Philadelphia, Wilmington, Baltimore, Washington, Richmond, Raleigh, Columbia, and Macon. Charlotte and Atlanta are located on rapid stretches of water farther inland on the Appalachian Piedmont itself.

1. What is the fall line? Why do streams fall rapidly along this line?
2. What is a break-in-bulk point?
3. Give three reasons why a city might benefit from location on the fall line.

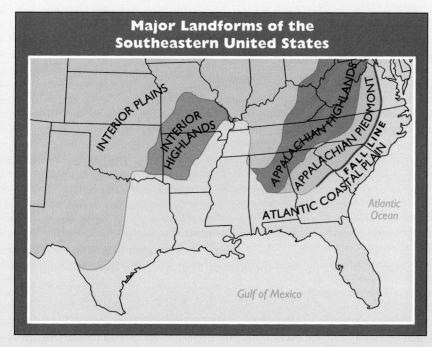

Major Landforms of the Southeastern United States

INTERIOR PLAINS

INTERIOR HIGHLANDS

APPALACHIAN HIGHLANDS

APPALACHIAN PIEDMONT

FALL LINE

ATLANTIC COASTAL PLAIN

Atlantic Ocean

Gulf of Mexico

◀ *This map defines major landforms of the Southeastern United States. Near what important city does the fall line disappear?*

▲ Because of a question about jurisdiction, the Mayflower Compact was drawn up and signed while everyone was still on board the ship. Do you recognize the names of any of these signatories?

▲ How does this 1640 engraving, showing the landing of the Pilgrims in Plymouth, Massachusetts, help you to understand who actually arrived on the Mayflower some twenty years before? Notice the clothing and the attitudes of the people.

66 other colonists eager to establish a colony "as a distinct body by themselves."

Before leaving England, the Separatists decided to settle north of the Jamestown Colony, where the Church of England was already established. But strong winds blew their ship, named the *Mayflower*, off course. When the passengers finally sighted land, they found themselves in the Cape Cod region, far north of their company's charter. Exhausted from their 67-day voyage, they determined to stay in the region and find a good site for settlement. They named their site Plymouth in honor of their funding company.

Because they were outside the boundaries of Virginia and under no European civil authority, the Pilgrims decided that before landing they would draw up a document stating their legal basis for governing themselves. This **Mayflower Compact** recognized James I as their king and stated that they would form a "civil body politic," which would "frame such just and equal laws . . . as shall be thought most right and convenient for the general good of the colony." The writers of the document did not intend to set up a nation of their own, but they did set a **precedent**, or important example. They formed a **compact**, or solemn agreement, promoting self-government. Women were not allowed to sign the compact because they were not considered able enough to take part in political affairs or to manage property on their own. That view reflected the general English practice of the time of denying political rights to women.

Plymouth Colony

Like Jamestown, the Plymouth Colony had a difficult beginning. The colonists had little time to provide themselves with adequate houses before the harsh winter set in. Their food supplies ran short, and illness took many lives. But spring brought relief in the person of **Tisquantum** (tee-SKWAHN-tum), called Squanto by the colonists. Six years previously,

This painting shows Governor John Winthrop landing with a group of Puritans from the ship Arabella *in Salem Harbor, Massachusetts, in June of 1630. What nation is represented by the flag?*

Squanto had been kidnapped by an English slave trader and carried to Europe. He learned English, escaped his captors, and found transport back home. In his absence, his entire tribe of Pawtuckets had died from an epidemic disease. Squanto then made himself a savior and friend of the Pilgrims.

Squanto, wrote Governor William Bradford, was "a special instrument of God. He directed [the colonists] to set their corn, where to take fish, and to procure other commodities, and was also their pilot to bring them to unknown places for their profit, and never left them until he died." Squanto also helped the Pilgrims to establish treaties with the surrounding Indians. These treaties would stay in effect for the next 50 years.

The Pilgrim colony survived, but it grew slowly. Eventually it was swallowed up by the more prosperous settlement of the Massachusetts Bay Colony, founded by a group of Puritans in 1630.

Massachusetts Bay Colony

Granted land by the Plymouth Company (by then called the Council of New England), the Puritans who founded the Massachusetts Bay Colony obtained a charter from the king before they left England. They intended to establish a "truly Christian community" that would serve as a model for the Protestant world. Governor John Winthrop declared, "We shall be as a city upon a hill, the eyes of the people are upon us." These Puritans set out to form a **commonwealth**—a community founded on law and united by agreement that the law would serve the common good. They intended to live according to Christian principles set out in a covenant, or a pact, with God. They felt themselves chosen to preserve the true faith in America so that later it could be transplanted back to Europe. But by the second generation, they had given up their original mission and had found a new purpose—the settlement of the wilderness of America.

In 1630, more than 1,000 Puritans set off from England, their 17 ships loaded with supplies. More prosperous than the Separatists, the Puritan immigrants included well-off merchants, farmers, and landowners, as well as college-educated ministers. They settled first along the Charles River and Boston Bay, organizing seven Puritan towns. By 1643, more than 20,000 English settlers had joined

Women Who Dared to Speak Out

Anne Hutchinson was a popular figure in Boston, acting as a midwife and providing herbal remedies for minor illnesses. More importantly, she opened her house on Wednesday afternoons so that 50 or 60 women could discuss the week's sermon and other religious matters. This activity got her into trouble with the church. She was accused of interpreting the Bible as only a minister was supposed to do. Because she claimed to receive direct revelation from God, Hutchinson was exiled to a neighboring colony.

Later, Mary Dyer, a close friend of Hutchinson, was appalled to hear that Anne and all but one of her children had been killed in an Indian attack. Dyer blamed both Governor Winthrop and the church for the deaths of her friends. She created a great scandal in Boston and was ordered to leave the city.

Dyer then went to London to study the religion of the Society of Friends, a group better known as Quakers because they were supposed to "tremble [quake] at the name of the Lord." The Quakers believed in absolute equality among people. They had no ministers, but anyone who wished, male or female, could become a "public Friend," discussing God's word and helping others who sought "inner light" or God's grace. Quakers re-

▲ *Howard Pyle chose to depict Dyer as a saint in this painting.*

fused to contribute to the Church of England, to take oaths in court, or to bear arms for the king. Many Quakers spent time in jail for defying the established order.

While in London, Dyer met Katherine Scott, Anne Hutchinson's sister, and Katherine's 11-year-old daughter Patience. The three women became Quakers and set off for Boston, determined to live among Puritans and to try to show them how narrow their beliefs had become. It was contrary to the laws of Massachusetts Bay for Quakers to preach their beliefs, so the women promoted their ideas by breaking bottles in a church to show how empty Puritan sermons

were. When Katherine Scott did that, she was publicly whipped.

Quakers in Boston were having their ears cut off and were being branded on the cheek. Young Patience sneaked off to Boston to protest, and she was promptly jailed. Dyer and Scott set off to rescue her, and they also were jailed.

After a visit to Providence, Mary Dyer and two male Quakers decided that they must return to Boston for more protests. They were arrested, and the two men were hanged. Dyer was released at the last moment. Once again she was ordered out of the colony, but once again her conscience would not let her rest. She returned to Boston a last time, carrying a roll of clean linen. Arrested for protesting, she was asked in court if she were not the woman who had once escaped the gallows. "I am," she stated. "This linen is for the wrapping of my body." This time Mary Dyer's sentence of hanging was carried out.

The statues of Hutchinson and Dyer flank the entrance to the Boston State House today, as reminders of their bravery.

---

1. Give one reason why the Puritans did not allow free discussion of religious matters.
2. Mary Dyer believed strongly enough to give her life for her cause. Do you think her actions were justified?

them, establishing more towns that radiated out from the original settlements. Only about half of these new colonists were Puritans, but the Puritans controlled the society.

The founders of the Massachusetts Bay Colony had no Squanto to help them, but they did receive indirect aid from previous Indian inhabitants. Those Indians had died of a disease that had probably been caught from European fishermen who had put to shore for a short time. The Indians' farmland had been cleared before the epidemic had struck, and it was ready for planting.

Even with this start, Winthrop's "city upon a hill" was not entirely free from trouble. There were dissenters, but the people usually relied on the courts to resolve differences. They believed in the rule of law, and they believed that their ministers had moral—but not political—authority. Those dissenters whose points of view were not accepted left the colony.

▼ Although Roger Williams was banished from the Massachusetts Bay Colony, he found refuge with some of his supporters in Providence. What traits of Williams's character are shown in this engraving?

The colony that had been started to protect the Puritan faith and to serve as a model for the world was only partially successful. Dissension among the Puritans themselves and persecution of other religious groups finally convinced the king to force a new royal charter on Massachusetts. This meant that the king would appoint the colony's governor and that property ownership, not church membership, would be the requirement for voting. The colony would also be forced to extend recognition to other religious groups, such as Quakers, Anglicans, and Baptists.

More New England Colonies

Rhode Island   The next several colonies developed because of religious differences among the Puritans. In 1635, Rhode Island, which would be the smallest of the English colonies, became the haven of **Roger Williams** and his supporters. A personable and well-liked minister, Williams served as the assistant pastor in the village of Salem in the Massachusetts Bay Colony. Increasingly, Williams's way of thinking got him into trouble. He questioned the legality of the colony's charter, since the Indians had not been paid for their land. He believed the civil government of the colony had no right to punish religious dissenters. A Separatist of extreme convictions, Williams was eventually banished from the Massachusetts Bay Colony. With a group of followers, he founded Providence, the first village in what would become the colony of Rhode Island. In that colony, no one—Christian or Jew—was persecuted for his or her religious belief. Rhode Island received its charter in 1644, and became a haven for Protestants from Europe as well as from the Bay Colony.

Connecticut, New Hampshire, and Maine

The colonies of Connecticut and New Hampshire were also started by settlers who left the Massachusetts Bay Colony. **Minister Thomas Hooker** and some of his congregation established the village of Hartford on the Connecticut River in 1636. Other Puritans soon set up their own small villages in the region. For some of these groups, the desire for more and better land was at least as strong a motive for moving to the frontier as were religious concerns. In 1639, the residents of the new towns met to sign the **Fundamental Orders of Connecticut**, the first written constitution or plan of government in America. The document specified that citizenship would be based on land ownership, not on religious belief as in the Massachusetts Bay Colony. In the Bay Colony, only Puritan church members could vote or hold office.

In 1637, two residents of the Massachusetts Bay Colony—the **Reverend John Wheelwright** and his strong-minded sister-in-law, **Anne Hutchinson**—found themselves involved in heated religious discussions. Hutchinson believed that people could find inner truth and divine guidance without the help of the Bible or the ministry. The Puritan leaders, especially Governor John Winthrop, thought that such an opinion called the very justification for the colony into question. If one person's truth was as correct as anyone else's, there would be religious anarchy. Hutchinson was forced out of the church and banished from the Bay Colony for her views. She was killed later by Indians in New Netherland in 1643.

Wheelwright and his followers had better luck. They were allowed to settle in New Hampshire, setting up a government that was not church-related. New Hampshire received its charter in 1679.

A number of other groups left Massachusetts to settle in what would become Maine, but that region would be administered by the Massachusetts Bay Colony, and later by the state of Massachusetts, until 1820.

▲ *Although this painting by Howard Pyle shows Anne Hutchinson preaching in her house in Boston, it is unlikely that she actually did preach. She caused dissension because of her refusal to keep silent about religious views. What beliefs of Hutchinson's did Governor Winthrop find especially upsetting?*

SECTION 4 REVIEW

1. State the main religious difference between the Puritans and Pilgrims.
2. Explain why some New England colonists moved to new regions.
3. Identify the Mayflower Compact.
4. Evaluate by today's standards whether or not the Mayflower Compact would be considered a democratic document.
5. Explain why the Massachusetts Bay Colony was only partially successful in its role as a model for the world.

The Middle Colonies

Some 35 years after the founding of the Jamestown Colony, people were successfully producing tobacco on large plantations located along the rivers of Virginia. People in New England were also prospering. Those lessons were not lost on persecuted, discontented, adventurous, or ambitious Europeans. During the late seventeenth and early eighteenth centuries, Europeans of many nations read pamphlets advertising the benefits of living in the new colonies. Colonial servants, said one pamphlet, "being industrious ... have gotten good stocks of cattle and servants of their own; have built houses and exercised their trades." Not all immigrants would prosper as the pamphlets suggested. Still, by 1740, nearly a million mostly non-English Europeans had settled in America's English colonies.

What motives led to the founding of the middle colonies?

How did England obtain New Netherland as a colony?

In what ways did Pennsylvania differ from the other colonies?

New York and New Jersey

New Netherland had long been a source of concern to the English. The Dutch settlement split the northern English colonies from the southern. More importantly, Dutch ships that used the ports of New Netherland seized goods from English ships, competed with the English in the developing slave trade, and sold goods to English colonists. Engaged in almost continuous conflict in various parts of the world, the two nations fought three wars between 1648 and 1673. In 1664, the English king, Charles II, "gave" his brother, the duke of York, Dutch holdings in America, provided that his brother could take control of the lands. The duke of York

quickly dispatched a fleet to the harbor of New Amsterdam.

When English naval guns threatened the city, Peter Stuyvesant (STY-vuh-suhnt), the Dutch governor, tried in vain to resist. Unfortunately for Dutch interests in America, the city's residents cared little who ruled them, so long as they could practice their own religions and make money. The Dutch were forced to surrender all of New Netherland. The city of New Amsterdam was renamed New York, and Stuyvesant retired to his farm in what is now New York City, content to spend the rest of his life in a land he had come to love.

The duke of York was as generous with other noblemen as his brother Charles II had been with him. The duke gave the New Jersey area of his newly gained land to Lord John Berkeley and Sir George Carteret (KART-ur-et), who in turn sold their portions to Quaker merchants. East Jersey later became a Puritan settlement, while West Jersey maintained its Quaker population. In 1702, the two sections were joined to form the colony of New Jersey.

William Penn and the Quakers

With the official Dutch presence removed, the rest of the duke of York's holdings were opened for settlement. **William Penn** was anxious to have part of that land to start a colony for his fellow Quakers. He decided this was a good time to remind the king of a large debt owed to his father. Charles II granted Penn a huge tract of land, and probably felt relieved that he had gotten rid of both the debt and many dissident Quakers. It was founded in 1681 as a haven for religious **radicals**, people who wanted to make extreme changes. Pennsylvania was destined to become one of the most important of the English colonies. In 1682, Penn also obtained a grant for the lands that would become the colony of Delaware in 1704.

Although Penn himself spent less than two years in his colony, he made certain that in Pennsylvania there would be no restrictions placed on Quakers or on any of the other religious groups that were to come from France, Holland, Germany, Sweden, and

The English Colonies to 1763

New England Colonies

Colony and Date of Settlement	Founders or Early Leaders	Reasons for Founding	Primary Economic Base
■ Plymouth Colony (1620) ■ Massachusetts Bay Colony (1630)	■ William Bradford, Separatists ■ John Winthrop, Puritans	■ Religious freedom for Separatists ■ Set up a Puritan commonwealth	■ Agriculture ■ Trade, shipbuilding, whaling
New Hampshire (1623) (became a royal colony in 1679)	John Wheelwright	Trade, religious freedom	Logging, trade, fishing
Rhode Island (1636)	Roger Williams	Religious freedom for dissenters	Shipbuilding, trade, light manufacturing
Connecticut (1636)	Thomas Hooker	Establish a separate Puritan settlement, open up an internal trade route	Agriculture, furs

Middle Colonies

Colony and Date of Settlement	Founders or Early Leaders	Reasons for Founding	Primary Economic Base
■ New Netherland (1624) ■ New York (1664)	■ Dutch West India Company ■ Duke of York	■ Colonization (land), trade	■ Furs, logging, wheat, trade
Delaware (New Sweden) (1638)	Peter Minuit, William Penn	Colonization for land, trade	Trade, agriculture
New Jersey (1664)	Sir John Berkeley, George Carteret, Sir Richard Nicolls	Quaker refuge, trade	Trade, agriculture
Pennsylvania (1637)	William Penn	Religious freedom for Quakers	Light manufacturing, trade, agriculture

Southern Colonies

Colony and Date of Settlement	Founders or Early Leaders	Reasons for Founding	Primary Economic Base
Virginia (1607)	Virginia Company of London, John Smith	Colonization for land, gold	Tobacco, trade, furs
Maryland (1632)	George and Cecilius Calvert	Religious freedom for Catholics	Tobacco
The Carolinas (1663) ■ North Carolina (1712) ■ South Carolina (1712)	Sir Anthony Ashley Cooper, Sir John Colleton, and others	Colonization for land, refuge for small farmers	■ Trade, agriculture ■ Rice, indigo
Georgia (1732)	James Oglethorpe	Buffer against Spanish land, refuge for debtors	Rice, indigo, trade

▲ Penn's Treaty with the Indians *by Benjamin West immortalizes Penn's unusual act of paying American Indians living on the land that the king had granted to him. West was one of America's greatest painters. How does he characterize the Quakers and the Indians?*

Denmark. Penn developed a Frame of Government for the new colony that put control into the hands of a council and governor.

Penn exhibited more concern for the rights of Indians than most colonizers. He met with Indian leaders to explain his plans for the colony, and he paid them for the land to be used by colonists. During his stay in the colony, Penn laid out plans for what he intended to become the "great city of Philadelphia."

◄ *This table summarizes basic information about the early colonies. How were the motives for settlement different in the three Atlantic coast regions?*

SECTION 5 REVIEW

1. State ways that New Netherland became an obstacle to English plans for America.
2. Describe how the English gained control of New Netherland.
3. Name the two religious groups that controlled East and West Jersey.
4. Identify William Penn.
5. List three ways in which Pennsylvania was different from the other colonies.

Chapter 2 Review

Summary

The Spanish maintained their presence, in the face of threats from the French and the Russians, by establishing missions and presidios in Florida, Texas, and California. In spite of problems between them, Spanish and Indian groups mingled to form a uniquely American culture. The fur trade brought the French into a close relationship with the Indians in eastern Canada. There the French claimed considerable territory. In the end, the French presence was less permanent in the areas they explored west and south of Montreal and Quebec, though, by the 1760s, French speaking refugees from Canada had settled in Louisiana. The Dutch set up trading relationships with the Indians and also founded a thriving commercial center in the city of New Amsterdam. It was the English, however, who proved to be the most dedicated colonizers.

Over a period of 126 years, the English settled colony after colony. English settlers came with the goal of living out their lives in America. Some were religious visionaries; others were more concerned with making money. Whatever their motives for coming to America, all the colonists struggled to survive. While many perished during the first difficult years of colonization, most later colonists prospered and established themselves successfully in an environment far different from the one they had left in Europe.

Vocabulary

cash crop	patroon
commonwealth	precedent
compact	presidio
diplomatic alliance	privateer
dissenter	proprietor
hierarchy	radical
joint-stock company	trustee

On a separate paper, write the correct vocabulary term next to the number of its matching definition.

1. A fort connected with a mission
2. A Dutch landowner
3. An example that determines future actions or rulings
4. A group united by similar political goals
5. The legal owner of a firm or business
6. Many investors sharing risks and profits
7. A type of government emphasizing the common good
8. Someone who disagrees with a commonly held viewpoint
9. A graded or ranked series
10. Someone who has legal responsibility without legal ownership
11. A "pirate" operating with permission of the government
12. An individual with an extreme point of view
13. A solemn agreement
14. A product grown for sale as a source of income

Review Questions

1. List four reasons, or motives, that prompted Europeans to settle in North America.
2. Describe how the Spanish used missions and presidios to control Indian populations.
3. What was the major difference between the long-range colonization goals of the French and Dutch and those of the English?
4. List three major goals of the first English settlements in America.
5. How were the motivations of English colonists of New England different from those who settled the South?
6. What issue forced some colonists in Massachusetts Bay to break away to found new colonies?
7. Briefly describe how the English obtained the lands that became New York and New Jersey.
8. What two benefits did Charles II gain by granting land to William Penn?
9. In what ways were William Penn's policies different from those of other colonial governors?

10. Explain why England was said to be the most successful of the colonizing countries.

Critical Historical Thinking

Writing Answer each of the following questions by writing one or more complete paragraphs:

1. How did Spain's success in obtaining riches from the New World weaken its position in Europe?
2. For a time during the 1600s, the Dutch were the greatest sea power in the world. Explain why they did not become a great colonial power in the New World.
3. The Mayflower Compact is considered to be a cornerstone in American government. This document, which was a legal basis for self-government, was both democratic and restrictive of rights. How is this true?
4. Evaluate the following statement and decide if it is mostly true or mostly false: Most colonists came to New England seeking religious freedom.

Making Connections with Economics

European explorers of the Americas were adventurers who left a familiar world for an unfamiliar one. In that sense, they can be compared to our modern astronauts. Like our astronauts, they were backed by the productive resources of their respective countries. The real costs of exploration were the resources used in the act of exploration that would have been devoted to another purpose. For example, let's suppose that if Spain had not chosen to explore the new world, Spain would have devoted those same resources toward strengthening its army. In economic terms, this means that a stronger army was the *opportunity cost* of exploration for Spain. Opportunity cost is the most highly valued opportunity or alternative forfeited when a choice is made. The leaders (investors) weighed the opportunity costs and reasoned that there would be a pay-

off, a return on investment that would improve the economy of the country or the profits of the company and its investors in the near term. Likewise, the space program is an investment that is expected to pay a return on investment in the form of new technologies, communications, and discoveries.

- Use your school or community library to research one of the returns on investment gained in space exploration—such as medicines and products like Tang orange drink, freeze-dried foods, and Teflon. Present your findings to the class in brief oral reports, or prepare a visual report for the class bulletin board.

Additional Skills Practice

Identify an interesting photograph in a newspaper or magazine that tells a story. Then answer the following questions:

1. What is the atmosphere, or mood, of the picture?
2. Where and when was this picture taken?
3. Why do you think the photographer took this picture? What was his or her purpose?
4. Do you think the photographer shows a bias, or particular point of view, by what he or she has chosen to photograph?

The Growth of Colonial Society

In the late 1700s and early 1800s, heavy immigration and a sharply rising birthrate caused the colonial population to soar. In 1700, the population stood at about 250,000. By 1755, it passed a million. Settled territory also grew as families began to move farther inland. While most settlers still supported themselves by farming, both manufacturing and trade began to thrive. The American Indians were pushed from the coastal regions. An increase of agriculture in the South accelerated the growth of slavery. Some colonists began to concern themselves with intellectual pursuits, as well as the management of political and economic affairs. Many others were caught up in a great religious revival that shook up traditional ideas of worship and church organization. This was a period of enormous change, and, for all the hard times colonists experienced, most white settlers continued to believe that they were living in the "best poor man's country."

▲ *In colonial America, Valentine's Day was not the important holiday it was to become with twentieth-century advertising, but Henry Drinker's girlfriend, Elizabeth, was probably greatly pleased with this valentine sent to her in 1753. The couple finally married in 1761.*

Sectional Differences Emerge

One early immigrant to New York claimed that "the hopes of having land of their own and becoming independent of Landlords is what chiefly induces people to America." For many colonists of the late 1600s and early 1700s those hopes were realized. The way they utilized their land varied depending on the region in which they settled, its climate, the rules and regulations of each particular colony, and the time period during which it was settled. The colonists' religious beliefs and social status determined other aspects of their lives. By the mid-eighteenth century, the ways of life of colonists in the different regions were, as one observer put it, "as different as their climes."

Why did the American colonies in different regions develop in such diverse ways?

Why did so many different kinds of occupations develop in the colonies?

In what ways did increasing trade change the everyday life of many of the colonists?

▲ *These artisans are making beaver felt hats, an important colonial product. These hats were popular with men and women in both Europe and America. Why do you think they were needed? (Beaver hat courtesy of the Pilgrim Society, Plymouth, Massachusetts.)*

The Economy of New England

Settlers in New England established their economy in two ways: they sold furs and hides to England, and they traded with the steady stream of new immigrants, exchanging their surplus foodstuffs and livestock for clothing and manufactured goods. The Puritan immigrants came mainly from the eastern part of England, where they had been farmers and skilled workers. They were fairly well off and were able to bring with them the tools and utensils needed to begin a new life. They migrated to set up a society free from religious persecution by the Anglican church and to escape an economic depression in the cloth trade.

The Puritans traveled in family groups and settled in villages using the surrounding land for farming and for pasturing livestock. Their family-worked farms averaged 70 to 100 acres. The soil was rocky, and the growing season was short. The main crop, corn, provided a variety of family dishes and fodder for the livestock, primarily pigs, poultry, and dairy cattle. Families averaged seven or eight children before 1700, and declined in size as the land filled up and large farms were no longer available. All members of the family worked as soon as they were able. Only a few families kept slaves or hired laborers.

Some men in every community spent part of

their time working as artisans, for example, as black-smiths or barrel-makers, using skills they had learned in England. As time passed, they hired new-comers or took on apprentices to serve the growing economy. By 1647, a writer noted that Boston could claim "professional weavers, feltmakers, rope-makers, three kinds of leatherworkers, six kinds of woodworkers, and seven kinds of metal workers." Some New England colonists had set up both a cloth-making factory and an ironworks by 1650, but neither concern survived because raw materials and manufacturing tools had to be imported at a pro-hibitive cost.

Fishing and Shipbuilding

The waters off the Atlantic coast of North America had been fished by ships from many na-tions for a century before the English established their colonies. It took New England settlers only a few years to realize that the many small harbors along the coast were suitable for their own small fishing industry. Timber to build a fleet of fishing boats could be found just inland. Soon, some enter-prising colonists began to make good money from the abundant schools of codfish. Villagers up and down the coast of New England bought fresh fish. The colonists found markets in the West Indies or Europe for dried or salted catches. Sometimes these seagoing merchants sold not only their cargo of dried fish, but also the carrying ship itself. Colo-nial sailors returned home any way they could.

A large and profitable commercial network slowly evolved from those first small efforts. Colo-

nial merchants often had contacts with relatives or friends in England with whom they could become business partners. Commerce among those partners led, in turn, to trade with other European nations. Eventually, a network of shipping lanes lined the American coast and crisscrossed the At-lantic. Raw materials such as lumber, pine tar, and turpentine, and cash crops such as tobacco and foodstuffs were carried to England. Manufactured goods were returned to the colonies.

One part of that profitable commercial network remains infamous today. This part of the network has been called the **triangular trade**. Although the triangular trade accounted for only a small percent-age of colonial commerce, it is remembered today because it involved the inhumane traffic in enslaved Africans. There were three separate voyages involved in the triangular trade—the three sides of the trian-gle. Colonial merchants carried food and wood products to the sugar islands of the West Indies and sold them in exchange for molasses. Back in New England, distillers turned the molasses into rum, which was carried to West Africa, and traded for slaves. On the homeward voyage, the enslaved Africans would be sold in the West Indies or the mainland colonies. They might be exchanged for

▼ *What legs of Atlantic trade were part of the well-known triangular trade? Why do you think modern historians downplay the economic importance of the triangular trade?*

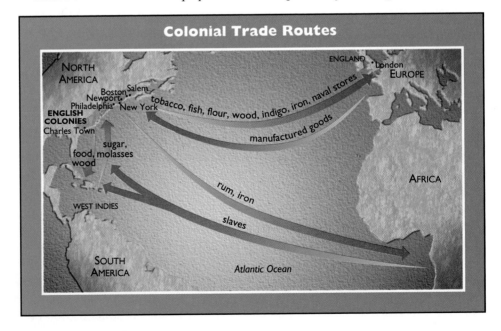

Life in Colonial Seaport Cities

The emergence of trade in the colonies brought with it a growth in seaport cities, such as Boston, New York, Philadelphia, and Charles Town. Trade was vital to the economic life of the colonies and the seaport cities were the centers of that trade. As such, they later became centers of culture, fashion, and political thought.

These seaport cities were relatively small in size and densely populated. In many ways these cities were like modern cities, complete with shopping, cultural, and employment opportunities. There were also traffic problems, and problems of homelessness and crime.

As trade centers, the seaport cities were the place to be if you needed to acquire a good or service. The cities bustled with the business of buying and selling. From the shops that fronted the street could be heard the clatter of hammers, saws, and mallets—all the tools used by artisans as they fashioned barrels, furniture, shoes, hats, guns, pewter plates, silver tea sets, and a wide variety of other goods. From taverns and coffeehouses, a babble of voices rose and fell as shipmasters, government officials, merchants, artisans, and newspaper publishers discussed the latest news from England.

▲ Why did visitors going from New York City to Brooklyn have to use a ferry?
▶

Which city had the greatest growth rate?

For the more wealthy, the cities offered lavish living with fine food, well-made clothes in the latest fashions, and wonderful entertainments. For the less fortunate, life in the cities could mean struggling for survival in filthy, deplorable conditions.

For people of all economic classes the cities meant traffic. Streets were easily jammed as horsedrawn carriages and wagons jostled herds of sheep and cattle being driven to the butcher. Stray dogs yapped at the heels of animals and pedestrians, while roaming pigs rooted through the rotting garbage that householders threw into the streets. Also filling the streets were peddlers hawking fresh vegetables, fish, eggs, and other goods for sale.

The Growth of Seaport Cities

	Estimated Population by Year	
	1700	1760
Boston	6,700	16,000
New York City	5,000	18,000
Philadelphia	2,200	24,000
Charles Town	2,000	8,000

These seaport cities were lively places to live, but they could also be dangerous. Robbery was a common crime and one often had to avoid dangerous drunken sailors. Epidemic diseases were often carried into the cities by sailors or immigrants. For example, in 1721, smallpox killed 14 percent of Boston's population of 12,000 and typhus and typhoid fever frequently swept through New York City and Philadelphia killing hundreds with each epidemic. Despite the dangers, however, these cities continued to attract newcomers throughout the colonial period.

1. Would you have liked to live in a colonial city? Why, or why not?
2. How did colonial cities differ from modern cities?

molasses, which the ship would carry back to New England, completing the triangle.

Atlantic trade spurred the development of seaport cities. Boston (the first port city in the English colonies) and Salem, Massachusetts, and Newport, Rhode Island, are some of the port cities that grew to accommodate the increasing trade.

Southern Colonies Expand

In contrast to the settlers of the New England area, who emigrated largely for religious reasons, the early settlers in the Chesapeake Bay region emigrated primarily for economic reasons. Like the New Englanders, they traded in furs and made their living by farming. Unlike the New Englanders, these farmers emphasized the production of tobacco, a crop that required intensive manual labor. Tobacco had become a very popular crop both in the colonies and in England. Because tobacco farming brought in large profits, planters cultivated more land and needed more labor. This was provided by **indentured servants**, who made up three-fourths of the population of the Chesapeake Bay region. Generally these were poor people, mostly from London and southern England, who sold themselves into servitude for a limited time in exchange for passage to the colonies.

Those settlers with wealth and high social position were granted or bought up all the land that lay along the navigable rivers. Riverfront locations allowed farmers to load their crops of tobacco directly onto oceangoing vessels for transport to market. Other colonists had to settle for small isolated farms, and they had to pay to have their crops transported and marketed by the wealthier planters.

High death rates and late marriages had kept the population relatively small in this region. After about 1674, the colonists had difficulty recruiting indentured workers. The birthrate in England had declined, and economic conditions in England had improved. This meant that fewer English workers were willing to move to the colonies. Enslaved Africans began to replace indentured servants as workers in the tobacco fields and later in the rice and indigo fields of South Carolina. More settlers had moved inland, away from the coast where mosquito-borne diseases had taken a heavy toll. The life expectancy of white settlers lengthened, and the population began to grow.

For the small farmers of the Chesapeake Bay and other regions of the South, the average cash crop was about 1,200 to 3,000 pounds of tobacco and a few bushels of corn. Farmers used the money they made to pay fees, required from members and non-members alike, to the established Church of England, and to buy small amounts of powder and shot, needles and thread, and coarse fabric for clothing. For families that were barely making a living, one bad tobacco crop could mean ruin, forcing

▼ *This is an early drawing of Charles Town, South Carolina. Why do you think so many houses were built close to the ocean?*

them to sell their land to pay their debts.

The lower southern colonies developed later than the Chesapeake Bay region. Until 1700, colonists in South Carolina traded metal tools and blankets for deerskins prepared by Indians. They later raised livestock that could be sold for a good profit in the West Indies. When first rice, and then indigo, became important cash crops, the population grew, but southern port cities never equaled the growth rate of those in the North. Of the southern port cities, Charles Town, South Carolina, experienced the largest growth. It grew from 2,000 people in 1700 to 8,000 in 1760. Savannah, Georgia, not established until the 1730s, would barely reach a population of 3,000 by the time of the American Revolution.

▲ *This painting by Edward Hicks is titled* The Residence of David Twining. *It depicts a farm in Pennsylvania and shows the neatness and peacefulness that were characteristics of those immigrants. What different ways of making a living from a farm are shown?*

Diversity of the Middle Colonies

In the middle colonies certain individuals—usually the favorites of the English crown—obtained huge grants of land. They could then farm their estates, rent them out, sell them outright, or hold them to sell later for huge profits. It made sense to hold land for several years. As the population increased, so did the value of land.

Even the smaller farmers in the middle colonies made a good living on their average holdings of 150 to 200 acres. The soil was much richer than in other colonies. While corn grew well and provided surplus crops, wheat was the crop that first made these farmers prosperous. Milled into flour, this crop found a ready market in the southern colonies, in the emerging colonial towns of New England, and on the sugar plantations of the West Indies. By the early 1700s, flour milling became a principal industry of New York City, the name given New Amsterdam in 1664. The middle colonies were soon given the nickname "breadbasket of the colonies." Farmers there also raised good crops of fruits and vegetables sold locally, and flax and hemp grown for export. They also began a flourishing business in raising livestock. Philadelphia became an important port city, developing a brisk trade in foodstuffs which ships carried to the West Indies and southern Europe. It soon eclipsed both Boston and New York.

Protestant Immigration   From their beginnings, the middle colonies were more diverse than other regions. William Penn's emphasis on religious

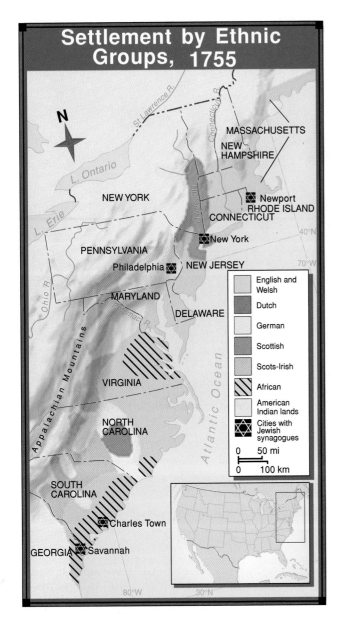

Settlement by Ethnic Groups, 1755

English and Welsh
Dutch
German
Scottish
Scots-Irish
African
American Indian lands
Cities with Jewish synagogues

0   50 mi
0   100 km

▲ *This map indicates major concentrations of ethnic groups, although often many different groups were present in any one area. Why do you think Scottish, Scots-Irish, and German immigrants settled in upstate New York, Pennsylvania, and western Maryland?*

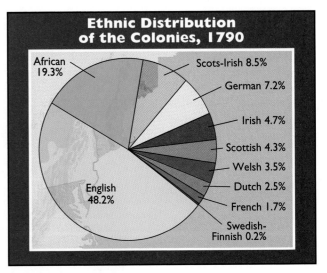

Ethnic Distribution of the Colonies, 1790

African 19.3%
Scots-Irish 8.5%
German 7.2%
Irish 4.7%
Scottish 4.3%
Welsh 3.5%
Dutch 2.5%
French 1.7%
Swedish-Finnish 0.2%
English 48.2%

▲ *What were the four largest population groups in the colonies in 1790?*

settlers. Their large, fruitful fields, gardens, and orchards and their carefully tended livestock provided a good living. Later, large numbers of Lutherans immigrated to Pennsylvania. They were not seeking religious freedom; they had that at home. Rather, they were hoping to improve their economic status.

The German immigrants were often called **Pennsylvania Dutch** because the English confused the name of their language, *Deutsch* (meaning German), with *Dutch*, meaning from Holland. Arriving in Pennsylvania after about 1717, the Germans accounted for more than one-third of Pennsylvania's population by 1766.

The largest group of non-English immigrants during the colonial period were some 250,000 Scots-Irish. They came from northern Ireland, where large groups of Scots had been settled by the English government during the seventeenth century. Most entered the colonies through the port of Philadelphia, and then made their way to the western sections of Pennsylvania, Maryland, Virginia, and the Carolinas. Poor people, the Scots could not afford to purchase expensive land. Proud people, they would not work long for others. In the backcountry they found good unsettled land and established their small farms without clear legal title to the land. Sometimes forced off the land they had claimed by

tolerance and his recruitment of colonists from the German states of Europe brought over a variety of Protestant sects whose members were fleeing religious persecution. These immigrants, mostly Mennonites and other Protestant groups whose views were similar to those of the Quakers, settled in the fertile valleys of Pennsylvania away from other

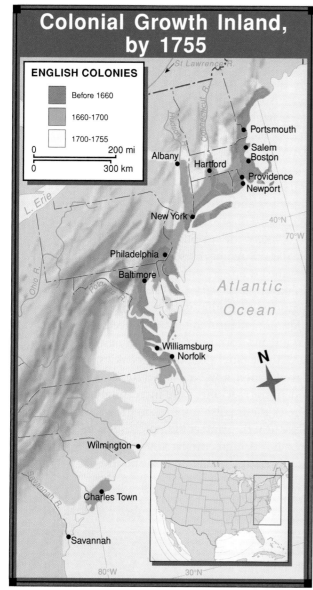

Colonial Growth Inland, by 1755

ENGLISH COLONIES

- Before 1660
- 1660–1700
- 1700–1755

0   200 mi
0   300 km

St Lawrence R.
Portsmouth
Salem
Boston
Albany
Hartford
Providence
Newport
New York
40°N
70°W
Philadelphia
Baltimore
Atlantic Ocean
Williamsburg
Norfolk
N
Wilmington
Charles Town
Savannah
80°W
30°N
L. Erie
Hudson R.
Connecticut R.
Ohio R.
Potomac R.
Savannah R.

▲ *Continued immigration to the colonies forced newcomers to settle further inland. In what time period was the movement inland greatest?*

▲ *At the local tavern, people received news of the happenings in other colonies and in England.*

squatter's rights, they simply packed up their goods and moved farther out on the frontier. For these land-hungry colonists, no hardship seemed too great.

As the frontier regions began to be populated by white settlers, small towns grew up along the **fall line**, the point where coastal rivers became navigable for transporting goods to coastal ports. Many of

the new immigrants, Germans and Scots-Irish, moved into those regions. In Richmond, Virginia; Raleigh, North Carolina; and Augusta, Georgia, enterprising merchants built warehouses. There they stored manufactured goods brought upriver from the coast, as well as farm goods brought downriver by western settlers. From miles around, settlers carried furs, animal skins, grains, flour, whiskey—any goods they could gather to sell. They came by horseback, pack train, and wagon. They took home more than manufactured goods. Newspapers from different colonies and conversations in shops alerted them to affairs outside their own colonies.

The rise in commerce began to change the character of the colonies. Each region developed its own economic pattern, but established few ties among or between other colonies. By the mid-1700s, the coastal trade brought some merchants into temporary association, but most found their Atlantic trading partners more important to their economic well-being than people from other colonies.

SECTION 1 REVIEW

1. Explain why the early settlers were so eager to obtain land in the colonies.
2. State why farms in New England were often smaller than farms in other regions.
3. List the obstacles that faced farmers in the Chesapeake Bay region.
4. List the reasons that made farmers in the middle colonies so successful.
5. Name some common colonial occupations other than farming.

SECTION 2

The Growth of Slavery

In the early 1760s, slave traders kidnapped **Olaudah Equiano** from his West African village and forced him to board a slave ship. The white-skinned crew terrified him, and he later wrote that he believed he "had gotten into a world of bad spirits that were going to kill me." Kept below deck during the voyage to America, Equiano complained that "with the loathsomeness of the stench and the crying together, I became so sick and low that I was not able to eat." Shipped to Virginia and set to work clearing rocks from fields, Equiano found himself "constantly grieving and pining and wishing for death." Equiano was more fortunate than most slaves. Bought by an English sea captain, he learned to read and write English. In 1762 he bought his freedom, and in 1789 he published his autobiography.

Why did southern planters so readily adopt the institution of slavery?

How did enslaved Africans react to their condition of bondage?

In what ways did slaves develop their own particular culture?

Slavery in the Colonies

In 1650, records show 720 enslaved people lived in the southern colonies, most of them purchased in the Caribbean to work in the tobacco fields of Virginia and Maryland. By 1770, the number of enslaved people had increased to more than 400,000. Many of them were brought directly from Africa, and others were born into slavery in the colonies. They were made to cultivate rice and indigo, as well as tobacco.

One of the reasons for this growth was that plantation owners preferred slaves to indentured servants. White indentured servants who ran away, unlike enslaved Africans, could move to a different region and blend in with the white population. In addition, indentured servants were usually in service for just five to seven years. Then new servants would have to be taught the necessary skills. The skills a slave learned, however, lasted for a lifetime. Finally, indentured servants were increasingly difficult to hire as the English population growth slowed down. To southern planters the purchase price of a slave, which was high compared to the cost of an indentured servant, seemed worth the investment.

Because their crops did not require intensive manual labor, settlers in the middle colonies were not interested in slaves as agricultural workers. The Dutch had used them on their farms, but most were bought to act as house servants or to work as artisans. In New York, the number

▲ *Olaudah Equiano (c. 1750–1797)*

of enslaved Africans increased slowly—from 2,170 in 1698 to nearly 20,000 by 1771, out of a total population of 168,000. There were even fewer slaves in New Jersey, Delaware, and Pennsylvania. Many of the inhabitants of those colonies—especially a majority of the Quakers and Mennonites in Pennsylvania after 1750—believed that owning slaves was morally wrong.

The New England colonies had even fewer enslaved people. Their small farms were family affairs, and the families had many children. If they needed more help, they tended to use neighbors as hired hands. The majority of enslaved people in the North worked as household servants or as artisans, mostly in the growing seaports. In New England, slaves had a somewhat better life than those in

other colonies. They seldom had to work on Sundays. They could attend church services, own property, and have trials by jury. But even this more lenient treatment did not alter the fact that they were not free.

Few Rights for Free Black People

A few free black people lived in each of the colonies. Most were descendants of black indentured servants, members of families that had never been slaves. Other black people had been given

▼ *The growing demand for laborers to work plantations brought a rapid growth in the slave trade after 1600. Why were the slave trading forts located at the mouths of Africa's great rivers?*

▲ *Why would the firm selling these slaves make such a point of stating that they were free of smallpox?*

▲ *This overview of a typical slave ship shows that slaves were forced to lie as close to each other as possible. The death rates on slave ships often reached 30 percent. Why would owners of slave ships take a chance on losing as much as 30 percent of their profit?*

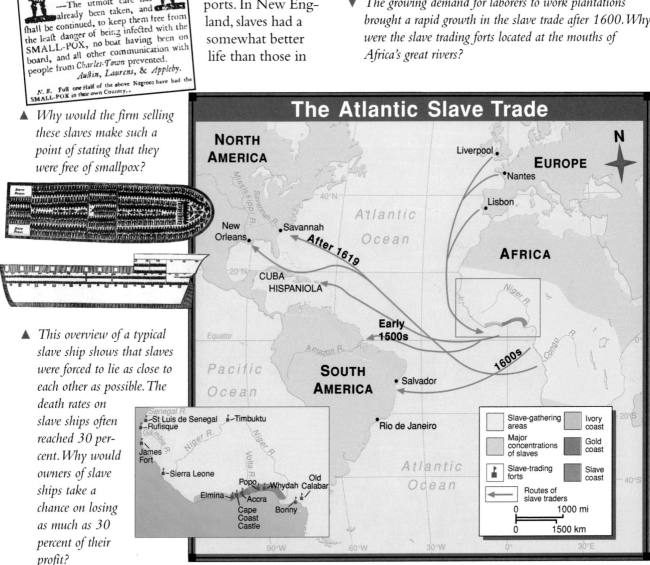

The Atlantic Slave Trade

their freedom by appreciative or sympathetic owners, or they had been allowed to buy their freedom with money saved when their owners allowed them to work for wages.

Being free did not guarantee equal treatment with white people. They were forced to live in certain sections of towns and cities, or on farms removed from those of white settlers. Even free black men with substantial amounts of property could not vote. Considered by most white colonists to be inferior beings, they suffered from prejudice and discrimination.

Enslaved Africans Adapt

No one distinctive African American culture developed during the early years of slavery. Slave masters purposely mixed slaves from different parts of Africa, feeling that those who could communicate with others would be more apt to plot dissension or worse. The slaves who survived the grueling voyage to America (about 70 to 80 percent) found themselves among people who were unlike the people they had known in their homelands.

While many Africans had experience in the jobs they were now forced to perform, they had to use unfamiliar methods and tools. They had no possessions to remind them of home, and no one to comfort them in a language they could understand. Enslaved Africans learned English, or in the case of those in South Carolina, they combined their several African languages with English to form a new mixed language known as **Gullah** (GUH-luh). This language is still spoken on the Sea Islands off the South Carolina coast.

Kinship ties were—and still are today—of special importance in most African cultures. Fearing they would never again be with their own relatives, enslaved blacks established close relationships with other slaves. Even shipboard, they began to call

▶

This painting by Thomas Coram, View of Mulberry Plantation (House and Street), *shows the owner's mansion and a street lined with slave quarters. Do you think this view of a plantation is typical?*

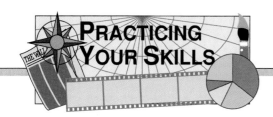
Reading a Map

Maps are visual representations of real places or events. In order to read a map successfully, you must know how to interpret the coded information on it. You have been reading maps for many years, but a brief review of the necessary tools should be helpful.

- **Read the title.** The title will tell you the subject and purpose of the map. It will indicate the part of the world being shown, or the theme of the map. It may also indicate a date or time period.

- **Read the key (map legend).** Maps use symbols to show important or frequently occurring data. Colors highlight important information. Circles or dots are frequently used to show cities and towns and their relative populations. A star might indicate a state or national capital. The key will explain all symbols, colors, and lines.

- **Study the map scale.** Scale is the relationship between distances on a map and the actual distance on Earth's surface. Although scale can be expressed as a fraction or a ratio, most maps use a bar scale to indicate the relationship. To use a bar scale, measure the distance on the map in inches or centimeters with a ruler. Then hold the ruler against the bar scale. The number on the bar scale is the actual distance in miles (or kilometers). You may have to do some estimating! Remember, the smaller the scale, the larger the distance being represented, and the larger the scale, the smaller the distance being represented.

- **Study the grid.** By using lines of latitude and longitude, you can find the absolute location of

places on Earth's surface. Many of the maps in this book use the grid system to indicate degrees of latitude (distance north and south of the equator) and longitude (distance east and west of the prime meridian). To locate a particular place, you need to determine the grid address that is made up of two coordinates—degrees latitude (N or S) and degrees longitude (E or W).

- **Find the map's orientation.** Some maps have a compass with arrow symbols to determine orientation, or direction. Most maps, by custom, are oriented with north at the top, south at the bottom, east to the right, and west to the left. There is no physical reason for this. In fact, early Arabian maps were drawn with east at the top in recognition of Muhammed's birthplace.

Part A—Study the map on page 77 of your text and answer the following questions:

1. What is the title of this map?
2. What do the symbols in the map key represent?
3. Using the map scale, determine the distance from Boston to Philadelphia.
4. (a) Which region has the largest number of cities? (b) Which region has the fewest cities?

Part B—Use the data presented on the map to infer the answers to these questions:

5. Why is there more settlement along the rivers?
6. Why are the densely settled areas largely confined to the coastal regions, even after 150 years?

friendly people "brother" or "sister." Those on the same plantation began to teach their children to regard their former shipmates and other older people as "aunt" and "uncle." In Africa, kin relationships brought with them certain responsibilities, and in America slaves took on these responsibilities for kin—either real or adopted.

As far as possible, enslaved Africans also retained their African religious practices, sometimes blending them with Christianity. On large plantations, slave quarters were set apart from the plantation house. This gave the enslaved people some opportunity to practice their own customs from sundown to sunup.

Resistance to Slavery

Slaves did not accept their bondage willingly. The more they developed a sense of belonging to a group, the more they dared to use methods of resistance. Slaves showed their hatred for their condition in many ways: by refusing to work, breaking tools, destroying other property, pretending to be unable to learn new skills, stealing from the white owners, and practicing work slowdowns. The most common form of resistance for slaves was to run away. But rarely did they escape for good. Sometimes they managed to join Indian tribes, or even to form their own communities. In 1728, near present-day Lexington, Virginia, runaway slaves established a village with dwellings like those they had known in Africa and a tribal government under a chief who had once been a prince. They farmed their land with typical African tools and agricultural techniques. This village lasted a full year, until whites killed the chief and returned the other villagers to the plantations.

During the colonial period, some slaves also organized rebellions. One uprising took place in New York in 1712, when a group of 25 slaves set fire to buildings, killed nine whites, and wounded several others. The slaves were quickly caught, and just as quickly executed. In 1741, also in New York, several fires and robberies were said to have been the work of slaves. Even though the evidence of guilt was never clear, 101 black people were convicted of the crimes, with 18 of these hanged and 13 burned alive.

Stono Rebellion The most serious slave revolt of the eighteenth century erupted in South Carolina. Early one morning in September 1739, about 20 slaves, many from the Portuguese colony of Angola in Africa, raided a store on the Stono River south of Charles Town. These slaves killed the storekeepers, stole guns and ammunition, killed some planter families, and then, joined by about 100 slaves from the neighborhood, headed south toward Spanish Florida where they would be free. The rebellion was short-lived. A white militia captured the slaves and killed most of them on the spot.

The **Stono Rebellion** terrified the colonists. In South Carolina, the proportion of enslaved people in comparison to the white population was high. A real possibility of revolt existed at all times. South Carolinians and other southern colonists, aware of what had happened at Stono River, passed harsher and more restrictive laws. These slave codes ruled that slaves could not leave plantations without passes, congregate in groups, marry whites, or be taught to read and write. Any disobedience could be punished by whippings, brandings, or by "appropriate maiming." In Virginia an additional law read, "If any slave . . . shall happen to be killed in such a correction [whipping], it shall not be counted as a felony; but the master shall be free . . . as if such an accident had never happened." Throughout the colonial period, the number of slaves continued to grow, and treatment of them became increasingly harsh.

SECTION 2 REVIEW

1. **Explain** why the practice of slavery became so much more widespread in the southern colonies than in the rest of colonial America.
2. **Discuss** why southern planters preferred the use of slaves over the use of indentured servants.
3. **Describe** how enslaved Africans in America struggled to maintain kinship ties.
4. **Identify** the Stono Rebellion.
5. **List** ways in which Africans showed their hatred of slavery.

Difficult Times for American Indians

"The Indians must be Christianized," claimed an early English settler. According to this settler, the first thing Indians had to do was to show respect for "Order, Industry, and Manners." Order demanded obedience to monarchs, parliament, and the army. Industry meant the Indians needed to quit their "scattered course of life," stop being "lazy lords of the universe," and give up their practice of "always removing from one place to another for conveniency of food." To achieve manners, according to the settler, the Indian men were to stop treating their wives as slaves who worked in the fields, and the men were to quit moving from place to place to hunt and fish. To the English, Christianizing meant more than changing the religious beliefs of the Indians. It meant rejection of the Indians' traditional ways of life.

In what ways did attempts by Europeans at Christianizing or enslaving Indians influence relationships between them?

How did using English technology change traditional Indian ways of life?

Why did some white settlers find Indian culture preferable to their own?

Missionary Efforts and Conflict

Generally speaking, the English were not zealous missionaries. Among the Puritans, however, there were several efforts to convert American Indians to Christianity. In southern New England, Puritans set up **praying towns**, which were organized so that Indians would live like English colonists. Ironically, the lands the colonial legislature provided for these towns were the same ones that had previously been taken away from the Indians. Sometimes called *reserves*, these areas were early versions of In-

dian reservations. In the praying towns, Indians governed themselves, running their own churches, schools, farms, shops, and jails. But they had white overseers, or trustees, appointed by the General Court of Massachusetts. They seldom had their own pastors and were served by missionaries, or neighboring clergymen. By the end of the seventeenth century, 22 such Puritan-Indian towns had been established.

Christianity did not greatly influence many New England Indians who lived beyond Puritan settlements. In other colonies, few settlers attempted to convert the Indians from their own religions. A few tribal leaders did send their sons to newly established Indian schools in order for them to learn about the English way of life. Some Indians accepted certain ceremonial aspects of Christianity, which they fit into their traditional religions. Most retained their own animistic beliefs, which generally emphasized the dependence of human beings on supernatural (that is, above nature) spirits that controlled all of life. Christianity, which appeared to elevate human beings above nature, seemed arrogant to most Indians.

▲ *Which elements of the dress of King Philip seem correct for a Wampanoag Indian and which seem to be invented by the painter?*

King Philip's War Missionary efforts were only one source of conflict between the English colonists and the Indians. A greater source of frustration for the Indians was the loss of their lands. These two problems combined to ignite a conflict known as **King Philip's War** (1675–76). The conflict was named after the leader of the Wampanoag (wahm-puh-NOH-ag) tribe, **Metacomet**, who was called King Philip by the colonists. Throughout the early 1670s, Metacomet and the Wampanoags had suffered as the colonists used both their religion and their system of courts to subjugate the Indians. The spark that set off King Philip's War

As this map indicates, the peoples known as American Indians comprised many different cultures. The Eastern Woodland Indians and the Indians of the Southeast were the first to feel the effects of British colonial policies. What natural geographic boundary parallel to the Atlantic seaboard would have protected some Indian nations before 1763?

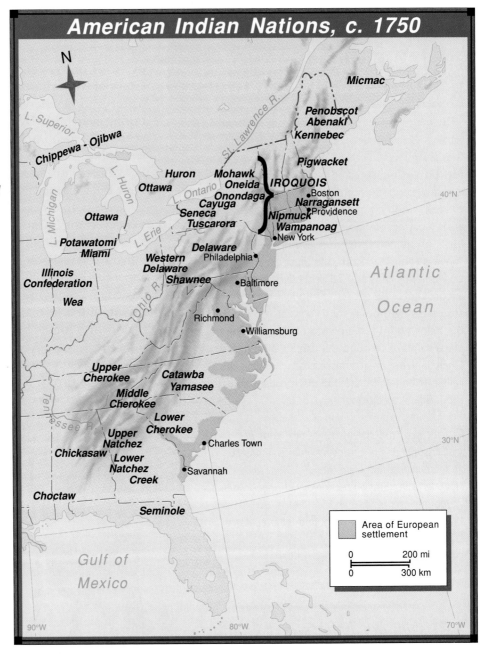

American Indian Nations, c. 1750

N

L. Superior

Chippewa - Ojibwa

L. Huron

L. Michigan

St. Lawrence R.

Micmac

Penobscot
Abenaki
Kennebec

Pigwacket

Huron
Ottawa
Mohawk
Oneida
Onondaga
Cayuga
Seneca
Tuscarora
IROQUOIS
•Boston
Narragansett
•Providence
Nipmuck
Wampanoag
•New York

L. Ontario

Ottawa

Potawatomi
Miami

Illinois
Confederation

Wea

L. Erie

Ohio R.

Delaware
Western
Delaware
Shawnee
•Philadelphia
•Baltimore
•Richmond
•Williamsburg

40°N

Atlantic
Ocean

Upper
Cherokee
Middle
Cherokee
Catawba
Yamasee

Tennessee R.

Lower
Cherokee

Upper
Natchez
Chickasaw
Lower
Natchez
Creek

•Charles Town

•Savannah

30°N

Choctaw

Seminole

Gulf of
Mexico

Area of European
settlement

0   200 mi
0   300 km

90°W   80°W   70°W

came in 1675 when authorities in Plymouth hanged three Indians for murdering a Christian Indian named Sassamon. Sassamon had attended Harvard, left Christianity to serve with Metacomet, and then returned to the Christian fold. The execution of the three Wampanoags led Metacomet and the Wampanoag tribesmen to retaliate by attacking the settlement of Swansea on the outskirts of Plymouth.

King Philip's War soon spread as members of the Nipmuck and Narragansett tribes joined Metacomet's forces. Other Indians, including members of the Mohawk tribe, fought with the colonists. Six hundred colonists and 3,000 Indians died as a result of the war, which raged for 11 months. Near the end of the war, Metacomet was killed, and his head was taken back to Plymouth where it was displayed for the next 25 years. At the close of the war, the colonists executed some of the surviving Indian leaders and sold others (including Metacomet's wife and son) into slavery in the West Indies. King Philip's War diminished New England's Indian population by 40 percent and effectively ended Indian resistance in New England.

Indian Resistance to Slavery

A good deal of colonial warfare sprang from the practice of enslaving Indian captives. Although the total number of Indians forced into slavery is unknown, it must have been in the tens of thousands. A census taken by the General Court of South Carolina in 1708 reported the presence of 1,400 Indian slaves among 1,000 white families. Other colonial records indicate that thousands more Indians were sent into slavery in the West Indies. The practice of enslaving Indians was sufficiently widespread to provoke retaliatory attacks by Indians, especially those south of Virginia.

One such attack, which set off the **Yamasee Border War**, took place in 1712 in North Carolina. The Tuscarora and several other tribes attacked and killed 130 English and German traders who had been cheating some of their Indian customers and enslaving others. In reprisal, the slave traders destroyed a Tuscarora fort, burning alive several Tuscaroras, killing 166 men regarded as unsuitable for slavery, and sending 392 others, mostly women and children, to the Charles Town slave market. The remaining Tuscaroras, the Yamasees, and other Indians representing 14 separate tribes began a series of counterattacks throughout the Carolinas, killing more than 400 white settlers. Some settlers escaped death only because the Indians could not maintain their alliance.

One by one, the allied tribes stopped their raids. The remnants of the Tuscarora, expelled from North Carolina by the English, sought asylum with the Oneidas of the Five Iroquois Nations. Later, the Tuscaroras became the sixth nation in the Iroquois confederacy. The end of the Yamasee Border War came in 1718 when some of the Indians realized that their only chance for survival was to move south to uninhabited regions of Spanish Florida, out of reach of the English colonists.

Technology Brings Changes

The greatest transformation in most Indians' traditional way of life came not as a result of English religious ideas, warfare, or enslavement, but as a result of English technology and trade goods. At first, the Indians hungered for English goods that made life easier or more pleasant. Metal tools—axes, hoes, knives, and guns—became substitutes for stone, bone, or wooden tools. Women welcomed iron kettles and awls, pointed tools for marking surfaces or piercing holes. When the weather was warm, "a good coarse blanket" or a piece of "broade cloth" felt more comfortable as a coat or a bed cover than a fur robe. Mirrors, rings, and Venetian glass beads gained popularity because they were both novel and decorative.

In the early days, as the fur trade dominated the colonial export economy, the Indians' dependence on English goods grew steadily. This was because the more time that Indians spent hunting for fur-bearing animals, the less time they had for providing for daily needs. Killing large numbers of animals for the fur trade also changed many Indians' attitudes toward wildlife.

The use of guns also brought great changes to the Indians' way of life. Before the 1600s, wars between tribes had been ritualistic encounters fought with bows and arrows or war clubs and had caused few deaths. By the end of that century, wars had become more deadly, fought with guns to capture, enslave, or destroy enemies. Some Indian societies also developed the type of centralized political leadership needed for large-scale military encounters. Occasionally, several tribes joined to fight against colonists. More often, however, Indian groups allied themselves with colonists against other Indian tribes. These alliances were set up for economic reasons or to obtain captives who would be adopted to replace tribal members killed in battle or sold into slavery.

Indian Cultural Influences

The colonists' culture was also affected by encounters with the Indians. Colonists adopted many Indian techniques for farming and hunting, for building temporary shelters, and for making leather clothing. A great number of Indian words became part of the emerging American English language. Because English had no names for animals native to American soil, such as the moose, the skunk, and the chipmunk, colonists used Indian words usually from the Algonquian (al-GAHN-kwee-uhn) family of languages. The colonists also used Indian words for food such as maize, hominy, and succotash. They learned to call certain trees tamarack, or hickory, or pecan.

Some settlers found Indian life so attractive that they adopted much more than just words. These colonists embraced the entire Indian way of life. Called "white Indians" by other colonists, they either lived with Indian tribes or near them, and practiced a way of life indistinguishable from that of their Indian friends. Some colonists captured during Indian raids and adopted into tribes refused to return to their families when they had the opportunity. French immigrant **Hector St. John Crèvecoeur** (krev-KUR) reported, "Thousands of Europeans are Indians, and we have no examples of even one of these Aborigines having from choice become European!"

Although some groups of European colonists and American Indians maintained friendly relationships, other groups became increasingly hostile toward one another throughout the late 1600s and early 1700s. In the end, it was the Indians who would move out of their traditional territories, displacing other Indian peoples. The early encounters between the Indians and the European settlers set up patterns of interaction. These patterns would be repeated for a long time.

SECTION 3 REVIEW

1. **Describe** two features about the Indian praying towns established by New England settlers.
2. **Explain** the significance of King Philip's War.
3. **Identify** the Yamasee Border War of 1712.
4. **Name** trade goods that appealed to the Indians.
5. **Summarize** briefly ways in which Indian culture affected the lives of European settlers.

SECTION 4

Intellectual and Religious Developments

Flashes of lightning on a rainy night in 1752 revealed a short, stocky figure scampering along holding tightly to the string of a flying kite. **Benjamin Franklin** was trying to prove that lightning was an electrical discharge. He tied a key to his kite string, and when threads of the string stood erect and repelled each other, he gingerly brought his knuckle up to touch the key. He expected a shock, and he received one. Franklin was lucky that he didn't kill himself. To his great satisfaction, however, he did prove that both the kite and the string had become electrified.

During the same period, **Benjamin Banneker**, a free black farmer, experimented successfully with clock designs, and taught himself calculus and trigonometry. For seven years he published an astronomical almanac.

Such personal experimentation to establish scientific principles and the use of such principles for practical inventions (such as the lightning rod) were typical not only of Benjamin Franklin and Benjamin Banneker, but also of many other colonists who valued knowledge and understanding.

Why did most colonists value an education?

How did the American Enlightenment set the stage for America's later interest in science and technology?

In what ways was the Great Awakening both divisive and cohesive?

Colonists Value Education

As a group, the American colonists were well educated compared to European populations of the same time period. Estimates suggest that by the mid-1700s about 90 percent of white males and 40 to 50 percent of white females in New England could read. Puritans believed that all individuals should read the Bible for themselves. To make that possible, Massachusetts lawmakers decreed in 1647 that every town of 50 families must provide a schoolmaster to teach all children—boys and girls alike—to read and write. The formal education of girls was usually brief, although a few towns set up academies where females could study sewing or music, the "lighter" subjects. The majority of Puritan men apparently believed as John Winthrop did: a woman who read too much would go insane, because women's brains were weaker than men's.

Towns larger than 100 families established Latin grammar schools, or secondary schools, to prepare young men who "may be fitted" for university training. Designed initially for the education of ministers, Harvard College was founded in 1636 to teach courses in theology, Latin, Greek, Hebrew, logic, and rhetoric. By the mid-1700s, Dartmouth College (first opened in 1767 as an Indian college), Yale, and Rhode Island College (later to become Brown University) had been established. By that time colleges were no longer meant just to train ministers, but were also open to gentlemen and professionals of all types.

In the middle and southern colonies, the literacy rate among white males was about 30 to 50 percent by the 1720s, about the same as in England. Those colonies had no publicly funded schools, but all boasted some private schools where students could study languages, surveying, bookkeeping, arithmetic, music, and even dancing. Several middle and southern colonies also provided higher education for their ministers. The Presbyterians founded New Jersey College (Princeton University), and the Dutch Reformed Church established Rutgers University. King's College (Columbia) in New York and the College of William and Mary in Virginia began to train ministers for the Episcopal, or Anglican, Church. Despite the number of colleges, only a small percentage of men actually attended and no women.

Only a very few Indians and Africans in the colonies received a formal education. For the most part, Indians found an English education of little use for their way of life. Many black people wanted an education. Boston poet **Phillis Wheatley** showed such great intellectual promise that her owners provided her with a tutor. Most colonists felt, however, that educated slaves would be a threat. Some free black people obtained an education in special schools, such as the one set up in Massachusetts by the black Quaker and sea captain Paul Cuffe.

▲ *Phillis Wheatley (c. 1753–1784)*

The Printed Word

Early Puritan literature reflected the colonists' deep religious faith. Sermons were listened to, read, and discussed at great length. The first book published in the colonies was *The Bay Psalm Book*, a collection of Old Testament psalms translated into rhythmic prose so they could be sung during church services. Poetry was almost always religious in nature. The best-known Puritan poet, **Anne Bradstreet**, did write of her love for her husband and children and her natural surroundings, but always within a religious framework. Phillis Wheatley, the first published black female author in the colonies, also emphasized religious themes in her poetry. Even children's textbooks carried religious messages. One New England primer used couplets to teach the alphabet: "Time cuts down all, Both great and small," and "Zacheus he did climb the Tree, his Lord to see."

Enduring Constitution

Peter Zenger and Freedom of the Press

Imagine you are the editor of a small town newspaper that has been publishing articles about the corruption and illegal activities of the state governor. You have indisputable proof of these activities. Nonetheless, you are arrested, thrown into jail for nine months, and brought to trial for treason—a crime punishable by death. Under the law, it does not matter if what you printed was true or not, only that it made the state officials look bad.

In November of 1734, **Peter Zenger** found himself in just such a situation. Zenger was a German immigrant hired by a group of colonial New York lawyers to act as editor and publisher for the *New York Weekly Gazette*, a publication that printed articles critical of William Cosby, the corrupt and thoroughly disliked royal governor.

In England, the spoken and written word had always been subject to censorship. Treasonous statements, even such careless slips as a "toast to better days," could be punished by imprison-

Peter Zenger joyfully recounts his acquittal from charges of seditious libel. Was Zenger innocent of the charges against him?

▲ *This rendition of Zenger's trial shows only part of the courtroom, but enough for us to realize that it was very different from today's courtrooms. What are some of the differences?*

ment, mutilation, or death. English common law held that it was a crime to publish any information or express any ideas that criticized the government. Speaking or writing against the monarchy, Parliament, or the king's ministers was called *seditious libel*. Whether or not the statement was accurate did not matter. Simply making the accusation was a crime.

In colonial America, censorship was not as strictly enforced

Enduring Constitution

(continued)

as in England, but the threat of censorship had always been present. The particular issue that sparked Zenger's arrest concerned the right to control the governor's salary. The governor was unable to arrest the authors of the articles, because, during the long months of his imprisonment, Zenger refused to reveal his sources.

At the trial, the jury had only to rule on the identity of whoever had published the statements. The truth of the charges was not decided by the jury.

Zenger's lawyer was Andrew Hamilton, a brilliant and respected resident of Philadelphia. Having no way to win the case as the law was interpreted, he boldly admitted his client's guilt as publisher and challenged the jury to find Zenger innocent on the basis that what he had printed was the truth. "The question before the Court and you gentlemen of the jury," Hamilton said, "is not of small nor private concern . . . It may in its consequences affect every freeman that lives under a British government on the main of America. It is the best cause. It is the cause of liberty; . . . every man who prefers freedom to a life of slavery will bless and honor you as men who have baffled the attempt of tyranny . . . . have given us the right—the liberty—both of exposing and opposing arbitrary power (in these parts of the world, at least) by speaking and writing truth."

Swayed by Hamilton's arguments, the jury found Zenger innocent. Eventually, the concept of freedom of the press was enshrined in the Bill of Rights to our enduring Constitution.

1. Why do you think the British government feared any criticism of its actions?
2. Making untrue spoken statements is called slander. Writing untrue statements is libel. Do you think one is more serious than the other? Why, or why not?

Not all colonial writing was religious, however. Almanacs were by far the most popular colonial publications, with Benjamin Franklin's annual *Poor Richard's Almanack* selling 10,000 copies a year. First printed in 1732, this almanac contained such practical information as calendars, planting guides, and recipes, as well as jokes, poems, and proverbs. "Early to bed, early to rise makes a man healthy, wealthy, and wise" is one example.

Weekly newspapers appeared in the early 1700s. People often gathered in groups to hear the newspaper read aloud. The first page printed news from England or other parts of Europe. The second page included news reprinted from other colonial newspapers, and the last two pages carried advertisements. There were few illustrations, but sometimes an editor would include a humorous poem or a short story. Because of the information about events in other colonies, and because colonists carried newspapers with them when they traveled, these publications became an important communication link among the various colonies.

The Enlightenment During the eighteenth century, Americans also read books and essays describing new ideas that were sweeping through Europe. Called by historians the **Enlightenment**, or the Age of Reason, this intellectual revolution suggested that the universe was orderly and governed by natural laws that could be understood by humans. Some European philosophers maintained that a benevolent God had set the world in motion like

Although Benjamin Franklin sold his almanac under the pseudonym of "Poor" Richard Saunders, it was his own work. Note the table of contents. Would you have liked to read this work?

a giant clock. He had then left it to human beings to use their reason to fashion institutions such as governments and churches for the improvement of the human condition. Many colonists ignored the religious implications of the Enlightenment. They did, however, take part in the energetic search for practical knowledge and useful inventions.

▲ *What do you think the artist was trying to say about Franklin in this portrait? What is the significance of what shows through the window?*

Scientific Studies

Benjamin Franklin was perhaps the most brilliant of colonial American thinkers; certainly he was one of the best known. He made a good deal of money in the printing trade, and retired from business in his early forties. He then began the most productive part of his life as scientist, statesman, and diplomat. Franklin tirelessly promoted humanitarian and cultural institutions. He founded the Society for the Relief of Free Negroes, Unlawfully Held; the first American lending library; and the American Philosophical Society, a forum where men could talk over their scientific investigations.

Franklin's own work included charting the routes of hurricanes and the flow of the Gulf

Stream. He conducted many other studies of electricity besides the famous kite experiment. He was the first scientist to understand the concept of negative and positive electrical currents. The lightning rod was only one of his many practical inventions. Franklin also developed the energy-efficient Franklin stove, bifocal glasses, a watering trough for horses, and a fan for his chair that would keep off flies. Franklin let others copy his inventions, suggesting that "as we enjoy great advantages from the inventions of others, we should be glad of an opportunity to serve others by any invention of ours."

Other American colonists studied natural history, astronomy, and medicine. Many plants and animals in the colonies were unknown in Europe. By collecting and describing these, several Americans aided Carl Linnaeus of Sweden as he developed his

Rittenhouse invented the orrery, at left, as a mechanical model of Newton's theory that equal but opposing forces hold the solar system in place.

▲ *How did the rational approach of scientists like David Rittenhouse lead to the modern scientific method?*

famous taxonomy, the orderly classification of the species of living things. John Bartram, a Quaker farmer in Pennsylvania, was one example of such a self-taught naturalist. David Rittenhouse, a clockmaker and university lecturer, studied astronomy and built a working model of the solar system.

Congregationalist minister **Cotton Mather** successfully inoculated his family and volunteer friends against smallpox when an epidemic broke out in Boston in 1720. Mather had read about the benefits of inoculation in an English publication and had the courage to try it out even when most doctors of the time spoke against it.

What distinguished the members of the Enlightenment, especially the early American scientists, was their firm belief that with enough thought and study all the world could be explained rationally and logically. Like Franklin and Mather, they experimented, and, certain of their convictions, they dared to act.

The Great Awakening

While some colonists were engaged in expanding their knowledge of science, many others were caught up in a burst of religious enthusiasm known as the **Great Awakening**. The movement spread across the northern and middle colonies from 1730 through 1740. By the 1750s and 1760s, the Awakening had spread into Virginia. Many ministers were worried about declining church membership, the decay in family authority, dishonest business practices, and an increase in swearing, lying, and young people staying out late at night. Several churchmen, like **Jonathan Edwards**, a Congregational minister in Massachusetts, believed that sinners needed to be brought back to the church. To reawaken religious devotion, these ministers held **revival meetings** in their churches.

During one such meeting, Edwards, who claimed he was not given to the emotional preachings of some other ministers of the time, still managed to put "the fear of God" into his listeners. His sermon "Sinners in the Hands of an Angry God" was reprinted many times and circulated throughout the colonies. People were chilled as they read:

> The God that holds you over the pit of hell, much as one holds a spider . . . over the fire, abhors you, and is dreadfully provoked; his wrath towards you burns like fire; he looks upon you as worthy of nothing else but to be cast into the fire. . . . There is reason to think that there are many in this congregation now hearing this discourse that will actually be the subjects of this fiery misery to all eternity.

Faced with such a vivid image, many backsliders returned to their churches.

◄ *Although pictured here inside a church, Whitefield is best known for enthralling huge outdoor audiences. According to some historical accounts, as many as 20,000 people attended his sermons.*

preach at churches all along his route to Georgia. He gathered such huge crowds that no church could hold all his listeners. Speaking in open fields, this small dynamic man with deep-set piercing eyes would pace back and forth and wave his hands as he made his points. His religious fervor and highly dramatic preaching style enticed thousands to come forward to confess their sins and throw themselves on God's mercy.

Soon other traveling ministers began to hold revival meetings, with people coming from near and far to listen to thunderous sermons. These sermons succeeded in reviving an interest in religion among many who had become indifferent. Puritan Congregationalists, the German sects, the Scots-Irish Presbyterians, and members of Baptist churches made up the largest audiences. Everywhere these zealous ministers spoke, they found many ready to

▼ *A Russian artist captured the rite of baptism in this drawing. New Light factions such as the Methodists and Baptists grew rapidly as a result of the Great Awakening.*

Traveling Ministers Spread the Gospel   A second notable minister of the Great Awakening was Englishman **George Whitefield**. In 1739, he stopped in Philadelphia on his way to Savannah, where he had been hired as a minister and planned to open an orphanage. Whitefield was a disciple of John Wesley, the founder of the evangelical Methodist movement within the Church of England. Invited to preach in Philadelphia before starting his trip, Whitefield made such an impression that he received invitations to

accept their message: to escape damnation, people had to cleanse themselves of sin, surrender to God's will, and accept the salvation of Jesus Christ. Many who converted went back to their old ways in short order, but for others their conversion became a life-long commitment.

The Great Awakening placed renewed emphasis on religion, but it was also divisive in some ways. Those who adopted the teachings of Edwards and Whitefield became known as New Lights; those who rejected them became known as Old Lights. Some of the most effective revivalists had not been trained as ministers, and most educated ministers did not believe that a revival's "bitter Shrieking, and Screaming; Convulsion like Tremblings and Agitations, Struggling and Tumblings" brought about true conversion to the faith. The congregations of established churches began to take sides on the issue, with some churches splitting into two groups. In New England, many Congregationalists left their church to become members of Baptist churches. The social position of ministers declined as people flocked to churches where a minister's education was considered less important than his preaching.

The Great Awakening had other results. New Lights reached out to include slaves in their services, and some slaves even became members of white churches. After a period of religious conflict and competition, people began to realize that they could make choices about how to practice religion. While this undermined the established churches, it also encouraged religious tolerance.

SECTION 4 REVIEW

1. **Describe** the connection between education and religion.
2. **List** the types of scientific study the colonists undertook.
3. **Identify** the Enlightenment.
4. **State** why some ministers of established churches opposed the New Lights.
5. **Explain** how the Great Awakening divided colonial society.

SECTION 5

Political and Economic Changes in the Colonies

When William Penn was organizing his colony in the late 1660s, he found that the political leaders of Pennsylvania spent much of their time arguing. In despair, Penn chided the political leaders of Philadelphia: "Cannot more friendly and private courses be taken to set matters right in an infant province? . . . For the love of God, me, and the poor country, be not so governmentish!" What Penn meant by "governmentish" was too much discussion over small items of business and too much control over what could be handled privately. But the people of Pennsylvania and the other colonies continued to be quarrelsome and "governmentish" throughout the colonial period. Politics were sometimes reduced to a state of chaos. There was competition among branches of the colonial governments and among economic, social, and regional groups. It seemed everybody was competing to have his or her personal and group interests served. Most seventeenth- and eighteenth-century governors at one time or another must have agreed with Penn: the colonists were "noisy and open in dissatisfactions."

Was the English system of government appropriate for the colonies?

What conflicts arose between those who governed and those who were governed?

How did the organization of the colonial governments provide a good model for colonists who would soon adopt their own government?

The English Model

From the beginning, the governments within the colonies reflected the English political system. The colonists considered themselves under the rule of the king and the two houses of Parliament. They believed that only adult male property owners should vote and that only the wealthy and wellborn should have power. As English subjects, they felt they had the certain right to freedom.

Colonial governors were the king's representatives and were responsible for overseeing the colonial government and enforcing laws. Councils advised the governor and assisted in running the colony. Council members were usually chosen from the ranks of wealthy merchants or planters and took on duties similar to those of the members of the English House of Lords. There was also an elected assembly modeled after England's House of Commons.

The assembly had power to make laws. This body had control over raising money through taxes and deciding how that money was to be spent. In effect, the assemblies represented the will of the majority of colonists. But the council, as well as the governor, had power to revoke any laws made by the elected assembly. They seldom canceled laws, however, because they feared the anger of the ordinary people. Intended to be the weakest part of colonial government, the assemblies eventually became the strongest part.

In many colonies, most free white adult males owned enough property to meet the qualifications for voting. They expected their representatives to act on their wishes. In New England, for example, citizens took part in **town meetings**, where they discussed issues and instructed assemblymen as to how they should vote. Overall, this system of government worked well until the mid-eighteenth century. There were, however, internal conflicts that tested colonial society.

Colonial Rebellions

Bacon's Rebellion was a serious conflict that disrupted colonial society in Virginia. In that colony, many freed indentured servants, as well as other poor immigrants, had settled in the backcountry. These frontier people suffered attacks by Indians who had not given up their own claims to that land. They were angry because the **House of Burgesses**, the Virginia assembly established in 1619, did not make sufficient efforts to protect them. In 1676,

Nathaniel Bacon, a prosperous new immigrant to the colony, demanded that the governor punish the Indians. When Governor Berkeley refused, Bacon organized 300 men, including many unemployed and homeless colonists, to act on their own. Bacon's backwoods army attacked the first Indians they encountered. As it happened, those Indians were not only peaceful, but they were also fur-trading partners of the governor and his wealthy and powerful friends. Furious with Bacon, Berkeley wanted to arrest him and all his men, but feared to do so because of favorable public reaction to Bacon's raid. Public pressure forced Berkeley to hold an election for the House of Burgesses. Bacon was elected, and he pushed through the reforms that he and his followers advocated.

The assembly itself soon called for Bacon to lead another expedition against the Indians. While Bacon was away from Jamestown, Berkeley raised his own army, hoping to attack Bacon on his return and thus retain power and control for the wealthy. A virtual civil war quickly unfolded. Upon his return Bacon attacked and set fire to Jamestown. The governor fled across Chesapeake Bay, and Bacon then set up his own government. It is impossible to know if Bacon would have retained his power because he became ill and died. His followers disbanded. Governor Berkeley was restored to power and quickly executed 33 of Bacon's followers. Berkeley, too, soon lost his power. He was recalled to England by King Charles II, who was tired of the conflict in Virginia and called Berkeley an "old Fool." The new governor accepted most of Bacon's reforms, which gave

Early on it became clear that colonial governments were not able to protect the rights of all their people. In Virginia, Nathaniel Bacon (left) demanded a commission from the military governor so that he and his neighbors could retaliate against Indian attacks. How do you think Governor Berkeley is responding?

The Salem Witch Hunt

Fear abounded in Salem Village, Massachusetts, in 1692. The village's agricultural way of life was changing forever, as the region's economic emphasis shifted toward trade. Commercial competition from nearby Salem Town and the threat of attacks from Indians facing encroachments by white settlers added to the general fears that came with changing times. There was also the fear of the devil, a theme that was woven throughout the sermons of Boston's minister, Dr. Cotton Mather.

Whether fear was the main cause of the terrible events of that year remains a point of controversy. There have been many theories developed over the years to explain the troubles that gripped Salem Village and led to the deaths of 20 people and the imprisonment of more than 100 citizens. One thing, however, is clear: Fear may not have started the events that have come to be known as the Salem Witch hunt, but fear certainly fed the fires of hysteria that burned in Salem Village in 1692.

The troubles began early in 1692, when two girls began to exhibit wild, strange behavior, including shouting and barking for no reason. The girls claimed that they had been bewitched by Tituba, a slave from the West Indies, whom the girls had earlier

▲ The Trial of George Jacobs for Witchcraft, 1692, *painted in 1855, shows a chaotic courtroom. How realistic do you think it is?*

befriended. Soon other girls began to act strangely and make accusations. Within weeks, dozens of people had been accused of witchcraft and locked in jail. In May of 1692, Royal Governor William Phips arrived from England. Phips immediately ordered a special court be convened to try the accused "witches," under a British law against witchcraft that had been passed by King James I in 1603. By the fall of 1692, the court had condemned twenty villagers to death for practicing witchcraft. Nineteen of these people were hanged outside of town on what was called Witches Hill. One man, 80-year-old Giles Corey, was also condemned to death at the trial. He was pressed, or crushed, to death under heavy stones.

Soon, however, the officials and the townspeople began to question the accusations. The accusers especially began to feel a backlash when they accused some of the more prominent townspeople of witchcraft. By May of 1693, the witch hunt was over, but for the twenty people who had been executed, it was too late. For historians and sociologists, the Salem witch hunt remains an event to be studied—a lesson in mass hysteria.

1. Why would Salem villagers believe the young girls were bewitched?
2. Do you think a bout of hysteria could occur in your own community today? Why, or why not?

more power to the House of Burgesses. That action furthered a general movement toward stronger local self-government.

The Dominion of New England   In the North, a second rebellion tested English control of the colonies. Increasingly, colonists in New England ignored taxes due on colonial export goods. The English Parliament reacted by placing the northern colonies into an association known as the Dominion of New England. Its appointed governor, Sir Edmund Andros, proved at once to be a dictatorial and inept leader. He refused to pay attention to the councils of the colonies, and he issued laws, including tax laws, on his own authority. Neither Andros nor his king retained power for long. Always unpopular, James II was forced to relinquish the crown to his daughter Mary and her husband, William of Orange, in a bloodless revolt. When news of this "Glorious Revolution" reached Boston in 1689, a furious crowd cheered and then arrested Andros and his aides and turned control of the government back to the council. The other colonies in the Dominion of New England followed Massachusetts and restored their local governments.

William and Mary did take away some of the colonists' rights. Massachusetts lost its earlier charter and was made a royal colony. They gave the new governor the power to veto Massachusetts council members. They also ordered that voting rights be granted on the basis of personal property, rather than on church membership. These new restrictions brought instability to the colony and its Puritan population.

Local Control of Government

During the 1700s, the concept of local control over local concerns drew many supporters. More people were allowed to vote than in earlier times, and many people took a keen interest in political affairs. Voting rights had expanded to include most property owners and, although qualifications for voting differed among the colonies, many people who would not have been able to vote in England could do so in the colonies. Even so, Jews, slaves, free blacks, indentured servants, Indians, women from any class, and all adult males who did not own property were excluded from voting in the colonies.

Because of their larger populations and more diverse occupations, the cities needed more government officials, local laws, and greater regulation of businesses. Although it was true that rural towns and communities also had to build and maintain roads and bridges, operate criminal courts, and provide for the poor, these tasks were more complicated in the cities. The sheer volume of work undertaken by city government made its functions more visible. This, in turn, encouraged closer scrutiny by the voters.

In the cities, as everywhere else in the colonies, the rich and wellborn tended to be elected to the important municipal offices. City dwellers reacted more strongly than rural colonists to the misuse of power. Street crowds, made up of the very poor who could not vote, influenced city politics through open protests. Sometimes these mobs took control of city offices to show their anger at a particular piece of legislation or at a regulation they disliked. Called the "unthinking multitude, the rabble" by the elite, these crowds were to become increasingly influential during the early 1700s, and they would later play a large role in the events that led to revolution.

The Mercantile System

In the early 1600s, the English had wanted colonies for the prestige they would bring to their country. During the next fifty years, the English Parliament began to realize that colonies also could be used to increase the economic well-being of the mother country. Like other European nations of the time, the English developed an economic policy known as **mercantilism**. The theory of mercantilism assumed that the entire world contained a limited amount of wealth and that the wealth of one nation represented lost wealth for all other nations. Under mercantilism the goals of a nation were:

■ to become as economically self-sufficient as possible, therefore limiting its dependence on the resources and goods of other nations.

- to acquire and maintain plentiful supplies of gold and silver by selling more goods to other nations than were bought from them.
- to acquire and maintain colonies as sources for raw materials and as markets for the nation's manufactured goods.

Under this system, colonies existed solely for the profit of the mother country. To assure themselves of that profit, parliament passed the **Navigation Act of 1651**. Under this act, Dutch traders who had been actively trading with the English colonies could no longer sell or buy goods in America. More Navigation Acts were passed in 1660 and 1663, and they were amended throughout the next hundred years. These acts stated that colonial cargoes were to be carried in British or colonial ships with crews that were at least three-quarters British or colonial. Foreign ships carrying goods destined for the colonies had to be routed to England or Scotland. This extra landing increased the price of foreign goods, thus making them less attractive to colonists.

Colonists could sell certain specific goods such as tobacco, rice, indigo, furs, and naval supplies only within the British Empire. These were called enumerated goods, and members of the empire could not buy those goods from other nations. Grain, livestock, lumber, fish, and rum (items that made up 60 percent of colonial exports) were never restricted because Britain had its own supplies. The colonists were encouraged to produce iron ore, hemp, lumber, dyes, and silk, because these goods had to be imported by Britain. Finally, the Navigation Acts forbade colonists to develop their own cloth-making or iron-making industries on a large scale that would compete against the British industries. Neither of these prohibitions hurt the colonies very much in the short run. British cloth was very cheap, and the British were happy to import pig iron from American smeltry works and send back to America manufactured iron tools.

In many ways, the Navigation Acts benefited the colonists. They provided farmers and merchants with a steady market in England and her other colonies. They also gave colonists opportunities to develop skills in shipbuilding and shiphandling. The English tended to ignore the acts for long periods of

▲ Boat building became an important industry in the seacoast colonies. What region would have benefited most from this industry?

time. The colonists learned to take advantage of the acts when it was to their benefit and to ignore them when it was not. This casual attitude toward English laws would continue to grow in the 1700s.

SECTION 5 REVIEW

1. **Describe** the ways in which the colonial governments were modeled after the system of government in England.
2. **Justify** King Charles II calling Governor Berkeley an "old Fool."
3. **List** two examples of actions that angered New England colonists opposed to Governor Andros.
4. **Identify** mercantilism.
5. **List** three basic requirements of the Navigation Acts passed by the British government.

Summary

From the time of the first settlement until the mid-1750s, the colonists moved from nearly complete dependence on agriculture to an economy that also included commercial fishing, small-scale manufacturing, and a growing Atlantic trade. Seaport cities grew to support that trade, and small towns were established to handle the trade that developed in the western regions of the colonies.

The increasing production of tobacco, rice, and indigo accelerated the growth of slavery. In every way possible, slaves demonstrated their reluctance to accept their condition. Members of many Indian tribes were also enslaved. Their traditional ways of life were destroyed both by forced moves and by the changes that took place in their society as they adopted English technology.

Intellectual affairs preoccupied some colonists in the early eighteenth century. Colonial scientists made solid contributions to scientific knowledge as they conducted observations and experiments. In religious matters, the Great Awakening changed many church practices and won many converts.

The English model of government began to give way to the idea of local control, especially among city dwellers. England's mercantile policies restricted the colonists from competing with British industries, but American skills and industries flourished.

By the mid–eighteenth century, the colonies were beginning to find their own identities, and they were starting to feel they were part of a region. But it would be some time before they had any sort of national identity.

Vocabulary

Enlightenment

Great Awakening

indentured servant

mercantilism

praying town

revival meeting

squatter's rights

town meeting

triangular trade

Below are short descriptions of situations or scenarios. On your paper, write the vocabulary term from the list that is illustrated or defined by each statement.

1. John disliked public speaking, but he wanted his assemblyman to know exactly how he felt.
2. This was not the first time they had been forced to move, but until they could afford to buy the land outright there was nothing they could do.
3. The colony's shopkeepers were forced to charge their customers higher prices for tea since they could import only English goods.
4. Her family had lived on the land for generations, but now the town had an unfamiliar feel. The church stood in the center of town.
5. The Winthrops were worried about the last shipment to England. The family had little faith in the ability of the captain to negotiate a profitable cargo in Africa.
6. A few minutes of listening had her both trembling with fear and fired up with passion.
7. It was a long time and hard work, but eventually Samuel would realize the day when he could be his own master.
8. This belief in a rational explanation for the universe strongly influenced her writings.
9. The town's renewed interest in religion gratified the Reverend Whitely.

Review Questions

1. Describe how soil fertility, climate, and labor resources affected farming practices in the colonies.
2. Describe some ways settlers who did not farm could make a living.
3. Explain how the development of fishing and shipbuilding stimulated trade.
4. What was the triangular trade?
5. Why did southern planters prefer slave labor over indentured servants?

6. Describe some methods enslaved Africans used to fight their enslavement.
7. List at least four items of European technology adopted by American Indians.
8. What was the chief accomplishment of the American Enlightenment?
9. Describe two ways that colonial society was affected by the Great Awakening.
10. Explain two ways in which the Navigation Acts helped the colonists.

Critical Historical Thinking

Writing Answer each of the following questions by writing one or more complete paragraphs:

1. The meeting of the European and the different American Indian cultures generally resulted in conflict. Do you think this conflict was inevitable? Why, or why not?
2. How did the different social and economic characteristics of the northern and southern colonies later play a crucial, and tragic, role in American history?
3. Compare the treatment that Indians and enslaved Africans received at the hands of the American colonists.
4. Read the selection in the Unit 1 Archives entitled "Indentured Servants." Whom do you think this arrangement favored more, the colonial employer or the immigrant looking for a new life? Give reasons for your answer.

Making Connections with Folk Traditions

Benjamin Franklin was well known to colonists for publishing *Poor Richard's Almanack*, which featured many maxims (sayings) from the folk traditions of various peoples and countries. The maxims

dealt with virtues of the idealized common man, such as honesty, hard work, independence, and thrift. You will probably recognize the following offerings from the *Almanack*:

God helps them that help themselves.
Honesty is the best policy.

Many of the sayings were humorous or biting:
Fish and visitors stink in three days.
Three may keep a secret if two of them are dead.

Some of the maxims have come down to us in a slightly different form:
A penny saved is two pence cleared. (A penny saved is a penny earned.)
Don't throw stones at your neighbors, if your own windows are glass. (People who live in glass houses shouldn't throw stones.)

▪ Write three maxims that might appear in a "modern" *Poor Richard's Almanack*. An example might be "Share a disk, share a virus."

Additional Skills Practice

Refer to a political map of the United States in an atlas. Answer the following questions about your state:

1. (a) What is the ratio of inches to miles on the map scale? (b) How many miles would be represented by 2 inches? How many by 3½ inches?
2. What is the approximate distance from the state capital to the northernmost point within the state?
3. What symbol represents (a) major highways, (b) rivers, (c) airports?
4. Does the map represent physical features (relief) such as mountains or lakes? If yes, what does the map key tell you about relief?
5. How many states are contiguous (touching or bordering on your state?

Unit 1 Review

Unit Review Questions

Write a brief paragraph in answer to each of the following prompts:

1. What evidence do we have that the Americas were first populated by migrants from Asia?
2. Explain why Europeans wanted to find a new trade route to the Orient.
3. Explain why France was more successful in dealing with the Indians in North America than were England and Spain.
4. Why did the English settlement of North America become permanent, whereas the Dutch and French settlements failed?
5. Explain the reasons for the introduction of the slave trade into America.
6. Comment on the effect of European exploration and colonization on the societies of American Indians.
7. Describe the fatal economic mistake made by Spain while she was the richest, most powerful country in Europe.
8. If you wanted to study Spanish influence in North America, explain what would provide you with the best avenue of study.
9. How were New England settlers able to move away from their dependence on agriculture?
10. How did the Great Awakening affect the social history of America during this period?

Personalizing History

Twenty Questions Pretend you are a colonist in the early 1700s. Write a paragraph describing your situation, including the conditions in your home country that motivated your emigration, and indicating where in America you will be settling. Select

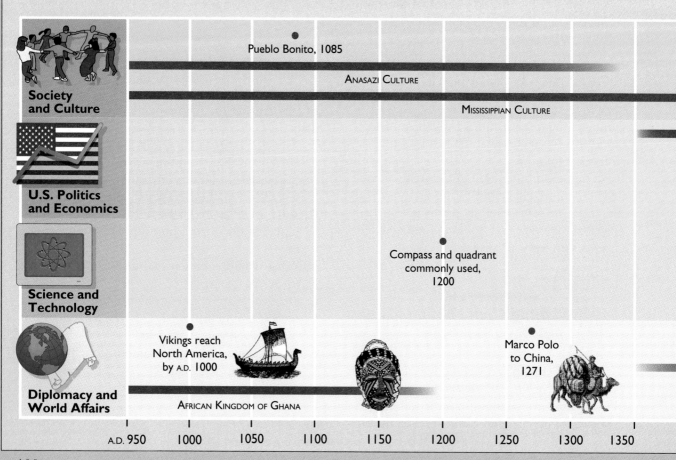

Pueblo Bonito, 1085

ANASAZI CULTURE

MISSISSIPPIAN CULTURE

Society and Culture

U.S. Politics and Economics

Science and Technology

Compass and quadrant commonly used, 1200

Vikings reach North America, by A.D. 1000

Marco Polo to China, 1271

Diplomacy and World Affairs

AFRICAN KINGDOM OF GHANA

A.D. 950   1000   1050   1100   1150   1200   1250   1300   1350 an occupation that would best suit you. (Remember to choose from careers available in the 1700s.) Describe your social status (gentry, middle class, indentured servant, enslaved African, etc.).

▪ Use this profile to take turns playing "Twenty Questions" with your classmates. See if they can guess who you are in less than twenty questions by asking questions that can only be answered "yes" or "no."

Linking Past and Present

Documenting History with Art An art form known as "social graffiti" has recently emerged in the inner cities. In an effort to reduce the costs of cleaning up illegal and unsightly graffiti, young urban artists are being encouraged by some city officials to create murals that both beautify the city and make important cultural statements.

For centuries, American Indians have been subject to geographic, political, and social upheaval. In your class, create a wall mural that illustrates some of the effects of the clash of the different European and native American cultures. Use the material in Unit 1 as well as data on early tribal histories, reservation life, and present-day problems to present different perspectives.

Time Line Activity

Select one of the scientific and technological events shown on the time line that occurred before A.D. 1600. Explain how it contributed to the Age of Exploration.

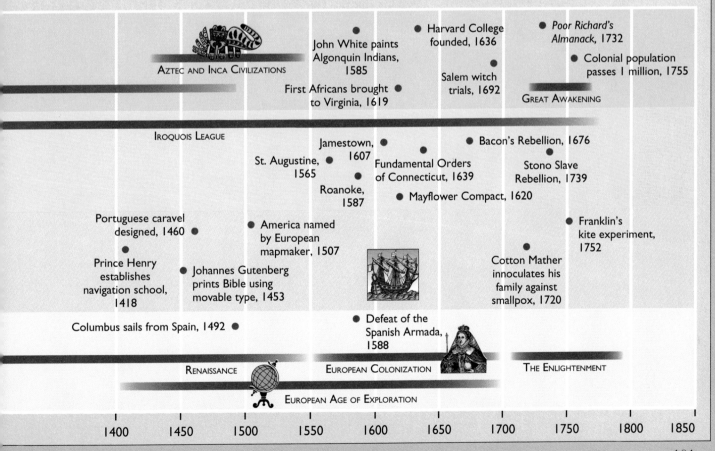

AZTEC AND INCA CIVILIZATIONS

John White paints Algonquin Indians, 1585

Harvard College founded, 1636

Poor Richard's Almanack, 1732

Colonial population passes 1 million, 1755

Salem witch trials, 1692

First Africans brought to Virginia, 1619

GREAT AWAKENING

IROQUOIS LEAGUE

St. Augustine, 1565

Jamestown, 1607

Fundamental Orders of Connecticut, 1639

Bacon's Rebellion, 1676

Stono Slave Rebellion, 1739

Roanoke, 1587

Mayflower Compact, 1620

Portuguese caravel designed, 1460

America named by European mapmaker, 1507

Franklin's kite experiment, 1752

Prince Henry establishes navigation school, 1418

Johannes Gutenberg prints Bible using movable type, 1453

Cotton Mather innoculates his family against smallpox, 1720

Columbus sails from Spain, 1492

Defeat of the Spanish Armada, 1588

RENAISSANCE

EUROPEAN COLONIZATION

THE ENLIGHTENMENT

EUROPEAN AGE OF EXPLORATION

1400   1450   1500   1550   1600   1650   1700   1750   1800   1850

UNIT 2

Making a New Nation, 1750–1815

The period from 1750 to 1815 saw the United States strengthened by the struggle for independence, the forging of a new form of government, the birth of political parties, and successful resolutions of the nation's first constitutional challenges. The Louisiana Purchase doubled the size of the new nation, directed national attention to the West—away from Europe—and provided almost limitless possibilities for adventurous immigrants. Finally, the declaration of war against a major European power alerted the world to the growing strength of the fledgling nation.

Chapter 4
Moving Toward Independence, 1750–1781

Chapter 5
Creating a Republic

Chapter 6
Testing the New Nation

◀ *Independence Hall, in Philadelphia, was the site of some of the most significant events in United States history. Built in 1741, it served as the State House for the colony of Pennsylvania. From 1753 to 1976, it housed the Liberty Bell. What other events can you name that took place within its historic framework?*

Themes

- **Democracy and Citizenship** Colonial Americans wrestled with the very meaning of republican democracy. The founders asked how government should be organized, who should be represented, and how individual rights could be safeguarded.
- **Economics** Issues of taxation, currency, a national bank, and private and public debt led some citizens to open rebellion and also gave rise to the birth of political parties.
- **Geography and the Environment** The demands of the growing population for resources and land disrupted forever the lives of the American Indians of the Atlantic coastal plain and the Southeast.
- **Arts and Humanities** Architecture in the nation's capital reflected the ideology of the new nation. Artists and writers began to foster a sense of American patriotism.

The British Colonies: Two Views of the Future

A Nation of Their Own

Peter Kalm, a Swedish naturalist who visited America in 1750, made the following observation about future possibilities for the British colonies.

It is however of great advantage of the crown of England that the North American colonies are near a country, under the government of the French, like Canada. There is reason to believe that the king never was earnest in his attempts to expel the French from their possessions there; though it might have been done with little difficulty. For the English colonies in this part of the world have increased so much in their number of inhabitants, and in their riches, that they almost vie with Old England. . . . .

I have been told by Englishmen, and not only by such as were born in America but also by those who came from Europe, that the English colonies in North America, in the space of thirty or fifty years, would be able to form a state by themselves entirely independent of Old England. But as the whole country which lies along the seashore is unguarded, and on the land side is harassed by the French, these dangerous neighbors in times of war are sufficient to prevent the connection of the colonies with their mother country from being quite broken off.

Peter Kalm, *Travels in North America* (1770), vol. I., p. 140.

The Obstacles to Unity

Andrew Burnaby, an English clergyman who visited North America in 1759, questioned whether the colonies would ever be able to unite in a common cause.

America is formed for happiness, but not for empire: in a course of 1,200 miles. . . I saw insuperable causes of weakness, which will necessarily prevent its being a potent state. . . .

JOIN, or DIE.

▲ *Popular pre-Revolutionary War image*

A voluntary association or coalition, at least a permanent one, is . . .difficult to be supposed: for fire and water are not more heterogeneous than the different colonies in North America. Nothing can exceed the jealousy. . .which they possess in regard to each other. The inhabitants of Pennsylvania and New York have an inexhaustible source of animosity, in their jealousy for the trade of the Jerseys. Massachusetts Bay and Rhode Island, are not less interested in [the trade] of Connecticut. . . . Even the limits and boundaries of each colony are a constant source of litigation. In short, such is the difference of character, of manners, of religion, of interest, of the different colonies, that. . .were they left to themselves, there would soon be a civil war from one end of the continent to the other; while the Indians and negroes would, with better reason, impatiently watch the opportunity of exterminating them all together.

Rufus Rockwell Wilson, ed., *Burnaby's Travels Through North America* (New York, 1904), p. 154.

The Death of General Braddock

Benjamin Franklin, who talked with General Edward Braddock on his way to Fort Duquesne, wrote this description of the general and of his final hours.

The general was, I think, a brave man, and might probably have made a figure as a good officer in some European war. But he had too much self-confidence, too high an opinion of the validity of regular troops, and too [low] a one of both Americans and Indians. . . .

In conversation with him one day, he was giving me some account of his intended progress. "After taking Fort Duquesne," says he, "I am to proceed to [Fort] Niagara, and having taken that, to [Fort] Frontenac. . . for Duquesne can hardly detain me above three or four days. . . .

Having before revolved in my mind the long line his army must make in their march by a very narrow road. . . I had conceived some doubts and some fears for the event of the campaign. But I ventured only to say. . . "The only danger I apprehend of obstruction to your march is from [ambushes] by Indians. . . ."

He smiled at my ignorance, and replied, "These savages may, indeed, be a formidable enemy to your raw American militia, but upon the King's regular and disciplined troops, sir, it is impossible they should make any impression." I was conscious of an impropriety in my disputing with a military man in matters of his profession, and said no more.

The enemy. . .attacked [Braddock's] advanced guard by a heavy fire from behind trees and bushes, which was the first intelligence the General had of an enemy's being near him. . . .

The General, who was wounded, was brought off [the field] with difficulty. . . and out of 86 officers, 63 were killed or wounded, and 714 men killed out of 1,100. . . .

Captain Orme, who was one of the General's aides-de-camp. . .continued with him to his death. . . told me that he was totally silent all the first day, and at night only said, "Who would have thought it?" That he was silent again the following day, saying only at last, "We shall better know how to deal with them another time;" and died in a few minutes after.

John Bigelow, ed., *Autobiography of Benjamin Franklin* (Philadelphia, 1868), pp. 309–313.

Taxing the Colonies

The following statements represent positions taken in 1765 concerning Parliament's attempt to tax the colonies.

Not Having a Choice

James Otis complained that the colonists were not allowed to decide for themselves how to raise money for defense.

If an army must be kept up in America at the expense of the colonies, it would not seem quite so hard if after the Parliament had determined the sum to be raised, and apportioned it, to have allowed each colony to assess its quota and raise it as easily to themselves as might be. But to have the whole levied and collected without our consent is extraordinary.

James Otis, *The Rights of the British Colonies Asserted and Proved* (3rd. ed., London, 1766).

No Taxation Without Representation

The delegates attending the Stamp Act Congress in 1765 took the following position on the question of Parliament levying taxes on the colonies.

The Congress met. . .and upon mature deliberation agreed to the following declarations of the rights and grievances of the colonists, in America. . . .

1. That His Majesty's subjects in these colonies owe the same allegiance to the Crown of Great Britain that is owing from his subjects born within the Realm, and all due subordination to that august body, the Parliament of Great Britain.

2. That His Majesty's liege subjects in these colonies are entitled to all the inherent rights and liberties of his natural-born subjects within the Kingdom of Great Britain.

3. That it is inseparably essential to the freedom of a people, and the undoubted right of Englishmen, that no taxes be imposed on them but with their own consent, given personally or by their representatives.

4. That the people of these colonies are not, and, from their local circumstances, cannot be represented in the House of Commons in Great Britain.

5. That the only representatives of the people of these colonies are persons chosen therein by themselves, and that no taxes ever have been or can be constitutionally imposed on them but by their respective legislature.

Proceedings of the Congress at New-York (Boston, 1765).

Virtual Representation

Soame Jenyns, a member of Parliament, attacked the colonists' arguments that they were not represented in Parliament. He insisted they were "virtually" represented.

The right of the legislature of Great Britain to impose taxes on her American colonies, and the expediency of exerting that right in the present conjuncture, are propositions so indisputably clear that I should never have thought it necessary to have undertaken their defense. . . .

That no Englishman is or can be taxed without the consent of the majority of those who are elected by himself and others of his fellow subjects to represent them. . . is certainly. . . false. . . for every Englishman is taxed, and not one in twenty represented. . . . Manchester, Birmingham, and many more of our richest and most flourishing trading towns send no members to Parliament. . . .

If the towns of Manchester and Birmingham, sending no representatives to Parliament, are notwithstanding there represented, why are not the cities of Albany and Boston equally represented in that assembly? Are they not alike British subjects? Are they not Englishmen? Or are they only Englishmen when they solicit for protection, but not Englishmen when taxes are required to enable this country to protect them?

Soame Jenyns, *The Objections to the Taxation of our American Colonies. . . Briefly Consider'd* (London, 1765).

Internal vs. External Taxation

Parliament also attempted to raise revenue by imposing duties on goods imported into the colonies. Some in Britain argued that import duties were "external" taxes that did not require the consent of colonial assemblies. James Otis opposed that point of view.

If the Parliament have an equitable right to tax our trade, 'tis indisputable that they have as good a one to tax the lands and everything else. . . . There is no foundation for the distinction some make in England between an internal and an external tax on the colonies. By the first is meant a tax on trade, by the latter a tax on land and the things on it.

James Otis, *The Rights of the British Colonies Asserted and Proved* (3rd. ed., London, 1766).

A Tory Tarred and Feathered

The treatment given one Boston Tory was described by Ann Hulton, who was herself a Tory.

The most shocking cruelty was exercised a few nights ago, upon a poor old man, a tidesman, one

▲ *Victim of tarring and feathering*

Malcolm. . . . A quarrel was picked with him. He was afterward taken, and tarred and feathered. There's no law that knows a punishment for the greatest crimes beyond what this is, of cruel torture. . . . He was stripped stark naked, one of the severest cold nights this winter, his body covered all over with tar, then with feathers, his arm dislocated in tearing off his clothes. He was dragged in a cart, with thousands attending, some beating him with clubs and knocking him out of the cart, then in again. They gave him several severe whippings, at different parts of the town. This spectacle of horror and sportive cruelty was exhibited for about five hours.

Ann Hulton, *Letters of a Loyalist Lady* (Cambridge: Harvard University Press, 1927), pp. 70–71.

Shays's Rebellion

Henry Knox

General Henry Knox saw the uprising led by Daniel Shays as a declaration of war by poor farmers against the owners of property. His reports from Massachusetts persuaded many of his contemporaries, including George Washington, that a grave crisis was at hand.

The people who are the insurgents have never paid any or but little taxes. But they see the weakness of government. They feel at once [the lack of] their own property, compared with the opulent, and their own force, and they are determined to make use of the latter in order to remedy the former. Their creed is that the property of the United States has been protected from the confiscations of Britain by the joint exertions of all, and therefore ought to be the common property of all. . . .

This dreadful situation has alarmed every man of principle and property in New England. They start as from a dream, and ask what has been the cause of our delusion? What is to give us security against the violence of lawless men? Our government must be braced, changed or altered to secure our lives and property. We imagined that the mildness of our government and the virtue of the people were so correspondent that we were not as other nations, requiring force to support the laws. But we find that we are men, actual men, possessing all the turbulent passions belonging to that animal, and that we must have a government proper and adequate for him. . . .

Something is wanting, and something must be done or we shall be involved in the horror of faction and civil war without a prospect of its termination. . . . Unless this is done we shall be liable to be ruled by an arbitrary. . . armed tyranny, whose want and will must be law.

Henry Knox to George Washington, Oct. 23, 1786.

Thomas Jefferson

Jefferson, then the American minister to France, saw Shays's Rebellion in a much different light. He wrote the following in a letter to James Madison.

I am impatient to learn your sentiments on the late troubles in the eastern states. So far as I have yet seen, they do not appear to threaten serious consequences. Those states have suffered by the stoppage of the channels of their commerce, which. . . make the people uneasy. This uneasiness has produced acts absolutely unjustifiable; but I hope they will provoke no severities from their governments. . . . [Republican government] has its evils. . . the principal of which is the turbulence to which it is subject. . . . Even this evil is productive of good. It prevents the degeneracy of government, and nourishes a general attention to public affairs. I hold it that a little rebellion now and then is a good thing, and as necessary in the political world as storms in the physical. Unsuccessful rebellions indeed generally establish the encroachments on the right of the people which

have produced them. An observation of this truth should render honest republican governors so mild in their punishment of rebellion as not to discourage them too much. It is a medicine necessary for the sound health of government.

Thomas Jefferson to James Madison, Jan. 30, 1787.

Slavery and the Declaration of Independence

The statement in the Declaration of Independence that all men are created equal was contradicted by the existence of slavery. Individuals and states responded to this dilemma in different ways.

Vermont Abolishes Slavery

Vermont's Constitution contained the following clause.

That all men are born equally free and independent, and have certain natural, inherent, and unalienable rights, amongst which are the enjoying and defending life and liberty. . . . Therefore, no male person, born in this country or brought from over sea, ought to be holden by law to serve any person as a servant, slave, or apprentice after he arrives to the age of twenty-one years, nor female, in like manner, after she arrives to the age of eighteen year, unless they are bound by their own consent, after they arrive to such age or bound by law, for the payment of debts, damages, fines, costs, or the like."

Vermont Constitution, 1777.

Patrick Henry on Slavery

Patrick Henry, the Virginia patriot who opposed British rule with the cry "Give me liberty or give me death" took the following position in regard to slavery.

Is it not amazing that at a time when the rights of humanity are defined and understood with precision, in a country, above all others, fond of liberty, that in such an age and in such a country we find men professing a religion the most humane, mild, gentle and generous, adopting a principle as repugnant to humanity as it [slavery] is inconsistent with the Bible, and destructive to liberty? Every thinking, honest man rejects it in speculation [theory]; how few in practice from conscientious motives!

Would anyone believe I am the master of slaves of my own purchase! I am drawn along by the general inconvenience of living here without them. I will not, I cannot justify it. . . .

I believe a time will come when an opportunity will be offered to abolish this lamentable evil. . . . Let us transmit to our descendants, together with our slaves, a pity for their unhappy lot and an abhorrence of slavery.

Patrick Henry to Robert Pleasants, Jan. 18, 1773.

Massachusetts Declares Slavery Unconstitutional

In 1783, the Massachusetts Supreme Court made slavery illegal in that state with the following ruling.

. . . Our Constitution of Government, by which the people of this Commonwealth have solemnly bound themselves, sets out with declaring that all men are born free and equal—and that every subject is entitled to liberty, and to have it guarded by the laws, as well as life and property—and in short is totally repugnant to the idea of being born slaves.

Massachusetts Historical Society, *Proceedings* (1873–1875), p. 293.

The Articles of Confederation or the Constitution?

At the center of the debate in 1787 over the ratification of the Constitution was the question of whether a new government was necessary. Following are some of the arguments made on both sides of that question.

Alexander Hamilton Argues for a Stronger Government

Alexander Hamilton, a patriot leader from New York and delegate to the Constitutional Convention, gave the following reasons for adopting the new Constitution.

We may indeed. . . be said to have reached almost the last stage of national humiliation. There is

scarcely any thing that can wound the pride or degrade the character of an independent nation which we do not experience. . . . Do we owe debts to foreigners and to our own citizens. . . that we contracted for the preservation of our political existence? These remain without any proper or satisfactory provision for their discharge. Have we valuable territories and important posts [frontier forts] in the possession of a foreign power [Britain] which, by express stipulations, ought long since to have been surrendered? These are still retained. . . . Are we in a condition to resent or to repel the aggression? We have neither troops, nor treasury, nor government. . . . Are we entitled by nature and compact to a free participation in the navigation of the Mississippi? Spain excludes us from it.

The Federalist, No. 15, Dec. 1787.

Why the Constitution Should Be Ratified

▼ *Portable writing desk*

This newspaper painted a grim picture of the future should the document be rejected.

Let every well-wisher to his country carefully consider the following questions. . . .

Whether in the present situation of public affairs it is not *absolutely necessary* that some form of government should be immediately established for the United States, distinct from that which is formed by the Confederation? . . .

What will be the consequence of a refusal of this Constitution? What will become of our public creditors? How will our commerce be regulated, or people employed, and poverty and extreme distress be prevented? Will not anarchy take place, and the people, driven to despair, seize upon each other's property, and at length submit to some aspiring chief, who, by taking advantage of our situation, will become a king or a tyrant?

The Massachusetts Centinel, Oct. 20, 1787.

Was a Change in Government Necessary?

An opponent of the Constitution questioned whether a change in government was necessary.

I have read. . . several publications which have lately appeared in favor of the new Constitution; . . . the arguments. . . of most weight. . . may be reduced to the two following:

1st. That the men who formed it were wise and experienced; . . . that they were four months deliberating on the subject, and therefore it must be a perfect system.

2nd. That if the system be not received, this country will be without any government, and of consequence will be reduced to a state of anarchy and confusion, and involved in bloodshed and carnage. . . .

It is readily admitted that many individuals who composed this body were men of the first talents and integrity in the union. It is at the same time well known to every man who is but moderately acquainted with the characters of the members, that many of them are possessed of high aristocratic ideas, and the most sovereign contempt of the common people; that not a few were strongly disposed in favor of monarchy; that there were some of no small talents and of great influence, of consummate cunning, and masters of intrigue, whom the war found poor. . . and left with princely fortunes. . . .

In answer to the second argument, I deny that we are in immediate danger of anarchy and commotions.

The country is in profound peace, and we are not threatened by invasion from any quarter. The governments of the respective states are in the full exercise of their powers; and the lives, the liberty and property of individuals are protected. . . . It is true, the regulation of trade and a competent provision for the payment of the interest of the public debt is wanting; but no immediate commotion will rise from these; time may be taken for calm discussion and deliberate conclusions.

The New York Journal and Weekly Register, Nov. 8, 1787.

Patrick Henry Opposes Ratification

Patrick Henry, one of Virginia's patriot leaders, defended the Articles of Confederation on the following grounds.

The [Articles of] Confederation, this despised government, merits in my opinion the highest encomium [praise]—it carried us through a long and dangerous war; it rendered us victorious in that bloody conflict with a powerful nation; it has secured us a territory greater than any European monarch possesses—and shall a government which has been thus strong and vigorous, be accused of imbecility and abandoned for want of energy? Consider what you are about to do before you part with the government. . . .

The Federal Convention ought to have amended the old system; for this purpose they were solely delegated; the object of their mission extended to no other consideration.

Speech of Patrick Henry before the Virginia Ratifying Convention, 1788.

Washington's Inauguration

A Dutch diplomat, Rudolph Van Dorsten, described George Washington's inauguration as first president of the United States in a report to his government.

On Thursday, April 30th, General Washington was inaugurated President of the United States. . . . After the President, pursuant to the new Constitution, had publicly taken the oath of office, in [the] presence of an innumerable crowd of people, his Excellency was led into the Senate-chamber and there delivered an oration. . . . By this address this admirable man made himself all the more beloved. The coaches, in which were seated gentlemen of Congress, were drawn by two horses and the presidential coach by four. His Excellency was dressed in plain brown clothes, which had been presented to him by the mill at Hartford, Connecticut. At night there was a display of fire-works at the State-House. . . . The next day the President received congratulations. The President adopts no other title than simply President of the United States. He receives visits twice a week, Tuesdays and Fridays, from two to three o'clock, and not at other times. . . . . This gentleman alone, by his courteous and friendly demeanor and still more so by his frugal and simple mode of living, is able to unite the parties in America and make the new Government effective and regular in execution, if such be possible.

The History of the Centennial Celebration of the Inauguration of George Washington as First President of the United States (New York, 1892), pp. 49–50.

Hamilton vs. Jefferson

Ideological differences led to disagreements between Alexander Hamilton and Thomas Jefferson during President Washington's administration and, eventually, to the formation of the Federalist and Republican political parties.

The Two Parties

Men by their constitutions [temperament] are naturally divided into two parties: 1. Those who fear and distrust the people, and wish to draw all powers from them into the hands of the higher classes. 2. Those who identify themselves with the people, have confidence in them, cherish and consider them as the most honest and safe, although not the most wise depository of the public interest. In every country these two parties exist, and in every one where they are free to think, speak, and write, they will declare themselves. Call them, therefore, Liberals and Serviles, Jacobins and Ultras, Whigs and Tories, Republicans and Federalists, Aristocrats and Democrats, or by whatever name you please, they are the same parties still, and pursue the same object. The last appellation of Aristocrats and Democrats is the true one expressing the essence of all.

Thomas Jefferson to Henry Lee, Aug. 10, 1824; Adrien Koch and William Peden, eds., *The Life and Selected Writings of Thomas Jefferson* (New York, 1944), p. 715.

Hamilton on Popular Rule

All communities divide themselves into the few and the many. The first are the rich and well born; the other, the mass of the people. The voice of the people has been said to be the voice of God; and however generally this maxim has been quoted and believed, it is not true in fact. The people are turbulent and changing; they seldom judge or determine right. Give therefore to the first class a distinct, permanent share in the government. They will check the unsteadiness of the second, and as they cannot receive an advantage by a change, they therefore will ever maintain good government.

Alexander Hamilton, speech to the Constitutional Convention, 1787.

Hamilton on the Whiskey Tax Riots

When riots broke out in western Pennsylvania against the collection of a tax on whiskey in 1794, Hamilton urged President George Washington to restore order by the use of armed force.

I have the honor to submit my opinion as to the course which it will be advisable for the President to pursue, in regard to the armed opposition recently given in the four western counties of Pennsylvania to the execution of the laws of the United States laying duties upon spirits distilled within the United States, and upon stills. . . .

What in this state of things is proper to be done? . . .

A competent force of militia should be called forth and employed to suppress the insurrection, and support the civil authority in effectuating obedience to the laws and punishment of offenders.

It appears to me that the very existence of government demands this course, and that a duty of the highest nature urges the Chief Magistrate to pursue it.

Alexander Hamilton to President Washington, Aug. 2, 1794.

Jefferson on the Government's Response to the Whiskey Tax Riots

Jefferson was convinced that the government had overreacted to the riots and that Hamilton and his friends had used the occasion and their influence with the president to strengthen the federal government at the expense of individual liberty.

Employing military force for civil purposes, when it has been impossible to produce a single fact of insurrection. . . and when the ordinary process of law had been resisted indeed in a few special cases but by no means generally [was a mistake.] But it answered the favorite purposes of strengthening government and increasing public debt; and therefore an insurrection was announced and proclaimed and armed against, but could never be found. And all this under the sanction of a name [George Washington] which has done too much good not to be sufficient to cover harm also.

Thomas Jefferson to James Monroe, May 26, 1795.

Jefferson's Inaugural Address

At his inauguration in 1801, Thomas Jefferson gave an address that included the following call for harmony and frugal government.

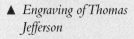

▲ *Engraving of Thomas Jefferson*

Let us then, fellow citizens, unite with one heart and one mind. . . . Let us then pursue with courage and confidence our own federal and republican principles, our attachment to union and representative government. Kindly separated by nature and a wide ocean from the exterminating havoc of one quarter of the globe; too high-minded to endure the degradations of the others; possessing a chosen country, with room enough for all descendants to the 1,000th . . . generation; . . . with all these blessings, what more is necessary to make us a happy and prosperous people? Still one thing more, fellow citizens, a wise and frugal government, which shall restrain men from injuring one another, shall leave them otherwise free to regulate their own pursuits of industry and improvement, and shall not take from the mouth of labor the bread it has earned. This is the sum of good government, and this is necessary to close the circle of our felicities. . . .

Paul I. Ford, ed., *The Works of Thomas Jefferson* (New York, 1905), vol. IX, pp. 194, 199–200.

Jefferson on Washington

You expect to discover the difference of our party principles in General Washington's valedictory, and my inaugural address. Not at all. General Washington did not harbor one principle of federalism. He was neither an Angloman, a monarchist, nor a separatist. He sincerely wished the people to have as much self-government as they were competent to exercise themselves. The only point on which he and I every differed in opinion, was, that I had more confidence than he had in the natural integrity and discretion of the people, and in the safety and extent to which they might trust themselves with a control over their government.

Thomas Jefferson to John Melisk, Jan. 13, 1813. Adrien Koch and William Peden, eds., *The Life and Selected Writings of Thomas Jefferson* (New York, 1944), p. 624.

WORKING WITH THE ARCHIVES

Reaching a Valid Conclusion

This skill exercise gives you practice using a "supported induction organizer" to help you make valid conclusions from primary source documents. The process of *induction* involves using particulars to make a general conclusion. This is different from making a deduction, where you start with a generality and make inferences (conclusions) about particulars.

For example, if you read that the colony of Pennsylvania was settled primarily by Quakers from England, Lutherans from Germany, and Calvinists from Scotland, you might *induce* that William Penn was a man of religious tolerance. If you learned, however, that the Oneida Indians lived in upper New York State, you might *deduce* that they lived by fishing, hunting small game, and trading beaver pelts with the French, practices common to many of the American Indian tribes of the Northeast.

Read the two documents entitled "A Nation of Their Own" and "The Obstacles to Unity" on page 104. Organize the particulars (facts) found in these primary source excerpts to answer the following question: Why would unification of the American colonies have been difficult prior to 1776?

CHAPTER 4

Moving Toward Independence, 1750–1781

In less than 30 years, the colonists changed from English subjects who would toast their king to Americans who celebrated their successful revolution against that king. The colonists fought for England during the French and Indian War. They did not rebel against British policies until they believed their rights as English subjects were being violated.

Part of this dramatic change in colonial loyalties came as a result of misguided administration by the British government. Then, in a brief space of time remarkable for its emphasis on political issues, Americans from all walks of life came to support the democratic ideas of the small band of defiant men now recognized as the founders of the United States of America. John Adams explained that the war itself was not really a part of the revolution. "It was only an effect and a consequence of it. The Revolution was in the minds of the people, and this was effected from 1760 to 1775, in the course of fifteen years before a drop of blood was drawn at Lexington."

▲ *On this teapot, colonists expressed their opposition to British laws.*

Rivalries over the Western Frontier

Both the British and the French laid claim to the rich lands in the Ohio River Valley. By the 1750s, when the population in the English colonies, had reached more than a million, land speculators planned to make money by selling lands along the Ohio River. The French, with only about 60,000 people in New France, did not want to start colonies there, but they wanted to protect their fur trade and their access to the Mississippi River Valley. To discourage English settlement, they began to build forts in the Ohio Valley.

Young **George Washington** was sent by Virginia Governor Dinwiddie to tell the French that their actions aroused "surprise and concern," and that they must withdraw from British territory. Washington wrote of his meeting with the French: "They told me it was their absolute design to take possession of the Ohio, and by God, they would do it.... They pretend to have an undoubted right to the river from a discovery made by one La Salle sixty years ago, and the rise of this expedition is to prevent our settling on the river or waters of it."

That both the French and the British were quarreling over lands rightfully inhabited by American Indians did not come to the attention of either power.

How did frontier rivalry lead to the French and Indian War?

What did Britain gain from the war?

In what ways did the conflict affect American Indians?

Frontier Skirmishes

From 1689 to 1763, European nations in their desire to build empires engaged in a series of wars. Generally, these wars were between the French and the British. When the wars spilled into North America, the colonists took the side of their mother country, and their Indian allies joined them. Colonial involvement was greatest in the **French and Indian War** (1754–1763). This conflict began in America but spread to Europe in 1756 where it became known as the Seven Years' War.

The war was sparked in 1754 when George Washington returned from his trip to the Ohio Valley with the news that the French were constructing Fort Duquesne (doo-KAYN). This was bad news for Governor Dinwiddie and other land speculators of the Ohio Company, who owned a 200,000-acre tract of wilderness land. They were already moving families onto this frontier. The governor asked Washington to lead his Virginia militia against the French. With 40 men, Washington attacked a small French camp, killing 10 men and taking 21 others prisoner. One man escaped and carried word of the attack back to Fort Duquesne.

To prepare for the French attack that was sure to come, Washington and his men began to build Fort Necessity, a stockade some 40 miles south of Fort Duquesne. Before construction was completed, the French attacked and routed the Virginians. Since war had not been officially declared, Washington and his defeated troops were allowed to return to Virginia with the unwelcome news that the French now had firm control of the Ohio Valley.

The Albany Plan of Union

Frightened by this French movement, representatives from seven colonies met in Albany, New York, in June 1754 to seek a new alliance with the Iroquois and to plan for their common defense. Neither venture turned out well. The Iroquois preferred to remain neutral, and the British and the colonies rejected the **Albany Plan of Union** drawn up by their delegates to the conference. That plan provided for a council that would levy taxes, raise armies, build forts, found new settlements, wage war, and make peace with the Indians. Unfortunately, both England and the colonial assemblies believed the Albany Plan would give the council too much power.

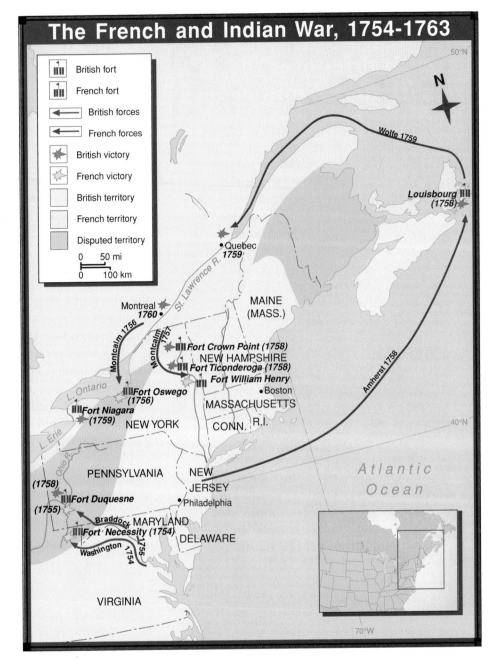

The French and Indian War ended with Great Britain temporarily driving the French from the mainland of North America. The British conquest of French Canada was widely applauded by the colonists. Why was the capture of Fort Duquesne vital to winning the war?

The French and Indian War, 1754–1763

British fort
French fort
British forces
French forces
British victory
French victory
British territory
French territory
Disputed territory

0   50 mi
0   100 km

Wolfe 1759

Louisbourg (1758)

Quebec 1759

MAINE (MASS.)

Montreal 1760

Montcalm 1756

Montcalm 1757

Fort Crown Point (1758)

NEW HAMPSHIRE

Fort Ticonderoga (1758)

Fort William Henry

Boston

Fort Oswego (1756)

MASSACHUSETTS

L. Ontario

Fort Niagara (1759)

NEW YORK

CONN.   R.I.

Amherst 1758

L. Erie

St. Lawrence R.

PENNSYLVANIA

NEW JERSEY

Philadelphia

40°N

Atlantic Ocean

Ohio R.

(1758)

Fort Duquesne

(1755)

Braddock 1755

MARYLAND

Fort Necessity (1754)

DELAWARE

Washington 1754

VIRGINIA

50°N

N

70°W

Had the plan been accepted, it might have prevented many of the problems that led to the American Revolution. Benjamin Franklin, Pennsylvania's delegate and author of the plan, complained, "Everyone cries a union is necessary, but when they come to the manner and form of union, their weak noodles are perfectly distracted."

The French and Indian War

Events moved rapidly after the Albany conference failed. Still smarting from the defeat at Fort Necessity, the British decided that colonial militia

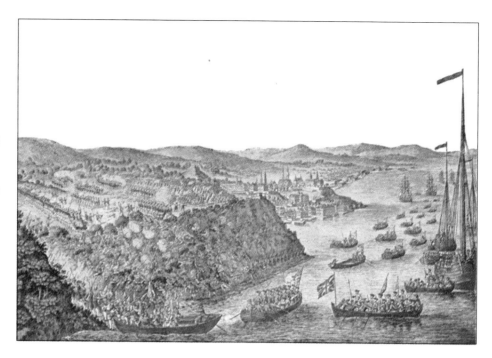

This view shows the capture of Quebec by the British in 1758. The attack was the turning point of the war in North America. For three months, General Wolfe studied the defenses of the city to find the best method of attack. The British Royal Navy prevented French troops from crossing the Atlantic to reinforce the city. What other methods of attack did the British use?

forces alone could not repel the French and their numerous Indian allies. In 1755, General Edward Braddock and 1,400 red-coated British troops landed in Virginia. With Washington as his aide and with 1,000 colonial militiamen joining the British troops, Braddock set out to clear the French from the Ohio Valley. As the troops marched on Fort Duquesne, they were surprised by 900 Frenchmen and their Indian allies. Caught in a deadly cross fire, two-thirds of the British and colonial troops were killed or wounded.

During the first years of the war, the British experienced defeat after defeat. The French and their Indian allies seized British forts in western New York. During this time, the French were also winning battles in Europe and the Mediterranean. British fortunes finally changed when William Pitt became chief minister and took charge of the war. Pitt hired German **mercenaries** (soldiers for hire) to fight England's European battles. This freed British forces to fight at sea and in North America.

In 1758, under Pitt's direction, British ships and British troops laid a successful siege against Louisbourg, the French outpost guarding the entrance to the St. Lawrence River Valley. British troops could then move on to attack Quebec. The same year,

British forces, including a regiment of Virginians under Washington's command, seized Fort Duquesne, which was quickly renamed Fort Pitt (now Pittsburgh). Colonial soldiers also played a role in victories over the French at Fort Niagara and Crown Point, New York, and at Quebec. Montreal fell in 1760, and New France surrendered. The fighting in other parts of the world continued until 1763.

The Treaty of Paris

Signed in February 1763, the **Treaty of Paris** marked the official end of the French and Indian War. France ceded to Britain all of Canada and all of its lands east of the Mississippi River, except for the seaport of New Orleans. The Spanish, who had entered the war against Britain in 1762, surrendered both East and West Florida to Britain, but received in exchange all French lands west of the Mississippi, as well as New Orleans. France retained two small fishing islands off the coast of Newfoundland and valuable sugar islands in the West Indies.

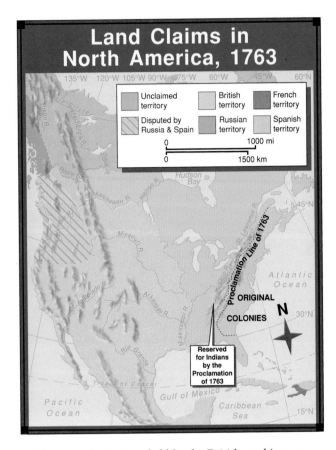

Land Claims in North America, 1763

Legend:
- Unclaimed territory
- British territory
- French territory
- Disputed by Russia & Spain
- Russian territory
- Spanish territory

0 1000 mi
0 1500 km

Proclamation Line of 1763

ORIGINAL COLONIES

N

Reserved for Indians by the Proclamation of 1763

▲ *Compare the territory held by the British on this map with the territory of the French and Spanish settlements shown on the map on page 42. Identify the territory claimed by Britain in 1763 that was claimed by France in 1750.*

Britain was now the ruling power in North America, in Europe, and on the seas. American colonists celebrated the victory with as much enthusiasm as the people in England. They hailed the young King George III as a great and virtuous monarch, drank toasts to the wisdom of William Pitt, and composed poems in honor of such brave heroes as James Wolfe, who died during the capture of Quebec. The colonists felt themselves to be very much a part of the great and glorious British Empire. It seemed, declared one colonist, that nothing could dim the love the colonists held for "their own nation, their Great Britain."

Despite the apparent unity of the colonists and the British government, the French and Indian War substantially changed their relationship. The colonists expected to return to the period of **salu-**

tary neglect, a time when, with the exception of the Navigation Acts to control trade, Parliament had made few laws that affected the colonies. Even those laws were loosely enforced. But now the British found themselves facing staggering war debts and needed the colonists to help pay for the post-war defense of the Empire. The British also became concerned about the loyalty of some colonists who had engaged in smuggling and trading with the French throughout the war.

British Policy on the Western Lands

American Indians did not celebrate the Treaty of Paris. For them, too, the old balance of power had changed. Few Indians still lived in New England, but the Iroquois counted 2,000 warriors in New York. There were several thousand fighting men in the Ohio Valley, and at least 14,000 Cherokee, Creek, Choctaw, and Chickasaw warriors in the South. Before the French and Indian War, the Iroquois had maintained neutrality pacts with both the British and the French for 50 years. The Creeks, in the South, had put some of their villages under the protection of the British and others under the protection of the Spanish, but they often joined other Indians in fighting either or both powers. With the French removed from Canada and the Spanish from Florida, skillful American Indian diplomats realized they could no longer play one European nation against another when bargaining.

All along the frontier, the Indians fought against the continued takeover of their lands and the dishonest practices of the traders now under British authority. The largest Indian uprising took place in the spring of 1763. **Pontiac**, chief of the Ottawa Indians and former ally of the French, led hundreds of Indians from several tribes in attacks that destroyed all but three of the frontier forts the British had captured from the French. The fighting raged all summer, with about 2,000 colonists and Indians killed. Smaller battles erupted over the next three years. In October 1766, the British negotiated peace treaties with the Indians. The British now realized how difficult it was going to be to control the vast lands won from France.

The **Procla-mation of 1763**, issued by the king, came as an unpleasant surprise to the colonies. It was meant to prevent further Indian wars. The Proclamation declared all lands west of the Appalachian Mountains to be Indian reserves and prohibited colonists from buying Indian lands. However, it did not really solve the problems of western land policy. Because the

▲ *Chief Pontiac was an important spokesman for the Ottawa Indians.*

Proclamation Line was carelessly drawn, some established settlers found themselves living in Indian territory. In addition, land speculators refused to give up their chance to make a fortune. The presence of several thousand British troops kept the situation under control for a time, but the colonists' desire for land conflicted with the British desire to stabilize western land policy and Indian affairs. Most colonists probably agreed with George Washington, who was himself a heavy speculator in western lands. He claimed that the Proclamation was "a temporary expedient to quiet the minds of the Indians." The British saw the conflict over the western land policy as growing evidence that the colonies required strict regulation.

SECTION 1 REVIEW

1. **Explain** why the French and British could not peacefully coexist in the Ohio Valley.
2. **List** several ways the Albany Plan of Union would have helped the colonists.
3. **Identify** William Pitt.
4. **List** the changes to the map of North America brought about by the Treaty of Paris.
5. **Describe** briefly how the French and Indian War affected the American Indians.

British Taxation and Problems of Control

The colonists bitterly resented the new British attempts to control colonial affairs. For example, in August 1765, riots forced a Massachusetts distributor of tax stamps to resign out of fear. Mobs attacked and burned the houses of upper-class Bostonians who were thought to be too friendly with British authorities. **Josiah Quincy Jr.**, a lawyer and member of the colonial upper class, recorded both these events in his diary: "The destructions, demolitions, and ruins caused by the rage of the Colonies . . . at that singular and ever memorable Stamp Act, will make the present year one of the most remarkable eras in the annals of North America. And that peculiar inflammation, which fired the breasts of the people of New England in particular, will always distinguish them as the warmest lovers of liberty; though undoubtedly, in the fury of revenge . . . they committed acts totally unjustifiable." Although he could not condone the destructive acts of the mobs, Quincy's words did reflect a widespread belief that the colonists would not tolerate offensive regulations such as the Stamp Act.

What actions of the British Parliament infuriated the colonists?

Why did the British feel their actions were justified?

What were the effects of the Stamp Act and the Townshend Acts?

The Search for Revenue

The British government was struggling under the burden of an extremely high debt. The costs of the French and Indian War, Pontiac's Rebellion, protection for the newly gained North American territory, and economic problems at home had doubled Britain's debt between 1754 and 1765. From Parliament's point of view, the colonies in America

Major Pre-Revolutionary Legislation

1763 ■ **Proclamation of 1763** limits western expansion.

1764 ■ **Sugar Act** sets higher duties on sugar, lower duties on molasses.
■ **Currency Act** prohibits colonies from issuing paper money.

1765 ■ **Quartering Act** requires colonists to provide housing and some provisions to British troops.
■ **Stamp Act** provides for stamps to be placed on documents; British appoint n stamp distributors.

1766 ■ **Stamp Act** is repealed.
■ **Declaratory Act** restates British sovereignty over colonists.

1767 ■ **Townshend Acts** put duties on tea, glass, paper, paint, and other goods.

1770 ■ Townshend duties are repealed except on tea.

1773 ■ **Tea Act** reduces price of tea but includes new tax. It gives monopoly to East India Company (resulting in the Boston Tea Party).

1774 ■ **Coercive Acts:**
Boston Port Bill closes harbor of Boston.
Administration of Justice Act sends military trials to England.
Massachusetts Government Act restricts local government in Massachusetts.
Quartering Act sends more troops to Boston.
■ **Quebec Act** places trans-Appalachian region north of Ohio under government of Quebec.

▲ *This table summarizes major acts passed by Parliament before the War of Independence. Why did these acts lead to the meeting of the First and Second Continental Congresses?*

benefited from the removal of the French and from the efforts taken for the colonies' defense and, thus, should pay a fair share of the costs. A series of attempts to tax the colonists began.

British Prime Minister George Grenville was charged with developing a plan to raise the needed revenue. It quickly became obvious to Grenville that the traditional methods of obtaining revenue from customs duties and taxes were not working. Previously enacted duties and taxes, such as the Navigation Acts and the **Molasses Act of 1733**, were failing to raise revenue for a variety of reasons, including inefficiency, corruption, and well-run smuggling operations. When the Molasses Act of 1733 was passed to discourage colonial trade with the French West Indies, the colonists began the practice of large-scale smuggling. This smuggling flourished in part because very little effort was made to actually enforce the Molasses Act.

Grenville, knowing that enforcement of the Molasses Act would be extremely unpopular, proposed a replacement called the **Sugar Act**. The Sugar Act, enacted by Parliament in 1764, imposed new duties on sugar, coffee, and other imports but reduced the duties on molasses. Originally the tax was set at half the amount specified in the old Molasses Act; later this was further reduced to one-sixth the original amount. Grenville hoped to make it cheaper for the colonists to pay the tax than to avoid it by smuggling. He also expected this act to be much better enforced than the Molasses Act.

To enforce the Sugar Act, the British established naval patrols to halt and inspect all ships entering colonial harbors. The British gave customs inspectors the right to use **writs of assistance**. These were a type of general warrant that allowed British inspectors to search any warehouse, or even private home, that might contain illegal goods. (Writs of assistance had also been used by the British during the French and Indian War.) A colonist, found to be in possession of illegal goods, would be tried by a British judge of the Admiralty Court, not by a jury of his peers.

More Restrictive Acts Follow   The Sugar Act was soon followed by more unpopular legislation. In 1764, Parliament passed the new **Currency Act**. This act barred the colonists from printing their own paper money. The British insisted that the colonists use gold or silver to pay their debts, even though the colonists had little of these precious metals. Then, in 1765 came the **Quartering Act**, which stated that the colonists had to provide barracks and supplies for the British troops stationed in the colonies. This was, in effect, another tax since the cost of providing these quarters and supplies was borne by the colonists.

The restrictive laws and taxes soon spurred the colonists to action. Individual colonists, as well as legislatures from eight colonies, bombarded Parliament with letters of protest. Colonial representatives even went to London to petition Parliament to stop passing revenue-raising acts. However, it seemed that these angry voices were not heard.

▲ *Stamps such as that shown above right varied in denomination. They were to be affixed to a great variety of papers and documents. What are the colonists doing to show their resentment of the Stamp Act?*

The Stamp Act

Despite the objection of the colonists, Parliament passed the **Stamp Act** in March 1765. The Stamp Act placed a tax on a wide variety of legal documents and printed matter, therefore affecting nearly every colonist. For example, the act taxed anyone who purchased a newspaper, obtained a marriage license, made a will, transferred land, bought playing cards or dice, accepted a government position, or even borrowed money. In each of these cases, a tax stamp was affixed to the legal document or bill of sale as evidence that the tax had been paid.

As similar taxes had been in place in England since 1694, Grenville and the Parliament were not prepared for the strong reaction against the Stamp Act. Throughout the colonies, the Stamp Act was met with protest. Many of the protests were spearheaded by newspapers and pamphlets. Articles were filled with angry declarations against the British, who had "invited despotism to cross the ocean, and fix her abode in this once happy land." Colonial assemblies passed resolutions asking Parliament to rescind, or cancel, the act. **Patrick Henry** declared in Virginia's House of Burgesses that the Stamp Act was a conspiracy against the colonies.

Henry also stated that the colonists had a right to be taxed only by their **direct representatives**. The colonists, however, had no Parliamentary representatives elected directly by votes cast by the colonists. Instead their interests were supposed to be looked after by a system known as **virtual representation**. In this system, all members of Parliament represented all English citizens, not just those in the locality from which they were elected. In this way, the interests of all British subjects, including the colonists, were supposedly represented.

Henry spoke for many other colonists when he asserted that Americans were not represented in the House of Commons in the same manner as were other English subjects. Some Americans rejected completely the idea of virtual representation. They claimed that all people, regardless of where they lived, should be directly represented.

In response to the Stamp Act, the mobs described earlier by Josiah Quincy became more organized. They took on the name **Sons of Liberty**. The Sons of Liberty included many different groups in different colonies. The Sons of Liberty were inspired by wealthy colonists, but in most cases were led by shopkeepers and artisans from the lower middle class. These men, from many different groups in different colonies, organized protests against the Stamp Act. On occasion, they went too far in their protests. As Quincy recorded, the Sons of Liberty "did great damage in destroying . . . houses, furniture, &c., and irreparable damage in destroying their [agents'] papers." In addition, groups of women, the Daughters of Liberty, promoted boycotts of all British goods.

▲ A newspaper announces the repeal of the Stamp Act. Why might British merchants have been as happy at the repeal as the colonists?

The Stamp Act Congress

Soon, Massachusetts called for a **Stamp Act Congress** at which colonists could discuss their mutual problems. Delegates from nine colonies responded. In the other colonies, royal governors denied the colonial assemblies the right to select and send delegates.

The Stamp Act Congress met in New York in October 1765. The delegates called for a unified position opposing the Stamp Act and decrying the treatment of the colonists at the hands of the British government. One delegate claimed, "There ought

to be no New Englanders, no New Yorkers, known on the continent, but all of us Americans." The delegates quickly drafted a Declaration of Rights and Grievances. This document stated that the colonists accepted the authority of the British government by acknowledging "all due subordination" to the king and Parliament. More importantly, however, it claimed that the colonists could not be taxed by any but their elected representatives in colonial assemblies (direct representation).

In England, this petition was met with mixed responses. While many members of the British government felt that the Stamp Act was just and called for, British merchants tended to side with the colonists. The colonial boycotts had reduced exports to the colonies by 40 percent in just a few months. This affected the livelihood of English merchants, manufacturers, shippers and laborers. After much discussion and pressure from British merchants, Parliament withdrew the Stamp Act in March 1766. On the same day, however, Parliament passed the **Declaratory Act**, which clearly restated Parliament's right to legislate for the colonies "in all cases whatsoever," including taxes.

News that the Stamp Act had been repealed brought great joy to the colonists. They realized that a boycott could be an effective political tool. **John Adams** wrote, "Such a day has not been seen in Boston before or since . . . . Music was heard in the streets . . . . The whole town was splendidly illuminated. The common was covered with multitudes. Rockets blazed in every quarter." But the colonists' celebration was to be short-lived. In the excitement over the repeal of the Stamp Act, many colonists overlooked the warning nature of the Declaratory Act. Parliament had neither given in nor given up.

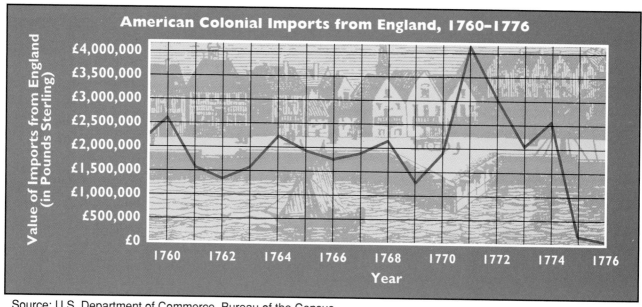

American Colonial Imports from England, 1760–1776

Source: U.S. Department of Commerce, Bureau of the Census.

▲ *The first dip in American imports came with the recall of British troops to England at the end of the French and Indian War. What events may have caused the other dips?*

The Townshend Acts

By the next year, serious problems plagued Britain. An economic depression caused widespread unemployment, more money was needed for the army and navy, and there were still large unpaid war debts. The British government remained convinced that the colonists should pay their share of the costs of administering and defending the colonies. To this end, Parliament passed the **Townshend Acts** between June 15 and July 2, 1767. The Townshend Acts, which included a new set of duties on such items as cloth, lead, glass, paper, and tea, were another attempt to tax the colonists. To help prevent the colonists from smuggling the items to be taxed, the new acts gave customs officers the authority to issue writs of assistance as they saw fit.

Once again the colonists were quick to mobilize against the new acts. New boycotts were started, but this time fewer people were allowed to make up their own minds about joining in. The Sons of Lib-

erty destroyed the property of some merchants who did not comply with the boycott, and mobs in Boston harassed and even tarred and feathered customs collectors. The Sons of Liberty asserted that Parliament must be made to understand that Americans would never accept the British government's restrictive legislation.

There was a provision to the Townshend Acts that particularly disturbed the colonists. Under the acts, some of the revenue raised was meant to be used "for defraying the charge of the administration of justice, and the support of the civil government" in the colonies. This meant that the salaries of governors and judges would be paid by the British government rather than by colonial assemblies. The colonists believed they should maintain control over internal taxation and pay the salaries of their own elected officials, as they had always done. The colonists felt the power to make economic decisions—to levy some internal taxes and pay the salaries of government officials—was vital. Losing this power would mean losing an important political weapon for limiting the power of the British

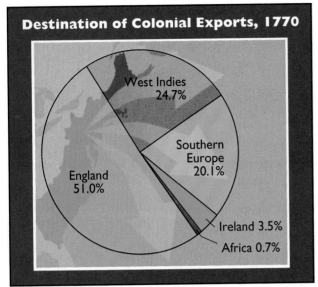

Destination of Colonial Exports, 1770

West Indies 24.7%

Southern Europe 20.1%

England 51.0%

Ireland 3.5%

Africa 0.7%

Source: U.S. Department of Commerce, Bureau of the Census.

▲ *More then 75 percent of colonial exports went to England and mostly British-controlled islands in the West Indies. Why would you expect nations in southern Europe to be the next major trading partners?*

▶ *Colonists were asked to boycott certain importers of British goods as a protest to the Townshend Acts. How was this like the Stamp Act protest?*

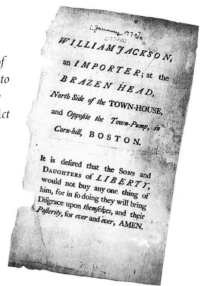

government. To many colonists, the Townshend Acts appeared to be a direct threat to their political independence, and thus their liberty.

Protests Bring British Troops   The situation grew especially tense in Massachusetts. In 1768, the Massachusetts House of Representatives drafted and sent a **circular letter** to other legislatures denouncing the Townshend Acts. A circular letter was a statement or argument written by one colonial assembly to be circulated to all the other assemblies. The circular letter stated that the Townshend Acts were a clear violation of the principle of no taxation without representation. The circular letter also requested suggestions on how best to circumvent the Townshend Acts. Angered by its contents, the British government ordered the Massachusetts House to revoke the circular letter. The House voted 92 to 17 to defy the order. The British governor of Massachusetts then dismissed the colony's elected assembly.

The dissolution of the Massachusetts assembly served to heighten resistance to the Townshend Acts. The primary means for opposing the Townshend Acts was to refuse to import British goods.

The merchants of Philadelphia, Boston, Charleston, and New York soon made nonimportation agreements. Additionally, the Townshend Acts once again led the colonists to form mobs and resort to violence. Boston illegally ordered its inhabitants to arm themselves and then called for a convention of town delegates. British government customs officials found it impossible to enforce regulations under such riotous conditions, and they asked for military help. By October 1768, British troops had begun to arrive in Boston. By 1769 there were nearly 4,000 British soldiers in a town of 15,000. The massing of British troops was a turning point in relations between the British and the colonists. For the first time, the British government had sent soldiers to enforce their law in the colonies.

SECTION 2 REVIEW

1. **Explain** why the British needed to raise money from the colonies.
2. **Describe** how a writ of assistance might aid in tax collection efforts.
3. **List** reasons that made the Stamp Act seem so unfair to the colonists.
4. **Define** the term *virtual representation.*
5. **Evaluate** the role of the Townshend Acts in weakening Britain's control of the colonies.

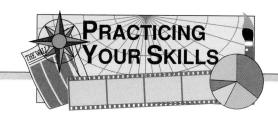

Understanding Graphs

One way to present a large amount of information clearly is to use a graph. The relationship between items of numerical information can be shown more quickly in graphs than in sentence format. With graphs, it is easier to make inferences and conclusions about the data.

There are three common kinds of graphs: line graphs, circle graphs, and bar graphs. Line graphs show changes that take place over a period of time. The lines are created by connecting points of data that are plotted on a grid. Sometimes more than one change, or trend, is marked on the same graph. A line graph can make comparisons between events by using a new line for each event. Here are some important steps to follow when analyzing a line graph:

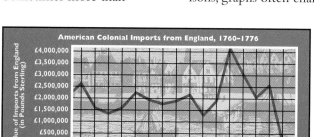

American Colonial Imports from England, 1760–1776

Value of Imports from England (in Pounds Sterling)

£4,000,000
£3,500,000
£3,000,000
£2,500,000
£2,000,000
£1,500,000
£1,000,000
£500,000
£0

1760 1762 1764 1766 1768 1770 1772 1774 1776
Year

Source: U.S. Department of Commerce, Bureau of the Census.

- **Read the title of the graph.** The title will tell you what the graph is about and may also give you a time period.
- **Try to determine the source of the data presented in the graph.** Often, the graph will have a source line at the bottom telling you how, when, or where the data was gathered. It may also explain any exceptions or unusual statistics by using asterisks or footnotes. Knowing the source may help you evaluate the accuracy of the data, or at least make you aware of any possible bias.
- **Read the vertical and horizontal axes.** The vertical axis usually gives a scale for measuring quantities. The horizontal axis usually shows time on a scale of days, months, or years.
- **Note whether the numerical information is in percentages or whole numbers.** Graphs that use whole numbers often save space by eliminating zeros. This will be explained in a phrase such as "in thousands of dollars," meaning the last three zeros of all numbers have been dropped.
- **Read the key carefully to know what the different colors and types of lines (broken or solid) represent.** When making comparisons, graphs often change the appearance of the line to make it easier to follow. This is especially necessary when the lines cross each other.

Examine the graph on page 121, and answer the following questions:

1. Write the type of graph, its title, and its source.
2. What are the beginning and ending years marked on the horizontal axis?
3. What does the vertical axis represent?
4. What was the value of goods imported in 1763?
5. Why do you think this graph begins in 1760 and ends in 1776?
6. What year showed the highest import value?
7. What year showed the lowest import value?
8. List two conclusions you can make from your study of this graph.

American Resistance, 1770–1775

Even after British troops were quartered in Boston, the city remained the center of protest. Nowhere was the worsening nature of the relationship between the British authorities and British colonial citizens more apparent. On the evening of March 5, 1770, an angry street mob composed mostly of laborers, seamen, and young boys threw rocks and snowballs and shouted insults at British soldiers. Although crowds had gathered before to taunt the "lobster backs," as the red-coated British soldiers were called, the crowds had always dispersed as darkness fell. On this evening, disturbed by a scuffle earlier that day between a British soldier and a ropemaker, the crowd was rowdier and more threatening than usual. The redcoats, either panicking or simply unable to take the abuse any longer, fired into the club-wielding crowd. When it was over, five colonists (including Crispus Attucks, a mulatto seaman who had escaped from slavery) were dead, and several others were wounded. The soldiers suspected of firing the shots were arrested, but that did not cool the colonists' anger. Paul Revere created a celebrated engraving depicting what he called "A Bloody Massacre." Radical **Samuel Adams**, cousin of John Adams and a leader of the Sons of Liberty, immediately saw the propaganda value of the incident. He made sure that all colonists heard of the incident. Since 1768, Adams had been publishing the *Journal of the Times*, which described the abuses of the British soldiers and customs officials. In this publication, he made use of his gift for fiery words to stir up the people and played up the **Boston Massacre** for all it was worth.

What incidents provoked the colonists to consider rebellion?

How did the British justify their actions?

What was the significance of the Continental Congress?

Protests Continue

While Samuel Adams saw the Boston Massacre only as a symbol of British tyranny, John Adams was more reflective. He felt it was vital that the arrested British officers receive a fair trial. The colonists, who revered liberty and justice, should show that their ideals applied to all people. He and another prominent patriot, Josiah Quincy Jr., acted as lawyers for the accused soldiers. After listening to Adams's arguments, the jury acquitted six soldiers and gave a light sentence—branding on the thumb—to the two found guilty.

After the trial had relieved some of the tension provoked by the Boston Massacre, colonists learned that the British Parliament had already repealed the Townshend Acts, keeping only the tax on tea. The new British prime minister, Lord Frederick North, realized that the taxes Grenville and Townshend had imposed did not raise much money, and that they had angered the colonists. North also let the Quartering Act expire.

▼ *This is one of the most famous engravings in American history. Do you think the engraving helped to inflame the colonists?*

For two years, there was relative calm in the colonies, but then, in 1772, another incident provoked colonial anger. A British naval vessel, the *Gaspee*, went aground as it was pursuing colonial smugglers. Rhode Island colonists boarded and burned the ship. The British announced that those who had committed this crime would be sent to England for trial, a clear violation of the principle of trial by one's peers. The British commission investigating the crime found no evidence, and there were no arrests. Still, the colonists were uneasy.

▲ *Above is the Boston Tea Party as shown in a Currier lithograph. Do you think the destruction of the British tea was justified?*

Shortly after the *Gaspee* incident, Massachusetts governor Thomas Hutchinson, a Tory, or supporter of the king, decided to enforce the provision of the earlier Townshend Acts which declared that his salary and those of colonial judges should be paid from customs revenues rather than by the Massachusetts assembly. By taking this action, Hutchinson believed that royal officers would be free from control by the colonists. Samuel Adams spoke out again. He asked a Boston town meeting to appoint a **Committee of Correspondence** to communicate with other towns and other colonies. Everyone should know, he felt, what the British were doing.

Within a few months, nearly every town in Massachusetts had established its committee. Thereafter, other colonies had committees, too, creating a communication network that was the first step toward united political action. A renewed confrontation seemed likely as Lord North was determined to uphold the sovereignty of Parliament over the colonies.

The Boston Tea Party The **Tea Act of 1773** provided the spark for the confrontation. This law was passed to help the financially troubled British East India Company, a trading corporation that imported tea from Asia and India. In order to save the company from bankruptcy, Parliament gave it the exclusive right to sell tea in North America. Some American merchants would be hurt by this **monopoly**, because only favored merchants would be granted licenses to retail the tea. The really serious opposition to the Tea Act, however, came from colonial radicals who saw it as a way to get Americans to accept another hated tax. Even though the price of the British East India Company tea was actually lower, the radicals reminded the colonists that the new, lower price included a tax levied by Parliament without the consent of the colonies. The idea of a royally imposed monopoly was also cause for alarm.

The Sons of Liberty decided that no British East India tea should be sold in the colonies. In Charleston, the tea was unloaded, but it was locked up in a warehouse. In both New York and Philadelphia, the Sons of Liberty would not allow the ships to land. In Boston, on the night of December 16, 1773, Sons of Liberty, dressed as Indians, boarded three ships and threw 342 chests of tea into Boston harbor. The violence of the **Boston Tea Party** frightened some colonists, but it had the support of many others.

The Intolerable Acts

The British Parliament was furious over this direct challenge to its right to legislate for the colonies. In the spring and summer of 1774, Parliament passed four **Coercive Acts**—known throughout the colonies as the **Intolerable Acts**. These acts were intended to punish Massachusetts and to make it an example to other colonies that might resist Parliament's decisions. The Boston Port Bill closed the harbor until the tea was paid for. The Administration of Justice Act provided that any British official (including any soldier) charged with a capital offense in Massachusetts would be taken to England for trial. The Massachusetts Government Act annulled the Massachusetts charter and stated that town meetings could only be held with the consent of the governor and that juries would be chosen by the sheriff. A new Quartering Act would put British troops into private homes if barracks were not available. Finally, Massachusetts was given a military governor, General Thomas Gage, with troops sufficient to enforce Parliament's orders.

If most colonists were not directly affected by the Coercive Acts, they were concerned about what such British actions implied for every colony. Their worries about British use of power were further aroused when Parliament passed the **Quebec Act** in 1774. The Quebec Act dealt with the administration of the defeated French subjects in Canada. It not only recognized the boundaries of the Province of Quebec as extending to the Ohio River, but also legalized the practice of Catholicism in this region. The act did not establish a representative assembly nor allow for trial by jury in civil cases. The law greatly angered nearly every type of colonist—Protestants, traders, settlers, and land speculators.

Colonists everywhere were shocked by the Quebec Act and by the harshness of the Coercive Acts. Committees of Correspondence called for all colonists to support Boston in its time of trouble. With the harbor closed, Bostonians were suffering from shortages of food and almost total unemployment. Support for the Bostonians blossomed everywhere in the colonies. Nothing, claimed Virginian **Thomas Jefferson**, united the colonies so much as their belief that the people of Boston were being deprived of their rights as Englishmen. He and other Patriot leaders believed it just a matter of time before all colonists would suffer.

Call for a Continental Congress

In September of 1774, delegates from all the colonies but Georgia assembled in Philadelphia as the **First Continental Congress**. The Congress first discussed an appropriate response to the Coercive Acts. Then it passed resolutions asking for an immediate change in British policies. The Congress asked for rights to "life, liberty, and property," and the renewal of the boycott on trade with the British. The Congress appointed Committees of Safety and Inspection to publish the names of those who violated the boycott. Finally, anticipating further trouble, the delegates vowed to meet again in the spring if, by then, the British had not repealed the Coercive Acts.

When the Continental Congress adjourned near the end of October, colonists in Massachusetts were already preparing for war. They were certain the British would use the powers of the Declaratory Act to maintain their policies. Forming special military units called **minutemen**, the colonists began to stockpile weapons. They also set up a communication network so they could respond at a "minute's notice" to protect their rights.

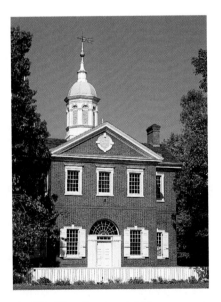

▲ *The First Continental Congress met in Carpenter Hall, in Philadelphia.*

The British reacted to these events immediately. They sent orders to General Gage to arrest the Patriot leaders. At first, Gage delayed his response to these orders, fearing such action would start a war, but when his spies told him there were collections of guns and ammunition in nearby towns, he acted.

Lexington and Concord

Wanting to make a surprise attack to discover the hidden weapons, General Gage ordered his troops to march through the night of April 18, 1775, to the town of Concord to find the weapons. At dawn on April 19, British troops arrived at the green in Lexington on their way to Concord. Facing them were 70 armed minutemen who had been warned of British plans through the efforts of Paul Revere, William Dawes Jr., and Dr. Samuel Prescott. The British commander, Major John Pitcairn, ordered the minutemen to drop their guns and leave the area. The colonials did turn to leave, but they held on to their weapons. Then someone fired a shot. Within seconds, the British troops opened fire. When the smoke cleared, eight colonists lay dead, and another ten were wounded.

Marching on to Concord, the British found few guns but exchanged shots with minutemen who were pouring in from the countryside. (This encounter was the subject of Ralph Waldo Emerson's famous poem "Concord Hymn" which tells of "the shot heard round the world.") Knowing they could not defeat the British in a head-on fight, the Patri-

▲ A View of the Town of Concord, *April 19, 1775, was based on an eyewitness account. Why would Ralph Waldo Emerson later write that the fighting in Concord represented "the shot heard round the world"?*

ots hid behind walls and trees, firing on the frantically retreating British soldiers. By the time the redcoats reached Boston, 73 had been killed and 174 wounded. The pursuing colonists could do little more at that time, but they camped in a circle around Boston, setting bonfires, shutting off land routes to the city, and beginning a siege of English troops in Boston.

Militia from nearby towns joined the ranks of the Patriots. Other colonists also took action. Within three weeks, the Green Mountain Boys, led by **Ethan Allen**, marched from their Vermont homes to Fort Ticonderoga and Fort Crown Point on Lake Champlain, capturing British ammunition and cannons. These arms were later sent to help the militia troops surrounding Boston. Finally, General Gage withdrew his troops from the outlying areas, concentrating them on the peninsula around Boston. For a time, there was a standoff and all was quiet.

1. Explain how Lord North brought a period of calm to the colonies.
2. Describe the role Samuel Adams played in inciting the colonists to political action.
3. List the actions taken by the colonists in response to the Coercive Acts and the Quebec Act.
4. State how the British responded to the actions of the Continental Congress.
5. Explain why Emerson called the conflict at North Bridge in Concord the "shot heard round the world."

SECTION 4

The Decision for Independence

With the shots fired at Lexington and Concord fresh in their memories, the delegates to the **Second Continental Congress** met in Philadelphia on May 10, 1775. Many had hoped that this session would not have to take place. Others were now sure that relations with Britain could never be repaired. Representing the **conservative** members, John Dickinson urged Congress to send a message to the king, telling him they "had not raised armies with ambitious designs of separating from Great Britain." In July, the delegates sent off the **Olive Branch Petition**, which proclaimed loyalty to the king and blamed his "cruel" ministers for colonial problems. At the same time, more radical delegates, such as Samuel Adams and Patrick Henry of Virginia, urged Congress to declare independence. Throughout the debate, delegates were keenly aware that, whatever the outcome, their actions would be judged by future generations.

What motives drove the Second Continental Congress to declare independence from Great Britain?

Why did many formerly loyal colonists support the rebellion?

Was war with Great Britain inevitable?

The Second Continental Congress

The delegates to the Second Continental Congress were well aware that they were heading toward what some called a civil war. Wrote one scholar, "The sudden vehemence with which the Americans moved into rebellion astonished contemporaries, and it has astonished historians ever since." Patriotic leaders and critics of the British acts and taxes insisted they were preserving the principles of English constitutionalism, not rebelling against them. They called themselves **Whigs**, after the British political group that had long claimed that the king's ministers, by wielding excessive executive power, were corrupting Parliament and English society. These Americans saw the attempts by the king's ministers to develop workable mechanisms to run the empire as having an altogether different purpose. Thomas Jefferson declared that they were part of "a deliberate systematical plan of reducing us to slavery."

As delegates at the Congress discussed and debated what action to take against British abuses, dramatic news arrived. After two months of quiet, fighting had erupted in Boston. More than 10,000 American colonists had surrounded the city. Militiamen set up a fortification on Breed's Hill, a spur of Bunker Hill. On June 17, 1775, under General William Howe, British forces made three attacks straight up the hill toward the Americans, finally dislodging them, but at a terrible cost. At this first formal battle of the Revolution, misnamed the **Battle of Bunker Hill**, British casualties were the heaviest of the entire war, numbering 1,000 men, or more than 40 percent of the British troops.

Washington Appointed Commander in Chief
The news prodded the Second Continental Congress into taking on the responsibilities of a central government for all the colonies. The Congress formed a committee to negotiate with foreign countries and issued paper money to support the colonial troops. It appointed George Washington as commander in chief of the newly created Continental army. Then 43 years old, the Virginia planter had never commanded more than 1,200 men, and that had been more than 20 years earlier. However,

▼ *Would history have been different if King George III had accepted the colonists' Olive Branch Petition?*

▲ *After the fighting at Lexington and Concord, the Massachusetts Committee of Public Safety called for an army to defend their wives and children from "an in-human soldiery." Militia groups gathered near Breed's Hill, a spur of Bunker Hill. How does this drawing suggest the frantic pace of the Patriots who built a defensive position on the hill?*

Washington was an aristocrat and a wealthy man of outstanding character, who could be counted on to secure Virginia's support for the war. What is more, suggested John Adams in recommending the appointment of Washington, he was a moderate Patriot. Washington believed in the colonists' right to protest their treatment by the British crown and Parliament, but he continued to drink to the king's health every evening. The present crisis had not yet changed his sense of identity as an Englishman, but he was willing to keep on fighting until the British government consented to find a remedy for the colonists' complaints.

In late August 1775, King George III, ignoring the Olive Branch Petition, declared the colonies to be in open rebellion. In December, he closed the colonies to all trade and ordered American ships under sail to be seized.

In the meantime, the Patriots decided to invade Canada to head off an expected attack from Sir Guy Carleton. It was rumored that Carleton planned to invade New York from his base in Quebec. General Richard Montgomery and 1,200 American troops set out from Fort Ticonderoga toward Quebec.

General Benedict Arnold, with another 1,100 troops, set out from Maine. The two armies met outside Quebec, and, during a raging blizzard on December 30, they assaulted the city. This time the Americans were badly defeated, with 100 soldiers killed (including General Montgomery) and 300 taken prisoner.

The Americans fared better the next spring in Boston. Early in 1776, they erected batteries on Dorchester Heights. On March 17, short of supplies and exposed to bombardment, the British decided to evacuate the city. The Patriots were ecstatic, but remained uneasy. They realized that the British would regroup and strike again.

The Final Break

The Patriot cause had many forceful supporters. Daniel Dulany and Thomas Jefferson wrote pamphlets in support of independence. **Mercy Otis Warren** and others continued to write political

The Power of the Written Word

Much of the support for revolution came from the words of fiery speakers or writers. As a member of the revolutionary convention of Virginia in 1775, Patrick Henry believed war was inevitable. He offered a resolution supporting an armed militia. His blazing speech was much reported and later printed in many colonial newspapers. The words of his challenge have thrilled freedom lovers ever since:

> Sir, we have done everything that could be done, and we have been spurned, with contempt, from the foot of the throne. . . . We must fight! I repeat it, sir, we must fight. Is life so dear, or peace so sweet, as to be purchased at the price of chains and slavery? Forbid it, Almighty God! I know not what course others may take; but as for me, give me liberty, or give me death!

Mercy Otis Warren of Plymouth, Massachusetts, was a tireless writer of poetry, plays, and political tracts. Her social circle included her brother, James Otis, who was known as "the Patriot," and John and Abigail Adams. Warren used her literary talents for the Patriot cause. She had a particular talent for satire, which she directed against the Massachusetts governor and council members.

▲ *This portrait of Mrs. James Warren (Mercy Otis) was painted by John Singleton Copley about 1763. What role did Warren play in the Patriot cause? (Bequest of Winslow Warren, Courtesy of Museum of Fine Arts, Boston.)*

Her other particular targets were native-born Americans who sided with the British. *The Group*, a play printed just two weeks before the confrontation at Lexington, suggested that bloodshed was about to occur. Her deep concern for the republican ideals of the Patriots' cause lasted all her life:

> The people may again be reminded, that the elective franchise is in their own hands. . . . They therefore cannot be too scrutinous on the character of their executive officers. No man should be lifted by the voice of his country to presidential rank, who may probably forget the republican designation, and sigh to wield a sceptre, instead of guarding sacredly the charter from the people.

Thomas Paine had only been in America since 1774. While still in London, he met Benjamin Franklin, who gave him letters of introduction to the best-known Patriots in Pennsylvania. Paine impressed these men, and, in 1776, they urged him to publish the essay *Common Sense*. This essay was considered a powerful statement for republicanism and summed up the feelings of many:

> Volumes have been written on the subject of the struggle between England and America. Men of all ranks have embarked in the controversy, from different motives, and various designs: but all have been ineffectual and the period of debate is closed. . . . Every quiet method for peace hath been ineffectual. Our prayers have been rejected with disdain; and have tended to convince us that nothing flatters vanity or confirms obstinacy in kings more than repeated petitions. . . . A government of our own is a natural right. . . . O ye that love mankind! Ye that dare oppose not only tyranny but the tyrant, stand forth!

1. Explain how the writing style of these excerpts might arouse the colonists.
2. Describe a time when you heard or read a speech that used emotional language. Was it effective?

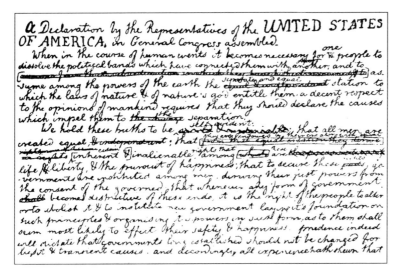

▼ It is believed that Jefferson wrote the first draft of the Declaration of Independence on this portable writing desk.

▲ The Declaration of Independence has influenced dozens of nations and remains an important reminder of our heritage of freedom. What contract does the document make between the government and the American people?

tracts, poems, and plays that dramatized the cause. **Thomas Paine's** pamphlet, entitled *Common Sense*, provided a thoughtful set of reasons for independence. "Everything that is right or reasonable pleads for separation. The blood of the slain, the weeping voice of nature cries, 'Tis time to part.'" Patriots throughout the colonies applauded Paine's words. George Washington claimed that *Common Sense* "is working a powerful change in the minds of men." Within a few months, 120,000 copies of the pamphlet had been printed, and they were read with care.

During the spring of 1776, the Second Continental Congress reacted to the increasing support for independence by commissioning privateers to attack British merchantmen. Delegates also decided to open American ports to foreign shipping, and suggested that colonial assemblies write constitutions and establish state governments. In June, the delegates listened closely as Richard Henry Lee rose to offer a resolution:

> RESOLVED: That these United Colonies are, and of right ought to be, free and independent States, that they are absolved from all allegiance to the British crown, and that all political connection between them and the State of Great Britain is, and ought to be, totally dissolved.

The Declaration of Independence

Lee's resolution was not voted on immediately. Instead, the Congress formed a committee to write a more thorough justification for independence. Benjamin Franklin, John Adams, Roger Sherman, and Robert Livingston gave advice, but Thomas Jefferson wrote the document. Based on ideas proclaimed by the scholars of the Enlightenment and the colonists' experiences with British rule and self-government, the **Declaration of Independence** was short and explicit. The first section used moral and legal reasons, based on natural rights, to explain the colonists' demand for freedom. The second section included a long list of injuries the colonists had suffered and explained how the colonists were being abused by a cruel king. This section also spoke against "our British brethren . . . who have been deaf to the voice of justice." The actual declaration of independence came near the end of the document. It echoed Lee's resolution: "These United Colonies are, and of Right ought to be, FREE AND INDEPENDENT STATES."

On July 2, 1776, the Congress voted to accept Lee's resolution. Then, after spending a day making a few changes in Jefferson's version of the declaration, those delegates present at the Congress signed the document. Their signatures represented their pledge of "our Lives, our Fortunes, and our sacred Honor" to the cause. Now there was no turning back. Now the rebellion had become a war for independence.

Not all colonists approved of the Declaration of Independence. Some, known as Loyalists or Tories, believed that as English subjects they had to support the homeland. About 55,000 Loyalists eventually joined the British army or militia, about 100,000 emigrated to other British-controlled lands, and another 300,000 or 400,000 did their best to remain neutral during the war. Historians estimate that no more than two-fifths of the colonists openly joined the revolution. Most soldiers were hardworking farmers, but some were poor men who found army service a way to improve their lot in life. Among the most active rebels were many of the best educated and most articulate of the colonial leaders.

▲ *This 1786 painting by John Trumbull depicts the signing of the Declaration of Independence. Can you locate George Washington, Thomas Jefferson, and Benjamin Franklin?*

SECTION 4 REVIEW

1. **Explain** why the colonists believed their rebellion supported English constitutional law.
2. **Name** the first formal battle of the Revolution.
3. **Identify** Thomas Paine.
4. **Name** the document that justified the American fight for self-rule.
5. **Decide** whether you would have been a Patriot or a Loyalist in 1776, and give your arguments for choosing that side.

The War of Independence

Neither the army of the United States nor its commander in chief did well during the 1776 campaign in New York. Forced to evacuate New York City, General George Washington asked two brigades of troops to engage the enemy while his other troops retreated. Instead, as one observer described, "they run off without firing a gun, tho Genl. Washington himself was present. . . . The General was so exasperated that he struck several officers in their flight, three times dashed his hat on the ground, and at last exclaimed, 'Good God, have I got such troops as those!' "

What problems did George Washington have with the Continental army?

For what reasons did the French enter the war on the American side?

In what ways did the British overrate their support in the South?

War Begins

British and American forces had been fighting for a year before delegates at the Second Continental Congress signed the Declaration of Independence. The revolution would go on for almost eight years, making it the longest war in America's history until the Vietnam conflict nearly 200 years later.

After evacuating Boston on March 17, 1776, the British withdrew to Halifax to consider their strategy. They decided to renew the battle by striking at New York City, where Washington had taken control. That city had a superb port and was in a more central location than Boston. The British believed

▼ *The British controlled the port city of New York until 1783, when the war ended. Why did the British need to keep control of at least one major port? George Roger Clark's victory at Vincennes (in present-day Indiana) secured control of the Ohio River Valley for the American forces.*

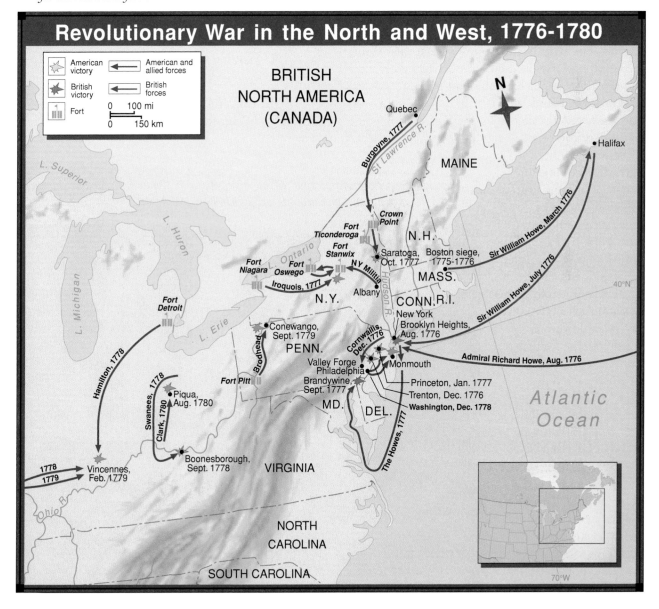

Revolutionary War in the North and West, 1776-1780

American victory
British victory
Fort
American and allied forces
British forces

0   100 mi
0   150 km

BRITISH NORTH AMERICA (CANADA)

Quebec
Burgoyne, 1777
St. Lawrence R.
MAINE
Halifax

Crown Point
Fort Ticonderoga
Fort Stanwix
Fort Niagara
Fort Oswego
Iroquois, 1777
NY Militia
Saratoga, Oct. 1777
Boston siege, 1775-1776
Sir William Howe, March 1776
Sir William Howe, July 1776

L. Superior
L. Huron
L. Michigan
L. Ontario
L. Erie

N.H.
MASS.
CONN. R.I.
Albany
N.Y.
Hudson R.

Fort Detroit

Conewango, Sept. 1779
Brodhead
PENN.
New York
Brooklyn Heights, Aug. 1776
Cornwallis, Dec. 1776
Monmouth
Admiral Richard Howe, Aug. 1776

Hamilton, 1778
Swanees, 1778
Clark, 1780
Fort Pitt
Piqua, Aug. 1780
Valley Forge
Philadelphia
Brandywine, Sept. 1777
Princeton, Jan. 1777
Trenton, Dec. 1776
Washington, Dec. 1778

Atlantic Ocean

40°N

1778
1779
Vincennes, Feb. 1779
Boonesborough, Sept. 1778
MD.
DEL.
The Howes, 1777

VIRGINIA

Ohio R.

NORTH CAROLINA

SOUTH CAROLINA

70°W

New York's population would be more sympathetic to their cause than the New England "rabble." In the summer of 1776, Sir William Howe, then commander of the British army in North America, landed 30,000 troops. Determined to cut New England off from the other colonies, Howe meant to defeat Washington's army in a decisive battle.

Howe began his campaigns on July 2 by placing some of his British and Hessian troops (German mercenaries) on Staten Island. Soon his brother, Admiral Lord Richard Howe, brought in naval reinforcements. By the end of August, the British had landed 20,000 of their troops on Long Island, where Washington had stationed most of his soldiers. The British quickly pushed the Americans back to Brooklyn Heights. There, they were caught in a trap. The British land troops were at their front; the British navy was at their backs. Washington prodded his troops to cross the East River to safety on Manhattan Island. The British quickly followed. After a few small-scale battles, the British took control of New York City.

With the winter of 1776–1777 coming and a shortage of food and supplies facing him, Washington retreated across New Jersey to the Pennsylvania shore of the Delaware River. There, he and his troops could spend the winter in safety. Congress moved from Philadelphia to Baltimore, but left no orders for reinforcements for Washington, who had been losing soldiers at an incredible rate. Only 1,500 troops had been killed in the engagements in New York, but desertions occurred every day. The Continental army never had more than approximately 18,000 men at any one time. The portion of the Continental army com-

manded personally by Washington seldom exceeded 5,000 soldiers. By the time the retreat was over, only about 3,000 troops of that army were left.

Knowing he had to take action before the enlistment time of his troops was up, Washington led a bold attack on Hessian troops stationed in Trenton, New Jersey. Crossing the icy Delaware River on Christmas night, he surprised the enemy and captured over 1,000 soldiers. A week later, Washington forced the British to withdraw from Princeton. Now totally exhausted, the American troops pulled back to the hills near Morristown, New Jersey, for the rest of the winter.

A Turning Point at Saratoga

The British, embarrassed by their defeats at Trenton and Princeton, determined to end the war

▼ *This painting portrays Washington rallying his troops at the Battle of Princeton. Do you think Washington really appeared this way in battle?*

George Washington

Dozens of biographies, scores of history books, and hundreds of articles have attempted to explain why George Washington so quickly became a figure of adoration, almost reverence. He was not as well educated as many other colonial leaders. He was not completely successful as a military man nor as a president. As Jefferson said, he had a heart that was "not warm in its affections." Yet this man of somewhat ordinary talents, but great determination, was transformed into the new nation's first genuine hero.

Was this man simply a symbol, or was he a real hero? The answer lies in the man himself and the society in which he lived. The society had respect for political leaders, but also a great fear of the

▲

George Washington, first president of the United States.

powers such leaders might hold. Washington took power reluctantly and relinquished it with enthusiasm. This was taken as a sign of humility and integrity. In the perilous time of the Revolution and the founding of the nation, Ameri-

cans saw in Washington what they wanted to see: a serious, steadfast representative of the deeply held values that were incorporated into the Declaration of Independence. When the Revolution succeeded, they felt justified in their choice of a leader. Praise for Washington was partly a kind of self-congratulation for their own brilliance in choosing a president who would lead them to success. In fact, it might be said that the idea of George Washington, not always the man himself, was what counted.

1. Look closely at the paintings of Washington in this feature and list the symbols used to provide the viewer with a sense of Washington's greatness.
2. Name some of the values Washington's image might evoke for the American people.

▶

How does this Emanuel Leutze painting, Washington Crossing the Delaware, *present Washington as a symbol?*

The subjects of patriotic pictures were often copied. This oil on canvas, entitled The Surrender of Burgoyne's Army at Saratoga, *is based on a John Trumbull painting. What was the important result of this battle?*

in 1777. Once again, they set out to cut New England off from the rest of the colonies. Their first objective was to recapture Fort Ticonderoga. Lieutenant Barry St. Leger and his Indian allies were to march from Oswego on Lake Ontario to the east along the Mohawk River. The main army under General John Burgoyne was to move south from Canada along the Lake Champlain corridor. It was expected that General Howe would send troops up the Hudson River to meet Burgoyne at Albany. These three armies would then destroy the Americans.

The plans went awry. On August 4, St. Leger stopped to surround Fort Stanwix on the Mohawk River and to demand surrender. The Americans sent a relief force of New York militia under General Nicholas Herkimer. These troops forced St. Leger to turn back. General Howe decided to attack Washington's troops in Pennsylvania rather than send an expedition to Albany. He succeeded in defeating Washington once again at Brandywine Creek, and then went on to take Philadelphia. But because General Howe had not left enough troops at New York to complete the march up the Hudson River Valley, General Burgoyne found himself in deep trouble. As Burgoyne marched south, he was constantly attacked by local militia units. Having already lost nearly half his troops by October, he was then set upon by General Benedict Arnold and his militia. Stopping at the town of Saratoga in New York, Burgoyne suffered five days of attacks by a second unit of the American army under General Horatio Gates. Burgoyne was forced to surrender his army of 6,000 in October 1777. The British defeat at the **Battle of Saratoga** had important results.

The French, eager to avenge their humiliating defeat in the Seven Years' War, had all along been secretly supplying money and arms to the Americans. They also opened their ports in Europe and the West Indies to American privateers, and French military officers joined Washington's army. In February 1778, a group of American diplomats, headed by Benjamin Franklin, asked France to recognize the new American Republic, sign a treaty promoting trade, and agree to a military alliance. Franklin let the French know that the British were negotiating to see if the Americans would now accept a return to their status of 1763—what the Americans had originally asked for. The victory at Saratoga convinced the French that the Americans did not need to accept those terms; they had a chance to win the war.

Winter at Valley Forge   In spite of the morale boost provided by the victory at Saratoga, Washington's army soon faced one of its greatest trials. From December 1777 through June 1778, Washington camped with his men at Valley Forge, Pennsylvania. It was a winter of despair. Poorly clothed and badly housed, more than 2500 soldiers died from starvation and disease. Then, on February 6, 1778, the French committed themselves to help the American side, and Spain soon became an ally of the French. Altogether, the French contributed some $2 million to the Patriot cause, as well as supplies, troops, and military commanders. A 20-year-old Frenchman, the **Marquis de Lafayette**, became one of Washington's most effective aides. Other Europeans were attracted to the Patriot cause. Baron Friedrich von Steuben taught Prussian military methods to the Continental soldiers at Valley Forge. Polish engineer, Thaddeus Kościuszko (kawsh-CHUSH-koh), helped build fortifications. This kind of aid was important to the war effort, but even more encouraging to the Americans was the knowledge that people from other nations respected their cause and believed their war could be won.

The Battleground in the South

The American victory at Saratoga and the intervention of the French caused the British, in 1778, to adopt a new military strategy. Having failed in the North, the British decided to strike next in the southern colonies. The new British commander, General Henry Clinton, was convinced that most southerners were Loyalists and would rush to join the British as they marched through the South. Leaving part of his army in New York City to protect his position there, Clinton set out to establish a new base of operations.

In December 1778, the British took Savannah, Georgia. Within a month, they had established a

▼ *The name of this painting is* The March to Valley Forge. *It captures the exhaustion and low morale of Washington's troops as they sought the safety of Valley Forge. How does the painting reflect the mood of the soldiers? (Courtesy of Valley Forge Historical Society.)*

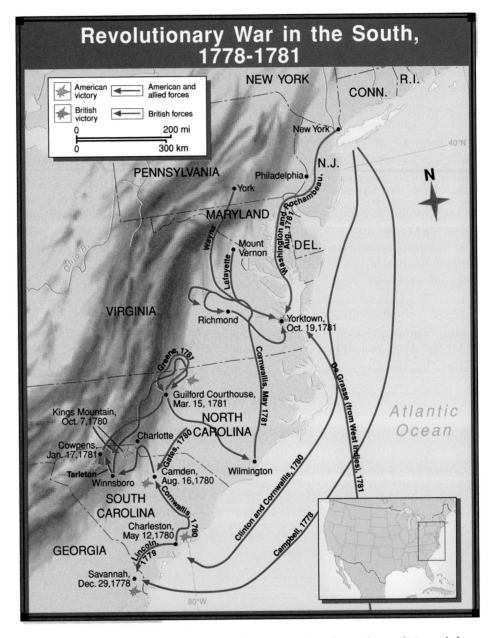

In escaping General Greene's troops, Cornwallis led his army into Virginia. Here he was within striking distance of George Washington's forces and the French, who had allied with the colonists. What other reason made Yorktown a poor choice for Cornwallis to select as a base?

Revolutionary War in the South, 1778-1781

American victory

British victory

American and allied forces

British forces

0   200 mi
0   300 km

NEW YORK
CONN.
R.I.
New York
40°N
N.J.
PENNSYLVANIA
Philadelphia
York
Washington and Rochambeau, Aug. 1781
MARYLAND
DEL.
Wayne
Mount Vernon
Lafayette
VIRGINIA
Richmond
Yorktown, Oct. 19,1781
Ohio R.
Greene, 1781
Cornwallis, May 1781
De Grasse (from West Indies), 1781
Atlantic Ocean
Guilford Courthouse, Mar. 15, 1781
Kings Mountain, Oct. 7,1780
NORTH CAROLINA
Charlotte
Gates, 1780
Cowpens, Jan. 17,1781
Tarleton
Camden, Aug. 16,1780
Wilmington
Winnsboro
Clinton and Cornwallis, 1780
Cornwallis, 1780
SOUTH CAROLINA
Charleston, May 12,1780
Campbell, 1778
Lincoln, 1779
GEORGIA
Savannah, Dec. 29,1778

royal government there, and for over a year there were no decisive battles. Then, in a campaign that lasted from February to May in 1780, the British took Charleston, South Carolina. Now convinced that the South could be secured, Clinton left General Charles Cornwallis in charge of southern campaigns and returned to New York. There, he would plan the final struggle to retake the rebellious colonies.

But Clinton had misjudged the strength of southern Patriots. On October 7, 1780, at Kings Mountain, South Carolina, Virginia, and North Carolina militiamen isolated Loyalist militia and defeated them. This battle, in which Americans fought against Americans was a bitter reminder that the war was as much a civil war as a revolution. Under the leadership of General Nathanael Greene and General Daniel Morgan, the Patriots used guerrilla warfare to wear down the British and Loyalist troops. The same style of fighting had helped the Americans in the West, in 1778–1779, where George Rogers Clark and his militia had captured British forts in territory that is now Illinois and Ohio.

▲ *A French officer who fought in the Revolution sketched these men in colonial militia uniforms. Shown from left to right are an African American infantryman with a light rifle, a musketman, a rifleman, and an artilleryman. Why do you think the uniforms differ?*

With French support in North America, and Britain being forced to fight on many fronts, the tide of war was beginning to turn in favor of the Americans. Morale was improving, although setbacks occurred. One such blow was the desertion, in 1780, of General Benedict Arnold to the British cause. A trusted aide and friend of George Washington, Arnold felt he was not being given the recognition and authority that his skills demanded. Fortunately for the Patriot cause, his plot to turn over the stronghold of West Point on the Hudson River to the British was accidently uncovered. Arnold had turned traitor in return for a commission in the British army and for money. When his plan was discovered, he escaped to join the British. In 1781, he waged two separate campaigns against the colonial forces. His name became synonymous with treason.

The Battle of Yorktown   During the summer of 1781, Cornwallis moved his troops north to Yorktown, Virginia. With his base on the peninsula between the York and James Rivers, he could be supplied by British vessels sailing out of New York City. While Lafayette, von Steuben, and General Anthony Wayne kept a watch on Cornwallis, Washington and allied French troops watched Clinton's garrison in New York City. Then Admiral de Grasse, commander of the French fleet in the West Indies, offered to help the Americans. Washington immediately asked de Grasse to place his fleet at the mouth of Chesapeake Bay so that Cornwallis would be cut off from supplies from New York. Washington's army and several thousand French troops then began a ten-day forced march toward Yorktown to block the escape of Cornwallis by land.

By September 28, 9,000 Americans and 7,800 French soldiers had trapped Cornwallis and his 8,000 British and Hessian troops. After a three-week siege, Cornwallis was forced to surrender on October 19, 1781. Although the war dragged on for more than a year, most people understood that the British defeat at Yorktown meant that the War of Independence had been won.

▲ *John Trumbull, who served as an aid to General Washington, celebrated the surrender of Lord Cornwallis in this twelve-by-eighteen-foot painting. Washington is shown just to the left of the flag and Cornwallis in the center. Why was the surrender of Cornwallis so important? What technique does the artist use to draw attention to the figure of Washington?*

American Advantages

That the Americans actually won the war seemed miraculous to most observers of that time. The British population numbered 11 million. Americans were only about 2.5 million, and of those, 20 to 30 percent were Loyalists, and another 20 percent were enslaved Africans. The British had an experienced army and the money to buy the services of the well-trained Hessians. Britain could claim the world's largest and most effective navy. The Americans had only a few ships.

The Americans did have some advantages. While the British had to deal with a 3,000-mile supply line, the Americans were outfitted from their own countryside. The British were superbly trained to fight on open fields and, indeed, had defeated the Americans in almost every formal battle. The British, however, were too few to occupy the countryside after winning their victories. When they marched on, the American militia merely took over again. Further, while the Americans had a good deal of help from European nations, they also had the advantage of fighting on their home ground and the knowledge they were protecting their own property and the lives of their families.

► Benjamin West planned to paint a portrait of the American and British commissioners at a preliminary treaty meeting. He was unable to persuade the British to sit for the portrait, but he captured the likenesses of Americans Benjamin Franklin, John Jay, and John Adams. Why might the British have refused to sit?

Independence Gained

While the victory at Yorktown ensured the American victory, the war was not officially ended until a treaty was signed in Paris in 1783. The British were ready for peace. They had suffered reverses in other parts of their empire as well as in America. In 1782, the Tory government, under Lord North, was replaced with a Whig ministry. This government favored the Americans and was eager to renew trade with them. Finally, the British government feared that if it did not give the Americans liberal terms for peace, the French-American alliance might continue and strengthen.

American negotiators Benjamin Franklin, **John Jay**, and John Adams, aware of the British concerns, asked for and received more than they could have expected. The British recognized American independence and ceded their right to all lands east of the Mississippi River, from the Great Lakes to the northern boundary of Florida. They opened the Mississippi River for use by both Americans and British, and stipulated that Americans would hold fishing rights off the coast of Newfoundland. In return for these concessions, the Americans were pledged to recommend to their government that Loyalists could make claims through the new American courts for property seized during the war.

SECTION 5 REVIEW

1. **List** three reasons why General Howe attacked New York rather than Boston.
2. **Explain** the significance of the British defeat at the Battle of Saratoga.
3. **Explain** why the French would be eager to see the American colonies win the War of Independence.
4. **List** some of the advantages that were held by the Americans in the war.
5. **State** two reasons the British were willing to negotiate a peace favorable to the Americans after the war.

Summary

Rivalries among European powers dragged Americans into a number of international wars. The French and Indian War finally pushed the French from the North American continent and brought vast new lands under the control of the British. Problems arising from the need to control these lands and to pay the costs of the wars caused British troops to be stationed in America.

British efforts to collect badly needed revenues brought increasing resistance from colonists, who felt they were losing their rights as English subjects. The more the British insisted that the Americans should pay their share of the costs of the war, the more the colonists dug in their heels and insisted on their right to resist. The Sugar Act, Writs of Assistance, the Currency Act, the Stamp Act, the Townshend Acts, the Tea Act, and finally the Coercive Acts brought forth indignation and bitterness. Delegates met at a Continental Convention in 1775 to debate what actions to take. Writers such as Thomas Paine persuaded many Americans to support the Patriot cause for independence.

The fighting of the war began even before the colonists signed their Declaration of Independence. At first, colonists were badly beaten, but British mistakes at Saratoga and stronger-than-expected Patriot resistance in the South began to turn the tide. With French help, the Americans were triumphant at Yorktown, and the long, hard-fought war was near an end. Skillful negotiations and various British problems produced a peace treaty favorable to the Americans.

Vocabulary

circular letter	monopoly
conservative	salutary neglect
direct representative	virtual representation
mercenaries	writ of assistance
minutemen	

On a separate piece of paper, write sentences using the vocabulary terms. Relate them by using two or more of the terms in each sentence or a short paragraph to bring out the meaning. If you do not feel a particular term should be paired or linked with any other term, use it by itself.

Review Questions

1. Why did the French and the British quarrel over the Ohio River Valley?
2. How did the quarrel lead to the French and Indian War?
3. Why did the outcome of that war lead the British to take strict measures against the colonists?
4. How did the British justify their several revenue-raising acts?
5. Why did the duties and taxes imposed by the British anger colonists so deeply?
6. Explain virtual representation and why it was at the root of the colonial anger with Britain.
7. How did Boston become the hub of Patriot resistance?
8. List two political and two economic causes of the War of Independence.
9. Why do you think the colonists waited more than one year to declare their independence?
10. Why is it surprising that the Patriots won their War of Independence?

Critical Historical Thinking

Writing Answer each of the following questions by writing one or more complete paragraphs:

1. Read again the chapter introduction. What did John Adams mean when he stated that the real revolution was over before a shot was fired?
2. Write a paragraph from the point of view of a Loyalist condemning the actions of the Second Continental Congress.

3. Some historians believe that the War of Independence could have been avoided if Britain had agreed with the colonists that virtual representation was not a valid principle. Do you believe the colonists would have been satisfied with direct representation in Parliament? Give reasons for your answer.

4. Support or refute this statement: The colonies only won the War of Independence because France and other European countries attacked Britain at the same time.

Making Connections with Popular Culture

How do you identify with those who might like the same type of music and parties as you? Perhaps the most obvious way is with clothing. Teens who like certain types of music tend to wear clothing that serves as an outward means of identification with that lifestyle or cultural expression. Using clothing as a means of group identification was no less important during the War of Independence than it is today. Until the colonists began to boycott English goods, English fashions were popular throughout the colonies. With the boycotts, Patriot women began making clothing out of cotton cloth spun at home. Wearing "homespun" soon became a symbol of opposition to British policies in the colonies. Homespun served to identify the colonial Patriots from the British Loyalists.

Writing Look in fashion magazines and other sources, study various clothing styles from different times in American history (World War I, the "Roaring Twenties," the Great Depression, and World War II). Try to draw some conclusions about the social conditions of whatever period you discuss based on such clues as colors and type of material, length of dresses, and accessories. How did clothing fashions reflect the times? Present your findings in a written report.

Additional Skills Practice

Line graphs plot two sets of information—one set on the vertical axis and one set on the horizontal axis. The horizontal axis is usually divided into time periods of days, months, years, or centuries. It has a label that explains the purpose of the horizontal axis. The vertical axis also is labeled. It runs up the left side of the graph and usually shows such data as amount of production, growth of population, or the rising price of automobiles.

Use the data below to create a line graph depicting the population in the colonies from 1660 to 1760. Be sure to label both axes and give the graph a title.

Year	Population
1660	90,000
1680	160,000
1700	270,000
1720	480,000
1740	910,000
1760	1,190,000

Creating a Republic

Military battles were only one part of the Revolution. Even while fighting raged across the land, the delegates to the Second Continental Congress planned for peace. They sought to develop a framework for a new form of government that would carry out the ideals of the Declaration of Independence. This government would need to ensure the "unalienable rights" of "Life, Liberty, and the Pursuit of Happiness" referred to in the Declaration.

In addition, the government would justly claim the right to rule by deriving its "powers from the consent of the governed." From 1776 through 1791, Americans worked to develop state and national governments that would honor and reflect their values and that would also provide the necessary mechanisms for conducting the day-to-day business of government.

▲ *This silver Syng inkstand is now displayed in Independence Hall. The quill pen may be the one used to bring into being a new government.*

Forging New Governments

The birth of the new government was marked by a process of trial and error. "We are, I think on the right road to improvement, for we are making experiments." So wrote Benjamin Franklin, who himself knew quite a bit about both experiments and political affairs. Americans saw their successful rebellion as an opportunity to establish new and more perfect governments. They had often discussed what a government should and should not do. They had examined the literature on political philosophy looking for useful models. Their knowledge of the Roman Republic, which was based on the ideal of virtuous citizens, led them to believe that a republic would be the best type of government. As Thomas Paine explained, "The word *republic* means the public good of the whole, in contra-distinction to the despotic form which makes the good of the sovereign, or of one man, the only object of government." As colonists, Americans had accepted a limited monarchy and professed loyalty to the king. As citizens of a new nation, they were determined to reject the concept of a king heading the government and also to establish a republic. The exact form such a republican government should take was less clear.

Why did the republican model appeal to the founding fathers?

What governmental reforms were written into the new state constitutions?

How did the new constitutions reflect a belief in inalienable rights?

Republican Ideals

Even before the delegates to the Continental Congress signed the Declaration of Independence in July 1776, they asked the separate colonies to form new governments "under the authority of the people." This meant the beginning of a new political order in which **sovereignty** (political authority) was derived from the people. As yet, there was no real national government. The United States of America was still an informal military alliance of former colonies which shared a common enemy, Britain, and a common goal of independence. Yet, there were large areas of agreement among Americans about what characteristics the citizens of these new republics should share. Above all, they ought to be *virtuous*, that is, public-spirited and self-sacrificing. Being virtuous in this sense means more than being good. It means setting aside personal interests and private concerns for the sake of the common good. In a republic, wrote Benjamin Rush, the citizen is "public property. His time and talents—his youth—his manhood—his old age—nay more, life, belong to his country."

Republicanism is a belief that supreme power, or sovereignty, resides in a body of citizens entitled to vote and that such a power is exercised by elected officials or representatives. In a republic, the citizens must possess **civic virtue**. They must be conscientious, active, responsible, and patriotic. So strong was this sentiment that in several new state constitutions, some states called themselves commonwealths to indicate their devotion to the public welfare.

Owning property was central to the idea of republican citizenship. Republicans connected voting with property ownership. They thought that the poor might sell their votes or vote against their own judgment out of fear of displeasing their employers or landlords. Property ownership indicated permanence and investment in a particular community. Consequently, those who had no property could be denied the vote.

Although the idea of equality was also central to republicanism, this did not mean that everyone should be equal in wealth, rank, and position. The republican leaders at the time of the Revolution believed that social distinctions would inevitably exist. In fact, these leaders had little use for democracy in the sense of mob rule. Instead, they believed that political leaders should come from a "natural aristocracy." Leaders would be distinguished from others based on their ability rather than on inheritance. People would only move up the social ladder through their own natural talent and efforts, not because they had inherited great amounts of land.

In many states inheritance laws were enacted to break up large hereditary landholdings. These laws banned **primogeniture**, or the right of the eldest child, usually the eldest son, to inherit the entire estate of one or both parents. In practice, because land was so readily available in the colonies, most large landholders already provided a living for all their children.

Equality Denied Some People Republican ideals and social reality were often in conflict. Slavery was present in ancient Greece and Rome, the birthplace of republicanism. Yet, slavery was incompatible with republican ideals of liberty as well as equality. In those states where slavery did not represent a major economic investment, there was no need or desire to reconcile the contradiction. Some of those states passed laws that restricted the slave trade; other states made it easier to free slaves. Vermont's constitution specifically outlawed slavery. In Massachusetts, slavery ended when the state court took the side of a slave who claimed he should be free because the state constitution said that "all men are born free and equal."

In the southern states, no such laws were passed. While some southern plantation owners did free their slaves as a republican gesture, most felt economic need outweighed antislavery sentiment. In the South, therefore, political equality came to mean equality among white property owners.

▲ *The original caption of this drawing noted that it showed women voting in the late 1700s. What state is represented? Why do you think the editor chose to run this picture in November of 1864?*

The status of women in late eighteenth-century America was also inconsistent with the belief in equality before the law and equality of opportunity. Women had supported the Revolution and were very much engaged in the discussions on the new state constitutions. They gained respect for such efforts, but none of the new constitutions, except New Jersey, gave serious consideration to women's rights. (For a short time, property-owning women were allowed to vote in New Jersey.)

Some women resented their situation. South Carolinian Eliza Wilkinson wrote, "The men say we have no business [with politics], but I won't have it thought that because we are the weaker sex as to bodily strengths we are capable of nothing more than domestic concerns. They won't allow us liberty of thought, and that is all I want." Other women accepted the traditional role of managing the household and rearing virtuous children who would become good citizens. This seemed to many to be a natural way to use their abilities.

Freedom of conscience was another important part of republicanism. In the South, this meant that people were no longer forced to pay taxes to support the Church of England—now renamed the Episcopal Church. However, in some parts of New England, the descendants of the Puritan settlers continued to require tax support of the Congregational Church and would allow only Protestants to vote. In several states, Catholics, Jews, and atheists could neither vote nor hold office.

New Structures of Government

Republicans strongly believed that the powers of government should be limited. One method of limiting power is to divide it up so that no one individual can become a tyrant or despot. In the new state constitutions the three branches of government were the legislative, the executive, and the judicial.

The colonists' unhappy experiences with a despotic king and his appointed governors led many states to design an executive branch with few powers allotted to the governor. Unlike the former colonial governors, most state governors did not have the authority to control meetings of the legislatures, appoint council members, appoint courts, coin money, grant favors, or issue pardons. Instead, most states limited governors' terms to one year and elected councils that could control the governors' power. For a time, Pennsylvania abolished the office of governor altogether, and an elected council of 12 members took over the administrative functions.

The legislature was meant to be the principal representative of the will of the people. All but two states, Georgia and Pennsylvania, created **bicameral**, or two-house, legislatures. The elected

legislators took over most of the duties previously performed by the colonial governor. To ensure that these bodies would more fully represent the wishes of property owners, the drafters of the state constitutions pulled out all their old arguments against virtual representation and developed a new system for actual representation. The states developed electoral districts equal in size, called for annual elections, and broadened voting rights. Most state legislators were chosen to represent geographic districts, but in Maryland and South Carolina they were elected on a statewide basis.

Most of the new state constitutions included a declaration of natural rights that the government could not infringe upon or violate. Most of these rights were ones the colonists felt the British government had abused. Spelling out such rights in the early state constitutions was an act that would profoundly affect the federal Constitution when it was written. The rights listed usually included:

- protection of property
- trial by jury
- freedom of worship, speech, and assembly
- freedom from unreasonable punishments
- freedom from general search warrants
- freedom from forced service or the support of standing armies.

Most state constitutions also included clauses stating that if the state government should prove to be inadequate or inclined to act against the wishes of the voters, it could be abolished, reformed, or altered.

The Articles of Confederation

The Second Continental Congress was convened because of the urgent need to manage the war with Britain. The Congress had no legal basis for its actions, but took upon itself the authority to issue the Declaration of Independence, to establish and maintain an army, to frame rules for commerce, to issue continental currency, to enact a military code, to define crimes against the Confederation, and to call on the states to write constitutions. In short, it wielded an extraordinary degree of military, political, and economic power. Some Americans feared—while others eagerly anticipated—that once the war was won, these powers would be lost. An English clergyman spoke for many when he suggested that after winning the Revolutionary War, "the Americans will have no Center of Union among them. . . . the Americans can never be united." At the close of the War of Independence, no one knew whether or not these words would prove true.

How was the national government under the Articles of Confederation different from the governments of the new states?

What were the achievements of the government under the Articles of Confederation?

What were the government's failures?

A New Federal Government

In 1776, shortly after the states began writing their constitutions, the Continental Congress appointed a committee to develop a plan for a central government which took the form of a confederation, or loose alliance of members with common interests. The resulting **Articles of Confederation** were quickly written, but **ratification**, or official approval, was held up until 1781, chiefly because of

quarrels over western lands claimed by several of the states. The colonial charters of some states had given them claims to lands west of the Appalachian Mountains. The six states without such claims, led by Maryland, argued that the West should become public land owned by the national government. Maryland refused to ratify the Articles of Confederation until this was done. Virginia was reluctant to give up claims to its huge landholdings, but when the British general Cornwallis and his large army moved toward Virginia, the state decided that land was less important than a united force to oppose the British. In the end, however, Virginia only released claim to the lands north of the Ohio River, and retained its claim to the Kentucky country into which settlers had actually moved. Moreover, Virginia demanded that the lands it ceded to the **jurisdiction**, or control, of the Congress should "be settled and formed into distinct republican states."

The Articles of Confederation created a union of states called the United States of America. Basically a continuation of the Second Continental Congress, the new government used Benjamin Franklin's Albany Plan of Union as a guide to establish a "firm league of friendship" among sovereign states. An assembly of delegates acted jointly on behalf of the states they represented. Because of fear that the larger states might try to dominate the

▶

This is the cover of the official copy of the Articles of Confederation. What does the full title suggest? How have state names changed?

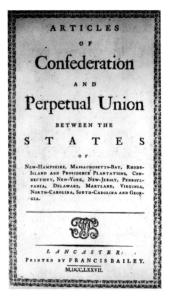

ARTICLES
OF
Confederation
AND
Perpetual Union
BETWEEN THE
S T A T E S
OF

NEW-HAMPSHIRE, MASSACHUSETTS-BAY, RHODE-ISLAND AND PROVIDENCE PLANTATIONS, CONNECTICUT, NEW-YORK, NEW-JERSEY, PENNSYLVANIA, DELAWARE, MARYLAND, VIRGINIA, NORTH-CAROLINA, SOUTH-CAROLINA AND GEORGIA.

LANCASTER:
PRINTED BY FRANCIS BAILEY.
M,DCC,LXXVII.

smaller states, each state, no matter the size of its population, had one vote in the Confederation Congress. Any act of Congress required the approval of nine of the thirteen states. The Congress claimed the powers that had traditionally been the king's: to make war or peace, conduct diplomatic relations, requisition men and money from the states, coin and borrow money, regulate Indian affairs, and settle disputes between the states. But Congress's authority stopped short of enforcing laws, regulating commerce, administering justice, and levying taxes. Those powers were reserved to the states. The Articles of Confederation forbade anyone from serving more than three years in the Congress, out of fear that an elite group of politicians might develop.

The Confederation Congress could cite some important achievements. Under the Articles of Confederation, Americans signed the **Treaty of Paris (1783)**, which officially ended the Revolutionary War. Peace talks were conducted by Benjamin Franklin, John Jay, and John Adams. Although they were strong bargainers, even these diplomats were somewhat surprised by the good terms they were able to obtain. Not only did the British recognize American independence, they also recognized American jurisdiction of all lands from the Atlantic Coast to the Mississippi River. The United States of America was now ten

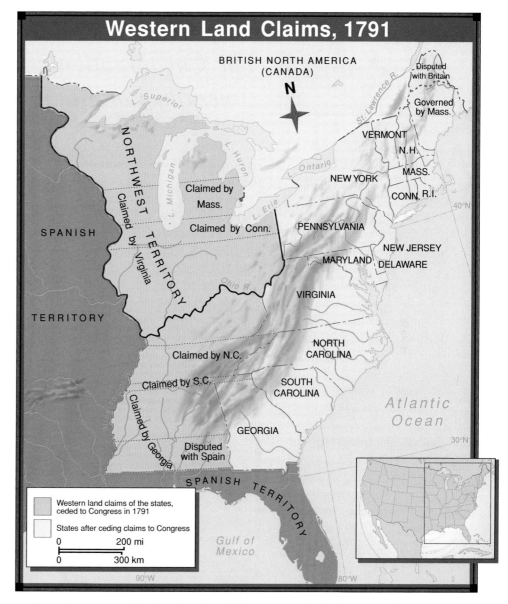

▲ One achievement of the Articles of Confederation was the development of rules for governing territories and for admitting new states. Compare this map with a modern map of the United States and determine which states were created from the Northwest Territory.

times the size of Great Britain and four times the size of France.

The Northwest Ordinances

The Confederation Congress also took up the problems of the western territories. Even before the

The Organization of the American Landscape

At the end of the Revolutionary War, the United States was deeply in debt. It had, however, gained from the British all lands located between the Appalachian Mountains and the Mississippi River. To pay its debts, the Confederation Congress decided to sell some of this land located north and west of the Ohio River, an area then called the Old Northwest. Under the Land Ordinance of 1785, this area was prepared for sale.

Two major systems of surveying and land allocation were used during the colonial period. In New England, the **township and range** system was used. Land was divided into **townships** six miles square, each of which was subdivided into 36 **sections** that were one mile square (or 640 acres each). Only after these townships were surveyed and mapped was land granted to groups or individuals. This led to a compact and orderly checker-board division of the land.

In the South, by contrast, the **metes and bounds** (literally measures and boundaries) system was used. Under this system, individuals were granted a certain amount of land, travelled into the interior seeking out the best land, and then recorded a survey of its

▼ *Under the metes and bounds system, the South was settled in bits and pieces.*

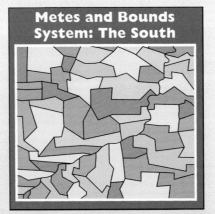

Metes and Bounds System: The South

landmarks and property lines. A typical survey read:

> Start at the large oak tree on the first fork of the river, thence due east to a large sandstone outcrop. South for 325 paces to the top of the knoll, then return west to a spot 510 paces below the fork.

Using this system, land in the South was settled in bits and pieces because settlers excluded swamps and other unusable land from their plot. Settlements, therefore, were often separated by large blocks of unclaimed land. Land boundaries were irregular, and land disputes were frequent.

Congress decided to use the more orderly township and range system from New England in laying out settlement in the Old Northwest. The principal surveyor of the first party was Augustus Porter, an experienced "gridder." His aide, Seth Pease, was a compe-

Revolution, Daniel Boone had opened the Wilderness Road to the lands south of the Ohio River. By 1780, more than 100,000 people were living in what would become Kentucky and Tennessee. These settlers expected to be able to use the courts of law and receive protection from the Indians whose lands they had seized. To develop a process for the orderly disposal of lands that were now considered public domain, the Congress passed the two Northwest Ordinances.

The **Land Ordinance of 1785** provided for the survey and orderly sale of the lands known as the Northwest Territory—a region bounded by the Ohio River, the Great Lakes, and the Mississippi River. The Congress divided these lands into townships—areas of land six miles square. Each township was further divided into 36 sections, with each section measuring 640 acres. Land was sold by section at one dollar per acre. One section from each township was designated to support a public school. The

tent mathematician. Together they laid out the baselines upon which this grid-pattern division of land was based.

Two centuries after the original surveyors completed their work, the impact of the township and range and the metes and bounds systems of land division on property lines in the country remains. The distinctive human geometry of these systems is a permanent feature of the cultural landscape of much of the United States.

———————

1. How does the township and range system differ from the metes and bounds system?
2. Could you describe the location of a specific piece of land to a fellow classmate using each system?

▶

Viewed from above, farms and cities in a region subject to the township and range system look as if they have been placed on a giant checkerboard.

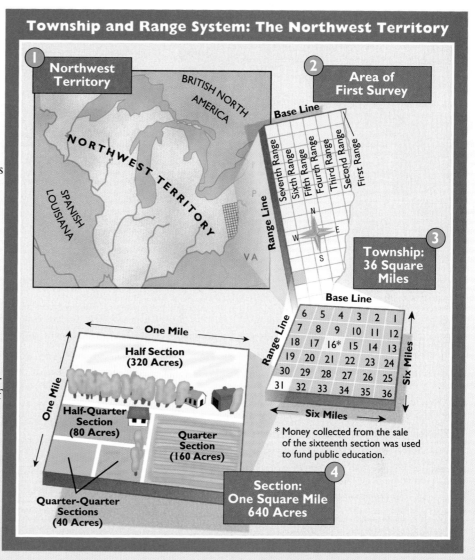

Township and Range System: The Northwest Territory

1 Northwest Territory

BRITISH NORTH AMERICA

NORTHWEST TERRITORY

SPANISH LOUISIANA

VA

2 Area of First Survey

Base Line

Seventh Range · Sixth Range · Fifth Range · Fourth Range · Third Range · Second Range · First Range

Range Line

3 Township: 36 Square Miles

Base Line

6	5	4	3	2	1
7	8	9	10	11	12
18	17	16*	15	14	13
19	20	21	22	23	24
30	29	28	27	26	25
31	32	33	34	35	36

Range Line · Six Miles · Six Miles

* Money collected from the sale of the sixteenth section was used to fund public education.

One Mile

Half Section (320 Acres)

One Mile

Half-Quarter Section (80 Acres)

Quarter Section (160 Acres)

Quarter-Quarter Sections (40 Acres)

4 Section: One Square Mile 640 Acres

money collected from the sale of this section was used to fund the school. The other sums collected from the sale of the lands went to support the national government.

To provide political control over these lands, the Confederation Congress passed the **Northwest Ordinance of 1787**. This law set up a three-stage process for establishing governments in the regions of the territory that would become states. As soon as a region had 5,000 free white adult males, these men could elect their own legislature and send a nonvoting member to meetings of the Congress. When a region had grown to 60,000 people, it could draft a constitution and become a state. There were to be no more than five states and no fewer than three states carved from the territory. Eventually, the states of Ohio, Indiana, Illinois, Michigan, and Wisconsin emerged from the Northwest Territory.

All of the constitutions for these states forbade slavery. It had been forbidden even while the states

▲ *George Caleb Bingham (1811–1879) gained a reputation as painter of the Mississippi Valley. His interest extended to the entire westward movement. Why do you think this 1851 painting of Daniel Boone (1734–1820) escorting pioneers is one of his best-known works?*

were still territories. Each new state also had a bill of rights that guaranteed settlers the right to trial by jury, **due process** (the right to fair and reasonable treatment under the law), and freedom of religion.

The Need for a Stronger Government

The successful negotiation of the 1783 Treaty of Paris and the plans for settling the western lands were the main achievements of the Confederation government. Other issues were not so easily solved. The Confederation was simply not strong enough to deal with the problems left over from the war. For example, the Second Continental Congress had borrowed money during the war and owed heavy debts to France, Holland, and Spain, as well as to American citizens who had lent money to the United States. But when Congress tried to levy an import tax to raise money, some states vetoed the plan. They wanted that source of income for themselves. Britain, once the chief trading partner of the

colonies, now put up barriers to trade with the states. For example, they refused to allow dried and salted fish from New England to be sold in the British West Indies.

Since the Confederation Congress could not force the states to pay back war debts or to restore property to Loyalists, Britain had the excuse it needed to refuse to give up its military forts in the West, including Fort Detroit and Fort Niagara. The Confederation could do nothing about it. Spain quarreled with the United States over the boundary of Florida and, in 1784, closed New Orleans, at the mouth of the Mississippi River, to American traffic. Settlers in Kentucky and Tennessee needed the river to transport their produce to New Orleans for sale.

As troublesome as these international problems were, economic chaos within the Confederation during the period 1784 to 1786 caused even more concern. Neither Congress nor the states were able to establish a currency with a stable value. Both the states and Congress had issued paper money during the war, but neither had been able to back it with silver or gold. The result was a bewildering variety of currencies in circulation, all of them inflated, and all carrying different values. Creditors did not want loans paid back in paper money, which was soon worth less than the original loan. Debtors, of course, were pleased to pay a debt with money of less value. States often refused to accept other states' currencies, which made trade between the states difficult. Increasingly, traders, manufacturers, and creditors came to the conclusion that Congress needed some power to control commerce.

A Call for Reform

Throughout the life of the Confederation, almost every state had a crisis over money. A problem in one state might not have been enough to shake the Confederation, but when farmers in several states demonstrated against high taxes and high interest rates, the situation could not be ignored. Things were especially tense in Massachusetts. In 1781, that state's legislature had outlawed the use of paper money and raised taxes in hopes of paying off

▲ Shown above is paper money from Georgia valued at eight Spanish milled dollars. The front and back of the Rhode Island currency for the same amount appears at immediate right and above right. Few states actually backed their paper money with gold or silver, even though the Rhode Island bill suggested that the United States insured it.

► This engraving shows Shays's followers arguing with officials at a courthouse door. How did this rebellion spark a call for a stronger government?

its large war debts. These new laws were especially hard on farmers who were having a difficult time as the wartime demand for food declined and food prices fell. Many farmers in the central and western part of the state, unable to pay their taxes or their private debts, lost their farms. Some were even imprisoned for debt. Many farmers felt the new government was no better than the one they had fought against to gain their freedom.

Shays's Rebellion In 1786, mobs of farmers in Massachusetts marched on the county courts to stop the sale of farms for nonpayment of taxes and debts. Daniel Shays, a former Continental army captain and leader of one of these groups, wore his old uniform as he led a mob some 1,000 strong to a munitions arsenal in Springfield to try to get more guns. Faced with the threat of Shays's Rebellion, the Confederation Congress found that its hands were tied. It had neither the funds to support an army nor the authority to send an army into a state, except in the event of an Indian uprising. In the end a group

of wealthy Bostonians raised a private army of 4,000 to put down Shays and his followers, as well as other such ragtag mobs. Shays's Rebellion made many people fear that lawlessness was a real threat to the country. It also fuelled the fear of mobocracy, or mob rule. George Washington wrote, "We have probably had too good an opinion of human nature in forming our Constitution [the Articles]. Experience has taught us, that men will not adopt and carry into execution measures the best calculated for their own good, without the intervention of a coercive power."

As unrest continued to spread throughout the states, many well-to-do Americans were frightened by the increasing power of the state legislatures and their majority factions. These shifting factions, claimed **James Madison**, passed more laws in the ten years after the Revolution than had been passed throughout the entire colonial period. "A spirit of *locality*," wrote James Madison, was destroying "the aggregate interests of the community." Different uses of power by the state legislatures, as much as flaws in the Articles themselves, brought on calls for altering the Articles of Confederation.

Several congressional delegates tried to solve the problems in a piecemeal fashion. They first called for a meeting in Annapolis, Maryland, on several issues related to interstate trade. Only five states sent delegates to the September 1786 meeting, so little action could be taken. Nevertheless, the delegates did discuss such problems as Shays's Rebellion and the debts owed by the states and the Confederation government. **Alexander Hamilton**, a 31-year-old delegate from New York, persuaded the delegates to call for another convention the next year in Philadelphia to discuss the regulation of commerce and other mechanisms that would make the new nation stronger. All states but Rhode Island sent delegates to the May 1787 meeting "for the sole and express purpose of revising the Articles of Confederation."

SECTION 2 REVIEW

1. **State** why quarrels over western lands held up ratification of the Articles of Confederation.
2. **List** the ways the Northwest Ordinances solved problems connected with western lands.
3. **Explain** briefly how the Massachusetts legislature failed to meet the farmers' needs.
4. **Describe** the main problems that led to the calling of a convention to revise the Articles of Confederation.
5. **Evaluate** the overall effectiveness of the Articles of Confederation.

SECTION 3

The New Constitution

There were many opinions on what a convention could do to solve the nation's problems. Some believed that minor adjustments to the Articles of Confederation were all that was necessary. Others refused to attend the **Constitutional Convention**. Patrick Henry was among them, saying, "I smelt a rat." He believed the members of the Convention would undermine the powers of the states and replace them with a great "consolidated government" like that of Great Britain.

Still others, displeased with the weaknesses of the Articles of Confederation, saw the Convention as an extraordinary opportunity. They believed it was a chance to correct the mistakes made in formulating the Articles of Confederation. George Washington was of two minds. He had pressing business at home, he was tired from the rigors of the war, and he feared his reputation might suffer if the Convention failed. On the other hand, as the time neared, he found that men of good reputation had already been selected as delegates, and he wondered how his own reputation would fare if delegates made great and important decisions without him. In the end, he decided that since "to see this nation happy . . . is so much the wish of my soul," he would agree to lead the Virginia delegation.

How did the large and the small states disagree over the structure of the new government?
What compromises were made for the benefit of the southern states?
How were presidents to be chosen to lead the new government?

The Virginia and New Jersey Plans

Twelve states sent delegates to Philadelphia. Only Rhode Island declined to take part. Most of

▶ *Shown here is the assembly room of Independence Hall, birthplace of the Declaration of Independence.*

▲ *This picture of Independence Hall in Philadelphia in 1776 was drawn after a lithograph. What evidence can you find in the drawing that Philadelphia was a growing commercial city?*

the 55 men who met in Philadelphia beginning on May 25, 1787, were relatively young, but they were experienced in questions of government. Most of the delegates were lawyers or had studied law, and half were college graduates in a country in which fewer than one percent finished college. Three-fourths had served in the Continental Congress. Many had worked on the drafts of their state constitutions and had been representatives to their state legislatures. Small farmers, city laborers, and frontiersmen were not represented, although they made up the bulk of the population of the country.

None of the delegates was as thoroughly prepared as James Madison. By the time the convention met, he had already drafted a design for a new government that he hoped would win the agreement of the delegates.

As soon as the convention began its meeting, Virginia Governor Edmund Randolph presented Madison's plan for a new structure of government. This plan, which became known as the **Virginia Plan**, called for a national government with three branches: executive, legislative, and judicial. The point of having three branches of government was

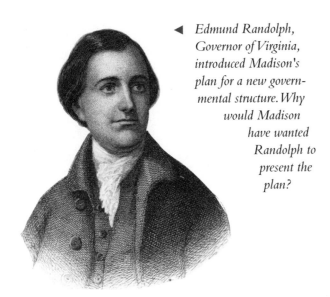

Edmund Randolph, Governor of Virginia, introduced Madison's plan for a new governmental structure. Why would Madison have wanted Randolph to present the plan?

egates could not agree on either the Virginia Plan or the New Jersey Plan. They were weary of discussion and worn out by the heat of the Philadelphia summer. George Washington, president of the convention, was so discouraged that he wrote a friend that he had lost all hope that agreement could be reached and that he was sorry he had anything to do with the convention.

Convention Compromises

As the arguments continued, it became clear that the delegates were doing more than making amendments to the Articles of Confederation. They were writing a whole new constitution. This undertaking began on July 16, when the deadlock in the convention was broken through a series of compromises. The most important, the **Great Compromise** (Article I, Section 2, paragraph 3), was developed by a committee and presented to the assembly by Roger Sherman of Connecticut. Under this Connecticut plan, Congress would have a bicameral legislature: a Senate with an equal number of representatives from each state, and a House of Representatives with representation based on each state's population.

The delegates accepted this compromise, but fresh disagreement broke out over how to determine the representation by population for the House of Representatives. The southern states wanted to include enslaved African Americans in their population total. If only free people were counted,

to separate the powers of government. Each branch would act to check the powers of the other two branches. After much debate, the convention agreed to use this model as the basis for further discussion.

Members representing the small states reacted in alarm and anger over Madison's concept of a bicameral legislature. He had proposed a lower house elected directly by the people of the states and an upper house elected by the members of the lower house. Both houses would base representation on population, which would mean that the larger states would have more delegates and more power than the smaller states.

"New Jersey will never [agree to] the plan," declared New Jersey delegate William Paterson. "She would be swallowed up! If we are to be considered as a nation, *all* state distinctions must be abolished." No single state, Paterson claimed, should have more power than another. His state, he assured the convention, would "rather submit to a monarch, to a despot, than to such a fate." He then called for simple **amendments**, or changes, to the Articles of Confederation. These amendments would give the Confederation Congress added powers to levy taxes and regulate commerce, and would give each state a single vote in a single legislative house. Paterson's position was known as the **New Jersey Plan**.

Debate on the two plans, which are sometimes called "the large-state plan" and "the small-state plan," raged all through June and into July. The del-

Roger Sherman of Connecticut presented the Great Compromise. What problem did this resolve?

Slave Population of the Original Thirteen States, 1790

State	Total Population	Slave Population
Connecticut	237,946	2,764
Delaware	59,096	8,887
Georgia	82,548	29,264
Maryland	319,728	103,036
Massachusetts	378,787	0
New Hampshire	141,885	158
New Jersey	184,139	11,423
New York	340,120	21,324
North Carolina	393,751	100,572
Pennsylvania	434,373	3,737
Rhode Island	68,825	948
South Carolina	249,073	107,094
Virginia	691,737	292,627

▲ *Which colonies had the largest and which the smallest slave populations? Why did the North and the South have different perspectives on counting slaves for representation and taxation?*

the South would have far fewer representatives than the northern states. Southerners, however, did not want the enslaved African Americans to be counted in figuring the amount of taxes to be collected. The northern states argued that if enslaved people were legal property, as southerners claimed, then they should not be counted for representation, but should be counted for taxation. The resulting compromise, called the **Three-fifths Compromise** (Article I, Section 2, paragraph 3), again brought the two sides together. Each enslaved African American would be counted as three-fifths of a person for *both* representation in the House of Representatives and for tax purposes. After much discussion, the southerners accepted this compromise.

The slave trade was also hotly debated. Even though the First Continental Congress had called for its end and several states had abolished the slave trade as well as the institution of slavery, southern delegates, especially those from Georgia and South Carolina, maintained that it was vital to their economy. Southerners feared that if Congress were given the power to regulate trade, it could, if it chose, outlaw the slave trade or place taxes on slaves brought into the country. Again the delegates accepted a compromise. Congress could not make any law affecting the importation of slaves for 20 years, until 1808 (Article I, Section 9, paragraph 1). Then it could, but did not have to, enact such legislation. Also, under this compromise, runaway African Americans would have to be returned to their masters. Those who suggested the compromise felt that slavery as an institution would die out if no more slaves entered the country.

Both of these latter compromises, though essential to the Constitution, came at the expense of enslaved African Americans.

The Executive and Judicial Branches

The next topic to be debated was the form that the executive branch should take. Many feared investing executive authority in a single man, who they thought might become a popularly elected dictator. Yet their experiences under the Articles had shown them the ineffectiveness of a weak executive branch. After extensive debate, the delegates decided that a president and a vice president would be elected every four years by an **electoral college**. The college would be comprised of electors, chosen by local elections, equal in number to the representatives and senators from each state. The person winning the most electoral votes would become president, and the person with the second largest vote would become vice president. If no candidate won a majority vote, or if there were a tie, the House of Representatives would select the president. This plan reflected the delegates' fears that if the people voted directly for the president instead of electors, they might make poor choices.

There was less discussion about the judicial branch of government. The Supreme Court would supervise the judiciary in all the states, and Congress could set up additional courts as it thought

Instead of revising the Articles of Confederation, the Constitutional Covention drafted a new document. What major weakness of the Articles of Confederation were corrected by the Constitution?

Comparing the Articles of Confederation and the Constitution

The Articles	The Constitution
The Executive Branch	
■ Congress has exclusive power to govern ■ Executive Committee acts for Congress when it is not in session ■ No executive branch to enforce legislation	■ President administers and enforces federal laws ■ President chosen by electors who have been chosen by the states
The Legislative Branch	
■ A unicameral or one-house legislature ■ Each state has one vote ■ Nine votes needed to pass legislation	■ A bicameral or two-house legislature ■ Each state has equal number of representatives in the Senate ■ Representation in the House determined by state population ■ Simple majority required to enact legislation
The Judicial Branch	
■ No national court system ■ Congress to establish temporary courts to hear cases of piracy	■ National court system directed by the Supreme Court ■ Courts to hear cases related to national laws, treaties, the Constitution; cases between states, between citizens of different states, or between a state and citizens of another state
Other Provisions	
■ Admission to the Confederation requires nine votes ■ Amendment of the Articles must be unanimous	■ Congress to admit new states ■ All states must have a republican form of government ■ Amendment of the Constitution by two-thirds vote of both houses of Congress, or by a national convention and ratified by three-fourths of the states

necessary. Judges would serve "during good behavior," or for life. The Supreme Court would hear cases affecting international treaties, trials of ambassadors, and treason, and it would also settle disputes between the states. The **supremacy clause** (Article VI) ensured that the Constitution would be the highest, most important law of the land. Laws and treaties of the United States must be observed by the states, and if a state law contradicted a law passed by Congress, the state law would be considered void.

The Completed Constitution

By autumn, the arguments were over. The document went through several drafts, and the Committee on Style touched it up. The most important change was in the Preamble, or the introduction, which now read "We the People" rather than "We the States." The new wording reflected a change in the idea of where sovereignty lay. The

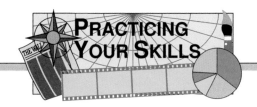

Reading Tables

Statistics play an important part in helping historians interpret events. Tables are a way of presenting a great deal of information in a limited space. They present facts and figures in a clear visual format. Once you learn the strategies for reading a table, you should be able to make comparisons and draw conclusions more easily. The data is gathered in one place in a format that is easy to read and understand.

Here are some general strategies for reading a table:

▪ **Read the title, and make note of any footnotes or additional information provided.** The title will tell you what the table is about. As with the line graph, always look to see if a source for the data has been listed.

▪ **A table presents information both vertically and horizontally.** Rows run horizontally, and columns run vertically. Both rows and columns should be labelled.

▪ **As with the graph, note whether the numerical information is in percentages or whole numbers.** Tables also save space by dropping off zeros, and presenting data as briefly as possible.

State	Total Population	Slave Population
Connecticut	237,946	2,764
Delaware	59,096	8,887
Georgia	82,548	29,264
Maryland	319,728	103,036
Massachusetts	378,787	0
New Hampshire	141,885	158
New Jersey	184,139	11,423
New York	340,120	21,324
North Carolina	393,751	100,572
Pennsylvania	434,373	3,737
Rhode Island	68,825	948
South Carolina	249,073	107,094
Virginia	691,737	292,627

Slave Population of the Original Thirteen States, 1790

Source: U.S. Department of Commerce, Bureau of the Census.

Examine the table on page 157, and answer the following questions:

1. Using the guidelines suggested above, determine the title and source of the information in this table. What is listed in the middle column? What is listed in the third column?

2. (a) Which state has the largest total population? Which state has the smallest? (b) Which state has the largest population of enslaved African Americans? (c) Which state has the smallest?

3. What percentage of the total population of Virginia was made up of enslaved African Americans? (Hint: The enslaved population of Virginia divided by the total population of Virginia equals the percentage of the total population of Virginia who were enslaved.)

4. Based on the information given in this table, make a comparison statement about the location of the states (North or South) and the size of their African American populations.

5. From your text reading, class discussion, and the information given on this table, explain why the North and the South had different viewpoints on counting and taxing enslaved African Americans.

▲ *This painting by Albert Herter captures a historic moment during the Constitutional Convention. Compare this to the painting of the signing of the Declaration of Independence. How many of the people can you identify?*

framers were making it clear that the new government's authority would come from the will of the people. Government power had previously been considered indivisible. The Constitution created a federal form of government with power shared between the states and the central governments.

On September 17, 1787, the document was read to the 42 delegates still at the convention. Some hesitated to sign it. Benjamin Franklin admitted, "I confess that there are several parts of this Constitution which I do not approve, but I am not sure that I shall never approve them." He went on to explain that over his long life (he was then 81) he had learned that his judgment had not always been correct, and he doubted that a different convention could do a better job.

Another delegate spoke of the essential point of the document. "In all our deliberations on this subject we kept steadily in our view that which appeared to us the greatest interest of every true American—*the consolidation of the Union*—in which is involved our prosperity, felicity [happiness], safety,

and perhaps our national existence." In the end, 39 delegates signed the document and notified the Congress that their work was finished. Congress, in turn, submitted the document to the states for ratification. The Congress adjourned on September 17, less than four months after convening.

SECTION 3 REVIEW

1. **Explain** why James Madison is regarded as the "Father of the Constitution."
2. **List** the major differences between the Virginia and New Jersey Plans.
3. **Describe** the compromise that answered the question of how to count enslaved African Americans for representation and taxation.
4. **Define** the term *supremacy clause*.
5. **Explain** how the electoral college was a protection against mobocracy.

Ratification

Initial reactions to the Constitution were expressed by two Massachusetts farmers with different points of view. One, from western Massachusetts, saw it as an instrument designed by the rich to oppress the poor. He described it as a device created by "lawyers and men of learning, and moneyed men that talk so finely ... to make us poor illiterate people swallow down the pill." Government, he insisted, should be kept simple so that people could not use it to further selfish ambition. The other farmer, who was better off and who had been terrified by Shays's Rebellion, disagreed. He warned that "anarchy leads to tyranny.... These lawyers, these moneyed men, these men of learning, are all embarked in the same cause with us, and we must all swim or sink together." Rufus King, who was a signer and a strong supporter of the Constitution, summarized in a letter to James Madison what appeared to worry the ordinary people: "An apprehension that the liberties of the people are in danger, and a distrust of men of property and education have a more powerful effect on the minds of our opponents than any specific objections against the Constitution."

What criticisms did the Anti-Federalists have of the Constitution?

Why did the Federalists promise that a bill of rights would be added to the Constitution?

Why was the battle for ratification in New York so difficult?

Reactions to the Constitution

Following a bold strategy that favored its ratification, the framers of the Constitution stated that nine state conventions had to approve the Constitution before it could go into effect. The Articles of Confederation had stipulated that the approval of all 13 states was needed to ratify any changes. Ratifica-tion by the necessary nine states took less than one year. In the nine long months of discussion and debate, two camps were quickly formed. The **Federalists** supported the Constitution and the **Anti-Federalists** opposed ratification of the Constitution. The name Anti-Federalist is somewhat misleading because the term **federalism** describes a relationship of independent states that share power with a central government. What the Anti-Federalists were really opposed to was a central government that might dominate the local, or state governments. The Constitution, they charged, gave too much power to the central (national) government at the expense of the power of the states. The Anti-Federalists did not want another level of government with the power to tax the people. Finally, the Anti-Federalists believed that without a bill of rights, the Constitution did not adequately protect individual liberties. As Rufus King had recognized, many people were worried that those freedoms gained at such a high cost would be lost through the government's abuse of power.

Many Anti-Federalists were doubtful that a centralized republican government could adequately govern the vast territory and diverse people who then made up the United States. Never had a republican government been applied to circumstances such as existed in the new nation. For example, the Roman republic had been confined to a small territory and had become a dictatorship when Rome built its empire. In 1649 England had abolished its monarchy in favor of a commonwealth, only to fall into a military dictatorship until the monarchy was restored after 1660. The only modern republics—Holland and some Italian and Swiss city-states—were small and compact with little cultural diversity. None of them provided a pattern for the United States. With no real model to follow, how could the framers of this Constitution be sure that it would endure?

The new government was different from other republics. It was no longer a confederation of sovereign states, nor was it simply the merging of states into a national government. It was somewhere in between. Patrick Henry, the persuasive orator who was violently opposed to the new Constitution, called it "horribly defective, horribly frightful, [because] it squints toward monarchy." He went on to say, "This government is so new, it wants a name."

The Federalists, who backed the new form of government, effectively campaigned to ease the worries of the Anti-Federalists on several issues. They promised that a bill of rights would be added to the ratified document. It was not that the Federalists objected to the rights being sought. Rather, they noted that many rights were already specified in the Constitution, and they were concerned that a listing of specific rights might not be inclusive enough and might actually limit rights to only those listed.

Bill of Rights Proposed The most pressing concern among the common people, however, was just this lack of protection of individual rights. Even a supporter like Thomas Jefferson, who approved of a national government strong enough to support itself "without needing continual recurrence to the state legislatures," worried about the lack of a bill of rights to guarantee the liberties of the people. Jefferson wrote, "A bill of rights is what the people are entitled to against every government on earth, . . . and what no government should refuse."

A bill of rights had been proposed during the final days of the convention by George Mason of Virginia. The demand for a bill of rights was the expression of a belief that no government could be trusted to protect the liberties of it citizens. Mason's motion had been quickly defeated. Many delegates felt that the Constitution itself provided a sufficient guarantee of rights. Others, such as James Madison, explained that the checks and balances in the Constitution would be a much better way to ensure people's rights. "I have seen the [Virginia] bill of rights violated in every instance where it has been exposed to a popular current," Madison said. Some delegates feared that discussion about a bill of rights would inevitably bring about another quarrel over slavery. South Carolina delegate Charles Cotesworth Pinckney spoke only the truth of the time when he later said candidly, "Such bills generally begin with declaring that all men are by nature born free. Now, we should make that declaration with very bad grace when a large part of our property consists in men who are actually born slaves." In spite of these arguments against a bill of rights, it appeared that those delegates who supported the idea were more in touch with the will of the people.

▲ *Patrick Henry was violently opposed to the new Constitution. How does the artist convey Henry's powerful oratorical style?*

The Ratification Process

Delaware became the first state to ratify the Constitution, with Pennsylvania, New Jersey, Georgia, and Connecticut following in fairly short order. Heated discussion arose in Massachusetts, Maryland, and South Carolina, but all those states approved the document within a few months. (Massachusetts narrowly voted for it—187 votes for and 168 against.) In June of 1788, New Hampshire became the ninth state to ratify, and the Constitution went into effect. Among supporters, there was less jubilation than one might expect. The states that had not yet voted, including New York and Virginia, contained 40 percent of the country's population and were among the most powerful. It seemed vital to the future unity of the country that those states vote for the Constitution.

In Virginia eloquent spokesmen campaigned on both sides of the argument. Powerful voices such as

James Madison

Nearly 50 years after the signing of the Constitution, James Madison overheard someone mention to a friend that there is "*the* writer of the Constitution of the U.S." Madison is recorded as replying, "You give me a credit to which I have no claim, for the Constitution was not . . . the off-spring of a single brain. It ought to be regarded as the working of many heads and many hands." Madison was too modest. He had earned his titles: the "Sage of His Time," "the Great Little Madison," and "Father of the Constitution." Although several others did help to develop the final document, the core of the Constitution was Madison's own Virginia Plan.

More than anyone else, Madison was prepared for the Constitutional Convention. In some ways that preparation began when he was a child. The oldest of 12 children, he was small for his age, sickly and frail, and he suffered from epilepsy, or what he called a "falling sickness." Although he loved to be outdoors roaming the 5,000 acres that he knew would someday be his, he had to spend many days in bed. There, he read everything he could get his hands on. Before he was 11, he had read his father's entire collection of 85 books, and he begged to go to school. He enjoyed five years at a nearby private school, and then was tutored until he was 18. Next, he set off for Princeton College,

▲ *Madison at age 32.*

▲ *Madison in his later years.*

where he studied the works of the great political philosophers of the Enlightenment. After his graduation, he continued to study the workings of past governments.

After attending the Annapolis Convention, Madison talked the Virginia General Assembly into issuing a national call to send delegates to Philadelphia in 1787. He wrote letters to potential delegates, convinced George Washington that it was his duty to attend, and persuaded his fellow Virginia delegates to back the plan he had drafted earlier that year.

After the Constitution was completed, Madison went on to support it, through writing many of *The Federalist* essays and through private letters and conversations. His painstaking notes of all the meetings of the Constitutional Convention make up the only record we have of much of the debate.

Madison continued his public service after the Constitution was ratified. He was elected to the first session of Congress as a representative from Virginia. He compiled the amendments, or additional changes, that state ratifying conventions had proposed for the Bill of Rights, served as secretary of state under Thomas Jefferson, and as fourth president of the United States.

Throughout his career, Madison remained a modest man. He was ill at ease at public functions, especially if they were held in his honor. He once commented, "I would rather be in bed." He died well respected and loved at the age of 85.

1. What do the titles Madison was given tell you about him?
2. Not remembered as an outstanding president, Madison is still regarded as a great statesman. Why is that so?

► This portrait of Alexander Hamilton was painted by John Trumbull. James Madison and John Jay aided Hamilton in the fight for ratification of the Constitution in New York. Why did New York think it could easily exist without being part of the United States?

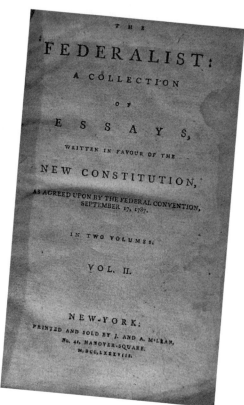

► Title page of The Federalist, Volume II.

those of George Washington and James Madison spoke for ratification, while Patrick Henry was absolutely opposed. When the vote was taken, the Constitution was approved by a mere ten votes. It was the promise that a bill of rights would be added to the document that swung the vote.

The battle for ratification was intense in New York. If that large state did not ratify the document, the prestige of the Constitution would be weakened. Governor George Clinton led the opposition, arguing that a state as large and wealthy as New York could get along by itself, with no need of a central government. Both Federalists and Anti-Federalists flooded newspapers with articles defending their positions and seeking votes for or against the document.

One Anti-Federalist writer questioned whether a republic could adequately secure the liberty of the citizens. He noted that the Greek and Roman republics had been small and that as soon as they took over large territories, they had exchanged their free government for "those of the most tyrannical that ever existed in the world." Even the present territory of the United States was vast, he went on to say, and "now contains near three millions of souls, and is capable of containing more than ten times that number. Is it practicable for a country, so large and so numerous . . . to elect a representation, that will speak their sentiments, without becoming so numerous as to be incapable of transacting public business? It certainly is not."

The Federalist Papers   Along with Alexander Hamilton, New York's sole signer of the Constitution, the brilliant and popular John Jay led the fight for ratification. With help from James Madison, together they bombarded New York newspapers with essays that presented well-thought-out arguments in favor of ratification. Eventually collected and published in booklet form, these essays were published in 1788 as *The Federalist* and are often referred to as *The Federalist Papers*. Today they stand out as early statements of American political theory. In *The Federalist* Number 9, Hamilton explained how the states and national governments could work together:

The proposed Constitution, so far from implying an abolition of State Governments, makes them constituent parts of the national sovereignty by allowing them a direct representation in the Senate, and leaves in their possession certain exclusive and very important portions of sovereign power. This fully corresponds . . . with the idea of Federal Government.

▶ In August 1788, North Carolina voted against ratification of the Constitution by a vote of 184 to 84. Why do you think the people of that state decided to hold another election? What would have happened if Rhode Island's vote had been 32 for ratification and 34 against?

▼ Americans have always loved a parade and this celebration of ratification of the Constitution was a day for fun and excitement. Why do you think Hamilton's name is on the float?

Dates of Ratification of the Constitution

State	Date	For	Against
Delaware	December 7, 1787	30	0
Pennsylvania	December 12, 1787	46	23
New Jersey	December 18, 1787	38	0
Georgia	January 2, 1788	26	0
Connecticut	January 9, 1788	128	40
Massachusetts	February 6, 1788	187	168
Maryland	April 28, 1788	63	11
South Carolina	May 23, 1788	149	73
New Hampshire	June 21, 1788	57	46
Virginia	June 25, 1788	89	79
New York	July 26, 1788	30	27
North Carolina	November 21, 1789	194	77
Rhode Island	May 29, 1790	34	32

The Federalist Number 10, written by James Madison, is generally considered the most important document for describing how a large republic has advantages over a small one:

"The smaller the society, the fewer probably will be the distinct parties and interests composing it . . . the more easily they will concert and execute their plans of oppression. Extend the sphere and you take in a greater variety of parties and interests; you make it less probable that a majority of the whole will have a common motive to invade the rights of other citizens . . . ."

In other words, individual rights could and would be better protected.

Other articles painstakingly met every point the opposition proposed. Just how much influence these essays had on the New York ratification convention members is uncertain, but as the debate raged on, news came that Virginia had ratified. That news, along with the promotion of the Constitution by The Federalist, tipped the scales. New York would be isolated if it did not join the union. When the vote took place, those favoring ratification won by 30 to 27 votes. Later both North Carolina (1789) and Rhode Island (1790) ratified the Constitution. All the states had finally agreed to a federal union.

SECTION 4 REVIEW

1. **State** three reasons why the Anti-Federalists distrusted the Constitution.
2. **Explain** how the size of the United States increased the Anti-Federalist distrust of the Constitution.
3. **Relate** why people like Madison and Pinckney opposed a bill of rights.
4. **Predict** what might have been the consequences if New York had not ratified the Constitution.
5. **Identify** *The Federalist Papers*.

SECTION 5

The Constitution Examined

The Constitution that took so long to ratify was never meant by its framers to stand for all time without alteration. George Washington noted the need for continual examination of the document. He wrote that "the warmest friends and the best supporters the Constitution has do not contend that it is free from imperfections. . . . I do not think we are more inspired, have more wisdom, or possess more virtue than those who will come after us." Even the "Father of the Constitution," James Madison, believed it might need to be altered in the future: "In framing a system which we wish to last for all ages, we should not lose sight of the changes which ages will produce."

Over the two centuries since its ratification, many changes have been made to the Constitution. However, the basic premises on which the Constitution was framed—republicanism, federalism, and attention to the rights of the people—remain at the heart of the document.

Why did the framers include methods for change in the Constitution?

How has the scope of the Bill of Rights changed since it was ratified?

What are the four basic principles of our constitutional government that continue to make it functional?

The Bill of Rights

As promised, the first Congress to serve under the new Constitution altered that document by adding a bill of rights that would protect individual liberties on a national level. Many ideas for amendments had been submitted by the states and by individuals to the Congress. James Madison organized these ideas into 19 amendments and submitted them for Congress to consider. After a good deal of debate, Congress accepted 12 of those amendments and sent them to the states for ratification. The states, in turn, ratified ten amendments, and these make up the **Bill of Rights**. The last two of the original thirteen colonies—North Carolina and Rhode Island—joined the Union once the Bill of Rights had been ratified. Vermont became the fourteenth state in 1791.

The Separation of Powers

Like the state governments, the national government had three specific functions and three branches. Congress was to make the laws, the president was to carry them out, and the judiciary was to create the courts. This division of responsibility was meant to provide a system of **checks and balances** to guarantee a balance of power, and to make certain that one branch could not control the others. Each derived its authority directly from the Constitution.

This system of checks and balances reflects the framers' fear that government could become too powerful. The "accumulation of all powers, legislative, executive, and judiciary, in the same hands," Madison wrote, is "the very definition of tyranny." Over the years, there have been many times when Americans have felt that this separation of powers, with its checks and balances, has become unwieldy and inefficient. For example, the business of government can often be stalled or slowed when the president is a member of one political party and the Congress has a majority of members from the other party. Others argue that the system is still needed to protect people from the abuse of government power.

The Bill of Rights (Ratified in 1791)

First Amendment	Guarantees freedom of religion, speech, press, assembly, and petition.
Second Amendment	Guarantees the right to keep and bear arms, since a state requires a well-equipped citizen army for its own security.
Third Amendment	Prohibits the lodging of soldiers in peacetime, without the dweller's consent.
Fourth Amendment	Prohibits unreasonable searches and seizures of persons or property.
Fifth Amendment	Guarantees the right to trial by jury, due process of law, and fair payment when private property is taken for public use, such as in eminent domain; prohibits compulsory self-incrimination and double jeopardy (trial for the same crime twice).
Sixth Amendment	Guarantees the accused in a criminal case the right to a speedy and public trial by an impartial jury and with counsel; allows the accused to cross-examine witnesses against him or her, and to solicit testimony from witnesses in his or her favor.
Seventh Amendment	Guarantees a trial by jury for the accused in a civil case involving $20 or more.*
Eighth Amendment	Prohibits excessive bail and fines, as well as cruel and unusual punishments.
Ninth Amendment	Establishes that the people have rights in addition to those specified in the Constitution.
Tenth Amendment	Establishes that those powers neither delegated to the national government nor denied to the states are reserved for the states.

* Federal trials today involve large sums of money.

▲ *The Bill of Rights originally applied only to the federal government. States were not constitutionally bound by these amendments. Why do you think the framers were more concerned with restricting the powers of central government?*

Federal Rights Versus States Rights

The federal system, as developed by the framers of the Constitution, dictates that powers are to be shared by the national government and the states. Each of these bodies may directly govern through its own officials and laws. Both derive their authority and legitimacy from the Constitution, and each exercises power within certain specific areas of government. Changes in the Constitution can only be made through agreement by three-fourths of the states. Through the Tenth Amendment of the Bill of Rights, the states are guaranteed all powers not designated to the national government. Each state has a right to equal treatment, and, in the Senate, each state has an equal number of representatives. However, each state does not have equal political power

The Federal System: Division of Powers

Powers Delegated to the Federal Government	Powers Shared by Federal and State Governments	Powers Reserved to the States
■ Declare war	■ Enforce laws	■ Establish local governments
■ Regulate interstate and foreign trade	■ Borrow money	■ Regulate commerce within a state
■ Maintain armed forces	■ Levy taxes	■ Provide for public safety
■ Coin money	■ Charter banks	■ Create corporation laws
■ Establish post offices	■ Establish courts	■ Establish schools
■ Set standards for weights and measurements	■ Provide for general welfare	■ Make marriage laws
■ Admit new states		■ Assume all powers not granted to the federal government or prohibited by the Constitution
■ Establish foreign policy		
■ Establish laws for citizenship		
■ Regulate patents and copyrights		
■ Pass laws necessary for carrying out its powers		

▲ *In government, federalism is the distribution of power between a central authority and the constituent elements (or states). Some powers are exclusive while others are shared. What is one power that belongs to the federal government alone?*

since the number of members each state has in the House of Representatives is based on state population.

Amendments are not the only way in which the Constitution and the government have been altered. Other changes have come from the application of two statements embedded in the document itself: (1) the Preamble to the Constitution states that it is to "provide for the general welfare," and (2) Article I, Section 8, Clause 18, gives power to Congress "to make all laws which shall be necessary and proper." This clause is often called the **elastic clause**, or the **necessary and proper clause.** It is the basis for **implied powers** or those powers considered necessary to carry out specified powers. The federal government has also gained power through amendments to the Constitution. For example, the Bill of Rights originally was meant to protect the **civil liberties**, or those basic rights protected by the Constitution, against the powers of the government. But the Fourteenth Amendment, passed after the Civil War, mandated that *states* may not deprive anyone of due process of law or equal protection. In effect, this incorporated the Bill of Rights into state as well as federal law.

The tensions between state governments and the national government often erupt into disagreements over the question of personal liberty and civil rights. Issues such as privacy rights, discrimination, and due process have tended to increase the power of the federal government at the expense of the states. Another example of the increasing power of the national government is the Income Tax Amendment of 1913, which led to the national government's collecting the largest proportion of tax revenue. This weakened state power.

Judicial Review

Interpretations of the meaning of specific articles and amendments of the Constitution have changed over the years. These interpretations are a result of the process known as **judicial review**. Judicial review is based on three concepts:

- the Constitution is the supreme law of the land
- any legislative, executive or state acts or actions contrary to the Constitution are null and void
- the courts have the responsibility of determining if acts violate the Constitution.

When the Constitution was written, most people accepted that the federal courts would have the power to declare state laws unconstitutional. Some even believed the Supreme Court should have and use the right to review acts of Congress or of the president. In fact, the Court was not to test this power of judicial review until *Marbury v. Madison* (1803), when Chief Justice **John Marshall** declared one part of the Judiciary Act of 1789 unconstitutional.

Seldom used in the early years of the republic, judicial review has come to be a powerful mechanism in preserving the intent of the Constitution. At the same time, it allows for interpretation that accommodates changing times and needs.

The Constitution Endures

Constitutional scholars agree that four principles of the American form of constitutional government are central to its success. These principles include:

- protection of individual rights and liberties
- limited government with the separation of power and checks and balances
- the federal system
- judicial review.

None of these principles appeared in definite form when the Constitution was ratified. Rather, they

▲ *The original Constitution is displayed in the National Archives building in Washington, D.C.*

have come to be the guiding principles through changes that have been made based on specific controversies. Often, these controversies involved two or more levels of government or branches of the federal government. In many cases, it has been the Supreme Court, through its power of judicial review, that has crystallized what is now meant by each of the principles. Through the same process the Constitution has been strengthened and altered in important respects, and it is indeed, as many scholars claim, a "living" document.

SECTION 5 REVIEW

1. Name the term given to the basic rights incorporated into the Constitution.
2. Restate Madison's definition of tyranny.
3. Define the term *judicial review*. Why is it so important?
4. Evaluate the following: The separation of powers is the heart of the Constitution.
5. List the four most important enduring principles of our constitutional government.

Summary

Even as the Revolutionary War was being fought, Americans realized the need to shape new governments that would turn the colonies into states and would provide for more central control. The ideology of republicanism and the experiences of the colonists shaped these new governments.

The revolutionaries took care to limit the powers Congress could exercise under the Articles of Confederation. In some areas, Congress under the Articles of Confederation succeeded brilliantly. Nothing, however, could be done to enforce laws, regulate commerce, or levy needed taxes. These powers were necessary for an independent nation to grow in the confusing times following the war. Americans turned to the idea of a stronger central government.

At the Constitutional Convention, the delegates worked out compromises necessary to support a new government. The Federalists and Anti-Federalists engaged in a battle during the ratification process, and the differences of opinion would continue to be important. In the end, the promise that a bill of rights would be amended to the original document convinced many legislatures and ratifying conventions to accept the Constitution.

On a separate piece of paper write the term from the vocabulary list that correctly completes each sentence. Not all terms will be used.

1. Quarrels among the states held up |||||||||| of the Articles of Confederation until 1781.
2. The |||||||||| makes the Constitution the highest law of the land.
3. Interpreting the meaning of specific articles of the Constitution is called |||||||||| .
4. Basic rights that are protected by the Constitution are known as |||||||||| .
5. The proceedings which guarantee the right to fair and reasonable treatment under the law are called |||||||||| .
6. The |||||||||| , also known as the |||||||||| , gives power to Congress "to make all laws which shall be necessary and proper."
7. In the new political order of the United States, |||||||||| was derived from the people.
8. |||||||||| is the sharing of power between independent states and a central government.
9. A patriotic citizen who behaves conscientiously and responsibly possesses |||||||||| . A country of such citizens acts according to principles of |||||||||| .
10. A major debate in American history was between |||||||||| who opposed a stronger central government and |||||||||| who favored it.

Vocabulary

amendment
Anti-Federalists
bicameral
checks and balances
civic virtue
civil liberties
due process
elastic clause
  or necessary and
    proper clause
electoral college

federalism
Federalists
implied powers
judicial review
jurisdiction
primogeniture
ratification
republicanism
sovereignty
supremacy clause

Review Questions

1. How did the ideology of republicanism influence the new governments of the states?
2. In what ways did the state constitutions reflect unhappiness with colonial governments?
3. What political value was put on the rights of women and enslaved persons?
4. How effective was the national government under the Articles of Confederation?
5. What kinds of compromises were necessary for agreement among the large and small states in forming the new government?

6. Why were enslaved African Americans in the South to be counted as three-fifths of a person?
7. Why was there discussion over who should head the government?
8. Why did the Bill of Rights become an important issue in ratification campaigns?
9. What were the basic disagreements between the Federalists and the Anti-Federalists?
10. What are the four guiding principles of the Constitution?

Critical Historical Thinking

Writing Answer each of the following questions by writing one or more complete paragraphs:

1. Explain why many historians believe that it was necessary for the colonists to experience government under the Articles of Confederation in order to create the Constitution.
2. Discuss the effect that the compromise regarding the slave trade had on the future of the nation.
3. Examine the Preambles to the Declaration of Independence and the Constitution. Discuss common principles in both of these writings.
4. Read "Why the Constitution Should Be Ratified" and "Was a Change in Government Necessary?" in the Unit 2 Archives. Identify the main arguent of each selection. Which piece of writing do you believe is more persuasive? Why?

Making Connections with Politics

Lawmakers attempt to write laws in very specific language in order to avoid the possibility that a law will be applied in ways they did not intend. Still, more than one meaning can often be drawn from a statement, no matter how carefully written. For example, if a sign says "You must be 18 years old to enter," does that mean you can't enter if you are 19? Soon after the ratification of the Constitution, uncertainty of this sort was the source of a major controversy, the core of which has remained with the nation to the present.

Article I, Section 8, of the Constitution grants Congress the power to pass whatever laws are "necessary and proper" for carrying out its constitutional powers. Thus, Congress is specifically empowered to declare war but not to institute a draft to raise an army. Article I, Section 8, the so-called elastic clause, considers that raising an army is a necessary and proper function of the power to declare war. Therefore, Congress may pass laws to create a draft. The necessary and proper powers of the government were at the heart of the argument between Alexander Hamilton and Thomas Jefferson over the scope and powers of the new federal government.

▪ Investigate and report on an instance of the use of the elastic clause by Congress in American history.

Additional Skills Practice

Refer to "The Federal System: Division of Powers" chart on page 168 to answer the following questions:

1. What information does this chart present?
2. What is the advantage to organizing the information in this way?
3. Which levels of government—federal, state, or both—have these powers?

   a. collect taxes
   b. set standards for weights and measures
   c. establish citizenship requirements
   d. charter banks
   e. admit new states
   f. coin money
   g. borrow money
   h. assume powers not specified in the Constitution

Constitution of the United States of America

The short Preamble originally read, "We the States." The final version was changed to read, "We the People." Note that there are six purposes for writing the Constitution.

ARTICLE I. LEGISLATIVE BRANCH

Article I explains how the legislative branch of government is to be organized, and details the powers of Congress.

SECTION 2. HOUSE OF REPRESENTATIVES

Clause 1: Note that persons who have the right to vote for members of the larger house of their own state legislature also have the right to vote for that state's representatives in the House of Representatives (and, under the Seventeenth Amendment, for that state's U.S. senators).

Clause 2: Each member of the House must be at least 25 years of age, have been a U.S. citizen for at least seven years, and be a resident of the state in which he or she is elected.

Clause 3: This clause includes what has been called "the three-fifths compromise." In this clause, "those bound to Service for a Term of Years," refers to indentured servants, who were to be counted as "free Persons." As used here, the phrase "all other Persons" refers to slaves, who were to be counted as three-fifths of a person.

A number of amendments have changed these provisions. All the people of a state are now

The Preamble

We the People of the United States, in Order to form a more perfect Union, establish Justice, insure domestic Tranquility, provide for the common defence, promote the general Welfare, and secure the Blessings of Liberty to ourselves and our Posterity, do ordain and establish this Constitution for the United States of America.

Article I. Legislative Branch

SECTION 1. LEGISLATIVE POWERS

All legislative Powers herein granted shall be vested in a Congress of the United States, which shall consist of a Senate and House of Representatives.

SECTION 2. HOUSE OF REPRESENTATIVES

Clause 1: Composition and Election of Members. The House of Representatives shall be composed of Members chosen every second Year by the People of the several States, and the Electors in each State shall have the Qualifications requisite for Electors of the most numerous Branch of the State Legislature.

Clause 2: Qualifications. No Person shall be a Representative who shall not have attained to the Age of twenty five Years, and been seven Years a Citizen of the United States, and who shall not, when elected, be an Inhabitant of that State in which he shall be chosen.

Clause 3: Apportionment of Representatives and Direct Taxes. Representatives and direct Taxes[1] shall be apportioned among the several States which may be included within this Union, according to their respective Numbers which shall

[1]Modified by the Sixteenth Amendment.

be determined by adding to the whole Number of free Persons, including those bound to Service for a Term of Years, and excluding Indians not taxed, three fifths of all other Persons.[2] The actual Enumeration shall be made within three Years after the first Meeting of the Congress of the United States, and within every subsequent Term of ten Years, in such Manner as they shall by Law direct. The Number of Representatives shall not exceed one for every thirty Thousand, but each State shall have at Least one Representative; and until such enumeration shall be made, the State of New Hampshire shall be entitled to chuse three, Massachusetts eight, Rhode Island and Providence Plantations one, Connecticut five, New York six, New Jersey four, Pennsylvania eight, Delaware one, Maryland six, Virginia ten, North Carolina five, South Carolina five, and Georgia three.

Clause 4: *Vacancies.* When vacancies happen in the Representation from any State, the Executive Authority thereof shall issue Writs of Election to fill such Vacancies.

Clause 5: *Officers and Impeachment.* The House of Representatives shall chuse their Speaker and other Officers; and shall have the sole Power of Impeachment.

Section 3. The Senate

Clause 1: *Term and Number of Members.* The Senate of the United States shall be composed of two Senators from each State chosen by the Legislature thereof,[3] for six Years; and each Senator shall have one Vote.

Clause 2: *Classification of Senators.* Immediately after they shall be assembled in Consequence of the first Election, they shall be divided as equally as may be into three Classes. The Seats of the Senators of the first Class shall be vacated at the Expiration of the second Year, of the second Class at the Expiration of the fourth Year, and of the third Class at the Expiration of the sixth Year, so that one third may be chosen every second Year; and if Vacancies happen by Resignation, or otherwise, during the Recess of the Legislature of any State, the Executive thereof may make temporary Appointments until the next Meeting of the Legislature, which shall then fill such Vacancies.[4]

Clause 3: *Qualifications.* No Person shall be a Senator who shall not have attained to the Age of thirty Years, and

[2]Modified by the Fourteenth Amendment.
[3]Repealed by the Seventeenth Amendment.
[4]Modified by the Seventeenth Amendment.

counted to determine how many representatives a state can have. One member can be chosen for every 30,000 persons in the nation, but every state has the right to one representative no matter how small its population might be. The limit of 435 representatives was set by Congress in 1929. Note that if each member of the House currently represented only 30,000 people, there would be more than 6,000 representatives. "Enumeration" refers to the census, or the counting of the population, that has taken place every ten years since 1790.

Clause 4: When a representative resigns, the governor may call an election to fill the vacancy.

Clause 5: Members of the House can choose their own officers, including the Speaker of the House. Only the House can impeach, or bring charges against, an American official.

Section 3. The Senate

Clauses 1 and 2: The Seventeenth Amendment changed this procedure so that senators are now elected by the people rather than by the legislature. All senators serve terms of six years, but only one-third are elected in any particular election.

Clause 3: Each senator must be at least 30 years of age, have been a U.S. citizen for at least nine years, and be a resident of the state in which he or she is elected.

Clause 4: The only duty of the vice president listed in the Constitution is to act as president of the Senate and to vote in case of a tie. Modern presidents have given many more duties to their vice presidents.

Clause 5: The Senate elects one of its members to preside when the vice president is absent. This senator is called the president pro tempore of the Senate because of the temporary nature of the office.

Clause 6: The House has the power to impeach, or bring charges against, an official of the American government, but the Senate acts as jury for the case, which, when the president is tried, is presided over by the chief justice of the Supreme Court. A conviction, or guilty verdict, requires the agreement of two-thirds of the senators present. Upon a conviction, the Senate can only force the official to leave office and bar him or her from ever holding federal office again. The individual, then, is also open to be tried in the appropriate regular court.

SECTION 4. CONGRESSIONAL ELECTIONS: TIMES, MANNER, AND PLACES

Clauses 1 and 2: In 1845, Congress set the first Tuesday after the first Monday in November in even-numbered years as election day. The Twentieth Amendment states that Congress will begin its yearly sessions on January 3 of each year.

SECTION 5. POWERS AND DUTIES OF THE HOUSES

Clause 1: Under this clause, Congress, until 1969, had the authority to act as the sole judge of the qualifications of its members. Then, the Supreme Court ruled that Congress could not exclude duly elected candidates if they met all the requirements listed in Article I, Section 2.

Clause 2: Each house of Congress may adopt its own rules guiding proceedings. Each house may also discipline its members for unacceptable conduct. No member may be expelled without a two-thirds majority.

Clause 3: Each house of Congress keeps a journal of its proceedings. In addition, the *Congressional Record* is published daily during sessions. Congress can withhold from the record information that the members believe should be kept secret.

been nine Years a Citizen of the United States, and who shall not, when elected, be an Inhabitant of that State for which he shall be chosen.

Clause 4: *The Role of the Vice President.* The Vice President of the United States shall be President of the Senate, but shall have no Vote, unless they be equally divided.

Clause 5: *Other Officers.* The Senate shall chuse their other Officers, and also a President pro tempore, in the Absence of the Vice President, or when he shall exercise the Office of President of the United States.

Clause 6: *Impeachment Trials.* The Senate shall have the sole Power to try all Impeachments. When sitting for that Purpose, they shall be on Oath or Affirmation. When the President of the United States is tried, the Chief Justice shall preside: And no Person shall be convicted without the Concurrence of two thirds of the Members present.

Clause 7: *Penalties for Conviction.* Judgment in Cases of Impeachment shall not extend further than to removal from Office, and disqualification to hold and enjoy any Office of honor, Trust, or Profit under the United States: but the Party convicted shall nevertheless be liable and subject to Indictment, Trial, Judgment, and Punishment, according to Law.

SECTION 4. CONGRESSIONAL ELECTIONS: TIMES, MANNER, AND PLACES

Clause 1: *Elections.* The Times, Places and Manner of holding Elections for Senators and Representatives, shall be prescribed in each State by the Legislature thereof; but the Congress may at any time by Law make or alter such Regulations, except as to the Places of chusing Senators.

Clause 2: *Sessions of Congress.* ~~The Congress shall assemble at least once in every Year, and such Meeting shall be on the first Monday in December, unless they shall by Law appoint a different Day.~~[5]

SECTION 5. POWERS AND DUTIES OF THE HOUSES

Clause 1: *Admitting Members and Quorum.* Each House shall be the Judge of the Elections, Returns, and Qualifications of its own Members, and a Majority of each shall constitute a Quorum to do Business; but a smaller

---

[5]Changed by the Twentieth Amendment.

Number may adjourn from day to day, and may be authorized to compel the Attendance of absent Members, in such Manner, and under such Penalties as each House may provide.

Clause 2: Rules and Discipline of Members. Each House may determine the Rules of its Proceedings, punish its Members for disorderly Behaviour, and, with the Concurrence of two thirds, expel a Member.

Clause 3: Keeping a Record. Each House shall keep a Journal of its Proceedings, and from time to time publish the same, excepting such Parts as may in their Judgment require Secrecy; and the Yeas and Nays of the Members of either House on any question shall, at the Desire of one fifth of those Present, be entered on the Journal.

Clause 4: Adjournment. Neither House, during the Session of Congress, shall, without the Consent of the other, adjourn for more than three days, nor to any other Place than that in which the two Houses shall be sitting.

SECTION 6. RIGHTS OF MEMBERS

Clause 1: Compensation and Privileges. The Senators and Representatives shall receive a Compensation for their services to be ascertained by Law, and paid out of the Treasury of the United States. They shall in all Cases, except Treason, Felony and Breach of the Peace, be privileged from Arrest during their Attendance at the Session of their respective Houses, and in going to and returning from the same; and for any Speech or Debate in either House, they shall not be questioned in any other place.

Clause 2: Restrictions. No Senator or Representative shall, during the time for which he was elected, be appointed to any civil Office under the Authority of the United States, which shall have been created, or the Emoluments whereof shall have been encreased during such time; and no Person holding any Office during such time; and no Person holding any Office under the United States, shall be a Member of either House during his Continuance in Office.

SECTION 7. LEGISLATIVE POWERS: BILLS AND RESOLUTIONS

Clause 1: Revenue Bills. All Bills for raising Revenue shall originate in the House of Representatives; but the Senate may propose or concur with Amendments as on other Bills.

Clause 4: Neither house of Congress can adjourn for more than three days, nor go to a city other than that where the other house is sitting, without the consent of the other house.

SECTION 6. RIGHTS OF MEMBERS

Clause 1: Senators and representatives are paid from federal rather than state funds. This provision was meant to strengthen the federal government. This section also includes what is known as the immunity privilege.

The immunity privilege means that members cannot be prosecuted for anything they say in Congress. They cannot be arrested while Congress is in session, except for treason, major crimes, or breaking the peace. This immunity applies to them while in the Capitol Building itself and not in their private lives.

Clause 2: This clause bars a member of Congress from holding an office in the executive or judicial branches of the federal government if that office was created or if its salary was increased during his or her term in Congress. This clause also reinforces the separation of powers by preventing a member of Congress from holding office in the executive or judicial branches during his or her term in Congress.

SECTION 7. LEGISLATIVE POWERS: BILLS AND RESOLUTIONS

Clause 1: All tax laws must originate in the House of Representatives. The reasoning was that since those members of Congress are elected every two years, they would listen to the public and be more attentive to its approval. The Senate may amend tax bills.

Clause 2: A bill becomes a law when it is passed by both houses of Congress and signed by the president. If the president vetoes the bill, it is returned to the house in which it originated, along with a statement of why the president objects to the bill. To override a presidential veto, two-thirds of the members of each house must vote for it. If the president does not sign or veto a bill within ten days, it becomes law. If, however, Congress adjourns during the ten-day period (excluding Sundays), the bill does not become law This is called a "pocket veto." The veto power of the president and the ability of Congress to override such a veto are two of the important checks and balances written into the Constitution.

Clause 3: The president must either approve or veto everything that Congress passes, except votes to adjourn and resolutions not having the force of law.

SECTION 8. THE POWERS OF CONGRESS

Clause 1: This clause gives Congress the power to establish and collect various types of taxes. *An impost* is a type of tax.

Clause 2: Congress has the power to borrow money, and the Constitution places no limit on the amount of money Congress may borrow. Congress usually borrows money through the sale of U.S. Treasury bonds on which interest is paid.

Clause 3: This clause, known as the Commerce Clause, is the basis for much of what Congress does. The Commerce Clause gives Congress the power to regulate interstate commerce and foreign trade.

Clause 4: Congress has the authority to establish the naturalization process, or the process by which the citizens of other countries become citizens of the United States, and to ensure that this process is uniform in all states. Congress also may make laws with respect to bankruptcy.

Clause 5: Congress has the power to mint coins and print paper money. Congress also has the power to establish uniform measures of weight, time, distance, etc.

Clause 6: Congress is responsible for punishing those who produce counterfeit, or forged, U.S. money. Agents of the treasury department investigate and arrest counterfeiters.

Clause 7: This clause gives Congress the power to establish a post office and the roads (including

Clause 2: The Presidential Veto. Every Bill which shall have passed the House of Representatives and the Senate, shall, before it becomes a Law, be presented to the President of the United States; If he approve he shall sign it, but if not he shall return it, with his Objections to the House in which it shall have originated, who shall enter the Objections at large on their Journal, and proceed to reconsider it. If after such Reconsideration two thirds of that House shall agree to pass the Bill, it shall be sent together with the Objections, to the other House, by which it shall likewise be reconsidered, and if approved by two thirds of that House, it shall become a Law. But in all such Cases the Votes of both Houses shall be determined by Yeas and Nays, and the Names of the Persons voting for and against the Bill shall be entered on the Journal of each House respectively. If any Bill shall not be returned by the President within ten days (Sundays excepted) after it shall have been presented to him, the Same shall be a Law, in like Manner as if he had signed it, unless the Congress by their Adjournment prevent its Return in which Case it shall not be a Law.

Clause 3: Actions on Other Matters. Every Order, Resolution, or Vote to which the Concurrence of the Senate and House of Representatives may be necessary (except on a question of Adjournment) shall be presented to the President of the United States; and before the Same shall take Effect, shall be approved by him, or being disapproved by him, shall be repassed by two thirds of the Senate and House of Representatives, according to the Rules and Limitations prescribed in the Case of a Bill.

SECTION 8. THE POWERS OF CONGRESS

Clause 1: Taxing. The Congress shall have Power To lay and collect Taxes, Duties, Imposts and Excises, to pay the Debts and provide for the common Defence and general Welfare of the United States; but all Duties, Imposts and Excises shall be uniform throughout the United States;

Clause 2: Borrowing. To borrow Money on the credit of the United States;

Clause 3: Regulation of Commerce. To regulate Commerce with foreign Nations, and among the several States, and with the Indian Tribes;

Clause 4: Naturalization and Bankruptcy. To establish a uniform Rule of Naturalization, and uniform Laws on the subject of Bankruptcies throughout the United States;

Clause 5: Money and Standards. To coin Money, regulate

the Value thereof, and of foreign Coin, and fix the Standard of Weights and Measures;

Clause 6: *Punishing Counterfeiters.* To provide for the Punishment of counterfeiting the Securities and current Coin of the United States;

Clause 7: *Roads and Post Offices.* To establish Post Offices and post Roads;

Clause 8: *Patents and Copyrights.* To promote the Progress of Science and useful Arts, by securing for limited Times to Authors and Inventors the exclusive Right to their respective Writings and Discoveries;

Clause 9: *Lower Courts.* To constitute Tribunals inferior to the supreme Court;

Clause 10: *Punishment for Piracy.* To define and punish Piracies and Felonies committed on the high Seas, and Offences against the Law of Nations;

Clause 11: *Declaration of War.* To declare War, grant Letters of Marque and Reprisal, and make Rules concerning Captures on Land and Water;

Clause 12: *The Army.* To raise and support Armies, but no Appropriation of Money to that Use shall be for a longer Term than two years;

Clause 13: *Creation of a Navy.* To provide and maintain a Navy;

Clause 14: *Regulation of the Armed Forces.* To make Rules for the Government and Regulation of the land and naval Forces;

Clause 15: *The Militia.* To provide for calling forth the Militia to execute the Laws of the Union, suppress Insurrections and repel Invasions;

Clause 16: *How the Militia is Organized.* To provide for organizing, arming, and disciplining the Militia, and for governing such Part of them as may be employed in the Service of the United States, reserving to the States respectively, the Appointment of the Officers, and the Authority of training the Militia according to the discipline described by Congress;

Clause 17: *Creation of the District of Columbia.* To exercise exclusive Legislation in all Cases whatsoever, over such District (not exceeding ten Miles square) as may, by Cession of particular States, and the Acceptance of Congress, become the Seat of the Government of the United States, and to exercise like Authority over all Places purchased by the Consent of the Legislature of the State in which the Same shall be, for the Erection of Forts, Magazines, Arsenals, dock-Yards, and other needful Buildings;—And

highways, railways, waterways, and airways) needed to deliver the mail.

Clause 8: This clause gives Congress the authority to establish laws governing copyrights and patents. Copyrights protect the original works of authors, composers, etc., and patents protect the inventions of inventors, engineers, etc.

Clause 9: Congress has the power to establish lower courts, or all federal courts other than the Supreme Court, which is established by the Constitution.

Clause 10: Congress has the authority to make piracy, or the robbing of a ship on the high seas, a federal crime, even if this crime occurs outside U.S. waters. Congress also has the authority to punish those who violate international law.

Clause 11: Only Congress has the power to declare war. A letter of "Marque and Reprisal" was a commission granted by Congress that authorized private individuals to capture and destroy enemy ships during wartime. Letters of marque and reprisal were prohibited by international law under the Treaty of Paris of 1856.

Clause 12: Congress has the authority to create and fund an army. There is a two-year limit on spending for the army; this gives ultimate control of the army to voters.

Clause 13: This clause gives Congress the power to create a navy.

Clause 14: Congress has the authority to establish the rules for the armed forces. Most of these rules are contained in the Uniform Code of Military Justice, which was passed by Congress in 1950.

Clauses 15 and 16: The militia here refers to each state's militia, or volunteer army. Since 1916 the militia has been known as the National Guard. Normally, the National Guard in each state is under the command of the state's governor. Under Clause 15, the Congress has the power to call the militia into federal service. The Constitution also gives this power to the president (see Article II, Section 2). Clause 16 states that Congress has the authority to make rules for the National Guard while it is acting in federal service.

Clause 17: Under this clause, Congress has the authority over the United States capital, which will not be in the jurisdiction of any one state. Congress established the District of Columbia as the nation's capital in 1791.

Clause 18: The last sentence in Section 8 is called the "elastic clause" of the Constitution and is one of its most important provisions. *Necessary and proper* are the key words. Much of what Congress does is done under the justification that such action is necessary and proper. Powers given to the government by the elastic clause are called "implied" powers. When Alexander Hamilton proposed the establishment of a national bank, he said the bank was necessary and proper in order to carry out such powers of Congress as borrowing money and regulating currency. Thomas Jefferson said that the Constitution did not say anything explicit about a national bank, so it would be unconstitutional to establish one.

Section 9. The Powers Denied to Congress

This section lists those powers denied to Congress.

Clause 1: This clause reflects the compromise the framers reached regarding the slave trade. This clause denied Congress the authority to pass any law restricting the slave trade until 1808. Note that the word *slave* is used neither here nor in the earlier three-fifths compromise.

Clause 2: Habeas corpus means "produce the body." A writ of habeas corpus is a court order directing a sheriff, warden, or other government official who is detaining someone, to produce that person before the court so the court can determine the legality of the detention.

Clause 3: A bill of attainder is a law that inflicts punishment without a trial. An ex post facto law is a law that inflicts punishment for an act that was legal when it was committed.

Clause 4: Capitation tax refers to a "head tax," or a tax levied on a per-person basis. Direct tax is a tax paid directly to the government, such as income tax or property tax. This provision was modified by the passage of the Sixteenth Amendment, which authorized Congress to tax "incomes, from whatever source derived."

Clause 5: This clause forbids Congress from taxing any good exported from one state to another or from one state to another country. Congress does have the authority to tax goods imported from other countries.

Clause 6: Congress must treat all ports within the United States the same in terms of taxing and commerce. Congress may not levy a tax on goods

Clause 18: The Elastic Clause. To make all Laws which shall be necessary and proper for carrying into Execution the foregoing Powers, and all other Powers vested by this Constitution in the Government of the United States, or in any Department or Officer thereof;

Section 9. The Powers Denied to Congress

Clause 1: Question of Slavery. The Migration or Importation of such Persons as any of the States now existing shall think proper to admit, shall not be prohibited by the Congress prior to the Year one thousand eight hundred and eight, but a Tax or duty may be imposed on such Importation, not exceeding ten dollars for each Person.

Clause 2: Habeas Corpus. The privilege of the Writ of Habeas Corpus shall not be suspended, unless when in Cases of Rebellion or Invasion the public Safety may require it.

Clause 3: Special Bills. No Bill of Attainder or ex post facto Law shall be passed.

Clause 4: Direct Taxes. ~~No Capitation, or other direct, Tax shall be laid, unless in Proportion to the Census or Enumeration herein before directed to be taken.~~[6]

Clause 5: Export Taxes. No Tax or Duty shall be laid on Articles exported from any State.

Clause 6: Interstate Commerce. No Preference shall be given by any Regulation of Commerce or Revenue to the Ports of one State over those of another; nor shall Vessels bound to, or from, one State, be obliged to enter, clear, or pay Duties in another.

Clause 7: Treasury Withdrawals. No Money shall be drawn from the Treasury, but in Consequence of Appropriations made by Law; and a regular Statement and Account of the Receipts and Expenditures of all public Money shall be published from time to time.

Clause 8: Titles of Nobility. No Title of Nobility shall be granted by the United States: And no Person holding any Office of Profit or Trust under them, shall, without the Consent of the Congress, accept of any present, Emolument, Office, or Title, of any kind whatever, from any King, Prince, or foreign State.

Section 10. Those Powers Denied to the States

Clause 1: Treaties and Coinage. No State shall enter into any Treaty, Alliance, or Confederation; grant Letters of Marque and Reprisal; coin Money; emit Bills of Credit; make any Thing but gold and silver Coin a Tender in

[6]Modified by the Sixteenth Amendment.

Payment of Debts; pass any Bill of Attainder, ex post facto Law, or Law impairing the Obligation of Contracts, or grant any Title of Nobility

Clause 2: Duties and Imposts. No State shall, without the Consent of the Congress, lay any Imposts or Duties on Imports or Exports, except what may be absolutely necessary for executing its inspection Laws; and the net Produce of all Duties and Imposts, laid by any State on Imports or Exports, shall be for the Use of the Treasury of the United States; and all such Laws shall be subject to the Revision and Controul of the Congress.

Clause 3: War. No State shall, without the Consent of Congress, lay any Duty of Tonnage, keep Troops, or Ships of War in time of Peace, enter into any Agreement or Compact with another State, or with a foreign Power or engage in War, unless actually invaded, or in such imminent Danger as will not admit of delay.

Article II. Executive Branch

SECTION 1. THE NATURE AND SCOPE OF PRESIDENTIAL POWER

Clause 1: Four-Year Term. The executive Power shall be vested in a President of the United States of America. He shall hold his Office during the Term of four Years, and, together with the Vice President, chosen for the same Term, be elected, as follows.

Clause 2: Choosing Electors From Each State. Each State shall appoint, in such Manner as the Legislature thereof may direct, a Number of Electors, equal to the whole Number of Senators and Representatives to which the State may be entitled in the Congress; but no Senator or Representative, or Person holding an Office of Trust or Profit under the United States, shall be appointed an Elector.

Clause 3: The Former System of Elections. ~~The Electors shall meet in their respective States, and vote by Ballot for two Persons, of whom one at least shall not be an Inhabitant of the same State with themselves. And they shall make a List of all the Persons voted for, and of the Number of Votes for each; which List they shall sign and certify, and transmit sealed to the Seat of the Government of the United States, directed to the President of the Senate. The President of the Senate shall, in the Presence of the Senate and House of Representatives, open all the Certificates, and the Votes shall then be counted. The Person having the greatest Number of~~

shipped via water from one state to another nor give one state's ports any legal advantage over those of another state.

Clause 7: This clause specifies that no federal money can be spent unless authorized by an act of Congress. This gives Congress the "power of the purse" and is a significant check of presidential power.

Clause 8: No title of nobility, such as duke or duchess, will be granted to an individual by the United States. This clause also forbids government officials from accepting any title, office, or gift from an official of a foreign government without the consent of Congress.

SECTION 10. THOSE POWERS DENIED TO THE STATES

Clause 1: This clause denies states the power to conduct foreign relations or coin money; these powers are exclusive to the federal government. Additionally, this clause denies to the states several powers that are also denied to the federal government.

Clause 2: This clause explains that states cannot tax goods entering or leaving their borders. States do have the power to charge a fee for inspecting goods, but the profit from such activity must be turned over to the federal government. Congress can alter the inspection laws of a state.

Clause 3: States may not keep an army or a navy, or go to war unless the state is directly attacked. States may not collect fees from foreign ships or make treaties with foreign nations. Such powers are reserved to the federal government.

ARTICLE II. EXECUTIVE BRANCH

SECTION 1. THE NATURE AND SCOPE OF PRESIDENTIAL POWER

Clause 1: The president is granted the "executive Power," which is the power to carry out the laws made by Congress. The framers of the Constitution wanted the terms of the president and vice president to be different from those of members of Congress. The framers settled on a four-year term of office for the president and vice president. The Twenty-second Amendment limits the number of times an individual may be elected president.

Clause 2: The "Electors" are more commonly known as the electoral college. The president is elected by electors—that is, representatives chosen by the people—rather than directly by the people. A state has the same number of electors as the combined total of that state's members of Congress (both the House and the Senate).

Clause 3: The original system of electing the president and the vice president outlined in this clause was replaced by a new system outlined in the Twelfth Amendment. The problems with this system were made clear in the elections of 1800 and 1804.

Clause 4: Congress is authorized to set the day on which the electors are chosen and the day on which the electors cast their ballots. Congress set the Tuesday after the first Monday in November every fourth year as the date for choosing electors. The electors cast their ballots on the Monday after the second Wednesday in December of that year.

Clause 5: The president must be a natural-

A NEW LEADER FOR THE 60's

KENNEDY FOR PRESIDENT

born citizen, be at least 35 years of age when taking office, and have resided within the United States for at least 14 years. The youngest elected president was John F. Kennedy, who was 43 years old when he took office. Theodore Roosevelt was 42 when he assumed the office of president after President William McKinley was assassinated in 1901. Ronald Reagan, at 69, was the oldest elected president.

Clause 6: This clause was extensively modified by the Twenty-fifth Amendment. The order of presidential succession after the vice president was established by the Presidential Succession Act (1947). This act declares that after the vice president, the Speaker of the House followed by the president pro tempore of the Senate, and then members of the cabinet (beginning with the secretary of state) in the order of the creation of the departments, would become president.

Clause 7: Emolument means salary or wages. Originally set at $25,000 per year, the president's

~~Votes shall be the President, if such Number be a Majority of the whole Number of Electors appointed; and if there be more than one who have such Majority, and have an equal Number of Votes, then the House of Representatives shall immediately chuse by Ballot one of them for President; and if no Person have a Majority, then from the five highest on the List the said House shall in like Manner chuse the President. But in chusing the President, the Votes shall be taken by States, the Representation from each State having one Vote; A quorum for this Purpose shall consist of a Member or Members from two thirds of the States, and a Majority of all the States shall be necessary to a Choice. In every Case, after the Choice of the President, the Person having the greater Number of Votes of the Electors shall be the Vice President. But if there should remain two or more who have equal Votes, the Senate shall chuse from them by Ballot the Vice President.~~[7]

Clause 4: The Time of Elections. The Congress may determine the Time of chusing the Electors, and the Day on which they shall give their Votes; which Day shall be the same throughout the United States.

Clause 5: Qualifications for President. No person except a natural born Citizen, or a Citizen of the United States, at the time of the Adoption of this Constitution, shall be eligible to the Office of President; neither shall any Person be eligible to that Office who shall not have attained to the Age of thirty five Years, and been fourteen Years a Resident within the United States.

Clause 6: Succession of the Vice President. ~~In Case of the Removal of the President from Office, or of his Death, Resignation or Inability to discharge the Powers and Duties of the said Office, the same shall devolve on the Vice President, and the Congress may by Law provide for the Removal, Death, Resignation or Inability, both of the President and Vice President, declaring what Officer shall then act as President, and such Officer shall act accordingly, until the Disability be removed, or a President shall be elected.~~[8]

Clause 7: The President's Salary. The President shall, at stated Times, receive for his Services, a Compensation, which shall neither be encreased nor diminished during the Period for which he shall have been elected, and he shall not

[7]Changed by the Twelfth Amendment.
[8]Modified by the Twenty-fifth Amendment.

receive within that Period any other Emolument from the United States, or any of them.

Clause 8: The Oath of Office. Before he enter on the Execution of his Office, he shall take the following Oath or Affirmation: "I do solemnly swear (or affirm) that I will faithfully execute the Office of President of the United States, and will to the best of my Ability, preserve, protect and defend the Constitution of the United States."

SECTION 2. POWERS OF THE PRESIDENT

Clause 1: Commander in Chief. The President shall be Commander in Chief of the Army and Navy of the United States, and of the Militia of the several States, when called into the actual Service of the United States; he may require the Opinion, in writing, of the principal Officer in each of the executive Departments, upon any Subject relating to the Duties of their respective Offices, and he shall have Power to grant Reprieves and Pardons for Offences against the United States, except in Cases of Impeachment.

Clause 2: Treaties and Appointment. He shall have Power, by and with the Advice and Consent of the Senate, to make Treaties, provided two thirds of the Senators present concur; and he shall nominate, and by and with the Advice and Consent of the Senate, shall appoint Ambassadors, other public Ministers and Consuls, Judges of the supreme Court, and all other Officers of the United States, whose Appointments are not herein otherwise provided for, and which shall be established by Law; but the Congress may by Law vest the Appointment of such inferior Officers, as they think proper, in the President alone, in the Courts of Law, or in the Heads of Departments.

Clause 3: Vacancies. The President shall have Power to fill up all Vacancies that may happen during the Recess of the Senate, by granting Commissions which shall expire at the end of their next Session.

SECTION 3. DUTIES OF THE PRESIDENT

He shall from time to time give to the Congress Information of the State of the Union, and recommend to their Consideration such Measures as he shall judge necessary and expedient; he may, on extraordinary Occasions, convene both Houses, or either of them, and in Case of Disagreement between them, with Respect to the Time of Adjournment, he may adjourn them to such Time as he shall think proper; he shall receive Ambassadors and other public Ministers; he

salary has been $200,000 per year since 1969. The president also has an expense account of an additional $50,000 per year. The president pays taxes on both amounts.

Clause 8: The president is "sworn in" prior to beginning the duties of the office. The ceremony is called inauguration. Traditionally the oath of office is administered by the chief justice of the Supreme Court. Because President Washington followed his oath of office with the words, "so help me, God," all succeeding presidents have done likewise.

SECTION 2. POWERS OF THE PRESIDENT

Clause 1: This clause names the president, an elected civilian, as commander in chief of the military, thus placing the armed forces under civilian control. The mention of the "principal Officers" of each of the executive departments is the only hint of the president's cabinet in the Constitution. Cabinet members are appointed by the president, but must be confirmed by the Senate. The president's clemency powers extend only to federal cases. In those cases, the president may grant a full or conditional pardon, or reduce a prison term or fine.

Clause 2: Many of the major powers of the president are identified in this clause. Included in it are the power to make treaties with foreign governments (with the approval of two-thirds of the senators present) and the power to appoint ambassadors, Supreme Court justices, and other government officials. Most such appointments require Senate approval.

Clause 3: If the Congress is not in session, the president has the power to appoint temporary officials to fill vacant federal offices without Senate approval. These temporary appointments automatically expire at the end of the Senate's next session.

SECTION 3. DUTIES OF THE PRESIDENT

Each year, the president reports to Congress on the state of the union. The president proposes a federal budget and presents an economic report. The president is also given the power to call special sessions of Congress and can adjourn Congress if the two houses cannot agree on a time of adjournment. The president is authorized to receive diplomatic representatives of other governments and to ensure the execution of all federal laws.

SECTION 4. IMPEACHMENT
Treason here refers to giving aid to the nation's enemies. The definition of high crimes and misdemeanors is usually given as serious crimes or abuses of political power.

ARTICLE III. JUDICIAL BRANCH

SECTION 1. JUDICIAL POWERS, COURTS, AND JUDGES
The Supreme Court is given the judicial power, as are the lower federal courts that Congress creates. Federal judges serve for life unless they are impeached and convicted by Congress. The salary of a federal judge may not be reduced during that judge's time in office.

SECTION 2. JURISDICTION
Clause 1: The federal courts take cases that concern the meaning of the Constitution, all federal laws, and all treaties. They can also take cases involving citizens of different states and citizens of foreign nations.

Clause 2: In cases that involve a representative from another country or in which a state is a party, the Supreme Court acts as a trial court and has original jurisdiction. In all other situations, cases

shall take Care that the Laws be faithfully executed, and shall Commission all the Officers of the United States.

SECTION 4. IMPEACHMENT
The President, Vice President and all civil Officers of the United States, shall be removed from Office on Impeachment for, and Conviction of, Treason, Bribery, or other high Crimes and Misdemeanors.

Article III. Judicial Branch

SECTION 1. JUDICIAL POWERS, COURTS, AND JUDGES
The judicial Power of the United States, shall be vested in one supreme Court, and in such inferior Courts as the Congress may from time to time ordain and establish. The Judges, both of the supreme and inferior Courts, shall hold their Offices during good Behaviour, and shall, at stated Times, receive for their Services a Compensation, which shall not be diminished during their Continuance in Office.

SECTION 2. JURISDICTION
Clause 1: Cases Under Federal Jurisdiction. The judicial Power shall extend to all Cases, in Law and Equity, arising under this Constitution, the Laws of the United States, and Treaties made, or which shall be made, under their Authority;—to all Cases affecting Ambassadors, other public Ministers and Consuls;—to all Cases of admiralty and maritime Jurisdiction;—to Controversies to which the United States shall be a Party;—to Controversies between two or more States;— between a State and Citizens of another State;[9]— between Citizens of different States;— between Citizens of the same State claiming Lands under Grants of different States, and between a State, or the Citizens thereof, and foreign States, Citizens or Subjects.[10]

Clause 2: Cases for the Supreme Court. In all Cases affecting Ambassadors, other public Ministers and Consuls, and those in which a State shall be a Party, the supreme Court shall have original Jurisdiction. In all the other Cases before mentioned, the supreme Court shall have appellate Jurisdiction, both as to Law and Fact, with such Exceptions, and under such Regulations as the Congress shall make.

Clause 3: The Conduct of Trials. The Trial of all Crimes, except in Cases of Impeachment, shall be by Jury; and such

[9]Modified by the Eleventh Amendment.
[10]Modified by the Eleventh Amendment.

Trial shall be held in the State where the said Crimes shall have been committed; but when not committed within any State, the Trial shall be at such Place or Places as the Congress may by Law have directed.

SECTION 3. TREASON

Clause 1: The Definition of Treason. Treason against the United States, shall consist only in levying War against them, or, in adhering to their Enemies, giving them Aid and Comfort. No person shall be convicted of Treason unless on the Testimony of two Witnesses to the same overt Act, or on Confession in open Court.

Clause 2: Punishment. The Congress shall have Power to declare the Punishment of Treason, but no Attainder of Treason shall work Corruption of Blood, or Forfeiture except during the Life of the Person attainted.

Article IV. Relations Among the States

SECTION 1. FULL FAITH AND CREDIT

Full Faith and Credit shall be given in each State to the public Acts, Records, and judicial Proceedings of every other State. And the Congress may by general Laws prescribe the Manner in which such Acts, Records and Proceedings shall be proved, and the Effect thereof.

SECTION 2. TREATMENT OF CITIZENS

Clause 1: Privileges and Immunities. The Citizens of each State shall be entitled to all Privileges and Immunities of Citizens in the several States.

Clause 2: Extradition. A Person charged in any State with Treason, Felony, or other Crime, who shall flee from Justice, and be found in another State, shall on Demand of the executive Authority of the State from which he fled, be delivered up, to be removed to the State having Jurisdiction of the Crime.

Clause 3: Fugitive Slaves. No person held to Service or Labour in one State, under the Laws thereof, escaping into another, shall, in Consequence of any Law or Regulation therein, be discharged from such Service or Labour, but shall be delivered up on Claim of the Party to whom such Service or Labour may be due.[11]

---

[11]Repealed by the Thirteenth Amendment.

must be tried first in the lower court and can then be appealed to the Supreme Court. In these cases the Supreme Court has appellate jurisdiction. Congress, however, may make exceptions. Today, the Supreme Court rarely acts as a trial court of first instance.

Clause 3: In all cases, except impeachments, any person accused of a federal crime is granted the right to a trial by jury. This trial is to be held in a federal court in that state in which the crime was committed.

SECTION 3. TREASON

Clause 1: Treason is defined here as making war against the United States or giving aid to the enemies of the United States.

Clause 2: This authorizes Congress to establish the punishment for treason. Congress has provided that the punishment ranges from a minimum of five years in prison and/or a $10,000 fine to a maximum of death. The phrase "no Attainder of Treason shall work Corruption of Blood" prohibits punishment of the traitor's heirs.

ARTICLE IV. RELATIONS AMONG THE STATES

SECTION 1. FULL FAITH AND CREDIT

All states are required to respect the laws, court decisions, and records of other states. There are exceptions, however. For example, a state does not have to recognize another state's grant of divorce if the person obtaining the divorce did not establish legal residence in the state in which it was given.

SECTION 2. TREATMENT OF CITIZENS

Clause 1: This clause makes it clear that a resident of one state may not be discriminated against unreasonably by another state.

Clause 2: Any person accused of a crime who flees to another state must be returned to the state in which the crime occurred.

Clause 3: This clause, requiring the return of any persons who had escaped from slavery, was nullified by the Thirteenth Amendment, which abolished slavery in 1865.

Section 3. Admission of States

Clause 1: This clause gives Congress the power to admit new states into the union. No new state may be created by taking territory from an existing state without the consent of the existing state's legislature.

Clause 2: This clause gives Congress the authority to make all laws and administer U.S. territories, public land, and all other property of the United States.

Section 4. Republican Form of Government

This section guarantees to each state a republican form of government. It also makes it clear that the federal government must defend the states against any attack by foreigners and, at the request of the state's legislature or governor, must protect the state during times of internal disorder.

Article V. Methods of Amendment

Constitutional amendments may be proposed by either of two methods: by a two-thirds vote of each house of Congress or by a majority vote at a convention called by Congress at the request of two-thirds of the states. Constitutional amendments may be ratified by either of two methods: by the legislatures of three-fourths of the states or by the voters in three-fourths of the states. This article exempted two clauses dealing with slavery (Article I, Section 9, Clauses 1 and 4) from the amendment process until 1808. Further, the amendment process cannot be used to deny any state equal representation in the Senate.

Article VI. National Supremacy

Clause 1: This clause pledged that the new government created by the ratification of the Constitution would assume all the financial obligations of the Confederation government.

Clause 2: This is called the Supremacy Clause. It declares that federal law takes precedence over all forms of state law. No state or local government may make or enforce any law that conflicts with any provision of the Constitution, act of Congress, treaty, or order, rule, or regulation issued by the president or other officials of the executive branch.

Clause 3: Every federal and state official must take an oath of office promising to support the

Section 3. Admission of States

Clause 1: The Process. New States may be admitted by the Congress into this Union; but no new State shall be formed or erected within the Jurisdiction of any other State; nor any State be formed by the Junction of two or more States, or Parts of States, without the Consent of the Legislatures of the States concerned as well as of the Congress.

Clause 2: Public Land. The Congress shall have Power to dispose of and make all needful Rules and Regulations respecting the Territory or other Property belonging to the United States; and nothing in this Constitution shall be so construed as to Prejudice any Claims of the United States, or of any particular State.

Section 4. Republican Form of Government

The United States shall guarantee to every State in this Union a Republican Form of Government, and shall protect each of them against Invasion; and on Application of the Legislature, or of the Executive (when the Legislature cannot be convened) against domestic Violence.

Article V. Methods of Amendment

The Congress, whenever two thirds of both Houses shall deem it necessary, shall propose Amendments to this Constitution, or on the Application of the Legislatures of two thirds of the several States, shall call a Convention for proposing Amendments, which, in either Case, shall be valid to all Intents and Purposes, as Part of this Constitution, when ratified by the Legislatures of three fourths of the several States, or by Conventions in three fourths thereof, as the one or the other Mode of Ratification may be proposed by the Congress; Provided that no Amendment which may be made prior to the Year One thousand eight hundred and eight shall in any Manner affect the first and fourth Clauses in the Ninth Section of the First Article; and that no State, without its Consent, shall be deprived of its equal Suffrage in the Senate.

Article VI. National Supremacy

Clause 1: Existing Obligations. All Debts contracted and Engagements entered into, before the Adoption of this Constitution shall be as valid against the United States under this Constitution, as under the Confederation.

Clause 2: Supreme Law of the Land. This Constitution, and the Laws of the United States which shall be made in Pursuance thereof; and all Treaties made, or which shall be made, under the Authority of the United States, shall be the supreme Law of the Land; and the Judges in every State shall be bound thereby, any Thing in the Constitution or Laws of any State to the Contrary notwithstanding.

Clause 3: Oath of Office. The Senators and Representatives before mentioned, and the Members of the several State Legislatures, and all executive and judicial Officers, both of the United States and of the several States, shall be bound by Oath or Affirmation, to support this Constitution; but no religious Test shall ever be required as a Qualification to any Office or public Trust under the United States.

Article VII. Ratification

The Ratification of the Conventions of nine States shall, be sufficient for the Establishment of this Constitution between the States so ratifying the Same.

Done in Convention by the Unanimous Consent of the States present the Seventeenth Day of September in the Year of our Lord one thousand seven hundred and Eighty seven and of the Independence of the United States of America the Twelfth. In witness whereof we have hereunto subscribed our Names.

Go. WASHINGTON
Presid't and deputy from Virginia

Attest
WILLIAM JACKSON
Secretary

CONNECTICUT
Wm. Saml. Johnson
Roger Sherman

DELAWARE
Geo. Read
Gunning Bedfordjun
John Dickinson
Richard Basset
Jaco. Broom

NEW YORK
Alexander Hamilton

NEW JERSEY
Wh. Livingston
David Brearley.
Wm. Paterson.
Jona. Dayton

MASSACHUSETTS
Nathaniel Gorham
Rufus King

Constitution. Religion may not be used as a qualification to serve in any federal office.

ARTICLE VII. RATIFICATION
Nine states were required to ratify the Constitution. Delaware was the first state to ratify and New Hampshire the ninth. However, its success was not assured until Virginia and New York (tenth and eleventh) also voted for ratification.

PENNSYLVANIA
B. Franklin
Thomas Mifflin
Robt. Morris
Geo. Clymer
Thos. FitzSimons
Jared Ingersoll
James Wilson.
Gouv. Morris

NEW HAMPSHIRE
John Langdon
Nicholas Gilman

MARYLAND
James McHenry
Dan of St. Thos. Jenifer
Danl. Carroll.

VIRGINIA
John Blair
James Madison Jr.

NORTH CAROLINA
Wm. Blount
Richd. Dobbs Spaight.
Hu. Williamson

SOUTH CAROLINA
J. Rutledge
Charles Cotesworth
    Pinckney
Charles Pinckney
Pierce Butler

GEORGIA
William Few
Abr. Baldwin

Amendments to the Constitution of the United States

Amendment I.
RELIGION, SPEECH, ASSEMBLY, AND POLITICS
Congress shall make no law respecting an establishment of religion, or prohibiting the free exercise thereof; or abridging the freedom of speech, or of the press; or the right of the people peaceably to assembly, and to petition the Government for a redress of grievances.

Amendment II.
MILITIA AND THE RIGHT TO BEAR ARMS
A well regulated Militia, being necessary to the security of a free State, the right of the people to keep and bear Arms, shall not be infringed.

Amendment III.
THE QUARTERING OF SOLDIERS
No Soldier shall, in time of peace be quartered in any house, without the consent of the Owner, nor in time of war, but in a manner to be prescribed by law.

Amendment IV.
SEARCHES AND SEIZURES
The right of the people to be secure in their persons, houses, papers, and effects, against unreasonable searches and seizures, shall not be violated, and no Warrants shall issue, but upon probable cause, supported by Oath or affirmation, and particularly describing the place to be searched, and the persons or things to be seized.

Amendment V.
GRAND JURIES, SELF-INCRIMINATION, DOUBLE JEOPARDY, DUE PROCESS, AND EMINENT DOMAIN
No person shall be held to answer for a capital, or otherwise infamous crime, unless on a presentment or indictment of a

---

THE BILL OF RIGHTS (AMENDMENTS I–X)

On September 25, 1789, Congress transmitted to the state legislatures twelve proposed amendments, two of which, having to do with Congressional representation and Congressional pay, were not adopted. The remaining ten amendments became the Bill of Rights.

AMENDMENT I.
RELIGION, SPEECH, ASSEMBLY, AND POLITICS

Congress may not create an official church or enact laws that limit the freedoms of religion, speech, the press, assembly, and petition. It is important to note that these guarantees, like the others in the Bill of Rights, are not absolute—each may be exercised only with regard to the rights of other persons.

AMENDMENT II.
MILITIA AND THE RIGHT TO BEAR ARMS
To protect itself, each state has the right to maintain a "well regulated" volunteer armed force. Individual states and the federal government regulate the possession and use of firearms by individuals.

AMENDMENT III.
THE QUARTERING OF SOLDIERS
Before the Revolutionary War, it had been common British practice to quarter, or house, soldiers in colonists' homes. Military troops do not have the power to take over private houses during peacetime.

AMENDMENT IV.
SEARCHES AND SEIZURES
Here the word *warrant* means "justification" and refers to a document issued by a magistrate or judge indicating the name, address, and possible offense committed. Anyone, such as a police officer, asking for a warrant must be able to convince the

magistrate or judge that an offense probably has been committed.

AMENDMENT V.
GRAND JURIES, SELF–INCRIMINATION, DOUBLE JEOPARDY, DUE PROCESS, AND EMINENT DOMAIN

There are two types of juries. A grand jury considers physical evidence and the testimony of witnesses, and decides whether there is sufficient reason to bring a case to trial. A petit jury hears the case at trial and decides it. "For the same offence to be twice put in jeopardy of life or limb" means to be tried twice for the same crime. A person may not be tried for the same crime twice or forced to give evidence against herself or himself. No person's right to life, liberty, or property may be taken away except by lawful means, called the due process of law. Private property taken for public use must be paid for by the government.

AMENDMENT VI.
CRIMINAL COURT PROCEDURES

Any person accused of a crime has the right to a fair and public jury trial in the state in which the crime took place. The charges against that person must be so indicated. Any person accused of a crime has the right to a lawyer to defend him or her and to question those who testify against him or her, as well as the right to call witnesses to speak on his or her behalf.

AMENDMENT VII.
TRIAL BY JURY IN CIVIL CASES

Either party in a dispute may request a jury trial in any case involving more than $20. If both parties agree to a trial by a judge without a jury, the right to a jury trial may be put aside.

AMENDMENT VIII.
BAIL, CRUEL AND UNUSUAL PUNISHMENT

Bail is money that a person accused of a crime may be required to deposit with the court as a guarantee that she or he will appear in court when requested. The amount of bail required or the fine imposed as punishment for a crime must be reasonable for the crime involved. Any punishment judged to be too harsh or too severe for a crime is prohibited.

Grand Jury, except in cases arising in the land or naval forces, or in the Militia, when in actual service in time of War or public danger; nor shall any person be subject for the same offence to be twice put in jeopardy of life or limb; nor shall be compelled in any criminal case to be a witness against himself, nor be deprived of life, liberty, or property, without due process of law; nor shall private property be taken for public use, without just compensation.

Amendment VI.
CRIMINAL COURT PROCEDURES

In all criminal prosecutions, the accused shall enjoy the right to a speedy and public trial, by an impartial jury of the State and district wherein the crime shall have been committed, which district shall have been previously ascertained by law, and to be informed of the nature and cause of the accusation; to be confronted with the witnesses against him; to have compulsory process for obtaining witnesses in his favor, and to have the assistance of counsel for his defence.

Amendment VII.
TRIAL BY JURY IN CIVIL CASES

In Suits at common law, where the value in controversy shall exceed twenty dollars, the right of trial by jury shall be preserved, and no fact tried by jury, shall be otherwise re-examined in any Court of the United States, than according to the rules of the common law.

Amendment VIII.
BAIL, CRUEL AND UNUSUAL PUNISHMENT

Excessive bail shall not be required, nor excessive fines imposed, nor cruel and unusual punishments inflicted.

Amendment IX.
THE RIGHTS RETAINED BY THE PEOPLE

The enumeration in the Constitution, of certain rights, shall not be construed to deny or disparage others retained by the people.

Amendment X.
RESERVED POWERS OF THE STATES

The powers not delegated to the United States by the Constitution, nor prohibited by it to the States, are reserved to the States respectively, or to the people.

Amendment XI.
SUITS AGAINST STATES
(RATIFIED ON FEBRUARY 7, 1795)

The Judicial power of the United States shall not be construed to extend to any suit in law or equity, commenced or prosecuted against one of the United States by Citizens of another State, or by Citizens or Subjects of any Foreign State.

Amendment XII.
ELECTION OF THE PRESIDENT
(RATIFIED ON JUNE 15, 1804)

The Electors shall meet in their respective states, and vote by ballot for President and Vice President, one of whom, at least, shall not be an inhabitant of the same State with themselves; they shall name in their ballots the person voted for as President, and in distinct ballots the person voted for as Vice President, and they shall make distinct lists of all persons voted for as President, and of all persons voted for as Vice President, and of the number of votes for each, which lists they shall sign and certify, and transmit sealed to the seat of the government of the United States, directed to the President of the Senate;—The President of the Senate shall, in the presence of the Senate and House of Representatives; open all the certificates and the votes shall then be counted;—The person having the greatest number of votes for President, shall be the President, if such number be a majority of the whole number of Electors appointed; and if no person have such majority, then from the persons having the highest numbers not exceeding three on the list of those voted for as President, the House of Representatives shall choose immediately, by ballot, the President. But in choosing the President, the votes shall be taken by States, the representation from each State having one vote; a quorum for this purpose shall consist of a member or members from two-thirds of the States, and a majority of all States shall be necessary to a choice. ~~And if the House of Representatives shall not choose a President whenever the right of choice shall devolve upon them, before the fourth day of March next following, then the Vice President shall act as President, as in the case of the death or other constitutional disability of the President.~~[12]—The person having the greatest number of votes as Vice President, shall be the Vice President, if such number be a majority of the whole number of Electors appointed, and if no person have a majority, then from the

[12]Changed by the Twentieth Amendment.

AMENDMENT IX.
THE RIGHTS RETAINED BY THE PEOPLE

This amendment makes it clear that many civil rights not expressly mentioned in the Constitution are still held by the people.

AMENDMENT X.
RESERVED POWERS OF THE STATES

Those powers not delegated by the Constitution to the federal government or expressly denied to the states belong to the states and to the people. This clause in essence allows the states to pass laws under its "police powers."

AMENDMENT XI.
SUITS AGAINST STATES

This amendment has been interpreted to mean that a state cannot be sued in federal court by one of its citizens, by a citizen of another state, or by a foreign country. Any suit against a state must be tried in the courts of that state.

AMENDMENT XII.
ELECTION OF THE PRESIDENT

The original procedure set out for the election of president and vice president in Article II, Section 1, resulted in a tie between Thomas Jefferson and Aaron Burr in the election of 1800. This amendment changed the procedure, providing for separate ballots for president and vice president.

two highest numbers on the list, the Senate shall choose the Vice President; a quorum for the purpose shall consist of two-thirds of the whole number of Senators, and a majority of the whole number shall be necessary to a choice. But no person constitutionally ineligible to the office of President shall be eligible to that of Vice President of the United States.

Amendment XIII.
PROHIBITION OF SLAVERY

Some enslaved persons had been freed during the Civil War. This amendment freed all enslaved persons in the United States and abolished slavery as well as involuntary servitude, or labor done against one's will. Section 2 of this amendment gave Congress the power to enact legislation needed to enforce the prohibition of slavery.

Amendment XIV.
CITIZENSHIP, DUE PROCESS, AND EQUAL PROTECTION OF THE LAWS

Under Section 1 of this amendment, states cannot make or enforce laws that take away rights given to all citizens by the federal government. States cannot act unfairly or arbitrarily toward, or discriminate against, any person.

Section 2 of this amendment struck down the three-fifths clause from the Constitution.

Section 3 of this amendment forbade former state or federal government officials who had acted in support of the Confederacy during the Civil War to hold office again. This section also limited the president's power to pardon those persons. Congress restored the rights of former confederate officials in 1898.

Amendment XIII.
PROHIBITION OF SLAVERY
(RATIFIED ON DECEMBER 6, 1865)

SECTION 1.
Neither slavery nor involuntary servitude, except as a punishment for crime whereof the party shall have been duly convicted, shall exist within the United States, or any place subject to their jurisdiction.

SECTION 2.
Congress shall have power to enforce this article by appropriate legislation.

Amendment XIV.
CITIZENSHIP, DUE PROCESS, AND EQUAL PROTECTION OF THE LAWS
(RATIFIED ON JULY 9, 1868)

SECTION 1.
All persons born or naturalized in the United States, and subject to the jurisdiction thereof, are citizens of the United States and of the State wherein they reside. No State shall make or enforce any law which shall abridge the privileges or immunities of citizens of the United States; nor shall any State deprive any person of life, liberty, or property, without due process of law; nor deny to any person within its jurisdiction the equal protection of the laws.

SECTION 2.
Representatives shall be apportioned among the several States according to their respective numbers, counting the whole number of persons in each State, excluding Indians not taxed. But when the right to vote at any election for the choice of electors for President and Vice President of the United States, Representatives in Congress, the Executive and Judicial officers of a State, or the members of the Legislature thereof, is denied to any of the male inhabitants

of such State, being ~~twenty-one~~[13] years of age, and citizens of the United States, or in any way abridged, except for participation in rebellion, or other crime, the basis of representation therein shall be reduced in the proportion which the number of such male citizens shall bear to the whole number of male citizens twenty-one years of age in such State.

Section 3.

No person shall be a Senator or Representative in Congress, or elector of President and Vice President, or hold any office, civil or military, under the United States, or under any State, who having previously taken an oath, as a member of Congress, or as an officer of the United States, or as a member of any State legislature, or as an executive or judicial officer of any State, to support the Constitution of the United States, shall have engaged in insurrection or rebellion against the same, or given aid or comfort to the enemies thereof. But Congress may by a vote of two-thirds of each House, remove such disability.

Section 4.

The validity of the public debt of the United States, authorized by law, including debts incurred for payment of pensions and bounties for services in suppressing insurrection or rebellion, shall not be questioned. But neither the United States nor any State shall assume or pay any debt or obligation incurred in aid of insurrection or rebellion against the United States, or any claim for the loss or emancipation of any slave, but all such debts, obligations and claims shall be held illegal and void.

Section 5.

The Congress shall have power to enforce, by appropriate legislation, the provisions of this article.

Amendment XV.
THE RIGHT TO VOTE
(RATIFIED ON FEBRUARY 3, 1870)

Section 1.

The right of citizens of the United States to vote shall not be denied or abridged by the United States or by any State on account of race, color, or previous condition of servitude.

[13]Changed by the Twenty-sixth Amendment.

AMENDMENT XV.
THE RIGHT TO VOTE

Section 1 of this amendment made it clear that no citizen can be refused the right to vote simply because of race or color or because that person was once enslaved. Section 2 of this amendment gave Congress the power to enact legislation to enforce the amendment.

AMENDMENT XVI.
INCOME TAXES

This amendment allows Congress to tax income without sharing the revenue so obtained with the states according to their population. This amendment modified Article I, Section 9, Clause 4.

AMENDMENT XVII.
THE POPULAR ELECTION OF SENATORS

This amendment modified portions of Article I, Section 3, that related to election of senators. Senators are now elected directly by the voters in each state rather than by the state legislators. When a vacancy occurs, either the state may fill the vacancy by a special election, or the governor of the state may appoint someone to fill the seat until the next election.

AMENDMENT XVIII.
PROHIBITION

This amendment made it illegal to manufacture, sell, and transport alcoholic beverages in the United States. It was nullified by the Twenty-first Amendment, which was ratified in 1933. This amendment was the first amendment to include a time limit (seven years in this case) for ratification.

SECTION 2.

The Congress shall have the power to enforce this article by appropriate legislation.

Amendment XVI.
INCOME TAXES
(RATIFIED ON FEBRUARY 3, 1913)

The Congress shall have power to lay and collect taxes on incomes, from whatever source derived, without apportionment among the several States and without regard to any census or enumeration.

Amendment XVII.
THE POPULAR ELECTION OF SENATORS
(RATIFIED ON APRIL 8, 1913)

The Senate of the United States shall be composed of two Senators from each State, elected by the people thereof, for six years; and each Senator shall have one vote. The electors in each State shall have the qualifications requisite for electors of the most numerous branch of the State legislatures.

When vacancies happen in the representation of any State in the Senate, the executive authority of such State shall issue writs of election to fill such vacancies: *Provided*, That the legislature of any State may empower the executive thereof to make temporary appointments until the people fill the vacancies by election as the legislature may direct.

This amendment shall not be so construed as to affect the election or term of any Senator chosen before it becomes valid as part of the Constitution.

Amendment XVIII.
PROHIBITION
(RATIFIED ON JANUARY 16, 1919)

SECTION 1.

After one year from the ratification of this article the manufacture, sale, or transportation of intoxicating liquors within, the importation thereof into, or the exportation thereof from the United States and all territory subject to the jurisdiction thereof for beverage purposes is hereby prohibited.

SECTION 2.

The Congress and the several States shall have concurrent power to enforce this article by appropriate legislation.

Section 3.

This article shall be inoperative unless it shall have been ratified as an amendment to the Constitution by the legislatures of the several States, as provided in the Constitution, within seven years from the date of the submission hereof to the States by the Congress.[14]

Amendment XIX.
WOMEN'S RIGHT TO VOTE
(RATIFIED ON AUGUST 18, 1920)

The right of citizens of the United States to vote shall not be denied or abridged by the United States or by any State on account of sex.

Congress shall have the power to enforce this article by appropriate legislation.

Amendment XX.
THE LAME DUCK AMENDMENT
(RATIFIED ON JANUARY 23, 1933)

SECTION 1.

The terms of the President and Vice President shall end at noon on the 20th day of January, and the terms of Senators and Representatives at noon on the 3d day of January, of the years in which such terms would have ended if this article had not been ratified; and the terms of their successors shall then begin.

SECTION 2.

The Congress shall assemble at least once in every year, and such meeting shall begin at noon on the 3d day of January, unless they shall by law appoint a different day.

SECTION 3.

If, at the time fixed for the beginning of the term of the President, the President elect shall have died, the Vice President elect shall become President. If a President shall not have been chosen before the time fixed for the beginning of his term, or if the President elect shall have failed to qualify, then the Vice President elect shall act as President until a President shall have qualified; and the Congress may by law provide for the case wherein neither a

[14]The Eighteenth Amendment was repealed by the Twenty-first Amendment.

AMENDMENT XIX.
WOMEN'S RIGHT TO VOTE

This amendment made it against the law to deny anyone the right to vote on account of sex. Women were given the right to vote by this amendment, and Congress was given the power to enforce this right.

AMENDMENT XX.
THE LAME DUCK AMENDMENT

Section 1 of this amendment modified Article 1, Section 4, Clause 2, and other provisions relating to the president in the Twelfth Amendment. The taking of the Oath of Office was moved from March 4 to January 20.

Section 2 changed the beginning of the Congressional term to January 3. The reason the Twentieth Amendment is called the Lame Duck Amendment is because it shortens the time between the time when a member of Congress is defeated for reelection and the time when he or she leaves office. During this period of time the member of Congress is said to be a "lame duck."

Section 3 of the amendment deals with problem areas left ambiguous by Article II and the Twelfth Amendment. If the president dies before January 20 or fails to qualify for office, the presidency is to be filled in the order given in this section.

Congress has never created legislation subsequent to Section 4 of this amendment.

President elect nor a Vice President elect shall have qualified, declaring who shall act as President, or the manner in which one who is to act shall be selected, and such person shall act accordingly until a President or Vice President shall have qualified.

Section 4.

The Congress may by law provide for the case of the death of any of the persons from whom the House of Representatives may choose a President whenever the rights of choice shall have devolved upon them, and for the case of the death of any of the persons from whom the Senate may choose a Vice President whenever the right of choice shall have devolved upon them.

Section 5.

Sections 1 and 2 shall take effect on the 15th day of October following the ratification of this article.

Section 6.

This article shall be inoperative unless it shall have been ratified as an amendment to the Constitution by the legislatures of three-fourths of the several States within seven years from the date of its submission.

Amendment XXI.
The Repeal of Prohibition

The amendment repealed the Eighteenth Amendment but did not make alcoholic beverages legal everywhere. Rather, they remained illegal in any state that so designated them. Many such "dry" states existed for a number of years after 1933. Today, there are still "dry" counties within the United States in which alcoholic beverages are illegal.

Amendment XXI.
The Repeal of Prohibition
(Ratified on December 5, 1933)

Section 1.

The eighteenth article of amendment to the Constitution of the United States is hereby repealed.

Section 2.

The transportation or importation into any State, Territory, or possession of the United States for delivery or use therein of intoxicating liquors, in violation of the laws thereof, is hereby prohibited.

Section 3.

This article shall be inoperative unless it shall have been ratified as an amendment to the Constitution by conventions in the several States, as provided in the Constitution, within seven years from the date of the submission hereof to the States by the Congress.

Amendment XXII.
LIMITATION OF PRESIDENTIAL TERMS
(RATIFIED ON FEBRUARY 27, 1951)

SECTION 1.
No person shall be elected to the office of the President more than twice, and no person who has held the office of President, or acted as President, for more than two years of a term to which some other person was elected President shall be elected to the office of President more than once. But this Article shall not apply to any person holding the office of President when this Article was proposed by the Congress, and shall not prevent any person who may be holding the office of President, or acting as President, during the term within which this Article becomes operative from holding the office of President or acting as President during the remainder of such term.

SECTION 2.
This article shall be inoperative unless it shall have been ratified as an amendment to the Constitution by the legislatures of three-fourths of the several States within seven years from the date of its submission to the States by the Congress.

Amendment XXIII.
PRESIDENTIAL ELECTORS FOR THE DISTRICT OF COLUMBIA
(RATIFIED ON MARCH 29, 1961)

SECTION 1.
The District constituting the seat of Government of the United States shall appoint in such manner as the Congress may direct:

A number of electors of President and Vice President equal to the whole number of Senators and Representatives in Congress to which the District would be entitled if it were a State, but in no event more than the least populous State; they shall be in addition to those appointed by the States, but they shall be considered, for the purposes of the election of President and Vice President, to be electors appointed by a State; and they shall meet in the District and perform such duties as provided by the twelfth article of amendment.

SECTION 2.
The Congress shall have power to enforce this article by appropriate legislation.

AMENDMENT XXII.
LIMITATION OF PRESIDENTIAL TERMS
No president may serve more than two elected terms. If, however, a president has succeeded to the office after the halfway point of a term in which another president was originally elected, then that president may serve for more than eight years, but may not serve for more than ten years.

AMENDMENT XXIII.
PRESIDENTIAL ELECTORS FOR THE DISTRICT OF COLUMBIA
Citizens living in the District of Columbia have the right to vote in elections for president and vice president. The District of Columbia has three presidential electors; before this amendment it had none.

AMENDMENT XXIV.
THE ANTI-POLL TAX AMENDMENT

A poll tax is tax on voting. This amendment states that no government shall require a person to pay a poll tax in order to vote in any federal election.

Amendment XXIV.
THE ANTI-POLL TAX AMENDMENT
(RATIFIED ON JANUARY 23, 1964)

SECTION 1.

The right of citizens of the United States to vote in any primary or other election for President or Vice President, for electors for President or Vice President, or for Senator or Representative in Congress, shall not be denied or abridged by the United States, or any State by reason of failure to pay any poll tax or other tax.

SECTION 2.

The Congress shall have power to enforce this article by appropriate legislation.

AMENDMENT XXV.
A PRESIDENTIAL DISABILITY AND VICE PRESIDENTIAL VACANCIES

Whenever a president dies or resigns from office, the vice president becomes president.

Whenever the office of the vice presidency becomes vacant, the president may appoint someone to fill this office, provided Congress consents.

Whenever the president believes he or she is unable to carry out the duties of the office, he or she shall so indicate to Congress in writing. The vice president then acts as president until the president declares that he or she is again able to properly carry out the duties of the office.

Whenever the vice president and a majority of the members of the Cabinet believe that the president cannot carry out his or her duties, they shall so indicate in writing to Congress. The vice president shall then act as president. When the president is able to resume the presidential duties, he or she shall so indicate to the Congress. If, though, the vice president and a majority of the cabinet do not agree, Congress must decide by a two-thirds vote within three weeks who shall act as president.

Amendment XXV.
A PRESIDENTIAL DISABILITY AND VICE PRESIDENTIAL VACANCIES
(RATIFIED ON FEBRUARY 10, 1967)

SECTION 1.

In case of the removal of the President from office or of his death or resignation, the Vice President shall become President.

SECTION 2.

Whenever there is a vacancy in the office of the Vice President, the President shall nominate a Vice President who shall take office upon confirmation by a majority vote of both Houses of Congress.

SECTION 3.

Whenever the President transmits to the President pro tempore of the Senate and the Speaker of the House of Representatives his written declaration that he is unable to discharge the powers and duties of his office, and until he transmits to them a written declaration to the contrary, such powers and duties shall be discharged by the Vice President as Acting President.

SECTION 4.

Whenever the Vice President and a majority of either the principal officers of the executive departments or of such other body as Congress may by law provide, transmit to the President pro tempore of the Senate and the Speaker of the

House of Representatives their written declaration that the President is unable to discharge the powers and duties of his office, the Vice President shall immediately assume the powers and duties of the office as Acting President.

Thereafter, when the President transmits to the President pro tempore of the Senate and the Speaker of the House of Representatives his written declaration that no inability exists, he shall resume the powers and duties of his office unless the Vice President and a majority of either the principal officers of the executive department or of such other body as Congress may by law provide, transmit within four days to the President pro tempore of the Senate and the Speaker of the House of Representatives their written declaration that the President is unable to discharge the powers and duties of his office. Thereupon Congress shall decide the issue, assembling within forty-eight hours for that purpose if not in session. If the Congress, within twenty-one days after receipt of the latter written declaration, or, if Congress is not in session, within twenty-one days after Congress is required to assemble, determines by two-thirds vote of both Houses that the President is unable to discharge the powers and duties of his office, the Vice President shall continue to discharge the same as Acting President; otherwise, the President shall resume the powers and duties of his office.

Amendment XXVI.
THE EIGHTEEN YEAR OLD VOTE (RATIFIED ON JULY 1, 1971)

SECTION 1.
The right of citizens of the United States, who are eighteen years of age or older, to vote shall not be denied or abridged by the United States or by any State on account of age.

SECTION 2.
The Congress shall have power to enforce this article by appropriate legislation.

Amendment XXVII.
CONGRESSIONAL COMPENSATION CHANGES (RATIFIED ON MAY 7, 1992)
No law, varying the compensation for the services of the Senators and Representatives, shall take effect, until an election of Representatives shall have intervened.

AMENDMENT XXVI.
THE EIGHTEEN YEAR OLD VOTE
This amendment states that no person over eighteen years of age can be denied the right to vote in federal or state elections by virtue of age.

AMENDMENT XXVII.
CONGRESSIONAL COMPENSATION CHANGES
An intervening congressional election is required before any changes in congressional compensation may be instituted. That is, a congressional election must occur between the time in which Congress votes for a change in congressional pay and the time in which that change goes into effect.

Constitution Review

Vocabulary

Develop a definition for each of the following terms as they are used in the Constitution. See if you can determine a synonym for each.

1. requisite (Article I, Section 2, Clause 1)
2. pro tempore (Section 3, Clause 5)
3. amendment (Section 7, Clause 1)
4. enumeration (Article I, Section 9, Clause 4)
5. imposts (Article I, Section 8, Clause 1)
6. disability (Article II, Section 1, Clause 6)
7. impeachment (Article II, Section 2, Clause 4)
8. excises (Article I, Section 8, Clause 1)
9. delegated (Amendment X)
10. ratify (Article V)
11. treason (Article III, Section 3, Clause 1)
12. militia (Article II, Section 2, Clause 1)

Reviewing the Document

1. Which branch of government initiates legislation? Explain how a bill becomes law.
2. Explain why the census is important in deciding how many representatives a state may send to the House of Representatives.
3. What happens if a representative or a senator dies in office or resigns before his or her term is completed?
4. Explain the process of impeachment and the trial of a federal official.
5. Why do you think the framers of the Constitution thought it was important for each house of Congress to keep a journal, or record, of its actions?
6. Why do you think the writers of the Constitution decided that all representatives and senators should be paid out of the federal rather than state treasury?
7. Which house of Congress has the right to initiate legislation for raising revenue?
8. What happens if the president vetoes a bill? Explain how a veto can be overridden.
9. What is a pocket veto? Do you think this is a sensible provision?
10. List at least ten of the powers of Congress, and explain why you think they are important and appropriate powers for Congress to have.
11. Why do you think "provide for the general welfare of the United States" has become such an important provision of the Constitution?
12. What might be one reason the framers rejected titles of nobility for Americans?
13. How does Section 10 of Article I ensure that the federal government will have powers greater than those of the states? Do you think this was a good idea? Why, or why not?
14. List the qualifications a candidate for president must have.
15. What happens if a president dies in office, resigns, or becomes unable to discharge his duties? What happens if the office of vice president becomes vacant?
16. Why do you think the Senate was given the power to approve treaties and presidential appointments?
17. Name the circumstances under which the Supreme Court has original jurisdiction.
18. How does the Constitution define treason?
19. How are amendments to the Constitution initiated?
20. How are amendments ratified?

Critical Historical Thinking

Writing Answer each of the following questions by writing one or more complete paragraphs:

1. The framers of the Constitution wanted to create a strong government, but they also wanted to limit that government's power. Do you believe they were able to do this? Explain your answer.
2. How did the Constitution provide for the national supremacy of the Constitution and the federal government? Cite and explain at least

two provisions in the document that uphold
the idea of national supremacy.

3. Examine the 27 amendments to the Constitu-
tion. Then classify them according to the head-
ings below.
   Rights the British Abused
   Extending Rights
   Correcting Problems

4. You are a planter with a large landholding in
Georgia. Write a paragraph in which you state
and explain the reasons you would have, or
not have, voted for the ratification of the
Constitution.

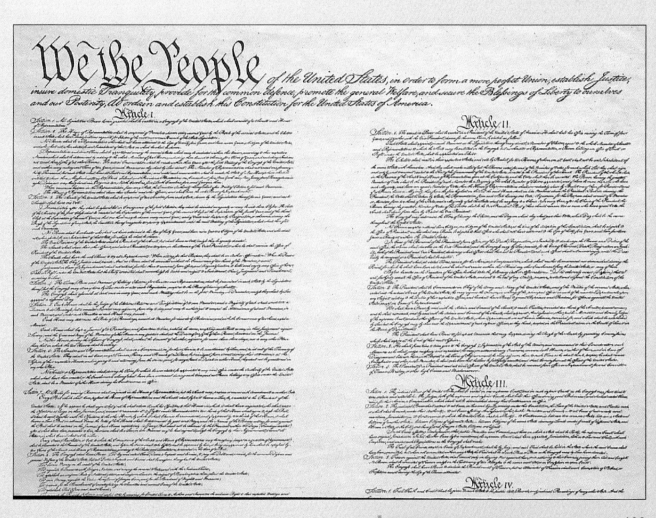

Testing the New Nation

With the new Constitution in place, Americans once again turned to George Washington for leadership. Although Washington himself was popular, his two terms as president were marked by sectional disputes and conflicting views on the proper functions of government. Factions soon developed into political parties that were deeply divided over monetary policy and foreign affairs. Actions taken by the second president, John Adams, magnified these differences between factions.

When Thomas Jefferson became president, he nearly doubled the size of the nation, but he could not solve the continuing problems with Great Britain. Then his successor, James Madison, led the nation through the inconclusive and generally unpopular War of 1812.

During this early national period, the people of the United States developed a culture that was American rather than colonial.

Front

Back

▲ *About 1,500 of these "halfdisme" pieces (worth 5 cents) were the first coins minted by the U. S. government. Our word* dime *comes from these pieces. What are the symbols shown?*

Organizing the New Government

Cheering crowds gathered along the wagon road from Virginia to New York to honor President-elect George Washington as he made his way to the temporary capital of the new nation. On April 30, 1789, thousands gathered in front of Federal Hall in New York City to watch in jubilation as Washington took the oath of office. As the first elected president, Washington was keenly aware of the effects his actions would have. By wearing a plain brown suit, Washington emphasized that he was now a civilian. By wearing his army dress sword, he emphasized the president's role as commander in chief. Washington knew that the new nation would face hardships. If necessary, he was willing to use military strength to preserve the new government.

Uneasy about the magnitude of his new office, Washington wrote to a friend that he had "feelings not unlike those of a culprit who is going to the place of his execution. My station is new. . . . I walk on untrodden ground, there is scarcely any part of my conduct which may not hereafter be drawn into precedent."

What tasks did Washington set for the new government?

Why were economic problems so difficult for the new nation?

How did the national bank issue help create political factions and prompt differing interpretations of the Constitution?

Launching the New Government

Among the first tasks President Washington undertook was the appointment of secretaries to head the three executive departments created in 1789 by the new Congress. Washington was careful in filling these posts. He wanted to be surrounded by friends he could trust, but he also wanted people who represented different regions of the country. The government must be, Washington felt, a government of *all* Americans. In fact, he split the appointments among strong men from three powerful states. From New York, he appointed Alexander Hamilton as secretary of the treasury. He also appointed another New Yorker, John Jay, to serve as secretary of state until Virginian Thomas Jefferson, who was in Europe, could assume the office. For secretary of war, he selected General Henry Knox of Massachusetts, a trusted friend from the Revolutionary War. His vice president, John Adams, also came from Massachusetts.

The Constitution made no direct provision for these secretaries to serve as a cabinet of presidential advisers, but Washington often sought their opinions. His need to hear the advice of others before he acted came from his prudence, which Jefferson described as "the strongest feature in his character." Washington seldom took action unless his advisers brought issues to his attention. Nonetheless, his reputation as a great leader and his choice of brilliant men as his secretaries strengthened the executive branch of government. He also established the tradition of forming a presidential cabinet.

▼ *How did Washington balance the appointed members of the first government under the Constitution? What feature of this engraving is most intriguing to historians?*

◄ *This illustration depicts Washington's inauguration on April 30, 1789. Do you think Washington was correct in saying that any part of his conduct or behavior could be interpreted as a precedent? (Collection of The New-York Historical Society.)*

▼ The Republican Court by Daniel Huntington provides a wonderful view of Martha Washington standing above the crowd as she welcomes people to a reception. The fine clothing of the Washingtons and their guests helps to create a royal image. Does this scene seem republican to you?

The Judiciary Act

Washington appointed judges in accordance with the terms of the **Judiciary Act of 1789**. That act provided for a chief justice and five associate justices to serve on the Supreme Court. They would have the power to reverse or uphold the actions of state courts in decisions regarding federal laws, treaties, or the Constitution. An attorney general was to represent the federal government in Supreme Court cases and provide legal advice to the executive branch of government.

The Judiciary Act also set up district courts in each of the 13 states and three circuit courts to hear disputes between citizens of different states, as well as appeals from the district courts. Two members of the Supreme Court were assigned to each of the circuits—northern, eastern, and southern. Washington appointed Virginian Edmund Randolph as the first attorney general and John Jay as the first chief justice of the Supreme Court. The courts had so little business during the first few years of the Republic that Jay soon resigned to take up the "more important" post of governor of New York.

Hamilton's Financial Plan

Alexander Hamilton, the new secretary of the treasury, was a brilliant lawyer who had served as Washington's aide-de-camp (military aide) during the Revolution. Even though he fought against the British, Hamilton admired English government and culture and hoped to forge close economic and diplomatic relationships with the British.

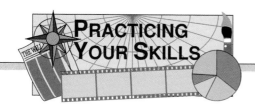
Examining Fine Art

Before the time of the camera, painters used their art to portray important historical events in the life of the new nation. Republican art emphasized the ideals of the new republic and helped to promote nationalism. It also inspired patriotism in the population. These paintings also are a mirror of the young nation for us. By analyzing and interpreting them, we can better understand what were the basic attitudes and ideals of Americans then.

Here are some important questions to ask when evaluating the historical role of fine art:

Collection of The New-York Historical Society.

- **What mood, or atmosphere, has the artist created?** How does the artist use color, light, style, and content to get the effect he or she wanted? How does the artist use composition (the placement of people and objects) to draw your eye to what is important?

- **What is the story being told in the painting?** Look carefully at the details. How does the artist use symbols to add to the story?

- **What is the purpose of the artist in creating the painting?** Does the picture reflect a political or social bias? What was the artist's intention? Was the artist paid for the work, and if so, by whom?

- **When was the painting done?** How long after the event being portrayed was the work created? Was the artist actually present at the time? Or was the artist painting from stories and second-hand reports?

The painting on page 202 (left) is entitled *First in War, First in Peace, First in the Hearts of his Countrymen, Inauguration of George Washington.*

1. How would you describe the scene depicted? Is it relaxed or formal, happy or sad, indoors or outdoors?
2. Locate George Washington. What does he appear to be doing? What do his position and the lighting in the painting say about George Washington?
3. Look at the other people in the painting. Notice how some of them are grouped in the painting. (a) How does the artist use them to direct your eye throughout the painting? Notice also the people in the windows of the building in the upper left. (b) What do they appear to be doing? (c) Based on today's inaugural ceremonies, which people are missing from this picture?
4. What basic attitudes about the role of the president in the new republic does this picture portray?
5. In what ways does this painting support the opening words of the Preamble to the Constitution, "We, the People . . ."?

Debt was one of the most pressing problems facing Hamilton. The national debt was roughly $54 million. The debt included certificates offered as pay to revolutionary soldiers, bond certificates issued during the war, debts incurred by the Confederation government, and loans from foreign nations. Similar debts, totaling about $25 million, were owed by state governments. Most people thought that the domestic part of the national debt (all debt other than that owed to foreign creditors) would be lowered by discounting the face value of bonds and certificates. Speculators had bought certificates at less than face value when bad times had forced owners to sell. If the debts were paid off at face value, these speculators stood to make huge profits.

With so much unpaid debt, the nation had virtually no credit. Hamilton believed his first duty was to reestablish the nation's credit. He insisted that all debts be paid at face value. Otherwise, he claimed, the government would never be able to borrow in times of need. Hamilton also proposed that the federal government should pay state debts to the extent of approximately $21,500,000. Hamilton wanted to create a permanent national debt, with new bonds being issued as old ones were paid. He argued that this would help creditors gain faith in the national government. The wealthy class would have an ongoing interest in seeing the government survive. Paying these debts and reestablishing credit was, he wrote, "the price of liberty."

The national government's decision to assume state debts and to pay off debts at face value to the present owners of bonds and certificates was hotly contested. Those states that had not paid their debts favored the plan, but states such as Virginia, Maryland, North Carolina, and Georgia, which had already paid most of their debts, objected to it. Because most of the debtor states were in the North, Hamilton cleverly tied his plan to another issue. Knowing that southerners wanted the national capital to be located in the South, Hamilton told Jefferson and Madison that he would back their proposed location of the capital on the Potomac River between Maryland and Virginia. Philadelphia would be the temporary capital until Washington, D.C., was built. In return, he asked for southern support for the national government's assumption of state debts. Congress accepted this compromise, and the two parts of Hamilton's plan for a sound credit policy were in place.

The National Bank

To put his plans into action, Hamilton proposed that Congress establish a national bank with a charter that would last 20 years. At that time, there were only a few banks in the country, primarily in the large eastern cities, such as Boston, Philadelphia, and New York. The national bank would be privately owned, but would operate as a part of the federal government. It would act as a collecting and disbursing agency for the Department of the Treasury, and, when necessary, it would lend money to the government. It would also issue currency to be used in payment of federal taxes. This ensured that the currency would maintain its value while it was in circulation.

Jefferson and Madison were outraged at the idea of a national bank. They claimed such an institution was absolutely unconstitutional. As **strict constructionists**, they believed that the government had only those powers specifically mentioned in the Constitution. Hamilton, as a **loose constructionist**, argued that the Constitution's elastic clause permitted Congress to take those actions deemed necessary and proper to carry out specified powers. According to Hamilton and other loose constructionists, the Constitution allowed the establishment of a bank as a necessary step for coining money, collecting taxes, and borrowing money. Hamilton won his case, established the credit of the nation, and strengthened the influence of the national government. The debate over strict versus loose construction of the Constitution continues to this day.

The Whiskey Rebellion

With the national assumption of state debts and with the national bank in place, Hamilton worked to find the revenue needed to pay off the debts and run the government. Some income was guaranteed because the national government had the right to regulate commerce with American Indian tribes. It

▲ The Whiskey Rebellion was the first serious test of the federal government's ability to enforce federal law. These farmers from western Pennsylvania were angry over the government's excise taxes. What is happening to the federal tax collector?

also received money from the sale of the public lands in the Northwest Territory, which had been obtained for a very low cost through treaty agreements with American Indians. But most of the federal revenues came from tariffs on imported goods, and the amount was not sufficient for Hamilton's program.

Hamilton then tried to raise money for the new government through an **excise tax** on liquor. An excise tax is a type of indirect tax on the manufacture, sale, or consumption of a product within a country. The liquor tax was passed by Congress in 1791. Large distillers in the North and farmers in the West were outraged; they felt this excise tax would cut into their profits. It was too expensive for most farmers to carry bulk grains to market. Those same grains, distilled into more easily transported liquor, could make them a profit. Recalling the successful tactics used in preventing British agents from collecting the hated Stamp Act revenues, farmers from western Pennsylvania terrorized tax collectors and refused to pay the tax. President Washington

was alarmed at this defiance of federal law, and in 1794 he led nearly 13,000 militiamen to put down the **Whiskey Rebellion**. The farmers had never really mounted a full-scale, armed rebellion, but they had been intimidating the tax collectors. The militia arrested only 20 men, but this action established the government's power to enforce its laws and to raise needed revenue.

SECTION 1 REVIEW

1. **Explain** how George Washington strengthened the executive branch of government.
2. **Describe** the structure of the judicial branch of government.
3. **State** what Hamilton offered to the South in return for support of federal assumption of state debt.
4. **Compare** Jefferson's and Hamilton's arguments on the founding of a national bank.
5. **State** what Hamilton considered to be "the price of liberty."

Factions and Parties

Thomas Jefferson once stated that he and Alexander Hamilton were pitted against each other every day in the cabinet. It seemed to him that Hamilton was too eager to forge a strong national government tied primarily to the fortunes of the rich and wellborn. Ordinary people, Hamilton had once claimed, "seldom judge or determine what is right." However, if the government would provide aid to such economic interests as trade, manufacturing, and finance, those interests would back strong government. Then, declared Hamilton, the "great Federal Republic" would be "noble and Magnificent."

Jefferson felt that a strong central government was unnecessary, something to be dreaded. He wanted to put his trust in the state government and the same ordinary, common people whom Hamilton seemed to scorn. Jefferson knew that human beings had selfish impulses, but he felt that farmers who supported themselves by their own toil somehow had more integrity than merchants and manufacturers who used others to do their work. "Those who labor in the earth," he wrote, "are the chosen people of God, if ever he had a chosen people." The difference of opinion between these two men reflected an ideological battle that would soon lead to the formation of political parties.

In what ways did Hamilton and Jefferson differ in their attitudes toward the functions of government?

How did factions turn into political parties?

How did President Washington deal with difficult foreign problems?

Emergence of Political Parties

By late 1792, those who had worked together so hard to adopt the new Constitution now found themselves sharply divided over practical issues of government. Jefferson and Madison were alarmed at the power the national government was acquiring through the activities of Alexander Hamilton. Madison had not liked Hamilton's plan to manage the debt, but he had gone along with those plans to maintain harmony in the new government. When Hamilton called for a charter for a national bank, Madison balked. He joined Jefferson in becoming a spokesperson for the opposition. Madison, now serving in the House of Representatives, attacked Hamilton's plan by writing critical newspaper articles. Hamilton struck back at Jefferson and Madison by voicing his position in the pages of another newspaper.

By the time of the 1792 national election, those who sided with Jefferson called themselves Democratic-Republicans, while supporters of Hamilton took the name Federalists. The Federalists were most popular in the large commercial centers of the Northeast. The Democratic-Republicans were more numerous in the rural South and West. Neither group was a political party in the modern sense, since they had no national committees or conventions. In fact, the Democratic-Republicans did not consider running a presidential candidate because it was a foregone conclusion that Washington, whom they still admired, would run and win. The Democratic-Republicans did put up Governor George Clinton of New York as a candidate for vice president, but the **incumbent**, or current office holder, John Adams was reelected. It became clear from the events surrounding the election of 1792, however, that when Washington retired, elections would become much more hotly contested.

Proclamation of Neutrality

When the French Revolution began in 1789, many Americans felt that it was inspired by their own republican revolution of 1776. In the beginning, Americans generally supported the anti-aristocratic, democratic aims of the revolution. As the rebellion progressed, however, the French king, queen, and, later, 20,000 other French people were executed. French revolutionary leaders set out to destroy the power of European kings while monarchs all over Europe set out to destroy the French republicans. By 1793, France was at war with the major European nations, including Great Britain and Spain. These conflicts brought more problems to Americans and divided public opinion. Under the Alliance of 1778 with France, the United States had agreed to defend the French West Indies "forever against all other powers." What if now the British or the Spanish attacked the French West Indies and the United States was expected to give aid? The British were firmly settled in Canada. The Spanish controlled lands to the west and south of the United States. Actions that provoked attacks from either of those nations could destroy the young American republic.

In spite of these fears, some Democratic-Republicans, by now often referred to as Jeffersonian Republicans, or just Republicans, continued to support the French. Some even adopted the dress and manners of the revolutionaries, calling each other "citizen" and "citizeness." They felt that only the destruction of European monarchs would bring political power to the ordinary citizens of all nations. Then, too, the Republicans still felt a strong obligation to the French for their vital support of the American Revolution.

The Federalists did not deny the French contribution to the American Revolution, but they were horrified at the excesses of the French Revolution. They tended to side with the more stable governments of Europe, generally the monarchies. Hamilton wanted to revoke the alliance with France and side with Great Britain, but Washington preferred not to back either side. In the **Proclamation of Neutrality** issued on April 22, 1793, Washington declared that the United States would "pursue a course friendly and impartial to both belligerent powers."

Avoiding Foreign Entanglements

The French reacted to Washington's statement by sending Edmond Genêt (zhuh-NAY) as minister of the French Republic to America. Citizen Genêt's goal was to influence Americans in support of the

▲ *Many believed that the American Revolution was a model for the French Revolution. There were, however, great differences in how the wars played out. What does this drawing tell you about the differences in the way the enemy was treated?*

French against the British. Originally welcomed by many pro-French Americans, Genêt later antagonized almost everyone when he recruited Americans in a French attempt to take over Florida and Spanish Louisiana. Then it became known that Genêt was also commissioning privately owned American ships to prey on British shipping. This action could easily have provoked a war between Great Britain and the United States. At this point, even Genêt's early supporters asked for his recall to France. Meanwhile, a more radical group had taken over the French government and recalled Genêt. Fearing he would be beheaded if he returned, Genêt sought political asylum in the United States, married the daughter of New York's governor, and vanished from public life.

Britain caused difficulties for the United States by violating the principle of freedom of the seas. To blockade France, the British navy seized American merchant ships carrying weapons and food to French ports. The British stopped over 600 United States ships in 1793 and 1794, sending some 250 of them to England as prizes of war. They also forced thousands of American sailors into the British navy, an act known as **impressment**. American shipping was being "kicked, cuffed, and plundered all over the Ocean," declared one American. Americans were also angry that the British had still not evacuated their forts in the Northwest Territory. They believed the British were inciting American Indians in that area to fight against Americans settling on Indian lands.

Jay's Treaty   Washington decided to act to protect American neutrality. He sent Chief Justice John Jay to Britain, hoping Jay could convince the British to leave the United States out of European squabbles. Jay's Treaty, signed on November 19, 1794, did win a pledge to remove the British from the Northwest Territory, and it opened some British colonies in Asia to American trade. The treaty also included a promise that Britain would compensate owners of American ships seized in the West Indies. The treaty angered many Americans because it did not contain a pledge that the British would stop seizing American ships and impressing American sailors. Still, President Washington was pleased with Jay's work, believing he had achieved all that was possible. He used all his influence to get the treaty ratified by the Senate. Jay's Treaty did accomplish two goals. It kept the United States out of war with Britain, and it set the stage for the Pinckney Treaty signed the next year with Spain.

Pinckney Treaty   In 1795, Washington sent a different delegation to secure a treaty with Spain. Thomas Pinckney, earlier a minister to England and then special envoy to Spain, obtained a treaty that was far more popular than Jay's Treaty. The **Treaty of San Lorenzo**, or Pinckney's Treaty, was generous to the Americans because the Spanish feared that Jay had forged a second, secret treaty with the British. The treaty with Spain allowed Americans to ship their goods down the Mississippi River through Spanish territory and deposit them in New Orleans to await shipment. The treaty also made the 31st parallel the southern boundary between the United States and Spanish Florida. Spain had never recognized American ownership of Florida. Both nations agreed to try to keep the Indians in their territories from attacking each other's citizens.

▲ *In cities throughout the nation, John Jay was burned in effigy over the 1794 treaty with Britain. Was the colonists' reaction justified?*

Washington's Farewell Address   By the time Washington was ready to retire in 1796, he felt the nation was gaining in prosperity and could remain at peace. In his Farewell Address, printed in newspapers on September 19, 1796, Washington spoke as "a parting friend." He advised Americans to "steer clear of permanent Alliances with any portion of the foreign world," and warned of the "continual mischiefs" of party politics. Washington was keenly aware that the new nation needed time to develop. He believed America should not waste its energies on European conflicts. To develop a strong nation, all people would need to work together. Factions or political parties would only distract from that main task.

SECTION 2 REVIEW

1. **Describe** philosophical differences that made Hamilton and Jefferson political adversaries.
2. **Explain** how the Federalists and Democratic-Republicans viewed the French.
3. **Define** impressment.
4. **Explain** why George Washington was fearful of political parties and factions.
5. **Evaluate** the advice that Washington gave the nation in his Farewell Address.

SECTION 3

Changes in the Presidency

Washington's retirement, wrote one congressman, was "a signal, like dropping a hat, for the party racers to start." In spite of the president's warnings against factions, political parties increased their efforts to win support and power. The Federalists chose John Adams as their candidate for president, and the Republicans backed Thomas Jefferson. At this time the Constitution specified that electors could cast two votes each for president. There were no votes actually cast for vice president, as the man who received the second highest number of votes was elected vice president. In 1796, Adams was elected president and Jefferson vice president. Adams had long been concerned that such a division of leadership could occur. It would be, he declared, a "dangerous crisis in public affairs if the president and vice president should be in opposite boxes." As it turned out, Adams respected Jefferson, and Jefferson conceded that Adams would make a good president. Other events, however, worked against long-term cooperation between the Federalists and the Republicans.

Did Adams and Jefferson work well together? How did they express their political differences? What role did John Marshall play in strengthening the national government?

The XYZ Affair

The first major problem that faced President Adams was the angry reaction of France to Jay's Treaty. Feeling that the treaty was basically a British-American alliance against France, the French had recalled their minister and for a time refused to receive the American minister. The French seized American ships trading with Great Britain, and treated as spies or traitors any captured Americans who served on British ships. Provoked by these acts of aggression, Adams sent a special bipartisan commission, including Charles Pinckney, the recently rejected minister, John Marshall, a Federalist and later chief justice of the Supreme Court, and Elbridge Gerry, a Massachusetts Republican, to France to try to work out a settlement.

On October 8, 1797, four days after the commission arrived, the French foreign minister Charles-Maurice de Talleyrand told the Americans that discussions with the French government would not begin for a time. A few days later, three French secret agents called on the Americans to tell them that negotiations would take place only if the Americans paid a $250,000 bribe. Pinckney is supposed to have cried out to the agents, "No, no, not a sixpence!" In describing this event, Adams did not name the French agents; instead, he called them simply X, Y, and Z. The **XYZ Affair**, as it then became known, caused a sensation. When the special commission returned home, Marshall offered his

◀ *Federalist John Adams became the nation's second president and Republican Thomas Jefferson the second vice president. Did the fact that these men were in opposite camps result in a division of leadership in the government?*

The Marshall Court and the Doctrine of Judicial Review

John Marshall was one of the towering figures in American judicial history. Appointed chief justice of the United States Supreme Court in 1801 by President John Adams, he served on the Court for 34 years, retiring during Andrew Jackson's presidency. Marshall, a staunch Federalist, led the Court during an era when the executive and legislative branches were dominated first by Republicans and later by Jacksonian Democrats. Marshall used his intelligence, charm, and keen political sense to make a reputation as a great chief justice.

In a series of landmark decisions written by the chief justice, the Court greatly strengthened its authority. Its decision in *Marbury v. Madison* (1803), which asserted the principle of judicial review, also helped to establish the Court as an independent and equal partner with the president and Congress.

Marbury v. Madison involved a complaint by William Marbury, one of the "midnight appointees" whom John Adams had appointed during the final hours of his presidency. In the

period between the November election of 1800 and the day when the Republicans actually assumed power, the Federalist majority in Congress created several circuit courts and increased the number of federal courts to 16. Adams appointed Federalists to the new judgeships just before he left office. He also appointed justices of the peace for the District of Columbia. Because Adams signed the papers for these appointments on his last day in office, not all of the commissions were delivered before Jefferson took his oath of office.

Angry that Adams would try to pack the courts with members of the Federalist party, Jefferson

ordered James Madison, the new secretary of state, not to deliver the remaining commissions, including one appointing Marbury a justice of the peace in the District of Columbia.

Marbury petitioned the Supreme Court for a *writ of mandamus*—an order issued by a court to force a government official to do something, in this case, to force Madison to deliver the commission.

At that time, the independence of the federal judiciary was under attack by the Republicans in Congress. They viewed the entire federal court system with deep suspicion, considering it the last stronghold of a Federalist system that favored a power

(continued)

ful central government. The Republicans in Congress succeeded in repealing the Federalist legislation that had created the new circuit courts. In 1803 they turned their attention to the Supreme Court. They attempted to remove Supreme Court Justice Samuel Chase, an abrasive Federalist, for reasons that were purely political. That attempt nearly succeeded. It was in this hostile environment that Marshall acted to protect the Supreme Court's independence, skillfully doing so in a way that did not invite Republican retaliation.

Marshall faced a most difficult decision. The Supreme Court could order Secretary of State Madison to release the commission to Marbury, but it had no constitutional power to enforce its order. Jefferson likely would have chosen to ignore it. If the Court decided against Marbury, the Republicans would have demonstrated that the legislature and executive were free from judicial control.

The decision that Marshall wrote in *Marbury v. Madison* appeared to hand the Republicans a victory. After criticizing James Madison for not handing over the appointment papers, the Supreme Court refused Mar-

bury's request that it compel the secretary of state to do so. The Court said that Congress had exceeded its constitutional authority when it gave the Court the power to issue writs of mandamus that did not involve original case jurisdiction. Marshall wrote, "All those who have framed written constitutions contemplate them as forming the fundamental . . . law of the nation, and consequently the theory of every such government must be, that an act of the legislature, repugnant to the Constitution is void."

Rid of one more Federalist appointee, Republicans breathed a sigh of relief. They failed to recognize that the Court had won a significant victory in asserting its right to declare acts of Congress unconstitutional.

The victory went largely unnoticed because the Supreme Court used the right of judicial review sparingly at first. By 1864, it had declared only two acts of Congress unconstitutional. Moreover, Marshall did not claim the Supreme Court alone had such authority.

The significance of *Marbury v. Madison* was realized after the Civil War, when the Supreme Court assumed its modern stance as the sole and final arbiter on constitutional issues. Marshall's decision in 1803 was

the Court's most important precedent.

1. Do you think Thomas Jefferson would have refused a Supreme Court order to deliver the commission? Why, or why not?
2. If the right of judicial review were limited to state laws, would it be an effective check to the legislative or executive branch?

This political cartoon about the XYZ Affair shows staunch Americans resisting threats and demands for money from the "wicked," revolutionary French. How is this different from modern editorial cartoons?

much-quoted statement: "Millions for defense, but not a cent for tribute."

Public opinion turned sharply against France. The majority of Americans would probably have supported a war against France. Agreeing with Washington that the nation needed time to grow stronger, Adams would not risk it. Still, knowing that the nation was unprepared if war should come, Adams did ask Congress for money to increase the size of both the army and the navy. Republicans and French citizens living in the United States sharply criticized President Adams. Although upset by the XYZ Affair, Republicans still valued a friendship with France and hoped to avoid war by opposing the military buildup.

The Alien and Sedition Acts

President Adams was seriously worried that if France declared war on the United States, some Republicans and French citizens living in the United States might side with France. In June and July of 1798, the Federalists pushed through Congress a series of laws called the **Alien and Sedition Acts**, designed to stop the activities of those friendly to

France and to maintain the Federalists' power in government by crushing their opposition. These laws were to be in effect for two years. The Naturalization Act increased from 5 to 14 years the time a foreigner had to live in the United States before being eligible for citizenship. This act was meant to reduce the influence of recent Irish immigrants, who tended to support the Republicans. The Alien Enemies Act allowed the president to deport aliens in time of peace and to deport or arrest aliens during time of war. Since the sea battles with France never led to a declared war, this act had little effect. The Alien Friends Act allowed the president to deport all aliens at any time he thought they were "dangerous to the peace and safety of the United States." Adams never invoked this law, but many aliens left the country in fear that he might.

The last of the new laws was the Sedition Act, which made it a crime "to impede the operation of any law," to instigate a riot or insurrection (revolt), or to publish or state orally any "false, scandalous, and malicious" criticism of the president and Congress. It did not mention the office of vice president held by Jefferson. The Federalists used this law to suppress Republican newspapers, and ten publishers, convicted of sedition, received fines and jail sentences. Ironically, instead of weakening the Democratic-Republican party as intended, public outrage over the Alien and Sedition Acts actually strengthened it.

The Kentucky and Virginia Resolutions

Jefferson, Madison, and other Republicans were infuriated by the Alien and Sedition Acts and believed them to be unconstitutional. In 1798, Jefferson, writing secretly because of his position as vice president and because of the power of the Sedition Act, drafted a resolution for the legislature of the new state of Kentucky. This resolution argued that each of the states had the right to declare null and void any acts of Congress they believed were violations of the Constitution. Madison, also secretly, drafted a similar resolution for the Virginia legislature. The Republicans appealed to state legislatures in this way because they believed that the states and not the Supreme Court should have the right to review the legality of congressional decisions. Together, the **Kentucky and Virginia Resolutions** laid the basis for the later **doctrine of states' rights**. This doctrine held that since the states had contracted to create the federal government, the states could declare acts of Congress unconstitutional. But, in 1798, Kentucky and Virginia took no further steps. Eventually, the hullabaloo died down, and the Alien and Sedition Acts were allowed to expire or were repealed when Jefferson became president.

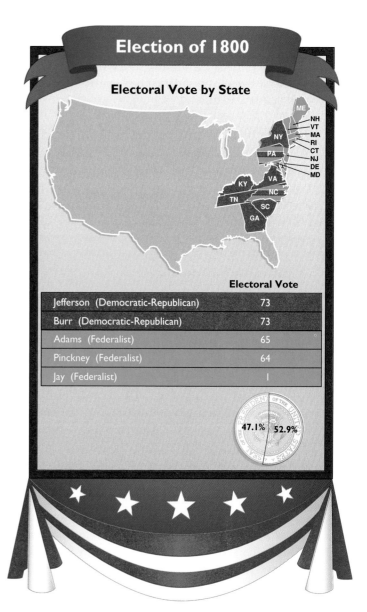

Election of 1800

Electoral Vote by State

	Electoral Vote
Jefferson (Democratic-Republican)	73
Burr (Democratic-Republican)	73
Adams (Federalist)	65
Pinckney (Federalist)	64
Jay (Federalist)	1

47.1%   52.9%

▲ *What generalizations can you make about the geographic location of each party's main support?*

The Jefferson Presidency

In 1800, the Federalists again nominated Adams for the presidency. The Republicans nominated Jefferson for president and **Aaron Burr** for vice president. When the ballots of the electors were counted, Adams had 65 votes, and Jefferson and Burr tied with 73 votes each. The tie meant that the Federalist-dominated House of Representatives had to choose which Republican they wanted for presi-

dent. On February 17, 1801, after seven days of deliberation and 36 ballots, Jefferson became president because Alexander Hamilton threw his influence against Burr. Hamilton distrusted Burr, describing him as "a dishonest schemer" and "an unprincipled man." Burr became vice president. In later years, Hamilton's and Burr's disagreements came to a head in a duel between the two men. Hamilton was mortally wounded, and Burr fled.

In his inaugural address, Jefferson tried to put dissension aside by stating, "We are all Federalists, we are all Republicans." But the differences between the parties were too great to be resolved by a few conciliatory words.

The Republicans now had a chance to carry out what they believed was the original aim of the Revolution of 1776: reducing the power of government over human affairs. They hoped to shape a national republic with limited executive power. President Jefferson set the tone by reducing to "republican simplicity" the formal and almost regal ceremonies the Federalists had built up around the presidency. He wanted no parades, no fancy parties or balls, no formal visits by the president to Congress, and no excessive **protocol** (a formal code of etiquette) at state functions.

Jefferson's idea of limited government amounted to a less active government. He believed the federal government should care only for external affairs and relations between the states. Other concerns were to be left to the states. To reduce government to what he deemed an appropriate level, Jefferson reduced the number of federal employees, cut the military budget in half, eliminated internal taxes, and lowered the federal debt by nearly half.

Jefferson believed that the will of the people was best expressed through the legislative branch of government. Although the Constitution provided for judicial review of state laws, it was not specific on the role of the Supreme Court in reviewing federal laws. In the case of *Marbury v. Madison* (1803), however, the brilliant legal decision of Chief Justice John Marshall increased both the prestige and the authority of the Supreme Court.

Jefferson, Madison, and Foreign Relationships

In April 1802, Robert R. Livingston, United States minister to France, offered the French government $2 million for West Florida and the port of New Orleans. To Livingston's surprise, the French minister Talleyrand countered this offer. How much, he asked, would the Americans pay for all of Louisiana? When Livingston mentioned the sum of $5 million, Talleyrand rejected it as too low. The next day, James Monroe arrived in Paris to help Livingston with the negotiations.

Although Jefferson had stated in his inaugural address that the United States had all the land it would use in a thousand generations, he had always dreamed that someday the lands west of the Mississippi River would become part of the "American empire of Liberty." It seemed that now, with the **Louisiana Purchase**, his dream could come true.

Why was the addition of the Louisiana Territory a matter of good luck?

Why did the U.S. Congress declare war against Great Britain?

What gains were made by the United States through the War of 1812?

The Louisiana Purchase

In 1800, a weakened and impoverished Spain had turned Louisiana over to France. Jefferson feared the French leader Napoleon Bonaparte might build an empire in the Americas and prevent western farmers from shipping their goods through the seaport of New Orleans.

A slave revolt in 1801 led by **Toussaint-L'Ouverture** (too-SAN loo-vair-TUER) stopped Napoleon's plans for an American empire and pushed the French out of Haiti on the Caribbean

---

1. List the major effects of the XYZ Affair.
2. State reasons why President Adams wanted Congress to enact the Alien and Sedition Acts.
3. Name the political philosophy that was the basis of the Kentucky and Virginia Resolutions.
4. Define protocol.
5. State reasons for the importance of *Marbury v. Madison*.

▲ *Toussaint-L'Ouverture led a successful revolution of the black population of St. Domingue (Haiti) against the French. How did that event help the Americans acquire Louisiana?*

Exploration of Louisiana

Despite his constitutional misgivings, Jefferson was wildly excited by the acquisition of this western territory. His only knowledge of these vast lands came from reports of ship captains who had sailed along the Pacific shore of Oregon and from the tales of fur trappers. Jefferson chose his friend, **Captain William Clark**, and his private secretary, **Meriwether Lewis**, to explore some of the lands west of the Mississippi River. The overall objectives were to discover an overland route to the Pacific, describe how the Americans could challenge British fur trade in the Northwest, and map as much of the territory as possible. His instructions to the explorers were precise. They were to

- find the source of the Missouri River
- cross the mountains and reach the Pacific Ocean
- provide records of the location of rivers, waterfalls, rapids, and islands
- provide descriptions of the weather, minerals, furs available, and Indians and their customs
- send to Washington specimens of the plants and animals they observed.

island of Hispaniola. The deaths of thousands of French troops from yellow fever prevented the French from retaking the island. Napoleon decided that without sugar producing islands he had no need of Louisiana as a source of food for the island's residents. He would rather put his energies and money into the war against Britain. The Americans met with French negotiators and settled on the incredibly low price of $15 million for lands nearly equal in size to the rest of the United States. The negotiators were stunned at such a bargain, but they eagerly accepted it.

Jefferson now faced a dilemma. As a strict constructionist he realized the Constitution said nothing about buying new territory. Had there been time, he would have asked for an amendment to the Constitution to provide for territorial acquisitions. The French wanted an answer in six months, and Livingston wrote from Paris that Napoleon already was having second thoughts about the sale. Jefferson, therefore, used the treaty-making power specified to the president in the Constitution to make the purchase. For a time, New England Federalists in the Senate thought of blocking passage of the treaty, but with such a great bargain, no one really wanted to play politics over the means by which Louisiana was acquired.

Setting out from St. Louis in the spring of 1804, the exploring party followed the Missouri River to its source. After wintering in present-day North Dakota with Mandan Indians, Lewis and Clark traveled westward over the Rocky Mountains. Guided part of the way by a Shoshone woman, **Sacajawea** (sak-uh-juh-WEE-uh), and her French fur-trader husband, the explorers finally sighted the Pacific Ocean on November 17, 1805. They then split up for the return to St. Louis, both of them drawing maps of the land they traveled through and gathering specimens of rocks, plants, and animals.

In 1805–1806, an expedition led by Zebulon Pike explored the territory near the headwaters of the Mississippi. The following year, Pike's group ventured into the land that became Colorado. Accounts of these expeditions made clear that not only had the United States doubled in size, but also it had doubled its population of Indians.

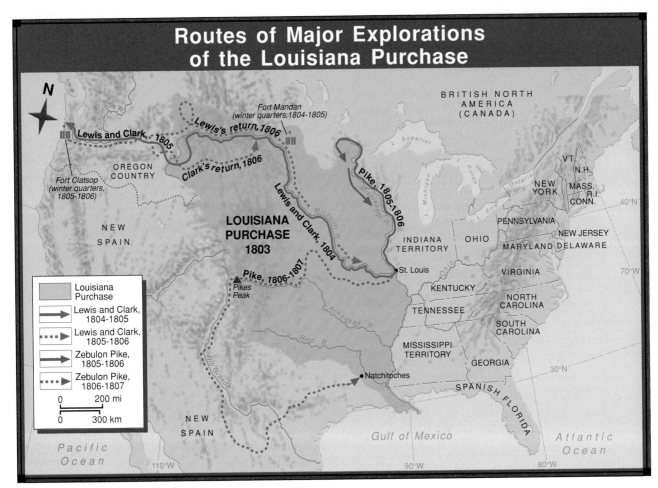

Routes of Major Explorations of the Louisiana Purchase

BRITISH NORTH AMERICA (CANADA)

Lewis and Clark, 1805

Lewis's return, 1806

Fort Mandan (winter quarters, 1804-1805)

Clark's return, 1806

Pike, 1805-1806

OREGON COUNTRY

Fort Clatsop (winter quarters, 1805-1806)

Lewis and Clark, 1804

NEW SPAIN

LOUISIANA PURCHASE 1803

Pike, 1806-1807

Pikes Peak

St. Louis

INDIANA TERRITORY

OHIO

KENTUCKY

TENNESSEE

MISSISSIPPI TERRITORY

GEORGIA

Natchitoches

NEW SPAIN

VT
N.H.
NEW YORK
MASS.
R.I.
CONN.

PENNSYLVANIA

NEW JERSEY

MARYLAND DELAWARE

VIRGINIA

NORTH CAROLINA

SOUTH CAROLINA

SPANISH FLORIDA

40°N

70°W

30°N

80°W

90°W

110°W

Louisiana Purchase

Lewis and Clark, 1804-1805

Lewis and Clark, 1805-1806

Zebulon Pike, 1805-1806

Zebulon Pike, 1806-1807

0   200 mi
0   300 km

Pacific Ocean

Gulf of Mexico

Atlantic Ocean

▲ *Information gathered by Lewis and Clark and Zebulon Pike stunned the American people. Many had no idea of how large the Louisiana Purchase really was. Why do you think Lewis and Clark took separate routes on their return from Fort Clatsop?*

▶

Sacajawea, a member of the Shoshone tribe, captured the imagination of the American public. Why would an Indian guide be useful to explorers such as Lewis and Clark?

The Hope for Indian Unity

▲ *Tenskwatawa was said to have knowledge of the future.*

◀ *The Dying Tecumseh by Ferdinand Pettrich was created in marble in 1856 out of the artist's imagination—no one saw Tecumseh's death. Despite brilliant efforts, Tecumseh could not protect his culture against the on-rushing white settlers.*

Throughout the early 1790s, conflict increased between settlers moving into the northwest regions of the country and the American Indians who claimed that land as their own. Devastating raids across western Pennsylvania, and in Ohio and Indiana, virtually cleared those regions of white settlers. After the American army suffered several defeats at the hands of the Shawnee, the Miami, and their allies, President Washington in 1792 had sent a strong force into Ohio. At the Battle of Fallen Timbers in 1794, General Anthony Wayne scored a decisive victory. Following this battle, Wayne forced the routed Indians to sign treaties giving the Americans rights to the southern two-thirds of Ohio. Similar treaties involving other western lands were signed in subsequent years.

Two Shawnee leaders set out to try to organize all the region's tribes into a single force that might be strong enough to defeat the Americans for good. Between 1809 and 1811, the Shawnee chief **Tecumseh** and his brother **Tenskwatawa** known as the Prophet, traveled and preached a message calling for united Indian resistance to a force that was destroying Indian civilization. Tecumseh reminded his listeners that "the White race is a wicked race," and their mere presence brings evil. "These lands are ours," he said. "No one has a right to remove us, because we were the first owners. The Great Spirit has appointed this place for us, on which to light our fires, and here we will remain."

Tecumseh was able to persuade over 1,000 Indian soldiers to gather at an old Indian town, Kithtippecanoe, renamed Prophetown, in Indian Territory. In 1811, while Tecumseh was in the South trying to recruit the Creeks into his confederacy, **General William Harrison** surrounded the Indian troops, killing some 150 of them and burning the village to the ground. Harrison was to use that modest victory in a campaign slogan for the presidency, "Tippecanoe and Tyler, Too!" Using this slogan, he won the presidential race in 1840. Tecumseh and his warriors fought on, finally casting their lot with the British in the War of 1812. During an American victory on the Thames River in Canada, Tecumseh was killed. His confederacy of Indian allies broke up, and by 1815 American settlers had once more taken over lands in the West that had once belonged to the Indians.

Despite his defeat, Tecumseh is remembered as a great leader who displayed courage, intelligence, and commitment to his people. He was described by Harrison as "one of those uncommon geniuses, which spring up occasionally to produce revolutions and overturn the order of things."

1. Why were Americans determined to move Indians out of the Northwest Territory?
2. Why would Tecumseh travel as far as the Creek towns in Georgia to recruit allies?

Continuing International Problems

During this period, Jefferson also had to deal with the pirates who preyed on commercial shipping off the Barbary Coast of North Africa. These pirates were sponsored by the rulers of the Barbary States of Morocco, Tunis, Algiers, and Tripoli. Most European nations paid a tribute each year to avoid having their ships raided, and the United States had previously followed that time-honored practice. In 1801, however, Tripoli demanded more tribute, and Jefferson decided that Americans should no longer pay these demands. He sent a small fleet to the Barbary Coast. One American ship, the *Philadelphia*, was captured, and it took a $60,000 ransom to free the crew. The Barbary pirates planned to use this vessel to attack other ships, but it was burned in a daring night raid by American lieutenant Stephen Decatur. Americans did launch a successful assault on Tripoli, but it was their naval blockade that finally forced the Barbary States to sign a peace treaty in 1805.

This small victory helped Jefferson begin his second term on a wave of good feelings. He did not have long to savor his success, however. The British

▼ *The snapping turtle, Ograbme (embargo spelled backward), is after a tobacco smuggler who is defying Jefferson's trade embargo. Do political cartoons usually reflect popular thinking?*

were at war with France and by 1807 were blockading French ports. American ships carrying goods to Europe were ordered to stop in Britain to pay a fee before moving on. The French threatened to seize any ship that stopped on British shores. With both of these great nations seizing American ships, and with Great Britain continuing to impress American seamen, any attempt to trade on the seas was risky.

When, in 1807, the British ship *Leopard* fired on the American warship *Chesapeake*, killing or wounding 21 Americans and impressing four others, many Americans called for a declaration of war against the British. Jefferson, realizing the country was in no position to fight a war, instead asked Congress for an embargo on all overseas trade. The 1807 **Embargo Act** ended commerce with foreign nations. No American ships could leave port, and foreign ships could not take cargo out of the United States. Jefferson believed that both France and Britain would moderate their policies if they could not obtain American merchandise.

The Embargo Act was disastrous to parts of the American economy. Exports fell from $108 million in 1807 to $22 million in 1808. Imports also declined dramatically. Virginian John Randolph claimed that it was like "trying to cure the corns by cutting off the toes." Wholesale smuggling began, and, in seaport towns, juries would not convict anyone accused of violating the Embargo Act. Jefferson finally admitted that his policy was a failure, and the act was repealed three days before he left office.

The War of 1812

In spite of Jefferson's unpopularity over the Embargo Act, his hand-picked successor, James Madison, easily won the election of 1808. Madison had no better luck in stopping the attacks against American shipping. More Republicans began to call for war. The western farmers wanted war because they still blamed Britain for their problems with some American Indian tribes, who continued to block their westward expansion.

The "**War Hawks**," as Congressmen **Henry Clay** of Kentucky, **John Calhoun** of South Carolina, and their supporters were called, cited the British-

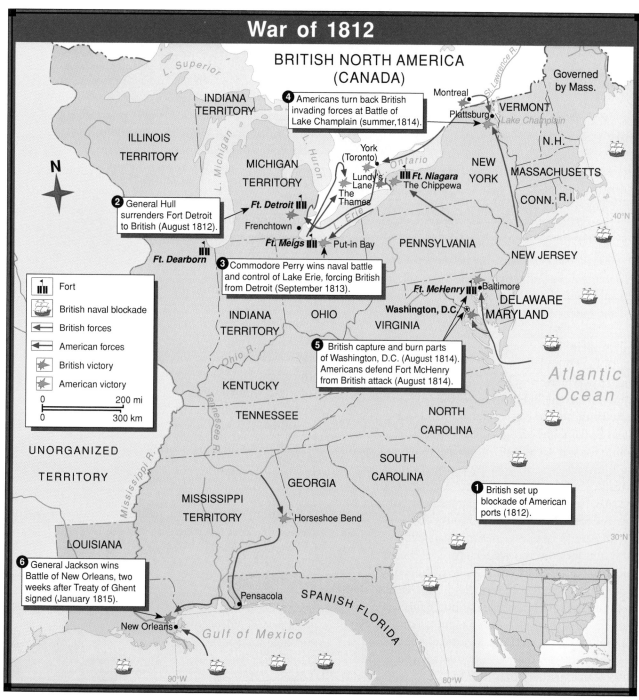

War of 1812

BRITISH NORTH AMERICA (CANADA)

4 Americans turn back British invading forces at Battle of Lake Champlain (summer, 1814).

INDIANA TERRITORY

ILLINOIS TERRITORY

Montreal

VERMONT

Plattsburg · Lake Champlain

Governed by Mass.

N.H.

York (Toronto)

MICHIGAN TERRITORY

Lundy's Lane

||| Ft. Niagara

The Chippewa

NEW YORK

MASSACHUSETTS

CONN. R.I.

2 General Hull surrenders Fort Detroit to British (August 1812).

Ft. Detroit **|||**

Frenchtown ·

The Thames

L. Erie

Put-in Bay

PENNSYLVANIA

NEW JERSEY

Ft. Dearborn **|||**

Ft. Meigs **|||**

3 Commodore Perry wins naval battle and control of Lake Erie, forcing British from Detroit (September 1813).

Ft. McHenry **|||** · Baltimore

DELAWARE

Washington, D.C. ⊛

MARYLAND

Legend

|||	Fort
🚢	British naval blockade
←	British forces
←	American forces
✦	British victory
✦	American victory

0 ——— 200 mi
0 ——— 300 km

INDIANA TERRITORY

OHIO

VIRGINIA

5 British capture and burn parts of Washington, D.C. (August 1814). Americans defend Fort McHenry from British attack (August 1814).

Atlantic Ocean

KENTUCKY

TENNESSEE

NORTH CAROLINA

UNORGANIZED TERRITORY

SOUTH CAROLINA

GEORGIA

1 British set up blockade of American ports (1812).

MISSISSIPPI TERRITORY

Horseshoe Bend ✦

LOUISIANA

6 General Jackson wins Battle of New Orleans, two weeks after Treaty of Ghent signed (January 1815).

Pensacola ·

SPANISH FLORIDA

New Orleans ·

Gulf of Mexico

▲ *Most of the fighting in the War of 1812 was inconclusive. Neither the British nor the Americans made lasting gains from the important battles of the war. Areas around the Gulf of Mexico, the Chesapeake Bay, the Great Lakes, and Lake Champlain, however, saw significant fighting. Why do you think British strategy included plans to achieve goals through naval victories?*

▲ *After Admiral Perry's flagship was destroyed during the Battle of Lake Erie, he was taken to the Niagara. Here he continued his fight and routed the enemy. Why do you think Perry's exploits made him such a hero?*

Indian alliances as cause for war. However, those New Englanders who had been economically hurt by the seizure of American ships were against war. They knew that in the long run the economic success of New England was closely tied to good relations with Great Britain. New Englanders suspected that those calling for war were really more interested in expanding United States territory by conquering Canada than they were in protecting American freedom of the seas. Eventually the War Hawks won out, and war was declared on June 18, 1812.

In August of that year, American armies focused their attention on the western forts of the British, but they had little success. General William Hull's army was attacked at Detroit, and Hull surrendered to the British without firing a shot. American armies that were supposed to capture Fort George, on the Niagara River, and Montreal failed because the militia troops that were to aid them refused to enter Canada where they would face well-trained British forces. Americans fared better on Lake Erie. There, **Captain Oliver Hazard Perry** led a small American fleet in a three-hour battle against British ships. To announce his victory, Perry sent a message that thrilled and gave courage to other American troops, "We have met the enemy, and they are ours!" Perry's victory in September 1813 secured control of Lake Erie for the United States and forced the British to leave Detroit.

The Treaty of Ghent

Most of the fighting in the War of 1812 was inconclusive. In 1814, Americans stopped a British land and water invasion from Canada near Lake Champlain, but they were not able to protect the national capital. In August, British ships carried 4,000 troops up Chesapeake Bay. The British burned several public buildings in Washington, including the president's house, which was later repaired and painted white to cover the smoke stains. Fleeing the city, first lady Dolley Madison had the foresight to take with her important government documents and a painting of George Washington. The British then moved on to attack Baltimore, Maryland, and to shell Fort McHenry, located on an island in the harbor. The Americans at Fort McHenry refused to surrender the fort, and the battle was an American victory. It was after witnessing this night-long shelling that Francis Scott Key was inspired to write the verses of a poem that was later set to music and became known as "The Star Spangled Banner."

By the end of 1814, both sides were weary of a war that seemed to be going nowhere. British and American representatives agreed to hold peace talks in Belgium. On Christmas Eve, 1814, the **Treaty of Ghent** ended the fighting, but it did not resolve the issues that had led to the war. It did not address the

▶

This portrait of Dolley Madison was painted by Rembrandt Peale. A great favorite of Washington society, Dolley was respected for her courage and loved for her sense of fun.

British violation of neutral rights on the high seas and the impressment of American seamen. The treaty simply provided for the return of all occupied territory, restoring the prewar boundaries between Canada and the United States. A joint commission was later to settle disputed land claims.

The Hartford Convention   Meanwhile, New England Federalists had met in October to discuss their opposition to what they termed "Mr. Madison's war." Convening in Hartford, Connecticut, the 26 delegates proposed a number of amendments to the Constitution including one which prohibited embargoes lasting more than 60 days and another which required a two-thirds vote of Congress to declare war. More significantly, the delegates also asserted the right of a state to "interpose its authority" against "unconstitutional" acts of the government. Because the war ended before the delegates to the Hartford Convention had taken action, nothing came of its deliberations. However, like the Kentucky and Virginia Resolutions, the proposed resolutions of the Hartford Convention struck a blow for states' rights. This convention established the potential for **secession**, or withdrawal, from the republic that would be remembered when sectional differences began to split the North and the South. But the Federalists involved in the Hartford

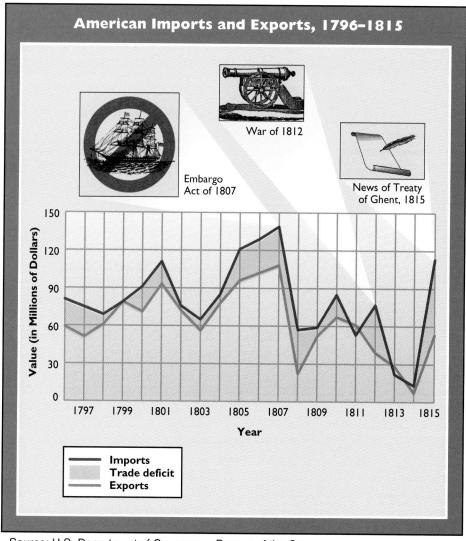

American Imports and Exports, 1796–1815

War of 1812

Embargo Act of 1807

News of Treaty of Ghent, 1815

Value (in Millions of Dollars)

150
120
90
60
30
0

1797 1799 1801 1803 1805 1807 1809 1811 1813 1815

Year

Imports
Trade deficit
Exports

◄ *If the War of 1812 was ended by the Treaty of Ghent in 1815, why did imports and exports already begin to increase by 1814?*

Source: U.S. Department of Commerce, Bureau of the Census.

▲ *Why was the Battle of New Orleans called the "battle that should never have been fought?" Does the painting give you enough information to predict the winner of the battle?*

Convention were not heard from after the war, and the Federalist Party soon lost much of its backing.

News of the Treaty of Ghent took a while to reach the armies in America, and meanwhile another battle gave heart to the Americans. The **Battle of New Orleans** of January 15, 1815, produced a great American victory. Led by **General Andrew Jackson**, the Americans killed or wounded more than 2,000 British troops and suffered only 71 soldiers killed, wounded, or missing. The news of the Treaty of Ghent arrived almost simultaneously in Washington, D.C., with the news of Jackson's victory. It was easy for people to assume that the battle for New Orleans had been a contributing factor. Although the battle did not affect the outcome of the war, it did give Americans something to celebrate. It also made General Andrew Jackson the "hero of New Orleans."

SECTION 4 REVIEW

1. **Explain** why buying the Louisiana Territory was a political problem for Jefferson.
2. **Identify** Sacajawea.
3. **List** the major causes of the War of 1812.
4. **State** reasons why the War of 1812 was inconclusive.
5. **Explain** the major outcome of the Hartford Convention.

SECTION 5

The American Way of Life, 1780–1815

Classical architecture, asserted Thomas Jefferson, should be used "to improve the taste of my countrymen, to increase their reputation, to reconcile them to the rest of the world, and procure them its praise." He believed that public buildings ought to be a visual reflection of the ideology of the new nation. An architect himself, Jefferson believed that just as the Constitution represented an attempt to build a social order based on rational principles, the architecture of the nation's capital should reflect the rational order shown in ancient Greek and Roman buildings. Jefferson was persuasive. Washington, D.C., did eventually become a grand capital that symbolized the vitality of the republic.

How did architecture and other arts represent a new social order?

In what ways did changes in government affect ideas about education?

How were people in the newly opened western lands affected by the new Americanism?

Architecture and Painting

Although Thomas Jefferson chose the sites for the nation's Capitol Building and the president's house, the major planning for the city of Washington, D.C., was the work of **Major Pierre-Charles L'Enfant** (lahn-FAHN). In 1801, he designed a city of sweeping boulevards that met in a series of circles. Public spaces were set aside for government buildings, parks, and magnificent monuments that would glorify the nation's heroes. Because of his fierce temper, L'Enfant was fired before his work was completed, but his aide, a free African American mathematician named Benjamin Banneker, completed the survey work. An Irish

The Federal Style of Architecture

After the Revolution, most Americans still felt strong cultural ties with Europe and looked for inspiration to the architectural styles popular in the great cities of Europe. Factors were present, of course, that worked against copying European styles. These included the need to deal with different climates and raw materials, and a feeling that the cities of this country should be as new and wonderful as the republic so recently fashioned. These opposing influences would come together and be expressed in a type of classical revival architecture known as the Federal style.

Thomas Jefferson was influential in popularizing the classic revival style. He looked back for inspiration to the buildings of a time when the seeds of democracy were being sown in ancient Greece and Rome. Jefferson believed that the buildings of the new republic should teach people about democracy, and that this classical style should dominate not only the capital city, but cities all over the nation.

The closely related Federal style, strongly influenced by Scottish architect Robert Adam, also relied on Greek and Roman designs. It was used extensively by architect Charles Bulfinch. In 1817, Bulfinch was summoned to Washington, D.C., to help rebuild the capital—burned during the War of 1812. Characteristics of the Federal style include the use of white building materials, slender columns, delicate fanlights (half-circle windows with bars in the shape of a fan) and an overall majesty that suggests light and volume rather than darkness and mass.

◀ Columns were important architectural features in classical designs.

▶ What classical revival features do you see on this door?

▲ What is symbolized by the architecture of the Supreme Court building?

▶ Doors and windows of Federal style buildings often had both fanlights above the door and sidelights. The center portion of this window is an elaborate arrangement called a six-over-six.

1. Find photographs of your own county and state government buildings. Do they reflect the classical style?

2. Note the fan-shaped windows above the doors of these buildings and the small columns at the entries. These are typical of the Federal style. Do these elements appear on buildings in your own community?

immigrant, James Hoban, won a $500 prize for his design of a president's house, and Dr. William Thornton's plan was chosen for the Capitol. These structures and the other public buildings of the nation's capital reflected Jefferson's belief that the city's appearance should be inspirational. This type of architecture, based on a revival of Greek and Roman styles of building and ornamentation, came to be known as the Federal style.

Painters also reflected the new nationalism. Among important artists of the period were **Gilbert Stuart**, John Trumbull, and Charles Willson Peale. Stuart painted portraits of the outstanding political, social, and economic leaders of his day. Among his most famous works are his several portraits of George Washington. The ruddy complexion that Stuart gave Washington in these paintings reflects Stuart's belief that other painters of the time made their subjects look "like putrid veal, a little brown with green flies."

John Trumbull fought in the Revolutionary War. When he later took up painting, he concentrated on what he called his "national work," the glorious depiction of important historical events. His enormous canvases, commemorating important events in American history, include *The Battle of Bunker Hill*, *The Surrender of the British at Saratoga*, *The Surrender of Lord Cornwallis at Yorktown*, and *The Declaration of Independence*. Like many Americans of his time, Trumbull held a deep belief that nationalism and patriotism should dominate the artistic as well as the political life of the day.

Charles Willson Peale was as much a practical man as an artist. He was a taxidermist, and he also repaired watches, made boots, invented a corn planter, and made dentures for George Washington. He operated a natural history museum where, among other items, he exhibited the bones of a mastodon he had discovered. He was a founder of the Pennsylvania Academy of the Fine Arts, which pledged to "unfold, enlighten, and invigorate the talents" of the new Americans.

Literature and Education

Writers also fostered American patriotism. An article in the *Columbian Magazine* urged Americans to produce their own republican literature, as opposed to copying European styles. **Noah Webster** worked from 1783 until 1828 to develop a dictionary of American English in which the "fancy English spelling" of many words was simplified. Webster also produced *The American Spelling Book*, which eventually sold over 100 million copies. In 1789, Jedediah Morse wrote *The American Geography*, which told students that the "astonishing" progress of the United States was due to the "natural genius of Americans." He hoped to impress young scholars with "the superior importance" of their own country.

A popular women's magazine, *All Lady Repository*, begun in 1792, published not only household hints but also moralistic accounts of the unique courage displayed by American women. Other writers stirred patriotism through fiction. Joel Barlow intended his 1787 *Vision of Columbus* to show that America was "the noblest and most elevated part of the earth." Royall Tyler's play, *The Contrast*, favorably compared an American, Colonel Manly, to decadent British men.

The development of republican virtues depended on an educated citizenry. Between 1776 and 1800, 16 new colleges were founded, and many more were established in the early years of the nineteenth century. Lower levels of education did not fare so well. Even though the Northwest Ordinance of 1787 set aside land to support public education, money was scarce, and dreams of a publicly supported educational system across all the states and territories were not to be realized until the mid–nineteenth century. Still, the republican idea that it was the state's responsibility to educate all citizens became an established doctrine during this early national period.

Changes in Society

All the talk of equality and the call for a bill of rights left a mark on society. Children were no longer regarded solely as a source of labor for their families. They were encouraged to seek a life better than that of their parents. No longer were older sons legally favored in the inheritance of property. Romantic love, rather than family arrangement and economic gain, became the basis for many marriages.

Mothers gained status as the caretakers of family virtue, since they now had the charge of rearing republican-minded children. Some women could add to the family income by selling handicrafts made in the home. In the early 1800s, some young unmarried women took their places as workers in newly built factories and as teachers in schools.

The Population Moves Westward

The greatest change of the early national period was the rapidly growing population. In 1790, the population was approximately four million. By 1810, it had grown to over seven million, and by 1815 it was nearly nine million. Much of this population growth took place in the newly acquired western lands. By 1810, the zone of white settlement extended from New York, along the Ohio River, and then west to St. Louis. From St. Louis, the line ran southeastward through Tennessee and Georgia. This great triangle of populated lands had pockets of heavy settlement and vast areas where only a few people lived.

People in the western frontier regions often moved three or four times during a lifetime. Their daily lives were little different from those of the backcountry farmers of the colonial era. They farmed, built their own houses, and made their own clothes. Most were unaware of the great government buildings in Washington. They had probably never heard of Gilbert Stuart, John Trumbull, or Charles Willson Peale, and few of them ever thought of reading a novel or seeing a play. Yet they felt themselves to be the sturdy, honest yeomen farmers that Jefferson believed were the "chosen people of God," the people who would maintain a true republic, an "empire of Liberty."

SECTION 5 REVIEW

1. **Describe** how the layout and the architecture of the new national capital reflected the concept of a republic.
2. **Explain** how nationalism affected painters and writers of this period.
3. **Describe** how women perceived their roles in the new republic.
4. **State** how republicanism helped the spread of education.
5. **Explain** how westward movement changed the demographics of the nation.

Summary

The first 25 years after the Constitution was adopted was a period of trying and testing the strength of the new nation. America was fortunate to have the most respected man in the nation, George Washington, as its first president. Because of his prudence and quiet strength, George Washington moved the nation forward when it might have faltered. It was his support for Hamilton and the opposition of Madison and Jefferson that led to the rise of political factions.

Washington's successors in office faced difficult times. Factions developed into opposing political parties, and the constant warfare between France and Great Britain made peace in America difficult to maintain. Both Adams and Jefferson strove to keep the nation out of war. When war came during Madison's presidency, the nation was strong enough to persevere.

Americans worked hard during this period and developed an identity as a people different from those in the rest of the world. They were Americans, and they tried to develop a way of life that properly reflected that designation. By 1815, the nation was well established and ready to face whatever the future might bring.

Vocabulary

doctrine of states' rights
excise tax
impressment
incumbent
loose constructionist
protocol
secession
strict constructionist

Pair the vocabulary term with its matching definition and write them on a separate piece of paper.

1. current office holder
2. theory that guarantees supremacy of states over the federal government
3. voluntary withdrawal
4. code of etiquette
5. Hamilton's interpretation of the Constitution
6. being forced into naval service
7. Jefferson's interpretation of the Constitution
8. internal commodity tax

Review Questions

1. In what ways did Alexander Hamilton establish a sound monetary policy for the new nation?
2. Describe the main difference between a loose constructionist and a strict constructionist.
3. How did political parties in the United States first develop?
4. Give one reason why Republicans and Federalists held different attitudes toward the French.
5. In what ways were Americans caught in the middle of the war between France and Britain?
6. Describe how the XYZ Affair turned public opinion against France.
7. What was the main purpose of the Alien and Sedition Acts?
8. Why was the *Marbury v. Madison* Supreme Court case so important to the development of the nation's governmental structure?
9. Why was the Embargo Act so disastrous to the American economy?
10. Identify some of the republican values included in the "American" way of life of this period.

Critical Historical Thinking

Writing Answer each of the following questions by writing one or more complete paragraphs:

1. Extreme measures often provoke extreme responses. Discuss how the Alien and Sedition Acts were related to the Kentucky and Virginia Resolutions.
2. Although Thomas Jefferson was a believer in limited government, one of his actions eventually helped to create a strong judiciary. Discuss how *Marbury v. Madison* was able to increase the power of the Supreme Court, while apparently giving in to Jefferson's administration.
3. How did the direction of the United States change after the War of 1812? In what way was the war a turning point?
4. Why was the development of a national identity important in 1815? Is it still important today to have a shared sense of what it means to be an American?

Making Connections with Art and Architecture

Art historian and critic Robert Hughes has said, "One of the great projects of art is to reconcile us with the world." While this is not the only aim of art, it is a fitting one to consider when looking at the nationalistic art produced from 1780 to 1815. The group of American artists and architects who are best known from that period produced art meant to raise our consciousness about the glories of a republic. Their ideal, of course, was taken from the republics of ancient Greece and Rome. Their aim was to create a physical environment that would evoke the spirit of republican values. To that end, their work emphasized harmony of line and form. Artists portrayed American heroes and events clothed in classical Greek and Roman imagery. Architects developed the Federal style of architecture, monumental colonnaded buildings patterned after the Parthenon and other Greek and Roman structures.

▪ Find books in your school or city library that illustrate the art and architecture of Washington, D.C. What features (columns, reliefs, materials) appear frequently on the public buildings? Make sketches of the most popular features to include in your report.

Additional Skills Practice

A work of art can focus attention on important historical and social issues. Artists often paint pictures that chronicle, or tell the story of, a nation. The paintings are often *allegorical*, meaning they use characters and objects that have hidden meanings. Usually an allegory relies on *symbols* to convey messages. A symbol is something that stands for, or represents, something else. Historians should be familiar with a culture's folklore and social values in order to fully appreciate what its artists are saying about that culture.

Create symbols for the following events or situations. You should be able to explain the reason why you selected or created the symbol that you did.

1. exploration of the New World
2. colonial New England
3. the Great Awakening
4. colonial resistance to British attempts to levy taxes
5. the Constitution
6. the Republican (Jeffersonian) party.

Unit Review Questions

Write a brief paragraph in answer to each of the following prompts:

1. Explain why most Indian tribes allied with the French during the French and Indian War.
2. How did the salutary neglect of King George III toward his American colonies contribute to the American Revolution?
3. What prompted colonial leaders to try to change the government that had been organized under the Articles of Confederation?
4. What logistics lessons did the colonists learn during the French and Indian War that helped them during the War of Independence?
5. What was the first major source of disagreement among delegates to the Constitutional Convention and what process was used to resolve this conflict?
6. Describe one way in which the American Revolution changed the lives of the former colonists.
7. What was the constitutional dilemma faced by President Jefferson in purchasing the Louisiana Territory from France?
8. Describe two important results of the Lewis and Clark expedition.
9. Explain how the debate over ratification of the Constitution affected all Americans.
10. Why might the Treaty of Ghent have been considered a failure?

Personalizing History

Webster's Words For many years most books read in the colonies were printed in England. Noah Webster wanted American writings to reflect the attitudes of the new nation, including spelling and pronunciation. Before standardized spelling, people

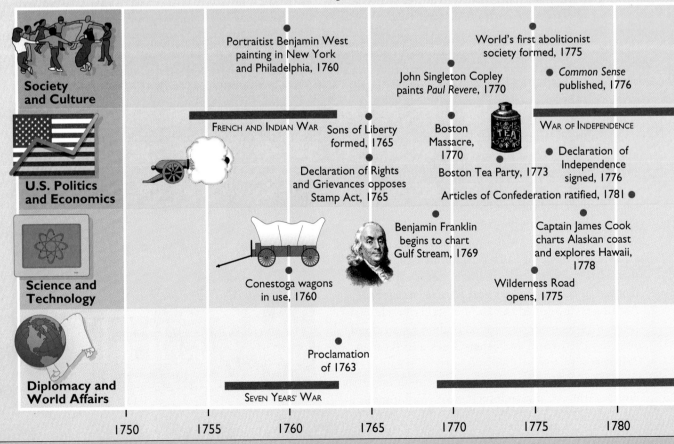

Society and Culture

Portraitist Benjamin West painting in New York and Philadelphia, 1760

World's first abolitionist society formed, 1775

John Singleton Copley paints *Paul Revere*, 1770

Common Sense published, 1776

U.S. Politics and Economics

FRENCH AND INDIAN WAR Sons of Liberty formed, 1765

Boston Massacre, 1770

WAR OF INDEPENDENCE

Declaration of Rights and Grievances opposes Stamp Act, 1765

Boston Tea Party, 1773

Declaration of Independence signed, 1776

Articles of Confederation ratified, 1781

Science and Technology

Benjamin Franklin begins to chart Gulf Stream, 1769

Captain James Cook charts Alaskan coast and explores Hawaii, 1778

Conestoga wagons in use, 1760

Wilderness Road opens, 1775

Diplomacy and World Affairs

Proclamation of 1763

SEVEN YEARS' WAR

1750   1755   1760   1765   1770   1775   1780

often spelled phonetically. *Ocean* and *route* might be *ocian* and *rout*.

Webster wanted to standardize spellings and add American meanings to the vocabulary. Today's dictionaries are based on his lexicon (collection of words). Americans continue to adapt their vocabulary, reflecting new discoveries and attitudes.

■ In small groups, brainstorm common phrases and words used by teenagers today. Do any members of the group know the origin of these words? Did they come from a movie, song, or other form of entertainment? Create a dictionary of terms used mostly by young people, possibly in actual book form and illustrated. Continue to add to your dictionary throughout the school year.

Linking Past and Present

Boycotting and Politics   Colonists frequently resorted to boycotts. They protested the Stamp Act by this method.

Such means have often achieved change. In the 1960s, César Chávez organized a successful boycott of California table grapes. In the 1980s, consumers successfully boycotted music companies whose packaging of CDs and tapes was wasteful. Citizens have also organized boycotts of products advertised by companies who sponsor violent television shows.

■ Find out if any group in your community is currently sponsoring a boycott. If not, try to find out about a nationally-sponsored boycott. Prepare a position paper for or against these efforts.

Time Line Activity

List chronologically five events from the time line which contributed to America's transformation from thirteen separate colonies into a new republic. Use items from different categories and explain your choices.

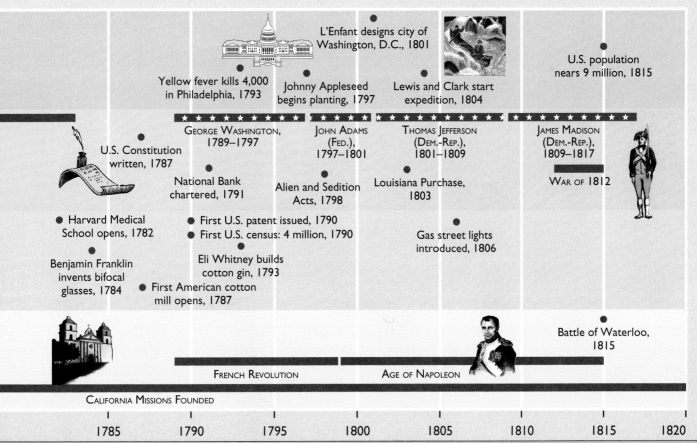

L'Enfant designs city of Washington, D.C., 1801

U.S. population nears 9 million, 1815

Yellow fever kills 4,000 in Philadelphia, 1793

Johnny Appleseed begins planting, 1797

Lewis and Clark start expedition, 1804

GEORGE WASHINGTON, 1789–1797

JOHN ADAMS (FED.), 1797–1801

THOMAS JEFFERSON (DEM.-REP.), 1801–1809

JAMES MADISON (DEM.-REP.), 1809–1817

U.S. Constitution written, 1787

National Bank chartered, 1791

Alien and Sedition Acts, 1798

Louisiana Purchase, 1803

WAR OF 1812

Harvard Medical School opens, 1782

First U.S. patent issued, 1790
First U.S. census: 4 million, 1790

Gas street lights introduced, 1806

Benjamin Franklin invents bifocal glasses, 1784

Eli Whitney builds cotton gin, 1793
First American cotton mill opens, 1787

FRENCH REVOLUTION

AGE OF NAPOLEON

Battle of Waterloo, 1815

CALIFORNIA MISSIONS FOUNDED

1785   1790   1795   1800   1805   1810   1815   1820

The Nation Transformed

The small republic founded by George Washington and Benjamin Franklin's generation became the world's largest democracy. The extension of the vote to all adult, white males occurred during the period included in this unit. During this time, the young republic also became a mighty nation that extended from sea to sea. This final phase of territorial expansion saw the American flag raised over Texas, Oregon, California, and the Southwest. But expansion was a mixed blessing for Americans. Westward expansion gave African American slavery a new lease on life. It brought misery and death to countless American Indians and made Mexican Americans aliens in their own land. During these years, Americans also became more interested in spiritual salvation and social reform.

Chapter 7
Politics, Reform, and Conflict

Chapter 8
Westward Expansion

Chapter 9
The North and the South

◀ *This bird's-eye view of New York City in the 1850s is a detail from a hand-colored lithograph. At that time, what were the most distinctive features of the city's skyline?*

Themes

- **Democracy and Citizenship** More people were eligible to participate in American politics than ever before. The election of Andrew Jackson to the presidency was symbolic of the growth of democracy.
- **Arts and Humanities** The growth of democracy was also reflected in American art, as artists looked to common people and everyday scenes for inspiration.
- **Geography and the Environment** The westward movement of the frontier and territorial acquisitions greatly expanded the geographical horizons of the American people.
- **Everyday Life** The growth of the factory system in the North and the expansion of slavery in the South made evident the growing sectional differences in the everyday lives of the American people.

The Nature of the Federal Union

Chief Justice John Marshall

Did the Constitution grant political sovereignty to the federal government or to the states? John Marshall, chief justice of the Supreme Court, answered that question.

That the United States form, for many, and for most important purposes, a single nation, has not yet been denied. In war, we are one people. In making peace, we are one people. In all commercial regulations, we are one and the same people. In many other respects, the American people are one; and the government which is alone capable of controlling and managing their interests in all these respects, is the government of the Union. . . . The constitution and laws of a State, so far as they are repugnant to the constitution and laws of the United States, are absolutely void.

Cohens v. Virginia. Wheaton's Reports,
vol. 6 (New York, 1821).

John Taylor of Caroline

John Taylor, a Virginia Republican who wrote extensively on political issues, presented an alternative view.

The appellation adopted by the Declaration of Independence, was, "The United States of America." The first confederation declares, that the style of this confederacy shall be, "The United States of America." And the union of 1787, ordains and establishes the Constitution for "The United States of America." The three instruments, by adhering to the same style, co-extensively affirmed the separate sovereignties of these states. It was a style proper to describe a confederacy of independent states, and improper for describing a consolidated nation."

John Marshall, *New View of the Constitution of the United States* (Washington City, 1823), pp. 237–241.

James Tallmadge Denounces Slavery

In February 1819, Representative James Tallmadge defended his amendment prohibiting slavery in Missouri despite threats of civil war from southern members.

Sir, the honorable gentleman . . . from Georgia [Representative Thomas Cobb] . . . has said "that, if we persist, the Union will be dissolved"; and, with a look fixed on me, has told us, "we have kindled a fire which all the waters of the ocean cannot put out, which seas of blood can only extinguish." Sir, language of this sort has no effect on me; my purpose is fixed . . . it is a great and glorious cause, setting bounds to a slavery the most cruel and debasing the world ever witnessed.

Sir, if a dissolution of the Union must take place, let it be so! If civil war, which gentlemen so much threaten, must come, I can only say, let it come! . . . If blood is necessary to extinguish any fire which I have assisted to kindle . . . I shall not forebear to contribute my might.

You boast of the freedom of your Constitution and your laws; you have proclaimed, in the Declaration of Independence, "That all men are created equal" and yet you have slaves in your country. . . . If you allow slavery to pass into territories where you have the lawful power to exclude it, you will justly take upon yourself all the charges of inconsistency.

Annals of the Congress of the United States, 15th Cong., 2nd Sess., pp. 1204–1206, 1211.

Jacksonian Democracy

Inauguration Day

A Washington, D.C., resident described the White House reception following Andrew Jackson's inauguration.

What a scene we did witness. . . . What a pity! What a pity! No arrangements had been made, no police officers placed on duty, and the whole house had been inundated by the rabble mob. . . . Cut glass and china to the amount of several thousand dollars had been broken in the struggle to get the refreshments. . . . Ladies fainted, men were seen with bloody noses, and . . . those who got in could not get out by the door again but had to scramble out of windows. At one time the President, who had retreated and retreated until he was pressed against the wall, could only be secured by a number of gentlemen forming round him and making a kind of barrier of their own bodies. . . . It was then the windows were thrown open and the torrent found an outlet, which otherwise might have proved fatal.

Gaillard Hunt, ed., *The First Forty Years of Washington Society, Portrayed by Family Letters of Mrs. Samuel Harrison Smith* (New York, 1906).

Andrew Jackson on Rotation in Office

In his first annual message to Congress, Andrew Jackson defended his removal of office holders to provide federal jobs for the Democrats who helped to elect him.

The duties of all public officers are, or at least admit of being made, so plain and simple that men of intelligence may readily qualify themselves for their performance. And I cannot but believe that more is lost by the long continuance of men in office than is generally to be gained by their experience.

In a country where offices are created solely for the benefit of the people, no one man has any more intrinsic right to official station than another. Offices were not established to give support to particular men at the public expense. No individual wrong is, therefore, done by removal, since neither appointment to, nor continuance in, office is matter of right.

James D. Richardson, ed., *A Compilation of the Messages and Papers of the Presidents* (Washington, D.C., 1896), vol. II, pp. 448–449.

Jackson on the Bank of the United States

In his message vetoing the bill to extend the charter of the Bank of the United States, Andrew Jackson explained why he considered such legislation inappropriate.

It is to be regretted that the rich and powerful too often bend the acts of government to their self-ish purposes. Distinctions in society will always exist under every just government. Equality of talents, of education, or of wealth cannot be produced by human institutions. . . . Every man is equally entitled to protection by law; but when the laws undertake . . . to make the rich richer and the potent more powerful, the humble members of society—the farmers, mechanics, and laborers—who have neither the time nor the means of securing like favors to themselves, have a right to complain of the injustice of the Government. . . . If [government] would confine itself to equal protection, and as Heaven does its rains, shower its favors alike on the high and the low, the rich and the poor, it would be an unqualified blessing.

James D. Richardson, ed., *A Compilation of the Messages and Papers of the Presidents* (Washington, D.C., 1897), vol. II, pp. 1153–1154.

Martin Van Buren on the Proper Role of Government

During the financial panic and depression of the late 1830s, many people appealed to Congress for aid. In a message to Congress in 1837, President Martin Van Buren responded to those appeals.

Those who look to the action of this Government for specific aid . . . , lose sight of the ends for which it was created, and the powers with which it is clothed. It was established to give security to us all. . . . It was not intended to confer special favors on individuals. . . . All communities are apt to look to Government for too much. Even in our own country, where its powers and duties are so strictly limited, we are prone to do so, especially at periods of sudden embarrassment and distress. The framers of our excellent Constitution. . . wisely judged that the less Government interferes with private pursuits, the better for the general prosperity. It is not its legitimate object to make men rich, or to repair, by direct grants of money or legislation in favor of particular pursuits, losses not incurred in the public service.

Congressional Globe, 25th Cong., 1st Sess., vol. 5 (1837), p. 9.

A Revival Preacher

Frances Trollope, an English visitor who found little that was likeable about Americans, wrote the following description of a revival meeting in Cincinnati.

The sermon had considerable eloquence, but of a frightful kind. The preacher described, with ghastly minuteness, the last feeble fainting moments of human life, and then the gradual progress of decay after death, which he followed through every process up to the last loathsome stage of decomposition. Suddenly changing his tone, which had been that of sober accurate description, into the shrill voice of horror, he bent forward his head, as if to gaze on some object beneath the pulpit.... The device was certainly a happy one for giving effect to his description of hell. No image that fire, brimstone, molten lead, or red hot pincers could supply with flesh, nerves, and sinews quivering under them, was omitted. The perspiration ran in streams from the face of the preacher; his eyes rolled, his lips were covered with foam, and every feature had the deep expression of horror it would have borne, had he, in truth, been gazing at the scene he described. The acting was excellent.

It was some seconds before the congregation could join [in hymn singing] as usual; every upturned face looked pale and horror-struck.

Frances Trollope, *Domestic Manners of the Americans* (1832).

Promoting the West

A British immigrant who settled in the Ohio Valley wrote a letter home to encourage his brother to join him.

This is the country for a man to enjoy himself: Ohio, Indiana, and the Missouri Territory.... I measured Indian corn in Ohio State last September more than fifteen feet high.... I believe I saw more peaches and apples rotting on the ground than would sink the British fleet. I was at many [farms] in Ohio where they no more knew the number of their hogs than myself.

The poorest families adorn the table three times a day like a wedding dinner—tea, coffee, beef, fowls, pies, eggs, pickles, good bread; and their favorite beverage is whisky or peach brandy. Say, is it so in England?

If you knew the difference between this country and England you would need no persuading to leave it and come hither.

Samuel Crabtree to his brother, *Important Extracts from Original and Recent Letters Written by Englishmen, in the United States of America, to Their Friends in England, Second Series* (Manchester, 1818).

Frontier Life

Pioneer Life in Ohio

William C. Howells, who settled in Ohio in 1813, looked back in later years at the way frontier settlers pitched in to help one another with their work.

I can hardly realize how greatly things have changed since that period.... Particularly remarkable was the general equality and the general dependence of all upon the neighborly kindness and good offices of others. Their houses and barns were built of logs, and were raised by the collection of many neighbors together on one day, whose united strength was necessary to the handling of the logs.... It was the custom always to send one from a family to help, so that you could claim like assistance in return....

This kind of mutual help of the neighbors was extended to many kinds of work, such as rolling up the logs in a clearing, grubbing out the underbrush, splitting rails, cutting logs for a house, and the like. When a gathering of men for such a purpose took place, there was commonly some sort of mutual job laid out for women, such as quilting, sewing, or spinning up a lot of thread for some poor neighbor. This would bring together a mixed party, and it was usually arranged that after supper there should be a dance or at least plays which would occupy a good part of the night and wind up with the young fellows seeing the girls home in the short hours.

The flax crops required a good deal of handling, in weeding, pulling, and dressing, and each of these processes was made the occasion of a joint gathering of boys and girls and a good time.

William Cooper Howells, *Recollections of Life in Ohio from 1813 to 1840.*

On the Indiana Frontier

The author of this account was a woman who settled in Indiana in the 1820s.

February 15, 1826, we started for our new home.... The weather was cold. We built a log-heap in our new [unfinished] cabin, but still we almost froze.... We were nearly three miles from our nearest neighbor. We brought cornmeal with us, sufficient, as we thought, to last until after planting; but it gave out, and I had to pound corn in an iron pot ... and sift it through a basket lid. We got our corn planted about the first of June.... I was taken sick about the first of July, and both our children. I shook forty days with the ague [fever].... I never saw a woman, except one ... for three months.... One night our dog fought some animal near the door, which had no shutter but a quilt. I was very much frightened, and our faithful dog was almost killed.

James H. Stewart, *Recollections of the Early Settlement of Carroll County, Indiana* (Cincinnati, 1872), pp 77–80.

Frontier Life in Illinois

A British visitor to the United States described the frontier farm of a British immigrant family that settled in Illinois in the early 1830s.

The house which Mr. Killam's family have erected is merely a temporary one... but they have made it very comfortable. They have put up a large plated iron stove... and their furniture is as shining and neat as possible. Their farming stock is as yet small;—two pairs of oxen ... and three cows.... They have considerable patches of wheat, maize, beans, peas, and potatoes.... His cattle cost him nothing for food ... and he has also a quantity of fine barn-door fowls, which support themselves entirely upon the prairie. His sons kill abundance of wild turkeys and prairie hens without any restriction. There are still a few wolves in the neighbourhood; but they do no mischief where three or four good dogs are kept.

James Stuart, *Three Years in North America* (Edinburgh, 1833), vol. II, pp. 345–350.

Removing the Potawatomi

The author of this account watched the Potawatomi Indians leave northern Indiana in 1838 on their way to reservations beyond the Mississippi.

It was a sad and mournful spectacle to witness these children of the forest slowly retiring from the home of their childhood.... They felt that they were bidding farewell to the hills, valleys and streams of their infancy.... All these they were leaving behind them to be desecrated by the plowshare of the white man. As they cast mournful glances back toward these loved scenes that were rapidly fading in the distance, tears fell from the cheek of the downcast warrior, old men trembled, matrons wept, the swarthy maiden's cheek turned pale, and sighs and half-suppressed sobs escaped from the motley groups as they passed along, some on foot, some on horseback, and others in wagons—sad as a funeral procession.

▲ *Cherokee on the "Trail of Tears"*

Sanford C. Cox, *Recollections of the Early Settlement of the Wabash Valley* (Lafayette, Indiana, 1860), pp. 154–155.

The Two Labor Systems Compared

In Defense of Slavery

In 1858, James Henry Hammond, a senator from South Carolina, defended slavery in a speech to the Senate.

In all social systems, there must be a class to do the menial duties, to perform the drudgery of life. That is, a class requiring but a low order of intellect and but little skill. Its requisites are vigor, docility, fidelity. Such a class you must have or you would not have that other class which leads [to] progress, civilization, and refinement. It constitutes the very mudsill [foundation] of society and of political government; and you might as well attempt to build a house in the air, as to build either the one or the other, except on this mudsill. Fortunately for the South, she found a race adapted to that purpose to her hand.

The Senator from New York said yesterday that the whole world had abolished slavery. Aye, the *name*, but not the *thing*. . . . Your whole hireling class of manual laborers and "operatives," as you call them, are essentially slaves. The difference between us is, that our slaves are hired for life and well compensated; there is no starvation, no begging, no want of employment among our people, and not too much employment either. Yours are hired by the day, not cared for, and scantily compensated, which may be proved in the most painful manner, at any hour in any street in any of your large towns. Why, you meet more beggars in one day, in any single street of the city of New York, than you would meet in a lifetime in the whole South.

"Speech on the Admission of Kansas," U.S. Senate, Mar. 4, 1858.

The Two Systems Compared

Orestes A. Brownson, a northern labor reformer and social critic, also compared the wage system to slavery.

In regard to labor, two systems obtain: one that of slave labor, the other that of free labor. Of the two, the first is, in our judgment, except so far as the feelings are concerned, decidedly the least oppressive. If the slave has never been a free man, we think, as a general rule, his sufferings are less than those of the free laborer at wages. As to actual freedom, one has just about as much as the other. The laborer at wages has all the disadvantages of freedom and none of its blessings, while the slave, if denied the blessings, is freed from the disadvantages.

We are no advocates of slavery. We are as heartily opposed to it as any modern abolitionist can be. But we say frankly that, if there must always be a laboring population distinct from proprietors and employers, we regard the slave system as decidedly preferable to the system at wages.

One thing is certain: that, of the amount actually produced by the operative, he retains a less proportion than it costs the master to feed, clothe, and lodge his slave. Wages is a cunning device of the devil, for the benefit of tender consciences who would retain all the advantages of the slave system without the expense, trouble, and odium of being slave holders.

Boston Quarterly Review (1840), pp. 368–370.

An Abolitionist's View of Slavery

Abolitionist Theodore Weld wrote a best-selling pamphlet attacking the slave owners' claim that slaves were well treated. It contained testimony by former slaves.

Reader, what have you to say of such treatment? Is it right, just, benevolent? Suppose I should seize

▼ *Slaves working on a Mississippi cotton plantation*

you, rob you of your liberty, drive you into the field, and make you work without pay as long as you live, would that be justice and kindness, or monstrous injustice and cruelty? Now, everybody knows that the slave holders do these things to the slaves every day, and yet it is stoutly affirmed that they treat them well and kindly, and that their tender regard for their slaves restrains the masters from inflicting cruelties upon them.

...We will prove that slaves in the United States are treated with barbarous inhumanity; they are overworked, underfed, wretchedly clad and lodged, and have insufficient sleep; that they are often made to wear round their necks iron collars armed with prongs, to drag heavy chains and weights at their feet while working in the field, and to wear yokes, and bells, and iron horns; . . . that they are frequently flogged with terrible severity . . . ; that they are often hunted with blood hounds and shot down like beasts, or torn in pieces by dogs; that their ears are often cut off, their eyes knocked out, their bones broken, their flesh branded with red hot irons. . . . All these things, and more, and worse, we shall prove. . . .

Theodore Dwight Weld, *American Slavery As It Is: Testimony of a Thousand Witnesses* (New York: American Anti-Slavery Society, 1839), pp. 7–10.

Slave Labor

A Slave Market
Louis Hughes, a former slave, wrote the following passage describing a slave market in his autobiography.

The trader's establishment consisted of an office, a large showroom and a yard in the rear enclosed with a wall of brick fifteen feet high. . . . . The women were placed in a row on one side of the room and the men on the other. Persons desirous of purchasing them passed up and down between the lines looking the poor creatures over, and questioning them in about the following manner: "What can you do?" "Are you a good cook? seamstress? dairymaid?"—this to the women, while the men would be questioned as to their line of work: "Can you plow? Are you a blacksmith? Have you ever cared for horses? Can you pick cotton rapidly?" Sometimes the slave would be required to open his

mouth that the purchaser might examine the teeth and form some opinion as to his age and physical soundness; and if it was suspected that a slave had been beaten a good deal he would be required to step into another room and undress. If the person desiring to buy found the slave badly scarred by the common usage of whipping, he would say at once to the foreman: "Why! this slave is not worth much, he is all scarred up. No, I don't want him; bring me in another to look at." Slaves without scars from whipping and looking well physically always sold readily.

Thirty Years a Slave: The Autobiography of Louis Hughes. (New York: Negro Universities Press, 1970).

The Overseers
A former slave, Mary Ella Grandberry, recalled the harsh treatment received from overseers.

De overseers was terrible hard on us. Dey'd ride up and down de field and haste you so till you near about fell out. Sometimes and most generally every time you behind de crowd you got a good lickin' with de bull whip dat de driver had in de saddle with him. I heard Mammy say dat one day dey whipped poor Leah till she fall out like she was dead. Den dey rubbed salt and pepper on de blisters to make 'em burn real good. She was so sore till she couldn't lay on her back nights, and she just couldn't stand for no clothes to touch her back whatsoever. . . .

Federal Writer's Project, *Slave Narratives.*

A Southern Teacher's View of Slavery
The following account appeared in a book published in 1835 by Joseph Holt Ingraham, a native of Maine who spent most of his life living and teaching in the South.

Planters, particularly native planters, have a kind of affection for their Negroes, incredible to those who have not observed its effects. . . . In health they treat them with uniform kindness, in sickness with attention and sympathy. . . . Every plantation is supplied with suitable medicines, and generally to such an extent that some room or part of a room in the planter's house is converted into a small apothecary's shop. These, in the absence of the physician in any sudden emergency, are administered by the planter. Hence, the health of the slaves, so far as medical skill is concerned, is well provided for.

Joseph Holt Ingraham, *The South-West by a Yankee* (1835).

A Plantation Hospital

This account of health care for slaves was written by a British actress who married a wealthy southern planter and lived for several years on a Georgia plantation.

In the afternoon I made my first visit to the hospital of the estate, and found it . . . so miserable a place for the purpose to which it was dedicated I could not have imagined on a property belonging to Christian owners. The floor (which was not boarded, but merely the damp hard earth itself) was strewn with wretched women, who, but for their moans of pain and uneasy restless motions, might very well have each been taken for a mere heap of filthy rags. . . . By degrees I was able to endure for a few minutes what they were condemned to live their hours and days of suffering and sickness through. . . .

Frances Anne Kemble, *Journal of a Residence on a Georgian Plantation* (1838–1839).

The Mill Workers

A Labor Contract

Workers hired by a New Hampshire textile mill in 1832 were required to sign a labor contract.

We, the subscribers [the undersigned], do hereby agree to enter the service of the Cocheco Manufacturing Company, and conform, in all respects, to the regulations which are now, or may hereafter be adopted, for the good government of the institution.

We further agree to work for such wages per week, and prices by the job, as the Company may see fit to pay, and be subject to the fines as well as entitled to the premiums paid by the Company.

We further agree to allow two cents each week to be deducted from our wages for the benefit of the sick fund.

We also agree not to leave the service of the Company without giving two weeks' notice of our intention, without permission of an agent. And if we do, we agree to forfeit to the use of the Company two weeks' pay.

We also agree not to be engaged in any combination [union] whereby the work may be impeded or the Company's interest in any work injured. If we do, we agree to forfeit to the use of the Company the amount of wages that may be due to us at the time.

Seth Luther, *An Address to the Working-Men of New England* (Boston, 1833), p. 36.

The Lowell Mill Workers

Charles Dickens, the British novelist, visited a textile mill at Lowell, Massachusetts, in 1842, and wrote the following description of the young women who worked there.

I happened to arrive at the first factory just as the [lunch] hour was over, and the girls were returning to their work; indeed the stairs of the mill were thronged with them as I ascended. They were all well dressed.

The rooms in which they worked were as well ordered as themselves. In the windows of some there were green plants, which were trained to shade the glass; in all, there was as much fresh air, cleanliness, and comfort as the nature of the occupation would possibly admit of. Out of so large a number of females, many of whom were only then just verging upon womanhood, it may be reasonably supposed that some were delicate and fragile in appearance: no doubt there were. But I solemnly declare, that from all the crowd I saw in the different factories that day, I cannot recall or separate one young face that gave me a painful impression; not one young girl whom, assuming it to be matter of necessity that she should gain her daily bread by the labour of her hands, I would have removed from those works if I had had the power.

▲ *Lowell mill dress, c. 1840*

Charles Dickens, *American Notes* (London: Chapman and Hall, 1846), pp. 30–32.

The Daily Work Routine

In 1846, a social reform magazine published this less favorable account of working conditions in the New England textile mills.

The operatives work thirteen hours a day in the summer time, and from daylight to dark in the winter. At half past four in the morning the factory bell rings, and at five the girls must be in the mills. A clerk, placed as a watch, observes those who are a few minutes behind the time, and effectual means are taken to stimulate to punctuality. This is the morning commencement of the industrial discipline—(should we not rather say industrial tyranny?) which is established in these Associations of this moral and Christian community. At seven the girls are allowed thirty minutes for breakfast, and at noon thirty minutes more for dinner, except during the first quarter of the year, when the time is extended to forty-five minutes. But within this time they must hurry to their boardinghouses and return to the factory, and that through the hot sun, or the rain and cold. A meal eaten under such circumstances must be quite unfavorable to digestion and health, as any medical man will inform us. At seven o'clock in the evening the factory bell sounds the close of the day's work.

 Harbinger, Nov. 14, 1846.

WORKING WITH THE ARCHIVES

Making Generalizations with Primary Source Materials

This skill lesson will help you understand how historians make generalizations and draw conclusions from primary sources, a process known as *supported induction*. Read the four archive selections about frontier life in the early nineteenth century: "Promoting the West," "Pioneer Life in Ohio," "On the Indiana Frontier," and "Frontier Life in Illinois." As you read, take note of the characteristics that describe frontier life in America's early nineteenth century. You will be asked to record these characteristics. Look for common patterns, and then draw a conclusion from those common patterns. To help you reach a conclusion about frontier life, you will complete a three-step supported induction graphic organizer.

Steps for Making a Supported Induction Graphic Organizer

1. Ask yourself "What exactly am I reading? What are the details?" From the four readings, select characteristics which describe frontier life. In short phrases, or quoting the primary resources without including your personal beliefs, record the information which describes each individual characteristic. An example might look like this: Solitude of frontier life—people lived miles apart and sometimes rarely saw other people.

2. Ask yourself "How can I put these details together?" Interpret the information by looking for patterns which create conclusions about frontier life. Combine two or more of the characteristics which create a pattern. For example, combine solitude of frontier life with dangers of frontier life and record the specific information about the two characteristics.

3. Ask yourself "What main idea does this information tell me?" Write down one or more conclusions about frontier life in America's early nineteenth century. Support your conclusion(s) with your notes from Step 1 and Step 2.

Politics, Reform, and Conflict

The two decades following the War of 1812 were an exciting period in American public life. Not since the election of Thomas Jefferson in 1800 had national politics generated so much interest. New political parties were organized, and new party leaders appeared on the scene. One man above all others left his mark on the politics of that age: Andrew Jackson. His loyal followers called him Old Hickory, and to them he represented the triumph of democracy. His opponents saw him as a tyrant and called him King Andrew. Whatever people thought of him, Jackson made politics exciting again.

So did the reform movements of the period, which drew men and women out of their homes into meeting halls and street demonstrations. It was a time of reform, of involvement in the important affairs of the nation, a time for crusades. Yet over it all hung the dark shadow of conflict between North and South. The issue that most seriously divided the two sections was slavery. The political crisis over slavery that erupted in the dispute about the admission of Missouri to statehood in 1820 almost tore the Union apart.

▲ *This image of John C. Calhoun—vice president, senator, and orator from South Carolina—captures the energy and forcefulness with which he presented his views.*

The Rise of Nationalism

The period immediately following the War of 1812 was a time of intense national pride in the United States. The American victory at New Orleans and the favorable peace treaty focused attention on the federal government and its leaders. After 1815, a national economic policy emerged along with a national culture. Postwar prosperity led to a general feeling of well-being. The prestige of the government improved with the economy. "Americans . . . rejoice!" the editor of the Richmond *Enquirer* newspaper wrote in 1815. "Thank your warriors who have given you Glory and your ministers who have given you Peace!" Countless Americans shared the editor's feelings of national pride, and for a time most people forgot about sectional and party loyalties. The war and the postwar policies of the federal government strengthened the bonds of national unity.

How would appeals to national pride help Republicans enact economic legislation?

In what ways did the spirit of nationalism influence American foreign policy?

How did decisions of the Supreme Court encourage a more nationalist outlook?

▲ *James Monroe was president from 1817 to 1825. Why was Monroe reelected in 1820 without opposition candidates?*

An Era of Good Feelings

National unity was strengthened after 1815 by the decline in the loyalty Americans felt toward political parties. This made American politics less divisive, and for a time the two-party system virtually disappeared. Because the Federalists had opposed the war, they lost most of their support. Only a small remnant of the party survived, mainly in New England. Elsewhere the Republicans, as the followers of Thomas Jefferson were now called, governed without opposition. In 1816, James Monroe, the Republican candidate for the presidency, easily defeated his Federalist opponent, Rufus King. In 1820, the Federalists did not even bother to run a candidate against Monroe. When the president made a tour of the country early in his first administration, he was greeted as warmly in Federalist New England as he was elsewhere. Monroe's reception in Boston led a local newspaper to announce that an "era of good feelings" had replaced the party battles of the past.

Growing interest in the national welfare also helped blur party lines. For example, Republicans as well as Federalists saw the need for a healthy economy. To help promote the growth of manufacturing and trade, the Republicans abandoned their earlier preference for a weak central government and adopted many of the measures once supported by the Federalists. These economic measures included high **tariffs**, or taxes, on foreign-made goods, the establishment of a Bank of the United States, and federal construction of roads and canals. To encourage broad support, Henry Clay, a Republican member of Congress from Kentucky, called these economic measures the **American System**. All patriotic Americans, Clay implied, should support these measures. Thus, the name itself helped to place this program beyond the reach of **partisan** (political party) conflict.

By appealing to national pride, the Republicans enacted much of this economic program. The Republican Congress passed the Tariff of 1816 to protect American-made goods and chartered the second Bank of the United States. The first Bank of the United States had closed its doors in 1811, when its 20-year charter expired. By permitting the second Bank of the United States to open branch banks in major cities and to issue a national currency, Congress, in effect, created a national banking system. In 1817, Congress also authorized the use of federal funds to help the states build roads and canals, but President Madison vetoed that bill shortly before leaving office. He did not think the Constitution gave Congress the authority to build roads.

◄ *As secretary of state, John Quincy Adams was the principal author of the Monroe Doctrine. What did this statement tell European powers?*

Bold Foreign Policy

The vigorous foreign policy of the Monroe administration also contributed to the nationalist spirit of the decade after the war. The chief architect of that policy was Monroe's capable secretary of state, **John Quincy Adams** (son of John Adams). Adams was determined to reduce Spanish holdings in North America. He first turned his attention to Florida. Adams's hand in negotiating with Spain was strengthened by chaotic conditions along the border between Florida and Georgia. The Seminole Indians of Florida posed a threat to the Georgia frontier. In fact, in 1816, United States troops had crossed into Florida pursuing runaway slaves and warring Seminole Indians.

In April 1818, General Andrew Jackson led an army across the border and occupied Spanish East Florida. Although other members of the Monroe administration criticized Jackson for this rash act, Adams saw it as an opportunity. He explained to the Spanish minister, Luis de Onis, that conflict could be avoided only if Spain sold Florida to the U. S.

Afraid that the Americans might be planning to take Florida by force, the Spanish government agreed to **cede** (grant by treaty) the territory to the United States. In the **Adams-Onis Treaty** of 1819, Spain relinquished Florida. In return the United States agreed to settle American citizens' claims against Spain—claims that totaled $5 million. The treaty also established a new boundary between United States and Spanish territory in the West, with Spain abandoning all claims to the area north of California. By obtaining Florida and ending Spain's claims to the Oregon country, Adams achieved a major diplomatic victory for the United States. The Adams-Onis Treaty raised Americans' pride in their government to new heights.

The Monroe Doctrine   Adams also wanted to limit the influence that European nations had in the Western Hemisphere. The main area of concern for Adams was Latin America, where Mexico and countries of Middle and South America were winning their independence from Spain. The Monroe

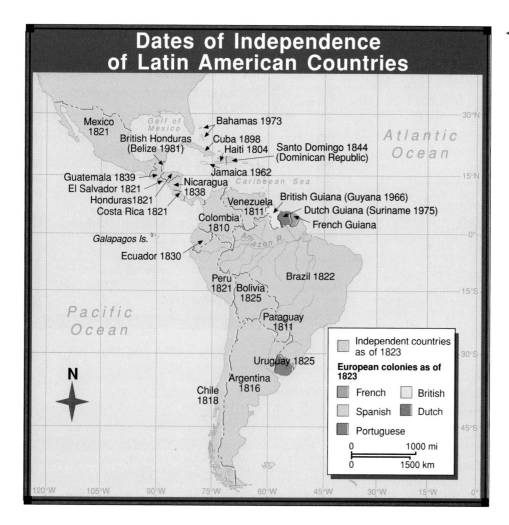

Dates of Independence of Latin American Countries

Mexico 1821
Gulf of Mexico
British Honduras (Belize 1981)
Bahamas 1973
Cuba 1898
Haiti 1804
Santo Domingo 1844 (Dominican Republic)
Atlantic Ocean
Guatemala 1839
El Salvador 1821
Honduras 1821
Costa Rica 1821
Jamaica 1962
Nicaragua 1838
Caribbean Sea
Venezuela 1811
Colombia 1810
British Guiana (Guyana 1966)
Dutch Guiana (Suriname 1975)
French Guiana
Galapagos Is.
Ecuador 1830
Amazon R.
Peru 1821
Bolivia 1825
Brazil 1822
Pacific Ocean
Paraguay 1811
Uruguay 1825
Argentina 1816
Chile 1818
N

Independent countries as of 1823
European colonies as of 1823
French   British
Spanish   Dutch
Portuguese

0 _____ 1000 mi
0 _____ 1500 km

◄ Latin American countries became independent over a period of years, beginning with Haiti in 1804. Independence for Spain's colonies took more than two decades to accomplish. Unlike Britain's North American colonies, the Spanish colonies did not declare independence all at one time. What consequence did this have for the future of Latin America?

administration applauded these colonial revolutions, viewing them as the continuation of the struggle for liberty begun by the American Revolution. The administration also saw that these newly independent countries could be future trade partners for the United States.

However, President Monroe and Secretary of State Adams were afraid that European nations would intervene to help Spain regain its American colonies. They were also concerned about the extension of Russian influence in the Pacific Northwest. It would be easy for the Russians to move south from their base in Alaska to establish colonies in the Oregon country.

In 1823, Secretary of State Adams saw an opportunity to make a bold new policy statement re-garding the Western Hemisphere. Great Britain had recently proposed a joint British-American declaration against European intervention in the newly independent nations of Latin America. The British, too, saw possibilities for developing trade with these countries. Adams advised Monroe against making a joint statement with Britain, and he proposed instead that the United States should make such a declaration on its own. "It would be more candid, as well as more dignified," Adams said to Monroe, "to avow our principles explicitly to Russia and France, than to come in as a cockboat [a small rowboat] in the wake of the British man-of-war."

The **Monroe Doctrine**, written mainly by Adams, declared that the United States opposed any further colonization in the Americas by European powers or any attempts by European powers to exert political influence in the Western Hemisphere. In return, President Monroe pledged that the United States would stay out of European affairs. This declaration became known as the Monroe Doctrine, a landmark of American foreign policy.

Nationalism Fostered by the Supreme Court

During this time, the United States Supreme Court also contributed to the growth of American nationalism. In the first place, the Court helped strengthen the national government by a series of decisions that restricted the powers of the state legislatures. Under the guidance of Chief Justice John Marshall, the Court strengthened the authority of Congress to regulate interstate trade. It did so by expanding the definition of **interstate commerce** to include goods transported on rivers, as well as goods shipped overland from one state to another. Marshall's decisions encouraged merchants and manufacturers to look to the federal government and federal courts to protect their businesses from restrictive regulations on trade imposed by the states.

The first of these cases, *Dartmouth College v. Woodward* (1819), limited the power of the states to control corporations. The case concerned an attempt by the state of New Hampshire to make a private school, Dartmouth College, into a state university. The college resisted. In presenting the college's case before the Supreme Court, attorney Daniel Webster argued that Dartmouth's royal charter of 1769 could not be swept aside by the state. The charter, Webster insisted, was a valid contract protected by Article I, Section 10, of the United States Constitution, which stated that no state could pass any law "impairing the Obligation of Contracts. . . ." In agreeing with Webster, the Court preserved Dartmouth's status as a private college. In doing so, it extended the protection of the Constitution to any charter granted to a private corporation. This limited the power of state governments

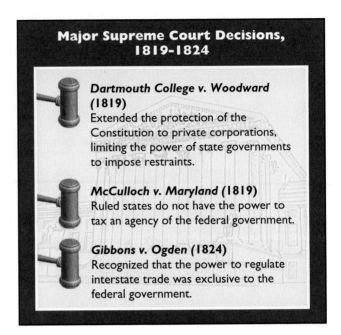

Major Supreme Court Decisions, 1819–1824

Dartmouth College v. Woodward (1819)
Extended the protection of the Constitution to private corporations, limiting the power of state governments to impose restraints.

McCulloch v. Maryland (1819)
Ruled states do not have the power to tax an agency of the federal government.

Gibbons v. Ogden (1824)
Recognized that the power to regulate interstate trade was exclusive to the federal government.

▲ *How do these Supreme Court rulings reflect the growth of American nationalism?*

to impose restraints, or checks, on business corporations and private colleges.

In two later decisions, the Marshall Court upheld the supremacy of the federal government over the states and restricted the powers of the state legislature. In the case of *McCulloch v. Maryland* (1819), the Supreme Court ruled that the state of Maryland could not tax the Baltimore branch of the second Bank of the United States. The Court maintained that the power to tax was the power to destroy. The Constitution, the justices concluded, did not give states the power to destroy an agency of the federal government.

Finally, in the case of *Gibbons v. Ogden* (1824), the Court recognized that the power to regulate interstate trade was exclusive to the federal government. In this case, it struck down a New York law that granted monopoly rights to a New York steamboat company to carry passengers to New Jersey. Again, the Court reinforced the supremacy of the federal government in freeing trade from state-imposed constraints. By striking down restrictive state laws, it extended greater freedom to American business.

1. **State** the main reason for the decline of the Federalist Party after the War of 1812.
2. **Explain** why the period following the War of 1812 is called the Era of Good Feelings.
3. **Define** partisan.
4. **Identify** the Monroe Doctrine and explain why Adams refused to make a joint declaration with the British.
5. **Describe** how the decisions of the Marshall Court strengthened the national government.

SECTION 2

Slavery and the Missouri Crisis

In 1819, the slavery question threatened to destroy the spirit of national harmony. The threat came quite unexpectedly with a petition for statehood from the territory of Missouri. Since slavery had existed in the territory, Missouri asked to be admitted as a slave state.

Up to that time, the admission of new states had been an uneventful process. The Northwest Ordinance of 1787 laid out the steps that settlers had to take to organize territorial and state governments. By the time of Missouri's petition, eight new states had been created west of the Appalachian Mountains, with few questions raised about the status of slavery. Five of these eight states had been admitted as slave states. But times were changing. A growing number of people, especially in the Northeast, wanted to stop the expansion of slavery. For that reason, the issue of admitting Missouri quickly became a major crisis. Americans for the first time saw how serious a threat the slavery issue was to the future of the Union.

Why did a growing number of northern people oppose the expansion of slavery?

What was the Missouri Compromise?

Did the Missouri Compromise permanently settle the issue of slavery in the territories?

The Slavery Question in Congress

The controversy over Missouri statehood centered on the status of slavery in that future state. A growing number of people in the North, both in and out of Congress, objected to admitting Missouri as a slave state. Some opposed slavery on principle and were determined to stop its expansion. Others worried about the political balance of power between slave and free states. Up to that time, an equal number of slave and free states (11 each) had been admitted to the Union. This gave the two sides equal representation in the United States Senate. Missouri's admission as a slave state would upset this balance.

Congress had just taken up the bill enabling the people of Missouri to form a state when a member of Congress from New York introduced an antislavery amendment. Congressman James Tallmadge's amendment, introduced on February 13, 1819, provided that Missouri would be admitted only if the further introduction of slaves into that state were prohibited. The slaves already there would remain in slavery, except that all slave children born after the territory became a state would be freed when they reached the age of 25. Eventually the Tallmadge Amendment would make Missouri a free state. The House of Representatives approved this amendment, but it was rejected by the Senate. Congress adjourned for the summer without taking further action, but the issue was far from settled.

During the summer of 1819, the Missouri statehood bill became the center of attention in the North. In Trenton, Boston, New York, and several other cities, public meetings were held to rally support for the Tallmadge Amendment. Many of the meetings were organized by antislavery reformers who simply wanted to stop the expansion of slavery. Others were organized by Federalists who hoped to use the slavery issue to divide the Republicans and to revive their own party. As a result of the meetings and a great deal of newspaper publicity, all eyes were on Washington, D.C., when Congress met again that winter.

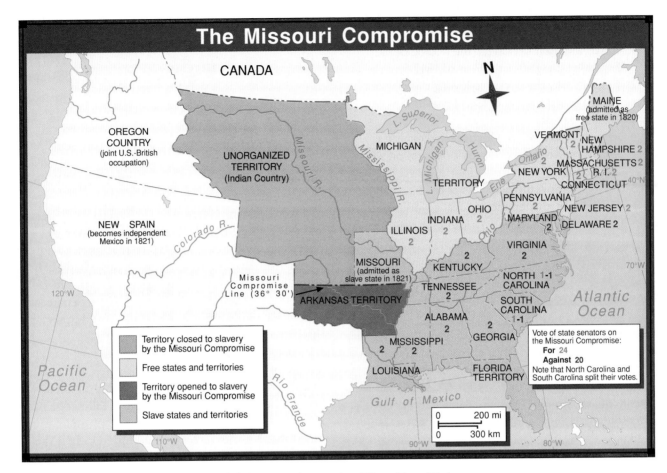

The Missouri Compromise

The Missouri statehood question divided Congress along sectional lines. How did the vote in the U.S. Senate reflect that division? How did the Missouri Compromise resolve the question of slavery in the territories?

Seats in the public gallery of the House and Senate were packed as the Missouri debate got under way. Many of the spectators were African American residents of the capital. The question of slavery was of far more immediate concern to them than to the congressmen taking part in the debate. Congressmen from free states warned that only by limiting the expansion of slavery could the North free itself from control by Virginia and the slave states. Every president since Jefferson had been a native of Virginia. With equal fervor, southern speakers took the position that any interference with slavery was a violation of the South's constitutional rights. A few even argued that restricting slavery would be grounds for the slave states to leave the Union.

The Missouri Compromise

As the debate grew more intense in the winter of 1820, several congressmen began to work out a compromise. Their solution was to admit Maine as a free state at the same time Missouri entered the Union as a slave state. That would maintain the balance between free and slave states. Senator Jesse B. Thomas of Illinois also proposed an amendment to the Missouri statehood bill that would settle the question of slavery in the remainder of the Louisiana Territory. The Thomas Amendment drew a line at 36 degrees 30 minutes (36° 30') latitude west from the boundary of Missouri to the frontier with Mexico. Slavery was prohibited in the territory north of that line and permitted south of it. Together, these provisions became known as the **Missouri Compromise**.

The compromise package had solid support in the Senate, but its chances seemed doubtful in the House. The great majority of northern congressmen still opposed the admission of Missouri as a slave state. The Missouri statehood bill finally passed after Speaker of the House Henry Clay managed to persuade 14 northern congressmen to vote with the South. The passage of the bill by the narrow margin of 90 to 87 was a testament to Henry Clay's skill as a politician. On March 3, 1820, Congress voted to admit Missouri as a slave state, to admit Maine as a free state, and to ban slavery from the Louisiana Purchase north of the 36° 30' line. This was the Missouri Compromise that President James Monroe signed into law three days later.

The Missouri Compromise of 1820 ended the crisis at hand but only temporarily settled the question of slavery in the West. Many Americans realized that slavery was the most dangerous issue ever to confront the nation. Senator Freeman Walker of Georgia warned that the slavery issue could mar the future by "feuds, civil wars, . . . a brother's sword crimsoned with a brother's blood, . . . our houses wrapt in flames, and our wives and infant children driven from their homes." The power of the slavery issue to tear the nation apart also alarmed the aging Thomas Jefferson. "This momentous question, like a fire bell in the night, awakened and filled me with terror," Jefferson wrote. The Missouri crisis, many Americans realized, had pushed the nation to the brink of disunion.

SECTION 2 REVIEW

1. **Explain** how Missouri's petition for statehood provoked a crisis.
2. **Identify** the Tallmadge Amendment.
3. **Identify** Senator Jesse Thomas (Illinois).
4. **List** the provisions of the Missouri Compromise of 1820.
5. **Explain** how the slavery issue created a threat of civil war.

SECTION 3

The Revival of Party Conflict

In the autumn of 1824, James Monroe was preparing to leave Washington, D.C., to return to private life. The president, once described as "a plain quiet man with a deeply reflective face," must have found little joy in the thought of retirement. His years in public service had left him bankrupt. He would have to sell his house to pay his debts. But Monroe could at least look back with satisfaction on his years in office and point to many solid accomplishments. During his administration, the national government had gained new stature both at home and abroad. Above all else, Monroe's presidency brought peace with foreign nations and relative harmony at home.

How did the election of 1824 bring the Era of Good Feelings to an end?

How did the revival of political conflict affect John Quincy Adams's presidential administration?

Why did the tariff become a source of sectional conflict?

An End to the Era of Good Feelings

As the election of 1824 approached, the question of who would succeed Monroe as president became a new source of conflict. Five prominent Republicans announced that they were candidates. Among them were three members of Monroe's cabinet: Secretary of the Treasury William H. Crawford of Georgia, Secretary of State John Quincy Adams of Massachusetts, and Secretary of War John C. Calhoun of South Carolina. Adams, an able administrator and intellectual, lacked the gift of being at ease among strangers. Calhoun was the youngest of the candidates. The other contenders were Congressman Henry Clay of Kentucky and General Andrew Jackson, the military hero from Tennessee.

Each candidate could count on support from his own region, but none had a large enough national following to carry the entire country. Calhoun, the youngest of the candidates, decided to settle for the vice presidency and served in that office under both Adams and Jackson. Consequently, the vote in the election of 1824 was split four ways, with no candidate receiving a majority. In such a case, the Twelfth Amendment required the House of Representatives to select a president from among the top three candidates. The three candidates with the most votes were Andrew Jackson, who received 99 votes in the electoral college; Adams, with 84 electoral votes; and Crawford, with 41 votes.

The House of Representatives cast a majority of its votes for John Quincy Adams. He won largely because Henry Clay, who ran fourth with 37 electoral votes, persuaded his supporters to vote for Adams. When Adams later named Clay as his secretary of state, the Jackson supporters, or Jacksonians, raised an outcry. They accused Adams and Clay of making a "corrupt bargain," which they claimed defeated the real wishes of the American people. Jackson, they pointed out, had the most electoral votes. No evidence exists that Adams struck a bargain of any kind with Clay, but by appointing him secretary of state—a traditional stepping stone to the presidency—Adams created the impression that the two men had made a deal.

The growth of democracy in the United States gave added emphasis to the Jacksonians' complaint. More eligible voters were participating in politics than ever before. In 1800, the voters in most states had not had the opportunity to vote for the president. The electors who cast their votes for president and vice president in the electoral college that year were chosen by state legislatures in 11 of the 16 states. By 1824, the voters themselves chose the electors in a majority of the states. Most of the states had also dropped the requirement that only property owners could vote. White male **suffrage** (the right of voting) was becoming the standard nationwide. As the political process became more open and democratic, elections at every level became more responsive to the popular will. But the Jacksonians insisted that had not been the case in the election of John Quincy Adams.

Adams's National Proposals

Shortly after he was inaugurated in 1825, John Quincy Adams presented Congress with an ambitious program for national development. To promote American manufacturing and to increase federal revenues, he asked Congress to raise the tariff rates on imported goods. The increased rates would bring more revenue into the U.S. Treasury. Higher tariff duty on imports also would help keep foreign-made goods out of the American market and stimulate American manufacturing. The growth of manufacturing towns and cities, in turn, would provide farmers with a larger domestic market for their crops. President Adams also proposed that Congress create a national observatory and a national university, and provide funds for scientific research. Finally, he recommended the adoption of a new standard of weights and measures based on the metric system used in Europe, a more effective patent law to encourage new inventions, and the creation of a Department of the Interior. This new department was to oversee the sale of public land and the orderly settlement of the West. Few presidents had come into office with such a clear vision of the nation's future and such a carefully thought-out plan for translating that vision into reality.

Despite his ambitious plans, John Quincy Adams accomplished very little. Andrew Jackson's supporters in Congress opposed Adams and his program at every turn. Bitter about their candidate's defeat, they launched an attack against the Adams administration and kept it up for four years. They denounced Adams's proposals as extravagant and aristocratic. Although a well-educated man with much experience in public life, John Quincy Adams was not a very good politician. He considered the presidency to be above politics, and refused to go to Congress to lobby for his proposals. He also did not try to rally popular support for his program. Unfortunately for Adams, public support for a stronger national government was waning, especially in the South. As a result, Adams would have little to show for his four years in office.

Sectional Conflict Revived

In 1828, Congress did enact a new and controversial tariff law. It was drafted by the Jacksonians in Congress in an effort to win votes for their candidate in the upcoming presidential election. They knew that both the Middle Atlantic states and the Midwest wanted tariff rates increased on certain items. The factory owners of New York and Pennsylvania wanted higher duties on manufactured goods to protect them from foreign competition. Midwestern wool growers wanted high tariffs to keep out cheap foreign wool. To gain support among these groups for their candidate, Jackson's supporters introduced a tariff bill that would raise import duties sharply. But they did not really expect such a high tariff bill to pass. They were much more interested in electing a president than in imposing high tariffs. Much to their surprise, the bill passed and the Tariff of 1828 became law.

The new tariff act was widely denounced, especially in the South, where it was called the **Tariff of Abominations**. Southern congressmen had once supported higher tariffs as a national good. But they had since lost most of their nationalist feelings. By 1828, they were far more concerned about protecting southern interests. Tariffs, they argued, benefited the North at the expense of the South. The South had few manufacturers, as it had concentrated its efforts on raising cotton. High tariff duties meant that southern cotton planters would have to pay more for the goods they had to import.

The publication of a pamphlet entitled *South Carolina Exposition and Protest* gave the debate over the tariff a new and more serious turn. Although published anonymously, the pamphlet was written by Vice President John C. Calhoun. In this piece, Calhoun argued that Congress had exceeded its

▲ *The caption for this cartoon reads: "Jackson is to be president, and you will be **HANGED**."*

powers in enacting a tariff. Moreover, he declared that states had the power to nullify, or refuse to enforce, any act of Congress that they decided had violated the Constitution. This became known as the **doctrine of nullification**. The states, and not the federal government, Calhoun argued, were supreme. This was the strongest assertion yet of the doctrine of states' rights.

Victorious Jacksonians

The election of 1828 was an abusive, mudslinging political campaign. The Jacksonians continued their attack against the "aristocratic Adams," going so far as to claim that Adams was a royalist who wanted to become king. The government, they charged, had fallen into the hands of an "aristocracy of officeholders," a privileged class that had lost touch with the American people. They promised to restore the government to the people.

President Adams's supporters launched a vicious counterattack. They portrayed Jackson as a drunk, a gunfighter, and a bully. They accused his wife of adultery, having discovered that she had married Jackson before she was legally divorced from her first husband.

Both sides engaged in mudslinging, but the Jacksonians were more successful in generating popular support. Jackson won a resounding victory, with 178 votes in the electoral college versus 83 for Adams.

The election of 1828 saw the emergence of a new political party. It was called the Democratic Party. Although organized solely to elect Andrew Jackson to the presidency, the party became a permanent fixture in American politics. It was strongest in the West and South, where Jackson drew most of

States' Rights and the Theory of Nullification

Before the Supreme Court's power of judicial review was confirmed by *Marbury v. Madison* (1806), states' righters declared their support of the doctrine of nullification, or in legal language, *interposition*. This doctrine allows for states to nullify, or cancel, laws and acts enacted by the federal government.

Both Thomas Jefferson and James Madison believed that the federal government existed only as an agent of the various states. Madison wrote, ". . . in case of a deliberate, palpable, and dangerous exercise . . . of powers not granted by the [Constitution], the States . . . have the right and are in duty bound to interpose for arresting the progress of the evil, and for maintaining within their respective limits the authorities, rights, and liberties appertaining to them." In plain language, this meant that the States had a duty to stop the federal government when it attempted to take on powers not specifically listed in the Constitution.

Then, in 1828, in response to the detested Tariff of Abominations, John C. Calhoun of South Carolina proposed that a majority of people within a state could veto federal actions and block enforcement of a federal law. This theory of the *concurrent majority* was tested in 1832 when South Carolina adopted the Ordinance of Nullification in response to another detested tariff. The ordinance not only declared the tariff "null, void, and no law," but forbade its citizens to appeal to federal courts, demanded that state officials swear an oath to support the ordinance, and declared the right of the state to secede from the Union should the federal government attempt to collect any tariffs.

President Andrew Jackson met this challenge to federal authority head on. He declared Calhoun's ordinance treasonous and stated that "The Constitution of the United States, then, forms a *government,* not a league . . . in which all the people are represented, which operates directly on the people individually."

The Union victory in the Civil War eventually settled the nullification issue, and the supremacy of the federal government over the states was firmly

▲ *This controversial tariff sharply increased import duties and became known in the South as the "Tariff of Abominations."*

established. Upon occasion, however, echoes of the old debate would be heard again. The cry of the states' righters against federal intrusion into local affairs would be raised again during the desegregation battles of the 1950s—this time, to no avail.

————◆————

1. What was James Madison's attitude toward states' rights?
2. Why do you think the Constitution did not declare the federal government supreme over state governments in all areas?

his support. John Quincy Adams and Henry Clay continued to lead the party established by Thomas Jefferson and his supporters, which was now called the National Republican Party.

SECTION 3 REVIEW

1. **Explain** how the candidate with the largest number of popular votes failed to win the election of 1824.
2. **Define** suffrage.
3. **List** five projects or proposals John Quincy Adams hoped to accomplish as president.
4. **Explain** why Adams accomplished so little.
5. **Name** the two major political parties involved in the election of 1828.

SECTION 4

Jacksonian Democracy

The inauguration of Andrew Jackson in March 1829 set the tone for his administration. Washington was packed with people who had come to watch the new president take office. "I never saw such a crowd here before," said Senator Daniel Webster of Massachusetts. "Persons have come 500 miles to see General Jackson." Fifteen to twenty thousand people gathered at the east portico of the Capitol to see Jackson take the oath of office. The reception that followed at the White House was a mob scene. The building was jammed with people who were hoping to shake the president's hand. The horde of well-wishers overturned the punch bowls, smashed the china, and stood with muddy boots on satin-covered chairs in order to catch a glimpse of their hero. It was a spontaneous outpouring of loyalty and affection unlike anything the nation's capital had ever seen before. It was truly a democratic inauguration.

How did Andrew Jackson respond to South Carolina's nullification of the Tariff Act?

Why did Jackson attack the Bank of the United States?

What were the economic consequences of the president's bank veto?

Jackson Takes Office

The new president moved quickly to fulfill his campaign promise to bring new people into the federal government. His first step was to remove from office several hundred clerks and government officials, mainly those who were suspected of working against his election. He replaced them with loyal Democrats and campaign workers. This policy of rewarding campaign workers and supporters with government jobs became known as the **spoils system**. The term comes from a phrase in a speech to the Congress by William L. Marcy: " . . . to the victor belong the spoils . . . ." Marcy was a member of the New York Democratic political organization headed by **Martin Van Buren**, who became Jackson's secretary of state. Altogether, Jackson replaced about 20 percent of the federal employees with his own followers. Although he did not make a clean sweep of the federal offices, Jackson removed enough officeholders to provide federal jobs for many of his supporters.

To Andrew Jackson, restoring government to the people also meant reversing the trend toward bigger government. He was convinced that the recent trend toward a more active federal government was dangerous and corrupting. He agreed with Thomas Jefferson that government is best (or at least most democratic and virtuous) which governs least. The government, he charged, had fallen into the hands of bankers, owners of corporations, and

▶

Andrew Jackson's supporters called him "Old Hickory." Did Jackson, as president, live up to this name?

◀ *In his reply to Senator Robert Y. Hayne of South Carolina in 1830, Daniel Webster stated that the Constitution made the federal government, not the states, the sovereign power. What tragic event finally settled this basic disagreement?*

wealthy people. They benefited from high tariffs and other government favors. Jackson was determined to trim back the power of the federal government.

Defending the Federal Union

Although Jackson wanted the federal government to be less active, he did not share the radical views about the rights of the states that were then becoming popular in the South. He did not agree with the position that Senator Robert Y. Hayne of South Carolina had defended in 1830 in a debate with Senator Daniel Webster of Massachusetts. In a speech about public lands, Hayne argued that a state had the right to declare federal laws null and void. The speech touched off a major debate in the Senate, with Webster arguing that the national government was supreme and that federal laws could not be set aside at the whim of a state government. He insisted that the federal government, not the states, was the great protector of American liberty. "Liberty *and* Union, now and forever, one and inseparable!" Webster exclaimed, in one of the most celebrated speeches in American history.

A nationalist at heart, Jackson was much closer to Webster's position than to Hayne's. Hayne's ideas were a restatement of John C. Calhoun's doctrine of nullification. At the annual Jefferson Day dinner in April 1830, Jackson confronted Calhoun directly in an exchange of toasts: "Our *federal* Union—it *must* be *preserved*." Vice President Calhoun, standing his ground, toasted in reply: "The Union—next to our liberty the most dear."

Nullification and Tariffs

The issue of nullification finally came to a head in 1832, when Congress enacted a new tariff law. Southern planters and farmers, pushed to the edge of bankruptcy by falling cotton prices, blamed many of their troubles on the tariff. The duties or taxes imposed by the tariff law increased the cost of the imported goods they bought. The tariff, they complained, robbed them of what little money they had. Many Southerners had wanted their state governments to nullify the existing tariff of 1828, but Calhoun had advised them to be patient. Congress might accomplish the same result by passing a new and lower tariff act. Much to the South's dismay, the Tariff Act of 1832 kept duties high.

The state of South Carolina responded to the new tariff legislation by holding a nullification convention. The assembled delegates declared that the tariff acts of 1828 and 1832 were "unauthorized by the Constitution" and were "null, void, and no law, nor binding upon this State, its officers or citizens." In so doing, the delegates placed themselves above the authority of Congress.

The Compromise Tariff Jackson responded quickly to South Carolina's act of defiance. By an executive proclamation, he denounced the state's attempt to nullify federal law. State nullification, he asserted, was "incompatible with the existence of the Union . . . and destructive of the great object for which it was formed." When South Carolina replied that it would "repel force with force," Jackson brought the crisis to a head by placing the forts in the Charleston harbor on alert and by putting an officer whom he could trust, General Winfield Scott, in command of all U.S. Army forces in South Carolina. Senator Hayne resigned from the Senate to return to South Carolina, where, as the newly appointed governor, he began preparations for war. The state legislature, in turn, elected Vice President John C. Calhoun to take Hayne's seat in the Senate. Calhoun thereupon resigned the vice presidency.

In January 1833, Jackson asked Congress for authority to use federal troops to collect the tariff. This led to a battle in Congress over the Force Bill, a measure which gave the president the authority that he wanted. Calhoun led the opposition to the bill in the Senate. As the crisis deepened, Henry Clay came to the rescue. He introduced a new tariff bill into Congress that would reduce the duties on imports. At this point, South Carolina backed down. No other state had come to its aid, and it was in no position to take on the federal government alone. Accepting a compromise solution, South Carolina promised to repeal its act of nullification in return for the reduction of the tariff provided by Clay's tariff bill. Thus, on the same day that Congress passed the Force Bill, it also enacted the so-called Compromise Tariff of 1833, which reduced tariff rates. South Carolina kept its promise, but it refused to concede that nullification was wrong. To emphasize this point, the state promptly nullified the Force Bill.

Jackson and the Bank of the United States

When the nullification issue came to a head in 1832, Jackson was already engaged in a battle against the Bank of the United States. This was the second Bank of the United States, created by Congress in 1816, which had replaced the earlier bank created by Alexander Hamilton. To many Jacksonians, the second bank had come to symbolize the special interests that were corrupting the government. It was the nation's most powerful financial institution and largest depository of federal funds. Certain that the bank used its funds to influence Congress, Jackson saw it as a grave threat to democratic government. He even suspected that the bank had given money to candidates who opposed his election in 1828. Jackson was determined to prevent the renewal of the bank's charter, which was due to expire in 1836.

In his war with the Bank of the United States, Jackson had the support of other enemies the bank had made. Chief among them were the rival banks chartered by the states and the customers of these banks. Less carefully managed than the national bank, the state banks had printed large quantities of paper money. Their paper dollars were supposed to be backed by gold, but the state banks had issued far more paper dollars than they had gold in their vaults. These state bank notes, in turn, were loaned to farmers and land speculators. They used them to buy land, which they hoped to sell later at a higher price. They profited from easy credit. To keep land speculation in check, the Bank of the United States would from time to time present bundles of state bank notes to the banks and ask for payment in gold. Such requests would force the state banks to call in loans, reducing, or contracting, the amount of bank credit available. Thus land speculators who had borrowed money to buy land had to sell it for whatever it would bring in order to repay their loans. New loans were harder to get. Such a contraction in 1819, caused partly by the Bank of the United States, had plunged the nation into a major depression.

The Democratic Spirit in Art

The democratic spirit of the Age of Jackson was reflected in American art. A new generation of painters who came of age after 1830 looked to common people and everyday scenes for inspiration. They turned away from the historical and literary themes that were the fashion in painting at that time. Instead, they painted pictures with everyday settings, such as barnyards, general stores, and the interiors of farmhouses and inns. They portrayed people doing such ordinary things as hunting, talking politics, and bargaining for a horse. These American artists were influenced by the realistic pictures of Dutch painters from the seventeenth century, whose paintings they had seen in museums. But unlike the Dutch masters, the American painters used subject matter that was purely American.

The first and one of the best of these new painters was William Sidney Mount (1807–1868), who painted rural Long Island scenes depicting the routines of country life. Mount, who grew up on a farm on Long Island, had set out to become a portrait painter in New York City. Forced by an illness to return home, he began painting scenes from everyday life instead. Other artists followed in Mount's footsteps. Among them was Richard Caton Woodville

▲ *This painting by George Caleb Bingham is entitled* The Verdict of the People. *It was painted about 1855.*

(1825–1856), who grew up in Baltimore. Woodville's subjects were city dwellers.

Perhaps the best known of the Americans who painted pictures of this kind was George Caleb Bingham (1811–1879). Having spent most of his youth on the Missouri frontier, Bingham used western settings for most of his paintings. Among the most popular of his paintings is *The Verdict of the People*, an election-day scene set in a western town. It captures the most dramatic moment of a local election: the announcement of the results. The winner is celebrating in the street. The loser looks on, sad-faced and glum. Although in politics Bingham was a member of

the Whig Party, the party that had emerged by 1840 to oppose the Democrats, his paintings captured the spirit of Jacksonian democracy.

1. Name the new subjects that the artists of this generation chose for their paintings.
2. In what ways did the paintings of Mount, Woodville, and Bingham reflect the democratic spirit of the Age of Jackson?

Controlled by eastern bankers, the Bank of the United States was especially resented in the West and South, where people often blamed the bank for hard times. In these sections of the country, Jackson found support for his campaign against the bank.

The confrontation between Jackson and the bank took place sooner than he had anticipated. In 1831, Nicholas Biddle, the bank's president, asked Congress for an early charter renewal. Biddle was advised to do so by Henry Clay, who planned to run against Jackson in the 1832 presidential election. Clay wanted to force Jackson to veto the bank's charter before the election, hoping it would cost him votes.

Andrew Jackson accepted the challenge. "The bank is trying to kill me, but I will kill it," he remarked. When Congress passed the bill renewing the bank's charter in July 1831, Jackson vetoed it. In his veto message, the president lashed out against special interests. Chartering the bank and granting it special privileges, Jackson wrote, only made "the rich richer and the potent more powerful." Only by getting rid of such institutions could the nation return to a simple republican government that "shower[s] its favors alike on the high and the low, the rich and the poor." Clay had made the bank an issue, but Jackson had quickly turned the issue to his advantage.

The bank veto helped Jackson win the presidential election of 1832. Clay had badly misjudged the attitude of farmers in the South and West toward the bank. Jackson's bank veto was especially popular in those sections. Clay finished with only 49 votes in the electoral college to Jackson's 219.

▲ This 1832 cartoon shows Jackson destroying the Bank of the United States by withdrawing the government's deposits. How does the cartoon support Jackson's charge that the bank was a corrupt influence in American politics?

The Specie Circular Jackson's bank veto, however, had unfortunate economic results. After he was reelected, Jackson withdrew government deposits from the bank and placed them in several dozen state banks. With these new deposits of gold on hand, many of the state banks printed new paper money, much of which they loaned to land speculators. The speculators used the dollars to buy public land from the federal government, which they would then try to resell to settlers at a handsome profit. This rapid expansion of credit drove up land values. To bring down the soaring price of land, Jackson was forced in July 1836 to issue an executive order called the **Specie Circular**, which demanded payment in **specie** (gold and silver coin) for public lands. Unable to make payments in the more plentiful paper money, many land speculators went broke, and land values collapsed. The sudden deflation of land values helped bring on the depression of 1837. Jackson had completed his second term by that time, but the depression made the presidency of his successor, Martin Van Buren, one of deepening gloom.

Van Buren's Administration President Van Buren was confronted with economic disaster shortly after his inauguration, as land values collapsed and the price of cotton fell by 50 percent. In the cities, unemployment rates soared, and many businesses went bankrupt. Van Buren could do little in response, as the Democratic Party was firmly committed to a policy of *laissez-faire*. Those who favored this policy, favored a minimum of government interference. Van Buren did manage to take federal funds out of weak state banks before they collapsed. He also proposed a "subtreasury" system independent of the banks in which to deposit federal funds. Opposed by those who preferred to recharter the Bank of the United States, even this limited measure was stalled in Congress for three years. It finally passed in 1840, the final year of Van Buren's administration. Although a capable man and an astute party politician, Van Buren accomplished little as president.

A New Opposition Party

During Jackson's second administration (1833–1837), a new opposition party emerged. At first, it was only a loose coalition of Adams and Clay followers, who called themselves National Republicans. By 1840, they had put together a new organization called the Whig Party. They borrowed the name Whig from the eighteenth-century English Whig party that had fought to limit the power of the king. The opponents of Jackson decided that Whig was an appropriate name for the party opposing "King Andrew," as they referred to the president after his bank veto.

The Whigs stood for a more active use of the federal government, including such economic policies as a high tariff to help protect American manu-

▲ *This political cartoon shows Jackson as "King Andrew the First."*

facturers from foreign competition, a national bank, and federal assistance for road and canal building. Much of their support came from the industrializing Northeast, from the urban middle class, and from prosperous farmers and planters.

In 1840, the Whigs dealt the Democrats and Van Buren a crushing defeat. They chose as their presidential candidate **William Henry Harrison**, a popular military hero. Harrison's defeat of the Shawnee Indians and their allies at the Battle of Tippecanoe made him a favorite in the West. The Whigs appealed to southern voters by nominating **John Tyler** of Virginia as Harrison's running mate. Their favorite campaign slogan was "Tippecanoe and Tyler, Too." Using torchlight parades and noisy political rallies, the Whigs turned out the largest number of voters for any presidential election up to that time. Seventy-eight percent of the eligible voters went to the polls (compared to 56 percent in

1828), giving Harrison a majority in the electoral college of 234 votes to Van Buren's 60 votes. The Whig party had emerged as a major force on the American political scene. From this time on, the two-party system became a permanent feature of national elections. Never again was only one party represented as during the Era of Good Feelings.

SECTION 4 REVIEW

1. **Explain** Andrew Jackson's position on nullification.
2. **State** Jackson's reasons for vetoing the bill that would have renewed the charter of the Bank of the United States.
3. **Explain** briefly why the Bank of the United States was unpopular in the South and West.
4. **Define** the term *laissez-faire*.
5. **Describe** the strategy that allowed the Whigs to defeat the Democrats in 1840.

SECTION 5

Religion and Reform

In the spring of 1831, the town of Rochester, New York, was buzzing with excitement. Charles G. Finney, the most stirring evangelist of his day, was preaching at the Third Presbyterian Church. Finney's message was simple and clear. By sinning no more, Christians could save themselves from the eternal fires of hell. By joining together, they could remake the sinful earth into the perfect Kingdom of Christ in as little as three months' time. Finney's powerful message electrified his listeners. "You could not go upon the streets," one Rochester citizen recalled, "and hear any conversation, except upon religion." Even the high school stopped classes to pray. Such was the beginning of the Great Revival.

How did the Great Revival generate support for social reforms?

How did the new movement to abolish slavery differ from earlier antislavery efforts?

How did the movement to abolish slavery create support for women's rights?

Religion and Reform

The wave of religious fervor that historians have called the **Second Great Awakening**, or the Great Revival, swept through the Northeast in the early 1830s. This **revival**, or renewal of religious interest, began in the towns of upstate New York, swept east to New York City and Boston, and west into Ohio and neighboring states. During the Second Great Awakening, church membership in the Northeast nearly doubled. Dozens of new churches were built. The spirit of religion transformed people's lives. Men and women who were heavy drinkers, who were habitually late for work, and who made life miserable for spouses and children became—at least for a time—sober, punctual, kind, and model Christians. The Second Great Awakening was, said **Lyman Beecher**, a Connecticut minister, "the greatest work of God, and the greatest revival of religion, that the world has ever seen."

The Second Great Awakening was also a powerful force for reform. It inspired many Americans who lived in the towns and cities of the Northeast to work for the perfection of society as well as for the perfection of individuals. Dozens of reform societies, many of them women's associations, were organized to uplift society. Among them were organizations devoted to keeping the Sabbath as a day of religious observance, to ending prostitution, and to outlawing gambling. Charitable organizations were founded to improve the condition of the urban poor. Other groups worked to provide better treatment of prisoners and of the insane. Perhaps the best

▶

Charles G. Finney, a Presbyterian minister, was a leader of the Great Revival of the 1830s. How did religion influence social reform?

▶ *This illustration shows a revival leader preaching at a Methodist camp meeting. What needs besides religious did these meetings fulfill?*

publicized of the reform efforts spawned by the revival was the **temperance movement** which aimed to reduce the use of alcohol.

The Temperance Movement

The temperance movement tried to persuade Americans to be more moderate in their consumption of alcohol. It was a monumental task. The United States of the early nineteenth century was a nation of hard drinkers. European visitors were astonished at the volume of beer, wine, and liquor that Americans consumed. As Englishman William Cobbett reported, "You cannot go into hardly any man's house without being asked to drink wine, or spirits, even *in the morning*." For some years, physicians had spoken out against excessive drinking as harmful to health, urging Americans to be more temperate in their use of alcohol. But their words had little effect.

By the 1830s, temperance leaders had taken up the methods of the Second Great Awakening to get their message across. They set out to convince Americans that liquor was an invention of the devil. Thus, they transformed the temperance movement into a moral crusade. At temperance meetings across the country, speakers warned that alcohol was a de-stroyer of homes and a cause of poverty, crime, and immorality. Their national organization, the American Temperance Society, had no fewer than 5,000 state and local chapters by 1834. Hundreds of thousands of Americans took the pledge to avoid alcohol, to be a "cold-water man," a "teetotaler."

Temperance reformers also worked to outlaw the sale of liquor. By 1855, the sale of alcohol was illegal throughout New England, in New York State, and in many places in the Midwest. Most of these laws were later repealed or struck down by the courts, but the legal prohibition of alcohol in this period set an important precedent for the temperance movement in the early 1900s.

Reformers Attack Social Problems

The belief that individuals and society were "perfectible" was a powerful force for social reform. Educational reformers argued that providing children with better schools would lead to a more perfect world. Perhaps the best-known school reformer was Horace Mann, who expanded the public school system of Massachusetts, making it a model for other states. Several states passed compulsory attendance laws to bring children under the good influence of the schools. To expand educational

►

Temperance leaders got their message across with pictures as well as words. What social class was the target of this message?

opportunities for girls, Emma Willard opened the Troy Female Seminary, a girls' high school.

In a similar spirit, social workers set out to eliminate poverty in the urban slums by trying to persuade the poor to be more virtuous, thrifty, and temperate.

While they failed to eliminate poverty, other social reformers did succeed in improving the treatment of the insane. Before the nineteenth century, people who suffered from mental illness were kept in poorhouses and in jails. In 1843, Dorothea Dix investigated the treatment of the insane in Massachusetts. She was shocked to discover that the insane were confined in "cages, closets, cellars, stalls, pens! Chained, naked, beaten with rods, and lashed into obedience!" She prodded the Massachusetts legislature to expand its state hospital for the insane. By 1854, she had traveled more than 30,000 miles to help reformers from New England to Louisiana pass legislation to create asylums for the insane.

Model Communities Built

To provide models for a more perfect society, reformers also founded a number of experimental

▼ *This 1868 woodcut depicts an "insane asylum" in New York.*

communities. Some, like the Harmony settlement in southern Indiana, were the work of religious groups. Harmony was founded in 1815 by a group that broke away from the German Lutheran Church. These Germans had immigrated to the United States under the leadership of George Rapp to live according to his strict religious teachings. They turned over their private property and wealth to the community as part of their attempt to live in harmony with one another. Social order was also maintained by the strong will of "Father" Rapp, who insisted, for example, that all quarrels be settled before the end of each day.

Other model communities were founded on ideas about equality and cooperative living. Several were based on the ideas of Charles Fourier (foor-YAY), a French social thinker. In the Fourier communities, the highest wages were paid to those with the least attractive rather than the most glamorous jobs. At Brook Farm, a Fourier community near Boston, manual labor was divided equally among all the inhabitants. When New England author Nathaniel Hawthorne arrived at Brook Farm in 1841, he was immediately handed a pitchfork and asked to clean out the stables. Most of the nonreligious communities, including Brook Farm, failed after a few years. Although born of a desire to create a better world, they usually fell victim to poor management, internal disputes, and unrealistic expectations.

The Abolitionist Movement

By the early 1830s, many whites in both the North and the South had come to see slavery as a serious blemish on American society. The enslavement of African Americans obviously contradicted the doctrine expressed in the Declaration of Independence that all people are created equal. Some Americans also opposed slavery on moral grounds, especially those who belonged to the Quaker religion. By 1805, all of the northern states had either outlawed slavery or had provided for the gradual **emancipation**, or freeing, of slaves. Becoming in-

creasingly more important in the South, slavery was dying out in the North.

In 1817, people who supported the emancipation of slaves in the South founded the American Colonization Society. It called for the gradual emancipation of the slaves, with the freed slaves to be sent to colonies in Africa. This, however, promised to be a long and expensive process, as slave owners would have to emancipate their slaves voluntarily and be compensated for their financial loss.

Not everyone accepted the idea of gradual emancipation and colonization. It met serious resistance among African Americans, especially those who had already gained their freedom. Among them was David Walker, a free African American who was born in North Carolina to parents who were former slaves. In 1829, Walker moved to Massachusetts. Shortly after his arrival, he published a pamphlet that urged African Americans to use violent means, if necessary, to win their freedom. *David Walker's Appeal*, as the pamphlet was commonly known, sent shock waves through the South, where it was condemned as "the diabolical Boston Pamphlet." Walker died in 1830, but the idea of an immediate **abolition**, or end, of slavery continued to gain ground.

The most outspoken white advocate of immediate abolition was **William Lloyd Garrison**. In January 1831, Garrison published the first issue of the *Liberator*, a radical antislavery newspaper. The Boston editor, who was only 26 years old, took sharp issue with the colonization movement. In contrast to that gradual and voluntary approach, Garrison demanded the immediate and unconditional abolition of slavery. Slavery was such a great evil, he argued, that gradual emancipation was an immoral choice. "Tell the mother to gradually extricate her babe from the fire into which it has fallen, but urge me not to use moderation in a cause like the present." He denounced slave owners as tyrants, "man-stealers," and immoral people. He was impatient and unbending. "I will be as harsh as truth, and as uncompromising as justice," he proclaimed.

Among Garrison's earliest supporters were free African Americans who lived in the northern states. One of Garrison's most famous contributors was **Frederick Douglass**, an escaped slave who earned enough money from lectures and writing to pur-

▲ *William Lloyd Garrison, publisher of* The Liberator.

▶

The Appeal, *written by an African American, was the first pamphlet published in the United States calling for the abolition of slavery.*

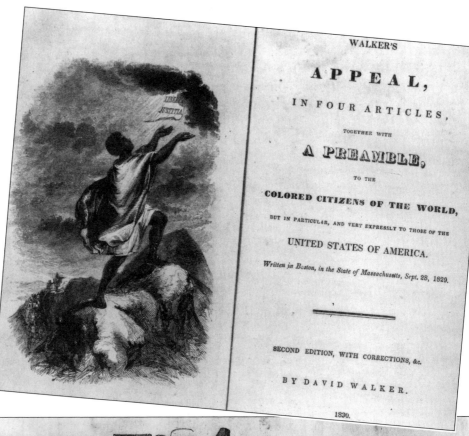

WALKER'S

APPEAL,

IN FOUR ARTICLES,

TOGETHER WITH

A PREAMBLE,

TO THE

COLORED CITIZENS OF THE WORLD,

BUT IN PARTICULAR, AND VERY EXPRESSLY TO THOSE OF THE

UNITED STATES OF AMERICA.

Written in Boston, in the State of Massachusetts, Sept. 28, 1829.

SECOND EDITION, WITH CORRECTIONS, &c.

BY DAVID WALKER.

1830.

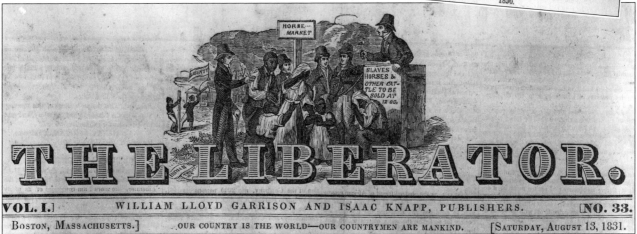

▲ The Liberator *was an antislavery newspaper. Why did the abolition of slavery attract white reformers such as Garrison as well as African Americans?*

chase his freedom. Although they numbered only about 130,000 people in a population of more than 6 million in the North, African Americans played a major role in the abolitionist movement. They were among the first to subscribe to the *Liberator*, and they organized the first local societies to support the abolitionist cause.

Those who supported the new antislavery movement were dedicated and well organized. In 1833, the abolitionists organized the American Anti-Slavery Society, which sent lecturers and organizers out to speak in every available church, community hall, and city auditorium. By the mid-1840s, the movement had some 1,300 local societies with a total membership of 250,000. It extended from Boston to New York City and across the state of New York to Ohio. Since many local societies restricted their membership to men, women organized their own antislavery groups.

White support for abolition came from the same people attracted to other reform movements. Abolitionists tended to come from religious families that had been influenced by the revival movements of recent years.

Resistance to the Movement

The abolitionist movement met with strong and sometimes violent opposition. In Charleston, South Carolina, a mob broke into the post office to seize and burn antislavery literature that was being sent through the mail. Even in the North, abolitionist meetings were broken up and antislavery speakers attacked. In Boston, a mob dragged William Lloyd

People Who Made a Difference

Frederick Douglass

By the 1840s, Frederick Douglass was the best known African American abolitionist in the United States. He was born in 1817 in Baltimore with the name Frederick Augustus Washington Bailey, the son of an enslaved African American and a white father. As a house servant in Baltimore, he had learned to read and write. He also worked in a local shipyard. At the age of 21, he escaped, made his way north, and changed his name to Frederick Douglass. He settled in New Bedford, Massachusetts, where he took a job as a common laborer.

In 1841, three years after his escape from slavery, Douglass attended a convention of the Massachusetts Anti-Slavery Society. There he delivered a speech that so deeply moved the society's leaders that they immediately hired him as an antislavery lecturer. Thereafter, Douglass devoted a

▲ *Frederick Douglass.*

great deal of time to the antislavery movement. He spoke frequently at abolitionist rallies throughout the North, and he was often attacked by proslavery mobs. In 1845, he published *A Narrative of the Life of Frederick Douglass*, an account of his experiences as a slave. Afraid that he would be captured as a runaway slave, Douglass lived in England from 1845 to

1847. He made enough money there as an antislavery speaker to buy his freedom when he returned to the United States.

Although Douglass wrote articles for the *Liberator*, he and Garrison disagreed over the tactics abolitionists should use. Garrison emphasized moral persuasion. Douglass thought the abolitionists should use every means at their disposal, including political action. In 1847, he broke with Garrison and founded his own abolitionist newspaper, the *North Star*, which he published in Rochester, New York. This journal gave African Americans their own voice within the antislavery movement.

1. What factors do you think made Douglass a sought-after speaker for abolitionist rallies?
2. What caused Douglass and Garrison to go their separate ways, although they were both abolitionists?

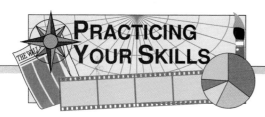

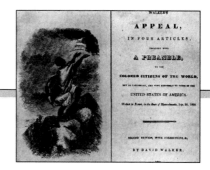

Identifying Propaganda

Words are powerful forces for change. When Thomas Paine wanted to convince others of the justice of the Patriot cause in colonial America, he used the cheapest and most effective means of reaching the greatest number of people at that time. His pamphlets entitled *Common Sense* and *The American Crisis* became "overnight best sellers." Although written for a worthy cause, they are good examples of propaganda literature. Below are some excerpts from *The American Crisis*:

> "These are the times that try men's souls."
> "Tyranny, like hell, is not easily conquered."
> "Every Tory is a coward; for servile, slavish, self-interested fear is the foundation of Toryism; and a man under such influence, though he may be cruel, never can be brave."

The term *propaganda* today has mostly negative associations. Many people believe that propaganda consists of untrue and biased statements. This is often the case, but not always. Propaganda is any information that is presented with the purpose of persuading to a particular point of view. When looking at a pamphlet to determine whether or not it is propaganda, ask the following:

- **What is the intention of the author?** Does the author state openly his or her purpose? Is the pamphlet sponsored by an organization that is closely allied with a particular political party or cause?
- **Are statements of opinion presented as facts?** Opinions are expressions of belief. Facts can be proven to be true or false. Learn to recognize when an opinion is presented as fact.
- **Does the pamphlet present both sides of the issue fairly?** Often a piece of writing will appear to present both sides, but will only present the weakest arguments of one side and the strongest points of the other side.
- **Does the writing style appeal more to emotions than to rational argument?** It is easier to convince people if you involve their emotions in the process.

David Walker urged enslaved African Americans to rise up against the institution of slavery:

> America is more our country than it is the whites'— we have enriched it with our blood and tears . . . . The whites want slaves, and want us for their slaves, but some of them will curse the day they ever saw us.

Look carefully at the reproduction of Walker's pamphlet on page 261. Study the *frontispiece* (illustration preceding the title page) then read again the excerpt from the *Appeal* before you answer these questions.

1. How does the writing style of the title page differ from the excerpt? In what way are the two styles similar? Would this title encourage you to read the pamphlet? Why, or why not?
2. Examine the frontispiece engraving. Notice how symbols are used to create an artistic style. What symbols can you identify? What concepts or moods are these symbols meant to convey? (Hint: Look for religious and classical themes.)
3. Walker knew that most of his intended audience was illiterate (could neither read nor write). How would that fact influence the style of his writing?
4. What facts or figures might Walker have included in his pamphlet if his main purpose had been to prove his point rationally rather than to compel his listeners to action?

Garrison through the streets by a rope tied around his body. The violence reached its peak in 1837 in Alton, Illinois, when a mob broke into an antislavery newspaper office and killed the editor, Elijah P. Lovejoy.

The defenders of slavery often succeeded in denying abolitionists the right of free speech. They smashed printing presses, disrupted meetings, and shouted down antislavery speakers. The national government also denied abolitionists a hearing. On May 26, 1836, the House of Representatives passed a resolution, the so-called **gag rule**, banning the discussion of antislavery petitions submitted to Congress. The rule was a clear violation of the First Amendment's guarantee that citizens have the right to petition the government, as John Quincy Adams and other antislavery congressmen pointed out. Nevertheless, it remained in effect for eight years, renewed at the beginning of each new session of Congress until 1844. (In 1830, ex-President John Quincy Adams had been elected to the House of Representatives, where he served his country for the next 16 years.)

▲ *Angelina (left) and Sarah Grimké (right) worked for the abolition of slavery and for women's rights. Why did they conclude that slaves and women had interests in common?*

Abolitionism As a Political Force

By 1840, abolitionism had become a political as well as a moral crusade. Most antislavery leaders recognized that they needed political influence to purge slavery from the land. The majority tried to work within the Whig Party, which was the dominant party in the Northeast. They supported Whig candidates who shared their views. Neither the Whig nor the Democratic Party had taken a stand on the slavery issue. Consequently, some abolitionists turned away from both parties. They founded a new party, called the Liberty Party, dedicated to the abolition of slavery. In its first presidential campaign in 1840, the Liberty Party won 3 percent of the popular vote for its candidate, James G. Birney. Although this was not an impressive showing, the birth of the Liberty Party did mark the beginning of abolitionism as an organized force in national politics.

Equal Rights for Women

In nineteenth-century America, women lacked full legal and political rights. Married women had no identity of their own in the eyes of the law. Laws prohibited women from voting. Public life, the legal and medical professions, and business careers were, for the most part, closed to women. Men and women who belonged to the middle class increasingly occupied separate spheres: men went off to the office or shop to work, while their wives remained at home. The popular media, including women's magazines, insisted that the home was women's proper sphere. Women's role, it was argued, was to obey their husbands and care for their children. In public, they should associate only with other women and not get involved in men's affairs. Many working-class women had to take jobs outside the home to help support their families, but they received only one-third to one-half the wages paid to men. The wages they earned belonged to their husbands by law. Many women accepted the limitations imposed on them, but others found them stifling and intolerable.

A growing number of women, especially those involved in the antislavery movement, refused to accept such limitations on their freedom. "The investigation of the rights of the slave has led me to a better understanding of my own," wrote Angelina Grimké, a well-known abolitionist. She and her sister, Sarah Grimké, had shocked the New England clergy by giving antislavery lectures before mixed audiences of men and women. The clergymen reminded them that a woman's duty was to obey men, not to lecture to them. That did not stop the Grimké sisters from lecturing. Instead, they devoted more of their time to defending the rights of women. In 1848, **Elizabeth Cady Stanton**, **Lucretia Mott**, and other advocates of full rights for women met at Seneca Falls, New York, to hold the first women's rights convention. The **Seneca Falls Convention** marked the beginning of the women's rights movement in the United States.

▲ *Elizabeth Cady Stanton addressed the first women's rights convention at Seneca Falls, New York, in 1848.*

The issue of women's rights split the abolitionist movement. William Lloyd Garrison openly championed the cause of equality for women. He and his followers supported the Grimké sisters' right to lecture to mixed audiences. They also favored admitting women as delegates to the annual meetings of the American Anti-Slavery Society. Many male abolitionists disagreed with Garrison. Some felt strongly that women should not meddle in men's affairs. Others agreed with Garrison but thought his timing was wrong. They cautioned that to raise the controversial issue of women's rights at that time would distract attention from the antislavery cause. The test came in 1840, when the American Anti-Slavery Society elected Abby Kelly to its all-male governing committee. A large number of male delegates walked out. The dissident group organized the American and Foreign Anti-Slavery Society, which divorced itself from the question of women's rights. In fact, most male abolitionists who supported women's rights considered this issue less important than the abolition of slavery.

SECTION 5 REVIEW

1. **Define** revival.
2. **Name** the major social reform movements that were under way in the 1830s.
3. **Describe** how the Second Great Awakening contributed to the movement for social reform.
4. **Explain** briefly how the abolitionist movement differed from earlier efforts to emancipate slaves.
5. **Explain** how involvement in the abolition movement often helped the women's rights movement.

Chapter 7 Review

Summary

The decade or so following the War of 1812 is often referred to as the Era of Good Feelings. The war and its successful conclusion had stimulated nationalist feelings that created an emotional bond among most citizens. What Americans had in common seemed more important than those things that divided them. National unity was reinforced by a series of Supreme Court decisions, which strengthened the federal government at the expense of the states. This mood of national unity made it easier for Congress to enact legislation designed to foster national economic development, such as the Tariff of 1816 and the bill chartering a new Bank of the United States. In the process, the Republican party adopted much of the economic program once identified with the Federalist party. This contributed to the downfall of the Federalist party.

The slavery issue briefly revived sectional conflict in 1819–1820, when Missouri petitioned for admission as a slave state. That crisis was settled by the Missouri Compromise of 1820. The election of 1824 and its aftermath produced a new era of political party conflict. The supporters of Andrew Jackson declared political warfare against President John Quincy Adams's administration. In 1828, Jackson won the presidency, but the political feuding continued. The major political battles of Jackson's two administrations were his fight against the Bank of the United States and against South Carolina's attempt to nullify federal tariff laws. Jackson left such an imprint on national politics that historians call this period the Age of Jackson or the Jacksonian Era.

A commitment to social progress and a belief in the possibility of individual and social perfection triggered a variety of reform movements during the Jacksonian Era. The temperance movement tried to change the drinking habits of the American people. Reformers worked to improve the treatment of the insane and of inmates in prisons. Other reformers attempted to develop new communities that would serve as models for a more perfect society. The two most controversial reform crusades of the period were the abolitionist and the women's rights movements. Both posed serious threats to the existing social order.

Vocabulary

abolition	partisan
American System	revival
cede	specie
doctrine of nullification	spoils system
emancipation	suffrage
gag rule	tariff
interstate commerce	temperance movement
laissez-faire	

On a separate piece of paper write the following headings: Politics and Government; Economics; and Social Movements. Write each of the vocabulary terms listed above under the appropriate heading.

Review Questions

1. Why do you think that the period following the War of 1812 was called the Era of Good Feelings?
2. How did the Supreme Court strengthen the federal government at the expense of the states?
3. Explain why a high protective tariff was generally favored by the northern states and opposed by southern states.
4. What prompted John C. Calhoun to write the pamphlet *South Carolina Exposition and Protest*?
5. Why did the Jacksonians charge John Quincy Adams and Henry Clay with striking a "corrupt bargain" in 1824?
6. What reasons can you offer for the lack of political success for John Quincy Adams?
7. What did Andrew Jackson mean when he accused the Bank of the United States of being a threat to democratic government?
8. What actions were taken by the abolitionists of this period to further their cause?

9. Describe the efforts made in this period to improve education.
10. Why did many people of the Jacksonian Era consider both abolitionism and women's rights to be radical movements?

Critical Historical Thinking

Writing   Answer each of the following questions by writing one or more complete paragraphs:

1. Americans became divided by a number of issues in the 1820s. Do you think the federal Union was more affected by the tariff and other economic issues or by the slavery issue?
2. Could the Missouri Compromise of 1820 have permanently settled the issue of slavery in the territories? Consult the map on page 246 as you consider your answer to this question.
3. Justify characterizing Jackson's presidency as an era of increased democracy in America.
4. President Jackson used the spoils system to place his supporters in appointed offices. Read the selection of the archives section entitled "Andrew Jackson on Rotation in Office." How did he defend removal of federal office holders?

Making Connections with Economics

We commonly think of banks as keepers and lenders of money. Banks have *reserves*, money they are required to keep on hand in case we want to withdraw funds. But *commercial banks*, unlike savings banks, create the majority of the money supply through the expansion of credit. When commercial banks lend money to their customers, they expand the money supply; when they withhold money by raising interest rates, the money supply contracts. The fact that commercial banks have the power to expand and contract the money supply is at the heart of Jackson's bank war. During a period of

prosperity, such as was occurring in the 1820s and 1830s, there was a strong demand for investment funds. However, if too much money flows into the economy, *inflation* is the result. Some investors would have overestimated *demand* for their goods and services. In other areas the *market* would soon be unable to absorb more investment. In both cases borrowers would find themselves unable to repay their loans. Thus, it is the job of the central bank to control the money supply by controlling the commercial banks. Today, the Federal Reserve Bank plays the role of the Second U.S. Bank in Jackson's day.

Writing   Using the school or public library, research the role of the Federal Reserve Bank in monitoring the money supply. Write a paragraph to answer the following question: What would be the effect on the money supply if the Federal Reserve Bank were to raise the prime lending rate?

Additional Skills Practice

Collect five or six pamphlets from a variety of sources, such as local and federal government offices, churches, stores, banks, street vendors, offices, hospitals, etc. Sort them according to the following purposes: (1) Persuasion (to convince others) (2) Advertising (to sell something) (3) Informational (to inform or educate). Analyze the style of the pamphlets in each category. Does one style do a better job than others of getting the message across? What effect does presentation have upon content? Are you more likely to believe something if you are impressed by its presentation? Create a display that presents your findings.

Westward Expansion

The West was a magnet that drew the American people by the thousands. It was a land of opportunity for every free, white American family that needed a new start in life and that could afford the cost of transportation. The settlement of the American West began in the woodlands of the Ohio and Mississippi River valleys, which were easily reached from the East by wagon roads and rivers. Later, settlers moved in wagon trains across the plains to Texas, California, and Oregon.

The West was a land of promise, but it was also a scene of tragedy.

American Indians paid a high price for the opportunities seized by white Americans. Indians were removed by force from their homelands. They, too, went West, but not by their own choice. They were resettled beyond the Mississippi River in places that white people thought unfit for civilized life.

Mexico also paid dearly for American expansion westward, losing its northern provinces through a war with the United States. Thus, the American West was a land of both hope and despair, victory and defeat.

▲ *Buckskin jackets like this were worn by fur trappers in the Rocky Mountains between 1806 and 1840.*

SECTIONS

1	2	3	4	5
The Westward Movement After 1812	Indian Removals	Texas and New Mexico	The Rockies, Utah, and the Oregon Country	Territorial Annexation and the Mexican War

The Westward Movement After 1812

Since the 1770s, restless families had made their way across the Appalachian Mountains, attracted by the West's abundance of cheap and fertile land. They settled first in Kentucky, following the Wilderness Road that legendary frontiersman Daniel Boone had opened to that frontier region. Next, they settled on land north of the Ohio River. But this early stream of migration was merely a trickle compared to the great numbers of emigrants heading west after the War of 1812. Travelers on the road from Philadelphia to Pittsburgh were amazed by what they saw. Morris Birkbeck, an Englishman on his way to Illinois, found himself "in the very stream of emigration.... We are seldom out of sight, as we travel on this grand track towards the Ohio, of family groups, behind and before us." For over 300 miles, the road was heavy with the traffic of people on horseback, families in light wagons, and lumbering Conestoga freight wagons. The scene on other major roads going west from Maryland and Virginia was much the same. "Old America," Birkbeck concluded, "seems to be breaking up, and moving westward."

What major roads led to the West?

What means of transportation, other than horseback and wagon, did Americans use to travel west?

Why were so many Americans moving west after 1812?

Major Highways to the West

Most westward-bound emigrants traveled by roads and **turnpikes** during the first phase of their journey. The turnpikes were privately built toll roads. This type of road got its name from a pole, or pike, at the tollgate. This pike was turned to admit

▲ *This Thomas Birch painting shows a Conestoga wagon on a turnpike in Pennsylvania around 1814. Why were people moving west willing to pay money to travel on turnpikes?*

traffic after the toll was paid. The major routes to the West were the Mohawk and Genesee Turnpike to Lake Erie, the Catskill Turnpike to the Allegheny River, the Forbes Road from Philadelphia to Pittsburgh, and the Cumberland and Wilderness Roads from Virginia and Maryland.

Although the private turnpikes were kept in good repair, the same could not always be said for the public roads. The roads in the western parts of Pennsylvania and Virginia were little more than forest trails. The Forbes Road, named for the British general who built it as a military road before the Revolution, still had low tree stumps standing in the roadway. One historian described the Wilderness Road, laid out by Daniel Boone, as "the longest, blackest, hardest road of pioneer days in America." The only road in reasonably good shape was the Cumberland Road, which extended from eastern Virginia and Maryland to the Ohio River town of Wheeling, Virginia (now a part of West Virginia). It was better known as the National Road after 1811, when it was taken over and maintained by the federal government. Despite the poor quality of these roads, they were still the major highways west to the Ohio River.

Steamboats Venture onto Western Rivers

In the American West of the 1830s, steamboats represented the cutting edge of transportation technology. A steamboat churning its way upriver presented unforgettable sights and sounds, with its engine pounding, its twin funnels or smokestacks belching smoke, and its decks standing high above the water.

To be a steamboat captain, Mark Twain would write, was every young man's ambition. It was also a hazardous occupation. Nearly 30 percent of the steamboats built before 1830 were destroyed in accidents. Some burned to the water level after their boilers exploded, often scalding the crew and passengers to death. Many had their hulls ripped open by snags, or submerged tree stumps, that had been carried downriver by the spring floods. But many people thought the risk of death and destruction a price worth paying for the benefits of working and traveling on the steamboat. The economic development of the West depended upon the rapid and cheap upriver transportation provided by the steamboat.

Steamboats were ideally suited to the American West, where rivers were the major routes of transportation. They brought dry goods and hardware up the Mississippi and Ohio Rivers and took soldiers and provisions to western army

▲ Robert Fulton's steamboat, the *Clermont*, traveled on the Hudson River in 1813. How much credit does Fulton deserve for the invention of the steamboat?

forts on the Missouri and Yellowstone Rivers. On their trip downriver, they carried pork, lead, and cotton to New Orleans, which oceangoing ships would then deliver to the markets of the world.

Although steamboats were widely used in the West, they were first developed in the eastern United States and in Great Britain. John Fitch had demonstrated a steam-powered paddleboat to the delegates attending the Constitutional Convention in Philadelphia in 1787, but its top speed was only three miles per hour. One of the onlookers was John Stevens, a New Jersey merchant. He built a successful steamboat in 1803, but it could only carry two or three people at a time. In England in 1801, John Symington built a paddle-wheel steamboat for a company that owned a canal, or man-made

waterway. It worked well, but the company refused to use it, afraid the wake from the paddle wheel would erode the banks of the canal.

Robert Fulton, who built the *Clermont* in 1807, had seen Symington's boat in England. Using a high-pressure steam engine imported from England, Fulton's boat greatly reduced the travel time between New York City and Albany. Thus, the invention of the steamboat was not a single event, but a process to which many people contributed.

1. Explain why steamboats were important to the commerce of the American West.
2. What can be learned about the process of invention from the development of the steamboat?

The Ohio River

Beyond the towns of Wheeling and Pittsburgh, the most heavily used "highway" to the West was the Ohio River. Most of the traffic going down the river was carried on flat-bottomed craft called flatboats. They floated downstream propelled by the current of the river. When they reached their destination, the boats were broken up and sold for lumber.

During the height of the emigration season, which lasted from May to November, the cargo carried by the flatboats that drifted down the Ohio River was amazingly diverse. Traveling downriver in the early 1820s, Timothy Flint saw one boat that carried a tinsmith's workshop. "In it all the different articles of tin-ware were manufactured and sold by wholesale and retail. . . . When they had mended all the tin, and vended [sold] all that they could sell in one place, they floated on to another." Such floating factories were not unusual, according to Flint. "A still more extraordinary manufactory, we were told, was floating down the Ohio," he continued. "Aboard this were manufactured axes, scythes, and all other iron tools of this description, and in it horses were shod. In short, it was a complete blacksmith's shop. . . . I have frequently seen in this region a dry goods shop in a boat, with its articles very handsomely arranged on shelves." During those emigration years, the Ohio River carried a floating cross section of American society.

A major improvement in western river travel took place in 1811 with the introduction of the steamboat. America's first commercially successful steamboat was built in 1807 by Robert Fulton. The *Clermont*, as it was officially named, although commonly known to a skeptical public as "Fulton's Folly," made its maiden voyage up the Hudson River that year. Unlike the flatboat, which could be poled against the current only with great difficulty, the steamboat could easily go upriver. These shallow-draft boats rode high in the water and could navigate all but the most shallow of the West's rivers. By 1830, nearly 200 steamboats were in use on the western rivers, with the number more than dou-

bling during the next ten years. By hauling goods quickly and cheaply, the steamboats cut transportation costs, brought increased profits to western farmers and merchants, and contributed to the growing prosperity of the West.

Cheap Transportation by Canal

Goods and people also went west by canal boat. The Erie Canal was the most famous of the canals to link the West with the eastern part of the United States. Completed in 1825, it provided an all-water connection between the Hudson River at Albany, New York, and Lake Erie. Financed by the state of New York at a cost of $7 million, the Erie Canal played an important role in the development of upstate New York. It also made New York City a major port for exporting farm products from the upper Midwest.

The success of the Erie Canal prompted other states to undertake their own canal projects. Canal promoters in Pennsylvania, Maryland, and Virginia built waterways from the seaboard to the western parts of those states. Canal projects in Ohio and Indiana were soon under way to connect the Great Lakes to the Ohio River. All these canals gave the

▼ *This scenic drawing of the Erie Canal was based on historical research. Why did canal boats become a popular way to travel west?*

American Landscape

Tying the Nation Together: The Conquest of Distance

By 1860, Americans had a country that extended from the Atlantic to the Pacific. Great chunks of land had been added to the nation. In 1803, the United States doubled its land area by buying the land between the Mississippi River and the Rocky Mountains from France. Texas, Oregon, and California joined the Union in the 1840s and 1850s. In 1853, the Gadsden Purchase of southern Arizona and southern New Mexico rounded out the frontiers of the continental United States.

Americans gradually built roads, canals, and railroads to tie this huge country together. In 1800, only farmers located on navigable rivers could transport grain, cotton, tobacco, or timber to coastal markets. The cost of moving goods 30 miles over local roads was as high as shipping goods 3000 miles across the Atlantic. Roads

were so inadequate that news of the signing of the Declaration of Independence in Philadelphia in 1776 took twenty-nine days to reach Charleston, South Carolina. Small wonder that Americans remained pinned to the Atlantic coast for nearly two centuries.

In the early 1800s, turnpikes were built to link east coast cities with the agricultural interior. The most ambitious of these turnpikes was the National Road, a federal highway that ran from Cumberland, Maryland, westward to Vandalia, Illinois. These turnpikes reduced the cost of short hauls, but, given the long distances involved, roads could not effectively connect the agricultural lands of the Middle West with population centers on the Atlantic coast.

Soon canals were built to connect bodies of water and the towns and cities located on them. In 1825, the Erie Canal connected

the Hudson River and New York City with Lake Erie. In the Middle West, canals joined the Ohio River and Mississippi River systems with the Great Lakes. Steamboats made it possible to transport goods thousands of miles along these inland waterways. By 1860, a thousand steamboats carried goods and people up and down the Mississippi, Missouri, and Ohio Rivers.

Steam railroads, however, were needed to overcome the huge distances that existed in the United States. By 1860, railroad lines bridged the Appalachian Mountains and connected the Atlantic coast and the Middle West. Chicago became the railroad hub of the interior plains. The first transcontinental railroad to California was completed in 1869. By 1883, four rail lines crossed the continent.

These improvements reduced the time and cost of transportation in the United States. Each region

West an inexpensive way to ship its surplus agricultural products and lumber to market.

Travel by canal was cheap and reasonably pleasant. On the Erie Canal, the fare on packet boats, as the first-class boats were called, was four cents per mile, with meals included. On the most inexpensive boats, which carried freight as well as passengers, the cost was as little as a penny a mile. The horse-pulled canal boats, which glided along at four miles per hour, provided a leisurely way to travel. As one Erie Canal traveler reported, "I walked-read-talked-sung-

fiddled-eat [sic]—very good meals we had, too—and looked upon the scenery of the Mohawk." During the daytime, the passengers usually sat on the deck atop the cabin roof. At night, benches inside the cabin were made into beds. All meals were served in the cabin. The boats stopped only to change horses every 12 to 15 miles and to navigate the canal locks. The locks were chambers that could be flooded or drained to lift or lower the boats, as the elevation of the canal changed a full 650 feet over the distance from Albany to Buffalo.

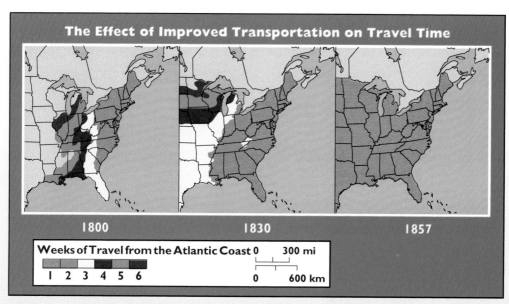

The Effect of Improved Transportation on Travel Time

1800   1830   1857

Weeks of Travel from the Atlantic Coast

1 2 3 4 5 6

0   300 mi

0   600 km

◀ *What transportation improvements between 1800 and 1857 contributed to this reduction in travel time?*

could now specialize in its most prosperous activities, because all of the country's markets were tied together by efficient and inexpensive transportation. The changes in travel time were dramatic. In 1800, it took four weeks to get from New York to New Orleans; by 1830, two weeks; by 1857 five and a half days. Technology had now conquered time and distance, and bound Americans together in one nation.

1. What was the best-known turnpike built by the federal government?

2. The Erie Canal proved to be a profitable venture. Why? What economic areas did it connect?

Government's Role in Settlement

The United States government played an active role in opening western land for settlement. First, it signed treaties with the Indians to secure clear ownership of the land, as described in the next section of this chapter. The government also used the army to explore and map much of the West beyond the Mississippi River. Its first major exploration, as we saw earlier, was the Lewis and Clark Expedition of 1804–1806. Thus, the fur trappers and settlers who followed the paths of the explorers had maps to guide them. Finally, Congress adopted a western land policy designed to make this land available at a reasonable cost.

Beginning in 1785, Congress passed legislation to make western land available for purchase. Initially, buyers had to purchase large 640-acre tracts, which limited land sales to well-financed land companies and wealthy speculators. However, by 1815, public land was sold at auction to the highest bidder in plots of 160 acres, with two dollars an acre the minimum price. After making a 25 percent down payment, the buyer could pay off the balance of the purchase price over a four-year period. Even then, much of the best land was bought by speculators, who resold it to settlers for more than two dollars an acre. But the speculators also contributed to the rapid settlement of the West by subdividing the land into smaller plots that poor farmers could afford.

Congress also encouraged the settlement of the West by providing a system for organizing new state governments. In the Northwest Ordinance of 1787, the Confederation Congress had worked out a process for admitting new states. The inhabitants of a region first had to petition Congress to recognize the region as a territory. During the territorial stage, the area was administered by a governor appointed by Congress and a legislature elected by the people. When the population reached 60,000, the inhabitants could draw up a state constitution and petition for statehood. If Congress approved the new constitution, the state would enter the Union on an equal basis with the existing states.

The first states west of the Appalachians to be admitted to the Union were Kentucky (1792) and Tennessee (1796). The Northwest Territory, as the area north of the Ohio River was known, yielded

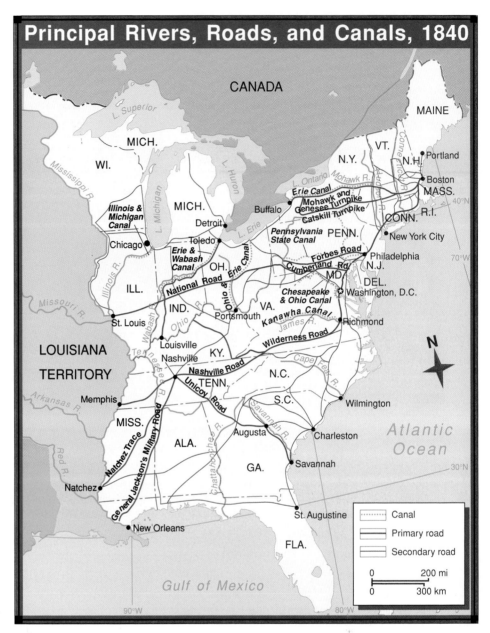

Principal Rivers, Roads, and Canals, 1840

▲ *Waterways and roads were the most important means of transportation in the early 1800s. Many states built canals to extend river transportation. Why were most canals located in northern states?*

three more: Ohio (1803), Indiana (1817), and Illinois (1818). The admission of Louisiana (1812), Mississippi (1817), and Alabama (1819) gave the West three more states. Other states would eventually be carved out of the Missouri, Michigan, and Arkansas territories. The growing number of western representatives in Congress gave that region increased political as well as economic importance.

1. Identify the Wilderness Road.
2. Identify where the Cumberland (National) Road began and ended in 1812.
3. Name the different types of boats used on western waterways.
4. Explain why steamboats were well suited to rivers in the West.
5. List three ways in which the federal government contributed to the settlement of the West.

SECTION 2

Indian Removals

The basic Indian policy of the federal government was to remove the eastern tribes from their homelands to land west of the Mississippi that was not yet occupied by whites. Policymakers mistakenly believed European settlement would not soon cross the Mississippi. Although it was supposed to be voluntary, removal became mandatory whenever the federal government felt it was necessary. How this policy was carried out varied from one presidential administration to the next, but few white Americans questioned its wisdom. "The savage must ever recede before the man of civilization," noted one writer of the 1830s. "The square mile which furnishes game to a single family of hunters will support a thousand families by agriculture and the mechanic[al] arts." Many white settlers assumed that their ability to use the land more productively gave them a natural right to own it. In return for Indians relinquishing their claims to the land, the government paid them an annuity, or yearly installment of money, and helped transport them to the West.

What was the government's policy toward Indian tribes that lived north of the Ohio River?

How did President Andrew Jackson's approach to Indian removals differ from that of his predecessors?

What effect did Jackson's removal policy have on the Indian tribes?

The Removal Policy

The Indian tribes north of the Ohio River were the first to be removed. They did not always leave willingly. The Miami and nearly a dozen other tribes in Ohio resisted the government's efforts to remove them, which led to open warfare. These tribes suffered a crushing defeat by the regular army and militia troops, or short-term volunteers, in 1794 at the Battle of Fallen Timbers near present-day Toledo, Ohio. A year later, these tribes reluctantly signed the Treaty of Grenville, which turned over their lands to the government. In Indiana, the Shawnee, under the leadership of their able chief **Tecumseh**, had also resisted. Their hope of turning back the wave of white settlement ended in defeat and in Tecumseh's death at the Battle of the Thames in 1813. Indian claims to most of Indiana and Illinois

▼ *Black Hawk was an important chief of the Sauk and Fox Indians. Although defeated in the Black Hawk War (1832), he remained a proud leader of his people.*

Sequoya created a written Cherokee language based on the 86 syllables shown on this tablet. Why did he say that a written language had given white society a powerful weapon to use against Indians?

were ended by treaties in 1818 and 1819, with the tribes moved to **reservations**, or land reserved for each tribe, beyond the Mississippi River. Once the tribes left, there was no coming back. In 1832, a band of Sauk and Fox Indians, led by a warrior named Black Hawk, made an unsuccessful effort to return to Illinois. Most of the group, which included many women and children, were massacred during an outbreak known as the **Black Hawk War**.

Indian removal in the South went more slowly. In 1830, millions of acres of farm and forest land in Georgia, Alabama, Mississippi, and Florida were still inhabited by American Indians. Land speculators and farmers were anxious to get their hands on that land, but the major southern tribes had successfully resisted. Among them were the Creek, Cherokee, Chickasaw, Choctaw, and Seminole peoples, called the Five Civilized Tribes by some European Americans. They had kept control of tribal lands partly by adopting European ways. The Creek Indians in Alabama and Georgia, for example, used European farming methods, and owned livestock. Most Cherokees became literate when **Sequoya**, a tribal member, developed a Cherokee alphabet. These American Indians were hardly standing in the way of the progress of "civilization." Many were completely familiar with American laws and knew how to protect claims to their land.

When the Georgia legislature threatened Cherokee control of tribal lands in 1828, the tribe filed suit in the United States Supreme Court. The tribe argued that the state had no jurisdiction over the Cherokee, as they were a separate nation with rights protected by treaties signed by the United States government. In *Cherokee Nation v. Georgia* (1831), the Supreme Court ruled in favor of the Cherokee. It declared the Indian tribes to be "domestic dependent nations" and stated that they were entitled to the protection of the federal government. A year later, the Court held, in *Worcester v. Georgia* (1832), that the Cherokee nation had distinct political boundaries within which the laws of Georgia had no force.

Andrew Jackson and the Southern Tribes

The fate of the southern tribes, however, depended less on the Supreme Court than on the person occupying the presidency. Each president from Thomas Jefferson to John Quincy Adams had favored removing the Indians, but none was willing to force them to leave against their will. This was not the case with President Andrew Jackson. Elected in 1828 largely by southern and western voters, he gave their demand for Indian removal his full support. In 1830, he persuaded Congress to pass the Removal Act, which gave him the authority to set up Indian reservations in the West. Congress also provided money for the cost of moving the southern tribes. In 1831, Jackson ignored the Supreme Court's ruling and insisted that the Indians relinquish their claims to the land. One by one, the tribes signed treaties in which they agreed to move to reservations in the West.

An indication of what was in store for the Indians moving to reservations came in 1831 with the Choctaw removal. The tribe had agreed, in a treaty signed in 1830, to move to what is now the state of Oklahoma. It was then largely uninhabited country, part of the hunting ground of Plains Indian tribes. Delay in getting funds from Washington held up the start of the Choctaw removal until winter. During that very cold and harsh winter, a great number of the ill-clothed and poorly sheltered Indians died of

▶ *Over a 30-year period (1820 to 1850), the United States government removed most of the Indian tribes living east of the Mississippi River. They were resettled on land west of the Mississippi. What major changes in lifestyle would the Indians have had to make to adjust to new climates?*

exposure. A European traveler who witnessed the Choctaw crossing the Mississippi at Memphis wrote that he would never forget the sight of "the sick, newborn babies, and the old men on the point of death." This was only one part of the tragedy of the removal of Indians from the South.

The Trail of Tears

The Cherokee fared even worse than the Choctaw. When the tribe refused to sign a removal

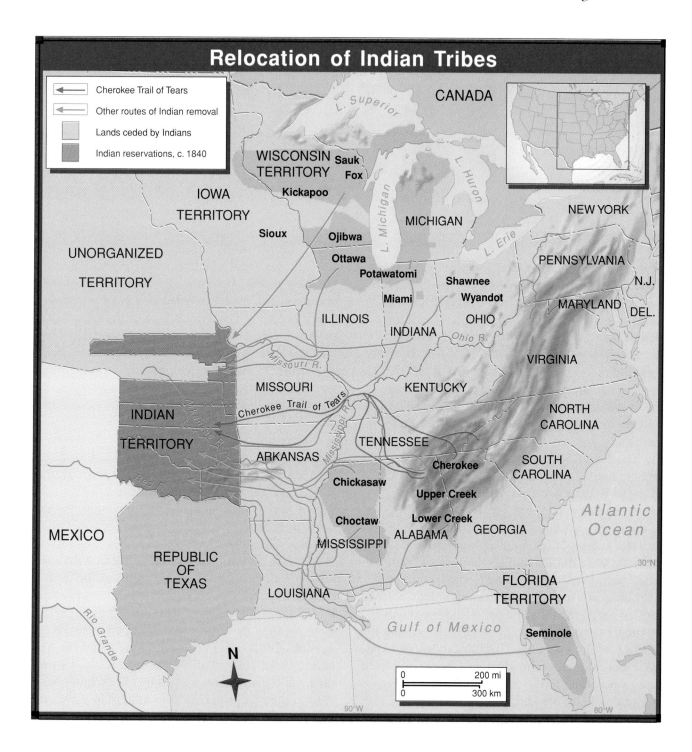

Relocation of Indian Tribes

Cherokee Trail of Tears

Other routes of Indian removal

Lands ceded by Indians

Indian reservations, c. 1840

CANADA

L. Superior

L. Huron

L. Michigan

L. Erie

NEW YORK

WISCONSIN TERRITORY

Sauk
Fox
Kickapoo

MICHIGAN

PENNSYLVANIA

N.J.

IOWA TERRITORY

Sioux

Ojibwa
Ottawa
Potawatomi
Miami

Shawnee
Wyandot

MARYLAND

DEL.

UNORGANIZED TERRITORY

ILLINOIS

INDIANA

OHIO

Ohio R.

VIRGINIA

Missouri R.

MISSOURI

KENTUCKY

NORTH CAROLINA

INDIAN

TERRITORY

Arkansas R.

Cherokee Trail of Tears

Mississippi R.

TENNESSEE

Cherokee

SOUTH CAROLINA

ARKANSAS

Chickasaw

Upper Creek

Red R.

Choctaw

Lower Creek

GEORGIA

Atlantic Ocean

MEXICO

MISSISSIPPI

ALABAMA

REPUBLIC OF TEXAS

LOUISIANA

FLORIDA TERRITORY

30°N

Rio Grande

N

Gulf of Mexico

Seminole

0   200 mi
0   300 km

90°W

80°W

The Cherokee traveled to their reservation over a "Trail of Tears." Does the evidence in this painting support the view that the Cherokee were a primitive people standing in the way of civilization?

treaty, the government found a way to force them to move. Although the vast majority of the Cherokees were opposed to leaving their tribal lands, a small number were willing to do so. The Jackson administration signed a removal treaty with the leaders of this minority group and then insisted that the treaty was binding on the entire tribe. Most of the 17,000 members of the tribe refused to leave by the date of the treaty deadline in 1838. The government sent in soldiers and Georgia volunteers to remove them by force.

The forced removal of the Cherokee tribe was a terrible human tragedy. In their attempt to escape from the soldiers, the Cherokees fled from their cabins, leaving everything they owned behind. Most of them were ruthlessly hunted down and forced into stockades. Many Cherokee women were raped and men were murdered. The violence was remembered years later by one of the Georgia volunteers who took part in it: "I fought through the Civil War and have seen men shot to pieces and slaughtered by the thousands, but the Cherokee removal was the cruelest work I ever knew." The forced march to the West that followed—the **Trail of Tears**—was even more devastating to the tribe. Thousands of men, women, and children died from exposure and disease on the trail.

Other tribes also resisted removal to the West, but with as little success as the Cherokee. In Alabama, the Creek Indians refused to sign a removal treaty. In response, the Jackson administration sent in the army with orders to remove the Creeks as a military measure. "We were drove off like wolves," said one Creek, ". . . and our people's feet were bleeding with long marches. . . . We are men. . . . We have women and children, and why should we come like wild horses?"

When the Seminole people in Florida also resisted removal, the government again used force. The Seminole were finally removed after a war that lasted from 1835 to 1843. In the Seminole War, the Indians, led by **Osceola** [oh-see-OH-luh] until his death in 1838, were assisted by former slaves who had escaped to Florida.

During his two terms in office, Andrew Jackson removed more Indians to reservations in the West than had any previous president. In eight years, he removed nearly 46,000 Indians. Another 50,000 were required by treaties to move at a future date. As a result of its Indian policy, the United States acquired about 100 million acres of Indian land. In return, the Indians were given some 32 million acres west of the Mississippi and $68 million in payments. For European Americans, this was indeed a bargain.

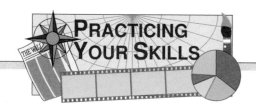

Special Purpose Maps: Looking at Movement

Human beings have always been on the move. From the beginning of recorded time, they have moved for reasons of survival, and later to find better opportunities somewhere else. The ancestors of all of us came here from other parts of the globe, some a long time ago, and some more recently. Today, modern transportation and technology make it inevitable that human beings and ideas will continue to travel around the world.

When one group of people moves, they frequently come into contact with other people from a different culture. New learning and fresh ideas can result, but conflict can also occur. Sometimes people are moved by force to some other place. African Americans were brought by force from their homelands in Africa to work for others in the New World. As settlers moved west, Native Americans were forced out of their ancestral lands. The forced removals resulted from the combination of the economic needs of white settlers and a deep-rooted prejudice against American Indians and their cultures.

Below are some steps to follow when analyzing special-purpose maps:

- **Read the title and any additional information including sources and footnotes.** This will tell you the purpose of the map and usually the time period.

- **Study the map key carefully.** The legend is extremely important in special purpose maps. Know what each line, arrow, color, shading, and symbol represents.

- **Know the map scale.** The scale of miles (or kilometers) is especially important in special-purpose maps that illustrate movement.

- **Finally, refer back to the map when reading the text.** When learning about the event, it is helpful to be able to associate the details of the event with the map.

Examine the map on page 277 and answer the following questions:

1. Where did the Trail of Tears begin and end?
2. Which tribe had the longest journey?
3. Name the river that all of the tribes had to cross. What are the advantages and disadvantages of having water on your route?
4. How did mountains, rivers, and other bodies of water affect the travel route?
5. What time of year would be better for traveling, and why?
6. How is the climate of the states where the tribes originated mainly different from the climate at their final destinations?
7. Why do you think the Indian Territory was chosen for the tribes' new homes?

▲ *Osceola was a Creek Indian who became a leader of the Seminole Indians of Florida.*

At that time, the land the Indians received was too far from transportation and markets to be of much value to anyone. As Alexis de Tocqueville, a Frenchman visiting the United States, remarked, "In this way, the Americans cheaply acquire whole provinces that the richest sovereigns in Europe could not afford to buy."

SECTION 2 REVIEW

1. **Name** the American Indian tribes that were part of the "Five Civilized Tribes."
2. **Describe** how President Andrew Jackson's implementation of Indian policy differed from that of previous presidents.
3. **State** the main reason American settlers and speculators supported the policy of Indian removal.
4. **Identify** the Trail of Tears.
5. **Explain** what happened when tribes resisted removal to the West.

SECTION 3

Texas and New Mexico

Across the Red River from the Arkansas Territory was a vast expanse of land called Texas. It was part of New Spain in 1820, when Moses Austin first sought permission from the authorities in Mexico City to settle there. From his farm on the United States side of the Red River, Austin could gaze out over Texas and see golden opportunities. A business promoter as well as a farmer, Austin had visions of getting rich. He applied to Spanish authorities for a land grant, which was awarded on condition that Austin settle 300 families in Texas. By charging the settlers only a few cents per acre, he counted on making $18,000 from land fees alone. Austin died before he could organize his colony, but his vision of making a fortune in Texas lived on after him. The newly formed government of Mexico, which gained its independence from Spain in 1821, would continue the Spanish policy of encouraging United States citizens to settle in Texas. Thousands of Americans would take advantage of this opportunity.

On what terms were U.S. citizens permitted to settle in Texas?

Why did the new settlers declare their independence from Mexico?

How did the Mexican government respond to the Texans' decision to establish a republic?

Hispanics Settle Texas, New Mexico, and California

The northern half of New Spain, which included Texas, was already thinly settled when Moses Austin received his land grant. In addition to the native Indian population, it had approximately 75,000 Spanish-speaking inhabitants. Most of them were mestizos, or people of mixed Spanish and Indian blood. The Spanish Americans lived in several

▲ *Serapes, like the one shown above, were hand-woven blankets worn as coats in winter.*

pockets of settlement. The majority of them, about 60,000 in all, lived in villages along the upper Rio Grande in present-day New Mexico. There were similar settlements in western Texas, in southern Arizona, and in California.

Most of the Spanish-speaking inhabitants lived in closely knit village communities. The houses were usually laid out around a central plaza or courtyard, which was enclosed to protect the residents from Indian raids. (Tribes that depended partly on raiding for their living, such as the Comanche and Apache, harassed the Spanish villages and those of the Pueblo Indians.) The people of the Spanish villages led simple lives. Most of their furniture, tools, and farming implements were homemade out of leather and wood. Their clothes were also hand-woven. They spent their days tending sheep, working small plots of irrigated farmland, and taking part in community and religious activities. Most of them were Catholic, and they had a culture distinctly their own.

United States Citizens in Texas

The newly independent government of Mexico awarded generous grants of land to several promoters. Among them was **Stephen F. Austin**, the son of Moses. Each family that Austin brought to Texas received 4,428 acres of land. In return, the colonists had to agree to become citizens of Mexico, to join the Roman Catholic church, and to free at the age of 14 the children of any slaves brought into Texas. They also had to pay Austin about $120 and pay the government a $30 fee. The offer was so attractive that by 1834 Texas had an Anglo American population of nearly 21,000.

It is difficult to say whether the majority of the American settlers intended to become loyal citizens of Mexico or whether they secretly hoped that the United States would **annex** Texas (bring it into the Union). Although most of them probably just wanted to be left alone, some American settlers advocated rebellion from the outset. They complained that they had little influence in the government of the Mexican state of Coahuila-Texas, the capital of which was located over 400 miles away at Saltillo. They also found Mexican customs, laws, and court procedures different and irritating. The courts, for example, did not provide for trial by jury.

Other settlers, including Stephen Austin, urged patience. Austin reminded the settlers that the Mexican government had been generous to the Americans. He was willing to accept separate statehood for Texas within a Mexican federal system.

Any hope for a peaceful solution was lost in the autumn of 1835, when the government in Mexico City tried to tighten its control over Texas. **General Antonio López de Santa Anna**, who had recently seized control of the government, rejected the Texans' plea for separate Mexican statehood. The government also banned further emigration from the United States and imposed taxes on goods imported from the U. S. The Texans, including moderates like Stephen Austin, reacted strongly to these measures. In October 1835, they took up arms and prepared to fight for their independence. On March 2, 1836, they signed a formal Declaration of Independence, which created the new Republic of Texas.

The Mexican government refused to recognize Texas's independence. Instead, General Santa Anna set out with an army to put down the rebellion. It seemed likely that he would succeed. Santa Anna marched north from Mexico City with nearly 5,000 troops. Facing him was an ill-equipped and unpaid army of Texas volunteers. Its officers were independent-minded men so lacking in military discipline that they refused to obey orders from their own commander in chief, **General Sam Houston**.

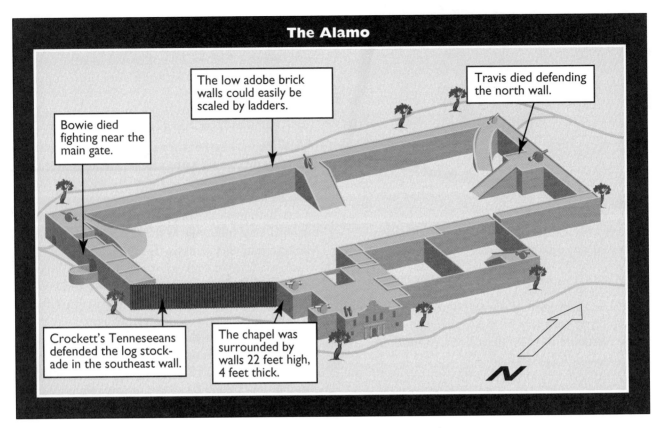

The Alamo

Bowie died fighting near the main gate.

The low adobe brick walls could easily be scaled by ladders.

Travis died defending the north wall.

Crockett's Tenneseeans defended the log stockade in the southeast wall.

The chapel was surrounded by walls 22 feet high, 4 feet thick.

N

▲ *Badly outnumbered, a detachment of Texas volunteers boldly tried to defend the Alamo against Mexican troops.*

The advancing Mexican army wiped out two separate detachments of Texas volunteers. One was led by William B. Travis and Jim Bowie, credited with inventing the Bowie knife, a weapon widely used on the Western frontier. Houston had ordered them to blow up the Alamo, an abandoned mission in San Antonio that the Texans used as a fort. The Alamo was of little military importance to the new republic. Instead, they occupied the fort with a detachment of 188 men and tried to hold off some 2,000 Mexican troops. Most of the defenders of the Alamo were slaughtered when the troops overran the fort. Seven men who surrendered were executed at Santa Anna's orders. The only known survivors were Suzanne Dickinson, the wife of a Texas soldier, her child Angelina, a slave named Joe, and a servant named Ben. Among the dead were Bowie and Tennessee frontiersman Davy Crockett. By military standards, the defense of the Alamo was a rash and futile act. Yet its defenders' courageous stand against impossible odds has been remembered ever since as one of the great examples of American heroism.

The cost to Mexican forces, too, was high. When Santa Anna announced his glorious victory,

◀ *Sam Houston led the Texas army to victory at the Battle of San Jacinto. Why did Texans want their independence from Mexico?*

► The decisive encounter in this war was the Battle of San Jacinto. Why did the Texans win that battle?

Texas War of Independence, 1835-1836

UNORGANIZED UNITED STATES TERRITORY

MO.

ARK.

LA.

Texas-Mexico boundary as claimed by Mexico

REPUBLIC OF TEXAS

Texas-Mexico boundary as claimed by Texas

Washington-on-the-Brazos

San Antonio (The Alamo)

Houston

San Jacinto

Gonzales

San Felipe

Goliad

Refugio

San Patricio

Gulf of Mexico

Santa Anna

Urrea

MEXICO   Matamoros

Disputed area claimed by Texas and Mexico

Mexican forces

Texan forces

Mexican victory

Texan victory

0   200 mi
0   300 km

his aide, Colonel Juan Almonte, privately noted: "One more such 'glorious victory,' and we are finished." His words soon proved prophetic.

Another detachment of Texas volunteers had assembled at the town of Goliad. Houston ordered its commander, Captain James W. Fannin, to abandon that position and join forces with him. Fannin, too, disobeyed Houston's orders. He waited too long to leave Goliad and was overtaken by the advancing Mexican army. Quickly overwhelmed, the Texans surrendered. They were taken back to Goliad as prisoners, where 350 of the men, including Captain Fannin, were executed.

Houston's army of untrained volunteers was all that was left to defend Texas. It was never larger than 900 men and sometimes fell to half that number as volunteers came and went. Houston's men wanted

to attack Santa Anna, but he wisely decided to retreat. As the Texans withdrew to the San Jacinto River in eastern Texas, Santa Anna committed a fatal blunder. He mistook Houston's caution for cowardice. Assuming that the Texans were afraid to fight, he advanced toward the San Jacinto with only a small part of his army. This Mexican force still outnumbered Houston's troops by two to one. The Texans met Santa Anna's army on the west bank of the San Jacinto River and prepared for battle. When the Texans failed to attack in the early morning of April 21, 1836, the Mexicans grew still more confident. They failed to post lookouts in the area separating the two armies. Late in the afternoon, when Santa Anna least expected it, the Texans attacked, shouting, "Remember the Alamo! Remember Goliad!" They routed the surprised Mexican troops in a

Sam Houston, wounded at the Battle of San Jacinto, is shown here accepting Santa Anna's surrender. Why is this decisive moment in Texas history presented in this painting in such an informal way?

battle that lasted barely 20 minutes. Santa Anna was captured alive the next day while he was trying to escape disguised as a common soldier.

As the price of his release, Santa Anna signed a treaty that recognized the independence of Texas. The Mexican government disowned the treaty as soon as Santa Anna was free, but it made no further attempt to regain Texas. Proclaiming themselves an independent republic, the Texans elected Sam Houston as their first president and Lorinzo de Zavala as their first vice president. The Republic of Texas remained an independent nation until December of 1845, when it was annexed to the United States.

Trade with New Mexico

By the 1820s, Americans had also turned their attention to the Spanish American settlements in New Mexico. Merchants in the frontier towns of Missouri saw possibilities for profitable trade with Santa Fe, Taos, and the villages along the upper Rio Grande. Trade had failed to develop earlier because Spain had prohibited it. However, the newly independent Mexican government encouraged trade

▲ *This woodcut from the 1860s shows a main street in Santa Fe, New Mexico. Why were merchants from the United States attracted to Santa Fe?*

with the Americans. After 1822, caravans of wagons loaded with merchandise left Independence, Missouri, each summer headed for Santa Fe. Their path across the plains became known as the Santa Fe Trail. Although most of the merchants returned to the United States after selling their goods, a few settled permanently in New Mexico and married into Mexican families.

SECTION 3 REVIEW

1. **List** the terms to which United States citizens agreed in order to receive land from the Mexican government.
2. **State** reasons why American settlers in Texas rebelled against Mexico.
3. **Identify** General Santa Anna.
4. **Describe** how the Mexican government attempted to retain Texas.
5. **Analyze** why that attempt failed.

SECTION 4

The Rockies, Utah, and the Oregon Country

While Stephen Austin and his colonists were settling in Texas, other Americans headed northwest up the Missouri River and its tributaries. These adventurous people were the fur trappers who became known as "the mountain men." They lived in constant danger of being buried in avalanches, attacked by Indians, or mauled by grizzly bears. Among them were men of extraordinary courage, such as "Peg Leg" Smith. After being accidently shot in the leg in a remote mountain valley, Smith faced certain death from his infected wound. He earned his nickname and survived by having a fellow mountain man amputate his leg without benefit of an anesthetic. In their search for beaver pelts and other valuable furs, these trappers explored much of the West from the Rocky Mountains to the Oregon country. They became the pathfinders of the West for the settlers who would come after them.

What role did the fur trappers and traders play in the development of the West?

Why did the Mormons establish a colony in Utah?

How did missionary activity help promote the settlement of the Oregon country?

The Western Fur Trade

Since colonial times, the quest for beaver and other valuable pelts had lured fur traders into the wilderness of North America. The Dutch in New Amsterdam, the French and British in Canada, and the Americans in the western regions of the United States profited from the commerce in furs. John Jacob Astor, a German immigrant to the United States, established a trading post in the Oregon Country in 1811. It was called Fort Astoria. For several years, Astor's American Fur Company controlled the fur trade of the western United States. His traders on the upper Missouri River did a brisk business exchanging knives, blankets, and other goods for the pelts that Indian hunters brought in.

In 1822, William H. Ashley challenged the American Fur Company's monopoly. Instead of trading with the Indians, as Astor's company did, Ashley decided to send out his own trappers. The mountain men were as diverse a group of adventurers as the West ever produced. Among them were Kit Carson, a European American who was married to a Cheyenne woman; the French American, Étienne Provost; and James Beckwourth, a man of African American descent who later became a chief of the Crow Indian tribe. In their quest for beaver pelts, the mountain men pushed into the Rocky Mountains and beyond to the Columbia River basin.

The trappers worked from late fall to early spring, the season when beaver grow their thick

▶

James Beckwourth was a fur trapper, explorer, and frontiersman. How was he an example of the multicultural character of the Rocky Mountain fur trade?

winter fur. The men who survived the hardships of winter in the Rockies met each summer at a designated place to sell their furs to Ashley's agents. This meeting, called a **rendezvous**, was the only contact with outsiders that most mountain men had for months at a time. After conducting their business, they spent several weeks visiting, drinking whiskey, and gambling away their profits. Then they returned to the mountains to begin the cycle again. The annual rendezvous continued for nearly 20 years, until changing fashions in men's hats reduced the demand for beaver pelts. The replacement of beaver felt hats with silk hats finally brought the trade in beaver furs to an end.

▲ *This wooden-geared "roadometer," invented by a Mormon, recorded the number of miles a wagon traveled.*

Mormon Settlements in Utah

Among the first American settlements in the vast area tramped over by the fur traders were those established by the Mormons in Utah. The Mormons were members of the Church of Jesus Christ of Latter-day Saints, a religion founded in New York in 1830 by **Joseph Smith**. The teachings of the new religion were contained in the *Book of Mormon*, which Smith claimed to have discovered in the form of messages written on golden tablets. Continually harassed by their non-Mormon neighbors, who were alarmed by the rapid spread of the new religion, the Mormons tried to establish communities of their own. After immigrating to Ohio and then to Missouri, they established a settlement in Illinois. There Joseph Smith was murdered by an anti-Mormon mob. Forced to move again, the Mormons this time withdrew completely from the United States. Under the leadership of Brigham Young, they set out during the winter of 1846–1847 for Utah, which was at that time still Mexican territory. There they established the town of Salt Lake City and a number of smaller agricultural settlements. The Mormons also added to their theology the practice of plural marriage, or polygamy, by which a man could have several wives. The Mormon church eventually abolished polygamy.

The Mormon colony in Utah grew and prospered. Under the centralized leadership of **Brigham Young** and the church, the Mormons were able to pool their resources as few frontier communities had done. Working for the good of the community as well as for themselves, they quickly built an irrigation system, planted fields, and made the Utah desert bloom. Birthrates were high, as the Mormons placed a strong emphasis on marriage and motherhood. They also built a temple that became the center of Mormon life in Utah. Mormon farms

▼ *This group portrait is of Brigham Young and his family. It was painted shortly after they arrived in Utah.*

supplied westward-bound emigrants and western miners with foodstuffs. Strongly committed to missionary activity, the Mormon community grew rapidly. Missionaries sent to the eastern states, England, and Europe made numerous converts each year, many of whom immigrated to Utah. With a steady stream of new settlers, the Mormon colony prospered.

The Oregon Country

The most remote area reached by the mountain men in the 1820s and 1830s was the Oregon Country. Consisting of the present states of Washington and Oregon, it was then a region inhabited by Indians. The only white residents were British fur traders who lived at Fort Vancouver, the Hudson Bay Company's trading post on the Columbia River. Washington and Oregon were claimed by both Britain and the United States. As neither nation had been able to make good its claim by actually settling these territories, the two countries had agreed in 1818 to joint occupation. This left the territory open to both British and American citizens. Ten years later, in 1828, the agreement was renewed indefinitely, with the provision that either country could end it by giving a year's notice. The claims of the United States were greatly strengthened during the 1830s and 1840s, as permanent American settlers made their way to Oregon.

Americans living east of the Mississippi River in the 1830s began to hear about the Oregon Country from missionaries who had moved there. After reports were published that the Indians in Oregon were eager to learn about Christianity, missionaries were sent there by several religious groups. The

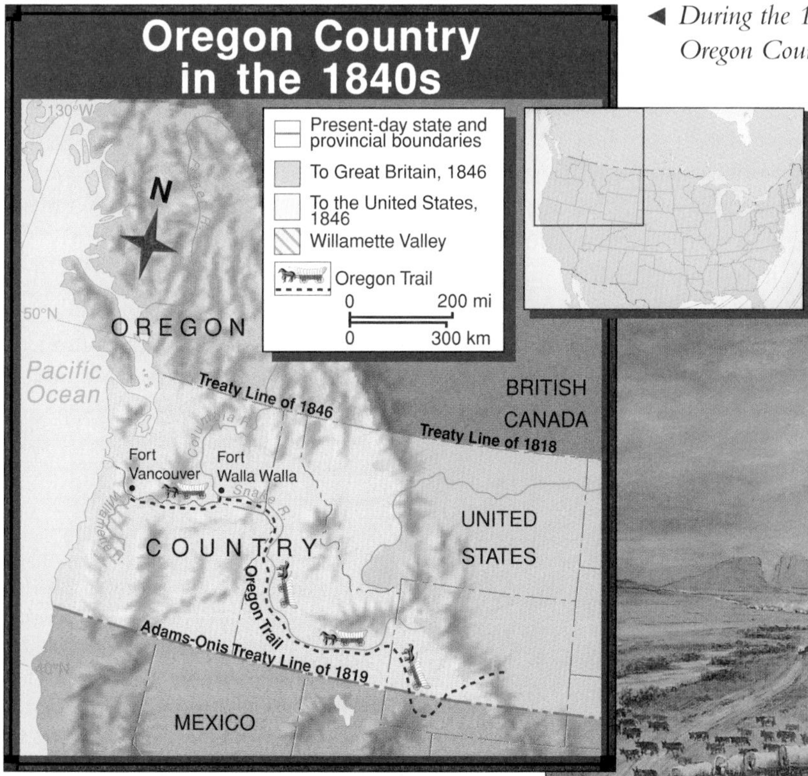

Oregon Country in the 1840s

- Present-day state and provincial boundaries
- To Great Britain, 1846
- To the United States, 1846
- Willamette Valley
- Oregon Trail

0   200 mi
0   300 km

OREGON

Pacific Ocean

Treaty Line of 1846

Treaty Line of 1818

Fort Vancouver   Fort Walla Walla

BRITISH CANADA

UNITED STATES

C O U N T R Y

Adams-Onis Treaty Line of 1819

MEXICO

◄ *During the 1840s, thousands of settlers reached the Oregon Country over the Oregon Trail. Why was the meeting point of the Willamette and Columbia Rivers a likely spot for the town of Portland to develop?*

► *This wagon train on the Oregon Trail was camped at Independence Rock, in present-day Wyoming. Why were the wagons arranged in a circle?*

Towns and Cities of the Frontier

Brigham Young later said that as he looked out across the Great Basin of Utah for the first time in July 1847, he heard the voice of God speaking to him. "This is the place where my people Israel shall pitch their tents," the voice said. The place in question was the future site of Salt Lake City, which became the center of the Mormon settlement in Utah. A prosperous town grew up around the Mormon temple at Salt Lake City to provide the urban services that every frontier community needed. In this respect, the Mormons had much in common with the early Puritans in Massachusetts. John Winthrop, too, had heeded a divine call to plant cities in the wilderness. Like Winthrop, Brigham Young was a pioneer of an urban, as well as an agricultural, frontier.

Towns and cities played a major role in shaping the life of the Midwest and the West. Villages consisting of at least a few houses and stores emerged in every frontier community. Most village settlements had a blacksmith shop, a flour mill, and a general store. Villages located on major rivers sometimes grew into towns or became thriving cities. As the Ohio Valley was settled, both Cincinnati and Louisville became major port cities. Cincinnati began as a cluster of houses around a military fort. Louisville started off as a village located by a waterfall in the Ohio River, where flatboats had to unload and then reload below the falls.

Some towns grew into centers of manufacturing. Pittsburgh emerged as the major manufacturing city of the Ohio Valley, as ironworkers, glassblowers, and other craftspeople set up shops and factories to produce goods for people on their way to lands further west.

Of the frontier cities of the nineteenth century, Chicago was the most remarkable. A newly laid-out town of 3,200 people in 1830, it had 30,000 inhabitants by 1850. It had the double advantage of being a port on Lake Michigan and the end point of a canal that linked the lake to the Illinois River. Its merchants controlled much of the trade of a large and rapidly developing agricultural region. In less than a generation, Chicago was transformed from a frontier settlement into the transportation hub and financial center of the Midwest.

1. Why were frontier settlements dependent on villages and towns?
2. What conditions allowed some frontier villages to grow into major cities?

▼ *The Mormon town of Salt Lake City was six years old when this lithograph was made in 1853.*

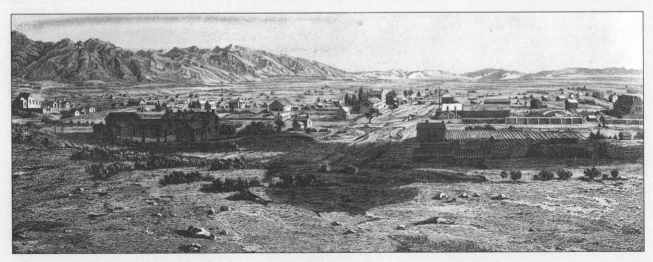

Reverend Jason Lee, a Methodist, opened a mission in the Willamette Valley of Oregon. Dr. Marcus Whitman and Narcissa Prentice Whitman, his wife, established a mission at Fort Walla Walla east of the Cascade Mountains in what is now the state of Washington. Father Pierre Jean de Smet, a Jesuit priest, represented the Catholic Church in this new territory. The reports about the Indians' craving for religion were not accurate, and the missionaries had little success in Christianizing them. (In fact, much of the Indian population was devastated by a measles epidemic.)

The missionaries did send letters home filled with glowing praise for the fertile land of the Northwest. As a result of this publicity, the Oregon Country attracted widespread public attention. Beginning in 1843, caravans of covered wagons set out each summer from Independence, Missouri, headed for the Northwest. Among the accounts describing life along the Oregon Trail and the scenery of the West was Francis Parkman's *The Oregon Trail* (1849), which became a classic of American literature. Most of the immigrants traveled in family groups. While men often found the trip to be an exciting adventure, this was not always the case for women. Moving to such a remote place as Oregon was usually not the women's idea, as their diaries and letters make clear. They went, as one woman wrote, "doing their best for affection's sake but too often in heartsickness and weariness."

Interest in the Oregon Country grew with each passing year. Each year the emigrants sent a new batch of flowing accounts back to be published in eastern newspapers and magazines. Their enthusiasm was highly contagious. "Woah ha! Go it, boys!" wrote one Missouri newspaper editor in 1845. "We're in a perfect *Oregon fever*." The white American population of Oregon increased each year. From about 1,500 people at the end of 1843, it reached 6,000 in 1845 and 9,000 in 1849. The settlers there were soon asking for a territorial government. However, an American territorial government could not be established until the British and Americans agreed which nation owned the region. The two nations had settled disputes about the U.S.–Canada border east of the Rocky Mountains in the Webster-Ashburton Treaty of 1842. But the northern boundary of the Oregon Country was still in question.

SECTION 4 REVIEW

1. **Identify** the mountain men.
2. **Identify** Joseph Smith.
3. **State** the reason that the Mormons established a colony in Utah.
4. **Describe** the role played by the missionaries in promoting the settlement of the Oregon country.
5. **Explain** why the increasing numbers of American settlers in Oregon were unable to set up a territorial government.

SECTION 5

Territorial Annexation and the Mexican War

Many Americans in the 1840s believed that the United States had a God-given right to push its boundaries west to the Pacific Ocean. An all-knowing deity, they believed, had reserved Texas, Oregon, and California for American settlement.

The United States gained more than 1 million square miles of new territory in the 1840s. By 1850, the country extended from the Atlantic to the Pacific coast.

As John L. O'Sullivan, editor of the *United States Magazine* and *Democratic Review*, wrote in 1845, it was the United States' "**manifest destiny** to overspread the continent allotted by Providence for the free development of our yearly multiplying millions." It was only a matter of time, O'Sullivan and other **expansionists** thought, until that manifest destiny would be fulfilled. They believed that the United States would and should extend across the whole continent. They intended to do everything they could to hasten that day.

How did the Democratic Party turn territorial expansion into a winning political issue?

How did the United States get involved in the Mexican War?

What did the United States gain from the war with Mexico?

The Annexation of Texas and Oregon

The expansionists focused their attention on Texas and Oregon, two areas that they thought the United States could easily acquire. Texas had asked to be annexed in 1836, but Congress was reluctant. It knew that annexation would antagonize Mexico, which did not recognize Texas's independence. The expansionists demanded that Texas finally be annexed and admitted as a state. However, when President John Tyler presented the Senate with a treaty to annex Texas in April, 1844, it voted the treaty down. The expansionists also insisted on the acquisition of all of the Oregon Country up to the latitude 54 degrees, 40 minutes—the boundary of Russian Alaska. Their slogan for Oregon was "54-40 or fight." They argued that the rush of settlers to Oregon after 1840 had tipped the balance in favor of the United States' claim to the area and against that of Britain.

In the election campaign during the fall of 1844, expansion finally became a national political issue. Sensing growing public support for the expansionists' demands, the Democratic Party that year endorsed both the annexation of Texas and the acquisition of Oregon. It also nominated as its presidential candidate **James K. Polk**, an ardent expansionist. Polk ran against Henry Clay, the Whig candidate, and James G. Birney, the candidate of the antislavery Liberty Party, both of whom opposed the annexation of Texas. Polk's election that fall was a victory for the expansionists.

Viewing the election results as a vote for expansion, Congress moved quickly to annex Texas. This was done by a joint resolution of both houses of Congress, which President Tyler signed into law shortly before he left office. In December 1845, Texas accepted the terms of annexation and was admitted as a state.

The Polk administration then took up the question of Oregon. Rather than risk a war with Britain by demanding all of the disputed territory, Polk proposed a compromise. He suggested a division of the region along the 49th parallel. Although reluctant at first, the British finally agreed. In June 1846, the

President James K. Polk was one of the few American presidents who achieved all of his foreign policy goals. How did he do it?

Senate ratified the treaty that fixed the 49th parallel as the permanent boundary in the West between the United States and British Canada.

War with Mexico

By the spring of 1846, the United States and Mexico were moving toward war. The Mexican government saw the United States' annexation of Texas as a hostile act, and it responded by breaking off diplomatic relations. That did not stop President Polk, who was determined to acquire New Mexico, California, and the area that is now Arizona. In August, 1845, he sent Ambassador John Slidell to Mexico City with an offer to purchase those territories. The Mexican government saw this as further evidence of American hostility. The president was furious when the Mexican authorities refused even to see Slidell.

Matters were further complicated by a dispute over the boundary between Texas and Mexico. The Texans claimed the Rio Grande as the boundary, although Mexico insisted that Spanish Texas had never extended beyond the Nueces River. The Polk administration upheld the Texans' claim and sent American troops commanded by **General Zachary Taylor** into the disputed zone. Mexico responded in April 1846 by sending soldiers across

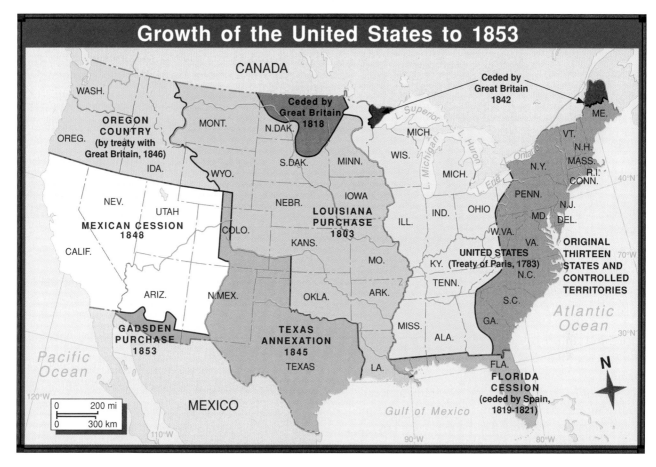

Growth of the United States to 1853

CANADA

WASH.

OREGON
COUNTRY
(by treaty with
Great Britain, 1846)

OREG.

IDA.

NEV.

UTAH

MEXICAN CESSION
1848

CALIF.

ARIZ.

GADSDEN
PURCHASE
1853

Pacific
Ocean

MEXICO

MONT.

WYO.

COLO.

N.MEX.

TEXAS
ANNEXATION
1845

TEXAS

N.DAK.

Ceded by
Great Britain
1818

S.DAK.

NEBR.

KANS.

OKLA.

MINN.

IOWA

LOUISIANA
PURCHASE
1803

MO.

ARK.

MISS.

ALA.

LA.

MICH.

WIS.

MICH.

ILL.

IND.

OHIO

TENN.

N.C.

S.C.

GA.

FLA.

FLORIDA
CESSION
(ceded by Spain,
1819–1821)

L. Superior

L. Michigan

L. Huron

L. Erie

L. Ontario

Ceded by
Great Britain
1842

ME.

VT.

N.H.

MASS.

R.I.

CONN.

N.Y.

PENN.

N.J.

MD.

DEL.

W.VA.

VA.

KY.

UNITED STATES
(Treaty of Paris, 1783)

ORIGINAL
THIRTEEN
STATES AND
CONTROLLED
TERRITORIES

Atlantic
Ocean

Gulf of Mexico

N

0   200 mi
0   300 km

120°W   110°W   90°W   80°W   70°W   40°N   30°N

▲ *The present-day boundaries of the continental United States were complete by 1853.
What different methods had the United States used to gain control of the new territory?*

the Rio Grande to drive out the "invaders." The clash that followed, in which 11 United States soldiers were killed and 6 wounded, led directly to war.

The Mexican attack came as a relief to President Polk. Unable to acquire additional territory from Mexico by purchase, he had already decided to do it by force. The attack was the provocation, or excuse, that he needed to justify a war. As he explained in a hastily written message to Congress, "Now after reiterated menaces, Mexico has passed the boundary of the United States, has invaded our territory and shed American blood on the American soil. War exists . . . by the act of Mexico herself." Unconcerned about the validity of Mexico's boundary claim, Congress responded two days later, on May 13, 1846, with a formal declaration of war.

United States Troops in New Mexico and California

The principal reason the United States went to war was to occupy New Mexico and California. This goal was quickly accomplished. An army under the command of Colonel Stephen W. Kearny set out from Fort Leavenworth, Kansas, to invade New Mexico. This army marched into Santa Fe on August 18, 1846, and raised the American flag. After leaving troops stationed in the major towns and villages, Kearny (now General Kearny) marched on to California. American occupation there began with an uprising at Sonoma, the Bear Flag Rebellion. This uprising of United States citizens who had

▲ *What role did Captain John Charles Frémont and the 60 United States soldiers under his command play in the conquest of California? (*Frémont at Monterey *by W. H. D. Koerner.)*

settled in California was led by the explorer John C. Frémont. No blood was shed. A naval force, commanded by Commodore John D. Sloat, sailed from the port of Mazatlán to aid the rebellion. Sailors from United States naval ships landed and occupied the principal towns from San Francisco to Los Angeles. American settlers in California welcomed the arrival of Kearny's army.

The Hispanic population of California and New Mexico did not welcome the Americans. As Spanish-speaking Catholics, they preferred Mexican rule. They had little in common with the English-speaking Protestants who had suddenly taken charge. In a short-lived revolt, the resident Californians drove the Americans out of Los Angeles. It was recaptured only after hard fighting. In New Mexico, 20 Americans were killed in a similar uprising on January 19, 1847. American authorities there quickly regained control. In both territories, resentment toward the English-speaking Americans continued for many years.

The War Drags On

Resistance ended in the occupied areas, but the war with Mexico continued. General Zachary Taylor led a U.S. army from Corpus Christi, Texas, to the Mexican town of Monterrey, which he cap-

tured in September 1846. Reinforced by troops led by General John E. Wool and Colonel Alexander W. Doniphan, Taylor engaged a Mexican army led by General Santa Anna at Buena Vista in February 1847. After suffering heavy losses, General Santa Anna withdrew his troops and returned to Mexico City. Efforts to negotiate a peace failed, as Mexico refused to accept their territorial losses.

Americans were divided in their support of the war. Although the war was popular in the South, it aroused intense opposition in the Northeast. Northern abolitionists and antislavery Whigs opposed the war on moral grounds. In the first place, they denounced it as an attempt by southern Democrats to bring in new slave territories. They also accused Polk of provoking Mexico into war. A young Whig congressman from Illinois, **Abraham Lincoln**, demanded to know "the spot" where blood had been shed on American soil. He contended that Mexico had the better claim to the area along the Rio Grande, where the first skirmish took place. Whig politicians also hoped to gain political advantage by blaming a Democratic president for the costly war.

The Defeat of Santa Anna

To force the Mexicans to the peace table, Polk assembled the largest American army of the war and ordered an attack against Mexico City. After landing at and capturing the Mexican port of Veracruz, this force of nearly 9,000 soldiers won a major battle against Santa Anna at the town of Cerro Gordo. The army then marched west to the Mexican capital. Commanded by General Winfield Scott, the American army fought its way into Mexico City on September 13, 1847. Still, it took President Polk another five months to get the peace treaty that he wanted, even with American troops camped in Mexico City.

The **Treaty of Guadalupe Hidalgo**, signed on February 2, 1848, finally brought the war to an end. In this treaty, Mexico gave up its claim to Texas and to all of its territory north of the Rio Grande. It also established the present boundary between Mexico and the United States (except for a thin

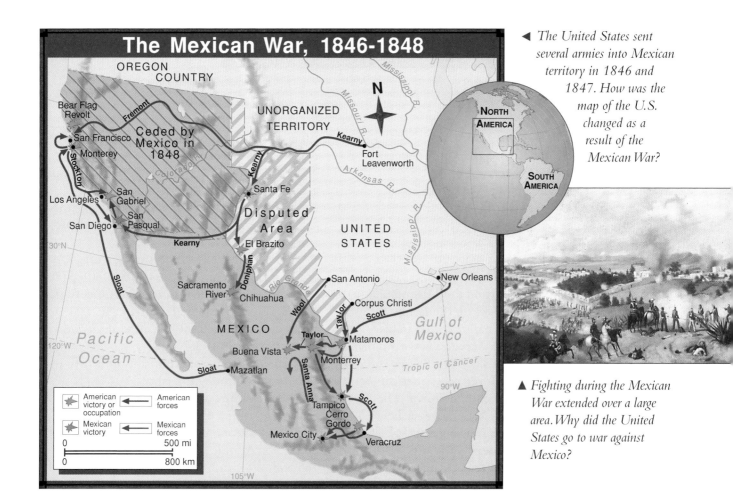

The Mexican War, 1846-1848

OREGON COUNTRY
UNORGANIZED TERRITORY
Bear Flag Revolt
Fremont
San Francisco
Monterey
Ceded by Mexico in 1848
Stockton
Colorado
Los Angeles
San Gabriel
San Diego
San Pasqual
Kearny
El Brazito
Kearny
Fort Leavenworth
Santa Fe
Disputed Area
UNITED STATES
Doniphan
Sacramento River
Chihuahua
Rio Grande
Wool
Taylor
San Antonio
Corpus Christi
Scott
New Orleans
MEXICO
Taylor
Matamoros
Gulf of Mexico
Buena Vista
Monterrey
Tropic of Cancer
Sloat
Mazatlan
Santa Anna
Tampico
Cerro Gordo
Scott
Mexico City
Veracruz
Pacific Ocean
Sloat

American victory or occupation
American forces
Mexican victory
Mexican forces
0   500 mi
0   800 km

NORTH AMERICA
SOUTH AMERICA

◄ *The United States sent several armies into Mexican territory in 1846 and 1847. How was the map of the U.S. changed as a result of the Mexican War?*

▲ *Fighting during the Mexican War extended over a large area. Why did the United States go to war against Mexico?*

strip of land in what is now southern New Mexico and Arizona that was added in 1853 by the Gadsden Purchase). The United States agreed to pay Mexico $15 million for the newly acquired territory. This was a payment of about five cents an acre—hardly more than a token for the 529,017 square miles the United States received. The treaty gave the native inhabitants of the newly acquired areas a year in which to resettle in Mexico, should they choose to remain Mexican citizens. The vast majority chose to stay where they were and thus automatically became citizens of the United States.

The Mexican War had far-reaching consequences for the United States. Acquiring the northern provinces of Mexico added greatly to the nation's physical resources. The discovery of gold in 1848 in California was only the first indication of the region's untapped wealth. As a result of the war, the United States also acquired new ethnic and cul-

tural minorities—the Spanish-speaking people of the Southwest and the peoples of the resident Indian tribes. Finally, the war left a political legacy of great importance. The acquisition of new territory revived the debate over the expansion of slavery, a debate that would occupy much of the attention of Congress for the next decade.

SECTION 5 REVIEW

1. **Name** the territories the expansionists wanted to annex in 1844.
2. **Identify** the underlying reason for the war with Mexico that began in 1846.
3. **Explain** how the United States gained control of California.
4. **Identify** General Zachary Taylor.
5. **List** two reasons some Americans opposed the war with Mexico.

Summary

The settlement of the West from 1815 to 1848 was a dramatic and important chapter in American history. In 1812, most of the territory between the Appalachian Mountains and the Mississippi River was still Indian country. However, many Americans believed it was the "manifest destiny" of the United States to expand to the Pacific. The expansionist policies of the Tyler and Polk administrations led to a war with Mexico. By the end of the Mexican War in 1848, the frontier was far beyond the Mississippi, extending from the plains of Texas to the fertile valleys of California and Oregon. For wagon trains of emigrants headed west, these were the new lands of opportunity.

As white settlement moved west, the American Indian tribes were forced to give up their land. They were defeated in battle and forced to move farther west. Thousands of Indians died resisting removal or from disease and malnutrition during the trip west.

The United States acquired Texas, California, and the Oregon Country during this period. Texas remained independent for ten years after its war with Mexico. It was the annexation of Texas by the United States and President Polk's desire to obtain New Mexico and California that prompted the outbreak of the Mexican war. This expansion would have serious consequences for the nation in the next decade.

Vocabulary

annex   rendezvous
expansionist   reservation
manifest destiny   turnpike

On a separate piece of paper, write a sentence using each of the six terms listed above. Your sentences should demonstrate your understanding of the historical importance of each term.

Review Questions

1. What motivated so many Americans to move west after the War of 1812?
2. Name two developments in transportation that made it easier for people to move west.
3. How did Andrew Jackson change the way the federal government's Indian policy was implemented?
4. What were the consequences of Jackson's policy for American Indians and for settlers?
5. What terms did the Mexican government offer Americans who wanted to settle in Texas?
6. What conditions led the Texans to declare their independence in 1836?
7. In what ways were the Mormons similar to the early settlers of New England?
8. How did eastern Americans learn about the fertile land of the Oregon Country?
9. Name at least one important effect of manifest destiny on American foreign policy in the 1840s.
10. How did the Mexican War intensify the sectional conflict over slavery?

Critical Historical Thinking

Writing Answer each of the following by writing one or more complete paragraphs:

1. In your opinion, why would Mexico have continued the Spanish policy of encouraging United States citizens to settle in Texas?
2. Describe the theory of manifest destiny and the classes of Americans that supported this theory.
3. Support or refute this statement: The war between Mexico and the United States could have been avoided.
4. Read the selection in the Archives for Unit 3 entitled "The Two Systems Compared" by Brownson. What is surprising about the theory of this northern reformer? What reasons does he give for his opinions on slavery?

Making Connections with Art

When the Louisiana Purchase doubled the territory of the United States, President Jefferson commissioned Captains Meriwether Lewis and William Clark to explore this vast new land. Because the places described seemed too fantastic to believe, artists often were asked to accompany these expeditions and provide visual documentation. In this way, painters such as Samuel Seymour, Karl Bodmer, Alfred Jacob Miller, George Catlin, and Albert Bierstadt brought the West to a curious world. The reports were enthusiastically read, and the paintings viewed, by Americans for whom the West represented the promise of rich resources, cheap land, and a way out of economic difficulties in the East.

But to what extent did the very size and grandeur of the Western landscape overwhelm even the artists? They seldom completed their work while on the expedition. Instead, they made sketches, watercolors, and took notes. They used these sources, and their imaginations, to complete their paintings. Schooled in the Romantic tradition, which saw the natural world as a paradise in contrast to the manmade world, these painters of the American West could not help but exaggerate the wonders that they had seen. Clarence King, a writer and explorer, once complained that Bierstadt had done nothing but, "twist and skew and distort and discolor and belittle and be-pretty this whole doggoned country[.] Why, his mountains are too high and too slim; they'd blow over in one of our fall winds. I've . . . [spent] two summers in Yosemite, and honest now, when I stood right up in front of his picture, I didn't know it."

■ At your school or public library, locate books on American art and find pictures by Albert Bierstadt and other painters of the West. Compare them to photographs of the same places. For example, compare Bierstadt's painting of Half Dome in Yosemite to Ansel Adams's famous photograph of Half Dome, or look at early paintings of the Grand Canyon and photographs of the canyon. Pay special attention to shape and scale. Do you think the charge of having exaggerated their landscapes is justified? Organize a display of paintings and photographs for the class to demonstrate your points.

■ Gather advertising photographs of items sold in fast-food restaurants and compare them with the products sold. Do the photographs of hamburgers and other items look like the product, or are they exaggerated? Report your findings to the class.

Additional Skills Practice

The map below depicts the Old Santa Fe Trail, opened in 1821 and used almost continuously until 1880, when a railroad was built.

1. Describe the major geographical features that would be of concern to migrants planning their route across the country.
2. Besides geography, what other factors would early migrants have needed to consider when planning their routes?
3. Examine the map below. What do you think primarily accounts for the location of those trail cities?

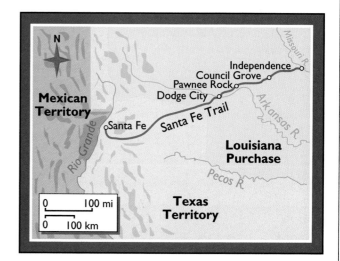

The North and the South

The first half of the nineteenth century was a period of remarkable economic growth for the young American nation. Throughout the northern states, rural villages were becoming thriving market towns. Larger towns were growing into cities. In New England, manufacturing towns were springing up almost overnight. A new urban society was emerging in places that had once been farming communities.

The economy and way of life of rural America were also changing. From the Great

▲ *This lunch pail from the 1800s may have been carried by a busy mill hand.*

Lakes to the Gulf of Mexico, forests were being cut down to make room for new farms, fields, and meadows. Work routines were changing, as planting, cultivating, and reaping became mechanized.

All this growth was not without its hazards and complications. The nation was headed along two diverging paths, one moving toward free labor on farms and in factories, and the other, toward a slave-labor system on large commercial plantations. Could people moving in divergent directions survive as one nation?

The Growth of Manufacturing

Oliver Evans was an American businessman and inventor. In 1785, he created a flour mill that ran by itself. At that time, milling flour was backbreaking work. The grain and flour had to be shoveled by hand from one place in the mill to another. Evans built a mill that used conveyor belts to move the grain. Evans's system of belts and machines carried the wheat from the farmers' wagons, cleaned it, ground it into flour, sifted out the hulls, and packed the flour into barrels. His techniques were so widely copied that his brother wrote to him in 1816, "I find mills in my travels manufacturing flour without any miller and all done by machinery and shut up.... I have walked through these mills calling for the miller and found none and the whole process of grinding, elevating, cooling and bolting going on and no miller." Evans continued to invent new machines and improved methods of production well into the nineteenth century. In time, such new methods of machine production would bring sweeping changes to nearly every aspect of American economic life.

How would machines change the way goods are produced?

What were the advantages of machine production?

What effect would machine production have on the meaning people found in work?

▲ *This New England woman is working at a spinning frame, a machine that made cotton yarn or thread. What earlier hand-powered device did the spinning frame replace?*

Manufacturing Methods Change

At the heart of the Industrial Revolution that Oliver Evans helped bring about were new methods of production that relied on steam and water power, and machines housed in mills and factories. The **factory system** of production brought machines and the workers who tended them together under a single roof. Until the nineteenth century, most man- ufactured items were made by skilled artisans working at home or in small shops. The mechanical devices they used were few and simple, and included potters' wheels, spinning wheels, and weaving looms. Most of these tools were worked by hand. Much of what these artisans produced was custom-made—that is, made specially for the customer who had placed the order. During the early decades of the nineteenth century, in one industry after another, new and more complicated machines began to make the old methods of production obsolete. Clothes, shoes, and dozens of other items could be made more cheaply by machines in standardized shapes and sizes, rather than by hand. With the introduction of machines, work was moved from homes and small shops to factories where dozens or even hundreds of workers were employed.

Textile manufacturing was the first major industry to be converted to factory production. In the late 1700s, manufacturers in Great Britain had developed the first machines for spinning thread. These machines eventually made the spinning wheel obsolete. Power-driven looms were invented for weaving thread into cloth. The British tried to keep a monopoly on factory production by passing laws that prevented the export of textile machinery. Machinists who knew how to build textile-making machines were forbidden to leave Great Britain. But the British could not keep these inventions to themselves forever. A British machinist, **Samuel Slater**, emigrated illegally to the United States. In 1791, he helped two Rhode Island merchants build a cotton yarn spinning mill. The New England countryside was soon dotted with yarn mills.

▲ *These machines prepared cotton for spinning. Why were most of the workers in New England textile mills women?*

In 1813, a Boston merchant named **Francis Cabot Lowell** built the first textile mill that brought machines for spinning thread and weaving cloth under the same roof. Previously, textile manufacturers had sent the machine-made thread out to weavers, who wove it into cloth on their hand looms at home. During a visit to England in 1810, Lowell discovered that the British had developed powered looms for weaving cloth. But they had not yet brought together these two stages of machine production. Lowell decided that the most efficient way to produce textiles was to put all the steps of production in a single factory.

After returning to the United States, Lowell called together a group of merchants who had money to invest. Together, they created the Boston Manufacturing Company. The new company built factories at Waltham, Lowell, and other towns in Massachusetts to produce finished cloth from raw cotton. The spinning, weaving, bleaching, dying, and printing of cotton cloth all took place within one factory, in an almost continuous process. The mills manufactured cloth so cheaply that the call for cloth spun and woven at home rapidly declined. By 1860, the making of homespun cloth had largely disappeared in the United States, except in remote frontier areas.

The American System of Manufacture

The United States was a latecomer to the Industrial Revolution. For the most part, American manufacturers borrowed, adapted, and modified machines and techniques developed by more advanced countries, especially Great Britain. However, this was not always the case. The United States also made major contributions to the new methods of industrial production.

▲ *These workmen are making parts for guns. How did machines permit guns to be made more cheaply than before?*

Chief among them was a method of production that the British called the **American system of manufacture**.

This system was based on the principle of manufacturing things with interchangeable parts. The American system of manufacture was developed in the 1790s by New England firearms manufacturers, among them inventor Eli Whitney. Under the old system of production by hand, gunsmiths often divided up the work of making the steel parts for a musket. It was most efficient for each craftsperson to concentrate on making a single part. But because these parts were made by hand, it was rare for any two of these parts to be exactly alike. When it came time to assemble the different pieces, they seldom fit together exactly. Each piece had to be further shaped with steel files, rasps, and other hand tools. This time-consuming and costly stage of production was largely eliminated by the system of interchangeable parts.

The new system used patterns or jigs to guide the workers' tools as they cut out and shaped the parts for muskets. Using this process, the workers made parts so identical that the weapons could be taken apart, the pieces mixed together, and the muskets reassembled in perfect working order. Even more important, musket parts could be made and assembled by workers who were less skilled than the gunsmiths. This had not been possible with the old way of making firearms. Manufacturers could pay these unskilled workers a lower wage, so firearms could now be made more cheaply than before.

Although pioneered by the makers of firearms, the system of interchangeable parts was quickly adopted by other manufacturers. It was soon used to produce clocks, watches, locks, reapers, sewing machines, and dozens of other items.

The Assembly Line By 1850, the meat-packing industry was using the basic principle of the **assembly line**. This is an arrangement of machines,

▼ *In this pork processing plant, each worker performed a separate task. How did the production line change the way manufactured goods were produced?*

equipment, and workers in which work passes from operation to operation in a direct line until the product is assembled.

This arrangement reduces the time and cost of manufacturing. On an assembly line, each worker performs one step in the manufacturing of a product. In slaughtering houses in Cincinnati, each worker performed a single operation as the carcasses of pigs, suspended from overhead tracks, moved past. The first worker would split open the carcass, the next would remove the entrails, another would flush the animal with a water hose, while others along the line did their assigned tasks in taking the carcass apart. In the twentieth century, this process of worker specialization would be used to put together such products as automobiles, televisions, and computers.

▶
The Baltimore and Ohio Railroad helped to take manufactured goods to the West and bring processed meat products to the East.

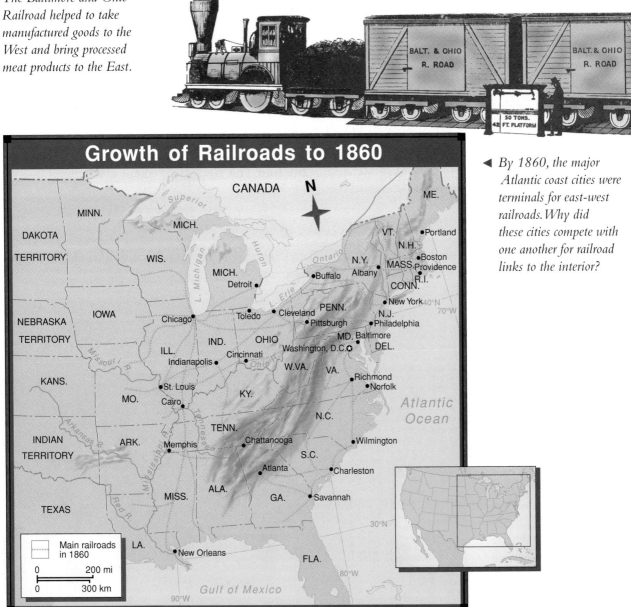

Growth of Railroads to 1860

◀ *By 1860, the major Atlantic coast cities were terminals for east-west railroads. Why did these cities compete with one another for railroad links to the interior?*

Changes in Work and Transportation

The new methods of production changed the way people worked. Factory work was unlike any kind of work the new employees had done before. It was monotonous and exhausting, and the workday was regulated by the clock. Employers insisted on punctuality and regular work habits in order to maximize their profits. Textile workers, for example, worked 12½ hours a day, beginning at 5:00 A.M. At 7:00, they took off exactly half an hour for breakfast, then worked until 12:30, when they stopped for lunch. At 1:30, they returned to work and stayed there until 7:00 P.M., which was quitting time.

The factory itself ran like a clock. "Who has not been delighted with the clockwork movements of a large cotton factory?" asked Henry Clay, senator from Kentucky. Although the regularity of factory work impressed outsiders such as Clay, it took much of the joy out of life for those on the inside. But it was more regular and better-paying work than being hired as a farm laborer or house maid.

Economic growth in the northern states was also stimulated by improvements in transportation. The states of New York and Pennsylvania built canals to link their coastal cities with the interior of the country. Worried about losing their trade with the West to New York City and Philadelphia, the merchants of Baltimore promoted the use of a new transportation technology—the railroad. They sent a delegation to England to take a look at a steam locomotive, which, like most of the machines of the early nineteenth century, was a British invention. (The first railroad, the Stockton and Darlington Railroad, began operating in England in 1825.) In 1828, the Baltimore merchants organized the Baltimore and Ohio Railroad Company and began construction of a railway. The first 13-mile stretch of the railroad was opened in 1830, making the Baltimore and Ohio the first commercial railroad in the United States. In a short time, railroads connected other coastal cities, such as Boston and Charleston, with towns and rural areas in the interior. By 1860, the United States had 30,627 miles of railroad track in operation.

SECTION 1 REVIEW

1. **Define** the term *factory system*.
2. **Explain** why the British refused to let machinists emigrate.
3. **Identify** the industry first converted to factory production.
4. **Explain** briefly the American system of manufacture.
5. **Describe** how machine production changed the way people worked.

SECTION 2

Social Change in Industrializing America

The factory system of production brought far-reaching social changes. It lured men, women, and children from the farms of the Northeast, as well as immigrants from abroad, into mill towns and factory cities. The factory system turned farm boys and kitchen maids into "mill hands," as textile workers were called. It gave hundreds of thousands of people a new way of life. "I can see myself now, racing down the alley, between the spinning frames, carry in front of me a bobbin-box bigger than I was," Harriet Robinson wrote, remembering her experience as a young girl in a textile mill. She especially remembered the hardship of getting up early enough to be at work at 5:00 A.M. "To this habit, I never was and never shall be reconciled, for it has taken nearly a lifetime for me to make up the sleep lost at that early age." The factory system changed Harriet Robinson's life and that of thousands of other Americans of her time.

How did the factory system affect the lives of American women and children?

How did the factory system produce sharper class and ethnic distinctions in the United States?

How did the expanding industrial economy increase social conflict in the United States?

How did the factory system produce sharper class and ethnic distinctions in the United States?

How did the expanding industrial economy increase social conflict in the United States?

Women and Children in the Factories

The Industrial Revolution in the United States created new work roles for women and children who previously worked at home. Women contributed to the family economy through kitchen and garden work and by spinning, weaving, and sewing. Children took care of a variety of household and barnyard chores. As a result of the new methods of production, large numbers of women and children left the home and went to work in factories. They were an essential part of the workforce in the growing textile industry.

New England textile manufacturers were faced with a severe shortage of labor. Unlike Great Britain, the United States had no large cities with a surplus of people who could be attracted to factory work. The yarn manufacturers of Connecticut and Rhode Island solved the problem by relying on whole families to provide workers for their mills. They advertised in the newspapers for rural families who would be willing to move to the mill site, where they promised work for everyone. The impoverished families who responded to these ads tended to have many children. These children, who worked for pennies a day and typically received as little as a dollar a week, made up a large percentage of the yarn-mill workers. The textile industry was the first of many industries in the United States to take unfair advantage of children.

The textile mills at Waltham, Lowell, and other towns in northern New England developed a different kind of workforce. Many of the machines in these large and highly mechanized factories were too complicated for children to operate. These manufacturers turned to a largely untapped pool of labor in rural New England: young women in their late teens and twenties. Mill owners attracted thousands of young farm women to the textile mills, offering them better wages than they could get as housemaids or teachers. The employers also promised them good working conditions. Most of the young women worked in the mills for only two or three years. They used the opportunity to contribute to their family's income, to buy what they needed to set up housekeeping when they married, or to send a brother to college. (At that time, colleges did not accept women.) The young women lived in company boardinghouses under the watchful eye of a housekeeper or matron. Their wages averaged about $1.90 per week, after deducting the cost of room and board. While not much by present-day standards, it was much better than the 75 cents a week earned in the 1830s by female servants.

Factory Worker Strikes

By the late 1830s, working conditions in the textile mills had begun to deteriorate. Increasing competition within the industry was the cause. As more mills were built and competition increased, manufacturers were forced to sell their goods for lower prices. They tried to keep their profits high by cutting costs, especially the cost of labor. They reduced wages, but that was only the beginning. To increase the productivity of each worker, the mill owners also introduced "speed-up" and "stretch-out" practices. They increased the speed of the machinery and stretched out the workforce by making each worker responsible for more machines. As a result, each person's workload more than doubled in many textile mills. Individual factory workers could easily be replaced, so unless they banded together, they were powerless to prevent such changes in their work routines.

In the textile and other industries, workers organized strikes to restore their original wages and to improve working conditions. In May 1824, the workers in Samuel Slater's mills in Pawtucket, Rhode Island, walked off their jobs to protest a wage reduction and an increase in working hours. The mill women at Lowell also "turned out," or walked away from their machines, in February 1834 and in October 1836 to protest wage cuts. These protests did the women little good; their original wages were not restored. The largest of these pre–Civil War labor upheavals was the Great Shoemakers' Strike of 1860. Nearly 20,000 men and

women walked off their jobs in the shoe factories of Massachusetts in response to wage reductions. The strike lasted for six weeks before the workers, hungry and with their savings exhausted, called it off and returned to work.

Although most of these early strikes were short-lived, the workers did achieve some successes. By 1860, most textile manufacturers had shortened the workday to 11 hours, and workers in some skilled trades had a 10-hour day.

Class Distinctions Sharpen

Industrialization sharpened class distinctions in the United States by widening the gap between the rich and the poor. Most people in preindustrial America were neither very rich nor very poor. The majority were farmers and skilled craftspeople, who stood on the middle rungs of the social ladder. The growth of the factory system created a new working class at the lower end of American society and made other people, especially the factory owners, much richer than ever before.

The most visible social change was the expansion of the urban working class. Each year, thousands of people moved to the factory towns of the Northeast, looking for work. "Operatives [workers] are pouring in as fast as room can be made for them," reported a Lynn, Massachusetts, newspaper. Some were "floaters" who moved from town to town trying to sell their labor wherever they could. Others were more stable, settling into cheap apartments and boardinghouses near the factories. Among them were both native-born Yankees just off the farms of New England and immigrants recently arrived in the United States. Although a diverse group, these workers had much in common. They all worked long hours at manual labor; they barely earned enough to keep homes and families together; they lived in overcrowded and often unsanitary quarters. Unskilled factory workers were the new lower class of industrial America.

The expanding industrial economy made other Americans very wealthy, including the owners of factories and railroads. Often, it was the rich who got richer. A great many families that were already wealthy, through shipping or trade, made new fortunes by investing in industrial enterprises. In other cases, skilled workers moved up from the middle class to become factory or mill owners. For example, many of the men who owned the machine

Working in the Textile Mills

In the 1830s, young women came by the thousands to Lowell and other Massachusetts textile mill towns. When Michael Chevalier, a French government official, visited Lowell in 1834, he found 5,000 "mill girls," as they were called, employed in that town alone. Most were between the ages of 17 and 24. "In France, it would be difficult to conceive of [such] a state of things," he observed, as young French women were not permitted to leave home without family supervision. Yet, Chevalier noted, these young women's morals seemed to suffer no ill effects. They were carefully supervised by their employers while at work and by the boardinghouse keepers in the evenings.

Mill work was hard. The young women worked more than 12 hours each day and spent most of that time on their feet. "It makes my feet ache and swell to stand so much," wrote one newly arrived Lowell employee, "but I suppose I shall get accustomed to that, too. The girls . . . almost all say that when they have worked here a year or two they have to procure shoes a size or two larger than before they came." The work was monotonous, the noise of the machinery was almost deafening, and the air was polluted with cotton dust. But that did not prevent

▲ *Lowell mill dress from the 1840s.*

thousands of young women from taking jobs in the textile mills.

Why did they do it? "There are girls here for every reason," one young woman wrote in the *Lowell Offering*, a local magazine. "One, who sits at my right hand at table, is in the factory because she hates her [stepmother]. . . . The one next to her has a wealthy father, but, like many of our country farmers, he is very [stingy], and he wishes his daughters to maintain themselves." Another wanted to wear prettier clothes than her mother would buy for her, so she went to work to buy her own. Still another was tired of the abuse she had suffered as a housemaid. "The next has left a good home because her lover, who has gone on a whaling voyage, wishes to be married when he returns, and she would like more money than her father will give her. . . . The next is here because her beau came, and she did not like to trust him alone among so many pretty girls."

▲ *The* Lowell Offering *published articles written by young women who worked at Lowell.*

Above all else, the wages were good. Most of the young women made at least $3.00 per week, before the cost of room and board was deducted. Few European women, Chevalier wrote, made more than a dollar per week doing comparable work. After four years in a factory, he noted, these young women "may have a little fortune of $250 or $300. When they have a dowry, they quit the factory and get married."

———————

1. Briefly describe what it was like to work in a textile mill.
2. Why would young women want to work under such hard conditions?

▲ *Poor children in Philadelphia often found it necessary to beg for meat scraps. Why did the number of poor people in American cities grow as a result of industrialization?*

▲ *Children in well-off families had servants to wait on them. How did industrialization increase the wealth of the upper classes?*

shops and locomotive works in Paterson, New Jersey, were skilled ironworkers or machine-shop foremen who had worked their way up. Although moving up in society was possible in industrial America, few ordinary laborers ever got to be factory owners. At most, they might move up to a better-paying job by acquiring a skill. Rags-to-riches success stories were rare.

Immigration Transforms American Society

Immigrants provided much of the labor needed by industrial America. Between 1820 and 1860, nearly 5 million immigrants entered the United States. Close to 90 percent settled in the North, usually in the industrial towns and cities of the Northeast. By 1860, immigrants willing to work for lower wages had largely replaced the young farm women in the New England textile mills. They also wielded the picks and shovels that dug canals and

▼ *Why did immigration to the United States increase dramatically from 1846 to 1855?*

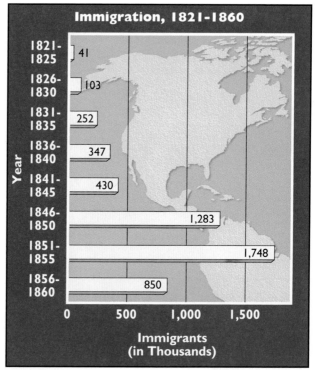

Immigration, 1821–1860

Year	Immigrants (in Thousands)
1821–1825	41
1826–1830	103
1831–1835	252
1836–1840	347
1841–1845	430
1846–1850	1,283
1851–1855	1,748
1856–1860	850

Source: U.S. Department of Commerce, Bureau of the Census.

Before 1840, the population of the United States was largely Anglo-American. What changes took place in the ethnic makeup of American society during the next two decades?

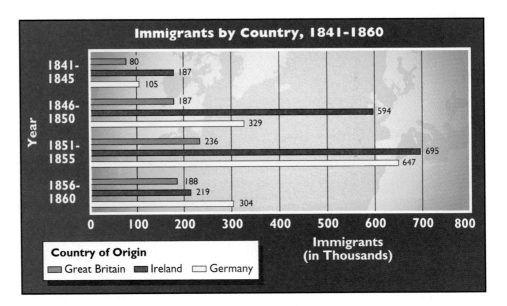

Immigrants by Country, 1841–1860

Year	Great Britain	Ireland	Germany
1841–1845	80	187	105
1846–1850	187	594	329
1851–1855	236	695	647
1856–1860	188	219	304

Immigrants (in Thousands)

Country of Origin
☐ Great Britain ■ Ireland ☐ Germany

built railroads throughout the North. Immigrants were an indispensable part of the workforce.

They came for many reasons. Skilled machinists, carpenters, and miners from England and Wales were attracted by the high wages paid in the United States, where skilled laborers were always in short supply. Irish immigrants in the 1840s fled from a famine caused by crop failures. During the famine years of 1845 and 1846, when the potato crops rotted in the ground, nearly a million Irish people died of starvation. Many of the survivors who could afford to leave the country did so. Most of the Irish families that emigrated settled in the United States, mainly in the port cities and mill towns of the

Northeast. They were too poor to pay the transportation cost of moving inland. Immigrants from other nations, especially those from Germany and Scandinavia, came to buy farmland in the Midwest.

Increased immigration created sharp divisions in American society along ethnic lines. In many cities of the Northeast, native-born Americans felt threatened by the growing numbers of immigrants and reacted with increasing hostility. The new immigrants brought with them religious and cultural values different from those of the native-born, Protestant majority. Most were either Irish Catholics or non-English-speaking Europeans. While ethnic differences enriched American culture, they were also a source of conflict. In some cities, **nativist** (anti-immigrant) clubs, newspapers, and political parties were organized. In 1844, the American Republicans, a nativist party, were strong enough to elect the mayor of New York City.

The anti-Catholic sentiment that swept through the cities in which the Irish settled often led to violence. Protestants burned St. Mary's Catholic Church in New York City in 1831 and destroyed a convent in Charleston, Massachusetts, three years later. Anti-immigrant riots were common. The most serious occurred in Philadelphia in May 1844. Clashes between Protestants and Irish Catholics killed 13 people.

SECTION 2 REVIEW

1. List the new sources of labor New England manufacturers tapped for their textile mills.
2. List the changes in the textile industry that produced worker discontent and strikes.
3. Describe the major change in American society produced by the factory system.
4. Identify the class of workers known as floaters.
5. Explain why many native-born Americans felt threatened by the growing number of immigrants.

◀ *State militia companies were sent to Philadelphia in 1844 to put down an anti-Catholic riot led by native-born Protestants. How were the nativists represented in the illustration?*

The Economy and Society of the Old South

In 1793, **Eli Whitney** built a machine that would radically change the economy of the South. It was a machine, or "engine," as mechanical appliances were called in those days, for cleaning the seeds out of cotton. A native of Connecticut, Whitney developed his cotton "gin," as it was commonly called, during a visit to Georgia. There he heard planters talk about the potential profits that could be made from growing cotton. But the handwork involved in picking the seeds from the cotton fibers, or lint, made cotton growing unprofitable. Cleaning a single pound by hand was a day's work. Other people had attempted to devise a machine to do this work, but they had not succeeded. Whitney's machine was a simple device, with rollers that separated the fibers from the seeds. Using the cotton gin, a good worker could clean 50 pounds of cotton a day. Because almost any blacksmith could make these machines, the gins quickly multiplied. So, too, did the number of cotton fields, slaves, farmers, and planters in the South. Partly because of the cotton gin, the South remained largely agricultural.

What effect did the expansion of cotton production have on the economy of the South?

How did the social structure of the South reflect the importance of cotton growing?

What effect did the growth of large-scale agriculture have on the institution of slavery?

The Agricultural South

Unlike the industrializing Northeast, the South remained a predominantly agricultural society throughout the nineteenth century. Manufacturing lagged far behind farming in economic importance in the South. The manufacturing establishments that

▲ The cotton gin was patented by Eli Whitney in 1793.

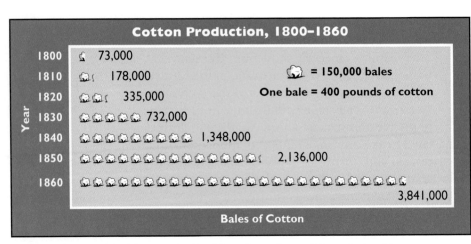

Cotton Production, 1800–1860

Year	Bales of Cotton
1800	73,000
1810	178,000
1820	335,000
1830	732,000
1840	1,348,000
1850	2,136,000
1860	3,841,000

= 150,000 bales
One bale = 400 pounds of cotton

▲ By 1860, cotton had become the South's major cash crop. What relationship between the invention of the cotton gin and increased cotton production does this graph suggest?

did exist were small, and they existed mainly to serve the rural society. The technology of greatest interest to the South was the technology of agricultural implements—cotton gins, planters, plows. The South's shops and factories produced ironware, hoes, material made of hemp for bagging cotton bales, and the cheap cotton cloth used to make slaves' clothing. Rural villages in the South did not grow into factory towns. Except for seaports such as Charleston and New Orleans, the South had few cities or large towns. Thus the South's social and economic development was quite unlike the North's.

Cotton was the South's major cash crop. It eventually outsold all other staples put together. From 3,000 bales in 1790, production increased to nearly 4 million bales by 1859, a bale containing 400 pounds of cotton. Cotton flourished in the long, hot growing season of the deep South. Cotton monopolized the best farmland in a wide belt extending from the Carolina hill country to the plains of eastern Texas. It assumed major economic importance far beyond the geographical limits of the South. Cotton made up 60 percent of the total exports of the United States in 1859. The remainder provided the basis for a thriving cotton textile industry in New England. Cotton, as southern politicians liked to say, was "king."

Cotton was not the South's only agricultural product. Farms and plantations throughout the region raised corn, a major source of food for both humans and livestock. Virginia, North Carolina, and the states of the upper South grew tobacco. Kentucky and Missouri grew hemp. Plantations in the coastal areas of South Carolina specialized in growing rice. Many of the plantations along the lower Mississippi River in Louisiana raised sugarcane. The South also led the nation in the production of livestock, producing 90 percent of its mules, 60 percent of its swine, and more than half of its poultry. Still, although all these products were important, they never rivaled cotton as the South's major source of income.

The Upper Classes of the Old South

The most influential social class in the Old South consisted of merchants and large plantation owners. Together with the bankers who kept them afloat financially, these were the wealthiest people in the South. However, few planters or merchants were rich enough to lead lives of leisure. Most planters invested their profits in slaves, borrowed money to buy more land, and worked hard to get out of debt. Merchants likewise had to work hard, buying and shipping cotton, and keeping the planters provided with the supplies they needed. Many of the merchants and bankers also owned plantations, investing their profits in land and slaves.

This painting depicts a cotton plantation on the Mississippi River. How was the expansion of slavery in the South related to the increased production of cotton?

The plantations that raised most of the South's major crops depended heavily on the labor of enslaved people. By 1860, nearly four million African American slaves lived in the South, concentrated in Virginia, the Carolinas, and the cotton-producing states of Georgia, Alabama, and Mississippi. Louisiana, which grew sugarcane as well as cotton, also had a large slave population. Slave labor produced 90 percent of the South's cotton and nearly all of its sugar and rice. Slaves did most of the work on southern plantations. They grew the corn and raised the chickens and hogs. After picking cotton in the fall, they picked and shucked the corn and gathered in the vegetables. During the winter, slaves slaughtered hogs, cut wood, mended fences, cleaned out ditches, and spread manure on the fields. In the spring, they plowed the fields and planted cotton, corn, and vegetables. They weeded the fields throughout the summer, until it was time to begin harvesting again. Other slaves labored as household servants or as blacksmiths, carpenters, and other skilled craftspeople. The number of enslaved people living on a farm or plantation varied from one or two to several hundred.

Relatively few white southerners owned large numbers of enslaved Africans. In 1860, only 12 percent of southern slave owners had 20 or more slaves. Most owners had fewer than 10. The typical slave owner was a farmer who had one or two slave families to help with the hard labor. The owner usually worked in the fields alongside his slaves.

Small Farmers and Poor White Southerners

Most white farmers in the South did not have slaves. By 1860, at least three-fourths of all southern white families did not own slaves. Most were self-sufficient farmers engaged in subsistence agriculture. That is, they grew crops of corn, wheat, or oats mostly for their own use. They kept gardens, and often raised patches of sweet potatoes. They made most of the things they needed. A small field of cotton provided the cash required for such necessities as salt, sugar, gunpowder, and lead. They hunted for meat, and they raised razorback hogs that were allowed to search for food in the woods. Living in the backcountry and hilly areas not suited for large-scale plantation agriculture, these farmers were the "plain folks" of the Old South.

In sharp contrast to the landowning farmers and planters was a landless and impoverished class of people usually referred to as poor whites. They made up about 10 percent of the South's population. Middle- and upper-class white southerners called them "hillbillies" or "sand hillers." Even the slaves, who called them "poor white trash," looked down on them. Not all mountain and hill people were poor whites, but this class usually lived on the least productive, hilly land in the South. They depended on hunting, fishing, and raising livestock for a living. Some worked as agricultural laborers at wages that were among the lowest in the nation. Except in the frontier areas of the South, where labor was scarce, white farmhands could not compete with slave labor and make a living wage.

Poor white people were often accused of being lazy, but their lack of energy and ambition was mostly due to an inadequate diet and the hookworm disease. The hookworm parasite, which entered the body through the skin of the feet, caused a fever that eventually weakened the body. It was widespread among poor white southerners.

African Americans

Enslaved African Americans and freed slaves were at the bottom of southern society. The nearly four million slaves who lived in the South in 1860 made up more than one-third of the region's population. Although the slaves were of African descent, few knew anything about Africa from firsthand experience. In 1808, Congress outlawed the importing of slaves into the United States. While thousands were still smuggled in after that time, by 1860 the vast majority of the enslaved people in the South were native-born. Many could claim a longer ancestry in North America than could the white families who owned them.

Although the vast majority of African Americans in the South were slaves, some 250,000 were free. These free African Americans were former slaves or the descendants of slaves who had gained their freedom. Occasionally, a planter would state in his will that his slaves should be freed when he died. A few slaves were able to save enough money to buy their own freedom. This was almost impossible

for a plantation slave, but urban slaves were frequently allowed to make money for themselves during their free time. Denmark Vesey, a slave who lived in Charleston, South Carolina, bought his freedom after winning $1,500 on a lottery ticket.

Although free African Americans were no longer in bondage, their social status was not much higher than that of slaves. Most southern states passed laws that severely restricted liberties of free African Americans. In some states, free African Americans could not assemble in large groups unless a white person was present. They were also excluded from occupations that would involve frequent contact with slaves, out of fear of slave revolts. Throughout the South, free African Americans were second-class citizens.

African Americans in the North   Free African Americans who migrated North were only a little better off. They still faced racial prejudice. Only in New England and in the upper Midwest, which was mainly settled by New Englanders, did the abolition of slavery and the idea of racial equality find much support. The lower Midwest was settled largely by people who had moved from the South, and they held the same racial attitudes as most white southerners. In the Lower Midwest, local customs and even state laws supported open discrimination against African Americans. In Indiana, African Americans were barred from voting, serving on juries, marrying white people, or attending white schools. Illinois had similar laws.

Still, northern African Americans did have basic civil rights that were lacking in the South. They could protest against slavery by publishing newspapers and printing books. An African American newspaper entitled *Freedom's Journal*, founded in 1827, regularly published articles calling for an end to slavery in the South. Northern African Americans also founded their own churches, which helped unite their communities. The African Methodist Episcopal Church, founded in Philadelphia in 1787, had become a national religious denomination by 1816. Beginning in 1830, national conventions brought free African Americans from throughout the North together to forge a common identity and to protest slavery.

▶ *Harriet Tubman was a "conductor" on the underground railroad. How large a role did free African Americans play in helping slaves escape?*

The Underground Railroad   Free African Americans in the North were also in a position to take direct action against slavery. They played a major role in the operation of the **underground railroad**, as the escape route for runaway slaves was called. Former slaves, such as **Harriet Tubman**, risked their lives on secret missions to bring slaves north to freedom. Many of the "conductors" who helped to move runaways along the underground railroad were free African Americans. Although some European Americans sympathized with the slaves' efforts to escape, the underground railroad was primarily an African American undertaking.

SECTION 3 REVIEW

1. **Discuss** the importance of the cotton gin to the southern economy.
2. **List** the South's major agricultural products.
3. **Name** the seven southern states that had the largest slave population.
4. **Explain** why slaves were no longer imported legally from Africa by 1860.
5. **Describe** two ways slaves could legally gain their freedom.

Slavery and the Slave Community

Slavery was a harsh way of life. Just how harsh it was depended partly on the owner of the enslaved person. Many slave owners were cruel, ordering their slaves to be lashed with whips for the slightest reason. William Wells Brown, who grew up as a slave, remembered years later the shock of seeing his mother whipped for arriving late in the cotton field. "The cold chills ran over me, and I wept aloud." Some owners and overseers were kind and gentle people. But no matter how individuals were treated, all enslaved African Americans experienced grinding toil, frustration, and fear. Each one faced the same struggle to keep a sense of self-worth while living a life that demanded obedience and self-denial.

What was life like for enslaved African Americans?
What kind of family life did slaves have?
What benefits did the slaves receive from their communities on larger plantations?

Hard Physical Labor

A slave's day consisted of long hours of physical labor. For a field hand, the workday began well before dawn and ended after sunset. Many free white farmers in the South also put in long hours in the fields. But unlike them, enslaved African Americans had no control over their work time. Slaves also worked under the constant threat of physical punishment.

Many slaves were brutally treated by their owners and overseers. The experience described by John White, a slave on a Texas plantation, was not uncommon,

The mistress was the best white woman I ever know, but Master Presley used his whip all the time, reason or no reason, and I got scars to remember by! . . . One day the master finds a soapy streak in his shirt [White did the plantation's laundry]. Then he finds me. The Military Road goes by the place and the master drives me down the road and ties me to a tree. First he tears off the old shirt and then throws the bullwhip to me. When he is tired of beating me more torture is a-coming. The saltwater cure. It don't cure nothing but that's what the white folks call it. 'Here's at you,' the Master say, and slap the saltwater into the bleeding cuts. 'Here's at you!' The blisters burst every time he slap me with the brine.

Slave owners could beat their slaves for the slightest reason whenever they wished. The courts of the South placed only one restriction on the slave owner's rights. An owner could not kill a slave without "good cause." Otherwise, the slave could be used or abused as the owner saw fit.

Despite these conditions, slaves did find ways to exert some control over their working lives. When driven too hard, they could deliberately slow down the pace of their work or pretend that they were ill. When all else failed, they could secretly break tools or damage crops. These tactics sometimes succeeded against an overseer who was too demanding, as the overseer had to answer to the planter for the amount of work done and for the condition of equipment and crops. Some planters listened to complaints against harsh overseers, realizing that well-treated slaves did more and better work than slaves who were mistreated.

Slave revolts were the most extreme form of resistance. Uprisings were not frequent, but the few that did occur and the fear that there would be others were sources of continual worry for white southerners. In August 1800, a Virginia slave named Gabriel Prosser organized an uprising that included plans for burning the city of Richmond and for capturing the state governor. The revolt was exposed before it could take place, and the principal leaders, including Prosser, were executed. Denmark Vesey, the Charleston slave who had bought his own freedom, planned a similar rebellion that was discovered in 1822. The most bloody uprising of all was the revolt in August 1831 led by **Nat Turner**, a slave on a plantation in Southampton County, Virginia. Turner and a small band of followers went from plantation to plantation killing nearly 60 white people. The revolt was quickly put down. Some 40 slaves were killed in retaliation. Turner was arrested, put on trial, and executed.

Primitive Living Conditions

Slaves might resist work demands that were too harsh, but they could do little about their living conditions. Field slaves usually lived in overcrowded, one-room cabins or in larger sheds that were little better than stables. It was common for 7 or 8 slaves to live and sleep in a single room, with the number sometimes reaching 10 or 12.

The slaves' diet consisted mainly of salt pork and cornmeal, from which cornbread and other starchy

▶
What clues does this painting provide as to the limited freedoms enslaved African Americans had over their own lives?

The Spoken Arts—African Influences in the South

The South had two cultural traditions, one European American, the other African American. Enslaved Africans were forced to adopt a European American way of life, raising cotton, sugar, rice, and other commodities for world markets. But they kept many elements of their traditional African cultures and lifestyles.

The West African cultures were preliterate, which means that they did not have written languages. Consequently, as historian Lawrence W. Levine notes in his book *Black Culture and Black Consciousness*, these cultures "assigned a central role to the spoken arts." Because of the slaves' African heritage, songs and folktales were an important part of their lives in the United States.

Music played a major role in the lives of enslaved African Americans. Like their African ancestors, slaves used songs to express their feelings and to establish a rhythm for their work routines. "They have magnificent voices and sing without instruction," a white southerner wrote. "They go singing to their daily labors. The maid sings about the house, and the laborer sings in the field." Singing helped the slaves get through long days of hard work. "I used to pick 150 pounds of cotton

▲ As these lyrics explain, slaves were expected to pick 100 pounds of cotton a day.

every day," one former slave remembered. "We would pick cotton and sing, pick and sing all day."

The spoken arts of the South also included the tales told in the slave community. The best known are the Uncle Remus stories that Joel Chandler Harris collected after the Civil War. These stories feature Br'er Rabbit, an animal trickster with a talent for outwitting his stronger and more powerful enemies. Slaves could easily identify with the trickster rabbit. They, too, outwitted their owners and overseers when the need arose. Some of the slave tales were adaptations of folktales from West Africa. Others

▲ In this drawing, Br'er Rabbit is passing on his tricks (wisdom) to the next generation.

were adapted from European folk traditions or were created by the slaves themselves.

The character of the easygoing Uncle Remus was later used to create an unfavorable stereotype of African Americans. This was an unfortunate misuse of a major figure in southern slave culture. It distracted attention both from the importance of the storyteller in African American slave culture and from Br'er Rabbit's message. His message was that cleverness can be a potent weapon in the hands of otherwise powerless people. The slaves lived in a world in which the oppressed had to use their wits to get the better of their oppressors.

1. What important roles did music play in the lives of slaves?
2. What does the popularity of trickster tales reveal about the slaves' view of the world?

dishes were made. The slaves tried to supplement this diet with greens, garden vegetables, and wild game animals. Still, this diet was dangerously low in protein and vitamins. Consequently, slaves often lacked the energy to do the hard work demanded of them. Dietary deficiencies also produced skin diseases.

The slaves' clothing was as inadequate as their food. The usual clothing ration for a field slave was one outfit for winter and one for summer, with one pair of shoes each year. Household slaves were dressed somewhat better, as they had to be presentable to the owner's houseguests and visitors. These slaves also had better food than field slaves.

Enslaved Families Provide Support

Although the law did not recognize slave marriages, many slaves married and had families. "The family, while it had no legal existence in slavery, was in actuality one of the most important survival mechanisms for the slave," historian John

Blassingame has written. "In his family he found companionship, love, sexual gratification, sympathetic understanding of his sufferings." The slave family served many needs. Children learned from their parents how to avoid the overseer's lash. Family roles gave mothers and fathers the status and respect that they did not have in the world outside.

Slave families were allowed to exist because they also served the interests of slave owners. Slave owners found that slaves who had wives, husbands, and children on the plantation were less likely to run away or cause trouble. Slaves with families were also easier to discipline. The threat of separating the family was an effective way to control behavior.

The selling of family members posed the greatest danger to the slave family. Historians estimate that 3 out of every 10 slave marriages were broken up by the sale of husband or wife. Every slave family was exposed to this danger. Even compassionate planters who tried to keep slave families together did not always manage to do so. A poor crop year might force the planter to sell slaves. Or the planter might die, leaving his heirs to divide up the property. Enslaved families lived in constant fear of being separated.

▶

*Enslaved African Americans were bought and sold at slave auctions. (*Slave Market, Richmond, Virginia, *1862, by Eyre Crowe, collection of Jay P. Altmayer, photograph courtesy of Kennedy Galleries, Inc., New York.)*

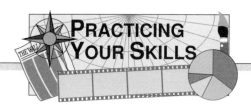

Analyzing Fine Art

Pictures are one of the pieces of evidence historians use to reconstruct the way people lived in the past. When you and your friends produce a yearbook, you are making a record of everyday life in your high school. Its pictures of teams, clubs, classes, and other activities reflect what you and your friends think are important. Someday these pictures may give others a clue to your values, customs, and beliefs.

Every society and culture has its own values, customs, and beliefs. They are expressed in its art, religion, and politics, and are reflected in its everyday life. Pictures of ordinary events often give us a revealing glimpse into the values and viewpoints of people in the past.

A review of the steps, introduced in the Chapter 2 Practicing Your Skills, to analyze pictures will help you complete this skill exercise:

- **Determine if the artist has a point of view or bias to express.** Did the artist have a particular purpose or reason for creating the work?
- **Determine when the picture was made.** Scenes generally become less accurate as the time between the actual event and the portrayal increases.
- **Study the details of the picture.** How has the artist used light, placement of figures, colors, and symbols?

- **Does the content of the picture support or contradict what you already knew about the event or time?** Is the image a reliable source of information? What knowledge or information did you gain from the picture that you didn't have before?

Examine the picture on page 314 and complete the following steps:

1. List three specific activities taking place in this picture.
2. What story does this picture tell?
3. Make a list of adjectives that you think describe this scene.
4. What attitudes about the respective roles of enslaved African Americans and the white slave owners are shown in this picture?
5. How do you think this artist viewed the institution of slavery? Give reasons for your answer.
6. Write two questions that came to mind while studying this scene.

Community Life

Slaves on the larger plantations also lived in a community that extended beyond the family. This community had its center in the slave quarters, the cluster of cabins and sheds that was a part of every large plantation. The slave quarters provided one of the few places where slaves could be more or less free from constant supervision. Congregating there at night or on Sunday, the enslaved African

Americans could share their hopes, fears, and complaints with one another. They could listen to the folktales passed down from their African ancestors, or they could pour out their sorrows in song and prayer. Slaves without families might find stand-in aunts, uncles, or other relatives to provide companionship and support.

Slave quarters were part of a still larger community that included slaves on other nearby plantations. It was common for slaves to visit friends or relatives on neighboring plantations, usually with a written pass provided by their owner. Visits were also made in the dark of night without permission. At busy times of the year, slaves from several plantations were sometimes brought together in work gangs. These events, especially at corn-shucking time, were social occasions as well as work.

Shucking parties added some excitement to the routine on southern plantations. As corn was harvested during the busy cotton-picking season, it had to be shucked, or stripped out of its husks, at night after the slaves had come in from the cotton fields. To make this extra work a little easier, slave owners often made it a festive time. "On these occasions," a former slave from Alabama remembered, "we all got together and had a regular good time." The planter would send word to neighboring plantations and butcher a hog for a barbecue. Turning the work into a contest, the slaves would appoint two leaders, the "corn generals," who would choose teams. Both teams would attack the piles of corn already brought in from the fields to see which side could shuck the most. During an evening of eating, drinking, and merriment, the corn was shucked, gossip and news were exchanged, and the bonds of the slave community were strengthened.

Slaves Adapt Christianity

Religion was a vital force in the slave community. The slaves combined elements of Christianity and traditional African religions. Alongside Christian tenets, the slaves maintained beliefs in spirits and magic. In most places, the slaves kept control over their own religious lives, meeting for services at their own "praying ground" on the plantation, apart from the owner's family. Although these were Christian services, praise meetings were very different from the white church services. The rhythmic music accompanying the slave services was complex and intense, strongly influenced by the old cultures and present-day needs. As one former slave described them,

> The way in which we worshiped is almost indescribable. The singing was accompanied by a certain ecstasy of motion, clapping of hands, tossing of heads, which would continue without cessation about half an hour; one would lead off in a kind of recitative style, others joining in the chorus. The old house . . . rang with their jubilant shouts, and shook in all its joints.

Slaves preferred the **spirituals**, or religious folk songs, that they composed on the spot to the church hymns they learned from white people. Painful memories of old friends and relatives who were sold to the slave traders might be eased with a verse such as this:

> When we all meet in Heaven,
>   There is no parting there.
> When we all meet in Heaven,
>   There is no parting there.

Community and culture provided part of the support that helped make slavery endurable. They strengthened enslaved African Americans' sense of identity, belonging, and support. With shared values and a sense of community, enslaved African Americans no longer felt as isolated or as if they were merely pieces of property belonging to someone else. They had become a people with a unique identity, a nation within a nation.

SECTION 4 REVIEW

1. **Describe** briefly what living conditions were like for enslaved African Americans.
2. **Detail** the forms that slave resistance took.
3. **Explain** why slaves were permitted and encouraged to have families.
4. **Describe** the role religion played in African American slave culture.
5. **Identify** praise meetings.

The Nation at Midcentury

When the British writer Charles Dickens toured the United States in 1842, he paid a visit to Lowell, Massachusetts. The young city, founded only 20 years earlier, was known on both sides of the Atlantic as a model factory town. Dickens was especially impressed by how fresh and new the town looked. "Nothing in the whole town looked old to me.... In one place there was a new wooden church, which, having no steeple, and being yet unpainted, looked like an enormous packing-case without any direction upon it." Even the river, the source of power for the machinery in the factories, seemed to acquire a youthful character from the new buildings of bright red brick and freshly painted wood that lined its banks. For Charles Dickens and many other European visitors of that time, Lowell represented the bright future that lay ahead for the young and rapidly industrializing American nation.

Why was industrial growth more rapid in the North than in the South?

Why did the South resent northern industrial growth?

How was the status of women changing in the northern states?

Industrial Growth in the North

The town of Lowell was an appropriate symbol for the rapid industrial growth of the United States during the second quarter of the nineteenth century. A village of 2,500 people in 1825, Lowell had become a bustling city of 33,000 by 1850. By then, nearly 100,000 workers were employed in the textile mills of New England and more than half of them were women.

The shoe industry also grew rapidly. Machines for cutting out leather and for sewing shoes togeth-

▲ *Both railroads and canals serviced the Oswego Starch Factory in Oswego, New York. Why did Americans of the 1800s think of smoke stacks as a sign of progress rather than as a source of pollution?*

er began to replace hand labor, just as machines had in the textile industry. Other lines of manufacturing, including the making of tools, farm implements, clocks, and other consumer goods, were becoming mechanized. By midcentury, the northeastern United States was well on the way to having a modern economy based on manufacturing and commerce.

The industrialization under way in the United States by midcentury was confined largely to the North. The New England states were the most industrialized region of the country, with the textile industry leading the way. However, the middle states, especially New York, Pennsylvania, and Ohio, were also experiencing rapid growth in manufacturing. The South lagged far behind.

Industrial growth was stimulated by many of the same factors that had made factory production possible in the first place. The North had a growing labor force made up of wage earners who were free to move from one factory town to another. The workforce had increased rapidly during the 1840s, due to immigration from Ireland and Germany. Successful merchants provided the initial investment capital. These merchant-manufacturers reinvested their profits in new and larger factories. The economic growth of the 1840s and 1850s was also stimulated by improvements in transportation.

The newly built canals and railroads opened up markets in the West for eastern manufactured goods and reduced the cost of shipping farm products to the East. The railroad mileage in the United States increased nearly tenfold from 1840 to 1860. The cost and time of overland travel fell dramatically. The time required to ship goods from Cincinnati to New York, for example, was reduced from 50 days in 1817 to 6 days in 1852. Passenger travel time between those cities was reduced from three weeks to two days. Wholesale prices declined nearly 40 percent during that period, partly as a result of savings in shipping costs. Falling prices, in turn, stimulated the demand for more goods.

Southern Resentment of the North

In industrial growth, the South lagged far behind the Northeast. Pennsylvania alone produced almost twice the volume of manufactured goods as all the southern states combined. Most of the wealth of the South was tied up in cotton and in slaves. One observer remarked:

> To sell cotton in order to buy negroes—to make more cotton to buy more negroes, "ad infinitum" is the aim and direct tendency of all the operations of the thoroughgoing cotton planter.

As a result, the South was heavily dependent on the North for manufactured goods.

Many southerners resented this growing dependence on the North. An Alabama newspaper noted in 1851,

> Northerners abuse and denounce slavery and slaveholders, yet our slaves are clothed with

▶

This illustration provides a great deal of information about public schools in the mid-nineteenth century. What things do you see in the woodcut that you would not see in schools today? What things have not changed?

▶ *A woman works in her well-equipped kitchen of the mid-nineteenth century. What factory products are visible here?*

Northern manufactured goods, have Northern hats and shoes, work with Northern hoes, ploughs, and other implements. . . . The slaveholder dresses in Northern goods, rides in a Northern saddle . . . sports his Northern carriage . . . reads Northern books.

During the years to come, these feelings would fuel the conflicts between the two sections.

Changes in Women's Status

By midcentury, the economic growth of the United States had also had an effect on the status of women. Northern women, especially working-class women, played a larger role outside the home than ever before. In 1850, almost 24 percent of the nearly 1 million manufacturing workers were women. Most of them worked in textiles, clothing, shoes, and millinery. More women were also working in such middle-class occupations as teaching, nursing, printing, and bookbinding. A few women had discovered that they could earn a living as novelists. Periodicals and newspapers of the early 1850s frequently carried weekly and monthly installments of novels written by Catherine Sedgwick, Fanny Fern, and other female writers. Consequently, some women questioned the traditional idea that they should be content with being homemakers and nothing more.

Other women still regarded homemaking as a legitimate occupation, but insisted that it be given greater respect. In a widely read book entitled *Treatise on Domestic Economy* (1841), Catherine Beecher argued that the home was still woman's proper sphere. Within that sphere, Beecher insisted, women should be assertive and powerful. She wanted to "render each department of woman's true profession as much desired and respected as are the most honored professions of men." While women's work was different from men's, Beecher wrote, it should not be considered inferior.

SECTION 5 REVIEW

1. **Name** five lines of manufacturing that were part of the rapid industrial growth in the northern United States.
2. **Detail** the improvements in transportation that stimulated industrial growth.
3. **Explain** why the North experienced more rapid industrial growth than the South.
4. **State** one reason the South resented their dependence on northern industrialization.
5. **Describe** the relationship between industrial growth and the changing status of women.

Summary

During the first half of the nineteenth century, the North and the South developed in different ways. The North, especially New England and the northeastern states, began to industrialize. More and more people went to work in textile mills and other factories, where they used machines to make a variety of manufactured goods. Factory towns grew in size and importance, attracting native-born Americans from rural areas and immigrants from abroad. The South, on the other hand, developed an economy based on cotton growing with the use of slave labor. The boardinghouses of Lowell, Massachusetts, and the slave quarters on southern plantations were worlds apart. These different labor systems—one free, the other enslaved—came to symbolize the diverging paths of the two regions.

As we have already seen, the Missouri Compromise of 1820 postponed, but did not settle, the issue of slavery. That compromise extended the dividing line between free and slave states to the Rocky Mountains, which was then the frontier with Mexico. By 1850, as we will see in the next chapter, the American frontier had moved all the way to the Pacific. What would be the status of slavery in the new territories acquired from Mexico? Would slavery be permitted or excluded in favor of the system of free labor? By midcentury, these questions were still unanswered.

Vocabulary

American system of   nativist
manufacture   spirituals
assembly line   underground railroad
factory system

Below are short descriptions of situations, or scenarios. On your paper write the vocabulary term from the list above that is illustrated, or defined, by each description.

1. That day in March 1844 the newspaper had two articles pointing out the dangers of hiring an Irish-Catholic worker. Patrick knew he would encounter some angry people when he went out looking for work.
2. The singing from the slave quarters echoed softly through the plantation at the end of the day. To the white children it sounded like holy singing, but the songs did not sound like any hymn they had heard in church.
3. Betty no longer spun her yarn at home in familiar surroundings. She went with all the other workers to the mill where everything was provided for her work.
4. Mary was worried about the family trailing wearily behind her. It had been a long, dangerous, and exhausting trip from the plantation.
5. The workers all had their individual stations. The carcasses of animals were suspended on tracks above them. Joseph wielded the cleaver all day, Peter the tongs, and Edward the hose.
6. Ben worried a little about the watches he was putting together. In the old days all the parts had needed individual attention. Now he and the other workers just took the parts off a pile, and the job was done in no time. It seemed almost too easy.

Review Questions

1. Briefly describe the American system of manufacture.
2. List three ways that the factory system of production changed people's work patterns.
3. Why did the textile mills of Lowell and other Massachusetts towns develop a workforce composed of young women?
4. How did working conditions in the textile industry change in the 1830s?
5. What were the South's major cash crops?
6. What percentage of southern whites owned slaves?

7. In what ways were slaves able to exercise some control over their own lives?
8. How did enslaved African Americans adapt Christianity to meet their needs?
9. How did the South respond to the North's industrial success?
10. What factors were responsible for the change in the status of women by 1850?

Critical Historical Thinking

Writing Answer each of the following questions by writing one or more complete paragraphs:

1. Samuel Slater has been called the "father of the American factory system." In your opinion, why does he deserve such recognition? Explain your answer.
2. Explain why the invention of the cotton gin, by Eli Whitney in 1793, played an important role in radically changing the economy of the South.
3. Aside from the slave issue, Americans began to divide along other ethnic lines, primarily because of increased immigration from Europe. Explain why you think this occurred in a country that had been founded on principles of democracy and understanding.
4. In the Unit 3 Archives, read "A Southern Teacher's View of Slavery" and "A Plantation Hospital." How could these two accounts be reconciled? What bias might have influenced each author?

Making Connections with Anthropology

Changes in society's attitudes and beliefs have an impact on the ways in which historians depict the past. For example, before the 1960s most historians would describe the institution of slavery from the point of view of the white slaveholder, either as an economic arrangement or as a social institution. Seldom did they describe slavery from the enslaved person's point of view. Following the Civil Rights Movement of the 1960s, historians worked to give African Americans a place in American history. But how does one write the history of a people who left few written records?

Anthropologists have developed techniques for investigating living societies, and historians have found their methods to be useful in reconstructing past societies. The picture historians have drawn gives us a far fuller picture of slave life. Using sources such as songs, stories, and the remains of houses and tools, historians have shown that far from being the simple victims of the white slaveowners, enslaved African Americans created their own systems of cultural values. Sometimes they presented one face to their owner and another to their friends and family. It was these values that gave slaves the ability to make a life for themselves when slavery came to an end.

■ To create an oral history, decide on an event that had a significant impact on your town, community, or school. (For example, you may have just had an anniversary celebration of the founding of your city.) Collect such examples of oral history as songs, stories, and tall tales from local citizens or from research in the library or with the historical society. Present your oral history project to the class.

Additional Skills Practice

Write a paragraph that interprets the photograph on page 298 documenting the women at work in the factory. Discuss possible bias, motivation, and intent. What social values are implied?

Unit Review Questions

1. Explain why the decade following the War of 1812 was called the Era of Good Feelings.
2. What changes occurred in the United States after 1815 that prompted historians to name that period the Age of Jackson?
3. List the major causes of the Mexican War.
4. Explain how the southern economy caused the resettlement of American Indians.
5. Describe how geographic features determined economic development of the North and the South.
6. What was the economic basis of the close relationship between England and the South?
7. Describe how the lives of southern Indians and enslaved African Americans were similar.
8. Explain why many northerners viewed the issue of nullification as a major threat.
9. Why was the war with Mexico popular in the South but strongly opposed in the Northeast?
10. Was northern opposition to the plantation system political, moral, or economic? Why?

Personalizing History

Honoring the Past   The period from 1815 to 1848 was a time of great achievements for the nation. The country as a whole grew larger, wealthier, and stronger. This tremendous effort was not without tragedy, however. Many people paid for this growth with their freedom, land, or opportunities to live on equal terms with other Americans.

■ Make as complete a list as possible of groups or individuals who suffered greatly during this period. Select one name from that list as your topic for research. Investigate libraries, museums, and other community sources to see if there are any displays,

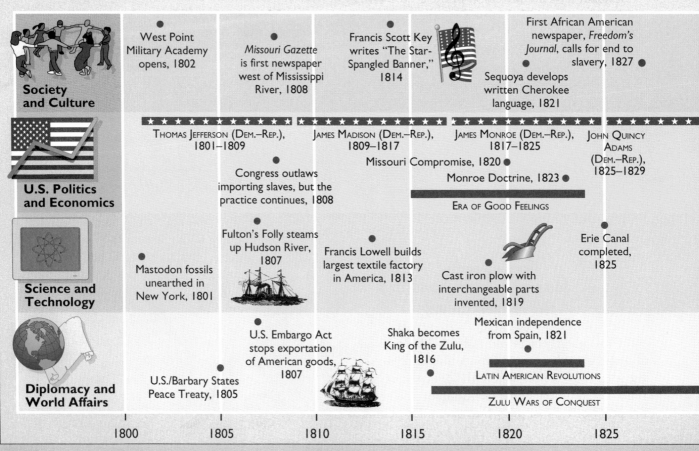

Society and Culture

West Point Military Academy opens, 1802

Missouri Gazette is first newspaper west of Mississippi River, 1808

Francis Scott Key writes "The Star-Spangled Banner," 1814

First African American newspaper, *Freedom's Journal*, calls for end to slavery, 1827

Sequoya develops written Cherokee language, 1821

U.S. Politics and Economics

THOMAS JEFFERSON (DEM.–REP.), 1801–1809

JAMES MADISON (DEM.–REP.), 1809–1817

JAMES MONROE (DEM.–REP.), 1817–1825

JOHN QUINCY ADAMS (DEM.–REP.), 1825–1829

Congress outlaws importing slaves, but the practice continues, 1808

Missouri Compromise, 1820

Monroe Doctrine, 1823

ERA OF GOOD FEELINGS

Science and Technology

Mastodon fossils unearthed in New York, 1801

Fulton's Folly steams up Hudson River, 1807

Francis Lowell builds largest textile factory in America, 1813

Cast iron plow with interchangeable parts invented, 1819

Erie Canal completed, 1825

Diplomacy and World Affairs

U.S./Barbary States Peace Treaty, 1805

U.S. Embargo Act stops exportation of American goods, 1807

Shaka becomes King of the Zulu, 1816

Mexican independence from Spain, 1821

LATIN AMERICAN REVOLUTIONS

ZULU WARS OF CONQUEST

| 1800 | 1805 | 1810 | 1815 | 1820 | 1825 |

exhibits, or perspectives that provide historical information about your choice. Visit the center and report back to class on your experience. If you can't find any local sources, you may be able to get permission from your teacher or parent to visit an on-line Internet source for information.

Linking Past and Present

What Does the Public Really Have a Right to Know?   As you learned in Chapter 7, the 1828 presidential election campaign became especially personal when Andrew Jackson's opponents made public allegations and accusations about his marriage. They claimed that Jackson had married Rachel before her divorce was final. Rachel's character became a topic for gossip, and Andrew Jackson blamed her death, which occurred shortly after the election, on the scandal.

Today, the privacy issue continues to be a difficult one for public figures to deal with. Newspapers, tabloids, and talk shows reveal the most intimate details about public figures, both politicians and celebrities. How much does the public need to know about a candidate for public office? Does the general public have the sophistication to decide what is fact and what is gossip? Is this "need to know all" a recent development?

■ Consider the topic of privacy and public officials. Summarize in two or three well-worded sentences your position on this topic.

Time Line Activity

Drawing from at least two categories on the time line, list five items that prompted or reflected America's westward expansion. Give reasons for your answers.

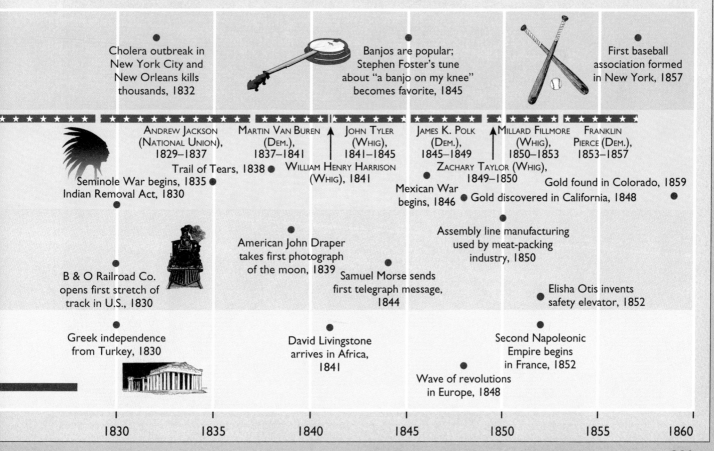

Cholera outbreak in New York City and New Orleans kills thousands, 1832

Banjos are popular; Stephen Foster's tune about "a banjo on my knee" becomes favorite, 1845

First baseball association formed in New York, 1857

ANDREW JACKSON (NATIONAL UNION), 1829–1837

Trail of Tears, 1838

Seminole War begins, 1835
Indian Removal Act, 1830

MARTIN VAN BUREN (DEM.), 1837–1841

WILLIAM HENRY HARRISON (WHIG), 1841

JOHN TYLER (WHIG), 1841–1845

JAMES K. POLK (DEM.), 1845–1849

ZACHARY TAYLOR (WHIG), 1849–1850

Mexican War begins, 1846

MILLARD FILLMORE (WHIG), 1850–1853

FRANKLIN PIERCE (DEM.), 1853–1857

Gold found in Colorado, 1859
Gold discovered in California, 1848

Assembly line manufacturing used by meat-packing industry, 1850

B & O Railroad Co. opens first stretch of track in U.S., 1830

American John Draper takes first photograph of the moon, 1839

Samuel Morse sends first telegraph message, 1844

Elisha Otis invents safety elevator, 1852

Greek independence from Turkey, 1830

David Livingstone arrives in Africa, 1841

Second Napoleonic Empire begins in France, 1852

Wave of revolutions in Europe, 1848

1830   1835   1840   1845   1850   1855   1860

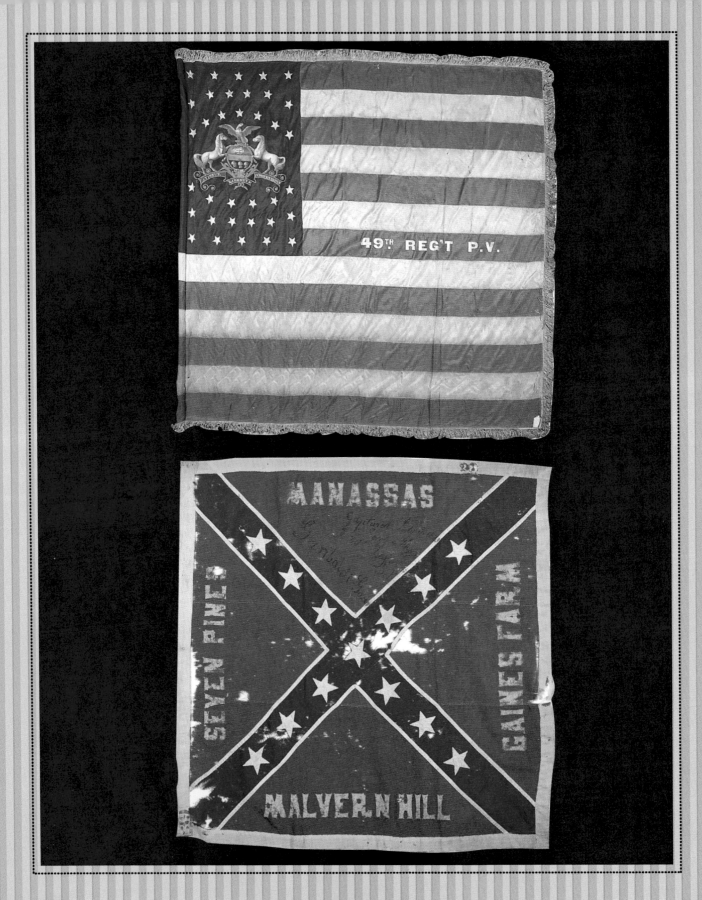

UNIT 4

A Nation Divided, 1848–1876

In 1861, the United States reached its greatest crisis. At the heart of the crisis was a dispute over the status of slavery in the territories. The South refused to accept any limitations on its right to take slaves into the new territories. The North was determined to exclude slavery from those areas. Several attempts to settle this issue by political compromise failed. Eleven states seceded from the Union in 1861, provoking a costly and bloody civil war. Almost as many Americans were killed in that war as in all of the nation's other wars combined. Although the nation survived that crisis, the South was devastated. The physical reconstruction of the war-torn South was an enormous task that took many decades to complete. Social reconstruction, including the extension of full citizenship to African Americans, would take a century.

Chapter 10 A Time of Crisis	**Chapter 11** The Nation at War	**Chapter 12** Reconstruction

◀ *Civil War troops carried state, regimental, and national flags into battle. The battle flag of Pennsylvania (top) shows the state colors. The state coat of arms is set on a field of stars. The 11th Mississippi Infantry flag (bottom) shows the names of Civil War battles involving the regiment.*

Themes

- **Democracy and Citizenship** The Civil War settled the question whether a government of the people, for the people, and by the people could survive in America. It was the most severe crisis for democratic government in this nation's history.
- **Technological Developments** The use of modern transportation and weapons technology made the Civil War the first modern war.
- **Economics** The Civil War also represented a clash of two economic systems. The industrial North was in a much better position than the agrarian South to fight a modern war.
- **Multicultural Society** Issues concerning slavery and civil rights indicated the extent to which the United States was a multiracial as well as a multicultural society.

The Issue of Slavery in the Territories

David Wilmot Opposes Slavery in the Territories

David Wilmot, a representative from Pennsylvania, led the opposition in Congress to the extension of slavery into California and New Mexico.

▲ *Slave leg iron*

The issue now presented is not whether slavery shall exist unmolested where it now is, but whether it shall be carried to new and distant regions, now free, where the footprint of a slave cannot be found. This, sir, is the issue. Upon it I take my stand, and from it I cannot be frightened or driven by idle charges of abolitionism.

I ask not that slavery be abolished. I demand that this government preserve the integrity of free territory against the aggressions of slavery—against its wrongful usurpations.

Speech of David Wilmot (Feb. 8, 1847), *Congressional Globe*, 29th Cong., 2nd Sess., Appendix, p. 315.

The Southern Argument in Favor of Slavery Extension

Robert Toombs, a congressman from Georgia, argued that the South had a right to take slaves into the new territories.

If by your [free soil] legislation you seek to drive us from the territories of California and New Mexico, purchased by the common blood and treasure of the whole people, and to abolish slavery in [the District of Columbia], thereby attempting to fix a national degradation upon half the states of this Confederacy, *I am for disunion.*

The Territories are the common property of the people of the United States, purchased by their common blood and treasure. You [members of Congress] are their common agents. It is your duty, while they are in a territorial state, to remove all impediments to their free enjoyment by all sections and people of the Union, the slaveholder and the non-slaveholder.

Speech of Robert Toombs (Mar. 4, 1850), *Congressional Globe,* 31st Cong., 1st Sess., p. 453.

Wilmot Attacks the Proslavery Argument

Speaking for northern Free-Soilers, David Wilmot denied that excluding slavery from California and New Mexico was unfair to the South.

Sir, I was in favor of the annexation of Texas. . . . Yes, sir, here was an empire larger than France given up to slavery. Shall further concessions be made by the North? Shall we give up free territory, the inheritance of free labor? Must we yield this also? Never, sir, never, until we ourselves are fit to be slaves.

We are told that the joint blood and treasure of the whole country [are] being expended in this acquisition, therefore it should be divided, and slavery allowed to take its share. Sir, the South has her share already. . . . We are fighting this war for Texas and for the South. . . . For this, sir, Northern treasure is being exhausted, and Northern blood poured upon the plains of Mexico. . . . Slavery is there; there let it remain.

Now, sir, we are told that California is ours, that New Mexico is ours—won by the valor of our arms. They are free. . . . Shall these fair provinces be the inheritance and homes of the white labor of freemen or the black labor of slaves? . . .

Shall the South be permitted . . . to wrest these provinces from Northern freemen? . . .

This is the question.

Speech of David Wilmot (Feb. 8, 1847), *Congressional Globe,* 29th Cong., 2nd Sess., Appendix, p. 315.

Civil War in Kansas

Axalla John Hoole, a proslavery immigrant in Kansas, wrote a letter home to his mother in South Carolina, which included the following account of a fight with the Free-Soilers.

[The Free Soilers] came against us last Friday.... We came in gunshot of each other, but the regular soldiers came and interfered, but not before our party had shot some dozen guns, by which it is reported that five of the Abolitionists were killed or wounded. We had strict orders from our commanding officer (Gen'l Marshall) not to fire until they made the attack, but some of our boys would not be restrained. I was a rifleman and one of the skirmishers, but did all that I could to restrain our men though I itched all over to shoot, myself. I drew a bead a dozen times on a big Yankee about 150 yards from me, but did not fire.... I firmly believed that we would have whipped them, although we would have lost a good many men.... I for one, did not feel as nervous as I am when I go to shoot a beef or a turkey.

Axalla John Hoole to Mrs. Elizabeth Stanley Hoole, Lecompton, Kansas Territory (Sept. 12, 1856).

What Caused the Civil War?

A Conflict over Political Principles

Alexander H. Stephens of Georgia, who served as vice president of the Confederacy, wrote that secession and the Civil War had resulted from opposing principles of government.

That the War had its origin in *opposing principles* ... may be assumed as an unquestionable fact.... The contest was between those who held it to be strictly Federal in its character, and those who maintained that it was thoroughly National. It was a strife between the principles of Federation, on the one side, and Centralism or Consolidation, on the other.

Slavery, so called, was but *the question* on which these antagonistic principles, which had been in conflict, from the beginning ... were finally brought into actual and active collision with each other on the field of battle.

Alexander H. Stephens, *A Constitutional View of the Late War Between the States* (Philadelphia, 1868–1870), vol. 1, p. 9.

South Carolina's Ordinance of Secession

The secession ordinance adopted by South Carolina on December 20, 1860, emphasized the threat posed by Lincoln's election.

On the 4th of March next ... [a sectional] party will take possession of the Government. It has announced that the South shall be excluded from the common [Western] territory, that the Judicial tribunal [Supreme Court] shall be made sectional, and that a war must be waged against Slavery until it shall cease throughout the United States.

The guarantees of the Constitution will then no longer exist; the equal rights of the States will be lost. The Slaveholding States will no longer have the power of ... self-protection, and the Federal Government will have become their enemy.

We, therefore, the people of South Carolina, by our delegates in Convention assembled ... have solemnly declared that the Union ... is dissolved.

Frank Moore, ed., *The Rebellion Record* (New York, 1861–1868), vol. I, pp. 3–4.

Lincoln's Pledge to Defend the Union

In his inaugural address on March 4, 1861, President Abraham Lincoln tried to reassure the South that his only purpose was to defend the Union.

Apprehension seems to exist among the people of the Southern States that by the accession of a Republican Administration their property and their peace and personal security are to be endangered. There has never been any reasonable cause for such apprehension.... The property, peace, and security of no section are to be in any wise endangered by the now incoming Administration....

In your hands, my dissatisfied fellow countrymen, and not in *mine*, is the momentous issue of civil war. The Government will not assail *you*.... You have no oath registered in heaven to destroy the Government, while I shall have the most solemn one to "preserve, protect, and defend it."

I am loath to close. We are not enemies, but friends. We must not be enemies. Though passion may have strained, it must not break our bonds of affection. The mystic chords of memory, stretching from every battlefield and patriot grave to every living heart and hearthstone all over the broad land, will yet swell the chorus of the Union, when again touched, as surely they will be, by the better angels of our nature.

James D. Richardson, ed., *A Compilation of the Messages and Papers of the Presidents* (Washington, D.C., 1897), vol. VI, pp. 5–12.

Two Civilizations in Conflict

William H. Herndon, Abraham Lincoln's Illinois law partner, explained his views about the cause of the sectional crisis.

Liberty and slavery—Civilization and barbarism are *absolute* antagonisms. One or the other must perish on this Continent. . . . Compromise—Compromise! Why I am sick at the very idea.

There is no dodging the question. Let the *natural* struggle, heaven high and "hell" deep, go on. . . . I am thoroughly convinced that two such civilizations as the North and the South cannot co-exist on the same soil and be co-equal in the Federal brotherhood. To expect otherwise would be to expect the Absolute to sleep with and tolerate "hell."

William H. Herndon to Charles Sumner, (Dec. 10, 1860).

Sectional Hatred

A southern senator acknowledged the hatred that existed between the people of the North and the South.

Sir, disguise the fact as you will, there is [a hatred] between the northern and southern people that is deep and enduring, and you never can eradicate it—never! . . . We are enemies as much as if we were hostile States. I believe that the northern people hate the South worse than ever the English people hated France; and I can tell my brethren over there that there is no love lost upon the part of the South.

Speech of Senator Alfred Iverson of Georgia (Dec. 4, 1860).

Billy Yank Meets Johnny Reb

Union and Confederate troops sometimes declared informal truces to exchange food, tobacco, and news, as these Union and Confederate soldiers did along the Rappahannock River in Virginia. The narrator was a Confederate soldier.

The sound of the gentle ripple of waves upon the sand was broken by a faint "halloo" which came from the other side.

"Johnny Reb; I say, J-o-h-n-n-y R-e-b. Don't shoot!"

Joe Reid shouted back, "All right!"

"What command are you?"

The spoken words floated clear and distinct across the water, "The Black Horse Cavalry. Who are you?"

"The Second Michigan Cavalry."

"Come out on the bank," said our spokesman, "and show yourselves; we won't fire."

"On your honor, Johnny Reb?"

"On our honor, Billy Yank."

In a second a large squad of blue-coats across the way advanced to the water's brink. The Southerners did the same; then the former put the query.

"Have you any tobacco?"

"Plenty of it," went out our reply.

"Any sugar and coffee?" they questioned.

"Not a taste nor a smell."

"Let's trade," was shouted with eagerness.

"Very well," was the reply.

. . . We shouted over to the Yanks that we had about twenty pounds of cut plug [chewing tobacco], and asked them what we must do? They hallooed back to let one of us swim across. . . . Then I volunteered. . . .

Alexander Hunter, *Johnny Reb and Billy Yank* (New York, 1905), pp. 429–30.

The Face of Battle

The Cornfield at Antietam

The bloodiest day of fighting during the war took place on September 17, 1862, during the Battle of Antietam. Some of the heaviest fighting took place in a cornfield, as described in the following account.

At the front edge of the cornfield was a low Virginia rail fence. . . . As we appeared at the edge of the corn, a long line of men in butternut and gray rose up from the ground. Simultaneously, the hostile battle lines opened a tremendous fire upon each other. Men, I can not say fell; they were knocked out of the ranks by dozens. But we jumped over the

▲ *Battle of Bull Run*

fence, and pushed on, loading, firing, and shouting as we advanced. There was, on the part of the men, great hysterical excitement, eagerness to go forward, and a reckless disregard of life, of everything but victory. . . .

Everybody tears cartridges, loads, passes guns, or shoots. Men are falling in their places or running back into the corn. The soldier who is shooting is furious in his energy. The soldier who is shot looks around for help with an imploring agony of death on his face. After a few rods of advance, the line stopped and, by common impulse, fell back to the edge of the corn and lay down on the ground behind the low rail fence.

Another line of our men came up through the corn. We all joined together, jumped over the fence, and again pushed out into the open field. There is a rattling fusillade and loud cheers. "Forward" is the word. The men are loading and firing with demoniacal fury and shouting and laughing hysterically, and the whole field before us is covered with rebels fleeing for life, into the woods. Great numbers of them are shot while climbing over the high post and rail fences along the turnpike. We push on over the open fields half way to the little church. The powder is bad, and the guns have become very dirty. It takes hard pounding to get the bullets down, and our firing is becoming slow. A long and steady line of rebel gray, unbroken by the fugitives who fly before us, comes sweeping down through the woods around the church. They raise the yell and fire. It is like a scythe running through our line. "Now, save, who can." It is a race for life that each man runs for the cornfield. A sharp cut, as of a switch, stings the calf of my leg as I run. Back to the corn, and back through the corn, the headlong fight continues.

 Rufus R. Dawes, *Service with the Sixth Wisconsin Volunteers* (Marietta, Ohio, 1890), pp. 90–92.

The Battle of Chancellorsville

The poet Walt Whitman, who served with the Union army as a male nurse, wrote this description of the battle at Chancellorsville.

There was part of the late battle at Chancellorsville, . . . a little over a week ago, . . . I would like to give just a glimpse of. . . . The fighting had been very hot during the day, and after an intermission the latter part, was resumed at night, and kept up with furious energy till 3 o'clock in the morning. . . . The night was very pleasant, at times the moon shining out full and clear, all Nature so calm in itself . . . yet there the battle raging, and many good fellows lying helpless . . . the red lifeblood oozing out from heads or trunks or limbs upon that green and dew-cool grass. Patches of the woods take fire, and several of the wounded, unable to move, are consumed—quite large spaces are swept over, burning the dead also. . . . The flashes of fire from the cannon, the quick flaring flames and smoke, and the immense roar—the musketry so general, the light nearly bright enough for each side to see the other—the crashing, tramping of men—the yelling—close quarters . . . and still the woods on fire.

Then the camps of the wounded—O heavens, what scene is this? . . . One man is shot by a shell, both in the arm and leg—both are amputated—there lie the rejected members. Some have their legs blown off—some bullets through the breast—some indescribably horrid wounds in the face or head, all mutilated, sickening, torn, gouged out—some in the abdomen—some mere boys.

 Walt Whitman, *Specimen Days* (1882–1883).

Sherman Shows No Mercy

They Must Reap the Whirlwind

In this letter to his wife, Union General William T. Sherman described the hatred expressed by the women of the

South toward his troops. Although a native of Ohio, Sherman had served as president of Louisiana's state university before the war.

I doubt if history affords a parallel to the deep and bitter enmity of the women of the South. No one who sees them and hears them but must feel the intensity of their hate. Not a man is seen; nothing but women with houses plundered . . . servants all gone and women and children bred in luxury, beautiful and accomplished, begging with one breath for the soldiers' ration and in another praying that the Almighty or Joe Johnston will come and kill us. . . . Why cannot they look back to the day and hour when I, a stranger in Louisiana, begged and implored them to pause in their career, that secession was death, was everything fatal? . . . I will treat them with kindness, but they have sowed the wind and must reap the whirlwind. Until [the Confederates] lay down their arms and submit to the rightful authority of the government, they must not appeal to me for mercy or favors.

▲ *Ruins of Richmond, Virginia*

William T. Sherman to his wife, Vicksburg (June 27, 1863).

Sherman in South Carolina

The following diary entries were written by Emma LeConte of Columbia, South Carolina, in February 1865. The town, where the first ordinance of secession was adopted in 1860, was anxiously awaiting the arrival of Sherman's army.

February 12 or 13th. Father brought in some news this morning. First and worst, the Yankees are skirmishing at Orangeburg. Second and more encouraging, Gen. Hampton says Sherman *will not* come to Columbia.

February 14. Tuesday. What a panic the whole town is in! I have not been out of the house myself, but Father says the intensest excitement prevails on the streets. The Yankees are reported a few miles off on the other side of the river. . . . It is true some think Sherman will burn the town, but we can hardly believe that.

February 16. Thursday. How can the terror and excitement of today be described! . . . "Wouldn't it be dreadful if they should shell the city?" someone said. "They would not do that," replied Mother, "for they have not demanded its surrender." Scarcely had the words passed her lips when Jane, the nurse, rushed in crying out that they were shelling. We ran to the front door just in time to hear a shell go whirring past. It fell and exploded not far off.

February 17th. Friday. Well, they are here. I was sitting in the back parlor when I heard the shouting of the troops. I was at the front door in a moment. Jane came running and crying, "Oh, Miss Emma, they've come at last! She said they were then marching down Main Street, before them flying a panic-stricken crowd of women and children who seemed crazy. . . . I ran upstairs to my bedroom windows just in time to see the U.S. flag run up over the State House. Oh, what a horrid sight! What a degradation! After four long bitter years of bloodshed and hatred, now to float there at last! That hateful symbol of despotism! . . .

Strange as it may seem, we were actually idiotic enough to believe Sherman would keep his word! A *Yankee*—and *Sherman!* It does seem incredible, such credulity, but I suppose we were so anxious to believe him—the lying fiend!

The wretched people running from their burning homes were not allowed to keep even the few necessaries they gathered up in their flight—even blankets and food were taken from them and destroyed. . . . The wind blew a fearful gale, wafting the flames from house to house with frightful rapidity. By midnight the whole town . . . was wrapped in one huge blaze.

Earl Schenk Miers, ed., *When the World Ended: The Diary of Emma LeConte* (Lincoln: University of Nebraska Press, 1957), pp. 29, 30–31, 32, 33, 35–36, 39, 40, 41–42, 44, 45.

The African Americans' Civil War

The New York Draft Riot

John Torrey, a New York doctor, wrote this firsthand description of the draft riots in that city.

New York, July 13th, 1863

Dear Doctor:

We have had treat riots in New York today & they are still in progress. . . . I had made arrangements for visiting Eliza . . . but just as I was starting Mr. Mason came in & said that he saw a mob stop two 3rd Ave. [street]cars to take out some Negroes & maltreat them. This decided me to return home, so as to protect my colored servants. . . . I found the streets full of people, & when I reached the terminus. . . I found the whole road way & sidewalks filled with rough fellows (& some rough women) who were tearing up rails, cutting down telegraph poles, & setting fire to buildings. . . . Toward evening the mob, furious as demons, went yelling over to the Colored-Orphan Asylum in 5th Avenue a little below where we live—& rolling a barrel of kerosene in it, the whole structure was soon in a blaze, & is now a smoking ruin. What has become of the 300 poor innocent orphans I could not learn. They must have had some warning of what the rioters intended; & I trust the children were removed in time to escape a cruel death.

Ever yours,
John Torrey

 Dr. John Torrey to Asa Gray (July 13, 1863).

The First Regiment Louisiana Native Guard

William Wells Brown, a former slave, described the attack by an African American regiment at the Battle of Port Hudson.

Although the [Union army's] First Louisiana had done well, its great triumph was reserved for the 14th of June, when Capt. Howard and his associates in arms won for themselves immortal renown. Never, in the palmy days of Napoleon, Wellington, or any other general, was more true heroism shown. The effect of the battle of the 27th of May, is thus described in "The New-York Herald," June 6 [1863]:

The First Regiment Louisiana Native Guard, Col. Nelson, were in this charge. *They went on the advance, and, when they came out, six hundred out of nine hundred men could not be accounted for. It is said on every side that they fought with the desperation of tigers. . . .* There are other incidents connected with the conduct of this regiment *that have raised them very much in my opinion as soldiers. After firing one volley, they did not deign to load again, but went in with bayonets; and, wherever they had a chance, it was all up with the rebels.*

. . . Humanity should not forget, that, at the surrender of Port Hudson, not a single [Union] colored man could be found alive, although thirty-five were known to have been taken prisoners during the siege. All had been murdered.

 William Wells Brown, *The Negro in the American Rebellion: His Heroism and His Fidelity* (Boston: Lee and Shepard, 1867), pp. 167–176.

Demanding Equal Pay

During the first years of the war, African Americans who enrolled in the army were classified as laborers, who received less pay and benefits than soldiers. By 1864, over 100,000 blacks were fighting as soldiers, but still receiving laborers' wages. Democrats in Congress opposed Republican attempts to equalize combat pay, despite a chorus of protests from African Americans. Equal pay legislation was finally enacted, retroactive to January 1, 1864, but not before. The following is taken from an editorial protest published in an African American church newspaper.

Will you accept us upon equal terms with white men in the service of our country? . . . That is the question. We ask for equal pay and bounty, not because we set a greater value upon money than we do upon human liberty, compared with which, money is mere trash; but we [seek] equal pay and bounty upon the principle, that if we receive equal pay and bounty when we go into the war, we hope to receive equal rights and privileges when we come out of the war.

Is that an unreasonable hope, or an unjust claim? It takes as much to clothe and feed the black man's wife as it does the white man's wife. It takes as much money to go to market for the black man's little boys and girls. We have yet to learn why it is that the black soldier should not receive the same compensation for labor in the service of his country that the white soldier receives.

A.M.E. Christian Recorder (Mar. 19, 1864).

Celebrating Victory

The following account about how the Civil War ended was written by Felix Haywood, a former slave who lived in Texas.

The end of the war, it come just like that—like you snap your fingers.

Soldiers all of a sudden, was everywhere—coming in bunches, crossing and walking and riding. Everyone was a-singing. We was all walking on golden clouds. Hallelujah!

> Union forever,
> Hurrah, boys, hurrah!
> Although I may be poor,
> I'll never be a slave—
> Shouting the battle cry of freedom.

Everybody went wild. We felt like heroes, and nobody had made us that way but ourselves. We was free. Just like that, we was free.

We knowed freedom was on us, but we didn't know what was to come with it. We thought we was going to get rich like the white folks. We thought we was going to be richer than the white folks, 'cause we was stronger and knowed how to work, and the whites didn't, and they didn't have us to work for them any more. But it didn't turn out that way. We soon found out that freedom could make folks proud, but it didn't make 'em rich.

B. A. Botkin., ed., *Lay My Burden Down: A Folk History of Slavery* (Chicago: University of Chicago Press, 1945), pp. 65–66.

The Freedmen During Reconstruction

J. W. Alvord was the General Superintendent of Education in the Freedmen's Bureau. In January 1870, he traveled through Georgia and South Carolina observing conditions among the freedmen and in their schools. The following are excerpts from his reports.

Augusta, Georgia

One half of the population of Augusta, numbering in all 12,000, is colored. With much to struggle against . . . the freedmen here are fully meeting our expectations. . . .

Just out of the city is a settlement of about one hundred families . . . where small homesteads have been purchased and are being paid for; average value of each from $100 to $500. These families are joyously cultivating their own gardens and provision grounds, also finding work in the city.

Further in the interior the freedmen are buying or renting land and raising their own crops. A community of such families, about thirty miles out, (in South Carolina) came in, a few days since, to market their crops for the season. They had chartered a railroad car for $140 the round trip, and loading it with cotton, corn, &c. exchanged the same for clothing, furniture, implements of husbandry, and supplies for putting in their next crop. They came to us on returning, and begged very hard that a teacher might be sent to their settlement, promising to pay all expenses. These are indications of the *drift* of these people towards independent home life and profitable labor.

▲ *Freedmen's school*

Columbia, South Carolina

I have been much interested in witnessing the social elevation of the freemen at this place. The Governor, General R. K. Scott, in his receptions makes no distinction among the members of the legislature, (125 of whom are colored). . . . All alike, on such occasions, crowd around his luxurious refreshment tables.

You will remember at the dinner party given on your account by the governor, and at which I had the honor of being a guest, his secretary of state, the Hon[orable] F. L. Cardozo and lady, (both colored), received equal attention with other officials, and ladies and gentlemen of the highest standing. I could but feel as I looked around upon that agreeable circle that *equality of character and culture were the true conditions of equality in social life.*

[The governor's] opinion is that in our higher institutions of learning *cultured* youth of both colors will come, at length, to associate on equal terms, and that scholarship and general refinement on each side will gradually settle the whole question of mixed schools.

Charleston, South Carolina

Alvord noticed changes in the clothing worn by the former slaves of Charleston.

In this advancing civilization, nothing is more apparent than the altered *apparel* of the freedmen. From linsey wolsey, ragged garments, clumsy brogans, or bare feet of former times, we notice the change to clothes of modern material; shoes or gaiters on the feet of boys and girls; whole schools

as tidily dressed as most of the common schools at the North. While the same make of clothing, bought with their own money from the shops, or skillfully made with their own hands, is everywhere to be seen. It gives the adult population in the streets and churches an air strikingly in contrast with the menial raiment with which slavery had clothed them. It is the costume of freedom, each choosing his or her dress, according to taste, and all mainly in the respectable [clothing] of society around them.

J. W. Alvord, *Letters from the South, Relating to the Condition of the Freedman* (Washington: Howard University Press, 1870), pp. 5–28.

WORKING WITH THE ARCHIVES

Analyzing Persuasive Arguments in Primary Sources

In this skill exercise you will learn to identify basic persuasive techniques. The four basic persuasive techniques (or appeals) are personality, tradition, rhetoric, and reason.

Personality. When the appeal is through personality, the speaker or writer tries to get you to like him or her. To accomplish this, he or she may use many personal stories or act very interested in you. Friendliness is a common element of this appeal.

Tradition or Accepted Beliefs. The power of this argument comes from the general acceptance over time of the values or beliefs being discussed. Often, the writer will urge you to "do the right thing."

Rhetoric. This appeal persuades through the beauty and style of language and the power of the construction of the argument. It relies on impressive phrases, idioms, or gestures.

Reason. An appeal to reason is an appeal to logic. The speaker makes claims systematically and provides evidence for the claims.

Directions: Read the archive selections entitled "The Southern Argument in Favor of Slavery Extension," "Wilmot Attacks the Proslavery Argument," "South Carolina's Ordinance of Secession," and "Lincoln's Pledge to Defend the Union." For each of the selections, answer the following questions:
1. What issue is being discussed?
2. Is the writer a proponent or opponent of the issue?
3. What are the main points of the argument?
4. Is the writer suggesting a course of action? If so, what is it?
5. Identify the persuasive techniques you think have been used by the writer. Describe the reasons for your choice, such as recording the impressive phrases or idioms used.
6. Which selection did you think was the most persuasive? Why?

A Time of Crisis

As the Mexican War drew to a close in 1848, public attention was focused on the West. A vast expanse of territory beyond the Mississippi, including the area from New Mexico to California that had recently been acquired from Mexico, was waiting for settlement. There, as Senator Stephen A. Douglas would say, "is the hope of this nation—the resting place of the power that is not only to control, but to save, the Union." The discovery of gold in California was just one sign of the untold wealth to be found in the West.

Yet the West was also a cause of deepening concern. The South insisted on its right to extend slavery into the new territories, while the North demanded an end to the expansion of slavery. The survival of the nation depended on how the American people resolved this issue. During the decade of the 1850s, the slavery issue would put the Union to its most critical test.

▲ *Leg irons like these were forced upon many enslaved African Americans. (Putnam Museum of History and Natural Science, Davenport, Iowa.)*

The Slavery Issue Is Revived

During an evening session of Congress in August 1846, David Wilmot, a congressman from Pennsylvania, rose from his seat to introduce a resolution. Congress was working late that night, hoping to complete its work before adjourning the next day for several months. In their haste to wind up the session, few members paid much attention as the congressman read what became known as the **Wilmot Proviso.** It stated that "as an express and fundamental condition to the acquisition of any territory from the Republic of Mexico ... neither slavery nor involuntary servitude shall ever exist in any part of the said territory."

Suddenly it became clear what Wilmot had done. He had brought back into Congress the question of the expansion of slavery. Twenty-five years earlier, when Missouri had applied for admission as a slave state, that issue had divided Congress along North-South lines. It had nearly torn the nation apart. Wilmot's resolution forced Congress to confront the issue of slavery again.

How did the Whig and Democratic parties deal with the issue of slavery in the territories?

How did the discovery of gold in California in 1848 give new urgency to the slavery issue?

How did Congress respond to California's petition for statehood?

Slavery and the New Territories

The Wilmot Proviso demonstrated once again the power of the slavery issue to divide the nation along sectional lines. In the House of Representatives, northern Whigs and Democrats joined together to pass Wilmot's resolution. Southern Whigs and Democrats cast all but three of the 64 votes against the measure. The Senate did not have time to vote on the proviso before the session ended, leaving this divisive question still unsettled. But the Senate, too, was divided over the issue along sectional lines.

People in the North opposed the expansion of slavery for a variety of reasons. Abolitionists condemned slavery as an immoral institution and wanted to get rid of it everywhere. They had opposed the Mexican War from the beginning, warning that it was an attempt by the "slave power" (the slave states) to extend slavery's evil influence by annexing New Mexico and California. In *The Bigelow Papers*, abolitionist James Russell Lowell had his cracker-barrel philosopher, Hosea Bigelow, point out:

> They jest want this Californy
> So's to lug new slave-states in
> To abuse ye, an' to scorn ye,
> An' to plunder ye like sin.

Many others who opposed the expansion of slavery simply wanted to contain slavery to the South. They wanted to protect free labor from unfair competition with slave labor in the new western territories.

Still others saw the expansion of slavery primarily as a racial issue. Many northern whites, especially Democrats, supported the Wilmot Proviso as a way to keep African Americans out of the western territories. For them, the resolution was desirable more for racist reasons than for its antislavery stance. Wilmot himself described his resolution as "the white man's proviso." It was designed to preserve the land acquired from Mexico for white settlement.

▶

James Russell Lowell was a Boston poet, writer, and magazine editor. Why did he and other northern authors oppose the Mexican War?

Regions: Where Is the South?

Regions are parts of Earth's surface which have one or more characteristics distinguishing them from surrounding areas. Geographers divide the world into regions to show similarities and differences among areas, just as historians divide time into periods.

The division of some regions is based on a single, identifying characteristic; others have many. These unifying characteristics may be political, cultural, economic, or environmental. Texas, for example, is a *political region* within whose borders the laws of the state of Texas apply. The Great Plains is a less clearly bounded *environmental region* whose landforms, climate, soil, and vegetation distinguish it from the Rocky Mountains to the west and the more humid parts of the Central Plains to the east.

Some names of regions, however, are used to describe very complex combinations of culture, economy, and environment. This is the case when we use terms like *New England,* the *South,* or the *Midwest* to describe parts of the United States. These names are powerful. They call to mind the customs of a specific people, the environments in which they live, their heritage, economic activities, and literature.

Geographers discovered how difficult it is to identify the boundaries of these complex *culture*

regions when they attempted to find out exactly where "the South" was located. Most often people think of the South as including the eleven states that seceded from the Union and fought for independence in the Civil War. But there are actually degrees of "southernness." People frequently identify the Deep South, the Upland South, the Ozarks, French Louisiana, and the Bluegrass Country as subregions within the South.

The map below shows how often the term *Dixie* appeared in selected telephone directories as compared with the term *American.*

According to this criterion, East Texas identifies less with Dixieland than most of Missouri, West Virginia, Maryland, and Delaware, four slave states that remained in the Union during the Civil War. Virginia and most of North Carolina and Florida also identify less with Dixieland.

———————◆———————

1. Describe the personality characteristics of a typical region, such as New England, the Midwest, or the West.
2. Can you think of another method by which you might be able to identify the South?

▼ *Language, or what terms are in popular usage, is only one measure of a culture region.*

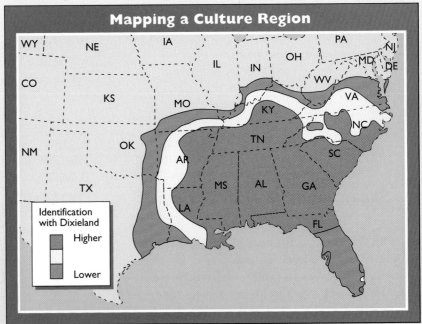

Mapping a Culture Region

Identification with Dixieland
- Higher
- Lower

"The negro race already occupy enough of this fair continent," Wilmot added. Bigotry of that type was widespread throughout the North.

The South was determined to keep the territories open to slavery. John C. Calhoun, the South's most illustrious spokesman, insisted that every citizen had the right to transport personal property into the territories. That right included the transporting of slaves into the territories, he argued, as slaves were the personal property of their owners.

Congress made several attempts to organize new governments in the western territories. In 1847, the settlers in Oregon petitioned for territorial status. Southern Democrats and Whigs objected. Each attempt to organize the territories simply led to more debates over slavery. The issue, complained an Ohio senator, "meets you in every step you take, it threatens you what way so ever you go."

▼ *This Whig party campaign poster from the 1848 presidential election portrays both the presidential and vice presidential candidates. Why was Taylor dressed in a military uniform?*

The Election of 1848

The Whigs and the Democrats did their best to prevent slavery from becoming an issue in the 1848 presidential election. Both parties chose candidates who had not taken a strong stand on the slavery question. The Whigs nominated Zachary Taylor, a Mexican War hero, as their presidential candidate. Although a slaveholder from Louisiana, Taylor was not an outspoken proslavery advocate. The Democrats nominated Lewis Cass, a United States senator from Michigan. They hoped Cass would be acceptable to the South as well as the North, as he had not taken a strong position against slavery.

The issue was brought back to the center of attention in 1848 by antislavery Whigs and Democrats who organized a third party, the Free-Soil Party. They nominated former President Martin Van Buren as their candidate to run on a platform that promised to exclude slavery from the territories. Although Taylor and the Whigs won the election, Van Buren received over 10 percent of the popular vote, and the Free-Soilers elected ten antislavery representatives to Congress. The Free-Soilers' gains were evidence of the North's growing concern about slavery.

The California Statehood Crisis

The discovery of gold in California in 1848 finally brought the slavery issue to a head. Working in a sawmill owned by John Sutter, James Marshall discovered gold along the American River. The word quickly spread, and by 1849, a major gold rush was under way. By the end of that year, 100,000 people had arrived in California. Each mining camp enacted its own rules to maintain law and order, but the region lacked a uniform system of laws and courts. A formal legal system could not be created until a territorial government had been established.

Each attempt to organize a territorial government for California was blocked in the U. S. Congress. Northern congressmen, reflecting the wishes of California's new residents, proposed legislation

▲ *Miners who panned for gold in California streams came with high expectations, but few skills.*

that would exclude slavery from the territory. Congressmen from the slave states used their influence to prevent that from happening. To break the deadlock, President Zachary Taylor urged the people of both California and New Mexico to bypass the territorial stage and to apply immediately for statehood. Unlike territories, states had the right to determine the slavery question for themselves. In October 1849, Californians drafted a state constitution that excluded slavery. Taylor submitted this constitution to Congress, requesting that it be quickly approved.

The president's actions provoked a crisis. Southern congressmen were shocked that Taylor, a slave owner himself, would agree to excluding slavery from California. They denounced him as a traitor to his native section. Most northern members of the House and Senate supported Taylor, but they lacked the majority of votes needed to pass the bill admitting California to statehood. Fistfights broke out in

Congress. Southern threats to withdraw from the Union became commonplace. "If by your legislation, you seek to drive us from the territories of California and New Mexico, *I am for disunion*," Senator Robert Toombs of Georgia warned northern congressmen. In mass meetings throughout the South, speakers echoed Toombs's threat of **secession**, or official withdrawal, from the Union. To consider that and other courses of action, nine southern states elected delegates to a protest convention to be held in Nashville. The Nashville Convention was an ominous sign, even though the delegates who met in June 1850 did not call for secession. Instead, they proposed extending the Missouri Compromise line to the Pacific.

The advocates of slavery expansion warned that the admission of California as a free state would lead to the destruction of the South. At that time, the number of free-state and slave-state senators in the Congress was evenly divided. Southerners were afraid that antislavery settlers in Oregon and other frontier regions would follow California's example and apply directly for statehood. This could produce a rush of new free states joining the Union, which would overturn the sectional balance in the Senate. Maintaining the balance in the Senate was vital to the South. It enabled southern Senators to block tariff bills and other legislation that might benefit the North at the expense of the South. However, the South's greatest fear was that a free-state majority in Congress would try to abolish slavery. If that happened, southern spokesmen predicted a "holocaust of blood."

SECTION 1 REVIEW

1. **Identify** the Wilmot Proviso.
2. **List** reasons people in the North opposed the expansion of slavery into the territories.
3. **Describe** how the Whig and Democrat Parties dealt with the issue of slavery in the territories in the election of 1848.
4. **Explain** how President Taylor tried to resolve the slavery issue in the case of California.
5. **Relate** how the South responded to California's request for admission as a free state.

The Compromise of 1850

As the year 1850 began, Congress faced its most serious crisis in two decades. Not since the nullification crisis of 1833 had the bonds of the Union been stretched so thin. In that crisis, South Carolina had defied federal authority by attempting to nullify the tariff. Henry Clay had helped put together the compromise that ended the crisis. Clay had also helped to design the Missouri Compromise of 1820, when Missouri had petitioned for statehood as a slave state. In January 1850, Clay rose from his seat in the Senate once again to play the role of the "Great Compromiser." Hollow-cheeked, his throat wracked with a chronic cough, the aged Clay offered a set of proposals designed to resolve this crisis as well. The purpose of this compromise, he explained, was "an amicable arrangement of all questions in controversy between the free and the slave States, growing out of the subject of slavery." With these resolutions placed before the Senate, Clay began the final act of his long and distinguished political career.

How did Henry Clay propose to end the crisis over the slavery issue?

What arguments did Daniel Webster and John C. Calhoun make for and against the proposals?

What was Stephen A. Douglas's role in passing the Compromise of 1850?

Clay Proposes a Compromise

The proposals that Clay introduced in January, which became known as the **Compromise of 1850**, consisted of four pairs of resolutions. Each pair would give something to each faction. In the first place, he proposed that California be admitted as a free state, which he paired with a resolution that allowed the remainder of the territory acquired from Mexico to be organized without any restrictions on slavery. It was unlikely that the remaining territory, which consisted of present-day New Mex-

ico, Arizona, Nevada, Utah, and part of Colorado, would become slave territories. Still, Clay hoped to win support from the South by at least keeping that possibility alive.

The second pair of Clay's proposals focused on Texas and New Mexico. The state of Texas, annexed in 1845, claimed much of what is now New Mexico, including the town of Santa Fe. The Hispanic people of New Mexico protested that claim. They pointed out that their ancestors had first settled in that region more than 200 years before Anglos had arrived in Texas. The outcome was important to the South, as some proslavery Congressmen hoped to create still another slave state out of the disputed territory. Clay proposed settling the boundary dispute in favor of New Mexico. To compensate Texas, the United States would agree to pay off Texas's $10 million state debt. Financially broke, Texas was unable to pay back the money it had borrowed through the sale of bonds. Many of the Texas bonds were held by southerners. While the boundary proposal displeased southern leaders, they approved of

▼ *The Great Compromise had provisions to please both the North and the South. Which pair of resolutions would have been most harmful to freed African Americans?*

The Compromise of 1850	
Resolutions Favoring the North	**Resolutions Favoring the South**
California to be admitted as a free state	No slavery restrictions on remaining territory acquired from Mexico
Boundary dispute between Texas and present-day New Mexico settled in favor of New Mexico	Federal government assumes Texas's $10 million state debt
Buying and selling of slaves banned in Washington, D.C.	Previously bought slaves could be brought into Washington, D.C.
	Local enforcement of fugitive slave laws required; Congress denied the power to regulate interstate slave trade

the federal government's paying off Texas's debt.

In two additional sets of resolutions, Clay again took up the issue of slavery. He proposed an end to the slave trade in the nation's capital, which northern abolitionists had long demanded. He balanced this proposal with a resolution guaranteeing the continued existence of slavery in Washington, D.C. In other words, southern slave owners could bring their slaves with them to the district, but they could not buy and sell slaves in the nation's capital.

Up to this point, Clay's compromise seemed to favor the North. This was not the case for the final set of resolutions, which represented a victory for the South. The first of these resolutions made it easier for slave owners or their hired agents to reclaim slaves who had fled to the North. The fugitive slave resolution required U.S. marshals to help. It gave the marshals the power to demand help from bystanders if necessary. In other words, local citizens who detested slavery could be deputized and forced to help recapture runaways. This proposal was paired with a resolution that denied Congress the power to regulate interstate trade in slaves.

The Great Debate The debate in 1850 over Clay's resolutions is still regarded as one of the great debates in American history. It brought together for a final performance three of the greatest statesmen of that era—Henry Clay, John C. Calhoun, and Daniel

▲ *Henry Clay is shown presenting the Compromise of 1850 to an attentive United States Senate. The ensuing debate is still considered to be one of the most significant ever held in the Senate. Why did John C. Calhoun oppose Clay's proposal?*

Webster. Clay began with a speech in February urging the North and the South to settle their differences by adopting his proposals. Early in March, Calhoun, ill and with less than a month to live, sat silently wrapped in flannel, while a Virginia senator read Calhoun's response to Clay. The growing power of the North had destroyed the balance between the

▼ *Henry Clay, Daniel Webster, and John C. Calhoun were the three strongest orators of their time.*

sections, Calhoun pointed out, and now threatened to destroy the Union. It could be preserved only if the North stopped its agitation over slavery and guaranteed slavery equal rights in the territories, which Clay's proposals failed to do.

Webster replied to Calhoun in his famous "Seventh of March" speech. "I wish to speak today," he began, "not as a Massachusetts man, nor as a Northern man, but as an American. I speak today for the preservation of the Union. Hear me for my cause." He urged the North not to insist on a law excluding slavery from New Mexico. Many of Webster's antislavery constituents demanded such a law, and Webster risked losing their support by advising against it. Slave owners, he pointed out, were not likely to move to New Mexico anyway. Then he cautioned the South about its thoughts of secession. The South, he warned, would never be allowed to secede peacefully from the Union. He urged both sections to accept Clay's proposals as a reasonable compromise.

Clay's compromise package met with strong opposition from both sides. Northern abolitionists did not like the fugitive-slave resolution. Southern advocates of slavery expansion opposed it for its failure to protect slavery in the territories. When it came to a vote, antislavery and proslavery senators combined to defeat the measure. Assuming that all hope of compromise was lost, Clay left Washington a worn-out and disappointed man. However, the drama was not yet over. Later that summer, **Stephen A. Douglas**, a Democratic senator from Illinois, revived Clay's proposals. Douglas tried a new strategy, dividing the package into separate resolutions. He then put enough pressure on northern Democrats to get each measure through the Senate separately. The resolutions were quickly approved by the House of Representatives and signed into law by President Millard Fillmore. Fillmore, the vice president, had become chief executive when President Taylor died in July.

Slavery Remains a Divisive Issue

The Compromise of 1850 removed the slavery question from Congress, but it did not end the

▼ *Senator Stephen A. Douglas was able to gain Senate approval for the Compromise of 1850. Why did Douglas succeed while Henry Clay failed?*

▼ *Boston's night watchmen and police were authorized and expected to catch runaway slaves, as this broadside pointed out. Why were all African Americans in Boston warned to avoid the police?*

CAUTION!!
COLORED PEOPLE
OF BOSTON, ONE & ALL,
You are hereby respectfully CAUTIONED and advised, to avoid conversing with the
Watchmen and Police Officers of Boston,
For since the recent ORDER OF THE MAYOR & ALDERMEN, they are empowered to act as
KIDNAPPERS
AND
Slave Catchers,
And they have already been actually employed in KIDNAPPING, CATCHING, AND KEEPING SLAVES. Therefore, if you value your LIBERTY, and the Welfare of the Fugitives among you, Shun them in every possible manner, as so many HOUNDS on the track of the most unfortunate of your race.
Keep a Sharp Look Out for KIDNAPPERS, and have TOP EYE open.
APRIL 24, 1851.

▼ *Harriet Beecher Stowe, a strident abolitionist, wrote* Uncle Tom's Cabin. *Why did that novel become a best seller?*

public debate over the issue. The enforcement of the **Fugitive Slave Act**, more than any other single factor, kept attention focused on slavery. The census of 1850 reported about 1,000 slaves as runaways. To the slave owners, each person that managed to escape the inhumanity of slavery represented "lost property." While 1,000 was not a great number in an enslaved population of just over 3 million, it did represent a significant loss of investment to individual slave owners. As soon as the act was passed, slave owners sent agents north to retrieve runaways. They took with them arrest warrants issued by southern courts. Once they had captured the fugitive, they brought the person before a federal commissioner. If the captured African American matched the de-scription in the warrant, the commissioner had no choice but to hand the person over.

The arrival of slave catchers in northern cities spread terror through the African American neighborhoods. To protect their newly gained freedom, hundreds of people who had escaped slavery promptly left for Canada. Many who did not leave in time were apprehended. Slave catchers in southern Indiana captured a former slave who had lived in freedom for 19 years. Free African Americans who had never been enslaved feared for their freedom, as there were instances of free persons being mistaken for runaway slaves. Under the Fugitive Slave Act of 1850, at least 300 runaway slaves were captured and returned to their owners.

AMERICAN SCENES

Abolitionists Rescue Fugitives

In Boston on February 15, 1851, a Virginia slave catcher seized a fugitive slave named Shadrack. The fugitive, who had escaped from slavery in Virginia in 1850, was employed as a waiter in the Cornhill Coffee House. The slave catcher, accompanied by a deputy U.S. marshal with an arrest warrant, took Shadrack to the courthouse. During a recess in the court proceedings, a crowd composed mostly of African Americans broke into the courtroom, seized Shadrack, and carried him away. The cheering crowd escorted him out of Boston, sending him eventually to Montreal, Canada.

Abolitionists also succeeded, in 1851, in rescuing fugitives from

▲ Runaway slaves Anthony Burns and Thomas Sims were caught in Boston. Townspeople watched as soldiers led them to a ship waiting to take them to South Carolina. Some runaway slaves were returned in neck yokes like the one at left, as well as in leg irons.

jails in Syracuse, New York; Christiana, Pennsylvania; and Ottawa, Illinois. In the future, antislavery groups would make other attempts to rescue fugitive slaves.

The slave rescues of 1851, the year following the Compromise of 1850, had wide repercussions.

The seizing of escaped slaves, often with the assistance of federal marshals, enraged northern abolitionists. In several instances, the abolitionists broke into jails to free captured fugitives, in open resistance to the law. At Cristiana, Pennsylvania, a slave owner and three local African American residents were killed in a riot sparked by such an attempt. To help protect themselves, free African Americans set up **vigilance committees** that kept a lookout for slave catchers. They also helped African Americans who were trying to escape slavery make their way to Canada.

Northern states also used legal means to resist the fugitive slave law. Nine states passed personal liberty laws that prevented local officials from taking part in the capture of runaways. These state laws also guaranteed fugitives a jury trial, which the federal law did not do. In an unusual reversal of roles, northern states used state legislation in an effort to defeat the purpose of a federal law, while the South—normally committed to defending states' rights—insisted on the supremacy of federal authority. Interfering with the Fugitive Slave Act, southerners said, violated property rights guaranteed by the Constitution.

The country's attention was also riveted on slavery by the publication in 1852 of **Harriet Beecher Stowe's** novel, *Uncle Tom's Cabin*. This story, about a fictitious slave family, did what no abolitionist or antislavery politician had yet been able to do. It paint-

When news of the Shadrack rescue reached Washington, D.C., President Millard Fillmore was furious. Committed to enforcing the Fugitive Slave Law, he demanded the arrest of everyone involved in the escape. He placed both the army and the navy at the disposal of the Boston authorities. Three of the participants were indicted, but their trial ended in a hung jury, that is, the jurors could not agree on a verdict. The escapes also angered southern congressmen and proslavery leaders. They concluded that the North did not intend to enforce the Fugitive Slave Act, which was the part of the Compromise of 1850 that most benefited the South.

In fact, the Fugitive Slave Act of 1850 was vigorously enforced. In his book, *The Slave Catchers* (1968), historian Stanley W. Campbell reports that of 191 cases tried in northern federal courts, 157 individuals were judged to be fugitives and returned to the South. There were 11 instances of mistaken identity, and all of them were released from custody. (At least another 150 individuals were captured and returned without due process of law.) Whatever they thought of the law, the northern marshals and federal commissioners charged with enforcing it did their duty. By and large, the northern public did not interfere. However, that was not the southern perception at the time. The South paid far more attention to the few dramatic and widely reported instances of slave rescues than to the routine obeying of the law.

Most rescue attempts ended in failure. In 1854, for example, an abolitionist mob in Boston tried to rescue Anthony Burns, a young fugitive from Virginia. They broke down the courthouse door with axes, but were turned back by club-wielding marshals. The next day, Burns was marched with a military escort to the wharf, placed on an armed ship belonging to the U.S. revenue service, and returned to Virginia.

But the attempts that succeeded became fixed in the minds of southerners. These rescues seemed to provide clear evidence of what a growing number of southerners had come to believe—that the North was a hotbed of abolitionism. These incidents fed the southern fear that slavery was no longer safe in a federal Union dominated by northern antislavery leaders.

1. Was the Fugitive Slave Act generally well enforced?
2. Why did the South perceive that the North had failed to enforce the act?

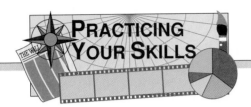
Recognizing Persuasive Writing

You have already learned about *The Federalist Papers,* a very famous collection of persuasive writings. Persuasion is a common tactic used by teachers, preachers, advertisers, political leaders, parents, friends, and ourselves to win over other people to our way of thinking, to get them to follow certain courses of action. Many people think persuasion (propaganda) is a dishonest tactic, but it can be used in both positive and negative ways.

Here are some general questions to ask to determine if a piece of writing uses persuasion tactics.

- **What belief or proposition are you asked to accept?** Restate the main argument or idea in your own words. This process forces you to think carefully about the content. Are you being asked to take any action?
- **Does the document use persuasion tactics?** These tactics may include name calling (big spender, trouble maker); speaking in generalities or using stereotypes; testimonials such as "All of the Olympic athletes drink Hi-Power;" card stacking (listing only the good facts); transferring a good or bad reputation to someone else, and urging everyone to get "on the band wagon."

CAUTION!!
COLORED PEOPLE
OF BOSTON, ONE & ALL,
You are hereby respectfully CAUTIONED and advised, to avoid conversing with the
Watchmen and Police Officers of Boston,
For since the recent ORDER OF THE MAYOR & ALDERMEN, they are empowered to act as
KIDNAPPERS
AND
Slave Catchers,
And they have already been actually employed in KIDNAPPING, CATCHING, AND KEEPING SLAVES. Therefore, if you value your LIBERTY, and the *Welfare of the Fugitives* among you, *Shun* them in every possible manner, as so many *HOUNDS* on the track of the most unfortunate of your race.
Keep a Sharp Look Out for KIDNAPPERS, and have TOP EYE open.
APRIL 24, 1851.

- **Does the document use visual symbols that many people feel strongly about?** For example, the flag is linked with patriotism, the dove to peace movements, and an eagle to Americanism.

Examine the broadside headed "CAUTION!" on page 341 and answer the following questions:

1. What is the purpose of this broadside? To whom is this broadside addressed? Who do you think wrote this?
2. What course of action does this broadside recommend?
3. What arguments are used to back up this recommendation? Do you find these arguments convincing? Why, or why not?
4. What is the tone of this broadside?
5. Why do you think this broadside was written and distributed?
6. Do you think this broadside is an effective piece of persuasion? Why, or why not?

---

ed a picture of slave life in human terms. Its main characters, Uncle Tom and Eliza, brought the dehumanizing reality of slavery home to countless readers in the North. The book sold 300,000 copies the first year of publication. By the end of the second year, this tremendously popular novel had sold over a million copies. In addition, thousands of people saw the play that was based on the novel. With slavery so much on the minds of the people, it was unlikely that this issue would remain long out of the halls of Congress.

SECTION 2 REVIEW

1. **List** the major provisions of the Compromise of 1850.
2. **Explain** why Clay's proposals were unpopular in both the North and the South.
3. **Identify** Stephen Douglas.
4. **Describe** how the Fugitive Slave Act heightened rather than eased sectional tensions.
5. **State** why *Uncle Tom's Cabin* became one of the best-selling novels of all time.

The Kansas-Nebraska Act

In 1854, Stephen A. Douglas introduced into the Senate a bill to organize the area of Kansas and Nebraska into new territories. Douglas knew that the bill would plunge the nation into another debate over slavery in the territories. Many northern congressmen would demand that slavery be excluded from Kansas and Nebraska. Southern senators and representatives would consider any further limit to the expansion of slavery as an insult to the South. Douglas knew that the bill would stir up controversy, but he thought it was worth the risk.

Douglas considered it his duty to promote the settlement of the West. He was the chairman of the Senate Committee on Territories and was the Democratic Party's leading spokesman for western interests. "There is a power in the nation greater than either the North or the South," Douglas proclaimed in the Senate. "That power is the country known as the Great West.... There, sir, is the hope of this nation."

He also realized that establishing territorial governments in Kansas and Nebraska was also essential to the building of a transcontinental railroad. A railroad to the Pacific would help bind California to the eastern states. A central route would connect the Far West to Chicago, the commercial hub of Douglas's home state. Douglas also had Chicago real estate investments that would benefit if a transcontinental railroad passed through that city.

In promoting the West and Chicago, Douglas provoked a crisis that wrecked the Whig Party, divided the Democrats, and nearly ruptured the bonds of union.

How did Douglas win southern support in Congress for his bill?

Why were many people in the North outraged by the Kansas-Nebraska bill?

How was the Kansas-Nebraska Act related to the founding of the Republican Party?

Repeal of the Missouri Compromise

In preparing his Kansas-Nebraska bill, Douglas faced a dilemma. He needed southern support to get the bill through Congress, but the South opposed bringing more free-soil territories and states into the Union. Kansas and Nebraska lay north of the 36° 30′ line, so they were in territory from which slavery had been excluded by the Missouri Compromise of 1820. An earlier generation of southern leaders had agreed to that compromise, knowing that plantation agriculture and the slave-labor system would probably not flourish that far north. However, southern attitudes toward excluding slavery from the territories had shifted dramatically since then. Following John C. Calhoun's lead, proslavery leaders in Congress had come to insist, as a matter of principle, that slavery and free labor be treated equally in all the territories. Southern Democrats in Congress agreed to support Douglas's bill only if it included a repeal of the Missouri Compromise. They also realized that repealing that compromise would give the South a major political victory over the antislavery forces in the North.

To make sure the bill would pass in Congress, Douglas rewrote it to satisfy the South. He agreed to erase the Missouri Compromise line. Instead, he applied the principle of **popular sovereignty** to Kansas and Nebraska. Popular sovereignty meant that the inhabitants of each territory could decide many issues for themselves. This included deciding the slavery question by popular vote when they organized a territorial government. Douglas did not want slavery introduced into Kansas and Nebraska, but he was not worried about the results of a vote based on popular sovereignty. He was convinced that the northern farmers who would settle those territories would vote to exclude slavery. "I think I am safe in assuming that each of these will be free territories and free states, whether Congress shall prohibit slavery or not," he remarked. But he also knew that repeal of the Missouri Compromise would be highly unpopular. In the North, it had become a cherished landmark of freedom.

The Kansas-Nebraska bill provoked outrage in the North. It was denounced in the Senate as "a

The Beecher Family

▲ *This photo of the Beecher family was taken in 1859. Standing from left to right are Thomas, William, Edward, Charles, and Henry. Seated from left to right are Isabella, Catharine, Lyman, Mary, and Harriet.*

The Beechers were one of the most remarkable American families of the nineteenth century. As the Reverend Leonard Bacon said in the 1860s, "this country is inhabited by saints, sinners, and Beechers." The head of the family, Lyman Beecher, was a Congregationalist minister and a popular revival preacher. He had 11 children. He carefully tended to their education and had remarkable success in handing down to them his own vitality, moral fervor, and skillful use of words. At least five of them became nationally known writers and public speakers. Altogether, the Beechers wrote well over 100 books. They also played a role in several of the major reform movements of the nineteenth century.

Two of the Beecher daughters were active in the movement for women's rights. The eldest, Catharine, devoted much of her life to providing better educational opportunities for women. She founded several girls' schools and helped open the teaching profession to women. Catharine Beecher also wrote a widely read book on home management—*Treatise on Domestic Economy for the Use of Young Ladies at Home and at School.* Her younger sister, Isabella Beecher Hooker, also became involved in women's causes. She wrote newspaper editorials and books on the importance of family planning and sex education. After the Civil War, she was a leader of the movement to extend to women the right to vote.

Several Beechers were involved in the antislavery movement. Edward Beecher, a college president in Illinois, was a close friend and supporter of abolitionist editor Elijah P. Lovejoy. He was with Lovejoy in 1837 at Elton, Illinois, the day the editor was murdered by a proslavery mob.

Harriet Beecher Stowe, the author of *Uncle Tom's Cabin*, contributed as much as any single individual to the spread of anti–slavery sentiment in the North. When President Abraham Lincoln met her in 1862, he reportedly said, "So this is the little lady who made this big war."

Her younger brother, Henry Ward Beecher, a Brooklyn minis-ter, had urged his congregation to send the rifles to Kansas that became known as Beecher's Bibles. As spellbinding a preacher as his father, Henry reached a wide audience with his antislavery sermons, newspaper articles, and lectures.

It is seldom that one family has made such a deep imprint on American culture and life. The founding father, Lyman Beecher, deserves much of the credit. Lyman Beecher, said his friend Theodore Parker, was "the father of more brains than any man in America."

1. Name several reform causes of the nineteenth century that the Beechers supported.
2. Name other families that have had important impact on our history.

gross violation of a sacred pledge, a criminal betrayal of precious rights," and as a plot to turn the northern plains into "a dreary region of despotism, inhabited by masters and slaves." Protest meetings were held throughout the North as the measure was being debated in Congress. Douglas later said that he could have traveled all the way to Chicago at night by the light of burning effigies of himself.

The Senate passed the Kansas-Nebraska bill in March of 1854, with the House of Representatives approving it in May.

Slavery Divides the Parties

The reopening of the slavery question in 1854 divided the major parties. There were antislavery factions of both the Whig and Democrat Parties in the North who strenuously objected to the repeal of the Missouri Compromise. Some northern Democrats agreed with Douglas that popular sovereignty would effectively exclude slaves from Kansas and Nebraska. In the South, Whigs and Democrats favored slavery expansion. They were overjoyed that the area north of the 36° 30′ line would be opened to the possible expansion of slavery. These internal party differences threatened to tear apart two of the most important institutions that bridged the chasm between North and South.

The Kansas-Nebraska bill produced an immediate political upheaval. Rallies in the North protesting Douglas's proposal brought together Free-Soilers, antislavery Whigs, and antislavery Democrats in a new political coalition. Those involved in the "anti-Nebraska movement" would eventually organize a new political party dedicated to preventing the expansion of slavery. They would call it the Republican Party.

In the midterm congressional elections of 1854, the anti-Nebraska movement defeated those Democrats who had supported Douglas. They carried all but 2 of the northern states. Only 7 of the 44 northern Democratic congressmen who voted for the Kansas-Nebraska bill were reelected. For the rest of the decade, northern Democrats were a minority in a party largely controlled by the South.

The Whig party was in even more trouble. In 1852, the northern Whigs had pushed through the nomination of General Winfield Scott as the party's presidential candidate. Scott was unpopular in the South because he refused to endorse the Fugitive Slave Act. Southern Whigs left the party in droves and helped to elect the Democratic candidate, **Franklin Pierce**.

With the passage of the **Kansas-Nebraska Act**, large numbers of northern Whigs also abandoned their party to join the anti-Nebraska movement. A few Whigs stayed with the party in 1854, among them Abraham Lincoln, who that year ran for the state legislature in Illinois. By 1856, when the Whigs nominated their last presidential candidate, the remaining antislavery Whigs (including Lincoln) had joined the Republican Party. The Whig Party, the old party of Clay and Webster, was collapsing.

The Growing Strength of the Republican Party

The Republican Party would benefit most from the Whig decline, but in 1854 it faced stiff competition from another new party. The nativist American Party appealed to ex-Whigs and northern Democrats who were as alarmed about the influx of Irish Catholics as they were about the expansion of slavery. They were called Know-Nothings because when asked about their anti-immigrant activities, they replied, "I know nothing." The Know-Nothings elected a mayor of Philadelphia, won state elections in Massachusetts in 1854, and helped to elect many anti-Nebraska movement congressmen that year.

The Republicans finally overcame this threat by absorbing the nativists into their own party. In 1856, they persuaded the American Party to endorse the Republican presidential ticket. While this marked the end of the Know-Nothings as a separate political force, it gave the Republican Party a nativist outlook that drove most Catholic immigrants into the Democratic Party.

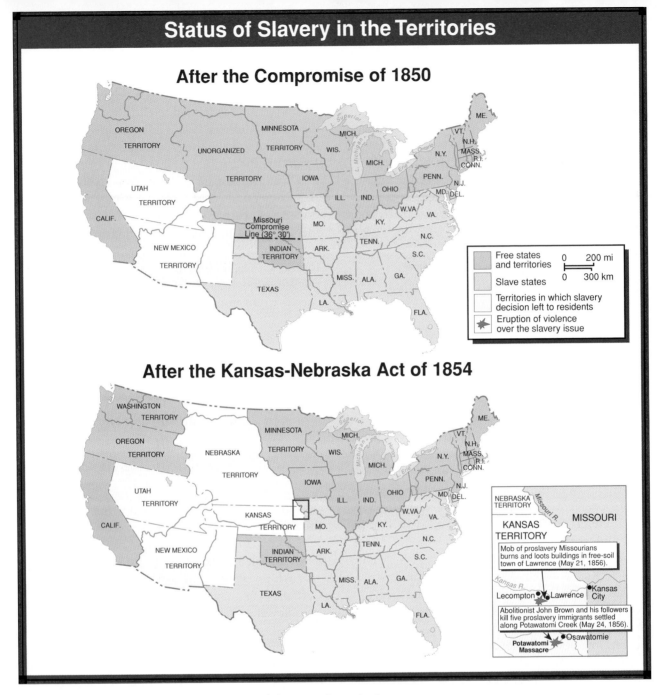

Status of Slavery in the Territories

After the Compromise of 1850

OREGON TERRITORY
UNORGANIZED TERRITORY
MINNESOTA TERRITORY
UTAH TERRITORY
CALIF.
NEW MEXICO TERRITORY
Missouri Compromise Line (36° 30')
MICH.
WIS.
IOWA
ILL. IND. OHIO
MO.
KY.
ARK. TENN.
INDIAN TERRITORY
TEXAS
MISS. ALA. GA.
LA.
VA.
W.VA.
N.C.
S.C.
FLA.
ME.
VT. N.H.
N.Y. MASS.
CONN. R.I.
PENN.
N.J.
MD. DEL.

Free states and territories	0 200 mi
Slave states	0 300 km
	Territories in which slavery decision left to residents
★	Eruption of violence over the slavery issue

After the Kansas-Nebraska Act of 1854

WASHINGTON TERRITORY
OREGON TERRITORY
NEBRASKA TERRITORY
UTAH TERRITORY
CALIF.
NEW MEXICO TERRITORY
KANSAS TERRITORY
MINNESOTA TERRITORY
MICH.
WIS.
IOWA
ILL. IND. OHIO
MO.
KY.
ARK. TENN.
INDIAN TERRITORY
TEXAS
MISS. ALA. GA.
LA.
VA.
W.VA.
N.C.
S.C.
FLA.
ME.
VT. N.H.
N.Y. MASS.
CONN. R.I.
PENN.
N.J.
MD. DEL.

NEBRASKA TERRITORY
KANSAS TERRITORY
MISSOURI
Mob of proslavery Missourians burns and loots buildings in free-soil town of Lawrence (May 21, 1856).
Lecompton — Lawrence — Kansas City
Abolitionist John Brown and his followers kill five proslavery immigrants settled along Potawatomi Creek (May 24, 1856).
Potawatomi Massacre — Osawatomie

▲ *The Kansas-Nebraska Act altered the status of slavery in the territories.*

The Election of 1856   The Republicans made an impressive showing in the elections of 1856, which was their first presidential campaign. To broaden the party's appeal, they chose as their candidate John C. Frémont, a well-known army officer and explorer. His Democratic opponent was **James Buchanan** of Pennsylvania, one of the few Democrats still acceptable to both the North and the South. Serving during the previous three years as minister to England, Buchanan had avoided taking a stand on the Kansas-Nebraska issue.

Although Buchanan won the election with 174 electoral votes to Frémont's 114 (with eight electoral votes going to Millard Fillmore, the Whig candidate), the Republicans carried all but five northern states. Had they been able to carry

▲ *The first state Republican convention was held outdoors on July 6, 1854, in Jackson, Michigan. Candidates were nominated for both state and congressional elections.*

▶ *In this formal portrait by Charles Fenderich, President James Buchanan is shown in his study. Why was Buchanan one of the few candidates in 1856 who was acceptable to both northern and southern Democrats?*

Pennsylvania and Illinois, the Republicans could have won the election without support in a single southern state. It was hardly an encouraging victory for either the Democrats or the South. Increasingly, the South found itself politically isolated from national affairs.

Bleeding Kansas

With the passage of the Kansas-Nebraska Act, attention shifted from Congress to the prairies of Kansas. Antislavery leaders in the North worked hard to send settlers to Kansas who would vote against slavery when the territorial elections were held. The Massachusetts Emigrant Aid Company helped to send 650 free-soil settlers to Kansas in 1854 and 1,000 more the following year. Proslavery forces were equally determined to make Kansas a slave territory. Armed bands from the neighboring slave state of Missouri, called Border Ruffians, repeatedly crossed into Kansas to terrorize the free-soil settlers. Kansas quickly became divided into

two hostile camps. Every settler who went there had to choose sides.

In Kansas, the democratic process broke down in this heated political atmosphere. When the first territorial election was held in March 1855, twice as many votes were counted as there were voters in the territory. On election day, proslavery voters from Missouri had crossed over into Kansas to vote illegally. They cast enough votes to give the first

▼ *Armed Missourians called Border Ruffians attacked free-soil towns in "Bleeding Kansas." Why did Missourians want Kansas to become a slave territory?*

Congressman Preston Brooks of South Carolina attacked Charles Sumner on the floor of the U. S. Senate. Senator Sumner of Massachusetts was a leader of the northern abolitionists in Congress.

territorial legislature a large proslavery majority. The free-soil forces promptly set up a rival government and declared Kansas a free territory. Both sides were armed. The **Reverend Henry Ward Beecher** urged his Brooklyn, New York, congregation to send rifles to Kansas. Rifles, he said, "are a greater moral agency than the Bible." Soon, boxes of rifles were on their way to the free-soil settlers in Kansas marked "Bibles," and every free-soil rifle in Kansas was called a "Beecher's Bible."

Violence broke out in the spring of 1856, with an attack on the free-soil town of Lawrence by an armed band of Missourians led by a proslavery Kansas sheriff. The mob destroyed two antislavery printing presses, burned the Free State Hotel, and went on a rampage of looting. Three days later, **John Brown**, an antislavery fanatic, led an attack against proslavery immigrants who had settled along Pottawatomie Creek. In the Potawatomi Massacre, Brown and his men stabbed or shot to death five proslavery settlers. "Bleeding Kansas," as the newspapers called the territory, had become a dress rehearsal for civil war.

Assault in the Senate   The violence in Kansas was echoed in the halls of the United States Senate in the spring of 1856. On May 22, Congressman Preston Brooks of South Carolina entered the Senate chamber, walked over to Charles Sumner, an antislavery senator from Massachusetts, and began clubbing him over the head with a cane. Two days before, in a fiery speech entitled "The Crime Against Kansas," Sumner had made insulting remarks about Brooks's relative, Senator Andrew P. Butler. After the beating, Sumner collapsed on the floor. Very seriously injured, he would remain away from the Senate for the next two and a half years. His vacant seat was a silent testimonial to the chasm that was widening between North and South.

SECTION 3 REVIEW

1. State why Stephen A. Douglas, an antislavery Democrat, agreed to the repeal of the Missouri Compromise.
2. Explain the principle of popular sovereignty.
3. Identify the anti-Nebraska movement.
4. Name the groups that joined together in 1854 to form the Republican Party.
5. Explain how the territorial legislature in Kansas had a proslavery majority in 1855.

The Crisis over Slavery Deepens

Dred Scott saw more of the United States than most enslaved African Americans. Raised in Virginia, he spent 11 years on a farm in Alabama before moving with his owner to St. Louis in the slave state of Missouri. There, Scott was sold to John Emerson, a medical doctor. Commissioned as a United States Army surgeon in 1833, Dr. Emerson took Scott with him to his new post in Illinois. Some years later, Scott and his owner moved again, this time to Fort Snelling, on the west bank of the Mississippi in the Wisconsin Territory. Two years later, Scott (now with a wife and child) was brought back to St. Louis. There, Scott sued for his and his family's freedom. In the suit, his lawyers argued that residence in the free state of Illinois and in a free territory while at Fort Snelling had made Scott and his family free people. Having once lived in freedom, they insisted, Scott could not be returned to slavery.

What was the Supreme Court ruling in the Dred Scott case?

How did the decision call into question the principle of popular sovereignty?

How did Stephen A. Douglas defend the idea of popular sovereignty after the Dred Scott decision?

Dred Scott, an enslaved African American, claimed that residence in a free territory made him and his family free. Did the United States Supreme Court agree with him?

Chief Justice Roger B. Taney wrote the majority opinion in the Dred Scott decision. How did the sectional loyalties of the justices influence the decision in this case?

The Dred Scott Decision

The Dred Scott case slowly made its way through the court system. In 1850, a local court in St. Louis decided in favor of the Scotts, with the jury declaring the family to be free. The decision was overturned two years later by Missouri's state supreme court. Scott sued again, this time in a federal court. The United States Supreme Court finally agreed to hear the case and decided to use it as a means of deciding the status of slavery in the territories.

In March 1857, the Supreme Court handed down its decision in the Dred Scott case. Speaking for the majority of the Court, which was dominated by southern Democrats, Chief Justice Roger B. Taney ruled that Scott was still a slave. He reasoned that Scott's residence north of the 36° 30′ line had not changed his status, because the Missouri Compromise was unconstitutional. The Court ruled that Congress had exceeded its authority in 1820 by restricting the expansion of slavery. The ruling also brought the legality of popular sovereignty into question. If Congress could not exclude slavery from a territory, how could a territorial legislature that derived its power from Congress legally do so? The Court did not address that question, but there was little doubt that it would rule against popular sovereignty should the occasion arise. Finally, Chief Justice Taney added that Scott should not have sued in the courts because African Americans, whether free or slave, had no rights of citizenship.

The Dred Scott decision was denounced in the North as a political decision and as a proslavery ruling handed down by proslavery justices. The members of the Court had divided along sectional lines in their decision. Five of the six justices who agreed to overturn the Missouri Compromise were southern Democrats. The justices who voted to uphold the Compromise were from the North. Abolitionists were also upset by Taney's statement that even free African Americans could not be citizens of the United States. Although the Court had hoped to settle the issue of slavery with its decision, it only succeeded in stiffening resistance in the North to what many people saw as a slave-power conspiracy.

The Lecompton Constitution

Many northerners believed that slaveholders and their allies in the Democratic Party meant to impose slavery on the territories whether or not the people wanted it. Events in Kansas in 1857 strengthened this perception. Antislavery (free-state) settlers outnumbered proslavery settlers by two to one. Still, proslavery legislators who had been fraudulently elected in 1855 controlled the territorial legislature.

The legislature held a convention at the town of Lecompton to draft a state constitution. Dominated by proslavery delegates, the convention adopted a constitution that protected slavery in Kansas. The **Lecompton Constitution** was then submitted to a public **referendum**, or special election, and approved by a majority of the popular vote. It won approval because antislavery forces, suspecting the election was rigged, refused to take part. Shortly thereafter, in a new election, the free-soil people won control of the legislature and submitted the Lecompton Constitution to a second referendum. It was rejected by a landslide. Nevertheless, President James Buchanan, yielding to pressure from southern Democrats, submitted the Lecompton Constitution to Congress and urged that it be approved.

The debate over the Lecompton Constitution plunged the nation and the Democratic Party into a new crisis over slavery. The opposition in the Senate was led by Stephen A. Douglas, who saw that the new constitution made a mockery of popular sovereignty. Buchanan opposed Douglas and made support for Lecompton a test of party loyalty. Kansas, he declared, "is at this moment as much a slave state as Georgia or South Carolina."

The fate of the Lecompton Constitution became a highly emotional issue. Northern state legislatures passed resolutions opposed to Lecompton. Several southern states threatened to secede if the constitution were rejected. "Rather than have Kansas refused admission under the Lecompton Constitution, let [the Union] perish in blood and fire," a spokesman for South Carolina said.

The proslavery constitution was approved by the Senate in 1858. It failed in the House, where northern antislavery forces were stronger. Kansas would finally be admitted as a free state, but not until 1861, after the South had seceded from the Union.

The Lincoln-Douglas Debate

Stephen A. Douglas returned to Illinois after the Lecompton debate to fight for reelection to the Senate. Although Douglas was a Democrat, his break with the Buchanan administration had earned him powerful enemies within the Democratic Party, especially in the South. He also faced a serious Republican challenge in Illinois. To oppose Douglas, the Republicans chose Springfield lawyer and former Whig Abraham Lincoln. Although Lincoln lacked Douglas's national reputation, having served only a single term in Congress from 1844 to 1847, he was well known in Illinois. The two men agreed to a series of joint debates in August and September 1858. These debates gave the voters a chance to compare the candidates' views on the status of slavery in the territories.

The debates also gave Douglas a chance to defend popular sovereignty. He reassured free-soil Democrats that slavery could be excluded from the territories despite the Supreme Court's ruling in the Dred Scott case. When Lincoln, during the debate at Freeport, Illinois, asked how that was possible, Douglas replied that the Dred Scott decision need not stand in the people's way. "In my opinion, the people of a territory can, by lawful means, exclude slavery from their limits," he replied. Douglas explained that they could refuse to pass the local laws and police regulations essential for the existence of slavery. The Freeport Doctrine, as Douglas's position became known, satisfied the antislavery Democrats of Illinois that popular sovereignty could still keep slavery out of the territories. It helped the Democrats win the state elections in Illinois, but it turned southern Democrats against Douglas. Two years later, that split in the Democratic Party would dash Douglas's hopes of being elected president.

Lincoln used the debates to emphasize the difference between the Democratic and Republican views on slavery. "The real issue in this controversy . . . is the sentiment on the part of one class that looks upon the institution of slavery *as a wrong*, and of another that *does not* look upon it as wrong. . . . The Republican Party . . . look upon it as being a moral, social and political wrong." Lincoln emerged from the debates as his party's most articulate spokesman on the issue of slavery.

The fall elections of 1858 in Illinois gave the Democrats a majority in the state legislature, which voted to return Douglas to the Senate for another term. (United States senators were not elected by the direct vote of the people until the adoption of the Seventeenth Amendment in 1913.) Although Lincoln was defeated in his race for the Senate, he became a major contender for the Republican Party's 1860 presidential nomination.

▲ *Abraham Lincoln and Stephen A. Douglas debated the question of slavery during their 1858 election campaign for the U. S. Senate.*

The Deepening Slavery Crisis

During the following months, sectional conflict paralyzed Congress at nearly every turn. President Buchanan tried to expand the nation's boundaries and reunite the Democratic Party by a proposal to annex Cuba. This proposal received wide Democratic support, but the Republicans saw annexation as an attempt to add another slave state, and they blocked the measure.

The southern Democrats, in turn, defeated a Republican proposal to provide settlers in the West with 160-acre homesteads. This proposal would not have benefited most slaveholders, who needed larger tracts of land. They also countered Douglas's Freeport Doctrine by demanding a federal slave code for the territories, which would protect slaveholders even if local governments refused to do so. A senator from Mississippi warned that failure to pass a federal slave code would be grounds for his state to secede from the Union. Talk of secession filled the air in Washington, especially after the news arrived of John Brown's raid at Harpers Ferry.

John Brown's Raid   On October 16, 1859, John Brown, the leader of the Potawatomi massacre in Kansas, led an attack against the federal arsenal at Harpers Ferry, Virginia. He was accompanied by a band of 18 men, including five African Americans. Brown hoped to take enough weapons from the arsenal to arm thousands of slaves for a bloody revolt against their owners. The plan had the support of some northern abolitionists, a few of whom had even contributed money to the cause. Brown and

John Brown, who led the Potawatomi massacre, also led an attack against the federal arsenal at Harpers Ferry, Virginia. Why did Brown's raid at Harpers Ferry terrify southerners?

▲ This musket and pike were used in John Brown's raid on Harpers Ferry in December 1859. What did Brown hope to accomplish by the raid?

his followers seized control of the arsenal. The federal government dispatched United States Marines to recapture it. The marines, commanded by Colonel Robert E. Lee of Virginia, defeated Brown and his men, killing ten of them, including two of Brown's sons. Brown and six other survivors were tried under the laws of Virginia for murder, treason, and insurrection (a revolt against a civil authority). The jury found them guilty, and the men were hanged.

John Brown's raid sent a shock wave throughout the South. Although not a single enslaved person had joined Brown voluntarily, the raid symbolized the South's deepest fear: the fear of slave insurrection. The prospect of slaves murdering slave owners in the darkness of night was a nightmare that haunted southern slave owners. While northern conservatives deplored the raid, radical abolitionists hailed Brown as a martyr who had died for the cause of freedom. Northern support for a slave rebellion, even if this support only came from extreme abolitionists, added to the South's trauma. Brown's raid had pushed the nation one step closer to disunion.

Other Issues Divide the Nation   The slavery issue was splitting the nation apart, but it was not the only source of sectional conflict. The North and South also had serious disagreements about economic policies. The South opposed the high tariffs that the Northeast wanted to protect its young industries from foreign competition. Tariffs increased the price of the clothing, tools, furniture, rifles, and other items that southern planters and farmers had to buy from northern manufacturers. Southerners deeply resented their growing dependence on northern manufacturers.

Congress also was divided along sectional lines over the route for a transcontinental railroad. A railroad to link California to the rest of the nation would be too costly for private companies to build without help from the federal government. Southern congressmen wanted a southern route. Northern congressmen insisted on a central route that would benefit the North.

Finally, southerners had begun to think of the South as a separate nation whose honor was at stake in this conflict with the North. The rise of southern nationalism made compromise on any issue more difficult. But of all the issues dividing the two sections in 1850, slavery aroused the most intense emotions. More than any other issue, it had the potential to tear the nation apart.

SECTION 4 REVIEW

1. **Explain** why opponents of slavery denounced the Dred Scott decision.
2. **Define** referendum.
3. **Explain** how the Lecompton Constitution violated the principle of popular sovereignty.
4. **Identify** the Freeport Doctrine.
5. **Name** three issues, other than slavery, that divided the North and the South.

The South Secedes

In the winter of 1859–1860, the nation moved rapidly toward its greatest crisis yet. The issue of slavery had all but paralyzed the national government. The House of Representatives was deadlocked for two months over the election of a Speaker, or presiding officer. Northern and southern Democrats blocked the Republican candidate, but they could not agree on a Democratic candidate. The Congress was bitterly divided over what the Dred Scott decision meant for slavery in the territories. In both the House and the Senate, tempers flared and blows were exchanged. James Hammond of South Carolina, like many other senators, kept a loaded revolver in his Senate desk. "I keep a pistol now in my drawer in the Senate," he wrote, "as a matter of *duty* to my section & to reinforce it in either House." The upcoming presidential election also cast a dark shadow over national politics. Congressmen from southern states talked about seceding if the Republicans won the election. Congress produced little that session but threats and ill-tempered speeches.

How successful was the Democratic Party in 1860 in resolving its differences over the slavery issue?

What was the South's reaction to the election of a Republican president?

What was President Lincoln's response to the secession of southern states?

Splits in the 1860 Democratic Convention

As the year 1860 began, the South was in a state of near panic. The South was truly alarmed by the radical abolitionists' support for John Brown's raid. Many southerners jumped to the conclusion that the entire North shared those views, which was not

▲ *In 1860, the Democrats held their nominating convention in Charleston. Why did the party fail to nominate a presidential candidate at this convention?*

the case. Republican gains in the North were equally disturbing, as many southerners suspected that abolitionists controlled the Republican Party. The South looked toward the presidential election of 1860 with growing apprehension. Their only hope to counter Republican strength in the North and in Congress was to elect a Democratic president who shared their views on slavery.

The southern Democrats went to the Democratic convention in Charleston in April 1860 determined to maintain their control of the party. To do that, they had to prevent the nomination of Stephen A. Douglas, whose Freeport Doctrine had won him a large following among Free-Soil Democrats in the North. But the Douglas forces at the convention were stronger than the South had anticipated. The Douglas delegates soundly defeated a southern motion to include in the party's platform a call for a federal slave code. With that, the most radical proslavery delegates walked out of the convention. Enough anti-Douglas delegates remained to prevent his receiving the nomination for the presidency. On the tenth day of the convention, after 57 ballots in which no candidate had received the two-thirds majority then required for a Democratic party nomination, the convention recessed. The delegates planned to meet again in Baltimore in July.

The Democrats were even more sharply divided in Baltimore. By discarding the two-thirds majority rule, the Free-Soil Democrats finally won the nomination for Douglas. Having failed to stop Douglas, about a third of the delegates, mainly from the South, withdrew to nominate their own ticket, with John C. Breckinridge, Buchanan's vice president, as their presidential candidate. The slavery issue had split the Democratic Party, virtually ensuring a Republican victory in 1860.

Lincoln Nominated by Republicans

At their convention in Chicago in May, the Republicans made the most of this opportunity. They used the convention to broaden their base of support. The delegates passed over the leading contender for the party's presidential nomination—Senator William H. Seward of New York—afraid that his radical antislavery views would alienate conservative voters. Seward had opposed the Compromise of 1850, arguing that slavery should not be allowed to exist anywhere as it was condemned by a higher law than the U.S. Constitution. Instead, the convention nominated Abraham Lincoln, whose views on slavery were more in tune with the major-

ity of northern voters. He opposed letting slavery expand into the territories, but was willing to tolerate slavery where it already existed. Moreover, his homespun image as "Honest Abe," the "rail-splitter from Illinois," would help attract western voters. The party's platform promised western farmers a homestead act that would make public land available for settlers at little cost. It also endorsed a transcontinental railroad. To improve their chances of carrying industrial states, the Republicans called for tariff protection for American manufactured goods. Northern voters, still trying to recover from the depression in 1857, would find the economic planks in the Republican platform attractive. Thus, the Republicans entered the election campaign of 1860 with an attractive candidate and a party platform with broad public appeal.

Still another party convention was held that summer. Former Whigs, mainly from the border states, who refused to support either the Democrats or the Republicans, organized the Constitutional Union Party. It nominated John Bell of Tennessee and Edward Everett of Massachusetts on a platform that avoided the slavery issue, calling for unity and respect for the Constitution. This new party's appeal for unity would have little chance of success.

▶

Supporters of presidential candidate Abraham Lincoln marched in this 1860 torchlight parade in New York City.

▼ *This glass lantern torch was used in the 1860 Republican election campaign.*

The South Secedes

The prospect of a Republican victory in the 1860 election created even more fear in the South. Convinced that Lincoln would try to abolish slavery, southern leaders warned that their states would secede and risk civil war if he were elected. As an Atlanta newspaper declared, "Let the consequences be what they may, whether the Potomac is crimsoned in human gore, and Pennsylvania Avenue is paved ten fathoms deep with mangled bodies . . . the South will never submit to such humiliation and degradation as the inauguration of Abraham Lincoln." It did not seem to matter that Lincoln had said repeatedly that as president he would have no power to abolish slavery where it already existed. The South was certain that if Lincoln were elected, his administration would be dominated by the most radical antislavery element in the Republican party.

Lincoln did win the election in November. He received a clear majority of the electoral vote: Lincoln, 180; Breckinridge, 72; Bell, 39; and Douglas, 12. He did not, however, win a majority of the popular vote. He polled 40 percent of the vote, compared to 29 percent for Douglas, 18 percent for Breckinridge, and about 13 percent for Bell. Moreover, Lincoln's support came entirely from the North. The Republicans had won the presidency without the South, confirming the long-standing fear of many southerners that the South was becoming a powerless minority section.

The rush toward disunion took place more rapidly than anyone had foreseen. A week after the election, the South Carolina legislature called for the election of delegates to a secession convention. Other states followed its lead. In each instance, the secessionists moved quickly, before passions cooled and Unionist sentiment could be organized. Within three months after Lincoln's election, seven states in the lower South had seceded from the Union. They included South Carolina, Georgia, Florida, Alabama, Mississippi, Louisiana, and Texas. These states, in turn, sent delegates to a convention in Montgomery, Alabama, to draft a constitution for the **Confederate States of America**. By March 1861, the new Confederacy had ratified this constitution

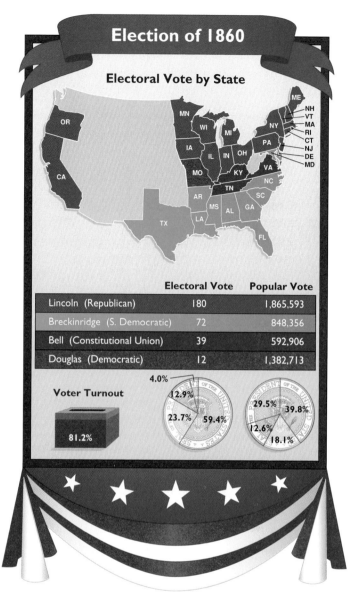

Election of 1860

Electoral Vote by State

	Electoral Vote	Popular Vote
Lincoln (Republican)	180	1,865,593
Breckinridge (S. Democratic)	72	848,356
Bell (Constitutional Union)	39	592,906
Douglas (Democratic)	12	1,382,713

Voter Turnout: 81.2%

4.0% 12.9% 23.7% 59.4%

29.5% 39.8% 12.6% 18.1%

▲ *In 1860 Abraham Lincoln won a clear majority of the electoral vote. Why was the South alarmed by the results of this election?*

and elected **Jefferson Davis** of Mississippi as the first Confederate president. The eight slave states in the upper South, where Unionist sentiment was stronger, hesitated. They waited to see if the crisis could be resolved by compromise.

The Crittenden Compromise Congress had considered several compromise plans that winter,

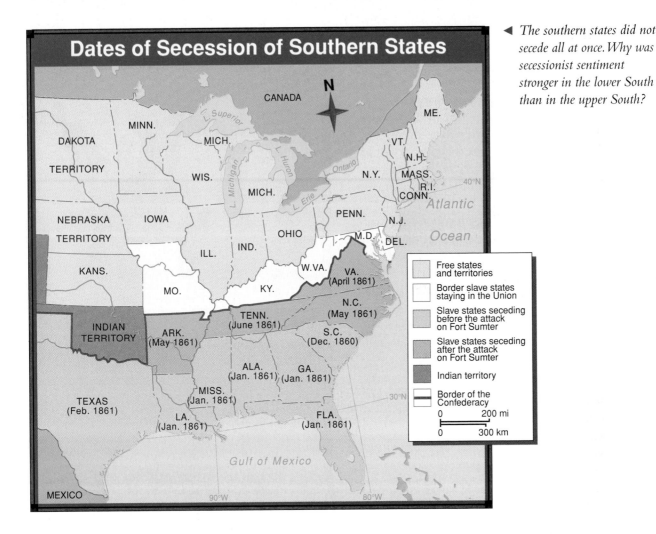

Dates of Secession of Southern States

CANADA

MINN.

DAKOTA
TERRITORY

MICH.

WIS.

MICH.

ME.

VT.
N.H.

N.Y.
MASS.
R.I.
CONN.

Atlantic

NEBRASKA
TERRITORY

IOWA

ILL.

IND.

OHIO

PENN.

N.J.

M.D.
DEL.

Ocean

KANS.

MO.

KY.

W.VA.

VA.
(April 1861)

INDIAN
TERRITORY

ARK.
(May 1861)

TENN.
(June 1861)

N.C.
(May 1861)

S.C.
(Dec. 1860)

TEXAS
(Feb. 1861)

MISS.
(Jan. 1861)

ALA.
(Jan. 1861)

GA.
(Jan. 1861)

LA.
(Jan. 1861)

FLA.
(Jan. 1861)

MEXICO

Gulf of Mexico

40°N

30°N

90°W

80°W

N

Legend:
- Free states and territories
- Border slave states staying in the Union
- Slave states seceding before the attack on Fort Sumter
- Slave states seceding after the attack on Fort Sumter
- Indian territory
- Border of the Confederacy

0   200 mi
0   300 km

◀ The southern states did not secede all at once. Why was secessionist sentiment stronger in the lower South than in the upper South?

but none received wide enough support in either the North or the South. The most popular was a proposal by Senator John J. Crittenden of Kentucky. It would have guaranteed the future status of slavery by a series of amendments to the United States Constitution. The new amendments would have:

- restored the Missouri Compromise, extending its dividing line to California and creating slave territories to the south of it
- protected the slave trade from federal interference
- prevented the abolition of slavery in the District of Columbia.

President-elect Lincoln opposed the Crittenden Compromise and advised Republican congressmen to "entertain no proposition for a compromise in regard to the extension of slavery." Committed to stopping the expansion of slavery, Republicans voted down the only plan that had a chance for success. In the meantime, President James Buchanan did little to stem the crisis. In his annual message to Congress in December, the president deplored the disruption of the Union. But in his opinion, the federal government could do nothing to prevent secession. As hope for a peaceful solution faded, the nation waited for Lincoln's inauguration to see what the new president would do.

Although determined to save the Union at all cost, Lincoln hoped to do so without provoking a civil war. In his inaugural address in March 1861, he vowed to enforce the laws and to "hold and possess" property owned by the federal government in every

► On April 12, 1861, Confederate guns in Charleston harbor fired on Fort Sumter. Why did President Lincoln maneuver the Confederacy into firing the first shot in the Civil War?

state. But he said nothing about retaking the forts and arsenals in several southern states that were already in Confederate hands. Trying to avoid any action that might give the upper South grounds for secession, Lincoln promised not to use force unless the government was attacked first.

The Fall of Fort Sumter

Lincoln's most urgent problem was Fort Sumter, the major federal fort in the South not yet taken by the Confederates. Located in Charleston harbor and cut off from land, it was rapidly running out of supplies. Its commander, Major Robert Anderson, warned the War Department that he would have to evacuate if he were not resupplied soon. The danger was that any attempt to bring in new supplies by sea would provoke the very war that Lincoln hoped to prevent, or at least to delay. Lincoln decided to send unarmed merchant vessels to resupply the fort. If the Confederates attacked the ships, they—and not the federal government—would bear the responsibility for starting the war.

In fact, Lincoln had left the Confederacy with little choice but to fire the first shot in the American Civil War. The Confederacy could not permit Fort Sumter to survive as a symbol of federal sovereignty within its own national borders. After Anderson refused a Confederate demand to surrender the fort before the supply ships arrived, Confederate guns opened fire on Fort Sumter on the morning of April 12, 1861. Anderson surrendered after a 34-hour bombardment that left the fort heavily damaged. Ironically, not a single person was killed in the first engagement in what was to be the bloodiest war in American history.

SECTION 5 REVIEW

1. **Explain** why the Democrats were unable to nominate a candidate at Charleston.
2. **List** two reasons why the Republican party selected Abraham Lincoln as its presidential candidate.
3. **Identify** Jefferson Davis.
4. **Describe** the two general reactions in the South to Lincoln's election.
5. **Explain** why Lincoln sent *unarmed* supply ships to Fort Sumter.

Summary

The revival of the conflict over slavery in the territories threatened to tear the nation apart. After lying dormant since the Missouri Compromise in 1820, the issue arose again during the Mexican War. The Wilmot Proviso to ban slavery from the territory acquired from Mexico found wide support in the North, but met with intense opposition in the South. A crisis developed when California applied for admission as a free state. While that crisis was finally resolved by the Compromise of 1850, the issue of whether slavery should be permitted in the territories remained unsettled. It divided the nation again in 1854 when Congress passed the Kansas-Nebraska Act. Stephen A. Douglas hoped to resolve the question by leaving the status of slavery up to the inhabitants of the territories. This doctrine became known as popular sovereignty. The violence in Kansas and the emergence of a new antislavery party, the Republican Party, kept the slavery issue very much alive.

As the decade of the 1850s drew to a close, the United States moved rapidly toward disunion. The South, bolstered by the Supreme Court's Dred Scott decision, insisted on its right to extend slavery into the territories. It denounced Douglas's Freeport Doctrine, which provided a method for settlers to exclude slavery and demanded the approval of the proslavery Lecompton Constitution for Kansas. Free-soil Democrats and Republicans alike opposed any further expansion of slavery. The slavery issue split the Democratic Party in 1860, leaving the southern Democrats an isolated political minority. Always distrustful of the Republican Party and stunned by Abraham Lincoln's election, the leaders in seven southern states withdrew their states from the Union and organized the Confederate States of America.

The first crisis that President Lincoln faced was the Confederate threat to Fort Sumter. The firing on Fort Sumter marked the beginning of the American Civil War. That war, which is described in the next chapter, would be the most tragic and costly war in terms of human lives ever waged by the American people.

Vocabulary

popular sovereignty   secession
referendum   vigilance committees

Match each vocabulary term above with one of the numbered terms below. Write a brief description of the relationship between each pair of words.

1. Lecompton Constitution
2. extension of slavery
3. Fugitive Slave Act of 1850
4. Senator Robert Toombs of Georgia

Review Questions

1. In what way did the Wilmot Proviso revive sectional conflict?
2. Summarize the method used by President Zachary Taylor to try to settle the California statehood question.
3. List the provisions of the Compromise of 1850.
4. Describe how northern antislavery leaders tried to prevent the enforcement of the Fugitive Slave Act.
5. Why did Stephen A. Douglas introduce the Kansas-Nebraska bill, knowing it would reopen the issue of slavery in the territories?
6. What effect did the Kansas-Nebraska Act have on the Whig Party?
7. What was the Dred Scott decision and how did it bring the principle of popular sovereignty into question?
8. What was the Republican view on slavery as stated by Lincoln in the 1858 debates?
9. Why did some southern states secede from the Union after Lincoln's election?
10. Explain why Lincoln opposed the Crittenden Compromise.

Critical Historical Thinking

——◁∿Writing Answer each of the following by writing one or more complete paragraphs:

1. Although Lincoln lost the Illinois Senate race to Stephen Douglas in 1858, the exposure allowed him to win the presidency two years later. Explain how this happened.
2. How could Lincoln have captured the presidency in 1860 with only 40 percent of the popular vote?
3. What further steps, if any, might have been taken to avoid war in 1861? Or do you feel, given the circumstances, civil war was inevitable?
4. In the Unit 4 Archives, read "David Wilmot Opposes Slavery in the Territories," and "Lincoln's Pledge to Defend the Union." Explain how the ideas of Wilmot and Lincoln concerning slavery were similar.

Making Connections with Politics

Politics in a democratic society is the art of compromise. This is especially true in the United States where two parties serve as umbrellas for a variety of political and sectional interests. Because the issue of slavery was so divisive, politicians generally avoided addressing the issue of slavery in Congress. The South could have its "peculiar institution." But,

as you have read, acquisition of the Mexican lands in the Southwest and the opening of Nebraska Territory for settlement inevitably raised the question of slavery's extension. Congressmen hoped to avoid a fight over slavery by proposing to allow the settlers themselves to decide the issue by voting whether or not their state should be a slave or free state. This solution ultimately satisfied no one. One of the problems was that whether or not the settlers exercised popular sovereignty, Congress still had to vote on the state's admission. Thus a Congressional floor fight was unavoidable.

——◁∿Writing Using your textbook, list the steps by which a territory becomes a state under the Northwest Ordinance of 1786. Write a paragraph explaining why Congress could not avoid confronting the issue of slavery in the territories. State at exactly which point in the statehood process slavery was likely to become a political issue.

Additional Skills Practice

Imagine your best friend is running for class president. Write a paragraph using one or more of the following persuasion tactics to convince your other friends to vote for her (or him):

- name calling
- speaking in generalities
- using stereotypes
- using testimonials
- card stacking
- urging to get on the bandwagon.

◀

This pro-Union symbol was used on the campaign banners of the Constitutional Union Party in 1860. The emblem did not achieve much success as the Constitutional Union Party carried only three border slave states.

The Nation at War

The Civil War was the greatest crisis the United States ever faced. For four years, the nation was on trial and its future in question. Would the republic endure, or would the South establish its own independence? Was the United States one nation or a temporary alliance of sovereign states? This crisis cost billions of dollars and the lives of more than half a million people. In the process, the issue of slavery was finally put to rest. The advancing Union armies, Abraham Lincoln's Emancipation Proclamation, and the Thirteenth Amendment to the Constitution (ratified after the war) freed nearly 4 million people from inhumane bondage. The human and economic costs of the war were staggering, but the United States of America emerged from this tragic trial wounded but whole.

▲ *This jacket and cap are believed to have belonged to a Union infantry colonel of the Fifth Connecticut regiment.*

▲ *This frock coat and cap belonged to a Confederate whose unit surrendered with General Lee at Appomattox Courthouse.*

SECTIONS

1	2	3	4	5
Union and Confederate Advantages	The First Battles	Behind the Lines	The Turning of the Tide	The End of the War

Union and Confederate Advantages

The South went to war in 1861 in a mood of celebration. The Union surrender of Fort Sumter was an electrifying event, ending the suspense that had gripped the South during the winter months. Thousands of southern men rushed to join Confederate regiments. The secession of the upper South—Virginia, North Carolina, Tennessee, and Arkansas—also boosted southern morale. Winning these states greatly strengthened the Confederacy. Battlefield successes early in the war pushed morale even higher. A British visitor in the South saw huge crowds with "flushed faces, wild eyes, screaming mouths," as bands played the southern anthem "Dixie." Southern morale and sectional loyalty remained high during the first months of the war.

What advantages did the Confederacy have in the Civil War?

What did President Lincoln do to mobilize the North for war?

What economic advantages did the North have over the Confederacy?

Weaknesses and Advantages of the South

Despite the general level of enthusiasm, the new Confederate government was not prepared for a major war. In 1861, it had no treasury, almost no navy, and few of the resources needed for modern warfare. With a much smaller population than the North, the South was able to enlist only a total of 800,000 men in the Confederate army compared to the Union army's total of 2,100,000. It also lacked the industrial base to keep these men adequately supplied.

◄ *Jefferson Davis was elected president of the Confederate States of America in 1861.*

Newly elected Confederate President Jefferson Davis of Mississippi had great difficulty mobilizing his nation for war. First of all, he was hampered by the South's attitude toward government—namely, its insistence on states' rights. For example, the governor of Georgia insisted that only Georgia officers should command Georgia troops. President Davis also had difficulty persuading the states to tax themselves to pay for the war. For financing, the Confederacy relied mainly on borrowing and on printing paper money. This created runaway inflation, as the price of men's shoes soared to $125 a pair.

The Confederacy did have certain advantages. At the beginning of the war, the South probably had the better army. The Confederate army certainly had more talented officers than did the Union army, perhaps because the culture of the South had stressed the importance of leadership and of martial values. Confederate **General Robert E. Lee** was the most capable military strategist of the war. Southern farm boys who had learned to ride and to shoot early in life probably made better soldiers than their more urbanized northern opponents. Union **General William T. Sherman** had no doubt about the superior quality of southern cavalry troops. He described them as "the young bloods of the South; sons of planters, lawyers about town, good billiard-players and sportsmen. . . . They are splendid riders, first-rate shots, and utterly reckless. . . . They are the best cavalry in the world."

Like Washington's army during the Revolution, the Confederate troops fought on familiar ground. In battles fought in their home states, Confederate

▲ *Already a distinguished officer, Lee declined a command in the Union army, choosing instead to lead Confederate troops.*

to keep from being defeated. A stalemate or a draw was enough to ensure Confederate independence. The North, on the other hand, had to fight an offensive war. It had to occupy Confederate territory and destroy the South's army, which was a far more difficult task. The editor of the London *Times* wrote,

> It is one thing to drive the rebels from the south bank of the Potomac, or even to occupy Richmond, but another to reduce and hold in permanent subjection a tract of country nearly as large as Russia in Europe.... Just as England during the revolution had to give up conquering the colonies, so the North will have to give up conquering the South.

Lincoln Mobilizes the Army

Following the attack on Fort Sumter, Lincoln set out to mobilize the North for war. It was a gigantic task, as the federal government was unprepared for a major conflict. The regular army had fewer than 16,000 men, most of whom were stationed in forts in the West. It was woefully short of officers, nearly a third of them having resigned to join the Confederate army. The president acted quickly, expecting Congress to ratify what he had

generals knew every back road and country lane. They could move troops down roads that did not even appear on the Union army's maps.

The South also had the advantage of fighting a defensive war. All it had to do to "win" the war was

▶ *John Singleton Mosby conducted guerrilla warfare against the Union army, attacking outposts and ambushing wagon trains. Was this an effective tactic for the South in the Civil War?*

Northern Railroads Help to Win the War

In 1861, railroads were the latest development in transportation technology. Both the Union and Confederate armies were quick to adapt this new technology to military purposes. Troops that were moved quickly by railroad could give an army a decisive advantage. In the First Battle of Bull Run, the initial battle of the Civil War, the Confederates gained an edge by moving an army to Manassas by railroad.

Both armies discovered early in the war that railroads could move military supplies further and faster than mule-drawn wagons. Railroad supply lines were especially critical to Union forces, as these invading armies were operating over long distances from their source of supplies.

As Union armies invaded the South, the War Department took over captured southern railroads and kept them in repair. To operate these railroad lines, the government created an agency called the United States Military Rail Roads. Its most spectacular achievement was to keep General Sherman's army supplied during his march to Atlanta. The agency used a single railroad line to keep Sherman's army of 100,000 men and 60,000 animals in the field for six months. When it finally reached Atlanta, the army was 360 miles from its base of supply. "The Atlanta campaign,"

▲ *This locomotive dates from the Civil War era. Why were the railroads so vital to both armies?*

Sherman wrote in his memoirs, "would simply have been impossible without the use of the railroads." By the end of the war, the United States Military Rail Roads Agency was operating 419 locomotives and 6,330 cars over 2,000 miles of track, making it larger than any of the nation's private railroad operations at that time.

Dependence on railroads also made the Union armies operating in the South vulnerable to guerrilla attacks. Confederate cavalry troopers became experts at railroad demolition. "Railroads are the weakest things in war," General Sherman said. "A single man with a match can destroy and cut off communications." Cavalry raids and individual acts of sabotage resulted in "bridges and water-tanks burned, trains fired into, track torn up" and "engines run off and badly damaged." The use of iron-plated armored cars attached to the front

of locomotives and equipped with revolving guns and cannon gave Union trains some protection.

The Union army also used railroads to remove the wounded from the battlefields to hospitals in the rear. In July 1863, trains made up of baggage carts with straw-covered floors carried wounded Union soldiers from Gettysburg to hospitals in Washington, D.C., and Harrisburg. By the war's end, the Union army had specially designed hospital cars outfitted with cots and stretchers to move wounded soldiers to hospitals. Railroads saved lives by reducing the time it took to transport seriously wounded soldiers to medical facilities.

1. Explain why railroads were important to the Union and Confederate armies.
2. How did dependence on railroads make an army more vulnerable?

done. First, he authorized an increase in the size of both the army and the navy. In April, Lincoln called for 75,000 90-day volunteers, and the response was enthusiastic. In addition, he asked for 42,000 more men to serve for three years in a volunteer army raised by the states. To prevent the South from importing arms from Europe, Lincoln also imposed a naval blockade of the southern coastline. From the outset of the war, Lincoln's skillful leadership was one of the North's major assets.

The loyalty of the border states deeply concerned Lincoln. After the fall of Fort Sumter, four states in the upper South (Virginia, North Carolina, Tennessee, and Arkansas) seceded from the Union. The future of four other slave states was still undecided. These were the border states of Delaware, Maryland, Kentucky, and Missouri. Lincoln discovered how crucial it was to hold Maryland in the federal Union when, on April 19, 1861, a pro-Confederate mob in Baltimore attacked several companies of Massachusetts militia on their way to Washington. If Maryland should secede, Washington, D.C., would be cut off from the North.

Lincoln was determined to keep the wavering border states in the Union. He helped ensure Maryland's loyalty by putting the state under **martial law**, or temporary rule by military authorities, and sending troops to Baltimore. The status of Kentucky and Missouri remained in doubt throughout the summer of 1861. In these states, Confederate and Union supporters were almost equally divided. The Unionists finally gained the upper hand, but both states went into the Civil War with families divided and brothers fighting against brothers. Delaware also remained in the Union. Finally, the Union regained the western counties of Virginia, which broke away to set up their own government. In 1863, these counties became the new state of West Virginia.

Superior Resources in the Industrial North

In a test of economic strength, the North had obvious advantages. It had six times as many factories and workshops as the South. The North had more than 70 percent of the nation's railroad tracks, most of its banks and financial resources, and more than double the South's population. Northern factories had little difficulty filling the War Department's orders for cannons, rifles, tents, uniforms, overcoats, blankets, canteens, wagons, horse harnesses, and the thousands of other items necessary to outfit an army. A campaigning army of 100,000 men consumed 600 tons of food and supplies each day. The food came from the bountiful harvests of northern farms. The Union government spent more than one billion dollars on war contracts alone, which it paid for by taxing the people, borrowing money, and issuing a new paper currency popularly called **greenbacks**.

▼ *The United States government paid for the war partly by printing paper money. Unlike earlier paper dollars, these greenbacks were not redeemable in gold. What were the economic results of circulating these paper bills?*

Front   Back

▲ *This colored lithograph depicts the battle of the* Monitor *and the* Merrimack. *What effect did this battle have on the future of naval construction?*

The Union government built a modern navy during the Civil War. In 1861, the United States Navy consisted of just 42 warships, most of them on patrol far from the United States. By 1865, the navy had grown to a fleet of 671 vessels—the largest navy in the world at that time. It was equipped with the latest in naval technology, including ships armored with sheets of iron. On March 8, 1862, in one of the most famous battles of naval history, the navy's first ironclad battleship, the *Monitor*, dueled with another ironclad, the *Merrimack*. The *Merrimack* was a captured federal vessel that the Confederate navy department had rebuilt and rechristened the *Virginia*. After battling for hours, the ships broke off the engagement. This battle of the ironclads marked the end of the era of wooden warships.

The Union navy played an important part in the war. Warships enforced the blockade of southern ports, making it difficult for the South to market its cotton. The blockade also sharply reduced imports of manufactured goods. The navy supported the Union army with its fleet of river **gunboats**, especially in the West. These flat-bottomed, steam driven "floating forts" allowed Union cannons to be carried up the shallow rivers of the Confederate states.

┌─────────────────────────────┐
│   SECTION 1 REVIEW   │
└─────────────────────────────┘

1. **List** the military advantages the South had in the Civil War.
2. **Name** the weaknesses of the Confederacy at the start of the war.
3. **List** the steps taken by Lincoln to mobilize the North for war.
4. **Name** the slave-holding states that remained in the Union.
5. **Identify** the major advantages held by the North in fighting the war.

SECTION 2

The First Battles

The attack on Fort Sumter united northern sentiment in favor of going to war to save the Union. "We must settle this question now," Lincoln said, "whether, in a free government, the minority have the right to break up the government whenever they choose." The vast majority of northern Democrats as well as Republicans rallied behind the president. As Stephen A. Douglas, the Democratic senator from Illinois, declared, "There can be no neutrals in this war; only patriots—or traitors." The ailing Douglas, who died that summer, gave his full support to Lincoln. Within weeks of Lincoln's call for volunteers, enthusiastic regiments of untrained militia were marching off to defend Washington, D.C., and other strategic points. The editor of the New York *Tribune* called for an immediate invasion of the Confederacy. "FORWARD TO RICHMOND! FORWARD TO RICHMOND!" its headlines declared. Other newspapers echoed that call.

How successful was General McClellan as a field commander?

What did Confederate armies hope to accomplish during the first year of the war?

Why was the Battle of Antietam a defeat for the Confederacy?

The Battle at Bull Run

Lincoln expected the war to be over quickly, as did most people in both the North and the South. In July 1861, he tried to put down the rebellion with one blow by ordering an attack against the Confederate army in northern Virginia. When General Irvin McDowell, the commanding officer of the Union army, asked for more time to train his men, Lincoln refused the request: "You are green, it is true, but they are green also; you are all green alike." Lincoln fully expected McDowell to defeat the Confederates and march on to Richmond. He assumed that capturing the rebel capital would end the war.

The Confederate army halted the Union advance 30 miles southwest of Washington at a stream called Bull Run, near Manassas. Expecting an easy

▲ *In 1861, Confederate troops overran the Union line at the first Battle of Bull Run. How did General Thomas Jackson earn his nickname during this battle?*

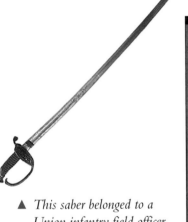

▲ *This saber belonged to a Union infantry field officer of the 154th Illinois Volunteers. Why did officers carry swords, while troops serving under them carried rifles?*

▶

During the early part of the war, most of the fighting in the East took place in Virginia. Why did McClellan fail to capture Richmond?

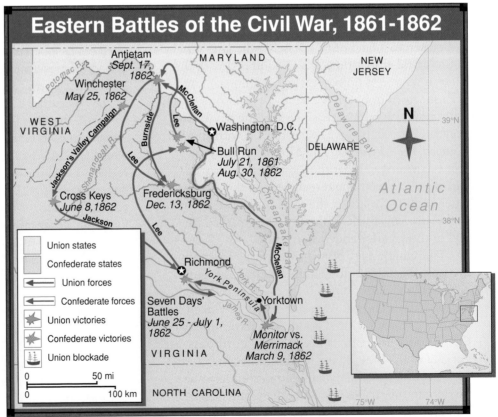

Eastern Battles of the Civil War, 1861-1862

MARYLAND
NEW JERSEY

Antietam
Sept. 17, 1862

Winchester
May 25, 1862

WEST VIRGINIA

Jackson's Valley Campaign

Washington, D.C.

Bull Run
July 21, 1861
Aug. 30, 1862

DELAWARE

Cross Keys
June 8, 1862

Fredericksburg
Dec. 13, 1862

Jackson

Atlantic Ocean

Richmond

York Peninsula

Seven Days' Battles
June 25 - July 1, 1862

Yorktown

Monitor vs. *Merrimack*
March 9, 1862

VIRGINIA

NORTH CAROLINA

Union states
Confederate states
Union forces
Confederate forces
Union victories
Confederate victories
Union blockade

0   50 mi
0   100 km

N

39°N
38°N
75°W   74°W

Union victory, civilians and newspaper reporters came out from Washington to watch the battle. McDowell ordered an attack that almost routed the rebel forces. But they held on, partly due to the courage of Confederate **General Thomas Jackson.** "Look," cried out a Confederate officer in the midst of battle, "there is Jackson standing like a stone wall. Rally behind the Virginians." Stonewall Jackson, as he was known thereafter, was to become one of the Confederacy's best field commanders.

At the **Battle of Bull Run** one attack followed another in a battle that raged for 14 hours. Finally, the Confederate army launched a massive counterattack that sent 18,000 men surging forward. As they were driven backward, McDowell's untrained troops panicked and fled all the way to Washington. A congressman who observed the battle noted, "Off they went, one and all; off down the highway, over across fields, towards the woods, anywhere, everywhere, to escape." Fortunately for the fleeing Union troops, the Confederates were too disorganized to pursue them. Both armies still had a lot to learn.

The Union defeat at Bull Run taught Lincoln and the North a lesson. They discovered that the rebellion could not be put down by green troops marching off to capture Richmond. Defeating the Confederacy would take much longer than first anticipated. It would also take all the patience, resources, and manpower that the Union government could muster.

Union Victory in the West and Stalemate in the East

The Union army won its first victories in the West. In February 1862, Lincoln received good news from **General Ulysses S. Grant.** With the help of the Union gunboats, his army had captured two western forts held by the Confederates. These were Fort Henry on the Tennessee River and Fort Donelson on the Cumberland. These victories forced the Confederates to abandon all of western Tennessee. That month, the North also celebrated the capture of Nashville, the first Confederate state capital to fall. Union forces also won a costly victory at the **Battle of Shiloh**, the bloodiest battle fought thus far on American soil.

◀ *This military saddle was used by General Ulysses S. Grant. How does it differ from a western saddle?*

◀ *General Grant was one of the Union army's most successful field commanders.*

▲ *Cannon balls and artillery shells were staples of Civil War arsenals. Each artillery shell contained an explosive charge and metal balls.*

▶

Union forces in the West tried to defeat Confederate armies and regain control of the upper South. What other objective did the Union armies have in the West?

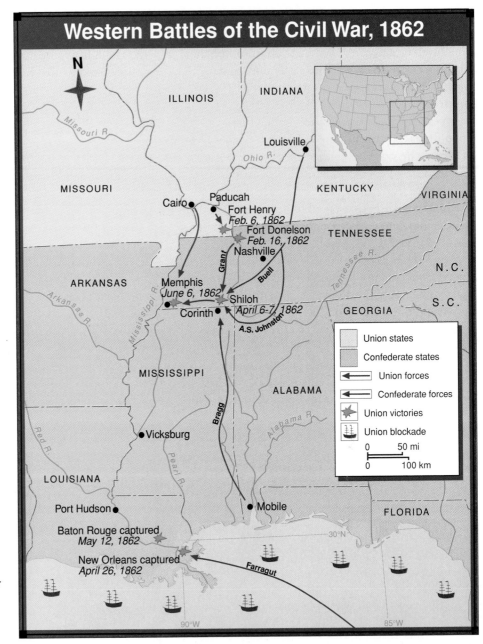

Western Battles of the Civil War, 1862

Cairo
Paducah
Fort Henry
Feb. 6, 1862
Fort Donelson
Feb. 16, 1862
Nashville
Grant
Buell
Memphis
June 6, 1862
Shiloh
April 6-7, 1862
Corinth
A.S. Johnston
Bragg
Vicksburg
Port Hudson
Mobile
Baton Rouge captured
May 12, 1862
New Orleans captured
April 26, 1862
Farragut

ILLINOIS
INDIANA
Louisville
Ohio R.
MISSOURI
KENTUCKY
VIRGINIA
Missouri R.
ARKANSAS
TENNESSEE
Tennessee R.
N.C.
S.C.
GEORGIA
Arkansas R.
Mississippi R.
MISSISSIPPI
ALABAMA
Alabama R.
Red R.
Pearl R.
LOUISIANA
FLORIDA
30°N
90°W
85°W

Union states
Confederate states
Union forces
Confederate forces
Union victories
Union blockade

0   50 mi
0   100 km

In the spring of 1862, a Union fleet of gunboats, under the command of Admiral David G. Farragut fought its way from the Gulf of Mexico up the Mississippi. It captured New Orleans and Baton Rouge, the second Confederate state capital to fall. Another fleet moved down the river from St. Louis and captured Memphis. By midsummer, complete Union control of the Mississippi was only prevented by the strong Confederate defenses at Vicksburg, Mississippi, and Port Hudson, Louisiana.

That spring, the war also resumed in the East. Lincoln had replaced McDowell with **General George B. McClellan,** one of the most popular officers in the army. McClellan spent the fall and winter expanding the Army of the Potomac to 150,000 men and putting it in fighting trim. He was a genius at organizing men and building morale. However, he tended to misjudge the strength of opposing forces, generally thinking that they were stronger and better prepared than he was. After delaying any move against the Confederacy for nine months, he finally took his army by sea to the York Peninsula of Virginia for an attack against Richmond.

After landing his army in Virginia in April, McClellan moved up the peninsula to Yorktown. The Union troops outnumbered the Confederates 70,000 to 17,000. Again, McClellan misjudged the enemy's strength and refused to attack. When McClellan asked Lincoln for still more troops, the president begged him to fight. "It is indispensable to you that *you* strike a blow. . . . *But you must act.*" In delaying, McClellan gave the Confederates time to rally more troops. When he reached the defensive lines five miles from Richmond in May, McClellan stopped again. This time his army of 100,000 faced 60,000 Confederates. Again, he demanded that Lincoln send more men. Stonewall Jackson kept the Union armies that might have come to McClellan's aid occupied by staging a series of daring attacks in northern Virginia. As McClellan stalled, the Confederates took the offensive. In seven days of brutal fighting (the Seven Days' Battles) from June 25 to July 1, an army commanded by General Robert E. Lee pushed McClellan back down the peninsula. Although the Confederates suffered heavy losses, the Union army had had enough. McClellan was ordered to withdraw his army from Virginia.

The summer of 1862 ended with another Confederate victory in the **Second Battle of Bull Run.** On August 28 and 29, Stonewall Jackson, with Lee's help, once again bloodied the Union troops on this northern Virginia battlefield. After a summer of campaigning, the Union forces had accomplished nothing. Their superior numbers were more than offset by inferior leadership.

Through the summer of 1862, the Confederacy followed a defensive strategy. It had used its army to stop McDowell's advance at Bull Run in 1861 and saved Richmond from McClellan's army the following year. But this strategy had its limitations. It meant fighting a long, drawn-out, and costly war, the very kind of war the Confederacy could least afford. The hope of ending the war quickly prompted Confederate leaders to wage offensive campaigns.

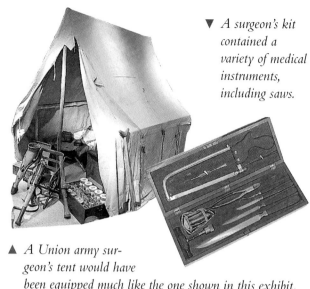

▼ A surgeon's kit contained a variety of medical instruments, including saws.

▲ A Union army surgeon's tent would have been equipped much like the one shown in this exhibit. What objects can you identify?

The Confederate Offensive

In the fall of 1862, Davis and the Confederate military command launched a double offensive. In the East, Lee marched north into Maryland with an army still weary from the Second Battle of Bull Run. A decisive victory in Maryland might bring that state into the Confederacy and cut off Washington. At the least, Lee hoped to draw the Union armies out of Virginia and give the farmers there time to harvest their crops. In the West, Confederate armies advanced toward Kentucky and western Tennessee.

Jefferson Davis was convinced that Kentucky remained in the Union against the will of most of its people. Military success in the West might add that state to the Confederacy and regain control of Tennessee. The Confederate officials also hoped that success would lead quickly to foreign recognition of Confederate independence. It might even bring about the intervention of Britain and France to end the war. It was a bold plan designed to bring about early negotiations for peace and for Confederate independence.

The 1862 fall offensive in the West went badly. Although a Confederate army under General

Braxton Bragg did invade Kentucky and briefly occupied the state capital at Frankfort, the mass uprising against the Union that Davis had hoped for failed to take place. The people of Kentucky remained loyal to the Union. After Bragg's army was stopped at the Battle of Perryville by a much larger number of federal troops, he was forced to withdraw from the state. The army moving into western Tennessee was also turned back with heavy losses. And in the East, Lee's invasion of Maryland was in trouble from the outset.

Lee and McClellan at Antietam

When Lee invaded Maryland, McClellan set out with a much larger Union army to stop him. Lee had divided his own troops into five columns for a broad sweep through the western part of the state. By a stroke of rare good luck, McClellan was given the chance to destroy the Confederate army one piece at a time. In an abandoned camp, a Union soldier found a paper wrapped around three cigars that a careless Confederate officer had mislaid. The paper was a copy of Lee's marching orders, giving the exact location of each column of troops. McClellan was delighted. "Here is a paper with which if I cannot whip 'Bobbie Lee,' I will be willing to go home." But McClellan estimated that Lee's army was two and a half times larger than it really was, and he moved slowly. By the time he caught up with Lee near Antietam Creek, the Confederate forces were reunited and ready for battle.

The two armies clashed near the town of **Sharpsburg, Maryland,** on September 17, 1862, in what became the bloodiest single day of fighting during the Civil War. McClellan's army advanced along a three-mile front, facing Confederate soldiers who had taken cover in groves of trees, behind stone walls, and in cornfields. Men died by the thousands. General Joseph Hooker later recalled the Union attack on a 40-acre cornfield in which Confederate troops were hiding:

> In the time I am writing, every stalk of corn in the northern and greater part of the field was cut as closely as with a knife, and the slain lay in rows precisely as they had stood in their ranks a

▲ *General McClellan's Union forces attacked the Confederate army at Antietam. What factor contributed to making this the bloodiest battle in American history?*

few minutes before. It was never my fortune to witness a more bloody, dismal battlefield.

Attacks and counterattacks carried waves of Confederate and Union troops back and forth across the open fields, littering the countryside with bodies. Even the groves of trees offered little protection. A British visitor who saw the battlefield ten days later noted, "In about seven or eight acres of wood there is not a tree which is not full of bullets and bits of shell. It is impossible to understand how anyone could live in such a fire as there must have been." At the end of this daylong ordeal, both armies were exhausted. Two days later, Lee marched his battered army back toward Virginia. His invasion of the North had come to an end.

More American soldiers died in the **Battle of Antietam** than in any single day of warfare before or since. Union deaths totaled 2,100; Confederate deaths, 2,700. The number of wounded on both sides amounted to 18,500, of whom 3,000 later died. On that one day, more than twice as many Americans were killed as in the War of 1812, the Mexican War, and the Spanish-American War of 1898 combined. Four times as many died as would

◀ *President Abraham Lincoln met with Union army officers following the Battle of Antietam.*

lose their lives in the June 6, 1944, invasion of Normandy during World War II.

Civil War battles like Antietam turned into mass slaughters because military thinking had not kept up with technological changes. The nineteenth century saw a major breakthrough in military technology, as rifled weapons replaced smoothbore muskets. (A rifle has spiraled ridges inside the barrel, which spin the bullet, making it shoot straighter than a projectile from a weapon with a smooth bore.) Frontal attacks by infantry were often successful in earlier days, when armies fought with smoothbore muskets. But muskets were not effective beyond 80 yards, which gave the defenders time to load and fire only once or twice before being overrun by an infantry attack. The modern rifles used by both sides during the Civil War could be fired with deadly accuracy from up to 400 yards away, giving the defenders a much greater advantage. They could fire round after round into the charging infantry, cutting them down before they ever got close. Yet the generals of both armies continued to order frontal assaults as if nothing had changed. As a result, casualty rates soared during the Civil War.

Although neither army clearly won the Battle of Antietam, the engagement was a serious setback for the South. It marked the beginning of what Jefferson Davis called "the darkest and most dangerous period we have yet had." Britain and France were awaiting the battle's outcome before deciding whether to recognize the Confederacy as an independent state. Lee's retreat to Virginia made the decision for them, ending the Confederacy's hope of gaining foreign recognition.

SECTION 2 REVIEW

1. **Explain** why McClellan's peninsula campaign was a failure.
2. **Write** the reason that convinced the Confederate generals to take the offensive in 1862.
3. **Compare** the casualties from Antietam to the losses suffered in the 1944 invasion of Normandy.
4. **Explain** why Civil War battles had such high casualty rates.
5. **Describe** the result of the Battle of Antietam on British and French foreign policy.

Behind the Lines

The vast majority of the Unionists who went to war in 1861 did so for the purpose of saving the Union. They did not go to war to free the slaves. President Lincoln reassured the people that his main objective was to restore the federal Union. "My paramount object in this struggle *is* to save the Union, and is *not* either to save or to destroy slavery," he said. "If I could save the Union without freeing *any* slave I would do it, and if I could save it by freeing *all* the slaves I would do it; and if I could save it by freeing some and leaving others alone, I would also do that." At that time, only a minority of people in the North supported the abolition of slavery. Although the Civil War began as a struggle to reunite a nation in which slavery would still exist, it gradually became a war for **emancipation**, a war to free people from slavery.

What was the significance of the Emancipation Proclamation?

What effect did the Civil War have on women's roles?

Why did the North reap larger economic benefits from the war than the South?

Slaves Liberated by the War

The logic of the war itself pushed the North toward favoring emancipation. As the army advanced into the South, thousands of slaves came across the Union lines. The federal government had to decide what to do with them. It could hardly return the slaves to their owners, as that would aid the Confederate war effort. Congress passed a law stating that all slaves coming within Union lines "shall be deemed captives of war and shall be forever free." Advancing Union armies brought with them freed African Americans, who were given food, clothing, and work to do in the Union cause. Some assisted the Union armies directly as guides or scouts. Others took jobs with the army as wagon drivers and

woodcutters, nurses and laundresses. Still other freed African Americans were put to work on plantations owned by southerners who had remained loyal to the Union. They did many of the same tasks that they had done as slaves. The big difference was that they were now free laborers who worked for wages.

As the Union armies advanced, many former slaves dreamed of owning their own farms. Rumors flew that the federal government would divide up the plantations, giving each African American family "40 acres and a mule." Freed African Americans on the islands off the coast of South Carolina and Georgia did claim farms for themselves when those islands were captured early in the war. At the end of the war, General William T. Sherman also resettled some 40,000 freed African Americans on small farms along the coast of South Carolina. However, in very few instances did the African Americans' dream of land ownership become a reality. Congress refused to recognize the former slaves' title to the land Sherman had given them in South Carolina. After the war, much of the land was returned to its former Confederate owners. The North's failure to support land reform was a great disappointment to the freed African Americans.

The Emancipation Proclamation

As the war against the South dragged on, public opinion began to shift toward emancipating the slaves. By the summer of 1862, Congress had abolished slavery in the District of Columbia and prohibited slavery in the western territories. These actions paved the way for Lincoln's **Emancipation Proclamation.**

On September 22, 1862, shortly after the Battle of Antietam, Lincoln issued a preliminary proclamation about emancipation. He had been waiting for a Union victory to strike a major blow against slavery, as that would strengthen the government's position. He declared that on the first day of January 1863 he would emancipate all slaves in states that "shall then be in rebellion against the United States." This was partly a tactic of war, an invitation to the Confederacy to lay down its arms before that date if it wished to preserve slavery. In a second proclamation on January 1, Lincoln declared that slaves in all the areas still under Confederate control were freed.

The Emancipation Proclamation was largely a symbolic act. It freed few slaves, as it did not apply to slaves in the border states or in parts of the Confederacy already occupied by Union troops. As one Republican complained, "we show our sympathy with slavery by emancipating slaves where we cannot reach them and holding them in bondage where we can set them free." The Proclamation did not go beyond the steps that Congress had already taken to free slaves as the Union army advanced. However, symbolic acts are often important in the affairs of nations. The Emancipation Proclamation announced to the world that the abolition of slavery had become a major purpose of the Civil War. It helped transform a war to preserve the Union into a war for human freedom. In that sense, the Emancipation Proclamation was a turning point.

▲ *This lithograph by Currier and Ives depicts the charge at Fort Wagner by the 54th Massachusetts Regiment in July 1863.*

African Americans in the Union Army and Navy

The emancipation of slaves created a new issue. Should the freed slaves be permitted to serve in the Union army? The Emancipation Proclamation mentioned the possibility of enlisting black soldiers and sailors for duty behind the front lines. At first, the idea of enlisting African Americans met with strong opposition, especially from northern Democrats. They saw it as a move toward racial equality, which they feared. Strong prejudice against African Americans also existed within the Union army itself. White soldiers questioned whether the freed slaves would make good soldiers.

Support for enlisting African Americans came from Republican abolitionists, who saw military service as the shortest route toward full citizenship. "Once let the black man get upon his person the brass letters, U.S.," said abolitionist Frederick Douglass, "let him get an eagle on his button, and a musket on his shoulder and bullets in his pocket, and there is no power on earth which can deny that he has earned the right to citizenship." The most compelling argument for enlisting African Americans, however, was the Union's need for manpower. That argument carried the day.

▼ *This musket belonged to James Peters, shown in the picture. Peters was a former slave from Virginia who served in the Union army.*

In time, white troops came to accept the presence of African Americans in the Union army. As one Union soldier wrote home,

> An honest confession is good for the soul. . . . A year ago last January I didn't like to hear anything of emancipation. Last fall, accepted confiscation of rebels' Negroes quietly. In January took to emancipation readily, and now . . . am becoming so [color] blind that I can't see why they will not make soldiers. . . . I almost begin to think of applying for a position in a [black] regiment myself.

He had in mind a position as an officer, as **segregated** (restricted to one race) regiments of black soldiers were always commanded by whites.

By the end of the war, 179,000 African Americans had served in the Union army and about 20,000 in the navy. They made significant contributions to the eventual Union victory. Robert Smalls, who had been a slave in South Carolina, singlehandedly captured a Confederate boat in Charleston harbor and delivered it to the Union fleet that was blocking the port. He became a pilot in the Union navy. The most celebrated African American regiment, the 54th Massachusetts, distinguished itself in July 1863 by its bloody assault against Fort Wagner, an earthen barrier guarding Charleston harbor. Although the attack failed, the regiment fought with extraordinary bravery, losing nearly half of its men. This battle, noted the New York *Tribune*, "made Fort Wagner such a name to the colored race as Bunker Hill had been for 90 years to the white Yankees." By the time the war was over, 16 black men had won the Congressional Medal of Honor, the nation's highest military honor.

Black women had also played an important role as nurses. Among them was Susie King Taylor, who taught black soldiers how to read and write while she worked in the camp.

▶

Susie King Taylor, who served as a Civil War nurse, was one of the few African American women who were directly involved in the war effort.

New Roles for Women

The war affected the lives of those who remained at home as well as the lives of the soldiers on the battlefields. The enlistment of nearly two million men in the Union and Confederate armies created severe labor shortages. About half the men of military age in the North served in the Union army. In the fall of 1862, one township in Iowa reported that it had "only two men between 18 and 45 remaining." In the South, nearly four out of five white men in that age group went to war. As a result, new burdens were placed on those who remained at home.

Having husbands and fathers away at war changed the pattern of life in countless homes. It was especially hard on the poorer families in the war-torn South. A woman from Virginia wrote to her husband:

> Christmas is most hear again, and things is worse and worse. Everything me and children's got is patched. . . . We haven't got nothing in the house to eat but a little bit o' meal. I don't want you to stop frighten them yankees till you kill the last of them, but try and get off and come home and fix us all up some and then you can go back and fight them a heep harder.

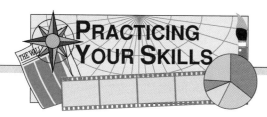

Practicing Your Skills

Interpreting a Lithograph

Civil War photographer Mathew Brady called pictures "the eye of history." Although he and others produced a photographic record of the Civil War, the images were difficult and expensive to reproduce. As a result, newspaper engravings and lithograph prints were among the few depictions of the war available to most people at home. Even 25 years after the war, colored lithographs like the one on page 375 were still popular. A middle class was emerging that could afford to buy cheap, machine-made goods. In response to this demand, two New York City entrepreneurs, Nathaniel Currier and James Ives, mass produced many inexpensive pictures of heroic or landscape subjects to decorate the homes and offices of average Americans.

From these popular pictures we can gather information about the attitudes and values of Americans in the late nineteenth century. Historians look at the choice of the subject, the atmosphere created in the picture, the way in which people and objects are grouped, and the relationships between people to get clues about how Americans viewed these events.

Review the guidelines in Practicing Your Skills on page 53 for help in analyzing the lithograph on the top of page 375. Then answer the following questions:

1. Describe the scene. What is the story told in this picture? What mood is being communicated? Why do you think this event was chosen?
2. (a) How does this picture depict discrimination against African Americans? (b) Using this picture as evidence, what might you conclude about the black soldier's role and conduct in the battle?
3. How are the activities of African American soldiers in this picture different from what you have learned about the early activities of black soldiers first assigned to the Union army?
4. What impression is given about who won this battle? Who did win the battle of Fort Wagner?
5. Which groups of Americans do you think would have purchased this lithograph to display?
6. Do you think this lithograph supports or rejects Douglass's prediction about black soldiers fighting in the Union army? Why, or why not?
7. What attitude towards war and death is conveyed in this picture?

This man did come home, deserting his Confederate regiment. When he returned, he was arrested, convicted of desertion, and would have been executed had the Confederate government not declared a general **amnesty**, or pardon, for this offense because so many others had done the same.

Women were thrust into a variety of new roles. In Richmond and in other Confederate cities, southern women became "government girls," replacing men in state and Confederate offices. Others became schoolteachers, which until then was a man's occupation. In the North, more women found work in factories than ever before. In rural areas everywhere, women shouldered more of the hard work of farming. As an Illinois clergyman wrote in 1863, "Yesterday, I saw the wife of one of our parishioners driving the team in a reaper; her husband is at Vicksburg." Planters' wives in the South suddenly found themselves selling cotton and managing slaves.

Women also contributed directly to the war effort. It has been estimated that at least 400 women served and fought in the armies, disguised as men. Scores of others worked as spies and scouts. **Harriet Tubman,** a former slave, guided Union troops in raids on southern plantations, freeing hundreds of slaves. In the North, thousands of women served as volunteers to collect food and medical supplies for the army. Others worked for the United States Sanitary Commission, a private agency created to improve medical care for Union soldiers. Women in the South contributed to the Confederate war effort in much the same way, sending food and clothing to the soldiers and caring for the wounded in battlefield hospitals.

The Civil War helped nursing gain recognition as a respected profession. Taking care of sick and wounded soldiers was of vital importance during the Civil War, as the number of men who died of disease was twice the number killed in battle. The best-known Union army nurse was Mary Ann Bickerdyke, a widow from Illinois whom the soldiers called Mother Bickerdyke. Clara Barton, who later founded the American Red Cross, also worked in Union battlefield hospitals. The Union army had at least one woman surgeon, Mary Walker, whom the Confederates captured in Georgia. They were shocked that "the debased and depraved Yankee nation" should permit a woman to perform surgery on men.

Although women primarily served in rear-area hospitals, many did lend a hand nearer the battlefield. Women helped prepare food in field hospitals, especially the diets for badly wounded soldiers who could not eat regular army rations. After the Battle of Gettysburg in July 1863, women volunteer nurses descended on the town to care for the wounded. The Union government also allowed southern women to come to Gettysburg to take care of wounded Confederate soldiers.

Serving as a Civil War nurse was a transforming experience for many women. The wife of George Templeton Strong insisted on going to the Virginia peninsula in the summer of 1862 to serve as a volunteer nurse. The experience changed her life and her image in her husband's eyes. "The little woman has come out amazingly strong," he wrote in his diary. "Have never given her credit for a tithe of the enterprise, pluck, discretion, and force of character that she has shown. God bless her." Women's service as Civil War nurses helped alter American men's perception of women.

▲ *Women volunteers raised money for Union wartime hospitals by auctioning Rose Percy dolls, like the one shown here.*

The Wartime Economy

The industrial economy of the North prospered during the war years. The manufacturers of cannon, rifles, and gun powder benefited directly from the war effort. So did the makers of wagons, horse harnesses, and horseshoes. An army of 100,000 men needed 2,500 supply wagons and 35,000 horses and mules to keep it in the field. The production of ready-made clothing rapidly expanded, as orders for army uniforms poured in. Cotton textile manufacturing was the only major northern industry that did not prosper during the war, as shipments of southern-grown cotton to northern factories stopped. The economic loss to the North of peacetime goods was more than made up for by new orders for woolen goods, ironware, and farm implements.

Northern agriculture also thrived during the Civil War. The production of corn, wheat, and pork increased to meet the demands of the War Department. Union soldiers consumed more food per person than any previous army in history. Crop failures in Europe also led to an increase of farm product exports during the Civil War years. With fewer men to work in the fields, northern farms needed to become more mechanized. In 1861, farm-implement factories produced 20,000 mowing machines for cutting hay. By 1864, that number increased to 70,000. With the aid of a mowing machine, or a reaper, one woman could do the work of several men. As a result, farm production increased in the North during the war years despite the shortage of farm labor.

The war also stimulated the growth of the canned-food industry in the United States. Canned milk had only recently been introduced to American consumers, with Gail Borden building his first condensed-milk plant in 1859. By the end of the war, Borden's company produced 17,000 quarts of canned milk a day, and the War Department was a major customer. Army contracts also led to the increased production of canned fruits and vegetables, which rose from 5 million cans in 1860 to 30 million by the end of the decade.

▲ *John Ferguson Weir's painting,* The Gun Foundry *(1866), shows workers in an iron foundry making cannon. What other northern industries flourished during the Civil War?*

The Southern Economy Suffers   While the war stimulated the northern economy, it brought economic ruin to the Confederacy. The prewar South had depended heavily on imported manufactured goods, which it paid for by exporting cotton. The Union naval blockade almost stopped the flow of imports and sharply reduced the South's cotton sales. Cut off from its source of new locomotives and replacement rails, the Confederacy's railroads quickly deteriorated. This made it more difficult to keep the armies supplied. The Confederate troops often fought in tattered uniforms, without shoes and on nearly empty stomachs. The South produced enough food to feed itself, but during the war it had difficulty getting food to the armies. Food rotted while the army starved. The daily food ration in Lee's army in Virginia during the winter of 1862–1863 was four ounces of bacon and two cups of cornmeal.

The Confederacy did succeed in creating a new industry to manufacture firearms. By the end of the war, the South made all of its own rifles, pistols, and ammunition. However, Confederate munitions makers often had to comb the battlefields looking for lead to make new bullets.

Shortages and wartime inflation in the South drove prices up to fantastic levels. A sack of salt worth $1.25 in the North sold for $60 in the South. Food shortages in the cities led to price increases of 700 percent over prewar levels. In 1863, food riots broke out in several cities. By the end of the war, prices had increased by 9,000 percent. This meant that the Confederate currency was almost worthless.

Wartime Governments Assume Powers

The Civil War greatly expanded the role of government in American life. Generally speaking, the withdrawal of the southern Democrats from Washington in 1861 gave the Republicans a free hand to pass whatever legislation they wanted. They enacted a far-reaching economic program that included a

Wartime Nurses

Women, as well as men, responded to President Lincoln's call for volunteers in April 1861 by offering their services as military nurses. Hundreds of would-be nurses poured into Washington, among them Dorothea Dix, who was widely known for her humanitarian work and for the insane asylums she had founded. The secretary of war promptly appointed her Superintendent of Female Nurses, creating a new position for her and a new profession for American women.

At the time of the Civil War, nursing, especially military nursing, was a man's occupation. Army hospitals gave that duty to ordinary soldiers, men either temporarily released from front-line duty or invalids—"nurses by accident"— who were recovering from their own wounds. In either case, the men had no training and were often too weak themselves to be of much help in the hospital wards.

The Civil War helped open nursing to American women. In August 1861, Congress authorized the surgeon general to substitute female nurses in rear-area or general military hospitals. A year later, the Confederate government also began to recruit female nurses. The Union government's surgeon general was so impressed by female nurses that he signed an order in July 1862 requiring at least one-third of all nurses in general mili-

▲ *This photo shows the bodice of a dress worn by Clara Barton.*

◄ *Clara Barton worked as a nurse in the Union army. She continued to be active in humanitarian work after the war, founding the American division of the Red Cross.*

tary hospitals to be women. Nevertheless, these nurses had to contend with a strong public prejudice against women attending men in hospitals.

The role model to whom these women looked was Florence Nightingale, who had modernized British medical service during the Crimean War of 1853–1856. She did more than any other single individual to make nursing a respectable occupation for women. At the same time, Florence Nightingale helped raise nursing from low-status labor to the level of a profession. She created the first school of nursing at St. Thomas's Hospital in London.

The first sight of a wartime hospital was a shock to the women volunteers. Kate Cumming served as a Confederate volunteer nurse after the Battle of Shiloh. She wrote about the hotel that served

as the Confederate army hospital, "Nothing that I had ever heard or read have given me the faintest idea of the horrors witnessed here," she wrote in her diary. "I sat up all night, bathing the men's wounds, and giving them water. The men are lying all over the house, on their blankets, just as they were brought in from the battlefield. . . . The foul air from this mass of human beings at first made me giddy and sick, but I soon got over it. We have to walk and when we give the men anything kneel, in blood and water; but we think nothing of it."

1. Why were women in demand as nurses during the Civil War?
2. Describe how Dorothea Dix and Florence Nightingale changed the status of nursing.

A recruiting poster for an Irish Brigade of the 23rd Regiment of Illinois Volunteers promised significant rewards for men who volunteered to serve in the Union army. What did the poster say would happen to men who waited too long to enlist?

The decorated jacket front helped Union officers find their buglers in the smoke of battle. These signalers sounded important commands such as "charge" and "retreat."

new national banking system and increased tariff protection for industry. The Republican Congress passed the **Homestead Act of 1862**, which provided cheap land in the West for settlers. This act granted 160 acres of public land to anyone who would settle on it for five years. Congress also provided land grants to railroads for building a rail line to California, and it gave tracts of land to states to help them found state colleges.

Limited by its states' rights philosophy, the Confederate government in Richmond played a less active role. Nevertheless, Jefferson Davis did persuade southern farmers to increase food supplies, by producing more meat and grain, and to cut back on the growing of cotton.

The Civil War also brought government into the lives of ordinary people more directly than ever before. In April 1862, the Confederate Congress passed a **conscription law** to draft white men between the ages of 18 and 35 into the army. A year later, the Union government passed its own draft law. The major effect of both laws was to prod men into volunteering, with relatively few soldiers being drafted outright. Volunteering was the more patriotic thing to do, and volunteers were paid a bounty. In 1863, the Union army paid each volunteer $300 to enlist.

In addition, northern consumers felt the heavy hand of government through increased taxes. To help finance the war, the Union government taxed a wide range of consumer items. It also adopted the nation's first income tax. The Confederacy collected taxes in the form of cotton, corn, and other produce, often taken from unwilling farmers.

SECTION 3 REVIEW

1. **List** ways in which the war hastened the abolition of slavery.
2. **Name** some ways in which freed African Americans assisted the war effort.
3. **Describe** ways women contributed to the war effort.
4. **Discuss** how northern industry and agriculture benefited from the Civil War.
5. **Describe** the effect the war had on the southern economy.

▲ *Confederate soldiers died behind this stone wall while resisting the Union advance at Fredericksburg. Who suffered greater casualties here, the Confederate or Union forces?*

The Turning of the Tide

For two years, Abraham Lincoln searched for a general who could give the North a decisive victory. In November 1862, Lincoln removed McClellan as commander of the army in the East because he was too cautious. He replaced McClellan with General Ambrose Burnside. Burnside was not cautious enough. He pursued Lee's army to Fredericksburg, Virginia, where he led his troops into a massacre. The **Battle of Fredericksburg,** fought on December 13, 1862, was one of the worst Union disasters of the war. Lincoln then replaced Burnside with General Joseph Hooker. In May 1863, Hooker was defeated at the Battle of Chancellorsville by a much smaller and less well-equipped Confederate force. (The South also suffered a serious loss at Chancellorsville when General Stonewall Jackson was mistakenly killed by his own men.) The defeat at Chancellorsville was a major blow to Lincoln. "My God! My God!" he exclaimed. "What will the country say?" Despite the Union's larger and better-equipped armies, Lincoln could not find the key to victory.

Why was the Battle of Gettysburg a turning point in the war?

Why were Union victories at Vicksburg and Port Hudson a serious blow to the Confederacy?

How did Union victories in 1863 affect the United States' relations with Great Britain?

Gettysburg and Vicksburg

The gloom that settled over Washington finally lifted in July 1863 when news arrived from the battlefield at Gettysburg. Made confident by their recent victories, the Confederate leaders had sent Lee north to invade Maryland again. Lee advanced through Maryland and into Pennsylvania. There, he clashed with Union forces under General George Meade near the quiet country town of Gettysburg.

The **Battle of Gettysburg** was called by one historian "the most crucial battle in American history." For three days, the fighting raged on the hills and ridges south of the town. In one desperate gamble on the third day, Lee massed 13,000 troops under General George Pickett for a frontal attack at Cemetery Ridge. Although one of his officers cautioned that "no 15,000 ever arrayed for battle can take that position," Lee ordered the assault. More than half of Pickett's troops died.

Gettysburg was a decisive Union victory. In the three days of fighting, Lee lost 25,000 killed or wounded; Meade had 3,155 men killed and 14,529 wounded. Meade, like McClellan after the Battle of Antietam, let Lee escape to Virginia with what remained of his army. But having led the best of the Confederate troops to their slaughter, Lee would never again be able to mount a major offensive.

The victory at Gettysburg was quickly followed by news that General Ulysses S. Grant had taken Vicksburg, the most important of the Confederacy's strongholds on the Mississippi River. Grant had failed to capture the city by direct assault, located as it was on a 200-foot bluff above the river and surrounded by swamps. He had worked all through the previous winter to surround the city and cut it off from its line of supply. During two weeks in April

▲ *The Battles of Gettysburg (top) and Vicksburg (bottom) were crippling defeats for the Confederacy. The naval scene shows Rear-Admiral David Porter's Union gunboats in front of Vicksburg.*

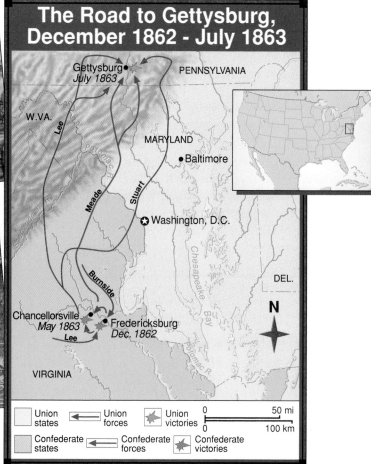

The Road to Gettysburg, December 1862 - July 1863

| Union states | Union forces | Union victories |
| Confederate states | Confederate forces | Confederate victories |

0   50 mi
0   100 km

▲ *Lee's invasion of the North ended at Gettysburg. Why do historians consider the Battle of Gettysburg the most important battle of the Civil War?*

1863, Grant won four hard-fought battles against Confederate defenders and got his army through the swamps. With Vicksburg surrounded, its food exhausted, and with no hope of relief, the Confederate garrison of 30,000 surrendered on July 4, 1863. The fall of Vicksburg and the capture of Port Hudson four days later were serious blows to the Confederate cause. Now the Union navy had complete control of the Mississippi River, cutting off the Confederate states to the west.

Northern Resistance to the Draft

Despite the North's willingness to sacrifice money and blood in the Union cause, support for

the war was not universal. Many northern Democrats had opposed the war from the outset. Even loyal Unionists became disheartened after the defeat of federal troops at Fredericksburg and Chancellorsville. Resistance to the war increased during the summer of 1863. Much of it was focused on the state militia drafts. To help states fill their enlistment quotas, Congress had authorized the drafting of young men into state militia companies. State drafts were met with violence in the Pennsylvania coalfields, in Wisconsin, and especially in New York City, where an antidraft riot broke out on July 13, 1863.

The New York rioters were mainly Irish immigrants. Competing daily with the city's free African Americans for unskilled jobs, the Irish were the most anti-black ethnic group in the city. Many refused to be drafted into a war to free more African Americans. In protest, Irish mobs burned the New York City draft office, looted the homes of Republican leaders, and lynched at least a dozen African Americans. The riot, which lasted for four days, was finally put down by the arrival of Union troops from Gettysburg. Scores of rioters were killed.

The New York City draft riot, one of the worst riots in American history, marked the height of resistance to the war. The quick dispatch of troops to New York may have discouraged other potential rioters. The Union victories at Gettysburg and Vicksburg also helped to restore morale and dampen antiwar sentiment.

▲ *Federal troops were pulled from the battle zone at Gettysburg to disperse New York City's draft rioters. How did ethnic conflict spark the violence in New York?*

Looking Toward Victory

The North's relations with Great Britain improved after the Emancipation Proclamation and successes on the battlefield. In 1861, the two nations had been on the brink of war. A United States naval ship had stopped the British mail ship *Trent* and removed James Mason and John Slidell, two Confederate diplomats on their way to England. The British had demanded an apology and threatened

to dispatch troops to Canada. This crisis passed after Lincoln released Mason and Slidell, but the threat that Britain would recognize Confederate independence remained. Lincoln's Emancipation Proclamation strengthened pro-Unionist sentiment in Britain. The Union victories of 1863 removed any further question of Britain's intervention on the Confederate side.

No one was more pleased with the news from Gettysburg and Vicksburg than President Abraham Lincoln. He knew that these Union victories had dealt the Confederacy a serious blow. Lincoln, how-

▼ *Members of the Signal Corps are shown relaxing during a lull in the war.*

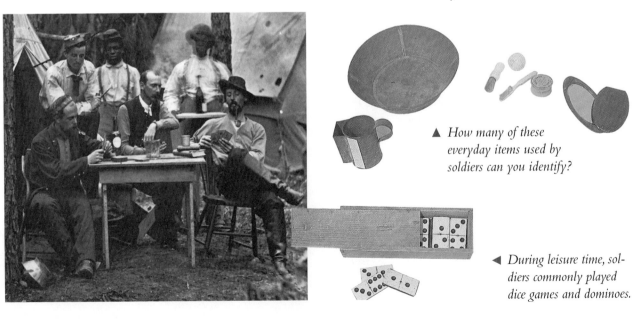

▲ *How many of these everyday items used by soldiers can you identify?*

◄ *During leisure time, soldiers commonly played dice games and dominoes.*

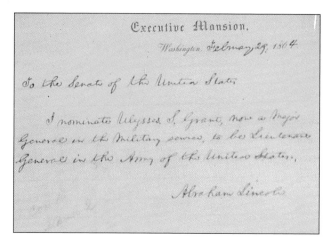

▲ *In this handwritten letter, Lincoln authorized Grant's promotion to lieutenant general. George Washington was the last officer before Grant to hold that rank.*

ever, was disappointed that Meade had let Lee's army escape to Virginia after Gettysburg, when Meade had Lee within his grasp.

The key to success, Lincoln realized, was General Ulysses S. Grant. In Grant, Lincoln found a general who would fight. In October 1863, Lincoln created a new Division of the Mississippi, and placed Grant in charge. It included all the armies between the Appalachian Mountains and the Mississippi River. Within a month, Grant had pushed the Confederates out of Tennessee, winning a stunning victory at the Battle of Chattanooga. Early in 1864, Lincoln promoted Grant to lieutenant general, a rank last held by George Washington, and placed him in charge of all the Union armies. Grant promptly moved his headquarters to Virginia, where he spent the remainder of the war fighting Robert E. Lee.

SECTION 4 REVIEW

1. **Explain** how the defeat at Gettysburg influenced Confederate military strategy.
2. **List** the ways in which the Union victory at Vicksburg weakened the Confederacy.
3. **Discuss** ways in which the New York City draft riot reflected competition in American society.
4. **Explain** why Union victories in 1863 improved the North's relations with Great Britain.
5. **State** reasons Lincoln preferred General Grant over General Meade as commander of the armies.

SECTION 5

The End of the War

The summer of 1864 was a trying time for Abraham Lincoln. For nearly a year, most of the news that he received from the battlefields was bad. General Sherman had set out from Tennessee to capture Atlanta, but his advance was stopped dead in its tracks. In Virginia, Grant's army was suffering heavy losses as it battled Lee's entrenched soldiers. As the war dragged on, Lincoln came under increasing attack from his political opponents. His administration, the Democrats charged, was incapable of ending the war. Although the Republicans had nominated Lincoln for a second term, his chances of winning the election that November seemed bleak. "This morning, as for some days past," he wrote on August 23, "it seems exceedingly probable that this Administration will not be re-elected." The future for Lincoln and for the Union did not look bright.

How did General Sherman's military campaign contribute to Lincoln's reelection?
What terms of surrender did Grant offer to Lee?
How high a price did the South pay for secession?

Lincoln's Reelection

The slow progress made by Union armies in 1864 was largely the result of a new Confederate strategy. From the fall of 1862 through the following summer, Lee and other southern generals had waged an aggressive war, trying to destroy Union armies in open battle. It was a war of rapid troop movements, big battles, and decisive results. After the heavy Confederate losses at Gettysburg, Lee could no longer take the offensive. He had to dig in his troops and fight defensively from fortified positions. The resulting trench warfare inflicted heavy losses on the attacking Union forces, but produced few victories. Lee's strategy was to wear down the North

Four score and seven years ago our fathers brought forth, on this continent, a new nation, conceived in Liberty, and dedicated to the proposition that all men are created equal.

Now we are engaged in a great civil war, testing whether that nation, or any nation so conceived, and so dedicated, can long endure. We are met on a great battle-field of that war. We have come to dedicate a portion of that field, as a final resting-place for those who here gave their lives, that that nation might live. It is altogether fitting and proper that we should do this.

But, in a larger sense, we can not dedicate — we can not consecrate — we can not hallow — this ground. The brave men, living and dead, who struggled here, have consecrated it far above our poor power to add or detract. The world will little note, nor long remember what we say here, but it can never forget what they did here. It is for us the living, rather, to be dedicated here to the unfinished work which they who fought here have thus far so nobly advanced. It is rather for us to be here dedicated to the great task remaining be-

▲ *Union troops destroyed mile after mile of railroad track during General William T. Sherman's march to the sea. Why did Sherman deliberately and completely destroy the property of Confederate civilians?*

▲ *Seen here in Lincoln's own handwriting is the first page of the Gettysburg Address. It was brief, lasting only three minutes. It was not the keynote address at the Gettysburg ceremony, nor did it receive much public attention at the time. Why do you think it is so famous?*

with mounting losses and to break its will to continue the war.

As war weariness grew in the North, the Confederate strategy seemed to be succeeding. In 1864, opposition to the war in the North reached new heights. Hoping to turn this opposition to their political advantage, the Democrats nominated General George B. McClellan for the presidency on a platform calling for peace negotiations. This platform, said Alexander Stephens, the vice president of the Confederacy, was "the first ray of light I have seen from the North since the war began." Confederate agents in the North spent several hundred thousand dollars to encourage the peace movement. They used the money to support Democratic newspapers, to organize peace rallies, and to pay campaign costs of antiwar candidates for public office.

The Union cause was saved once again by good news from the battlefield. Just as support for the war

and for Lincoln reached its low point, word arrived that Sherman had captured Atlanta. "Atlanta is ours, and fairly won," Sherman said in his telegram of September 2, 1864. The North was jubilant. Northern cities celebrated with 100-cannon salutes and fireworks. Atlanta was the Confederacy's strategic western railroad hub. The fall of the city struck a fatal blow to Confederate hopes for peace and independence, and brought an end to talk of peace without victory in the North.

The fall of Atlanta guaranteed the reelection of Abraham Lincoln. In November, he carried 55 percent of the popular vote, defeating McClellan in every state but New Jersey, Kentucky, and Delaware. It was a stunning victory for Lincoln and for the Union.

Sherman and Grant Crush the Confederacy

After taking Atlanta, Sherman was determined to carry the war directly to the southern people. "We cannot change the hearts of these people of

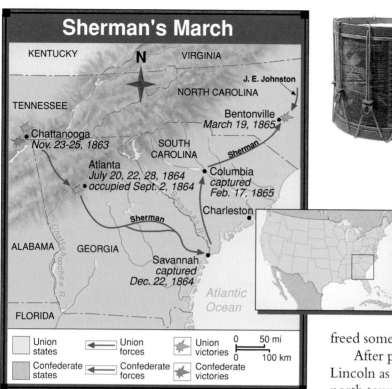

Sherman's March

KENTUCKY

N

VIRGINIA

J. E. Johnston

NORTH CAROLINA

TENNESSEE

Bentonville
March 19, 1865

Chattanooga
Nov. 23-25, 1863

SOUTH
CAROLINA

Sherman

Atlanta
July 20, 22, 28, 1864
occupied Sept. 2, 1864

Columbia
captured
Feb. 17, 1865

Charleston

Sherman

ALABAMA

GEORGIA

Savannah
captured
Dec. 22, 1864

Atlantic
Ocean

FLORIDA

			0 50 mi
Union states	Union forces	Union victories	0 100 km
Confederate states	Confederate forces	Confederate victories	

▲ *After capturing Atlanta, Sherman's army marched to the coast. From there, it turned north to invade the Carolinas. Use the map scale to estimate how far Sherman's army marched from July 1864 to March 1865.*

◀ *This regulation drum came from the 10th U. S. Infantry Regiment.*

the South," he remarked, "but we can make war so terrible . . . [and] make them so sick of war that generations would pass away before they would again appeal to it." He proposed to Grant that he be allowed to "move through Georgia, smashing things to the sea. . . . I can make the march, and make Georgia howl." Grant approved the request. On November 15, Sherman and his army of 62,000 men set out on his notorious march to the sea, an epic of destruction and pillage that the South would long remember.

Sherman's army moved through Georgia cutting a path of destruction 50 miles across. Moving at 10 miles per day, the army consumed or destroyed everything of value in its path. "We had a gay old campaign," recalled one soldier. "Destroyed all we could not eat . . . burned their cotton & gins, spilled their sorghum, burned & twisted the R. Roads and raised Hell generally." The army reached Savannah and the sea on December 21, leaving in its wake

enormous damage. Sherman estimated the cost "at $100,000,000; at least $20,000,000 of which has inured [contributed] to our advantage, and the remainder is simply waste and destruction." During the course of their journey, the soldiers also freed some 25,000 enslaved African Americans.

After presenting the capture of Savannah to Lincoln as a Christmas present, Sherman turned north toward the Carolinas. The army made good time crossing the swamps of South Carolina, building its own roads as it went. A Confederate general remarked:

> When I learned that Sherman's army was marching through the Salk swamps, making its own corduroy roads [logs laid side by side] at the rate of a dozen miles a day and more, and bringing its artillery and wagons with it, I made up my mind that there had been no such army in existence since the days of Julius Caesar.

Sherman's army left a trail of devastation in South Carolina that was even more complete than the destruction in Georgia. The soldiers placed the primary blame for the war on South Carolina, the first southern state to secede from the Union. "Here is where treason began, and, by God, here is where it shall end," said one Union private. After capturing Charleston and burning Columbia, the state capital, the army marched on into North Carolina. Since leaving Atlanta, it had covered a distance of more than 700 miles, leaving a path of ruin through the heart of the Confederacy.

While Sherman paused to rest his troops in North Carolina, Grant began the final attack against

Lee's army near Richmond. He finally succeeded in driving the Confederates out of their entrenched positions. This left Richmond open to attack. After setting fire to arsenals, factories, and government property, Lee's troops abandoned the burning city on April 3, 1865. The following day, President Lincoln visited the Confederate capital and was cheered through the streets by the city's African American population.

Surrender at Appomattox Courthouse   In the meantime, Lee, with 35,000 troops, tried to escape to the West. Grant followed in pursuit, with a Union army of 80,000 men. He finally cut off and surrounded Lee's army on April 9 near the village of **Appomattox Courthouse.** Lee spared his soldiers a last suicidal attack by arranging a meeting with Grant. There he surrendered. The meeting took place in the house of Wilmer McLean, who had moved to Appomattox to escape the devastation of war. His former house near Manassas had been taken over as a Confederate headquarters during the First Battle of Bull Run. Thus, the fighting in Virginia had literally begun and ended in McLean's front room. Grant offered Lee generous surrender terms. His mounted troops could keep their horses and mules "to put in a crop." The Confederate soldiers were paroled and sent home.

Lee's surrender to Grant brought organized Confederate resistance to an end, even though it would take another six weeks for the last rebel soldiers in the West to lay down their arms. The surrender at Appomattox Courthouse signaled the beginning of a joyful celebration throughout the North. A Union soldier in Virginia wrote:

> The air is black with hats and boots, coats, knapsacks, shirts and cartridge boxes. They fall on each other's neck and laugh and cry by turns. Huge, lumbering, bearded men embrace and kiss like schoolgirls, then dance and sing and shout, stand on their heads and play leapfrog with each other.

The news and the celebration quickly spread north. After four years, the most tragic and costly war in American history was finally over.

Immense Costs of War

It is impossible to measure fully the human cost of the Civil War. It caused hardship and suffering

► *General Lee surrendered to General Grant at Appomattox Courthouse on April 9, 1865, bringing the formal, organized war effort to an end. What terms did Grant offer Lee for surrendering?*

beyond anyone's ability to imagine. Millions of people grieved for the loss of a relative or friend. The war directly cost the lives of 620,000 soldiers (360,000 Union and 260,000 Confederate). The number killed and wounded on both sides exceeded one million. Many of the wounded were maimed for life. The number of dead from the Civil War almost equals the number killed in all other American wars combined up to the present time.

The financial cost, which was also staggering, is somewhat easier to calculate. Government loans and tax revenues spent on the war totaled nearly $3 billion for the Union government. The Confederacy spent over $2 billion. Twenty years after the end of the war, the United States was still spending over 60 percent of the federal budget for interest on the war debt and veteran's benefits. Yet government spending amounted only to a fraction of the $20 billion or so of the total cost of the war. Much of the rest represented the physical destruction of the South.

Advancing Union armies destroyed much of the wealth of the South. Farm buildings, mills, and factories were reduced to smoking ruins. The war reached into every corner of the Confederacy and devastated vast areas. The heavy fighting that took place in Tennessee, Virginia, and elsewhere left the countryside scarred for years. Large sections of Georgia, South Carolina, Virginia, and Alabama were laid waste by Union armies and raiding parties.

Grant had instructed General Philip Sheridan to destroy the crops in Virginia's Shenandoah Valley so completely that "crows flying over it for the balance of the season will have to carry provender [food] with them." After driving General Jubal Early's Confederate army out of the Shenandoah Valley, Sheridan reported back to Grant,

I have destroyed over 2,000 barns filled with wheat, hay, and farming implements; over 70 mills filled with flour and wheat; have driven in front of the army over 4,000 head of stock, and have killed and issued to the troops not less than 3,000 sheep.

Southern railroads suffered heavy damage. Railroad tracks were torn up, and locomotives and cars were demolished. In one cavalry raid through Alabama, 600 locomotives and freight cars were de-

▲ *The devastation to the South caused by the Civil War was without parallel, as these ruined buildings in Richmond show.*

stroyed. In Georgia, the Union soldiers made "Sherman neckties" out of the iron rails by heating them over a bonfire and bending them around trees.

In all, the South lost two-thirds of the assessed value of its wealth (including the value of freed slaves), more than half of its farm equipment, two-fifths of its livestock, and one-fourth of its white men between the ages of 20 and 40. The South would take decades to recover.

SECTION 5 REVIEW

1. **Describe** how Sherman's capture of Atlanta affected the election of 1864.
2. **Summarize** the results of Sherman's march through the heart of the Confederacy.
3. **Name** the event that symbolizes the end of the Civil War.
4. **Compare** the loss in lives between the Civil War and other wars in which Americans have fought.
5. **Explain** why it would take so many years to recover from the war.

Summary

The firing on Fort Sumter in 1861 united the people in the North behind the Union cause and in the South behind the Confederate cause. One side went to war to preserve the Union; the other to secure southern independence. In the beginning, neither side had a clear advantage. The North had more people and a larger industrial base, but the South had the better army and could fight a defensive war on familiar ground. The Confederate leaders ordered an invasion of the North in 1862, hoping to achieve a quick victory. The failure of this campaign, especially Lee's defeat at the Battle of Antietam, made certain that the country would face a long and exhausting war.

The Civil War brought sweeping social and economic changes to the millions of people behind the lines. It created a shortage of manpower that thrust women into new roles. More women took jobs in industry, government, and teaching than ever before, and women did more of the work on farms. The Union army freed thousands of African Americans as it moved into the South. Lincoln's Emancipation Proclamation announced to the world that the abolition of slavery had become a major goal of the war. In the North, industry thrived and farm production increased despite the shortage of labor. Mowers, reapers, and other farm machines replaced the men who had gone to war. Meanwhile, in the Confederacy, the war years brought severe inflation, food shortages, and hard times.

The superior resources of the North finally wore the Confederacy down. Lee's army suffered heavy losses at Gettysburg, and the South could not replace them. The fall of Vicksburg and Port Hudson gave the Union forces control of the Mississippi and split the Confederacy. In 1864, Sherman cut a swath of destruction through the heart of the South. Finally, in April 1865, Lee surrendered to Grant at Appomattox Courthouse, bringing this tragic era of American history to an end. Both the North and the South paid a heavy price for the four years of war. The South lost two-thirds of the assessed value of its property and wealth. The toll in human misery for both sections is beyond calculation.

Vocabulary

amnesty   gunboats
conscription   martial law
emancipation   segregated
greenbacks

Write a sentence for each of the above terms that includes a contextual definition of the word. For example: When the president signed the general *amnesty* after the war, Peter was able to return home and resume the life he led before enlisting.

Review Questions

1. Describe the early actions Lincoln took to mobilize the North.
2. List the economic advantages the North had over the South during the Civil War.
3. Name the strategic advantages of the Confederacy.
4. Why were casualty rates so high in the Civil War?
5. Describe various ways the Civil War changed women's roles in both the North and the South.
6. In what ways did government play a larger role in the lives of citizens during the war years?
7. List two immediate results of the Emancipation Proclamation.
8. Why was the Union victory at Gettysburg an important turning point in the war?
9. How were railroads important to the Union war effort?
10. List three reasons why the North won the Civil War.

Critical Historical Thinking

──◦⌁⋀**Writing** Answer each of the following by writing one or more complete paragraphs:

1. The border states of Delaware, Maryland, Kentucky, and Missouri were of critical importance to the Union during the war. What difficulties do you think would have arisen for the North if these states had seceded in 1861?

2. Discuss how the role of women in warfare has changed since the Civil War. Draw on what you know or have heard about women serving in Vietnam and in the Gulf War.

3. Compare and contrast the American Revolution and the Civil War. In what ways were they similar? How were they different?

4. It took a long time to heal the wounds between the North and South. What factors influence the healing process a nation undergoes after a civil war?

Making Connections with Literature

Authors writing before the Civil War identified with the Romantic authors of Europe. Romantic Era (1819–1868) writers such as Washington Irving, James Fenimore Cooper, Nathaniel Hawthorne, Edgar Allan Poe, Herman Melville, and Walt Whitman wrote stories set in distant times and places. The public avidly read gothic novels and mysteries. But the Civil War saw such battles as Antietam with 20,000 casualties in a day. Union armies, according to a typical southern account, "destroyed everything which the most infernal Yankee ingenuity could devise means to destroy; hands, hearts, fire, gunpowder, and behind everything, the spirit of hell, were the agencies which they used." After the war, the scariest scenes of Edgar Allan Poe

seemed more believable; the misty and romantic lands of knights and chivalry seemed less believable. Herman Melville observed that the war had opened "new and ominous [frightful] potentialities" for him. Melville's poems *Battle Pieces* (1866) and Walt Whitman's poems on war mark the divide between the Romantic Era and the Age of Realism (1860–1900). The industrialization that followed the Civil War also played a major role in shaping the new literature, but the Civil War convinced writers that the world itself would become a place radically different from what it had been before.

──◦⌁⋀**Writing** Write two or three complete paragraphs comparing the poems of William Cullen Bryant ("Thanatopsis" or "To a Waterfowl"), Edgar Allan Poe ("Annabelle Lee" and "The Raven"), and Walt Whitman ("Scented Herbage of My Breast" and "Song of Myself") with Stephen Crane's poems (from *The Black Riders and Other Lines*) or William Vaughn Moody ("An Ode in Time of Hesitation"). These poems are readily located in anthologies of American poets. Focus on the issues of romanticism and realism.

Additional Skills Practice

Lithographs were a relatively inexpensive way to mass produce original art. Today, many young people decorate their rooms with inexpensive posters of famous musicians, movies, or celebrities. The choice of posters may reveal important information about the heroes and values of a segment of society.

Take an informal survey of the posters or artwork owned by three or four of your friends. List and categorize the pieces according to content. Are there any generalizations that you can make about the interests or values of your friends based on this list? How reliable do you think these generalizations would be? What factors would affect the accuracy or reliability of your conclusions?

Reconstruction

The end of the fighting in 1865 brought new problems to the American nation. First and foremost was the task of restoring the southern states to the federal Union. Creating loyal state governments in the South was going to be difficult enough. Even more difficult was the challenge of economic recovery, which southerners would face largely alone. The economy of the region was in a shambles. Much of the South's wealth had been destroyed; its fields and factories were in disrepair. Hardly less imposing was the task of rebuilding southern society. Emancipation had radically altered the status of nearly four million freed African Americans. Their future place in the social organization of the South was very much in question.

▲ *Carpetbags were cheaply produced traveling bags made of carpet fabric. Southerners used the word* carpetbagger *to describe Northerners who went south to work in the Reconstruction effort. Although some carpetbaggers took advantage of local governments, most were well-educated people from the middle class who looked to settle permanently in the "New South."*

The Beginning of Reconstruction

In the final weeks before Lee's surrender at Appomattox, Lincoln thought more about peace than about war. The final sentences in his inaugural address, the shortest ever given by a president of the United States, looked beyond victory to the peace that would come: "With malice toward none, with charity for all, with firmness in the right as God gives us to see the right, let us strive on to finish the work we are in, to bind up the nation's wounds, to care for him who shall have borne the battle, and for his widow, and his orphan—to do all which may achieve and cherish a just and lasting peace among ourselves and with all nations."

As this speech shows, Lincoln had begun to think about the process of "binding up the nation's wounds." This process gave a name to the period following the war: it was called **Reconstruction**.

What was Lincoln's plan for Reconstruction?

How did the Radical Republican plan for Reconstruction differ from Lincoln's?

Why did Republicans oppose Andrew Johnson's attempt to reconstruct the Union?

Reconstruction Plans

The primary task of Reconstruction, as Lincoln saw it, was to restore governments loyal to the Union in the South. He had first addressed that task in December 1863, when he announced that southern states would be readmitted to the Union as soon as 10 percent of their voters had taken an oath of loyalty to the United States. He promised a full presidential pardon to each person who took such an oath, except for high-ranking political and military officials of the Confederate government. The only other requirement was that the state's new constitution had to abolish slavery.

This announcement provided a quick and relatively painless way for former Confederate states to rejoin the Union. It mainly affected states already occupied by Union troops, including Tennessee, Louisiana, Arkansas, and Mississippi. By April 1865, these four southern states had met Lincoln's requirements and were waiting to rejoin the Union.

Lincoln had hoped to accomplish two things with his "10 percent plan," as his lenient approach to Reconstruction was called. In the first place, he wanted to persuade the Confederate states occupied early in the war to abolish slavery. (The Emancipation Proclamation applied only to those areas *not* controlled by Union troops in January 1863.) Lincoln also hoped that the reconstructed states would give civil and political rights, such as **suffrage**, to those freed African Americans who had fought for the Union, but he did not insist on it. Second, his plan was a wartime strategy designed to encourage weary Confederate troops to stop fighting and to reaffirm their loyalty to the United States. He also hoped that a lenient approach to Reconstruction would shorten the war.

Radical Republicans Most Republicans in Congress opposed Lincoln's conciliatory approach. They wanted stronger guarantees that Unionists would be in control of the newly restored states, and they insisted on safeguards for the rights of African Americans. The most extreme element in the Republican party, the **Radical Republicans**, also demanded that land be distributed to freed slaves and that they be given the right to vote. They needed both, the Radicals argued, to protect their newly won freedom.

In 1864, Congress presented its own plan for Reconstruction in the Wade-Davis bill. Under this plan, 50 percent of the population of each state had to take the loyalty oath before Reconstruction could begin. Only those male citizens who had never willingly aided the rebellion could vote and hold office. The bill stopped short of the Radicals' demand for land reform and for giving freed slaves the right to vote. Instead, it would rely on the federal courts to protect the freedom of African Americans.

Congress passed the Wade-Davis bill in July 1864, but Lincoln let it die by a **pocket veto**. A

▲ *John Wilkes Booth shot President Abraham Lincoln with the pistol shown above left, in Ford's Theater in Washington, D.C., on April 14, 1865. Lincoln was the first American president to be assassinated.*

president can kill a bill during the final ten days of a session of Congress by refusing to sign it. Lincoln vetoed the Wade-Davis bill in this way. Furious at Lincoln's veto, Congress, in turn, blocked the president's efforts toward Reconstruction. It refused to let the newly elected congressmen from Louisiana, Arkansas, and Tennessee take their seats. The result was a stalemate between the president and Congress that promised trouble for the Republican party.

This conflict was still unresolved when Abraham Lincoln was assassinated on April 14, 1865. The president was mortally wounded by a gunshot as he watched a performance at Ford's Theater in Washington. His assassin was John Wilkes Booth, an actor who sympathized with the South. Lincoln died the following day, and his death was mourned throughout the North. Vice President Andrew Johnson became the new president, inheriting Lincoln's disagreement with Congress over Reconstruction.

Andrew Johnson's Reconstruction Plan

Andrew Johnson had his own views about Reconstruction. They were partly the product of his southern background. Johnson had been born in

North Carolina into a poor white family. After moving to Tennessee as an adult, he entered politics as a Jacksonian Democrat, championing the common man. His political opponents came from the wealthy planter class. Johnson was also a staunch Unionist. He opposed secession and was determined to crush the planters who had led the South into rebellion. However, as Johnson shared the racial prejudice of many whites of his time, he had even less sympathy for the African Americans. He hoped to use Reconstruction to shift power in the South to those poor white people and independent farmers who had not taken an active part in the rebellion.

With Congress in recess during the summer and fall of 1865, Johnson implemented his version of Reconstruction. He granted a general pardon to all who took an oath of loyalty. Wealthy planters and prominent leaders of the Confederacy were excluded from this privilege. However, they could apply individually for special presidential pardons. The president also required each state to revoke its secession ordinance and to ratify the **Thirteenth Amendment,** which abolished slavery. Each state also had to agree not to make payments on the Confederate war debt. Under Andrew Johnson's guidance, new state governments were organized throughout the South. However, they were not yet readmitted to the Union.

Republicans Oppose Johnson's Program

Few Republicans liked Johnson's Reconstruction program. They were disturbed by his lenient terms and by the failure of some states even to abide by those terms. Mississippi and Texas, for example, refused to ratify the Thirteenth Amendment. Republicans were also concerned that none of the states granted African Americans the right to vote. The provisional governor of South Carolina said, "This is a white man's government, and intended for white men only." That attitude seemed typical of the new state governments that Johnson had installed in the South.

The National Peace Jubilee

In June 1869, a gala celebration called the National Peace Jubilee took place in Boston. Conceived by its promoter in a vision, its purpose was to commemorate the return of peace and the reconstruction of the Union. The jubilee reflected America's fondness for band concerts. In those days, every town had a band that performed on special occasions. Composed of brass, wind, and percussion sections, the bands played military marches and belted out the tunes of waltzes and polkas. But no previous concert had been as lavish as the extravaganza that Patrick Gilmore planned for the National Peace Jubilee.

Patrick Gilmore, the inspiration for the stage play "the Music Man," was the most prominent bandmaster of his day. His band, the Boston Brigade Band, had performed at the Republican National Convention in Chicago in 1860 to celebrate Lincoln's nomination. With the outbreak of war the following year, Gilmore had marched his band through the streets of Boston to help recruit soldiers for the Massachusetts 22th Volunteer Regiment. In 1864, Gilmore went to New Orleans to help celebrate

▲ *In 1869, bandmaster Patrick Gilmore (at left) organized a massive extravaganza in Boston to celebrate the return of peace.*

the Union victory over Confederate troops in Louisiana. For that occasion, he assembled a chorus of 5,000 voices and a 500-piece band for a concert hailed as the greatest musical spectacle of its day. But even that concert was eclipsed by the Peace Jubilee he organized in Boston.

The National Peace Jubilee was advertised as "the Grandest Musical Festival Ever Known in the History of the World." The city of Boston built a new coliseum in St. James Park to house the festival. To ensure a large audience from all parts of the country, Gilmore persuaded the railroad companies to offer half-priced tickets for the excursion to Boston.

The highlight of the concert was a special rendition of Giuseppe Verdi's *Anvil Chorus*. In addition to

a 1,000-piece orchestra and 10,000-member choir, it featured 100 local firemen dressed in blue and red flannel uniforms banging on anvils. It was such a rousing performance, according to one spectator, that audience members all "rose to their feet, jumped up and down, and nearly dislocated their arms by waving handkerchiefs, fans, hats, parasols, even babies. . . . Fifty thousand people in a wooden building can sure make noise." Those present long remembered that gala occasion when thousands of Americans gathered to celebrate peace and to help usher in a new era of national growth.

1. What was the purpose of the National Peace Jubilee?
2. What do you think was one of Gilmore's motivations for the concerts?

The Reconstruction Amendments

Amendment	Date of Passage in Congress	Date of Ratification (3/4 of all States)	Main Provisions
Thirteenth	January 1865	December 1865	Prohibited slavery in the United States
Fourteenth	June 1866	July 1868	■ Defined conditions of national citizenship ■ Guaranteed equal protection of the laws ■ Reduced congressional representation for disfranchised voters ■ Denied former Confederate officials and military leaders the right to hold office ■ Declared the Confederate war debt invalid
Fifteenth	February 1869	March 1870	Stated the right to vote could not be denied due to race, color, or past servitude

▲ *The amendments passed during Reconstruction were designed primarily to establish and protect the freedom of African Americans. How did the Fourteenth Amendment affect all Americans?*

Unionists throughout the North were even more alarmed as they watched the South elect former Confederate leaders to high public office. Despite his long-standing dislike of the planter class, Johnson granted many presidential pardons to former Confederate leaders. He may have thought that his generosity would win their support in the next presidential election. Among the senators and representatives elected to Congress were four Confederate generals, four colonels, numerous members of the Confederate Congress, and the vice president of the Confederacy, Alexander H. Stephens. Republicans questioned whether such men would be loyal to the Union they had so recently tried to destroy.

Northern Republicans were also concerned about the so-called **black codes** that every new southern legislature enacted. Although extending basic rights of citizenship to African Americans, these laws restricted their freedom in various ways. A new state law in South Carolina restricted African Americans to household and farm work, thus effectively excluding blacks from businesses and skilled trades. Several states required them to sign labor contracts as plantation workers. In some instances, the contracts bound them to one planter for an extended period, imposed nighttime curfews, and required former slaves to have a pass from their employer before they could leave the planter's property.

Antislavery Republicans reacted strongly to the black codes. The codes seemed to impose a new kind of slavery in place of the old. As the editor of the *Chicago Tribune* warned, "tell the white men of Mississippi that the men of the North will convert the state of Mississippi into a frog pond before they will allow any such laws to disgrace one foot of soil in which the bones of our soldiers sleep and over which the flag of freedom waves." The new codes raised doubts about the South's acceptance of one of the major outcomes of the Civil War.

SECTION 1 REVIEW

1. **Summarize** the two main points of Lincoln's plan for Reconstruction.
2. **List** the terms of the Wade-Davis bill.
3. **Define** the term *pocket veto*.
4. **Explain** why Congress opposed Andrew Johnson's plan for Reconstruction.
5. **State** an example of how the South showed it had not accepted the abolition of slavery.

Congressional Reconstruction

Thaddeus Stevens, a leader of the Radical Republicans in the House of Representatives, was deeply disturbed by the black codes. Like other Radicals, he insisted that African Americans be granted full rights of citizenship. Andrew Johnson's willingness to accept the black codes made it appear to Stevens that the president did not care what happened to the freed slaves. Stevens decided that it was time for Congress to take charge of Reconstruction. At the opening session of Congress in December 1865, Stevens proposed that the House and Senate create a Joint Committee on Reconstruction to produce its own plan for reconstructing the South. Although Republicans close to Andrew Johnson denounced Stevens as "ignorant and vicious," many others looked to him for leadership. The young Rutherford B. Hayes, who would later be president, wrote to his wife from Washington that Stevens was "witty, cool, full and fond of 'sarcasms,' and thoroughly informed. . . . He is [the] leader." So many Republicans were displeased with Andrew Johnson's measures that Stevens's resolution easily passed.

What was the congressional plan for Reconstruction?
What was the Fourteenth Amendment?
Why was Andrew Johnson impeached?

Congress's Reconstruction Plan

While the Republicans in Congress were determined to protect the African Americans' newly won freedom, they did not agree on how to go about it. The Radical Republicans insisted that the very least Congress could do was to give the freed men the right to vote. Armed with the ballot, African Americans could protect themselves. Thaddeus Stevens, who became the chairman of the Joint Committee on Reconstruction, doubted that the ballot was sufficient. He argued that the right to vote would provide little protection unless the blacks were also economically independent. He proposed confiscating plantations and dividing up the land to give the freed African Americans their own farms. Property ownership was believed to be a sacred right by most of the Radicals. This threat to the private property rights of the plantation owners found little support.

The majority of Republicans in Congress also rejected the Radicals' demand that African Americans be given the vote. Republican congressmen were not willing to grant the former slaves political equality with white citizens. Instead, the Republican majority searched for a middle way between Johnson and the Radicals.

The Freedmen's Bureau Moderate Republicans made a serious effort to work with the president. As a compromise measure, they proposed extending the life of the **Freedmen's Bureau,** a temporary agency created in 1865. Its purpose was to assist in the care and feeding of refugees in the war-torn South. Although the bureau helped white people as well, it was especially important to the freed slaves. It supplied them with food and medicine, and set up schools staffed by volunteers from the North. The bureau also provided African Americans with legal advice about labor contracts. Moderate Republicans proposed that military courts, at the request of the Freedmen's Bureau, intervene to protect black people from the most serious forms of racial discrimination.

Andrew Johnson was a stubborn and unbending man who refused to compromise with Congress. When the new Freedmen's Bureau bill was passed in February, he vetoed it. The bill, he said, unnecessarily continued the government's war powers in time of peace. Angry at Johnson, Congress quickly passed a bill that made it a federal offense to violate **civil rights,** or those rights that people have by virtue of being citizens. This civil rights bill guaranteed African Americans the "equal benefit of laws enjoyed by white citizens." Johnson also vetoed that bill, turning all but the most conservative Republicans against him. With support from both the moderate and the Radical Republicans, Congress

Enduring Constitution

The Fourteenth Amendment

The end of the Civil War did not end the problems of African Americans in the southern states. The Thirteenth Amendment freed the slaves, but it had not placed them or their civil rights under federal protection. The Constitution had not defined citizenship nor expressly granted Congress the authority to prevent the states from violating the rights of citizens. The Fourteenth Amendment was designed to solve problems that Congress faced during Reconstruction.

In broad, sweeping language, the Fourteenth Amendment set forth three principles. First, it declared that "all persons born or naturalized in the United States" were citizens of the United States and of the states in which they resided. It also said that no state could make or enforce any law that would abridge the rights of citizens. The amendment changed the relationship of the national government and the states, making Americans citizens of the United States first and foremost. Second, the amendment provided that no state could deprive any person of life, liberty, or property

without *due process of law*. Third, it said that no state could deny or deprive any person *equal protection* of the laws.

The new amendment did not specifically give freedmen the right to vote, but it did reduce the representation in Congress of any state that withheld voting rights in state and federal elections. Other provisions temporarily barred former Confederates from holding state or federal office and disclaimed federal responsibility for the Confederate war debt.

The House of Representatives and the Senate approved the Fourteenth Amendment in June 1866 and submitted it to the states for ratification. Within two years, three-fourths of the states had ratified it. The amendment became part of the Constitution on July 28, 1868, providing Congress with the constitutional justification that it needed for Radical Reconstruction.

Like other political weapons, the Fourteenth Amendment proved to be a two-edged sword. At first, conservative judges were using the amendment to prevent states from establishing minimum wages and maximum hours for industrial laborers. Such regulations, they reasoned, deprived workers of the *freedom of contract* without due process of

▲ *While the Fourteenth Amendment encouraged all states to extend voting rights to African Americans, the Reconstruction Acts gave African Americans that right in the southern states.*

law. As time passed, however, the real impact of the Fourteenth Amendment became clear.

So far-reaching were the implications of the Fourteenth Amendment for civil liberties that it has been called "the second American Revolution." The due process clause would be used in future Supreme Court decisions to extend protections guaranteed in the Bill of Rights to citizens of the various states. By 1966, some 100 years later, the amendment would protect citizens from actions by federal and state governments that endangered life, liberty, or property.

1. What did the Fourteenth Amendment address?
2. Do you agree that the Constitution should be amended as needed?

overrode the president's veto, passing the **Civil Rights Act of 1866** by a two-thirds majority vote. Two weeks later, Congress voted on the Freedmen's Bureau Bill a second time, and this time it successfully overrode the president's veto. Congress and the president were fighting a major battle over Reconstruction.

The Fourteenth Amendment

In April 1866, Congress introduced its own plan for Reconstruction in the form of the **Fourteenth Amendment** to the United States Constitution. At that time, there was still some question as to whether African Americans, free or enslaved, were citizens. Less than ten years earlier, in the Dred Scott case, the Supreme Court had ruled that they were not. The amendment did not guarantee that African Americans would have the right to vote. It did, however:

- make African Americans United States citizens by defining as citizens "all persons born or naturalized in the United States"
- protect citizens from state laws that might discriminate against them by declaring that no state could deny any person equal protection of the laws
- reduce the representation in Congress of states that prevented African Americans from voting
- restrict the right of former Confederate officials and military officers to hold public office
- declare the Confederate war debt to be invalid and void, meaning the federal government would not repay loans to the Confederate government.

Passage of the Fourteenth Amendment became the next battleground in the contest between Andrew Johnson and the Republicans in Congress. Johnson opposed the amendment and urged southern states not to ratify it. As the approval of three-fourths of the states was required for ratification, the amendment could not be passed without some support in the South. Tennessee was the only former Confederate state to vote for it. As a reward, Congress promptly readmitted Tennessee to the Union.

The remaining ten states of the Confederacy followed the president's advice and voted overwhelmingly against the amendment.

As the congressional midterm elections of 1866 approached, the contest over Reconstruction became even more heated. To win support for his position, the president organized a National Union Convention, which met in Philadelphia in August. He used this gathering to organize a new National Union Party composed of Democrats and conservative Republicans. With this coalition behind him, Johnson hoped to turn the moderate and Radical Republicans out of office. That autumn, Johnson traveled throughout the Midwest campaigning for candidates who supported him. Voters had a clear choice between the president, supported mainly by Democrats and former Confederates, and Republicans pledged to the Fourteenth Amendment. The outcome in November was a major defeat for Andrew Johnson since the voters returned a large Republican majority to Congress.

The Reconstruction Acts   Following the election, Congress worked out a more detailed plan for Reconstruction. Its first order of business was to replace the state governments in the South that had refused to ratify the Fourteenth Amendment. With this in mind, Congress passed the Reconstruction Act of March 1867 and three other Reconstruction Acts in 1867 and 1868. The acts returned the South to military control until new governments could be installed. The South was divided into five military districts to be administered by generals of the army. These military commanders were given the power to hold constitutional conventions and to arrange for the election of new state officials. To guarantee the southern states' future loyalty, the Reconstruction Acts stated that the new state constitutions had to exclude former Confederate officials from voting or running for public office. The constitutions also had to extend full political rights to African American males over the age of 21. After each state had ratified the Fourteenth Amendment, it could apply to Congress for readmission to the Union.

The Reconstruction Acts were a major victory for the Radical Republicans. Unable to think of any other way to ensure a voting majority that would be loyal to the Union, the moderate Republicans in

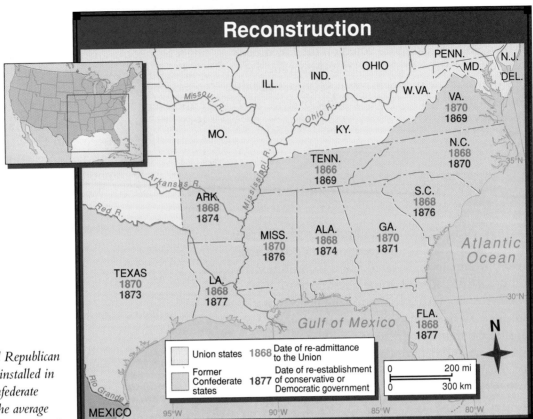

Reconstruction

VA.
1870
1869

W.VA.

N.C.
1868
1870

TENN.
1866
1869

S.C.
1868
1876

ARK.
1868
1874

MISS.
1870
1876

ALA.
1868
1874

GA.
1870
1871

TEXAS
1870
1873

LA.
1868
1877

FLA.
1868
1877

OHIO

PENN.

MD.

N.J.

DEL.

ILL.

IND.

MO.

KY.

Atlantic Ocean

Gulf of Mexico

N

| Union states | 1868 | Date of re-admittance to the Union |
| Former Confederate states | 1877 | Date of re-establishment of conservative or Democratic government |

0   200 mi

0   300 km

MEXICO

▶

By 1870, Radical Republican governments were installed in all the former Confederate states. What was the average life span of these governments?

Congress had finally agreed to give African Americans in the reconstructed states the right to vote. The new state officials were elected by black voters, who became the backbone of the Republican Party in the South. African Americans held public offices at every level. Two African American men, Blanche K. Bruce and Hiram Revels, served in the United States Senate from Mississippi. However, most officeholders in the newly reconstructed states were either white northern Republicans who had recently settled in the South or white southerners who had not actively supported the Confederacy. Both groups were bitterly denounced by former Confederates excluded from politics under the Reconstruction Acts.

White southerners denounced the northern Republicans as **carpetbaggers**, a name that came from the carpetbags or satchels popular at that time. The implication was that they were short-term visitors who had come only to exploit the South. In

fact, many were teachers, lawyers, former Union soldiers, and investors who saw a future for themselves in the postwar South. The former Confederates also heaped scorn on the **scalawags**, white southerners who cooperated with the Republicans. For the most part, scalawags were ordinary farmers and planters who were willing to work with the Republicans to rebuild the war-torn South.

Impeachment

By 1867, the Republicans in Congress had taken control of Reconstruction. However, they discovered that Johnson could still influence events in the South by using his powers as commander in chief of the army. The president removed from duty those military commanders who, according to him,

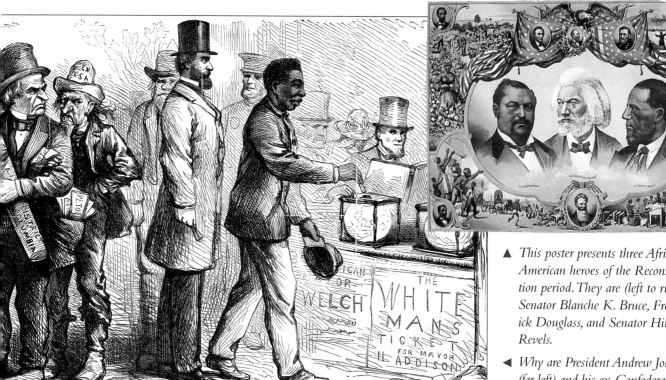

▲ *This poster presents three African American heroes of the Reconstruction period. They are (left to right) Senator Blanche K. Bruce, Frederick Douglass, and Senator Hiram Revels.*

◄ *Why are President Andrew Johnson (far left) and his ex-Confederate companion frowning in this 1867 Thomas Nast political cartoon?*

were too sympathetic to the Republicans. He also helped former Confederates regain the right to vote by ordering military officials not to ask them if they had ever been disloyal. Alarmed by the way Johnson used his presidential powers, the Radical Republicans worked for the **impeachment** of the president.

The Constitution grants Congress the power to remove a president from office for committing "treason, bribery, or other high crimes and misdemeanors." The power of impeachment is divided between the House of Representatives and the Senate. The House has the authority to impeach, or bring to trial, any federal officeholder, while the Senate, acting as a court of law, has the power to convict. The Radicals found grounds for impeachment in the summer of 1867, when Johnson removed Secretary of War Edwin M. Stanton from office. They charged that this action violated the Tenure of Office Act, which Congress had passed earlier that year. This act stated that officials whose appointment required the consent of the Senate could not be removed during the term of the president who appointed them without the Senate's approval. It was not clear that the act protected Stanton, as he had been appointed by Lincoln rather than by Johnson. By duly notifying the Senate of his action, Johnson had acted as if he was complying with the law when he removed Stanton. Whether Stanton's removal was legal or not, it was important to Congress to keep him in office. Stanton was the last member of Johnson's cabinet who was still friendly to the Republicans. Johnson, on the other hand, wanted a secretary of war more sympathetic to his policies. Alarmed by Stanton's removal, even many moderate Republicans favored impeachment.

The impeachment of Andrew Johnson was an historic occasion. Never before had Congress tried to remove a president during his term of office. The House of Representatives voted to impeach Johnson on February 24, 1868. He was then tried by the Senate and almost convicted. The Radicals in charge of the proceedings failed by a single vote to get the necessary two-thirds majority. Several moderate Republicans were afraid to give the Radicals more power than they had already, and voted against

▶ *A Congressional committee drafted articles of impeachment against President Andrew Johnson, which the House of Representatives approved in February 1868. What role does the Senate have in the impeachment process?*

conviction. Johnson's removal would have placed Benjamin Wade, a Radical Republican who was the acting president of the Senate, in the presidency. Wade supported women's suffrage as well as political rights for African Americans, which made him one of the extreme radical thinkers of that day. When the Senate voted on the articles of impeachment in May, enough Republicans preferred Andrew Johnson to Benjamin Wade to tip the balance. Congress's failure to remove Johnson from office preserved the independence of the executive branch of the federal government.

The Election of 1868   Five days after the vote in the Senate, the Republicans nominated General Ulysses S. Grant as their candidate for the 1868 presidential election. The Democrats nominated Horatio Seymour, a former governor of New York. The outcome was never in doubt. Grant was a war hero running on a platform that endorsed Radical Reconstruction and condemned Andrew Johnson. The Radicals controlled six states in the South that would normally have voted Democratic. The three southern states that were not yet reconstructed did not participate in the election. Grant carried 26 of the 34 participating states.

Reconstruction was finally completed in 1870, when the last of the former Confederate states rejoined the Union. By that time, the required number of states had also approved the Fourteenth and Fifteenth Amendments. The **Fifteenth Amendment** stated that the right to vote could not be denied on account of race, color, or previous condition of servitude. As black southerners already enjoyed the right to vote, its most immediate effect was to give African Americans throughout the North the right to vote.

SECTION 2 REVIEW

1. **Name** the action taken by President Johnson that turned many moderate Republicans against him.
2. **List** three provisions of the Fourteenth Amendment.
3. **Describe** how the Reconstruction Acts protected the rights of formerly enslaved African Americans.
4. **Explain** how the power to remove a president is divided between the houses of Congress.
5. **Identify** the main reason the Radicals failed to convict Andrew Johnson.

Women's Rights

Elizabeth Cady Stanton watched with growing dismay as the battle over Reconstruction took shape. As an ardent abolitionist, she favored civil rights for African Americans, including the right to vote. As a leader of the women's rights movement, she wanted women to be given the right to vote as well. By the autumn of 1865, Mrs. Stanton realized that most Republican leaders, including abolitionists, had turned their backs on women's suffrage. "I would not mix the movements," advised Wendell Phillips, a Radical Republican who had once supported the cause of women's rights. "I think such mixture would lose for the Negro far more than we should gain for the woman." Alarmed at this turn of events, Stanton hurried off a letter to her friend **Susan B. Anthony,** who was on a speaking tour in Kansas. "Come back and help," she pleaded. "I have argued constantly with Phillips and the whole fraternity, but I fear one and all will favor enfranchising the Negro without us. Woman's cause is in deep water."

Why did the Radical Republicans ignore the issue of women's suffrage?

Why did some leaders of the women's rights movement attempt to defeat the Fifteenth Amendment?

What caused the division in 1869 in the women's suffrage movement?

▲ *Why did Susan B. Anthony and Elizabeth Cady Stanton oppose the Fifteenth Amendment?*

They focused on the issue of women's suffrage. If freed slaves were to enjoy the full rights of citizenship, why not women? Stanton and Anthony were convinced that the time was ripe for securing equal rights for women as well as African Americans. They suspected—correctly as it turned out— that it would be the last opportunity for a long time for women to win the right to vote.

Both Stanton and Anthony were dismayed by the Fourteenth Amendment, which encouraged the South to give African Americans the vote, but said nothing about women's right to the ballot. In fact, the amendment clearly stated that a state's representation in Congress would be reduced only if male inhabitants were denied the vote. This was the first use of the term *male* in the Constitution. Stanton and Anthony felt even more betrayed by the Fifteenth Amendment, which enfranchised African Americans but not women. "I will cut off this right arm of mine," Anthony declared, "before I will ever work for or demand the ballot for the Negro and not for women." Furious about the gender bias of the Fifteenth Amendment, Stanton and Anthony made a valiant but vain effort to prevent its ratification.

In drawing up the Fourteenth and Fifteenth Amendments, Congress had deliberately avoided the question of women's suffrage. Many Republican congressmen shared the popular belief that involving women in the sordid world of politics would undermine the stability of the American home.

The Fight for Women's Suffrage

During the war years, Elizabeth Cady Stanton and Susan B. Anthony had put the women's movement aside to work for the greater cause of national survival. They had also devoted time and energy to the abolitionist movement. With the Union preserved and emancipation accomplished, these women activists turned their attention once more to the question of women's rights.

Even Radical Republicans who favored women's suffrage backed away from the issue. They were afraid that they would lose the opportunity to secure political equality for African Americans if that issue were linked to the unpopular cause of women's suffrage. The Radicals argued that helping African Americans protect themselves through the ballot was far more urgent. "When women, because they are women, are dragged from their homes and hung upon lamp posts," said Frederick Douglass, the black abolitionist, ". . . then they will have an urgency to obtain the ballot." This was the "Negro's hour," the Radical Republicans insisted, and the opportunity to secure the vote for African Americans should not be thrown away. The loss of the Radicals' support was a serious blow to the women's suffrage movement.

▲ *This Currier and Ives lithograph mocks the women's rights movement. Why did the movement arouse such bitter opposition?*

Splits in the Women's Rights Movement

A split also developed among the women who led the women's rights movement. Although disappointed with the Fifteenth Amendment, some leaders of the movement supported it as a step in the right direction. Among them were Lucy Stone, Julia Ward Howe, and other members of the American Woman Suffrage Association. Stanton, Anthony, and others who opposed the amendment went their separate way in 1869, founding the National Woman Suffrage Association. Distrustful of male leadership, they decided to limit the membership of the new organization to women. The National Woman Suffrage Association advocated other women's issues besides suffrage, including the right of women to control their own earnings and the right to divorce. The American Woman Suffrage Association, in contrast, appealed to more conservative women. Avoiding such controversial questions as divorce, the group concerned itself solely with the right to vote. This division within the women's movement continued for the next 20 years.

Such internal divisions weakened the women's suffrage movement, but they were not the principal reason for its failure. More important was the solid wall of opposition that its leaders encountered wherever they turned. At the heart of this opposition were strong traditional beliefs about gender roles. An overwhelming majority of American men shared that view. In 1866, the United States Senate voted down a bill to give women the right to vote in the District of Columbia by a margin of 37 to 9. When women's suffrage was put to a vote in Kansas in 1867, it received only 9,000 out of 30,000 votes cast. By the end of Reconstruction, women had achieved the right to vote only in Wyoming and Utah. And these were sparsely settled western territories far removed from the centers of political power.

SECTION 3 REVIEW

1. **Name** two prominent leaders of the women's suffrage movement.
2. **Identify** the focus of the women's rights movement during the Reconstruction era.
3. **State** why many Republicans who wanted to give African Americans the right to vote opposed women's suffrage.
4. **List** the reforms, besides women's suffrage, that the National Woman Suffrage Association demanded.
5. **Explain** briefly why the women's suffrage movement of the 1860s failed.

Social and Economic Factors

At the end of the Civil War, much of the South lay devastated. Farms and plantations that were in the path of advancing armies suffered most heavily, with barns and fences destroyed and farm animals carried away. The war destroyed half of the farm machinery and one-third of the mules and horses in the Confederate states. The once-prosperous Tennessee Valley, noted an English traveler who visited the area shortly after the war, "consists for the most part of plantations in a state of semi-ruin, and plantations of which the ruin is for the present total and complete.... The trail of the war is visible throughout the valley in burnt up gin-houses, ruined bridges, mills, and factories, of which latter the gable walls only are left standing, and in large tracts of once cultivated land stripped of every vestige of fencing." The defeated South faced an enormous task of social and economic reconstruction.

How did the South revive its agricultural production?
What social changes occurred in African American communities during Reconstruction?
Why did most white southerners oppose the new state governments?

Agriculture in the South

The South's most urgent task was to restore agricultural production on its farms and plantations. Four years of war had crippled southern agriculture. The problems resulting from the destruction of wealth and property were compounded by the absence of cash and credit. Many planters lacked the money to buy seeds or to pay wages to their former slaves. In desperation, they improvised a system that put their former slaves to work as **tenant farmers**. Tenant farmers paid rent while **sharecroppers** paid the landowner a share of the crop at harvest time.

The planters divided their land into smaller farms, giving each tenant a plow, mules, and a cabin to live in. This system spread so rapidly throughout the South that by 1910, the majority of farmers in eight southern states were tenants or sharecroppers. Among them were many poor whites as well as former slaves.

The credit that the farmer needed to buy seed and food was provided by a **crop lien**, an agreement that pledged the farmer's crop to the merchant to pay off the debt. This meant that a local merchant, often the major landowner, would advance the sharecropper the needed supplies. The cost of these supplies would be deducted at harvest time. A sharecropper who entered into such an agreement became wholly dependent on the merchant. Without cash, he could trade only with the merchant who held the crop lien on his crop. This dependency allowed the merchant to charge high prices. It was a vicious system that often forced the sharecropper deeper into debt each year.

Tenant farming and sharecropping were a blight on the southern economy. The lien system created a form of **peonage**, a system in which debtors are bound to their creditors in servitude. Destitute

▼ *In this photograph, farmers wait in line, their wagons filled with cotton to be weighed and processed at the cotton gin. Why did southern farmers concentrate so heavily on growing cotton?*

farmers could not leave the land until their debts were paid. The crop lien also locked the South into a one-crop system of agriculture. Merchants and landowners insisted that their tenants plant cotton only, a crop for which there was always a market. Tenants were "forced to raise it to get credit," as one Alabama farmer complained. As a result, the South produced a surplus of cotton, which drove down the market price. The more cotton the sharecroppers produced, the further the price of cotton fell. One-crop tenant farming kept the South locked in the grip of poverty.

African American Families and Communities

While struggling to make a living as sharecroppers, black southerners went about the task of rebuilding their family life. Many used their newly won freedom to search for family members from whom they had been separated. Husbands and wives who had once lived on separate plantations now were able to live together. They were also free from the constant supervision of slave owners. Some families were quickly reunited; others spent years searching for missing wives, husbands, and children. For families that were intact, emancipation brought a new sense of family solidarity. Parents, for the first

▼ *A sharecropper family in western North Carolina gathered for a photograph in 1896. What does the photograph tell you about family life in African American communities in the rural South?*

▲ *This picture of a religious service in Washington, D.C., shows that an African American middle class was developing in some cities in the country.*

time, had complete control over their children.

Emancipation also brought new forms of community life. The slave quarters ceased to be the center of the African American community, as black people moved off the plantations to cabins of their own. In some instances, they built clusters of houses in all-black settlements. They also built new churches, which served as a focal point for African American community life throughout the South. The schools founded by the freed slaves or by the Freedmen's Bureau served a similar purpose. During the Reconstruction years, thousands of ex-slaves, adults as well as children, enrolled in these schools. Denied an education as slaves, they placed a high value on the ability to read and write. Literacy was a badge of freedom.

Race Relations

The freedmen's efforts to find a new place in southern society met with stubborn resistance. Many white people were reluctant to acknowledge that slavery had ended. On some remote plantations, African Americans did not learn about emancipation until months after the Civil War was over. In some places in Texas, enslaved African Americans

The Freedmen's Schools

The most enduring legacy of Reconstruction was the schools for freedmen that were established throughout the South. Several schools opened during the Civil War, often at the initiative of the freed slaves themselves. Northern charitable organizations founded other freedmen's schools, providing them with money, textbooks, and teachers. With the beginning of Reconstruction, the newly established Freedmen's Bureau took over the operation of the freedmen's schools. By 1869, the Bureau had under its wing over 3,000 schools that enrolled over 150,000 pupils.

The rapid spread of freedmen's schools throughout the South demonstrated the value that former slaves placed on education. Adults as well as children gathered to attend classes in abandoned churches, deserted hotels, and private homes. The first freedmen's school in New Orleans opened in the building that had been the city's slave market. A Freedmen's Bureau agent in Mississippi reported that when he announced to a gathering of freedmen that they "were to have the advantages of schools and education, their joy knew no bounds. They fairly jumped and shouted in gladness." African Americans went to school to learn how to read the Bible and

◀ Classrooms were crowded in the freedmen's schools with students of all ages. Why were these schools so well attended?

newspapers, to write letters, and to learn how to keep business accounts. Schools were solid proof of their newly gained freedom and independence.

A great variety of people served as teachers in the freedmen's schools. At first, many were freed slaves themselves, men and women who had learned to read and write during slavery. By the end of Reconstruction, the majority were "Yankee schoolmarms," which was the nickname given to the young women recruited by northern freedmen's aid societies. They were dedicated women, usually from Massachusetts, New York, or Ohio. They typically came from abolitionist families and were active in the women's rights movement. They were well educated; most of them had at least completed high school. Among them was Charlotte Forten, the daughter of James Forten, a wealthy African American from Philadelphia. A few teachers were sympathetic white southerners who stood up to the intense social pressures

against cooperating with the Freedmen's Bureau.

The schools operating under the supervision of the Freedmen's Bureau were the first step toward a system of public education in the South. When the bureau ceased operations in 1870, the Radical Republican state governments took responsibility for the freedmen's schools. They became part of the public school systems that the Radical governments established throughout the South. They provided a free public education for both black and white children, although in most localities the schools were racially segregated. Funding for public education was sharply reduced after southern Democrats returned to power, but the idea of publicly supported schools survived.

1. Why did the number of freedmen's schools increase so rapidly during Reconstruction?
2. Why was the creation of the freedmen's schools of lasting significance to the South?

did not learn that they were free until June 19. "Juneteenth" celebrations are held to this day in Texas by African Americans to celebrate the end of slavery. Throughout the South, African Americans faced open discrimination. Those few who could afford to buy farms were often denied the opportunity. White people feared they would lose control should African Americans become property owners. They were also alarmed by the new political role that African Americans had begun to play during the time of Reconstruction.

White resistance to Reconstruction focused on the Republican-controlled state governments. As some officeholders were former slaves, southern whites accused carpetbaggers and scalawags of forcing "Negro rule" on the South. In fact, white people made up the majority of southern state legislatures and congressional delegations during Reconstruction.

White property owners also objected to Republican-sponsored state legislation that resulted in higher taxes. The Republicans raised taxes to provide schools and social services for African Americans and other poor people. To discredit such policies, southerners accused Reconstruction state governments of waste and corruption.

Some Radical officeholders did accept bribes and steal public funds, which left the reconstructed state governments open to criticism. However, this was a period of widespread corruption in state and local government. The Radical governments were no more corrupt than many governments in other parts of the United States. Southern whites were actually bothered less by corruption than by the loss of power to Republicans who were supported by African American voters.

SECTION 5

The End of Reconstruction

The Radical Republican governments in the former Confederate states were short-lived. Beginning in 1869, the Democrats regained control in state after state. In the upper South, they organized the white majority and voted Republicans out of office. They resorted to violence in those areas where African Americans were in the majority. Bands of white racists rode through the night, hauling Republican leaders out of bed, beating or killing them, and spreading terror among African American voters and their white allies. "Of the slain there were enough to furnish forth a battlefield," wrote Albion W. Tourgee, a superior court judge in North Carolina, "and all from those three classes, the negro, the scalawag, and the carpetbagger—all killed with deliberation, overwhelmed by numbers, roused from slumber at the murk midnight ... shot, stabbed, hanged, drowned, mutilated beyond description, tortured beyond conception."

Many Republican voters went to the polls despite threats to their lives, but the days of Reconstruction were numbered. No political party could long survive such violent opposition.

How did former Confederates regain the right to vote?
What was the Compromise of 1877?
How was racial segregation accomplished in the South?

SECTION 4 REVIEW

1. **Describe** briefly the sharecropping system during this period.
2. **Identify** consequences of the crop lien system.
3. **Describe** ways in which African American family and community life changed after emancipation.
4. **Identify** Juneteenth.
5. **List** some reasons southern whites opposed the new state governments.

White Rule in the South

The former Confederates who were excluded from government during Reconstruction were determined to regain control. They resented being governed by freed slaves, northern carpetbaggers, and scalawags. They detested Radical programs that taxed white property owners to provide services to African Americans and the poor. They set out to redeem the South, and called the process of restoring power to native-born whites **Redemption**. In states in which white voters were in the majority, the Redeemers relied on the power of the ballot. White voting strength was substantially increased in 1872, when Congress passed the general Amnesty Act. This restored full political rights to all but a few hundred of the highest-ranking Confederate officials. In places with heavy concentrations of African Americans, places where the Redeemers could not count on outvoting the Republicans, they relied on terrorist tactics.

Terrorist groups were organized throughout the South to intimidate African Americans and to keep Republican voters from the polls. The best publicized of these groups was the Ku Klux Klan, whose hooded horsemen paid nighttime visits to the cabins of both white and black Republicans. Whippings, beatings, and lynchings by Klansmen became common occurrences.

Congress did not approve of the increasing violence in the South. In 1870 and again in 1871, it passed legislation that permitted the president to impose military authority over civilians and to use federal troops to put down violence. President

▼ *Members of an African American family are attacked in their home. Why did hooded klansmen of the Reconstruction period terrorize African Americans?*

Grant used these laws sparingly. Few northern Republicans favored returning the South to military control, although that may have been the only way to protect African American voters and to ensure the continuation of Republican rule. Other Republicans actively opposed Grant, charging that he had intervened too much in the affairs of the South. The majority of northern Republicans were obviously growing tired of the problems of Reconstruction.

By 1872, northern support for Radical Reconstruction was waning, as the passage of the Amnesty Act that year indicated. Many of the Radicals who had championed military-controlled reconstruction were no longer in Congress. Their leader, Thaddeus Stevens, had died in 1868. Democratic election victories in several northern states had cost other Radicals their seats in Congress. The growing evidence of corruption in the reconstructed state governments embarrassed northern Republicans. To show their opposition to Radical Reconstruction and to corrupt government in both the North and South, a group of reform-minded Republicans organized a new Liberal Republican Party in May 1872. They nominated Horace Greeley, the editor of the *New York Tribune*, on a platform pledged to abolishing the spoils system and to ending Radical control in the South. Taking advantage of this split in the Republican ranks, the Democrats endorsed the Greeley ticket. But Grant, still a popular war hero to most Republicans, won reelection to a second term despite the slipping away of support for Radical Reconstruction.

The Election of 1876

Until the presidential election of 1876, Radical Republicans still held Florida, Louisiana, and South Carolina. The fate of Reconstruction in those states depended on the outcome of the election that year. The Republicans nominated Ohio's Governor **Rutherford B. Hayes.** The Democrats chose Governor Samuel J. Tilden of New York as their candidate. The election results in the three states controlled by the Radicals were contested. Both

◄ *Ohio governor Rutherford B. Hayes was elected president in 1876. Why was the outcome of this election in dispute?*

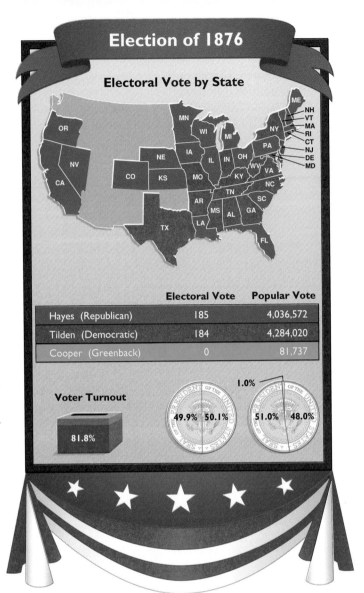

Election of 1876

Electoral Vote by State

	Electoral Vote	Popular Vote
Hayes (Republican)	185	4,036,572
Tilden (Democratic)	184	4,284,020
Cooper (Greenback)	0	81,737

Voter Turnout

81.8%

49.9% 50.1%

51.0% 48.0%

1.0%

▲ *The electoral votes of Florida, South Carolina, and Louisiana were disputed. How did the Republicans finally win these states for Hayes?*

parties claimed they had won the 20 electoral votes of these states. Without them, Tilden was one electoral vote short of a majority, as the totals from the other states gave Tilden 184 votes to 165 for Hayes. Hayes needed all 20 of the contested votes to win. Fraud and intimidation of voters had been so widespread in those states that it was unclear which party had won an honest majority of the votes.

As Hayes needed all three states to become president in this very close election, the national Republican party leaders struck a deal. They agreed to turn over the three southern states to Democratic control in return for the electoral votes necessary to make Hayes president. After his election, President Hayes completed the deal, known as the Compromise of 1877, by withdrawing the remaining federal troops from the South. Without military support, the last of the Republican governments in the South collapsed, effectively marking the end of Reconstruction.

The Republicans' attempt to reconstruct the South on the basis of political equality between the races had failed. Perhaps it was an effort doomed to failure from the outset, given the racial attitudes of that time. Many people of that time believed the white race was superior to all others and that economic and political power properly belonged under white control. This belief in white supremacy blocked all efforts to integrate African Americans into white society. As one historian has written, "the wonder is not that the Southern Republicans were ousted from power after only a few years, but that they ever held power at all." African Americans made up more than 80 percent of the Republican

voters. Lacking property, wealth, or any other source of power, they were an easy target for white supremacists, who would stop at nothing to reestablish their control.

Democrats Regain Power

The era of Reconstruction ended in 1877, with the Democrats in control throughout the South.

They proceeded to use every means possible to guarantee the continuation of their political power. The new state governments made it more difficult for poor and illiterate African Americans to vote. Thousands were disfranchised or deprived of the right to vote. As one Tennessee legislator admitted, "I believe in the law of revenge. The Radicals disfranchised us, and now we intend to disfranchise them." To accomplish this, the white Redeemers made use of such devices as literacy tests, property requirements, and **poll taxes**. A poll tax was a tax paid in some states before a person was allowed to vote. Although in theory these requirements had to be met by both black and white voters, the southern states devised ways to exempt most white voters. **Grandfather clauses** stated that any man whose father or grandfather had the right to vote as of January 1, 1867, was automatically entitled to vote. The "understanding clause" permitted the local registrar to judge each voter's understanding of the Constitution, a requirement of the literacy test. Although some African Americans could meet these requirements, the black vote was reduced to a fraction of its former size. Voting fraud, including the stuffing of ballot boxes, further reduced Republican strength. The Democratic Party, the "white man's party," would remain the dominant party in the South for decades to come.

The end of Republican rule also brought an end to many of the programs and public policies sponsored by the Radicals. To reduce expenditures and taxes, the new Democratic governments cut back social services to the poor. In state after state, budget cuts crippled the public school system.

Although pledged to saving the taxpayers money, the Democratic state governments were as corrupt as the Republican governments of Reconstruction. The state treasurer of Tennessee, a former Confederate officer, disappeared in 1883 with $400,000 of the state's funds. Scandals involving Democratic state treasurers also occurred in Alabama, Arkansas, Louisiana, and Mississippi. In Louisiana, the treasurer, Major E. A. Burke, left for Honduras with $793,600 stolen from the state. The theft of such vast sums further reduced the services that these impoverished states could provide.

White Supremacy Restored

The Democrats imposed white supremacy throughout the South. Their principal goal, after disfranchising black voters, was the segregation of the races. State after state passed **Jim Crow laws** that extended racial segregation into every corner of southern life. The laws were named after Jim Crow, an African American character in a comedy act popular before the Civil War. These laws segregated theaters, hotels, cafés, railroad cars, and other public facilities. The result was a rigid caste system that served as a constant reminder to African Americans of white supremacy. The accommodations reserved for African Americans were seldom equal to those used by white people.

Lacking equal protection under the law, African Americans were exposed to constant danger. They were the victims of mob violence in cities across the South. After burning down an African American–owned newspaper office in Wilmington, North

▼ *This Thomas Nast cartoon satirizes Redemption, the period when white supremacy was restored in the South. What does Nast mean by "WORSE THAN SLAVERY"?*

Analyzing an Editorial Cartoon

Unlike a column of text that may take several minutes to read, a cartoon has an immediate impact on the viewer. This is one reason why newspapers and other periodicals regularly use cartoons to support or attack current issues and public figures. Editorial cartoonists rely heavily on symbols and words in their cartoons to expose what they consider to be foolish, wrong, or ignorant in people and governments.

One of the most famous American cartoonists was Thomas Nast. He was best known for his cartoons making fun of the corrupt "Boss" Tweed ring in New York City in the 1860s. Nast invented the idea of the elephant to represent the Republican Party and used the donkey to represent the Democratic Party. He also invented the costume that artists usually put on Santa Claus. Nast's cartoons appeared in illustrated magazines, such as the widely read periodical *Harper's Weekly*. Such periodicals were the main source of information in the late nineteenth century.

When looking at editorial or political cartoons, follow these guidelines:

- **Look carefully for labels, captions, and other words.** Cartoonists use words sparingly, but they are important for identification and scene setting.
- **Identify the symbols used.** Often, the point of the cartoon is not clear unless a figure is correctly identified. Think about the possible meanings of all the symbols used.

- **Determine if the cartoonist's point of view is positive (supportive) or negative (critical).** What is the general tone or mood of the cartoon? Is it severely critical or gently mocking?
- **Finally, make a verbal statement that summarizes the cartoonist's message.** Overall, what political or social purpose motivated the drawing? What message was the cartoonist trying to get across?

Study the Thomas Nast cartoon on page 411 and complete the following steps:

1. List the objects and people you see in the cartoon. Which of the objects on your list are symbols? What do you think each of the symbols means?
2. Identify the cartoon title. List the words or phrases used by the cartoonist to identify objects or people within the cartoon and tell what they represent.
3. List adjectives that describe the emotions portrayed in the cartoon by the different figures.
4. Why do you think Nast chose to show the faces of the African American family but hide the faces of the white supremacists?
5. Terrorism is the use of threats and violence against people and property in order to make them meet demands they would not normally agree to. What evidence (symbols) of terrorist activity do you see in this cartoon?

Carolina, in 1898, a mob killed 11 African Americans and injured many more. For several days in July 1900, white mobs roamed the city of New Orleans, looting, burning, and shooting black people. As a New Orleans newspaper noted, "it is evident that the grand idea of white supremacy has become the stalking horse of anarchy in this part of the Union." Ten African Americans and two white people were killed in 1906 in a race riot in Atlanta.

Riots and incidents of racial violence also occurred in the North, but they were more concentrated in the South. During the years 1880 to 1918, more than 2,400 blacks were lynched by white mobs in the South. About 100 lynchings of African Americans took place in the North during that period. In the South especially, the belief in white supremacy became a license for murder.

Advocates of white supremacy were aided by a series of Supreme Court decisions. The Court ruled in 1873 to limit the rights protected by the Fourteenth Amendment. State governments would not be required to guarantee due process of law to its citizens. In 1883, the Court struck down the 1875 Civil Rights Act. This act had guaranteed equal access to hotels, theaters, and other public places for black and white people. The Court ruled that the Fourteenth Amendment prevented states, but not private individuals such as hotel owners, from discriminating on the basis of race.

In 1876, the Court ruled in the case of *United States v. Reese* that the Fifteenth Amendment did not guarantee every male citizen the right to vote. A state could deny that right for any reason it chose other than "race, color or previous condition of servitude." In effect, this made the literacy tests used to disfranchise African Americans constitutional. During the 1880s, several lower courts ruled that states could impose segregation as long as the separate facilities were equal. In its ruling in *Plessy v. Ferguson* (1896), the Supreme Court approved the **separate-but-equal doctrine**, which segregated black facilities. Three years later, in *Cumins v. Richmond County Board of Education*, the Court extended the doctrine to include school segregation. With those decisions, the nation's highest court gave its blessing to the full range of segregation in the South.

SECTION 5 REVIEW

1. **Describe** two ways in which former Confederates regained political control in the South.
2. **List** two major terms of the Compromise of 1877.
3. **Explain** how grandfather clauses disfranchised black voters.
4. **List** three ways the Redeemer governments in the South reduced the number of black voters.
5. **Summarize** briefly how the United States Supreme Court ruled during this period in cases concerning racial segregation.

Summary

The political recovery of the South was the most pressing problem facing the nation at the end of the Civil War. Loyal governments had to be organized in the South, and the former Confederate states had to be restored to the Union. The task was made more difficult by a bitter political contest between President Andrew Johnson and Congress. The Republican Congress questioned the loyalty of the governments restored under Johnson's lenient approach to Reconstruction. Congress also objected to the black codes used by the South to control the labor of the freed slaves. Congress devised its own plan for Reconstruction, which excluded former Confederates from public life and gave African Americans the right to vote. Johnson's continued opposition to Congress led to his impeachment. Reconstruction was finally completed, with the former Confederate states restored to the Union. During this time the Thirteenth, Fourteenth, and Fifteenth Amendments to the Constitution were approved.

The Reconstruction period also saw a revival of the movement for women's rights. Its leaders focused attention on the question of women's suffrage. They were disturbed that Congress had extended the right to vote to African Americans, but not to women. The majority of the Republicans in Congress refused to support women's suffrage. Some opposed giving women the right to vote on principle. Others were afraid that linking the two demands would prevent African Americans from getting the right to vote. Although unsuccessful in securing the franchise in the 1860s, women did create two national organizations that continued to work for this cause.

The Republicans in Congress were unsuccessful in their attempt to build a new political order in the South based on equality. In less than a decade, white factions regained control in every southern state. White people, in turn, disfranchised African Americans and reduced them to the status of second-class citizens. To emphasize white supremacy, white people also imposed racial segregation on nearly every aspect of southern life. Tired of struggling with the problem of Reconstruction, the North accepted this new order in the South. In a series of important decisions, the United States Supreme Court upheld segregation and African Americans' loss of political rights.

Vocabulary

Reconstruction/Redemption
Jim Crow laws/black codes
tenant farmers/sharecroppers
crop lien/peonage
civil rights/separate-but-equal doctrine
carpetbaggers/scalawags
pocket veto/impeachment
grandfather clause/poll tax

Use each of the above pairs of vocabulary terms in a sentence. Your sentence should describe the relationship between the words in each pair.

Review Questions

1. Briefly describe Abraham Lincoln's approach to Reconstruction.
2. Why did the Radical Republicans oppose Johnson's plan for Reconstruction?
3. What was the main provision of the Radical plan for Reconstruction?
4. What events led the Radical Republicans to impeach Andrew Johnson?
5. What reason did Elizabeth Cady Stanton give for opposing the Fifteenth Amendment?
6. What issues divided the women's movement by 1869?
7. Why did the South turn to the sharecropping system?
8. Explain how the lien system imposed one-crop farming on the South.

9. Describe the methods southern Democrats used to regain control of state governments.
10. Give two reasons Radical Reconstruction failed to protect the rights of freedmen.

Critical Historical Thinking

Writing Answer each of the following by writing one or more complete paragraphs:

1. Predict what course Reconstruction might have taken if Lincoln had not been assassinated.
2. Explain why the South remained bitter for many years after Reconstruction ended, and tell how this resentment was apparent in politics in the former Confederate states.
3. Do you think abolitionists were justified in separating the issue of civil rights for women from that of civil rights for African Americans? Why, or why not?
4. Discuss why you think women achieved the right to vote in the western states of Wyoming and Utah before they did in the New England states.

Making Connections with Economics

The Civil War was a total war in the sense that all of the nation's resources were bent to the war effort. The United States government spent more in those four years of war than it had in all the previous years of the nation's existence. Besides taxes, there were two means of raising revenue: *borrowing* money and *issuing* money. (Selling government bonds is a way of borrowing money, because when you buy government bonds you are lending the government money and receiving a promissory note, or bond, that the money will be paid back with interest.)

Beginning in 1862, the government began issuing greenbacks to help cover the costs of war. The money the government issued during the war, however, was not backed by silver or gold specie.

What to do with the greenbacks became a major problem by 1868. Those who advocated *hard money* (money backed by gold or silver) wanted the greenbacks retired, and the government began doing so in 1866. Had all the greenbacks been retired, the result would have been to contract the money supply. This favors creditors, or those who loan money. Debtors, those who borrow money, wanted an expanded money supply to help them pay off their debts. The *soft money* advocates, as these debtors were called, wanted the greenbacks kept in circulation.

Hard money and soft money advocates clashed over how the government was to repay the debt owed to those who bought government bonds during the war. Soft money proponents argued that the debt should be repaid in greenbacks. Hard money proponents argued that the debt should be paid in specie in order to protect the nation's credit. The government voted to pay off the bonds in specie.

The greenback controversy continued for several more years. At the heart of the matter was the impact of expansion and contraction of the money supply on those who loan money (creditors) and those who borrow money (debtors).

■ Work with a partner to present arguments for and against a contracted money supply. One person should role play an indebted farmer; the other should be an Eastern banker. Be prepared to debate your position in front of the class.

Additional Skills Practice

Find a political cartoon in a newspaper or news magazine and cut it out. Mount it on a sheet of paper, and include a short explanation of the artist's purpose in drawing the cartoon. Share your cartoon with other class members. Note the main topics. Does any one topic appear often? Why do you think cartoons deal most often with current topics?

Unit Review Questions

1. Define the term *popular sovereignty*, and explain why it had little chance of solving the question of expansion of slavery.
2. What was the importance of the Supreme Court's Dred Scott decision?
3. Why were most Civil War battles fought on southern soil?
4. Briefly describe the effect of the war on the everyday lives of women.
5. Explain how southerners could point to the American Revolution as an argument for their right to secede.
6. Why did the South hope that England would support them during the Civil War?
7. Was Reconstruction a success or failure? Why?
8. Did Reconstruction have any major effect on the women's rights movement?
9. What long-term effect did the assassination of Lincoln have on the South and on Reconstruction?
10. Why did Congress take Reconstruction out of Andrew Johnson's hands?

Personalizing History

Recruiting Poster   The Civil War, also known as the War Between the States, stirred up strong emotions. Research the position your town or county took during the war. Are there Civil War memorials in your area? Many local libraries have retained personal journals from war veterans which you can read. Did the war create controversy in your area?

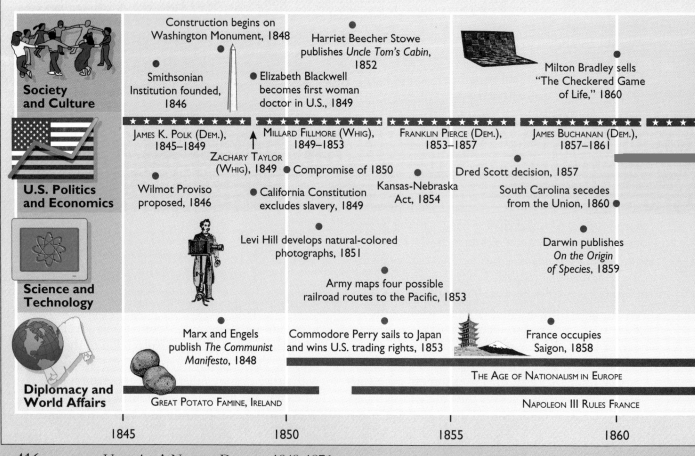

Society and Culture

Smithsonian Institution founded, 1846

Construction begins on Washington Monument, 1848

Elizabeth Blackwell becomes first woman doctor in U.S., 1849

Harriet Beecher Stowe publishes *Uncle Tom's Cabin*, 1852

Milton Bradley sells "The Checkered Game of Life," 1860

U.S. Politics and Economics

JAMES K. POLK (DEM.), 1845–1849

ZACHARY TAYLOR (WHIG), 1849

MILLARD FILLMORE (WHIG), 1849–1853

FRANKLIN PIERCE (DEM.), 1853–1857

JAMES BUCHANAN (DEM.), 1857–1861

Wilmot Proviso proposed, 1846

California Constitution excludes slavery, 1849

Compromise of 1850

Kansas-Nebraska Act, 1854

Dred Scott decision, 1857

South Carolina secedes from the Union, 1860

Science and Technology

Levi Hill develops natural-colored photographs, 1851

Army maps four possible railroad routes to the Pacific, 1853

Darwin publishes *On the Origin of Species*, 1859

Diplomacy and World Affairs

Marx and Engels publish *The Communist Manifesto*, 1848

Commodore Perry sails to Japan and wins U.S. trading rights, 1853

France occupies Saigon, 1858

THE AGE OF NATIONALISM IN EUROPE

GREAT POTATO FAMINE, IRELAND

NAPOLEON III RULES FRANCE

1845   1850   1855   1860

■ Create a colorful recruiting poster for the Union or Confederate army that reflects your county during the war. Include at least three reasons given at the time to encourage young men to join the cause. Present your poster to the class. Do you agree with the ideas on the poster you have created? Explain your opinion.

sination of President McKinley, that the Secret Service assumed the job of protecting the president. Today, its members are constant companions to the "First Family."

■ Find out the qualifications for becoming a member of the Secret Service. What branch of government controls it? What are the responsibilities of the agents? Then write a "help wanted" advertisement that would answer the above questions.

Linking Past and Present

Protecting the President On April 14, 1865, President Lincoln attended a play at Ford's Theater, where he was assassinated by John Wilkes Booth. The Secret Service had been established that year to uncover counterfeiters, smugglers, and illegal liquor manufacturers. It was not until 1901, after the assas-

Time Line Activity

Use the time line to find six specific events affecting or describing the political status of African Americans between 1845 and 1875. Avoid the broad headings "The Civil War" and "Reconstruction."

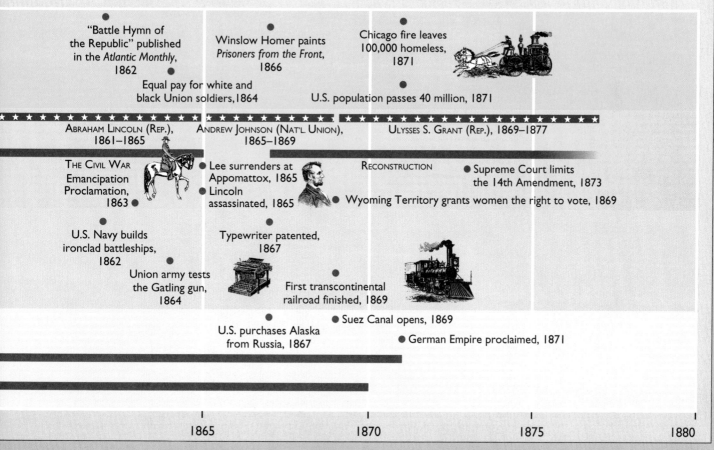

"Battle Hymn of the Republic" published in the *Atlantic Monthly*, 1862

Winslow Homer paints *Prisoners from the Front*, 1866

Chicago fire leaves 100,000 homeless, 1871

Equal pay for white and black Union soldiers, 1864

U.S. population passes 40 million, 1871

ABRAHAM LINCOLN (REP.), 1861–1865

ANDREW JOHNSON (NAT'L. UNION), 1865–1869

ULYSSES S. GRANT (REP.), 1869–1877

THE CIVIL WAR

Emancipation Proclamation, 1863

Lee surrenders at Appomattox, 1865

Lincoln assassinated, 1865

RECONSTRUCTION

Supreme Court limits the 14th Amendment, 1873

Wyoming Territory grants women the right to vote, 1869

U.S. Navy builds ironclad battleships, 1862

Typewriter patented, 1867

Union army tests the Gatling gun, 1864

First transcontinental railroad finished, 1869

U.S. purchases Alaska from Russia, 1867

Suez Canal opens, 1869

German Empire proclaimed, 1871

1865   1870   1875   1880

UNIT 5

The Emergence of Industrial America

The decades following the Civil War saw the United States emerge as a major industrial nation. Old industries expanded and many new ones emerged, such as petroleum refining and electrical power transmission. Railroads reached out to bring even remote parts of the country into a national marketing system. This industrial growth transformed American society and created a truly national economy. It produced an expanded blue-collar working class and a new class of wealthy industrialists. The labor force that made industrial expansion possible was made up largely of immigrant workers. Immigrants played a larger role than ever before in American politics. Not everyone shared in the economic prosperity of this period. Many immigrant workers were unemployed much of the year. American farmers also faced hard times, as increased production resulted in falling prices for farm produce.

Chapter 13 The Nation Transformed	**Chapter 14** Society and Politics of Industrial America	**Chapter 15** A Time of Discontent	**Chapter 16** The United States Emerges as a World Power

◀ *This woodcut shows passengers on a Kansas Pacific Railroad train shooting buffalo for sport—an activity that led to the demise of the great buffalo herds.*

Themes

- **Multicultural Society** The immigrant workers who arrived in large numbers after the Civil War added new dimensions to the multicultural society of the United States.
- **Global Interactions** Both the immigrant labor force and much of the industrial technology that made American industrial expansion possible came from many parts of the globe.
- **Technological Developments** American industrial expansion was based on technological developments created by people from many nations.
- **Geography and the Environment** The plowing up of the semiarid Great Plains caused environmental damage as well as economic difficulties for the farmers involved.

419

Mechanization: Some Contemporary Views

Machines on the Farm

This writer was amazed by the changes that had taken place in farming during his own lifetime.

The introduction of machinery has revolutionized almost every branch of work on farms, and has greatly reduced the number of laborers required. In the great grain-producing sections of the country, farming has almost become a sedentary occupation. The soil is turned by a gang plow drawn by four horses, while the driver is mounted on a spring seat covered with a cushion. . . . Haymaking, once the most laborious occupation on the farm, has been rendered the easiest by the introduction of machines that cut the grass, spread it over the surface of the ground, rake it together when it has become dry, raise it upon the wagon, and carry it to the hay loft or stack. The [threshing] flail has been laid aside with the distaff, the hand loom, and the spinning wheel. The steam propelled threshing machine surpasses any other labor-saving device ever invented.

Rodney Welch, "The Farmer's Changed Condition," *The Forum,* vol. X (1891), p. 697.

Machinery as Labor-Saving Devices

The use of machinery greatly increased the productivity of American workers and reduced the cost of manufactured goods.

In the manufacture of agricultural implements, specific evidence is submitted showing that six hundred men now do the work that, fifteen or twenty years ago, would have required 2,145 men—a displacement of 1,545.

The manufacture of boots and shoes offers some very wonderful facts in this connection. In one large and long-established manufactory, the proprietors testify that it would require five hundred persons, working by hand processes, to make as many

women's boots and shoes as a hundred persons now make with the aid of machinery—a displacement of eighty percent.

Quoted in David A. Wells, *Recent Economic Changes* (New York: D. Appleton and Co., 1889), p. 91.

A Tailor's View of the Sewing Machine

Conrad Carl compared life before and after sewing machines were introduced into the clothing trade.

Before we had sewing machines we worked piecework with our wives, and very often our children. We had no trouble then with our neighbors, nor with the landlord, because it was a very still business, very quiet; but in 1854 or 1855, and later, the sewing machine was invented and introduced, and it stitched very nicely, nicer than the tailor could do; and the bosses said: "We want you to use the sewing machine; you have to buy one." Many of the tailors had a few dollars in the bank, and they took the money and bought machines. . . . Later, when the money was given out for the work, we found out that we could earn no more than we could without the machine; but the money for the machine was gone now, and we found that the machine was only for the profit of the bosses; that they got their work quicker, and it was done nicer. . . . The machine makes too much noise in the place, and the neighbors want to sleep, and we have to stop sewing earlier; so we have to work faster. We work now in excitement—in a hurry. It is hunting; it is not work at all; it is a hunt.

Conrad Carl, testimony taken by the Senate Committee upon the Relations between Labor and Capital (1883).

A Union Official on the Subdivisions of Labor

Horace Eaton, a labor leader, gave the following testimony at a congressional hearing in 1899 on the conditions of working people. He focused on the shoe industry.

QUESTION: Taking the material as it is prepared for the shoemaker, how many hands does a gentleman's finished shoe pass through in the process of manufacture?

ANSWER: To answer that question in another way, there are about one hundred subdivisions of labor in the manufacture of a shoe. . . .

Q: Now let me ask, in connection with that, what effect has that specializing, if it might be so termed, upon the workman? Has it a beneficial effect or otherwise?

A: Oh, it has been detrimental to the workman.

Q: The workman only knows how to perform the labor of one department?

A: That is all, and he becomes a mere machine.

 Testimony of Horace Eaton (Sept. 21, 1899). U.S. Cong., House, *Report of the Industrial Commission on the Relations and Conditions of Capital and Labor* (Washington, D.C., 1901.)

Feeding and Watching the Great Machine

In this article written in 1883, R. Heber Newton compared the condition of skilled labor in the 1700s with that of the factory workers in his own time.

The whole condition of industrial labor has changed in our century. Contrast the state of such labor a century ago with what it is now. Then the handicraftsman worked in his own home, surrounded by his family, upon a task, all the processes of which he had mastered, giving him thus a sense of interest and pride in the work being well and thoroughly done. Now he leaves his home early and returns to it late, working during the day in a huge factory with several hundred other men. The subdivision of labor gives him now only a bit of the whole process to do . . . whether it be the making of a shoe or of a piano. He cannot be the master of a craft, but only master of a fragment of the craft. He cannot have the pleasure or pride of the old-time workmen, for he *makes* nothing. . . . Steam machinery is slowly taking out of his hands even this fragment of intelligent work, and he is set at feeding and watching the great machine which has been endowed with the brains that once was in the human toiler.

 R. Heber Newton (1883).

Was This a Golden Age?

In 1890, Andrew Carnegie wrote the following assessment of progress during the previous half century.

Touching the material condition of the great mass of the people between 1889 and 1890, we may

▲ *Bicycle advertisement, 1897*

safely say that no nation ever enjoyed such universal prosperity. The producers, in agriculture and manufacturers, have not made exceptional gains. Indeed, these have not been as prosperous as usual, owing to the great fall in the prices of products. But the masses of the people have never received compensation so high or purchased commodities so cheaply. Never in any country's history has so great a proportion of the products of labor and capital gone to labor and so little to capital. And this furnishes the best proof of a most satisfactory condition of affairs. It is probable that in many future decades the citizen is to look back upon this as the golden age of the Republic and long for a return of its conditions.

 Andrew Carnegie, *Triumphant Democracy: Sixty Years March of the Republic* (New York, 1890).

Social Mobility: A Two-Way Street

Social Mobility in the Textile Mills

Textile mills, according to Frederick Smyth, provided a means for each new immigrant group to work its way up in American society.

All the [workers], at first, were Yankees. Then the Irish came directly from Ireland with their families, and . . . we commenced gradually working them into the mills . . . So then we had first the Irish, and we had no other; then came the Germans. There were not yet any French [Canadians]. As the foreigners worked in, the Yankees worked out; ... while some remained, and what we call the "second hands" worked up to first, and then by and by the third hands worked up. As the Irish came in they took the under work and gradually rose up till they had places of importance. That has been going on gradually till the Germans commenced coming, and the French. It is going on all the time, until this day, for, as you know, a very large part of the help now is foreign.

 Frederick Smyth, testimony taken by the Senate Committee upon the Relations between Labor and Capital (1883).

Social Mobility and the Skilled Machinists

An official for the machinists union gave the following testimony about the social status of machinists.

QUESTION: What is the social condition of the machinists in New York and the surrounding towns and cities?

ANSWER: It is rather low compared to what their social condition was ten or fifteen years ago.

Q: Do you remember when it was better?

A: When I first went to learn the trade a machinist considered himself more than the average workingman; in fact he did not like to be called a workingman. He liked to be called a mechanic. Today he recognizes the fact that he is simply a laborer the same as the others. Ten years ago he ... felt he belonged in the middle class; but today he recognizes the fact that he is simply the same as any other ordinary laborer, no more and no less.

Q: I am requested to ask you this question. Dividing the public, as is commonly done, into the upper, middle, and lower classes, to which class would you assign the average workingman of your trade at the time when you entered it, and to which class would you assign him now?

A: I now assign them to the lower class. At the time I entered the trade I should assign them as merely hanging on to the middle class; ready to drop out at any time.

 Testimony of John Morrison (Aug. 28, 1883), U.S. Cong., Senate, *Report of the Committee of the Senate Upon the Relations between Labor and Capital* (Washington, D.C., 1885), vol. I, p. 757.

Ethnic Diversity and Cultural Conflict

A Riot in New York

The following item appeared in a newspaper in New York City, where the Irish were the dominant immigrant group. Working-class Italian immigrants were just beginning to arrive.

Sheriff Conners says that for some time past the bitterest feelings of hatred have been manifested between the Irish and Italian laborers employed in grading and laying out the Grand Park. ... Crowds of Irishmen, who had been collecting along the railroad, rushed upon the Italians, and a bloody and desperate conflict ensued. Sticks, stones, bludgeons, knives—indeed every imaginable weapon was used. The Italians, nearly all of whom were armed with knives, fought like tigers. But, the Irishmen being constantly reinforced, the Italians were at last forced to fall back.

 New York Sun (Aug. 15, 1870).

Job Wanted

The following job-wanted ad appeared in a New York newspaper.

Situations Wanted Females: CHAMBER MAID. — By a respectable Protestant girl, as chamber maid and waitress, or as nurse and seamstress in a private family; city or country; good reference. Can be seen for two days at No. 321 West 42nd St.

COOK. — By a Protestant American woman, having excellent recommendations for capability, sobriety, honesty; is punctual and obliging; will go city or country; wages moderate. Can be seen at the Institute, No. 138 6th Av., above 10th St., over the drug store.

 New York Times (June 28, 1873).

Oath of the American Protective Association

New members of the American Protective Association, an anti-immigrant organization, were required to take the following secret oath.

I do most solemnly promise and swear ... that I will use my influence to promote the interest of all Protestants everywhere in the world that I may be; that I will not employ a Roman Catholic in any capacity, if I can procure the services of a Protestant.

 American Protective Association (1893).

Police Brutality

The following complaint against the New York City police was published in a Jewish immigrant newspaper.

Many complaints have also been laid before us that the police have for a long time past been insulting and brutal in their treatment of the Jews of the lower East Side. ... We find that instances of uncivil and even rough treatment toward the people of this district by individual policemen are inexcusably common.

 American Hebrew (Sept. 12, 1902).

The Concentration of Wealth and Power

Henry George, the author of this piece, was an economic theorist and reformer of the post–Civil War era.

Concentration is the law of the time. The great city is swallowing up the little towns; the great merchant is driving his poorer rivals out of business; a thousand little dealers become the clerks and shopmen of the proprietor of the marble-fronted [department store]; a thousand master workmen, the employees of one rich manufacturer, and the gigantic corporations, the alarming product of the new social forces which Watt and Stephenson introduced to the world, are themselves being welded into still more titanic corporations. ... Of the political tendency of

▲ *Gilded Age home*

[these developments], it is hardly necessary to speak. To say that the land of a country shall be owned by a small class, is to say that that class shall rule it; to say—which is the same thing—that the people of the country shall consist of the very rich and the very poor, is to say that republicanism is impossible. Its forms may be preserved; but the real government which clothes itself with these forms, as if in mockery, will be many degrees worse than an avowed and intelligent despotism.

 Henry George, *Our Land and Land Policy, National and State* (San Francisco, 1871), pp. 34–35.

The Crow Aid General Crook

This account was dictated by Plenty-Coups, a Crow warrior whose band aided General Crook in a fight against the Sioux shortly before the Custer massacre. The Sioux were the Crow's traditional enemies.

We came to the hills that looked down on the flat on Goose Creek. I shall never forget what I saw there. It was nearly midday, and countless little tents were in straight rows in the green grass, and there were nearly as many little fires. Blue soldiers were everywhere. I could not count the wagons and horses and mules. They looked like the grass on the plains—beyond counting. ... Even before we dismounted to dress up and paint ourselves for war, a bugle sang a war song in the soldiers' village, after which many blue men began running about. Then, under our very eyes and so quickly we could scarcely believe them, countless blue legs were walking together; fine horses in little bands that were all of one color were dancing to the songs of shining horns and drums. Oh, what a sight I saw there on Goose Creek that day in the sunlight!

Many of us had cartridge guns now, and the soldiers gave us whole boxes of cartridges, cans of power, and more balls than we could carry. I had never before seen plenty of ammunition. My own people were always out of either powder or lead. We could make arrows for our bows, but we could not make powder or lead for our guns. But now everybody had more than he needed, more than he could use. And besides cartridges and powder, the soldiers gave us hard bread and bacon—too much of it. They had wagons filled with such things, and the soldiers were generous men.

From Frank B. Linderman, *American* (New York: The John Day Company, 1930).

Industrial Conflict: The Homestead Strike

A Contemporary Account

This account appeared in Harper's Weekly *shortly after the lockout and violence at Andrew Carnegie's steel mill at Homestead.*

One of the most serious and disastrous riots that has ever occurred in America happened on the 6th of July at Homestead, Pennsylvania, where are located the mills of the Carnegie Steel and Iron Company, of which Mr. Andrew Carnegie is the chief owner. This company, through its president, Henry C. Frick, arranged a scale of wages some time ago, and announced that the workmen of the company must agree to this scale by the 24th of June. It was decided by the workmen that the scale, which was a serious reduction of rates, was unfair, and they refused to accede to it. . . . [The workmen] had been shut out of the mills after declining to accept the reduction of wages.

Meantime, Pinkerton's Detective Agency of Chicago had employed several hundred men to act as watchmen of the mill. These men, engaged in New York, Philadelphia, and Chicago, were taken quietly to Pittsburg. . . . Having arrived in Pittsburg, these men were taken to boats that had been prepared for them. . . . As soon as they had embarked, the boats were towed away towards Homestead. This was Tuesday night.

At four o'clock Wednesday morning three horsemen galloped into Homestead, and immediately there was a cry heard throughout the town: "To the river! to the river! The Pinkertons are coming!"

Now there was a frenzy of excitement in the town, and the men, armed with pistols, muskets, rifles, shot-guns, and clubs, hurried to the river-front.

There was a brief parley between the men on the boats and the workmen on the riverbank. While this was in progress some one from the boat fired a Winchester rifle, and then a serious battle begun [sic]. . . . At the first fire several men in the mob fell, killed and wounded, and there were casualties also on the boats, the leader of the Pinkerton watchmen being the first to be struck.

While the crowd of millhands were still discussing the situation, a white handkerchief was waved from one of the boats. This was a signal of surrender.

Then the Pinkerton men disembarked, and were placed under guard, and moved toward the jail. . . . The progress toward the jail was like running the gauntlet. Men, boys, and women broke through the guards, and stabbed and clubbed the disarmed prisoners. Stones were thrown at them as they staggered hurriedly along. It was a cruel and cowardly business this, and scarcely a single man of all those who surrendered escaped unhurt.

Harper's Weekly, vol. XXXVI (July 16, 1892), pp. 676–678.

The Company's View

After the riot, Henry Clay Frick justified the hiring of Pinkerton men. Frick was the president of the Carnegie Steel and Iron Company.

We did not see how else we would have protection. We only wanted them for watchmen to protect our property and see that workmen we would take to Homestead—and we have had applications from many men to go there to work—were not interfered with.

Testimony of Henry Clay Frick, Senate Report, 52nd Cong., 2nd Sess.

What the Homestead Workers Thought

Hugh O'Donnell, a spokesman for the workers, gave an explanation for the workers' actions.

Mr. Hugh O'Donnell . . . writes what is probably the real fact: "The strikers thought that as there were two barges, one contained scabs and the other their Pinkerton Guard." He also says that a German among the Pinkertons told him after their surrender that he was an old iron worker, and that, like many others of the 300, he had been engaged to work in the mills. Probably the chiefs of the Pinkerton force would deny this latter point, which was not referred to in the official investigations.

 Senate Report, 52nd Cong., 2nd Sess.

An Ironworker's Explanation for the Battle

W.T. Roberts, an ironworker, described the attitude of the Homestead workers.

Now the men at Homestead were in a peculiar condition. The most of them . . . had started to build their own little homes. Some of them had them about half paid for under the conditions that existed prior to this time. . . . To be forced into accepting a reduction that they didn't think was right or just at that time, and then to be confronted with a gang of loafers and cutthroats from all over the country, coming there, as they thought, to take their jobs, why they naturally wanted to go down and defend their homes and their property and their lives, with force, if necessary.

 Senate Report, 52nd Cong., 2nd Sess.

An English View of Homestead

A writer in the English journal Blackwood *defended Carnegie and Frick.*

Blackwood thinks that Mr. Carnegie had no option but to take this course. . . . The issue had come to this: "Are we, the proprietors of these works, to have the control of them; or are they to pass out of our control into the hands of a trades union?" When matters get to that pass any employer who has a spark of manhood in him will spend his last breath and his last shilling before he will make an ignoble surrender to a set of agitators.

 Review of Reviews (Sept. 1892), p. 336.

Mary E. Lease Makes a Speech

The following is an excerpt from a Populist speech that Mary E. Lease made during the 1890 election campaign in Kansas.

Wall Street owns the country. It is no longer a government of the people, by the people, and for the people, but a government of Wall Street, by Wall Street, and for Wall Street.

The great common people of this country are slaves, and monopoly is the master. The West and South are bound and prostrate before the manufacturing East.

Money rules. . . . Our laws are the output of a system which clothes rascals in robes and honesty in rags.

The parties lie to us and the political speakers mislead us. We were told two years ago to go to work and raise a big crop, that was all we needed. We went to work and plowed and planted; the rains fell, the sun shone, nature smiled, and we raised the big crop that they told us to; and what came of it? Eight-cent corn, ten-cent oats, two-cent beef, and no price at all for butter and eggs—that's what came of it.

Then the politicians said we suffered from overproduction. Overproduction, when 10,000 little children, so statistics tell us, starve to death every year in the United States, and over 10,000 shopgirls in New York are forced to sell their virtue for the bread their niggardly wages deny them. . . .

We will stand by our homes and stay by our fireside by force if necessary, and we will not pay our debts to the loan-shark companies until the government pays its debts to us. The people are at bay; let the bloodhounds of money who have dogged us thus far beware.

 W. E. Connelley, ed., *History of Kansas, State and People* (Lewis Historical Publishing Company, 1928), vol. II, p. 1167.

Breaking the Railroad Strike by Injunction

Eugene V. Debs testified at a congressional hearing about how the courts in several states used the power of injunction to break the railroad strike of 1894.

On the second day of July, I was served with a very sweeping injunction that restrained me, as president of the union, from sending out any telegram or any letter or issuing any order that would have the effect of inducing or persuading men to withdraw from the service of the [railroad] company. . . . From Michigan to California there seemed to be concerted action on the part of the courts in restraining us from exercising any of the functions of our offices. . . . Following the issuance of that injunction by a few days, I have forgotten the exact date, a special grand jury was convened for the purpose of examining into my conduct as president of the American Railway Union in connection with this trouble. The grand jury was in session very briefly, but found a bill upon an information that was filed, and I was ordered to be arrested. A warrant was issued and placed in the hands of a United States marshal for that purpose. On the 7th day of July, if I am not mistaken, I was arrested.

▲ *Promontory Point,*
Utah, 1869

 From the testimony of Eugene V. Debs (Aug. 20, 1894), U.S. Cong., House, United States Strike Commission.

Colonial Expansion: The Philippines

In Defense of Colonial Expansion
Albert J. Beveridge, a Republican senator, defended the acquisition of colonies in a speech to the Senate.

Today we are raising more than we can consume. Today we are making more than we can use. Today our industrial society is congested; there are more workers than there is work; there is more capital than there is investment. . . . Therefore we must find new markets for our produce, new occupation for our capital, new work for our labor.

Think of the thousands of Americans who will pour into Hawaii and Puerto Rico when the re-

public's laws cover those islands with justice and safety! Think of the tens of thousands of Americans who will invade mine and field and forest in the Philippines when a liberal government protected and controlled by this republic . . . shall establish order and equity there! . . .

What does all this mean for every one of us? . . . It means that the resources and the commerce of these immensely rich dominions will be increased as much as American energy is greater than Spanish sloth; for Americans henceforth will monopolize these resources and that commerce.

 Congressional Record, 56th Cong., 1st Sess. (Jan. 9, 1900), p. 708.

Anti-Imperialists Oppose Keeping the Philippines
Opponents of colonial annexation met in Chicago in 1899 to organize the American Anti-Imperialist League. Their statement of principles included the following.

We hold that the policy known as imperialism is hostile to liberty and tends toward militarism. . . . We regret that it has become necessary in the land of Washington and Lincoln to reaffirm that all men, of whatever race or color, are entitled to life, liberty, and the pursuit of happiness. We maintain that governments derive their just powers from the consent of the governed. We insist that the subjugation of any people is "criminal aggression" and open disloyalty to the distinctive principles of our government.

We earnestly condemn the policy of the present national administration in the Philippines. It seeks to extinguish the spirit of 1776 in those islands.

We demand the immediate cessation of the war against liberty, begun by Spain and continued by us. We urge that Congress be promptly convened to announce to the Filipinos our purpose to concede to them the independence for which they have so long fought and which of right is theirs. . . . A self-governing state cannot accept sovereignty over an unwilling people.

 Platform of the American Anti-Imperialist League, adopted Oct. 17, 1899.

Why the United States Should Keep the Philippines

Senator Henry Cabot Lodge took issue with the opponents of Philippine annexation.

Our opponents put forward as their chief objection that we have robbed these people of their liberty, and have taken them and hold them in defiance of the doctrine of the Declaration of Independence in regard to the consent of the governed. As to liberty, they have never had it, and have none now, except when we give it to them protected by the flag and the armies of the United States.

The taking of the Philippines does not violate the principles of the Declaration of Independence, but will spread them among a people who have never known liberty.

The next argument of the opponents of the Republican policy is that we are denying self-government to Filipinos... The Filipinos are not now fit for self-government.... The form of government natural to the Asiatic has always been a despotism.... You cannot change race tendencies in a moment.

We shall also find great profit in the work of developing the islands. They require railroads everywhere. Those railroads would be planned by American engineers, the rails and the bridges would come from American mills, the locomotives and cars from American workshops. The same would hold true in regard to electric railways, electric lighting, telegraphs, telephones, and steamships for the local business.

Congressional Record, 56th Cong., 1st Sess. (Mar. 7, 1900).

Bryan Opposes Colonial Annexation

In the following speech, William Jennings Bryan opposed the annexation of colonies on economic grounds.

The opponents of imperialism are fortunate in having upon their side the dollar argument as well as the arguments based upon fundamental principles.

The forcible annexation of the Philippine Islands ... would prove a source of pecuniary loss rather than gain.

Who can estimate in money and men the cost of subduing and keeping in subjection eight millions of people, six thousand miles away, scattered over twelve hundred islands and living under a tropical sun?

If this question is to be settled upon the basis of dollars and cents, who will ensure the nation that the receipts will equal the expenditures?... Who will place a price upon the blood that will be shed?

In his essay on the West Indies, Lord Macaulay denies that colonies are a source of profit even to European countries.... Shall we refuse to profit by the experience of others?

William Jennings Bryan, et al., *Republic or Empire? The Philippine Question* (Chicago, 1899).

WORKING WITH THE ARCHIVES

Identifying Bias in Primary Sources

Industrial conflict was a major theme of United States history throughout the second half of the nineteenth century.

Directions: Read the five selections from "Industrial Conflict: The Homestead Strike" beginning on page 424. (You may also wish to refer to pages 494 and 495 for an overview of this incident.) Then answer the following questions:

1. According to the account published in *Harper's Weekly*, what was the source of the conflict that led to the Homestead Strike and the role played by the Pinkerton Detective Agency in the ensuing riots?
2. Why did the strikers believe they could succeed?
3. How did Henry Frick justify his actions in his testimony before the Senate?
4. How did the workmen respond to Frick's assertions that he was acting within his rights?
5. Write a short response, from the workers' viewpoint, to the English journal *Blackwood*.
6. Had you lived in Pittsburgh at that time, do you think you would have supported or opposed the Homestead Strike and the workers? Why?

The Nation Transformed

The Civil War had stimulated the growth of some industries in the United States. Such war-related industries as shipbuilding and firearms manufacturing had prospered.

With the end of the war, the United States entered a period of still more impressive economic growth. With the victory at Appomattox hundreds of thousands of young men became available

▲ *This telegraph key is a symbol of the communications revolution that took place in nineteenth-century America. This pocket-sized key was properly called a Canton Pocket sounder. It was used in 1861, the first year of the transcontinental telegraph, at Leavenworth, Kansas. With this instrument an operator in the field could tap into a telegraph line to send messages.*

for more productive employment. Iron furnaces and foundries where cast iron was made were put to work making railroad locomotives rather than cannonballs. Work crews began building railroads rather than finding ways to destroy them. The war-torn South was slow to recover, but the rest of the nation entered a period of growth and prosperity.

The Railroad Era

When Nevada entered the Union as a state in 1864, it placed on its great seal (the official emblem of the state) an object that captured the imagination of its citizens. It was not the American eagle or the mountain lion native to that western state. The seal showed a Virginia & Truckee Railroad train crossing a high trestle that spanned a mountain canyon. The steam-driven locomotives of the 1860s, with their diamond-shaped funnels, pointed cowcatchers, and clattering train of freight or passenger cars, were the noisiest, most powerful and imposing machines that Americans had ever seen. They left a deep impression on the minds of that generation. The railroad had an impact on popular culture and folklore, as well as on American economic and social life. It was the era of Casey Jones, a locomotive engineer who became a celebrated folk hero. It was truly the Age of the Railroad.

How were the transcontinental railroads financed?
How did railroads spur economic growth after the Civil War?
How did railroads contribute to new sales and marketing approaches?

The Nation's Railroad System

At the beginning of the Civil War, railroads were a relatively new form of transportation. The nation's railroad system in 1860 totaled only 30,000 miles. Railroads running from Boston to Washington, D.C., linked the major eastern cities together. The larger cities had feeder lines that extended to nearby towns. Railroads also ran from New York, Philadelphia, and Baltimore to cities in the Midwest. However, the outbreak of the war had brought railroad construction nearly to a standstill. The United States government laid new track to move troops and supplies into the South, but little civilian construction was undertaken.

The state of Nevada included a railroad train on its great seal. Why was the railroad an appropriate symbol for a western state?

After the war, railroad companies resumed construction at a frenzied pace. In eight years, they doubled the mileage of track in the nation's railroad system. Although railroad building was slowed by an economic depression during the mid-1870s, another surge of construction began near the end of the decade. By 1893, the nation's railroad network was nearly completed, with 181,000 miles of track in operation. That was more than six times the amount of track that had existed when the Confederates fired on Fort Sumter.

Railroad travel also became safer and more comfortable. In 1868, George Westinghouse patented the air brake, which used compressed air to bring railroad cars to a stop. The air brake greatly improved the safety of high-speed rail travel. In 1867, George Pullman founded the Pullman Palace Car Company to build railroad cars with specially constructed sleeping spaces. The company also built luxury cars for wealthy industrialists who wished to travel in style. The addition of dining cars and Pullman's sleeping cars made long-distance rail travel more comfortable and convenient.

The most impressive feat of postwar railroad construction was the building of the transcontinental routes. In 1862, Congress passed the Pacific Railway Act, which authorized the construction of the first transcontinental railroad. The act authorized the Union Pacific Railroad to build west from Omaha, Nebraska, and the Central Pacific Railroad to build east from Sacramento, California. The two railroads came together at Promontory Point, Utah, on May 10, 1869. Thirty years later, five major railroads spanned the Great Plains to connect the eastern states with the Pacific Coast. The Union Pacific and Central Pacific crossed the central plains. The Northern Pacific Railroad and the Great Northern Railroad opened up the rich farmlands of Minnesota and North Dakota to settlement. The Santa Fe and the Southern Pacific railroads linked the southern plains to eastern markets.

▶ *This chart illustrates the growth of railroads in the 1800s. Why do you think the graph shows relatively little growth during the years 1861 to 1870 compared to the years 1851 to 1860?*

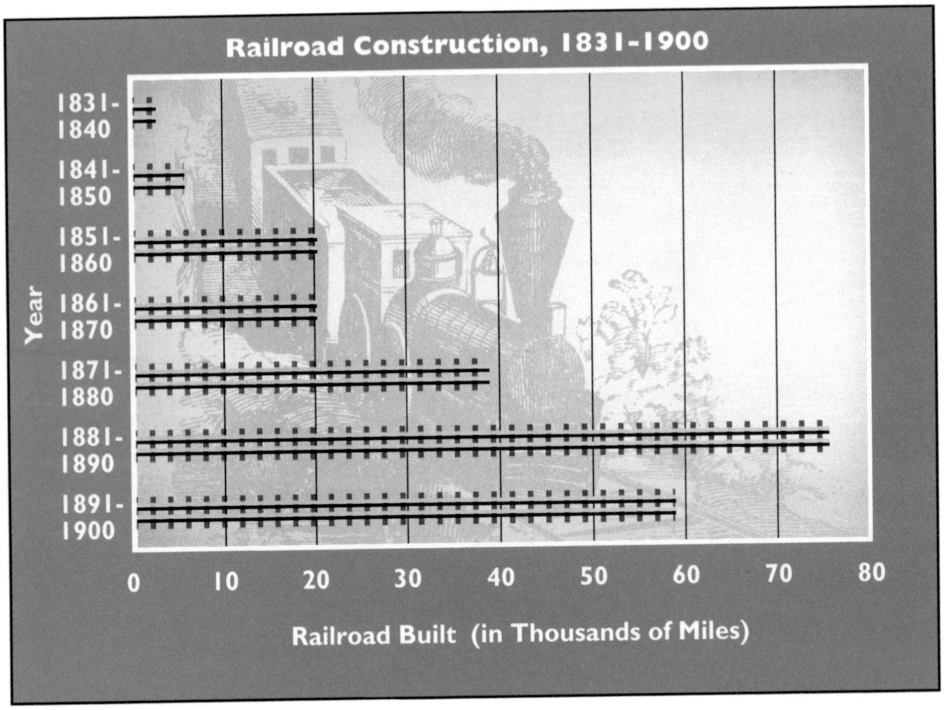

Railroad Construction, 1831-1900
Year
1831-1840
1841-1850
1851-1860
1861-1870
1871-1880
1881-1890
1891-1900
0
10
20
30
40
50
60
70
80
Railroad Built (in Thousands of Miles)

▼ *This engraving shows Benjamin Harrison in his presidential observation car. Luxury cars such as this were built by the Pullman Palace Car Company.*

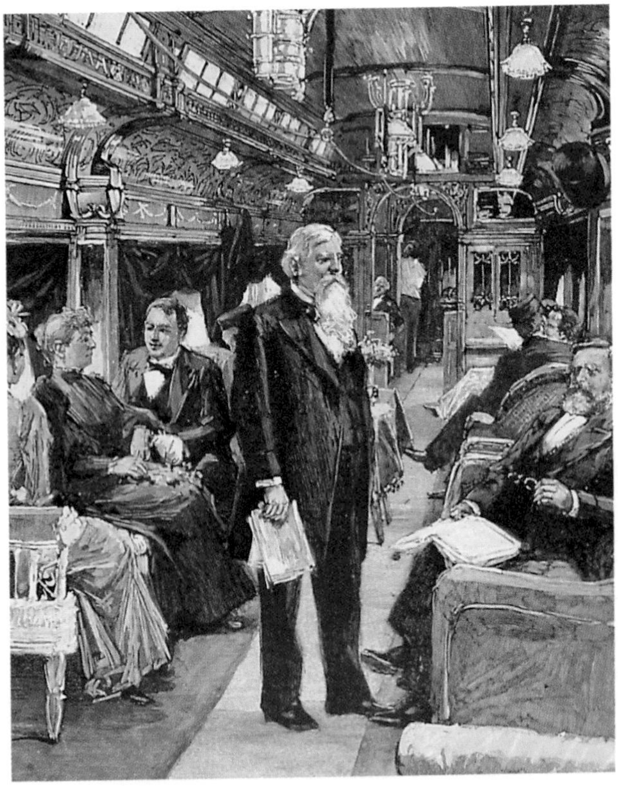

Four of the five transcontinental railroads were built with help from the federal government. Private banks were reluctant to loan money to railroad companies building across the largely unsettled West, as it would take a long time for the railroads to pay off their debts. Congress stepped in to provide assistance in the form of loans and grants of public land. These **land-grant railroads** received millions of acres of public land. The railroad companies, in turn, sold the land to raise money, which sped up the settlement of the West.

The last of the Pacific railroads to be completed was the Great Northern, which was the only transcontinental railroad built without federal aid. The building of the Great Northern was the masterwork of James J. Hill, one of the great railroad leaders of the era. As a young man, Hill had emigrated from Canada to St. Paul, Minnesota, where he began his career as a merchant and coal dealer. In 1878, he and a group of Scottish Canadian friends bought a bankrupt local railroad for a fraction of its original cost. After extending the line north into Canada and making it a paying railroad again, Hill announced that he would build west to the Pacific. The business people of St. Paul scoffed at the idea, calling it "Hill's Folly." They doubted that Hill

▲ *The Central Pacific (left) and Union Pacific (right) railroads were joined together at Promontory Point, Utah, on May 10, 1869, at the "Golden Spike" ceremony. How did the federal government aid the construction of transcontinental railroads?*

could finance such an undertaking. Instead of immediately building all the way to the Pacific, as other transcontinental railroads had done, Hill slowly extended the railroad west, keeping pace with agricultural settlement. This enabled Hill to pay for construction with income generated by the railroad. With this conservative approach, Hill built his Great Northern Railroad into one of the finest railroads of its day. The Great Northern reached Puget Sound at Everett, Washington, in 1893, and connected with Seattle and Portland a few years later.

Railroads Spur Economic Growth

The railroads constructed after the Civil War were a major spur to economic growth. In the first place, railroads were consumers of the products of the nation's mines, mills, and factories. As one historian has noted, "the railroads, too, became large users of machine tools, of copper, glass, India rubber, felt, and animal and mineral oils." The railroads' demand for longer lasting rails also gave birth to the modern steel industry. The iron rails first used by the railroads wore out quickly and unexpectedly, driving

up costs and creating safety hazards. By the 1870s, railroads had begun to use more durable steel rails, which provided the first market for American-made steel. The timber industry benefited from railroad orders for the wooden ties on which the rails were laid. Coal mines were kept busy supplying fuel for railroad locomotives.

The railroads also stimulated economic growth by opening up vast areas of the West to settlement. Farming and ranching on the Great Plains were profitable because the railroads provided a cheap and efficient way to get wheat and cattle to market. This, in turn, created new flour-milling and meat-packing industries, processing the farmers' grain into flour and the livestock into meat ready for the market. The westward expansion of settlement also benefited city merchants, since the volume of their business increased because of the growing rural demand for consumer goods.

Nationwide Marketing

Railroads enabled merchants and manufacturers to create the first nationwide marketing and sales

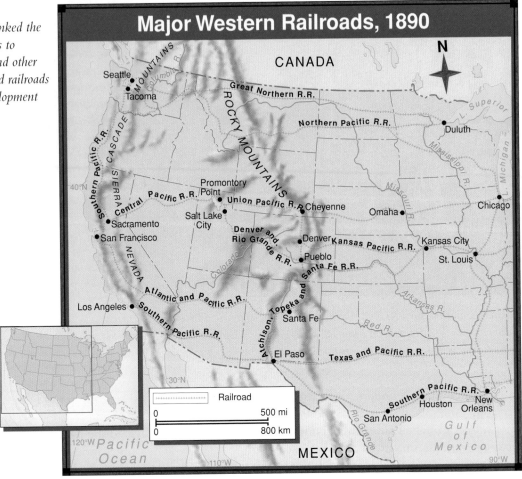

By 1890, railroads linked the western United States to Chicago, St. Louis, and other eastern cities. How did railroads contribute to the development of the West?

Major Western Railroads, 1890

organizations. In 1872, **Aaron Montgomery Ward** used the improved mail service provided by the railroads to create a direct-mail retailing company. He began by mailing to consumers in rural America a one-page notice that advertised his wares and guaranteed satisfaction. By 1886, Ward was producing a 304-page catalog that offered a variety of goods to farmers and small towns. These goods had previously been available only to shoppers in large cities. Soon, Ward had a competitor in mail-order sales. Richard W. Sears, a railroad clerk turned merchant, founded the Sears, Roebuck Company. But the most impressive feat of all was the marketing revolution begun by **Gustavus Swift** in the meat-packing industry.

Gustavus Swift used the growing railroad network to create an entirely new marketing system for distributing dressed meats. A butcher by trade, Swift had moved from his native Massachusetts to

▼ James J. Hill (fifth from right) and friends posed in front of his company's first locomotive. The Great Northern was the only transcontinental railroad built without federal aid.

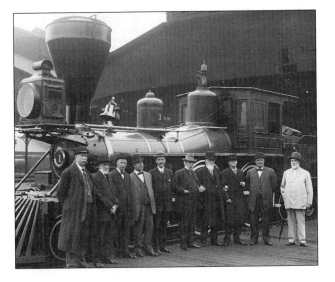

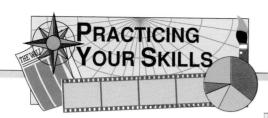
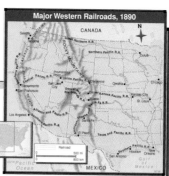

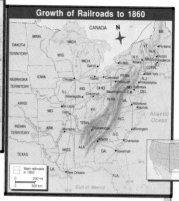

Special Purpose Maps: Looking at Regions

Today, cars, buses, subways, and planes handle most of the needs of our mobile society. Rush hour traffic, noise, and air pollution are undesirable side effects of all this movement, but getting from one place to another is relatively easy. However, until the development of the railroads—the first mass transit ground system—travel was slow, tiring, and often dangerous. While a stagecoach trip from St. Louis to San Francisco took three weeks, the railroad could get a traveler from Philadelphia to San Francisco in just one week. Americans embraced rail travel enthusiastically. Railroads moved people, goods, and supplies. With them came the exchange of ideas and cultures that accompanies all movement and defines the nature of places and regions.

Review the guidelines for reading a map on page 81. With special purpose maps, it is important that you ask yourself the following additional questions:

- **What special information does the map illustrate?** What is the specific purpose of the map? Often, special purpose maps record economic or demographic information.
- **Does the map represent a particular point in time, or does it trace changes over time?** Changes over time will allow you to make historical comparisons.
- **Does the map support or contradict previous knowledge?** How does the map add to your understanding of the topic? Is the visual format of the map an effective means of presenting the information?

Examine the maps on pages 300 and 432 to help you answer the following:

1. Through which states and territories did the Great Northern Railroad pass on its way from Duluth to the Pacific Ocean?
2. Name four major cities that were connected by railroads to St. Louis.
3. What geographic features in the West might have caused construction problems for the builders of the transcontinental railroads?
4. If you lived in Chicago, Illinois, what would be the shortest railroad route for you to take to Los Angeles, California?
5. What benefits might people in the East enjoy from the building of the transcontinental railroads? What benefits might westerners enjoy from it?
6. Why do you think there are so few tracks in Texas and what is now Oklahoma?
7. How would the building of the railroads have affected the American Indian tribes in the Great Plains?
8. Why might the location of a railroad nearby be of concern to the following people: a farmer, a miner, a housewife, a cattleman, a factory owner?

▲ *Preparing meat for shipping to distributors is called "dressing." In this colored engraving, workers in a meat-packing house are dressing beef. How did Gustavus Swift change the way American consumers were provided with meat?*

▲ *Mail-order catalogs helped Sears, Roebuck and Company create a national market for its retail goods. What role did railroads play in direct-mail retailing?*

Chicago shortly after the Civil War. He knew from firsthand experience that the butchers of New York, Boston, and other eastern cities were exhausting their local meat supplies. With the increasing population, the demand for meat was growing faster than the supply. Swift was also aware that railroads brought thousands of head of Texas cattle each year to the stockyards of Chicago. Moving to Chicago, Swift established a slaughterhouse there that would prepare beef for shipment east in refrigerated railroad cars. To a population dependent on local butcher shops, this was a novel—and slightly dangerous—idea. No one had ever dreamed of eating meat from animals killed a thousand miles away. After overcoming the initial reluctance of eastern consumers, Swift expanded his business by opening branch plants in numerous American cities. Other Chicago meat packers, such as Armour and Compa-

ny, followed his example. They created a major new industry for Chicago and brought about a nation-wide marketing revolution.

Society, Culture, and the Railroads

The impact of the railroads extended far beyond the factories and slaughterhouses. They enriched the American language. Railroad terms such as highball, going at full speed, main line, and asleep at the switch became popular slang. Railroad themes produced a new generation of American folk songs, such as "The Wreck of Old 97" and "I've Been Working on the Railroad." Casey Jones, a locomotive engineer who was killed in a train wreck, was added to the gallery of American folk heroes. So, too, was an Iowa farm girl named Kate Shelly, whose timely warning saved a Chicago and North Western train from plunging off a washed-out bridge.

The railroads even affected the way Americans kept time. Before 1883, the time kept within each region of the country varied from one community to another. In that year, the country was divided into four time zones to help the railroads prepare train schedules. Thus, railroads influenced almost every aspect of American life.

SECTION 1 REVIEW

1. Describe the ways the federal government assisted in the construction of transcontinental railroads.
2. List the industries that were stimulated by railroad purchases of goods and materials.
3. Explain how the opening of the West for settlement stimulated American economic growth.
4. Identify Gustavus Swift.
5. Explain why the period after the Civil War might be called the Age of the Railroad.

SECTION 2

The Growth of Industry

On May 10, 1876, the Centennial Exhibition was held in Philadelphia to celebrate the 100th anniversary of the signing of the Declaration of Independence. It opened with a speech from President Ulysses S. Grant and cheers from the multitude of visitors. The fair became a celebration of a century of American industrial progress. Nearly 50 foreign countries and 26 states contributed exhibits in technology and the arts and sciences. The main attraction was the huge Machinery Hall. The most imposing object in the hall was the American-made Corliss engine, a giant stationary steam engine that supplied power for the entire fair. Novelist William Dean Howells described it as rising "loftily in the center of the huge structure, an athlete of steel and iron." The Corliss engine impressed everyone who saw it. "The mighty walking-beams plunge their pistons downward, the enormous flywheel revolves with a hoarded power that makes all tremble," Howells wrote. For the novelist and for thousands of his fellow Americans, the Philadelphia exposition's Corliss engine became a powerful symbol of the nation's industrial progress.

How did machines change the way people worked?
What new industries emerged after 1860?
How successful was the postwar South in attracting industry?

Machines Take Command

The machinery at the exhibition was impressive evidence of the nation's recent industrial growth. At the heart of the industrial process was the mass production of goods by machines, a process first developed in the eighteenth century by British textile manufacturers. After a century of industrial progress, machines had replaced skilled craftspeople in one industry after another. American clothing manufacturers of the 1870s relied on machines to knit stockings and to sew the seams of shirts and dresses. Shoemakers had machines that cut out the leather for boots and shoes. Steel manufacturers used machines to spew out nails and screws by the hundreds of thousands. By reducing the need for skilled hand

▼ *The Corliss engine was the showpiece of the 1876 Centennial Exposition in Philadelphia.*

The Power of Electricity

▲ *In March 1877, Alexander Graham Bell gave a public demonstration of his telephone. This telephone in Boston was connected to a second phone in the town of Salem.*

Harnessing the power of electricity was the result of a truly international collaboration of ideas and efforts. Working independently in 1831, Joseph Henry, an American scientist, and Michael Faraday of Great Britain demonstrated that electric current could be produced by moving a magnet through coils of wire. Shortly after that, Samuel F. B. Morse, an American portrait painter, invented the key-operated telegraph that used electric current to communicate over a distance. For the first time, almost instant communication over vast empty distances such as found in the West was possible.

The next challenge was to use electric current to transmit the human voice. By 1860, Philipp Reis in Germany had developed a device that transmitted tones, but not voice. He called his apparatus a telephone. Alexander Graham Bell, whose family had emigrated from Scotland to Canada, took the next step. In 1876, he developed a telephone that used a vibrating diaphragm to create voice waves. These sound waves were then transmitted by electric current to a listening device, which converted the impulses back into sound. At that time, Bell was working as an instructor in a school for the deaf in Boston. He later became an American citizen.

The development of electric lighting was also an international collaboration. In 1808 in England, Humphry Davy demonstrated that electricity could produce light, either by making an electric current create an arc of light between two conductors or by heating a filament until it glowed. The arc was too bright for interior use. Pursuing Davy's second alternative, Thomas Alva Edison devised a light bulb suitable for both interior and exterior use.

In 1882, Edison built the first commercial generating station in New York City to provide power to his electric light customers. However, the direct current (DC) that Edison's generators produced flowed in only one direction and could not be transmitted over a great distance. Long-distance transmission was made possible by the use of alternating current (AC), a current that reversed directions at regular intervals, invented by a European named Nikola Tesla. Tesla developed the first AC power system in Budapest in 1882. He later immigrated to the United States, worked briefly with Edison, and then set up his own lab in New York City. By 1888, Tesla had also developed a motor that made it possible to power industrial machinery by electricity. Tesla's patents were the basis of George Westinghouse's success as an electrical manufacturer.

By the end of the century, the industrial nations of the Western world had harnessed the power of electricity through a transatlantic exchange of people, ideas, and technology.

1. How does the process of invention reach beyond national boundaries?
2. How was American leadership in electrical manufacturing in the nineteenth century related to the United States' liberal immigration policy?

labor, machines lowered production costs and the prices to consumers.

While **mechanization**—using machines to do work formerly done by humans or animals—produced an abundance of new goods, it had other less desirable consequences. Machines changed the way people worked by subdividing the manufacturing process into dozens of separate tasks. Skilled craftspeople of earlier days had the satisfaction of seeing a piece of work through from the beginning to the finished product. They had a sense of accomplishment that was rarely experienced by the men and women who tended the machines of industrial America. "He cannot have the pleasure or pride of the old-time workmen, for he *makes* nothing," noted one observer. "He sees no complete product of his skill growing to finished shape in his hands. What zest can there be in this bit of manhood?" Although workers benefited from machine-made cheaper goods, they often complained that work had lost much of its meaning.

With mechanization, the pace of work also changed. How fast the machine could be operated determined how fast the workers had to perform their tasks. "It is a constant race from morning to night after this machinery," complained a New England textile worker. Much the same was true in the shoe industry. A shoe worker explained:

> Now take the proposition of a man operating a machine to nail on forty to sixty . . . cases of [pairs of] heels in a day. That is 2,400 pairs, 4,800 shoes, in a day. One not accustomed to it would wonder how a man could pick up and lay down 4,800 shoes in a day, to say nothing of putting them on a jack into a machine and having them nailed on. That is the driving method of the manufacture of shoes under these minute subdivisions.

Mechanization also affected personal relationships in the workplace. The factory system brought workers together in large shops and factories, where machines could be most efficiently used. In most factories, work was supervised by a foreman or overseer, not directly by the owner. Workers in large factories seldom saw the officers and owners of the company. "I never do my talking to the hands," a New England textile mill owner explained. "I do all my talking with the overseers." As a result, much of the personal contact that had once existed between the owners of small workshops and their employees was lost. A brass worker remarked in 1883:

> Well, I remember that fourteen years ago . . . it was just as easy and free to speak to the boss as anyone else, but now the boss is superior, and the men all go to the foreman. . . . The average hand growing up in the shop now would not think of speaking to the boss, would not presume to recognize him, nor the boss would not recognize him either.

In the impersonal world of the factory, the gap between owners and workers rapidly widened.

The Iron and Steel Industry

The industrial era was an age of iron and steel. For centuries, human beings had used iron to make tools and weapons, but steel was a rare commodity. Steel, an alloy of iron with a low carbon content, was difficult and expensive to produce. However, in the 1860s, Henry Bessemer in Britain and William Kelly in the United States independently developed a cheaper way to make steel. The Bessemer process, as it was called, used a blast of air to burn the excess carbon and other impurities out of molten iron in order to produce steel quickly and efficiently. This new technique, along with a growing demand for steel rails by the railroads, led to a dramatic increase in steel production in the United States. In 1877, American steel mills produced 7,156,957 tons of steel, compared to only 1,643 tons a decade before. The United States was well on its way to becoming the world's major producer of iron and steel.

The nation's foremost steel maker was **Andrew Carnegie**, a Scottish immigrant whose family had settled in Pittsburgh. As a telegraph operator and later as the Pittsburgh division manager for the Pennsylvania Railroad, he discovered that railroads had a huge need for iron and steel. His early investments in a sleeping-car company, an ironworks, and an iron bridge building company paid him large

▲ Steelworkers here are operating a Bessemer converter. How did the Bessemer process greatly reduce the cost of producing steel?

▶ Scottish immigrant Andrew Carnegie built the world's most efficient steel mills. Has the role of the entrepreneur changed since Carnegie's time?

▼ This illustration shows Edison's first success with an incandescent lamp at his lab in Menlo Park. Why did Edison call his lab an "invention factory"?

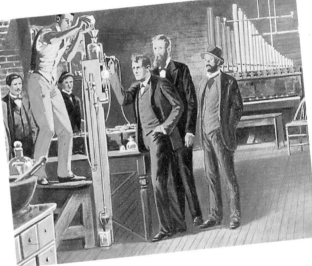

dividends. Resigning from the railroad, Carnegie founded his first steel company in 1872. Carnegie was well aware of the advantage of steel rails over iron. Using the new Bessemer method and taking care to keep the cost of production as low as possible, he was soon producing steel rails more cheaply than any other American steel maker. Carnegie's steel mills were the most cost-effective and productive mills in the world.

New Industries Emerge

In the decades after the Civil War, the invention of new products for American homes and offices produced several entirely new industries. At his research laboratory in Menlo Park, New Jersey,

Thomas Alva Edison developed the incandescent light bulb, the phonograph, and other electrical devices that became commonplace in American homes, offices, and factories. He thought of his laboratory as an "invention factory," and his goal was to produce "a minor invention every ten days and a big thing every six months or so."

Edison was not the only one with the drive to create new machines and consumer products. Other inventive Americans created the carpet sweeper, the electric iron, and the fountain pen. In the year 1897 alone, the United States Patent Office granted 22,000 patents for new inventions. Patents protected the inventor's rights to his or her invention.

The modern industry that produces office and business machines emerged during the post–Civil War era. The typewriter, invented in 1867, became widely used during the next decade. For writers and

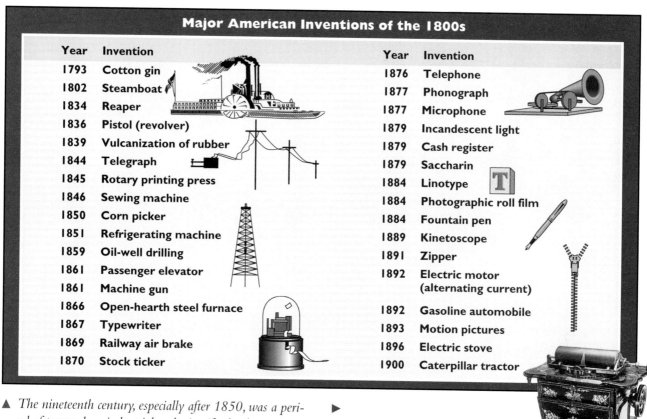

Major American Inventions of the 1800s

Year	Invention	Year	Invention
1793	Cotton gin	1876	Telephone
1802	Steamboat	1877	Phonograph
1834	Reaper	1877	Microphone
1836	Pistol (revolver)	1879	Incandescent light
1839	Vulcanization of rubber	1879	Cash register
1844	Telegraph	1879	Saccharin
1845	Rotary printing press	1884	Linotype
1846	Sewing machine	1884	Photographic roll film
1850	Corn picker	1884	Fountain pen
1851	Refrigerating machine	1889	Kinetoscope
1859	Oil-well drilling	1891	Zipper
1861	Passenger elevator	1892	Electric motor (alternating current)
1861	Machine gun	1892	Gasoline automobile
1866	Open-hearth steel furnace	1893	Motion pictures
1867	Typewriter	1896	Electric stove
1869	Railway air brake	1900	Caterpillar tractor
1870	Stock ticker		

▲ *The nineteenth century, especially after 1850, was a period of tremendous industrial and scientific development. New inventions changed the way Americans both lived and earned a living.*

▶

Remington manufactured a hugely successful typewriter line in 1873. Mark Twain used a machine like this one.

secretaries who had used only pencils and steel-tipped pens, it was an amazing invention. Author Mark Twain liked it, he explained, because it "piled an awful stack of words on one page." Twain's *The Adventures of Tom Sawyer* (1876) was the first book to be published from a typewritten manuscript. The decade from 1876 to 1886 produced the cash register, the adding machine, and the skyscraper. The telephone, patented in 1876 by Alexander Graham Bell, created a new system of business communications. (The communications revolution that the telephone created in American homes was largely a twentieth-century development.)

On the eve of the Civil War, Samuel Kier discovered a new use for the crude oil that seeped out of the ground on his farm in western Pennsylvania. Until then, he had bottled it and sold it as a patent medicine. Through distillation, he discovered it could also be refined into kerosene, a cheap substitute for the expensive whale oil then used in lamps. The new petroleum-refining industry that emerged

almost overnight soon caught the attention of **John D. Rockefeller**. He was a Cleveland merchant willing to risk investing money in a new and uncertain field. Rockefeller brought most of the nation's refineries under the control of his own refining company, Standard Oil. He made kerosene refining an orderly and highly profitable new industry.

Industry in the South

Impressed by northern industrial progress, southern political and business leaders tried to rebuild southern railroads and to attract industry. They hoped to build a "New South" that would someday rival the North in wealth and power. As a Kentucky newspaper editor declared, "the ambition of the South is to out-Yankee the Yankee." They achieved

▲ John D. Rockefeller founded the Standard Oil Company in 1870.

▲ *Nests of oil derricks sprang up almost overnight and developed into oil towns such as Red Hot, Pennsylvania, pictured above. Two years later, the town had disappeared but the deserted derricks remained. How did John D. Rockefeller make money from oil fields like this one?*

some success. Rich iron ore and coal deposits near Birmingham, Alabama, provided the basis for a southern iron- and steel-producing center. Manufacturers took advantage of the region's cheap labor and nearby cotton fields to create a southern cotton textile industry. The number of cotton mills in the South increased from 161 in 1880 to 400 in 1900. The promoters of the New South also exploited the region's timber resources. Sawmills sprang up throughout the South, and great stretches of its pine forests were reduced to lumber.

The New South's most impressive industrial success story was the creation of the cigarette industry. At the heart of this new industry was a machine invented by a Virginian in 1880 for rolling cigarettes. Before then, tobacco was used primarily for chewing and for smoking in pipes and hand-rolled cigars. The cigarette-rolling machine revolutionized the industry. "Everything from the stemming of the leaf to the payment of wages to the employees of the factory is done by machinery," reported one observer. Most of the tobacco factories were concentrated in North Carolina, the state that gave the South its most notable industrialist, James Buchanan Duke. Founder of the American Tobacco Company, Duke became the nation's largest manufacturer of cigarettes. "I had confidence in myself," Duke declared. "I said to myself, 'If John D. Rockefeller can do what he is doing for oil, why should not I do it in tobacco?'"

Industrialists as successful as Duke were rare in the South. The backward and war-torn southern economy failed to catch up with that of the North. By 1900, the South still had few industrial centers. Most of the factories and mills were small locally-owned businesses that survived by exploiting poorly paid workers. Forced to buy necessities in company-owned stores and to live in company-owned houses, mill workers were hardly better off than they had been as sharecroppers. Much of the wealth from the lumber industry and from Birmingham's iron and steel industries flowed out of the region into the pockets of northern investors. At the end of the century, the South remained the most rural and impoverished section of the United States. Creating thriving cities and new industries in that impoverished region would be a slow and painful process.

SECTION 2 REVIEW

1. **Describe** how mechanization changed the nature and pace of work.
2. **Explain** how factory production altered traditional personal relationships in the workplace.
3. **Identify** Andrew Carnegie.
4. **Name** three new industries that emerged in the United States after the Civil War.
5. **List** three reasons the South lagged behind the North in industrial growth.

The Industrial Workforce

In one industry after another, machines, tended by workers with few skills, began to take the place of highly skilled craftspeople. John Morrison, a skilled mechanic, watched this change take place in the machine shops of New York City. "When I first went to learn the trade," he reported in 1883, "a machinist considered himself more than the average workingman; in fact, he did not like to be called a workingman. He liked to be called a mechanic." With mechanization, "he recognizes the fact that he is simply a laborer the same as the others." By the end of the nineteenth century, skilled laborers had become a small minority of the workforce. Most industrial workers were unskilled and poorly paid.

How much pay did industrial workers receive?

Why did manufacturers hire women and children whenever possible?

How did industrial workers respond to the way they were treated?

Reports of daily wages and piecework rates are somewhat misleading, as workers were not guaranteed continuous work on a regular schedule and the employer was free to lower the amount paid per piece. In 1885, 30 percent of the wage earners in Massachusetts were out of work during four months of that year. This cost them one-third of their potential income.

Wage rates in the nineteenth century seem astonishingly low compared to modern wages. It must be kept in mind that modern-day wages reflect the inflation of consumer prices that has occurred since then. The skilled machinist who made $2.45 per day in 1880 typically paid less than $20.00 per month for rent. Even so, factory workers were poorly paid in relation to the value of the goods they produced. Unskilled factory workers faced a desperate struggle just to keep a roof over their heads and food on the table. Even skilled workers had to live frugally to make ends meet.

Working conditions in most industries were hard and often dangerous. The steelworkers in Andrew Carnegie's mills labored 12 hours a day in the intense and exhausting heat of the furnaces. "And everywhere is the danger of accident from constantly moving machinery, from bars of glowing steel, from engines moving along the tracks in the yard," noted one observer. "The men, of course, grow used to these dangers, but a new peril lies in the carelessness that results from such familiarity."

Industrial Wages

Industrial wages depended on the amount of skill required for a particular job. In 1880, skilled machinists averaged $2.45 a day, common laborers $1.32, and textile workers in the South $0.75 a day. Earnings also depended on how fast or how many hours a person worked, as employees in many industries were paid by piecework, that is, by the amount each worker produced.

▼ *Industrial workers of the nineteenth century were poorly paid. What might be one reason for the decline in average earnings between 1860 and 1865?*

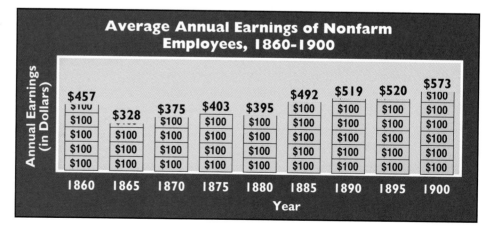

Average Annual Earnings of Nonfarm Employees, 1860–1900

Annual Earnings (in Dollars)

1860	1865	1870	1875	1880	1885	1890	1895	1900
$457	$328	$375	$403	$395	$492	$519	$520	$573

Year

▲ *This 1873 woodcut shows workers filling an iron furnace. What does the illustration say about industrial safety in the nineteenth century?*

Industrial accidents were common hazards in mills, mines, and on the railroads. Thousands of people died each year. From 1900 to 1917, 230,000 workers were killed and over 2 million other workers were injured in the railroad industry alone. Such tragic losses of life and limb were made even more difficult for the workers' families, as they had also lost their major source of income. Employers did not compensate workers who were injured. When a worker was killed, the family received no money or benefits from the company.

Women and Children in the Workforce

During the last decades of the nineteenth century, more women than ever before took jobs outside their own homes. The 1.9 million women employed in 1870 increased to over 5 million by 1900. At least half of that number were employed as domestic servants. Large numbers also worked in offices as secretaries and typists and as clerks in shops and stores. However, more than a million women were employed in factories. They continued to find jobs, as women had since the 1820s, in the textile industry. In some instances, textile mills hired women in preference to men, as women could be paid lower wages for the same work. A weaver in

Lawrence, Massachusetts, noted, "I know of a number of men who are compelled to stay at home, do the housework, and attend to the children because they can get nothing to do . . . owing to this unreasonable demand [by factories] for women." The expansion of the textile industry into the South after the Civil War also brought thousands of southern women into the workforce.

Women held the least skilled industrial jobs and were among the lowest paid of American workers. In 1900, the few women who found skilled industrial jobs, including the 45 women employed as railroad engineers and stokers or locomotive fire tenders, were rare exceptions. The vast majority of women workers held unskilled factory jobs, which earned the lowest wages. In 1899, men in manufacturing industries averaged $587 a year compared to $314 for women. Black women, still rarely hired in industry, made about half of what white women earned.

In their never-ending search for cheap labor, employers also hired large numbers of children. By

▼ *Children working in textile mills were supervised by foremen who ensured the children worked hard. Why did mill owners want to hire children?*

1900, some 1.7 million children between the ages of 10 and 15 were gainfully employed. That figure represents about one out of every five children in that age group. Nearly half of them worked in industry. The textile industry depended heavily on child labor to do the simple repetitive tasks involved in tending the spindles and looms. Rose Ferrigno, for example, quit school in the fifth grade to help support her five brothers and sisters when her father became too ill to work. By age 15, she was working eight hours a day in a New York City shirtwaist factory. Her income was five dollars a week.

Laborers Form Unions

By 1865, the iron molders, carpenters, machinists, and other craftworkers had organized craft or **trade unions** to improve wages and working conditions. One of their chief demands was an eight-hour work day for labor. In 1866, the trade unions formed the National Labor Union (NLU), the first national federation of unions. It called for the organization of women workers as well as men, and supported equal pay for equal work. Although it failed to secure the eight-hour work day, the NLU did persuade Congress to repeal a wartime law that permitted cheap labor to be imported under contract from Europe. The NLU was short-lived. It collapsed in 1872, after its Labor Party ticket was defeated in the presidential election of that year. However, individual trade unions remained an important force in the movement for better conditions and pay.

The **Knights of Labor**, a new labor organization, was founded in 1869 by garment workers to protect its members against abuse from employers. It was the first union to organize unskilled as well as skilled workers into one centralized union. By the mid-1880s, it had attracted about 700,000 members, making it the largest industrial union of its time. Unlike trade unions, the Knights accepted women and African Americans as members. Women made up about 10 percent of its membership.

The Knights of Labor grew largely as the result of several successful strikes that its local unions had organized. This was ironic, as its national leader, Terence V. Powderly, disapproved of strikes. He warned that strikes for higher wages brought "at best . . . only temporary relief." Instead, he urged laborers to organize **cooperatives**, which were workshops and stores owned by the workers. Only by becoming self-employed, he insisted, could workers regain their freedom and dignity. During the 1880s, members of the Knights did form at least 100 such cooperatives, including retail stores, newspapers, workshops, and a coal mine in Indiana. The problem with this strategy was that few laborers had any money to invest in workshops and stores. After losing a series of strikes in 1886–1887, the Knights' membership quickly declined. After the Haymarket Square Riot of 1886, the Knights also suffered by being identified in the public mind with anarchism and labor violence.

Strikes became the most common form of labor protest. In the year 1886 alone, half a million workers in 10,000 places of employment went on strike. However, strikes were not effective in industries that relied largely on unskilled laborers. The striking workers could easily be replaced by other unskilled people. When the textile workers at Fall River,

▼ *Labor strikes and demonstrations against factory owners and industrialists were not uncommon in the late 1800s. What were some of the major grievances of industrial workers?*

Massachusetts, complained to their foreman about working conditions, they were simply told, "If you don't like it, get out!" Skilled workers were more successful in using strikes to get their demands met, as they were more difficult to replace.

Although the Knights of Labor rapidly lost ground after 1887, the organization was not a total failure. Its demand for better and safer working conditions triggered a movement that would, in the years to come, produce state legislation to make factories and mines safer, and to limit child and female labor. Its effort to organize all workers, unskilled as well as skilled, women as well as men, created a vision of solidarity that would guide future leaders of organized labor. The Knights of Labor organization was also an early supporter of women's suffrage. While its moment of triumph was short-lived, the Knights left an important legacy.

The decline of the Knights of Labor left the individual trade unions as the dominant force in organized labor. These unions concentrated on such "bread-and-butter" issues as higher wages, shorter hours, and accident and health benefits for union members. As a result, their membership gradually increased. In 1886, the trade unions tried again, this time successfully, to organize a national federation of unions. The result was the **American Federation of Labor** (AFL). **Samuel Gompers**, its forceful president, was the major spokesperson for organized labor for the remainder of the century. Yet neither Gompers nor the AFL spoke for all American labor. The masses of industrial workers—the factory, mill, and mine workers—were not highly skilled. They remained outside the unions.

SECTION 4

The Frontiers of America

In the fall of 1858, the frontier towns of Kansas and Missouri were electrified with the news that prospectors had discovered gold near the Rocky Mountains. One local newspaper announced the event with this headline: "THE NEW ELDORADO!!! GOLD IN KANSAS TERRITORY!! THE PIKE'S PEAK MINES! FIRST ARRIVAL OF GOLD DUST AT KANSAS CITY!!!" The accompanying story in the *Kansas City Journal of Commerce* noted that one man had arrived in Kansas City with "three ounces which he dug with a hatchet in Cherry Creek and washed out with a frying Pan. Mons[ieur] Richard, an old French trapper, has several ounces of the precious dust, which he dug with an axe.... Kansas City is alive with excitement, and parties are already preparing for the diggings." News of the new gold strike quickly spread across the nation.

Why did gold and silver mining become industrial enterprises?

Where was the cattlemen's frontier?

How was the frontier of the plains farmers different from the earlier frontiers in the eastern woodlands?

Gold and Silver Discoveries

The discovery of gold in the vicinity of present-day Denver, Colorado, marked the beginning of a new wave of western settlement. Until 1859, the only permanent white settlers in the Pikes Peak region were a few mountain men who had stayed on after the fur trade ended. Otherwise, the area was inhabited by Plains Indians. The gold rush that began in 1859 brought thousands of prospectors to the Pikes Peak region. They discovered rich gold deposits in many of the mountain valleys. During the next decade, miners fanned out from the Colorado diggings to make other gold strikes in Idaho, Montana, and Utah. As the gold deposits ran out, prospectors in 1877 discovered silver in Leadville, Colorado. This created a new Rocky Mountain mining boom that would continue until the 1890s. Each discovery brought new waves of people, with mining camps and towns springing up almost overnight.

The year 1859 also saw a gold and silver rush to the mountains of what is now Nevada. Prospectors from the California mines made their way across the Sierra Nevada range to discover the rich mineral deposits of the Comstock Lode. The area was named after Henry T. P. Comstock, one of the early prospectors. It became one of the most productive gold and silver mining districts in the United States. By 1880, the Comstock Lode had produced $300 million worth of precious metals.

The Mining Frontier   The mining frontier was an urban frontier from the outset. The first miners to arrive pitched their tents along the mountain streams where the first discoveries were made. If the nearby gulches and hills contained enough paying ore, the campground developed into a mining town. The first structures were log cabins, followed by frame houses made with boards cut by nearby sawmills. Although located in remote mountain valleys, the mining towns were much like towns anywhere at that time. "We have churches, chapels, schools, and [a] new large hotel, in which a very polite dancing party assembled the other evening," wrote a resident of Central City, Colorado, in 1872. Some mining towns grew into small cities. The twin cities of Gold Hill and Virginia City, built on the Comstock Lode, had a combined population of 20,000 at their peak. It took the camp at Leadville just over two years to become the second largest city in Colorado, with a population of nearly 15,000 people.

▲ *The town of Leadville, Colorado, looked like many mining settlements of the time. Why was the mining frontier an urban frontier?*

Most mining districts passed very quickly from the prospecting stage to the industrial stage of mining. The first prospectors used simple devices such as pans and sluice boxes to remove the flakes of gold found in streambeds and surface soil. The next task was to find the layer of gold-bearing rock from

▼ *This 1871 Currier and Ives lithograph shows various techniques of placer mining, including mining with a pan, a cradle, and a sluice box, or Long Tom.*

◀ *This balance scale for weighing gold was used in California and Nevada in the 1860s. Miners were on the lookout for scales rigged to give inaccurate readings.*

which the flakes had crumbled away and washed down into the streams. The loose rock nearest the surface could be taken out by pick and shovel, but the hard quartz rock underneath was a different matter. It had to be drilled and blasted out with dynamite, and then broken up in huge stamp mills or crushing mills. As the miners tunneled deeper into the mountains, water pumps and air blowers were needed to drain and ventilate the mines. This required more money than most miners had. As a result, entrepreneurs organized mining companies, and mining became an industrial enterprise. Eventually, most of the miners found themselves working for a mining company for hourly wages. When a mining town reached this stage of development, it more closely resembled an eastern factory town than the mining camp of the early days.

The Cattlemen's Frontier

During the 20 years following the Civil War, a great ecological transformation took place on the western plains. The vast expanse of grassland that extended from southern Canada to Texas had once supported enormous herds of bison, commonly called the American buffalo. The buffalo, in turn, had provided the Plains Indians with food and other necessities of life. By 1870, the great buffalo herds were nearly gone, and Indians no longer roamed the plains. But the grasslands did not go unused. Huge herds of cattle and sprawling cattle ranches soon filled the plains. The buffalo range and the Indians' hunting ground became the cattlemen's frontier.

Spanish settlers brought the first cattle to the plains of Texas and northern Mexico. After Mexico gained its independence from Spain, Mexican ranchers continued to build their herds. In time, the Spanish cattle became interbred with farm cattle that American settlers had brought to the Texas plains. The Texas longhorns retained the long horns and wiry toughness of the original breed. Vast herds of these cattle ran wild over the plains of western Texas.

The problem was how to get these Texas longhorns to eastern markets. In the 1850s, a few herds were driven to Iowa and Illinois. Long-distance cattle drives resumed after the Civil War, but not for long. The farmers who had settled in western Missouri and eastern Kansas did not want their dairy cows infected with the dreaded "Texas fever" carried by the longhorns. They turned back the herds. Joseph G. McCoy, an Illinois stock buyer, finally found a solution to the problem. He persuaded the Kansas Pacific Railroad to build cattle-shipping pens

▼ *This 1923 oil painting by W. H. D. Koerner is titled* And So, Unemotionally, There Began One of the Wildest and Strangest Journeys Ever Made in Any Land. *Do you think this title is appropriate? (Buffalo Bill Historical Center, Cody, Wyoming.)*

Western Cattle Trails

Forested lands
Arid lands
Grasslands
Cattle trail
Railroads
Cattle-raising country

0 200 mi
0 300 km

▲ *This map details the major cattle trails used to drive Texas longhorns to shipping points along the railroads and to northern ranges. Why was Abilene ideally situated to become an important cattle town?*

at the frontier town of Abilene, Kansas, which was located on the railroad line. The longhorns could be driven from Texas to the railroad at Abilene over open plains without passing through farm country.

Driving Texas cattle over the trails to Kansas became a booming industry. Hundreds of trail herds set out each summer, reaching Abilene or other shipping towns like Wichita and Dodge City two or three months later. Some of the herds contained as many as three or four thousand cattle. By 1880, over four million cattle had been driven to the shipping towns of Kansas.

The Open-Range Cattle Industry

The cattle drives from Texas also laid the foundation for the open-range cattle industry. By the mid-1870s, ambitious cattle ranchers were buying large Texas herds to stock the central and northern plains. Because the plains were public land that could be used by anyone, they provided a vast open range for cattle grazing. The cattleraisers established a "home range" by buying or filing a homestead claim for land along a stream. This gave each water for a herd and a place for a ranch house and corrals. The cattle wandered far beyond this home range, grazing freely over the unfenced plains. Their owners kept track of which livestock belonged to them

► *Western artist Charles M. Russell entitled this watercolor* A Bronc to Breakfast. *It was good fun for everyone but the cook.*

◀ *Vaqueros, or Mexican cowboys, might have worn a pair of fancy spurs such as these from the Spanish colonial period in California. The spurs were made of iron inlaid with silver.*

by marking each animal with a distinctive brand. Twice each year, the cattlemen rounded up the cattle, branded the new calves, and sent part of the herd off to market. Most of the work, however, was done by hired laborers, or cowboys.

The first cowboys were the Spanish vaqueros, who had introduced cattle to Mexico in the sixteenth century. Two centuries later, Mexican and Indian cowboys were herding cattle at the Spanish missions established in California and Arizona. Many of the terms and tools that the American cowboy would use on the Great Plains were Spanish or Mexican in origin. The term *lariat* for the cowboy's rope came from the Spanish *la reata*. Leather *chaps,* the short name for what the Mexican cowboys called *chaparreras,* protected his legs. Nearly one-sixth of the cowboys of the open-range period were Mexican. Perhaps another one-sixth were African American.

In the folklore of the American West, cowboys often appear as heroic figures. In reality, their life was anything but heroic. Cowboys worked long hours. During roundups and trail drives, they often spent eighteen hours a day in the saddle. Yet when winter came, many were laid off. They

THE NORMAN FILM MFG. CO.
PRESENTS

BILL PICKETT
WORLD'S COLORED CHAMPION...IN
'THE BULL-DOGGER'
Featuring The Colored Hero of the Mexican Bull Ring in Death Defying Feats of Courage and Skill.
THRILLS! LAUGHS TOO!
Produced by NORMAN FILM MFG. CO.
JACKSONVILLE, FLA.

▲ *Bill Pickett was a working cowboy, a Wild West show performer, and a rodeo athlete. Pickett was best known for his skill in bulldogging, or wrestling steers to the ground.*

survived the winter by doing odd jobs in the nearest town. Or they killed wolves for the cash bounties paid by ranchers, as wolves sometimes killed cattle. The typical cowboy was young and single—and poor. After a few years on the open range, most cowboys quit to take a job in town or to settle down on a farm. A fortunate few made money by performing in rodeos, such as Bill Pickett, an African American rodeo star. But well-paid performers like Pickett were the exception.

In the 1880s, the open-range cattle industry expanded rapidly. As people realized that money could be made by fattening Texas cattle on free public grass, more and more ranchers got into the business. East Coast and European investors organized corporations and invested capital in cattle-raising operations. The open-range cattle industry became a big business, with millions of head of cattle grazing on the central and northern plains. It was because of this rapid expansion that the open-range cattle industry declined.

During the years 1885–1886, the open-range phase of the cattle industry came to a disastrous end. By that time, the plains had too many cattle for the grass that was available. During the harsh winter of 1885, weakened and hungry cattle died by the thousands. The following summer was unusually dry, providing the herds with even less grass than before. Then came the disastrous winter of 1886, when severe blizzards covered the plains with ice and snow. Cattle starved or froze to death by the hundreds of thousands. Ranchers went broke, and companies went bankrupt.

By the end of the century, cattle raising on the open range had given way to modern cattle ranches. The cattlemen who survived the blizzards and drought learned new techniques of raising cattle. They limited the size of their herds, built fences to keep the cattle closer to home, and fed them hay in the wintertime. The problem of fencing cattle ranges on the treeless plains was solved in 1874 by Joseph F. Glidden, who marketed his first barbed wire in that year. Farmers would also find barbed-wire fences useful for keeping range cattle off their land.

Farmers Adapt to the Frontier

The **frontier line** is defined as the line of settlement indicating fewer than two people per square mile. In 1865, it extended from northern Minnesota down through eastern Kansas to central Texas. Generally speaking, that line also marked the boundary between the woodlands of the Midwest and the open prairies and plains. To the west, as far as the eye could see, were rolling plains unbroken by trees except for isolated stands of timber along the streams. West of the 100th meridian, the plains became a semiarid region, with less than half the annual rainfall of the more humid East. Much of the prairie and plains region was opened for settlement by the Homestead Act of 1862, which granted 160 acres of public land to anyone who would settle on it for five years.

Settlers who arrived on the frontier in the 1860s found the land different from anything they had encountered in the East. To adapt to that land, they had to make many adjustments. In the first place, they had to learn new farming techniques that compensated for the lack of rainfall. In time, they developed **dry farming** methods that conserved the moisture content of the soil by deep plowing

MERITS of the Glidden Steel Barb Fence.

FIRST. "Cheapness." Three lines, at a cost of 75 cents per rod, make a fence that no cattle, however unruly, can pass.

SECOND. It can be put up with the same ease and quickness as the old plain wire.

THIRD. It cannot be burned.

FOURTH. It will not cause snow-drifts, and is alike unaffected by falling snow, wind or flood.

———

The Glidden Steel Barb Fence transforming the Defects of Plain Wire into Advantages.

FIRST. It is *Steel*, and of *two strands*, and will hold 1400 pounds to each line of wire, without breaking, or 4200 pounds in a fence of three lines; hence practically cannot be broken.

SECOND. Is *easily seen*, each line being composed besides the two strands, of barbs projecting at right angles.

THIRD. Cattle, after once coming in contact with the Barb Fence, ever after *avoid it*.

▲ *A trade catalog produced around 1875 describes the merits of Glidden's new barbed wire fence. Why did cattle raisers on the western plains use wire fences?*

and by letting fields remain **fallow** (unplanted) on alternate years. They also switched to more drought-resistant crops, planting more wheat and less corn. As timber was scarce on the Great Plains and lumber was expensive, the plains farmers built their first houses out of sod and used barbed wire instead of wood for fences. These frontier farmers also encountered new hazards, such as grass fires that swept out of control across the plains and waves of grasshoppers that stripped their fields bare.

The farming that took place on the plains during the postwar decades was commercial; that is, farmers specialized in cash crops that they hauled to market. With their profits, they bought most of the supplies they needed. Like other commercial producers of the time, they found they could increase production by using machinery. The wheat farmers of the plains, noted one observer, did most of their work from the seat of a planting or harvesting machine:

The sower . . . rides on a grain drill and holds the reins. At harvest time the owner of the wheat fields mounts another cushioned spring seat, shaded by a canopy, and again takes the reins; the self-binding harvester does the rest. Corn is planted, cultivated, husked, and shelled by machines.

The large wheat farms in the Dakota Territory used modern industrial management techniques. Oliver Dalrymple owned or managed several large Dakota wheat farms in 1879, having a total of 10,000 acres of wheat in cultivation. Planting and harvesting this much wheat required 60 plows, 30 mechanical harvesters, and five steam-powered threshing machines. Fifty men were hired during

Highways Across the Plains

For a decade or so after the Civil War, wagon roads were the major routes across the Great Plains. During the spring and summer, they bore the heavy traffic of freight wagons, emigrant wagons, and stagecoaches. The two major roads across the plains were the Central Overland Road, which followed the Platte River, and the Smoky Hill Road across central Kansas. They were barely maintained dirt trails, but they were true highways across the plains.

Tons of freight crossed the plains each summer in Conestoga wagons pulled by five to seven teams of mules or yokes of oxen. Traveling from the towns of eastern Kansas to Denver took 45 days. The freight wagons carried food, farm tools, mining machinery, store merchandise, and even cases of French champagne for Denver's fancy hotel bars. Lumbering along at 14 to 18 miles a day, a caravan of 25 freighters was an impressive sight. At the lead was the wagonmaster, who set the pace and was the boss of the caravan. Mule skinners, as the drivers were called, kept the teams moving. The crack of their whips could be heard for miles across the plains. Young boys out for an adventure took jobs with the wagons as "swampers," which meant that they did odd jobs along the way.

▲ *Thomas Worthington Whittredge traveled west to find inspiration for his paintings. He was one of the few who were interested in accurately reflecting scenes from the plains.*

Others worked as "cavvy boys," tending the mules or oxen at night.

Stagecoach companies provided fast passenger travel to the West. Pulled by four or six hard-galloping horses, the stagecoaches maintained an average speed of ten miles per hour. They kept round-the-clock schedules. Major roads had stagecoach stations about every 15 miles. They were maintained by the stage companies to provide fresh teams of horses to pull the coaches and to offer meals for the passengers. The stagecoach stations were small, one-story buildings that served as ticket office, the agent's home, and dining room for the passengers. The coaches also carried the United States mail, as mail contracts added greatly to the profits.

Emigrant wagons called prairie schooners carried people to new homes in the West. The white canvas covering the wagon resembled the sails of the seagoing schooners. Inside were household items, a few pieces of furniture,

food, plows, and seed grain. The family's cows, sheep, and dogs trailed along behind. Services that emigrants needed sprang up alongside the major wagon roads. Travelers could buy supplies at trading posts, treat themselves to a meal at a stagecoach station, and exchange exhausted animals for fresh livestock at roadside ranches.

After the completion of the transcontinental railroad in 1869, railroads gradually took over the fast passenger service and long-distance hauling of freight across the plains. The railroads could haul more passengers and freight in less time, which sharply reduced passenger fares and shipping rates. Travel by train was more comfortable, especially for those who could afford to use their dining and sleeping cars.

1. Describe the vehicles used to transport goods and people across the plains before 1869.
2. What advantage did railroads have over wagon travel?

harvest time to operate the threshers. Each farm had its machine sheds and blacksmith shop, its foreman, and living quarters for hired hands. Dalrymple operated his farms as if they were modern factories, rather than wheat fields on the farmers' frontier.

The Closing of the Frontier

The United States census of 1890 noted an historic fact. For the first time in the nation's history, there was no longer a frontier *line* that represented the westward edge of white settlement. There was still public land to be settled, but it was broken up into isolated pockets. During the previous decades, farmers, ranchers, and miners had moved to occupy vast stretches of the western plains and mountains. Never had so large a region been settled so quickly. In fact, more land in the United States became farm land between 1870 and 1900 than during the preceding 250 years. Most of it was newly settled land in the West.

The area settled during those years yielded a dozen new states and territories. The first new state was Kansas (1861), followed by Nevada (1864), Nebraska (1867), and Colorado (1876). Four new states were admitted in 1889—North and South Dakota, Montana, and Washington—bringing the total of states to 43. Two new territories—Arizona (1863) and Oklahoma (1890)—were created that had not yet become states.

SECTION 4 REVIEW

1. **Compare** the development of western mining to the development of manufacturing in the eastern states.
2. **Explain** why the mining frontier could also be called an urban frontier.
3. **Identify** the Comstock Lode.
4. **Outline** the major reasons for the collapse of the open-range cattle industry.
5. **Name** two disasters faced by farmers of the Great Plains.

SECTION 5

The Plains Indians

In the summer of 1846, Francis Parkman arrived at Fort Laramie in present-day Wyoming. The young Harvard graduate was preparing to write a history of the French in North America and their early contacts with American Indians. He wanted to study Indian ways of life. At the fort, he encountered a band of Indians, members of the Oglala tribe of the Teton Lakota or Sioux. Parkman spent the next several weeks with the Oglala warriors, learning about their life. He was impressed by their skill as hunters, having gone with them on a buffalo hunt. "Amid the trampling and the yells, I could see their dark figures running hither and thither through clouds of dust, and the horsemen darting in pursuit," he wrote in *The Oregon Trail*, the now-classic account of his trip.

Parkman took this trip not a moment too soon. The lives of the Sioux would soon be changed forever by the intrusion of white people, who were about to descend on the Great Plains in vast numbers.

How did the discovery of gold and the opening of the West to settlement affect the Plains Indians?

What role did the army play in resettling Indians on reservations?

How successful was the government's reservation policy?

Indians of the Great Plains

At the time of Parkman's visit to Fort Laramie, several tribes of American Indians inhabited the Great Plains. The Cheyenne and the powerful tribes of the western Sioux nation dominated the northern plains. The Pawnee, Arikara, Arapaho, Comanche, and other tribes occupied the central and southern plains. These tribes were seldom at peace with one another. Warriors on horseback raided the villages of other tribes to steal horses and to display

This scene of a hunter pursuing a buffalo symbolizes the close dependence of the Plains Indians on the buffalo herds. How did the Indians utilize the buffalo they killed?

personal courage and bravery. Yet despite their traditional rivalries, the Plains Indians had much in common.

The Plains Indians were nomadic hunters. They subsisted mainly on buffalo and other animals, which they hunted with bows and arrows. They usually hunted buffalo on horses descended from those brought by the Spanish in the 1500s. The Plains Indians were skillful riders and hunters. Each tribe claimed an area of the plains as its hunting ground, which the hunters from other tribes either respected or violated at the risk of their lives. Within those tribal boundaries, the Indians moved their villages from one place to another following the buffalo herds. That great shaggy beast provided the Indians with food and many other necessities of life. They used the hides as lodge coverings, coverlets, and winter robes. The sinews, or tendons, were made into bowstrings. The bones were sharpened to make augers, or drills, and other tools.

Contest for the Plains

The Plains Indians' encounters with white people, which dated back to the days of the fur trade,

became more frequent after the opening of the Oregon Trail in the 1840s. These contacts also became more threatening. The wagon trains crossing the Great Plains brought diseases to which the Indians had no immunity. Entire villages were destroyed by smallpox, cholera, and other diseases. The discovery of gold in California brought even heavier wagon traffic across the plains. Until 1859, most of the white people the Plains Indians had encountered were travelers passing through to Utah, Oregon, or California. With the discovery of gold in the Rockies, that was no longer the case. The merchants who set up shop in Denver for the miners, and the farmers and ranchers who followed them, laid claim to the land itself. The needs of the miners, ranchers, merchants, and farmers with all their resources were pitted against the Indians' prior claims to the land. Open conflict was inevitable.

In the 1860s, a fierce and deadly Indian War swept across the plains. The heaviest loss of white lives took place in 1862, during the Sioux uprising in Minnesota. These Indians had given up their hunting grounds in return for a much smaller reservation and a cash settlement, but they were cheated out of most of the money promised them by dishonest government agents. The Sioux struck back with a fury that took the white settlers completely

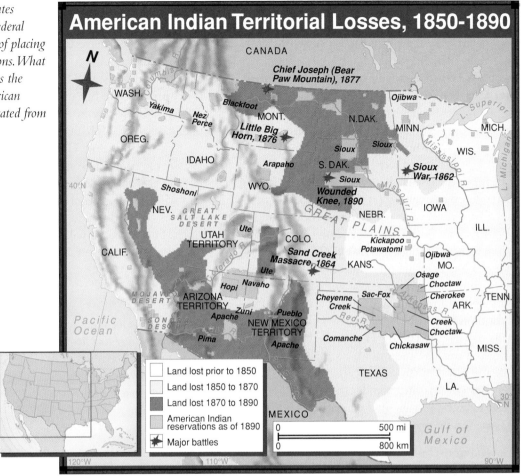

This map demonstrates the outcome of the federal government's policy of placing Indians on reservations. What present-day state was the home of many American Indians forcibly relocated from the East?

American Indian Territorial Losses, 1850-1890

CANADA

Chief Joseph (Bear Paw Mountain), 1877

WASH.

Yakima

Nez Perce

Blackfoot

MONT.

Little Big Horn, 1876

Ojibwa

N.DAK.

MINN.

MICH.

OREG.

IDAHO

Arapaho

Sioux

Sioux

WIS.

S. DAK.

Sioux

Sioux War, 1862

WYO.

Sioux

Wounded Knee, 1890

Shoshoni

NEV.

GREAT SALT LAKE DESERT

Ute

UTAH TERRITORY

COLO.

NEBR.

IOWA

ILL.

Kickapoo Potawatomi

Ojibwa

CALIF.

Ute

Sand Creek Massacre, 1864

KANS.

MO.

Osage

Hopi

Navaho

Cheyenne Creek

Sac-Fox

Choctaw

Cherokee

TENN.

MOJAVE DESERT

ARIZONA TERRITORY

Zuni

Apache

Pueblo

NEW MEXICO TERRITORY

Apache

ARK.

Pacific Ocean

SONORA DESERT

Pima

Comanche

Creek

Choctaw

Chickasaw

MISS.

TEXAS

LA.

MEXICO

Gulf of Mexico

Land lost prior to 1850
Land lost 1850 to 1870
Land lost 1870 to 1890
American Indian reservations as of 1890
★ Major battles

0   500 mi
0   800 km

by surprise. In their attacks the Sioux killed several hundred white people.

Sand Creek Massacre As warfare on the plains moved farther west, white people also murdered innocent Indians. One of the bloodiest massacres of Indians took place in the Colorado Territory in 1864. Several hundred Cheyenne and Arapaho Indians had come to Fort Lyons on the Arkansas River to accept peace terms offered them by the United States government. They set up their lodges on Sand Creek near the fort. Placing themselves under the protection of the fort, the Indians relaxed their defenses. They did not know that a regiment of Colorado volunteers had set out from Denver determined to kill every Indian in sight. The territorial governor, not the army officers at Fort Lyons, commanded the volunteer militia. In the early light

of dawn on November 19, 1864, the volunteers charged on the village at Sand Creek, killing at least 160 Indians. Of those, 110 were women and children.

The Reservation Policy

In a series of treaties signed in the late 1860s, the Plains Indian tribes agreed to settle on reservations. In return, the U.S. government promised them annual payments of money and supplies. The Indians did not adopt reservation life willingly, as it represented a radical change in their way of living.

In 1876, several bands of western Sioux refused to move to the reservation set aside for them. They had signed treaties years before that recognized their hunting rights on the northern plains. That area included the Black Hills, a sacred place that had special importance in the Sioux religion. In 1875, gold was discovered in the Black Hills, and the federal government decided to open the region to gold mining. Warrior bands led by **Chief Sitting Bull, Chief Crazy Horse**, and several other chiefs resisted. They refused to sign the treaty drawn up by the United States government requiring them to leave the Black Hills. In response, the government decided to remove them to a reservation by force.

In the summer of 1876, a large United States military force converged on the Big Horn Mountains of Montana, where the defiant Sioux and their Cheyenne allies had gathered. Among the troops was a detachment led by **Colonel George A. Custer**, a headstrong and reckless cavalry officer. Disregarding orders to proceed with caution, Custer led his troops into an attack against a village of several thousand Indians. In this engagement, called the **Battle of the Little Big Horn**, the Indians killed Custer and the 264 men in his command. The Sioux and Cheyenne had only a few months to enjoy their victory. Pursued by the rest of the army, the exhausted warriors finally broke off the fighting and were forced onto reservations. Sitting Bull and part of his band escaped to Canada, where they

stayed until 1881. At that time they returned to the U.S. and surrendered to authorities in Montana.

The United States government repeatedly called out the army to drive Indians to reservations. In the Southwest, the army hunted down bands of Apache Indians who resisted. The famous Apache chief, **Geronimo**, held out until 1886. By that time, 5,000 soldiers were in the field looking for Geronimo and his band of 36 warriors.

Like Sitting Bull, **Chief Joseph** and his band of Nez Percé tried to escape to Canada. The army chased his band, which consisted of 200 warriors and 450 women, children, and old people, for four months over a distance of more than a thousand miles. The soldiers finally caught the Nez Percé only a few miles from the Canadian border. Chief Joseph was exiled to Oklahoma.

▶

Chief Joseph of the Nez Percé attempted to lead his people to a safe haven in Canada. After the Battle of Bear Paw Mountain he declared, "From where the sun now stands I will fight no more forever."

◀ *The final moments of the Battle of the Little Big Horn were captured in this interpretive painting by Edgar S. Paxson (1852–1919). Why was Little Big Horn a short-lived victory for the Plains Indians? (Buffalo Bill Historical Center, Cody, Wyoming.)*

The date of this photograph of Cheyenne Indians on the Tongue River reservation in Montana is unknown. Why was it most likely taken after 1876?

The last major Indian-white engagement took place in 1890, after a band of Sioux left their reservation in the Dakotas. In a massacre of Indians at **Wounded Knee**, some 300 Sioux were either killed by soldiers or left to die of exposure in the freezing winter weather.

The decline of the buffalo herds left the Plains Indians no real alternative to living on reservations. They could no longer support their families and tribes by nomadic hunting. White hunters slaughtered buffalo in vast numbers. The first hunters were men hired by the railroads to kill game for their construction crews. In later years, hunting parties came from as far away as Russia to shoot buffalo for sport. By the 1870s, professional buffalo hunters slaughtered entire herds, doing so not for sport, but to sell the hides. It had become fashionable in the East to use buffalo robes to keep warm during winter carriage rides. Largely as a result of overhunting, the buffalo, with a population estimated at 12 to 15 million by the end of the Civil War, was nearly extinct by the 1880s. By destroying the Plains Indians'

This Osage wedding coat of blue wool, red satin, gold epaulets, and brass buttons was made sometime during the late nineteenth century. It is an example of the survival of distinctively Indian cultural forms even after the forced removal of many American Indian peoples to reservations.

American Landscape

People–Environment Relations: A Way of Life

Between 1784 and 1880 the United States government signed and broke 370 treaties with American Indian tribes. As the frontier moved west in the 1800s, millions of acres of land—two-thirds of a continent—were taken from various Indian tribes. Today, Americain Indians, with a population of 8.7 million, are the tenth largest ancestry group in the country. Their reservations comprise 2.2 percent of the total area of the United States.

The last major group of American Indians conquered by the United States government was the buffalo-hunting peoples who lived on the Great Plains. This region is a grassland that covers nearly a quarter of the continental United States. It slopes eastward from the Rocky Mountains to the Mississippi Valley and extends northward from Texas into western Canada. For the most part, the Great Plains is a level, treeless, and dry region. In an 1820 government report, it was labeled the "Great American Desert," and was generally believed to be unfit for cultivation. Indeed, in the 1850s, Congress allocated $30,000 to import two boatloads of camels into Texas in an effort to convert the Plains Indians into camel-herding nomads like those of the Middle East. Uncertain rainfall, scanty fuel, winter blizzards, and summer grass fires made the Great Plains unattractive to trappers, miners, and pioneers. Thus, it remained the domain of mounted buffalo-hunting tribes well into the 1800s.

In 1860, some 250,000 American Indians inhabited the Great Plains. The strongest and most warlike were the Sioux, Blackfoot, Crow, Cheyenne, and Arapaho in the north, and the Comanche, Apache, Ute, and Kiowa in the south. Trapped in a rapidly closing vise between cattlemen and farmers advancing from the east and miners rebounding from the gold fields of California, the Plains Indians still lived as nomadic hunters, migrating northward in summer andsouthward in winter, feeding off enormous herds of buffalo.

Some buffalo herds were made up of as many as 12 million animals. The Plains Indians relied on food supply, commercial hunters had made the government's reservation policy much easier to carry out.

Changes in the Indian Policy

By the 1880s, a growing number of white people, especially in the eastern states, began to sympathize with the plight of the American Indians. They knew that many Indian Bureau officials in charge of the reservations had abused the Indians. Reformers investigating the government's Indian policy had exposed many instances of fraud. In some cases, corrupt agents had stolen money that was intended for the support of the tribes. In 1881, Helen Hunt Jackson wrote a book that sharply criticized the federal government's Indian policy. Entitled *A Century of Dishonor*, the book traced the history of broken promises made to the American Indians. Sarah Winnemucca, a Paiute (py-OOT) Indian, wrote a book entitled *Life Among the Paiutes, Their Wrongs and Claims* (1883), which vividly described the tragedy of Indian life. Both books widened the public's awareness of the duplicity and failure of the government's Indian policy.

In 1887, Congress responded to the growing concern about the Indians. In that year, it passed the

▼ *Frederic Remington recorded the rapidly disappearing "Wild West" in his paintings and sculptures. This oil on canvas, measuring 35 x 20 inches, is entitled* Conjuring Back the Buffalo. *Do you think Remington conveyed the despair of the Plains Indians caused by the demise of the buffalo?*

them for food, shelter, and clothing. As the railroads penetrated the plains, buffalo hunters, farmers and cattlemen began to shoot buffalo for hides and to encroach on hunting grounds granted by treaty to the Plains Indians for "as long as water runs and grass grows."

The livelihood of the Plains Indians was directly threatened by this slaughter of the buffalo. Record kills of 120 buffalo in 40 minutes and 6,000 in 60 days were logged by skilled buffalo hunters. In the late 1860s, about 1 million animals were killed each year. By 1873, only one large buffalo herd in the Texas Panhandle was still intact. By 1876, few targets were left.

In desperation, American Indians fought back in hundreds of pitched battles with army troops. As each group was subdued, the survivors were herded onto reservations. Tribal lands were taken by theft or purchase. The Indian population was drastically reduced by army raids, disease, and hunger. Long before the pitiless massacre of a band of Sioux at Wounded Knee on New Year's Day 1891, the extinction of the buffalo had sealed the fate of the Plains Indians, and the last significant obstacle to westward settlement was removed.

1. What were the largest groups living on the Great Plains in the 1860s?
2. Why did the destruction of the buffalo herds have such a dramatic impact on the lives of the Plains Indians?

Dawes Act, which attempted to end the reservation policy. The purpose of the act was to break up the reservations and to integrate Indians into the mainstream of American life. It tried to accomplish this by making the Indians land-owning farmers. It allowed reservations to be divided up, with each Indian family receiving 160 acres of land. Any land left over after the Indian allotments was to be returned to the public domain and opened to settlement. The result was that vast tracts of reservation land were sold to white settlers. By 1934, the Indians had lost 90 million acres of land. The Dawes Act left Indian tribes worse off than before. They had less land and still were not integrated into the larger American

society. Many continued to live on reservations that had survived the Dawes Act.

SECTION 5 REVIEW

1. **Describe** how the buffalo contributed to Plains Indian life.
2. **Name** the discovery that sparked war between Indians and white people during the 1860s.
3. **Identify** the Sand Creek Massacre.
4. **List** three reasons why some Indian bands resisted moving to reservations.
5. **Summarize** the overall effect of the Dawes Act on the Plains Indians.

Summary

With the end of the Civil War, the United States resumed its remarkable economic growth. The expansion of the railroad network allowed farmers and ranchers to market their products more cheaply and helped to create a national market for manufactured goods. An increased demand by the railroads for locomotives, cars, and iron and steel rails also stimulated the growth of other industries. During the three decades after the war, the modern steel industry began to flourish. A number of new industries also emerged during those years, including the oil-refining and electrical-manufacturing industries. The South was the only section that lagged behind during this era of economic growth, and even it developed modern steel and cigarette manufacturing industries. Still recovering from the waste and destruction of the war, the South, at the end of the century, remained the most rural and impoverished section of the United States.

The postwar era also saw the rapid growth of labor unions. Skilled workers organized trade unions and in 1886 formed the American Federation of Labor. However, the labor leaders of the period were less successful in organizing the large, mass-production industries. The Knights of Labor failed in its attempt to organize all workers.

A new wave of western migration began in the 1860s, as thousands of white settlers moved into the western mountains and plains. Some were miners, who created a new mining industry. Others were farmers and ranchers, who transformed the ecology of the plains from a buffalo range into a land of cattle ranches and wheat farms. As the Plains Indians saw their buffalo-hunting grounds being occupied by white people, they resisted with open warfare. In the end, they were overwhelmed by the sheer numbers of white settlers and by the disappearance of the buffalo. The Indians were forced to live on reservations, where they had to depend on food and clothing supplied by the government.

Vocabulary

cooperatives

dry farming

fallow

frontier line

land-grant railroads

mechanization

trade union

Write three or four sentences explaining each of the vocabulary terms listed above. Include information on how each affected life on the Great Plains or in the city during this period.

Review Questions

1. Explain why the federal government became involved in building transcontinental railroads.
2. How did railroad construction after the Civil War stimulate American economic growth?
3. How did the mechanization of production affect personal relationships in the workplace?
4. Why did industrial growth after the war proceed more rapidly in the North than in the South?
5. How did the mechanization of production change the skills needed by workers in the American workforce?
6. How successful were labor unions representing skilled workers compared to unskilled workers?
7. Briefly explain the meaning of the term *urban frontier* as used in Section 4.
8. Name two events that brought the open-range phase of the cattle industry to an abrupt end.
9. Describe two methods that the federal government used to implement its policy of moving Indians to reservations.
10. What was the government's motivation for adopting the Dawes Act in 1887?

Chapter 13 Review

Critical Historical Thinking

Writing Answer each of the following by writing one or more complete paragraphs:

1. Drawing on what you know about transportation and communication patterns today, compare the importance of railroads to social and economic life in the late 1800s and today.

2. It is 1870 and you are considering a move from Philadelphia, where you do piecework in a shoe factory, to Omaha, Nebraska, where you will grow wheat. Discuss your concerns about the move, weighing the risks and benefits.

3. Helen Hunt Jackson's *A Century of Dishonor* exposed the mistreatment of the American Indians. Harriet Beecher Stowe's *Uncle Tom's Cabin* brought the evils of slavery to the attention of the nation. Discuss why you think these novels were so successful, and then discuss a situation existing today that you feel needs exposing. Describe how you would do this.

4. Read "Feeding and Watching the Great Machine" in the Unit 5 Archives. According to the author, why did he admire the eighteenth-century skilled laborers more than factory workers in industrialized America?

Making Connections with Popular Literature

Popular literature, or "pop lit," is often a better indicator of the general taste of a period than classical literature. The subjects of pop lit indicate what captures the imagination of the people.

Dime novels first became popular during the Civil War. Selling for about 10 cents each, they were short, highly exaggerated novels filled with lurid details and sensational action. Many focused on the American West and shaped the commonly held idea of frontier life. Two favorite series were about "Buffalo Bill" Cody (written by himself) and "Deadwood Dick" by Edward Wheeler.

For Americans growing up in the Industrial Age, pop lit provided simple lessons about how to get ahead in business and urban life. Horatio Alger wrote some 130 books on the theme of young boys' valiant struggles against poverty and temptation. Often they were rewarded with fame and riches (thus the term "rags to riches"). With titles like "Luck and Pluck," "Sink or Swim," "Work and Win," and "Struggling Upward," these novels told of poor youngsters who made their ways to the top through hard work, thrift, honesty, and luck. The luck often involved catching the boss's eye by rescuing his daughter from a runaway carriage, their falling in love, and his being promoted.

Writing Consider the reasons why dime novels and rags-to-riches stories were so popular. What needs did they meet? What fantasies did they create? Identify a form of literature that is popular today. What need does it meet? What fantasies does it provide for readers? How is computer technology influencing popular literature? Would you classify electronic games of today as popular literature? Why, or why not? Prepare your answers to these questions in a report or visual presentation.

Additional Skills Practice

Mass transit is the efficient movement of large numbers of people using a minimum of resources (such as energy and raw materials). Railroads were an early form of mass transit. Research and report on the types of mass transit available in your town. Good sources include the school or public library, city hall, the chamber of commerce, and friends or neighbors that don't commute to work in private cars. Discuss both the advantages and disadvantages of using a mass transit system today. Consider all factors, including safety and scheduling delays.

CHAPTER 14

Society and Politics of Industrial America

Americans who had reached middle age by 1870 would see enormous changes take place during their lifetime. They had lived through a sweeping technological revolution. They saw gas lamps replace candles, to be replaced in turn by kerosene oil lamps, which would then give way to the incandescent light bulb. They took the steam-engine revolution in stride and saw the introduction of electric motors. Born into an agricultural society, they lived through an industrial revolution that altered the way millions of people made their living. They watched while the prospect of industrial jobs lured more people to American cities than ever before.

With urban living came more leisure time, at least for the middle and upper classes. And the way these people spent time away from work also changed dramatically, as Americans developed new sports and devised new forms of recreation. At the same time, neighborhoods filled up with immigrants who brought with them distinct languages, foods, and cultures.

▲ *Immigrants, such as these tenement dwellers, played a very important role in industrial America. They provided the labor on which much of American industry was built.*

Industrial Society

Americans of the 1870s could see what industrial growth meant for the future of their society by looking at their own towns and cities. A resident of Paterson, New Jersey, remembered his town in 1850 as "an up-country hamlet, chiefly noted for its fine waterfall and valuable waterpower." Twenty years later, Paterson was a booming industrial center. Thousands of workers were employed in the foundries and mills powered by the city's hydroelectric plants. These workers far outnumbered the middle-class merchants and craftspeople who had been the bulk of the city's earlier residents. The factories and mills also attracted Irish laborers, French and German silk workers, and English weavers. Nearly one-third of the city's 33,581 residents in 1870 were foreign-born. Local society was dominated by a new upper class of well-to-do manufacturers that included prospering ironworkers and mechanics. It was a different city from the Paterson of 1850, one more like the industrial cities of the future than the hamlets of the past.

How well did working-class people live in industrial America?

Why was the middle class better off than before?

How did the rich industrial class make itself so visible?

American Society Reshaped

In Paterson and in other communities across the United States, economic change altered the very structure of American society. In earlier times, most white Americans had thought of themselves as more or less equal. Even though substantial differences in wealth and social status did exist, most households were headed by landowning farmers or by craftspeople and merchants who made a modest living. In that mainly middle-class society, few were either very rich or very poor.

The explosive industrial growth of the middle decades of the nineteenth century shattered the feeling of social equality. A wide gap opened between the mass of **blue-collar workers**, who were generally industrial workers paid hourly or by the piece and who lived on the edge of poverty, and an upper class whose wealth had greatly increased. Wedged in between was a middle class that was also becoming more affluent. Wherever they fit into the social structure, Americans were becoming more aware of social class and of their own social status.

While class differences were more visible, white American society remained remarkably open and fluid. An unskilled male laborer had a good chance of working his way up to a better job as a machine operator during his working career. His son might even find work in an office as a salaried bank clerk or bookkeeper, dressing for work in shirts and ties, thus becoming a **white-collar worker**. By hard work and frugal living, a skilled worker might save enough money to buy a small shop or become a saloon keeper.

Of course, not everyone found it so easy to move in American society. African Americans and single women were more likely to find themselves trapped for life in unskilled, lower-paying jobs.

Expansion of the Working Class

The most visible social change taking place in industrial America was the rapid expansion of the blue-collar working class. Manual laborers converged on the cities to work in factories, on construction sites, and in the railroad yards or along the docks. Once there, they crowded into rented houses and apartment buildings called tenements, creating new working-class neighborhoods in the less desirable sections of the cities.

How well a working-class family lived depended on the number of its wage earners and the level of their skills. Generally, unskilled workers led hard and miserable lives. Wages of $1.25 a day, with no promise of a full day's work, placed decent housing out of reach. Talking of the stench that reeked from the overcrowded tenements of New York City, one

Except during times of economic crisis, most tenement dwellers were among the "working poor," meaning one or more members of the family were employed most of the time. The poor living conditions reflected in this photograph were more the result of low wages than of unemployment.

resident complained, "The privies [toilets] are full to overflowing, the flooring is all broken, to give the odors better ventilation."

Skilled laborers and their families fared better. A carpenter or weaver earned $3.00 a day, and this wage provided rent for a four-room house, plain but adequate clothing for a family of five, and inexpensive carpets on the floor. But seldom was enough money left over for savings or for insurance payments to help in cases of accidental death. Among the laborers in Troy, New York, only the skilled ironworkers were able to save enough to own their own homes.

Living so close to the edge of poverty prompted many families to put their children to work in the mills and factories at as early an age as possible. A child's income might make the difference between barely getting by and a somewhat comfortable existence.

The Affluent Middle Class

Economic growth also swelled the ranks of the middle class. The lawyers, bankers, merchants, and other self-employed people of the old middle class shared in the prosperity that railroads and new industries brought to their towns and cities. Weavers, shoemakers, and other craftspeople were forced down into the working class as mechanization made their skills obsolete. New middle-class occupations had emerged by the end of the century, including salaried office workers, accountants, office managers, and corporate executives. They soon overshadowed the merchants and tradespeople in numbers as well as in their impact on American social life.

Taking great pride in the progress of American industry, this new middle class consumed as many products as its growing affluence could afford. These new white-collar workers set the tone and the style of living for much of middle-class America. They bought ready-made clothes, purchased food in tin cans, and filled their houses with the heavy, mass-produced furniture so popular in that period. The rapid expansion of the public school system and the passage by 1900 of compulsory school-attendance laws in most states reflected the commitment of middle-class Americans to education. They read books and subscribed to newspapers and magazines in numbers unheard of at any time before. Much of the reading was done by women. The rising in-

▶ *Economic growth created new white-collar jobs. How did white-collar office workers such as these set new standards for middle-class living?*

comes of middle-class families freed women from the need to work outside the home.

Within the homes of middle-class Americans, the roles of men and women became increasingly distinct. Many people viewed the earning of an income as solely the man's responsibility. A woman's highest calling, they argued, was to provide an orderly and comfortable home. Hers was the inside world of the home, sheltered from the harsher outside world where men worked. As one writer summed it up in the *Ladies' Home Journal* in 1893, "Every man knows as well as I do that this outside world, the business world, is a long scene of jostle and contention.... Oh, my good woman, thank God you have a home, and that in it you may be queen." Raising the children, directing the servants, and keeping the home organized as a soothing refuge for her husband were thought to be the middle-class woman's proper role.

The Rich Grow Richer

At the top of American society were the wealthy families of the new industrial elite. These

▲ *As middle-class families prospered, they moved to newer neighborhoods and built two-story houses like this one. How did middle-class Americans help redefine the role of women?*

were the people who controlled the railroad, steel, and manufacturing empires of industrial America. Their wealth and power even overshadowed that of the old upper-class families who had made their fortunes in shipping or real estate before the Civil War. Although these newly rich families represented only a small percentage of the total population, they made up an expanding and increasingly visible class in American society.

Jacob Riis's New York City

I n 1870, a 21-year-old Danish immigrant arrived in New York City. His name was **Jacob Riis**. For seven years, he drifted from one low-wage job to another, ending up penniless and homeless in New York City's worst slum. Riis finally landed steady work as police reporter for the *New York Tribune*. Hanging out at police stations, he reported on crime, greedy landlords, and accidents in the slum neighborhoods which he knew so well.

Realizing that words alone did not do justice to the human misery and degradation that he saw, Riis bought a camera. He rigged it with a flash device that burned magnesium powder so he could take pictures indoors and at night. Armed with this camera, he became America's first photojournalist.

In 1889, Riis published an article in *Scribner's* magazine entitled "How the Other Half Lives," which included 19 photographs of New York City slums. The next year he expanded this into a book with the same title. It was an illustrated documentary of the miserable conditions in New York's tenement district. Technically, his pictures—often blurred and overexposed—left much to be desired. "I came to take up photographing . . . not exactly as a pastime, . . ." he later wrote. "I had use for it, and

▲ *Jacob Riis was America's first photojournalist.*

▲ *How do you think the readers of Riis's books and articles reacted to his photographs?*

beyond that I never went. I'm downright sorry to confess here that I'm no good at all as a photographer." Nevertheless, the pictures had a jarring impact on his readers. His photographs of tenement children in soiled, tattered clothing were impossible to forget. As a reviewer in the *Nation* wrote, "his aim is to let you know the worst. . . . He allows us to see that there is another side." The book, a less friendly critic pointed out, had a "roughness amounting almost to brutality." *How the Other Half Lives* shocked New Yorkers into an awareness of the misery of slum life as nothing had before.

Riis published seven books documenting the poverty of New York's slum neighborhoods. Retiring from journalism in 1901, he spent the next 13 years on the lecture circuit, showing his pictures to

civic groups and public audiences. By the time Riis died in 1914, his body of work had helped inspire Theodore Roosevelt and a generation of reformers to attend to the problems of the slums.

1. Explain what prompted Jacob Riis to become America's first photojournalist.
2. Relate the importance of Jacob Riis's work in changing conditions in slum areas.

▲ *The room shown above is from the New York mansion of William K. Vanderbilt. The newly rich believed in conspicuous consumption, or the public show of great wealth.*

Their visibility resulted partly from the extravagant manner in which some of the newly rich spent their money. They built costly mansions and spent lavishly on fashionable clothing. One critic of the showy display of well-to-do women of the time placed much of the blame on their indulgent husbands. "The more recklessly money is lavished, the more they exult over the fact. 'You will find my wife a smart woman,' said a husband glorifying himself and his better half, 'quite an elegant lady. These 16 boxes are her luggage. She spent in Europe $30,000 on dress.' " It was an age of conspicuous spending.

SECTION 1 REVIEW

1. **Identify** ways that industrial growth altered the social structure of industrial America.
2. **Name** one difference between blue-collar and white-collar workers.
3. **Describe** the kind of housing in which working-class Americans lived.
4. **Generalize** briefly about the accepted role of middle-class women at this time.
5. **Describe** ways the newly rich called attention to themselves.

Immigration and Social Change

The arrival of an immigrant ship produced much the same scene in every port city from Boston to New Orleans. Long lines of immigrants with ragged bundles and children in tow filed past the checkpoints of the immigration authorities. Only those who were in good health and who were sound of mind were admitted; the others were either hospitalized or refused entrance. Those admitted soon walked out into the bustling streets of the promised land. "Here they found themselves in the chaotic confusion of this million-peopled city," wrote one observer in New York, "not knowing whither to betake themselves, and bewildered by cries of 'Cheap hacks!' 'All aboard!' 'Come to the cheapest house in all the world!' and invitations of a similar description." With such greetings were they welcomed to America by the notorious immigrant runners. These were the agents of cheap hotels, hustlers selling railroad or steamship tickets, and thieves looking for an unwatched satchel or trunk who met each immigrant ship at the wharf. The wonder is not that so many immigrants arrived here during the nineteenth century, but that so many survived their first day in an American city with their possessions intact.

From what countries did immigrants come?
What impact did immigrant voters have on city politics?
How did ethnic diversity lead to increased social tensions in American society?

Immigrants Pour into the United States

With the end of the Civil War, immigrants again flooded into the United States. During the years

▲ *This 1868 lithograph shows a characteristic scene at Castle Garden, New York City's center for receiving immigrants before Ellis Island was opened. Here, the immigrants are being welcomed to America by runners and thieves, as well as family and friends.*

from 1870 to 1900, 12 million immigrants arrived, more foreign-born people than had settled in this country during the preceding 70 years. Most of the newcomers during the 1870s and 1880s came from Germany, Ireland, and England, which were also the principal sources of immigration prior to the Civil War. By the 1890s, increasing numbers arrived from Italy, eastern Europe, Russia, Scandinavia, and French Canada. Immigrants truly came from all corners of the earth—Iceland, the West Indies, Mexico, Turkey, China, and Japan. Although most immigrants came to settle permanently in the United States, many worked for a few years and returned home with their savings. The majority of Chinese immigrants, for example, were single men who later returned to China. For every 100 Italians who arrived between 1892 and 1896, 43 returned to Italy. Although the farmlands of the West attracted some immigrant groups in large numbers, especially the Germans and Scandinavians, a much larger number settled in the growing industrial cities.

▼ *Since the 1840s, most immigrants from Europe had come from Great Britain and Germany. Which other European countries were contributing significant numbers of immigrants toward the end of the nineteenth century?*

Immigration, by Region of Origin, 1870–1900

Region of Origin	Number of Immigrants
Germany	2,794,809
Great Britain	1,731,245
Ireland	1,538,145
Central Europe (including Poland)	1,181,563
Southern Europe	1,086,511
Scandinavia	1,036,626
Canada and Newfoundland	798,251
Eastern Europe and Russia	783,541
Northwest Europe	446,868
China	215,451
West Indies	77,741
Japan	28,408
Mexico*	8,112

*Data not available for 1886 to 1893.

Source: U.S. Department of Commerce, Bureau of the Census.

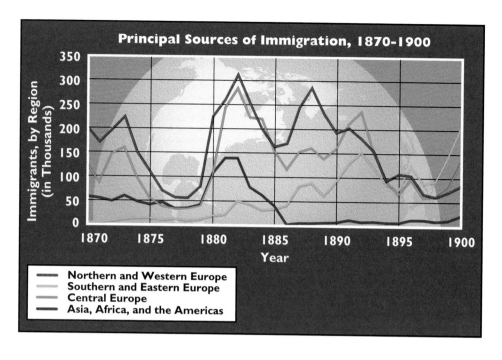

► *Immigrants came to the United States primarily to find work. What effect did the depressions in 1873 and 1893 have on immigration to the United States?*

Principal Sources of Immigration, 1870–1900

Immigrants, by Region (in Thousands)

Year

— Northern and Western Europe
— Southern and Eastern Europe
— Central Europe
— Asia, Africa, and the Americas

Immigrant communities, in both rural and urban settings, were held together by a network of social institutions. Churches provided religious services in the immigrants' native languages. The foreign-language press that flourished during the nineteenth century kept the newcomers informed about local and national news. In many cities, immigrants formed mutual-aid societies, such as the Polish National Alliance or the Order of Sons of Italy. These institutions helped immigrants during times of need. Banks were founded that catered to particular ethnic groups. They reassured immigrants that their savings were safe and loaned them money when they needed help. The New York Hebrew Free Loan Society made interest-free loans from $10 to $200. These and other institutions helped the immigrants adjust to American life and allowed them to maintain cultural links to the Old World.

Immigrants and City Politics

Immigrants had a large impact on urban politics after the Civil War, as the ethnic vote became increasingly important in city elections. Party politicians, especially Democrats, encouraged the immigrants to apply for citizenship so that they could gain the right to vote. In return for the immigrants' votes, the politicians helped them find jobs or provided aid during hard times with baskets of food and buckets of coal. In time, immigrant names also began to appear on party tickets at election time. In 1880, New York City elected its first Irish Catholic mayor, William R. Grace. Four years later, an Irish politician, Hugh O'Brien, became mayor of Boston. City politics provided ways for many immigrants to get ahead in society.

Within this system of ethnic politics, the **ward boss**, or local party leader played a highly visible role. It was his job to see that the majority of voters in his ward (neighborhood) or city voted for the party's candidates. He increased the chances that this would happen by doing favors for the voters. For Christmas of 1897, a ward leader in Chicago handed out six tons of turkeys—one to every family in his voting district. With influence at City Hall, ward bosses could also put in a good word with a judge if a potential voter got into trouble with the law. As Martin Lomasny, a ward boss in Boston, explained, "I think that there's got to be in every ward somebody that any bloke can come to—no matter what he's done—and get help. Help, you understand, none of your law and justice, but help." The boss system made big-city government more personal and probably more humane.

This system was also a source of corruption, as needy immigrants were not the only ones who came to the boss for help. Gamblers and prostitutes made payments to the local ward boss, who protected their illegal activities by bribing the police. Contractors found that "gifts" to the local party leader helped them get work from the city. **William Marcy Tweed** ran **Tammany Hall**, the Democratic party organization in New York City. Tweed allowed city contractors to pad their bills if they would hand over to him part of the amount added to the bill. This was known as a kickback. The notorious Tweed Ring, as the boss and his corrupt associates at City Hall were known, was finally exposed. Boss Tweed was sent to jail in 1871, after costing the taxpayers of the city millions of dollars. While reform movements led by taxpayers sometimes succeeded in rooting out corrupt politicians, much of the corruption of the era escaped public notice.

▼ *Boss Tweed gave $50,000 to the poor of his ward. What does cartoonist Thomas Nast suggest was the source of Tweed's money?*

TWEEDLEDEE AND SWEEDLEDUM
(*A new Christmas Pantomime at the Tammany Hall.*)
Clown (to Pantaloon). "Let's Blind them with *this*, and then take *some more.*"

Ethnic Diversity Produces Social Tensions

The mounting tide of immigration after the Civil War brought fundamental changes to American society. No longer could it be said, as John Jay had a century before, that Americans were "one united people—a people descended from the same ancestors, speaking the same language, professing the same religion, attached to the same principles of government, very similar in their manners and customs." The increasing numbers of Catholics, Russian and East European Jews, and non-English speakers making new homes in the United States shattered this basic cultural unity beyond repair. The result was a society diverse in its beliefs and values, conscious of its separate ethnic identities, and deeply divided.

Religion figured largely in the identity of ethnic groups and was a major factor in the growing ethnic tensions of the period. The Irish were targets of discrimination primarily because they were Catholics. Their arrival in large numbers activated American Protestants' long-standing fear and hatred of Catholicism. It culminated in the United States in the 1890s with the growth of the American Protective Association, an anti-Catholic organization that called for an end to immigration. The secret oath that members took included: "I do most solemnly promise and swear . . . that I will use my influence to promote the interest of all Protestants everywhere in the world that I may be; that I will not employ a Roman Catholic in any capacity, if I can procure the services of a Protestant."

With increased Jewish immigration by the end of the century, a wave of prejudice and discrimination against Jewish people, known as **anti-Semitism,** swept the eastern United States. Even successful Jewish businessmen found themselves excluded from New York's fashionable clubs.

Of all the recent immigrants, the Chinese were the most vulnerable. Attracted initially by the California gold rush, Chinese immigrants arrived in large numbers during the 1850s. They worked as agricultural laborers, on railroad construction crews,

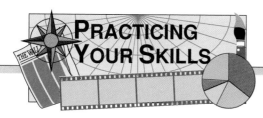

Understanding Mean, Median, and Mode

Historians often use historical data or statistics to help formulate theories or make inferences about why things happened. Because of the difficulty of working with large amounts of data, one of three figures is often used to represent the data. These figures are the *mean*, the *median*, and the *mode*.

The mean is the average of a series of items. It is found by adding up the items and then dividing by the number of items added. For example, if over the course of four days' work you earned $25.00, $18.50, $26.00, and $19.50, your mean (average) earnings for the four days would be: $25.00 + $18.50 + $26.00 + $19.50 = $89.00 ÷ 4 = $22.25.

The median is the midpoint in any series of numbers arranged in order. In the number list 5, 42, 57, 58, and 62, the median is 57. Note that the median number 57 is much closer to most of the numbers in the list than the mean of those same numbers (44.8). The median is used when there is a possibility of unusually low or high data points that would skew the average. (In a list with an even number of ordered numerals, the median is halfway between the middle two numbers. For instance, the median in the list 4, 7, 7, 9, 10, and 11 is 8.)

The mode is the most frequently occurring number in a list. In the set {6, 12, 11, 6, 5, 6, 3, and 6} the mode is 6. The mode is often used when a choice, or decision, among distinct options must be made.

Examine the graph on page 467, and answer the following questions:

1. What is the title of this graph? What is its source?

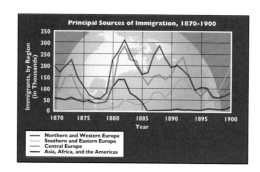

2. (a) What does the horizontal axis represent? (b) What is the beginning year? (c) What is the last year? (d) What does the vertical axis represent? (e) What is the lowest number on the axis? (f) What is the highest?

3. List the years of highest and lowest immigration for these groups: (a) northern and western Europe; (b) southern and eastern Europe; (c) Asia, Africa, and the Americas.

4. (a) In what years was immigration from northern and western Europe and from southern and eastern Europe the same? (b) In what year was it the same for southern and eastern Europe and for Asia, Africa, and the Americas? (c) What was the total immigration of all groups into the United States in 1900?

5. List the data points for immigrants from Asia, Africa, and the Americas for 1870, 1880, 1890, and 1900. Determine the mean, the median, and the mode. Which figure do you think presents the most accurate picture of actual immigration?

6. From your reading in the text and class discussion, what caused the dramatic drop in immigration from Asia, Africa, and the Americas after 1882? What economic conditions in the United States caused the drop in all immigration in the mid- 1870s and early 1890s?

▲ *The Chinese family above celebrated a wedding in their new hometown of Idaho City, Idaho. Why did Chinese immigration virtually stop in 1882?*

SECTION 2 REVIEW

1. **Name** the countries that sent the most immigrants to the United States between 1870 and 1900.
2. **Name** new social institutions that developed in the immigrant communities to assist the newcomers during times of need.
3. **Identify** Boss Tweed.
4. **Describe** briefly the impact of immigration on city politics.
5. **Explain** why ethnic differences increased social tensions.

and in low-paying industrial jobs. With the onset of hard times in the 1870s, unemployed European Americans began to compete for the jobs traditionally reserved for the Chinese. Racial hatred enflamed by economic competition led to anti-Chinese riots, the exclusion of Chinese children from San Francisco's schools, and pressure by California's congressional delegation for federal legislation to end Chinese immigration. The result was the Chinese Exclusion Act of 1882, which virtually ended Chinese immigration to the United States for nearly a century.

While large-scale immigration created social tensions, it also produced a new kind of society in the United States. During the post–Civil War era, American society emerged as the first truly multicultural society of modern times. By opening the door to immigrants, the United States tapped the creative resources of Europe, Latin America, and, for a time, Asia. This would soon pay dividends far beyond those paid to American industries where the newcomers found their first jobs. The newcomers made major contributions to science and brought a new vitality to the theater and the arts. They helped transform American society and culture, demonstrating that diversity, as well as unity, is a source of national strength.

SECTION 3

The Continued Growth of Cities

A steady stream of people attracted by jobs and by the advantages of city life poured into industrial cities and factory towns from farms and settlements in the countryside. "We cannot all live in cities, yet nearly all seem determined to do so," wrote Horace Greeley. " 'Hot and cold water,' 'bakers' bread, gas, the theater, and the streetcars ...indicate the tendency of modern taste. Away behind these is the country." Between 1880 and 1890, almost 40 percent of the townships in the United States lost population because of migration from the country and smaller towns to the cities. The factory town of Lowell, Massachusetts, grew from a town of 6,000 in 1830 into a city of over 40,000 people 40 years later. By 1890, 26 American cities had a population of 100,000 or more, while New York City, Philadelphia, and Chicago each had over a million. The rural America of Abraham Lincoln's split-rail fences was rapidly becoming an industrial society of brick smokestacks and crowded city streets.

What immigrant groups found urban living attractive?
How did population growth change the structure and appearance of American cities?
What were the major problems of nineteenth-century urban life?

Growth of the Cities

The population of American cities swelled partly because of the increase in immigration. More than 80 percent of the Irish, Romanian, Turkish, and Russian Jewish immigrants settled in cities. Over 70 percent of the Greeks, Hungarians, and Italians did so. As a result, New York City had more Irish than Dublin, more Hungarians than Budapest, and more Jewish residents than any city in the world. Only two cities in Poland had a larger Polish population than Chicago, and only one city in Sweden had more Swedish people.

The immigrants settled where they did for various reasons. The impoverished Irish stayed in the port cities of Boston, New York, or New Orleans

▼ *This busy street market was located on New York City's lower East Side, where many immigrants lived. Judging from this photograph, what do you think was one of the major urban problems of this period?*

because they could not afford to go further inland. Germans headed for Cincinnati, St. Louis, and Milwaukee because these were centers of previous German settlement in the farm country of the Midwest. Italian and Polish immigrants went to Buffalo or Chicago in large numbers because family and friends who had settled in these cities earlier to work in mills and factories helped them find work.

In the cities, the immigrants created a new ethnic geography. Streets and sometimes entire neighborhoods were settled by one ethnic group or another. **Jane Addams**, a noted reformer and social worker, described the inner city of Chicago in this way:

> Between Halsted Street and the river live about 10,000 Italians, Neapolitans, Sicilians, and Calabrians. . . . To the South on Twelfth Street are many Germans, and the side streets are given over almost entirely to Polish and Russian Jews. . . . To the north-west are many Canadians . . . and to the north are many Irish.

Much the same ethnic pattern developed across the country, as Chinatowns and Little Italys emerged in nearly every large American city.

The City Skyline

The explosion in the urban population during the nineteenth century changed the size and shape of American cities. Places that had once been small, compact cities grew outward. They encompassed dozens of square miles of urban settlement. As streetcar lines reached into the countryside, rural areas and neighboring towns were drawn into the orbit of the city and speedily joined to it. New York City added nearly a million people in the year 1898 by bringing Brooklyn, Queens, and part of Staten Island into a city of 3 million people.

The visual appearance of cities also changed. Skylines, once dominated by the spires of churches, became studded with smokestacks, bridge towers, and, by the end of the century, the first skyscrapers.

The skyline of New York City was dramatically altered by the building of the Brooklyn Bridge, one of the engineering marvels of the century. It was designed by John Roebling, who was fatally injured

The Brooklyn Bridge—over the East River between New York City and Brooklyn—was completed in 1883. The bridge was one of the engineering marvels of its time. It was the tallest structure in New York City. Why do you think it was necessary to make the bridge so tall?

while supervising the construction. Completed by his son, Washington A. Roebling, the bridge was opened to traffic on May 25, 1883. The bridge spanned the East River and connected New York with the city of Brooklyn. It was the most magnificent suspension bridge of its time. Residents and visitors alike were astounded by its size and amazed by the feat of engineering that put the bridge in place. "The impression upon the visitor is one of astonishment that grows with every visit. No one who has been upon it can ever forget it," remarked Seth Low, the mayor of Brooklyn. Its majestic towers, which rose 276 feet above the river, dwarfed every other structure in the city. For half a century, the Brooklyn Bridge remained New York City's most unforgettable landmark.

▲ *A New York City streetcar motorman of the early 1900s is shown posed above. How did streetcars contribute to the expansion of American cities?*

Central Business Districts

Next to the towering bridges and factory smokestacks, the change that most impressed city residents of the post–Civil War era was the growth of the central business district. "Downtown" had always been a center for wholesaling and trade. It now became the city's vital core in almost every respect. Clusters of downtown banks developed into major financial districts. Retail stores multiplied, turning downtown into the city's major shopping centers as well. Although the largest factories were being built on the outskirts of town, most manufacturing took place in small workshops located in inner-city warehouses and workshops. The downtown area was alive with activity, as laborers, bankers, store clerks, white-collar workers, shoppers, and visitors converged there each day.

The poet Walt Whitman marveled at the "rush of these great cities, the . . . lofty new buildings, facades of marble and iron, . . . the flags flying, the

► *The population of both urban and rural areas increased during this period. Which of the two areas had the more rapid rate of increase? Why did that part of the population grow more rapidly than the other?*

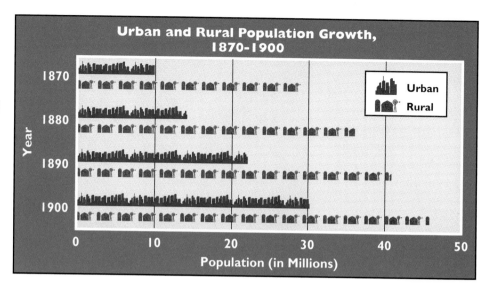

Urban and Rural Population Growth, 1870-1900

Urban
Rural

Year

1870
1880
1890
1900

Population (in Millions)

0   10   20   30   40   50

endless ships, the tumultuous streets, Broadway, the heavy, low, musical roar, hardly ever intermitted [interrupted], even at night." During a visit to New York City in 1867, Mark Twain noted, "There is something in this ceaseless buzz, and hurry, and bustle, that keeps a stranger in a state of unwholesome excitement all the time." Such was the throbbing life of the central business district of cities in the industrial era.

The principal magnet that attracted shoppers of that era to the downtown area was the department store. Combining several specialty shops—or departments—under one roof, it was the most important retailing invention of the century. Department stores rose four and five stories tall. They had painted cast-iron facades, and were listed in guidebooks as places to visit and things to see. Department stores like Macy's in New York, Marshall Field and Company in Chicago, and Wanamaker's in Philadelphia never ceased to amaze visitors who shopped there for the first time. "Forty-nine counters are here arranged, all loaded with garments—coats enough . . . to dress an empire," exclaimed a visitor to Wanamaker's third floor. Department stores were

▲ *This sketch shows bargain day in a busy dry goods store in 1889.*

the bargain or discount stores of their day, as their large volume of business permitted them to keep prices low. They attracted shoppers from every part of the city.

Problems Brought by Growth

While cities of the post–Civil War era were vital places, they also suffered a variety of ills. For urban dwellers of that time, the most serious problems were crowding and congestion. The narrow downtown streets had been laid out when the city was much smaller. The expansion of the central business district clogged the narrow streets with traffic. Getting around town became both difficult and dangerous. A New York journalist described the streets of that city as filled with "hacks, carts, and omnibuses choking the thoroughfares, their . . . drivers dashing through the crowd furiously, reckless of life; women and children . . . knocked down and trampled upon, and the ruffians drove on uncaught."

The Great Chicago Fire of 1871 swept through parts of the city, leaving almost 100,000 people homeless and causing millions of dollars in damage. Why were fires a major hazard in nineteenth-century cities?

It was difficult for most city residents to escape the continuous pressure of people, even at home, as housing was also overcrowded. It is not surprising that the more wealthy class fled to spacious homes uptown or to outlying areas as quickly as they could afford them.

Cheap wooden construction of buildings in the inner cities made devastating fires all too common. On October 8 and 9, 1871, a fire that supposedly started in a stable owned by Patrick O'Leary burned much of Chicago to the ground. The *Chicago Evening Post* quoted one of the city's unknown poets:

> One dark night,—when people were in bed,
> Old Mrs. O'Leary lit a lantern in her shed;
> The cow kicked it over, winked its eye, and said,
> "There'll be a hot time in the old town tonight."

The Chicago fire destroyed 17,500 buildings and laid waste to four square miles of the inner city. It was one of several great fires of the nineteenth century. Only a year later, a fire in Boston consumed 65 acres of buildings in that city. Fires continued to be a menace throughout most cities.

Disease posed other threats to city dwellers. Cholera and scarlet fever epidemics ravaged the cities during the middle decades of the century.

These problems mostly stemmed from the outdoor privies and open sewers that also gave big cities their characteristic smell. "The river stinks. The air stinks. People's clothing permeated by the foul atmosphere stinks," noted the *Chicago Times*, commenting on that city's smell in 1880. The unsanitary conditions that polluted the air also bred disease-carrying mosquitoes and made city drinking water impure. Until these conditions were improved around the turn of the century, cities remained unhealthy places in which to live.

SECTION 3 REVIEW

1. **Outline** the main reasons immigrants were attracted to American cities.
2. **Describe** briefly how the visual appearance of American cities changed during the nineteenth century.
3. **Name** some of the economic activities of the central business districts of American cities.
4. **Explain** why large fires were common in inner cities.
5. **Identify** some major problems of living in a large city in the 1880s.

▲ *By the 1800s, baseball in America had become a professional sport.*

SECTION 4

Industrial Society at Leisure

During the decades following the Civil War, people found new ways to spend leisure time. Some even had more leisure time to spend, as the ten-hour work day replaced the twelve-hour work day for white-collar employees. To devote more time to recreation, many Americans had to overcome their own Victorian attitudes toward play as time wasted. The easiest solution was to combine recreation with self-improvement, especially physical fitness. One result was the physical culture movement that swept the United States in the 1880s. Women, as well as men, embraced the physical fitness movement. Anne MacDonald of Rochester, New York, noted in her diary in 1885 that she and her friend Daisy were going to a "Methodist social where they are to swing clubs." Indian clubs—wooden clubs shaped like bowling pins—were especially popular among women. Anne and Daisy attended three other church meetings that month, where they put on performances with Indian clubs. MacDonald also regularly used a local gymnasium, as did thousands of Americans during the 1880s. The nation was caught up in its first physical fitness fad.

Why did baseball become a popular pastime?
Why did young Americans find bicycling so attractive?
How did Americans who were not sports lovers keep themselves entertained?

New Forms of Recreation

During the postwar years, baseball emerged as a popular sport. Based on an old English game called rounders, modern baseball was created in the 1840s as a sport played by members of well-to-do private clubs. New York City's Knickerbocker Base Ball Club wrote the basic rules for the game. The public became interested in the sport as clubs from various cities began to play against one another. The expanding railroad network made intercity play with regularly scheduled games possible. Requiring little in the way of special equipment or clothing, the game caught on quickly. By the end of the century, baseball was played by young men in ballparks and vacant lots in towns and cities across the nation.

Baseball became a professional sport during these years as players began to accept money to play for ball clubs. As cities competed to field the best team, competition for the best players increased. Boss Tweed, an ardent baseball fan, attracted good players to New York City by putting them on the city payroll. From 1869 to 1871, Tweed's fondness for the game cost New York's taxpayers an estimated $30,000. In 1869, Cincinnati dropped all pretense that big-time baseball was an amateur sport. That year, Cincinnati organized the first professional team, the Red Stockings. The players received a salary, and the fans paid an admission fee to watch them play. Other cities soon did the same, and the modern era of professional baseball was under way.

Baseball became big business. Owners of teams spent large sums of money on salaries and new ballparks. To protect their investments, the team owners in 1876 organized the National League of Professional Baseball Clubs. By organizing, the owners could limit the number of professional clubs and better control the salaries paid to their players. The National League was joined in 1899 by the American League. This led in 1903 to championship contests between the two leagues which were called the World Series.

Other new sports and recreational activities became popular during the postwar years. Among them was croquet, a French game brought to the United States by way of England. It was a lawn game played by knocking balls through semicircular wickets with wooden mallets. As one of the few sports in which men and women could compete against one another, it was an instant success in the United States. Virtually every middle-class family had its croquet set. Roller-skating, brought over from England in the 1870s, also became popular with both men and women. By the end of the century, nearly every town had a roller-skating rink. Boxing, football, ice hockey, and golf were other sports gaining popularity during this era.

The Bicycle Craze

In the 1890s, the bicycling fad swept the United States. The French velocipede, an early form of the bicycle, was introduced into this country in the 1860s. It had two wheels and a seat but no pedals. It did not catch on. The high-wheeler bicycle, introduced from Britain and first displayed at the 1876 Centennial Exhibition in Philadelphia, did somewhat better. It appealed especially to daring young men who often wore handlebar mustaches and who enjoyed the "strenuous life."

▼ *Croquet was a popular pastime in the 1870s because it was one of the few sports in which men and women could compete fairly.*

▶

How did the new safety bicycle advertised at right change the sport of cycling?

The bicycle that finally put masses of Americans on wheels was the safety bicycle, which was invented in 1884 by a British machinist. Patented in the United States in 1887 by A. H. Overman of Chicopee, Massachusetts, it had two wheels of the same size, a diamond-shaped frame, and pedals with a chain drive. By the end of the century, this machine, equipped with air-filled tires and a coaster brake, provided the model for the modern bicycle. The safety bicycle became immensely popular, as it could easily be ridden by women as well as by men. (The high-wheeler was too difficult to mount by women wearing dresses.)

The bicycle had a significant impact on American society. It provided a new sense of freedom and mobility for the young generation. They no longer had to depend on streetcars or their parents' horse-drawn carriages. Bicycling brought a new look to the wardrobe of the young American woman, adding lighter-weight sports clothes and shorter skirts that would not get caught in the chain. The bicycle also created a new category of sports heroes—the professional bike racers. Among the

▼ *Although Marshall "Major" Taylor was named the United States National Champion bicycle racer in 1891, he was barred from competing in future league events because of his race. He later became the first African American athlete in any sport to win a world professional championship.*

best-known racers of the 1890s was Marshall Taylor, an African American athlete. Taylor once earned $875 in a single day of racing—the equivalent of a year's wages for a blue-collar worker.

The bicycle fad subsided after the turn of the century, but lasted long enough to give Americans a taste for mobility. This hunger would be fed in 1909 by Henry Ford's Model T.

Time to Read

Increased leisure time also gave Americans more time to read. The most popular books of the postwar era were romantic novels about characters and times far removed from the harsh realities of industrial society. **Louisa May Alcott's** *Little Women* (1868–1869), a novel about four young women and their middle-class family, eventually sold more than 2 million copies. So did General Lew Wallace's *Ben-Hur* (1880), a novel set in the Roman Empire at the time of Christ. Zane Grey's novels about the American West and Edgar Rice Burrough's Tarzan tales also reached a wide audience. Boys read ten-cent thrillers called dime novels, which featured real and fictitious heroes such as Buffalo Bill Cody and Deadwood Dick.

More serious readers chose Mark Twain or the novels of William Dean Howells or Henry James. **Mark Twain**, the pen name of Samuel L. Clemens, poked fun at the hypocrisy of small-town America in *Huckleberry Finn* (1884), one of the classic works of American fiction. Both that novel and his earlier book, *Tom Sawyer* (1876), were widely read. Howells and James wrote realistic novels that appealed to a more limited audience. Breaking from the tradition of romantic fiction, Howells and James wrote novels that portrayed real-life, naturalistic situations. Howells explored the greed of American businessmen and the plight of industrial workers in *A Hazard of New Fortunes* (1890). In *The Bostonians* (1886) and other novels, James portrayed the lives of upper-class Americans, often Americans living in Europe.

This generation of Americans also kept itself informed through newspapers and magazines. More than 2,000 daily newspapers were being published in 1900, with a total circulation of over 15 million

Mark Twain's America

You don't know about me without you have read a book by the name of *The Adventures of Tom Sawyer*; but that ain't no matter. That book was made by Mr. Mark Twain, and he told the truth, mainly. There was things which he stretched, but mainly he told the truth.

T his frank opinion expressed by the young hero Tom Sawyer about his creator's honesty has probably been read by more young—and old—people than any other critique.

In his fiction and other writings, Mark Twain, as Samuel Langhorne Clemens was best known, left a record of life in America that is unmatched in its breadth in nineteenth-century writing. He wrote about a wide assortment of characters, nearly all of whom he had met in real life. Few other writers of his time had experienced as broad a sweep of American society. Born in 1835, he grew up in Hannibal, Missouri, a small town on the Mississippi River. It was town, farm, frontier, and border-state slave society all woven together. *Tom Sawyer* (1876) and *Huckleberry Finn* (1884), his two most important novels, captured the flavor of this segment of American life.

Although a midwestern village, Hannibal was no backwater. It was a Mississippi River town exposed to the varied human traffic of the nation's greatest waterway. As a young man, Mark Twain became a steamboat pilot on the Mississippi. The river introduced him to many different kinds of people. He described riverboat society and the scenery of the Mississippi in *Life on the Mississippi* (1883). He later said that in all of his travels, he never met anyone whose type he had not first encountered on the river. (He took his pen name from the expression *mark twain*, "by the mark two fathoms," used by riverboat pilots in measuring the depth of the river.)

Although he liked the profession of steamboat pilot, Mark Twain gave it up in 1861 to accompany his brother to the Nevada Territory. Twain spent the next five years absorbing the life of mining camps and the boomtown metropolis of San Francisco. He

◄ *Samuel Langhorne Clemens wrote under the pen name Mark Twain. He was the most widely read American humorist of his time.*

wrote about these backgrounds of American life in his first book, *The Celebrated Jumping Frog and Other Sketches* (1867), and in *Roughing It* (1872).

He left San Francisco in 1866 to travel to Europe with a group of American tourists, a trip that he recorded in *The Innocents Abroad* (1869). When he returned home, Twain divided his time among work as a newspaper editor, journalist, and lecturer. Each role brought him into contact with different facets of life in post–Civil War America. As a journalist in Washington, D.C., he observed firsthand the corruption of national politics. That experience became the basis for *The Gilded Age* (1873), a novel that he coauthored with Charles Dudley Warner. Twain spent much of his time lecturing in towns and cities throughout the United States, entertaining audiences with his dry humor.

1. Explain the importance of Hannibal, Missouri, to Twain's writings.
2. Create a list of the different occupations Twain held during his life. How do you think they aided him in his writing?

Popular literature of this period included novels about the adventures of William F. "Buffalo Bill" Cody, famous for his Wild West shows.

▲ *Saddles similar to this one used by Buffalo Bill were marketed in the 1880s with his endorsement.*

pany with that of James A. Bailey in 1881, the great Barnum and Bailey Circus toured the nation each summer. The traveling circuses brought their highly popular acts to hundreds of thousands of Americans.

The American theater also prospered during these years. In the cities, local acting companies offered a wide variety of theatrical fare. Most popular at the end of the Civil War were **melodramas** (always featuring a villain, an endangered heroine, and a hero), minstrel shows in which white comedians performed in blackface, and comedy routines. A more select audience watched such notable actors as Edwin Booth (brother of Lincoln's assassin, John Wilkes Booth) perform Shakespeare. They attended the works of European playwrights, such as Henrik Ibsen and Oscar Wilde. By the 1880s, a new form of popular theater had emerged called **vaudeville**, which consisted of variety shows that included comedy, song-and-dance, juggling, magic, and other acts. With the help of the railroads, advanced bookings, and traveling companies of professional actors, vaudeville reached a mass audience by the turn of the century.

copies. This represented slightly more than one newspaper per family. Newspapers brought political news, editorial comment, and news stories of general interest into virtually every American home. And with the news came advertisements for a wide range of consumer products. Large-circulation magazines, such as the *Ladies' Home Journal,* founded in 1883, flourished at this time. It gave useful advice to middle-class women about what they should wear and how they should furnish their homes.

► *Vaudeville comedy teams traveled with other performing acts to provide Americans with an early form of mass entertainment.*

Show Business

Professional entertainers reached a growing audience during the decades following the Civil War. Circus companies and theater troupes discovered the value of the railroad network in extending their reach beyond the major cities. In 1871, **Phineas T. Barnum**, one of the great showmen of his day, opened a three-ring circus, the "Greatest Show on Earth." The next year he converted his circus wagons into railroad cars. After the merger of his com-

1. **Describe** the role played by railroads in the development of professional sports and other forms of mass entertainment in the United States.
2. **List** the new sports and recreational activities that became popular in the United States after the Civil War.
3. **Explain** what impact the bicycle had on American society in the 1890s.
4. **Name** five American authors during the post–Civil War era.
5. **Identify** P.T. Barnum.

SECTION 5

Politics in Industrial America

In the presidential election of 1884, both parties pulled out all the stops. The Democrats praised the virtues of their candidate, **Grover Cleveland**, the governor of New York, and accused Republican candidate James G. Blaine of corrupt dealings with the railroads. The Republicans, in turn, defended Blaine, "the plumed knight from the state of Maine," and dug up a scandal in Cleveland's personal life involving his fathering a child out of wedlock.

That fall, there seemed to be no end to rallies, parades, marching bands, and political speeches. Banners and campaign buttons were everywhere. The election campaign was noted for mudslinging. However, Blaine angered many voters when he did not disavow a statement made by a fellow Republican that painted Democrats as lovers of "rum, Romanism, and rebellion." In November, Blaine was narrowly defeated, and Cleveland became the first Democrat to win the presidency since before the Civil War.

Why were political campaigns and elections such popular events?

Why were the two parties so evenly balanced?

What were the major differences between the two parties on economic issues?

The Great National Pastime

In nineteenth-century America, politics was the great national pastime. No sporting event generated as much popular enthusiasm as a presidential campaign. Politics was to Americans, one foreign observer noted, "what the theatre is to the French or the bull fight . . . to the Spanish." In fact, politics was one of the few forms of entertainment available to virtually every person in nineteenth-century America. Campaign parades and political "speakings" were more than political events. They were social and recreational occasions—the nation's first form of mass entertainment.

This intense interest in politics was reflected in a high voter turnout for elections. Normally, more than 80 percent of those eligible voted in local and national elections in the 1880s. (The turnout today is about 50 percent in most national elections.) The high turnout was partly the doing of the political parties. Party members worked hard to drum up enthusiasm and get out the vote. They did so because party victories were well rewarded. Success in a presidential election resulted in tens of thousands of well-paying government jobs becoming available to party workers. Under the spoils system, the winning party got to fill many of the nonelected public offices with its own people.

▶

President Andrew Jackson popularized the spoils system—the practice of rewarding campaign workers by appointing them to public office. Political cartoonist Thomas Nast criticized the abuses of the spoils system.

► President James A. Garfield was shot in a Washington, D.C., railroad station. How did his assassination help bring about civil service reform?

The spoils system came under attack during the 1870s. Its critics charged that it placed unqualified people in public office. They called for a professional **civil service** selected on the basis of competitive exams. Civil service reform had little success until 1881, when President James A. Garfield was assassinated by a disappointed office seeker. Garfield's death prompted Congress to enact a civil service reform law. In 1883, it passed the Pendleton Civil Service Act. This act, signed by **Chester Arthur**, Garfield's successor, required that some federal jobs be filled by competitive examinations, and it stated that officeholders could be removed only for good cause. Over the years more and more jobs were added to the civil service system, reducing the number of jobs that could be filled by party supporters.

Political Parties

The nearly even political balance between the two major parties in post–Civil War America also added excitement to elections, especially to presidential elections. Nationally, the voters were almost evenly divided between the Democratic and Republican Parties. Between 1877 and 1897, the Republicans captured the presidency for 12 years, the Democrats for eight. The Republicans were more successful than the Democrats in the electoral college, with wins in key states, but not once during those 20 years did they win a majority of the popular vote in a presidential election. Control of the national government was never certain for either party.

The Democrats made a quick political comeback after the Civil War. They regained control of the House of Representatives in 1874 and almost won the presidency two years later. In the presidential election of 1876, an election marred by fraud and corruption, Samuel J. Tilden, the Democratic candidate, lost to **Rutherford B. Hayes** by a single vote in the electoral college.

The Democrats did well at the polls, despite their party's identification in the public mind with the South and secession. They emphasized the party's commitment to limited government, individual initiative, and states' rights. In those days, the Democrats were opposed to active government, and this appealed to a large number of voters, including many in the North. The party also commanded the support of Irish immigrants, who associated the Republican Party with the nativist movements of the prewar era.

The Republican Party had strong support in the North, since this was the party that had saved the

Union. Its leaders did all that they could to identify the Republican Party with Union victory in the Civil War and to keep alive the public's fear of a solidly Democratic and disloyal South. "Our strong ground is the dread of a solid south, rebel rule, etc., etc.," Hayes wrote to a Republican Party leader in 1876. "I hope you will make these topics prominent in your speeches." Waving the bloody shirt, as this campaign strategy was called, won votes. However, the party could not rely forever on the fear of Democrats and fading memories of the Civil War.

Economic Issues Gain Importance

With the revival of Democratic strength in the 1870s, the Republicans looked for ways to broaden their support. James G. Blaine, a Republican leader in the Senate, urged party workers to focus on economic issues, especially the tariff. "Fold up the bloody shirt and lay it aside," he told a Republican campaign speaker in 1880. "It's of no use to us. You want to shift the main issue to [tariff] protection."

Blaine hoped that emphasizing the party's support for higher protective tariffs would give the Republicans a new winning issue.

The Republican Party tried to use the tariff issue to broaden its base of voter support. High tariffs had an obvious appeal to American manufacturers. Tariff duties on imported cloth, ironware, and other products made them cost more and made them less competitive in the American market. The Republicans also hoped to use the tariff issue to appeal to working-class voters. Protecting the domestic market for American-made products, they argued, produced more jobs and higher wages for American workers. The Republicans also appealed to the farm vote with the tariff issue, pointing out that prosperous industrial centers would consume more of the products of American farms. By hammering away on the tariff issue, Republican campaign speakers and newspaper editors tried to focus attention on their party's program for economic progress.

The Democrats responded to the tariff issue in the presidential election of 1888, launching the first full-scale debate over economic policy since the Civil War. In his annual message to Congress that

▼ *The period between 1865 and 1900 is sometimes referred to as the Gilded Age. During this time of rapid industrial expansion, great fortunes were made and displayed. Political campaigns were also showy and developed into the nation's first form of mass entertainment. During the Gilded Age, neither political party was dominant in New York or the states of the upper Midwest. How did this fact influence the parties' choices of presidential candidates?*

Presidents of the Gilded Age

Name	Party		Dates in Office	Home State
Ulysses S. Grant	Rep.		1869-1877	Illinois
Rutherford B. Hayes	Rep.		1877-1881	Ohio
James Garfield	Rep.		1881	Ohio
Chester A. Arthur	Rep.		1881-1885	New York
Grover Cleveland	Dem.		1885-1889 and 1893-1897	New York
Benjamin Harrison	Rep.		1889-1893	Indiana
William McKinley	Rep.		1897-1901	Ohio

year, President Cleveland declared that protective tariffs were the source of most of the nation's economic problems. During his campaign for reelection that fall, Cleveland and other Democratic leaders expanded on this theme. Tariffs, they argued, raised the price that consumers had to pay for many items they used every day and drove up the cost of living. The Democrats also pointed out that tariffs restricted competition. In 1888, the Democrats again nominated Cleveland as their presidential candidate. Although Cleveland lost the election in the electoral college to the Republican candidate, **Benjamin Harrison**, the Democrats had made a strong case for lower tariffs.

During Harrison's administration (1889–1893), the Republicans put their economic program into effect. The McKinley Tariff Act of 1890 raised tariffs higher than ever before. With majorities in both houses of Congress, they pushed through extensive economic legislation. Congress increased the amount of currency in circulation by issuing new paper money called treasury notes. The "Billion-Dollar Congress," as it became known, also voted millions of dollars in pensions for Civil War veterans. It spent millions more on river and harbor improvements, subsidies to steamship lines, and bonuses to government bond holders. The Republicans would lose control of Congress in 1890 and of the White House in 1892, but only briefly. Democratic candidate Grover Cleveland was reelected, the only U.S. president to serve two nonconsecutive terms. The Republicans regained control of both the presidency and the Congress in the election of 1896. By emphasizing economic issues and an active approach to government, the Republicans were building a coalition that would for the first time make their party the majority party in the United States.

SECTION 5 REVIEW

1. **Identify** the spoils system.
2. **Explain** how the spoils system contributed to high voter turnout in nineteenth-century elections.
3. **Explain** what the phrase *waving the bloody shirt* means.
4. **Contrast** Democratic and Republican positions on the tariff issue.
5. **Name** the major legislation passed by the Republican Party in the early 1890s.

Summary

Industrialization led to far-reaching social and economic changes in the United States. Class structure changed significantly. The ranks of the blue-collar working class expanded rapidly, as unskilled immigrants poured into industrial cities and factory towns. Industrial growth also created a new class of very wealthy Americans at the top of the social pyramid. A white-collar middle class emerged, composed of professional people who worked in or for the growing corporations. The new waves of immigration also made American society more ethnically diverse. And with diversity came an increase in ethnic tensions and social conflict. Industrialization involved significant social costs.

American cities grew rapidly. Both the size of cities and the percentage of the population living in towns and cities increased during these years. The growing downtown, or central business district, became the focus for much of the city's life.

Urban Americans found new forms of recreation to occupy their leisure time, including bicycling, baseball, the circus, the theater, and vaudeville. However, cities also had their problems. Congestion, fire, and disease made them unpleasant and sometimes dangerous places in which to live.

Politics continued to hold the interest of the American people. Election campaigns were social as well as political events. The political rewards made possible by the spoils system encouraged active party participation. The balance between the two parties also made elections exciting. However, during the 1880s, both parties began to focus more on economic issues.

Vocabulary

anti-Semitism
blue-collar worker
civil service
melodrama

vaudeville
ward boss
white-collar worker

Choose a term from the vocabulary list and write the term on your paper next to the number of the sentence that defines or explains it.

1. The "dastardly villain" is sure to get what he deserves.
2. He would need better working clothes now that he was salaried and working in an office.
3. There was no justification for the unfair treatment suffered by the recent Jewish immigrants.
4. If she could pass the written test given by the government, the job would be hers.
5. Fortunately for him, the coveralls protected his clothing and he would not have to buy a new shirt from his meager wages.
6. Vincent disliked the man, but needed his help. Without it, Vincent's brother might lose his job.
7. The troupe was a smash in Mobile, but the acts were not very popular in Hartford.

Review Questions

1. Explain how industrialization altered the structure of American society.
2. Describe how industrialization redefined the role of middle-class American women.
3. How had the sources of immigration to the United States changed by the 1890s?
4. How was immigration related to corruption in city government in the post–Civil War era?
5. How did industrialization alter the size and shape of American cities?
6. Describe the urban problems that resulted from the rapid growth of cities after the Civil War.
7. Why did baseball become such a popular sport in the United States?
8. What impact did the bicycle have on American society in the 1890s?
9. Why did such a large number of Americans participate in the political process during the late nineteenth century?
10. What important economic issue divided the major political parties in the 1890s?

Critical Historical Thinking

✐∿Writing Answer each of the following by writing one or more complete paragraphs:

1. While many Americans opposed immigration, others supported a nonrestrictive policy towards immigration. What classes or groups of Americans at this time might have supported open immigration? Why? Which groups would have opposed large numbers of immigrants? Why?
2. What factors do you think attracted immigrants to America? Do you think those factors still exist today?
3. People in the United States became better educated after the Civil War. How do you think the development of an industrial society may have contributed to this fact?
4. Read "Social Mobility and the Skilled Machinists" in the Unit 5 Archives. Explain why union official John Morrison felt as he did about the social status of machinists, amidst the tremendous growth of industrial America.

Making Connections with Art and Architecture

Many places and times are identified by their architectural symbols: the pyramids and Egypt, the Eiffel Tower and Paris, the Empire State Building and New York. The Brooklyn Bridge, connecting Brooklyn and Manhattan, is also such a symbol. When the Brooklyn Bridge opened on May 24, 1883, it was thought to be the grandest structure ever put together by human hands. The historian and critic Lewis Mumford once said of the Brooklyn Bridge, "if it isn't part of our life, if it doesn't add to the quality of our thought, it doesn't really exist." What he meant was that the bridge was more than a means to get from Brooklyn to Manhattan and back again. The Brooklyn Bridge stands as a symbol of human ingenuity and human artistry. The bridge, like the skyscraper, also stood for the industrial age

in America. It came to represent the spirit of an age of optimism and belief in the ability of science and technology to better human life. At least the middle class of America and many immigrants thought of the bridge and the technology it represented in such terms.

✐∿Writing Find an article on the Brooklyn Bridge in the *American Heritage* magazine in your library, or read from David McCullough's *The Great Bridge*. Make a report to the class on the difficulties of its construction.

✐∿Writing Read Hart Crane's poem "The Bridge" and look at a print of Frank Stella's "Brooklyn Bridge." Write an essay that discusses the role of the bridge in the imagination of American intellectuals in the 1920s.

Additional Skills Practice

1. Use the data below to create a line graph that shows the changes in the labor force in the listed occupations from 1890 to 1910.
2. Calculate the median and the mean for each category. Was the change over time an increase or decrease?
3. What trend does your line graph illustrate?

Year	Agriculture	Manufacturing
1890	51.0%	20.0%
1900	37.6%	24.8%
1910	31.4%	25.7%

Year	Mining	Trade	Other
1890	1.5%	7.0%	20.5%
1900	2.3%	10.3%	25.0%
1910	2.8%	14.2%	25.9%

A Time of Discontent

I ndustrial growth brought great benefits to the United States, but the resulting social and political changes it left in its wake also disturbed many Americans. The growing power of the railroads and other corporations alarmed some people. Others were concerned that all people had not shared equally in the blessings of industrial wealth. Farmers complained of falling crop prices that forced them deeper into debt. In-dustrial workers demanded higher wages and relief from long hours of labor. Countless Americans suffered from the recurring major economic slowdowns that went with industrial growth. During the 1890s, more people raised their voices in protest than ever before. That decade was a difficult time for industrial America, a time of trouble and of discontent.

◀ *Voters who favored the Republican Party and the gold standard wore gold bug pins, such as the one pictured here, during the 1896 presidential election campaign.*

Big Business and Its Critics

When **John D. Rockefeller** died in 1937 at age 97, the *New York Herald-Tribune* compared him to Napoleon. Like the French emperor, Rockefeller had created an empire, one that extended into nearly every community in the United States. It was an empire based on oil. When he founded the Standard Oil Company in 1870, there were dozens of oil-refining companies scattered throughout the Northeast. During the next 20 years, Standard Oil took over most of those companies or drove them out of business. Rockefeller built his oil empire partly by slashing the cost of refining petroleum through careful management. He also forced the railroads to pay Standard Oil **rebates** on its freight charges. Rebates were discounts from the published rates demanded by large volume shippers to keep their business. These rebates helped Standard Oil charge lower prices than its rivals. By 1898, this giant corporation produced 83 percent of all the oil used for lighting in the United States. John D. Rockefeller would long be identified with the rise of big business in the United States.

Why were industrial companies organized as corporations?

How did corporations try to eliminate competition?

How did Congress attempt to regulate railroads and abolish trusts?

Big Business Corporations

By the end of the century, most large businesses in the United States were corporations. Corporations were legal entities usually owned by large numbers of people rather than by an individual proprietor or a partnership. The corporate form of organization had several advantages. Through the sale of **stock** to hundreds or even thousands of people, a corporation could raise the large sums of money needed to build a railroad or a factory. Stock is a claim on the assets of a corporation that gives the stockholder, or shareholder, a share of the ownership and the profits of the corporation. Shareholders of corporations also enjoy **limited liability**. Personal assets of the shareholders cannot be seized to pay off corporate debts. Their losses are limited to the value of the stock. By 1900, corporations produced two-thirds of the nation's manufactured goods and were dominant in nearly every industry.

Large size was another trait that characterized American businesses at this time. Prior to the Civil War, most U.S. industries had been made up of a great many small companies. Each town or region had its own furniture makers, glassblowers, and flour millers, for example. As a result, business in nearly every field was highly competitive. No one company controlled the market. By 1900, that era of intense competition was nearing an end. Small businesses were merged into larger ones until a few large corporations controlled each major industry. What Standard Oil was to oil refining, U.S. Rubber and Goodyear were to the rubber industry, and Westinghouse and General Electric to electrical manufacturing. The nine sugar companies that had merged to form the American Sugar Refining Company held a near **monopoly** in that industry. A monopoly refers to a single company that has exclusive control of a market for a given product or service. Giant corporations had come to play a major role in nearly every industry.

Corporations and Trusts

This concentration of economic power was accomplished in several ways. The railroads tried to eliminate competition among themselves by agreeing to charge the same rates (price fixing) and by dividing up the freight among cooperating lines. But such **pooling agreements**, as they were called, did not last long. These agreements usually collapsed when one railroad tried to seize a larger share of the market by reducing its rates.

▼ This editorial cartoon shows the Standard Oil Trust as a grasping monster. What do the symbols in the tentacles of the octopus represent?

▲ This Standard Oil Company tank wagon was typical of those used to deliver kerosene to retail stores. This was a great improvement over the single-barrel delivery of earlier times.

To combine the oil refineries in the Northeast, Standard Oil turned to a device called the **trust**. A trust was a combination of companies that dominated an industry and could control prices and eliminate most, or all, competition. Trusts had boards of trustees that held the stock of companies that had once competed against one another. A board held the stock "in trust" for the owners while it managed the combined companies. After the courts declared this form of trust to be illegal, it was replaced by a new device called a **holding company**.

Holding companies were corporations created to own stock in other companies. They provided central management for several of these companies. Most of them were chartered in the state of New Jersey, which passed a law in 1888 making it legal for corporations to hold stock in other companies. As a result, that state became widely known as "the home of trusts." Although the trust form itself was no longer used, the term survived. It now referred to any big corporation that controlled much or all of an industry.

Business leaders saw many advantages to the concentration of economic power. Above all else, they argued, business mergers reduced costs and thus reduced the prices paid by the consumers.

Standard Oil, for example, lowered its operating costs by acquiring the oil fields that produced its raw materials, the tank cars that brought in the crude oil, and the pipelines that carried the kerosene to market. By reducing his operating costs, Rockefeller brought the price of kerosene down from around 19 cents per gallon in 1876 to about 8 cents per gallon a decade later. He also brought most of the refineries that produced kerosene under his control in order to eliminate competition. Corporate leaders, the "captains of industry," insisted that such consolidations were needed to bring order and stability to American industry.

Regulation of the Railroads

As the nation's first big businesses, the railroads were the first to demonstrate the dangers as well as the benefits of industrial growth. Americans recognized this and kept a wary eye on the railroads. A foreign observer noted, "The American people, although on the whole, I think, by no means unreasonable, are opposed to large corporations. . . . Hence the people are 'hard on the railways.'" Many Americans thought they had reason to be critical. They pointed to the growing political influence of the railroads in state legislatures. Handing out free passes and campaign contributions to politicians gave the railroads influence far beyond that of any private citizen. The railroads used this influence to defeat legislation that would limit the rates they could charge. Rumors linking the railroads with political corruption were widespread.

The most intense criticism of the railroads focused on the rates they charged shippers. Besides rebates demanded by favored shippers, large volume shippers tended to get more favorable rates than small shippers. Shipments over long distances often went for lower rates per mile than those going a shorter distance. The reason for this, the railroads claimed, was that the frequent loading and unloading of short hauls made these shipments more expensive. Farmers and local merchants complained of unfair discrimination. Farmers also protested against the high cost that grain elevators and warehouses charged for storing crops.

In the late 1860s, in response to the growing criticism against the railroads and grain storage elevators, the states began to enact laws to regulate railroads and storage facilities. These railroad regulation laws were called **Granger laws** because they had the support of the Granges, the most important farmers' organizations of that time. These laws also had the support of merchants and reform politicians. Usually the laws prohibited rate discrimination and rebates, and established the maximum rates that the railroads could charge. The railroads and warehouse owners appealed to the courts, arguing that the state legislatures had no authority to deprive them of potential profits. In 1877, the principle of state regulation was upheld in a series of decisions by the United States Supreme Court. In the first of these cases, *Munn v. Illinois*, the Court ruled that any private property that affected the public interest "must submit to be controlled by the public for the common good."

Although the courts upheld the principle of state regulation, Granger laws were less effective than the farmers had hoped. The commissions established to enforce the rates were often more sympathetic to the railroads than to the shippers. State laws were further weakened when the Supreme Court ruled in *Wabash v. Illinois* (1886) that Congress alone had the authority to regulate interstate trade. The national railroad network that was emerging by that time clearly needed federal rather than state supervision.

In 1887, Congress responded to demands for federal regulation of the railroads by passing the **Interstate Commerce Act**. This act outlawed rate discrimination and created the Interstate Commerce Commission to investigate complaints against the railroads. However, the Supreme Court ruled in 1897 in a case concerning maximum freight rates that the commission lacked the power to establish rates. To change an unfair rate, it had to file suit against a railroad and take it to court. As the courts usually ruled in favor of the railroads, the commission remained largely ineffective until strengthened by new legislation after the turn of the century. Nevertheless, public protest against the railroads had given the federal government a new regulatory function. It would lead in the future to other regulatory acts and to a vast expansion of federal responsibilities.

Attempts to Outlaw Trusts

By the late 1880s, public attention was shifting away from the railroads to trusts in other industries. Many Americans deeply feared the effect of declining competition on the prices they would have to pay for the necessities of life. Every price increase, whatever may have caused it, was blamed on the trusts. The editor of a Kansas newspaper complained about the plow trust. "As soon as it was perfected," he wrote, "the price of plows went up 100 per cent. . . . Who suffers? Who, indeed, but the farmer." The result was increased political pressure on Congress to do something about trusts.

In July 1890, Congress passed the **Sherman Antitrust Act**. It declared illegal "every contract, combination in the form of trust or otherwise, or conspiracy, in restraint of trade or commerce." The act made it illegal to combine individual business firms in ways that restricted competition. It further provided that any person or corporation that "shall monopolize, or attempt to monopolize" trade and commerce would be found guilty of a criminal act.

Congress had outlawed trusts, but the question remained how the courts would interpret the law. By the end of the decade, conservative justices on

Enduring Constitution

Separate but Equal: One Dissenting Voice

One day in 1892, Louisiana resident Homer Plessy bought a first-class railway ticket in New Orleans. He boarded an East Louisiana Railway train in a car reserved for white people. Homer Plessy was an octoroon. He looked like a white person, but one of his great-grandparents was black, making him one-eighth African, hence the word *octoroon*. Under Louisiana law in the 1890s, he was considered black. Louisiana was one of six states that had statutes requiring separate railroad accommodations for the races. Intending to challenge the constitutionality of the law, Plessy refused to vacate his seat when asked to do so by the conductor. He was arrested.

During the first few years after the Civil War, there was little state-imposed segregation of the races in public transportation or accommodations. Some states—Massachusetts, New York, and Kansas—specifically prohibited segregation. Though African Americans were often unable to afford a first-class ticket, American author George Washington

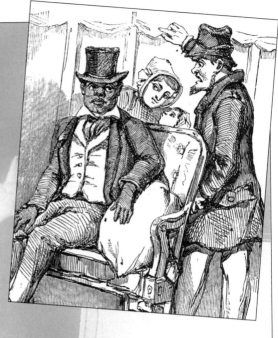

▶ *A railroad conductor orders an African American passenger from a "whites only" railroad car. How did the Supreme Court's ruling in* Plessy v. Ferguson *(1896) justify the segregation of public transportation?*

Cable noted that, in South Carolina, they rode in first-class cars as a right, and their presence excited no comment. However, during the 1890s one southern legislature after another passed laws, often referred to as Jim Crow laws, that segregated the black and white communities. These laws affected schools, housing, public transportation, restaurants, and other facilities.

Homer Plessy and the civil rights group with which he worked wanted to test these laws. The railroad officials, not liking the cost of the extra cars, were sympathetic. John H. Ferguson, a criminal court judge, conducted the trial and established that the law had been broken when Plessy failed to leave the car reserved for white people. Later, the Louisiana State Supreme Court upheld the law. Plessy then appealed to the Supreme Court, which, in *Plessy v. Ferguson* (1896), affirmed the decision of the state court.

Plessy had hoped that the Supreme Court would find the Louisiana statute contrary to the Thirteenth and Fourteenth Amendments. The Court's finding, however, was that these amendments were not infringed. Seven justices, headed by Justice Henry Billings Brown, voted for the decision. The Court claimed that while the Fourteenth Amendment's intention was to "enforce the absolute equality of the two races before the law... in the nature of things it could not have been intended to abolish distinctions based upon color, or to enforce social, as distinguished from political, equality... ." The states could require separate facilities, the court concluded, so long as the facilities were equal. For approximately 60 years, *Plessy v. Ferguson* stood as the precedent for the separate-

(continued)

but-equal doctrine governing much of public life, particularly in the South.

One justice, John M. Harlan, vehemently disagreed with the "separate-but-equal" principle. Justice Harlan's vigorous dissent is still one of the most widely quoted opinions in American constitutional law. A former Kentucky slave owner himself, he saw the "arbitrary separation of citizens on the basis of race," as "a badge of servitude" on African Americans. He asserted that "our Constitution is color-blind, and neither knows nor tolerates classes among citizens." Justice Harlan concluded that "the judgement this day rendered will, in time, prove to be quite as pernicious as the decision made by this tribunal in the Dred Scott case."

In time, the Supreme Court justices came to agree with Justice Harlan. His view finally prevailed in 1954, when the Supreme Court reversed the decision of *Plessy v. Ferguson*. In its decision in *Brown v. Board of Education of Topeka, Kansas,* the Court ruled that "separate facilities are inherently unequal." That was exactly Justice Harlan's point: "If a white man and a black man choose to occupy the same public conveyance on a public highway, it is their right to do so; and no government, proceeding alone on grounds of race, can prevent it without infringing the personal liberty of each." That was Homer Plessy's point, too.

1. What was the Supreme Court's justification for ruling against Plessy?
2. What did Justice Harlan mean when he said the Constitution is "colorblind?"

---

the Supreme Court had removed most of the teeth from the Sherman Antitrust Act. In 1895, the Court refused to allow the government to break up the sugar trust. It ruled in *United States v. E. C. Knight Co.* that the act outlawed combining companies in trade and commerce, but not in manufacturing (in this case, sugar refining). The Sherman Antitrust Act could only be applied to manufacturing, the Court decided in *Addystone Pipe and Steel Company v. United States* (1899), if the producers had a written agreement among themselves to fix prices. As most of the new trusts were the result of mergers rather than pricing agreements, the Court made the Sherman Act largely useless. Ironically, the courts continued to use the Sherman Act to prevent labor unions from using strikes, boycotts, and other tactics that were said to interfere with interstate trade.

The Inequality of Wealth

By the 1870s, the growing gap between the rich and the poor came under sharp criticism. Industrialization increased the wealth of the business and professional classes, while the working class sank deeper into poverty. "It is as though an immense wedge were being forced, not underneath society, but through society," wrote Henry George, a newspaper journalist and social critic. "Those who are above the point of separation are elevated, but those who are below are crushed down. . . . This association of poverty with progress is the great enigma of our times." Most Americans accepted the increasing inequality as the inevitable price of progress. A small but vocal minority raised their voices in protest,

▶ Edward Bellamy founded the Nationalist movement and wanted to replace the competitive capitalist system with a form of cooperative socialism.

◀ Henry George wrote a widely read book entitled Progress and Poverty. How did he propose to redistribute wealth in the United States?

BELLAMY.

and they demanded radical social change.

Henry George was the best known of these critics, and his book, *Progress and Poverty* (1879), was the most widely read nonfiction work of his generation. A few men had amassed great wealth, George explained, because they had established a near monopoly of land and property. His solution was to return this wealth to society by a "single tax" on land to replace all other taxes. This tax would be equal to the increase in the value of the land. Although widely denounced as dangerous and unworkable, especially by well-to-do landowners, George's single-tax movement attracted a wide following.

Still more radical was the solution proposed by American **socialists** to the unequal distribution of wealth. Under socialism, the government owns the means of production and distribution of goods. Influenced by the writings of such radical European thinkers as Ferdinand Lassalle and Karl Marx, socialists argued that inequality was inherent in the **capitalist** system, the economic system based on private ownership and unrestricted competition. Socialists insisted that factories, railroads, and other sources of wealth should be owned by the producers or workers who created the wealth. Their solution was to overthrow capitalism and replace it with a classless society. Socialists, however, did not agree among themselves about how this should be accomplished. **Political socialists** hoped to do away with capitalism peacefully, by way of the ballot. **Revolutionary socialists** supported the use of violence. Among them was a small group of **anarchists**, who called

for the abolition of all government. By 1900, socialists had attracted only a small following. The Socialist Labor Party, founded in 1877, drew its membership mainly from German immigrants who conducted their political meetings in German. The vast majority of working-class Americans expressed little interest in socialism. For them, the promise of economic success in the future outweighed the hardships of the present.

Many Americans were attracted to the "Yankeefied" socialism inspired by Edward Bellamy's *Looking Backward* (1888). This widely read novel was an account of life in a socialist **utopia**, or ideal community, in the year 2000. It portrayed a future in which the competitive struggle to survive was replaced by a cooperative society in which industry was owned by the state. Instead of socialist, Bellamy preferred the term *Nationalist* to describe his system. During the decade following the book's publication, thousands of people joined Nationalist clubs to discuss Bellamy's utopian ideas. The Nationalist movement proved, however, to be no more than a passing fad.

SECTION 1 REVIEW

1. **Define** the term *limited liability*.
2. **Describe** briefly the purpose of the Granger laws.
3. **State** Edward Bellamy's goal for the ideal community in the year 2000.
4. **Define** socialist.
5. **Explain** why Americans of the 1880s might have been alarmed by the concentration of corporate power.

An Era of Industrial Conflict

Although the 1880s was a period of rapid industrial growth, workers complained that few of the benefits were passed on to them. Wages in the mass-production industries remained at a bare survival level. Even skilled machinists made only $2.45 per day for ten hours of hard labor. "The machinists today are on such small pay, and the cost of living is so high," complained a New York City machine shop worker in 1883, "that they have very little, if anything, to spend for recreation." Wanting more from life than a drab existence, a growing number of workers demanded higher wages and shorter working hours.

Was justice served in the trial that followed the Haymarket Square Riot?

Why did the steelworkers lose the strike at Homestead?

How did Eugene V. Debs organize the railroad workers?

A Militant Labor Force

Unhappy about the growing extremes of wealth and poverty in the United States, an increasing number of workers joined unions and went on strike. When Jay Gould announced a 15 percent wage cut on his western railroads in 1885, workers who belonged to the Knights of Labor walked off the job and closed down the railroads. The old wage scale was immediately restored. The year 1886 saw a record number of labor disturbances, with over half a million workers on strike at one time or another. The strikes also became increasingly violent, as employers called in police and private detectives like the Pinkertons to protect the new workers they hired to break the strikes. In a clash between strikers and the police at the McCormick Harvester Works in Chicago on May 3, 1886, one worker was killed and several injured. But the worst was yet to come. The incident touched off the bloodiest riot in Chicago's history.

Haymarket Square Riot To protest the killing of the striker at the Harvester Works, a group of Chicago's anarchists called for a public meeting on the evening of May 4 at the city's **Haymarket Square**. Several of the speakers at the Haymarket rally were revolutionary socialists who had advocated the overthrow of the existing class system. Although no one called for violent action that evening, the rally ended in a bloodbath. When a column of police marched into the square to break up the meeting, an unknown person in the crowd threw a dynamite bomb. One policeman was killed and six others in the crowd were fatally injured by the blast. In the exchange of gunfire between the police and armed men in the crowd, four other people were killed and at least 60 injured.

Chicago and the nation were stunned by the Haymarket riot. The assault against police, the very symbol of law and order, was widely viewed as an attack against society itself. The Chicago authorities quickly arrested eight of the city's anarchists, accusing them of inciting the riot by their radical writings and speeches. It did not matter that many of the accused were not even present at the rally. "Convict these men," argued the prosecutor at their trial, "make examples of them, hang them, and you save our institutions." After a trial that captured national attention, the jury found the men guilty. Four were hanged, one committed suicide in his jail cell, and three were sentenced to prison. Although public support for the sentences was widespread, some saw the verdicts as a tragic miscarriage of justice. There was no evidence that the accused men had killed anyone that night at Haymarket Square. Six years later, a new governor of Illinois, John P. Altgeld, granted pardons to the three survivors.

The Eight-Hour Day The eight-hour day was the major issue besides wages in the labor upheavals of the 1880s. Blue-collar workers had long resented the demand that they work 10, and in many cases 12 or more, hours a day for low wages. Labor lead-

▲ The anarchist handbill pictured above announces the meeting at Haymarket Square. Why do you think it was repeated in German?

▲ This scene is one interpretation of the 1886 Haymarket Square Riot in Chicago. Why did many Americans view this riot as a dangerous attack against society?

ers launched a national movement for an eight-hour day, calling for a general strike (a nationwide walk-out) in May 1886 if their demands were not met. In response, nearly 200,000 workers walked off their jobs, but the results of the strike were disappointing. Skilled carpenters secured an eight-hour day in 137 cities by 1890, but most blue-collar workers had to wait another 25 years to enjoy that benefit.

The Homestead Steelworkers Strike

By 1892, the future of organized labor looked bleak. Union membership was down sharply from the decade before, as labor lost one major strike after another. During the summer of 1892, federal troops were called in to break a strike in the silver mines at Coeur d'Alene, Idaho, while state militia units put an end to strikes by railroad switchmen in Buffalo, New York, and coal miners in Tracy City, Tennessee. But the most serious setback to orga-

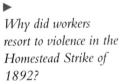
Why did workers resort to violence in the Homestead Strike of 1892?

nized labor and one of the most bitter strikes in American history was the breaking of the steelworkers union at Andrew Carnegie's steel mill in Homestead, Pennsylvania.

Henry Clay Frick, who would become president of the Carnegie Company in 1895, was deter-

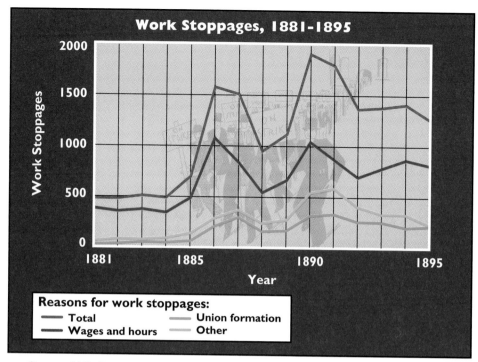

▶ *Labor protests and work stoppages increased dramatically during this period. What was the most common reason for striking?*

Work Stoppages, 1881-1895

Source: U.S. Department of Commerce, Bureau of the Census.

mined to smash the union that had organized the skilled workers at that plant. He wanted complete freedom to reduce wages when he saw fit, which he could not do under the wage contract that the company had earlier signed with the union. In order to oust the union, Frick decided not to renew the contract. When it expired in 1892, Frick locked the workers out of the Homestead plant and set out to hire a nonunion workforce in their place. He also hired some 300 guards from the Pinkerton Detective Agency to protect the mill and the new workers from the union members who went on strike.

The result was a violent showdown between capital and labor. When the Pinkerton men arrived at the plant on barges towed up the Monongahela River, they were met by an army of angry strikers. In a pitched battle on July 6, 1892, seven guards and nine strikers were killed. To protect the nonunion workers who were on their way to Homestead, Frick persuaded the governor of Pennsylvania to send eight thousand militiamen to guard the nonunion strikebreakers. National attention was focused on Homestead later that month when Alexander Berkman, an anarchist from New York, tried to assassinate Frick. Having read about the

plight of the locked-out workers, Berkman went to Homestead, burst into Frick's office, and shot him with a pistol. Frick was seriously wounded, but survived. By fall, the mill had resumed production, the strike was over, and the union was broken. Steel remained a nonunion industry for the next 40 years.

Eugene Debs and the Railroad Workers

Labor's only major success in the early 1890s was the organization of the railroad workers by the American Railway Union (ARU). Founded in 1893 by **Eugene V. Debs**, the ARU was an **industrial union** rather than a trade union. That is, the ARU was open to everyone who worked for a railroad, whether they were skilled or unskilled. (Since trade unions organized workers by craft, they enrolled only skilled workers.) Debs, a former official in the railroad firemen's union, set out to build a new kind of union that would represent all railroad workers.

The ARU scored an early success by winning a strike in 1893 against the Great Northern Railroad.

Mary Harris Jones

Mary Harris Jones became a living symbol of the American labor movement. "Mother" Jones, as her friends in the labor unions liked to call her, dedicated half of a very long life to improving the conditions of workers. Born Mary Harris in County Cork, Ireland, in 1830, her family immigrated to Canada when she was a young girl. She grew up in Toronto, where she became a teacher and dressmaker. Later she moved to the United States, where in 1861 she married an ironworker from Memphis, Tennessee. In 1867, she lost her husband and their four children in one of the Mississippi Valley's recurring yellow-fever epidemics. She then opened a dressmaking shop in Chicago, but lost everything in the great Chicago fire of 1871. While living there, she began attending meetings of the Knights of Labor and adopted the labor movement as a lifetime cause.

Mother Jones took part in virtually every major labor protest of the next half century. She was at the Haymarket Square Riot in 1886, took part in the Pullman Strike of 1894, and was an organizer for the United Mine Workers after the turn of the century. In 1905, she helped found the Industrial Workers of the World. Although the IWW became one of

▲ *Mother Jones, shown here at her desk in 1914, became a living symbol of the American labor movement.*

the most radical labor organizations of its time, Mother Jones was neither a socialist nor a supporter of women's suffrage. She was an outspoken labor agitator and a reformer. She actively supported legislation to prohibit child labor.

Growing old seemed to have little effect on Mother Jones. In her eighties, she traveled to Denver to protest the killing of coal miners in Colorado's infamous Ludlow Massacre. She was arrested in 1923 for supporting striking coal miners in West Virginia—at the age of 93.

She celebrated her 100th birthday by giving a speech, which was captured on film by a movie camera. Mother Jones died six months later. A union woman to the last, she was buried in a United Mine Workers' cemetery in Illinois.

1. How did Mother Jones become a symbol of the labor movement?
2. Why do you think union workers gave the nickname "Mother" to Mary Jones?

▲ *Eugene V. Debs headed the American Railway Union in 1893.*

When the unorganized workers on that line walked off the job to protest a series of wage cuts, Debs went to Minnesota to join them. He urged the strikers to avoid violence, which was the reason employers commonly used for requesting federal or state troops to break strikes. Under the skillful management of Debs, the workers won the strike in 18 days. The railroad restored almost the whole amount of three wage cuts, amounting to about $16 a month for each worker. The strike established the reputation of the ARU, which was soon gaining members at the rate of 2,000 a day. By 1894, its membership totaled 150,000, making it the nation's largest single union. Whether the ARU's remarkable success could be sustained remained to be seen.

SECTION 2 REVIEW

1. **List** the principal demands of organized labor in the 1880s.
2. **Describe** the immediate causes of the Haymarket Square Riot.
3. **Explain** why public opinion condemned the accused anarchists in the Haymarket Square Riot case.
4. **Describe** the methods used by Frick to break the steelworkers union at Homestead.
5. **Contrast** the membership of an industrial union and a trade union.

SECTION 3

Protests from Farmers

Farmers as well as laborers felt deprived of the benefits of the nation's economic growth. Prosperity had returned to the cities by the 1880s, but not to the farms. Industrial profits climbed to ever higher levels, while the price farmers received for crops fell. "There is something radically wrong in our industrial system," wrote the editor of a North Carolina farm journal in 1887. "There is a screw loose. . . . The railroads have never been so prosperous, and yet agriculture languishes. The banks have never done a better or more profitable business, and yet agriculture languishes. Manufacturing enterprises have never made more money or were in a more flourishing condition, and yet agriculture languishes." The editor spoke for many rural Americans, who thought of themselves as the real producers of the country's wealth. Yet in the struggle to make a living, the farmers seemed to be falling ever farther behind.

How did farmers organize to promote their economic interests?

What did the People's Party hope to accomplish?

Why did farmers find currency expansion an attractive issue?

The Farmers Organize

Like workers in American industry, farmers had tried over the years to cope with their problems through organization. They had set up a network of organizations in the 1870s throughout the South and Midwest called Grange chapters. This was the popular name for the Patrons of Husbandry, an organization founded in Washington, D.C., in 1867 to promote the interests of agriculture. Oliver Hudson Kelley, an official in the United States Department of Agriculture and chief organizer of the movement, saw the Granges mainly as social clubs to help combat the isolation of farm life. But these organizations addressed other problems as well. In addition to supporting railroad regulation, the Granges formed and supported cooperatives, or collectively-owned businesses, to help market farm produce. One Grange even attempted to manufacture its own harvesters. In time, most of the Grange businesses failed due to a shortage of capital and lack of managerial experience, or because of price slashing by their competitors. Even when the cooperative ventures were successful, the Granges' policy of cash-only sales kept them from aiding the farmers who needed help most.

▲ *According to the signs at this Grange protest meeting in Illinois, what problems brought farmers together to demand political action?*

By the 1880s, growing rural discontent produced a new network of organizations called the **Farmers' Alliance**. Beginning in Texas, where cotton farmers were sinking deeply into debt, the movement quickly spread throughout the South. A second organization, the Northern Alliance, also emerged in the plains states of Kansas, Nebraska, and the Dakotas. The Alliance movement, which included a Colored Farmers' Alliance for African American farmers in the South, focused on the economic problems of hard-pressed farmers.

The Alliance was especially concerned about the high cost of credit that kept farmers in debt. Southern tenant farmers, who mortgaged their crops each year to buy seeds and supplies, were especially hard pressed. In place of the crop liens and bank loans, the Alliance wanted to substitute low-interest loans provided by the federal government. It proposed the creation of a new subtreasury system empowered to make these loans. The loans would be secured either by crops stored in a government warehouse or by a mortgage on any land the farmer might own. Either way, the subtreasury system would free the farmers from the grip of the merchants and bankers. By placing more money in circulation through its loans to the farmers, the subtreasury system would also expand the money supply. The result, the Alliance hoped, would be inflationary, producing higher prices for farm products. Like the Granges, the Alliance also tried to organize marketing cooperatives so that farmers could avoid paying fees to the merchants who marketed their crops.

Agrarian Revolt and the Populist Party

In the summer of 1890, falling crop prices and a drought that ruined the wheat crop in the West touched off a major **agrarian** revolt. (Agrarian interests are those related to farmers, fields, and agriculture.) Throughout the South and West, farmers joined the Alliance and used it as a base for political action. In the primarily one-party South, the Southern Alliance tried to gain control of the powerful Democratic Party. In the plains states, the farmers worked to create new parties that would be more responsive to their needs than either the Democrats or the Republicans had proved to be.

Few of the leaders of this agrarian political revolt were well-established politicians. Most were plain country folk whose belief in their cause made up for their lack of political experience. Among them was Jerry Simpson of Kansas, a third-party candidate for Congress. He denounced the "silk-stocking," or well-to-do, Republicans and took pride in being so poor that he could not afford to wear socks at all. "Sockless Jerry," as the people called him, had a wide following among the poorer farmers in Kansas. So did Mary Elizabeth Lease, a lawyer and mother of four, who was a popular Alliance speaker. What the farmers of Kansas needed, she said, was to "raise less corn and more hell." In the same way that women were active in the settling and development of the Midwest, they took an active part in the new political movement. As one observer wrote, "women with skins tanned to parchment by the hot winds, with bony hands of toil and clad in faded calico, could talk in meeting, and could talk right straight to the point."

In the elections of 1890, the Alliance made substantial political gains. In Kansas, the People's Party, as the new party was called, elected one senator and five congressmen at the national level and controlled the lower house of the state legislature. Throughout the United States, the Alliance helped to elect 50 congressmen, 3 senators, and several governors. Encouraged by these successes, the Alliance members turned their attention next to the organization of a national party.

By 1892, a national People's Party (commonly known as the Populists) had taken shape. At a July convention in Omaha, Nebraska, the party nominated a presidential ticket and adopted a platform. Its candidates were James B. Weaver, an Alliance leader from Iowa, for president, and James G. Field of Virginia for vice president. The platform called for sweeping reforms designed to benefit American

▲ *Wooden noisemakers like this one were used by Grover Cleveland's supporters at political rallies during the 1892 presidential campaign.*

farmers and make the government more responsive to their needs. Among the Populists' demands were the government ownership of the nation's railroad, telegraph, and telephone systems, a federal income tax, and the subtreasury system of crop loans. The Populist platform also endorsed an expansion of the currency to make it easier for farmers to pay their debts. To make the government more democratic and responsive to people like themselves, the new party called for the direct election of United States senators. It also called for new procedures that would allow voters to propose and vote on new legislation. Finally, it endorsed the use of the **Australian ballot**, a printed ballot that contained all the candidates' names and which voters could mark in secret. At that time, voters cast ballots provided by the political parties, which let everyone know the party they had voted for. In an effort to attract the labor vote, the Populists also endorsed the eight-hour day.

Despite a hard-fought campaign for their ticket, the Populists made a poor showing in the elections of 1892. Grover Cleveland, the Democratic candidate, won a solid victory, with 46 percent of the popular vote to the Republican Benjamin Harrison's 43 percent. The Weaver-Field Populist ticket attracted only about 8 percent of the vote. Although the Populists did well in the silver-mining states (Nevada, Idaho, and Colorado) and in the plains states of Kansas and North Dakota, they did poorly in the industrial cities and in the South. Reluctant to abandon the Democratic Party, the party of white supremacy, most southern farmers voted for Grover Cleveland.

Currency Expansion

By calling for the unlimited purchase of silver by the U. S. Treasury, the Populists also endorsed a

Farmers in Distress

Farmers on the Great Plains complained that they were at the mercy of the banks, the railroads, and the weather. The banks and railroads charged interest rates and freight rates that farmers thought were excessively high. Yet often it was the weather, especially the recurring droughts, that finally broke them.

Unusually abundant rainfall in the mid-1880s enticed many thousands of settlers onto the high plains of Kansas, Nebraska, and eastern Colorado. During the years 1884–1886, an average of 10,000 persons a year filed claims for farm land under the terms of the Homestead Act in Nebraska alone. Farmers plowed up land once thought fit only as rangeland for buffalo and cattle. A Scandinavian farmer in North Dakota looked up from his plowing one day to find an elderly Sioux Indian watching in silence. The farmer watched as the Indian knelt, put his hand into the furrow, and fingered the broken sod. "Wrong side up," he said, then left. For some years, the farmer told the story as a joke on the Indian. Then the rains stopped, the customary dry years returned, and he discovered that the joke was on him. The winds that swept across the high plains blew the exposed topsoil away. Unlike the native grass, the farmer's wheat did not have enough roots to hold the soil in place.

▲ *This 1887 photograph shows poor but proud farmers standing in front of their sod house with their livestock and steel plow.*

Thomas Sisk was another of those high-plains farmers. As a contractor who graded the roadbeds for western railroads, he fell in love with the plains of eastern Colorado. "It was in the early summer and everything was green and thriving," he remembered. "Farmers were moving in there from the East and the government land was being rapidly taken up." He traded his grading equipment, worth $10,000, for cattle, lumber, furniture, and farming equipment, and settled down to farm. That was the first of five consecutive dry years. Nothing grew. He got rid of most of his cattle, as he and his neighbors had plowed up the best grassland. One by one, the neighboring families pulled out. "So, in 1893, I got a chance to sell out for $300.00 and took it. . . . I had put in five years of hard work and $10,000 and come out with $300.00. Besides that, there was no school for the children near. There were no books nor papers, no church. We were glad to leave." Sisk's experience was shared by thousands of others who had turned the grasslands "wrong side up."

1. How could better knowledge of the climate have benefited people like Thomas Sisk?
2. How could the settlers have made a living on the plains grasslands without turning the sod "wrong side up?"

▲ The front and back of an 1882 silver dollar are shown above. Why did western farmers and mine owners want Congress to purchase more silver and to coin more silver dollars?

▲ Above are the two sides of an 1894 ten-dollar gold piece. Many Americans of this period favored the gold standard and opposed the coinage of silver.

proposal that had long been a controversial issue in American politics. Most people in the nineteenth century believed that paper money had to be backed by gold or silver to have value. That is, confidence in the value of the dollar depended on the fact that a person could redeem it, or exchange it on demand, for its equivalent value in one of the precious metals. During most of its existence, the United States had backed its money by gold and silver, which was called a **bimetallic standard**. In 1873, however, the U.S. had dropped silver from its currency list and had gone to a gold standard. Currency expansionists would later call this the "Crime of 1873." The fact that gold was scarce severely limited the amount of currency in circulation. Going back to a bimetallic standard would permit an expansion of the currency. There would be more money in circulation. This in turn would lead to higher prices. For farmers faced with large existing debts, this meant that their crops would be worth more while the size of their debts remained the same. Thus, farmers joined the silver miners and mine owners in the West, who hoped that government purchases of silver would also reverse the decline in the price of that metal. Together, farmers and miners made currency expansion a major political issue.

The pro-silver forces had achieved some success by the 1890s, but they were still not satisfied. In 1878, Congress had passed the Bland-Allison Act, which provided for a set amount of silver to be purchased by the government and minted into coins. However, the $2 million of silver that the U.S. Trea-

sury purchased each month under the terms of the act was not enough to have a noticeable effect on prices. Still under pressure from the silver lobby, Congress acted again in 1890 by passing the Sherman Silver Purchase Act. This law required the U.S. Treasury to purchase 4.5 million ounces of silver each month at the market price. The purchases were to be paid for by new treasury notes—paper dollars—that could be redeemed either in gold or in silver. But the U.S. Treasury consistently redeemed these notes in gold, so the country, in effect, remained on the gold standard. And the actual dollar amount of silver purchased was not much greater than under the Bland-Allison Act. Still dissatisfied, the mine owners and currency expansionists waited for a better opportunity to bring about the unlimited coinage of silver. What they needed was an economic crisis that would make more voters feel the pinch of hard times. They did not have long to wait.

SECTION 3 REVIEW

1. **List** ways the Alliance movement tried to promote the interests of farmers.
2. **Outline** the principal demands of the People's Party.
3. **Define** the term *bimetallic standard*.
4. **Identify** the Crime of 1873.
5. **Explain** why farmers and mine owners demanded that the government increase its purchase of silver.

The Depression of 1893

On January 23, 1893, Charles G. Dawes, a young banker in Lincoln, Nebraska, and future vice president of the United States (1925–1929), was roused from his sleep at 6:00 A.M. by a bearer of bad news. One of the local banks, the Capital National Bank, had failed. The bank did not have enough cash on hand to meet its depositors' demands to withdraw their money. "It looks like a bad failure," he wrote in his diary that day, one that might cause jittery customers of other banks to panic and withdraw their deposits. By late spring, banks everywhere were going under, although Dawes's bank survived. All across the country, depositors were lining up to withdraw their savings. This created problems for banks since they loaned out most of their deposits while only keeping a relatively small portion in reserve. Banks that did not have enough cash in reserve closed their doors and went out of business. Dawes observed in July, "The country is passing through a great panic.... With many concerns each day has seemed their [the banks'] last."

Why were the 1890s a decade of labor unrest?
What role did the federal government play in the Pullman Strike?
How did President Grover Cleveland respond to the depression?

A Nationwide Depression

Businesses were already experiencing a slow-down when the banking panic swept through the nation in the spring of 1893. The economy worsened quickly. Industrial production declined sharply as orders from railroads and manufacturers virtually ceased. Factories closed down, and unemployment soared. Of the 4,500 workers normally employed by the Pullman Company in its railroad-car works, only 1,100 still had their jobs in November 1893.

By the next summer, 2.5 million workers, or about 20 percent of the nation's work force, were unemployed. A growing number of industrial firms and railroads went bankrupt as the nation slipped into its worst **depression** in 20 years. A depression is a major slowdown of economic activity with high rates of unemployment and business failures.

The depression of 1893 brought widespread distress to millions of Americans, especially workers in the industrial cities. In New York City alone, an estimated 20,000 homeless people wandered the streets, sleeping in police stations, temporary shelters, and doorways. Thousands of unemployed people became tramps, moving from one city to another in search of work or handouts of food. To help feed the destitute people of Detroit, Mayor Hazen Pingree turned vacant lots into potato patches. In some cities, unemployed laborers exchanged a day's work for the city for a bag of groceries. But neither the cities nor private charities had enough resources to meet the task. As a New York clergyman noted, "Never within my memory have so many people literally starved to death as in the past few months."

Coxey's Army The deepening depression brought demands for federal assistance for the unemployed. Among such plans was the "good roads" proposal

▼ *In 1894, Jacob S. Coxey led a protest march to Washington, D. C., to demand action on unemployment problems. How did he propose to put people back to work?*

▶ These children in New York City's lower East Side used the sidewalk as a playground. They lived in poverty even in good times.

advanced by Jacob S. Coxey, a businessman from Ohio. He called for Congress to issue $500 million in paper money to be used to put the unemployed to work building public roads. In 1894, when Congress refused to pass such a bill, Coxey led a protest march of several hundred unemployed people to the nation's capital to demand action. The march ended with Coxey's arrest on the steps of the Capitol for having ignored signs to keep off the grass. Not until the Great Depression of 1929 would Congress fund public works projects to provide jobs for the unemployed. Jacob S. Coxey was ahead of his time.

Labor Unrest

As the depression worsened, a new wave of labor unrest swept across the country. It reached its peak in 1894 with a major railroad strike. The strike began in the company town of Pullman, Illinois, which George Pullman had built to house employ-

ees of his railroad-car works. At the beginning of the depression, Pullman had slashed wages but had not reduced the rents on the company-owned houses. When the workers formed a committee to complain about the wage cuts, Pullman fired the leaders of the group. In May 1894, protesting Pullman workers walked off the job. Since many Pullman workers were also members of Eugene Debs's American Railway Union, they called on the union for support. The result was a decision by the ARU leaders to boycott trains carrying Pullman cars until the workers' demands were met.

The action by the ARU transformed the **Pullman Strike** into an epic battle between Debs's union and the railroads. Seeing an opportunity to smash the union, the railroads joined forces. They agreed to fire any railroad employee who supported the union's boycott, which quickly led to the dismissal of switchmen who had refused to handle Pullman cars. To protest these dismissals, the ARU called a strike against the railroads. The strike shut down much of the train traffic from Chicago to

▲ *National guardsmen and federal troops were involved in the violence during the railway strike of 1894.*

California. As the strike spread across the country, railroad officials urged President Cleveland to intervene. They pointed out that the strike interfered with the movement of the United States mail and would lead to violence and anarchy. Mobs roaming the railroad yards in Chicago had destroyed railroad property, including several boxcars that were turned over and burned. With the president's approval, Attorney General Richard Olney secured an **injunction**, or court order, demanding an end to the strike. Cleveland also sent 2,000 federal soldiers to Chicago to help enforce the injunction. Refusing to call off the strike, Debs and other ARU officials were arrested and jailed for disobeying the injunction. They were also charged with conspiracy to obstruct interstate commerce. Federal troops and marshals were promptly called out to protect the new workers who were hired to run the trains. The strike was broken, and the union was crushed.

When his efforts to organize the railroad workers proved unsuccessful, Debs looked for other means to improve the condition of the laboring class. While serving a six-month jail sentence for having disobeyed the injunction, he read much of the literature on socialism. "Government ownership of railroads," he noted that summer, "is decidedly better for the people than railroad ownership of the government." By 1897, Debs had converted to socialism, and for the next 20 years, he remained the most prominent spokesperson for socialism in the United States.

Cleveland Battles the Depression

Grover Cleveland took office in March 1893 in the midst of a serious financial crisis. The U.S. Treasury was losing millions of dollars in gold each month as banks redeemed the silver certificates issued under the Sherman Silver Purchase Act. The silver certificates were also being redeemed in gold, even though the value of silver relative to gold had declined. Heavy withdrawals by foreign investors contributed to the gold drain. If the rate of loss continued, the treasury officials would have to suspend gold payments. Cleveland was certain that the result would be economic disaster. It would take the United States off the gold standard, leaving everyone in doubt about the dollar's value. He was convinced that the resulting uncertainty would make the depression worse and would delay recovery for years. The president was also certain that the cause of the problem was the Sherman Silver Purchase Act. To remedy the situation, Cleveland called Congress into special session to repeal that act.

In having the act repealed, Cleveland nearly destroyed the Democratic Party. Eastern Democrats in the House and Senate who favored currency contraction joined with Republicans to provide the majority for repeal. Democrats from the South and West, wanting currency expansion, opposed the administration. They wanted more silver in circulation, not less. To make matters worse, repeal of the act did not stop the drain of gold. The U. S. Treasury had to shore up its reserves by arranging for the purchase of gold through private bankers. J. P. Morgan and other prominent bankers used their influence to stop demands on the Treasury. This convinced the public that Cleveland and the eastern bankers were working hand-in-hand. Critics pointed out that the administration was paying the large fees charged by these bankers while doing nothing to help destitute farmers and the unemployed. Cleveland's attack on silver had divided the party and had cost it badly needed support.

The Democrats' attempt at tariff reform was also a disaster. During his campaign, Cleveland had promised to help consumers by reducing the duties

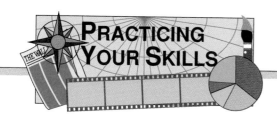

Analyzing a Photograph

By the late nineteenth century, many new immigrants as well as Americans from rural areas found themselves squeezed into overcrowded sections of our major cities. Sometimes ten or more members of a family might live in a couple of rooms in a crowded tenement in a whole block of similar tenements. In such conditions, life spilled out onto the streets. The street offered a place to sell goods from a pushcart, a bit of fresh air, a chance to visit with neighbors, or a playground for children. Streets were also dangerous, dirty, and unhealthy places.

The depression of 1893 worsened conditions in the cities. Many reformers documented their observations of life in the city slums with photographs. They hoped to gain support for reforms. Photographs such as these provide the historian with many concrete details of what life was like. However, as the photographer is not an entirely unbiased observer, photographs must be carefully analyzed for hidden meanings.

Review the guidelines for analyzing pictures on page 315 in the Practicing Your Skills feature. Then examine the photograph on page 503 and answer the following questions:

1. Describe this scene. What message is the photographer trying to send?
2. Do you think this is a candid or posed photograph? Why?
3. Name at least three situations in the photograph that identify this neighborhood as lower middle class.
4. What time of year do you think this is? What evidence can you give for your conclusion?
5. What is unusual about the figures in the photograph? (Hint: What group or groups of people are missing?)

---

on foreign imports. William L. Wilson of West Virginia did get a low tariff bill through the House of Representatives, but it was heavily amended in the Senate by members who supported protective tariffs. Cleveland failed to veto the Wilson-Gorman bill even though it actually raised some of the tariff rates. He also spoke out against the bill's most popular feature—a tax of 2 percent on incomes of $4,000 or more. The income tax provision was promptly struck down by the United States Supreme Court as unconstitutional. Congress did not gain the authority to collect an income tax until the Sixteenth Amendment was ratified in 1913.

In the congressional elections of 1894, the Democrats paid dearly for the administration's blun-

ders and for the party's inability to cope with the severe depression. The Republicans won an overwhelming victory, earning 244 seats to the Democrats' 105. Throughout the industrial East and the Midwest, the Republicans regained control of state legislatures and of city halls. In more than half the states, the Democrats did not elect a single candidate to national office. Although the Populists' showing improved, the Republicans were the big winners in 1894. They were well on the way to establishing the Republican Party as the majority party in the United States. The Democrats had lost all the ground they had recently gained. They were about to become a minority party for the first time since the Civil War.

1. **Explain** how low cash reserves contributed to the banking panic of 1893.
2. **Relate** how railroad officials justified their appeal to President Cleveland to intervene in the Pullman Strike.
3. **Describe** the actions taken to break the Pullman Strike.
4. **Summarize** why Cleveland feared the gold drain resulting from the Sherman Silver Purchase Act.
5. **Name** two events that helped the Republicans win the 1894 elections.

SECTION 5

The Politics of Depression

A new pamphlet was on the newsstands in 1894, a best-seller by William H. Harvey entitled *Coin's Financial School*. Its main character, an economist named Coin, was a specialist on the money question. Among the students at Professor Coin's imaginary school were the nation's top business leaders, who came to learn the truth about the currency issue. The business leaders learned that the unlimited coinage of silver was the only road back to prosperity. By increasing the number of dollars in circulation, Coin explained, "you make it possible for the debtor to pay his debts; business to start anew, and revivify all the industries of the country." The book offered a simple and easy way out of the depression. It sold hundreds of thousands of copies, while excerpts in newspapers reached millions of other readers. Its enormous appeal indicates once again this generation's perception that currency reform was the solution to its economic problems.

What positions did the major parties take on the currency issue?

Why did the Populists endorse the Democratic candidate in 1896?

What advantages did the Republican Party have in the 1896 election?

Currency Becomes a National Issue

By the presidential election year of 1896, the currency question was the most important issue in American politics. Harvey's book, and many imitations, brought the debate more sharply into focus. But the issue had surfaced largely because of widespread economic distress. The advocates of silver coinage insisted that an increase in the money supply was all that was needed to restore good times. Their opponents warned that business and agriculture would not revive so long as people remained uncertain about the value of the dollar. Supporters of the gold standard said that only a stable currency based on gold would restore public confidence. That, they insisted, was the key to recovery. But the argument for the gold standard found little favor in the South and the West, where falling crop prices and the price of silver made the distress most acute.

In both the South and the West, the leaders of the Democratic Party tried to recover from the crushing defeats of 1894 by embracing silver coinage. The survival of the party seemed to depend on its taking a stand for silver. Many western Democrats, including Congressman Richard P. Bland (coauthor of the Bland-Allison Act), had long advocated silver coinage. Others, such as **William Jennings Bryan** of Nebraska, were more recent converts. Bryan had spent months traveling in the West and in the South speaking out in favor of the silver standard and building his oratory skills. The only question by 1896 was whether the silver-supporting Democrats were strong enough to take control of the national Democratic Party.

▲ *Populist William Jennings Bryan was the Democratic candidate for president in 1896. He advocated the unlimited coinage of silver.*

The showdown came in July 1896 at the Democratic National Convention in Chicago. The Cleveland Democrats, or "goldbugs," were in control of the platform committee, and they presented a currency plank that upheld the gold standard. It was opposed by the "silverites," who insisted on debating the issue and putting it to a vote on the convention floor. In one of the most rousing speeches in the history of party conventions, William Jennings Bryan presented the case for silver coinage. Sensing the drama of the moment, Bryan concluded with a flourish:

> Having behind us the producing masses of the nation and the world . . . we will answer their [the urban bankers and businessmen's] demand for a gold standard by saying to them: You shall not press down upon the brow of labor this crown of thorns, you shall not crucify mankind upon a cross of gold.

Since they controlled a majority of the delegations, the silver Democrats carried the day. They voted down the gold plank and committed the party to the unlimited coinage of silver. On the final day of the convention, the Democrats nominated William Jennings Bryan for president and Arthur Sewall of Maine for vice president—a ticket pledged to support the silver coinage platform.

McKinley Nominated by Republicans

Bryan's Republican opponent in 1896 was **William McKinley**. He attracted working-class voters, eastern business interests, and the urban middle class. As a congressman and as governor of Ohio, McKinley championed the interests of labor, supporting high tariffs on the ground that protection for industry meant higher wages for workers. In 1890, the McKinley Tariff was passed. Although as concerned as Bryan about the plight of farmers and the unemployed, McKinley opposed the unlimited coinage of silver. The keys to recovery, he believed, were the gold standard and a higher protective tariff.

At its convention in St. Louis, the Republican Party had taken a strong stand in support of a currency backed by gold. It did so knowing full well that it would lose votes in the West by opposing silver. It counted on making up those losses in the Midwest and Northeast, where the party had made impressive gains in 1894. "We are unalterably opposed to every measure calculated to debase our currency," read the currency plank in the Republican platform. "We are therefore opposed to the free coinage of silver, except by international agreement with the leading nations of the earth." When this plank was adopted, Colorado Senator Henry M. Teller and other delegates from the mining states of the West walked out of the convention in protest. As an international agreement on silver was highly unlikely, the Republicans were pledged to defend the gold standard.

▲ *In 1896, the Republican Party nominated William McKinley on a platform supporting the gold standard.*

The Populist Dilemma

Holding their convention after both the Republicans and the Democrats, the Populists faced a dilemma. By nominating Bryan on a silver platform, the Democrats had stolen much of the Populists' thunder. Indeed, their leaders had even considered nominating Bryan themselves. But now if the Populist party also nominated Bryan, it would risk losing its own identity. Keeping the new party alive was important to them because silver was not the only issue that most Populists cared about. As mentioned earlier, they also demanded government ownership of the railroads, the subtreasury system of crop loans, and other reforms that the Democrats did not support. Yet if the Populist Party made a separate nomination, they would split the silver vote and help elect McKinley.

▲ *This editorial cartoon shows Uncle Sam turning his back on the foolish silverites, while relying on the gold reserve in the U. S. Treasury to pull the country through hard times.*

▲ *William Jennings Bryan took his message directly to the people across the United States. Where might you see similar scenes today?*

At their convention in late July, the Populists tried to escape this dilemma by compromising. To avoid splitting the silver vote, the party nominated Bryan as its presidential candidate. But to maintain the party's separate identity, it nominated its own candidate for vice president—Thomas E. Watson of Georgia. Voters would have a choice of casting their ballots for Bryan as a Democrat or as a Populist. The question remained whether enough people would vote for the Bryan-Watson ticket to keep the Populist Party alive.

McKinley Defeats Bryan

Few presidential campaigns in American history have aroused as much interest and excitement as the McKinley-Bryan contest of 1896. The issues were clear-cut, and the stakes were high. The economic future of the United States seemed to hang in the balance. Adding greatly to the excitement was the vigorous campaign that Bryan conducted. Perhaps

the greatest orator of his day, Bryan went directly to the people with his demand for silver coinage. He took advantage of the railroad network as no other political candidate had before. Altogether Bryan traveled 18,000 miles to reach some 5 million people in 27 states. Running a more traditional "front-porch" campaign, McKinley remained at home in Canton, Ohio, speaking to delegations of Republicans when they came to pay their respects. The Republicans relied on the press and on an army of campaign speakers and party workers to get McKinley's message across.

In both organization and financing, the Republicans had a clear advantage. Concerned that a Bryan victory would bring financial ruin, corporations and businesses contributed heavily to the Republican campaign chest. Altogether the party raised $3.5 million, the largest sum spent on an election campaign to that date. With the money, the Republicans flooded the country with documents presenting the virtues of protective tariffs and the gold standard. Speakers were sent into every corner of the nation. In contrast, the Bryan campaign was continually short of funds. Even so, the Democrats organized silver clubs, distributed thousands of copies of *Coin's Financial School*, and printed millions of pamphlets on the need for silver coinage.

Election day in November brought a resounding victory for the Republicans. McKinley defeated

▲ *William McKinley accepted the Republican nomination in a speech given from the front porch of his house in Canton, Ohio. How did McKinley's and Bryan's campaign styles differ?*

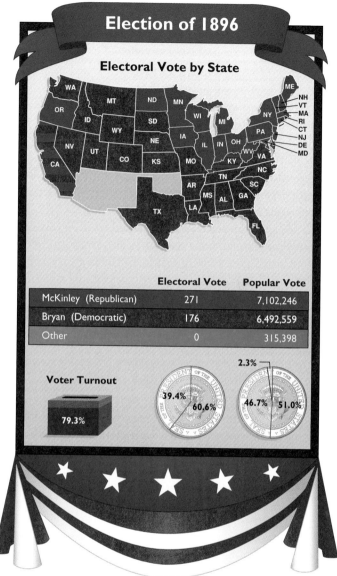

Election of 1896

Electoral Vote by State

	Electoral Vote	Popular Vote
McKinley (Republican)	271	7,102,246
Bryan (Democratic)	176	6,492,559
Other	0	315,398

Voter Turnout 79.3%

39.4% 60.6%

2.3% 46.7% 51.0%

▲ *What do the red and blue horizontal lines in California and Kentucky indicate?*

Bryan by more than 600,000 popular votes and a majority of 271 to 176 in the electoral college. As expected, the Democrats carried the South and did well in the plains and mountain states. But McKinley rolled up huge majorities in the Midwest and industrial Northeast. Bryan ran well in the most depressed rural districts, but McKinley carried the cities. Blue-collar workers as well as business and professional men decided they had more to gain from Republican tariffs and the gold standard than from Bryan and silver. In winning the industrial Northeast along with the Midwest, the Republicans had put together a voting coalition that would make theirs the majority party for the next 36 years.

As a major force in American politics, the Populist Party did not survive the defeat of 1896. It lingered on for another decade, but it had lost most of its support. Most of its voters returned to the Democratic Party in 1896, and remained with that party thereafter. However, many of the principles for which the Populist Party stood did survive. The direct election of United States senators, referendum, recall of office holders by popular vote, and the Australian ballot would in time become the law of the land.

SECTION 5 REVIEW

1. **Describe** the Democratic platform in 1896.
2. **Summarize** the Republican Party's position on the currency issue.
3. **Contrast** the presidential campaigns of Bryan and McKinley.
4. **Explain** why the Republicans won in 1896.
5. **Name** three measures backed by the Populists that eventually became law.

Chapter 15 Review

Summary

The postwar era was a time of industrial growth and consolidation. As large corporations came to dominate one industry after another, economic power became increasingly concentrated. Consequently, there was less competition in many key industries, which had traditionally benefited American consumers by keeping prices low.

Many Americans were alarmed by the growing power of the railroads and other corporations. They demanded government action to check that power. Some called for government ownership of railroads and other industries. Farmers called for a variety of reforms to aid agriculture, including an expansion of credit and currency. Industrial workers demanded higher wages and a shorter workday. By the early 1890s, many of these elements of discontent joined in political protest, which led to the founding of the Populist Party.

The depression in 1893 made the social problems of industrial America far more acute. In 1894, strikes nearly paralyzed the nation's railroads. Cities exhausted their relief funds and demands grew for federal assistance. The Democratic administration of Grover Cleveland responded with a series of highly unpopular measures. The president approved the use of troops to break the railroad strike. Cleveland also called for the repeal of the Sherman Silver Purchase Act. In the congressional elections of 1894, the Democrats suffered heavy losses.

The political discontent of that era reached its climax in the election of 1896. On one side were the Democrats and the Populists, who supported William Jennings Bryan. They were committed to the unlimited coinage of silver. On the other side were the Republican Party and its candidate, William McKinley. The Republicans won a resounding victory in 1896, partly because the industrial cities voted overwhelmingly for McKinley.

Vocabulary

agrarian
anarchist
Australian ballot
bimetallic standard
capitalist
depression
Granger laws
holding company
industrial union
injunction

limited liability
monopoly
political socialist
pooling agreements
rebate
revolutionary socialist
socialist
stock
trust
utopia

1. List the three terms that describe illegal or unfair business practices.
2. List the five terms that describe political parties or ideologies or their followers.
3. List the term relating to elections.
4. List the three terms describing organizations or business entities or their practices.
5. List the terms that describe aspects of corporations.
6. Which term is a type of court order?
7. Which term describes an idealized political state?
8. Which term indicates a severe economic slowdown?
9. Which term is an adjective relating to farming and agriculture?
10. Which term describes how paper money is backed?

Review Questions

1. What methods or devices did corporations use to eliminate competition?
2. How effective was Congress in abolishing the trusts?
3. How did industrial unions like the American Railway Union differ from trade unions?
4. What were the reasons for the bleak outlook for organized labor in 1892?

5. Why was currency a major issue in American politics during the 1890s?
6. Describe the dilemma faced by the Populist Party in the 1896 presidential election.
7. Explain why the Populist Party could be considered successful, although they never gained the presidency.
8. Describe measures taken by Cleveland in response to the depression of 1893.
9. What were the positions of the major parties in 1896 on the currency issue?
10. Identify reasons for the Republican success in the presidential election of 1896.

Critical Historical Thinking

Writing Answer each of the following by writing one or more complete paragraphs:

1. Explain how the growth of large corporations both helped and harmed American consumers.
2. Strikes were used with increasing frequency during the period that labor unions were developing. Do you think strikes today are an effective tool for use in determining wages and working conditions? Why, or why not?
3. Cleveland took action against the Pullman strikers on the grounds that the national security and essential federal services were threatened. Do you agree with his decision to intervene? Why, or why not?
4. In the Unit 5 Archives, read "Mary E. Lease Makes a Speech." Explain why she contends that Wall Street is like a slave master.

Making Connections with Economics

The value of the American dollar in today's world market is much more closely linked to the value of other world currencies than in the 1890s. Moreover, the dollars you carry are but a tiny fraction of the money supply. These facts lead to some interesting circumstances. For example, the McDonald's Corporation has fast-food restaurants in almost every country in Asia. The price of their Big Mac is calculated so that it is valued at the same amount throughout the world. For example, if the value of the foreign currency goes down against the dollar, the price charged for the hamburger will go up accordingly. At one time, the *Asian Wall Street Journal* established a "Mac Index" which listed the price of Big Macs in all Asian countries. The difference in the prices was a measure of the relative value of each country's currency.

Writing Although a strong dollar is good when traveling to another country, many merchants worry when the dollar becomes too strong or stays high for too long. Write two or three paragraphs explaining why exporters might fear a strong dollar.

Additional Skills Practice

Photojournalists prize candid photographs, those photos which are not posed or prearranged. Candid photographs taken during riots, natural disasters, or sports events are of great historical value. Others, because of the "staged" nature of the setting (grouping of the people, subjects focused on the camera, etc.), are obviously posed photographs. Public relations agents and politicians often go to great trouble to set up good "photo opportunities" for publicity reasons. Sometimes photos that look real are actually reenactments of historical events. The official photograph of the historic meeting of the Union Pacific and Central Pacific Railroads at Promontory Point, Utah, was taken after the event, when surrounding grounds were cleaned of debris and litter.

Bring to class photographs from magazines and newspapers that you believe represent each of the three categories: candid, posed, and recreated. (You may have to do some reading or researching to find out if a photo was recreated.)

The United States Emerges as a World Power

Before the 1880s, the United States was relatively isolated—both geographically and politically—from the rest of the world. By the last quarter of the nineteenth century, the Civil War and Reconstruction were over, the conquest and settlement of the West were virtually complete, and the transition to an industrial economy was well under way. As a result, many Americans began to turn their attention outward. Connecticut Senator Orville Platt sensed these changes. "A policy of isolation did well enough when we were an embryo nation," Platt asserted, "but today things are different. . . . We are 65 million people, the most advanced and powerful on earth, and regard to our future demands an abandonment of the doctrines of isolation." Others went even further. "Is America a weakling," Theodore Roosevelt asked, "to shrink from the work of the great world powers?" Americans had mixed reactions to the idea of world power, increased foreign involvement, and imperialism. Nevertheless, by the turn of the century, the United States—partly by accident, partly by design—emerged as a world power with imperial possessions overseas. Other nations, and Americans themselves, could no longer afford to ignore this fact.

▲ *This detail from the painting* Dewey? We do! *depicts a ship in Commodore Dewey's Asiatic Squadron steaming into Manila harbor to engage the Spanish fleet.*

The Roots of American Overseas Expansion

In 1880, the sultan of Turkey, looking for ways to cut government expenses, closed **diplomatic missions** in nations he thought were unimportant. A diplomatic mission is a foreign service office in another country that conducts economic and political relations with the host country. The sultan withdrew his ministers from Belgium, the Netherlands, Sweden, and the United States. Many nations at that time regarded the United States as a second-rate power. This perception, however, was rapidly changing. By 1892, every major power except Austria-Hungary had raised its diplomatic mission in Washington to **embassy** status. An embassy is a diplomatic mission staffed with an official ambassador. In addition, these embassies were beginning to be seen as important, and they were staffed by some of the world's ablest diplomats. All of this meant that the United States was beginning to be recognized as a world power by other nations.

Why had most Americans been so little concerned about foreign affairs?

How did the changing economy influence Americans' changing views of foreign affairs?

How did Social Darwinism affect Americans' views of foreign affairs?

▲ *Commodore Perry made his first visit to Japan in 1853. Was his expedition diplomatic or military in nature?*

Little Interest in Foreign Affairs

From 1815 to 1885, the United States had little involvement and few conflicts with other nations. Protected on two sides by oceans, the United States was geographically isolated from Europe and Asia. Europe during this period was relatively peaceful, and no attempts were made to draw the United States into alliances.

The United States had no rival in the Western Hemisphere. The conquest and settlement of new territories had created conflict with Canada and Mexico, but these countries were less of a threat to the United States' security than the United States was to theirs. The United States' interest in expansion rarely went beyond North America. However, some Americans did involve themselves in places beyond the nation's borders. Merchants had developed trading interests in Latin America and the Caribbean. In the early 1800s, missionaries had settled in Hawaii and other Pacific islands. Whalers and other seafarers stopped in these islands for rest, food, and water. In 1784, the *Empress of China*, a small New England merchant vessel, first traded with China. By the 1850s, American clipper ships were engaged in brisk trade with China. In 1853, U.S. Navy Commodore Matthew Perry forced Japan to open some of its ports to Western traders.

Still, the only people who really noticed such overseas contacts were those directly involved. When more ambitious plans for overseas expansion arose from time to time, most Americans opposed them. From the 1840s to the Civil War, southern planters sought to acquire Cuba and other areas in

Latin America to expand their slave-based economy. Opponents of slavery blocked these efforts. During and after the Civil War, William Seward, secretary of state under Presidents Lincoln and Johnson, tried without success to annex Cuba and Hawaii to serve as naval bases. Similarly, in the 1870s, President Grant proposed to annex Santo Domingo and other Caribbean islands for use by the navy. American expansionists also talked repeatedly of building a canal across Central America to link the Atlantic and Pacific Oceans.

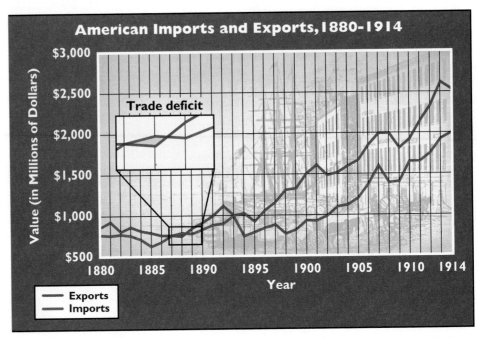

American Imports and Exports, 1880-1914

Legend: Exports / Imports

▲ *Because the United States was a developing nation through most of the nineteenth century, it usually imported more goods than it exported. By 1880, that general trend reversed. During what years did the U.S. again show a trade deficit?*

Such plans for overseas expansion won little support, and most failed. A notable exception was Seward's purchase of Alaska from Russia in 1867. Despite its bargain price—$7.2 million for over 600,000 square miles—many opposed the deal. Opponents called Alaska "Seward's Folly," "Seward's Icebox," and "President Andrew Johnson's Polar Bear Garden." Another exception was the annexation of Midway Island (about 1,000 miles northwest of Hawaii) in 1867 for use as a naval base.

The Search for New Markets

By the 1890s, the United States was a great power. American industrial output was increasing at a staggering pace. By 1900, the United States manufactured more goods than any single European country. Its farm machinery, machine tools, electrical equipment, and iron and steel products began to pour into foreign markets. Oil products also became important American exports. In 1890, Standard Oil Company controlled 70 percent of the world market in kerosene. Meanwhile, because of sharp de-

creases in ocean and railroad shipping costs, U.S. farm goods were flooding foreign markets.

The United States had long been an exporter of raw materials (chiefly cotton) and an importer of manufactured goods, paying in gold to make up the difference. American foreign trade had been small yet important, and it increased rapidly after the Civil War. In 1876, the value of American exports exceeded imports for the first time. In the two decades after 1880, American exports doubled.

The nation's vast production of farm and factory goods caused increasing alarm among Americans. Indeed, many politicians and economists believed that overproduction caused the severe depression of 1893. Indiana Senator Albert Beveridge declared, "American factories are making more than the American people can use; American soil is producing more than we can consume. Fate has written our policy for us; the trade of the world must and shall be ours."

Powerful industrial and agricultural interests began to lobby the government to keep foreign markets open for American goods. Government officials were responsive. In 1898, for example, a State Department report stated, "Every year we shall be confronted with an increasing surplus of manufactured goods for sale in foreign markets if American operatives and artisans are to be kept employed the year around." The State Department concluded that it should use diplomacy to encourage U.S. exports to keep factory workers employed and to avoid social turmoil at home.

Other concerns were propelling Americans outward. The Census Bureau reported that since 1890 the frontier line had disappeared. Many Americans mistakenly assumed that this meant there was no room left for expansion or growth, and that social tensions would build up to danger levels. The violence of the Homestead and Pullman Strikes fueled these fears of social unrest.

▲ *This satire of imperialism appeared on the cover of* Life *magazine on March 16, 1899.*

Overseas Expansion Justified

New ideas also promoted an interest in expansion. Americans had long believed that it was their manifest destiny to expand over the North American continent. This idea was given new life by the theory of **Social Darwinism**. Charles Darwin, in his book *On the Origin of Species* (1859), had proposed that nature, through the process of natural selection, allowed only the fittest to survive. Fittest meant being the strongest, smartest, fastest, or possessing whatever trait provided a winning edge in the struggle for existence.

English sociologist Herbert Spencer interpreted Darwin's ideas of the "struggle for existence" and the "survival of the fittest" as natural laws that accounted for all human progress. Competition in society, he explained, separated the strong from the weak. These ideas nurtured European racism and nationalism.

Many writers, politicians, and business leaders—including industrialist Andrew Carnegie—popularized Social Darwinism in the United States. The doctrine included Americans among the "fit." They were therefore destined to extend their institutions over "every land on the earth's surface." Following this theory, some religious leaders favored taking up the "white man's burden," that is lifting up other races through Christian missionary activity

throughout the world. Indeed, American missionary activity increased substantially in this period. Between 1870 and 1900, the number of Protestant missions abroad increased by 500 percent. American missionaries stimulated interest in foreign places in several ways. They exposed local peoples to American goods and often directly encouraged trade. Missionaries were certain that products of American technology, such as medicine and manufactured goods, would improve the quality of life for the native people. As missionaries raised funds at home to support their work, they appealed to their American congregations with alluring stories of exotic places.

A distinctly aggressive attitude colored the nationalism of the late 1800s. Visions of empires occupied the thoughts of both Europeans and Americans. Americans boasted of their political institutions, growing population, and expanding industrial might. Exclusive societies that reflected this intense patriotism were founded. These organizations, such as the Daughters of the American Revolution (1890) and the Society of Colonial Dames (1891), restricted membership to certain groups or classes of people. Churches, newspaper offices, and the floors of Congress resounded with calls for patriotism and Americanism. Few were immune to these nationalistic messages.

1. **List** two reasons for American isolation from foreign affairs before 1880.
2. **Identify** Seward's Folly.
3. **Describe** the economic changes that encouraged Americans to take more interest in overseas involvement in the late 1800s.
4. **Explain** the influence of Social Darwinism on American attitudes about foreign affairs.
5. **Describe** how nationalism encouraged expansionist thinking in the late 1890s.

SECTION 2

The Changing World Scene

Massachusetts Senator Henry Cabot Lodge was a tireless advocate of building national power through commerce and diplomacy. New developments in transportation and communication were making American foreign trade more profitable than ever. American manufacturers were ready to compete with European powers in the world market. Lodge wanted the nation to become more active in foreign affairs. In "Our Blundering Foreign Policy" (*Forum*, March 1895), he summarized his position: "Small states [countries] are of the past and have no future. The modern movement is all toward the concentration of people and territory into great nations and large dominions. The great nations are rapidly absorbing . . . all the waste places of the earth. It is a movement which makes for civilization and the advancement of the race. As one of the great nations of the world, the United States must not fall out of the line of march." Increasing numbers of Americans supported Lodge's views but gave little thought to the desires and interests of the native peoples of the so-called "waste places."

How did changing technology influence global relationships in the late nineteenth century?

How did European imperialism after 1880 affect the United States?

How did Alfred Mahan influence U. S. foreign policy?

The Race for Empire

Since the final defeat of Napoleon Bonaparte in 1815, Europe had maintained a **balance of power** that preserved peace on the continent. No one country or alliance felt strong enough to try to conquer the others. Rapid industrialization, however, created problems in Europe similar to those in the United States. By the 1880s, the overproduction of goods and widespread social unrest put stress on the governments of the major European powers. They adopted higher tariffs to keep competing foreign goods out of their domestic markets. They also sought new sources of raw materials and new markets for their finished products in Africa, Asia, South America, and the Pacific. European countries raced to gain control of other people and territories, and concentrated on building empires that would allow them trade and military advantages. These actions collectively were known as **imperialism**.

By the late nineteenth century, Europeans dominated almost the entire world. They carved up Africa, except for Ethiopia. The Europeans desired colonies and naval bases in the Pacific and wished to develop trade in Latin America as well. They also moved to control China from established bases in Asia. Meanwhile, Japan emerged as a major world power when it convincingly won the Sino-Japanese War in 1894. (*Sino* is a prefix that means Chinese.)

Henry Cabot Lodge, a long-time Republican senator from Massachusetts, was an active supporter of defense and foreign policies to make the United States into a major world power. What term describes this approach?

By 1900, European nations had established control of almost the entire continent of Africa. Which two European nations controlled the most territory? What other major European power controlled only small holdings in Africa?

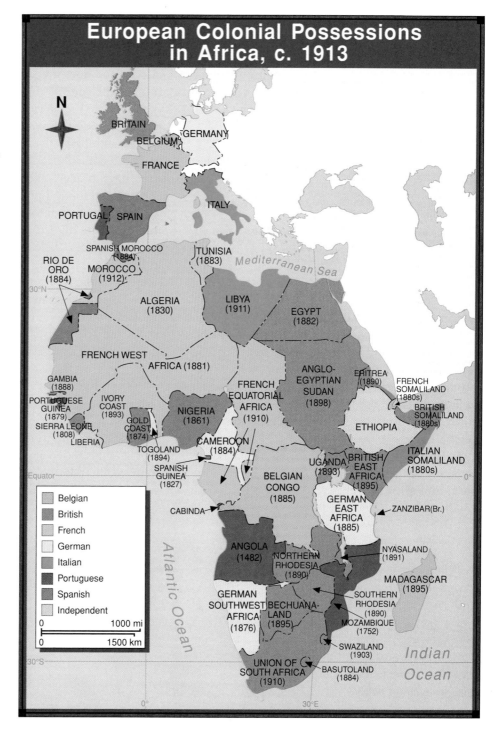

European Colonial Possessions in Africa, c. 1913

N

BRITAIN
BELGIUM
GERMANY
FRANCE
ITALY
PORTUGAL
SPAIN

SPANISH MOROCCO (1884)
RIO DE ORO (1884)
MOROCCO (1912)
TUNISIA (1883)
Mediterranean Sea
30°N
ALGERIA (1830)
LIBYA (1911)
EGYPT (1882)
FRENCH WEST AFRICA (1881)
GAMBIA (1888)
PORTUGUESE GUINEA (1879)
SIERRA LEONE (1808)
LIBERIA
IVORY COAST (1893)
GOLD COAST (1874)
TOGOLAND (1894)
NIGERIA (1861)
FRENCH EQUATORIAL AFRICA (1910)
CAMEROON (1884)
SPANISH GUINEA (1827)
ANGLO-EGYPTIAN SUDAN (1898)
ERITREA (1890)
FRENCH SOMALILAND (1880s)
BRITISH SOMALILAND (1880s)
ETHIOPIA
ITALIAN SOMALILAND (1880s)
Equator
UGANDA (1893)
BELGIAN CONGO (1885)
BRITISH EAST AFRICA (1895)
GERMAN EAST AFRICA (1885)
ZANZIBAR (Br.)
CABINDA
Atlantic Ocean
ANGOLA (1482)
NORTHERN RHODESIA (1890)
NYASALAND (1891)
MADAGASCAR (1895)
GERMAN SOUTHWEST AFRICA (1876)
BECHUANA-LAND (1895)
SOUTHERN RHODESIA (1890)
MOZAMBIQUE (1752)
SWAZILAND (1903)
Indian Ocean
30°S
UNION OF SOUTH AFRICA (1910)
BASUTOLAND (1884)
0°
30°E

	Belgian
	British
	French
	German
	Italian
	Portuguese
	Spanish
	Independent

0   1000 mi
0   1500 km

Japan, like the countries of Europe, sought to extend its influence in China, Korea, and Manchuria. Where actual colonization was not practical, nations sought to establish **spheres of influence**, areas of control informally recognized by other powers.

Within these spheres, they established military bases and trading posts.

Each power looked with fear and jealousy on the successes of its rivals in the race for empire. Military power was essential to get and guard imperial possessions. Thus, imperial rivalry in turn caused an **arms race**, a peacetime buildup of weapons, among the major powers. As one nation increased its military power, other nations increased their own military power, or they formed new alliances to reestablish the former balance of power. The nationalism of individual European countries fanned the fires of rivalry in virtually every imaginable way. The rivalries for empire were among the primary causes of the outbreak of World War I in 1914.

Foreign Policy Develops

The goal of a nation's foreign policy is to promote and protect its vital national interests. These include, for example, defending a nation's territory, promoting trade, and protecting its citizens' legal activities overseas. These goals may be accomplished by using such means as diplomacy, military power, and prestige. Until the late nineteenth century, the United States was ill-prepared to protect its national interests.

As late as the 1880s, the U.S. State Department had only 25 ministers posted to foreign capitals. It had no diplomats of ambassador rank until 1893. In 1889, the *New York Sun* claimed that the State Department had outlived its usefulness and called for its abolition. "It is a nurse to snobs," the *Sun* declared, "and does no good to anybody." Moreover, most of the nation's diplomats, including secretaries of state, were inexperienced amateurs. Many were political appointees whose diplomacy was often clumsy and ineffective. Washington officials often had little control over foreign policy. Instead, diplomats, naval officers, and sometimes even private citizens created foreign policy on the spot.

Other agents of foreign policy were no more impressive. In 1890, the U. S. Army ranked 13th in size in the world, below Bulgaria. Fighting Indians in the West, exploring and surveying land, and engineering public works projects occupied U.S. soldiers. Foreign governments were aware of America's military potential. During the Civil War, the United States had proved itself capable of raising, equipping, and leading massive armies. Yet, potential military power was not the same as actual military power.

Given the nation's geography and national interests, a strong navy was far more important than a large army. During the Civil War, the Union navy had expanded and modernized. After the war, however, its ships rotted at the docks. In terms of warship tonnage, in 1885 the U.S. Navy ranked 12th in the world, just behind Chile. A future secretary of the

▶

The light cruiser USS Newark *was built in the late 1880s and was part of the growing effort to reform and modernize the U.S. Navy. What role might this ship have played in the United States' new foreign policy?*

navy observed that the navy amounted to a bunch "of floating washtubs."

By the 1880s, many influential Americans were discussing the need for a coherent and effective foreign policy. Emerging foreign policy experts—including politicians, scholars, military strategists, and other opinion makers—realized the importance of the rapid changes in the world situation. They understood that rivalries among the major powers were making the world a much more dangerous place. They concluded that the United States could defend its own interests only by building up its national power and prestige.

◄ *Alfred Mahan's writings were influential in Europe as well as in the United States. How did his arguments promote a worldwide naval arms race?*

The Large Policy Navy Captain **Alfred Thayer Mahan** outlined a comprehensive plan to accomplish these ends. In *The Influence of Sea Power on History* (1890) and other writings, Mahan argued that sea power was the key to national survival in international relations. Echoing Social Darwinism, Mahan believed that nation-states were engaged in a ruthless struggle for survival and expansion. A nation with a powerful navy and the bases to support it was invulnerable in war and prosperous in peace. Mahan believed that the United States should:

- increase its exports
- gain new markets and sources of raw materials
- expand its merchant fleet
- set up bases to service its fleets
- construct a large modern navy to protect its shipping and bases
- build an interocean canal so the navy could move easily between the Atlantic and Pacific.

Mahan's thinking was very influential. His supporters included Massachusetts Senator Henry Cabot Lodge and future president **Theodore Roosevelt**, among many others. These advocates of national power and prestige worked tirelessly to implement Mahan's ideas and to create what they called the **Large Policy**. Large-policy advocates believed that a coherent foreign policy required new ways of thinking. They mobilized support for a modern steam-driven and steel-armored navy. By the close of the century, Congress voted funds to build 17 battleships, 6 armored cruisers, and an array

of smaller craft. The "floating-washtub" navy of 1885 became a formidable force by 1910.

Following the Large Policy meant clearly defining vital national interests and applying national policies consistently. Would Germany, Britain, or Japan take American interests in Asia seriously, for example, if the United States dealt meekly with Cuba or Spain over matters of vital national interest?

The Large Policy required government officials to adopt new practices. Supporters of a consistent foreign policy wanted foreign-policy decisions to be made by officials in Washington rather than by diplomats or naval officers in the field. Since most decision makers believed the American public did not understand the nation's vital interests, they became increasingly willing to influence public opinion through the news media. Over time, large-policy advocates were able to develop a more coherent foreign policy.

American Influence Overseas

American public opinion sometimes opposed, but at other times supported, greater U.S. involvement overseas. Most Americans, for example, opposed acquisition of Hawaii, at least until the late 1890s. Even so, by the mid–nineteenth century, American missionary families such as the Doles

Technology and Imperialism

In the 1870s, science fiction writer Jules Verne wrote a book entitled *Around the World in Eighty Days*. Most readers thought that the idea of actually traveling around the world as quickly as Verne's hero Phineas Fogg was sheer fantasy. But by the winter of 1889–1890 life had imitated fiction. *New York World* reporter Elizabeth Cochrane Seaman, who adopted the pen name "Nellie Bly" after a Stephen Foster tune, bettered Fogg's fictional time. She dashed around the world in 72 days, 6 hours, 11 minutes, and 14 seconds. "Nellie" had traveled 21,740 miles at an average speed of over 22 miles an hour. Clearly, technology had bound the world's people together more tightly than ever before.

Changes in technology profoundly affected the world situation. Technology was making even the most remote corners of the world accessible. Steam-driven ships sped up the pace of ocean voyages. Engineering feats like the Suez Canal (completed in 1869) significantly reduced travel time from Europe to regions bordering the Indian and Pacific Oceans. River steamers and railroads made travel into the interiors of every continent easier. Underwater telegraph cables spanning the oceans, such as the TransAtlantic Cable,

▲ *Journalist Elizabeth Cochrane Seaman, who wrote under the name "Nellie Bly," began her writing career at the age of eighteen.*

▲ *This 1866 lithograph depicts the arrival of the TransAtlantic Cable off Newfoundland's coast.*

quickened international communication. Cables and overland telegraphy expanded the scope, depth, and immediacy of people's knowledge of the world. News, military and diplomatic traffic, and business information traveled with ever-greater speed and increasing volume. Thus, technology fostered the growth of worldwide networks through which goods, people, and ideas could be exchanged.

Europeans discovered that taking quinine effectively reduced the dangers of malaria, allowing them to live in tropical regions. Europeans used new rapid-fire arms, including primitive machine guns, to defeat numerically superior native

peoples when they resisted European control. Finally, improved transportation and communications made conquest and control of colonial territory easier. Europeans had fashioned empires in the seventeenth and eighteenth centuries. Thanks to nineteenth-century technology, the major powers now governed and controlled their empires more tightly.

1. How did changes in technology influence communications and travel in the late nineteenth century?
2. How did improved technology aid the European powers in governing and controlling their empires?

In 1893, a group of American sugar planters and Christian missionaries, with the help of the U.S. Marines, drove Queen Liliuokalani from the throne. The U.S. government apologized to Hawaiians a century later. How did the overthrow of Queen Liliuokalani reflect American large-policy attitudes?

dominated Hawaii's economy and government. In 1875, Hawaii and the United States signed a treaty that allowed Hawaiian sugar to enter the U.S. without tariff in exchange for Hawaii's promise not to give territory or special trading privileges to any other country. The treaty encouraged vast growth in sugar production. But in 1890, the McKinley Tariff placed customs duties on Hawaiian sugar. This caused a major economic crisis in the islands.

Queen Liliuokalani (lee-lee-OO-oh-kah-LAHN-ee), the new ruler in Hawaii, greatly resented the influence of American merchants and sugar planters in Hawaii's affairs. She proclaimed a new constitution that gave her absolute political power. The Americans in Hawaii staged a revolution and sent a delegate to Washington to negotiate a treaty of annexation. In early 1893, President Benjamin Harrison sent this treaty to the Senate. Since Harrison's term was about to end, President-elect Grover Cleveland asked the Senate not to vote on the treaty. Once Cleveland took office, he withdrew the treaty and sent a commission to Hawaii to investigate the situation. Cleveland discovered that Hawaiians did not favor annexation by the United States, and he scrapped the treaty. Sanford Dole, president of the revolutionary government, proclaimed Hawaii an independent republic in 1894, but continued to lobby Congress to support annexation.

As a result of these large-policy attitudes, the United States became more assertive in foreign af-

fairs. The active search for a U.S. naval base in the Samoan Islands led to diplomatic, and nearly military, conflict with Germany and Britain. After wrangling over control of Samoa for more than ten years, the three powers established joint control there in 1889. In another case, the United States threatened war with Chile after 2 American sailors died and another 17 were injured in a riot in Valparaiso in 1891. The war scare passed when Chile apologized and paid an indemnity to the United States.

Americans' assertive mood and talk of war continued to mount in the 1890s. As E. L. Godkin, editor of *The Nation*, said in 1894, "Navy officers dream of war and talk and lecture about it incessantly. The Senate debates are filled with predictions of impending war and with talk of preparing for it at once." Even President Grover Cleveland, an opponent of military intervention abroad, was not immune, as his meddling in a conflict between Great Britain and Venezuela in 1895 showed. In that conflict, Cleveland tried to force Britain to **arbitrate** (negotiate with an impartial third party) the disputed border between British Guiana and Venezuela. Talk of war again filled the air. Theodore Roosevelt said, "I rather hope that the fight will come soon. The clamor of the peace faction has convinced me that this country needs a war." American interference was annoying to the British. Having no allies in Europe, however, Britain decided to court the Americans as a potential ally rather than create an enemy. They finally agreed to arbitration. Another war scare had passed, but a larger one was looming on the horizon.

The Spanish-American War

By the 1890s, 20,000 Cuban immigrants lived in the United States. Many were **refugees**, people who had fled the worsening economic and political conditions in Cuba. Cuba and Puerto Rico were Spain's last two colonies in Latin America. The refugees organized secret societies and clubs dedicated to freeing Cuba from Spanish control. They raised money and sent supplies to Cuban rebels. They also tried to create American public support for Cuban independence. In Chicago, the *Club Patriotico Cubano*, with the help of labor unions, churches, and American patriotic organizations, staged a pro-Cuba rally in late September 1895. Over 6,000 people attended the rally. The Chicago City Council even adjourned a meeting so its members could attend. The Committee of 100 was formed to keep Chicagoans' pro-Cuba enthusiasm alive. In the next few months, similar demonstrations took place in cities across the United States. By December, resolutions, petitions, and letters supporting Cuban independence were flooding Congress. As events unfolded in Cuba, American public opinion was clearly being shaped to support Cuban independence.

What caused the Spanish-American War?
What were the major influences on American public opinion concerning Spain and Cuba?
How did President McKinley handle the conflict with Spain over Cuba?

Revolt Against Spanish Rule

Cuban resentment over Spanish rule had smoldered for decades. After years of waiting for promised reforms, fighting broke out in 1895. Cuban rebels were no match for the 120,000 Spanish troops sent to put down the rebellion. The rebels resorted to nontraditional military tactics known as **guerrilla warfare**. These included surprise attacks by small, quick-hitting forces. They also used **terrorism**, violent acts aimed at civilians, such as blowing up passenger trains and public facilities and destroying both foreign- and native-owned property. Spanish troops, commanded by General Valeriano Weyler, responded in kind. Weyler began a campaign aimed at stopping the terrorist attacks that included arbitrary arrests and executions. He also began a "reconcentration" program that forced the inhabitants of suspected rebel areas into concentration camps. The camps were foul places where thousands of Cubans died of starvation and disease. The island became a slaughterhouse as terrorist acts by one side led to reprisals by the other.

Americans sympathized with the Cubans, who appeared to be fighting for liberty and democracy against an autocratic Old World power. Most American newspapers supported the Cubans. Sensational stories about the Cuban crisis became ammunition in the battles waged by newspapers for circulation and advertising. Such sensationalist reporting became known as **yellow journalism**, or the yellow press, probably because of the colored inks used in popular comic strips such as the "Yellow Kid." New York City became the center for the yellow press. The *Journal*, owned by **William Randolph Hearst**, and the *World*, owned by Joseph Pulitzer, took advantage of every opportunity to increase their readership. At the height of the Cuban crisis, both of these newspapers printed around 1.5 million copies a day. The *World*, for example, described "butcher" Weyler as a modern-day Genghis Khan who trailed "the corpses of bound victims" behind him. The *Journal*, not to be outdone, depicted Weyler as Spain's "most ferocious and bloody soldier . . . [and a] fiendish despot."

More important than the yellow press in influencing American public opinion, however, was the Cuban Junta. (A junta is a group of political conspirators.) This group supported the activities of Cuban exiles in the United States. They raised money, distributed stories supporting the rebels to newspapers, and lobbied tirelessly in Washington for American intervention.

Despite public pressures to intervene in Cuba, President Cleveland avoided action. His administration adopted a policy of neutrality to the extent that geography and Americans' sympathies would allow. Cleveland understood that Americans had significant economic interests in Cuba. These included investments of $40 million in Cuban sugar and mining. Even so, Cleveland had little sympathy for the rebels, who seemed to him lawless and unstable. Cleveland feared that an independent Cuba or a Cuba in the hands of another nation would jeopardize American interests.

President McKinley Acts

Americans elected William McKinley president in 1896 on a platform that supported the large policy and called for Cuban independence and "the eventual withdrawal of all European powers from the Western Hemisphere." McKinley hoped to achieve these policy goals peacefully, but he was willing to use force if necessary. He hoped to continue Cleveland's neutrality policy toward Cuba.

McKinley, however, would not accept, as Cleveland did, Spain's attempt to crush the rebellion by any means. The carnage in Cuba genuinely horrified McKinley, and he privately donated $5,000 toward Cuban relief. On June 26, 1897, McKinley sent a note to Spain to clarify his position. The note emphasized American interest in the restoration of peace. It condemned Spain's reconcentration policy and insisted that Spanish troops fight in Cuba in a "civilized" fashion. McKinley also warned that a solution to the Cuban crisis must be acceptable to the Cubans as well as to Spain.

McKinley put forward two solutions. First, he offered to purchase Cuba from Spain. Spain rejected this idea out of pride and nationalism. Second, McKinley tried to arbitrate a truce between the Spanish and Cubans, but neither side would settle for less than complete victory. Failing to achieve either solution, McKinley sent the battleship *Maine* to Havana harbor in January 1898 to protect Americans and their property and to pressure Spain into a settlement. At home, the president tried to divert Congress's attention from Cuba by introducing a bill for Hawaiian annexation. Congress passed a joint resolution for this purpose by large majorities, and McKinley signed it on July 7, 1898.

Two blows rocked Spanish-American relations in February 1898. On February 9, Hearst's *Journal* published a private letter written by Enrique Dupuy de Lôme (doo-PWEE duh-LOHM), Spanish envoy to the United States. De Lôme's letter contained a personal insult to McKinley, calling him a petty politician who was "weak and a bidder for the admiration of the crowd." Unruffled by the personal insult, McKinley was more concerned by de Lôme's suggestion that Spain's promised reforms in Cuba were not being carried out in good faith. De Lôme immediately resigned, and Spain officially apologized. Nevertheless, the incident offended the American public, and Spanish-American relations worsened.

Declaration of War Six days later, on February 15, the battleship *Maine* mysteriously exploded and sank in Havana harbor. Two hundred sixty American

▼ *This cartoon entitled* The Spanish Brute *was published in 1898 during the Spanish-American War. What was the aim of this cartoon?*

THE SPANISH BRUTE

sailors perished. Although there was little evidence to support the charge, Americans immediately blamed the incident on Spain. The slogan "Remember the *Maine*" echoed in the press throughout the nation.

Despite the anti-Spanish clamor, McKinley avoided quick action. Yet he soon sensed that Spain was merely stalling. Therefore, on March 27, 1898, McKinley issued an ultimatum. Spain must declare an immediate armistice, permanently abolish the reconcentration policy, and permit McKinley to mediate the dispute. Mediation would occur only if the Spanish and Cubans could not reach an agreement during the armistice. Finally, McKinley threatened to submit the matter to Congress if Spain did not accept his demands.

Since Spain recognized that the third demand was equivalent to freeing Cuba, they agreed only to the first two. Not satisfied with their response, McKinley on April 11 asked Congress for authority to end the Cuban rebellion. On April 19, Congress passed a joint war resolution. It proclaimed the end

of Spanish sovereignty in Cuba and gave McKinley authority to employ armed force to expel Spain from the island. In the **Teller Amendment**, Congress vowed that the United States would not annex Cuba. A few days later, Spain declared war on the United States. The nation found itself in a foreign war for the first time in over 50 years.

"Not Much of a War"

The actual fighting lasted only four months. As Theodore Roosevelt said, "It wasn't much of a war, but it was the only war we had." Informed observers fully expected the United States to win because Spain was a weak, second-rate power. Still, the speed and ease with which the United States defeated Spain astonished everyone. Much of the credit for this outcome went to the new navy.

Although the war occurred because of events in Cuba, the actual fighting began in the Spanish-

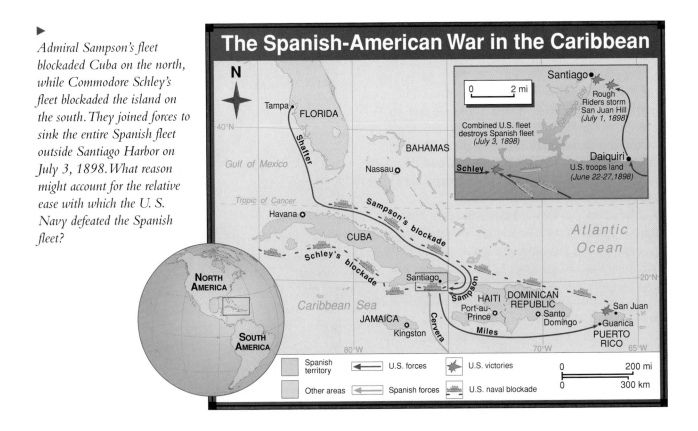

Admiral Sampson's fleet blockaded Cuba on the north, while Commodore Schley's fleet blockaded the island on the south. They joined forces to sink the entire Spanish fleet outside Santiago Harbor on July 3, 1898. What reason might account for the relative ease with which the U. S. Navy defeated the Spanish fleet?

"Remember the Maine"

The USS *Maine* arrived at Havana in late January 1898. Part of its mission was to ease tensions and promote Spanish-American goodwill. Spanish officials were cordial and showed the *Maine*'s officers and crew every courtesy. American and Spanish sailors mingled in town. Townspeople went to see the ship and to sell food and souvenirs to the crew. Then, on the evening of February 15, an explosion ripped through the *Maine*'s hull.

Official dispatches from Havana soon reported that the ship had sunk and almost the entire crew had perished. No one knew the cause of the explosion. Newspapers rushed extra editions to the streets. Under banner headlines, news stories—often as fanciful as factual—described the disaster and speculated about its causes. Many Americans, influenced by the reporting in the yellow press, assumed that the explosion was not accidental and that Spain was somehow at fault. For the next six weeks, the *Maine* was constantly in the news. The result, as the French ambassador reported, was that "a sort of bellicose [warlike] fury has seized the American people."

McKinley, hoping to cool public passions, quickly appointed

▲ *The* New York Journal *used the sinking of the USS* Maine *to fight its own war for readers and advertising dollars. What evidence of yellow journalism can be seen?*

a naval board of inquiry to investigate the disaster. As the inquiry went forward, Senator Lodge noted, "If it is found that the *Maine* was blown up from the outside, it will be difficult to restrain the American people." The *Cleveland Leader* agreed: "Nine out of every ten American citizens doubtless believe firmly that the explosion which destroyed the *Maine* was the result of the cowardly Spanish conspiracy, and the Report of the Court of Inquiry will not tend to destroy that belief."

In late March, the American commission reported that an external explosion had destroyed the *Maine*, but it assigned no blame. A simultaneous Spanish inquiry concluded that an internal explosion

had destroyed the *Maine*. Most Americans, however, were in no mood to listen.

Nearly eighty years later, a U.S. Navy inquiry headed by Admiral Hyman Rickover supported Spain's position. Such explosions were reasonably common on the modern naval vessels of that time. Coal dust occasionally caused spontaneous explosions, and faulty electrical wiring could have detonated the ship's ammunition stores.

1. How did the *Maine's* sinking influence American public opinion toward Spain?
2. Why were Americans so eager to blame the explosion on Spanish agents?

Bottled up in Santiago Bay by a superior U.S. naval force, the Spanish finally decided to leave the safety of the harbor. Within hours, the U.S. fleet sank all the Spanish ships. How did this sea battle affect Spain's hopes for victory in Cuba?

controlled Philippine Islands. As the Cuban crisis worsened, Theodore Roosevelt—then assistant navy secretary—cabled Commodore George Dewey to prepare to attack the Spanish fleet at Manila harbor. Dewey, in Hong Kong, was the commander of the United States Asiatic Squadron. On May 1, Dewey's squadron destroyed Spain's weak fleet without losing a single American life. Dewey then blockaded the harbor and waited for reinforcements.

U.S. volunteer soldiers, who eventually numbered 11,000, began arriving in the Philippines in late June. Although these troops captured Guam (Spain's possession in the Mariana Islands) on the way, they accomplished little in the Philippines be-

◄ *Frederic Remington, famous for his paintings and sculptures of the Old West, memorialized the charge of Teddy Roosevelt and the Rough Riders up San Juan Hill.*

fore the war ended. The Filipino people thought their islands would become independent if they helped the Americans fight the Spanish. Filipino rebel leader Emilio Aguinaldo helped Dewey organize and arm the Filipinos to fight the Spanish troops.

In Cuba the small American army was less prepared to fight a foreign war than was the navy. Two hundred thousand volunteers and National Guardsmen soon bolstered the regular army. Roosevelt resigned as assistant navy secretary to raise a volunteer regiment—which became known as the Rough Riders—and to fight in Cuba. U.S. troops landed near Santiago, Cuba, in late June. In the **Battle of San Juan Hill**, the Rough Riders and the Ninth Cavalry, a regiment of African American soldiers, stormed this strategic point on July 1. After they captured San Juan Hill, American artillery forced the Spanish fleet to flee Santiago harbor. It sailed into the hands of the powerful American fleet, which quickly sank all the Spanish ships. U.S. naval forces also soon captured Spanish-held Puerto Rico. Loss of life from battle casualties was relatively low (nearly 400); however, diseases such as malaria and yellow fever took nearly 6,000 American lives.

Spain requested peace terms in late July and signed an **armistice**, a mutual agreement to end hostilities, on August 12. McKinley's peace demands jolted the Spanish. Spain had fully expected to lose Cuba, but McKinley also demanded Puerto Rico and Guam. The fate of the Philippines was left to be decided at a later date. The Spanish, utterly defeated, had little choice but to sign the armistice.

SECTION 3 REVIEW

1. State reasons for American interest in Cuba during the 1890s.
2. List the major causes of the Spanish-American War.
3. Define the term *yellow journalism*.
4. Explain what Theodore Roosevelt meant when he said, "It wasn't much of a war, but it was the only war we had."
5. Describe the role played by Theodore Roosevelt in the Spanish-American War.

SECTION 4

The United States' Imperial Experiment

In January 1903, the *Christian Advocate* reported a story that described how McKinley reached his decision about Philippine annexation. "I walked the floor of the White House night after night until midnight," McKinley said, "and I am not ashamed to tell you, gentlemen, that I went down on my knees and prayed Almighty God for light and guidance more than one night. And one night late it came to me this way . . . :" McKinley decided it would be cowardly to give the Philippines back to Spain and that it would be bad business to leave the islands to Germany and France, America's business rivals in Asia. He believed the Filipinos were "unfit for self-government." He finally concluded that "there was nothing left for us to do but to take them all, and to educate the Filipinos, and uplift and civilize and Christianize them . . . And then I went to bed, and went to sleep and slept soundly. . . ." While McKinley's position had many supporters, his decision disturbed other Americans.

What were the most important results of the Spanish-American War?

What were the major arguments used by supporters and opponents of the Treaty of Paris?

What problems did U.S. policymakers face in the Philippines, Cuba, and other colonial possessions after the war?

Debate on the Merits of Empire

In October 1898, Spanish and American negotiators met in Paris to draft a peace treaty. McKinley sent five commissioners, including one Democratic and two Republican senators. As expected, Spain agreed to most of the terms outlined in the armistice agreement. However, the fate of the Philippines proved to be a thorny issue. Technically, Manila and the Philippines were not spoils of war because U.S. soldiers had captured Manila after the

Territorial Expansion of the United States, to 1904

Acquisition	Date of Acquisition	Area of Acquisition (Square Miles)	Manner of Acquisition
Original States and Territories	1783	888,685	Treaty with Great Britain
Louisiana Purchase	1803	827,192	Purchased from France
Florida Cession	1819	72,003	Treaty with Spain
Texas Annexation	1845	390,143	Annexed independent nation
Oregon Country	1846	285,580	Treaty with Great Britain
Mexican Cession	1848	529,017	Yielded by Mexico
Gadsden Purchase	1853	29,640	Purchased from Mexico
Alaska	1867	586,412	Purchased from Russia
Hawaii	1898	6,450	Annexed independent nation
The Philippines	1898	115,600	Yielded by Spain (granted independence, 1946)
Puerto Rico	1898	3,435	Yielded by Spain
Guam	1898	212	Yielded by Spain
American Samoa	1900	76	Treaty with Germany and Great Britain
Panama Canal Zone	1904	553	Treaty with Panama (returned by treaty to Panama, 1978)

▲ *During the nineteenth century, the United States grew to become one of the largest countries in the world. Which territories of the present United States were purchased?*

armistice. McKinley nevertheless instructed the peace commissioners to demand the Philippines. Spain finally agreed to the settlement after McKinley offered to pay $20 million for the islands. The Treaty of Paris was signed on December 10, 1898.

When McKinley sent the treaty to the Senate for ratification, its terms touched off a storm of debate. The treaty's supporters basically followed McKinley's line of reasoning. Above all, they feared that another major power would seize the islands for themselves. Germany, which had sent a naval squadron to Manila during the war, was especially suspect. American patriots argued that once the U.S. flag flew over the Philippines, it should remain there. Moreover, many business people thought the Philippines could serve as a base for selling American goods in the coveted Chinese market. These were strong arguments for annexation.

Opponents of the Treaty of Paris included many prominent people. Former Presidents Harrison and Cleveland, industrialist Andrew Carnegie, labor leader Samuel Gompers, writer Mark Twain, and reformer Jane Addams were among those who opposed the treaty in particular and expansionism in general. The anti-imperialists, as they called themselves, argued that the United States had previously acquired only thinly settled territory on the North American continent. These areas had been capable of statehood and full participation in the republic.

Treaty opponents doubted that the Philippines, alien in so many respects and 10,000 miles distant, could follow that pattern. They also argued that the Filipinos desired freedom and that American possession of the islands violated the cardinal principle of "consent of the governed." They argued that democracy and imperialism were contradictory principles. Despotism of this sort abroad, they thought, could produce despotism at home. Furthermore, the anti-imperialists thought that Philippine annexation would propel the United States into a great power rivalry in Asia, with unforeseen consequences.

It seemed that the treaty was doomed to fall short of the two-thirds vote necessary for ratification. At this point, William Jennings Bryan publicly stated his support for the treaty. Bryan, Democratic candidate for president in 1896, flatly opposed annexing the Philippines. Even so, he saw potential Democratic political advantage by branding the Republicans as imperialists. First, Bryan argued that to reject the treaty would leave the nation technically at war with Spain with the Philippine question undecided. Second, since the United States already had the islands, the sooner the Senate ratified the treaty, the sooner the Philippines could be freed. Ratifying the treaty would be a first step to independence for both the Philippines and Cuba. Finally, Bryan said the people should decide the issue " . . . not by a minority of the Senate but by a majority of the people." The next presidential election should be a referendum on Philippine annexation. With Bryan's support, the Senate ratified the Treaty of Paris on February 6, 1899, with only one vote to spare.

▼ *Under the leadership of General Emilio Aguinaldo, Filipino rebels inflicted heavy casualties on U.S. troops.*

The United States and Empire

The Filipinos assumed they would be freed after the war. The Senate, however, would not pass such a clear-cut pledge. Conflicts between the Filipinos and U.S. troops stationed there increased after the war. On February 4, 1899, Emilio Aguinaldo led the Filipinos into open rebellion against the Americans. The United States found itself in an imperial war *against* rule and consent of the governed—a principle this country had supported.

The struggle in the Philippines continued for over two years and involved far more savage fighting and many more casualties than the Spanish-American War. Since American troops usually defeated the ill-equipped Filipinos in formal battles, the rebels melted into the jungle to wage vicious guerrilla warfare. American troops were savage in turn. Stories of atrocities on both sides shocked Americans at home. The United States forced Filipinos into concentration camps, much as "butcher" Weyler had done in Cuba. The fighting ended in 1901 when American

▼ *By May 1900, over 70,000 U.S. soldiers were in the Philippines, trying to put down the Filipino rebellion against U.S. rule. Why did the United States want to control the Philippines?*

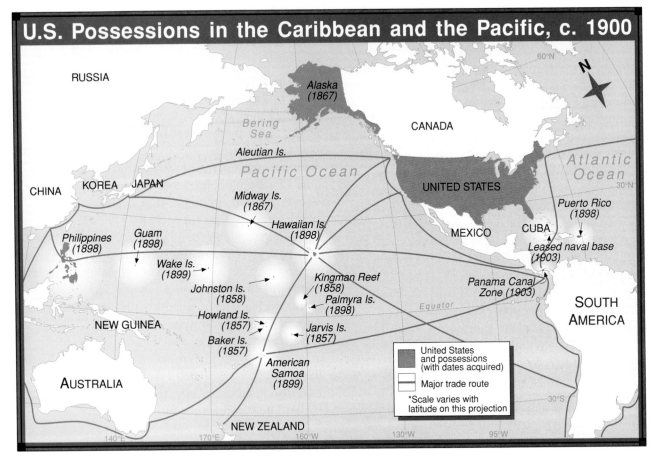

U.S. Possessions in the Caribbean and the Pacific, c. 1900

RUSSIA

Alaska (1867)

Bering Sea

CANADA

Aleutian Is.

Pacific Ocean

Atlantic Ocean

CHINA KOREA JAPAN

Midway Is. (1867)

UNITED STATES

Puerto Rico (1898)

Hawaiian Is. (1898)

MEXICO CUBA

Philippines (1898) Guam (1898)

Leased naval base (1903)

Wake Is. (1899)

Kingman Reef (1858)

Panama Canal Zone (1903)

Johnston Is. (1858)

Palmyra Is. (1898)

Equator

SOUTH AMERICA

NEW GUINEA

Howland Is. (1857)

Jarvis Is. (1857)

Baker Is. (1857)

American Samoa (1899)

United States and possessions (with dates acquired)

Major trade route

*Scale varies with latitude on this projection

AUSTRALIA

NEW ZEALAND

▲ *Alfred Mahan—author of the Large Policy—wrote that the United States should no longer regard the world's oceans as protective barriers, but as vast highways for carrying on world trade. Even though American colonial possessions were relatively few, how did they help the U. S. become a world power?*

troops captured Aguinaldo, although sporadic outbursts dragged on for months. In all, 4,200 Americans and thousands of Filipinos lost their lives in the fighting.

The anti-imperialists, horrified by these events in the Philippines, redoubled their protests over American involvement. At the same time, President McKinley tried to solve the problem of governing the islands. The United States poured millions of dollars into the islands, improving roads, public health, and sanitation. Sugar became the most important of many economic links binding the two countries. In 1899, McKinley had appointed the Philippine Commission to investigate the situation and make recommendations. The commission recommended Philippine independence, but at some future unspecified date.

The Foraker Act Important constitutional questions arose as a result of acquiring an overseas empire. McKinley set up military governments in the Philippines, Puerto Rico, and Cuba without specific congressional authority. In 1900, Congress passed the Foraker Act, which established civilian government in Puerto Rico. The act did not grant Puerto Ricans American citizenship or complete self-government. It placed tariffs on Puerto Rican goods imported into the United States. In *Downes v. Bidwell* (1901), the tariff issue came before the Supreme Court. The challengers argued that Puerto Rico was part of the United States and tariffs were therefore illegal. The Supreme Court, however, upheld the tariff. In this and other cases, the Supreme Court gave Congress and the president broad authority to develop colonial policy.

▲ *This photograph, dated around 1916, shows U.S. improvements to the naval station at Guantánamo Bay, Cuba. Who occupies Guantánamo Bay today?*

The Platt Amendment Cuba created even more headaches for American policymakers. When the first Americans arrived during the Spanish-American War, they found government, public services, and the economy at a virtual standstill. Conflict almost immediately broke out between American troops and the Cubans. Tensions increased after McKinley established a military government on the island in 1898. Congress had attached the Teller Amendment to the war resolution against Spain which denied "intention to exercise sovereignty, jurisdiction or control" over Cuba. Even so, many Americans, including military governor General Leonard Wood, thought annexation the best solution to Cuban problems. Moreover, U.S. economic interests, the strategic importance of Cuba to the United States, and political chaos on the island all suggested that America would not withdraw. The major powers expected the United States to annex Cuba and could scarcely believe it when the United States withdrew in 1902.

The United States, however, did not turn Cuba completely loose. Just as McKinley worried about Germany's designs on the Philippines, so he feared its meddling in the Caribbean. McKinley could not allow Germany or any other major power to secure a position only 90 miles from the United States. Therefore, the United States forced the Cubans to adopt the **Platt Amendment** in their new constitution (1901). The Platt Amendment restricted Cuban autonomy in foreign affairs. Cuba could not enter into a treaty with another power nor borrow foreign funds beyond its ability to repay. It granted the United States the right to intervene in Cuba in order to restore order "as necessary for mutual protection." The Cubans also agreed to lease a naval base at Guantánamo Bay to the United States, which it still operates. The agreement, which provided for Cuban self-government, protected American interests, and it could be revoked only with the consent of both parties.

SECTION 4 REVIEW

1. **Explain** why the U.S. agreed to pay $20 million for the Philippine Islands.
2. **Identify** three reasons that led the United States to annex the Philippines rather than grant them independence after the war.
3. **List** the reasons the anti-imperialists opposed annexing the Philippine Islands.
4. **Describe** the results of the Platt Amendment.
5. **State** the constitutional questions that arose as a result of the U.S. acquiring an overseas empire.

The United States as a World Power

In 1899, Assistant Secretary of State John Bassett Moore reflected on the events of the past decade. He noted that the United States had moved "from a position of comparative freedom from entanglements into the position of what is commonly called a world power. . . . Where formerly we had only commercial interests, we now have territorial and political interests as well." In addition, American policymakers were more willing to use force on behalf of their foreign policies. Between 1870 and 1890, no U.S. troops served outside the country, but by 1900 they were fighting, standing guard, and even performing governmental duties in Cuba, Puerto Rico, the Philippines, and China. For good or ill, these activities signified America's emergence as a major world power.

What events in China prompted the Open Door notes?

Why did the Boxer Rebellion lead Hay to send the second Open Door note?

Did Hay's Open Door notes accomplish what he hoped they would?

The Lure of China

One reason many Americans favored annexing the Philippines was because they lay close to China. Americans involved in commerce and industry had long dreamed of selling American goods to the Chinese. Since the 1840s, English merchants had dominated trade with China. Now other nations were threatening the British trade advantage. Japan, as a result of its decisive victory in the Sino-Japanese War (1894), had taken control of Formosa (Taiwan) and forced favorable trade concessions from China. Russia, France, and Germany, working together to lessen Japanese control in China, had established spheres of influence in port cities on the Chinese mainland.

The British were disturbed by the actions of the other powers and approached President McKinley with a proposal that would prevent the partition of China. McKinley decided not to join with the British, since he feared American public opinion would not support joint action with Britain. Moreover, McKinley and his secretary of state, John Hay, were planning to act alone. Hay sought to protect American interests while avoiding any entangling alliances with Britain or any other major power. Hay had been eager to act for some time. In 1899 the time seemed right because Japan, Germany, Russia, and Great Britain all wanted to protect their own trade and investments throughout China.

The Open Door Policy

On September 6, 1899, Hay addressed the first of two notes that would form the **Open Door Policy** to Britain, France, Germany, Russia, Italy, and Japan. He asked them to pledge that they would not close their spheres of interest in China to the other powers. For example, he wanted to prevent the powers charging unfair port fees and railroad freight rates in their own spheres of influence. Hay's objective was to ensure that America was able to trade freely in China. He did not intend to criticize the foreign nations' intervention in China.

Hay asked each power to cooperate with the United States in getting the other powers to recognize the Open Door principles. The powers, however, had mixed reactions to Hay's Open Door note. Their replies generally evaded agreement with Hay's position. Russia, resenting American meddling, sent the most negative reply. Hay nevertheless announced on March 20, 1900, that all the major powers had responded favorably to America's position.

Meanwhile, a wave of antiforeign violence, led by a secret society of Chinese nationalists known as the Righteous, Harmonious Fists (or Boxers), erupted in China. The crumbling Manchu dynasty, led by the dowager empress Tz'u-hsi (tsoo-shee), initially

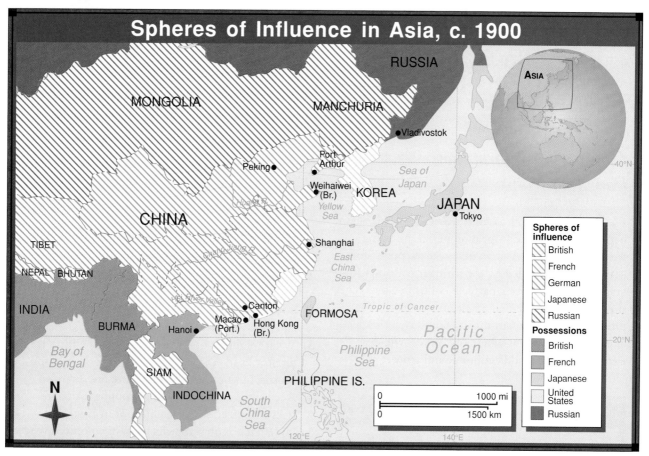

Spheres of Influence in Asia, c. 1900

Spheres of influence
- British
- French
- German
- Japanese
- Russian

Possessions
- British
- French
- Japanese
- United States
- Russian

▲ *By the end of the nineteenth century, the major European powers and Japan had established colonies in Asia and had carved out significant spheres of influence in China. What countries had possessions or spheres of influence bordering on the Yellow Sea?*

▼ *In 1900, foreign troops entered Peking (Beijing), the capital of China, to liberate missionaries there. What nations supplied soldiers for the rescue effort?*

encouraged the rebellion, hoping to loosen the foreigners' grip on China. The Boxers destroyed foreign-owned property, attacked foreign missionaries and businesspeople, and killed a number of foreigners, including German and Japanese diplomats. The Boxers then set siege to diplomatic missions in Peking (Beijing), where the foreigners had gathered for protection. The rival powers hastily organized a military force of 20,000, including 2,500 Americans. The force fought its way to Peking and rescued their citizens, who had been stranded there for 55 days.

The **Boxer Rebellion** put Hay's Open Door principles to the test. McKinley and Hay worried that the other powers would use the rebellion as an excuse for further partition of China. So on July 3, 1900, Hay issued a second Open Door note. Hay declared that American policy sought to safeguard

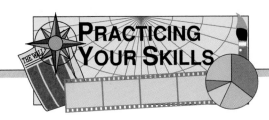

Comparing Information from Two Maps

In the nineteenth century, Africa and Asia again became targets for European imperialism. Some parts of Africa and Asia became *colonies*, possessions completely controlled by the stronger nations. Others became *protectorates*, partially controlled by a stronger power and dependent on that power for protection from foreign threats. Some were *spheres of influence*, territories where one power wielded exclusive political and economic influence.

Review the guidelines for reading maps in the Practicing Your Skills on page 81. Then examine the maps on pages 517 and 533 and answer the following questions:

1. (a) What time period is covered by these maps? (b) What is the subject of each map?
2. (a) Which colonial powers shown on these maps are European powers? (b) Which is an Asian power? (c) Which power is both a European and an Asian power?
3. What might be one reason that competition for territories in Asia led to war between Japan and Russia, but not between England and France?
4. According to the map, what country or countries colonized in Africa but not in Asia?
5. (a) What country appears to have colonized the largest area in Africa? (b) What country had the largest sphere of influence in Asia?
6. Why is there no color symbol for independent countries on the map of Asia?
7. What fact might account for the relatively few German possessions on both maps?

European Colonial Possessions in Africa, c. 1913

BRITAIN
GERMANY
BELGIUM
FRANCE
ITALY
PORTUGAL SPAIN

SPANISH MOROCCO (1884)
RIO DE ORO (1884)
MOROCCO (1912)
TUNISIA (1883)
Mediterranean Sea
ALGERIA (1830)
LIBYA (1911)
EGYPT (1882)

FRENCH WEST AFRICA (1881)
GAMBIA (1888)
PORTUGUESE GUINEA (1879)
IVORY COAST (1893)
SIERRA LEONE (1808)
LIBERIA
GOLD COAST (1874)
NIGERIA (1861)
FRENCH EQUATORIAL AFRICA
ANGLO-EGYPTIAN SUDAN (1898)
ERITREA (1890)
FRENCH SOMALILAND (1880s)
BRITISH SOMALILAND (1880s)
ETHIOPIA

TOGOLAND (1894)
CAMEROON (1884)
SPANISH GUINEA (1827)
UGANDA (1893)
BRITISH EAST AFRICA (1895)
ITALIAN SOMALILAND (1880s)
Equator
BELGIAN CONGO (1885)
CABINDA
GERMAN EAST AFRICA (1885)
ZANZIBAR (Br.)

ANGOLA (1482)
NORTHERN RHODESIA (1890)
NYASALAND (1891)
MADAGASCAR (1895)
Atlantic Ocean
GERMAN SOUTHWEST AFRICA (1876)
BECHUANA-LAND (1895)
SOUTHERN RHODESIA (1890)
MOZAMBIQUE (1752)
SWAZILAND (1903)
Indian Ocean
UNION OF SOUTH AFRICA (1910)
BASUTOLAND (1884)

Legend:
- Belgian
- British
- French
- German
- Italian
- Portuguese
- Spanish
- Independent

0   1000 mi
0   1500 km

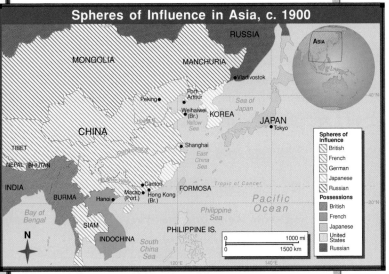

Spheres of Influence in Asia, c. 1900

ASIA

RUSSIA
MONGOLIA
MANCHURIA
Vladivostok
Port Arthur
Peking
Weihaiwei (Br.)
KOREA
Sea of Japan
JAPAN
Tokyo
CHINA
Shanghai
Yellow Sea
East China Sea
TIBET
NEPAL BHUTAN
INDIA
BURMA
Hanoi
Macao (Port.)
Canton
Hong Kong (Br.)
FORMOSA
Tropic of Cancer
Pacific Ocean
Bay of Bengal
SIAM
INDOCHINA
PHILIPPINE IS.
Philippine Sea
South China Sea

Spheres of Influence
- British
- French
- German
- Japanese
- Russian

Possessions
- British
- French
- Japanese
- United States
- Russian

0   1000 mi
0   1500 km

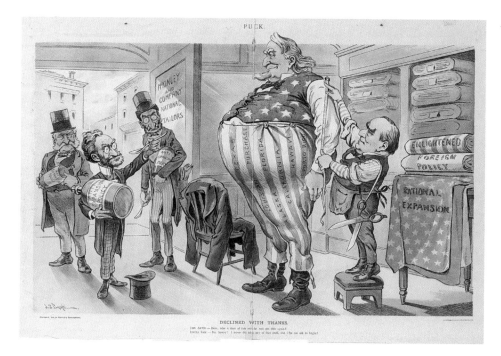

President William McKinley (the tailor) is measuring Uncle Sam for a new and larger suit of clothes. Meanwhile, Uncle Sam is declining the anti-imperialists' offer of a "fat-reducing" medicine. Why did the cartoonist include the names of various territories on the striped pants worn by Uncle Sam?

the Open Door throughout China and to preserve China's political integrity. China was forced to pay nearly a third of a billion dollars indemnity for the damage the Boxers caused, but was spared from further partition.

Americans hailed Hay's Open Door Policy as an important diplomatic victory. They believed that Hay's diplomacy had protected America's trading interests in China while also avoiding entangling alliances with other nations. At the same time, Hay had protected China from further partition. These outcomes, however, resulted mainly from the precarious balance among the major powers in Asia rather than from American diplomacy. While Hay's diplomacy was admirably cautious and an apparent success, the note of 1900 seemed to commit the United States not only to the Open Door, but also to preserving China's territorial and political in-

tegrity. Later administrations felt morally pledged to support China against Japan and other major powers. Over time, this moral commitment expanded even though America's available power and its actual interests in China were quite small.

SECTION 5 REVIEW

1. State the reason some Americans were interested in China.
2. Specify the intent of John Hay's first Open Door note to the major powers.
3. Relate why the Chinese empress encouraged the Boxer Rebellion.
4. Explain why Hay felt it necessary to send a second Open Door note.
5. Evaluate the effectiveness of Hay's Open Door Policy in protecting American interests.

Summary

From the War of 1812 to the early 1880s, the United States was relatively isolated from international affairs. After that time, however, dynamic economic growth forced Americans to look beyond their own shores. Farmers, merchants, and manufacturers wanted new markets for their vastly increasing volume of products. Meanwhile, imperial rivalries among the European powers threatened arms races, international stability, and trade, which in turn threatened America's vital national interests.

Between the early 1880s and the Spanish-American War in 1898, many influential Americans began to think more seriously about their nation's position in the world. They created ambitious foreign policy plans to ensure America's safety and prosperity. They also refashioned the nation's navy and the diplomatic corps. With better means at its disposal, the United States became more aggressive in asserting its interests around the world. The stunning victory over Spain in the Spanish-American War was more a symbol than a cause of the nation's rise to world-power status.

By 1900, the United States was recognized by all as a major world power. Its industrial output was second to none. Its armed forces had proved formidable in war. Its colonies extended from the Caribbean Sea across the Pacific to the shores of Asia. Moreover, the nation was now involved in the rivalries of the major powers as the Open Door Policy in China clearly revealed. Isolation from foreign involvement was over. While many Americans rejoiced in their newfound sense of power and prestige, others opposed U.S. imperialism or clung to isolationist traditions. These legacies would influence American diplomacy throughout the twentieth century.

Vocabulary

arbitrate
armistice
arms race
balance of power
diplomatic mission
embassy
guerrilla warfare
imperialism

Large Policy
Open Door Policy
refugees
Social Darwinism
spheres of influence
terrorism
yellow journalism

Examine the vocabulary terms grouped below and decide which term does not belong in each group. Then explain the relationships of the remaining terms.

1. Large Policy; Open Door Policy; arbitrate
2. diplomatic mission; embassy; Social Darwinism; imperialism
3. guerrilla warfare; arms race; yellow journalism; terrorism; armistice
4. balance of power; refugees; spheres of influence

Review Questions

1. Explain how the industrial and transportation revolutions encouraged imperialism on the part of industrialized nations.
2. Why was there an apparent lack of interest in imperialism in the United States until the late nineteenth century?
3. Compare the U.S. balance of trade before and after the Civil War.
4. Why was there concern in the United States as production of farm and factory products continued to grow?
5. Briefly summarize the large policy.
6. How did American journalists encourage support for the Spanish-American War?
7. Describe methods used by President McKinley to end the Cuban revolt and to protect American interests on the island.

8. Summarize arguments used by anti-imperialists against the Treaty of Paris in 1899.

9. Explain how the United States retained some control over Cuba in spite of the decision not to annex the island.

10. Summarize the main intent of Secretary of State Hay's Open Door Policy in China.

Critical Historical Thinking

Writing Answer each of the following by writing one or more complete paragraphs:

1. The perception that there was no longer a frontier for American expansion was one of the driving circumstances behind U. S. imperialism. What effect would the lack of frontiers have on immigrants, homesteaders, conservationists, and land speculators?

2. Compare and contrast the Monroe Doctrine with Hay's Open Door Policy, especially with regard to the United States' imperialism.

3. Yellow journalism played a large part in conditioning the American people to accept the Spanish-American War. Discuss whether newspapers today have as much influence in determining public opinion.

4. Read the selections "Why the United States Should Keep the Philippines" and "Bryan Opposes Colonial Annexation" in the Unit 5 Archives. Your own personal opinion aside, which writer is more persuasive? Why?

Making Connections with Social Psychology

When Bill Clinton ran for the presidency in 1992, his avoidance of military service was considered to be a liability. Could a president who protest-ed American military actions be a competent commander in chief?

It is often the case that those presidents who have experienced combat are the most reluctant to commit the nation to military action. Prior to the War of 1812, the War Hawks cried out for war with England. President Madison, however, could remember the anguish of the American Revolution and the miraculous American victory.

In the months leading up to the outbreak of war with Spain, a young Theodore Roosevelt thought President McKinley cowardly for not immediately declaring war. McKinley had fought in the Battle of Antietam, the bloodiest single day in American history, and in several other Civil War battles. He was reluctant to put the country and its young men through war unnecessarily.

Writing Read excerpts from Edmund Burke's (1729–1797) writings on British cruelties during the American War of Independence. Research and write an essay that answers the following question: Have the steps taken by international bodies such as the Geneva Convention and the United Nations to reduce the cruelty of war been effective?

Additional Skills Practice

Study the maps of North America and Europe in the Atlas located at the back of your textbook to answer these questions:

1. How has the location of the United States and Europe affected their participation in world events?

2. Why would you expect the attitude of Europeans toward isolationism to be different from that of North Americans?

3. How would this view be affected by ballistic missiles and instant global communications?

Unit Review Questions

1. Explain why the South did not share in the general economic prosperity following the Civil War.
2. List two reasons for the new wave of migration west after the Civil War.
3. Identify the major industries that made use of the land originally occupied by the Plains Indians and the great buffalo herds.
4. How did the lives of the Plains Indians change as a result of the westward migrations?
5. Describe briefly the effect of massive European immigration to the United States after the Civil War.
6. What were two of the major changes in American life caused by industrialization?
7. How did politics affect American life in the decades immediately following the Civil War?
8. Describe three concerns that led to the formation of the Populist Party.
9. Explain why American policies began to change from isolationism to active participation in global affairs after the Civil War.
10. Name three factors that contributed to America's being viewed as a major world power by 1900.

Personalizing History

Traveling Light The decision to emigrate to the United States was a difficult one for many families in the late nineteenth century. Life in Europe was marked by religious and political persecution. Farmland was becoming scarce as the population of Europe grew. Passenger ships were crowded and unhealthy. The decision to leave homeland and friends must have been very difficult. Furthermore,

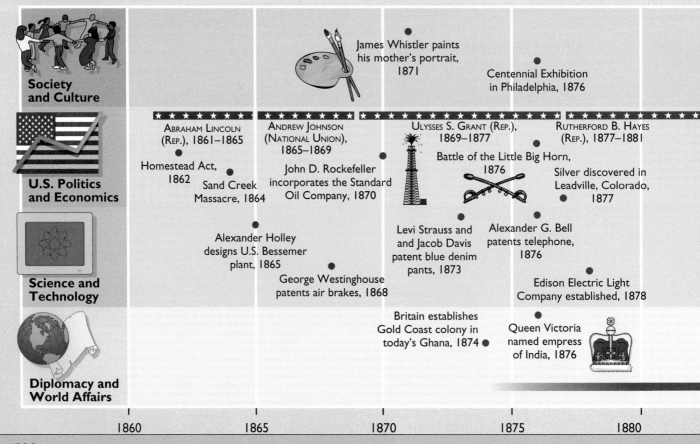

Society and Culture

James Whistler paints his mother's portrait, 1871

Centennial Exhibition in Philadelphia, 1876

U.S. Politics and Economics

ABRAHAM LINCOLN (REP.), 1861–1865

ANDREW JOHNSON (NATIONAL UNION), 1865–1869

ULYSSES S. GRANT (REP.), 1869–1877

RUTHERFORD B. HAYES (REP.), 1877–1881

Homestead Act, 1862

Sand Creek Massacre, 1864

John D. Rockefeller incorporates the Standard Oil Company, 1870

Battle of the Little Big Horn, 1876

Silver discovered in Leadville, Colorado, 1877

Science and Technology

Alexander Holley designs U.S. Bessemer plant, 1865

George Westinghouse patents air brakes, 1868

Levi Strauss and and Jacob Davis patent blue denim pants, 1873

Alexander G. Bell patents telephone, 1876

Edison Electric Light Company established, 1878

Diplomacy and World Affairs

Britain establishes Gold Coast colony in today's Ghana, 1874

Queen Victoria named empress of India, 1876

1860   1865   1870   1875   1880

families were able to bring very few possessions with them to America. What would you have taken with you if you had been in this position?

Pretend you must leave your home, never to return. What possessions would you take? Choose items that would fit in one paper bag, no larger.

■ Make a list of the belongings you have chosen and write an explanation. What would be the hardest custom for you to leave behind? Write a paragraph that states whether you could have done what these immigrant Americans did.

Linking Past and Present

City Living The period following the Civil War was one of great change in the United States. The nation was flooded with immigrants. Along with the growth of industry, railroads, and cities, increasing worker discontent and dissent

appeared. Labor began to speak out and newspapers spread the word, influencing public opinion. Today, inner city dwellers are still facing the problems brought on by poverty, overcrowding, and inefficient or corrupt local governments.

■ Design a poster that illustrates one of the problems facing the urban dweller. In the design, incorporate a creative idea for one way to begin solving the problem, however small the effort may seem to you.

Time Line Activity

Find a pair of items on the time line that demonstrates a cause-and-effect relationship or shows a correlation. Explain the nature of the relationship between the items.

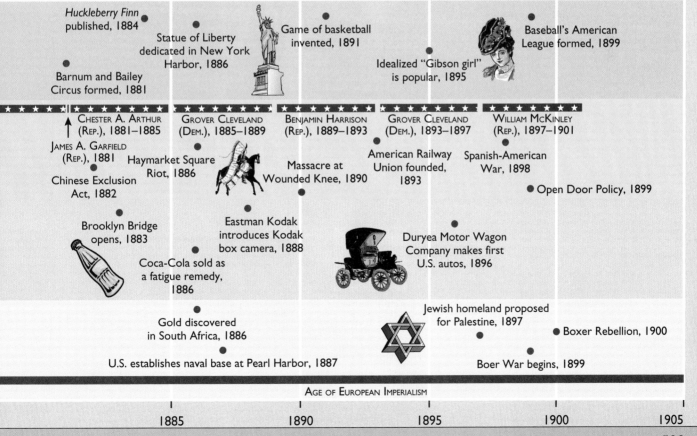

Huckleberry Finn published, 1884

Statue of Liberty dedicated in New York Harbor, 1886

Game of basketball invented, 1891

Idealized "Gibson girl" is popular, 1895

Baseball's American League formed, 1899

Barnum and Bailey Circus formed, 1881

CHESTER A. ARTHUR (REP.), 1881–1885

GROVER CLEVELAND (DEM.), 1885–1889

BENJAMIN HARRISON (REP.), 1889–1893

GROVER CLEVELAND (DEM.), 1893–1897

WILLIAM MCKINLEY (REP.), 1897–1901

JAMES A. GARFIELD (REP.), 1881

Haymarket Square Riot, 1886

Massacre at Wounded Knee, 1890

American Railway Union founded, 1893

Spanish-American War, 1898

Chinese Exclusion Act, 1882

Open Door Policy, 1899

Brooklyn Bridge opens, 1883

Eastman Kodak introduces Kodak box camera, 1888

Duryea Motor Wagon Company makes first U.S. autos, 1896

Coca-Cola sold as a fatigue remedy, 1886

Jewish homeland proposed for Palestine, 1897

Boxer Rebellion, 1900

Gold discovered in South Africa, 1886

Boer War begins, 1899

U.S. establishes naval base at Pearl Harbor, 1887

AGE OF EUROPEAN IMPERIALISM

1885   1890   1895   1900   1905

UNIT 6

The Progressive Era

The early twentieth century was an era of business expansion and of progressive reform. Big businesses kept getting bigger. This alarmed many Americans, who saw corporate power as a threat to democracy. Alarmed by a rash of corporate mergers, they strengthened antitrust laws and gave the federal government more power to regulate corporations. These progressives, as they called themselves, also worked to make American society a better and safer place in which to live. In addition, they worked to clean up corrupt city governments, to improve working conditions in factories, and to better living conditions in the slums. They brought about other reforms by amending the United States Constitution. This generation of Americans also hoped to make the world a more democratic place in which to live. The United States joined Britain and France, two democratic nations, in their war against autocratic Germany and Austria-Hungary.

Chapter 17 Stirrings of Reform	**Chapter 18** Progressive America	**Chapter 19** Progressive Era Diplomacy

◀ *This 1915 magazine illustration is titled* Retouching An Old Masterpiece. *A founding father looks over the shoulder of a suffragette as she amends the Declaration of Independence. Readers' interpretations of the image depended on their views about women's suffrage.*

Themes

- **Economics** The United States entered a period of rapid economic expansion, with big corporations becoming even bigger and more powerful.
- **Democracy and Citizenship** Progressives broadened the definition of democratic citizenship to include reforming American politics and helping working-class Americans to improve their living and working conditions.
- **Arts and Humanities** Novelists, journalists, and scholars helped to make Americans more aware of the social and political problems of industrial America.
- **Global Interactions** The United States also based its relations with other nations on progressive and democratic ideals. President Woodrow Wilson wanted to make the world safe for democracy.

Andrew Carnegie on Wealth

Andrew Carnegie's ideas about wealth and civilization were applauded and widely shared by industry leaders.

The Socialist or Anarchist who seeks to overturn present conditions is to be regarded as attacking the foundation upon which civilization itself rests. . . . Upon the sacredness of property, civilization itself depends—the right of the laborer to his hundred dollars in the savings bank, and equally the right of the millionaire to his millions. . . . Not evil, but good, has come to the [human] race from the accumulation of wealth by those who have the ability and energy that produce it.

> Andrew Carnegie, "Wealth," *North American Review* (June 1889), p. 656.

The Death of Kostanty Butkowski

In the following letter, the brother of an immigrant killed in a foundry informed his family in Poland of the tragedy.

Now I inform you, dearest parents, and you, my brothers, that Kostanty, your son, dearest parents, and your brother and mine, my brothers, is no more alive. It killed him in the foundry, it tore him in eight parts, it tore his head away and crushed his chest to a mass and broke his arms. But I beg you, dear parents, don't weep and don't grieve. God willed it so and did it so. It killed him on April 20, in the morning, and he was buried on April 22.

He was buried beautifully. His funeral cost $225, the casket $60. Now when we win some [money] by law from the company, we will buy a place and transfer him that he may lie quietly, we will surround him with a fence and put a cross, stone, or iron upon his grave. This will cost some $150. For his work, let him at least lie quietly in his own place. It is so, dear parents: Perhaps we shall re-

ceive from the [insurance] society $1,000. . . . Whatever we receive, after paying all the expenses I will send you the rest, dear parents, and I will come myself to my country.

> Antoni Butkowski to Dear Parents (Apr. 26, 1903). William Thomas and Florian Znaniecki, *The Polish Peasant in Europe and America* (5 vols., Chicago, 1918), vol. II, pp. 263–264.

The Concentration of Power in Corporate America

The Spread of Trusts

This description of the growth of trusts emphasized the unfair business practices of some of the trust builders.

In the course of the last two years trusts have been formed in sugar, pork, oatmeal, glass and wheat flour. At this very moment a great struggle is going on between the sugar trust and the legislature and courts of New York State. Up to now the trust has been the victor on all points, although the courts have succeeded in making public many facts about the internal workings, and more important, about the profits of this trust . . . that the ringleader, Havemeyer, made more than $12,000,000 in one year.

> Tverskoy [Peter A. Demens], *Urban America* (1895), pp. 352–354.

The Concentration of Financial Power

Two journalists listed the names of industrialists and bankers who held the power to create monopolies through their control of investment capital.

Seven men in Wall Street now control a great share of the fundamental industries and resources of the United States. . . . They dominate, with their allies and dependents, the national machinery for the making and holding of great corporate monopolies, into which a greater and greater part of the capital and business of the country must inevitably be drawn.

Three of these seven men—Pierpont Morgan, James J. Hill, and George F. Baker, head of the First National Bank of New York—belong to the so-called Morgan group; four of them—John D. and William Rockefeller, James Stillman, head of the National City Bank, and Jacob H. Schiff, of the private banking firm of Kuhn, Loeb & Co.—to the so-called Standard-Oil-City-Bank group.

They are one thing, and one only—makers and traders in monopoly; the oldest and most reliable makers of monopoly in America.

The active leadership in the movement of concentration is in the hands of Morgan. He and Baker and Schiff and Stillman control the machinery for the distribution of securities to the public. But Morgan himself by temperament is the one aggressive constructor of monopolies.

The individuals in the group are old men—all over sixty, all but two over seventy. They will soon be dead. But others will take their places. The group is the thing—the central machine for the control of corporate capital. When these men are gone, others will immediately arise to take control of it.

 John Moody and George Kibbe Turner, "Masters of Capital in America: The Seven Men," *McClures* (Aug. 1911).

The Growing Political Power of Corporations

Senator La Follette of Wisconsin was alarmed by the growing power of railroads and industrial monopolies.

The last thirty years of struggle for just and equitable legislation demonstrates that the powerful combinations of organized wealth and special interests have had an overbalancing control in state and national legislation.

For a generation the American people have watched the growth of this power in legislation.... They have observed that these great combinations are closely associated in business for business reasons; that they are also closely associated in politics for business reasons; that together they constitute a complete system; that they encroach upon the public rights, defeat legislation for the public good, and secure laws to promote private interests.

 Speech of Robert M. La Follette (Apr. 23, 1906), *Congressional Record*, 59th Cong., 1st Sess., pp. 5722–5723.

Drug Abuse, Consumer Fraud, and Impure Food

Urban Youth and Drugs

Jane Addams described the teenage drug problem that existed in the neighborhood of Hull House at the turn of the century.

For several years the residents of Hull House struggled with the difficulty of prohibiting the sale of cocaine to minors.... The long effort brought us into contact with dozens of boys who had become victims of the cocaine habit. The first group of these boys was discovered in the house of "Army George." This one-armed man sold cocaine on the streets and also in the levee [downtown] district by a system of signals so that the word cocaine need never be mentioned, and the style and size of the package was changed so often that even a vigilant police found it hard to locate it. What could be more exciting to a lad than a traffic in a contraband article, carried on in this mysterious fashion?

An investigation showed that cocaine had first been offered to these boys on the street by . . . an agent of a drug store, who had given them samples and urged them to try it. In three or four months they had become hopelessly addicted to its use, and at the end of six months, when they were brought to Hull House, they were all in a critical condition. At that time not one of them was either going to school or working. They stole from their parents, "swiped junk," pawned their clothes and shoes, —did any desperate thing to "get the dope," as they called it.

 Jane Addams, *The Spirit of Youth and the City Streets* (New York: Macmillan Co., 1909), pp. 64–65.

Patent Medicine Fraud

Patent medicines were among the most popular home remedies, although few users were aware of the dangerous nature of some of their contents.

A distinguished public health official and medical writer once made this jocular suggestion to me:

"Let us buy in large quantities the cheapest Italian vermouth, poor gin, and bitters. We will mix them in the proportion of three of vermouth to two of gin with a dash of bitters, dilute [with water] and bottle them by the short quart, label them 'Smith's Revivifyer and Blood Purifyer'."

"That sounds to me very much like a cocktail," said I.

"So it is," he replied. "But it's just as much a medicine as Peruna and not as bad a drink."

Peruna . . . is at present the most prominent [patent medicine] in the country. It has taken the place once held by Greene's Nervura and by Paine's Celery Compound, and for the same reason which made them popular. The name of that reason is alcohol.

Hostetter's Bitters contain . . . 44 percent alcohol; Lydia Pinkham appeals to suffering womanhood with 20 per cent of alcohol; Hood's Sarsaparilla cures "that tired feeling" with 18 percent; . . . and Paine's Celery Compound with 21 per cent.

One thing the public has a right to demand . . . that the government carry out rigidly its promised policy no longer to permit liquors to disguise themselves as patent medicines. . . . That they label every bottle with the percentage of alcohol it contains."

 Samuel Hopkins Adams, "The Great American Fraud," *Collier's* (Oct. 28, 1905).

Making Sausage in Chicago

The following passage from Upton Sinclair's The Jungle *(1906) described how sausages were made in a Chicago packinghouse. Although a fictional account, this description was based on fact.*

There was never the least attention paid to what was cut up for sausage; there would come all the way back from Europe old sausage that had been rejected, and that was moldy and white—it would be dosed with borax and glycerine, and dumped into the hoppers, and made over again for home consumption. There would be meat that had tumbled out on the floor, in the dirt and sawdust, where the workers had tramped and spit uncounted billions of consumption germs. There would be meat stored in great piles in rooms; and the water from leaky roofs would drip over it, and thousands of rats would race about on it. It was too dark in these storage places to see well, but a man could run his hand over these piles of meat and sweep off handfuls of the dried dung of rats. These rats were nuisances, and the packers would put poisoned bread out for them; they would die, and then rats, bread, and meat would go into the hoppers together. This is no fairy story and no joke; the meat would be shoveled into carts, and the man who did the shoveling would not trouble to lift out a rat even when he saw one—there were things that went into the sausage in comparison with which a poisoned rat was a tidbit. There was no place for the men to wash their hands before they ate their dinner, and so they made a practice of washing them in the water that was to be ladled into the sausage. There were the butt-ends of smoked meat, and the scraps of corned beef, and all the odds and ends of the waste of the plants, that would be dumped into old barrels in the cellar and left there. Under the system of rigid economy which the packers enforced, there were some jobs that it only paid to do once in a long time, and among these was the cleaning out of the waste barrels. Every spring they did it; and in the barrels would be dirt and rust and old nails and stale water—and cartload after cartload of it would be taken up and dumped into the hoppers with fresh meat, and shipped out to the public's breakfast.

▲ *Meat processing plant*

 Upton Sinclair, *The Jungle* (New York, 1906), pp. 160–162.

Women's Suffrage: Arguments For and Against

Women Should Have the Right to Vote

The editor of a major New York newspaper gave the women's suffrage amendment this endorsement.

Eliminating from the suffrage controversy all of its cant and twaddle, the question is a straight issue of whether all the adult citizens of the State shall be

entitled to a vote in making the laws to which all of them are subject, or whether this privilege should be the exclusive property of half of these citizens who gain their political power by the accident of sex.

▲ *Suffragette outfit*

"Women's Right to Vote," *New York World* (Mar. 14, 1915).

Women Will Benefit from Having the Vote

Suffrage advocates argued that having the vote would help women protect their own interests.

Women receive a smaller wage for equal work than men do, and . . . the smaller wage and harder conditions imposed on the woman worker are due to the lack of the ballot.

Equal pay for equal work is the first great reason justifying this change in governmental policy.

Robert L. Owen, in *Annals of the American Academy of Political and Social Science,* vol. XXXV (May 1910), Supplement, p. 6.

The Threat to the Home

Its opponents saw women's suffrage as the first step toward their deeper involvement in political life.

Woman's participation in political life . . . would involve the domestic calamity of a deserted home and the loss of the womanly qualities for which refined men adore women and marry them. . . . To children the political activity demanded as a "right"

would be a still greater wrong in often depriving them of a mother's care when most needed.

Henry T. Frick, "Are Womanly Women Doomed?" *The Independent* (Jan. 1901), pp. 269–270.

Not a Step Toward Reform

This female opponent questioned whether women's suffrage would have any benefit.

The question of woman suffrage should be summed up in this way: Has granting the ballot to women in the two suffrage states where they have had it for forty years brought about any great reforms or great results?

Have the saloons been abolished in any of the suffrage states? No.

Have the slums been done away with? Indeed no.

Have women purified politics? No, not in the least.

Have women's wages been increased because women vote? No, indeed.

Are women treated with more respect in the . . . suffrage states than elsewhere? Not at all."

Mrs. Gilbert E. Jones in *Annals of the American Academy of Political and Social Science,* vol. XXXV (May 1910), Supplement, pp. 16–21.

The New Nationalism vs. the New Freedom

Theodore Roosevelt's New Nationalism

In his speech accepting the Progressive Party's presidential nomination in 1912, Theodore Roosevelt addressed the trust issue as follows.

It is utterly hopeless to attempt to control the trusts merely by the antitrust law, or by any law the same in principle, no matter what the modifications may be in detail. In the first place, these great corporations cannot possibly be controlled merely by a succession of lawsuits. The administrative branch of the government must exercise such control. . . .

A national industrial commission should be created which should have complete power to regulate and control all the great industrial concerns engaged in interstate business—which practically means all of them in this country.

Theodore Roosevelt (Aug. 6, 1912).

The Progressive Party Platform

In its 1912 platform, the new Progressive Party included the following plank concerning trusts.

We . . . demand a strong national regulation of interstate corporations. The corporation is an essential part of modern business. The concentration of modern business, in some degree, is both inevitable and necessary for national and international business efficiency. But the existing concentration of vast wealth under a corporate system, unguarded and uncontrolled by the nation, has placed in the hands of a few men enormous, secret, irresponsible power over the daily life of the citizen—a power insufferable in a free government and certain of abuse.

We urge the establishment of a strong federal administrative commission of high standing, which shall maintain permanent and active supervision over industrial corporations engaged in interstate commerce, or such of them as are of public importance.

Such a commission must enforce the complete publicity of those corporate transactions which are of public interest; must attack unfair competition, false capitalization and special privilege.

Progressive Party platform, 1912.

Woodrow Wilson's New Freedom

Woodrow Wilson, the presidential candidate for the Democratic Party, attacked Roosevelt and the Progressive Party's position on the trust issue.

If you have read the trust plank in [the Progressive Party's] platform as often as I have read it, you have found it very long, but very tolerant. It did not anywhere condemn monopoly, except in words; its essential meaning was that the trusts have been bad and must be made to be good. You know that Mr.

Roosevelt long ago classified trusts for us as good and bad, and he said that he was afraid only of the bad ones. Now he does not desire that there should be any more bad ones, but proposes that they should all be made good by discipline, directly applied by a commission of executive appointment. All he explicitly complains of is the lack of publicity and lack of fairness; not the exercise of power, for throughout that plank the power of the great corporations is accepted as the inevitable consequence of the modern organization of industry.

If the government is to tell big business men how to run their business, then don't you see that big business men have to get closer to the government even than they are now? Don't you see that they must capture the government, in order not to be restrained too much by it?

Woodrow Wilson, *The New Freedom* (New York, 1913), pp. 200–203.

Progressive Jurisprudence: *Muller v. Oregon* (1908)

Influenced by the Brandeis Brief, the Supreme Court ruled on the constitutionality of an Oregon law that established maximum hours for women.

The legislation and opinions referred to [in Louis D. Brandeis's brief] . . . may not be, technically speaking, authorities . . . yet they are significant of a widespread belief that woman's physical structure, and the functions she performs in consequence thereof, justify special legislation restricting or qualifying the conditions under which she should be permitted to toil.

That woman's physical structure and the performance of maternal functions place her at a disadvantage in the struggle for subsistence is obvious.

Differentiated by these matters from the other sex, she is properly placed in a class by herself, and legislation designed for her protection may be sustained, even when like legislation is not necessary for men and could not be sustained.

Muller v. Oregon (1908), 208 U.S. 412.

Divorcing Business from Politics: A Prediction

William Allen White, a progressive newspaper editor, made this optimistic prediction about limiting business influence in politics.

The movement to divorce the corporation from politics is so general that a federal law has been enacted limiting campaign contributions. . . . No more important step toward government by the people, for the people, has been taken in this Republic since its beginning. It is true that in many states the law is a form only; but the fact that it is a law indicates a tendency in American thought which eventually will express itself in custom and usage. . . . And it is safe to say that the decree of divorce between business and politics will be made absolute within a few years.

William Allen White, *The Old Order Changeth* (New York, 1910), pp. 47–48.

Intervention in World War I

Wilson Asks Congress to Declare War Against Germany

On April 2, 1917, President Wilson spoke before a joint session of Congress, asking for a declaration of war against Germany.

With a profound sense of the solemn and even tragic character of the step I am taking and of the grave responsibilities which it involves . . . I advise that the Congress declare the recent course of the Imperial German Government to be in fact nothing less than war against the government and people of the United States. . . .

▲ *World War I triplane*

Neutrality is no longer feasible or desirable where the peace of the world is involved and the freedom of its peoples, and the menace to that peace and freedom lies in the existence of autocratic government.

We are glad . . . to fight thus for the ultimate peace of the world and for the liberation of its peoples, the German peoples included. The world must be made safe for democracy.

R.S. Baker and W.E. Dodd, eds., *The Public Papers of Woodrow Wilson: War and Peace* (New York, 1927), vol. I., pp. 6–16.

Senator Norris Speaks Against the Declaration of War

Senator George Norris of Nebraska spoke against the declaration of war in an impassioned speech in the Senate.

To my mind, what we ought to have maintained from the beginning was the strictest neutrality. If we had done this I do not believe we would have been on the verge of war at the present time. . . . We have loaned many hundreds of millions of dollars to the Allies in this controversy. . . . The enormous profits of munitions manufacturers, stockbrokers, and bond dealers must be still further increased by our entrance into the war.

Their object in having war and in preparing for war is to make money.

We are going into war upon the command of gold. We are going to run the risk of sacrificing millions of our countrymen's lives in order that other countrymen may coin their lifeblood into money.

Congressional Record, 65th Cong. 1st Sess. (Apr. 4, 1917), pp. 212–215.

A Republican Senator Supports Wilson

Senator Henry Cabot Lodge, the highest ranking Republican member of the Senate Foreign Relations Committee, supported President Wilson's request for a declaration of war.

Our future peace, our independence as a proud and high-spirited nation, our very security are at stake. There is no other way, as I see it, except by war to save these things without which national existence is a mockery and a sham. But there is a still higher purpose here as I look upon it. . . . We enter this war to unite with those who are fighting the common foe in order to preserve human freedom, democracy, and modern civilization. . . . This is a war, as I see it, against barbarism.

Congressional Record, 65th Cong., 1st Sess. (Apr. 4, 1917), pp. 207–208.

A Democrat in Congress Votes Against Going to War

Congressman Claude Kitchin of North Carolina, who was the Democratic floor leader in the House of Representatives, opposed Wilson's war measure.

I have come to the undoubting conclusion that I should vote against this resolution.

In my judgment, we could keep out of the war with Germany as we kept out of the war with Great Britain, by keeping our ships and our citizens out of the war zone of Germany as we did out of the war zone of Great Britain.

War upon the part of a nation is sometimes necessary and imperative. But here no invasion is threatened. Not a foot of our territory is demanded or coveted. No essential honor is required to be sacrificed. No fundamental right is asked to be permanently yielded or suspended.

We are [asked] to help fight out . . . a difference between the belligerents of Europe to which we were and are utter strangers.

Congressional Record, 65th Cong., 1st Sess. (Apr. 5, 1917), pp. 332–333.

A Republican Questions the Consistency of American Policy

Congressman William L. LaFollette, a Republican from Washington, questioned whether an alliance with Britain against Germany was fair.

Can we consistently declare war on Germany and enter into an alliance with [Britain], who . . .

laid down a prescribed zone in the Atlantic Ocean and the North Sea sowing those waters with deadly contact mines. Three of our vessels were sunk in this prescribed zone with attendant loss of life. . . .

Mr. Chairman, is a life lost by the destruction of a vessel, coming in contact with a floating mine less dear than one lost on a vessel sunk by a torpedo fired by a submarine? Is the water less cold or wet?

The floating mine in my judgment, is more despicable than the submarine, whose operators are at least taking some chances of losing their own lives. We are asked to go into partnership with the belligerent who prescribed a zone and sowed it full of mines to help it destroy the belligerent who prescribed a zone and in that zone uses submarines. Oh, consistency, thou art a jewel.

Congressional Record, 65th Cong., 1st Sess., pp. 207–208.

A Wartime Nation of Immigrants

They'll Forget Tolerance

Frank Cobb, a newspaper editor, reported this conversation with Woodrow Wilson shortly before the president asked Congress for a declaration of war.

He said when a war got going it was just war, and there weren't two kinds of it. It required illiberalism at home to reinforce the men at the front. We couldn't fight Germany and maintain the ideals of government that all thinking men shared.

"Once lead this people into war," he said, "and they'll forget there ever was such a thing as tolerance. To fight you must be brutal and ruthless, and the spirit of ruthless brutality will enter into the very fiber of our national life, infecting Congress, the courts, the policeman on the beat, the man in the street." Conformity would be the only virtue, said the President.

John L. Heaton, *Cobb of "The World"* (New York, 1924), pp. 268–269.

Wartime Hysteria

The author of this account was a commissioner of immigration at Ellis Island during the World War I years.

Hysteria over the immoral alien was followed by a two-year panic over the "Hun." Again inspectors . . . were given carte blanche to make arrests on suspicion. Again Ellis Island was turned into a prison. . . . During these years thousands of [resident alien] Germans, Austrians, and Hungarians were taken without trial from their homes and brought to Ellis Island.

From our entrance into the war until after the armistice my life was a nightmare. My telephone rang constantly with inquiries from persons seeking news of husbands and fathers who had been arrested. On my return home in the evening I would often find awaiting me women in a state of nervous collapse whose husbands had mysteriously disappeared. . . . I furnished them with such information as was possible.

Within a short time, I was branded [by coworkers] as pro-German. I had to war with the local staff to secure decent treatment for the aliens.

Frederick C. Howe, *Confessions of a Reformer* (New York, 1925).

A Close Call in Cleveland

Even pro-war immigrants sometimes found wartime America a dangerous place in which to live.

In Cleveland a few days ago a foreign-looking man got into a street car and, taking a seat, noticed pasted in the window next to him a Liberty Loan poster, which he immediately tore down, tore into small bits, and stamped under his feet. The people in the car surged around him with the demand that he be lynched, when a Secret Service man showed his badge and placed him under arrest, taking him in a car to the police station, where he was searched and found to have two Liberty Bonds in his pocket and to be a non-English [speaking] Pole. When an interpreter was procured, it was discovered that the circular which he had destroyed had had on it a picture of the German Emperor, which had so infuriated the fellow that he destroyed the circular to show his vehement hatred of the common enemy. As he was unable to speak a single word of English, he would undoubtedly have been hanged but for the intervention and entirely accidental presence of the Secret Service agent.

From Frederick Palmer, *Newton D. Baker* (New York, 1931), vol. 2, pp. 162–163.

WORKING WITH THE ARCHIVES

Analyzing Perspectives in Primary Sources

In this skill exercise, you will analyze primary source selections that reflect different perspectives on the issue of voting rights for women.

Directions: Read the archive selections entitled "Women Should Have the Right to Vote," "Women Will Benefit from Having the Vote," "The Threat to the Home," and "Not a Step Toward Reform." Two of the readings support women's suffrage and two oppose it. Next, create and complete a chart that will help you organize your responses to the questions below.

1. What is the large issue being discussed? Across the top of the chart, make a box that summarizes the issue. (In this case, the large issue is "Should women be allowed to vote, thereby taking part in national decision-making politics?")

2. What opinions (perspectives) are expressed on this issue? Set up and give a heading on your chart for each perspective on the large issue.

3. What are the reasons or explanations for the positions taken above? Examine the political, religious, and social beliefs behind the reasons given. Write these underneath the perspective headings.

4. What generalities can you make by bringing the perspectives together? In a box across the bottom of the chart, describe in general terms what you have learned about the times and about the people who wrote on this issue.

Stirrings of Reform

The United States of 1900 was a society undergoing rapid change. "My country in 1900 is something totally different from my own country in 1860," wrote the aging Henry Adams, who was 22 the year Abraham Lincoln was elected president. "I am wholly a stranger in it." A historian by profession, he found himself more at home in the past than in the present.

Unlike Adams, the younger generation who did not remember Abraham Lincoln embraced

▲ *This Ferris wheel was one of the memorable symbols of the 1893 Columbian Exposition.*

the changes taking place around them. To them, the year 1900 was a good time to be alive. They did not overlook the poverty, political corruption, and abuses of corporate power that surrounded them. They intended to change that, too. They faced the future with optimism and with a sense of responsibility for the shape it would take. They wanted to be remembered as a generation that would leave the world better than they found it. In many respects, they succeeded.

Turn-of-the-Century America

In 1900, middle-class Americans faced the future with confidence. They had weathered the depression and the strikes of the 1890s to enter a new era of peace and prosperity. The harvests were good, factory production was up, and businesses were booming. In 1904, the city leaders of St. Louis decided it was time to hold a world's fair. They called it the Louisiana Purchase Centennial and persuaded Congress to appropriate $5 million toward the costs. In fact, it was another celebration of American scientific and industrial progress, like so many other world's fairs held in the United States. In addition to railroad locomotives and industrial machinery, the St. Louis fair featured a large display of automobiles, making it the world's first auto show. It was a celebration of progress and prosperity. "We could not if we would stop this onward march of progress," said an Indiana banker, basking in the optimism kindled by the fair. "We might as well try to stop the ebb and flow of the ocean tide."

How well did the American economy perform in the period from 1897 to 1914?

Which Americans benefited from the return of prosperity?

Which Americans did not share in the benefits of economic growth?

▲ *The opening day ceremonies at the 1904 Louisiana Purchase Centennial Exposition in St. Louis attracted a huge crowd.*

Industrial America Prospers

The beginning of the new century brought a return to prosperity in the United States. The depression that had begun in 1893 had bottomed out by 1896, with signs of recovery becoming evident the following year. A steady rise in the price of corn, wheat, and other farm products after 1900 brought a higher standard of living for farm families. Better roads, increased use of machinery, and the introduction of the Model T also helped improve the quality of rural life. Factory output was up, and exports soared. The United States had become Europe's largest supplier of wheat. By 1900, American farm machinery, sewing machines, and petroleum products flooded the world markets.

The extent of the recovery could be seen in the increase of the **gross national product (GNP)**, the total of the goods and services that a nation produces each year. It is one indicator that economists use to measure economic growth. Between 1897 and 1914, the GNP increased by 6 percent a year. There was a brief financial panic on Wall Street in 1907, when a large New York investment bank failed. Alarmed that the panic might spread, healthy banks rushed to the rescue by loaning money to those in need. But the causes of the panic were bad banking practices, not a weak economy.

Benefits for the Urban Middle Class

The return of prosperity meant the revival of trade, and more money in the cash registers of storekeepers, shop owners, and small manufacturers in cities across the country. Accountants and chemists, lawyers and architects, and other professional people

The gross national product (GNP) is one measure of economic growth. What does the dip in the GNP in 1907–1908 indicate?

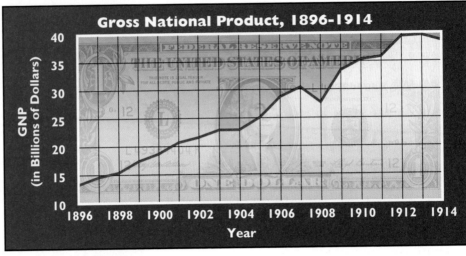

Gross National Product, 1896-1914

▲ By 1919, baseball was quickly becoming the "great American pastime," as attendance shows at this World Series game between the Chicago White Sox and the Cincinnati Reds.

were once again in demand. Businesses hired more women as typists and secretaries for clerical work. As their incomes generally grew faster than the rate of inflation, small-business owners and professional people enjoyed an improved standard of living. After those wealthy families who owned the railroads, banks, and factories, the urban middle class gained the most from the upswing of the economy.

The return of prosperity also gave middle-class men and women the benefit of more leisure time. Factory workers and farmers still worked long hours, but the eight-hour workday became com-

mon among white-collar workers. Congress legislated eight-hour workdays for employees of government contractors (1912) and workers on interstate railroads (1916). Summer vacations became commonplace for business and white-collar employees, although not yet for blue-collar workers. In 1910, the *New York Times* conducted a poll of prominent Americans to find out how much annual vacation time they thought was essential. Most of the recommendations ranged from two weeks to a month and a half. William Howard Taft, the easygoing president of the United States at that time, recommended two to three months.

The middle class occupied its new leisure time with a variety of recreational activities. By 1915, baseball was no longer merely a sandlot game or just another professional sport, like boxing and horse racing. It was evolving into the activity that would later cause French-born critic and historian Jacques Barzun to write, "Whoever wants to know the heart and mind of America had better learn baseball, the rules and realities of the game—and do it by watching . . . small town teams."

Fans packed the bleachers at ballparks, transforming baseball into "the great American pastime." As baseball became a national institution, it also became racially segregated. In the early years of baseball, several African American athletes played on predominantly white baseball teams, and all-black teams occasionally played against white teams in the same league. By 1900, the color line had been

▲ *Amusement parks of the early 1900s had much in common with those of modern times. Riding bumper cars is still popular.*

drawn, with African American players and teams excluded from major and minor league baseball. Black players later formed their own leagues, the Negro National League (1920) and the Eastern Colored League (1923).

Nearly every city had an amusement park, as well as a baseball field. These parks usually included a Ferris wheel, a roller coaster, and a carousel. County and state agricultural fairs attracted large crowds. By the turn of the century, the traditional livestock exhibits were overshadowed by concession stands, band pavilions, amusement rides, circus tents, and other amusements. County fairs were no longer just for farmers.

The newest type of entertainment was motion pictures. Invented by Thomas Alva Edison in the 1880s, the movies had become a form of mass entertainment by 1910. In that year, the nation's 10,000 movie theaters drew a weekly audience of 10 million people. With the price of a ticket at around 5 cents, movies attracted urban working-class as well as middle-class audiences. The first movie spectacular was D. W. Griffith's The *Birth of a Nation* (1915), an epic film about the Civil War and Reconstruction period. Although innovative in its use of such film techniques as close-ups and fade-outs, the film dealt a major blow to racial understanding in the United States. Its portrayal of black people during Reconstruction as a threat to American values strengthened the tide of racial prejudice sweeping the nation during the Progressive Era.

Americans also invested time in adult education and self-improvement. The most popular national adult education program was the Chautauqua movement, which brought adults and families

▼ *Wisconsin Governor Robert M. La Follette addressed many groups, such as this Chautauqua meeting in Decatur, Illinois, interested in improving themselves and the world around them.*

American Landscape

Movement in the United States: Going to Town

In 1900, the United States was rapidly becoming a nation of city dwellers. Although some Americans still moved westward in search of land and fortune, many more were now lured to the nation's expanding cities. By 1900, 30 million of America's 76 million people were urbanites (city dwellers). One-twelfth of the nation's population lived in New York, Philadelphia, or Chicago.

By 1910, America's great cities were swelling in size. New York's population had soared to 3 million, and the city dominated trade across the Atlantic. The building of the Erie Canal—which completed a link that ultimately connected New York to the Great Lakes—and the growth of railroads had made New York a focus for interior trade, as well. San Francisco, Los Angeles, and Seattle were major trading centers on the shores of the Pacific. In the interior, Pittsburgh and St. Louis were located at important river junctions. At either end of the Mississippi, Minneapolis-St. Paul and New Orleans were thriving cities. Chicago, the country's most active rail hub, was, in the words of poet Carl Sandburg, "hog butcher, tool maker, stacker of wheat, player with railroads, and freight handler to the nation."

After the Chicago Fire of 1871, the wealthy residents migrated south and formed exclusive neighborhoods. Immigrant neighborhoods in the west and north became well established by 1900 and took on a distinctively ethnic feel. The population grew to nearly 2 million by 1910—more than three-quarters of the population was foreign-born or had at least one parent who was foreign-born.

The rate of urbanization varied from one part of the country to another. In 1900, 19 American cities had populations of more than 250,000. Fourteen of these were located in the northern belt of industry that stretched from the Atlantic coast inland along the southern shores of the Great Lakes to Chicago and Milwaukee. Seven of every ten people in New England and the Middle Atlantic states lived in cities, as did half the Great Lakes population. These industrial centers drew large numbers of whites from rural farmlands and African Americans from the South. A comparable level of ur-

together for weeklong summer camps. Begun in 1878 at Chautauqua, New York, the program had spread throughout the United States by 1912. Chautauqua meetings usually took place in a large tent pitched at a local campground. People gathered to attend scientific demonstrations, musical performances, and lectures. Popular speakers such as William Jennings Bryan and labor leader Eugene V. Debs traveled from one Chautauqua to another, their engagements arranged by a national speakers' bureau. In one summer, Bryan gave 50 Chautauqua lectures in 28 days.

Few Benefits for the Working Classes

The return of prosperity was a mixed blessing. More jobs and higher wages placed additional money in the hands of consumers. However, the increased spending power also pushed up the price of consumer goods. Prices rose at the rate of about 3 percent a year, creating the first period of inflation since the Civil War. Many working-class families

banization was reached on the West Coast, where the population of San Francisco had reached 1 million in 1890 and Los Angeles would emerge as a center for finance and industry.

By contrast, the western plains region with its reliance on grain farming and cattle raising had far fewer cities of size. The lowest rate of urbanization was in the South, where only one of every five people lived in a city. It was the great-est of all American migrations—the country was determined to go to town.

1. What were the three largest cities in the United States in 1900?
2. What is urbanization? Are you an urbanite?
3. Give reasons why your city (or the city nearest you) grew in size and importance.

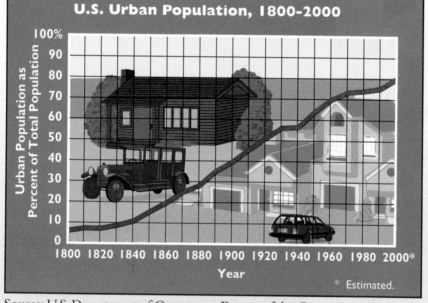

U.S. Urban Population, 1800–2000

Urban Population as Percent of Total Population

Year

* Estimated.

Source: U.S. Department of Commerce, Bureau of the Census

◀ *One of the most significant long-term population changes (demographic trends) in the United States was the movement of people from rural to urban areas.*

were worse off than before, as higher prices more than canceled out their increased income.

The wages of industrial workers lagged far behind the salaries of white-collar employees, and men working in industry earned more than women. Most industrial workers earned barely enough for survival. Unskilled workers in Chicago's meat-packing houses earned $7.40 a week and frequently faced layoffs when business was slack. Young women in New York City's clothing factories worked at sewing machines 70 hours per week at top speed to earn $4.00 to $5.00 per week. As food for a working-class family of six people cost about $5.00 per week in 1910, most families needed more than one wage earner. Wages remained low partly because labor unions had failed to organize unskilled workers. As described earlier, the failure of the Homestead and Pullman Strikes had crushed the steelworkers unions and railroad unions that existed in the 1890s.

Industrial work was still dangerous and unhealthy. In the year 1917 alone, 11,338 workers died in industrial accidents, and 1,363,080 were injured on the job. The courts provided workers little

▲ *Immigrant families worked from their tenement apartments finishing men's suits. From what countries did most immigrants come at the turn of the century?*

protection. Court rulings, based on English common law, held that employers were not at fault if they could demonstrate that an injury or death was the result of employee carelessness. Employers were also not liable if they could show that the employee knew that the occupation involved risks. Employers had little difficulty proving one or the other.

The return of prosperity did little to relieve the distress of the urban poor. Robert Hunter, author of a book entitled *Poverty* (1904), estimated that 10 million people in the cities of the United States were so poor that they were slowly starving to death. Thousands of poor families barely eked out a living earning just pennies a day by doing menial tasks. In New York City, whole families worked together in their tenement apartments making paper flowers or sewing buttons on clothing brought to them by manufacturers. Many of the urban poor were recently arrived immigrants. They were easily exploited by manufacturers looking for cheap labor.

New Urban Immigrants

Between 1900 and 1915, more than 15 million immigrants arrived in the United States. That was as many immigrants as had arrived during the preced-

ing 40 years. Seventy-six percent of New York's population in 1910 consisted of foreign-born people and first-generation Americans.

The source of immigration had also shifted dramatically. Unlike most earlier immigrants, the majority of the newcomers after 1900 came from non-English-speaking countries. Southern and eastern Europe produced several million new immigrants. Most of them came from Italy, Poland, and Russia. Different from other Americans in language and culture, the new immigrants faced a difficult task in adjusting to life in the United States.

American cities, in turn, had difficulty absorbing the new immigrants. The inner cities were overwhelmed by the torrent of newcomers. They crowded into four- and five-story tenement buildings, often with one room per family. City services failed to keep up with the population explosion. In 1900, two-thirds of Chicago's streets were unpaved, becoming rivers of mud when it rained. Many cities did not have adequate water facilities. The water pressure was so low in Washington, D.C., that toilets did not work in half of the city's schools. The stench of overcrowded tenements and the summer heat often forced New York's slum residents to spend the night on the roofs or in the streets.

▼ *John Sloan etched* Roofs, Summer Night *in 1906. The cool night air provided a break from the summer heat.*

This 1913 George Wesley Bellows painting is entitled Cliff Dwellers. *Why are the residents of these tenements gathering on the sidewalk and in the streets?*

Corrupt City Governments

City governments in the United States were still notoriously corrupt. In his book *The American Commonwealth* (1888), James Bryce, an English political scientist, called city government "the one conspicuous failure of the United States." He saw political party bosses and dishonest city officials as the principal villains. Bryce also charged that corrupt city officials lined their pockets by accepting bribes from corporations that wanted to do business with the city.

Although many city councils and urban bosses were corrupt, Bryce's judgment that city government was a failure may have been too harsh. The mayors and city councils that he condemned guided the cities through an era of extraordinary growth.

The corruption itself was partly a reflection of how fast the cities were growing. For example, as they expanded, cities outgrew their old water and sewer systems. City councils had to spend vast amounts of money on new streets, water lines, and sewers to keep pace with this growth. To win these valuable contracts, construction companies often bribed city councilmen. The councilmen also profited by awarding city contracts to companies that they personally owned. Corruption resulted from the expansion of other municipal services, as well. Most cities depended on private companies to provide such basic services as electric lighting and public transportation. To win a contract to operate streetcars in Chicago that was worth millions of dollars, Charles T. Yerkes spent thousands to bribe the Democratic party leaders who ran the city government. In Detroit, competing electric-light companies regularly bought the votes of city councilmen.

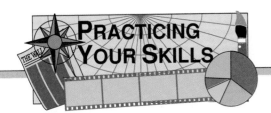

PRACTICING YOUR SKILLS

Interpreting Fine Art

By 1900, the city had become a dominant part of American life. It was the center of American wealth and growth. While reformers made Americans aware of the ugliness, dirt, and poverty of city life, there was another side to urban living. A group of artists, called the Ashcan school by their critics, began to paint scenes of everyday life in American cities. Although their painting technique was conventional—many were trained in Europe—the subjects they painted were startling to many Americans. Their paintings, often in subdued colors, were full of people going about their ordinary activities on the roof tops and fire escapes, and in the tenements, streets, back alleys, and bars of American cities. The Ashcan painters seldom dealt with reform or controversy. Their message seemed to be that the American city, in spite of its overcrowding and dirt, held a rich diversity of people and activities. The city, as well as the scenic countryside, had its own beauty and was a wonderful, exciting place to be.

Review the guidelines presented on page 315 of your text for analyzing fine art. Then examine the painting on page 557 and answer the following questions:

1. Why do you think this school of art was called the Ashcan school?
2. List 5 adjectives that describe the mood of this painting. What is the message of this painting?
3. Why do you think Bellows called this painting *Cliff Dwellers*? (Hint: Compare this painting to the Pueblo cliff dwellers of the Southwest on page 19. How are modern city apartments and Pueblo dwellings similar? How are they different?)
4. Name at least 10 activities that are going on in this painting. Are these strictly urban activities?
5. What colors predominate in the picture? Why do you think the faces of people are indistinct in this painting? Which is emphasized more in this painting, people or buildings? Why?

Although corrupt, party bosses also performed useful services. By putting immigrants on the city payroll, they helped give new ethnic minorities a stake in the community. John Powers, a party boss in Chicago, accepted a bribe for his role in getting Yerkes the streetcar contract. But he also won jobs on the streetcar line for the immigrants in his ward. He personally benefited, but he also eased the neighborhood's unemployment problem. In return, Powers and other city bosses expected the immigrants to vote for their candidates at election time. It seemed to them a fair exchange.

SECTION 1 REVIEW

1. **Describe** briefly the condition of the American economy between 1897 and 1914.
2. **Identify** which class or group of Americans benefited most from the return of prosperity.
3. **Name** the source of most immigrants to the U.S. after 1900.
4. **Explain** why American cities had difficulty absorbing the new immigrants.
5. **Outline** reasons for corruption in many of the city governments at the turn of the century.

The Growing Power of Corporate America

On a winter evening early in 1901, Charles Schwab, the manager of Andrew Carnegie's steel mills, paid a visit to J. P. Morgan. Schwab had come to New York City to make a proposal to Morgan, the nation's most powerful banker. He asked Morgan to finance a merger of the Carnegie holdings and several other major steel companies. How much did Carnegie want for his steel mills? Schwab wrote a figure on a piece of paper and handed it to Morgan: $492,000,000. Morgan looked back at Schwab and said, "I accept." That decision made possible the creation of the United States Steel Corporation, the largest corporation in the world at that time. It consisted of 156 mills and factories, extensive ore and coal deposits, and ore boats and railroad lines. The new company, with total shares valued at $1.4 billion, controlled 60 percent of the nation's steel production. The creation of the nation's first billion-dollar corporation was a fitting way for American business to usher in the new century.

Why did so many corporate mergers take place around the turn of the century?

Why were many Americans disturbed by these mergers?

How did large corporations gain political influence?

Corporate Mergers Increase

Economic recovery brought a rash of corporate mergers like that which created the United States Steel Corporation. The "great merger movement," as historians have called it, ushered in a new era in American business history. It resulted in a dramatic increase in the number of giant corporations and trusts. While the existence of trusts dated back to the rise of Standard Oil in the 1880s, only a few industries prior to the depression of 1893 were domi-

nated by big corporations. That was not the case a decade later, as each major industry came to be dominated by a few giant firms. Between 1897 and 1904, more than 3,000 companies, many of them quite large already, were combined into a few hundred supercorporations.

The managers hired to run the big corporations were a new breed of American businessman. Their approach to business management differed sharply from that of the men who had founded many of the companies. The captains of industry of Andrew Carnegie's generation had taken enormous risks. They thrived on cutthroat competition. The new corporate managers tried to minimize risk. They wanted to protect the millions of dollars stockholders had entrusted to their care. One way to do this was to eliminate competition and, therefore, control the market.

Their success varied from one industry to another. In oil, steel, and other industries in which large sums of money were invested, the age of unrestrained competition was ending. Prices were fixed by the producers. Usually, a major company would become the **price leader**. This company would set a profitable price that the rest of the industry adopted. During the 20 years before the creation of the United States Steel Corporation in 1901, the price of steel ranged from $16 to $85 a ton. The merger of the Carnegie holdings with other major steel companies in 1901 provided the industry with a new structure, which virtually eliminated price competition. For the next 15 years, steel remained at a predictable and highly profitable price of $28 a ton.

Competition survived in industries largely made up of small and medium-sized companies. In textiles, clothing, furniture making, and lumbering, manufacturers could organize new firms with only a modest investment. These industries, unlike steel or oil, stayed competitive because it was easy for potential competitors to get into the business. Competition also survived among retail stores in towns and cities across the country.

The great merger movement rekindled middle-class fears of big business. Many saw the supercorporations not as benevolent giants, but as a new generation of monster trusts. They served to remind the American public that earlier efforts to break up, or

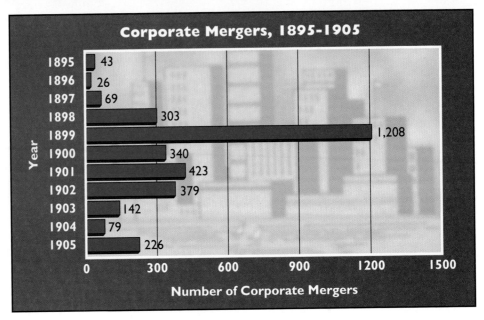

Corporate Mergers, 1895-1905

Year	Number of Corporate Mergers
1895	43
1896	26
1897	69
1898	303
1899	1,208
1900	340
1901	423
1902	379
1903	142
1904	79
1905	226

at least to regulate, corporate monopolies had not succeeded. The Interstate Commerce Act of 1887 had given the federal government the power to regulate the railroads. The Sherman Antitrust Act of 1890 had outlawed business "combinations in restraint of trade." Neither law had proved effective. When shippers complained of unfair rates, the Interstate Commerce Commission ruled mainly in favor of the railroads. The Supreme Court weakened the Sherman Antitrust Act by deciding, in the case of *United States v. E.C. Knight* (1895), that the act applied to commerce, but not to manufacturing. Even Congress seemed to lack the power to control the trusts.

The American public was alarmed by the growing political influence of corporations. The residents of Chicago, Detroit, and other large cities knew that streetcar and electric-light companies won favors from city government by bribing city council members. Corporations also bought influence in state legislatures. In California, it was common knowledge that the Southern Pacific Railroad practically owned the state legislature. Rival copper-mining companies battled for control of the Montana legislature. In Wisconsin, lumber companies, mining companies, and the railroads openly bought legislation that favored their interests. The nation's largest corporations also gained substantial influence in

Congress. They helped write tariff bills and managed to weaken regulatory legislation. Many people warned that the United States was becoming an aristocracy of corporate wealth, instead of a democracy.

▼ *Corporate interests that had gained undue influence in the United States Senate were depicted in this editorial cartoon entitled "Bosses of the Senate." Why do you think the cartoonist drew the corporate men so large?*

1. **Name** the movement that describes the dramatic increase in giant corporations.
2. **List** some of the corporate advantages gained by mergers.
3. **Contrast** the actions of corporate executives of 1900 with those of the captains of industry who had preceded them.
4. **Explain** why previous attempts to outlaw trusts and regulate corporations were unsuccessful.
5. **Describe** one way corporations tried to influence government.

SECTION 3

Progressivism in the Cities

In the early years of the twentieth century, a wave of reform activity swept across the United States. Historians call it the progressive movement, or **progressivism**. In fact, it was several different reform movements headed in more or less the same direction. Some progressive reformers focused on social injustice, others on corrupt government, and still others on the problem of big business. Unlike the leaders of the protest movements of the 1890s, the progressives were not poor farmers and workers on strike. They were middle class "to the core." In Kansas, progressivism was led by "the successful middle-class country town citizens, the farmer whose barn was painted, the well-paid railroad engineer and the country editor." In the larger cities, the reform movement drew heavily from the new middle class of college-trained engineers, lawyers, corporate executives, and white-collar professionals. The bond that united them was a firm belief in the possibility of social progress.

What role did settlement houses play in the progressive movement?

What reforms did progressives bring about in city government?

What was the muckrakers' role in achieving reform?

Settlement Houses and the Social Gospel

Among the first fruits of progressivism were the **settlement houses** that sprang up in New York, Chicago, and other cities. These were community centers opened in immigrant neighborhoods by young, middle-class volunteers, who also lived in the houses. The settlement houses provided places where people in slum neighborhoods could come together for community meetings, night classes, and social events. In turn, the young college graduates who lived there could learn firsthand about the problems of the urban poor and help the immigrants improve the quality of life in the slums. The volunteers provided vocational training and taught classes in nutrition and other practical subjects. They also worked to get bathhouses, libraries, playgrounds, parks, and kindergartens established in the inner city. Among them were many young college-educated women, who saw work in the settlement houses as a new way to take part in public life.

One of the earliest and best known of the settlement houses was Hull House, established in Chicago in 1889 by **Jane Addams**. A recent college graduate, she had visited settlement houses in London, where the idea originated. She saw settlement-house work as a chance for her to be useful to society. There were few such opportunities outside the home open to women, even to those with a college degree. Her religious upbringing was also a factor. Helping the unfortunate in the inner cities gave her an opportunity to apply Christian teachings to society. Historians have called this aspect of progressive reform the **social gospel**.

The settlement houses were ill prepared to attack the basic causes of urban poverty. Night classes for immigrants did not alter the unequal distribution of wealth in the United States. However, working with the urban poor did help the settlement workers become better informed about conditions in the industrial cities. Many young men and women took advantage of that opportunity. By 1900, the number of settlement houses had grown to 100, and to over 400 by 1910. Many settlement-house workers went on to careers as social workers

▲ *Jane Addams founded Hull House, the first settlement house in Chicago. Was she successful in improving conditions in immigrant neighborhoods?*

▲ *Settlement houses provided social and educational opportunities for immigrants. This singing class brought together neighbors of all ages.*

or lobbied for legislation that would improve living and working conditions in the cities. The settlement houses helped a generation of Americans understand the gap that was widening between the middle class and the urban poor.

Corrupt City Politics

Progressive reformers won their first political battles against corrupt city governments. By 1901, Detroit, Toledo, and Cleveland had elected reform mayors. This was not the first time that voters, shocked by the waste of their tax money, had tried to reform city government. Such taxpayer revolts dated back to 1871, when the voters of New York City overthrew the Tweed Ring. But earlier reform victories had been short-lived. The ward bosses always returned because they provided services that many city residents needed. For reformers to win lasting victories, they had to be able to compete with the bosses for popular support.

Ironically, the reform mayors of Detroit, Toledo, and Cleveland were not elected as reformers. They were businessmen, not unlike those who made a habit of bribing city officials. Hazen Pingree was a Detroit manufacturer. Toledo's Samuel Jones was an oil millionaire. Tom Johnson of Cleveland owned a streetcar company. What set these men apart from the businessmen who corrupted city governments was their commitment to social justice.

Once in office, these reform mayors tried to use city government to improve conditions for the working class. During his four terms as mayor, Pingree expanded public health services, reduced streetcar fares, and provided relief for the unemployed. In Toledo, Jones introduced an eight-hour day for city workers and built free playgrounds and kindergartens. Johnson reduced streetcar fares in Cleveland. He also developed model farms where the aged and people with mental disorders could live with dignity. But to accomplish these things, all three mayors had to fight both the politicians and the streetcar and utility companies that wanted to keep fares and rates high. Attacked by the party bosses and the corporations, they reached out to the common people for support. As Pingree explained, "I have come to lean upon the common people as the real foundation upon which government must rest."

To consolidate their gains, municipal reformers transformed city government. In Toledo, Cleveland, and other cities, reform mayors fought for city ownership of electric-light and streetcar systems. This was the only way to get the private utility corporations out of city politics. In other cities, reformers changed the very structure of local government. Many adopted new city charters that strengthened the mayor at the expense of corrupt city councils. In 1908, the Staunton, Virginia, city council hired a professional manager to oversee the city government. This **city-manager system** appealed to white-collar progressives, who placed a high value on efficient management and professional expertise. This system would spread to hundreds of other cities in the years to come. Reformers often succeeded in making city government less corrupt, more efficient, and less costly to taxpayers, especially in small and middle-sized cities.

In the largest cities, the boss system continued to thrive. Jane Addams fought a losing battle against John Powers, the boss of the Chicago ward in which Hull House was located. Like settlement-house workers elsewhere, Hull House residents supported reform candidates in local elections. However, Powers understood the needs of his immigrant constituents better than the settlement-house workers. He provided jobs on the city payroll and in the wintertime distributed coal, food, and clothing to those in need. The voters repaid Powers by electing the candidates he endorsed.

Investigative Journalism

The progressive movement was fueled by a growing public awareness of social injustice, corporate abuse, and political corruption. Public attention was focused on these issues by a flood of articles in mass-circulation magazines that appeared after the turn of the century. The articles uncovered a wide range of abuses. *McClure's* magazine published the first of these exposés with two series of articles that began in 1902. Ida Tarbell's account of the origins of Standard Oil explained how John D. Rockefeller had eliminated competition by persuading the railroads to give his Standard Oil Company rebates on freight rates. The other was Lincoln Steffens's series on corruption in city government, later published as a book entitled *The Shame of the Cities* (1904). Steffens documented the link between businessmen and corruption in city government. These articles marked the beginning of investigative journalism, reporting that publicized the need for reform.

Other publishers, realizing that these articles helped sell magazines, soon followed the lead of *McClure's*. A series entitled "Frenzied Finance," published in *Everybody's* magazine in 1904, exposed Wall Street financiers who had cheated investors out of millions of dollars. *Cosmopolitan* magazine published a series by David Graham Phillips entitled "The Treason of the Senate." It described the way corporations bought influence in the United States Senate. *Collier's Weekly*, *The Outlook*, and other periodicals began their own exposés of Congress, patent medicine fraud, and the liquor industry.

In a speech in 1906, President Theodore Roosevelt labeled the authors of articles calling for reform **muckrakers**, referring to a man in John Bunyan's *Pilgrim's Progress* who raked up filth from the floor. He thought journalists were spending too much time raking the muck. Despite the fact that Roosevelt had meant the remark as criticism, writers liked the term and proudly adopted it. The name stuck, and muckraking journalism became a powerful weapon in the fight for reform.

SECTION 3 REVIEW

1. **Describe** briefly the settlement houses of this period.
2. **Define** the term *social gospel*.
3. **Explain** why reform mayors wanted city ownership of utilities.
4. **List** some changes brought about by municipal reformers in the structure of city government.
5. **Discuss** the purpose of investigative journalism.

Investigative Journalism

The founding of *McClure's* magazine in 1893 marked the beginning of a new era in American journalism. At that time, monthly magazines sold for 35 cents a copy, a luxury that most people could not afford. Samuel S. McClure set the price of his new magazine at 15 cents (later dropping it to 10 cents) a copy. He cut costs by taking advantage of new printing methods, charging for commercial advertising, and relying on mass circulation to make a profit. He had a good instinct for what his readers wanted. In 15 years, circulation rose from 120,000 to 370,000.

By 1900, McClure knew that the time was ripe for hard-hitting exposures of what was wrong with American society. McClure told editor Lincoln Steffens to "get out of here, travel—go somewhere" and discover the mood of the country. He sent other writers out to investigate, too, insisting that their reports be thorough and accurate. He spared no expense on his writers. He put them on salary and gave them all the time they needed for research. Ida Tarbell, one of the first women to be successful in American journalism, spent five years writing her series on Standard Oil. *McClure's* set a standard for truth in journalism that few of its competitors ever

matched. And the competition was severe. By 1910, no fewer than 12 mass-circulation magazines had opened their columns to investigative reporters. It took a real commitment to reform just to keep up with what the muckrakers were publishing.

The muckrakers liked to tell a story about a rich Alaskan gold miner who tried to persuade an editor to support a new reform cause. He promised to provide all the evidence needed.

"You certainly are a progressive," the editor said.

"Progressive," the miner replied. "Progressive! I tell you I'm a full-fledged insurgent. Why, man, I subscribe to 13 magazines!"

The Insurgents, to whom he referred, were progressive Republicans in Congress who in 1909 rebelled against their party's conservative leadership.

Mass-circulation magazines like *McClure's* were vital to the success of the progressive movement. Their articles reached a wide audience, riveting national attention on corporate abuses and political corruption. They were the chief publicity agents for reform.

▲ *Ida Tarbell, one of the first successful female journalists, published in such periodicals as* McClure's. *How did muckrakers contribute to progressive reform?*

1. What innovations did Samuel S. McClure bring to magazine journalism?
2. How did magazines such as *McClure's* help the progressive movement?

Progressivism as a National Movement

One Christmas, the social workers at Hull House held a party for the neighborhood children. Much to the surprise of Jane Addams and her friends, the children refused the candy that was offered to them. When the social workers asked about this strange behavior, they learned that these children worked six days a week in a candy factory. They could not stand the sight of candy. The Hull House volunteers discovered that other children from the neighborhood worked near dangerous machinery. Evening classes for immigrant children were poorly attended, as the children did not have enough energy left to stay awake. It was probably inevitable, Jane Addams later explained, "that efforts to secure a child labor law should be our first venture into the field of state legislation."

How successful were reformers in regulating child and female labor?

How did reformers propose to improve the health and safety of industrial workers?

What reform legislation did progressives want Congress to enact?

America's Shame

The grueling labor of children in factories and mines was industrial America's most glaring social injustice. Middle-class Americans were outraged by stories about children who worked such long hours that the foreman had to splash cold water in their faces to keep them awake. Much of the groundwork to regulate child labor was provided by the investigations conducted by settlement-house workers. The reformers at Chicago's Hull House led the fight against child labor in Illinois. Their first major victory was the Illinois Factory Act of 1893, which prohibited the employment of children under age

14 at night or for longer than eight hours during the day. Illinois Governor John P. Altgeld appointed Florence Kelley, a Hull House resident, as the state's first factory inspector. New Jersey enacted a similar law in 1903. Pennsylvania raised the minimum age for work in coal mines from 14 to 16. Other states followed with similar legislation.

Getting child labor laws enacted was only the first step, as the reformers quickly discovered. The real challenge was to enforce the laws in the face of defiant factory owners and hostile courts. The Illinois courts ruled most of the 1893 Factory Act unconstitutional, which forced reformers to fight that battle all over again. In 1903, they succeeded in getting new and even stronger child labor legislation enacted. Reformers in other states also fought a continuing battle to enforce child labor laws.

The public school system proved to be the child labor reformers' most valuable ally. A growing number of parents realized that education was the best guarantee of economic success for their children. By 1917, the majority of states had enacted compulsory education laws designed to keep children in school until at least age 14. Attendance clerks and truant officers were hired to enforce these laws. As the daily school attendance figures rose, the number of young children in the workplace declined.

Legislation to Protect Other Laborers

The reformers who worked to regulate child labor also tried to limit the hours of women's work. "I do not know why it is that women and children are invariably classed together," wrote reformer Mary Simkhovitch. But she concluded that it was a good thing. It made little sense to protect a girl until she turned 16, only to free her to work "13 hours a day, 78 hours a week, for six dollars a week" thereafter. Reformers also believed that low wages and long hours of work forced women into prostitution and caused working mothers to neglect their children. Their goal was a ten-hour day for women and a minimum wage.

Child Labor

The coal mines of Pennsylvania hired boys to remove worthless slate from the newly mined coal. They worked crouched over the coal chutes picking out slate as the coal rushed past. "The coal is hard, and accidents to the hands, such as cut, broken or crushed fingers, are common among the boys," John Spargo wrote in *The Bitter Cry of the Children* (1906), a book that cataloged the horrors of child labor. "Sometimes there is a worse accident; a terrified shriek is heard, and a boy is mangled and torn in the machinery, or disappears in the chute to be picked out later smothered and dead." In one Pennsylvania town, 150 boys were employed in the mines. Among these, 45 were 12 years old, 45 were 11, 40 were 10, and 5 were only 9. The mine owners hired them because they worked for one-third the wages of adults.

In 1900, the American workforce included 1.75 million children between the ages of 10 and 15. Of the total number, 40 percent were employed in nonagricultural labor, which included manufacturing, mining, transportation, and common labor. The textile industry was the largest single industrial user of child labor, providing jobs for 44,000 children in 1900. Nearly 20 percent of textile

▲ *Many young boys were employed in Pennsylvania coal mines. Why did coal mining and other industries use child labor?*

mill employees were under the age of 16. Some mill owners only hired men who had young children who were willing to work for 30 to 40 cents per day.

While visiting Paterson, New Jersey, Spargo was struck by how quiet the streets were at midday. He saw mothers with babies and small children, "but the older children, whose boisterous play one expects in such streets, were wanting." When he asked where the children were, he was told to wait until the flax mills closed. "At six o'clock the whistles shrieked, and the streets were suddenly filled with people, many of them mere

children." Spargo had never seen such "tired, pallid, and languid-looking children." Industrial America, he concluded, was depriving children of their childhood.

1. What part did child labor play in the workforce in 1900?
2. Why do you think John Spargo focused his attention on children employed in non-agricultural labor rather than on those who were agricultural workers?

Their efforts brought mixed results. Reformers did succeed in limiting the hours of women's work. In 1903, Oregon passed the first effective ten-hour-day law for women, which became a model that many other states adopted. The reformers made less headway in securing minimum-wage laws for women. Although 15 states established such laws, the Supreme Court in 1923 declared them unconstitutional on the grounds that they violated **freedom of contract**. In this case, freedom of contract meant a woman's right to enter into any kind of labor contract that she chose.

White-collar reformers joined forces with labor leaders to pass laws to protect the health and safety of workers. At first, the relationship between the two groups was shaky. "The workers are not bugs to be examined under the lens of a microscope, by intellectuals on a sociological slumming tour," growled Samuel Gompers, the president of the American Federation of Labor. However, both groups recognized that workers needed protection from the shockingly high rate of industrial accidents and fatalities.

The Triangle Shirtwaist Company Fire The general public remained unsympathetic until 1911, when Americans were shocked by the news of New York's Triangle Shirtwaist Company fire. In that catastrophe, 146 workers, mostly young women, lost their lives inside the burning factory. They could not escape because the doors had been locked to keep the employees from leaving during working hours and to allow company officers to search employees for stolen materials. New York and several other states enacted building and safety codes soon thereafter.

Reformers also won battles in state legislatures to provide compensation for injured workers. In

▲ *The tragedy that occurred at the Triangle Shirtwaist factory building led to stricter building and safety codes.*

1902, Maryland had enacted the first workers' compensation law. Other northern industrial states followed. Typical was the New York Workmen's Compensation Act of 1914, which set up a schedule of payments to compensate for accidental injury or death without regard to whose fault it was. The only workers not entitled to compensation were those injured as a result of being under the influence of alcohol. By 1915, 30 states had enacted laws to provide at least some medical benefits to injured workers and death pensions for the families of workers killed on the job.

Progressivism and the Political Process

The progressives pushed reform legislation through state legislatures despite the political power of the corporations. They did this by making state government more responsive to the voting public. In 1898, voters in South Dakota adopted the nation's first **initiative** and **referendum** laws. The initiative allowed voters to propose legislation; the referendum gave them the power to pass or defeat laws put to the voters in statewide elections. Both measures allowed reformers to bypass the state legislatures and take issues directly to the people. Within 20 years, 14 states had adopted the initiative and the referendum. Some had also adopted **recall** procedures, which allowed voters to decide in special elections whether an elected officeholder should be removed from office.

Another device that made both state and national elections more democratic was the **direct primary.** Until now, candidates had been selected to run for public office at nominating conventions, which were often controlled by the party bosses.

The direct primary let the voters, rather than convention delegates, pick the candidates.

In several states, the movement for reform was led by progressive governors. Among them was **Robert La Follette** of Wisconsin, who pledged that he would support "anything that makes government more democratic, more popular in form, anything that gives the people more control in government." To achieve these ends, "Battling Bob," as he was called, created a team of experts that turned the state of Wisconsin into an experimental laboratory for progressive policies. With La Follette's leadership, Wisconsin passed direct-primary, initiative, and referendum laws. It enacted tax reform, which increased taxes on corporations. Wisconsin progressives also passed legislation to regulate working conditions. In time, other states with progressive governors, including Charles Evans Hughes in New York, Woodrow Wilson in New Jersey, and Hiram Johnson in California, enacted similar laws.

The Progressive National Agenda

Although the progressives focused on the state legislatures, they also sought national reform legislation. They recognized that a uniform federal law prohibiting child labor, for example, would be easier to enforce than a dozen different state laws. In 1904, the National Child Labor Committee began an organized campaign to end child labor in the factories. They used grassroots committees to spread propaganda and to collect documentation on the mistreatment of child laborers. In spite of their successes in getting many state laws passed, the abuses continued. In 1906, Albert Beveridge, a progressive senator from Indiana, introduced federal legislation to "prevent the employment of children in factories and mines." It was too radical a measure to win a majority in Congress at that time, but a federal child-labor law was passed ten years later.

As reform became a national issue, the progressives' agenda expanded. Progressive Democrats in Congress added tariff reduction to the list of reform causes. They blamed the skyrocketing cost of living on the highly protective McKinley Tariff of 1890. Progressive Republicans and Democrats alike de-

manded more effective regulation of the railroads. Progressives in Congress also worked for laws to protect consumers, including legislation to monitor the meat-packing and drug industries. In time, the list of reform demands included a graduated income tax, conservation of national resources, banking reform, and more forceful antitrust action by Congress and the courts.

Support for Prohibition

Prohibition, or prohibiting the sale and use of alcoholic beverages, also became part of the progressive reform agenda. The crusade to ban the drinking of alcohol had a long history. Religious revivalists since the 1830s had attacked liquor on moral grounds. They denounced drinking as a source of immoral behavior, family abuse, and broken homes. The temperance movement had emerged by the time of the Civil War. Rooted in rural and small-town Protestant America, it continued to oppose liquor on moral grounds. The urban prohibitionists of the Progressive Era were more concerned about industrial efficiency and good government. Excessive drinking, they argued, made workers less efficient, increased the number of industrial accidents, and shortened lives. Prohibiting the sale of liquor would also close down the liquor industry, which reformers denounced as a corrupting influence on politics. They associated saloons and bars in immigrant neighborhoods with political corruption. The saloon keeper often served as the local ward boss, and liquor flowed freely at election time. "Sobering up" politics, progressives believed, would help end the ward boss system and restore good government. With public sentiment aroused, the reformers began their campaign to pass a constitutional amendment to close the saloons forever.

Prohibition was a gradual process. By 1906, only a few states had statewide prohibition, but nearly 40 percent of the nation's population had already driven saloons from their local communities. Some states relied on high liquor license fees to reduce the number of saloons. A more widely used measure consisted of state laws that gave cities and counties the option to prohibit the sale of liquor locally.

▲ *Saloon poker chips, like those shown along the left, have become popular collector items. Why did the progressives of the early 1900s want to close saloons such as the one above?*

On a national level, all patent medicines transported across state lines had to label alcohol and morphine content to comply with the Pure Food and Drug Act of 1906. Two years later, Congress prohibited the use of the mails to ship liquor. In response to public pressure, even the United States Brewers Association began a campaign to close saloons that harbored prostitution and gambling or that sold liquor to minors. America was far from "bone dry" in the early 1900s, but these piecemeal reforms foreshadowed the vigorous movement that later would write prohibition into the highest law in the land.

SECTION 4 REVIEW

1. **Evaluate** how successful reformers were in regulating child labor.
2. **Define** the term *freedom of contract*.
3. **Name** one measure introduced by progressives to make government more democratic.
4. **Identify** Robert La Follette.
5. **Explain** one way progressives made elections more democratic.

SECTION 5

The Persistence of Inequality

Humorist Finley Peter Dunne wrote a newspaper column that was popular during the Progressive Era. It featured a comic caricature of an Irish immigrant named Mr. Dooley. Each day, Mr. Dooley offered up his opinions on current events. In a 1909 conversation with Mr. Hennessy, the neighborhood saloon keeper, Mr. Dooley commented, in his heavy Irish brogue:

> "It won't be long befure I'll be seein' ye and ye'er wife sthrollin' down th' sthreet to vote together."
>
> "Niver," said Mr. Hennessy with great indignation. "It will niver come. A woman's place is in th' home darning her husband's childher. I mean—"
>
> "I know ye mean," said Mr. Dooley.

What Mr. Hennessy really meant was that women did not yet enjoy full rights of citizenship in the United States. Neither did several other minority groups in American society. In guaranteeing democratic participation and civil equality for all citizens, Americans of the Progressive Era still had a long way to go.

What status did American women occupy at the beginning of the twentieth century?
Why did many African Americans think of northern cities as a promised land?
Who were the Red Progressives?

Unequal Treatment of Women

Women had made many gains by the opening of the new century, but economic and political equality with men was still a distant goal. Most industries employed women, but not in the better-paying positions. Sixty percent of all working women were employed as domestic servants. Gender still determined work roles in most occupations. For example, in the garment industry, men earned

▲ *Shown above is a young girl's play suit and an upper-class woman's Gibson Girl outfit of the 1890s. Why did women's journals call for dress reform?*

$16 a week cutting cloth, while women earned $6 sewing the finished product. Even when men and women did the same work, women were paid less.

The gender division was also apparent in leisure-time activities and clothing fashions. Men had comfortable clothing that allowed them to participate in sports, while women were confined in stiff petticoats and corsets, long skirts and high-collared blouses. By 1900, even the conservative *Ladies' Home Journal* proposed dress reform for women and urged them to get involved in activities such as bicycling, badminton, and golf.

Women had made some advances under the law. They could control their earnings, own property, and take custody of their children in case of divorce. They had the right to vote in four states (Wyoming, Utah, Colorado, and Idaho). However, changes were under way that held promise for greater equality in the future.

The women of 1900 had more educational opportunities than American women had ever had be-

fore. As girls were less inclined than boys to seek employment at a young age, they were more likely than boys to graduate from high school. Colleges had only begun to admit women during the decade following the Civil War. The founding of private women's colleges, such as Vassar and Bryn Mawr, paved the way. State colleges eventually followed their lead, but women's educational opportunities were still not equal to those of men. In 1895, Mary Whiton Calkins completed all of Harvard's requirements for a doctorate in psychology, yet the university did not award her the degree. Despite such gender discrimination, women were enrolled in more than 70 percent of the United States' colleges and universities by 1900.

Women were also entering the professions in greater numbers. However, gender determined most of the duties performed by women in law, medicine, and teaching. Female lawyers were given office tasks rather than courtroom trials, while women doctors typically treated other women and children. Most professional women worked in occupations that were rapidly becoming dominated by women rather than men. That is, once women made their presence felt in a particular profession, such as teaching school, men either moved up to supervisory roles or changed careers. As women entered the classrooms, for example, men typically left to become school administrators. As a result, occupations dominated

▼ *Why do you think there were more young women than young men in this high school graduating class of 1901? Can you spot a future president in this picture?*

by women lost status because the work came to be regarded as "women's work." In 1900, the United States had 110,620 men teachers and 325,022 women teachers. A decade later, the number of women teachers had increased by over 150,000, while the number of men in the profession had grown by fewer than 8,000. By the early years of the twentieth century, nursing and clerical jobs belonged to women and were no longer considered men's work. The occupations judged most suitable to women were still those most similar to their traditional duties at home.

Women's Organizations By the turn of the century, women were organizing into groups to exert more influence. In towns and cities across the nation, women joined clubs to work for better schools, the regulation of child labor, and women's suffrage. In 1890, many of these clubs formed a national organization called the General Federation of Women's Clubs (GFWC). African American women also joined clubs concerned with improving social conditions. In 1895, these clubs joined together to form the National Association of Colored Women. The women's clubs had a much different purpose than the literary societies in which women had traditionally met to discuss Dante's *Inferno* and other classics. "Dante is dead," exclaimed Sarah Platt Decker, the GFWC president, "and I think it is time that we dropped the study of his *Inferno* and turned our attention to our own." By 1910, the clubs represented by the GFWC had enrolled more than one million women.

Large numbers of women also worked through the Women's Christian Temperance Union (WCTU) to prohibit the sale and consumption of liquor. Like the women's clubs, the WCTU permitted women to address public issues in a sheltered setting. "Its manner is not that of the street, the court, the mart, or the office; it is the manner of the home," explained Frances Willard, the president of the WCTU. Even professional women of Frances Willard's stature upheld traditional values concerning the roles of women.

The weight of those values continued to deprive most women in the United States of the right to vote. The women's suffrage movement had made slow progress since the Civil War, partly because of

▲ *Clerical workers were commonly women by the early twentieth century. Name one striking difference between this office scene and one of modern times.*

internal disagreements. In 1890, the opposing factions of the movement finally joined together to form the National American Woman Suffrage Association (NAWSA). Julia Lathrop, a social worker and later director of the Children's Bureau, told the NAWSA convention in 1905, "that woman's suffrage is a natural and inevitable step in the march of society forward." But even many women disagreed. Women who upheld traditional gender roles argued that politics was an improper activity for women. Voting, some insisted, might even cause women to "grow beards." The challenge to traditional roles represented by the suffrage movement was as threatening to some women as it was to most men.

Second-Class Citizens

The prospects for equality in 1900 seemed even more remote for African Americans than for white women. In the South, African Americans were kept from voting, despite the guarantees of the Fifteenth Amendment. Stripped of political power, they had no way to stop the march of white supremacy. Racial segregation in hotels, theaters, streetcars, and other public facilities was virtually complete. Disheartened by these conditions and by economic hard times in the rural South, increasing numbers of African Americans migrated north.

Net Movement of African Americans by Selected States, 1900–1920

State	Loss (−)	Gain (+)
Alabama	92,900	
Arkansas	23,500	
Georgia	90,900	
Kentucky	38,900	
Louisiana	67,300	
Maryland	4,400	
Mississippi	160,500	
North Carolina	57,300	
South Carolina	146,500	
Tennessee	63,600	
West Virginia	30,800	
Illinois		93,300
Indiana		24,400
Michigan		50,600
New Jersey		43,000
New York		98,900
Ohio		80,600
Pennsylvania		115,400

▲ *By 1920, African Americans were leaving the South in large numbers. Why were they attracted primarily to the Midwest and Middle Atlantic states?*

Each year, thousands of southern African Americans made their way to Chicago, New York, and other northern cities. Work was easier to find there than in the South, and race relations were somewhat more relaxed. One of the nation's major African American newspapers, the *Chicago Defender*, urged African Americans to flee the South. "To die from the bite of frost is far more glorious than at the hands of a mob," its editor wrote. "I beg you, my brother, to leave the benighted land." Each year between 1890 and 1910, nearly 20,000 southern African Americans took the *Defender's* advice and headed north.

When they arrived, they found something less than the promised land that they had expected. African Americans were confined to the lowest-paying jobs, such as domestic servants and hotel porters. Only during World War I, when immigrant labor from Europe was cut off, did northern factories hire African Americans. Even then, they could find housing only in the most run-down urban neighborhoods. As their numbers increased, African Americans found themselves confined to segregated **ghettos**. The ghetto was a city within a city, isolated by white prejudice and locked into poverty by racial discrimination in hiring.

African American Leaders By the turn of the century, new leaders had emerged to represent the interests of African Americans. Among them was **Booker T. Washington**, the head of Tuskegee Institute in Alabama. He had founded Tuskegee in 1881 as a school to train young African Americans to become skilled workers. Washington urged young black people to get ahead by acquiring industrial skills and efficient work habits. "No race that has anything to contribute to the markets of the world is long in any degree ostracized," he wrote. Political privileges were important, he added, "but it is vastly more important that we be prepared for the exercise of these privileges." Washington advised African Americans to concentrate on material progress and not to press for social equality. His compromise with segregation earned Washington a great deal of criticism, but he gave up nothing that had not already been lost.

Northern black leaders eventually challenged Booker T. Washington, refusing to compromise any of the rights of African Americans. Among them was **William E. B. Du Bois** (doo BOYS), an African American sociologist, historian, and Harvard graduate. Du Bois and others argued that without full civil rights, including the right to vote, African Americans would never break the chains of inequality. At a meeting held near Niagara Falls, New York, in 1905, northern black leaders issued a manifesto demanding full civil and political rights and an end to every kind of racial discrimination.

▼ *Booker T. Washington (left) urged African Americans to work hard and gain industrial skills and an education. W. E. B. Du Bois (right) challenged Washington's economic approach to black advancement. How did Du Bois believe African Americans should achieve equality?*

Although begun by African Americans, the Niagara Movement gained the support of some white progressives. Jane Addams and other white reform leaders were disturbed by growing racial tensions in the North. In 1909, these white reform leaders joined the Du Bois group to form the **National Association for the Advancement of Colored People (NAACP)**. As editor of the new organization's journal, *The Crisis*, Du Bois kept up his fight against racial discrimination. The NAACP's strategy was to fight through the courts to regain the constitutional rights blacks had lost after Reconstruction. As we shall see in later chapters, the NAACP would eventually be successful.

The Forgotten Americans

For American Indians at the turn of the century, the future looked bleak. The vast majority were living in the most degrading poverty, either on reservations or on the land allotted them in 1887 under the Dawes Act. The allotment of individual landholdings had actually benefited white people more than the native Americans. Within 20 years, over half the Indians included in the allotment had sold or otherwise lost their land. Valuable timberlands, grazing lands, and mineral rights—including some of the richest oil deposits in Oklahoma—were sold by poor and desperate Indians at a fraction of their true value. Even those who kept their land had difficulty adjusting to a way of life that was alien to Indian values and tribal ways.

A high death rate among children and childbearing women and a low life expectancy due to poverty continued to reduce the American Indian population. From an estimated 5 to 10 million at the time of first European contact, their number was reduced by 1900 to about 250,000. Instead of assimilation into the mainstream of American life, Indians had become the "vanishing Americans."

Yet even in that dark hour, there were reasons for hope. Although still reluctant to accept Indian culture on its own terms, the Bureau of Indian Affairs had relaxed its effort to stamp it out completely. As Francis Leupp, commissioner of Indian affairs, remarked in 1905, "I like the Indian for what is In-

dian in him. . . . Let us not make the mistake, in the process of absorbing him, of washing out whatever is distinctly Indian."

An estimated 10 percent of the American Indian population had made their way into the middle class by 1910, although American Indian doctors and lawyers were still rare exceptions. Athletic programs at some of the Indian schools brought recognition to Indian athletes. Among them was Jim Thorpe, the legendary football and track star. Thorpe won gold medals in the 1912 Olympics at Stockholm in both the decathlon and the pentathlon.

The Indian middle class produced a small group of "Red Progressives." Included among this group were Dr. Carlos Montezuma, an Apache physician; Henry Roe Cloud, a Winnebago teacher; and Gertrude Bonnin, a Sioux writer and musician. Reaching beyond tribal boundaries, the Red Progressives established a Pan-Indian movement that called for industrial training for American Indian youths, pride in Indian culture, and respect for Indian rights. Although still weak and as yet ineffective, the Pan-Indian movement ensured that American Indians would not be forgotten completely during this era of progressive reform.

▲ *Jim Thorpe, an American Indian of Sauk and Fox descent, became the first president of the National Football League.*

SECTION 5 REVIEW

1. **List** areas in which women did not have equal rights with men in 1900.
2. **Name** the goal of temperance movements.
3. **Identify** which occupations became open to women at this time.
4. **Contrast** how Booker T. Washington and W. E. B. Du Bois differed in their approaches to securing equality for African Americans.
5. **Summarize** briefly the goals of the Red Progressives.

Summary

The United States at the turn of the century was a rapidly changing society. The economy was surging ahead, the cities were growing, and many Americans had more leisure time than ever before. But it was also a society beset with problems. The industrial cities were burdened with widespread poverty, dangerous and unhealthy working conditions, and corrupt governments. Large corporations had acquired vast economic power and political influence. To some, the future of American democracy itself seemed in danger.

Although aware of the problems created by rapid industrialization, Americans of this generation firmly believed in the possibility of progress. They rejected the idea that big corporations were beyond their control or that American politics had become hopelessly corrupt. Most Americans seemed convinced that people of goodwill acting together could reform American society. This idea was especially appealing to members of the well-educated professional class, people trained and skilled in the techniques of management. All they needed to do, they believed, was to apply those same skills to the nation's social and political problems.

The result was a series of reform efforts known as the progressive movement. Middle-class reformers reached out to the urban poor by establishing settlement houses in the slums. Reform mayors helped clean up municipal government in a number of cities. Other progressives worked to limit child labor and to regulate the working hours of women. Prodded by reformers, state legislatures enacted factory safety and workers' compensation laws. Progressives also made government more democratic by introducing changes to election processes.

Although progressives achieved major reforms, women, African Americans, and American Indians still occupied a minority status in American society. Despite the efforts of organizations that fought for political rights and the hard work of valiant and dedicated minority leaders, the reform movement still had a long way to go.

Vocabulary

city-manager system
direct primary
freedom of contract
ghetto
gross national product (GNP)
initiative
muckrakers

price leader
progressivism
prohibition
recall
referendum
settlement houses
social gospel

Write a brief paragraph of three or four sentences explaining each of the above vocabulary terms. Include important information about how these concepts relate to the progressive movement.

Review Questions

1. How equally shared were the benefits of economic recovery after 1900?
2. List reasons that led James Bryce to state that corruption in city government was the United States' most conspicuous failure.
3. Describe the effect of corporate mergers on business competition and prices.
4. Why did Americans have mixed feelings about these business consolidations?
5. What role did settlement-house workers play in bringing about progressive reforms?
6. Recount some developments in American journalism that were important to the success of progressivism.
7. How successful were reformers in regulating the conditions of female labor?
8. Why did progressives introduce measures that called for more direct democracy?
9. Describe two approaches to African American activism at this time.
10. Briefly outline the status of American Indians at the turn of the century.

Critical Historical Thinking

Writing Answer each of the following by writing one or more complete paragraphs:

1. Explain how great fortunes amassed by the industrial giants often led to political corruption.
2. Booker T. Washington and W. E. B. Du Bois were national leaders among African Americans at the turn of the century. They proposed different approaches to improve conditions for African Americans. Which of the two approaches was more likely to be accepted in the South among educated young African Americans? Why?
3. Explain why progressive reformers felt that voting reform would help to end corruption in the government.
4. Muckrakers had an extensive influence on bringing abuses to the attention of the public. Discuss how the media today deals with social and political exposés.

Making Connections with Environmental Science

The National Park Service, created in 1916, comprises three types of parks: (1) areas set aside for the preservation of natural geological and biological features, such as Yellowstone National Park and Everglades National Park in Florida; (2) areas preserved for historical and cultural reasons, including national monuments such as the Statue of Liberty, the White House, and the Liberty Bell; and (3) areas preserved for recreational use, such as Lake Mead in Arizona or Golden Gate Park in California.

Serious problems are now facing our national parks, including overuse by visitors, acid rain, chemical pollutants from rivers, and poaching of protected species. Economic concerns also threaten the national parks. Many parks were established at a time when the land was judged to be of little value other than for its beauty. Since then mining, log-

ging, and oil companies have identified these parks as potential sources of great wealth. The question now debated is "How much wilderness is enough?"

Writing Discuss the following scenario and thoroughly consider all sides of the issue. Then, write a paragraph supporting either the logging company or the conservationists, or proposing a compromise solution.

Anytown, USA, is a small rural community situated on the edge of a national forest preserve. The main employer has recently moved to another state where the taxes and costs of doing business are lower. The town faces financial ruin. A paper manufacturing company has offered to build a new plant if the federal government will provide a permit to do light logging in the park. The company has an environmental impact statement to say that a carefully managed logging project would not adversely affect the ecosystem of the park. The paper manufacturer has promised to reforest. The town supports the plan, but conservationists have expressed doubts about the reliability of the impact study. They cite noise pollution, traffic congestion, and danger to bird life as major problems.

Additional Skills Practice

Several artists who painted in the Ashcan style achieved national prominence. George Bellows, Robert Henri, John Sloan, George Luks, William Glackens, and Everett Shinn portrayed the everyday drama of city living. Visit your school library to see if these artists and their paintings are represented.

Then, imagine that you are an artist from the Ashcan School who has decided to paint a scene that would capture the essence of everyday life at your school. Make a list of the elements (situations, scenes, characters, buildings, mood, etc.) that you would include in your painting. Analyze your list. What do the contents tell you about your perception or attitude toward your school? Then compare your list with those of your friends. Do they include similar elements?

Progressive America

After the turn of the century, a new generation gained political influence in the United States. Their leader was Theodore Roosevelt, the first president who was too young to have served in the Civil War. Roosevelt's generation had a major impact on American politics and political institutions. Theodore Roosevelt, along with Woodrow Wilson, transformed the presidency. Most of Roosevelt's predecessors had been content to enforce laws passed by Congress. Presidents Roosevelt and Wilson overshadowed Congress, each becoming a great national leader in his own right.

This progressive generation also created the modern **regulatory state**. Government, they thought, should do more than maintain law and order. It should also play a regulatory role. That is, it should make sure that businesses and corporations did not engage in practices that endanger the public. It is difficult to imagine a time when government did not protect consumers from false advertising, laborers from the hazards of the workplace, and young children from excessive work. It is a tribute to the reformers of the Progressive Era that government offers such protections today.

▲ *In the 1800s, the right to vote was not considered a basic right of citizenship. Suffragettes led the fight to enfranchise women.*

Roosevelt and Progressivism

In September 1901, President William McKinley went to Buffalo to deliver a speech at the Pan-American Exposition. He used the occasion to remind other Americans of the importance of international trade to the United States. McKinley liked industrial expositions, with their displays of machinery and industrial wares. He called them "the timekeepers of progress." On September 6, the day after his speech, the president attended a reception given in his honor. As he stood in a receiving line shaking hands with guests, McKinley was shot in the chest by a man with a pistol concealed in his bandage-wrapped hand. The assassin, Leon Czolgosz, was an anarchist who wanted to rid the world of government, beginning with the president of the United States. Eight days later, a saddened nation received the news that McKinley had died. He was an admired and much-loved president, the third to be killed by an assassin's bullet since the Civil War. The assassination of McKinley made Theodore Roosevelt president of the United States.

What was Roosevelt's attitude toward the trusts?

How did Congress strengthen the Interstate Commerce Act?

How important was Theodore Roosevelt's contribution to progressivism?

Theodore Roosevelt and Politics

A member of an old and prominent New York family, Theodore Roosevelt was not a typical politician. He had a passion for politics at a time when most upper-class Americans had withdrawn from public life. He was elected to the New York State Assembly in 1881 at the age of 22. Depressed over the deaths of his wife and his mother on the same day in February 1884, Roosevelt quit politics to take up cattle ranching in the Dakota Territory. But the lure of public office proved irresistible.

In 1889, President Benjamin Harrison offered Roosevelt an appointment as head of the United States Civil Service Commission, and he quickly accepted. He resigned that position to become New York City police commissioner and later served as assistant secretary of the navy.

Capitalizing on fame won during the Spanish-American War as leader of the Rough Riders, Roosevelt ran successfully for governor of New York on the Republican ticket in 1898. As governor, he pushed through legislation that benefited labor and raised taxes on corporations. Thomas Platt, the Republican Party boss of New York, thought Roosevelt was too much of a reformer. Anxious to get him out of New York, Platt helped arrange Roosevelt's nomination for vice president on the McKinley ticket in 1900. Roosevelt accepted the nomination and was elected vice president of the United States. He assumed the presidency after McKinley's assassination.

Despite his reputation as a reformer, Roosevelt followed a moderate course during his first term in office. He followed the advice of a high-ranking Republican official who urged him to go slowly early in his term. He remained on good terms with the "Old Guard," as the Republican Party's conservative leaders in Congress were known, as well as with progressive Republicans. He did not attack the high protective tariffs that the Old Guard cherished, and he was always ready to compromise to get the legislation he wanted passed.

Roosevelt and the Square Deal

The coal strike of 1902 presented the new administration with its first crisis. Early that year, the United Mine Workers, the main coal miners' union, went on strike. The miners demanded higher wages, an eight-hour workday, and the mine owners' recognition of their union. A coal strike was a serious matter, as coal was industrial America's principal source of heat and energy. The strike continued through the summer with no sign of a

During the period from 1860 to 1900, three of the seven elected presidents were assassinated. This scene shows the attack on President William McKinley in Buffalo, New York.

settlement. The mine owners refused to recognize the existence of the union or to talk to its president, John Mitchell. By fall, schools began closing for lack of coal to heat classrooms. As entire industries prepared to shut down, Roosevelt acted.

In October, the president invited Mitchell and the mine owners to a conference at the White House. It was a fruitless effort, the owners pretending that Mitchell was not even present. Their lack of concern for the public welfare infuriated Roosevelt. After the meeting broke up, he threatened to send federal troops to take over and operate the mines. This alarmed other industrialists. They saw government operation of the coal mines as a first step toward socialism. Under pressure from the rest of the business community, the mine owners backed down. They agreed to let a commission appointed by the president settle the matter, and the miners went back to work. In the end, the miners got a 10 percent pay increase and reduced working hours, although they did not get recognition of their union. Because both sides gained by compromising, Roosevelt called the agreement a "square deal." The slogan became the trademark of his presidency.

Roosevelt's intervention in the coal strike was a historic departure. It was the first time a president had tried to settle a strike by sitting down with representatives of capital and labor. In 1894, Grover Cleveland had ended the great railroad strike by sending in troops to crush the American Railway Union. Roosevelt saw that unions had a legitimate role to play in protecting the workers. All that he wanted, he said, was a square deal for both the workers and the owners. He also intervened in order to protect the public interest. In doing so, he created a new role for the federal government as a mediator in labor-management disputes.

Roosevelt as Trustbuster

Although Roosevelt had promised to go slowly, he took swift action on the issue of trusts and giant corporations. In 1902, the major railroads serving Chicago from the Pacific Northwest had merged, creating a $400 million monopoly known as the

▶ President Theodore Roosevelt attempted to end the coal strike of 1902 by bringing mine owners and union leaders together. How successful was this attempt?

▼ This editorial cartoon presents President Theodore Roosevelt as a lion tamer. How accurately does it portray Roosevelt's policy toward trusts?

Northern Securities Company. By ending competition over freight rates, the new corporation would reap enormous profits. The merger was a clear violation of the Sherman Antitrust Act, as it created the kind of "combination in restraint of trade" outlawed by the act. The new company would place restraints on trade by increasing freight rates.

Alarmed by the threat this posed to the public interest, Roosevelt ordered Attorney General Philander C. Knox to file suit to dissolve the new railroad trust. The Wall Street bankers who had put the merger together pleaded with the attorney general to let them fix whatever the Justice Department did not like. "We don't want to fix it up. We want to stop it," Attorney General Knox replied. In 1904, the Supreme Court ruled that the Northern Securities Company was an illegal monopoly that had to be broken up. Using the Sherman Antitrust Act with renewed vigor, Knox also filed suits to break up the Standard Oil Company and the meat and tobacco trusts.

Roosevelt would be remembered as a trust-buster, but he did not oppose large corporations just because they were large. The president considered the trend toward bigness to be a natural result of the evolution of modern business. He thought it was sufficient in most cases for the government to permit mergers, while regulating those corporations that affected the public welfare. "The great corporations . . . are the creatures of the State," he remarked, "and the State . . . is in duty bound to control them wherever the need of such control is shown." As a first step toward building the **regulatory state**, Roosevelt persuaded Congress to set up a new Bureau of Corporations to investigate business practices. He saw the bureau as the government's friendly watchdog. It would warn corporations that got out of line and help them mend their ways. Those trusts that blatantly violated the Sherman Antitrust Act or that persisted in their illegal behavior became candidates for antitrust suits. In most cases, Roosevelt would rather regulate trusts than destroy them.

Reform Legislation

Roosevelt's promise to the Old Guard that he would go slowly was a shrewd political tactic. By 1904, they trusted him enough to give him the presidential nomination. In the election that November, Roosevelt defeated his Democratic opponent, Alton B. Parker, by a large majority. Eugene V. Debs, the Socialist candidate, ran a poor third. After being elected in his own right, Roosevelt felt free to develop his own political program.

After the election, Roosevelt proposed a series of new reform measures. He hoped that a program of moderate reform would help close the rift that was developing between the Old Guard and the progressive wing of the Republican Party. Roosevelt was also acutely aware of the mounting public demand for the reform of corporate abuses. He preferred to lead the movement for reform rather than be swept aside by it.

Railroad Reform The first issue Roosevelt addressed was that of unfair rates charged by railroads. Although Congress had set up the Interstate Commerce Commission (ICC) in 1887 to regulate rates,

the commission was too weak to have much effect. The railroads continued to set freight charges as they saw fit. The rate problem was partly solved in 1903 by the Elkins Act, which outlawed secret rebates to shippers. Even the railroads supported the Elkins Act, since the rebates reduced their profits. However, that still left the problem of excessive rates and fares in regions where shippers and passengers had little bargaining power. For example, railroads west of Chicago charged higher rates than eastern railroads because they faced less competition.

Roosevelt urged Congress in 1904 to attack the problem of excessive rates. Congress finally did so in 1906 by passing the Hepburn Act. This act gave the Interstate Commerce Commission the power to set a reasonable rate, although its rate decisions were subject to review by the courts. As the courts usually sided with the railroads, this turned out to be a serious flaw. The act also extended the commission's authority to set rates charged by sleeping-car companies and fees at railroad terminals. While the Hepburn Act strengthened the Interstate Commerce Commission, it did not go as far as many progressives wanted. Senator Robert La Follette and others insisted that the commission should have the final say in setting rates.

Consumer and Worker Protections Roosevelt also supported a campaign led by progressives to give consumers more protection. Americans had long been victims of mislabeled foods and worthless drugs. The muckraking exposés of the early 1900s made people aware of the seriousness of the problem. In 1904, the *Ladies' Home Journal* ran a series of articles exposing misleading advertisements for patent, or nonprescription, medicines. *Collier's Weekly* disclosed the enormous profits made by drug companies in selling harmful products. Two years later, the country was shocked by Upton Sinclair's novel, *The Jungle*. The book described in nauseating detail the unhealthy and filthy conditions of Chicago's meat-packing plants. The public outcry against the meat packers prompted Roosevelt to send a commission of experts to investigate the packing-houses and stockyards. The commission report confirmed the accuracy of Sinclair's fiction and the truth of the popular jingle:

THE JUNGLE
BY
UPTON SINCLAIR

DOUBLEDAY, PAGE & C.
NEW YORK

▲ *Upton Sinclair's novel shocked American readers by exposing the unsanitary conditions that existed in the meatpacking industry. Why do you think the publishers chose this cover illustration?*

> Mary had a little lamb,
> And when she saw it sicken,
> She shipped it off to Packingtown,
> And now it's labeled chicken.

Even the packers took steps to clean up their industry, realizing, as one executive commented, that "the sale of meat and meat products has been more than cut in two."

With support from the president, the public protest against impure and mislabeled food and drugs produced two landmark pieces of legislation. Less than six months after *The Jungle* was published in 1906, Congress passed the Meat Inspection Act. This law placed federal inspectors in packinghouses to inspect and approve meat. In 1906, Congress also passed the Pure Food and Drug Act, which imposed fines for the mislabeling of food and drugs.

By the end of his second term, Roosevelt had endorsed a wide range of reforms. In January 1909, he sponsored a White House conference that called for a national inquiry into the conditions of child labor. That conference led to the creation in 1912 of a federal Children's Bureau to compile information about child labor. Roosevelt also supported proposals for workers' compensation, labor protection for women, and graduated income and inheritance taxes.

Conservation   An avid outdoorsman, Roosevelt strongly supported the **conservation movement** which worked to preserve the nation's natural resources. Since the Civil War, land speculators and developers had removed large tracts of forests and grazing land from the public domain. They had also laid claim to waterpower sites and coal deposits. The developers did so by purchasing or leasing public land for a fraction of its real value. Conservationists called for federal supervision of such resources to preserve them for future use. Naturalists such as John Muir had also begun a campaign to preserve California's Yosemite Valley and other scenic areas as national parks.

When Roosevelt took office, the president had the authority to set aside timberlands as national forests. Gifford Pinchot (pin-SHOH), the chief of the federal Forest Division, urged Roosevelt to use this power more vigorously. Roosevelt followed

▶

Gifford Pinchot, the United States' chief forester, helped Roosevelt set aside national forest preserves. Do you think the preservation and management of public forests is a legitimate role of the federal government?

Pinchot's advice, even exceeding the letter of the law. He set aside waterpower sites in the West and coal lands in Alaska by declaring them protected forests. By the end of his administration, the president had added more than 100 million acres of public land to the national forest preserve.

Roosevelt expanded the nation's forest preserves, but he had no intention of halting the development of the West. In 1902, the president signed the Newlands Reclamation Act, which provided funds for irrigation projects in arid states. Its goal was to reclaim the desert, bringing large tracts of arid land into cultivation. With Roosevelt's support, Congress also expanded the Homestead Act of 1862 to permit land grants of 640 acres of desert land to farmers and ranchers. Conservation to Roosevelt did not mean slowing down western settlement and agricultural development.

Roosevelt left a lasting mark on the presidency. A vigorous and impetuous man, at age 42 he was the youngest man ever to become president. (John F. Kennedy in 1960, at age 43, became the youngest man ever to be *elected* president.) He was also one of the most active and energetic. "The president," said journalist Ray Stannard Baker, "ran full-speed on all the tracks at once." Roosevelt used the presidency as a "bully pulpit"—a platform from which he could publicize and promote causes dear to him. The pounding fist with which he drove home points in his presidential speeches delighted photographers, cartoonists, and the public at large. "While president I have *been* president, emphatically.... I believe in a strong executive; I believe in power," Roosevelt boasted. In carrying out those beliefs, Roosevelt helped transform the presidency from a weak administrative office into a position of political power and leadership.

SECTION 1 REVIEW

1. **Identify** the "Old Guard."
2. **Explain** why the Justice Department took action against the Northern Securities Company.
3. **Describe** how the Hepburn Act strengthened the Interstate Commerce Commission.
4. **List** the aims of the conservation movement.
5. **Evaluate** briefly Theodore Roosevelt's effect on the presidency.

The Taft Interlude

Theodore Roosevelt was delighted by the outcome of the 1908 presidential election. His handpicked candidate, **William Howard Taft**, had easily defeated William Jennings Bryan, who headed the Democratic ticket. Taft had a distinguished record, having served as a federal court judge, governor general of the Philippines, and secretary of war. Roosevelt assumed that Taft would carry on the battle for progressive reform that he had begun.

He assumed incorrectly. Although Taft was a progressive at heart, he was no Theodore Roosevelt. In many respects, the two men were total opposites. Roosevelt craved action. Taft, who weighed over 300 pounds, was slow moving and somewhat lazy. Roosevelt had relished the limelight of the presidency; Taft complained when he took office that he "felt like a fish out of water." Both Roosevelt and the progressives who liked his dynamic presidential leadership were soon disappointed with Taft.

How did President Taft disappoint the progressives?
Why did Theodore Roosevelt break with the Taft administration?
Why did the progressives form a new party in 1912?

Taft Disappoints the Progressives

The progressive Republicans in Congress looked to Taft for leadership. They needed his help to limit the power of Joseph Cannon, the conservative Republican Speaker of the House. His position as Speaker gave him the power to decide what bills would be introduced into the House of Representatives. Cannon was a major obstacle to reform legislation. Early in 1909, 30 Republican members of Congress publicly announced their opposition to Cannon. Initially, Taft also wanted to strip Cannon of much of his power. When Cannon threatened to block tariff legislation if the attack persisted, Taft

---

Why were progressive Republicans disappointed in President William Howard Taft?

made a deal. He agreed to support Cannon in return for a tariff reduction bill. The progressive Republicans, or Insurgents, were shocked that the president had abandoned them so quickly.

Taft called Congress into special session to deal with the tariff issue. During the election campaign, both progressive Republicans and Democrats in the House had called for tariff reductions. They blamed high tariff rates for the soaring cost of living, pointing out that merchants paid an average duty of 40 percent on imported goods. In response to the clamor for reform, the House of Representatives passed a bill that sharply reduced rates. However, it met with strong opposition in the Senate, where the conservative Republican Old Guard rewrote the bill. The result was the Payne-Aldrich Act, which raised rates higher than ever before.

In the battle over tariffs, the progressives again looked to Taft. They were disappointed. Taft wanted tariff reform and did not like the Payne-Aldrich bill, but he much preferred it to an open battle within the Republican Party. As the tariff debate grew more heated, Taft blamed the progressives for dividing the party, calling them "assistant Democrats." He was not opposed to reform, but he did not care much for reformers. A conservative by temperament, he preferred the company of corporation lawyers and bankers to crusading progressives. When the Senate finally passed the Payne-Aldrich bill, Taft signed it into law. Then he made the mistake of calling it "the best tariff measure the Republican party has ever passed."

A Setback for Conservationists

While the tariff battle raged, Taft turned his attention to the conservation issue. Roosevelt had set aside waterpower sites, oil lands, and coal deposits under the pretense that they were forest preserves. Western power companies and coal mine operators urged Taft to reopen these lands for private development. Gifford Pinchot, the government's chief forester, argued against it. Convinced that Roosevelt had gone too far, Taft removed large tracts from the Forest Service reserves. Meanwhile, his secretary of the interior, Richard A. Ballinger, awarded coal deposits in Alaska to developers who were personal friends. Pinchot discovered this and tried to use this information to force Ballinger from office. Taft viewed this as an attempt to discredit his administration and urged Pinchot to drop the matter. When Pinchot persisted, Taft fired him.

With the dismissal of Pinchot, most of the progressives lost faith in the president. They concluded that Taft had sold out to the western land developers. Even Roosevelt was alarmed. "We have just heard that you have been removed," he wrote to Pinchot from his hunting trip in Africa. "I cannot believe it. I do not know any man in public life who has rendered quite the service you have." The Ballinger-Pinchot affair drove the first wedge between the former president and Taft.

The Progressives Look to Roosevelt

In 1910, the progressive Republican Insurgents organized a full-scale revolt. They proceeded to strip Cannon of much of his legislative control. Once again, Taft let them down by sympathizing with Cannon. Disillusioned with the president, the Insurgents turned to Roosevelt. When the former president returned from his extended hunting trip to Africa and tour of Europe, they presented him with a full account of Taft's misdeeds. Although Roosevelt tried to avoid a break with Taft, he found it difficult to remain neutral. He was certain that Taft had betrayed the cause of conservation, for

The Progressive Party Convention

On August 5, 1912, more than 10,000 cheering delegates crowded into the Chicago Auditorium. They had come to create the new Progressive Party and to nominate Theodore Roosevelt as the party's presidential candidate. This was no ordinary political convention. Conspicuously missing were the politicians like those who had gathered in that same auditorium six weeks before to nominate William Howard Taft. Most of the delegates were young, middle-class, intensely earnest men and women who had paid their own expenses to get there. They represented the cream of the progressive movement.

The atmosphere of the Progressive Party convention was more like that of a religious revival meeting than a political party gathering. Again and again, the delegates broke into choruses of "Onward Christian Soldiers" and the "Battle Hymn of the Republic." Roosevelt himself had set the tone for this assembly in a speech earlier that summer, when he said, "We fight in honorable fashion for the good of mankind. . . . We stand at Armageddon and we battle for the Lord." In Roosevelt's eyes the progressives were like the force of good that the Bible said would battle the force of evil at the end of the world.

▲ *Theodore Roosevelt addressed the Progressive Party convention of 1912. Why was Roosevelt the logical candidate for this party's presidential nomination?*

The convention opened with a keynote address by Senator Albert Beveridge. He reminded his listeners that "we stand for a nobler America. . . . We enlist for the war." The next day, Roosevelt spoke, dismissing the Republican and Democratic Parties as "husks, with no real soul within either." He, on the other hand, felt as strong as a bull moose. At that point, the Bull Moose Party became the popular name for the Progressive Party. He pledged the new party to a platform "which shall be a contract with the people." Next came the platform itself, which included virtually every reform that progressives had advocated. It called for protective legislation for women and children, workers' compensation, women's suffrage, health insurance for industrial workers, an income tax, the limitation of warships, and

other reforms. Finally, the delegates nominated a presidential ticket headed by Roosevelt, with California's progressive Governor Hiram Johnson as his running mate.

The Progressive Party convention of 1912 was progressivism's finest hour. Its platform embodied the most advanced social thought of that era. No one deserved the honor of heading its presidential ticket more than Theodore Roosevelt, who had already done so much to advance the cause of progressivism.

1. How did the Progressive Party convention differ from other political nominating conventions?
2. How did this convention represent the high point of the progressive movement?

▲ *What point do you think the editorial cartoonist was making with this portrayal of Roosevelt and Taft?*

which his administration had done so much. In August 1910, Roosevelt announced a new reform program, which he called the **New Nationalism**. It proposed clear alternatives to Taft's policies, including conservation, social reform, and the strict regulation of corporations.

The break finally came in 1911, when the Taft administration filed an antitrust suit against the United States Steel Company. In 1907, this huge corporation had merged with one of its major competitors, the Tennessee Coal and Iron Company. Roosevelt considered Taft's antitrust suit an insult, as he had personally approved the merger four years earlier. In fact, Taft was only enforcing the Sherman Antitrust Act. In four years, he would break up more trusts than Roosevelt had in nearly twice that time. But all that Roosevelt saw was betrayal by the man he had elevated to the presidency. When progressives urged Roosevelt to run for president in 1912, they found him ready and willing.

The Progressive Party

Anxious to be back in the thick of politics, Roosevelt organized a campaign for the Republican nomination. To take advantage of his popular support, progressives in several states enacted laws allowing for presidential primary elections. Roosevelt

▼ *This chart shows the results of the presidential election of 1912. How did the split in the Republican Party affect the outcome of the election?*

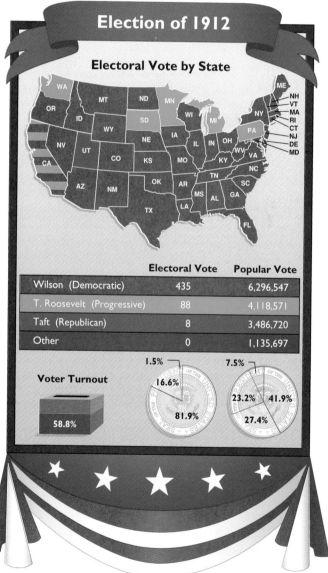

Election of 1912

Electoral Vote by State

	Electoral Vote	Popular Vote
Wilson (Democratic)	435	6,296,547
T. Roosevelt (Progressive)	88	4,118,571
Taft (Republican)	8	3,486,720
Other	0	1,135,697

Voter Turnout

58.8%

1.5%
16.6%
81.9%

7.5%
23.2% 41.9%
27.4%

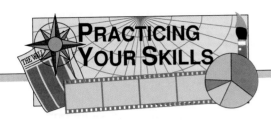

PRACTICING YOUR SKILLS

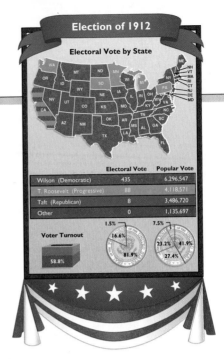

Election of 1912

Electoral Vote by State

	Electoral Vote	Popular Vote
Wilson (Democratic)	435	6,296,547
T. Roosevelt (Progressive)	88	4,118,571
Taft (Republican)	8	3,486,720
Other	0	1,135,697

Voter Turnout 58.8%

Special Purpose Maps: Interpreting Election Results

Maps can be very helpful in understanding statistics such as the results of elections. These special purpose maps not only provide the number of votes each candidate received, they also show the geographic distribution of the vote. Election maps usually show political boundaries rather than natural features.

In the electoral college system, each state's electoral vote is the total of the number of its delegates in the House of Representatives plus its two senators. The smallest states in population have three electoral votes; large states have many more. In order for a presidential candidate to get all of the electoral votes in a state, the candidate has to get only one more vote than the next highest candidate. This "winner takes all" system is called the *unit rule*. The unit rule allows for the possibility of a candidate with a minority of the total popular vote to win a majority of the electoral votes and thereby win the presidency. Refer to the election map of 1876 on page 410 for an example. Although the popular vote is important, a candidate becomes president by winning a majority of the electoral votes. The unit rule makes it important for a candidate to do well in the larger states since they have more electoral votes. This has had an important influence on the way campaigns are run.

Here are some important guidelines for interpreting presidential election results:

- **Check the figures for both popular and electoral votes.** Note how closely the number of electoral votes reflects the popular vote.
- **Check the trends.** What political parties were stronger or weaker in different regions of the country?

- **Study the results.** Consider what factors influenced the outcome of the election. Explain the reasons for the geographic location of each party's strengths and weaknesses. Compare these results with those of previous presidential elections.

Examine the map on page 585 and answer the following questions:

1. What is the title of this map? What information does the map provide?
2. (a) What was the total electoral vote of all 48 states in the 1912 election? (b) How many electoral votes did Wilson need to win in 1912?
3. Why is the popular vote between the candidates closer than the electoral vote? How did the unit rule make the splitting of the Republican Party more damaging?
4. What percentage of the popular vote did Wilson win?
5. How do you explain that Socialist Party candidate Eugene Debs won 900,000 popular votes, but does not appear on this map?
6. What are the consequences for a president who wins the election without a majority of the popular vote?

swept the presidential primaries, but it did him little good. Conservatives controlled the state parties that sent most of the delegates to the Republican National Convention. When the convention met in June, it refused to seat the Roosevelt delegates and nominated Taft by a large majority. Rather than accept defeat, Roosevelt and the progressives stormed out of the convention. They organized a new party called the Progressive Party, which held its own convention six weeks later. Amid great fanfare, the Progressive Party nominated Roosevelt as its presidential candidate.

The split in the Republican Party assured the election of a Democratic president. To add to their advantage, the Democrats nominated **Woodrow Wilson**, a former college professor and president of Princeton University. Elected governor of New Jersey in 1910, Wilson had quickly established a reputation as a champion of reform. In the campaign against Taft and Roosevelt, Wilson promised the country a **New Freedom**. By that he meant lower tariffs, an overhaul of the banking system to limit the power of Wall Street, and a relentless war against the trusts and giant corporations. He promised consumers, farmers, and small businesses a return to a free-market economy governed by open competition and an end to tariff-protected monopolies.

The outcome of the election was never seriously in doubt. Wilson won with 435 electoral votes to 88 for Roosevelt and 8 for Taft. The Socialist candidate, Eugene V. Debs, polled an impressive 900,000 popular votes, but won no electoral votes. Despite a landslide victory in the electoral college, Wilson received only 42 percent of the popular vote. Taft would have been reelected had it not been for the split in the Republican Party.

SECTION 2 REVIEW

1. **Identify** Joseph Cannon.
2. **State** reasons why Taft abandoned the tariff reformers.
3. **Describe** how Pinchot's firing affected Taft's relationship with the conservationists.
4. **Explain** why Roosevelt broke with Taft in 1911.
5. **Discuss** how Roosevelt's candidacy helped Wilson win the presidency.

SECTION 3

Woodrow Wilson and the Progressive Democrats

Dr. Thomas Woodrow Wilson was the first intellectual to be elected president since James Madison. Like Madison, he was a Virginian by birth and would bring southern views on race issues to the White House. At his inauguration, Wilson committed his administration to a renewal of reform. "This is not a day of triumph; it is a day of dedication. Here muster not the forces of party, but the forces of humanity. . . . I summon all honest men, all patriotic, forward-looking men, to my side. God helping me, I will not fail them." It was the most eloquent inaugural address in decades. Even Theodore Roosevelt liked it, calling it "the call of a prophet to a Nation to repent of its sins and return [to] . . . the spirit of the Fathers." The question remained whether this professor-turned-president could provide the leadership necessary to complete the task of reform.

How did Wilson view the office of president?
What reform legislation did Wilson and the progressive Democrats enact?
How did Wilson's position on the trust issue change after he became president?

Wilson's Vision of Leadership

Wilson brought to the White House a new and dynamic view of presidential leadership. As president, he saw himself not only as chief executive, but as chief policymaker and leader of his party in Congress. His vision of presidential leadership was based on the British system, in which the prime minister is a legislative leader in Parliament as well as the executive head of the government. The president, Wilson had once written, is the political leader of the nation. To provide that leadership, Wilson developed a legislative program and worked closely with

▲ *Woodrow Wilson was the Democratic Party's presidential candidate in 1912. He strongly influenced our modern views about presidential leadership.*

ceptable to both the House and the Senate. (Almost all important work on tax laws occurs in the House Ways and Means Committee.) When the tariff lobbyists tried to defeat the Underwood bill, Wilson appealed directly to the voters. The volume of mail that flooded Washington in response to this plea carried the bill through Congress.

The Underwood Tariff Act was the first major reduction of tariff rates since the Civil War. Partly to compensate for lost tariff revenues, Congress in 1913 passed the Sixteenth Amendment that allowed for a graduated income tax.

The Federal Reserve System Wilson and the Democrats in Congress next turned their attention to reforming the nation's banking system. A banking panic in 1907 had caused a brief, but sharp, recession, or temporary downturn, in the economy. The panic was caused by frightened depositors withdrawing savings from several banks that were rumored to be unsound. It demonstrated the need for some way to shift reserves from healthy banks to banks that were in trouble. The existing system also lacked a mechanism to increase the supply of currency to meet the expanding needs of business. Many of the nation's bankers wanted to create a privately owned central bank that would regulate other banks. Progressives of both parties insisted that the banks be placed under strict federal control.

Under Wilson's leadership, the Democrats in Congress worked out a compromise. The Federal Reserve Act of 1913 created the Federal Reserve Board and 12 regional **federal reserve banks**. The federal reserve banks could ease or tighten credit by lowering or raising the interest rate that they charged other banks for borrowing money. Lowering the interest rate would encourage banks to borrow money for reloaning to businesses and the public. They also had the power to expand or contract the supply of money in circulation. The banking system was still privately owned, but policies governing the federal reserve banks were set by the Federal Reserve Board, whose members were appointed by the president. Although modified over the years, the federal reserve system created in 1913 is still the basis for the modern banking system of the United States.

the Democratic majority in Congress to see that it was enacted. Like Roosevelt, he also effectively used the press to rally public support for his proposals. He invited newspaper reporters to the White House, inventing the modern presidential press conference.

On the day of his inauguration, Wilson called Congress into special session. At the opening of the session, Wilson addressed the House and Senate. He was the first president since John Adams to deliver a message to Congress in person. Wilson placed tariff reform at the top of his legislative agenda. Most Democrats thought that the high Republican tariffs, had succeeded too well in shielding business from foreign competition. As a result, consumers paid high prices, monopolies were created, and inefficient businesses thrived. Wilson called for tariff reform and worked with Oscar W. Underwood, Democratic chairman of the House Ways and Means Committee, to construct a low-tariff bill ac-

Oliver Wendell Holmes Jr.

Oliver Wendell Holmes Jr. (1841–1935) was one of the United States Supreme Court's most influential justices. During his 30 years on the Court (1902–1932), he was the leader of its progressive, or liberal, wing and usually in the minority.

Holmes left his mark on the Court by writing brilliant dissenting opinions, arguments of the justices that disagree with the decision of the majority of the Court. His dissent in *Lochner v. New York* (1905) exploded the fiction that justices were neutral agents who simply held up written laws against a written Constitution to see if they matched. In that opinion, he flatly accused the justices of reading their own conservative economic philosophy into the Constitution. "The Fourteenth Amendment does not enact Mr. Herbert Spencer's *Social Statics*," he wrote, referring to the British philosopher whose writings were widely used to justify the status quo. His rebuke may have been the deciding factor in the Court's reversing its position, when it declared a similar Oregon law constitutional in *Muller v. Oregon* (1908). When the Court struck down the Keating-Owen Child Labor Act in 1918, citing the principle of freedom of contract, Holmes again dissented.

▲ *Oliver Wendell Holmes Jr., "the Great Dissenter."*

A firm commitment to democracy was Holmes's guiding principle. He thought that the American people were wise enough to enact legislation appropriate to the times. In one of his many dissenting opinions, he criticized the Court for using the Constitution to prevent "the making of social experiments." Legislatures and not the courts, he insisted, should determine matters of public policy. Holmes firmly believed in the constitutional right to disagree: "If there is any princi-ple of the Constitution that more imperatively calls for attachment than any other it is the principle of free thought—not free thought for those who agree with us but freedom for the thought that we hate."

◆━━◆

1. Since Holmes was usually in the minority on the Supreme Court, how was he able to exert so much influence?
2. Who did Holmes think should create public policy?

President Woodrow Wilson signed the Keating-Owen Child Labor Act of 1916, which barred products made by child labor from interstate commerce. What other social reform legislation did Wilson support?

Regulating Trusts Finally, Wilson urged Congress to address the corporate trust issue. During the presidential campaign, he had called for breaking up trusts in order to support his New Freedom policy based on economic competition. During Wilson's first term, the Justice Department did take action against several large corporations. In 1913, Attorney General James C. McReynolds filed suit against the American Telephone and Telegraph Company, (AT&T). The company wanted to gain control of all the telephone and telegraph systems in the United States. In the final settlement, AT&T was forced to give up its telegraph monopoly and to restore phone competition in the Northwest. Wilson also worked for the passage of the Clayton Antitrust Act of 1914, which strengthened federal antitrust laws.

Although the Justice Department did break up some trusts, Wilson relied more on the regulatory approach that Theodore Roosevelt had favored. In 1914, he supported legislation that created the **Federal Trade Commission**, which in time became the federal government's most important regulatory agency. The commission could make businesses stop certain unfair practices by issuing **restraining orders**. Even the Justice Department preferred the role of police officer to that of trustbuster. The antitrust suits filed by the attorney general usually

were settled in federal courts by **consent decrees** rather than by trials. That is, the corporations agreed to follow the government's regulations in return for the government's dropping the suit.

Before the conclusion of his first term in office, Wilson endorsed a variety of social reforms. He sensed that the country was in the mood for change. Wilson was also afraid that the Roosevelt voters would return to the Republican Party in 1916 if the Democrats failed to provide them with an alternative. Although Wilson did little to advance women's rights and set back the cause of racial justice by segregating the federal buildings in Washington, D. C., he did prod the Democrats in Congress into passing several reform measures. In 1916, for example, Congress passed the Federal Farm Loan Act, which made it easier for farmers to get low-interest loans. Wilson also supported the Keating-Owen Child Labor Act, which restricted the use of child labor, and a workers' compensation law for federal employees.

By the eve of the presidential election of 1916, Woodrow Wilson had become the nation's foremost champion of progressive reform. He had helped Congress enact, in the words of one historian, "the most sweeping and significant progressive legislation in the history of the country up to that time."

1. Summarize Woodrow Wilson's approach to the presidency.
2. Explain the connection between the Underwood Tariff Act and the Sixteenth Amendment.
3. Describe how the Federal Reserve Act of 1913 affected the nation's banking system.
4. Identify the Clayton Antitrust Act.
5. Discuss Wilson's approach to the trust question.

SECTION 4

The Progressives, the Courts, and the Constitution

On May 20, 1895, the Supreme Court had declared the federal income tax to be unconstitutional. The Court at that time was dominated by justices favoring the defense of private property. The income tax was viewed as an attack on the property of the wealthy. In its decision in *Pollock v. Farmers' Loan and Trust Company*, it struck down the income tax provisions of the Wilson-Gorman Tariff Act (1894). In arriving at its decision, the Court ignored its own ruling in an earlier case that had upheld Congress's right to tax incomes. It was the Court's duty, wrote Justice Stephen J. Field, to protect the wealthy from attacks by the poor. "The present assault upon capital is but the beginning," he said. "It will be but the stepping stone to others, larger and more sweeping, till our political contests will become a war of the poor against the rich; a war constantly growing in intensity and bitterness." In striking down the income tax, the Court gave itself a new legislative role. It gave notice that it would strike down acts of Congress based on what it judged to be bad social policy.

On what grounds did the courts oppose progressive reform?

What arguments did progressive lawyers use to justify social legislation?

How successful were the progressives in amending the Constitution?

The Progressives and the Courts

The Industrial Revolution transformed the American judicial system into a protector of the property rights and interests of big business. The majority of the justices serving on the United States Supreme Court had been either conservative lawyers or corporation attorneys when they were appointed. This conservative Supreme Court discovered a new tool for protecting corporate interests in the **due process clause** of the Fourteenth Amendment. No state, that amendment said, shall "deprive any person of life, liberty, or property, without due process of law." Although the amendment had been added to protect former slaves from discriminatory state legislation, it served equally well to protect corporations from unwanted regulatory laws. In a series of decisions in the 1890s, the Supreme Court extended the protection of the due process clause to corporations as well as to individuals. Corporations also benefited from the Court's broad definition of the term *liberty*. Liberty, the Supreme Court said in *Allgeyer v. Louisiana* (1897), included the right of a person "to live and work where he will; to earn his livelihood by any lawful calling; to pursue any livelihood or avocation." It also included a worker's right "to enter into all contracts which may be proper, necessary, and essential to his carrying out to a successful conclusion the purposes above mentioned." States could not pass laws that might deprive workers of their freedom of contract, even when that only meant the freedom to work long hours for little pay in hazardous workplaces.

The Brandeis Brief Guided by the Supreme Court's conservative interpretation of the Fourteenth Amendment, state and federal courts were major obstacles to progressive reform. Illinois courts gutted that state's pioneering Factory Act of 1893, forcing Chicago progressives to begin the legislative process all over again. Laws regulating hours of labor were challenged in other states, and frequently were overturned. In *Lochner v. New York* (1905), the Supreme Court struck down a New York law that limited the hours of work for bakers. The state had

A New Model for Lawyers: The "Brandeis Brief"

Should state governments be allowed to regulate working conditions? By 1900, the United States Supreme Court had developed an answer to the question of how far states could go in regulating working conditions. In a series of cases, the Supreme Court had decided that the word *liberty* in the Fourteenth Amendment ("No State shall . . . deprive any person of life, *liberty*, or property, without due process of law") meant there existed a *liberty of contract* for workers. Workers could contract their services on their own with their boss. No state law could tell a worker how many hours he or she could work. The Fourteenth Amendment would not allow a state to interfere with the right of a worker to contract his or her labor. The state could not use its *police power*, that is, its power to protect its citizens against crime, to protect its citizens from long working hours, the Court said. Liberty of Contract was a right guaranteed by the Fourteenth Amendment.

These decisions raised many questions in the minds of pro-

▲ *Louis D. Brandeis, lawyer, reformer, and justice of the United States Supreme Court.*

gressive reformers of the time. Should workers be forced by greedy employers to work long hours around dangerous machinery and be injured? Could they be forced to permanently damage their health? Wasn't it wrong for women to work longer than men at hard physical labor? Why shouldn't a state government be able to pass a law to protect its citizens from abuse by powerful industries?

The growing industrialization of the United States, fed by available immigrant labor, led to the use of dangerous machinery for long periods of time. Progressive reformers encouraged states to pass laws regulating the workplace conditions and work-

ers' hours. Some states required employers of young people under 16 to obtain the permission of the state. Others required that women not be allowed to work as many hours as men.

The questions asked by reformers were finally answered in 1908 in *Muller v. Oregon*. Curt Muller, an Oregon laundry man, was arrested and convicted of violating the state's ten-hour-work-day law by employing women regularly for longer hours. Muller appealed to the United States Supreme Court.

The Oregon Consumers' League was a strong supporter of progressive labor laws regulating hours of work. A lawyer named Louis Brandeis was found to represent the League's interest. He was known as the "People's Attorney" because he supported the causes of the common people. He believed that you can improve society by upgrading local living and working conditions. He liked to use facts to prove legal arguments instead of abstract ideas of law. One observer stated he was an example of someone who believed in the famous legal saying "From the facts springs the law."

Brandeis set out to prove that the State of Oregon was correct in regulating working conditions that were dangerous

Enduring Constitution

(continued)

to all workers, including women. Brandeis used many assistants, including a medical student to help him understand the medical issues. Ten research assistants from Columbia University library looked into as many studies about working conditions as they could find. The legal papers they helped him produce included over ninety reports by committees, bureaus of statistics, commissioners of health, and factory inspectors in America and Europe dealing with working conditions and workers' health.

Supreme Court procedures called for each lawyer to submit a written argument, called a *brief.* One observer described the famous Brandeis Brief as "... only 2 pages about the law and 119 about working and health conditions of workers in Europe and 20 states in the United States." Never before had a Supreme Court brief relied more upon the social and medical facts surrounding a case than on legal or contractual precedents.

The written brief, and carefully prepared oral arguments based on the detailed information in the brief, overwhelmed the justices. They agreed with Brandeis's points. In the written

opinion of the Court, the justices said that public opinion, studies, research, etc., should not decide a case without relating all these things to the law. They admitted, though, that the facts of this particular case had to include the opinion of many of the studies and simply could not be ignored.

Brandeis was a good lawyer. He argued that there was enough factual evidence to allow the state of Oregon to modify the *liberty of contract* in the interest of the workers (in this case, women). The Supreme Court ruled there was insufficient evidence to overturn the law of Oregon dealing with workers' hours. In fact, there was ample medical and social evidence to show that this law was needed. This marked a change in subsequent court ideas about working conditions and the Fourteenth Amendment's interpretation.

The Brandeis Brief was distributed to hundreds of lawyers, law firms, libraries and judges. Many said it was the beginning of a new way to argue about the Constitution in law courts. Eight years later President Woodrow Wilson appointed Louis Brandeis to a seat on the United States Supreme Court.

The Supreme Court frequently used social, economic, and medical information to

reach its decisions while Justice Brandeis was a member. Now and then an important case would remind court observers of the use of social and medical facts made famous in the Brandeis Brief. In 1954, The National Association for the Advancement of Colored People (NAACP) used vast amounts of social, psychological, educational, and economic information in their brief in the famous *Brown v. Topeka Board of Education* case. The Supreme Court relied upon this information when it abolished separate schools for whites and African Americans. The development of a new way to argue about the Constitution, exemplified by the Brandeis Brief, is just another example of how our legal system adapts to the enduring Constitution.

1. What is a legal brief?
2. Which do you think is more important: the laws affecting a case or the facts surrounding a case?

Important Events of the Progressive Era

POLITICAL REFORM MOVEMENT

1900	Robert La Follette elected governor of Wisconsin
1902	Oregon adopts the initiative and referendum Mississippi adopts the direct primary Newlands Reclamation Act passed
1906	Pure Food and Drug Act passed Meat Inspection Act passed
1913	Dayton, Ohio, installs city-management government Federal Reserve Act passed to regulate banking industry Seventeenth Amendment (direct election of senators) ratified
1914	Federal Trade Commission Act passed to regulate businesses New York Workmen's Compensation Act passed
1917	Compulsory education laws passed in nearly all states
1919	Eighteenth Amendment (prohibition) ratified
1920	Nineteenth Amendment (women's suffrage) ratified

SOCIAL REFORM MOVEMENT

1874	Women's Christian Temperance Union founded
1881	Booker T. Washington founds Tuskegee Institute
1889	Jane Addams opens Hull House
1900	Salvation Army enlistment tops 23,000 members
1902 to 1906	Ida Tarbell begins to write her exposé of Standard Oil Lincoln Steffens publishes *Shame of the Cities* Upton Sinclair publishes *The Jungle*
1905	National Education Association founded
1909	National Association for the Advancement of Colored People (NAACP) founded

▲ *This chart describes some landmark pieces of progressive reform legislation.*

no constitutional ground, it ruled, to keep bakers from working 60 hours or more per week. Bakers, the Court concluded, were not "wards of the state." They had to take care of themselves.

The first break for the progressives came with the Court's ruling in *Muller v. Oregon* (1908), which concerned an Oregon law that set maximum hours for women. **Louis D. Brandeis**, the attorney for Oregon, based his argument on sociological evidence rather than on **legal precedent**, that is, on the way courts had ruled in the past. Brandeis argued that the Oregon law was a reasonable exercise of state power, even though the courts had not ruled in favor of such laws before. The law, he argued, was necessary to protect the health and morals of women. He backed up this argument with a mass of statistical evidence on female labor in the United States. The Brandeis Brief, as it is known, set the pattern for future legal arguments in defense of progressive legislation.

Never before had a lawyer relied so heavily on such evidence in an argument before the Supreme Court. It worked. The Court ruled in *Muller v. Oregon* that the Oregon law was constitutional. Supreme Court rulings after *Muller v. Oregon* brought mixed results. The Court upheld workers' compensation laws in New York and Washington in 1917. In *Bunting v. Oregon* (1917), it also upheld an Oregon maximum-hour law for men as well as women. However, a year later, in *Hammer v. Dagenhart* (1918), the Court struck down the Keating-Owen Child Labor Act of 1916. That act had outlawed interstate shipments of goods made with child labor. The Supreme Court held that the law violated eight-year-old Homer Dagenhart's freedom of contract by denying him the right to work 12 hours per day. In *Adkins v. Children's Hospital* (1923), it declared invalid a federal law establishing a minimum wage for women and children in the District of Columbia. The progressives had made some inroads, but the Supreme Court continued to overturn progressive laws enacted by both state legislatures and by Congress.

Amending the Constitution

The surest way to protect some reform legislation from conservative judges was to amend the United States Constitution. For example, reformers in the Progressive and Democratic Parties favored an income tax. In 1900, tariff duties collected on imported goods were the principal source of tax revenue for the federal government. Progressives saw the tariff as an unfair tax, since it passed the tax burden on to consumers in the form of higher prices for imported goods. Taxing incomes was not a new idea; the Union government had imposed an income tax during the Civil War. More recently, Congress had enacted an income tax as part of the Wilson-Gorman Tariff Act of 1894. However, the Supreme Court had declared the 1894 income tax unconstitutional. In *Pollock v. Farmers' Loan and Trust Co.* (1895), the Court, by a margin of only five to four, had sided with wealthy Americans who had denounced the tax as an attack on private property.

In 1909, progressives from both parties joined Democrats from agricultural states to try again to enact an income tax. They hoped the Supreme Court would reverse the *Pollock* decision. To prevent the bill's passage, conservative Republicans introduced an income-tax amendment, proposing that the constitutional issue be resolved first. They assumed that the amendment would never be ratified by the necessary three-fourths majority of the states. Much to their surprise, the states promptly acted on

it. The Sixteenth Amendment was declared ratified on February 25, 1913, becoming the first new amendment since Reconstruction. The amendment cleared the way for Congress to include an income-tax provision later that year in the Underwood Tariff Act.

Although tax rates were low and applied only to incomes above $4,000, the tax measure had great significance. It marked the beginning of the shift toward the income tax as the principal method of financing the federal government.

Direct Election of Senators The progressives also revived a long-standing campaign to make election to the United States Senate a more democratic process. The Constitution stated that senators were to be elected by the state legislatures, which assumed that the Senate, unlike the House, represented the states rather than the people directly. The indirect election of senators was also supposed to serve as a check against the more democratically elected membership of the House. Both ideas were badly outdated. The argument that the common people could not be trusted to elect senators had not survived the rise of Jacksonian democracy. The notion of state sovereignty had died in the Civil War. The House had attempted several times to change this provision of the Constitution, but each effort had been blocked by the Senate.

The states had discovered a way around the Constitution by enacting preferential primary laws. Such laws let the voters decide whom they preferred to be elected to the Senate. The state legislatures were required to elect the winner of the primary. By 1912, 29 states had enacted preferential primary laws. As more senators were elected by primaries, fewer were left to oppose a constitutional change. The process of change was also sped up by scandals involving senators elected indirectly and by the Senate's growing reputation as a millionaire's club controlled by corporate interests. An amendment providing for the direct election of senators was finally approved by both houses of Congress in 1911. The **Seventeenth Amendment** was ratified by the necessary number of states on May 13, 1913.

Prohibition Progressives also supported the movement for a constitutional amendment to prohibit the sale and use of alcoholic beverages. Since the turn of the century, this movement had gained wide support. It was championed as a moral reform by the Women's Christian Temperance Union, which had over 500,000 members by 1900. Rural temperance advocates worked for prohibition through the Anti-Saloon League, which attacked saloons as an evil of the big cities. The need to conserve grain for wartime purposes during World War I also made prohibition a patriotic cause. In 1917, Congress approved the **Eighteenth Amendment**, which outlawed the manufacture, sale, and transportation of intoxicating liquors. It was ratified by three-fourths of the states in January 1919. Prohibition took effect in October 1919 with the passage of the Volsted Act, which authorized the Bureau of Internal Revenue to enforce the Eighteenth Amendment.

▼ *The title of this cartoon is "Woman's Holy War: Grand Charge on the Enemy's Works." What did the cartoonist suggest was the most significant accomplishment of the temperance movement?*

Women's Suffrage In 1906, Susan B. Anthony celebrated her 86th birthday. She was swamped with congratulatory messages, including a telegram from

◀ *Susan B. Anthony was an early leader of the movement for women's suffrage. After the Civil War, she worked for a constitutional amendment to enfranchise women.*

▶
The masculine cut and dark color of this suffragette suit from 1912 was no accident. To persuade men of women's equality and to win the vote, suffragettes dressed like men as nearly as they could.

President Theodore Roosevelt. Anthony, a long-time leader of the women's suffrage movement, was not impressed. "When will men do something besides extend congratulations?" she remarked. "I would rather have President Roosevelt say one word to Congress in favor of amending the Constitution to give women the suffrage than to praise me endlessly." Anthony and other women's suffrage leaders had placed their hopes on securing a constitutional amendment, but the outcome was still very much in doubt.

By 1910, leaders of the women's suffrage movement were making headway in their campaign to amend the Constitution. Women's organizations worked hard to bring the issue to the attention of the nation. The National Woman's Party, led by Alice Paul, picketed the White House to persuade President Wilson to work for passage of the amendment. They had organized campaigns in 11 states to put a suffrage referendum on the ballot. These campaigns were beginning to show results. Women could vote in nine states by 1912—although all were states west of the Mississippi. The more populous states in the East were still opposed. But the women's suffrage cause was winning converts among progressives at the national level. By 1916, both the Progressive and the Republican Parties had endorsed women's suffrage. Within three years, the suffrage leaders had won over a majority in Congress. In 1919, Congress passed the **Nineteenth Amendment**, which stated that the right to vote "shall not be denied or abridged . . . on account of sex." It was ratified by the necessary number of states in August 1920, bringing the long campaign to enfranchise women to a successful conclusion.

While the passage of the Nineteenth Amendment gave women the right to vote, it also threatened their status as protected workers. In *Adkins v. Children's Hospital* (1923), the Supreme Court ruled that women's suffrage had ended the need to treat women as a protected class. Justice Holmes dissented, as he so often did. "It will take more than the Nineteenth Amendment to convince me that there are no differences between men and women and that legislation cannot take those differences into account," he wrote. Nevertheless, steps toward equality with men entailed risks as well as benefits to women in industrial America.

SECTION 4 REVIEW

1. **Describe** the approach of the Supreme Court in opposing progressive social legislation.
2. **Explain** the significance of *Muller v. Oregon.*
3. **Explain** why the Brandeis Brief is significant in American legal history.
4. **Name** the constitutional amendments passed during this period that made the political process more democratic.
5. **Summarize** how the Nineteenth Amendment affected the status of women in American society.

SECTION 5

The Legacy of Progressivism

The year 1916 was a presidential election year. With the Republican Party united again, the Democrats realized that they had to win votes from progressive Republicans to reelect Woodrow Wilson. One result, as we have seen, was a flood of progressive legislation that enacted most of the Progressive Party's platform of 1912. He supported a plank in the Democratic platform endorsing state action for women's suffrage and began to work closely with suffrage leaders. During the presidential campaign, Wilson endorsed women's suffrage. This helped him win women's votes in the states that already allowed women to vote in presidential elections. Wilson also promised to keep the United States out of the Great War that had broken out in Europe in 1914. The strategy worked. In November, the Democrats won in the electoral college by the slimmest of majorities (277 to 254). However, with much of the progressive legislative agenda already enacted into law, the movement for reform had passed its peak. By 1916, the nation was shifting its attention to other concerns, especially to the war in Europe.

In what areas was progressivism most successful?
How did progressive thinkers influence American philosophy, education, and the social sciences?
How was progressivism reflected in literature and art?

Successes and Failures of Progressivism

How successful were the progressives? In some areas, the reformers were highly successful. Progressivism was not a single movement, but several reform efforts moving in several directions. Those who campaigned against child labor would in time substantially reduce the number of children working in factories and mines. The Meat Inspection Act and the Pure Food and Drug Act were important first steps in consumer protection. Reformers also succeeded in making the political process more democratic, by use of the direct primary, the initiative and referendum, and the Seventeenth and Nineteenth Amendments. Nevertheless, candidates backed by corporate campaign funds still had a distinct advantage in primary elections. Well-organized pressure groups could influence the outcome of a referendum.

Progressivism had a lasting impact on American political thought and institutions. Prior to 1900, few people thought of government as an agency for solving social problems. The dominant view was that government should create an economic climate favorable to business, but otherwise keep its hands off. Free competition in the marketplace would resolve such questions as hours, wages, and conditions of work. The progressives changed all that. They helped create a new perception of government as a mediator between private interests and the common good. Government, they argued, had social responsibilities. The reform legislation of the Progressive Era laid the foundation for the modern regulatory state. In the future, regulatory agencies would become a "fourth branch" of the federal government.

Other reform efforts were less successful. The antitrust movement scored some notable victories, such as the breakup of Standard Oil. However, it left most of the corporate mergers untouched and failed to reverse the trend toward ever-larger concentrations of economic power. The settlement houses had less impact on immigrant neighborhoods than their founders had hoped. Yet these houses had a profound effect on many of the reformers who worked there. They helped prepare scores of young people for careers in social work and public service. Thus, success is not always easy to measure.

The Social Sciences

Intellectuals of the Progressive Era challenged the widely held beliefs of the Social Darwinists. These beliefs had left little room for social reforms. The most impressive challenge was the publication in 1890 of a book by William James entitled *Principles of Psychology*. A Harvard University psychologist and philosopher, James found Spencer's view of reality deeply unsatisfying. It left no place for the exercise of free will, the characteristic that James thought set humans apart from other beings. Humans, James observed, were not passive creatures who lived out their lives automatically responding to their environment. They also acted on and shaped nature. They had the same freedom to reshape political and social institutions. He called for a new understanding of reality, one that would free people from the constraints of Social Darwinism.

In one area after another, intellectuals revolted against those constraints. In the field of sociology, which studies human social behavior, Frank Lester Ward had already arrived at conclusions similar to those of William James. Ward argued in his book *Dynamic Sociology* (1883) that Herbert Spencer had

▶

William James, a Harvard psychologist and philosopher, helped give intellectual respectability to progressivism.

overlooked the fact that human beings had brains with which they could shape the future. In human society, he concluded, the law of mind had replaced the law of nature. Progressive economists also challenged Social Darwinism. Economist Richard T. Ely rejected the idea that inequality of wealth was natural and inevitable. It could be explained by an analysis of banks, corporations, and other institutions that helped concentrate wealth in the hands of the few. Progressive historians reexamined American and European history, applying critical methods of scholarship. The United States Constitution, argued Charles Beard, a Columbia University historian, was not an inevitable product of social evolution. It was, he wrote in *An Economic Interpretation of the Constitution* (1914), an economic document designed to protect men of property.

A broad movement for educational reform took shape during the Progressive Era. This movement was in large part inspired by philosopher John Dewey, who published his ideas about education in *The School and Society* in 1899. Dewey insisted that schools should help children cope with the world around them. Schools had failed in that mission because they paid more attention to subject matter than to children. They stuffed children's minds full of facts instead of helping them become useful citizens in the modern industrial world. Teachers who tried to put Dewey's ideas into practice created a more child-centered approach to education. In pro-gressive schools, memorizing facts gave way to student activities that emphasized personal growth and intellectual development. In the decades to come, Dewey and his followers would have a lasting impact on American education.

American Literature and Art

New ways of looking at reality also had an impact on American literature. The generation of American writers who came of age during the Progressive Era rebelled against the romantic literature of the post–Civil War period. They searched for new subjects in industrial cities and wrote in a more realistic manner. Among them were Stephen Crane, who wrote *Maggie: A Girl of the Streets* (1893), and Theodore Dreiser, the author of *Sister Carrie* (1900). Both dealt with the theme of sexual immorality and described the powerful effect city living had on people's minds and actions. Maggie was an

▼ *Jack London's realistic fiction was widely read during the Progressive Era.*

◄ *John Dewey founded the movement for progressive education.*

immigrant girl driven to sin and suicide by life in the city slums. Sister Carrie was a shop girl whose rejection of traditional middle-class morals paved the way to her success. The Progressive Era writers went beyond the earlier realism of William D. Howells and Henry James. They depicted the more brutal and seamy aspects of life, as Upton Sinclair did in *The Jungle* (1906). Even the animals that Jack London wrote about in *Call of the Wild* (1903) and *White Fang* (1906) were brutal and violent.

In the beginning, such realistic fiction was not warmly received. Readers who had grown up with *Little Women* were shocked by *Maggie*. It took time for public taste to catch up.

Abstract Art Americans who were shocked by naturalism in literature were equally astonished by new developments in art. Many Americans were first introduced to abstract or modern art by an exhibition in 1913 held at the 69th Regimental Armory Building in New York City. The Armory Show, as it is known, was the first major exhibition in the United States of abstract paintings. In **abstract art**, the painter intentionally distorts or rearranges forms and colors rather than trying to portray them realistically. While several American artists were represented, European paintings such as Marcel Duchamp's *Nude Descending a Staircase* received most of the attention. Viewers accustomed to landscapes, historical scenes, and portraits were

▼ *Marcel Duchamp painted* Nude Descending a Staircase, No. 2, *in 1912. Why were many Americans shocked by the work of the abstract painters?*

▼ Red Canna *by Georgia O'Keeffe (c. 1923) transformed a conventional subject into an abstract symphony of form and color. [Collection of The University of Arizona Museum of Art, Tucson, Gift of Oliver James. The Georgia O'Keeffe Foundation/Artists Rights Society (ARS), New York.]*

amused or disturbed by the new art. A small group of American artists was inspired by the Armory Show to create paintings and sculpture that did not follow conventional styles.

The most important sponsor of modern, or abstract, art in the United States was Alfred Stieglitz, a photographer who owned a gallery in New York City. He showed abstract paintings by French and American artists as early as 1907. Over the next decade, Stieglitz sought out the most promising of the young American painters. He displayed their work, sold their paintings, and put them in touch with their counterparts in Europe. Among these painters was John Marin, who painted semiabstract landscapes and urban scenes. Stanton MacDonald-Wright, another member of the group, moved beyond representational painting altogether. Typical of his work was *Synchronomy in Green and Orange*, a painting composed of abstract forms and color. Perhaps the best known artist today of the Stieglitz group is Georgia O'Keeffe. Although she began painting abstract compositions, her later paintings are of recognizable subjects, especially flowers and desert scenes.

SECTION 5 REVIEW

1. **Relate** how progressivism changed the perception of government's role.
2. **Identify** John Dewey.
3. **Describe** how William James's view of reality differed from that of Herbert Spencer.
4. **Explain** how the novels of Crane, Dreiser, and London differed from earlier novels that used similar themes.
5. **Name** one aspect of abstract art that was "progressive."

Summary

The reformers of the Progressive Era were the first generation of Americans to expand the role of the federal government into the affairs of everyday life. They looked to the federal government to resolve problems too big for local and state governments. They passed legislation that put federal meat inspectors in the packing plants and that forced food processors to label the contents of their products. At their insistence, Congress created the Federal Trade Commission to oversee the big corporations. Out of the progressives' belief in progress and social justice came the foundation for the modern regulatory state. This was a major legacy that progressive Americans of the turn of the century left to future generations.

Aware that the presidency was the only elected office that represented all the people, Roosevelt and Wilson found new ways to expand the powers of the office. They used the visibility of the White House and the power of the press to mold public opinion and to shape legislation.

Although the Court took a conservative approach to most of the progressive legislation (child labor and minimum wage laws), some reform legislation was upheld, including the right to make laws limiting the number of hours that women could be made to work.

Passage of the Sixteenth Amendment finally settled the question of whether or not an income tax was constitutional. The direct election of senators, Prohibition, and universal women's suffrage were other reforms that were gained in this period by amendments to the Constitution.

The influence of progressives was also felt in literature and art. Writers attacked Social Darwinism and began to write fiction using realistic settings and characters. Painters began to experiment with abstract art forms that influenced people's perceptions of reality.

Vocabulary

abstract art
consent decree
conservation movement
due process clause

federal reserve bank
legal precedent
regulatory state
restraining order

Write on a separate paper the word or term that best completes the following sentences. You will not use all the terms listed above.

1. The Federal Trade Commission issued a |||||||||| to prevent the company from giving the supplier a rebate.
2. The director was appalled by the examples of |||||||||| displayed in the exhibition.
3. Many progressives approved of the government assuming the powers of a ||||||||||.
4. After 1914, tightening of credit was a function of the ||||||||||.
5. Without admitting guilt, the corporation accepted the terms of the ||||||||||.
6. Corporations, as well as people, were protected under the |||||||||| of the Fourteenth Amendment.
7. Making a decision based on the finding of an earlier case is known as following a ||||||||||.

Review Questions

1. Name two important ways that Theodore Roosevelt differed from most earlier presidents.
2. How did Roosevelt gain his reputation as a trustbuster?
3. Explain why President Taft was a disappointment to the progressives.
4. How did the actions of progressive Republicans in 1912 contribute to the election of Woodrow Wilson?
5. Compare Woodrow Wilson's and Theodore Roosevelt's ideas about presidential leadership.
6. How did Wilson's New Freedom differ from Roosevelt's New Nationalism?
7. How did the Court block progressive reforms?

8. Which constitutional amendments date from the Progressive Era?
9. What did the novels of Crane, Dreiser, and London have in common?
10. Why was the Armory Show of 1913 a significant event in the history of American art?

Critical Historical Thinking

Writing Answer each of the following by writing one or more complete paragraphs:

1. Discuss why the Supreme Court does not necessarily reflect the dominant social or political attitudes of the times. Why does it make decisions that often do not agree with the opinions of the majority of people?
2. Discuss whether you believe government has gone too far in its regulatory role. Give specific examples to support your arguments.
3. Many people would like to elect the president directly and abolish the electoral college. Discuss whether or not you would be in favor of such an amendment. Give your reasons.
4. Read "Making Sausage in Chicago" in the Unit 6 Archives. Explain why you think that Upton Sinclair's novel, *The Jungle*, was instrumental in the passage of pure food and drug laws in the early 1900s.

Making Connections with Political Science

Today, in a world doing business on a global scale, it is difficult for us to imagine the degree to which Americans at the turn of the century feared the giant corporation and its powers.

Many Americans were enthusiastic about the Industrial Revolution in America and identified with its leaders: Rockefeller, Carnegie, Morgan, etc. But after the depression of the 1890s, Americans began to look at industrialization very differently.

They came to worry that too much power had become concentrated in the hands of a few corporations whose very operations seemed to deny the individualism and personal accountability they valued so highly.

The corporation in 1900 was not a *legal entity*. Legally speaking, only persons had "standing" before the law. How then was a corporation to be made accountable? A person who acted illegally could be arrested and brought to trial, and the injustice could be remedied in civil court. But what of a corporation? There simply was no means to sue something that was not a person, and the courts had not defined the constitutionality of regulating corporations and ensuring the safety of their products.

The first step in solving this dilemma was to define a corporation as a person for the purpose of legal representation. When the courts did this, it allowed a corporation to be held legally accountable for its actions just like a person. It also served to protect corporations from the excessive zeal of regulators, because the Fourteenth Amendment prohibits the government from depriving a person of property without due process of law. Profit is a type of property. The Fourteenth Amendment also guarantees people equal protection of the laws.

Writing Research the Fourteenth Amendment in your school or public library. Write a paper that addresses the following questions: Why was it enacted? To whom was it meant to apply? What would you say about the nature of the Constitution based on what you have learned about the Fourteenth Amendment and its application to corporations?

Additional Skills Practice

If you add up the number of electors of each state of the United States, the total number falls three short of the actual number of electors in the electoral college. Write an explanation for this discrepancy. If you need a hint, look carefully at the political map of the United States.

Progressive Era Diplomacy

I n 1898, the stunning victory of the United States in the Spanish–American War symbolized the nation's arrival as a major power on the world scene. The war not only demonstrated American military might, it also resulted in the nation's occupation of territories in Asia, in the Pacific, and in the Caribbean. Meanwhile, the United States had growing commercial and financial interests—and therefore political interests—in Asia, Europe, and Latin America. As a result, presidents Theodore

I WANT YOU

for the U.S. ARMY ENLIST NOW

▲ *James M. Flagg created this World War I army recruiting poster. It was so popular it was revised for use during World War II.*

Roosevelt, William Howard Taft, and Woodrow Wilson all pursued more active and aggressive foreign policies than presidents before them. American policymakers were exploring new ground, feeling their way along with few precedents about how best to define and to pursue vital national interests. Therefore, the style, values, policies, and actions of these three presidents —Roosevelt's taking the Panama Canal, Taft's economic-based diplomacy in Asia, or Wilson's leading the nation into the Great War—differed greatly from one another.

Theodore Roosevelt's Foreign Policies

Today Americans are accustomed to their president traveling overseas for goodwill visits or for meetings with foreign leaders. It was not always so. In 1906, for example, President Theodore Roosevelt told Andrew Carnegie that he wished "that we did not have the ironclad custom which forbids a president ever to go abroad." The occasion for Roosevelt's wishful thinking was a British request that he help reduce the naval arms race between Britain and Germany. Roosevelt was certain that if he could talk with them in person, he could persuade the German Kaiser and other European leaders to slow this arms race. But Roosevelt also believed that American public opinion would disapprove if he went to Europe to conduct diplomacy. Within months of this decision, however, Roosevelt broke with custom by leaving the United States to observe the construction of the Panama Canal. Roosevelt was sensitive to public opinion when he felt he had to be, but he also was willing to take action, even when his actions broke new ground.

What ideas guided Theodore Roosevelt's foreign policies?

What was Roosevelt's foreign policy toward Latin America?

What foreign policy goals did Roosevelt have in Asia?

Roosevelt and the Large Policy

President Theodore Roosevelt left a powerful imprint on the conduct of United States foreign relations. Roosevelt believed that "the average American [did not] take the trouble to think carefully or deeply" about foreign affairs. As a result, the United States needed strong leadership, which he was more than willing to provide. Roosevelt's approach to leadership in foreign affairs reflected his leadership

▲ *The battleship* Virginia, *with other ships of the "Great White Fleet," left Hampton Roads, Virginia, in December 1907. What was the purpose of the voyage?*

style in domestic affairs—he was skillful, daring, and had a flare for bending public and congressional opinion to his will. Roosevelt was prepared to act, without the knowledge of the American people, in what he assumed to be their best interests.

Roosevelt was by personality and belief well suited to undertaking an active foreign policy. A boxer in college, Roosevelt spoke fondly of the virtues of "the strenuous life." He believed that physical combat was a noble way to prove one's manhood. Indeed, his adventures in the Spanish-American War only increased his fondness for battle. He believed the United States had to be strong militarily to maintain and enlarge its economic and political stature.

In the decade before he became president, Roosevelt had joined his friends Admiral Alfred Thayer Mahan and Henry Cabot Lodge in advocating the large policy—greater U.S. military power and national prestige. Roosevelt's use of a West African proverb, "Speak softly and carry a big stick," reflected his attitude toward diplomacy and national power. As president, Roosevelt vigorously prodded Congress to vote funds to create a "bigger stick." During Roosevelt's presidency, Congress approved 10 new battleships and 21 other warships, making the U.S. Navy the third most powerful in the world—behind Britain and Germany. Roosevelt also persuaded Congress to reform the army, particularly to improve the training of its officers.

Roosevelt's Use of the Media

When Theodore Roosevelt became president, the office was not as powerful as it would one day become. Roosevelt vigorously pushed for more power for the office. He was probably the first president to fully enjoy the office and its limelight. He used every medium at his disposal to dramatize and promote himself, his office, and his ideas. He used newspapers, magazine articles, and personal appearances to accomplish his goals.

Roosevelt pioneered the art of using the press as a government news service. He set aside space in the White House for a press room, and he cultivated close relationships with Washington journalists. Roosevelt briefed reporters "off the record" and leaked information when it served his purpose. He tested ideas by publishing them in the press and then assessing public response. He also used the press to influence public opinion. As his aide Archie Butt later said, "Mr. Roosevelt understood the necessity of guiding the press to suit one's own ends."

Roosevelt's colorful personality made good newspaper copy. He welcomed stories, photographs, and even cartoons about himself. Republican conservatives thought him too unconventional, too outspoken, too undignified, and too energetic. Yet these very attributes

▲ Theodore Roosevelt, photographed at a Flag Day rally in 1910, was an animated public speaker. What was the occupation of the men seated below the former president?

endeared Roosevelt to reporters and public alike. Many people now view some of his beliefs—his racism and fervent nationalism for example—as outrageous. But these attitudes did little to damage his popularity then.

"Roosevelt's [combative spirit] was so much a part of the life of the period, was so tied up to the newspapers," journalist Mark Sullivan wrote, "as to constitute for the average reader . . . almost all of the passing show, the public's principal interest." Woodrow Wilson said it differently. "That part of the government," Wilson wrote in 1908, "which has the most direct

access to opinion has the best chance of leadership and mastery; and at present that part is the presidency." Roosevelt's use of the press broke new ground and expanded presidential influence and power.

1. Describe the methods used by Roosevelt to promote his ideas in the media.
2. What aspects of Roosevelt's personality might not be acceptable to the American public today?

For Roosevelt, military power was important because international relations were based on a struggle for existence. All nations used their military and economic power to pursue interests they thought vital to their survival. For each nation these interests included:

- security
- promoting the welfare of its citizens
- expanding trade and other commercial opportunities
- protecting its citizens and property overseas
- controlling immigration
- maintaining prestige among other nations.

Since there was competition among nations to meet these needs, one country's interests could easily conflict with those of another country.

Roosevelt took for granted the superiority of the United States and its leaders—whose roots and values came mostly from northern and western Europe. He believed there were important differences between "civilized" and "uncivilized" nations of the world. "Uncivilized" nations were primarily non-white, did not have Western cultures, and often provided raw materials to industrialized nations. In Roosevelt's view, the exception was Japan. Japan was "civilized" because it had adopted Western ways, was industrializing, and was a rising military power. It was the right and duty of the "civilized" nations to intervene in the affairs of "uncivilized" nations to ensure order and stability.

Roosevelt's general views about Britain and Germany influenced all of his specific foreign policies. Roosevelt thought the national interests of the United States often coincided with those of the British. Both nations wanted to promote trade and commerce throughout the world. The powerful British navy kept ocean lanes open for such trade. Since both countries possessed colonies they wanted to keep, both supported the existing balance of power throughout the world. British and American leaders should recognize their similar aims and look to each other for friendship and mutual support.

On the other hand, Roosevelt viewed Germany as a threat to the economic and political interests of the United States. Germany aggressively sought colonies in Africa, Asia, the Pacific, and even Latin America. It viewed with jealousy the power of the British navy and began to expand its sea force. As a result, Germany's foreign policies threatened British interests all over the world. Germany also posed a threat to American interests in Latin America and in the Pacific (especially the Philippines).

The Panama Canal Zone

Since the 1840s, Americans had dreamed of building a canal across Central America, connecting the Atlantic and Pacific Oceans. The Spanish-American War had increased this desire. When hostilities broke out in the Caribbean in 1898, it took 71 days for the battleship USS *Oregon* to steam from San Francisco, around Cape Horn, to its battle station in the Atlantic. A Central American canal would cut travel time by two thirds. Several obstacles, however, stood in the way.

One question was where to locate the canal. Both Roosevelt and Congress favored Nicaragua since a sea-level route that would not require a system of locks could be built there. Panama—then the northern province of Colombia—was another possible location. The Panama route was shorter but would require locks. In fact, a French company had begun construction of a canal across Panama in 1882, but technological problems and outbreaks of malaria caused it to go bankrupt. In 1894, a second French company, the New Panama Canal Company, took over the original company's operations.

Meanwhile, stockholders in the New Panama Canal Company, including Philippe Bunau-Varilla, began to lobby Washington to buy the company's rights and equipment. This lobbying, along with the eruption of a volcano in Nicaragua, influenced Congress's decision about which canal route to choose. In 1902, Congress authorized Roosevelt to buy the New Panama Canal Company's rights and equipment for $40 million—if Colombia would agree to a satisfactory canal treaty. By that time, the Panama Canal was 40 percent complete.

In January 1903, Secretary of State John Hay negotiated a canal treaty with Tomás Herrán, Colombia's ambassador in Washington. The Hay-Herrán Treaty granted the United States a 99-year lease to a six-mile-wide canal zone for a one-time payment of $10 million and $250,000 annual rent. The Senate quickly ratified the treaty, but Colombia refused. The country wanted more money for this valuable asset. Colombia's refusal irritated Roosevelt. He considered seizing the Panama route by force, but events soon made that unnecessary.

On November 3, 1903, the Panamanians revolted against Colombian rule. They succeeded in establishing their own government within two days with remarkably little bloodshed. The presence of the gunboat USS *Nashville* prevented the Colombians from landing troops to put down the rebellion. The arrival of additional U.S. ships ensured the survival of the new Panamanian government. On November 6, the U.S. State Department recognized the new government.

▲ *This photograph of the Pedro Miguel Locks under construction in November 1910 reflected the vast scale and difficulty of the Panama Canal project.*

▼ *A system of locks moves ships through the Panama Canal. Why are the locks necessary?*

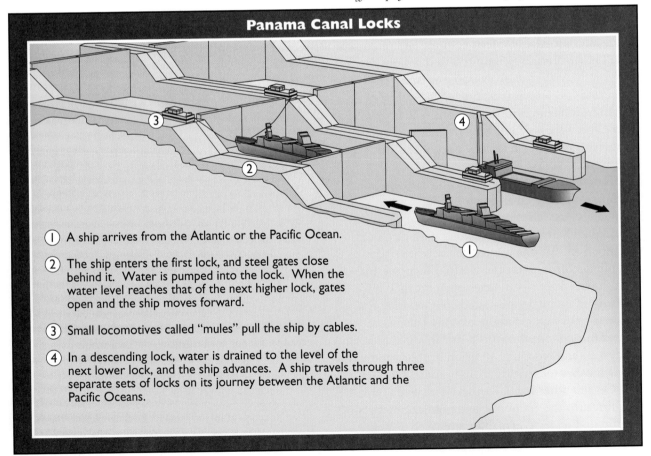

Panama Canal Locks

1. A ship arrives from the Atlantic or the Pacific Ocean.

2. The ship enters the first lock, and steel gates close behind it. Water is pumped into the lock. When the water level reaches that of the next higher lock, gates open and the ship moves forward.

3. Small locomotives called "mules" pull the ship by cables.

4. In a descending lock, water is drained to the level of the next lower lock, and the ship advances. A ship travels through three separate sets of locks on its journey between the Atlantic and the Pacific Oceans.

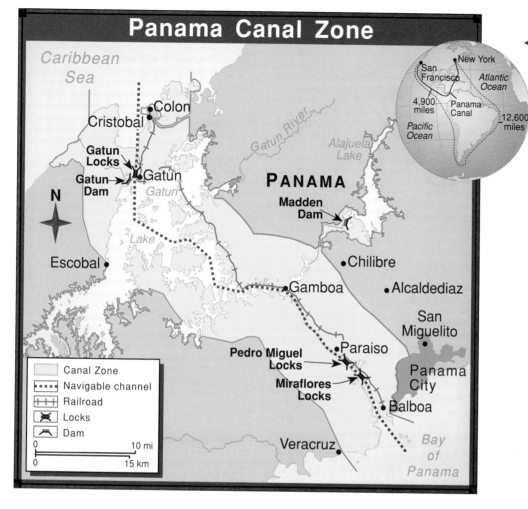

Panama Canal Zone

Caribbean Sea

Colon
Cristobal
Gatun Locks
Gatun Dam
Gatun
Gatun River
Escobal
Lake

PANAMA

Madden Dam
Alajuela Lake
Chilibre
Gamboa
Alcaldediaz
San Miguelito
Pedro Miguel Locks
Paraiso
Miraflores Locks
Panama City
Balboa
Veracruz
Bay of Panama

N

Canal Zone
Navigable channel
Railroad
Locks
Dam
0   10 mi
0   15 km

The opening of the Panama Canal cut thousands of miles off the sea route between the Atlantic and Pacific Oceans. What geographical reasons would have influenced the engineers to choose this location for the canal?

New York
San Francisco
Atlantic Ocean
4,900 miles
Panama Canal
Pacific Ocean
12,600 miles

Roosevelt and Hay acted rapidly. The resulting Hay–Bunau-Varilla Treaty granted the United States a permanent lease to a ten-mile-wide canal zone for the original $10 million and $250,000 annual rent. Although unhappy with the treaty's terms, Panama ratified the agreement. Canal construction resumed almost immediately. "I took the canal and let Congress debate," Roosevelt later boasted, "and while the debate goes on the canal does also." The canal was finished in 1914 at a cost of $400 million and with a great deal of bitterness on the part of many Latin Americans toward the United States.

The Roosevelt Corollary

U.S. interests in the Caribbean, including Puerto Rico, the Panama Canal Zone, and Cuba, created new responsibilities. In 1902, Venezuela's military

dictator refused to repay loans from Britain, Germany, and Italy. Those countries blockaded Venezuela's ports and collected the debts by force.

Roosevelt feared that further interventions of this kind might lead to permanent European control or even annexation. He wanted to prevent aggressive powers such as Germany from establishing military bases in the area. In December 1904, Roosevelt announced his corollary to the Monroe Doctrine. The Monroe Doctrine had warned Europe against meddling in the Western Hemisphere. The **Roosevelt Corollary** stated that the United States alone had the right to intervene in the domestic affairs of its Latin American neighbors if they proved unable to maintain order and stability on their own.

The Dominican Republic was the first test of the Roosevelt Corollary. The island nation had been unable to make payments on some foreign loans. Roosevelt, not wanting to annex the island, proclaimed: "I would have about the same desire to annex it as a gorged boa constrictor might have to swallow a porcupine wrong-end-to." Instead, he negotiated a treaty that gave the United States control of Dominican import taxes and finances. An American-appointed agent used 55 percent of the taxes to pay off the debt.

Anti-imperialist senators blocked ratification of the treaty, but Roosevelt outmaneuvered them by issuing an **executive agreement**. An executive agreement is similar to a treaty, but it is binding only for the duration of a specific president's term and does not need Senate approval. Recognizing defeat, the Senate ratified the treaty in 1907. Over the next 30 years, presidents

▲ *How is the Roosevelt Corollary illustrated here?*

used the Roosevelt Corollary to justify continuing intervention in Caribbean and Central American affairs.

A Balance of Power in Asia

In Roosevelt's view, America had few important interests and little actual military power in Asia. Trade with China was small and relatively unimportant. Governing the Philippines was costly and the islands were virtually impossible to defend. Roosevelt therefore used diplomacy rather than military intervention to protect America's few inter-

▼ *How many times were U.S. troops sent to Latin America during the period shown?*

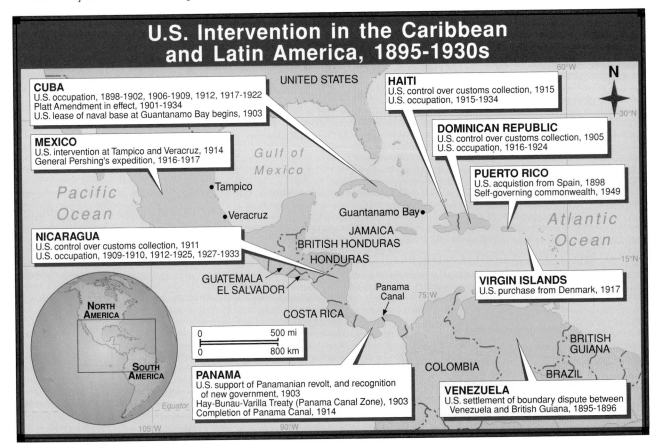

U.S. Intervention in the Caribbean and Latin America, 1895-1930s

UNITED STATES

CUBA
U.S. occupation, 1898-1902, 1906-1909, 1912, 1917-1922
Platt Amendment in effect, 1901-1934
U.S. lease of naval base at Guantanamo Bay begins, 1903

MEXICO
U.S. intervention at Tampico and Veracruz, 1914
General Pershing's expedition, 1916-1917

HAITI
U.S. control over customs collection, 1915
U.S. occupation, 1915-1934

DOMINICAN REPUBLIC
U.S. control over customs collection, 1905
U.S. occupation, 1916-1924

PUERTO RICO
U.S. acquistion from Spain, 1898
Self-governing commonwealth, 1949

Gulf of Mexico

Pacific Ocean

•Tampico

•Veracruz

Guantanamo Bay•

JAMAICA
BRITISH HONDURAS
HONDURAS

Atlantic Ocean

NICARAGUA
U.S. control over customs collection, 1911
U.S. occupation, 1909-1910, 1912-1925, 1927-1933

GUATEMALA
EL SALVADOR

Panama Canal

VIRGIN ISLANDS
U.S. purchase from Denmark, 1917

COSTA RICA

NORTH AMERICA

SOUTH AMERICA

Equator

0   500 mi
0   800 km

PANAMA
U.S. support of Panamanian revolt, and recognition of new government, 1903
Hay-Bunau-Varilla Treaty (Panama Canal Zone), 1903
Completion of Panama Canal, 1914

COLOMBIA

VENEZUELA
U.S. settlement of boundary dispute between Venezuela and British Guiana, 1895-1896

BRITISH GUIANA

BRAZIL

N

ests as best he could. Roosevelt's goal was to maintain a balance between Russia and Japan, the region's two major powers.

In spite of the Open Door Policy, Russia had moved aggressively to expand its commercial interests and political influence in China, Manchuria, and Korea. Meanwhile, Japan moved to balance growing Russian power in the region by forming an alliance with Britain. Roosevelt applauded the alliance since it confirmed Japan's recognition of the Open Door Policy. Because of Russia's continued successes, Japan launched a surprise attack on the Russian fleet at Port Arthur, Manchuria, in late 1904. The Japanese won a series of battles, and it appeared that Japan might win the Russo-Japanese War decisively. The war dragged on, however, and by early 1905 Japan was close to financial and military exhaustion.

Japan and Russia agreed to having Roosevelt mediate a peace settlement. The resulting Portsmouth (New Hampshire) Treaty pleased neither side entirely, and both blamed Roosevelt. Although Roosevelt received the Nobel Peace Prize for his efforts, the goodwill that had existed for years between the United States and Russia vanished almost overnight. Anti-Roosevelt riots broke

▼ *President Roosevelt, shown with delegates at the Portsmouth peace conference, negotiated an end to the Russo-Japanese War. How did Roosevelt's involvement affect his reputation?*

out in Japan, too, even though Japan was now the dominant power in Asia. Roosevelt sent William Howard Taft to Tokyo to negotiate the Taft-Katsura Agreement, which recognized Japan's dominance in Korea in exchange for Japan's promise not to invade the Philippines.

Japanese Immigration   U.S. domestic politics complicated diplomacy with Japan. A wave of Japanese immigration into the United States took place around the turn of the century. In 1890, America's Japanese population was 2,000. By 1910, it was 67,000, and many of these immigrants lived in California. Politicians and newspapers warned of a supposed "Japanese menace." In 1905, Californians organized a Japanese and Korean Exclusion League, and the legislature debated a bill excluding Asians. A year later, the San Francisco school board assigned all Asian students to one segregated school.

Japan formally protested, calling the segregation order a racial slur. Roosevelt did not believe the United States could afford to offend Japan. He called the school board's action a "wicked absurdity." In 1907, Roosevelt fashioned an informal agreement. The San Francisco school board retracted the segregation order. In exchange, Japan voluntarily restricted emigration of Japanese farmers and workers to the United States and Hawaii. Although the arrangement improved Japanese-American relations in the short run, it avoided the underlying issue of anti-Asian feeling. This issue would continue to plague relations between the two nations.

▶

Keikichi Aoki was one of the Japanese students who resisted being sent to an all-Asian school in San Francisco, California. How did the Japanese government react to this attempted segregation?

SECTION 1 REVIEW

1. **Explain** why President Roosevelt took an active role in foreign affairs.
2. **Describe** Roosevelt's foreign policy toward less developed nations.
3. **State** reasons for Roosevelt's wanting to build the Panama Canal.
4. **Define** the term *executive agreement*.
5. **Explain** why Roosevelt sought a balance of power in Asia.

SECTION 2

Dollar Diplomacy to Missionary Diplomacy

Roosevelt's immediate successors, William Howard Taft and Thomas Woodrow Wilson, could scarcely have been more unlike Roosevelt in foreign policy matters. Taft, although Roosevelt's handpicked successor, was passive rather than active and had little interest in foreign affairs. Wilson was an activist president, but he focused on domestic reform during his first term. When Wilson turned to foreign affairs, his moralism, idealism, and inexperience hampered his effectiveness. Still, the presidencies of Taft and Wilson, like that of Roosevelt, illustrated the powerful influence the chief executive could exert on the nation's foreign policies.

What was dollar diplomacy?
How did Wilson's idealism and moralism influence his Latin American policies?
What was Wilson's policy toward Mexico?

Taft's Dollar Diplomacy

As president, Taft broke sharply with Roosevelt's foreign policy in East Asia. Roosevelt had little respect for China because he saw it as weak and unstable. He thought American trade with China was insignificant. Roosevelt also admired Japan and generally sympathized with its special interests in China and Manchuria. He therefore thought America's Open Door policy in China and Manchuria "an excellent thing" if it could be maintained by a general agreement among the great powers. Still, Roosevelt would not risk war to defend either China or the Open Door policy if challenged by a major power in the region. In contrast, Taft decided to defend, and even expand, the Open Door policy in East Asia.

Taft encouraged not only trade, but also American investment opportunities overseas. Because of its emphasis on the benefits of financial investments, Taft's general approach to foreign policy became known as **dollar diplomacy**. He believed that dollar diplomacy would create common commercial interests among strong and weak powers alike. He also thought that economic interdependence would replace regional power rivalries that seemed constantly to threaten world peace. He therefore urged American bankers to invest in East Asia, especially in the railroad and mining industries. Since both Japan and Russia had dominated these industries for some time, they saw these actions as threats to their own interests in the region. The result, which could hardly have been farther from what Taft had intended, was to form a bond of friendship between the two formerly hostile nations.

Meanwhile, Taft aggressively pushed dollar diplomacy in Latin America. Protecting the Panama Canal Zone, stabilizing Latin American governments, and avoiding European interventions were still the primary goals of U.S. policy there. To achieve these goals, Taft urged U.S. bankers to fund the debts owed by Guatemala, Honduras, and Haiti to European financiers. American bankers profited from these activities, but the new loans did little to promote political stability or economic development in the debtor countries.

Dollar diplomacy proved even less effective in Nicaragua. In 1911, the United States began supervising Nicaragua's financial affairs in an attempt to restore political stability. When that objective proved impossible to achieve, a small detachment of U.S. Marines was stationed there from 1912 to 1933 to protect American interests.

Wilson's Missionary Diplomacy

Woodrow Wilson entered the White House in 1913 with little experience or interest in foreign affairs. His secretary of state, William Jennings Bryan, had even less. Yet both held firm convictions about how to conduct foreign policy. Both were keenly religious men whose missionary zeal shaped their foreign-policy views. Both had been outspoken opponents of American imperialism, and they distrusted balance of power diplomacy. They believed that international relations should rest on idealism and morality rather than on power and force.

It is hard to imagine an ideology (a systematic set of ideas) farther from Roosevelt's "big stick" politics. In fact, Roosevelt scorned Wilson's foreign policies. He accused Wilson of being spineless, unmanly, and a moralizing preacher who did not understand the realities of life.

Wilson intended his Latin America policy to reflect his beliefs in fairness and morality. He strongly desired to teach Latin American countries about democracy, constitutionalism, and the "orderly processes of just government based upon law, not upon arbitrary or irregular force." In applying **missionary diplomacy**, however, Wilson failed to grasp the complexities of the internal affairs of these countries. His plans to provide long-term stability to the governments of the Dominican Republic and Haiti resulted instead in the long-term occupation of these countries by American military forces.

A Volatile Mexico

By 1910, Americans had invested over a billion dollars in mines, railroads, and huge agricultural landholdings in Mexico. Although foreign investors and dictator Díaz's ruling circle thrived from these activities, the Mexican people were mired in poverty. The country seethed with revolution.

In 1911, Francisco Madero led a revolt that toppled Díaz's government. Madero called for genuine representative government, social reform, and de-

▲ *President Wilson lectures Mexico in this cartoon reprinted from the British journal* Punch. *What point was the cartoonist trying to make about Wilson's diplomacy in Latin America?*

creasing foreign control over Mexico's economy. U.S. business interests opposed Madero and actively encouraged a counterrevolt against his regime. In early 1913, General Victoriano Huerta overthrew Madero's government and then murdered Madero only weeks before Wilson took office.

American investors immediately pressured Wilson to recognize Huerta's regime. Traditionally, governments did not officially judge the morality of other governments. If a new regime came to power in a country, normal diplomatic relations usually began quickly. Wilson, however, refused on moral grounds to recognize Huerta's "government of butchers." Wilson even suggested that Huerta step aside and allow free elections. Huerta flatly rejected this proposal. And, despite Huerta's general unpopularity, the Mexican people reacted angrily to Wilson's interference.

Wilson stubbornly persisted. First, he asked European governments not to recognize Huerta's

▲ *Francisco "Pancho" Villa (center foreground) was one of the leaders in a revolution against a Mexican military regime. Why might Villa have been viewed as both a hero and a villain?*

regime. Second, he offered aid to Venustiano Carranza's anti-Huerta forces. Aside from arms, Carranza wanted no help from Wilson. Such help would do more harm than good, considering Mexicans' anti-Yankee feelings. Undaunted, Wilson seized on a trivial incident at Tampico, Mexico, in which Mexican officials mistakenly arrested several U.S. sailors. When Wilson asked for authority to act against Huerta, Congress agreed.

In mid-April 1914, Wilson ordered troops into Veracruz, Mexico's major eastern seaport. Wilson hoped to cut Huerta's primary source of income, import taxes, and topple him from power. Although Wilson assumed the intervention would be bloodless, a short battle ensued in which 126 Mexicans and 19 U.S. soldiers died.

Wilson's action deeply offended Latin Americans. Anti-Yankee riots broke out in Mexico and throughout Latin America. Newspapers in Europe and America roundly criticized Wilson's intervention. The bloodletting at Veracruz genuinely horrified Wilson. He quickly accepted the offer from Argentina, Brazil, and Chile (the "ABC powers") to arbitrate the dispute.

The conflict with Mexico was far from over. Huerta's regime fell, but civil war again erupted when one of Carranza's generals, Pancho Villa, revolted against him. Wilson initially considered supporting Villa, thinking him a sincere reformer. In October 1915, however, Wilson officially recognized Carranza's regime. This angered Villa. In January 1916, Villa's soldiers murdered 18 U.S. citizens on a train in northern Mexico. In March, Villa burned Columbus, New Mexico, and killed 17 Americans.

With Carranza's permission, Wilson responded to these outrages by sending General John Pershing and 11,000 U.S. troops to capture or destroy Villa's

▲ *General John J. "Black Jack" Pershing led expeditionary forces into Mexico. What major event on the other side of the world distracted American attention from this conflict?*

guerrilla band. Villa eluded Pershing's forces, but as U.S. troops drove deeper into Mexico, their presence inflamed Mexican nationalism. By April, Carranza withdrew his permission and threatened war if U.S. forces did not leave Mexico. In fact, Pershing's and Carranza's troops fought two skirmishes in which 40 Mexicans and 12 Americans died. Wilson agreed to mediation and began withdrawing U.S. forces. He now faced a larger problem: the United States was rapidly sliding toward involvement in the war in Europe.

SECTION 2 REVIEW

1. **Compare** Roosevelt's and Taft's policies in East Asia.
2. **Describe** dollar diplomacy.
3. **List** the important features of Wilson's Latin American policies.
4. **Relate** the steps taken by Wilson to defeat the Huerta regime in Mexico.
5. **Identify** Pancho Villa.

SECTION 3

The Great War

On June 28, 1914, Archduke Franz Ferdinand, heir to the throne of the empire of Austria-Hungary, visited Sarajevo, then a small town in Bosnia. His visit symbolized the empire's intent to continue controlling southeastern (Slavic) Europe. Serbian nationalists, hoping to create an independent Slavic nation, assassinated the archduke and his wife. The murders sparked a chain of events that plunged Europe into war. Most Americans were stunned when the major powers of Europe took up arms in August 1914. They simply could not imagine how the death of an obscure prince in a remote place could ignite a general European war. They had not considered the fear, the arms race, and the complicated system of alliances that had developed in Europe over the preceding three decades.

What were the causes of the Great War?

Why was American neutrality so difficult to maintain during the Great War?

How did Wilson's insistence on American neutral rights lead the United States to the brink of war by 1917?

Europe Marches Off to War

In the late nineteenth century, Germany and Austria-Hungary formed an alliance based on common cultures, enemies, and interests. When Italy joined, the partnership became the Triple Alliance, although Italy was a weak partner and ally. Austria-Hungary governed large portions of the Slavic Balkans and wanted to extend and consolidate that control. Germany wanted to extend its influence and trade in the Balkans and the Middle East. Both had reasons to oppose Slavic nationalism in southern Europe and to seek friendly relations with Turkey.

The aims of the Triple Alliance scared Russia and France. The German friendship with Turkey threatened Russian navigation between the Black Sea and the Mediterranean. Austria-Hungary's control of the Balkans threatened Russian leadership of the Slavic nationalist movement. France needed Russia as an ally in order to offset the growing power of Germany, its traditional enemy. If war should break out, Germany would have to fight a war on two fronts. France and Russia formed the Dual Alliance. Each promised to aid the other if attacked by Germany.

In addition, Germany's growing naval power and Kaiser Wilhelm II's ambitions for a global empire challenged Britain's interests throughout the world. Britain joined Russia and France to form the Triple Entente in 1907 and thus offset the Triple Alliance. As fears and antagonisms among European nations grew, both major alliances began to prepare for the war they now felt was inevitable. Archduke Ferdinand's assassination provided the spark that ignited this tinderbox.

After the assassination, leaders in both alliances made a series of choices that led to war. German leaders believed their own nation's security depended on Austria-Hungary remaining a great power. Germany prodded Austria-Hungary into going to war with Serbia. The German general staff thought war in Europe was inevitable and that Germany's chances of winning were better now than they would be later.

As Austria-Hungary went to war against Serbia, Serbia's ally Russia went to war against Austria-Hungary. Russian leaders, wishing to maintain their nation's own great power status, felt they could not abandon Serbia. France stood by its ally, Russia. Germany, fearing Russian mobilization and a two-front war, swept through neutral Belgium in order to strike France and try to knock it out of the war as quickly as possible. Britain, supporting Belgium, then declared war on Germany.

Over 30 nations eventually took part in the conflict called the Great War and, later, World War I. Germany, Austria-Hungary, and their allies were called the **Central Powers**. Russia, Britain, France, and their supporters became known as the **Allies**. Although military campaigns occurred in Asia, Africa, and the Middle East, most of the fighting occurred in Europe, on Germany's western and eastern fronts. In the West, France was the primary theater of war. Military planners on both sides thought that the war would be short and decisive and that their soldiers, sent to war in August, would be home by Christmas. But the German strategy of quickly knocking France out of the war failed, and the stalemated western front soon became a bloodbath. Both sides dug in, creating hundreds of miles of trenches from Belgium to Switzerland.

Meanwhile, on the eastern front, Russia and its lesser allies took a horrible beating from Germany and Austria-Hungary. Thousands of Russian soldiers died. Ineffective leadership, poor training, and obsolete equipment demoralized Russian troops, and they deserted in droves. Indeed, these military disasters were a primary cause of the collapse of the Russian government in March 1917.

American Neutrality

When war broke out in August 1914, President Wilson appealed to Americans to remain strictly neutral. Although most Americans wished to avoid involvement in the conflict, neutrality proved difficult to maintain. Many groups in the United States leaned toward one side or the other. Eleven million Americans of German, Austrian, and Hungarian ancestry favored the Central Powers. Irish Americans were anti-British, and eastern European Jewish Americans were anti-Russian. Both of these groups generally favored the Central Powers. Americans of British ancestry, including the nation's elite and many government officials, supported the Allies. They favored Britain because of financial ties and their admiration of British cultural and political institutions. Americans of Italian, Russian, and southeastern European ancestry tended to support the Allies.

Patterns of international trade made American neutrality difficult to maintain. Under the traditional rules of neutrality, the United States was allowed to trade with all the powers in the conflict. Tradition also allowed private citizens to export munitions and other war matériel. In theory, such trade was neutral if no side received special advantages. In practice, American war trade favored the Allies be-

World War I in Europe, 1914-1917

Legend:
- Allies
- Central Powers
- Neutral nations
- Allied offensive
- Central Powers offensive
- Farthest advance of Central Powers, 1917
- Eastern Front armistice line, December 1917
- Line of trench warfare, 1915-1917
- Allied mine barrier
- German submarine war zone
- Sinking of the Lusitania on May 7, 1915
- British naval blockade

Eastern Front

Western Front

Labeled locations: NORWAY, SWEDEN, DENMARK, GREAT BRITAIN, London, NETHERLANDS, Berlin, GERMANY, BELGIUM, LUXEMBOURG, Paris, FRANCE, SWITZERLAND, AUSTRIA-HUNGARY, Budapest, Sarajevo, ITALY, MONTENEGRO, SERBIA, ALBANIA, GREECE, ROMANIA, BULGARIA, RUSSIAN EMPIRE, OTTOMAN EMPIRE, PERSIA, ARABIA, EGYPT, LIBYA, TUNISIA, ALGERIA, SPANISH MOROCCO, PORTUGAL, SPAIN, Arctic Circle, Baltic Sea, North Sea, Atlantic Ocean, Black Sea, Mediterranean Sea

Scale: 0 – 500 mi / 0 – 800 km

▲ *By early August 1914, most European countries had joined complex alliances that drew them into war. According to the map, which nations were Central Powers?*

cause Britain controlled the Atlantic shipping lanes. Geography and British sea power made the United States a partner of the Allies.

At first, the war worsened a business recession that had begun in the United States in 1913. However, Allied purchases of American goods sparked the economy. When the Allies' ability to pay cash for goods ebbed in late 1914, Wilson feared that this new American prosperity would vanish. So he relaxed restrictions on loans and credits. By early 1917, U.S. bankers had loaned nearly $2.3 billion to the Allies, but only $27 million to Germany.

Germany thought Wilson was favoring the Allies. Equally important, business and financial interests had a growing stake in an Allied victory.

Traditional Neutral Rights

Wilson insisted that all **belligerents**, or nations at war, observe the traditional rights of U.S. neutrality. Neutrals could sell and ship non-war-related goods to any country without interference from those nations at war. Neutrals could sell actual war-related goods to anyone, but belligerents could seize such goods and settle accounts after the war. Belligerents were expected to observe certain rules concerning naval blockades and the searching of ships suspected of carrying war matériel. By right, citizens of neutral countries could travel freely, though not on belligerent ships. Yet many of these principles conflicted with methods of modern warfare. Asserting the rights of neutrality, as Wilson did, led to serious disputes with Britain and Germany.

Britain's military strategy emphasized using its navy to strangle trade with Germany. The British Royal Navy detained neutral ships, expanded the list of **contraband** (illegal or prohibited goods), and even seized cargoes destined for neutral countries. In November 1914, the Royal Navy effectively closed trade by sea with Germany by laying mines in the North Sea. Britain hoped to stop overland trade with Germany as well. In March 1915, Britain decreed a blockade of the Central Powers and their neutral neighbors. Wilson protested these actions, but not vigorously.

In striking contrast, Wilson showed little tolerance for German violations of neutral rights. With its surface fleet bottled up by Britain's superior navy, Germany turned to submarine, or U-boat, warfare. In early 1915, Germany drew a war zone around Britain. It declared that all Allied ships within the zone would be sunk on sight. Deadly from below, U-boats were quite vulnerable on the surface. Germany claimed that British antisubmarine tactics—flying neutral flags, disguising warships as freighters, and ramming surfaced U-boats—

prevented it from observing traditional rules of search and seizure. It therefore advised neutrals and their citizens to avoid the war zone.

Wilson warned that he would hold Germany to "strict accountability" for U-boat violations of American neutral rights. This position was risky, for it placed the American government in direct opposition to German naval strategy. As Wilson himself said, "any little German lieutenant [referring to U-boat commanders] can put us into the war at any time by some calculated outrage."

On May 7, 1915, a U-boat sank the British ship *Lusitania* off the coast of Ireland, killing over 1,200 people, including 128 Americans. Although a luxury passenger liner, the *Lusitania* also carried tons of small arms and munitions bound for England. As a result, it exploded and sank rapidly. Wilson condemned the sinking as a violation of international law, laws of morality, and neutral rights. He demanded that Germany abandon submarine warfare and pay for the losses it caused.

So stern was Wilson's response that Secretary of State Bryan resigned in protest. Bryan already thought Wilson's policies treated Germany and Britain unequally. Now he feared that Wilson's stance on U-boat warfare would plunge the nation into war. Bryan felt that defending neutral rights was a trivial concern compared to the prospect of war with Germany. Moreover, Bryan believed that Wilson could easily avoid incidents like the *Lusitania* crisis. The president simply needed to warn civilians that they traveled in war zones at their own risk. Wilson would not compromise on the issue of neutral rights. American newspapers savagely criticized Bryan for leaving his post during the crisis.

Additional incidents involving U-boats and neutral rights worsened German-American relations in 1915. Then on March 24, 1916, Germany sank the British steamer *Sussex*, killing 80 people. Wilson threatened to break diplomatic relations with Germany. In the "*Sussex* pledge," Germany vowed that it would attack no unresisting belligerent merchant vessel without giving warning and ensuring passenger safety. However, Germany notified Wilson that, unless he convinced Britain to observe the principle of freedom of the seas and allow other neutral nations to trade with Germany, it might revoke the pledge.

► *The* Lusitania *carried passengers and military contraband. Why were most Americans outraged that a German submarine had attacked the ship?*

"All the News That's Fit to Print."

The New York Times.

VOL. LXIV...NO. 20,923.

NEW YORK, SATURDAY, MAY 8, 1915—TWENTY-FOUR PAGES.

EXTRA
5:30 A.M.

ONE CENT

LUSITANIA SUNK BY A SUBMARINE, PROBABLY 1,260 DEAD; TWICE TORPEDOED OFF IRISH COAST; SINKS IN 15 MINUTES; CAPT. TURNER SAVED, FROHMAN AND VANDERBILT MISSING; WASHINGTON BELIEVES THAT A GRAVE CRISIS IS AT HAND

The Move Toward War

By early 1917, grueling warfare had pushed both the Central Powers and the Allies to the brink of disaster. All combatants had already lost too much, in blood spilled and treasure spent, to consider anything short of total victory. The desperate German military command feared starvation and certain defeat within a year unless something dramatic turned the tide. They planned a massive ground offensive in France. They also decided to renew unrestricted U-boat warfare in order to strangle Britain. German leaders were certain their decision would pull the United States into the war, but they hoped to win before America could mobilize and affect the outcome.

Wilson broke diplomatic relations on February 3, after Germany announced that it would resume U-boat warfare. Still, the president was uncertain about the next steps to take. He considered several options—arming merchant ships, fighting a limited sea war, and using warships to protect merchant vessels from U-boat attack. As Wilson struggled with these issues, British intelligence made public a telegram from German undersecretary of foreign affairs Arthur Zimmermann. The **Zimmermann Telegram** instructed the German ambassador in Mexico to persuade Mexico to declare war on the United States if the U.S. entered the war against Germany. In exchange, Germany would help Mexico recover California, Texas, and New Mexico, territory taken by the United States in the 1840s. The proposed alliance infuriated Americans. The incident convinced Wilson that Germany was "a madman that needed restraining."

NOTICE!

TRAVELLERS intending to embark on the Atlantic voyage are reminded that a state of war exists between Germany and her allies and Great Britian and her allies; that the zone of war includes the waters adjacent to the British Isles; that, in accordance with formal notice given by the Imperial German Government, vessels flying the flag of Great Britian, or of any of her allies, are liable to destruction in those waters and that travellers sailing in the war zone on ships of Great Britian or her allies do so at their own risk.

IMPERIAL GERMAN EMBASSY,
WASHINGTON, D. C., APRIL 22, 1915.

CUNARD

EUROPE VIA LIVERPOOL
LUSITANIA
Fastest and Largest Steamer now in Atlantic Service Sails
SATURDAY, MAY 1, 10 A. M.
Transylvania - Fri, May 7, 5 P.M.
Orduna, - - - Tues., May 18, 10 A.M.
Tuscania, - - - Fri., May 21, 5 P.M.
LUSITANIA, - Sat., May 29, 10 A.M.
Transylvania, - - - - - 5 P.M.

▲ *In 1915, the German government placed a notice directly next to a travel advertisement for the* Lusitania.

On April 2, 1917, Wilson asked Congress to declare war against Germany. He was enough of a realist to know that America's national security depended on a strong England and that Germany threatened that security. Even so, Wilson was by temperament a moralist and idealist. In his war message, he spoke not of the balance of power, of narrow national interests, or of limited objectives. America, Wilson said, would fight for neutral rights, for peace and justice, and for self-government for oppressed peoples. "The world must be made safe for democracy," he said. "Its peace must be planted upon the tested foundations of political liberty." The vote on the war resolution was 82 to 6 in the Senate and 373 to 50 in the House of Representatives.

Technology Revolutionizes Warfare

An unprecedented number of new machines and devices were first used on a large scale during World War I. These included submarines, airplanes, tanks, motor trucks, machine guns, rapid-fire artillery, barbed wire, and poison gas. The new technologies made conventional strategies and tactics of war as obsolete as the equipment they replaced. The net effect was a stalemated war.

Machine guns were invented in the late nineteenth century. American inventor Hiram Maxim demonstrated the first fully auto-

▼ The development of poison gas, machine guns, tanks, and airplanes changed the way war was fought. The Geneva Protocol of 1925 banned the use of poison gas after seeing its terrible consequences in World War I.

matic machine gun—which fired 666 rounds a minute—in England in 1887. A Chinese diplomat observed that the cost of bullets alone would make his nation a second-rate power forever. European military leaders failed to grasp the killing potential of this weapon. During the war, military leaders on both sides believed that the offense, rather than the defense, had the tactical advantage. Field commanders continued to send their troops on assaults of well-fortified defenses, even as machine guns mowed these troops down by the thousands.

Similar misunderstandings surrounded the use of poison gas and airplanes. When Germany first used poison gas in April 1915, the effect on Allied lines was so devastating that the Germans were not prepared to exploit their advantage. In December, they were bet-

ter prepared, but by then so were the Allies, with gas masks and poison gas of their own.

The military use of the airplane also evolved over time. At first, the belligerents usually used their airplanes for observation—pilots on both sides often waved to each other as they flew to their battle stations. As the war grew more intense, both sides found new uses for airplanes. They developed specialized types of planes—fighters, bombers, and scouts—and found new ways to use them. By the end of the war, Britain had 22,000 airplanes in Europe, the United States nearly 3,600.

---

1. What mistake did military leaders continue to make, though new technology had changed warfare?
2. Describe the evolution of the airplane during World War I.

SECTION 3 REVIEW

1. **Name** the event that sparked the outbreak of the Great War in 1914.
2. **Define** belligerents.
3. **Describe** problems faced by Russia during the war which eventually led to government collapse in 1917.
4. **Explain** why America had difficulty in staying neutral.
5. **State** in your own words what Wilson meant when he declared that "the world must be made safe for democracy."

SECTION 4

The Home Front

Shortly after Congress declared war against Germany, the Senate Finance Committee held hearings on a $3 billion War Department budget request. The committee called Major Palmer E. Pierce to testify about the huge and confusing budget. Committee Chair Thomas S. Martin, a Virginia Democrat, asked Pierce how the money would be spent. Pierce answered, "Clothing, cots, camps, food, pay . . . and we may have to have an army in France." Martin, startled by Pierce's response, interrupted, "Good Lord, you're not going to send soldiers over there, are you?" In the spring of 1917, many Americans would have shared Martin's astonishment. They, too, naively assumed that the nation's involvement in the war would be limited to goods and money. Americans would soon have to face the true costs of modern warfare.

How did war mobilization affect the United States?
Why did the war stimulate some social changes?
How did the war affect Americans' civil liberties?

Mobilization

The nation was surprisingly ill prepared for war. The economy was booming because of the war trade, yet American factories were producing little actual war matériel. In 1915, Wilson had begun a war-preparedness program to increase the size of both the navy and army. Although by 1916 the size of the army doubled to 310,000 soldiers, it was scarcely ready to fight in 1917. The Wilson administration soon discovered, however, that the Allies were in desperate shape and that fully mobilizing American society for war would be necessary.

The administration almost immediately proposed a draft that would require young men to serve in the military. Congress debated the draft issue for weeks. Advocates argued that a draft was necessary because volunteers would never provide enough soldiers as quickly as needed. Opponents feared the draft would lead to a nation dominated by the military. Congress finally passed a draft act in mid-1917 and another in 1918. Registration for the draft began on June 5, 1917, and, by midsummer, the first draftees arrived at camps for basic training.

The Wilson administration also began mobilizing farming and industry for war. Congress created the Food Administration to control food production. Directed by Herbert Hoover, it set farm prices high in order to stimulate farm production. Farmers not only produced more, but their real income shot up nearly 30 percent during the war. Hoover also persuaded civilians to conserve food by observing "wheatless" Mondays and Wednesdays, "meatless" Tuesdays, and "porkless" Thursdays and Saturdays. Between 1915 and 1918, food exports tripled while Americans faced few shortages at home.

In July 1917, Congress created the War Industries Board (WIB) to plan and control all aspects of industrial production. The WIB was ineffective until Wilson appointed Wall Street financier Bernard Baruch as director in March 1918. Baruch was given virtually dictatorial power to allocate scarce resources, standardize products, coordinate purchasing, fix prices, and grant exemptions from antitrust laws. Under Baruch, the WIB succeeded because businesspeople trusted him to protect business interests. Business leaders were involved in planning and decision making, and they could fix prices at levels that ensured large profits.

The government also regulated fuels, transportation, and labor in the name of the war effort. Just as industry groaned under the strains of wartime

▲ *Financier Bernard Baruch, head of the War Industries Board, coordinated the industrial war effort on the home front.*

production, the nation's fuel production and railroads were also stretched to capacity. Although energy conservation proved most difficult, the Fuel Administration rationed coal and oil and established Daylight Saving Time to conserve energy use. In December 1917, the government took over the railroads. The Railroad Administration pooled railroad equipment, centralized purchasing, standardized accounting practices, and raised passenger rates and laborers' wages. Meanwhile, the National War Labor Board set policy for all workers. It controlled wages and hours, encouraged collective bargaining and unionization, and helped workers find jobs in war industries.

Social Changes

With the armed forces drafting workers and immigration reduced to a trickle, unem-

ployment disappeared and workers' wages rose noticeably. War-induced prosperity created new opportunities for disadvantaged groups. African Americans from the rural South flooded northern industrial cities seeking work. They found work, but usually not the high-paying industrial jobs they wanted or expected. Discriminatory hiring policies pushed African Americans into low-paying service jobs. As their numbers grew in northern cities, they encountered poor housing conditions and hostility. Violent conflicts erupted as the races competed for jobs and housing. Wartime racial tensions led to major race riots in East St. Louis, Chicago, and other American cities between 1917 and 1919.

Because drunkenness hampered worker and soldier productivity, sobriety became a patriotic necessity. Grains used in processing alcohol were now needed for food exports. In 1917, sale of alcoholic beverages was prohibited around military bases. In 1918, Congress sent the Eighteenth Amendment to the U.S. Constitution to the states for ratification. When the states ratified this amendment in 1919, it outlawed the manufacture, sale, and transportation of alcoholic beverages nationally.

▼ *During the war, women filled jobs they had never before considered holding. For practical reasons, women began wearing trousers at work and, eventually, in the home.*

In which region of the country did women first gain full suffrage? What reason might there have been for this?

▶

▼ *This World War I poster suggested some ways women patriots could aid the war effort. Would you expect a recruitment poster today to look similar?*

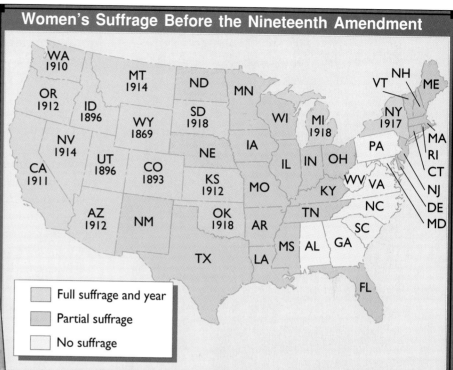

Women's Suffrage Before the Nineteenth Amendment

WA 1910
OR 1912
MT 1914
ND
MN
VT NH ME
ID 1896
SD 1918
WI
MI 1918
NY 1917
NV 1914
WY 1869
NE
IA
IL IN OH
PA
MA RI CT
CA 1911
UT 1896
CO 1893
KS 1912
MO
WV VA
NJ DE MD
AZ 1912
NM
OK 1918
AR
TN
KY
NC
TX
LA
MS AL GA
SC
FL

- Full suffrage and year
- Partial suffrage
- No suffrage

FEMININE PATRIOTISM

DOMESTIC ECONOMY   HOME DEFENSE   AID TO THE SUFFERING

The war also affected the condition and status of women. The demand for labor overcame traditional attitudes against women working outside the home. Women filled many jobs. They became factory assembly workers, trolley conductors, train engineers, mail carriers, and office workers. However, women received lower pay than men in similar jobs. Middle- and upper-class women who did not work for pay often redirected their volunteer work toward the war effort through the Young Women's Christian Association (YWCA) and other women's clubs.

The war affected women's political activities in diverse ways. On one hand, many women abandoned the peace movement because of the war. On the other hand, many women continued to assert their right to vote. Not allowing half the population to vote was an embarrassment for many Americans in a nation fighting for democracy. Women's suffrage received powerful support from the war. In 1918, Congress sent the Nineteenth Amendment to the U.S. Constitution granting women's suffrage to the states for ratification. The states ratified it by 1920.

War Stifles Civil Liberties

Although the war stimulated such progressive reforms as women's suffrage and prohibition, at other times government actions conflicted sharply with progressive values. Most progressives placed great faith in the free exchange of information and a well-informed citizenry. The Wilson administration violated these principles in the name of national security.

The Committee on Public Information (CPI) conducted a massive **propaganda** campaign by

▲ *This 1918 poster was designed to encourage the public to buy war bonds. What symbols on the poster appealed to American patriotism?*

spreading materials deliberately designed to promote public support for the war. Directed by journalist George Creel, the CPI deluged the nation with millions of pamphlets and thousands of speeches at theaters, churches, and civic clubs. The CPI described the war as a crusade for democracy against a warmongering, autocratic Germany. The CPI extolled the virtues of the Allies and exaggerated stories of German war atrocities.

The government also acted to limit free speech and to curb opposition to the war. In 1917, Congress passed the Espionage Act, which imposed $10,000 fines and 20-year prison terms on those convicted of aiding the enemy or disrupting the draft. The act banned sending antigovernment and antiwar materials through the mail. In 1918, Congress passed the Sedition Act, which forbade anyone to "utter, print, write, or publish any disloyal, profane, or abusive language" about the government, Constitution, or military uniforms. The Sedition Act passed the House by a vote of 293 to 1, with one congressman stating his regret that it did not carry the death penalty.

The government was swift in using these new powers. Attorney General Thomas Gregory advised war opponents to seek God's mercy, "for they need expect none from an outraged people and an avenging government." A court sentenced Eugene Debs, former labor leader and Socialist candidate for president in 1912, to ten years in prison for making an antiwar speech. The producer of the movie *The Spirit of '76* also received a ten-year prison term because the film was critical of British soldiers. In *Schenck v. United States* (1919), the Supreme Court upheld these actions, ruling that free speech had limits in wartime and could be restricted when the words presented a "clear and present danger" to public order.

Vigilantes took matters into their own hands when government action was not swift enough. Vigilante groups like the American Protective League ridiculed individuals who did not buy war bonds. German words dropped from common use; sauerkraut, for example, became "liberty cabbage." Local schools stopped teaching German language courses. In many communities, overzealous patriots persecuted German Americans, fired them from jobs, and boycotted their businesses. Local vigilantes also harassed, sometimes violently, socialists, pacifists, and radical labor organizations.

SECTION 4 REVIEW

1. **State** reasons why the United States was not prepared for war.
2. **List** four ways in which Congress mobilized for war.
3. **Explain** briefly how the war stimulated progressive reform.
4. **Define** propaganda.
5. **Describe** the effect of the war on American civil liberties.

A Dubious Peace

Wilson's aims in the Great War were very different from those of the Allies. He recognized that "peace without victory," rather than the victors taking vengeance on the losers, was the only real basis for lasting peace in Europe. He tried to mediate several times during the war, but neither side showed interest. Wilson's ideas for a lasting world peace were truly visionary, but he always found compromise extremely difficult. Once Wilson adopted an idea, he clung to it tenaciously, and this commitment sometimes clouded his political judgment. While teaching at Princeton, Wilson once got into an argument with another professor. His colleague said, "Well, Doctor, there are two sides to every question." Wilson answered, "Yes, a right side and a wrong side."

How did American and Allied opinions differ about how victory was achieved?

In what ways did the peace settlement imposed on Germany differ from Wilson's Fourteen Points?

Why did the U.S. Senate fail to ratify the Versailles Treaty?

The End of the War

When the United States finally joined the conflict, the Allies were in desperate shape. By 1917, every belligerent had fully mobilized its society for war and had raised heavy taxes and borrowed vast sums of money to sustain the war. In addition to human losses and physical destruction, their economies verged on bankruptcy and inflation mounted. Soldiers and civilians alike experienced appalling deprivations and made extreme sacrifices as the war dragged on. There was still no end in sight, and Germany began new offensives on the western front and at sea. Then, in November, revolution in Russia dramatically changed the war. The Russian Revolution was successful, in part, because the **Bolsheviks** (members of Lenin's radical Communist Party) promised to quit the war. Their call for mass revolt against all belligerent governments was nearly as frightening to Allied leaders as Russia's leaving the war.

▼ *U.S. soldiers, or "doughboys," charged over the top of this protective trench. What term describes the type of ground fighting perfected in World War I?*

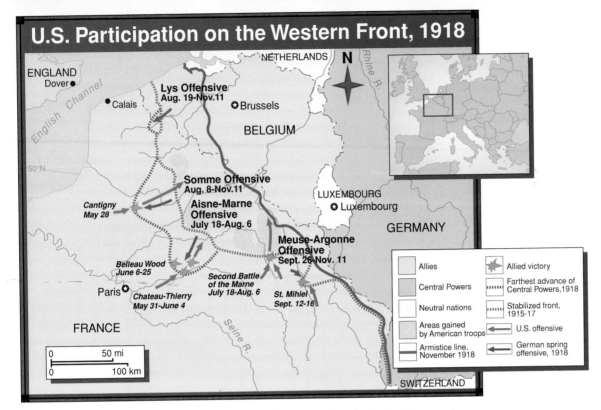

U.S. Participation on the Western Front, 1918

ENGLAND
Dover •
• Calais
NETHERLANDS
N
Rhine R.
• Brussels
BELGIUM
Lys Offensive
Aug. 19-Nov.11
LUXEMBOURG
• Luxembourg
GERMANY
Somme Offensive
Aug. 8-Nov.11
Cantigny
May 28
Aisne-Marne
Offensive
July 18-Aug. 6
Belleau Wood
June 6-25
Meuse-Argonne
Offensive
Sept. 26-Nov. 11
Paris ✪
Chateau-Thierry
May 31-June 4
Second Battle
of the Marne
July 18-Aug. 6
St. Mihiel
Sept. 12-16
FRANCE
Seine R.
50°N
English Channel
SWITZERLAND

Allies		Allied victory	
Central Powers		Farthest advance of Central Powers,1918	
Neutral nations		Stabilized front, 1915-17	
Areas gained by American troops		U.S. offensive	
Armistice line, November 1918		German spring offensive, 1918	

0 — 50 mi
0 — 100 km

▲ *The influx of American troops and supplies to the western front broke the Germans' spring offensive and allowed the Allies to take the offensive themselves. In what battles did American troops participate?*

In March 1918, the Bolsheviks signed a separate peace treaty with Germany. The Treaty of Brest-Litovsk had two major results. First, the Allies decided to intervene in Russia. They hoped to keep Russia in the war. They also hoped to topple the new Bolshevik regime by militarily aiding its opponents in the emerging civil war there. Second, now Germany no longer had to fight the Allies on two fronts and could transfer troops to France. Fortunately for the Allies, these transfers were delayed, and the Germans' planned 1918 spring offensive started slowly.

By the time Germany's offensive in France began, it was too late. Fresh American army units, arriving by the tens of thousands, helped turn the tide of war. By the end of the summer, the Allies had taken the offensive all along the western front and had begun to drive the German army toward its own borders. The Central Powers were soon exhausted. In early November, German military leaders convinced Kaiser Wilhelm that the war

was lost and that he should abdicate the throne. The new German government sued for peace. On November 11, 1918, an armistice ended the Great War in Europe.

The Terms of Peace

After the armistice, the Allies and the Americans had differing views about America's contribution to winning the war. This complicated Allied relations with the United States. The Allies' casualties had been staggering. They were virtually bankrupt and owed America huge debts. Americans, on the other hand, had suffered relatively few casualties in their brief military involvement. American prosperity during the war was due to Allied purchases. The Allies understandably believed that their sacrifices had paid for the victory. They were in no mood to be treated as junior partners by Wilson.

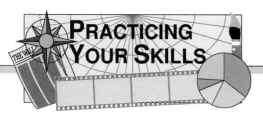

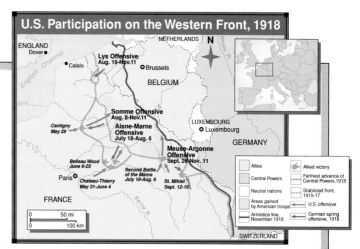

U.S. Participation on the Western Front, 1918

Special Purpose Maps: Analyzing Military Campaigns

Historians rely on military maps to help interpret and analyze the outcomes of major battles and war strategies. Complicated movements of troops and supplies are more easily understood when plotted on a map. Military maps can illustrate land gained or lost over many years or focus on particular battles—even a particular troop movement within a battle. Follow these steps when analyzing military maps:

- **Read the title of the map.** Along with the name of the war, battle, or event, the map should tell you when the event took place (the time frame covered).
- **Study the map key or legend.** What do the symbols mean? Are movements and actions indicated? Are colors used to indicate gains or losses in territories? How are broken and solid lines used? Are the physical features, such as canals, rivers, and mountain ranges, indicated?
- **Pay careful attention to the scale.** The scale of miles is especially important in military maps since distance is often crucial to planning military strategy.
- **Study the map itself, paying careful attention to the sequence of dates of battles, offensives, and movements of all types.** Understand the order in which events on the map

occurred. You can then relate this information to social and political events of the same time period.

Study the map on page 626 and answer the following questions:

1. (a) What was the westernmost point of the German advance of September 1918? (b) Approximately how many miles did the stabilized front of 1915–1917 extend? (c) What problems would the Germans have had in holding a line like this?
2. Make a time line of all the battles on this map.
3. (a) Approximately how far apart are the 1915–1917 line and the spring 1918 stabilized line at their widest point? (b) What generalization can you make about the extent of military action from 1915 to 1918 in France from this map?
4. Based on this map, write a generalization about the role of the American forces on the western front in 1918.

Americans felt that U.S. troops had arrived just in time to provide the push needed for victory. American loans and goods had kept the Allies afloat for three years. To Americans, the Allies seemed grossly ungrateful when they disagreed with American policy positions. In fact, the Allies could not

deny the Americans a significant role in drawing up the peace settlement. Wilson thought he could control the Allies. As he put it in July 1917, "When the war is over, we can force them to our way of thinking because by that time they will . . . be financially in our hands."

Casualties in World War I, by Country

Country	Number of Casualties*	
	Killed	Wounded
Allies		
Russia	1,700,000	4,950,000
France	1,357,800	4,266,000
British Empire	908,371	2,090,212
Italy	650,000	947,000
Romania	335,706	120,000
United States	116,516	204,002
Others	74,238	223,492
Total	**5,142,631**	**12,800,706**
Central Powers		
Germany	1,773,700	4,216,058
Austria-Hungary	1,200,000	3,620,000
Turkey	325,000	400,000
Bulgaria	87,500	152,390
Total	**3,386,200**	**8,388,448**
TOTAL	**8,528,831**	**21,189,154**

*Estimated deaths from all causes.

▲ *This chart summarizes the estimated casualties of the major belligerents during World War I. Which side had the higher number of casualties?*

Among other things, Wilson wanted Allied support for his **Fourteen Points** for peace in Europe. Had Wilson's Fourteen Points been more fully adopted, they might have resulted in a lasting peace in Europe. Taken as a whole, Wilson's proposal promised a new world order that would end secret alliances and reliance on balance-of-power politics. Freedom of the seas and an end to the build-up of weapons were two specific points listed in the plan. Another important point concerned national **self-determination**—allowing ethnic groups in former colonies and conquered territories to determine their own futures. Wilson also believed in **collective security**. In his view, countries should work together in an international organization for world peace and thus prevent world war from ever happening again. Except for most Allied leaders, people the world over applauded Wilson's vision for lasting peace.

Unfortunately, Wilson failed to secure Allied agreement to his war aims before America entered the war. Once American soldiers had tipped the balance of power and helped secure victory, such concessions were virtually impossible to get. In late 1918, the Allies did agree to use the Fourteen Points as the basis for discussing the peace settlement, but

▼ *The table below outlines President Wilson's plan for creating a lasting peace in Europe. Which of these points have become today's realities?*

Wilson's Fourteen Points

1. An end to secret diplomacy
2. Freedom of the seas in peace and war
3. Removal of economic trade barriers among nations
4. Reduction of armaments to levels needed for domestic security
5. Fair and impartial adjustment of colonial claims
6. Evacuation of Russian territory and acceptance of its government into the society of free nations
7. Restoration of Belgian sovereignty
8. Evacuation of all French territory and return of Alsace-Lorraine to France
9. Aligning Italian boundaries along clearly recognizable lines of nationality
10. Self-determination of national groups in Austria-Hungary
11. Restoration of the Balkans and unrestricted access to the sea for Serbia
12. Self-determination for minorities in Turkey and the former Ottoman Empire
13. Independence for Poland, including unrestricted access to the sea
14. Establishment of a League of Nations to ensure political and territorial integrities

▶ Seated left to right are the leaders of the Big Four powers at the Versailles peace conference: Vittorio Emanuele Orlando of Italy, David Lloyd George of Great Britain, Georges Clemenceau of France, and Woodrow Wilson of the United States. How did their negotiations violate the spirit of the Fourteen Points?

there were many problems. For example, France insisted that Germany should pay more than $200 billion in **reparations** (payments made by defeated nations for war damages). Britain would not negotiate freedom of the seas. Wilson discovered that other issues, too, contradicted the provisions of the Fourteen Points.

Wilson insisted on taking up the **League of Nations** first. In its final form, the League of Nations included an assembly of all member nations and a council of nine (five of its members were the United States, Britain, France, Italy, and Japan). A World Court was designed to arbitrate disputes among nations. A secretariat provided administrative functions, and a number of special commissions were designed to handle specific problems. The league's covenant, or constitution, contained many admirable objectives, including arms reduction, dispute arbitration, and collective security.

The Treaty of Versailles   The Versailles peace conference met outside of Paris, France, from January to May of 1919. Those who hoped the treaty would follow the Fourteen Points were sorely disappointed. Its very setting violated Wilson's call for a peace among equals and for open diplomacy. Leaders of the Big Four powers—Britain, France, Italy, and the United States—hammered out the treaty among themselves in secret sessions. Germany and Russia were not even allowed to attend.

The Treaty of Versailles did not usher in a new world order. In fact, it planted the seeds for an even greater conflict in Europe. The treaty was punitive and designed to crush Germany and exclude Soviet Russia from European affairs. It forced Germany to accept responsibility for starting the war and to pay huge reparations. By later agreement, these reparations amounted to $33 billion. The victors stripped Germany of some of its territory in Europe and of its entire overseas empire, including its colonies in Africa and strategic islands in the Pacific. Millions of Germans were either forced to move or to live in territory controlled by France, Poland, or Czechoslovakia. But rather than weakening Germany as France had intended, the long-range effect of the treaty was to cause fierce resentments among the German people. These resentments, in turn, created the climate in which Adolf Hitler rose to power in the 1930s.

Wilson was disappointed with the treaty. He especially objected to the harsh reparations forced on Germany and to some of the territorial settlements. Still, he went along with Britain and France to win their support for the League of Nations. He had faith that the league would correct some of the treaty's shortcomings.

Wilson Loses the Fight for Ratification

Although American public opinion initially favored ratification of the Versailles treaty, Wilson

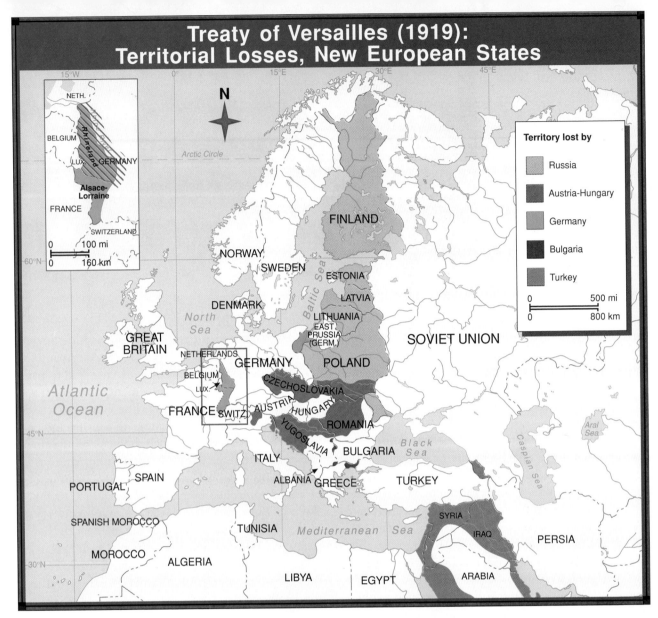

Treaty of Versailles (1919): Territorial Losses, New European States

Territory lost by
- Russia
- Austria-Hungary
- Germany
- Bulgaria
- Turkey

0 ___ 500 mi
0 ___ 800 km

0 ___ 100 mi
0 ___ 160 km

▲ *The Versailles Treaty altered the national boundaries of Europe and the Middle East.*
What nation states were created from territory that was once Austria-Hungary?

made several political mistakes. First, Wilson made the treaty a partisan issue during the midterm elections in 1918. He had urged voters to elect Democrats if they wanted to support him in achieving a just peace. When Democrats lost seats in both houses, critics charged that the voters had symbolically voted against Wilson himself. Second, Wilson's decision to attend the Versailles conference firmly identified the treaty with him personally. Third,

Wilson chose no notable Republicans and no senators as delegates to the peace conference. Finally, Wilson would allow no alterations to the treaty.

These were significant political mistakes, since the Senate, in Republican hands after the election of 1918, would decide the peace treaty's fate. The senators had diverse opinions about the treaty. One group of progressives condemned Wilson and opposed the treaty because he had failed to deliver a

▲ *After President Wilson suffered a major stroke in 1919, his wife Edith shielded him from the outside world.*

▲ *President Wilson took his case for the League of Nations to the people after the Senate voted to reject the Treaty of Versailles, as shown in this cartoon.*

treaty based on the Fourteen Points. One veteran reformer called the treaty "a terrible document; a dispensation of retribution with scarcely a parallel in history." A small group of isolationists opposed the treaty in any form because they thought it would lead to further U.S. involvement in European affairs.

Another group, led by Foreign Relations Committee Chair Henry Cabot Lodge, detested Wilson personally. This group would support the treaty only if certain reservations were added. Many senators were genuinely concerned about the treaty on constitutional grounds. The League of Nations and collective security presented especially vexing constitutional issues. Lodge held an unprecedented six weeks of hearings on the treaty, hoping the delay would erode public support.

Meanwhile, Wilson sought to pressure Senate action. He embarked on a national speaking tour to mobilize public support. In three weeks, Wilson traveled 8,000 miles and made 36 formal speeches. On September 26, Wilson collapsed in Colorado, and he suffered a near-fatal stroke on his return to Washington. Though incapacitated, Wilson refused to compromise with his Senate opponents.

Until the very end, Wilson had sufficient support in the Senate to ratify the treaty if he had been willing to make some compromises. When the French ambassador informed Wilson that the Allies were willing to accept the Senate's reservations, Wilson replied, "Mr. Ambassador, I shall consent to nothing. The Senate must take its medicine." Wilson himself doomed the treaty. In November 1919, the Senate defeated the original treaty by a vote of 55 to 39. Changes were made, but the Senate again rejected the treaty in March 1920 by a vote of 49 to 35. Ironically, 23 Democrats, at Wilson's insistence, joined the isolationists in defeating the amended treaty. For Wilson, defeat was better than compromise. Moreover, Wilson still believed that the public stood behind him. He hoped the presidential election of 1920 would be a "solemn referendum" on the treaty and would force Senate ratification. In fact, the election of Republican Warren G. Harding as president did settle the matter, but not as Wilson had hoped. In 1921, the United States signed a separate peace treaty "officially" ending the war with Germany, Austria, and Hungary.

SECTION 5 REVIEW

1. **Explain** why revolution in Russia in 1917 threatened the Allied cause.
2. **Compare** the American and Allied opinions concerning the contribution of the United States to ending the war.
3. **Evaluate** the argument that the Treaty of Versailles actually planted the seeds for later conflict in Europe.
4. **Define** the term *self-determination*.
5. **List** mistakes made by Wilson regarding the treaty ratification.

Summary

After 1900, whether Americans desired it or not, the nation could no longer avoid playing a significant role in world affairs. The progressive presidents—Roosevelt, Taft, and Wilson—clearly understood this new role. Yet each had different ideas about how to go about playing it.

These three presidents also brought very different styles, interests, and values to their conduct of international relations. Their specific policies reflected these differences. Roosevelt's balance-of-power diplomacy contrasted sharply with Taft's dollar diplomacy and Wilson's missionary idealism. Of the three, Roosevelt was probably most successful in accomplishing his foreign policy goals. Taft's dollar diplomacy met with little success. Wilson was probably least successful overall, because his idealism and vision exceeded what he could practically accomplish. How these progressive presidents' foreign policies are judged depends largely on a definition of national interests and how best to pursue them. Americans continue to debate these matters.

The desire to build empires plus complicated political alliances plunged Europe into the greatest war the world had yet seen. The United States tried to remain neutral, but such factors as German interference with American shipping and strong cultural and economic ties with England forced the United States into the Great War (World War I.) After the defeat of the Central Powers, the Allied powers imposed a peace settlement that many historians believe helped to bring about World War II.

Vocabulary

belligerents	executive agreement
Bolsheviks	missionary diplomacy
collective security	propaganda
contraband	reparations
dollar diplomacy	self-determination

Select the appropriate term from the vocabulary list to complete the following analogies. You will not use all the terms.

1. *Taft* is to *dollar diplomacy* as *Wilson* is to |||||||||||.
2. *Import* is to *goods* as *smuggling* is to |||||||||||.
3. *Roosevelt* is to *large policy* as *Taft* is to |||||||||||.
4. *Voting* is to *election* as *choice* is to |||||||||||.
5. *Congress* is to *legislation* as *president* is to |||||||||||.
6. *Analysis* is to *report* as *persuade* is to |||||||||||.
7. *Progressives* is to *Insurgents* as *Communists* is to |||||||||||.
8. *Accident* is to *compensation* as *war* is to |||||||||||.

Review Questions

1. List Roosevelt's major foreign policy accomplishments in Europe, Latin America, and Asia.
2. Give examples of how Roosevelt expanded the powers of the executive branch.
3. Why did building the Panama Canal cause bitterness among many Latin American countries?
4. Describe the role played by Roosevelt in the Russo-Japanese war.
5. Explain why Russia and Japan opposed the dollar diplomacy of Taft in East Asia.
6. What role did political alliances play in leading to the Great War in Europe in 1914?
7. Why was it difficult for the United States to maintain its neutrality from 1914 to 1917?
8. Explain why the Zimmerman Telegram upset Americans more than the sinking of the *Lusitania* and the *Sussex*.
9. Describe two effects the war had on women's social position in America.
10. Explain why the United States Senate failed to ratify the Treaty of Versailles.

Critical Historical Thinking

Writing Answer each of the following by writing one or more complete paragraphs:

1. Evaluate the success of Roosevelt's "big stick" policy in dealing with foreign nations. Include in your analysis a discussion of the goals of imperialism.
2. Explain the danger to civil liberties when dissent is treated as a treasonable act, as during the Wilson war years.
3. Explain why a more lenient Treaty of Versailles could have led to a more lasting peace in Europe.
4. Read "A Republican Senator Supports Wilson" in the Unit 6 Archives. What is ironic about the senator's speech, considering his role in the attempt to ratify the treaty?

Making Connections with Art

When it became evident that America would enter the war in Europe, public opinion had to be geared to the war effort. To this end, President Wilson created the Division of Pictorial Publicity, directed by Charles Dana Gibson, America's most famous illustrator. The organization enlisted most of the best-known illustrators in America. Their task was to create "pictorial publicity" for all aspects of the war effort, from recruiting ("Uncle Sam: I Want You!") to war relief ("Free Milk for France") to food and fuel conservation ("Food *is* Ammunition—*Don't Waste It*"). The efforts of the illustrators were enormously successful.

▪ Make an inventory of billboards and posters in your city or town, and describe how the illustrator has employed pictures as a means of persuasion.

▪ Locate a picture book of posters from World Wars I and II (an excellent source for World War I is Walton Rawls, *Wake Up, America! World War I and The American Poster*). Examine the pictures, and describe and categorize them by the persuasion tactics used.

Additional Skills Practice

Using information from the chapter and the list below, create a military map that records instances of submarine warfare carried on by Germany. Be sure to give your map a title and a key, and to use symbols to indicate the nationality of the ships. You will need to start with an outline map showing northern Europe, the North Atlantic, the Irish Sea, and the British Isles.

Date	Event
November 3, 1914	British plant mines in the North Sea, keeping the Strait of Dover clear of mines.
February 4, 1915	German U-boats ring British Isles, threatening to sink enemy merchant ships.
March 11, 1915	British blockade neutral ports to seize ships of German origin, destination, or ownership.
March 28, 1915	Germans sink the British steamer *Falaba* in the Irish Sea.
May 1, 1915	Germans sink American tanker *Gulflight* in the North Atlantic.
May 7, 1915	British liner *Lusitania* is sunk in the Irish Sea off the coast of Ireland.
August 19, 1915	German U-boat sinks British liner *Arabic* in the Irish Sea.
March 24, 1916	German U-boat sinks French steamer *Sussex* in the Atlantic off the coast of France.

Unit Review Questions

1. Describe important steps taken by progressive presidents for conserving natural resources.
2. Why were higher wages and increased job opportunities a mixed blessing for many American families?
3. Explain briefly how rapid industrialization prompted the progressive movement in America.
4. How did changes in art and literature reflect the influence of the Progressive Era?
5. Explain how American foreign policy changed under the progressive presidents.
6. What physical evidence of World War I might you see in France today?
7. Which groups of Americans did not benefit from progressive reforms?
8. How did progressive reforms affect the relationship between Americans and the federal government?
9. What factors drew America into World War I?
10. What direction in American foreign policy was actively pursued by all of the progressive presidents?

Personalizing History

Speaking Out   Women began to speak out for their rights even before independence had been won from Great Britain. In order to influence public opinion, women employed "nuisance tactics" such as disrupting public meetings, marching in pa-

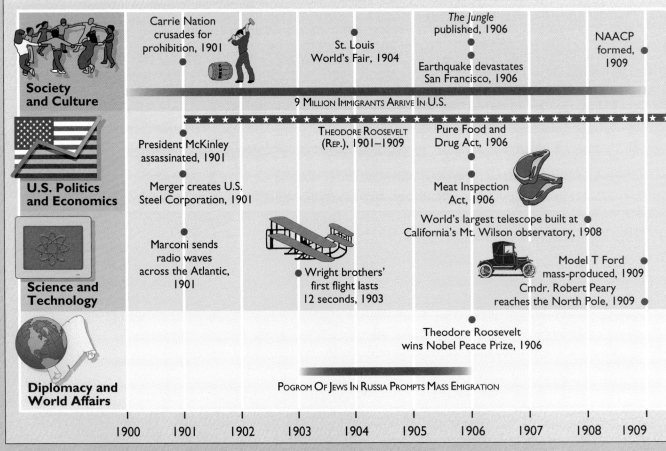

Society and Culture

Carrie Nation crusades for prohibition, 1901

St. Louis World's Fair, 1904

The Jungle published, 1906

Earthquake devastates San Francisco, 1906

NAACP formed, 1909

9 MILLION IMMIGRANTS ARRIVE IN U.S.

U.S. Politics and Economics

President McKinley assassinated, 1901

Merger creates U.S. Steel Corporation, 1901

THEODORE ROOSEVELT (REP.), 1901–1909

Pure Food and Drug Act, 1906

Meat Inspection Act, 1906

Science and Technology

Marconi sends radio waves across the Atlantic, 1901

Wright brothers' first flight lasts 12 seconds, 1903

World's largest telescope built at California's Mt. Wilson observatory, 1908

Model T Ford mass-produced, 1909

Cmdr. Robert Peary reaches the North Pole, 1909

Diplomacy and World Affairs

Theodore Roosevelt wins Nobel Peace Prize, 1906

POGROM OF JEWS IN RUSSIA PROMPTS MASS EMIGRATION

1900   1901   1902   1903   1904   1905   1906   1907   1908   1909

rades, and writing editorials. Many people were opposed to women's suffrage, fearing that it would weaken the family and social bonds of the nation. Although the Constitution forbids discrimination on the basis of sex, many women feel the fight for equal rights is far from over.

■ For the next several weeks, scan the newspapers of your local community for articles that address issues of women's rights. Cut them out and begin a bulletin board in your class as a forum for drawing attention to these problems.

Linking Past and Present

Investigative Journalism Today, muckrakers, or investigative journalists, continue to report on cor-

ruption or abuses in politics and business. Choose an incident that is currently being reported in a weekly periodical or daily newspaper. With a classmate, create a skit where one of you is playing the role of an interviewer and the other is the person being investigated. You may wish to watch a television news program such as *60 Minutes* or *20/20* to get a feel for this type of reporting.

Time Line Activity

Using the events from the time line below, create a "mini" time line that includes just those items relating to one of the following three categories: progressive reforms, consumer protection, or the regulatory state.

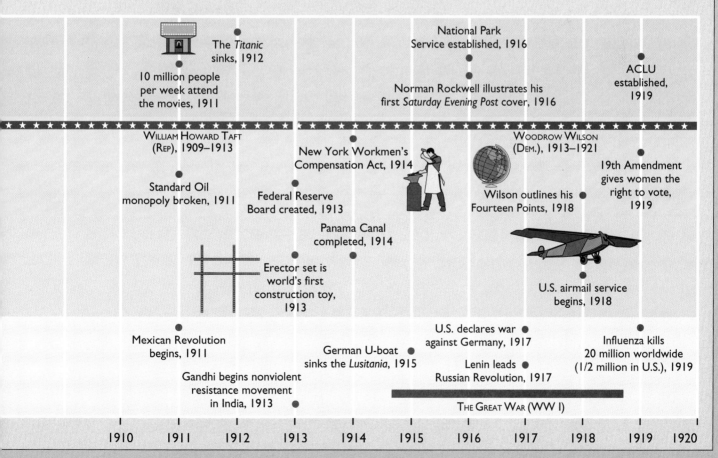

10 million people per week attend the movies, 1911

The *Titanic* sinks, 1912

National Park Service established, 1916

Norman Rockwell illustrates his first *Saturday Evening Post* cover, 1916

ACLU established, 1919

WILLIAM HOWARD TAFT (REP), 1909–1913

WOODROW WILSON (DEM.), 1913–1921

Standard Oil monopoly broken, 1911

New York Workmen's Compensation Act, 1914

Federal Reserve Board created, 1913

Panama Canal completed, 1914

Wilson outlines his Fourteen Points, 1918

19th Amendment gives women the right to vote, 1919

Erector set is world's first construction toy, 1913

U.S. airmail service begins, 1918

Mexican Revolution begins, 1911

German U-boat sinks the *Lusitania*, 1915

U.S. declares war against Germany, 1917

Lenin leads Russian Revolution, 1917

Influenza kills 20 million worldwide (1/2 million in U.S.), 1919

Gandhi begins nonviolent resistance movement in India, 1913

THE GREAT WAR (WW I)

1910   1911   1912   1913   1914   1915   1916   1917   1918   1919   1920

UNIT 7

From New Era to New Deal

The 1920s and 1930s were two dramatically different decades. The 1920s was a decade of economic growth and prosperity. This prosperity was widely shared, with the wages of blue-collar workers increasing as well as the incomes of middle-class families. The major growth industry was automobile manufacturing. Americans fell in love with the automobile, which radically changed their way of life. But the prosperity of the 1920s was not destined to last. It ended in the worst economic depression in American history. To recover from the depression, Americans turned for help to the federal government. During the New Deal era of the 1930s, the federal government played a larger role than ever before in the economic life of the nation.

> **Chapter 20**
> America in the Twenties

> **Chapter 21**
> The Great Crash and the Depression

> **Chapter 22**
> Franklin D. Roosevelt and the New Deal

◀ *The subject of this mural sponsored by the Works Progress Administration is a concert given by the African American opera singer Marian Anderson in 1939. Can you identify the building in the background?*

Themes

- **Technological Developments** The automobile, the latest development in transportation technology, had a major impact on American society and values.
- **Economics** The American economy took a roller-coaster ride during this period, plunging from widespread prosperity to the worst depression the United States had ever experienced.
- **Everyday Life** The quality of everyday life for Americans of this period was heavily influenced by the state of the economy. Both the widespread prosperity of the 1920s and the severe depression of the 1930s influenced the way millions of Americans lived.
- **Geography and the Environment** During the 1930s, Americans became more environmentally conscious as dust bowls and soil erosion added to the distress of impoverished farmers.

Henry Ford Introduces the Assembly Line

The key to mass production in the auto industry was the assembly line. In this passage from his autobiography, Henry Ford explained how the assembly line increased production.

Along about April 1, 1913, we first tried the experiment of an assembly line. We tried it on assembling the fly-wheel magneto.

That line established the efficiency of the method and we now use it everywhere. The assembling of the motor, formerly done by one man, is now divided into eighty-four operations—those men do the work that three times their number formerly did. In a short time we tried out the plan on the chassis.

About the best we had done in stationary chassis assembling was an average of twelve hours and twenty-eight minutes per chassis. We tried the experiment of drawing the chassis with a rope and windlass down a line 250 feet long. Six assemblers traveled with the chassis and picked up the parts from piles placed along the line. This rough experiment reduced the time to five hours fifty minutes per chassis. In the early part of 1914 we elevated the

▼ *The beach, 1920s*

assembly line. . . . The waist-high arrangement and a further subdivision of work so that each man had fewer movements cut down the labour time per chassis to one hour thirty-three minutes. Only the chassis was then assembled in the line. . . . Now the line assembles the whole car.

 Henry Ford, *My Life and Work* (New York: Doubleday, 1922), pp. 77, 80–82.

The Flappers

In the following article, the father of two flappers explained what he liked about the young women of this generation.

I am the father of two flappers: trim-legged, scantily dressed, bobbed-haired, hipless, corsetless, amazing young female things, full of pep, full of joy, full of jazz. They have been the despair of me for two or three summers; but if they don't fly off and marry and quit me before I'm a century old, I'm going to know those girls.

The young folks of this generation have very little faith in, or respect for their elders, because they think we elders are unsophisticated, unfair, and insincere. They have set us down as a lot of moral frauds and hypocrites who do not present the facts of life fairly and squarely to them, and they are determined to explore life for themselves. In their automobiles and in the open-air life that they lead, they see everything in the world and in nature that we have so foolishly tried to keep them from seeing.

Moving pictures bring to them every aspect of human

▲ *1920s flapper*

society, at its worst as well as its best. The newsstands are loaded with cheap and trashy magazines in which these young people find frank discussions of phases of life in which they are by nature intensely interested, and about which we older folks maintain a prudish silence in their presence.

These young people are thinking a lot about sex. I am astounded to find that my girls are familiar with the adventures of the leading female lights of history, from Cleopatra, Hypatia, and Theodora down to Marie Antoinette, Mary Stuart and Queen Elizabeth, and still on down to more modern times.

I have discreetly sounded them on the inside of the social life of our town, and found them cognizant of the indiscretions of every married woman who is not playing straight, and they know every unfair husband.

And so these amazing young folks with their superior educational advantages and a wealth of knowledge that was denied their parents, look down upon us older folks as a lot of old fogies. And having discovered much insincerity, much inconsistency and much hypocrisy in us as well, they flaunt our authority. They haven't given thought yet to the fact that some day they, too, will be old fogies in the eyes of a newer and even wiser generation.

W.O. Saunders, "Me and My Flapper Daughters," *The American Magazine*, vol. CIV (Aug. 1927), pp. 27, 121–125.

Advertising Comes of Age

A critic of advertising in the 1920s, Stuart Chase examined the amount spent on ads and the role of the advertising industry as a creator of illusions.

More than half of the output of the country's printing presses is advertising matter. In newspapers, the ratio of advertising space to total space runs from 40 to 75 percent. . . . It has been estimated that 80 percent of all mail matter consisted of advertising material.

In America one dollar is spent to educate consumers in what they may or may not want to buy, for every 70 cents that is spent for all other kinds of education—primary, secondary, high school, university.

And yet when all is said and done, advertising does give a certain illusion, a certain sense of escape in a machine age. It creates a dre[...] faces, shining teeth, schoolgirl com[...] feet, perfect fitting union suits, disti[...] wrinkleless pants, odorless breaths, reg[...] els, happy homes in New Jersey (15 m[...] Hoboken), charging motors, punctureles[...] fect busts, shimmering shanks, self-washing[...] backs behind which the moon was meant t[...]

Stuart Chase, "The Tragedy of Waste," *The New Republic* (Aug. 19, 1925).

The Ku Klux Klan
The Klan's Fight for Americanism
In this article, Hiram Wesley Evans, the Imperial Wizard of the Ku Klux Klan, presented the Klan's argument for white, Protestant supremacy in the United States.

We are a movement of the plain people, very weak in the matter of culture, intellectual support, and trained leadership. We are demanding, and we expect to win, a return of power into the hands of the everyday, not highly cultured, not overly intellectualized, but entirely unspoiled and not de-Americanized, average citizen of the old stock. Our members and leaders are all of this class.

This is undoubtedly a weakness. It lays us open to the charge of being "hicks" and "rubes" and "drivers of second hand Fords." We admit it.

The Klan, therefore, has now come to speak for the great mass of Americans of the old pioneer stock. . . . These are, in the first place, a blend of various peoples of the so-called Nordic race, the race which, with all its faults, has given the world almost the whole of modern civilization.

▲ *Ku Klux Klan march, 1926*

These Nordic Americans for the last generation have found themselves increasingly uncomfortable, and finally deeply distressed.

...came the moral breakdown that has ...going on for two decades. . . . The sacredness of ...r Sabbath, of our homes, of chastity, and finally even of our right to teach our own children in our own schools fundamental facts and truths were torn away from us. Those who maintained the old standards did so only in the face of constant ridicule.

Along with this went economic distress. The assurance for the future of our children dwindled. We found our great cities and the control of much of our industry and commerce taken over by strangers, who stacked the cards of success and prosperity against us. . . . So the Nordic American today is a stranger in large parts of the land his fathers gave him.

Hiram Wesley Evans, "The Klan's Fight for Americanism," *The North American Review* (Mar. 1926), p. 33.

A Typical Klansman

Gerald W. Johnson, a southern newspaperman, wrote the following description of a typical Klansman and why such people found the Klan appealing.

I think that my friend Chill Burton is an Exalted Cyclops, although he may be only a Fury, or a lesser Titan, for my knowledge of the nomenclature of the Ku Klux Klan is far from exact.

From the bottom of his soul he believes that the dominance of the Anglo-Saxon is hourly imperiled by the Negro; that if the Nordic strain is polluted by infusion of any other blood, American civilization will collapse and disappear; . . . and that secret agents of the Pope, infiltrating the Bureau of Engraving and Printing, strove treacherously to convert America to Catholicism by introducing crosses, snakes and pictures of His Holiness among the decorations on the dollar bill of 1917.

Chill is profoundly convinced that the Nordic Protestant is in imminent danger; what could be more natural, then, than for him to regard with tolerance, if not with approval, the extra-legal chastisement of any one who violates Nordic Protestant standards in particular?

Gerald W. Johnson, "The Ku-Kluxer," *The American Mercury,* vol. I (1924), pp. 846–849.

The Klan's Search for Conformity

This writer used insights from behavioral psychology to explain the mentality of people attracted to the Klan.

One finds on every page of Klan literature an insistent, imperative, and even intolerant demand for like-mindedness. It is, of course, the beliefs and traditions of the old native American stock that are to provide the basis for this like-mindedness. The Catholic is free to entertain his own ideas in religion but he must feel, think, and act in terms of pure and unadulterated Americanism. The foreign-born member of the community is tolerated only on the presupposition that he learns the American tongue, adopts the American dress and conventionalities, in a word assimilates as quickly and thoroughly as possible the traditions of the old American stock. The eternal quarrel of the Klan with the Jew and the Negro is that mental and physical differences seem to have conspired to place them in groups entirely to themselves so that it becomes to all intents and purposes impossible for them to attain with anything like completeness this like-mindedness synonymous with one hundred percent Americanism.

Back of the Klan's crude insistence upon like-mindedness, however, there is much shallow and superficial thinking. To the average Klansman what appears on the surface of things to be alike is alike, what appears unlike is unlike. The accident of a black skin is made an excuse for debarring from the charmed circles of one hundred percent Americanism a man who may be, in spite of his Negro blood, intensely, intelligently, and patriotically American. . . . The Klansman, like the mass of average Americans, lives and moves in a world of mental stereotypes.

John Moffat Mecklin, *The Ku Klux Klan: A Study of the American Mind* (New Hampshire, 1924) pp. 109–113, 115–120.

Herbert Hoover on Rugged Individualism

Herbert Hoover, the Republican presidential candidate in 1928, defined the Republican Party's economic philosophy in the following speech.

During 150 years we have builded up a form of self-government and a social system which is peculiarly our own. It differs essentially from all others in the world. It is the American system.

When the war closed . . . we were challenged with a peace-time choice between the American system of rugged individualism and a European philosophy of . . . paternalism and state socialism.

When the Republican Party came into full power [in 1921] . . . it freed and stimulated enterprise, it restored the government to its position as an umpire instead of a player in the economic game. For these reasons the American people have gone forward in progress while the rest of the world has halted, and some countries have even gone backwards.

By adherence to the principles of decentralized self-government, ordered liberty, equal opportunity, and freedom to the individual, our American experiment in human welfare has yielded a degree of well-being unparalleled in all the world. It has come nearer to the abolition of poverty, to the abolition of fear of want, than humanity has ever reached before. Progress of the past seven years is proof of it.

 The New York Times (Oct. 23, 1928).

Wall Street's Black Tuesday

This news article in the New York Times *described the stock market crash of October 1929.*

Stock prices virtually collapsed yesterday, swept downward with gigantic losses in the most disastrous trading day in the stock market's history. Billions of dollars in open market values were wiped out as prices crumbled under the pressure of liquidation of securities which had to be sold at any price.

From every point of view, the day was the most disastrous in Wall Street's history. Hysteria swept the country and stocks went overboard for just what they would bring at forced sale.

It was estimated that 880 issues, on the New York Stock Exchange, lost between $8 billion and $9 billion yesterday.

Yesterday's market crash was one which largely affected rich men, institutions, investment trusts and others who participate in the stock market on a broad and intelligent scale. . . . They went overboard with no more consideration than the little trader who was swept out on the first day of the market's upheaval.

The market has now passed through three days of collapse. . . . It started last Thursday, when 12,800,000 shares were dealt in on the Exchange. . . . This was followed by a moderate rally on Friday and entirely normal conditions on Saturday. . . . But the storm broke anew on Monday, with prices slaughtered in every direction, to be followed by yesterday's tremendous trading of 16,410,030 shares.

 The New York Times (Oct. 30, 1929).

The Homeless

Dead in the Arms of His Wife

The death of a roofing contractor caught the attention of a New York Times *reporter.*

After vainly trying to get a stay of dispossession until Jan. 15 from his apartment at 46 Hancock

▲ *Depression, 1930s*

Street, in Brooklyn, yesterday, Peter J. Cornell, 48 years old, a former roofing contractor out of work and penniless, fell dead in the arms of his wife.

A doctor gave the cause of his death as heart disease, and the police said it had at least partly been caused by the bitter disappointment of a long day's fruitless attempt to prevent himself and his family being put out on the street.

Just before he died Cornell had carried a bag of coal he had just received from the police upstairs.

Cornell owed $5 in rent in arrears and $39 for January which his landlord required in advance. Failure to produce the money resulted in a dispossess order being served on the family yesterday and to take effect at the end of the week.

 The New York Times (Jan. 16, 1932).

Life on the Road

Robert Carter spent much of 1932 and 1933 living as a tramp. He traveled through the South, living on odd jobs and handouts.

Greenville, N.C.: Arrived here on a freight train late at night, tired and dirty from train smoke and cinders. I slept in the tobacco warehouse with two other young tramps. . . . Next morning was cold, the wind hinted of winter. Leaving town I turned due south, walking the roads. All day I went steadily, getting an occasional ride from trucks or Fords. When dinnertime came I asked for work at a farmhouse for food and picked peas with the farmer's family for two hours.

Morehead City, N.C.: I have found the hobo's paradise, for here I am off the beaten track and therefore in an unbummed town. I live well for three days and nights. . . . I lie in the sun, for I am worn out by the months of hardships, suspicions, the bad food and hard words.

Charleston, S.C.: Charleston is full of homeless boys from the North and Northwest, brought by the delusion of palm trees and warm days. . . . The restaurants are bummed to death. Rarely does one find a man off his guard enough to utter a resentful "yes" when asked for food.

En Route: Leaving Atlanta with three other boys, youngsters going deeper South, we were rounded up in the railroad yards by five detectives carrying pistols and shotguns. They caught eighteen or twenty of us after beating the bushes about the yards. . . . I saw one of the cops go a short distance away, take all the cartridges from his pistol, then return and sit down close to a tough-looking young man. The cop's pistol butt was in easy reach of the boy's hand. Another cop was watching. Had the boy grabbed the empty pistol from the cop's holster he would have been shot to give the other tramps a lesson, to keep them out of Atlanta.

The New Republic, vol. LXXIV (Mar. 8, 1933), pp. 92–95.

Hoover Valley

The New York Times *printed the following account of the eviction of homeless squatters in New York's Central Park.*

Acting Captain George Burnell of the Arsenal station and a squad of patrolmen staged a police raid last night on the residents of a new suburban development. The policemen . . . arrested for vagrancy twenty-five inhabitants of Hoover Valley, the shantytown that sprang up in the bed of the old lower reservoir of Central Park near the Obelisk.

Hoover Valley—the name is officially recognized by Park Department heads—sprang up during the Summer months. . . . Seventeen shacks, all of them equipped with chairs, beds and bedding and a few with carpets, were erected.

The manor of the colony, a brick structure 20 feet high in front of a boulder, having a roof of inlaid tile, was built by unemployed bricklayers, who dubbed it Rockside Inn. . . . Another shack, built of fruit and egg crates, with a tattered American flag flying atop of it, bears a sign, "Radio City." That has the only radio in the "jungle" and all residents are welcome to lounge inside.

Police and park department officials said they believed that almost all the men are New Yorkers, and that none of them are hoboes. They repair in the morning to comfort stations to shave and make themselves look presentable and keep their shacks as clean as they can, it was explained, but because of sanitary conditions must leave before the Board of Health takes action.

The New York Times (Sept. 22, 1932).

Franklin D. Roosevelt's Philosophy

In her memoir of the Depression years, Frances Perkins wrote the following about President Franklin D. Roosevelt's economic ideas. Perkins served as secretary of labor under Roosevelt.

Roosevelt was entirely willing to try experiments. He had no theoretical or ideological objections to public ownership when that was necessary, but it was his belief that it would greatly complicate the administrative system if we had too much.

A superficial reporter once said to Roosevelt in my presence, "Mr. President, are you a Communist?"

"No."

"Are you a capitalist?"

"No."

"Are you a socialist?"

"No," he said, with a look of surprise as if he were wondering what he was being cross examined about.

The young man said, "Well what is your philosophy then?"

"Philosophy?" asked the President, puzzled. "Philosophy? I am a Christian and a Democrat—that's all.

Those two words expressed, I think, just about what he was. They expressed the extent of his political and economic radicalism. He was willing to do experimentally whatever was necessary to promote the Golden Rule and other ideals he considered to be Christian, and whatever could be done under the Constitution of the United States and under the principles which have guided the Democratic Party."

Frances Perkins, *The Roosevelt I Knew* (New York: The Viking Press, Inc., 1946), pp. 329–330.

Panic Times in Akron

This is a description of the mood in Akron, Ohio, the center of the rubber industry in the United States, during the banking crisis just before Franklin D. Roosevelt's inauguration.

March 2, 1933

Both newspapers reported flatly that business in Akron was paralyzed.

The blight which, from Monday, had been gradually falling over the city wormed its way into every back street, into every eddy and nook of Akron. Life slowed down. The rubber companies alone had money to meet week-end pay rolls. The department stores, the grocery stores, the streetcar company, a hundred other business places had no money to pay their employees. Coal companies, unable to meet C.O.D. freight charges, predicted a fuel shortage.

The city funds were frozen in the bank. Relief funds were frozen in the bank. The county funds were frozen in the bank.

Grocery stores refused credit to old customers. Even speakeasies told favored friends, "Sales for cash only. Nobody may ever get any money again. . . ."

Ruth McKenny, *Industrial Valley* (New York, 1939), p. 67.

The First Hundred Days

A New York Times *correspondent described the nation's capital during the first weeks of the Roosevelt administration.*

Wherever you go in Washington today you come upon crowds of people. All day they wait in long queues outside the public galleries of Congress. Or they huddle in little groups in the corridors of the Capitol, in the corridors of the State Department, in the White House waiting rooms. . . . Always they are eager, anxious; always they are talking. The place hums and buzzes and quivers with talk.

You feel the stir of movement, of adventure, even of elation. You never saw before in Washington so much government, or so much animation in government. Everybody in the administration is having the time of his life. So they say, and so you perceive as you watch the new officials, often young, often inexperienced in politics, settling into this great business of national reconstruction. They dash from conference to conference, from hearing to hearing, briefcases bursting with plans and specifications. They are going somewhere, this is plain, and with such momentum and élan . . . they go about reorganizing agriculture, reflating the currency, reforming the structure of business and industry.

It is a little as if at last America had marched on Washington, so that for the first time the capital feels like the center of the country.

Anne O'Hare McCormick, "Vast Tides that Stir the Capital," *The New York Times Magazine* (May 7, 1933), pp. 1–2, 19.

Profiles of WPA Workers

In 1936 Margaret Bristol interviewed men employed by Works Progress Administration federal work program.

Mr. Bright is thirty-two years old and has a wife and nine children. . . . Before applying for relief he spent fourteen years in various forms of auto mechanic work. He averaged about $20 a week. In 1933 the work became so scarce that he applied for public assistance. . . . He received relief intermittently as he secured work for short periods. During the latter part of 1934 he was given work relief, first as a laborer and then as a timekeeper, and earned about $40 a month. . . . In November 1935 he received an assignment to WPA as a timekeeper at a monthly wage of $85.... He says that he is earning more now than he could anywhere else and because of this is not trying to locate other work. He does not believe that politics enters into the WPA situation at all for he has tried to exert pressure to get a better job but failed. He considers the work... useful and says that all the men work hard and that most of the men who work need the jobs.

Mr. Panek was born in Czechoslovakia and came to this country in 1923 and is now fifty-two years of age.... Before the depression Mr. Panek earned $60 a week as a union cement-worker. In 1932, after several months of unemployment, he applied for relief.... In November 1935, he was assigned to WPA and worked until March 1936 as a cement-finisher at $94 a month. At this time he received a nonrelief PWA job at $14 a day. Mr. Panek was quite enthusiastic about WPA and said that the work was well executed and of value to the community.

Mr. Mason is fifty-one years old and has his wife and sixteen-year-old son to support. Since 1912 he has been in the tire-repair and vulcanizing business. He has earned as much as $55 a week.... In November 1935, he went to work for WPA as a laborer at $55 a month. When he told his foreman that he could not do heavy work [because of a weak heart and bad back] he was set to work painting the bleachers in Soldiers Field. He believes that politics is all mixed up with the administration of WPA and that "if you know the right kind of people you can get a better job." According to Mr. Mason their foreman is present every day but he is also drunk every day and uses vile language to the men, so it must be "pull that got him in and keeps him in."

Mr. Packard is a steam-hoist operator and at regular work earned about $70 a week. He was assigned as a laborer on work relief and earned his budget of $35 a month. He is now on WPA as a steam-hoist operator and earns $96 a month. In spite of the wage, the red tape, and the partisanship shown on the job, and the lateness of the checks cause him to dislike WPA.... He believes that if a private contractor had the present job it would go twice as fast.

Mr. Krause is just twenty-three years old and his mother is dependent upon him as his father died

fifteen years ago. He graduated from high school, where he had taken a science course together with aviation mechanics, but he has always done clerical work, earning $15 a week until he and his mother had to apply for assistance in 1932.... He was at a CCC camp for six months and liked it very much and would like to return, but the $25 a month which he earned in camp is insufficient for his mother to live on, and they find that the two of them can live more comfortably on the $55 which he earns on WPA. For the first ten months he did street-repair work and then was transferred to a gardening project in Lincoln Park. This latter job is preferable to the first for he believes it to be more useful and necessary. According to Mr. Krause, WPA work has helped his morale, for he was "pretty discouraged when WPA came along and steady work has helped me to be self-respecting once again."

Mr. Dakin is forty years old and has a wife and three children under fourteen years of age. He is a decorator by trade and has done his own contracting. Mr. Dakin applied for assistance in 1931 and a year later was assigned to work relief where he earned $47 a month as a painter. Later he was assigned to WPA as a painter and is now earning $85 a month. Mr. Dakin is working on a school project which he considers useful, and in addition to the usefulness of the project he enjoys it because he is working at his regular trade.... He likes his work for he considers that payment for the work done is much more self-respecting than accepting direct relief.

Margaret C. Bristol, "Personal Reactions of Assignees to WPA in Chicago," *Social Service Review* (Mar. 1938), pp. 84–87, 94, 95.

Two African American Farmers

Sam Bowers

Sam Bowers, an African American farmer, owned a farm on Cape Fear River in North Carolina.

Soon as I got married [1911] I begun thinkin' of ownin' a home fur myself an' wife. I worked for dat wid it in mind day an' night till I bought it.

My next mind wuz to buy a car. I saved up

money an' bought one. I paid cash fur it. It wuz a model T Ford. I kep' savin' an' when I could I traded fur a Buick car, de one I has now. I don't believe in goin' in debt fur things much. . . . Dere's no 'parison 'tween what I makes now an' when I fust started to work. I made twenty cents a day den an' one meal. Now I makes 'bout $3,000 a year—from two to three thousand, countin' what my wife makes [teaching school]. We makes plenty to meet our needs an' keep buildin' up our place.

We has some money fur lux'ries an' to give to de chu'ches an' other good organizations. We is satisfied wid life.

Federal Writers Project, *These Are Our Lives* (Chapel Hill: University of North Carolina Press, 1939, 1967).

Joe Fielding

Joe Fielding, a sixty-year-old African American, rented a farm in North Carolina. He had raised thirteen of his own children plus five others, with eight still living at home.

I run a three-horse farm and good years make about eighteen bales o' cotton. I rent for four bales and some money. This year I won't get over one bale. My peanuts is right good, but it'll take my whole crop to pay my rent. There won't be no cash money from this year's crop, and the whole crowd's needin' shoes and clothes. They can't wear their old clothes, 'cause they're wore out. I'll get by some sort o' how. . . .

I can't hardly get by on no less'n a hund'ed dollars a month, and I can't make that even good years. . . . Don't reckon old Santy Claus can get around this year; he ain't failed yet, but this year. . . .

What I rather have than anything is a home and a farm o' my own. I wouldn't care about a big one, just so it was mine. No mo'm, I can't say I see one ahead. Long as I keep my health I'll get by somehow though. I always have.

Federal Writers Project, *These Are Our Lives* (Chapel Hill: University of North Carolina Press, 1939, 1967), pp. 40, 43, 74–75.

WORKING WITH THE ARCHIVES

More Practice With Supported Induction

You learned in the Unit 3 Archives skill lesson that one of the complex thinking skills used by historians is called supported induction. By comparing the personal experiences of many individuals, certain patterns emerge that allow historians to make generalizations about how people responded to particular events and times.

In this activity, you will take the role of a Depression-era journalist and, based on your inductions from a selection of primary sources, write a story that describes a "typical" federal relief worker.

Directions: Read the six selections under the heading "Profiles of WPA Workers" about people who worked for the Works Progress Administration. Design a chart or table that will help you organize the information in these selections. Then, combine the information to make generalizations about the workmen's experiences. Use the generalizations to write a newspaper article about a fictitious WPA worker. Create a headline to accompany the article.

Keeping the following questions in mind may help you in your analysis of the archive selections:

- What generalizations can you make about the working men?
- What conclusions can you draw about how the government is affecting the lives of the working men?
- What are the emotional and psychological states of the men?
- How could you account for conflicting comments by the men?
- How might the workers' backgrounds and experiences influence their opinions of the WPA?

America in the Twenties

▲ *The automobile represented here, a 1914 Model T Ford, became a symbol for the twenties.*

Few periods of American history stand out as sharply as the 1920s. This decade is fondly thought of as the Golden Twenties, especially by those Americans who lived through it. The twenties seemed special to them, partly because of the hard times that followed during the depression of the 1930s.

But the reputation of the twenties is also based on the real achievements of those years. This was a time of economic growth and prosperity, a period of dramatic social and cultural change, and an era of creativity in literature and the arts. It was truly a remarkable decade.

SECTIONS				
1	**2**	**3**	**4**	**5**
A Decade of Prosperity	An Era of Social Change	The Politics of Normalcy	American Culture in Transition	Americans' Reactions to Change

SECTION 1

A Decade of Prosperity

Henry Ford, more than any other automaker of the 1920s, put America on wheels. Although he did not invent the automobile, his techniques of mass production did bring it within the range of the average American's budget. New Fords rolled off the assembly lines in vast numbers. On the record production day of October 31, 1925, Ford's plants produced 9,109 new Model Ts—one for every *ten seconds* of the working day! By reducing the time and labor involved in making the Model T, Henry Ford brought its price down from $850 in 1908 to less than $300 by 1926. To the American public, Henry Ford, more than any other American businessman, symbolized the economic revolution of the 1920s and its miracles of mass production. Henry Ford was hailed as the genius of his age and became a folk hero in his own time.

In what ways were the twenties a time of economic prosperity?

What new consumer products spurred economic growth?

Why were the benefits of prosperity not shared equally by all Americans?

▲ *Assembly lines helped reduce the cost of automobiles. Who pioneered the use of assembly lines in the auto industry?*

The Booming American Economy

When Henry Ford founded the Ford Motor Company in 1903, automobiles were an expensive luxury. Only the very wealthy owned cars. Ford wanted to produce an automobile for the masses, one that any farmer or worker could use "to enjoy with his family the blessing of hours of pleasure in God's great open spaces." He did this in 1908 by producing a simple, inexpensive automobile called the Model T and later by installing assembly lines in his automobile plants. Sales of Ford automobiles soared. Other car manufacturers copied Ford's methods, and automobile ownership increased dramatically. The number of cars registered in the United States grew from a million in 1913 to 26 million by 1929. By then, half of all American households owned an automobile.

Automobile manufacturing was only one of several growth industries of the twenties. A **growth industry** is a key industry whose rapid expansion contributes greatly to the economy. Among growth industry leaders was the construction industry, driven by the demand for residential homes. Throughout the United States, real estate developers were transforming meadows into new subdivisions, housing tracts for people who could now commute to work by automobile. The use of electric power tripled during the twenties—63 percent of American homes had electricity by 1926. Telephone communication nearly doubled during the twenties, with over half of the homes having a telephone. This increasing use of electricity in American homes and factories spurred the growth of the public utilities industry. The chemical industry also prospered during the twenties. Of significance to future decades was the emergence of a new synthetic fabric called rayon.

Manufacturing was stimulated by the production of new **consumer goods**—goods that people use in their daily lives and that can be a measure of

The Auto Comes to Middletown

"Why on earth do you need to study what's changing this country?" asked a resident of Muncie, Indiana, in 1924. "I can tell you what's happening in just four letters: A-U-T-O." He was talking to sociologists from the University of Chicago, who had selected Muncie for a case study on American city life. Robert S. and Helen Lynd, who directed the study, later published their findings in a book entitled *Middletown* (1929). (They disguised Muncie's name to protect the privacy of the people as much as possible.) This book, which became a classic work of American sociology, reported that the automobile had, indeed, changed the way Middletown's residents lived.

In the first place, automobile ownership had a dramatic impact on the family budget. The Lynds reported that half of the working-class families of Middletown owned a car, and most of these cars were bought with borrowed money. Many residents made the monthly car payments instead of buying clothing.

"We'd rather do without clothes than give up the car," said one mother of nine children.

"We don't have no fancy clothes when we have the car to pay for," another said. "The car is the only pleasure we have."

▲ *How did the automobile change the way Americans of the 1920s lived?*

Some even put the car ahead of food. "I'll go without food before I'll see us give up the car," one woman said emphatically. Some unemployed families who managed to keep up their car payments may actually have made that choice.

Middletown's ministers complained about the effect of the automobile on church attendance. Their churches had too many empty seats on Sunday mornings.

"The ministers ought not to rail against people's driving on Sunday," one elderly church member replied. "They ought just to realize that they won't be there every Sunday during the summer, and make church interesting enough so they'll want to come."

Middletown's parents were concerned about the impact of the automobile on their children. Mothers were worried about their teenage daughters, who spent less time with the family because they

were out motoring with their boyfriends. Young men who lacked cars were said to be responsible for over half of the 154 auto thefts in the town during 1923. When the Lynds asked young people about the most common causes of disagreement with their parents, use of the family car ranked high on the list.

Finally, car ownership had revolutionized the use of leisure time in Middletown. Out-of-town excursions, picnics in the countryside, and family vacations were more common than ever before. As one housewife summed it up, "We just go to lots of things we couldn't go to if we didn't have a car."

1. How did car ownership change what was bought in Middletown?
2. Name three ways automobiles affected family life.

▲ *Stores selling electrical appliances, such as this store in Louisville, Kentucky, found it necessary to enlarge their sales forces during the twenties. How did the expansion of electric power during the 1920s affect the American home?*

the standard of living. A variety of new household appliances came on the market, made possible by the larger number of homes using electricity. By 1929, about 80 percent of American homes had an electric iron, nearly 40 percent had a vacuum cleaner, and 25 percent had a washing machine. Nearly half of those homes owned a phonograph, and a great many had an electric refrigerator. Among other consumer items that became available during the twenties were cigarette lighters, wristwatches, and book matches.

Rapid industrial growth during the twenties helped fuel an unprecedented economic boom. From 1922 to 1929, industrial production in the United States nearly doubled. Real income increased by nearly 30 percent. (Real income is how much your money can buy after adjusting for inflation.) Unemployment fell to its lowest peacetime level in years. By 1929, only 4 percent of the workforce was unemployed.

Economic growth was partly the result of a dramatic increase in the **productivity**, or rate of output, of American workers. By 1929, each worker produced nearly 50 percent more goods than a worker had only a decade before. The increased efficiency of production largely sprang from new industrial technology and from the use of mass-production methods, such as the assembly line.

Higher Wages and Increased Profits

The productivity gains of the 1920s were quickly translated into an improved standard of living for millions of Americans. A part of the savings gained

▲ *Men's and women's bathing suits became popular in the 1920s.*

▲ *This photograph of a "sea of cars" shows one way automobiles changed how Americans spent their leisure time. Can you think of others?*

by a more productive workforce was passed on to workers in the form of higher wages. Because prices remained stable during the decade, these increases were not eaten up by higher prices. This meant that hundreds of thousands of working-class families experienced an increase in their purchasing power. They had more cash available to buy more goods. The urban middle class also benefited, since the incomes of merchants, professionals, and white-collar workers went up even more than those of factory workers. Increased vacation time and shorter workdays—the eight-hour day had become widely accepted in American industry on the eve of World War I—provided more leisure time for enjoying these higher incomes.

Although workers benefited from the gains in productivity, the largest rewards went to the owners of businesses and the stockholders of corporations. Most of the gains from increased productivity were not passed on as higher wages, but were converted into increased profits for the business and its owners. Wages in manufacturing increased 8 percent between 1923 and 1929, but profits rose by 38 percent. Part of the profits were reinvested in the businesses that created them, but billions of dollars

ended up in the savings accounts of wealthy Americans. Thus, the benefits of prosperity were not shared equally.

The Great Merger Movement Continues

The decade of the 1920s saw the continued growth of big business through corporate mergers. Between 1919 and 1930, about 8,000 separate firms that engaged in manufacturing and mining disappeared because they were absorbed by or combined with other companies. In the automobile industry, for example, mergers and business failures had reduced the 181 automobile manufacturing companies that existed in 1903 to only 11 by 1930. In that year, the "Big Three" of these firms—Ford, General Motors, and Chrysler—produced 83 percent of the cars. Corporate-owned chain stores accounted for more than 25 percent of the nation's grocery, clothing, and general merchandise sales by the end of the decade. The A & P grocery chain, one of the biggest, grew from 5,000 stores in 1922 to some 17,500 by 1928. The concentration of economic power was proceeding so rapidly that by 1929 the 200 largest business firms owned nearly half the corporate wealth of the United States.

The business mergers of the 1920s had far-reaching consequences for the American people. Consolidation sharply reduced competition in the marketplace. In an industry dominated by only a few large firms, it was easy for these companies to agree informally on the price they would charge for their products. Also, an increasing number of Americans were working for large companies. By 1929, more than half the wage earners in the United States worked for companies that employed over 250 workers.

The merger movement of the turn of the century had met with resistance, and the regulatory state had emerged. The merger movement of the 1920s, however, met with little resistance from the government. The Justice Department kept its hands off corporate affairs. The Supreme Court even encouraged business consolidations by applying and broadening the **rule of reason** in trust cases. Under this principle, the question was not whether a merger resulted in the outlawed restraint of trade, but whether the Court thought that the restraint was *reasonable* or *unreasonable*. In *United States v. U.S. Steel Corporation* (1920), the Court decided that U.S. Steel's control of half the nation's steel production was reasonable. This decision encouraged future mergers. No president stepped forward during the 1920s as Theodore Roosevelt had during the Progressive Era, to earn the title of "trustbuster."

SECTION 1 REVIEW

1. **Define** the term *consumer goods*.
2. **Name** some of the growth industries of the 1920s.
3. **Describe** the process developed by Henry Ford that was responsible for reducing the cost of manufacturing automobiles.
4. **Explain** what happened to the productivity gains not passed on as higher wages.
5. **Discuss** how the rule of reason helped the merger movement.

SECTION 2

An Era of Social Change

The age of Henry Ford was also the era of the **flapper**. The flapper, a liberated young woman with bobbed hair who wore short, straight dresses, became the most enduring image of the 1920s. She represented not only a break from the traditional styles of women's clothing, but also a departure from conventional behavior and ideas about women's place in society. The upholders of the old ways were shocked because the flapper seemed to do and talk as she pleased with whomever she pleased. To the young women who decided to finish high school, go to college, or move to the city to work before getting married, becoming a flapper was a gesture of independence. It was a way of saying they were different from the generations of women that had gone before.

How did the status of women change during the twenties?

What technological developments altered the shape of American cities?

Why did African Americans migrate north during this decade?

More Opportunities for American Women

The flapper's display of independence had its roots in longer-term changes in the economic role of women in American society. Since the turn of the century, women had been gaining an increasing measure of economic independence. Women aged 16 to 44 who were gainfully employed increased from 22 percent of the workforce in 1890 to 30 percent by 1930. Although working-class women had labored in the mills and factories since before the Civil War, middle-class women had usually remained at home. By the 1920s, large numbers of middle-class women were working outside the

▶ *This 1926* Life *magazine cover portrays a flapper and her partner performing a new dance step. Artist John Held Jr. helped popularize the "flapper look." To the far right is a lace and silk flapper evening dress with matching sequined cloche-style hat. The flapper look also called for a long, free-swinging necklace, such as the one above made of imitation pearl beads.*

home either to support themselves before marriage or to add to their husband's income.

Middle-class women worked at better jobs than most women had before. More women were entering white-collar and clerical fields, passing over traditional jobs as domestic servants. Women were becoming better educated as well. Eleven percent of women aged 18 to 21 were in college in 1930, compared to only 4 percent in 1910. By 1930, they made up over 40 percent of all enrolled students. Forty percent of the 10 million women employed outside the home in 1929 held white-collar jobs. Employed women worked as nurses, teachers, shop clerks, or in business offices as secretaries and typists. Such jobs had higher status and usually were better paying than factory or mill work.

The circumstances of housework had changed as well. The household appliances that came into wide use during the twenties reduced the time needed for daily chores. Electric washing machines, irons, stoves, and vacuum cleaners largely eliminated

the need for servants. Until then, even middle-class women had relied on hired help to assist with housework and child care. Although the work was now done more quickly, the dependence on appliances instead of on servants often placed a greater burden on the housewife. She spent more of her time and invested more of herself in washing, ironing, sewing, and cleaning house. According to government studies, in this decade married women spent over 60 hours per week doing housework.

The leaders of the women's movement remained active. After securing women's suffrage with the Nineteenth Amendment in 1920, they took up other causes of concern to women. Some worked for world peace, others for better educational opportunities for women. Still others devoted their energies to securing passage of an equal rights amendment to the Constitution. The proposed amendment would have banned discrimination on the basis of sex. The leader of the equal rights movement was Alice Paul, founder of the National

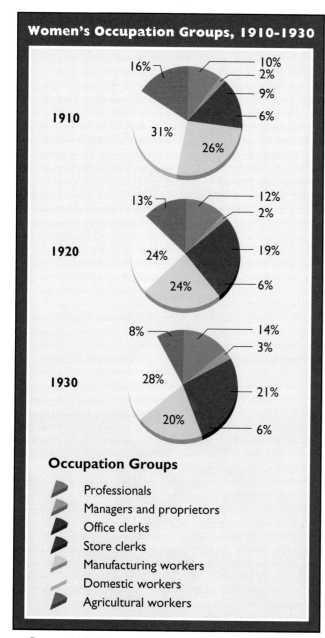

Women's Occupation Groups, 1910-1930

1910
- 16%
- 10%
- 2%
- 9%
- 6%
- 31%
- 26%

1920
- 13%
- 12%
- 2%
- 19%
- 24%
- 24%
- 6%

1930
- 8%
- 14%
- 3%
- 28%
- 21%
- 20%
- 6%

Occupation Groups

- Professionals
- Managers and proprietors
- Office clerks
- Store clerks
- Manufacturing workers
- Domestic workers
- Agricultural workers

Source: U.S. Department of Commerce, Bureau of the Census.

▲ *What categories of women's jobs had the greatest growth rates between 1910 and 1930? In what occupations were women less likely to be employed by 1930?*

Woman's Party. But few women and still fewer men of the 1920s were concerned about equal pay or equal rights for women. For the moment, winning the right to vote seemed enough.

An Urban Nation

By the 1920s, the United States was rapidly becoming an urban nation. According to the federal census of 1920, 51.4 percent of the population lived in communities that had 2,500 or more people. During the next ten years, some 6 million more people left farms and small towns to try urban living. Towns were transformed into cities, and big cities, like the auto city of Detroit, became sprawling metropolitan centers.

This spurt of urban growth caused a building boom in the cities. Towering office buildings and hotels changed the skyline of downtown areas. Increasing property values made it cheaper to build up than out. In 1920, buildings of 20 stories or more were still rare; by 1929, 377 skyscrapers existed. The Chrysler Building in New York City, a handsome building of steel and cadmium with electric elevators, rose 77 stories. It was surpassed by the Empire State Building, completed in 1930, which had 102 stories and for many years was the tallest building in the world.

▼ *The building boom in the cities during the twenties kept riveters and construction workers busy.*

During the twenties, cities grew outward as well as upward. New **suburbs**, or outlying neighborhoods, developed either where land was cheaper or along the highways and trolley lines extending out from the inner cities. Most suburbs offered brick and frame houses that middle-class and many working-class families could afford. Mass transit and the automobile made it possible for families with modest incomes to move out of the congested cities. More exclusive suburban communities were built for the wealthy, such as Beverly Hills near Los Angeles, Shaker Heights on the outskirts of Cleveland, and Grosse Pointe Park outside Detroit. Like the cities, the suburbs were segregated by income and social class. The migration of the middle and upper classes to the suburbs was transforming the inner cities into working-class and lower-class communities.

African Americans Move North

As white families moved from the inner cities to better neighborhoods in the suburbs, their places were taken by the newest immigrants to the cities—African Americans from the South. The mass migration from the rural South to northern cities begun on the eve of World War I continued at a brisk pace. The number of African Americans living in New York City, Chicago, and Detroit doubled, as 1.5 million black people made their way north during the 1920s. Large numbers also migrated to Atlanta and other cities of the South. African Americans were lured to these urban centers by the prospect of jobs. The shortage of labor opened more industrial jobs to African Americans, but

▼ *This is a reproduction of* The Migration of the Negro Series, Panel No. 1 *by Jacob Lawrence. Why did northern cities attract large numbers of African American migrants? (The Phillips Collection, Washington, D.C., provided courtesy of the artist and Francine Seders Gallery, Seattle, Washington.)*

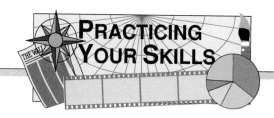

Using Graphs to Identify Historical Trends

Women's Occupation Groups, 1910-1930

1910
16%
31%
26%
10%
2%
9%
6%

1920
13%
24%
24%
12%
2%
19%
6%

1930
8%
28%
20%
14%
3%
21%
6%

Occupation Groups

▶ Professionals
▶ Managers and proprietors
▶ Office clerks
▶ Store clerks
▶ Manufacturing workers
▶ Domestic workers
▶ Agricultural workers

Source: U.S. Department of Commerce, Bureau of the Census.

The early twentieth century brought yet another surge in technological change for Americans. New weapons of warfare—machine guns, flame throwers, bombs dropped from airplanes, and tanks—were one indication of this. On the domestic front, everyday lives of many American families, especially women, began to change drastically. By the 1920s, automobiles made Americans more mobile, and electricity brought dozens of gadgets such as electric irons, vacuum cleaners, toasters, and washing machines into the home. Telephones, radio, and movies brought information, entertainment, and a national culture to every part of the United States. Trends, such as fewer children per family and more women working outside the home, continued into the 1920s.

Trends can be identified by looking at events in the recent past to see if they show a pattern or direction. Graphs of historical statistics are a useful way of identifying trends.

Here are some questions to help you identify trends on graphs. You may also want to review the guidelines for analyzing graphs on page 123 in Chapter 4.

- **What is the title of the graph?** What subjects are being compared? What is the source of the data?
- **What time period is covered?** Is it long enough to determine if a trend has been established?
- **Can you identify patterns or directions on the graphs?** Can you find a relationship among data points on various graphs?

- **Can you determine what might be some reasons for the trends shown on the graph?** For instance, does the outbreak of war coincide with a decrease in unemployment?

Examine the graphs on page 653 and answer the following questions:

1. What categories of women's employment are identified on the graphs?
2. (a) Which category is the largest on all three graphs? (b) Which category remained almost unchanged in the twenty years from 1910 to 1930? (c) Which category increased the most from 1910 to 1920? (d) Which category decreased the most from 1910 to 1920? (e) Which categories show constant decline from 1910 to 1930?
3. (a) Which categories of jobs do you think require the most education and skills training? (b) Which jobs require the least?
4. Looking at all three graphs, one might reasonably conclude that from 1910 to 1930 women made bigger gains in ‖‖‖‖‖‖ than in ‖‖‖‖‖‖ jobs.
5. What effect do you think the trends you have identified in these graphs had on American society in this period?

discrimination still limited them to the least-skilled and lowest-paying work.

The new migrants from the South settled in the emerging African American ghettos, the most crowded and run-down sections of the cities. Housing was poorly maintained. The major exception to the dismal conditions of the black districts was Harlem. Once a middle-class white suburb in uptown New York, Harlem had expanded too rapidly during a real estate boom. Rather than lose the houses through mortgage foreclosure, the builders subdivided them into smaller apartments and rented them to African Americans. It quickly became an all-black community. But the failure of the owners to keep up the rental properties soon reduced even Harlem to a slum.

Emerging African American Independence

Unlike white immigrants who had come before them, African Americans found it nearly impossible to escape the slums. White homeowners and realtors refused to sell property in white neighborhoods to African Americans. White property owners in adjoining neighborhoods resisted the expansion of ghetto boundaries, often with violence or threats of violence. They were determined to keep the black population confined to overcrowded ghettos. In large part, they succeeded.

African Americans responded by turning inward to develop social and economic institutions that reduced their dependence on the white city beyond. African American churches, hospitals, social clubs, and newspapers supported a vigorous community life. African American-owned businesses in the ghettos provided a limited measure of economic independence. The spirit of self-help was best represented by the Universal Negro Improvement Association (UNIA), led by **Marcus Garvey**. A Jamaican immigrant who settled in New York City, Garvey created a movement dedicated to self-reliance. Among other projects, Garvey founded a

▲ *Marcus Garvey, a Jamaican immigrant, advocated racial pride and self-reliance. He encouraged African Americans to establish a homeland in Africa.*

black-owned shipping line and tried to create a new nation in Africa to give black people a homeland free from white colonialism. The UNIA had about 600,000 followers by 1925, when it collapsed due to Garvey's conviction for mail fraud and the failure of his shipping line. Despite its disappointing results, Garvey's movement was a symbol of the impressive power of African American racial consciousness in the 1920s.

SECTION 2 REVIEW

1. **Summarize** the changing social and economic position of women during the 1920s.
2. **Name** a factor that caused the spurt of urban population growth.
3. **Name** two factors responsible for the growth of suburbs.
4. **State** a reason why African Americans migrated to northern cities during the 1920s.
5. **Explain** why African Americans found it more difficult than the European immigrants to move out of the slums.

The Politics of Normalcy

In the 1920 presidential campaign, the Republicans played it safe. They sensed that the voters were tired of crusades to make America progressive and the world safe for democracy. World War I had not produced a military hero of presidential stature, so they chose **Warren G. Harding** as their presidential candidate. Harding was a handsome, but undistinguished, senator from Ohio. "This man Harding is no world beater," one of the party's leaders acknowledged, "but we think he is the best of the bunch." Harding told the voters that what America needed was not heroics, but healings; not agitation, but adjustment. His only campaign promise was to return the country to "normalcy." The nomination for vice president went to **Calvin Coolidge**, the governor of Massachusetts who had opposed a police strike in Boston in 1919. No one, Coolidge had proclaimed, had the right to go on strike against the public safety. Adding him to the Republican ticket gave it an even more conservative tone. The Democrats nominated Governor James Cox of Ohio and **Franklin D. Roosevelt** of New York. Harding and Coolidge won with 16 million votes to their opponents' 9 million. "It wasn't a landslide," lamented a Democrat, "it was an earthquake."

What did Harding's slogan "less government in business, more business in government" mean?
How did corporations benefit from government policies?
How did American foreign policy help businesses?

Promoting American Business

Harding's election marked the beginning of an era of close cooperation between business and the federal government. The new president had little interest in social reforms that might interfere with the right of employers to manage their own affairs. Harding was flatly opposed to government regulation of business. What the country needed, Harding

President Warren G. Harding cultivated a strong presidential image.

said, was "less government in business, more business in government." (Or as Coolidge would later remark, "The business of America is business.")

The result was an economic policy that greatly benefited corporate America. It included a series of tax cuts proposed by Andrew Mellon, the wealthy industrialist whom Harding appointed as his secretary of the treasury. Tax laws enacted between 1922 and 1928 sharply reduced income taxes on corporations and wealthy individuals. The Republican majority in Congress also handed manufacturers a major windfall in 1922 in enacting the Fordney-McCumber Tariff. This protective tariff imposed high duties on imported chemicals, textiles, and a wide range of other items. It virtually cut out foreign competition and thus greatly increased the profits of American manufacturers.

Harding was more successful in setting a pro-business course for the federal government than in keeping his administration free from scandal. Although not a dishonest man, Harding made bad appointments and let dishonest men take advantage of him. Charles R. Forbes, whom Harding appointed to head the Veterans Bureau, defrauded the government of nearly $200 million. Forbes sold valuable government-owned hospital equipment as surplus goods to his associates at low prices and then bought the equipment back again at its full value,

Who Says a Watched Pot Never Boils?

▲ *The Teapot Dome scandal involved top government officials. In the cartoon, who is represented by the figures fleeing the flood?*

▲ *President Calvin Coolidge continued Harding's policy of favoring big business.*

sharing in the profits. In what became known as the **Teapot Dome scandal**, Albert Fall, the secretary of the interior, took $400,000 in bribes in return for illegally leasing to private oil companies public oil reserves at Elk Hills, California, and Teapot Dome, Wyoming. Harding died of a stroke on August 2, 1923, before the worst scandals caused by his bad appointments were exposed.

As the nation mourned Harding's death, Calvin Coolidge became the 30th president of the United States. Honest and far more careful than Harding, Coolidge quickly restored whatever public confidence the Republicans were losing due to the scan-

dals. Coolidge continued Harding's pro-business policies and took credit for the economic boom that coincided with his becoming president. Using "Coolidge Prosperity" as their campaign slogan in 1924, the Republicans easily defeated a Democratic ticket headed by John W. Davis and a Progressive Party ticket headed by Senator Robert La Follette of Wisconsin. Elected in his own right, Coolidge served a four-year term devoted to the promotion of American business at home and abroad.

Herbert Hoover Few of the public officials of the twenties did as much to promote business as Herbert Hoover, who served as secretary of commerce under Harding and Coolidge. Instead of regulating corporations and breaking up trusts, Hoover insisted that government should lend business a helping hand. His goal was "to change the attitude of government relations with business from that of interference to that of cooperation." Under Hoover, the Department of Commerce cooperated with business by sponsoring economic conferences, issuing business reports, and encouraging the formation of trade associations. Through these organizations, industrial leaders could come together voluntarily to exchange information, restrict production, and

▲ *As secretary of commerce, Herbert Hoover took part in an early transmission of television signals. Speaking over a telephone line from Washington, D.C., in 1927, Hoover was seen as well as heard by an audience in New York City.*

set prices. As food administrator during World War I, Hoover had learned the value of voluntary action to accomplish national goals, and he encouraged people in business to take the same approach.

When Coolidge announced that he would not run for a second full term in 1928, the Republican Party chose Hoover as its presidential candidate. Hoover faced a Democratic ticket headed by Alfred E. Smith, the governor of New York. Of German and Irish ancestry, Smith was the first Roman Catholic to be nominated for president by a major political party. Although Smith had wide support among the European ethnic groups in the eastern cities, his nomination was not well received by the rural Democrats, especially in the Midwest. With the Democratic Party badly divided over Smith's candidacy, Hoover won a landslide victory. The vote in the electoral college was 444 for Hoover to 87 for Smith. But Smith had carried the major eastern cities, bringing the European ethnic vote solidly into the Democratic Party. This gain was of great significance for the party's future.

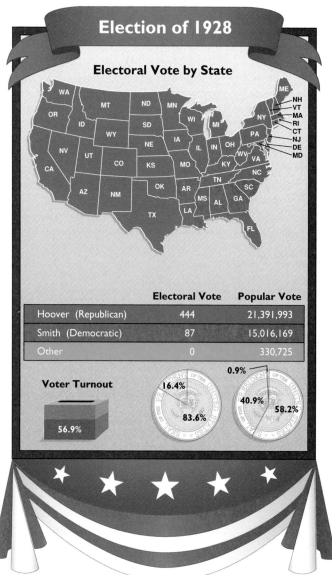

Election of 1928

Electoral Vote by State

	Electoral Vote	Popular Vote
Hoover (Republican)	444	21,391,993
Smith (Democratic)	87	15,016,169
Other	0	330,725

Voter Turnout

56.9%

16.4%
83.6%

0.9%
40.9%
58.2%

▲ *The Republicans carried all but six southern states in the election of 1928. What signs of hope for the future did the Democrats see in the election returns?*

Safeguarding American Business Interests Overseas

Republicans in the Senate had kept the United States out of the League of Nations by defeating the ratification of Wilson's treaty, but they had no intention of turning their backs on the world. In the first place, American business interests had too much at stake. Big business had regained respectability after the Progressive Era by expanding production during the war. American investments in Europe had greatly increased since the outbreak of World War I, making the United States a creditor nation—a lender rather than a borrower—for the first time. The Allied governments owed American banks more than $7 billion in war loans and $2 billion in postwar reconstruction costs. The Republican administrations were also committed to the expansion of American trade, especially in Europe and Latin America. Moreover, the nation had overseas possessions to protect and important strategic interests to promote, such as keeping sea-lanes open to American shipping. The Republicans charted an independent, but internationalist, course outside of the League of Nations. The cornerstone of Republican foreign policy was a series of treaties designed to limit armaments and to avoid another world war.

A conference held in Washington in 1921–1922 produced three major treaties. The Five-Power Agreement restricted the naval power of Britain, France, Japan, Italy, and the United States by allowing each a limited number of ships. The Four-Power Treaty, signed by the United States, Britain, Japan, and France, bound each of these nations to respect the others' rights in the Pacific and to settle further disputes at the conference table. The Nine-Power Treaty reaffirmed the Open Door Policy with China. In this treaty, the nations with an interest in China agreed to protect the "sovereignty, the independence, and the territorial administrative integrity of China." The signers included the signers of the Five-Power Agreement plus China, Belgium, Portugal, and the Netherlands.

The Kellogg-Briand Pact of 1928, which outlawed war as an instrument of national policy, was signed by the United States and 14 other nations. Although well intended, these agreements were little more than promises. With no means of enforcing them, they simply created, a fragile "paper peace."

The United States also played an active part in restoring a measure of financial stability to Europe. At the heart of the problem was a debt of $33 billion that Germany owed the Allied powers in war reparations. With its economy crippled by the war and burdened by soaring postwar inflation, Germany could barely make payments on the debt. Coming to the aid of the Germans in 1924, the United States produced the **Dawes Plan** proposed by Chicago banker Charles B. Dawes. It scaled down the debt and arranged for loans from American banks to help Germany make its payments. The Allies, in turn, used part of the German payments to make installments on the debts they owed to the United States. While this system would not withstand any serious financial crisis, it served for a time to keep Europe financially afloat.

The Republican administrations of the 1920s also did what they could to encourage American investments and trade in other parts of the world. The amount of American trade with Latin America tripled during the decade. Investments in Latin America increased from $1.26 billion in 1914 to $3.52 billion in 1929. The United States government, in turn, made every effort to see that American investments in railroads, banana and sugar plantations, oil fields, and public utilities were protected. For example, American troops were on duty in Haiti, the Dominican Republic, and Nicaragua during much of the decade. Less direct pressure was used to support friendly governments in Honduras and Cuba.

The Harding and Coolidge administrations also allowed American corporations to export machines and technology to the Soviet Union, although the United States refused officially to recognize the Soviet Communist government.

SECTION 3 REVIEW

1. **Describe** the general policy of the Harding, Coolidge, and Hoover administrations toward American corporations.
2. **Identify** the Teapot Dome scandal.
3. **Describe** how Herbert Hoover used his position as secretary of commerce to help American business.
4. **Explain** why Al Smith's defeat was a significant turning point for the Democratic party.
5. **Explain** briefly what is meant by the phrase "an independent, but internationalist," course in foreign policy.

American Culture in Transition

During the 1920s, American culture, like other aspects of American life, was caught up in a whirlwind of change. Traditional values, beliefs, and behaviors were questioned. Old standards of morality came under attack, especially by the younger generation. In a series of novels and short stories, **F. Scott Fitzgerald** depicted the cultural rebellion of the "flaming youth" of the 1920s. "None of the Victorian mothers—and most of the mothers were Victorian—had any idea how casually their daughters were accustomed to be kissed, . . ." he wrote in *This Side of Paradise* (1920). "Amory saw girls doing things that even in his memory would have been impossible; eating three-o'clock, after-dance suppers in impossible cafés, talking of every side of life with an air half of earnestness, half of mockery, yet with a furtive excitement that Amory considered stood for a real moral letdown." As Fitzgerald's character indicated, to the older generation the most disturbing of the cultural changes was this breakdown of Victorian morality among the young.

How did the urban prosperity of the twenties pose a threat to traditional values?

What changes occurred in the way Americans spent leisure time?

What sparked the literary and artistic creativity of the decade?

Traditional Values Threatened

People still associate the twenties with the rebellious youths of F. Scott Fitzgerald novels. Yet they were only the symbols of cultural changes in which a much larger segment of American society was involved. A substantial portion of the urban middle class took part in the revolt against traditional ways.

▲ *Refrigerators and other consumer goods became status symbols in the 1920s. What role did the mass media play in stimulating this market?*

Sharing in the prosperity of the decade, the middle class was making more money than ever before. The old values did not quite fit their new circumstances. Scrimping and saving had little appeal. Buying a new car, moving to a new house, or ordering a new refrigerator were far more satisfying. These possessions were also the marks of success. Success in the urban, industrial America of the 1920s was measured by the material things a family could buy. Consumption, not saving, brought social status.

The mass media publicized and promoted the rebellion against traditional values. Magazines, movies, and radio programs popularized a new set of values tailored to an economy that was based on the mass consumption of material goods. The advertising industry, another of the growth industries of the 1920s, urged Americans to spend rather than to save, and to enjoy life. Advertisements promoted new styles, urged women to spend money on cosmetics, and told them to give more time to themselves and less to the kitchen. This message was carried by the new communication media into small towns and into people's homes everywhere.

New Ways to Spend Leisure Time

The 1920s also saw changes in the way Americans spent their leisure time. In earlier years, time away from work had been spent mainly with the family or in the neighborhood. On Sundays, the principal day of leisure, families had typically gone to church, had a large noonday meal at home, and spent the afternoon in the parlor or visiting friends and relatives nearby. By 1929, leisure time was increasingly spent away from home and was less likely to be spent as a family. Mother and father went for a Sunday drive; young people attended the movies.

Like much else in American society, leisure itself was becoming a business. By the end of the decade, Americans were spending $4.3 billion each year to keep themselves amused. Some of this money was spent on fads. In 1923, for example, people rushed out to buy mah-jongg sets, a Chinese game played with ivory and bamboo tiles. The manufacturers could not keep up with the demand. That craze soon gave way to the crossword-puzzle fad. Although these word puzzles dated from about 1913, they were popularized by a new kind of book published in 1924 by Simon and Schuster. The *Cross-Word Puzzle Book*, which came with an attached pencil, was an instant best-seller. An observant traveler on a train between New York and Boston noted that 60 percent of the passengers and five of the waiters in the dining car were working on puzzles. As fads came and went, money spent on leisure activities steadily increased.

The movies were at the center of the booming entertainment industry in the twenties. Audiences packed the theaters to watch romantic feature-length films that cast Mary Pickford, Clara Bow, and other movie heroines in glamorous roles. Rudolph Valentino's dashing and romantic role in *The Sheik* (1921) made him the idol of American women. Sensuous love scenes also gave audiences new and more liberated role models. "Goodness knows," remarked a young woman, "you learn plenty about love from the movies. . . . You meet the flapper, the good girl, 'n' all the feminine types and their little tricks of the trade." Still, such movies continued to deliver the traditional message that winning a hus-

▲ *Most films in the twenties were silent. How did movies, such as this 1926 film starring Rudolph Valentino, challenge traditional values?*

band was the way to happiness. The comedies of Charlie Chaplin, Harold Lloyd, and Buster Keaton also drew large audiences, as did Westerns and historical dramas.

For most of the decade, movies lacked a soundtrack. They were flickering images on a silent screen. Moviegoers were amazed in 1927 to hear the voice of singer Al Jolson in *The Jazz Singer*. The first full-length, all-sound movie was *The Lights of New York*, released in 1928. Attendance at motion pictures reached 100 million a week in 1930, nearly twice the weekly attendance at church.

Sports Celebrities and Heroes

While films gave the public a galaxy of movie stars to admire, sports also produced popular heroes

Baseball legend Babe Ruth posed with Ray Kelly, the young mascot of the New York Yankees.

▼ The "Babe" gave his New York Yankees bat to President Warren G. Harding as a gift. Why was Ruth celebrated as a national hero?

and heroines. Baseball remained the great national pastime, with the World Series as its annual major event. The sports hero of the decade, whose fame rivaled that of any movie star, was George Herman "Babe" Ruth. His record of 60 home runs hit for the New York Yankees in 1927 was an impressive achievement that would stand for 34 years. Football was also rapidly gaining a mass following. The 1920s was the era of Knute Rockne, the famed football coach of Notre Dame, and of Harold "Red" Grange. A University of Illinois football star, Grange signed with the Chicago Bears in 1925 and was paid an amazing $42,000 for his first two games.

Boxing remained a popular sport. The 1921 match between Jack Dempsey and the French boxer Georges Carpentier drew an audience of 75,000. In 1926, Gertrude Ederle's feat of being the first woman to swim the English Channel (only five men had done so) gave the United States a sports heroine.

No single feat of individual skill and valor stirred the public as deeply as Charles Lindbergh's flight across the Atlantic. Flying alone in his plane,

▼ In 1927, Charles Lindbergh flew nonstop from New York to France in thirty-three and a half hours. Why were Americans so impressed by Lindbergh's achievement?

the *Spirit of St. Louis*, Lindbergh flew nonstop from New York to Paris on May 20–21, 1927, the first solo flight across the Atlantic. The flight was a milestone in aviation history, and it captured the imagination of the public. In an age of big corporations, organized sports, and mass participation, Lindbergh's solo feat rekindled the spirit of an earlier America, when individualism counted for more. Lindbergh returned to a hero's welcome on a cruiser that President Coolidge had sent to France.

A Golden Age for Writers

The 1920s was a time of unusual creativity in American literature. Few periods even approach these years in the outpouring of outstanding poetry and fiction. Three of the novelists who began writing during the 1920s, Ernest Hemingway, Sinclair Lewis, and William Faulkner, eventually won Nobel Prizes for literature, as did that decade's most important poet, T. S. Eliot. In addition to Eliot, the work of Ezra Pound, e. e. cummings, and Archibald MacLeish brought American poetry acclaim and respect. In 1924, political and social activist Edna St. Vincent Millay won the Pulitzer Prize for poetry. The American theater was enriched by the work of Eugene O'Neill and Maxwell Anderson. It was a golden age for American letters.

American fiction in the 1920s was written in the shadow of World War I. That war had left many writers disillusioned about human nature. Their generation had gone off to fight a "glorious war" to make the world safe for democracy, but had come home filled with bitterness and anger. "I had seen nothing sacred, and the things that were glorious had no glory and the sacrifices were like the stockyards at Chicago if nothing was done with the meat except to bury it," said one of Hemingway's characters in *A Farewell to Arms* (1929). It was difficult for young men to be idealistic after experiencing the horrors of war. Many American soldiers came home no longer believing in the ideals for which they had fought. They were convinced, wrote poet Ezra Pound in *Hugh Selwyn Mauberley* (1920), that ideals

were lies spread by old men. They had nothing left to believe in.

Gertrude Stein called the writers of the twenties the **Lost Generation** because of their disillusionment. It was true that few of these writers felt much at home in the America of the 1920s. They were dismayed by what Ezra Pound called the "Fordian" tendencies in American life—the worship of mechanical and material things. And they were put off by the smugness and self-satisfaction of the cities' business classes. The writers' contempt for these values was reflected in Sinclair Lewis's *Babbitt* (1922), in which the American businessman is caricatured in George F. Babbitt. The narrow-minded culture of the small town, which Lewis depicted in *Main Street* (1920), was equally unappealing. "It is an unimaginatively standardized background. . . . It is the Prohibition of happiness. . . . It is dullness made God," said Carol Kennicott, *Main Street*'s rebellious heroine. These writers felt disenchanted with urban and rural values of their time.

The writer most sympathetic to the materialism of the era was F. Scott Fitzgerald. He devoted a series of short stories and novels to the glittering, seemingly carefree life of the upper class. The income from his books—*This Side of Paradise* (1920), *The Beautiful and the Damned* (1922), and *The Great Gatsby* (1925)—permitted Fitzgerald to live on the fringe of that world. Although fascinated by the fast living, hard drinking, and heavy spending of fashionable society, he saw that they created a hollow life doomed to disaster.

► *Through his novels, F. Scott Fitzgerald helped create the image of the twenties as the Jazz Age, a carefree and materialistic era.*

Jazz Moves North

Jazz was born in New Orleans, where a mixture of African and European influences converged to produce this new musical style. It was a lively music created by the city's African American musicians, and improvisation was the main ingredient. Until World War I, jazz really flourished only in New Orleans. Here, artists created different tunes and arrangements each time they played. After that, traveling New Orleans musicians introduced jazz to other southern cities. With the coming of the war and the labor shortages in the North, large numbers of southern African Americans migrated to Chicago, New York, and other northern cities. Among them were many of the best jazz musicians from New Orleans.

By 1920, the center of jazz music had shifted to Chicago. King Oliver, the most widely acclaimed trumpet player of New Orleans, moved there in 1917. He organized the Creole Jazz Band, which came to represent Chicago jazz at its best. Oliver invited Louis Armstrong and other New Orleans musicians to Chicago to play in his band. In Chicago, New Orleans– style jazz bands got their first opportunity to make recordings. This, in turn, led musicians to pay greater attention to the technical details of their performances. Thus, Chicago jazz was New Orleans jazz carried to new technical heights.

▲ *King Oliver's jazz band played in Chicago in the early twenties. The young man with the cornet is Louis Armstrong. How did African American bands like King Oliver's help transform American music?*

▲ *Louis Armstrong played this cornet, an instrument similar to a trumpet but with a shorter range.*

In 1929, Louis Armstrong, arguably the best jazz trumpet player of all time, moved from Chicago to New York City. By then, New York, the center of the recording industry, had become the jazz capital of the nation. In New York, jazz went through another transformation. The small jazz bands of New Orleans and Chicago became large 15-piece ensembles that played in New York's huge Savoy Ballroom and Harlem's famous Cotton Club. New York's best-known jazz musicians were big-band leaders, such as African Americans Fletcher Henderson, Duke Ellington, and Count Basie. Their white counterparts included Paul Whiteman, Benny Goodman, and Glenn Miller.

Swing, the carefully composed arrangements played by the big bands of the 1930s, was one of the offshoots of jazz. By then, the original, highly improvised New Orleans–style jazz was played mainly in out-of-the-way nightclubs and bars. Polished up and toned down as swing, jazz became part of the mainstream of American culture.

1. How were audiences in the North introduced to New Orleans jazz?
2. How was the swing music of the 1930s related to jazz?

▲ *Langston Hughes, an African American writer, was a leader of the Harlem Renaissance. His writings conveyed a message of pride in race and self.*

The twenties also saw African American writers rebel against the dominant white culture. This movement, called the **Harlem Renaissance**, was led by a talented group of writers living in the ghetto of Harlem—Langston Hughes, Alain Locke, Zora Neale Hurston, Claude McKay, and others. These writers resisted the pressure to adopt white, middle-class values and ways of thought. "Why should I want to be white?" wrote Langston Hughes. "I am Negro—and beautiful." Jean Toomer's novel *Cane* (1923) and Alain Locke's essays carried the same message of racial pride. The Harlem Renaissance used literature and art to speak out against the racial injustice suffered by African Americans.

New Directions in Art and Music

The decade of the twenties was also a time of bold experimentation in American art. Much of the inspiration came from Europe, where painters and sculptors had already discarded the traditional approach in which art mimicked reality. During the twenties, New York produced its own community of artists devoted to modern art. Among these was Joseph Stella, a well-known American cubist painter. **Cubism** emphasized flat surfaces and geometric angles, with artists often fragmenting the figure and showing all sides at once. **Expressionist** artists, such as Georgia O'Keefe, did not try to portray real objects, but rather the feelings and emotions associated with objects. Edward Hopper painted stark urban landscapes that captured the loneliness of city life. The movement finally gained a measure of public recognition in 1929 with the opening in New York of the Museum of Modern Art. This was the first major gallery in the United States devoted exclusively to the newer forms of art.

American music also explored new avenues during the twenties. Black musicians migrating from the South to northern cities brought with them a new music called jazz. Jazz was fast-paced, blaring, and innovative. At first, it was played only in the African American nightclubs of Chicago's South Side and New York's Harlem. By the end of the decade, jazz had made its way into white dance halls, and had had a major impact on classical music. Searching for a distinctly American sound, composers such as George Gershwin and Aaron Copland incorporated elements of jazz into their work. "Jazz I regard as an American folk-music," Gershwin said. "I believe that it can be made the basis of serious symphonic works of lasting value." The result was Gershwin's *Rhapsody in Blue*, first performed in 1924, and his ballet *An American in Paris* (1928). Copland also incorporated the jazz motif into *Music for the Theatre* (1925) and *Piano Concerto* (1926). These compositions marked the arrival of a symphonic music with an unmistakable American style. Meanwhile, another black musical style, the blues, remained largely the province of African American female vocalists such as Billie Holiday.

SECTION 4 REVIEW

1. **Describe** some of the changes that took place in urban middle class values during the twenties.
2. **Describe** how leisure time activities changed during the twenties.
3. **Explain** why many American writers felt alienated from the traditional culture of the 1920s.
4. **Identify** the Harlem Renaissance.
5. **State** why you think the twenties were a period of literary and artistic creativity.

Americans' Reactions to Change

The American people had mixed feelings about the social changes taking place during the 1920s. Many Americans welcomed the technological changes. They applauded Henry Ford for making automobiles affordable, they went to the movies, and they bought new household appliances. Yet they also tried to keep a firm grip on traditional values. In some instances, these values were being undermined by the new technology. Small-town society, with its traditional way of life, seemed in danger of being swept away for good. "One by one, all our traditional moral standards went by the boards," remarked Hiram Wesley Evans, the head of the Ku Klux Klan, a white supremacist organization. Many Americans felt the need to slow down the rush of change.

How did rural and small-town Americans respond to the social changes of the twenties?

Why did many Americans want to restrict immigration?

Why did the Ku Klux Klan gain renewed popularity?

Politics and Change

The cultural values most directly threatened in the twenties were the traditional values of small-town and rural America. Most of the changes that had altered life in American cities since the turn of the century had not yet reached the countryside. The only major exceptions were the growing popularity of the automobile and small-town movie houses. In the towns and villages of the United States, social life still revolved around church socials, family reunions, county fairs, and holiday picnics. Women's place was still in the home, children treated their parents with respect, and most people worked hard and lived a frugal life. Rural Americans, for the most part, disapproved of the emerging values of the twenties.

Many Americans also felt threatened by the changes taking place in the world beyond the United States. Events in Russia were especially menacing. In 1917, the Russian Bolsheviks, or Communists, overthrew the czarist government. They imposed a dictatorship, executed many of their opponents, and abolished the private ownership of factories and banks. During the next two years, Communist parties took root in several European countries. A Communist government was established briefly in Hungary. Europe seemed to be a hotbed of political radicalism.

The federal government made it clear that it would not tolerate such extremism in the United States. In February 1919, the Justice Department rounded up 53 aliens on the West Coast and sent them to New York to be deported. The only charge against them was that they were Communists. Events that spring gave added weight to the fear that political radicals had selected the United States as their next target. On April 28, a bomb was discovered in the mailbox of the mayor of Seattle, who had recently earned the wrath of the labor movement by breaking a dockworkers' strike. The next day, the maid of Senator Thomas W. Hardwick of Georgia opened a package in the senator's mail. A bomb enclosed in the package blew her hands off. Investigators in the New York Post Office intercepted 16 other mail bombs. The packages were addressed to Attorney General A. Mitchell Palmer, Postmaster General Albert S. Burleson, and Supreme Court Justice Oliver Wendell Holmes, among other public officials. Bomb packages had also been addressed to banker J. P. Morgan and Standard Oil founder John D. Rockefeller.

The Red Scare   These threats to prominent Americans triggered the Red Scare of 1919–1920. Attorney General Palmer saw the mail bombs as proof of a Communist plot to overthrow the government. He ordered the Federal Bureau of Investigation (FBI) to infiltrate American Communist organizations. In December 1919, the government rounded up 249 known Russian Communists, or "Reds," and expelled them. On January 8, 1920, federal agents and local police swept down on Communist organizations in 33 cities, arresting some 4,000 suspects. Although radical immigrant aliens were the targets, many of the people jailed were American citizens and were not Communists. A third of those arrested were soon released for lack of evidence. Eventually 556 alien immigrants were deported because of their Communist Party membership. Even though Palmer never found proof of a plot to overthrow the government, the raids benefited him politically. He became a serious, but unsuccessful, contender for the 1920 Democratic presidential nomination.

▲ *The trial of Bartolomeo Vanzetti (left) and Nicola Sacco (right) attracted international attention. What factor complicated this murder trial?*

In the midst of the Red Scare, two Italian-born anarchists were arrested in South Braintree, Massachusetts, for the murder of a shoe-factory paymaster. The state of Massachusetts tried two known anarchists, Nicola Sacco and Bartolomeo Vanzetti, on murder charges. They were both convicted, even though little hard evidence of their guilt was ever produced. Many people were convinced that Sacco and Vanzetti were convicted because of their radical political views, on which the state prosecutor had focused during the case. Liberal and radical groups in Europe as well as in the United States protested the conviction, but without success. After a long delay to allow the state to reexamine the evidence, Sacco and Vanzetti died in the electric chair on August 23, 1927. By that time, the Red Scare had subsided, and Americans had turned their attention to other concerns.

Enforcement of Prohibition

The victory achieved by passage of the Eighteenth Amendment after World War I was more symbolic than real, as prohibition was impossible to enforce. In the larger cities, especially, the Volstead Act (the federal prohibition law enacted to carry out the amendment) was openly defied. Illegal saloons, or **speakeasies**, did a flourishing business. The small group of U. S. Treasury agents responsible for enforcing the law could not be everywhere at once, and local police usually looked the other way. "The old days when father spent his evenings at Cassidy's bar with the rest of the boys are gone, and probably gone forever," said Elmer Davis, a news reporter. "Cassidy may still be in business at the old stand and father may still go down there of an evening, but since prohibition mother goes down with him." In the cities, violating the Eighteenth Amendment became a new national pastime.

Although designed to improve the morals of the American people, prohibition had the ironic result of creating a crime wave. As the breweries and distilleries that had once legally supplied liquor stores and saloons were closed down, illegal ones took their places. Prohibition provided a golden opportunity for the criminal element in every American city. Gangsters like Al Capone in Chicago made enormous profits from the demand for illicit or "bootleg" beer, wine, and spirits. Fighting for control of this illegal business also led to a sharp increase in gangland violence. Prohibition created an illegal liquor industry that made crime more profitable than ever before.

▲ New York Speakeasy *is the title of this 1934 mural by Ben Shahn, sponsored by the Public Works Administration. Why was the Eighteenth Amendment a failure? (Museum of City of New York, Permanent Deposit of the Public Works Project through the Whitney Museum/©1995 Estate of Ben Shahn/Licensed by VAGA, New York, New York.)*

Immigration Restrictions

The most direct assault against the growing diversity of people and cultural values in urban America was the movement to restrict immigration. This movement was fueled in part by the dramatic increase in the number of immigrants since the 1890s. Some 650,000 immigrants entered the United States each year from 1907 to 1914. Although immigration declined during the war years, it resumed its previous level with the return of peace and was widely viewed as a problem. Labor unions complained that cheap immigrant labor cost American workers their jobs. Nativist (anti-immigrant) groups, such as the American Defense Society, warned that the new immigrants would be impossible to assimilate into American life. Unlike earlier waves of immigration, which had come mainly from England and northern Europe, the new immigrants were mostly Italians, Poles, and Jews from Russia and eastern Europe. With the Sacco and Vanzetti case still in the headlines, many Americans associated the new immigrants with radical politics. By 1921, the unions and the nativist groups had emerged as a powerful coalition determined to put an end to unrestricted immigration.

Under pressure to halt the flood of newcomers, Congress in 1921 passed the **Emergency Quota Law**. It marked a major departure from past policy by restricting the number of immigrants permitted each year from Europe. The Emergency Quota Law also established a precedent by setting an annual quota based on a percentage of the number of foreign-born already living in this country. The quota for Italy, for example, was 3 percent of the Italian-born population reported in the 1910 census, or about 42,000 immigrants per year. No longer would the United States be the unrestricted haven for Europe's "huddled masses yearning to breathe free," as American poet Emma Lazarus wrote.

Although the new law reduced the number of immigrants to a maximum of about 350,000 a year, there were those who wanted even tighter restrictions. They especially wanted to reduce the number of immigrants from southern and eastern Europe. Advocates of restriction urged using the 1890 census, when most immigrants still came from northern Europe, as the baseline for determining quotas. Using that census and allowing only 2 percent of each group based on national origin to enter would reduce Italian immigration, for example, from 42,000 to a mere 4,000 persons each year. In 1924, Congress incorporated that proposal into the new National Origins Act, which restricted the flow of

Enduring Constitution

Clear and Present Danger

The freedoms listed in the Bill of Rights were very important to the founders of the United States. But there is always a problem with freedom—how far does it go? Can a person cry "Fire!" in a theater when there is no fire and escape punishment for creating a panic?

In 1798, the Federalists had passed the Alien and Sedition Acts aimed at preventing false, scandalous criticism of the president and Congress. Other parts of the acts restricted the rights of aliens, or non-citizens.

When these acts were passed, no one challenged them in court as being unconstitutional. The Federalists argued that freedom of speech had to be limited because of the question of national security. These laws soon proved extremely unpopular and were not renewed in the next administration.

The conflict between freedom of speech and the need to maintain national security erupted again during Abraham Lincoln's presidency. Lincoln barred border-state critics of the Civil War by suppressing critical

▲ *Is the yelling of "Fire!" in a crowded theater when there is no fire a kind of free speech that is protected by the First Amendment?*

newspapers, mail, and pamphlets. He also made it difficult for public meetings to be held to criticize the northern efforts in the war. He argued that the nation's security was at stake and that he had to stop criticism of the war by northerners who sympathized with the South. After the Civil War, there was not a serious political dispute over freedom of speech until the next century.

The Espionage Act was passed by the United States Congress in 1917. It prohibited opposing the military draft and acts of speech by citizens that would adversely affect feelings toward the military. One of the

most famous freedom of speech cases dealing with the Espionage Act of 1917 was *Schenck v. United States.* Schenck was a socialist who thought the U.S. should not be in World War I. He printed some pamphlets that opposed the war and military drafts.

Schenck was tried and found guilty in a lower court. He appealed on the grounds that the Espionage Act violated the First Amendment's freedom of speech and press clauses. He argued that the First Amendment was absolute whether the country was at war or not. The government argued that the national security was at stake and, if Schenck was

Enduring Constitution

(continued)

successful in persuading others to avoid military service or harming the war effort, the security of the nation could be severely threatened.

The United States Supreme Court's ruling stated that, while the things which Schenck talked about and printed in his brochures would have been protected in peace time, the right to free speech depended upon the circumstances. One could not shout "Fire!" in a theater when there was none, cause a panic, and claim the shout didn't cause anything. The court then gave a rule or guide to use for future freedom of speech and national security cases. If the speech, or the circumstances in which it was uttered, created a *clear and present danger* to society, then the government had the right to regulate the speech.

The clear-and-present-danger test means that the speech has to clearly show that the speaker or writer wants to do things that are dangerous to the welfare of the country. It also means that the speaker or writer intends to do those things immediately, not sometime in the future. This test has not been as much a restriction on free speech as at first thought. It is hard to prove that merely speaking about issues and politics would cause a danger to the country. And, over time, the Court narrowed the range of discussion that could be considered dangerous. Professional advocacy groups, such as the American Civil Liberties Union, arose to act as watchdogs to preserve civil and political liberties.

This famous clear-and-present-danger test was used in many subsequent cases. But the important thing is that freedom of speech continues to be an integral part of our enduring Constitution.

1. In your opinion were the Alien and Sedition Acts constitutional?
2. In your own words, state what is meant by the clear-and-present-danger test.

---

immigrants still further. Immigration from eastern and southern Europe was reduced to a trickle. Immigration from Japan was prohibited completely, just as Chinese immigration had been outlawed since 1882. The Japanese viewed the new law as an insult, and it was a severe blow to Japanese-American relations.

Revival of the Ku Klux Klan

Among the groups that took credit for the passage of the National Origins Act of 1924 was the Ku Klux Klan. Like its namesake of the Reconstruction era, the Klan was a racist organization dedicated to white supremacy. Unlike the earlier Klan, it was strongly nativist. In many instances the Klan operated like a secret society, engaging in activities aimed at terrorizing "foreign and impure" elements in American society. When intimidation failed, the Klan often resorted to violence, including beatings, arson, and lynchings. At Klan rallies, speakers lashed out against Catholics, Jews, immigrants, and any alien influence that might threaten to undermine "100 percent Americanism." Its membership was limited to "native-born, white American citizens who believe in the tenets of the Christian religion." As a Klan spokesman declared, "The nation is Protestant and must remain so." The Klan felt that traditional Protestant beliefs served as a check against what Klan leader Hiram Wesley Evans called the "moral breakdown" of recent years.

From a modest beginning as a fraternal lodge founded in Atlanta in 1915, the Klan grew during the 1920s into a powerful movement. By 1925, it had over a million members. It especially appealed to the residents of small towns in the South and Midwest and to native-born whites who had migrated to the cities. Many of these people had experienced firsthand competition for jobs and housing from immigrants and African Americans. They were people who sensed that traditional values and the old-time religion were being overwhelmed by the forces of change.

For a brief time, the Klan achieved modest political influence. It was a force behind immigration restriction, and it helped to elect nativist candidates to public office. During the peak of its influence in 1924–1925, candidates endorsed by the Klan were elected governor of Indiana, mayor of Denver, and to a variety of municipal and county offices elsewhere. But the Klan's political impact was short-lived. By 1926, the Klan was in decline, embarrassed by scandals and reports of corruption among its leaders. By the end of the decade, the Ku Klux Klan had ceased to be a significant factor in American politics, without having slowed the pace of social and cultural change.

▲ *The Ku Klux Klan became politically influential during the 1920s. In 1926 they organized a parade in Washington, D.C. How do you think the public would react to such a parade today?*

The Scopes Trial

The most celebrated clash during the 1920s between traditional beliefs and modern ideas took place at the **Scopes trial** in Dayton, Tennessee. The trial concerned the teaching of the scientific theory of evolution in the public schools. **Fundamentalist** Christians, who believed in a literal interpretation of the Bible, opposed the teaching of evolution in the public schools. In 1925, Tennessee declared it unlawful for the public schools "to teach any theory that denies the story of the divine creation of man as taught in the Bible, and to teach instead that man has descended from a lower order of animals." By the end of the decade, Mississippi and Arkansas had

adopted similar laws. The state of Texas ordered the deletion of all references to evolution from state-adopted textbooks. To test the Tennessee law, John Thomas Scopes, a young biology teacher at Dayton's Central High School, agreed to violate the statute by openly teaching the evolution theory. Scopes was promptly arrested and a trial date set.

The trial that began in July 1925 became one of the most celebrated courtroom battles of modern times. At stake was a great deal more than the guilt or innocence of a teacher of biology. The Scopes trial was a contest between fundamentalist religion and modern scientific ideas. To help argue its case, the state enlisted William Jennings Bryan, three-time presidential candidate and a prominent fundamentalist. To defend Scopes's right to teach evolution in the classroom, the American Civil Liberties Union sent the famous trial lawyer Clarence Darrow to Dayton. Darrow had gained a

Clarence Darrow (left) and William Jennings Bryan (right) were the lead lawyers at the 1925 Scopes trial in Dayton, Tennessee. Why was this trial one of the most celebrated courtroom battles of the 1920s?

reputation for championing civil liberties and he often successfully defended his clients even when public sentiment ran strongly against them.

The climax of the trial came when Bryan took the stand to testify in support of divine creation. Bryan acknowledged his belief that Eve was created by God from Adam's rib, that Jonah was swallowed by the whale, and that the earth was created in 4004 B.C., as biblical evidence suggested. To his fundamentalist friends, Bryan was a hero. Rationalist thinkers who followed the Dayton trial in their newspapers thought Darrow had won by exposing what they saw as Bryan's simplistic views. Scopes was convicted and fined $100 for breaking the law. The evolutionists and the fundamentalists each claimed a resounding victory. This suggests how deeply Americans were divided over cultural values.

SECTION 5 REVIEW

1. **Identify** Sacco and Vanzetti.
2. **Name** an unintended negative result of prohibition.
3. **List** the provisions of the new immigration laws that were enacted during the twenties.
4. **State** reasons for the renewed interest in the Ku Klux Klan during this time.
5. **Explain** why supporters of both Clarence Darrow and William Jennings Bryan regarded the Scopes trial as a victory.

Summary

For most Americans, the decade of the 1920s was a time of prosperity. It was a time of rapid growth in American industry, with the construction, automobile, and public utilities industries leading the way. New methods of mass production made American workers more productive than ever before. The result was a higher standard of living for most workers and much higher profits for businesses and corporations. Profits were also increased by the tax and tariff policies of three successive Republican presidents. The administrations of Warren G. Harding, Calvin Coolidge, and Herbert Hoover pursued a foreign policy designed to extend and protect American overseas investments and trade.

The twenties were an era of dramatic social change in the United States. Women won the right to vote and went on to gain a greater measure of economic independence. Although European immigration declined with the passage of restrictive acts, migration of rural Americans to the cities continued. African Americans migrated from the rural South to northern industrial cities in large numbers. They were confined to low-paying jobs and to housing in the poorest neighborhoods. Racial discrimination made movement out of these ghettos nearly impossible. Cities grew upward and outward. Skyscrapers and suburban neighborhoods became common features of the landscape.

Many Americans were disturbed by the changes of the 1920s. They were alarmed that young people were rebelling against the Victorian standards of morality. Some Americans felt traditional values were being eroded as society was becoming culturally more diverse. The resurgence of nativism made groups like the Ku Klux Klan more popular.

Vocabulary

consumer goods

cubism

expressionism

flapper

fundamentalist

growth industry

productivity

rule of reason

speakeasy

suburb

Match the vocabulary terms with the definitions found below. Write the term on your paper next to the number of its descriptive phrase.

1. an illegal saloon operating during prohibition
2. criteria or test for determining if a merger is legal
3. important contributor to the economy
4. style of painting that emphasizes geometric planes and angles
5. liberated woman of the twenties
6. strict interpreter of biblical scripture
7. products that help to raise the standard of living
8. style of painting that emphasizes emotional responses to objects
9. residential area on the outskirts of a city
10. rate of worker output

Review Questions

1. Why were the 1920s a time of prosperity?
2. Explain why corporate profits rose faster than wages.
3. What contributed to the rapid growth of cities during the twenties?
4. Account for the growth of African American communities in northern cities.
5. How did Republican economic policies contribute to the economic boom of the twenties?
6. Describe the role played by the United States in the reconstruction of postwar Europe.
7. What changes occurred in the way Americans spent their leisure time during the twenties?
8. Give one explanation for the flowering of African American literature during the Harlem Renaissance.
9. How successful was the movement to restrict immigration during the twenties?
10. Account for the temporary popularity of groups such as the Ku Klux Klan.

Critical Historical Thinking

Writing Answer each of the following by writing one or more complete paragraphs:

1. Discuss the reasons many Americans felt laws restricting immigration were justified. Do you think that any of these conditions or reasons still exist today?

2. Consumerism (the frequent buying of goods and services) has its roots in the prosperous twenties. Discuss whether the trend of increased consumer buying has had overall positive or negative effects on the quality of life in America. How have lifestyles and working patterns been affected?

3. Do you think that it is generally helpful or harmful to have similar aims and goals for business and government? Give reasons and examples for your answer.

4. Read the selection entitled "The Flappers" in the Unit 7 Archives. Although written in 1927, the tone is such that it could have been written today. Have the complaints of the older generation toward the younger generation changed much since then? Discuss what you think would be the main criticisms against today's generation of young women. Write your answer mimicking the style of the father's lament.

Making Connections with Literature and Music

Harlem, a fashionable suburb of New York City in the 1880s, was the object of wild land speculation and overdevelopment in the 1890s. Harlem became one of the few places in America where African Americans had access to decent housing. For African Americans, Harlem became a political and cultural capital. African American writers such as Langston Hughes, Alain Locke, Countee Cullen, Claude McKay, Zora Lee Hurston, and many others addressed every aspect of the social, economic, and cultural conditions. Night clubs, such as the Cotton Club and Cafe Society became the center of New York's jazz scene, even though African Americans were not allowed in the Cotton Club except as entertainers. Musicians such as Duke Ellington, Fats Waller, Cab Caloway, and Count Basie met and worked in Harlem. While the Great Depression marked the end of the Harlem Renaissance, its legacy is to be found in all forms of contemporary jazz, the African American cultural revival of the 1970s, and the current popularity of African American artists, writers, and dancers.

■ Research one of the African American writers or musicians mentioned above and prepare a report, visual display, or oral presentation of his or her life and work.

Additional Skills Practice

Use the following data to create a bar graph that shows trends in immigration for the twenties. Then write a sentence that accurately describes the trend for immigrants from these regions during the 1920s.

Region	Number of Immigrants (in Thousands)		
	1921	1925	1930
Eastern and Southern Europe	335	15	25
Northern and Central Europe	305	125	115
Latin America	50	35	20
Asia	25	3	3

The Great Crash and the Depression

The prosperity of the 1920s ended abruptly in the most severe economic depression in history. Millions of Americans would remember the stock market crash of 1929 as the beginning of the worst years of their lives. Most did not even have money invested in stocks. Nevertheless, the depression threatened jobs, savings, and even people's homes. Unemployment soared to new heights, and "NO HELP WANTED" signs went up on factory gates across the nation. As savings ran out and banks foreclosed on mortgages, people became desperate. "What is going to become of us?" asked a resident of Arizona. "I've lost twelve and a half pounds this last month, just thinking. You can't sleep, you know. You wake up about 2:00 A.M., and you lie and think." For countless people, these were hard times, years of worrying and of wondering if things could get any worse.

▲ *This stock ticker machine printed out a tape that listed the current stock values.*

The Beginning of the Great Depression

For millions of Americans during the 1920s, the stock market was the symbol of wealth, success, and prosperity. Anyone could get rich by investing in stocks, said John J. Raskob, chairman of General Motors. "If a man saves $15 a week, and invests in good common stocks and allows the dividends and rights to accumulate, at the end of 20 years he will have at least $80,000 and an income from investments of $400 a month. He will be rich.... I am firm in my belief that anyone not only can be rich, but ought to be rich." With modern advertising techniques and the promise of getting rich quickly, stockbrokers lured more investors into the market than ever before.

What caused the boom in the stock market?
Why did the stock market crash in 1929?
Why did the Wall Street crash lead to a national depression?

▲ *Corporate stocks were bought and sold on the floor of the New York Stock Exchange. Why did the price of stocks increase dramatically during 1928 and much of 1929?*

Soaring Stock Values

When Raskob was being interviewed in 1929, the stock market was near the peak of rising stock prices. It was an extraordinary performance. After making steady gains over the previous six years, the market suddenly shot upward in the spring of 1928. For the next 18 months, stock prices soared. Radio Corporation of America (RCA), one of the glamour stocks of the 1920s, went from $94.50 a share in March 1928 to $505.00 by September 1929. During that same period, Montgomery Ward stock advanced from $132.00 to $466.00 and Westinghouse from $91.00 to $313.00. Most of the gains were purely speculative. In other words, the gains did not represent an increase in the real value of the nation's industrial corporations. The stock prices instead were pushed higher as investors kept putting more money into them, hoping that the prices would continue to go higher still. This cycle was called **stock speculation** because investors were taking a chance on making huge profits in the future.

No one knows for certain what started the mania of stock speculation in 1928. Decisions by major investors to take money out of their European investments and put it into American stocks were partly responsible. The ability of investors to buy stocks **on margin**—paying as little as 10 percent down and borrowing the rest from the stockbroker—made speculation easier. The Federal Reserve Board may have contributed to the fever of speculation by lowering the interest rate that it charged member banks to borrow money. This made it easier for the banks to loan money to stockbrokers, who, in turn, used it to let investors buy on margin. The cycle encouraged further speculation.

While all of these factors doubtless contributed to the stock market boom, the basic cause, historian Robert S. McElvaine argues, was "the notion that it was easy to get rich quickly." Investors once bought stocks largely for their earning power—their ability to reward the investor by paying dividends. This kept stock prices in check, as dividends were pegged not to the price of the stock but to the earning power of the company. Investors shied away from stocks with high prices that paid low dividends. However, by 1929, people bought stocks largely to

► *Wall Street—in New York's financial district—reacted with panic during the early days of the Great Crash.*

▼ *The front page of* The Boston Daily Globe *on Friday, October 25, 1929, predicted a rally in the stock market. How did investors react to this news during the following week?*

The Boston Daily Globe

BOSTON, FRIDAY MORNING, OCTOBER 25, 1929—FIFTY-SIX PAGES

BIG CRASH AND RALLY IN STOCKS

All Records for Severity of Decline Broken---12,894,650 Shares Traded In, a New High Mark---Tape 160 Minutes Behind at Close---Pool Formed at Morgan Office at Conference of Bankers Checks Headlong Break; Then Some Stocks Recover 10 to 20 Points---Banks and Brokers Sound

BALLOT PROBE IS STOPPED BY JUDGE

Defied by Curley and Ward Bolster Ends Hearing

Mansfield Signature Investigation May Result in Police Action

BURGESS IS GIVEN TEN TO TWENTY YEARS

Judge Fosdick Sentences Him Schoolmate

$100,000 FIRE LOSS TO HOME IN HINGHAM

Thayer Estate Destroyed by Blaze of Undetermined Origin—House Closed Wednesday For Winter

TIPSY DRIVING CASE SENTENCE DOUBLED

WALL ST WORKERS LABOR ALL NIGHT

Strive to Unravel Tangled Affairs Before Opening Today; Throngs Choke District

Wild Scenes on Exchange During Height of Selling Stampede, Extra Police Summoned

Thousands Ruined as Runaway Market Forces Brokers to Toss Their Holdings Over

BUSINESS IS SOUND BANKERS DECLARE

Review Stock Situation in Morgan Offices

---

reap profits by selling them later at a higher price. They bought on the speculation that the price would keep going up, no matter how small the dividend. RCA stock, for example, rose over 500 percent in less than two years, although it had never paid a dividend. Its price was based solely on investors' confidence that the stock price would con-

tinue to go up. All that was needed to puncture the bubble of confidence was a series of bad days when stock prices fell sharply. A general collapse in the value of stocks would almost certainly follow. That was exactly what happened in October 1929.

The Great Crash

After reaching a peak in early September 1929, stock prices began a moderate decline through mid-October. Then, during the last hour of trading on Wednesday, October 23, the value of stocks listed on the New York exchange suddenly dropped an average of $21.00 a share (or 21 points in stock market terminology). By the next morning, stockbrokers throughout the country were flooded with orders to sell. The rush of selling on Thursday, October 24, reduced stock values even more sharply. The plunge was halted only by the action of a group of Wall Street bankers, who combined to invest heavily in stocks as a show of confidence. On the following Monday and Tuesday, however, stock values utterly collapsed. On **Black Tuesday**, October 29, 1929, the average value of the stocks monitored each day by the *New York Times* fell an unprecedented 45 points, with 16.4 million shares changing hands.

Although Black Tuesday was the worst day of the Great Crash, the plunge of stock prices continued. By the end of the year, the *New York Times* stock exchange index was off 228 points from its early October high. In ten weeks, 50 percent of the value of stocks had been lost. The stock market would drop even lower during the three years to come, as the Great Crash of 1929 led to the Great Depression of the 1930s.

The Great Depression

The stock market crash led to a disastrous economic depression. It was not the first depression that Americans had experienced, but it was the most severe. During the next four years, the annual gross national product tumbled from $104 billion to $74 billion. As business declined, unemployment skyrocketed. By 1932, 12 million people, or nearly one-fourth of the workforce, were unemployed. Americans by the hundreds of thousands lost their life's savings as investments became worthless and banks failed. Although historians and economists are

not entirely certain why the stock market crash led to such a devastating depression, several factors seem to have been involved.

Recession The crash on Wall Street accelerated a recession, or downward turn in the economy, that was already under way. The housing industry, a growth industry of the early 1920s, was having trouble. The number of new houses built had been falling since 1926, creating rising unemployment in that industry. Automobile sales had dropped off in the spring of 1929 and had not recovered. Investment in manufacturing plants and equipment was declining, and inventories of unsold goods were growing. The stock market collapse helped to turn this recession into a major economic depression.

In trying to explain why the prosperity of the 1920s was so short-lived, historians have also pointed out that some areas of the economy were depressed long before 1929. The decade of the 1920s was not a good time for American farmers. Crop prices, which had risen during World War I, collapsed with the return of peace as European farms once again began to produce. Export sales of U.S. grain and meat dropped, huge agricultural surpluses were created, and crop prices fell. By 1924 average per capita farm income was only 37 percent of the average per capita national income. The railroads were also a "sick industry" during the 1920s. As people became more dependent on autos and trucks, passenger traffic declined, and freight

▶

What does this graph suggest about the relationship between the decline in the gross national product and the stock market crash of October 1929?

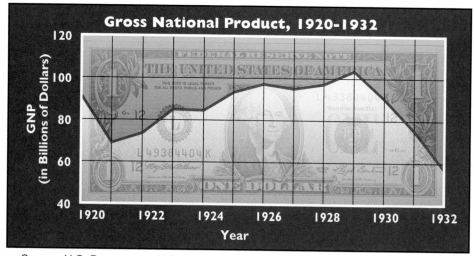

Source: U.S. Department of Commerce, Bureau of the Census.

American Landscape

People–Environment: The Dust Bowl

Farming the Great Plains. The last fertile region in the American West to be settled was the Great Plains, the dry western half of the Central Plains. The Great Plains is a semiarid grassland located between the 100th meridian and the Rocky Mountains. These treeless plains stretch from Texas to Canada and cover almost a quarter of the continental United States. Deeply matted turf, uncertain rainfall, scanty fuel, blizzards, and tornadoes discouraged early settlers. This region remained the province of buffalo-hunting Plains Indians while wagon trains moved across it to reach more promising land in Oregon and California.

Then Congress passed the Homestead Act in 1862, throwing an area as large as Texas open to settlement. Most of this land was located in the semiarid grasslands of the Great Plains.

In addition to cheap land, three newly-invented machines made farming the Great Plains practical. These were the steel plow, which turned the sod and exposed the soil; windmills, which pumped underground water to the surface; and barbed wire for keeping animals out of grain fields.

As 430 million acres of new land were settled, the population of the Great Plains increased rapidly. More homesteaders kept coming each decade. They plowed up the short grass prairies and planted wheat. In drier areas, they grazed cattle.

The great demand for wheat during World War I extended wheat cultivation deeper into the dry western margins of the Great Plains. Millions of acres of former grazing land were put to the plow.

Environmental Damage. Plowing the Great Plains tore up the root systems of the grasses that had anchored its fertile topsoil in place. Moreover, the land was left bare for several months after each harvest, exposing its surface to the fierce winds that often sweep over this region. In ranching areas, overgrazing destroyed large areas of grass. Gradually the land was laid bare. Unusually good rains in the 1920s disguised this environmental damage and encouraged homesteaders to plant even more.

But in the 1930s, drought struck. The Great Plains began to blow away. Crops died in the fields. Cattle starved. Winds ravaged the land and hurled great clouds of yellow dust high into the air. One such storm is described by the ballad singer Woody Guthrie:

The storm took place at sundown
It lasted through the night.
When we looked out next morning
We saw a terrible sight.

We saw outside our window
Where wheat fields they had grown,

Was now a rippling ocean
Of dust the wind had blown.

It covered up our fences,
It covered up our barns,
It covered up our tractors,
In this wild and dusty storm.

We loaded our jalopies
And piled our families in,
We rattled down the highway
To never come back again.

These "black blizzards" carried the fertile soil of the Great Plains to cities on the East Coast and far out into the Atlantic. Nineteen states in the heartland of America became a vast dust bowl. Twenty-foot sand dunes drifted across roads and buried homes. Farms were abandoned. Farm families piled into cars with their few possessions to escape to a better life. The "Okies" from Oklahoma and "Arkies" from Arkansas fled westward to become migrant laborers in California, a journey poignantly described in John Steinbeck's novel, *The Grapes of Wrath*. All told, some 400,000 people left the Great Plains, victims of a combination of severe drought and poor soil conservation practices.

1. What two factors led to dust-bowl conditions on the Great Plains in the 1930s?
2. Why did farmers cultivate the western margins of the Great Plains?

revenues leveled off. The cotton textile industry entered a slump because people began to wear more clothing made of synthetic fibers. Shipbuilding, coal mining, and leather-goods manufacturing were also ailing industries. While these weak areas did not cause the depression, they made matters worse once the depression was under way.

Income Distribution Some historians argue that an uneven distribution of income in the United States was the fundamental cause of the depression. Although wages and salaries had increased during the decade, 70 percent of American families in 1929 still lived on incomes below $2,500 a year. That placed a ceiling on how much they could spend.

A substantial increase in buying goods on installment plans did permit consumers to spend beyond the limits of their income. **Installment buying** allowed people to pay for expensive items by making monthly payments, usually with interest or a carrying charge added. By the end of the decade, three out of every five automobiles and four out of every five radios were bought with installment credit. But credit sales could not keep the wheels of industry turning forever. By 1929, many American families had reached the limit of their ability to take on new payments.

Much of the income that might have been spent on consumer goods ended up in the savings accounts of a small percentage of the population. By 1925, the 5 percent of people with the highest incomes received about one-third of all personal income. This placed a brake on continued economic expansion. Moreover, at least part of the money in the savings accounts of the wealthy was being used by 1929 for speculating in the stock market. The unequal distribution of income "was only one among many roots of the Great Depression," concluded historian Robert S. McElvaine, "but it was the taproot."

After the stock market crash, the recession steadily worsened. Consumer spending declined sharply in 1930, greatly reducing the market for manufactured goods. As sales declined, employers cut back on production and reduced their workforce. Unemployment rose from about 1 million in 1929 to 4 million a year later and to 8 million in 1931. The economic decline was accelerated in October 1930 by a **banking panic**. Depositors rushed to withdraw their savings from threatened banks, which forced the banks either to call in their loans or to close their doors. Bank failures and the general contraction of credit further reduced the supply of money available for the needs of business.

International and Federal Factors International factors contributed to the worsening of the depression. A rash of bank failures in Europe in 1931 led to a drain of gold out of the United States and to a further reduction of the money supply. The beginning of the depression in Europe crippled foreign trade and pushed down prices even more.

Policies of the federal government made the situation even worse. Republicans traditionally favored high tariffs to protect American producers from foreign competition. The crash of 1929 gave the tariff issue added urgency, as manufacturers clamored for tariff protection. The result was the Hawley-Smoot Tariff of 1930, which raised tariff duties substantially. However, as domestic spending continued to fall, it did little to help American manufacturers. They soon found it more difficult to sell their goods abroad, because European nations responded to the new tariff by imposing higher duties on American imports. Thus, the new tariff had the effect of decreasing international trade at the very time that it needed to be increased. The economic situation in the United States was further aggravated in 1932, when Congress passed a large income tax increase. Enacted to help balance the federal budget, the tax hike further reduced take-home pay and the purchasing power of consumers.

SECTION 1 REVIEW

1. **Describe** how buying stock on margin contributed to the stock market boom.
2. **Explain** why the Federal Reserve Board's decision to ease credit contributed to speculation in stocks.
3. **Name** sectors of the American economy that were in trouble before the stock market crash.
4. **Define** the term *banking panic*.
5. **Explain** briefly why some economists think that the federal government was partly responsible for the depression.

The American People in Hard Times

On May 3, 1932, a heavily bearded man in a faded brown suit was arrested in Brooklyn and charged with vagrancy. Langlan Heinz, age 44, had violated the law by sleeping in a vacant lot. At his appearance in court, Heinz told the judge that he was an unemployed civil engineer, a graduate of the University of Colorado. In recent years, he had worked for the city of New York, as a draftsman in Shanghai, and for an oil company in Venezuela. He had most recently been employed by a factory in Naples, Italy. He had arrived back in New York in January 1932, but could find no work of any kind. When his savings were used up, Heinz left his hotel in Manhattan and moved to the vacant lot. He lived on food given to him by the housewives and children in the neighborhood. When the police officer arrested him, Heinz had lived in that lot, sleeping on an improvised cot, for a month and a half.

How did the depression affect American families?
What special obstacles did women face?
How did minority groups fare during the depression?

▲ *This photograph captured the despair felt by many out-of-work people during the Great Depression.*

The Suffering of the Unemployed

For the 12 million workers unemployed by 1932, hard times had brought an end to the American dream. Langlan Heinz and thousands like him suddenly found themselves destitute. "We do not dare to use even a little soap, when it will pay for an extra egg or a few more carrots for our children," said an unemployed father in Oregon. Even those who kept their jobs found life more difficult than it was before. Many worked only part time and at sharply reduced wages.

Although the depression affected nearly everyone, the unemployed suffered the most. Shocked by the loss of their jobs, their first response was to look for a new one. At first, most were confident they could find work of some kind. That confidence faded as days of job hunting stretched into months. "You can get pretty discouraged and your soles can get pretty thin after you've been job hunting a couple of months," reported a man from Minnesota. A job hunter in Baltimore said he walked 20 miles in a single day searching for work. "I just stopped everyplace, but mostly they wouldn't even talk to me," he said. The unemployed felt guilty as well as discouraged. They had always been told that there was something wrong with a person who could not get a job. As a woman in Houston said, "I'm just no good, I guess. I've given up ever amounting to anything. It's no use." The unemployed were finally reduced to accepting charity or government handouts, which many found distasteful and humiliating.

Families Face Economic Crisis

The depression placed new pressures on the American family. For millions of households, unemployment or reduced wages brought sharp cutbacks in the standard of living. The depression threatened the very existence of some families.

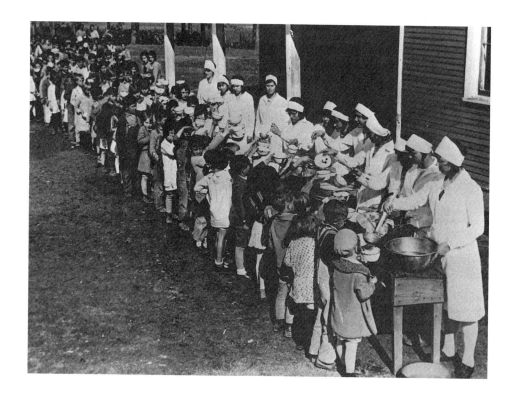

Charities and government agencies provided many children with free lunches during the depression.

How families responded to this crisis varied. Those families in which cooperation and sharing were commonplace helped each other through the hard times. The depression even brought some families closer together. "We got enough to get along on, and we got each other," said a shoe factory worker. "That should be enough to make anybody happy." On the other hand, husbands and wives who had problems before the depression often found those problems getting worse. Disharmony increased in many families, yet fewer marriages during the depression years ended in divorce. "I found a great many men and women who . . . stayed together mainly or merely for economic reasons," noted one observer, "figuring that apart they probably would even be worse off than they were together."

The depression put increased stress on those families that did stay together. Fathers who were unemployed and no longer able to support the family in comfort often lost status and sometimes respect. As one unemployed father explained to a social worker, "It's perfectly true that my word is not law around here as it once was. When they see me hanging around the house all the time and know

▼ *Apple vendors were commonly seen in New York City in 1932. Why did this man have to rely on selling apples to make a living?*

that I can't find work, it has its effect all right." Tensions sometimes developed between unemployed fathers and teenage sons who had found work selling newspapers or shining shoes. As the family's income earner, the son assumed that he and not the father should be looked up to as the head of the family. Working mothers also gained status at the expense of husbands, when the latter were unemployed. This was another potential source of conflict.

During the depression years, married women were caught in a double bind. Many had to go to work to help support the family. Yet they were also widely criticized for taking work away from

AMERICAN SCENES

Homeless Americans of the Great Depression

Early in the Great Depression, Thomas Minehan, a sociologist at the University of Minnesota, set out to discover how homeless people were faring. Disguised as a tramp, he talked to people standing in soup lines, visited camps of transient homeless people (known as hoboes), and hitched rides with the homeless on freight trains. It was, he discovered, a hard life, especially in winter. The transient homeless were hungry, suffered from frostbite, and risked being maimed in railroad accidents.

Large numbers of the homeless were boys and girls. Minehan estimated that the total number of homeless youth might be as high as 250,000, or one out of six of the estimated 1.5 million homeless Americans. They were outcasts from families that no longer could or would take care of them. "One woman asked me why did I leave home," said "Texas," a boy with whom Minehan shared a boxcar one day, "and I answers, 'Hard

▲ *Young hoboes ride a freight train.*

times, lady!' Just like that. 'Hard times, lady, hard times.'"

Many also came from broken or abusive homes. Either their parents had divorced or fathers had died or one or both of their parents were abusive. "Did I ever get a licking [beating] at home?" asked

one boy. "That's all I ever got. The old man would lick me if I did something. The old lady if I didn't."

The homeless youth of the Great Depression were part of a much larger number of homeless, unemployed Americans. They were like an army, camped out in shantytowns on the outskirts of cities or in shelters provided by local governments. One shelter, New York City's municipal lodging house, was a converted warehouse with 1,500 cots. The city proudly advertised it as "the world's largest bedroom." It was hardly a home, but it was more than most cities offered the homeless of the Great Depression.

1. Why were many young people among the transient homeless?
2. Explain why New York City boasted having "the world's largest bedroom" during the depression.

▲ *Nearly 5,000 people lined up at the New York State Labor Bureau the day the first federal relief jobs became available.*

ply fire the women, who shouldn't be working anyway, and hire the men. Presto! No unemployment. No relief rolls. No depression." Discrimination on the basis of sex in hiring did increase during the 1930s. For example, 77 percent of the school districts in the United States stopped hiring women. The depression gave a renewed vitality to the old notion that a woman's place was in the home. "We like our women to be at home," a Massachusetts fisherman said. It was widely assumed that the return of good times would see fewer women working outside the home. This attitude continued to be an obstacle for women who wanted to work in the years following the depression.

Hard-Hit Minorities

unemployed men. Women were resented for holding jobs for which men were qualified. Some people even insisted that the depression would be over quickly if women quit working. Journalist Norman Cousins described this commonly held view: "Sim-

Always among "the last hired and the first fired," African Americans suffered more than any other single group. Unemployment among blacks soared to about 50 percent by 1932, twice the national average. Unemployment was severe in the northern industrial centers to which many African Americans had migrated. The less desirable service jobs that

▶

Evicted from land they had farmed, sharecroppers settled in improvised camps. Why did the Great Depression hit African Americans especially hard?

were once reserved for African Americans—domestic servants, garbage collectors, elevator operators, bellhops—were now more sought after by white people. In many cities, the cry went up that African Americans should be fired from such jobs as long as white people remained unemployed.

The early 1930s saw a revival of racial violence, especially in the South. As a writer for the *New Republic* reported in 1931, "dust has been blown from the shotgun, the whip, and the noose, and Ku Klux [Klan] practices were being resumed in the certainty that dead men not only tell no tales but create vacancies." Lynchings increased from eight in 1932 to 28 in 1933.

Immigrants from Mexico also suffered during the depression. During the prosperous twenties, large numbers of Hispanic people entered the United States. By 1930 the total number had reached 1.5 million. Most worked as migrant farmworkers in the Southwest. As the depression began, the demand for their labor decreased. When the migrant workers were able to find work, the pay was extremely low. Pecan shellers in Texas had to support their families on an income of $1.50 to $4.00 per week. As a result, 88 percent of the workers had to receive assistance from charities in order to survive.

Nevertheless, immigrants continued to arrive from Mexico throughout the depression years. Although wages were low in the United States, economic conditions were much worse in Mexico. As the immigrants made their way north, they discovered that in many places they were not welcome. Local governments and federal authorities deported Mexican immigrants by the tens of thousands.

SECTION 2 REVIEW

1. **Describe** some problems faced by newly unemployed people.
2. **Explain** how the depression created stresses within the family.
3. **Name** ways that working women were affected by the depression.
4. **Explain** why the depression was hardest on African Americans.
5. **State** one reason racist acts increased in this period.

Herbert Hoover and the Depression

On the day after the great stock market crash of October 29, 1929, President Herbert Hoover held a press conference. As he met with the reporters, the nation was still dazed by the sudden collapse of stock values. No one was certain what the future held. When asked what effect the crash would have on the prosperity of the country, Hoover replied confidently that "the fundamental business of the country, that is production and distribution of commodities, is on a sound and prosperous basis." Although the president was quickly proved wrong, a great many Americans applauded his assurance that the economy was basically sound. Confidence, they insisted, was all the country needed to weather this economic storm.

What did President Hoover do to combat the depression?

How effective were local and state efforts to provide relief?

How did the depression create international problems for the Hoover administration?

Attempts to Restore Confidence

During the next several weeks, Hoover issued one confident press release after another. "Any lack of confidence in the economic future or the basic strength of business in the United States is foolish," Hoover said on November 15. In retrospect, it is Hoover's statements that seem foolish, as the recession was getting worse by the day. However, the president was convinced that he could help prevent a general depression by restoring confidence in the economy. He thought that the crisis could be confined to the stock market if businesspeople believed that it was still safe to conduct business as usual. Hoover felt it was his duty to exert presidential leadership to ward off economic disaster.

▲ *The need for food forced some people to desperate measures. What were the most difficult years of the Great Depression?*

▲ *Many farm families lost their land during the Great Depression. This uprooted Texas family was photographed in its pickup camper in 1936. What was the name given to the Great Plains drought of this period?*

Hoover did all that he thought he properly could do to shore up the faltering economy. He held a series of conferences with business leaders in November 1929. Among them were leaders in the fields of construction, agriculture, public utilities, railroad, and finance. Hoover asked for their voluntary cooperation to maintain current wage rates, to stabilize employment, and to increase construction activity. Believing strongly in a voluntary approach, he refused to use the power of the government to force businessmen to act. Unfortunately for Hoover and for the nation, his voluntary approach brought few results.

Struggles to Provide Relief

The nation's most urgent need by 1931 was to provide food and clothing for the growing number of families of the unemployed. Aiding the poor in times of depression was a responsibility that had always rested on local governments and private charities. That, Hoover insisted, was the way it should be.

He feared that federal aid would cause "degeneration of that independence and initiation which are the very foundation of democracy." Local and private funds were soon nearly exhausted, while the number of needy people continued to increase.

The inability of local agencies to provide adequate aid to the poor was well illustrated by the failure of Philadelphia's relief efforts. Private charities in that city launched a campaign in 1931 to raise $5 million to aid the 230,000 people who were unemployed. Although $5 million was a large amount to be raised by private donations in a depression year, the effort succeeded. But this huge relief fund lasted barely three months. When it was exhausted, the poor survived as best they could. A local investigator reported:

> One woman said she borrowed 50 cents from a friend and bought stale bread for 3 cents per loaf, and that is all they had for 11 days except for one or two meals.... Another family did not have food for two days. Then the husband went out and gathered dandelions and the family lived on them.

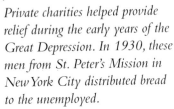

Private charities helped provide relief during the early years of the Great Depression. In 1930, these men from St. Peter's Mission in New York City distributed bread to the unemployed.

◀ *President Hoover held White House conferences with business leaders to ask for voluntary measures to combat the depression. Judging by today's standards, what is unusual about these conference members?*

In April 1932, the state came to the city's aid by supplying an additional $2.5 million for relief. That sum lasted only two months. By July, all relief aid for Philadelphia's unemployed was exhausted, and these people again faced the threat of starvation. In other cities the system of private charity and local relief was also rapidly breaking down.

It gradually became clear to President Hoover that voluntary action had failed to stop the economic decline. In 1930, he requested $150 million from Congress to spend on public works. The construction of new public buildings would provide jobs for some of the unemployed. In November

1931, the president agreed to support congressional legislation that would create the Reconstruction Finance Corporation (RFC). Established in 1932, this federal agency was empowered to loan money to banks and other financial institutions to make more credit available to American business. Easier credit, it was hoped, would bring about recovery. But Hoover drew the line at providing direct federal relief to individuals. He was afraid people would become too dependent on the federal government. Only after heavy pressure from Congress did he agree to sign a bill to loan money to the states for this purpose. The Emergency and Relief

Charles G. Dawes

◄ *A successful business-man, Charles G. Dawes was also a civic-minded American and public servant.*

In March 1932, President Herbert Hoover appointed Charles G. Dawes (1865–1951) as first director of the Reconstruction Finance Corporation. For Dawes, this was the high point of an extraordinary career as a businessman and public servant.

Dawes's career began in Lincoln, Nebraska, on the eve of the depression of 1893. He was a young lawyer and real estate buyer, who had also become a director of a local bank. By persuading Chicago and New York bankers to loan him money, Dawes saved the bank from failure while many others collapsed. This gave him a solid reputation among the nation's bankers.

In 1895, Dawes moved to Chicago and became active in the Republican party. He helped manage William McKinley's successful presidential campaign. As a reward, McKinley appointed him comptroller of the currency. This meant that Dawes, at the age of 31, had become the chief inspector of the nation's banks. He resigned four years later to resume his business career.

For the next 30 years, Dawes divided his time between business and public service. He was very good at both. When the United States went to war in 1917, Dawes volunteered his services. Within six months, he was promoted to the rank of brigadier general and was placed in charge of purchasing supplies in Europe for the entire American expeditionary force.

After the war, Dawes returned to Chicago, but not for long. Congress had passed a law in 1921 requiring the president of the United States to submit a budget each year. President Warren G. Harding appointed Dawes as the first director of the Bureau of the Budget. When he resigned 12 months later, Dawes had helped the administration cut expenditures by $1.7 billion and had balanced the federal budget. In 1923, he was appointed chairman of an Allied commission to devise a plan for Germany to pay war damages. The result was the Dawes Plan. It stabilized German currency, arranged a large U.S. loan to the German government, and created a schedule for Germany's war reparation payments.

In 1924, the Republicans looked to the Midwest for a running mate for Calvin Coolidge of Massachusetts, and they nominated Dawes. The ticket won by a landslide. After serving four years as vice president, Dawes was appointed United States ambassador to Great Britain. During the Great Depression, he resigned that position to head the Reconstruction Finance Corporation.

Finally, at 67, an age at which most men were retiring, Dawes left public life, returned to Chicago, and founded a new bank. He presided over the National City Bank and Trust Company until he was 85 years old, driving 14 miles each day from his home to his office. He died on April 23, 1951, sitting in his library, after a day spent organizing a meeting for a local civic committee.

1. How did Dawes's political party activities help advance his career in banking?
2. Describe the Dawes plan.

Construction Act of July 1932 provided $300 million in loans to be used for relief. This money enabled Philadelphia and other cities to extend public relief to the unemployed. Although Hoover was slowly moving toward an expanded role for the federal government, his conservative principles kept him from moving quickly enough to retain the support of the American public.

The Bonus Army   Hoover's handling of the **Bonus Army** of 1932 made him appear hardhearted about the needs of the unemployed. The Bonus Army consisted of 20,000 veterans of World War I, many with families, who had gathered in Washington, D.C., in the summer of 1932 demanding the immediate payment of a bonus not due to them until 1945. Lacking places to stay, the veterans made a camp just outside the city. The president was not sympathetic. He had already vetoed a bill that Congress had passed in 1931 (and enacted over his veto) allowing loans of up to 50 percent of the bonus to be made. In 1932, the House was impressed by the size of the demonstration and promptly approved the immediate payment of the full bonus. The bill was defeated in the Senate.

The veterans began leaving Washington in July, but not fast enough to suit some of the authorities. General Douglas MacArthur, army chief of staff, ordered his troops into the crowd of men, women, and children. The soldiers were armed with bayonets and tear gas. More than 60 people were injured before the veterans were driven from the capital. Although MacArthur exceeded the orders Hoover had given to him (to disperse veterans from the business district of the city and to return them to their camp), Hoover had to accept responsibility. The public looked on with disdain as the army drove the destitute veterans out of the nation's capital, seemingly with President Hoover's approval.

Hoover's Foreign Policy

The depression, which had become worldwide by 1931, cast its shadow over Hoover's foreign policies as well as his reputation at home. He had hoped to expand trade with Europe as one avenue toward recovery, but Congress made this difficult by passing the high Hawley-Smoot Tariff in 1930. Less able to sell goods in the United States because of the tariff duties, European countries then had less cash available to buy American-made products. In addition, the run on German banks in 1931 caused Germany to suspend its reparation payments to the Allies. That, in turn, forced the Allies to stop making debt

▶

With assistance from the military, the police broke up the camps of the Bonus Army outside Washington, D.C. Why was this action a political mistake for President Hoover?

payments to the United States. To remove some of the pressure, Hoover in 1931 declared a **moratorium**, or temporary suspension, on debt payments owed to the United States. Although widely acclaimed as a bold act of statesmanship, this merely recognized the obvious. Europe could no longer afford to pay its debts.

While worrying about the financial troubles of Europe, Hoover also had to respond to a crisis in China. In September 1931, the Japanese army launched an attack against the Chinese province of Manchuria. The victorious Japanese promptly made Manchuria into a Japanese colony. Although the attack violated the Open Door Policy and the Nine-Power Treaty of 1922, there was little that the administration could do. In 1932, a statement from Secretary of State Henry L. Stimson declared that the United States refused to recognize territorial change brought about by force. The Stimson Doctrine of Nonrecognition, like the debt moratorium, put the best face on a bad situation, but had no real effect.

Perhaps President Hoover's most important contribution was the improvement of relations with Latin America. His administration decided that the Monroe Doctrine did not justify military intervention in Latin America at the whim of the United States. By repudiating the Roosevelt Corollary to the Monroe Doctrine, Hoover set a precedent that other presidents would follow. Thereafter, United States intervention would take place only with the agreement of the nation concerned or with the consent of other Latin American states.

SECTION 3 REVIEW

1. List the actions that President Hoover recommended businesses take to combat the depression.
2. Name the actions taken by local and state governments in response to the depression.
3. Relate the reason given by President Hoover for not providing federal assistance to the unemployed.
4. Define moratorium.
5. Describe how President Hoover changed American foreign policy toward Latin America.

SECTION 4

American Values and the Great Crash

As the year 1931 drew to a close, Gerald W. Johnson surveyed the mood of his neighbors in Baltimore. Johnson, an editorial writer for the *Baltimore Sun*, described the people on his block as typical middle-class Americans. Their mood was grim. They were frightened by the economic collapse and disillusioned with the nation's business leaders. "Vast numbers of us actually believed the gospel of the New Economic Era," Johnson wrote, "actually believed that our postwar prosperity had been created by American businessmen," instead of being the product of economic circumstances. "Now," he concluded, "we realize that it was all an illusion." In cities across the nation, the depression shattered the faith that Americans had placed in business. Many of them now turned to new values that seemed better suited to the times.

What social values were dominant in the United States at the beginning of the Great Depression?

How did the depression bring these values into question?

How was the crisis in values reflected in the movies and other mass entertainment media?

Conflicting Values in America

The stock market crash and the depression brought the dominant social values of the 1920s into serious question. Among those tarnished truths was the notion of **rugged individualism**, an idea at the heart of the American business philosophy of the twenties. National economic growth and prosperity, according to this point of view, was the natural result of each individual's search for wealth. The more aggressive each individual was in acquiring wealth, the more prosperous the nation would become. The proper role of government was to provide the services the wealth-makers needed and to protect American producers from foreign competition through high tariffs. Otherwise, government should keep its hands off the economy. Except for the protective tariff policy, this was an old idea, borrowed from Adam Smith's *Wealth of Nations*. Smith's ideas, published a century and a half earlier, had never been so popular. Even many working-class people had found the notion of rugged individualism attractive during the twenties. On the eve of the depression, probably more Americans subscribed to it than ever before.

But not all Americans of 1929 accepted this point of view. The belief in rugged individualism coexisted along with other values, and some were in sharp conflict with it. While rugged individualism had always found strong support among the business class, rural and working-class Americans traditionally tempered their belief in individualism with a commitment to various forms of cooperation. The business ethic also ran counter to traditional values that emphasized justice and fairness. As the depression worsened, Americans increasingly drew on these other values to cope with hard times.

Rugged Individualism Questioned

By 1931, Americans far beyond Gerald W. Johnson's Baltimore neighborhood were questioning the value of systematic selfishness implied by rugged individualism. They considered the merits of other philosophies that seemed more humane. Some turned to socialism—the ownership of mines, factories, and railroads by the state—as the best guarantee of security. Most Americans, however, were not attracted to ideologies that called for a redistribution of wealth. Instead, they sought solutions that placed greater emphasis on cooperation.

As the Great Depression deepened, the White House was flooded with letters from ordinary people offering solutions. Many of them emphasized the value of cooperation. One man proposed that the unemployed and the people with jobs should change places for a while. "It seems fair that all get *some* of the pie." "The nation could be made an ideal place to live," wrote a man from Minnesota, "if every one would work together for the common good of every one instead of for selfish purposes." Years later, Americans would remember the spirit of cooperation that actually did emerge during the depression. "A lot of times one family would have some food," a woman recalled. "They would divide. And everyone would share."

This cooperative social ethic was neither radical nor new. It had deep roots both in rural America and in the organized labor movement. It was the basis for frontier barn raisings and for benevolent societies formed by urban immigrants to help families in times of distress. Urban workers had also joined together to form trade unions and social lodges that helped soften harsh economic realities. People remembered this tradition in the hard times of the depression years.

Popular Culture

Depression era values were reflected in the popular culture and the mass entertainment media. Many of the most popular films of the 1930s simply tried to help Americans forget their troubles. As a Paramount Pictures studio ad said, "There is a [movie] probably around the corner. See it and you'll be out of yourself, living someone else's life." People went to see the Marx Brothers in *Animal Crackers* (1930) and *Duck Soup* (1933) just to enjoy comic antics. Musicals were a novelty in the early 1930s, made possible by the recent introduction of talking films. The musical *The Gold Diggers of 1933* was an instant hit. Like the comedies, musicals were designed to help people escape reality.

But not all entertainment was escapist. It often showed sensitive expressions of the changes taking place in what Americans believed and valued. The extraordinary popularity of gangster movies is a good example. Gangsters, including such thugs as "Pretty Boy" Floyd, "Baby Face" Nelson, John Dillinger, and the team of Bonnie Parker and Clyde Barrow, were very much in the news during the depression. It is not surprising that Hollywood made movies about gangsters during the 1930s. What is noteworthy is the way in which gangsters were portrayed. For instance, perhaps the most successful gangster movie of the 1930s was *Little Caesar*

(1931). Its central character, Caesar Bandello (played by Edward G. Robinson), was a tough gangster who placed his own success above everything else. He was driven by greed and rampant individualism. Little Caesar was a thinly disguised version of the successful businessman of the 1920s, as moviegoers and critics clearly understood.

The movies directed by Frank Capra also had an unmistakable social message. In *Mr. Smith Goes to Washington* (1939), the hero (played by James Stewart) was an ordinary American elected to Congress. In Washington, Smith was shocked by the greed and selfishness of the businessmen and corrupt politicians he encountered. In response, Smith pleaded for "plain, ordinary, everyday kindness, a little looking out for the other fella, loving thy neighbor." Clearly, Frank Capra—and the moviegoers who made his movies popular—preferred the traditional values of small-town America to the individualism that was the hallmark of the twenties.

The rethinking of values was also evident in *The Grapes of Wrath* (1940), John Ford's classic movie about the Great Depression. Based on John Steinbeck's novel, it was the story of an uprooted family that made its way from Oklahoma to California in search of work. The Joad family was down and out, but not alone. They were helped out along the way by other migrants, truck-stop owners, waitresses, and truck drivers. The movie stressed the in-

▲ *The Marx Brothers starred in* Animal Crackers *(1930). Why were comedies especially popular at this time?*

justice of an economic system concerned only with profits, and it praised the benefits of cooperation.

The value of sticking together regained much of the respect it had lost during the 1920s. The depression convinced many Americans that the vision of a successful society based on rugged individualism was an illusion. Consequently, the 1930s would become, as historian Warren I. Susman has written, "*the* decade of participation and belonging." All that was needed by 1932 was a leader who could show the American people how to work together.

▼ The Grapes of Wrath *starred Henry Fonda. What social message did this classic American movie convey?*

▼ *Edward G. Robinson starred as a gangster in the film* Little Caesar. *What did many people believe movie gangsters had in common with business leaders of the 1920s?*

SECTION 4 REVIEW

1. **Explain** what American businesspeople meant by the term *rugged individualism.*
2. **Explain** why the depression led many people to question the value of rugged individualism.
3. **Name** traditional social values that Americans had as an alternative to rugged individualism.
4. **Relate** examples of when the cooperative social ethic was used.
5. **Summarize** the social messages of movies like *Mr. Smith Goes to Washington* and *The Grapes of Wrath.*

SECTION 5

Franklin D. Roosevelt and the Election of 1932

As the election year of 1932 approached, Hoover's approval rating reached an all-time low. Although Hoover had taken more forceful action to combat a depression than any president before him, he was still widely blamed for not doing enough to ease the distress and misery of the people. Hoover's name mockingly became associated with the effects of the depression. The shantytowns inhabited by the unemployed outside industrial cities were called "Hoovervilles." In the West, the jackrabbits and armadillos that became the mainstay of the diet for some poor people were known as "Hoover hogs." Newspapers became "Hoover blankets" when used for warmth by tramps on park benches.

Even though the Republicans were certain of defeat in 1932, they still nominated Hoover for a second term. The question became not whether the Democrats would elect the next president, but whom they would choose to try to lead the nation out of the depression.

Why did the Democrats win by such a large margin in 1932?

How did Franklin D. Roosevelt's approach to the depression differ from that of Hoover?

Why was there a banking crisis in 1933?

Franklin D. Roosevelt

At their convention in Chicago in the summer of 1932, the Democrats nominated **Franklin D. Roosevelt**, the governor of New York, as their presidential candidate. The Democratic convention passed over Alfred E. Smith, its candidate in 1928, and other contenders who seemed to be as well qualified as Roosevelt. Except for a stint as assistant secretary of the navy during World War I, Roosevelt had little experience at the national level. But he was a shrewd politician who had managed to unite much of the party around his candidacy, and he had an attractive personality. In the depression year of 1932, Roosevelt's buoyant, cheerful temperament proved to be an invaluable asset.

In accepting the Democratic nomination, Roosevelt left no doubt that he would provide the dynamic presidential leadership Hoover lacked. Breaking with tradition, Roosevelt went to Chicago to accept the party's nomination in person. In his acceptance speech, Roosevelt stated, "I pledge you, I pledge myself, to a new deal for the American people. Let us all here assembled constitute ourselves

▼ *Shantytowns and camps of homeless people were called Hoovervilles. Why were they named for President Hoover?*

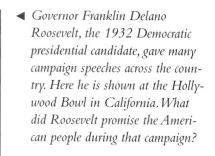

◀ Governor Franklin Delano Roosevelt, the 1932 Democratic presidential candidate, gave many campaign speeches across the country. Here he is shown at the Hollywood Bowl in California. What did Roosevelt promise the American people during that campaign?

▼ The election of 1932 swept the Democrats into the White House and gave them control of both houses of Congress.

◀ This bandanna was made for Roosevelt's 1940 reelection campaign.

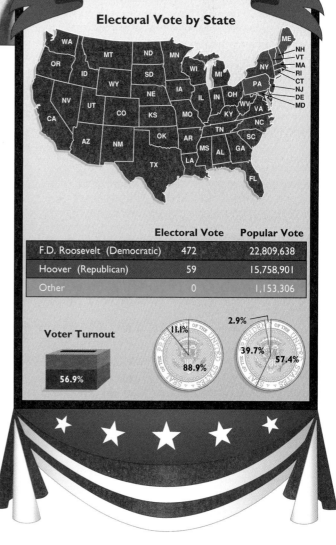

Election of 1932

Electoral Vote by State

	Electoral Vote	Popular Vote
F.D. Roosevelt (Democratic)	472	22,809,638
Hoover (Republican)	59	15,758,901
Other	0	1,153,306

Voter Turnout

56.9%

11.1%
88.9%

2.9%
39.7%
57.4%

prophets of a new order of competence and of courage. This is more than a political campaign, it is a call to arms." Roosevelt later borrowed from this speech the phrase "new deal" as the name for his plan of action to end the depression. This speech and others that would follow during the campaign were just what much of the American public wanted to hear. Here, at last, was a man who wanted to take charge, who was confident he could lead the American people out of the bleak depression.

In the election that fall, Roosevelt won by a landslide. He polled 22 million votes to Hoover's 15 million and carried all but six states. In the process, Roosevelt united the Democratic party, bringing together its warring urban and rural factions. He carried the rural South as well as the urban, ethnic voters of the Northeast. The "Roosevelt coalition," as this alliance is sometimes called, established the Democratic Party as the majority political party, ending a period of Republican dominance that had lasted 36 years. Roosevelt's election was more than just a victory for the Democrats. It was a political upheaval that would change the course of American politics for decades to come.

The New Deal

Between the election and his inauguration, the plans for the **New Deal** that Roosevelt had promised gradually took shape. The variety of programs that would emerge had one thing in common—they reflected the temperament and personality of the president-elect. Roosevelt's ideas about government were molded during the Progressive Era, when an earlier generation of Americans had called on government to help solve the problems of the day. But the social and political reforms of the progressive period provided few guidelines for dealing with a disastrous depression. Still, these reforms had given the federal government a larger role to play in national affairs. The new president would use the power of the federal government as vigorously, if not more so, than the progressives had earlier in the century.

The New Deal also bore the imprint of the advisers that Roosevelt called in to help him. As president-elect, he sought out a diverse group of people to help organize a plan for economic recovery. Roosevelt looked for advice to a group of professors, who became known as the Brain Trust. Roosevelt sought out individuals from various political and social backgrounds who gave him conflicting advice. This did not trouble Roosevelt. He preferred to surround himself with people who could offer contrasting views. He was then free to choose those opinions he liked best.

A Drifting Nation

Until the **Twentieth Amendment** was ratified on February 6, 1933, there was a four-month

▲ The New Yorker *magazine cover for March 1933 showed President Herbert Hoover and President-elect Roosevelt on the way to the inauguration. What does this caricature tell you about the personalities of the two men?*

interval between the time a new president was elected and the day he was installed in office. The new amendment provided that, thereafter, the president would take office on January 20 and the new Congress on January 3. Although Roosevelt was impatient to get the New Deal under way, he was unable to act until his inauguration in March. Hoover, too, could do little during that time, as he wielded little power. He was a **lame-duck** president. Lame-duck describes a defeated office holder who has not yet left office. Hoover did try to persuade Roosevelt to endorse the current administration's policies, insisting that only by doing so could he restore public confidence. But Roosevelt refused. He did not wish to commit himself to failed policies that the voters had rejected. With neither of the two leaders capable of acting, the government drifted.

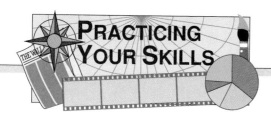

PRACTICING YOUR SKILLS

Mar. 4, 1933 THE NEW YORKER Price 15 cents

Peter Arno

Interpreting an Editorial Cartoon

Editorial (political) cartoons have been part of our nation's history from the very beginning. They are often funny, but they can present serious issues. Editorial cartoonists try to influence public opinion through their humorous and simple drawings.

Editorial cartoonists often use two techniques: *symbolism* and *caricature*. Symbolism uses an image to represent a larger idea, object, or feeling. For instance, the figure of Uncle Sam represents the whole concept of patriotism or nationalism; a dove stands for peace; and an elephant and a donkey represent the Republican and Democratic Parties. In caricature, the cartoonist exaggerates the physical features of the people in his drawing so that they are easily identified. Wide smiles, long noses, or ears that stick out are features that cartoonists find easy to exaggerate.

When looking at editorial cartoons, follow these guidelines:

- **Look carefully for labels, captions, and other words.** Cartoonists use words sparingly, but they are important for identification and scene setting.
- **Identify the symbols or caricatures used.** Often, the point of the cartoon is not clear unless a figure is correctly identified. Think about the possible meanings of all the symbols used.
- **Determine if the cartoonist's point of view is positive (supportive) or negative (critical).** What is the tone or mood of the cartoon? Is it severely critical or gently mocking?
- **Finally, make a verbal statement that summarizes the cartoonist's message.** Overall, what political or social purpose motivated the drawing? What message is the cartoonist trying to get across?

Examine the cartoon on page 696 and answer the following questions:

1. Why do you think you see no title, labels, or any words on this cartoon (aside from the name of the magazine, price, etc.)?
2. Does the cartoon present a positive or negative point of view of Hoover? How can you tell?
3. From their portrayal in this cartoon, contrast the personalities of Hoover and Roosevelt. What personal characteristics attracted voters to elect Hoover in 1928?
4. Do you think Hoover deserved the characterization of him in this cartoon? Why, or why not?
5. What part does personality and appearance play in the election and success of a president? Give some specific examples from the presidents we have studied to support your conclusion.
6. Three weeks before his inauguration, Roosevelt was riding in an open car in Miami when an unsuccessful assassination attempt on him resulted in the death of the mayor of Chicago. Why do you think *The New Yorker* never used this cartoon? Do you agree or disagree with its decision? What do you think an editor today would do in a similar circumstance? Why?

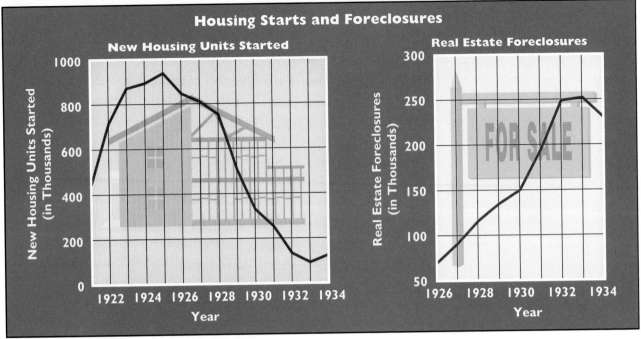

Housing Starts and Foreclosures

New Housing Units Started

(Line graph — vertical axis: New Housing Units Started (in Thousands), 0 to 1000; horizontal axis: Year, 1922 to 1934)

Real Estate Foreclosures

(Line graph — vertical axis: Real Estate Foreclosures (in Thousands), 50 to 300; horizontal axis: Year, 1926 to 1934)

Source: U.S. Department of Commerce, Bureau of the Census.

▲ *These graphs show the impact of the Great Depression on the housing industry and home mortgage foreclosures. When do these economic indicators begin to show improvement?*

The depression, in the meantime, grew steadily worse. Stock prices plunged to a new low in the early months of 1933. The gross national product decreased as consumer spending and business investment continued to fall. More workers were unemployed than ever before.

▶ *A rash of bank failures in 1931 led to many scenes like this across the nation. Why were people gathered on the sidewalk?*

Confidence in the banking system had ebbed and flowed since the beginning of the depression, but by March 1933, the United States faced its worst banking crisis yet. After a rash of bank failures in 1931, some 2,000 in all, the situation had improved. Creation of the Reconstruction Finance Corporation in 1932, which loaned more than $1 billion to banks and trust companies, had helped. Now, however, as more and more people withdrew their savings from questionable banks, a new crisis approached. Long lines of depositors waiting to make withdrawals threatened so many banks in Michigan by mid-February that the governor of the state declared a bank holiday, ordering the banks to close temporarily to prevent a complete collapse.

Other states soon followed this example. By inauguration day on March 4, 1933, the nation's banking system was on the brink of disaster.

SECTION 5 REVIEW

1. **Describe** the coalition that swept the Democrats to power in 1932.
2. **Identify** the Brain Trust.
3. **Explain** how Roosevelt's attitude toward using the power of the federal government differed from Hoover's.
4. **Define** the term *lame duck*.
5. **Explain** why several states declared a bank holiday in February 1933.

Summary

The depression that began in 1929 was the worst economic disaster that the United States has ever experienced. In trying to explain why the prosperity of the 1920s was so short-lived, historians have pointed out that agriculture and some industries were already depressed throughout that decade. The uneven distribution of income had also put a brake on further economic expansion. The depression grew progressively worse through 1933, with unemployment increasing each year. By March 1933, the economy was in desperate straits, with the banking system on the verge of collapse.

The depression was a shock to the American people. Although few escaped untouched, it was especially hard for the growing ranks of the unemployed. Many people were faced with mortgage foreclosures or the loss of their furniture or automobiles. For some, the loss of jobs also meant the loss of self-respect.

The depression brought some families closer together, but it caused problems for others. Unemployed fathers sometimes lost status and the respect of their wives and children. Although many married women had to find work to help support their families, they were resented for taking jobs away from men. Minorities were especially hard hit by the depression, with unemployment among African Americans climbing to twice the national average. The depression also led many Americans to question the value of rugged individualism, and to place greater value on mutual help and cooperation.

Herbert Hoover responded to the crash of 1929 by expressing confidence in the future and by urging American businesses to hold the line on investment, employment, and wages. A strong believer in voluntary action, the president refused to use the power of the government to force business to act. He believed that relief should come from local rather than federal sources. By 1932, however, local charities and governments were unable to provide relief to the growing numbers of unemployed. Hoover began to move cautiously toward a larger role for the federal government. He moved much too slowly to retain the confidence of most Americans. In the election of 1932, Hoover was defeated for reelection by Franklin D. Roosevelt, who inspired the voters by promising a "new deal" for the American people.

Vocabulary

banking panic	New Deal
installment buying	on margin
lame-duck	rugged individualism
moratorium	stock speculation

Write a sentence for each of the vocabulary terms that includes a contextual definition of the word. For example: As the *banking panic* spread and people rushed to withdraw money, "CLOSED" signs appeared on banks all over the city.

Review Questions

1. Describe the events that led to the stock market crash in 1929.
2. Why did the panic on Wall Street trigger a major economic depression?
3. How did the depression both strengthen and weaken American families?
4. Explain why minorities were hit harder by the depression than other Americans.
5. What actions did President Hoover first take in response to the depression?
6. Why did many Americans think that Hoover's response was inadequate?
7. Explain how the depression led to a questioning of values.
8. How did movies in the thirties reflect mainstream American values?

9. Why did such diverse groups as urban immigrants and southern farmers find Roosevelt an appealing candidate in 1932?

10. List the causes of the banking crisis in 1933.

Critical Historical Thinking

Writing Answer each of the following by writing one or more complete paragraphs:

1. Discuss what help was available for needy people in the 1930s and contrast it with options that are available today for people who need help. Consider such items as food stamps, workers' compensation, unemployment insurance, social security, etc. Tell whether you think these programs have been successful on a long-term basis.

2. How did President Hoover's reaction to the Great Depression reflect his belief in the philosophy of rugged individualism?

3. The Great Depression was felt all over the world. Many countries saw rioting and violence against the government. Why do you think that in the United States stability and order were the rule, not the exception?

4. In Roosevelt's inaugural address he said, "The only thing we have to fear is fear itself." What do you think he meant?

Making Connections with Sociology

Sociologists study the origins, development, organization, and functioning of human societies. Many sociologists turn to major events in history to gain insight into how humans cope with change and crisis. The shock of unemployment, the loss of one's life savings, the loss of self-confidence, and the loss of trust in the future had a lasting impact on those who lived through the Great Depression. It is difficult for later generations who have become used to relative economic security to understand the attitudes of the "depression generation."

Fortunately there are many excellent books and sources, such as oral history project tapes, on the Great Depression. The authors of these books and projects talked to hundreds of people who had experienced first-hand the effects of the depression. It is harder now to find *primary sources*, or people who themselves lived through that time. But it is still possible to find people who remember what others told them.

▪ In your class, create an oral history project on the Great Depression. Using a tape recorder, interview primary and secondary source people. Ask them if they have photographs or newspaper clippings they would be willing to lend to the project. Include the following questions in your interview: "Did the hardships of that period help to strengthen your family? Or did the strain of coping overly stress the family?" Choose the most descriptive and significant passages for transcribing and illustrating for display.

Additional Skills Practice

Indicate which of the descriptions below apply to political cartoons more than other forms of political commentary. Compare your answers with those of the rest of the class and discuss the differences.

1. uses exaggeration
2. uses symbolism
3. uses labels
4. uses humor
5. uses contrast
6. presents varying viewpoints
7. deals with social and political issues
8. tries to present unbiased points of view
9. deals with controversial issues

Franklin D. Roosevelt
and the New Deal

The era of the New Deal, as President Franklin D. Roosevelt's first two terms in office were known, was a time of optimism and hope in the United States. Although the nation was still in the depths of the depression, the darkest hours of despair had passed. They were dispelled in part by the president himself, whose dynamic personality and determination helped inspire the nation to have faith in the future.

"This great nation," FDR had said on taking office, "will endure as it has endured, will revive and will prosper. So first of all let me assert my firm belief that the only thing we have to fear is fear itself— nameless, unreasoning, unjustified terror." Roosevelt provided the leadership needed for a massive attack on the depression, and the majority of the American people placed their confidence in him.

▲ *This radio microphone was similar to those used by President Franklin D. Roosevelt when he broadcast his "fireside chats."*

The First Hundred Days

The New Deal that Roosevelt had promised the American people in his acceptance speech in Chicago was launched in March 1933 with a frenzy of activity. "This Nation asks for action, and action now," the president said in his inaugural address. The lights in the executive offices burned into the night as administration officials worked late drafting laws to cope with the economic crisis. Roosevelt called Congress into special session and urged it to act on these laws quickly. The first item on his agenda, an emergency banking bill, was introduced in Congress at noon on March 9, debated for 38 minutes in the House and for three hours in the Senate, and was signed into law by the president at 9:00 that night. This pace was typical of the **hundred days**, the beginning of Roosevelt's term when many programs of the New Deal were passed by Congress.

How did Congress provide immediate relief to the unemployed?

How did the Roosevelt administration address the problems facing farmers?

How did the New Deal promote industrial recovery?

Starting the New Deal

Roosevelt's first priority was to restore confidence in the nation's banking system. When depositors rushed to withdraw their money from checking and savings accounts, they had caused one bank failure after another at the beginning of 1933. To prevent a collapse of the system, Roosevelt declared a four-day banking holiday as soon as he took office. During these four days, Congress hurriedly passed the Emergency Banking Act. It provided federal funds to banks that could be saved and authorized the U.S. Treasury Department to close banks that did not have adequate cash reserves. The act also created the Federal Deposit Insurance Corporation,

(FDIC), which insured deposits up to $2,500. (Today that figure is $100,000.) The federal government promised to back a person's deposits in each bank up to that amount if a bank failed. On Sunday evening, March 12, the president went on the radio in the first of his informal "fireside chats" to assure the public that those banks that would be allowed to reopen were safe. Over half the banks, holding 90 percent of all bank deposits, reopened the next day. In the coming weeks, many others reopened with federal assistance. The crisis ended as confidence was renewed and deposits began to flow back into the banks.

The administration next turned to the problem of helping millions of needy families by providing federal relief. To shift the welfare burden from private charities and local governments to the national government, Congress, in May 1933, passed the Federal Emergency Relief Act (FERA). It provided an initial grant of $500 million to be used by cities and states for emergency relief. Another $400 million would be allocated in 1933 for the Civil Works Administration (CWA), which provided for **work relief** in the form of federally funded jobs for many of those able to work. Neither the Democrats nor the Republicans in Congress felt comfortable with relief programs that simply gave people money.

▼ *President Roosevelt gave informal radio speeches to reassure the American people. During this 1935 broadcast, he announced a new emergency relief program.*

The Radio

On March 12, 1933, President Franklin D. Roosevelt addressed the American people on radio in the first of his famous fireside chats. A new relationship became possible between a president and the 150 million citizens sitting at home whom he addressed as "my friends." The national conventions of 1924, a decade earlier, had been reported on the spot. The public was able to hear the actual proceedings as they occurred. The radio had brought about a new intimacy between political figures and the general public.

The technology that made Roosevelt's radio address to the American people possible was still relatively new. In 1887, Heinrich Hertz, a German physicist, discovered that electric sparks made

▲ This popular "cathedral model" radio was manufactured by the General Electric Co. during the 1930s.

waves that moved through the air. Five years later, a young Italian named Guglielmo Marconi demonstrated that Hertz's discovery could be used for the wireless transmission of Morse code. Most oceangoing ships were soon equipped with the new wireless telegraph. Then, on Christmas Eve of 1906, wireless operators on ships along the Atlantic coast who were used to receiving Morse code dots and dashes were stunned to hear the voice of a man singing "Oh, Holy Night." That was the first wireless transmission of the human voice.

At the heart of the radio sets tuned in to Roosevelt's fireside chats was a device called a grid-audion vacuum tube. This was a glass tube that contained a filament that amplified the strength of radio signals. It was called a vacuum tube because the air had been evacuated, or removed, from it. The grid-audion vacuum tube was developed in 1906 by an American named Lee De Forest. Edwin Howard Armstrong took this technology a step forward in 1913 by devising a vacuum tube that could receive radio signals over long distances. Ernst F. W. Alexanderson, a Swedish immigrant, invented an antenna that allowed broadcasters to select the direction they wanted to send the radio signal Thus, people from many countries worked together to perfect this invention.

The radio also represented a new stage in the process of invention. Many of the inventors of the

▲ Lee De Forest, developer of the radio vacuum tube.

radio began like Thomas Alva Edison, tinkering with crude apparatus in makeshift laboratories. Anderson did his early work at home. But once their ideas took shape, these inventors had access to well-equipped electrical laboratories. De Forest worked at the laboratory of the Western Electric Company in Chicago. Alexanderson worked for the General Electric Company. The inventors of the radio were much better educated than Edison. DeForest received a Ph.D. in engineering from Yale. Armstrong studied engineering at Columbia; and Anderson graduated from the Royal Technical University at Stockholm. It was a time of transition. Invention was moving out of the attic and into research laboratories staffed with university graduates.

1. How does the radio illustrate the cooperative nature of invention in modern times?
2. Why do you think corporations began to play a larger role in the inventing process?

▲ *In this photograph, a Civilian Conservation Corps crew is at work in Virginia. In addition to creating jobs, how did this program benefit society?*

Congress much preferred measures that satisfied the work ethic by providing people with jobs. By the end of the year, 4 million people were employed on CWA projects, repairing highways and building schools, parks, and airports. Being able to work for their relief checks was also important to the recipients. "At last I could say, 'I've got a job,'" remarked one CWA worker.

The administration also proposed a conservation program that created jobs while it helped preserve the nation's natural resources. The first of two major pieces of legislation created the Civilian Conservation Corps (CCC), which put young men between the ages of 18 and 25 to work digging reservoirs and ponds, planting trees, building fire towers, and helping farmers terrace fields to prevent soil erosion. By 1941, 2.5 million young men had spent time in CCC camps.

The second legislative measure focused on the Tennessee Valley, one of the most impoverished regions of the United States. Congress created the Tennessee Valley Authority (TVA), which set out to improve the area by building a series of dams and power plants. In addition to providing flood control and recreational facilities, the dams provided cheap electrical power to attract industry and jobs, and to improve the quality of life of the valley's residents. The TVA was the New Deal's boldest and biggest experiment in regional public planning and economic development.

Agriculture and Industry

During the hundred days, the Roosevelt administration turned its attention to the depressed condition of American agriculture. Boosting the purchasing power of the 30 percent of the U.S. population that lived on farms was essential to recovery. In May 1933, Congress passed the Agricultural Adjustment Act (AAA), aimed at raising the price of farm produce by helping farmers limit production. Farmers would receive payments from the government in return for raising less corn, cotton, pork, and other commodities. The program was to be paid for by a new consumer tax on food. Millions of acres were plowed under and some 6 million piglets were slaughtered in the spring of 1933 to reduce production for that year. Many people were shocked

▲ *A blue eagle was the symbol used by the National Recovery Administration. Businesses that conformed to NRA policies could display this poster in their windows.*

by such a waste of food when countless Americans went hungry. Although farm income remained below its 1929 level until the end of the depression, the AAA did help push up farm prices by about 50 percent. A second law, the Emergency Farm Mortgage Act, provided new mortgages at lower interest rates—thus lower monthly payments—to help landowners save their farms from foreclosure. Neither act provided much help for the poorest of rural Americans, the tenant farmers and sharecroppers who did not own their own farms.

With its farm program enacted, the administration turned next to the task of industrial recovery. The plan that it proposed, which became the National Industrial Recovery Act (NIRA) of 1933, had two parts. The first part allowed business firms to limit competition by working out industry-wide agreements on prices, wages, and production. This, it was hoped, would enable them to increase profits, expand production, and rehire laid-off workers. The act created a new agency to administer the law, the National Recovery Administration (NRA), and suspended the antitrust laws that made such price-fixing agreements illegal. The second part of the act set up the Public Works Administration (PWA) and appropriated $3.3 billion to stimulate the economy and increase employment by the building of public works projects such as parks, schools, and airports.

Interest-Group Democracy

Before the hundred days were over, the New Deal had provided something for nearly every special interest group in the nation. Historians have called this approach to government **interest-group democracy**. It was an attempt by Roosevelt to create broad political support for the New Deal by giving major interest groups at least part of what they wanted. In addition to aiding bankers, farmers, corporations, and the unemployed, Congress enacted legislation to help homeowners, stock investors, and the railroads. The Home Owners Refinancing Act provided $2 billion to refinance home mortgages facing foreclosure. The Federal Housing Administration (FHA) was created to help new home buyers secure low-interest mortgages. The FHA encouraged banks to lower their interest rates by guaranteeing repayment of home-mortgage loans. The Federal Securities Act required stockbrokers to provide investors with full information about new stock issues. The Emergency Railroad Transportation Act enabled bankrupt railroads to reorganize.

Roosevelt's approach to solving the nation's economic problems produced modest results. The number of unemployed fell from 13 million in 1933 to 11.4 million the following year. Farm income rose about 50 percent, although it remained well below its 1929 level. Industrial production and wages in manufacturing slowly moved upward. But despite these indications of progress, the nation remained caught in the grip of the worst depression in its history.

SECTION 1 REVIEW

1. **Define** the term *hundred days*.
2. **List** the actions Roosevelt and Congress took to restore confidence in the banking system.
3. **Explain** how the Agricultural Adjustment Act raised farm prices.
4. **Describe** how Congress encouraged businesses under the National Industrial Recovery Act.
5. **Summarize** the nature of Roosevelt's presidential leadership during the hundred days.

The Second New Deal

By 1934, it was clear that the honeymoon was over for the Roosevelt administration. Business and other interest groups, willing to overlook the faults of the New Deal during the crisis period of the first hundred days, were now taking a closer and more critical look at the administration. "Now that these people are coming out of their storm cellars they forget that there ever was a storm," Roosevelt remarked as his critics became more vocal. The broad support that the president had enjoyed at the beginning of his administration was eroding.

Why did the New Deal lose much of its early support from the business community?

Why did Roosevelt launch the Second New Deal in 1935?

How did the Second New Deal contribute to Roosevelt's reelection in 1936?

Criticisms of the New Deal

The New Deal came under increasing attack from the business community. Part of the criticism was focused on the mounting federal debt as Congress spent millions on relief and public works. Business leaders of that era believed firmly in a balanced budget, for government as well as for business firms. Many were also disturbed by the growth of federal regulations and government control, especially the NRA codes and regulations. Still others were shocked by the administration's monetary policy. By 1934, Roosevelt had persuaded Congress to devalue the dollar by about 40 percent in an effort to push up prices and inflate the economy. The cheaper dollar did produce some inflation, but it also lessened the value of existing savings accounts and investments.

The strength of the opposition from the business community surprised Roosevelt, who thought he had helped to save American business from its own self-destructive tendencies. "One of my principal tasks," he said in November 1934, "is to prevent bankers and businessmen from committing suicide!" The Emergency Banking Act and the National Industrial Recovery Act had rescued an economy that was on the verge of collapse. Yet many businesspeople hated Roosevelt because of his economic policies and wanted to abolish the New Deal. In response, they organized the Liberty League in 1934 to try to defeat pro-New Deal members of Congress who were running for reelection.

If business interests attacked the New Deal for being too radical, others criticized Roosevelt for not going far enough. Liberal Democrats who generally supported the administration did not agree with all of its policies. They criticized the Emergency Banking Relief Act for not bringing the banks under stricter federal control. On the extreme left, the Socialists and Communists called for even more radical changes in the economic system, including a government takeover of banks and industries. What was needed, said Minnesota's radical governor, Floyd B. Olson, was "not just a new deal, but also a new deck." Members of the Communist Party of the United States denounced Roosevelt for propping up a capitalist economic system they considered unworthy of saving.

▼ *Before his extremist views forced him off the air, Father Charles Coughlin used radio sermons to criticize the New Deal. On what grounds did he oppose President Roosevelt's policies?*

▲ *Dr. Francis E. Townsend criticized the New Deal for not doing enough for the elderly. He pioneered the idea of Social Security.*

▶

Senator Huey P. Long of Louisiana was President Roosevelt's most serious political rival in 1935. What was the basis for Senator Long's popular appeal?

Roosevelt was especially concerned about the charge that the New Deal had not done enough to redistribute wealth in the United States. Among these critics was Father Charles Coughlin, the "Radio Priest." By 1935, his radio sermons were heard by 30 to 40 million listeners. (Eventually his increasingly anti-Semitic, pro-Nazi bias forced the Catholic Church to stop his broadcasts.) Trying "to inject Christianity into the fabric of an economic system woven upon the loom of the greedy," Father Coughlin demanded the nationalization of banks and more equal sharing of wealth. Dr. Francis E. Townsend, a California physician, proposed a plan for redistributing wealth that also served a pressing social need. The Townsend Plan proposed giving every retired citizen over the age of 60 a monthly payment of $200. Although it would have been financially impossible to do this in depression America, Townsend's idea of old-age assistance became widely popular.

The growing popular appeal of Senator Huey P. Long of Louisiana was Roosevelt's most immediate concern. Long proposed "to break up the swollen fortunes of America and to spread the wealth among all our people." He would do this by giving $5,000 to each American family. To support his efforts, Long built a national organization called the Share Our Wealth Society, which had 27,000 local clubs by early 1935. It was generally understood that Long intended to use that organization and its voting power to prevent Roosevelt's reelection in 1936. He would have been a strong contender for either the Democratic or a third-party nomination had he not been cut down by an assassin's bullet on September 8, 1935.

In the spring of 1935, Roosevelt paused to rethink the direction of his administration. It was clear that interest-group democracy was not working. The large public spending necessary to fund welfare programs had only antagonized business. Yet the failure to do more for the unemployed, the aged, and the blue-collar workers played into the hands of people like Coughlin, Townsend, and Long. By trying to give something to everyone, Roosevelt was ending up with little support from anyone. He was in danger of losing the ability to lead. The prospect of being reelected to a second term looked dim.

The Second New Deal

Determined to regain the initiative, Roosevelt in 1935 sent Congress a new list of legislative

Working for the WPA

In 1936, afraid that government spending would cause inflation, the Roosevelt administration announced cutbacks in the Works Progress Administration's funding. The public response was immediate. "Please continue the W. P. A. program," wrote a worker from Michigan. "It makes us feel like an American citizen to earn our own living. Being on the dole or relief roll makes us lazy and funds are not enough to live decent on. So we as W. P. A. workers in Battle Creek, Michigan, appeal to you as our *Great Leader* to continue this great cause." This sentiment was widely shared, as demonstrated by the flood of mail received by the White House and members of Congress.

The WPA was a popular program because it put people to work. That much of the work consisted of manual labor in construction and other industries did not matter. Working was better than living on handouts. Accepting charity or public relief ran counter to a work ethic that was deeply engrained in the American character. Earning a daily wage was central to the self-respect of countless Americans.

The WPA projects not only provided jobs for millions of Americans, but also contributed directly to the welfare of the community. By 1943, WPA workers had constructed 5,900 new school

▲ *This mural in San Francisco was one of many art projects sponsored by the WPA during the Great Depression.*

buildings and nearly 13,000 playgrounds.

The WPA also created jobs for many white-collar employees. Thousands of unemployed novelists, journalists, and historians, for example, went to work for the WPA Federal Writers Project. They produced the first popular series of guidebooks to American states and cities.

The infusion of federal money through the WPA also helped the performing and fine arts survive during a difficult time. The Federal Theater Project hired actors, directors, and other performers to produce plays, variety acts, and dance performances. In April 1936, Los Angeles had six theaters showing Theater Project performances, in

cluding plays in English, French, Spanish, and Yiddish.

The Federal Arts Project provided similar employment for artists. The artists taught art classes, made sculptures, and painted murals in post offices and other public buildings across the country. Lewis Mumford, a well known critic of modern technological society, described the Federal Arts Project as "the salvation of the arts" in depression America.

1. Why was the WPA one of the most popular New Deal programs?
2. How did the WPA help creative artists survive the depression?

proposals. The result was a flurry of activity, similar to the hundred days of 1933. This new set of economic and social programs is sometimes called the **Second New Deal**.

The Second New Deal got under way in April 1935 with the passage of the Emergency Relief Appropriation Act. Providing no less than $4.8 billion for work relief, it was at that time the largest single congressional appropriation in American history. To administer the funds, Congress created several new agencies, including the Works Progress Administration (WPA), the National Youth Administration (NYA), and the Resettlement Administration (RA). The WPA put unemployed people to work on a variety of public projects. By 1943, it had employed more than 8.5 million Americans, who built 650,000 miles of roads and streets, 125,000 public buildings, and 8,000 public parks. The NYA provided work for young people of high school and college age, while the RA settled poor families on small farms. The Emergency Relief Appropriation Act also created the Rural Electrification Administration (REA), which helped provide electrical power to rural areas. Thus, the legislation not only put people to work, but also improved the quality of everyday life for millions of Americans.

During the Second New Deal, Roosevelt tried to identify his administration more with the working class and the poor and less with the business interests of the United States. The relief act was only the beginning. In the months to come, the president also called for legislation to regulate utilities (water, gas, and electric companies) and new taxes on large corporations and the wealthy. In 1935, Congress enacted two additional laws of far-reaching importance. One was the National Labor Relations Act discussed in the next section. The second was the Social Security Act.

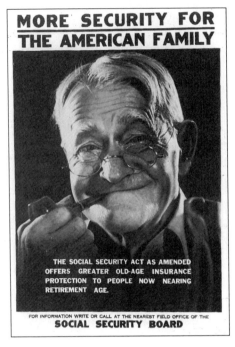

MORE SECURITY FOR THE AMERICAN FAMILY

THE SOCIAL SECURITY ACT AS AMENDED OFFERS GREATER OLD-AGE INSURANCE PROTECTION TO PEOPLE NOW NEARING RETIREMENT AGE.

FOR INFORMATION WRITE OR CALL AT THE NEAREST FIELD OFFICE OF THE
SOCIAL SECURITY BOARD

▲ *The Roosevelt administration launched its Social Security program with a poster campaign. This was one of a series of posters explaining the benefits of the Social Security Act of 1935.*

The **Social Security Act** of 1935 laid the foundation for the modern federal welfare system. It provided assistance to retired people, to the unemployed, and to the handicapped. Individuals covered by the Social Security Act qualified for monthly government payments if they had contributed to the system by payroll deductions over a period of years. The payments were to begin in 1941. The only groups excluded in the original legislation were domestic help and farmworkers. The act also provided federal aid to the states for the care of people with disabilities, mothers with dependent children, and for public health services. It attempted to establish an economic safety net for those Americans in need.

Widespread Support for the Second New Deal

The Second New Deal paid huge political dividends for the Roosevelt administration. It brought many wavering blue-collar voters back into the ranks of the Democratic Party. As a Philadelphian wrote to the president after his call for higher taxes for the wealthy, "I am now on your bandwagon again, after having slipped off." Any doubts about Roosevelt's renewed popularity were removed by the results of the 1936 presidential election.

Roosevelt again won by a landslide, polling over 60 percent of the popular vote. Running against a conservative Republican candidate, Governor Alf Landon of Kansas, the president carried every state but Maine and Vermont. The returns indicated that Roosevelt had welded together a voting coalition that included Democratic white southerners, blue-collar workers in the cities, and African American voters in every section of the country.

1. **Name** the New Deal measures attacked by the business community.
2. **Explain** why interest-group democracy was not successful.
3. **Describe** the ways in which the Second New Deal differed from the First New Deal.
4. **Name** the piece of legislation designed to act as a safety net for America's needy.
5. **State** reasons why the Democrats won by a landslide in 1936.

SECTION 3

The New Deal, Minorities, and Organized Labor

Roosevelt owed the impressive margin of his victory in 1936 partly to a historic shift of African American voters into the Democratic party. Since the Reconstruction Era, black voters who were not disfranchised had voted solidly Republican, because this was the party of Abraham Lincoln. But as a headline in the *Baltimore Afro-American* reminded its readers in 1936, "Abraham Lincoln Is Not a Candidate in the Present Campaign." The shift of African Americans toward the Democratic Party had begun in the 1934 congressional elections, when a majority voted Democratic for the first time. That year, African American voters in Chicago had elected Arthur Mitchell as the first black Democrat in Congress. African Americans went on to cast their ballots overwhelmingly for Roosevelt in 1936, giving him 76 percent of their vote. Winning over the African American vote marked a major turning point in the history of the Democratic party.

How did African Americans benefit from the New Deal?
How did the Roosevelt administration help American Indians?
How did the New Deal aid labor unions?

African Americans and the New Deal

African Americans in northern cities voted overwhelmingly for Roosevelt in 1936 in recognition of what the New Deal had done for them. Roosevelt had appointed African Americans to important positions in the administration. Among them were Robert C. Weaver in the Interior Department and Mary McLeod Bethune in the National Youth Administration. Mary McLeod Bethune, the daughter of former slaves, was a leading black educator. She headed several New Deal government agencies, founded the National Council of Negro Women and was vice president of the NAACP. The president also sought advice from the so-called black cabinet, an informal group that kept him aware of the needs and problems of African

▼ *Mary McLeod Bethune was a prominent African American appointed to office by President Roosevelt.*

Americans. Being among the poorest and most needy, African Americans benefited from the New Deal's relief and public works programs. Some 230,000 African Americans were on WPA payrolls by 1941, representing about 16 percent of the workers employed by that New Deal agency. (At that time African Americans made up 10 percent of the total population.)

Although the Roosevelt administration did more for African Americans than any administration since Reconstruction, its record was not unblemished. The New Deal did little for African Americans in the rural South. Black tenant farmers even lost ground as about 192,000 were pushed off the land by the AAA's crop reduction program. Southern cotton growers used cutbacks in production as an opportunity to get rid of African American tenant farmers and sharecroppers. Roosevelt, afraid that he would lose southern congressional support needed for other recovery legislation, did not protest. Roosevelt also did nothing to promote civil rights legislation. He failed to endorse proposed laws that would have made lynching a federal offense and that would have outlawed the poll tax—the major civil rights goals of the 1930s.

First Lady **Eleanor Roosevelt** was the administration's major champion of civil rights. She spoke out in favor of civil rights legislation and against racial segregation in public places. In 1939, the Daughters of the American Revolution (DAR) prevented Marian Anderson, an African American opera star, from singing at Constitution Hall in Washington, D.C. The DAR owned the hall and barred Anderson solely because of her race. Eleanor Roosevelt was among the first to protest. She resigned from the DAR and intervened to have Anderson's performance moved to the Lincoln Memorial. There, a much larger audience was able to hear the renowned vocalist.

Eleanor Roosevelt was involved in many reform causes. As first lady, she visited relief projects across the nation. She also wrote a syndicated newspaper column in which she discussed the issues facing the nation. She created a model of the first lady as political activist, although few of her immediate successors chose to follow it.

▼ *First Lady Eleanor Roosevelt gave her own weekly radio broadcasts entitled "Americans of Tomorrow." These talks about children were addressed to parents and teachers.*

▼ *Marian Anderson performed in 1939 on the steps of the Lincoln Memorial after the Daughters of the American Revolution had denied her permission to appear at Constitution Hall.*

Major New Deal Legislation

Date	Act or Agency	Description	Still in Effect?
March 1933	Emergency Banking Act	Fund some banks, close others	No
March 1933	Civilian Conservation Corps	Out-of-doors work relief for men 18-25	No
May 1933	Agricultural Adjustment Act	Regulate farm prices and production	No
May 1933	Tennessee Valley Authority	Develop resources in Tennessee Valley	Yes
May 1933	Federal Emergency Relief Act	Direct aid to cities and states	No
June 1933	Home Owners Refinancing Act	Relief for homeowners facing foreclosures	No
June 1933	National Industrial Recovery Act	Stimulate business and help raise wages and prices	No
June 1933	Public Works Administration	Provide employment on public works	No
June 1933	Federal Deposit Insurance Corporation	Guarantee individual bank deposits in insured banks	Yes
Nov. 1933	Civil Works Administration	Federally funded relief projects	No
June 1934	Federal Housing Administration	Loans for home repair and new housing	Yes
June 1934	Securities and Exchange Commission	Full disclosure of stock issues provided for investors	Yes
April 1935	Emergency Relief Appropriation Act		
	Works Progress Administration	Work relief on public works projects, especially fine and performing arts	No
	National Youth Administration	Work for high school and college youth	No
	Rural Electrification Administration	Provide electricity to rural areas	No
1935	National Labor Relations Act (Wagner Act)	Regulate and protect unions	Yes
1935	Social Security Act	Unemployment benefits, insurance, and retirement	Yes
1937	Farm Security Administration	Federal financing for tenant farmers and migrant workers	No

▲ *These legislative acts and programs were among the most important accomplishments of the New Deal. Many of the programs are still essential today.*

The New Deal and Other Minority Groups

The Roosevelt administration was more sensitive to the needs of American Indians. John Collier, the new commissioner of Indian affairs, was a long-time champion of American Indian rights. He was also an advocate of tribal rather than individual ownership of Indian lands. Under the Dawes Act of 1887, land held tribally by Indians had dwindled from 138 million acres to 48 million acres. Much of the best Indian land had ended up in the hands of non-Indian ranchers and farmers. At Collier's urging, Congress passed the Indian Reorganization Act of 1934, which reversed the government's Indian policy by bringing an end to the allotment of land to individuals. The act also permitted American Indians to organize local self-governments. As head of the Bureau of Indian Affairs, Collier encouraged instruction in Indian languages in reservation schools and insisted that agency employees respect Indian religion and culture.

In contrast, the New Deal did practically nothing for the thousands of Mexican immigrants in the Southwest who had entered the United States to work as migrant farm laborers. They had less political influence than some other ethnic minorities, as many were alien residents who could not vote. Moreover, the AAA could help farm owners, but had nothing to offer farmworkers. Unemployment among this group was extremely high, as farm production fell and the number of jobs diminished.

American Indian families endured much suffering in the Great Depression. How did the New Deal benefit American Indians?

The plight of the Mexican workers was made even worse by growers who gave most of the seasonal work that did exist to native-born workers. California growers did so partly to undermine the farmworkers' union, the Confederación de Uniones de Campesinos y Obreros Mexicanos (CUCOM), or Confederation of Mexican Farmers and Workers Unions, which Mexican migrant workers had organized. State governments were as unresponsive to their needs as the national government. Rather than provide welfare payments for resident aliens, California spent money to send them back to Mexico.

The New Deal and Organized Labor

At the depth of the depression in 1933, the future of organized labor in the United States seemed bleak. Union membership had declined from over 5 million in 1920 to fewer than 3 million. Most of the remaining members were skilled craftsmen who belonged to the trade unions affiliated with the American Federation of Labor (AFL). The unions had failed to organize the large mass-production industries, such as steel, textiles, and automobiles. These, not the skilled trades, were the growth industries of the twentieth century. Although the future of the unions looked unpromising at the beginning of the New Deal, they were actually on the threshold of the largest gains in the history of organized labor.

The gains were the result of a presidential administration sympathetic to organized labor and of pro-labor legislation enacted by Congress. Roosevelt had appointed Frances Perkins as his secretary of labor. Perkins, the first woman to serve in a cabinet position, was a long-time supporter of organized labor. She helped draft much of the New Deal labor legislation. Section 7a of the National Industrial Recovery Act of 1933 recognized the right of workers to join unions and, as a group, to negotiate hours, wages, and working conditions with their employers. This is called **collective bargaining**. Section 7a actually did little to help labor unions as many employers responded by organizing company unions that they controlled. Far more important was the **National Labor Relations Act** of 1935, which guaranteed workers a union of their own choice. This law was sponsored by New York Senator Robert F. Wagner Sr. and was commonly known

▶ *Frances Perkins was greeted by workers at a United States Steel plant during an information-gathering tour. What distinction was held by this secretary of labor?*

as the Wagner Act. It required employers to recognize and bargain in good faith with any union supported by a majority of their employees. The choice of unions was to be determined by an election supervised by the National Labor Relations Board, a new federal agency created by the Wagner Act. For the first time, labor organizers had the support of federal law.

The passage of the Wagner Act coincided with the emergence of new and more aggressive leadership within organized labor. In 1935, a split took place within the AFL. The rift was between the trade unions, which were mainly interested in organizing skilled workers, and the industrial unions. The latter, led by **John L. Lewis** of the United Mine Workers, were committed to organizing all workers within an industry, whether skilled or unskilled. Industrial unionism, they insisted, was the only basis on which the mass-production industries could be organized. When Lewis and the industrial unionists were expelled from the AFL in 1935, they formed a rival federation, the Congress of Industrial Organizations (CIO). This group was responsible for much of the growth in organized labor during the remaining years of the depression.

Lewis and the other organizers of the CIO were aided by a growing militancy among industrial workers. In 1936, rubber workers in Akron, Ohio, and autoworkers in Cleveland, Ohio, and Flint, Michigan, tried a relatively new weapon for bargaining with employers. It was called the **sit-down strike**. The striking workers sat down at their jobs

◀ *John L. Lewis, president of the United Mine Workers Union, was photographed addressing a national conference of labor and management leaders. Why were Lewis and the mine workers expelled from the American Federation of Labor?*

▲ *In 1937, auto workers in Flint, Michigan, staged a sit-down strike. Why was the sit-down strike such a powerful weapon for labor unions?*

The Waning of the New Deal

Franklin D. Roosevelt had great plans for his second administration. He intended to make the New Deal an instrument for social reform. "Wait until next year, Henry," Roosevelt had remarked to Henry Morgenthau, his secretary of the treasury in 1936, "I am going to be really radical. . . . I am going to recommend a lot of radical legislation." In his second inaugural address, Roosevelt announced that it was time to address the needs of the "one-third of a nation ill-housed, ill-clad, ill-nourished." With large Democratic majorities in both houses of Congress (328 to 107 in the House; 77 to 19 in the Senate), the president seemed to be in a good position to do almost anything that he wanted. Roosevelt could hardly have suspected that little would come from his resounding victory in 1936 and that the New Deal was almost over.

Why did Roosevelt attack the Supreme Court?
What consequences did the Court battle have for the New Deal?
What impact did the New Deal have on American society?

and refused to work or leave the plant until their demands were met. The more conventional method was for strikers to walk out and form a **picket line** in front of the factory. Loyal union members and union sympathizers would refuse to take a job that required crossing a picket line. In 1937, a wave of strikes swept through American industry. Many were successful, leading to union recognition and contracts with such firms as United States Steel and General Motors. Other strikes were broken, usually with the help of local law enforcement. In 1937, police broke a strike at Republic Steel in Chicago on Memorial Day by attacking a picket line, killing ten strikers and wounding many others. The unions eventually succeeded in organizing most of the major industries outside the South. The South, however, remained a stronghold of anti-union sentiment for years to come.

SECTION 3 REVIEW

1. **Describe** ways in which the New Deal benefitted African Americans.
2. **Explain** how the Indian Reorganization Act reversed the government's previous policy.
3. **State** reasons why labor unions were successful during the New Deal period.
4. **Identify** John L. Lewis.
5. **Contrast** the membership of the AFL and CIO.

Roosevelt and the Supreme Court

By 1936, a new threat had emerged that endangered the future of the New Deal. It came from the United States Supreme Court, which had already struck down two major pieces of New Deal legislation. In May 1935, the Court had ruled the National Industrial Recovery Act unconstitutional. By giving the executive branch the power to write the codes for this law, the Court decided that Congress had delegated too much of its authority. Under the Constitution, Congress alone has the power to regulate the interstate trade affected by the codes.

In January 1936, in the case of *United States v. Butler*, the Court also struck down the Agricultural

Adjustment Act. The Court declared the tax on food that financed payments to farmers unconstitutional, so the law itself was a misuse of Congress's power to tax. Following a strict interpretation of the Constitution, the Supreme Court again decided that Congress had given too much power to the executive branch.

Roosevelt viewed the matter in a different light. He saw the Supreme Court as the last stronghold of the Republican Party. He was afraid that the conservative justices (the "nine old men," as he called them) intended to dismantle the New Deal one law at a time.

Roosevelt was especially concerned about what the Supreme Court might do in the future. It did not matter to him that the NIRA and AAA were declared invalid, as neither had worked out as well as Roosevelt had hoped. After two years of NRA codes, the nation was still in a depression. Agriculture had fared little better under the AAA. But Roosevelt was worried that the Court would go on to strike down a battery of more recent legislation for which he did have high expectations. He decided that the Second New Deal was in danger.

In a message to Congress early in 1937, Roosevelt launched an attack against the Supreme Court. He called for legislation to reform the judiciary by allowing him to appoint a new judge, including up to six Supreme Court justices, any time an incumbent judge refused to retire after reaching the age of 70. His explanation was that the courts at every level were falling behind in their work because of aged and infirm judges. Roosevelt's explanation was less than candid. As six of the Supreme Court justices were older than 70, he clearly intended to use the proposed bill to appoint new justices who would be more favorable to the New Deal.

The judiciary reorganization bill that resulted

THE WASHINGTON POST: SATURDAY, FEBRUARY 6, 1937

"To Furnish The Supreme Court Practical Assistance."

THIS ACT SHALL TAKE EFFECT ON THE 30TH DAY AFTER THE DATE OF ITS ENACTMENT.

CONGRESS

▲ *This* Washington Post *editorial cartoon attacked Roosevelt's plan to reorganize the judiciary. Why did the cartoonist draw all six of the additional judges with Roosevelt's face?*

from Roosevelt's proposal led to a heated national debate. Conservatives accused the president of trying to "pack the Supreme Court." Even many supporters of the New Deal were disturbed by Roosevelt's attempt to impose his will on the judiciary. The judiciary reorganization bill threatened to upset the system of checks and balances provided in the Constitution. Although a revised reorganization bill passed, Congress voted down the court-packing proposal that Roosevelt wanted most.

Although Roosevelt lost the battle with the Supreme Court, he could claim that he had won the war to preserve the New Deal. In a series of decisions in 1937, the Court reversed direction and allowed important New Deal legislation to stand. The Wagner Act (NLRA) and the Social Security Act were upheld by votes of five to four. Seven justices resigned during the next four years, which allowed Roosevelt to appoint a majority that favored the New Deal.

Yet the Court battle had damaged Roosevelt more than he suspected. His program to aid the ill-housed and ill-nourished was stalled in Congress while the debate over the Court raged. This fight also drove a wedge into the Democratic Party, with conservative Democrats siding against the administration. The coalition of conservative Democrats and Republicans in Congress that opposed the court-packing bill remained intact to oppose other New Deal measures.

Losing Steam

It was clear by 1938 that the New Deal was losing momentum. Congress did pass the Fair Labor

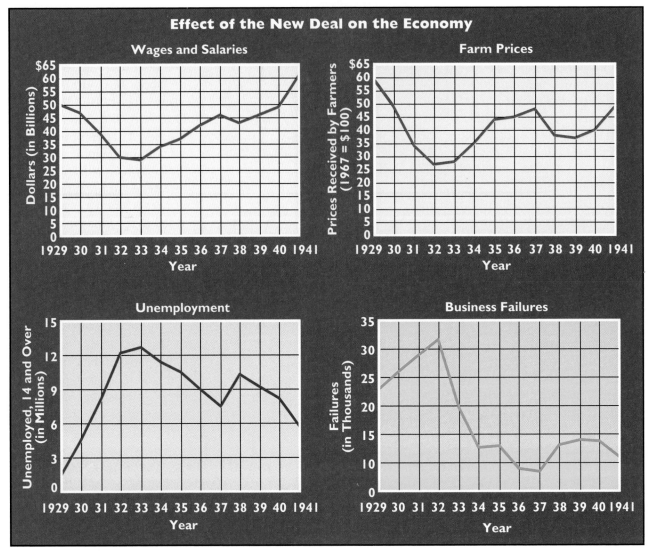

Effect of the New Deal on the Economy

Wages and Salaries

Dollars (in Billions)

1929 30 31 32 33 34 35 36 37 38 39 40 1941
Year

Farm Prices

Prices Received by Farmers (1967 = $100)

1929 30 31 32 33 34 35 36 37 38 39 40 1941
Year

Unemployment

Unemployed, 14 and Over (in Millions)

1929 30 31 32 33 34 35 36 37 38 39 40 1941
Year

Business Failures

Failures (in Thousands)

1929 30 31 32 33 34 35 36 37 38 39 40 1941
Year

▲ *These graphs chart four different measures of the health of the U.S. economy during the Great Depression. In what year did the recovery effort temporarily stall?*

Standards Act of 1938, which established a federal minimum wage and maximum weekly hours for certain classes of workers. The legislation also outlawed the use of child labor in interstate commerce. This bill passed only after its opponents managed to exclude domestic servants and agricultural workers from the wages and hours provision of the bill. A National Housing Act also passed in 1938, which authorized slum clearance and the building of public-housing apartments for the needy. However, few housing units were built because real estate interests lobbied against funding for the measure.

A new economic crisis also helped to sidetrack New Deal measures for reform. The economy showed sufficient signs of recovery from the depression by 1936 that economists feared runaway inflation unless government spending was reduced and credit tightened. The inflation never happened, and measures taken to combat it backfired. The nation was stunned in 1937 with a sudden downturn in the business cycle, the beginning of a sharp recession. The result was a contraction of economic activity. Most of the previous gains were lost. For the next two years, economic recovery was once again a

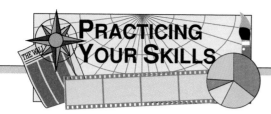
Making Inferences Using Multiple Graphs

You have already learned how to interpret data from a single graph. Comparing and contrasting data from more than one graph allows historians to suggest cause-and-effect relationships, and to make generalizations and inferences—much like a detective solving a mystery.

Review the guidelines for interpreting graphs presented in the Practicing Your Skills on page 123 and then read the following steps for comparing multiple graphs. When comparing two or more graphs ask yourself these questions:

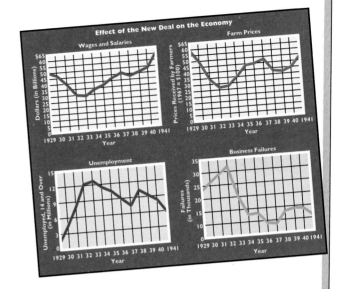

- **Are the graphs really comparable?** Are you trying to compare related information? You can't make valid inferences if there is no underlying connection or relationship between the graphs. On each graph read the title, purpose, time period covered, and information on the horizontal and vertical axes.
- **Are your measurements in common units (years, dollars, per thousand, etc.)?** You can't compare dollars with yen, or years with months.
- **Do the graphs cover related periods?** If you are looking for trends, the information should come from the same time periods. If you are trying to determine a cause-and-effect relationship, one graph should pre-date the other.

Examine the graphs on page 718 and answer the following:

1. (a) What is being compared on these graphs? (b) What do they have in common? (c) In what ways are they different? (d) Which of the four graphs concern characteristics of poor economic activity?
2. How does the graph of wages and salaries compare to the graph of unemployment? Relate the data on the wages and salaries graph to those on the unemployment graph.
3. How do you think an increase in business failures would affect unemployment and wages and salaries?
4. Identify the highest years for wages and salaries and for farm prices. Make a generalization about your findings.
5. From these graphs and from your reading in the text and class discussion, what inferences can you make about the economic recovery from 1929 to 1941?

▲ *A 1936 announcement to cut back on WPA programs such as this one in St. Louis brought a flood of protest mail to the White House and Congress. Why was the WPA one of the most popular of the New Deal programs?*

more pressing issue than social reform. Although most of the economic ground lost was regained by 1939, the question of reform was then being overshadowed by the concern for national defense.

Evaluating the New Deal Although almost over by 1939, the New Deal had already made a lasting impact on American life. Above all, the public programs of the New Deal era greatly expanded the responsibilities of the federal government. Government had assumed the responsibility of ensuring the social and economic health of the nation. It replaced local institutions as the principal source of social services and welfare relief. The legislation of the 1930s gave the federal government a much larger role in the economic affairs of the nation. The New Deal had established minimum standards for labor conditions and public welfare. By 1939, federal agencies regulated the stock market, insured savings accounts, made low-interest home mortgages possible, helped unions engage in collective bargaining, built school buildings, bridges, and public parks, and provided jobs for the unemployed. The Roosevelt administration had not brought the depression to an end by 1939, but it had made a great difference in the lives of those who had suffered through this period.

SECTION 4 REVIEW

1. **Explain** how the Supreme Court attempted to block the New Deal.
2. **Describe** Roosevelt's plan to weaken the power of the Supreme Court.
3. **State** how the recession of 1937 affected the momentum of the New Deal.
4. **Name** two groups excluded from the Fair Labor Standards Act of 1938.
5. **Describe** how the New Deal made a difference in the lives of Americans.

SECTION 5

The Foreign Policy of the New Deal

Roosevelt set the tone for his administration's foreign policy when he took office in 1933. He did not intend for the United States to retreat into isolation. Neither would the United States, in times of economic crisis, pursue a bold policy of world leadership. Rather, the United States would be a "good neighbor" in world affairs—"the neighbor who resolutely respects himself and, because he does so, respects the rights of others." Whether other nations would treat the United States as a friendly neighbor in return remained to be seen.

How did the Roosevelt administration change American policy toward Latin America?

How did Congress try to isolate the United States from troubles in Europe?

Why did the United States become the "arsenal of democracy?"

The Good Neighbor Policy in Latin America

The administration was highly successful in applying the **Good Neighbor Policy** toward Latin

America. Roosevelt continued Hoover's efforts to improve relations by avoiding military intervention. At the International Conference of American States in 1933, the United States agreed to a resolution stating that "no state has the right to intervene in the internal affairs of another." In keeping with this pledge, Roosevelt withdrew American troops from Nicaragua and Haiti, where they had been stationed since the 1920s. Congress also abolished the section of the Platt Amendment that gave the United States the right to intervene in Cuba. Under the Good Neighbor Policy, relations with Latin America steadily improved.

The withdrawal of the troops did not mean that the United States withdrew its presence from Latin America. It managed to protect its political and economic interests there by diplomacy, by extending economic aid to friendly governments, and by encouraging Pan-American cooperation. The United States still maintained its sphere of influence in Latin America.

► *The Italian dictator Benito Mussolini visited Hitler in Germany. What did these two leaders have in common?*

Security in an Unstable World

Although a degree of harmony had been restored in the Western Hemisphere, a crisis was developing in Europe. In 1933, Germany had elected a new chancellor, Adolf Hitler. Hitler was head of the National Socialist German Workers' Party, or the **Nazi Party**.

Hitler's Nazi Party capitalized on the discontent and suffering caused by the harsh peace settlement imposed by the Treaty of Versailles. Hitler quickly seized absolute power and turned Germany into a fascist state. **Fascism** was a dictatorship that merged the power of the state and German business interests. Intent on making Germany the dominant power in Europe, Hitler rebuilt the German army. Working together, Hitler and Germany's business leaders began re-arming Germany. Once again, Germany would become a threat to its neighbors.

Hitler also pursued an aggressive foreign policy. In 1936, German troops reoccupied the Rhineland, which the Treaty of Versailles had made a demilita-

rized zone in order to give France a secure border. In the fall of that year, Hitler made an alliance with Benito Mussolini, the fascist dictator of Italy, creating the Rome-Berlin Axis. Mussolini was known to his followers as *Il Duce*—meaning "the leader." With the help of his Black Shirt followers who terrorized all opposition, Mussolini made the Fascist Party supreme in Italy. In 1935, Mussolini began his own war of conquest by invading the East African nation of Ethiopia.

In 1938, the Germans invaded and annexed Austria, and demanded that Czechoslovakia surrender territory. At a series of meetings in Munich, Germany, with British Prime Minister Neville Chamberlain and Prime Minister Édouard Daladier of France, Hitler won agreement to annex Czechoslovakia's western border regions, the Sudetenland. Although Chamberlain and Daladier hoped to satisfy Hitler by giving in to his demands, a policy known as **appeasement**, others warned that he could not be stopped without a war.

In the face of the threatening events in Europe, the United States tried desperately to avoid getting involved. Public opinion was influenced by hearings

This poster was created by the America First Committee. Why did this group oppose sending military aid to Great Britain?

conducted from 1934 to 1936 by a congressional committee headed by Senator Gerald P. Nye of North Dakota. The Nye Committee concluded that the United States had been unnecessarily drawn into World War I in order to aid the "merchants of death" (weapon and munitions makers) and to help Wall Street bankers collect their loans to the Allied powers. Congress responded to the committee's findings with legislation designed to keep the United States neutral.

The neutrality laws of the 1930s tried to isolate the United States from European troubles. The Neutrality Act of 1935 prohibited the sale of arms to any nation at war. It was amended in 1936 to include the banning of bank loans to belligerent nations. The Neutrality Act of 1937 put a limited embargo on all other goods. A nation at war could

trade with the United States only on a cash-and-carry basis—that is, by paying for the goods and carrying them away in that nation's own ships. Finally, Americans were forbidden to travel on the ships of any nation at war.

War had already broken out in Asia, when Japan invaded mainland China in July 1937. Americans were shocked at the barbarity of the attack, especially the slaying of Chinese civilians. The United States became momentarily involved in December 1937, when Japanese war planes sank the American gunboat *Panay* on the Chang Jiang (Yangtze River). Japan apologized for its action, and the incident was forgotten. But the invasion of China reminded the United States that it might be difficult to remain neutral. The president warned the nation that if the world continued to drift toward war, "Let no one imagine America will escape."

◀ *Japanese troops invaded China in 1937. How did Japan's expansionist policies affect the United States?*

World War II Breaks Out in Europe

The rush of events in Europe in 1939–1940 confirmed Roosevelt's worst fears. German troops invaded Czechoslovakia in the spring of 1939. Then Italy attacked Albania. After signing a **nonaggression pact** in August 1939 with the Soviet Union agreeing not to invade each other's territory, Germany invaded Poland in September. The invasion of Poland brought a quick response from Poland's allies, Britain and France. Both nations promptly declared war against Germany.

By the next summer, Europe was engulfed in war. German armies invaded Denmark and Norway in April 1940 and overran the Netherlands, Belgium, and Luxembourg in May. From there, the Germans swept into France and quickly overpowered its armed forces. As a stunned world looked on, France surrendered on June 22.

American Neutrality Debated   With the German armies on the move, Roosevelt looked for ways to help the democratic nations of Europe. He urged Congress to revise the neutrality acts to permit arms sales to the nations at war with Germany. In November 1939, Congress did allow arms sales on a cash-and-carry basis.

With the fall of France in 1940, Roosevelt sought even more direct ways to aid Great Britain. That nation was the last remaining obstacle to

Hitler's control of Europe and the Atlantic. In July 1940, British Prime Minister **Winston Churchill** urgently pleaded for American destroyers, aircraft, and weapons. Roosevelt responded by exchanging 50 destroyers for 99-year leases on British bases in Newfoundland and the Caribbean. In doing so, he touched off a major foreign policy debate.

The issue was whether the United States should aid Britain or remain strictly neutral. On one side of the debate was the Committee to Defend America by Aiding the Allies, which advocated increased aid. Another vocal group, the America First Committee, opposed aid to the British as a violation of neutrality. It preferred isolation and a German victory to the threat of getting involved in another war in Europe. Although such isolationists as Charles Lindbergh and Herbert Hoover had little love for Hitler, they did not fear a Europe dominated by Germany.

▼ *In 1940, Roosevelt exchanged 50 American destroyers for long-term leases of British bases. Why did this deal cause a major foreign policy debate?*

Destroyers for Bases Deal

British bases leased to the United States in exchange for destroyers to aid Britain against Germany.

0   500 mi
0   800 km

The Arsenal of Democracy

Roosevelt still hoped to avoid direct American intervention in the war in Europe. The United States should serve as the "arsenal of democracy," the president said, letting Britain do the fighting. After accepting an unprecedented third presidential nomination in 1940, Roosevelt campaigned by pledging to keep the nation out of war. "I have said this before, but I shall say it again and again and again: your boys are not going to be sent into any foreign wars." Foreign policy was not a major issue in that campaign. Roosevelt's Republican opponent, Wendell Willkie, also supported aid to Britain short of actual intervention. That November, Roosevelt defeated Willkie by a vote of 27 million to 22 million. It was a general vote of confidence in Roosevelt and his policies.

Determined to support Britain's war effort, Roosevelt sent a new military-aid bill to Congress in January 1941. The **Lend-Lease Act**, as it was called after the bill was passed, discarded the cash-and-carry principle for arms sales. Churchill had warned Roosevelt in his latest appeal for help that Britain was nearly broke and that German submarines had taken a heavy toll on British ships. The act authorized the president to "lend, lease, or otherwise dispose of" arms and other supplies needed by any country whose security was vital to American defense. Although opposed by isolationists in Congress as a step toward war, the bill easily passed.

Roosevelt turned next to the problem of getting lend-lease supplies safely to Britain. To help British freighters avoid German submarines, he ordered the navy to extend patrols into the Atlantic. United States destroyers escorted merchant ships as far as Iceland. Roosevelt worked out an agreement with Iceland to establish a naval base there. He also got permission to station American troops in Danish-owned Greenland. Finally, in August of 1941, Roosevelt and Churchill met for four days on a ship anchored off the coast of Newfoundland. They discussed, among other things, their vision for the future which they spelled out in a document called the **Atlantic Charter**. This document, like Wilson's Fourteen Points, made known certain common principles and national policies to guarantee peace. Among the conditions eventually accepted by 26 nations in 1942 were the concepts of self-determination, freedom of the seas, an end to colonialism and "territorial aggrandizement," and an improvement in the living and working conditions of all peoples.

With its destroyers on patrol in the Atlantic, the United States had come close to the thin line separating aid for Britain from direct involvement in the war. How close became obvious on September 4, 1941, when the U.S. destroyer *Greer* gave chase to a German U-boat off the coast of Iceland. Unable to lose the *Greer*, the submarine tried to sink it with a torpedo. The *Greer*, in turn, attacked the submarine. Neither vessel was damaged. However, Roosevelt used the incident to announce a new defense policy that gave the navy a still larger role. In a radio address on September 11, he announced that American warships would patrol a wide area of the Atlantic between the East Coast and Iceland and would "shoot on sight" any German or Italian vessel encountered in that area. In effect, this was, as historian Arthur Link has written, "a declaration of undeclared war." On October 17, a German torpedo southwest of Iceland did strike a stalking destroyer, the *Kearney*, killing 11 American sailors. On October 31, the destroyer *Reuben James* was sunk off Iceland with the loss of 96 lives. The United States now found itself involved in an undeclared war in the Atlantic.

War in the Pacific

Japan's invasion of China in 1937 violated the Open Door Policy in China. The American government saw an aggressive Japan as a threat to the Philippine Islands and other American interests in the Pacific. It insisted that Japan cease its aggression and withdraw its troops from China. Intent on widening its sphere of influence in Asia, Japan refused to withdraw. Roosevelt tried to persuade the Japanese with economic sanctions. In September 1940, the United States placed an embargo on exports to Japan of strategic materials, including vital oil shipments and aviation gasoline. Roosevelt impounded Japanese assets in the United States and cut off all trade to Japan.

Cut off from its major source of petroleum and other strategic raw materials, Japan faced a crisis. It either had to withdraw from Asia or expand its conquests further by seizing the oil-rich Dutch East Indies. This would involve a war with the United States, as the Japanese would have to occupy the Philippine Islands in order to provide secure lines of communication in the western Pacific.

Attack on Pearl Harbor In a fateful decision, the Japanese government chose expansion. Preparations were made for a military operation that would overrun Southeast Asia, the Dutch East Indies, the Philippines, and other islands in the Pacific. To prevent an effective response by the United States, Japan decided to destroy the American Pacific fleet at its base in Pearl Harbor in the Hawaiian Islands. As the attacking forces were moving into position in November 1941, the Japanese government agreed to one final round of diplomatic talks. But neither side was willing to compromise the positions already taken. The talks ended on December 7, 1941, with Japan's surprise attack on Pearl Harbor.

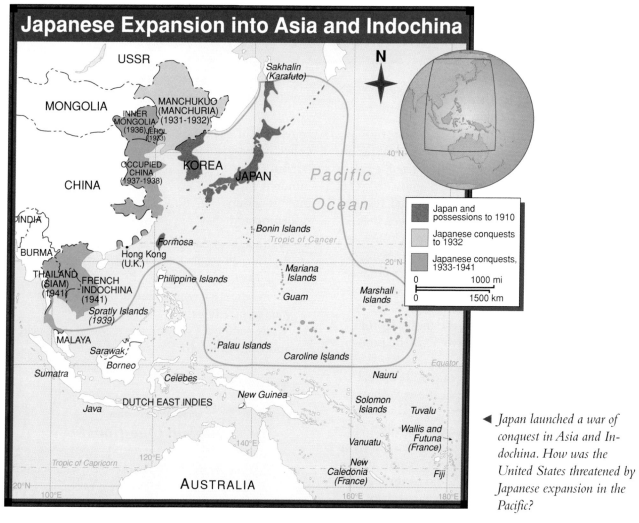

Japanese Expansion into Asia and Indochina

Map labels: USSR · MONGOLIA · INNER MONGOLIA (1936) · MANCHUKUO (MANCHURIA) (1931-1932) · JEHOL (1933) · Sakhalin (Karafuto) · OCCUPIED CHINA (1937-1938) · KOREA · JAPAN · CHINA · INDIA · Pacific Ocean · BURMA · Formosa · Hong Kong (U.K.) · Bonin Islands · Tropic of Cancer · THAILAND (SIAM) (1941) · FRENCH INDOCHINA (1941) · Philippine Islands · Mariana Islands · Guam · Marshall Islands · Spratly Islands (1939) · MALAYA · Sarawak · Borneo · Palau Islands · Caroline Islands · Equator · Sumatra · Celebes · New Guinea · Nauru · DUTCH EAST INDIES · Java · Solomon Islands · Tuvalu · Wallis and Futuna (France) · Vanuatu · New Caledonia (France) · Fiji · AUSTRALIA

Legend:
- Japan and possessions to 1910
- Japanese conquests to 1932
- Japanese conquests, 1933-1941

0 1000 mi
0 1500 km

◀ *Japan launched a war of conquest in Asia and Indochina. How was the United States threatened by Japanese expansion in the Pacific?*

By intercepting and decoding Japanese messages, the U.S. government knew that Japan was preparing for battle, but no one expected a surprise attack on Pearl Harbor. A message from officials in Washington warning that war with Japan was likely had been carelessly forwarded by commercial channels, and was not received in time at Pearl Harbor for the base to go on red alert. The base was caught completely off guard.

Using six aircraft carriers to transport more than 350 planes, the Japanese planes arrived at Pearl Harbor early Sunday morning while most American servicemen were still asleep. The targets were the American naval vessels and nearby airfields. When the attack was over, nearly 2,400 Americans were dead and 1,200 others wounded. Nineteen U.S. ships had been sunk or disabled. More than 120 U.S. planes were destroyed. In spite of these figures, the Japanese did not significantly affect the ability of the United States to wage war in the Pacific. Three aircraft carriers fortunately had been on a mission at sea and escaped the attack. These carriers would play a decisive role in the upcoming war. The Japanese had failed to destroy onshore oil tanks. Loss of that fuel would have crippled the remaining fleet and delayed mobilization in the Pacific. Finally, the attack outraged Americans and fueled their determination to enter and win the war.

SECTION 5 REVIEW

1. **Describe** the Good Neighbor Policy.
2. **List** the major provisions of the neutrality acts.
3. **State** reasons for the United States abandoning its isolationist position.
4. **Explain** the significance of the *Greer* incident.
5. **Summarize** the effectiveness of the attack on Pearl Harbor.

Summary

Congress, under Roosevelt's leadership, mobilized the resources of the federal government for a massive attack on the depression. It enacted legislation that rescued the banking system, provided relief for the poor and work for the unemployed, reversed the downward plunge of agricultural prices, helped homeowners save their homes from foreclosure, and attempted to get the wheels of industry moving again. Not all of the New Deal measures were successful. Some, the Supreme Court decided, were not even constitutional. But together the programs of the New Deal Era represented the most vigorous exercise of federal power to solve domestic problems in the nation's history.

The policies and programs of the New Deal also had far-reaching social implications. Congress passed the Social Security Act in 1935 to provide federal assistance for those too old or too disabled to work. Industrial workers were guaranteed the right to bargain collectively with their employers, and they were provided the means to do so through the National Labor Relations Act. Many minority groups benefited from New Deal programs, especially African Americans and American Indians. Public works projects that built new parks and schools made American cities better places in which to live.

In its foreign policy, the Roosevelt administration tried to chart a middle course between intervention in world affairs and isolation. Roosevelt developed the Good Neighbor Policy, committed to respecting the rights of other nations while protecting the interests of the United States. The policy was especially successful in Latin America, where it reversed a long-standing policy of military intervention. But the United States discovered that being a good neighbor with Germany and Japan was much more difficult. By 1939, each was at war with nations enjoying a special relationship with the United States—Britain and China. By 1941, the United States found itself at the very brink of war.

Vocabulary

appeasement
collective bargaining
fascism
hundred days
interest-group
  democracy

Lend-Lease Act
nonaggression pact
picket line
Second New Deal
sit-down strike
work relief

1. Write a short paragraph using the terms *hundred days*, *interest-group democracy*, *work relief*, and *Second New Deal*.
2. Write a sentence using the terms *collective bargaining*, *picket line*, and *sit-down strike*.
3. Write sentences relating the terms *appeasement* and *Lend-Lease Act*.
4. Write a sentence using the terms *fascism* and *nonaggression pact*.

Review Questions

1. What did Franklin D. Roosevelt try to accomplish during the first hundred days?
2. Evaluate how successful Roosevelt was in reaching his goal.
3. Explain why the business community was critical of the New Deal by 1934.
4. What was the Second New Deal?
5. Why did African Americans shift their political loyalty to the Democratic Party?
6. Why do you think the New Deal paid little attention to Mexican Americans?
7. Describe how the New Deal helped strengthen labor unions.
8. Evaluate the success of Roosevelt's attack against the Supreme Court.
9. How did the Good Neighbor Policy reverse the previous Latin American policy?
10. Describe methods used by the United States to aid certain European countries before 1941.

Critical Historical Thinking

Writing Answer each of the following by writing one or more complete paragraphs:

1. What problems would the government face today in trying to put the unemployed to work with New Deal-type programs?

2. There are now proposals that the age for retirement be raised so that workers do not start collecting Social Security until a later age. Do you think this is a good idea? Explain why, or why not.

3. In your opinion, was the New Deal good or bad for America? Did the benefits derived from the programs outweigh the negatives?

4. Read the selection entitled "Two African American Farmers" in the Unit 7 Archives. Explain why one farmer enjoys a comfortable life while another farmer is having a hard time.

Making Connections with Economics

Throughout the early twentieth century, the American farmer was faced with serious economic problems. The Agricultural Adjustment Act (AAA) was established under the New Deal with a series of programs to aid farmers.

Two economic factors affect farmers. First, without government intervention, farmers operate in a market with *perfect competition*—there are many producers, and no group of producers can control prices or production in the market. At the other end of the spectrum is *oligopolistic competition*—there are few producers who are potentially able to control prices and production either directly or indirectly.

Second, agriculture operates in a market with *inelastic demand*. For any given change in price there is only a small change in demand. If automobile manufacturers were suddenly to drop the price of their automobiles by one-third, demand would jump up as people rushed to take advantage of the bargain prices. Automobiles operate in a market with *elastic demand*. But, if the price of farm products were to fall by one third because it was a bountiful year, people would not rush out to buy more bread than they needed or other groceries just because the prices were lower. If it was a poor year, and there were crop failures that drove up the price of a product such as wheat, people would continue to buy about the same amount of bread and flour. They have little choice. This is what is meant by inelastic demand. The individual farmer can do little to affect the market price of his product. If the price is low because of a bumper crop, he must still meet all the costs of doing business. For these reasons, the AAA programs subsidized farm prices so that farmers could better participate in the economy.

▪ Research the AAA and make a list of programs, such as paying farmers not to grow certain crops or buying and storing surplus farm produce. Make a chart that shows how each of these programs helped farmers.

Additional Skills Practice

Cause-and-effect relationships occur when one event happens before, and causes or leads to, another event. For example, the tightening of credit and reduced federal spending in 1936 caused a recession in 1937.

Correlations are events that are related in some way, usually by sharing a common cause. For instance, there is a correlation between people under thirty and low voter turnout. Being under thirty is not the reason why a person does not vote; the lifestyle associated with young adults is more likely the reason why they don't vote as often as older adults. There is also a correlation between exercise and good health. A person who is healthy also tends to be more active. From the material in this chapter, identify two cause-and-effect relationships and two correlations.

Unit Review Questions

1. What was one reason that the 1920s was an era of prosperity for America?
2. Describe briefly the plight of African Americans during the prosperous years of the 1920s.
3. What were some of the changes in social values that occurred during the 1920s?
4. Describe some of the psychological problems that affected American families during the Great Depression.
5. How did the depression in the U.S. affect other countries?
6. What was a major long-term effect of Franklin Roosevelt's New Deal on American lives?
7. What path did the Roosevelt administration take on setting foreign policy in Latin America?
8. Explain why the depression was especially hard on families living in the Great Plains states.
9. Why did President Roosevelt want to increase the number of justices on the Supreme Court?
10. Tell whether the Great Depression helped or hindered the women's movement in America.

Personalizing History

The Generation Gap   By the 1920s, Americans had grown tired of progressive crusades. People had more time for recreation and leisure. For millions of Americans, movies and radio became very popular. Louis Armstrong was playing jazz and the dancers moved to the Charleston. There were new sports heroes in football and baseball, and popular fads spread quickly. Women bobbed their hair and chaperons were no longer considered necessary by dating couples or their parents. Young people read simplified versions of Sigmund Freud and frightened their parents with "modern" talk of sex.

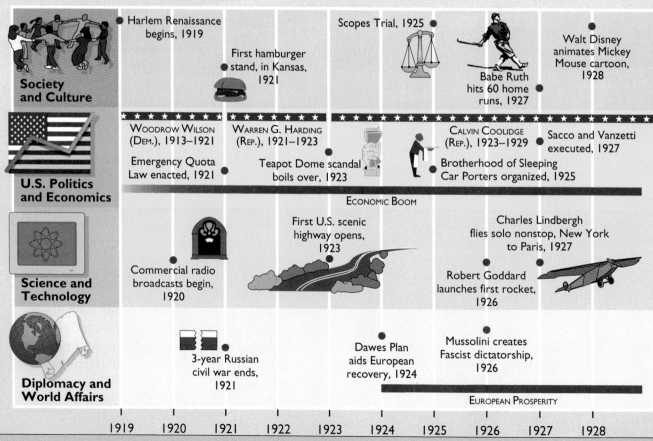

Society and Culture

Harlem Renaissance begins, 1919

First hamburger stand, in Kansas, 1921

Scopes Trial, 1925

Babe Ruth hits 60 home runs, 1927

Walt Disney animates Mickey Mouse cartoon, 1928

U.S. Politics and Economics

WOODROW WILSON (DEM.), 1913–1921

Emergency Quota Law enacted, 1921

WARREN G. HARDING (REP.), 1921–1923

Teapot Dome scandal boils over, 1923

CALVIN COOLIDGE (REP.), 1923–1929

Brotherhood of Sleeping Car Porters organized, 1925

Sacco and Vanzetti executed, 1927

ECONOMIC BOOM

Science and Technology

Commercial radio broadcasts begin, 1920

First U.S. scenic highway opens, 1923

Robert Goddard launches first rocket, 1926

Charles Lindbergh flies solo nonstop, New York to Paris, 1927

Diplomacy and World Affairs

3-year Russian civil war ends, 1921

Dawes Plan aids European recovery, 1924

Mussolini creates Fascist dictatorship, 1926

EUROPEAN PROSPERITY

1919 1920 1921 1922 1923 1924 1925 1926 1927 1928

■ People today—young and old—are still concerned about the "generation gap." Make a list of the complaints that parents from the 1920s made about their children that you believe would also appear on a list about today's generation of parents and young people. Why do you suppose these same concerns continue to be viewed so differently by teens and their parents?

Linking Past and Present

The Stamp of the Depression   Each year the United States Post Office issues a stamp commemorating significant events and people in American history. Only the most honored or those who have made significant contributions to American culture are chosen to have their likenesses on United States stamps. (The post office never selects people who

are living.) In your studies of the Great Depression you have read about the many sacrifices made by the nation and the people. You learned about the legislative commitment by Congress and the president, and the personal hardships faced by farmers, laborers, and families.

■ Review your text and select one person, event, or legislative act that you think deserves special recognition. Design, on unlined paper, a colorful postage stamp that honors that person or event from the time of the Great Depression.

Time Line Activity

Many of the events in the "Science and Technology" category could have been placed in one of the other categories. Identify three of these and move them. Explain why you placed them where you did.

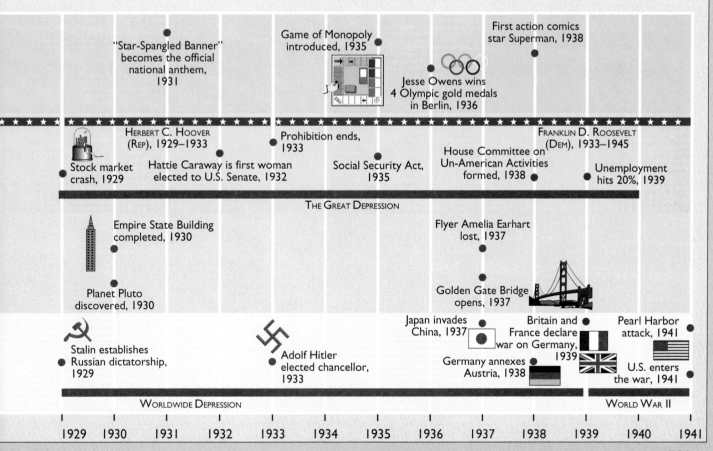

"Star-Spangled Banner" becomes the official national anthem, 1931

Game of Monopoly introduced, 1935

First action comics star Superman, 1938

Jesse Owens wins 4 Olympic gold medals in Berlin, 1936

HERBERT C. HOOVER (REP), 1929–1933

Prohibition ends, 1933

FRANKLIN D. ROOSEVELT (DEM), 1933–1945

Stock market crash, 1929

Hattie Caraway is first woman elected to U.S. Senate, 1932

Social Security Act, 1935

House Committee on Un-American Activities formed, 1938

Unemployment hits 20%, 1939

THE GREAT DEPRESSION

Empire State Building completed, 1930

Flyer Amelia Earhart lost, 1937

Planet Pluto discovered, 1930

Golden Gate Bridge opens, 1937

Japan invades China, 1937

Britain and France declare war on Germany, 1939

Pearl Harbor attack, 1941

Stalin establishes Russian dictatorship, 1929

Adolf Hitler elected chancellor, 1933

Germany annexes Austria, 1938

U.S. enters the war, 1941

WORLDWIDE DEPRESSION

WORLD WAR II

1929 1930 1931 1932 1933 1934 1935 1936 1937 1938 1939 1940 1941

UNIT 8

The United States in a Turbulent World

U.S. entry into World War II caused vast changes in virtually every aspect of American life. Flushed with the success of defeating Japan and Germany, Americans initially viewed their place in the postwar world with optimism and confidence. But within two years after the war, new challenges and perceived threats had emerged. By 1948, a new phenomenon—Cold War—had developed between the Soviet Union and the United States. The politics and policies of anti-Communism were pervasive both in foreign policy and at home. At the war's end, the U.S. economy was unrivaled in strength and potential. Building on that economic base, American society became affluent in the postwar years. The way in which Americans worked and lived underwent revolutionary changes. The fact that Americans did not benefit equally from such general affluence was a problem that received little attention in the 1950s.

Chapter 23 The Second World War	**Chapter 24** Harry S Truman and the Cold War	**Chapter 25** The Eisenhower Era	**Chapter 26** The Affluent Society

◄ Soldier's Homecoming *was one of over 300 paintings Norman Rockwell completed for the cover of the* Saturday Evening Post *during his career. Why do you think so many people admire Rockwell's paintings?*

Themes

- **Democracy and Citizenship** A majority of Americans after the war were politically conservative or centrist. The extension of civil rights was slow.
- **Everyday Life** The economic prosperity following World War II benefited the majority of Americans, raised living standards to astonishingly high levels, and changed day-to-day life.
- **Arts and Humanities** The United States became a world leader in the fine arts as expanding affluence revolutionized all levels of 1950s culture.
- **Global Interactions** Forced onto the world stage, the United States was the major power after the war. The nation assumed new and growing responsibilities in world affairs.

We Needed Pearl Harbor

Democratic Representative John W. Flanagan (Virginia) believed the war would unify the nation.

I do not know what happened at Pearl Harbor. It looks like we were asleep. . . . From the fragmentary accounts we pick up we evidently sustained a severe loss in armament and paid an appalling price in dead and wounded.

But by reason of Pearl Harbor, I do know what happened in America. . . . our very souls became so inflamed with righteous wrath, so fired with patriotism, that our differences and divisions and hates melted into a unity never before witnessed in this country. . . . probably we needed a Pearl Harbor . . . to arouse us from our self-sufficient complacency, to make us rise above greed and hate, to awaken us to . . . our spiritual duties and responsibilities, and unite us in defense of the God-given ideals of liberty, freedom, and equality, of peace, justice, decency, and morality, upon which this Republic rests.

Congressional Record, 77th Cong., 1st Sess. (Dec. 16, 1941).

War, Women, and Work

Sybil Lewis, a welder during World War II, talked about her on-the-job experiences.

I was an arc welder, I'd passed both the army and navy tests, and I knew I could do the job, but I found from talking with some of the men that they made more money. You'd ask about this, but they'd say, "Well, you don't have the experience," or "The men have to lift some heavy pieces of steel and you don't have to," but I knew that I had to help lift steel, too.

The war years had a tremendous impact on women. I know for myself it was the first time I had

▲ *World War II factory workers*

a chance to get out of the kitchen and work in industry and make a few bucks. This was something I had never dreamed would happen. In Sapulpa all that women had to look forward to was keeping house and raising families. The war years offered new possibilities. You came out to California, put on your pants and took your lunch pail to a man's job. In Oklahoma, woman's place was in the home, and men went to work and provided. This was the beginning of women's feeling that they could do something more.

Adele Erenberg found expression and self-confidence through her work.

For me defense work was the beginning of my emancipation as a woman. For the first time in my life I found out that I could do something with my hands besides bake a pie. I found out that I had manual dexterity and the mentality to read blueprints and gauges, and to be inquisitive enough about things to develop skills other than the conventional roles that women had at that time. I had the consciousness-raising experience of being the only woman in this machine shop and having the mantle of challenge laid down by the men, which stimulated my competitiveness and forced me to prove myself. This, plus working in the union, gave me a lot of self-confidence.

Mark Jonathan Harris, Franklin D. Mitchell, and Steven J. Schecter, *The Homefront: America During World War II* (New York: G. P. Putnam Sons, 1984).

Japanese American Internment

U.S. Representative Defends Action

California's attorney general testified concerning his views on how to handle "our alien enemy problem."

I am convinced that the fifth-column [e.g., spying, sabotage] activities of our enemy call for the participation of people who are in fact American citizens.... Many of our people and some of our authorities ... are of the opinion that because we have had no sabotage and no fifth column activities in [California] since the beginning of the war, that means that none have

▲ *Japanese internment, 1942*

been planned for us. But I take the view that this is the most ominous sign in our whole situation.... I believe that we are just being lulled into a false sense of security....

We believe that when we are dealing with the Caucasian [sic] race we have methods that will test their loyalty of them, and we believe that we can, in dealing with the Germans and Italians, arrive at some fairly sound conclusions because of our knowledge of the way they live in the community and have lived for many years. But when we deal with the Japanese we are in an entirely different field and we cannot form any opinion that we believe to be sound. Their method of living, their language, make for this difficulty.

 Testimony of Earl Warren in the U.S. House of Representatives, 77th Cong., 2nd Sess. (Feb. 1942).

What Kind of Americanism?

A Japanese American man was asked to sign a formal declaration of loyalty to the United States.

What do they know about loyalty? I'm as loyal as anyone in this country.... What business did they have asking me a question like that? I was born in Hawaii. I worked most of my life on the West Coast.

I have never been to Japan. We would have done anything to show our loyalty. All we wanted to do was to be left alone on the coast.... My wife and I lost $10,000 in that evacuation. She had a beauty parlor and had to give that up. I had a good position worked up as a gardener, and was taken away from that. We had a little home and that's gone now....

What kind of Americanism do you call that? That's not democracy. That's not the American way, taking everything away from people.... Where are the Germans? Where are the Italians? Do they ask them questions about their loyalty? ... Evacuation was a mistake, there was no need for it. The government knows this. Why don't they have enough courage to come out and say so, so that these people won't be pushed around?

 Michi Weglyn, *Years of Infamy: The Untold Story of America's Concentration Camps* (1976).

Personal Reflections on the War

In spite of bitter memories, this African American supported America's participation in World War II.

I do not like these 'race incidents' in the [military] camps. I do not like the world's not knowing officially that there were Negro soldiers on Bataan with General Wainwright. I do not like the constant references to the Japs as ... "yellow bellies" and "yellow monkeys," as if color had something to do with treachery, as if color were the issue and the thing we are fighting rather than oppression, slavery, and a way of life hateful and nauseating. These and other things I do not like, yet I believe in the war.

This is a war to keep men free. The struggle to broaden and lengthen the road of freedom—our own private and important war to enlarge freedom here in America—will come later. That this private, intra-American war will be carried on and won is the only real reason we Negroes have to fight. We must keep the road open. Did we not believe in a victory in that intra-American war, we could not believe in nor stomach the compulsion of this.

The very fact that I, a Negro in America, can fight against the evils in America is worth fighting for. This open fighting against the wrongs one hates is the mark and the hope of democratic freedom.

J. Saunders Redding, "A Negro Looks at This War," *American Mercury*, vol. 55 (Nov. 1942), pp. 585–592.

E.B. (Sledgehammer) Sledge was a much-admired Marine who wrote about his company's exploits in the Pacific.

There was nothing macho about the war at all. We were a bunch of scared kids who had to do a job. People tell me I don't act like an ex-marine. How is an ex-marine supposed to act? They have some Hollywood stereotype in mind. No, I don't look like John Wayne. We were in it to get it over with, so we could go back home and do what we wanted to do with our lives.

I was nineteen, a replacement in June of 1944. Eighty percent of the division in the Guadalcanal campaign was less than twenty-one years of age. We were much younger than the general army units.

The Japanese fought by a code they thought was right: *bushido*. The code of the warrior: no surrender. You don't really comprehend it until you get out there and fight people who are faced with an absolutely hopeless situation and will not give up. If you tried to help one of the Japanese, he'd usually detonate a grenade and kill himself as well as you. To be captured was a disgrace. To us, it was impossible, too, because we knew what happened in Bataan.

This is what we were up against. I don't like violence, but there are times when you can't help it. I don't like to watch television shows with violence in them. I hate to see anything afraid. But I was afraid so much, day after day, that I got tired of being scared. I've seen guys go through three campaigns and get killed on Okinawa on the last day. You knew all you had was that particular moment you were living.

Studs Terkel, *"The Good War": An Oral History of World War II* (Ballantine Books, a Division of Random House, 1984), pp. 56–59.

One person interviewed about the impact of World War II on the postwar U.S. observed the following.

I think that World War II was a great thing for America. It unified us—made a country out of us. Before the war, we were a bunch of vacillating isolationists displaying not much character. But the war and the victory showed us what we could do in the world. Showed us the role we could play. However, it is honest to admit that it did us some harm. The victory caused us to think that we could dominate the world. Ever since the war, in every part of the world, we've been trying to tell individual countries what to do and what not to do, and we still are. I think it's . . . foolishness, if you don't mind me saying so.

Oral history interview of Melville Grosvenor, by Ray Hoopes, *Americans Remember the Home Front* (New York: Berkley Books, 1977, 1992), pp. 248–249.

An Indefensible Moral Position

This Protestant journal strongly condemned Truman's dropping atomic bombs on Japan.

It is our belief that the use made of the atomic bomb has placed our nation in an indefensible moral position.

We do not propose to debate the issue of military necessity . . .

But there was no military advantage in hurling the bomb upon Japan without warning. The least we might have done was to announce to our foe that we possessed the atomic bomb; that its destructive power was beyond anything known in warfare . . . We could thus have warned Japan of what was in store for her unless she surrendered immediately. If she doubted . . . it would have been a simple matter to select a demonstration target . . . where the loss of human life would be at a minimum.

If, despite such warning, Japan had still held out, we would have been in a far less questionable position had we then dropped the bombs on Hiroshima and Nagasaki. At least our record of deliberation and ample warning would have been clear. . . . What the use of poison gas did to the reputation of Germany in World War I, the use of the atomic bomb has done for the reputation of the United States in World War II.

The Christian Century, Christian Cent. F. (Aug. 29, 1945).

Two Views on Korea

Truman Justifies His Actions
In April 1951, with a stalemated war in Korea, Truman sought to justify his decision not to widen the war.

The best time to meet the [Communist] threat is in the beginning. It is easier to put out a fire in the beginning when it is small than after it has become a roaring blaze.

If [peace-loving nations] had followed the right policies in the 1930s—if the free countries had acted together, to crush the aggression of the dictators, and if they had acted in the beginning, when the aggression was small—there probably would have been no World War II. . . . Since the end of World War II we have been putting that lesson into practice—we have been working with other free nations to check the aggressive designs of the Soviet Union before they can result in a third world war.

The aggression against Korea is the boldest and most dangerous move the Communists have yet made. . . . So far, by fighting a limited war in Korea, we have prevented aggression from succeeding and bringing on a general war. . . . But you may ask: Why can't we take other steps to punish the aggressor? Why don't we bomb Manchuria and China itself? Why don't we assist Chinese Nationalist troops to land on the mainland of China?

If we were to do these things we would be running a very grave risk of starting a general war. If that were to happen, we would have brought about the exact situation we are trying to prevent. . . . What would suit the ambitions of the Kremlin better than for our military forces to be committed to a full-scale war with Red China?

Harry S Truman, "Preventing a New World War," *Department of State Bulletin*, vol. XXIV (Apr. 16, 1951), pp. 603–605.

There Is a Deeper Reason
In a speech to the Senate in 1951, Senator Joseph McCarthy attacked Truman's Korean policy.

This administration, which has given us this caricature of a war, is now bent on an even worse horror—a phony and fraudulent peace. . . . I do not think we need fear too much about the Communists dropping atomic bombs on Washington. They would kill too many of their friends that way.

The people . . . recognize the weakness with which the administration has replaced what was so recently our great strength. They are coming to believe that [the decline in our strength] was brought about, step by step, by will and intention. They are beginning to believe that the . . . administration's indecently hasty desire to . . . arrive at a cease-fire in Korea instead of following the manly, American course prescribed by MacArthur, point to something more than ineptitude and folly. They witness the conviction of Hiss . . . and the others which have disclosed at the heart of government active Soviet agents influencing policy and pilfering secrets; they note the policy of retreat before Soviet assertion from Yalta to this day, and they say: This is not because these men are incompetents; there is a deeper reason.

Major Speeches and Debates of Senator Joe McCarthy (Washington, D.C.: 1951), pp. 218–219.

The Affluent Society

Private Prosperity, Public Squalor
In 1958, economist John K. Galbraith contrasted the shortcomings of private sector prosperity with the "squalor in the public sector."

The contrast was and remains evident . . . The family which takes its mauve and cerise, air-conditioned, power-steered, and power-braked automobile out for a tour passes through cities that are badly paved, made hideous by litter, blighted buildings, billboards, and post for wires that should long since have been put underground. They pass into a countryside that has been rendered largely invisible by commercial art. . . . They picnic on exquisitely packaged food from a portable icebox by a polluted stream and go on to spend the night at a park which is a menace to public health and morals. Just before dozing off on an air mattress, beneath a nylon tent, amid the stench of decaying refuse, they may reflect vaguely on the curious unevenness of their blessings. Is this, indeed, the American genius?

John Kenneth Galbraith, *The Affluent Society* (Houghton Mifflin, 1958), p. 251.

In the Cities, People Were Doing Things

Norman Hill contrasted life in the suburbs with what he had remembered about living in the Bronx.

Walking around the neighborhood grew less enchanting as the years passed. By ten in the evening, when dinner was over and the children in bed . . . there was not a living being to be seen. There was only the eerie, bluish flickering glow in every house signifying that someone inside was alive, presumably well and watching television. . . . A profound change had taken place in my life. I remember, as a young boy walking in the Bronx I loved, the limitless variety of colorful sights, sounds, smells, and most important, people . . . At night the Bronx streets teemed with life. . . . People came out to the streets, walked, stood about on corners. . . . There were people doing things. There were things happening. There was always something new and different. . . . I've now given up walking in the suburbs, for good I guess.

Norman Hill, "Ah, For Those Walks in the Bronx," *The New York Times* (June 7, 1970), Section VIII, pp. 1, 7.

If You Had a Fast Car, You Were a Big Man

Perhaps above all, the 1950s are associated in most people's minds with automobiles, as seen in this interview.

Ed: I think what we tried to do was make [our cars] as different as possible to what Detroit put out and it was neat to watch Detroit follow us. . . . Our interest [in cars] was stimulated by California, by the news we got from there and by the movies and songs that were prevalent then.

Boyd: The West Coast always led. . . . and it would take a year for that trend to move to the Midwest. In the early 1950s there was *Honk, Hot*

Rod, Rod and Custom, Car and Custom, just a whole stack of West Coast magazines.

Ed: We had a fairly large group of people [in a car club], 15, 16 guys, and the camaraderie was unbelievable. . . . Your importance in the club increased by your performance on the dragstrip. It didn't matter if you were a nerd; if you had a fast car and could make it down a quarter mile faster than anyone else, you were a big man.

George Lipsitz, "They Knew Who We Were: Drag Racing and Customizing," *Cultural Correspondence* (Summer/Fall, 1977).

A Vast Wasteland

Newton Minnow urged television executives to increase the quality of their programs.

I invite you to sit down in front of your television set . . . I can assure you that you will observe a vast wasteland. You will see a procession of game shows, violence, audience participation shows, formula comedies about totally unbelievable families, blood and thunder, mayhem, violence, sadism, murder, Western bad men, Western good men, private eyes, gangsters, more violence and cartoons. And, endlessly, commercials—many screaming, cajoling and offending. And most of all, boredom. True, you will see a few things you will enjoy. But they will be very, very few. . . . And most young children today, believe it or not, spend as much time watching television as they do in the schoolroom. . . . It used to be said that there were three great influences on a child: home, school and church. Today there is a fourth great influence, and you ladies and gentlemen control it.

Newton Minnow, *Equal Time: The Private Broadcaster and the Public Interest,* Lawrence Laurent, ed.

I Am Waiting

The following excerpt is from a poem by Beat poet Lawrence Ferlinghetti titled "I Am Waiting."

I am waiting
for my number to be called
and I am waiting
for the living end
and I am waiting
for dad to come home

his pockets full
of irradiated silver dollars
and I am waiting
for the atomic tests to end
and I am waiting happily
for things to get much worse
before they improve
and I am waiting
for the Salvation Army to take over
and I am waiting
for the human crowd
to wander off a cliff somewhere
and I am waiting
for Ike to act
and I am waiting
for the meek to be blessed
and inherit the earth
without taxes
and I am waiting
for forests and animals
to reclaim the earth as theirs
and I am waiting
for a way to be devised
to destroy all nationalisms
without killing anybody

"I Am Waiting," Lawrence Ferlinghetti,
A Coney Island of the Mind (New
Directions Publishing Company, 1958).

▲ *Segregated drinking fountains*

We conclude that in the field of public education the doctrine of 'separate but equal' has no
place. Separate educational facilities are inherently
unequal. Therefore, we hold that the plaintiffs and
others similarly situated for whom the actions have
been brought are, by reason of the segregation complained of, deprived of the equal protection of the
law guaranteed by the Fourteenth Amendment.

Brown v. Board of Education of Topeka,
347 U.S. 483, 74 S. Ct. 686, 1954.

Civil Rights in the Fifties

The *Brown* Decision

The decision of the Supreme Court in Brown v. Topeka
Board of Education *was both a cause and consequence
of a revolution in race relations in the United States.*

Segregation of white and colored children in
public schools has a detrimental effect upon the colored children. The impact is greater when it has the
sanction of the law; for the policy of separating the
races is usually interpreted as denoting the inferiority of the Negro group. A sense of inferiority affects
the motivation of a child to learn. Segregation with
the sanction of law, therefore, has a tendency to [re-
tard] the educational and mental development of
Negro children and to deprive them of some of the
benefits they would receive in a racial[ly] integrated
system. . . .

The Southern Manifesto

Some Americans strongly disagreed with the Brown *decision, as seen in this excerpt from the 1956 Southern
Manifesto.*

[The *Brown* decision] climaxes a trend in the
federal judiciary undertaking to legislate . . . and to
encroach upon the reserved rights of the States and
the people. . . . Though there has been no constitutional amendment or act of Congress changing this
established legal principle almost a century old, the
Supreme Court . . . undertook to exercise their
naked judicial power and substituted their personal
political and social ideas for the established law of
the land.

"Declaration of Constitutional Principles,"
Congressional Record, 84th Cong., 2nd Sess.
(Mar. 12, 1956).

Segregation Is a National Problem

Many African Americans recognized that segregation was not only a regional problem.

While the immediate problem is to secure desegregation in the public schools in the southern and border states, it should be remembered that segregation and other forms of racial prejudices present a national, not a regional problem. Northerners need to take a long look at their school systems and bend their efforts to eliminating segregation in their own public schools. One recognizes that here the defense is residential segregation, but that is really no answer. Surely we must have the ingenuity and skill to alleviate racial segregation in our schools without being required to await the long range leveling of racial barriers with respect to housing occupancy. If segregation in public schools is bad for our children in Atlanta, Georgia, it ought to be equally bad for them in New York City, Chicago, Philadelphia, or Boston.

Robert L. Carter and Thurgood Marshall, "The Meaning and Significance of the Supreme Court Decree," *The Journal of Negro Education*, vol. XXIV (1955), p. 404.

They Should Be Applauded

One African American newspaper praised the courage of the young people integrating Little Rock's Central High School in 1958.

Few incidents in recent American history can match the courage shown by the nine teenage Negroes of Little Rock. They risked their lives for the sake of establishing a principle: the right to attend an integrated high school. . . . This was the most severe test of the law. The federal courts paved the way; federal troops held the angry mob at bay. But the nine Negro pupils had to march through the guardsmen to enter Little Rock's Central High School. . . . How many of us would have had the fortitude to do what these youngsters have done? How often have we failed to take advantage of victories won for us? It is therefore the more remarkable that these young Negroes . . . fearlessly implemented the Court's action by their daily presence at Central High School. . . . The Supreme Court's integration ruling would have been meaningless had these Negro boys and girls failed to follow the course mapped out for them by the law. They should be applauded by all of us.

The Chicago *Daily Defender* (May 28, 1958).

The Domino Theory

At a press conference in April 1954, Eisenhower explained the domino theory as it related to Southeast Asia.

Question: Mr. President, would you mind commenting on the strategic importance of Indochina [Southeast Asia] to the free world?

Eisenhower: . . . Finally, you have broader considerations that might follow what you would call the 'falling domino' principle. You have a row of dominoes set up, you knock over the first one, and what will happen to the last one is the certainty that it will go over very quickly. So you could have a beginning of a disintegration that would have the most profound influences. . . . the loss of Indochina, of Burma, of Thailand, of the Peninsula . . . multiply the disadvantages that you would suffer through loss of materials, sources of materials, but now you are talking really about millions and millions and millions of people. . . . [it breaks] the so-called island defensive chain of Japan, Formosa, of the Philippines, and to the southward; it moves in to threaten Australia and New Zealand.

Eisenhower press conference (April, 7, 1954).

The Military-Industrial Complex

The following is an excerpt from Eisenhower's farewell address on January 17, 1961.

A vital element in keeping the peace is our military establishment. Our arms must be mighty, ready for instant action, so that no potential aggressor may be tempted to risk his own destruction. Our military organization today bears little relation to that known by any of my predecessors in peacetime, or indeed by the fighting men of World War II or Korea. Until the latest of our world conflicts, the

United States had no armaments industry. American makers of plowshares could, with time and as required, make swords as well. But ... we have been compelled to create a permanent armaments industry of vast proportions ... We annually spend on military security more than the net income of all United States corporations.

We must guard against the acquisition of unwarranted influence, whether sought or unsought, by the military-industrial complex. The potential for the disastrous rise of misplaced power exists and will persist. ... We must never let the weight of this combination endanger our liberties or democratic processes. We should take nothing for granted.

Public Papers of the President: Dwight D. Eisenhower, 1960–1961 (Washington, D.C.: National Archives and Records Service, 1961), pp. 1036–1039.

WORKING WITH THE ARCHIVES

Identifying Commonalities in Primary Source Documents

In this skill exercise you will compare two perspectives on United States foreign policy during the Korean War, with the purpose of finding common areas of agreement. The contrasting opinions are those of Truman and Joseph McCarthy.

To help you organize the data from these excerpts you will use a Venn Diagram, a type of graphic organizer. You will reproduce this diagram enlarged on a separate sheet of paper. In the oval labeled "A" you will record key ideas about Truman's perspective; key ideas from McCarthy's arguments will be written in the oval labeled "B." When A and B are complete, ideas appearing in both ovals can be shifted to the overlapping space that is labeled "Commonalities."

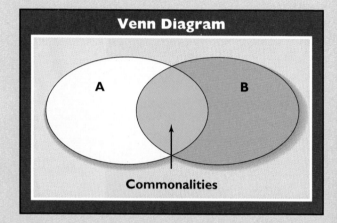

Venn Diagram

A   B

Commonalities

Directions:

1. Read the archive selections entitled "Truman Justifies His Actions" and "There Is a Deeper Reason." Use a Venn Diagram to record your answers to the following questions:

   a. According to each writer, who is the enemy in the Korean conflict?

   b. According to each writer, who is responsible for the acts of aggression in Korea?

   c. What does each writer believe is the correct military strategy to pursue in Korea?

   d. What does each writer believe to be the motivation behind the policy in Korea?

   e. What do you believe is the most important fear of each writer?

2. Write a brief essay summarizing the differences and commonalities in the opinions of Truman and McCarthy toward the Korean War policy.

The Second World War

World War II was an event of enormous significance in the twentieth century. It profoundly changed the lives of this nation and its citizens. At home, mobilizing the economy for war ended the Great Depression. With millions of men and women serving in the armed forces, most Americans—including women and minorities—had better job opportunities than ever before. Mobilization also led to extensive government involvement in the economy, and greatly increased the powers of the executive branch. Both of these developments would remain permanent fixtures in postwar America. At war's end, much of the industrialized world lay in shambles. Overseas, the war caused the death of nearly 50 million people and left millions more uprooted and homeless. Of the major world powers, only the United States emerged from the war prosperous, its factories and homes intact.

▲ *As this Red Cross poster suggests, almost everyone in the United States was involved, in one way or another, in World War II.*

A World at War

"Yesterday, December 7, 1941—a date which will live in infamy—the United States of America was suddenly and deliberately attacked by naval and air forces of the Empire of Japan." President Franklin Roosevelt's six-minute speech to a joint session of Congress continued, "Always will we remember the character of the onslaught against us. . . . I ask that the Congress declare that since the unprovoked and dastardly attack . . . a state of war has existed between the United States and the Japanese Empire." Later that day, Congress formally declared war on Japan. Three days later, Japan's Axis partners, Germany and Italy, declared war on the United States. The United States joined the conflict on the side of the Allies, and the Second World War truly became a global struggle.

Why did disagreements arise among the Allies?
How did Axis successes in 1942 threaten the Allies?
What Allied actions stemmed the Axis tide in 1942?

▲ *Smoke and flames poured from the USS* West Virginia *and the USS* Tennessee *after the Japanese attack on the U.S. Pacific fleet stationed at Pearl Harbor, Hawaii.*

tion among the Allies was essential to their survival, each country tolerated some differences. Yet suspicions lurked just below the surface, and they influenced the Allied war effort at every turn.

For example, the relations among the Big Three were sometimes strained because of differing war aims. Roosevelt's aims included upholding the principles of the Atlantic Charter and creating a new international organization for postwar collective

Difficult Times

Britain, the United States, and the Union of Soviet Socialist Republics (USSR)—the **Big Three**—would bear the primary burden of the war. The United States pledged to pursue a "Hitler-first" war strategy, since it agreed with the other Allied nations that Germany posed a greater overall threat than Japan. Thus, the United States agreed to fight a holding action against Japan until Hitler was defeated in Europe. Until 1945, only seven nations were involved in fighting Japan.

Alliances are always subject to the misunderstandings that result from differing values, goals, and methods. As Winston Churchill wrote, "The most difficult undertaking in war is to wage war with allies, except, of course, to wage war with no allies at all." Roosevelt and Soviet Premier **Joseph Stalin** surely agreed with him. As long as coopera-

QUIET!
LOOSE TALK CAN COST LIVES

◀ *During World War II, patriotic posters such as this one were displayed in factories and public places to urge Americans to be security-conscious. Whose arm is shown in the poster?*

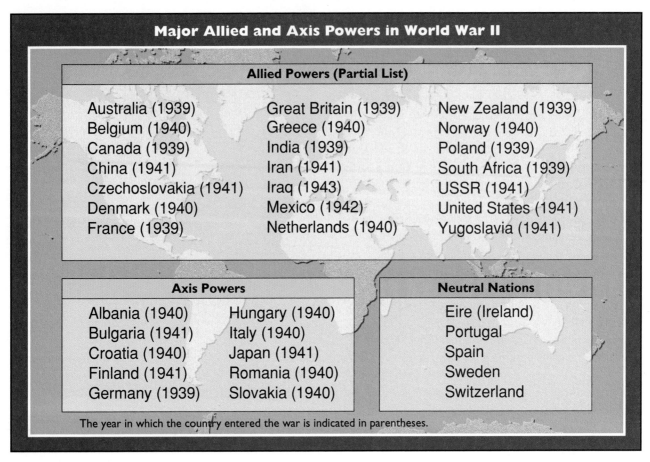

Major Allied and Axis Powers in World War II

Allied Powers (Partial List)

Australia (1939)	Great Britain (1939)	New Zealand (1939)
Belgium (1940)	Greece (1940)	Norway (1940)
Canada (1939)	India (1939)	Poland (1939)
China (1941)	Iran (1941)	South Africa (1939)
Czechoslovakia (1941)	Iraq (1943)	USSR (1941)
Denmark (1940)	Mexico (1942)	United States (1941)
France (1939)	Netherlands (1940)	Yugoslavia (1941)

Axis Powers

Albania (1940)	Hungary (1940)
Bulgaria (1941)	Italy (1940)
Croatia (1940)	Japan (1941)
Finland (1941)	Romania (1940)
Germany (1939)	Slovakia (1940)

Neutral Nations

Eire (Ireland)
Portugal
Spain
Sweden
Switzerland

The year in which the country entered the war is indicated in parentheses.

▲ *In addition to the countries listed, 28 nations eventually sided with the Allies against the Axis powers. What does this indicate about the extent of the conflict?*

security. In addition, he thought that cooperation among the major powers, especially the Soviet Union, was essential for postwar peace. Churchill's primary goals were to preserve and restore as much of Britain's overseas empire and international influence as possible. He also wanted to minimize Soviet influence in postwar Europe. Meanwhile, surviving as a country and relieving German pressure on the Eastern Front were Stalin's major war aims. His postwar aims included getting more territory and installing governments friendly to the USSR in Eastern Europe.

The West distrusted the Soviet Union and its Communist ideology that was dedicated to overthrowing the capitalist system. The Soviets, in turn, were suspicious of Western intentions. Relations between Britain and America were generally better. They even formed a joint military command

to coordinate war strategy, although conflicts arose over specific military actions and war aims.

Initially, the war did not go well for the Allies as the Axis powers—Germany, Italy, and Japan—scored many victories. In the first six months after Pearl Harbor, the Allies suffered one defeat after another. In June 1941, Hitler had launched Operation Barbarossa against the Soviets, and German armies had penetrated deep into Soviet territory. In 1942, the Nazis began another massive offensive on their Eastern Front, facing the Soviet Union. They were close to taking control of the USSR's industrial and oil resources. Nearly 200 German army divisions were fighting on the Eastern Front, and U.S. military planners feared that the Soviet Union might soon collapse.

The news from other battlefronts was no better. German U-boat warfare seriously damaged the Al-

German Offensives in World War II, 1939-1941

Legend:
- Axis Powers
- Axis-controlled area as of November 1942
- Vichy French-controlled area
- Allies
- Allied sphere of influence
- Neutral nations as of 1941
- German offensive
- Battle of Britain, July 1940-June 1941
- Farthest German advance as of November 1942

▲ *The height of Axis conquest in both Europe and North Africa occurred in 1942. Why did the Allies attack North Africa first?*

lied war effort between 1941 and 1943. German submarines made getting war supplies from America to the USSR and Britain difficult. U-boats hunted Allied vessels in "wolf packs" in the North Atlantic, the Caribbean, and the Gulf of Mexico. In the six months after Pearl Harbor, U-boats sank more than 650 Allied ships in the Atlantic alone. Not until 1943 did Allied tactics—convoying, using air patrols, and bombing U-boat bases—effectively neutralize German submarines.

Meanwhile, German General Erwin Rommel, known as the Desert Fox, raced his Afrika Korps across the North African desert toward Egypt. By June 1942, Rommel's forces were less than 60 miles from Alexandria. Rommel's offensive threatened the oil-rich Middle East and the Suez Canal, both vitally important to the Allies.

In Asia, Japanese forces captured many important Allied outposts. By the end of 1941, Wake, Guam, and Hong Kong had fallen. By early March 1942, the Japanese had captured the British fortress at Singapore and the Dutch East Indies (now Indonesia). By the end of April, they had overrun Burma and cut Allied supply lines to China by occupying the Burma Road. Japan also took strategic positions on New Guinea, New Britain, and the Solomon Islands, thus threatening Australia. By 1942, Japan had overcome organized Allied resistance and captured the Philippines. Japan now controlled much of the western Pacific and Asia.

European War Strategy

Serious disagreements emerged among the Allies in 1942 concerning war strategy in Europe. The primary conflict arose over launching a second front in France. Stalin insisted that the Allies invade France as soon as possible. Since Hitler had few reserve forces, an invasion of France would force him to shift forces to France from the Russian front. This would relieve pressure on Stalin's troops. American military planners also favored a direct attack on the Germans in France.

British leaders, however, opposed the invasion. They wanted to avoid a repeat of the terrible losses they had suffered in trench warfare during World War I. Churchill wanted to attack North Africa with the goal of reopening the Suez Canal to Allied shipping. Public opinion in the United States was pressuring Roosevelt to put greater military effort into the Pacific. Mindful of his "Germany-first" strategy, however, Roosevelt wanted U.S. troops to attack the Germans. The president was convinced North Africa was the only place such an attack could occur in 1942. Roosevelt and Churchill agreed to attack in North Africa instead of France. This decision bitterly disappointed Stalin.

In late October of 1942, British General Bernard Montgomery struck the Afrika Korps at El Alamein, Egypt, and began pushing Rommel's forces back across North Africa. Several days later, the Allies launched a coordinated attack behind Rommel's lines. Over 100,000 Allied soldiers, commanded by General **Dwight D. Eisenhower** landed in Morocco and Algeria. Allied forces met little initial resistance. Eisenhower obtained a cease-fire from Admiral Jean Darlan, the commander of Vichy French forces in North Africa. Since Vichy France had been a **puppet regime** under the control of Nazi Germany, and Darlan was a Nazi sympathizer, the Darlan deal was very controversial among the Allies and back home. Nevertheless, the deal allowed Eisenhower's forces to move rapidly against the German Afrika Korps. By April 1943, Allied forces had defeated the Axis forces in North Africa, and captured nearly 270,000 Axis soldiers.

The North African campaign was not what Stalin desired. He thought it a puny effort compared to his campaign on the Eastern Front, where Soviet fortunes finally improved in late 1942. At Stalingrad, Soviet forces surrounded the entire German Ninth Army and, after three months of vicious fighting, forced it to surrender. **The Battle of Stalingrad** marked an important turning point in the war in Europe. Afterward, German forces were on the defensive on the Eastern Front.

Allied achievements by early 1943 were many. The Allies had not only avoided defeat, they had begun offensives on most battlefronts. Allied military successes bought precious time for America to mobilize its economy for war. In modern warfare, whoever won the battle of industrial production would be likely to win the war.

SECTION 1 REVIEW

1. **Name** the countries referred to as the Big Three.
2. **Explain** why disagreements arose among the Allies.
3. **Describe** the initial successes of the Axis powers after Pearl Harbor.
4. **Explain** the strategic importance of North Africa.
5. **List** the Allied actions that stemmed the Axis tide in 1942.

American Mobilization for War

Even before America entered the war, President Roosevelt moved to make his nation "the great arsenal of democracy." To defeat the Axis powers, he declared, America had to make vast quantities of war matériel. He announced extremely high production goals; at the war's end, American industry had exceeded every one of them. By 1945, American factories had poured out 86,000 tanks, 296,000 warplanes, 64,000 landing ships, 6,000 naval vessels, hundreds of thousands of jeeps and trucks, millions of guns, and billions of bullets. America alone produced more war goods than all the Axis powers combined.

How did the federal government mobilize the nation for war?

How did the war affect the American economy?

How did the war affect American politics?

Mobilizing for War

Although Pearl Harbor was a tactical victory for Japan, it was also a serious blunder. Before Pearl Harbor, there had been sharp disagreement in the United States about whether to become involved in the war. After Japan attacked, such differences of opinion all but disappeared. Pearl Harbor underscored "the seriousness of the challenge confronting us," Virginia Representative John Flannagan observed, "and our very souls became so inflamed with righteous wrath, so fired with patriotism, that our differences and divisions and hates melted into a unity never before witnessed in this country." Unified public opinion helped the nation to begin mobilizing for war. But many other problems still required solutions.

▲ *This airplane plant in Fort Worth, Texas, had the longest straight assembly lines of the time.*

To mobilize as quickly as possible, FDR sought business cooperation. The federal government provided several incentives to businesses. These included liberal tax deductions for the construction of manufacturing plants for war matériel, suspending antitrust laws, and making contracts with businesses

▼ *Through rationing, buying war bonds, and recycling efforts such as this scrap metal drive, most Americans felt they were contributing to the war effort. Why would the government collect scrap metal?*

Corporate Income Taxes, 1938-1949

Source: U.S. Department of Commerce, Bureau of the Census.

► *This chart reflects two equally important trends. One trend is that the government increased the corporate income tax rate to help pay for the war. What is the other?*

▲ *What benefits were gained by the sale of these war stamps?*

that guaranteed them good profits. The federal government also built war plants and then leased them to companies on favorable terms. In addition, FDR turned to business leaders to run the war economy. This approach not only promoted cooperation but also ensured large profits.

Shortly after Pearl Harbor, Roosevelt established the War Production Board (WPB). The WPB supervised the conversion of industry to war produc-

tion and allocated scarce materials. Steel needed for tanks could not be wasted on automobiles, nor could aluminum needed for warplanes be used in pots and pans. The WPB thus limited or suspended the manufacture of many consumer goods. To help meet the production goals, the WPB usually awarded contracts to large, efficient corporations. The 10 largest companies received one-third of all war contracts. Three-fourths of all war contracts went to the top 56 companies. This approach concentrated production in the hands of a few businesses.

The government's role and size also grew dramatically during the war. In fact, the federal government grew far more during the war than during the New Deal. The number of federal civilian employees increased by nearly 400 percent from 1941 to 1945. These men and women staffed the many new agencies that oversaw the war effort.

The federal government spent a total of $364 billion—$290 billion on defense—during the war. To help pay these costs, the government raised taxes. The Revenue Act of 1942 laid the foundation for the nation's current tax system. The system of withholding payroll taxes began in 1943. The act also increased corporate income taxes to 40 percent. Taxes paid only half the cost of the war. Liberty Bonds and war loans paid the other half. The government designed bond drives not only to raise money, but also to allow purchasers to feel that they were doing their part for the war effort.

A booming economy, full employment, and a shortage of consumer goods created tremendous inflationary pressures. The need to fight inflation by taking money out of circulation was another reason the administration increased taxes and sold Liberty Bonds. Equally important for fighting inflation was the Office of Price Administration (OPA). In April 1942, the OPA set maximum prices on most consumer goods.

Since many consumer goods were scarce, the OPA used **rationing** to try to ensure that scarce items would be fairly distributed. The OPA issued ration stamps that were needed to purchase many items. Canned goods were rationed to conserve tin. Military and lend-lease needs made rationing meat, milk, and cheese necessary. The OPA rationed food according to family size. Gasoline was rationed not only to conserve fuel, but also to conserve tires and other rubber supplies. Ration stickers for gasoline were issued according to need. Most people got three gallons per week, but those who had to drive long distances to work or who used their cars in their work, such as ministers and doctors, received larger allotments. In general, rationing worked fairly well. Even so, some people traded ration stamps, and illegal blackmarketing (buying and selling) of scarce goods occurred from time to time.

▲ *Americans used ration stamps and books to buy scarce consumer items.*

The Return to Prosperity

Defense mobilization energized the economy after years of depression. Economic production more than doubled during the war. Defense mobilization created nearly 17 million new jobs during the war. There were jobs for nearly everyone who wanted to work. More people took home paychecks, and paychecks were larger than ever before. In real terms, average worker wages rose 22 percent during the war. Millions of workers could now pay off old debts and save large sums as well.

Labor union membership also rose dramatically. Between 1941 and 1945, membership jumped by

▶ *This chart summarizes annual expenditures and income in the years around World War II. Which category showed a greater percentage increase from 1940 to 1946—total expenditures or income?*

Government Spending, Income, and National Debt (in Billions of Dollars), 1940-1946

Year	Total Expenditures	Defense Expenditures	Income	Cumulative Debt
1940	9.6	1.5	6.9	43.0
1941	14.0	6.1	9.2	49.0
1942	34.5	24.0	15.1	72.4
1943	78.9	63.2	25.1	136.7
1944	94.0	76.9	47.8	201.0
1945	95.2	81.6	50.2	258.7
1946	61.7	44.7	43.5	269.4

Source: *Historical Statistics of the United States.*

over 50 percent. By the war's end, nearly one-third of the labor force (or about 15 million people) belonged to unions. Since the government imposed limits on wage increases, unions worked for fringe benefits and improved working conditions. They made these gains largely without resorting to strikes. Most unions observed the no strike pledges they made following Pearl Harbor. Workers, however, staged many **wildcat strikes** (strikes without union approval) during the war over such grievances as work speedups, safety, and employee discipline.

Farmers enjoyed unparalleled prosperity during the war. The crop surpluses and falling prices that had plagued farmers since World War I all but disappeared as military, lend-lease, and civilian demands increased. Net farm income doubled between 1941 and 1945. With their rising incomes, farmers bought more land and farm machinery. They needed more machines to offset labor shortages. Additionally, the use of better fertilizers and pesticides increased crop yields per acre. The overall result was a 30 percent increase in farm production during the war. America became the granary, as well as the arsenal, of democracy.

Coal Miners Suffer While most industrial workers had seen their wages rise since 1941, the real wages of miners actually went down. Moreover, coal miners had the highest rate of injury of any industrial workers in the country, a situation made worse by the wartime pressure to produce. Coal miners achieved record levels of production, but it cost them dearly. By May 1943, their total casualties since Pearl Harbor—including nearly 2,000 fatalities—were higher than those of the U.S. armed forces to that time. That year, the United Mine Workers went on strike. Because of the war, it was easy for businesses and the press to depict strikes as unpatriotic rather than as attempts to gain a fair share of the economic prosperity. The press reviled UMW President John L. Lewis. Congress soon passed strong legislation—the Smith-Connally Act—allowing the government to seize and run striking industries if they were judged essential to the war effort.

Wartime Politics

"Politics is out," Roosevelt told reporters in 1942, as he sought bipartisan support for his war policies. The appointment of such notable Republicans as Henry Stimson as secretary of war and leading business executives to his wartime administration served this purpose. Roosevelt's declaration in late 1943 that "Dr. Win-the-War" had replaced "Dr. New Deal" underscored his political priorities. "The overwhelming first emphasis," he said, "should be on winning the war." Social reform, a major goal of the New Deal, would be put on hold until the end of the war.

Delaying the reform effort was possible in part because the war solved problems that the New Deal could not. Full employment, a better standard of living, flourishing trade unions, and better farm prices all resulted from the war. "The honest-minded liberal will admit," noted one New Dealer in 1943, "that the common man is getting a better break [now] than he did under the New Deal." The war also weakened social reform efforts in other ways. Military needs led to longer working hours, a suspension of antitrust and child labor laws, and a delay in bringing electricity to rural areas. As one reformer said, "where a social service doesn't help to beat Hitler, it may have to be sacrificed. This may sound tough—but we have to be tough."

Despite President Roosevelt's hope to shelve politics for the duration, it was impossible to do so. In the 1942 congressional elections, Republicans had gained seats in both houses of Congress. A coalition of Republican and Democratic conservatives now controlled Congress. Using the war as an excuse, Congress curtailed or abolished many New Deal programs. The Civilian Conservation Corps, the Works Progress Administration, and the National Youth Administration were all abolished during this period. Wartime spending made Congress even less willing than usual to fund domestic programs. Congress did not enact proposed legislation to extend Social Security, unemployment insurance coverage, or a comprehensive health care plan.

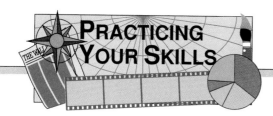

More Practice Reading Tables

Waging total war means waging war using all of a country's resources. In World War II, this mobilization of men and women, natural resources, and industrial output resulted in a tremendous increase in government spending from earlier years. The United States spent about $250 million per day to defeat the Axis powers. But economists do not figure costs in dollars only. The death of human beings means a loss to society of skills and productivity. Benefits paid to veterans extend into the future. Interest paid on money borrowed to fight the war must be paid by future generations. Thus, the total cost of war cannot be precisely calculated.

In completing this exercise, it will help to refer back to the guidelines for reading a table in Practicing Your Skills on page 159. Also, study the additional steps below:

- **Be sure you understand what is meant by the labels used for the columns or rows.** What is meant by the term *national debt?* What is meant by the heading Defense Expenditures? What figures are included in the column headed Total Expenditures?
- **Determine how all the numbers in the table are related.** How do all the parts go together? For example, what is the relationship

Year	Total Expenditures	Defense Expenditures	Income	Cumulative Debt
1940	9.6	1.5	6.9	43.0
1941	14.0	6.1	9.2	49.0
1942	34.5	24.0	15.1	72.4
1943	78.9	63.2	25.1	136.7
1944	94.0	76.9	47.8	201.0
1945	95.2	81.6	50.2	258.7
1946	61.7	44.7	43.5	269.4

Government Spending, Income, and National Debt (in Billions of Dollars), 1940-1946

among the Income, Total Expenditures, and Defense Expenditures columns?

- **Look the table over for any *anomalies—* unusual or unexplained data.** Are there any years missing from the data? Are there any inconsistencies in the data?

Examine the table on page 747 and answer the following questions:

1. (a) What is the title of this table? (b) What is the source of the data? (c)What years does the table cover?
2. (a) In what year was defense spending the highest? (b) By how much did total spending exceed income in 1945? (c) Which year saw the greatest increase in total spending?
3. (a) Which year saw the greatest increase in defense spending? (b) Which year saw the greatest increase in the national debt?
4. How do you account for the fact that in 1946 total spending dropped, although the national debt rose?

Roosevelt himself hardly seemed to have given up politics as he ran for his fourth presidential term in 1944. Rumors of Roosevelt's failing health underscored the importance of his possible successor. Conservative Democrats disliked liberal Vice President Henry Wallace. The party chose instead Missouri Senator Harry S Truman as FDR's running mate, since Truman was acceptable to all party factions.

Few issues actually distinguished Roosevelt from his Republican rival, Thomas Dewey. Although Dewey criticized New Deal programs for their wastefulness, he vowed to keep them. Despite the concerns Dewey raised about the president's declining health, Roosevelt won, but with a smaller margin than ever before.

SECTION 3

The Home Front

Americans suffered less than people of other nations because of the war. Still, most Americans' lives were changed by it. As a 1942 Office of Civilian Defense pamphlet stated it: "War changes the pattern of our lives. It cannot change our *way of life*, unless we are beaten. The kids still play baseball in the corner lot—but they knock off early to weed the victory garden, cart scrap paper to the salvage center, carry home the groceries that used to be delivered. The factory whistle blows—but it calls three shifts of workers instead of one." Another observer noted, "The whole pattern of our economic and social life is undergoing kaleidoscopic changes, without so much as a bomb being dropped on our shores."

How did wartime migration affect Americans' lives?
What social changes did wartime conditions create?
How did the war affect American minority groups?

Massive Migrations

The war affected virtually every aspect of American society. The most obvious was that 15 million men and several hundred thousand women left civilian life for military service. Individuals who had never ventured very far from home reported to bases scattered around the country and then served all over the world. They discovered unfamiliar ways

◀ *Nearly 40,000 women joined the WAVES (Women Accepted for Volunteer Emergency Service) or WACs (Women's Army Corps).*

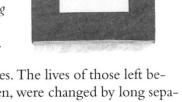

▶

Many homes displayed flags that showed blue stars for family members serving in the war and gold stars for people killed in action.

of life and new cultures. The lives of those left behind, especially women, were changed by long separations, new freedoms, and increased responsibilities.

The war caused massive population shifts among the civilian population. Families often moved with relocated soldiers. Millions more moved in search of new job opportunities. Centers of war production in the industrial Midwest and on the West coast grew at dizzying rates. Nearly 20 percent of the farm population moved to cities. These population shifts caused growth pains in many communities.

In 1943, American author John Dos Passos toured the United States to find out what impact

◀ *Scholastic newspapers encouraged school children to take part in the war effort. For what military conflict in the early 1990s might you have seen a similar picture?*

New Opportunities for Minority Groups

Millions of new war jobs and the draft of young men to be soldiers created many labor shortages on the home front. People with little or no prior experience in industrial work filled these jobs. Into the war plants and shipyards came thousands of young people, retirees, people with disabilities, rural dwellers, and women who had never before worked for pay outside their homes.

No group of people experienced greater changes as a result of the war than women. The number of women workers increased from 14 million to 19 million and made up about 35 percent of the civilian labor force by war's end. War industries actively recruited and hired women. In the process, women began working in many jobs that had long been closed to them. Although many people assumed that women were too weak or soft for industrial work, they proved capable of doing almost any job. Women worked as welders, riveters, engineers, and crane operators, among hundreds of other

the war was having on American society. Of Mobile, Alabama, Dos Passos wrote, "To be doing something towards winning the war, to be making some money, to learn a trade, men and women have been pouring into the city for more than a year now." This description fit many communities across the United States.

▼ *Rosie the Riveter became a symbol of women's participation in the war effort. What does the slogan "We can do it!" mean as used in this poster?*

▼ *Teams of women worked on assembly lines during the war making fuselages (the central body portions) of airplanes.*

occupations. The number of women belonging to unions grew fourfold, and their wages were better than ever before. Even so, they still earned only about 65 percent of men's wages for similar work.

Traditional attitudes also persisted. Married women had always worked for pay in smaller numbers than single women. Women continued to value marriage and families as central to their lives. Wives' decisions to work continued to cause conflicts with their husbands. Government and business leaders discouraged the labor of mothers with young children "unless all other supplies [of labor] are exhausted." Nevertheless, the number of married women who worked for pay outside their homes doubled during the war. In some regions with acute labor shortages, married women even outnumbered single women in the workforce.

African Americans were plainly missing from the new labor force early in the war. They had long faced discriminatory hiring practices, and many labor unions excluded them from membership. African Americans were virtually always among the last hired for well-paying jobs. Of the 100,000 workers in the aircraft industry in 1940, for example, only 240 were African Americans. In the face of these inequities, they grew more determined in their struggle for equal treatment. In mid-1941,

African Americans under the leadership of A. Philip Randolph, head of the Brotherhood of Sleeping Car Porters, threatened to march on Washington to pressure Roosevelt to end discriminatory hiring practices in defense industries. As a result, Roosevelt issued Executive Order 8802, which forbade discrimination in federal hiring, job-training programs, and defense industries.

Roosevelt also created the Fair Employment Practices Committee (FEPC) to investigate discrimination against African Americans in war industries. Since the FEPC had few powers, it did not cure deep-seated problems of discrimination in black employment and job training. Eventually, employers did hire African Americans in larger numbers. Altogether, nearly a million African Americans entered the labor force for the first time during the war. By mid-1945, they held 8 percent of all war industry jobs. (They comprised 9.8 percent of the population.) Opportunities for African American women also increased as they moved from jobs as domestic and farm laborers into better paying factory jobs.

Rising Social Tensions

Wartime conditions worsened a variety of social problems. Juvenile delinquency increased dramatically during the war. This was especially alarming because adult crime rates were declining. Experts blamed juvenile delinquency on several trends. Divorce rates rose during the war from 16 per 100 marriages to 27 per 100. Teenagers often worked rather than going to school. With many fathers away at war and a growing number of working mothers, there was less child supervision. Irregular work shifts and inadequate day-care facilities made child care a major problem for working mothers.

In some areas, competition for good jobs and scarce housing provoked racial and ethnic conflict during the war. In Detroit, Michigan, for example, racial friction sparked a horrible confrontation between black and white people. A major center for defense industries, Detroit attracted thousands of people who competed for war jobs and for the city's already scarce housing. On June 20, 1943, a swelter-

▼ *President Roosevelt forbade discrimination in government hiring. Why is A. Philip Randolph's name on the side of the model Pullman car?*

▲ *Social tensions caused by competition for housing and jobs erupted in a race riot in Detroit, Michigan, in June 1943.*

▲ *Friction between "zoot suiters" and white people resulted in race riots in some big cities.*

ing hot day, several petty fights broke out. That night, a violent riot left at least 25 African Americans and 9 white people dead. More than 800 people were injured and property damage was estimated at more than $2 million.

While few race riots of this size occurred elsewhere, the conditions that caused them were present in many cities. In Los Angeles, for example, Hispanic youths had organized "pachuco" gangs. Many wore "zoot suits," outfits that included broad-brimmed hats, baggy pegged-leg pants, and long gold watch chains. White hostility to these gangs had smoldered for some time. Then, in July 1943, rumors that a Hispanic gang had beaten a white sailor set off a four-day riot. White servicemen invaded Hispanic neighborhoods and attacked the zoot-suiters. Sometimes these attacks occurred within full view of white police officers, who did nothing to stop the violence.

Japanese Internment   The wartime experience of Japanese Americans was even worse. This group had long faced racial prejudice and discrimination in the United States. The hostility was especially strong in California, where most Japanese Americans lived. After Pearl Harbor, many Americans believed that Japan might next strike the West Coast.

Newspaper headlines such as "Jap Boat Flashes Message Ashore" and "Enemy Planes Sighted over California Coast" fanned these fears. FBI agents arrested more than 2,000 Japanese in the weeks after Pearl Harbor. Most were released after the Justice Department conducted loyalty hearings.

Citing military necessity as their reason, the army imposed a curfew on West Coast Japanese Americans. Then, on February 19, 1942, Roosevelt issued Executive Order 9066. The order announced the immediate evacuation of all Japanese Americans from the West Coast. Over the following six months, the government rounded up nearly 110,000 Japanese Americans—two-thirds of whom were American citizens—and confined them to **internment camps** in Wyoming, Colorado, Arkansas, Arizona, Utah, and inland California.

The Japanese Americans who had been moved suffered great hardships. Many had to sell their homes, businesses, and personal possessions at cut-rate prices. Conditions in the internment camps made daily life difficult. Rooms were small and without privacy. Bathrooms and kitchens were shared by many, and families were split up. Moreover, the forced relocation cast unfair shadows on the innocence and dignity of American citizens.

In *Korematsu v. United States* (1944), a divided Supreme Court upheld the constitutionality of the evacuation order, ruling that the government could set aside certain rights of citizens in wartime as military need required. One dissenter, Justice Frank Murphy, argued that the government had not produced sufficient evidence of military need or Japanese American disloyalty. Therefore, the evacuation order "fell into the ugly abyss of racism." Unknown to the justices at the time, an Office of Naval Intelligence investigation had already clearly sup-

Gordon Hirabayashi

On May 16, 1942, Gordon Hirabayashi arrived at the FBI office in Seattle, Washington. A native-born Japanese American and a senior at the University of Washington, Hirabayashi had defied a military order requiring "all persons of Japanese ancestry" to register for evacuation from the West Coast. He handed an FBI agent a four-page letter that explained why he had refused to heed the government's order.

Hirabayashi pointed out that, like himself, the majority of the evacuees were native-born American citizens. Their rights, he continued, were being "denied on a wholesale scale without due process of law and civil liberties. ... If I were to register and cooperate under those circumstances, I would be giving helpless consent to the denial of practically all of the things which give me incentive to live. ... Therefore, I must refuse this order." After reading the letter, the FBI warned Hirabayashi that he risked a year in prison. When he refused to change his stand, the FBI promptly jailed him. The FBI searched his briefcase and discovered that Hirabayashi had also violated the military's curfew order and added this charge.

A Washington court found Hirabayashi guilty of violating both the curfew and evacuation orders. He appealed his case, which

▲ *How did the Supreme Court rule on the constitutionality of Japanese internment?*

eventually found its way to the Supreme Court. The Court used this case to weigh the conflict between "war powers" and "due process of law." Chief Justice Harlan Fiske Stone stated that racial discrimination was "odious to a free people" and had "often been held to be a denial of equal protection" by the Supreme Court. During wartime, however, "the successful prosecution of the war" may justify measures that "place citizens of one ancestry in a different category from others." In ruling only on the curfew order, the Court held that military officials had simply responded to the "grave danger" of sabotage and es-

pionage by "disloyal members" of the Japanese American community. In 1987, however, the U.S. Court of Appeals vacated (voided) the criminal conviction of Gordon Hirabayashi, by then a retired college professor, holding that it was "based upon racism rather than military necessity."

———◦◦◦———

1. Why do you think the Supreme Court ruled only on the curfew order and not the evacuation order against Hirabayashi?
2. Do you agree that wartime conditions justify curtailing civil rights?

ported Murphy's position. The navy's Ringle report concluded that "less than 3 percent" of Japanese Americans posed any potential security threat, and these had already been arrested by the FBI. Circulated among army officials before the evacuation began, the Ringle report recommended individual loyalty hearings and argued against mass evacuation.

By 1944, the government allowed internees to leave the camps if they could prove their loyalty, get a job, or go to school away from the West Coast. Many young Japanese Americans joined the U.S. armed forces and served with distinction, most with the "Fighting 442nd" Division in Italy. On January 20, 1945, the government closed the camps. In 1983, a congressional task force finally condemned the relocation as a product of "war hysteria," "racial prejudice," and "failure of political leadership." In 1988, Congress voted a payment of $20,000 to each surviving internee.

Although there were more German, and Italian Americans living in the country than Japanese Americans, there was less cultural hostility displayed toward them. Americans tended to blame the political systems and leaders that had spawned Nazism and fascism for World War II more than they blamed the people themselves, which had not been the case in World War I. Ironically—as was noted by one resentful African American in Kansas—German prisoners-of-war, furloughed on work parties, enjoyed eating at a lunchcounter that would not serve African Americans.

SECTION 3 REVIEW

1. List ways wartime migration affected Americans' lives.
2. Examine briefly how the war changed women's work patterns.
3. Identify A. Philip Randolph.
4. Explain why Japanese Americans on the West Coast were sent to internment camps.
5. Describe how the Supreme Court justified abusing Japanese American civil rights.

SECTION 4

Closing the Ring on the Axis Powers

In January 1943, Roosevelt and Churchill met in Casablanca, Morocco. Stalin declined to attend the conference since the pivotal battle of Stalingrad was then reaching its climax. After long and heated discussions, the Western leaders agreed on their military priorities for the coming year. The most important decision was that they would again postpone a full-scale invasion of France. Roosevelt wanted to reassure Stalin about his allies' good intentions. At a press conference, he announced "Peace can come to the world only by the total elimination of German and Japanese war power . . . [which] means the unconditional surrender by Germany, Italy, and Japan." The unconditional-surrender policy was controversial from the beginning. Critics argued that it increased Axis resistance and prolonged the war. Moreover, the policy left Stalin unimpressed.

Why was the Casablanca Conference important?
What Allied offensives took place in Europe in 1943 and 1944?
What was the Allied strategy for fighting Japan?

Divisive Issues Among the Allies

Roosevelt and Churchill agreed on their 1943 military priorities at Casablanca. These included ridding the Atlantic of German U-boats, sending all possible aid to the Soviets, increasing the strategic bombing campaign against Germany, preparing for the 1944 cross-channel invasion of France, capturing Sicily after the North African campaign, and taking offensive opportunities against Japan as they arose.

When his allies told him of their decisions at Casablanca, Stalin wrote them that the "vagueness of your reply, . . . in regard to the opening of a second

▲ *An African American air squadron aided in the invasion of Sicily.*

▲ *How did American Indian "code talkers" prevent the enemy from eavesdropping on secret communications?*

front in France, provokes alarm which I cannot suppress." Stalin soon informed the Allies that Hitler had recently transferred 36 more army divisions to the Eastern Front. "I must give a most emphatic warning, in the interest of our common cause," Stalin wrote, "of the grave danger with which further delay in opening a second front in France is fraught." Roosevelt and Churchill wondered if Stalin was warning them that he might make a separate peace with Germany and leave them to face Hitler alone.

In July 1943, shortly after the Allies defeated the Afrika Korps in Tunisia, they attacked Sicily. Clearing that island of its Axis forces would secure the Mediterranean Sea for Allied shipping and provide a base for invading Italy. After five weeks of fighting, Allied forces overran Sicily. The Sicilian campaign had one unexpected result. On July 25, war-weary Italians overthrew the government of Fascist dictator Benito Mussolini.

Hitler soon rushed German troops to Italy and rescued Mussolini from his Allied captors. In early September 1943, Allied forces attacked Italy. During the next nine months, Allied troops slowly advanced up the Italian peninsula against strong German resistance. Heavy fighting on the beaches near Anzio

delayed the capture of Rome until June 1944. The Italian campaign displeased Stalin since it diverted Allied soldiers and supplies from other uses. Still, it tied down 25 German army divisions that might otherwise have fought on the Eastern Front.

Meanwhile, the Allies stepped up their bombing campaign against Germany. The Allies' goals were to reduce German industrial capacity and weaken Germany's will to fight. During 1943 and 1944, American planes bombed by day, British planes by night. In 1942, the Allies dropped 48,000 tons of bombs on Germany. In 1943, the total was 207,000 tons. These attacks hampered German industrial output, but that output continued to grow through 1944. The Allies eventually discovered that bombing specific targets, or pinpoint bombing, was difficult in daylight and impossible at night. So they began saturation bombing, or dropping bombs over a wide area. The main effect was to kill German civilians (over a million perished), and may have increased the Germans' will to continue the war.

In November 1943, Roosevelt, Churchill, and Stalin met in Tehran, Iran. Issues the Big Three discussed included postwar Europe, the establishment of the United Nations, and Soviet participation in the war against Japan after victory in Europe. The major issue remained the invasion of France. Stalin insisted that only a direct Allied assault in France could defeat the Nazis. Army Chief of Staff George C. Marshall and the U.S. War Department also strongly supported the invasion of France. Soon

Roosevelt and Churchill notified Stalin that they would attack France no later than May 1944.

Allied Invasion of Normandy

The cross-channel attack on France (code-named Operation Overlord) was a massive undertaking. Many of the soldiers and most of the equipment and supplies—from tanks to tooth fillings—had to be shipped from North America to England. Successfully reducing the German U-boat menace in the Atlantic made this job safer, if no less overwhelming. The use of radar and specially equipped aircraft swept the U-boats from the At-

lantic. By May 1944, only three U-boats remained in service in the Atlantic.

D-Day for the invasion of France was June 6, 1944. Extreme measures and subterfuges had been taken to ensure that German intelligence agents did not identify Normandy as the invasion site. On the evening before, under the orders of General Eisenhower, supreme commander of the Allied forces, thousands of vessels of all sizes, military and civilian, left English ports. They carried an assault force of 156,000 Allied soldiers. Thousands of warplanes strafed and bombed all approaches leading to the invasion beaches. An armada of warships bombarded German fortifications along the coast. In just a few days, the Allies had secured their beachheads, or landing points, on the Normandy coast of northern France. In the months that followed, thousands

▼ *General Dwight D. Eisenhower gave many pep talks to encourage servicemen such as these paratroopers. What was Eisenhower's full rank in 1944?*

Allied Offensives in World War II, 1942-1945

Normandy Invasion

Legend:
- Allied-controlled area as of 1942
- Area gained by Allies as of May 1945
- Axis-controlled area as of May 1945
- Neutral nation
- Allied offensive

U.S. forces
British and Canadian forces
Allied airborne forces
Code-named assault area

0   30 mi
0   40 km

0   500 mi
0   800 km

▲ *The arrows on this map show the major Allied offensives against the Axis between 1941 and 1945.*

of troops and millions of tons of equipment poured into France.

In July 1944, the Allies broke through German lines around the Normandy beachheads. General George Patton's Third Army began a lightning advance through France. Allied troops liberated Paris in August. By September, 2 million Allied troops were in France. The German army was in chaos and had begun to retreat. On July 20, some German officers, convinced that the war was lost, tried to assassinate Hitler. The attempt failed and hundreds of suspected conspirators were put to death.

At the same time, the Soviets began a crushing offensive in the East. They liberated Warsaw in July. By August, they had taken Rumania and Bulgaria. By October, the Soviet army had freed Belgrade, Yugoslavia, and was advancing on Hungary.

In a desperate attempt to avoid defeat, Hitler launched a surprise offensive in the Ardennes forest region in France and Belgium in December. Using troops from the Eastern Front and his last reserves, Hitler hoped for a decisive victory to force the British and Americans to sign an armistice. Aided by surprise and winter weather, the Germans drove 60 miles deep into Allied positions. The Battle of the Bulge was the scene of bitter fighting. When it was over in early 1945, Allied forces had recaptured all the ground they had lost. Yet the price was high. The Allies suffered 75,000 casualties, the Germans over 100,000. Meanwhile, Soviet troops had advanced to less than 40 miles from Berlin.

The Allies Take the Offensive in Asia

FDR initially had high hopes for China's participation in the fighting against Japan. The administration and press believed that General **Chiang Kai-shek**, head of the Chinese Nationalist government, was a strong leader who could rally his nation against its Japanese invaders. Chiang was more concerned, however, with crushing **Mao Zedong's** Communist forces and possible postwar control of China than with fighting Japan. As a result, Chiang contributed little to the war effort in Asia.

Allied strategy for fighting Japan therefore focused on the Pacific rather than on the Asian mainland. The strategy had two major dimensions. First, combined navy and marine troops, commanded by Admiral Chester Nimitz, would attack strategic Japanese-held islands in the Central Pacific. Second, General Douglas MacArthur's forces would strike Japanese positions along the northern coast of New Guinea and other islands in the Southwest Pacific leading toward the Philippines.

Military actions in the Pacific in 1942 were pivotal to the war's outcome. In April of that year, the **Battle of the Coral Sea** blocked Japan's offensive drive toward Australia. The Japanese fleet had moved to capture Port Moresby at the extreme northern tip of New Guinea, but was stopped. This naval battle was the first in which participating ships exchanged no direct gunfire. Carrier-based aircraft did all the fighting.

The decisive **Battle of Midway** was fought in early June. The Japanese wanted Midway Island as a base for another attack on Pearl Harbor. They also hoped to lure American aircraft carriers into a fatal trap. Forewarned of their plan by decoding secret Japanese messages, the Americans instead trapped the Japanese. In the battle that followed, the United States lost one aircraft carrier and 150 planes. Japan lost four carriers, one cruiser, and 322 planes. Midway marked an important turning point. Japan would be on the defensive for the remainder of the war in the Pacific.

To protect Allied lines of supply to Australia, United States navy and marine units under the command of General MacArthur attacked the Solomon Islands in August of 1942. Guadalcanal, where the Japanese were trying to complete an air base from which they could attack Allied supply lines to Australia, was the focus of the fighting. After bitter ground combat and spectacular naval battles, the marines captured Guadalcanal in February 1943. They secured the Solomon Islands by year end.

In November 1943, Admiral Nimitz began his thrust through the Central Pacific using a strategy known as "island hopping," targeting strategic Japanese bases. Fighting was fierce when marines landed on Tarawa, the largest of the Gilbert Islands. Of the 5,000 marines who struggled ashore, more than 1,000 perished and 2,000 suffered wounds. Of the 4,500 Japanese defenders, only 17 survived. This bloody experience taught American military planners several lessons they used in later island assaults. The marines refined their landing equipment and techniques. The navy learned how to soften Japanese defenses by using air and naval bombardment first. Nonetheless, U.S. casualties were even higher in subsequent island invasions.

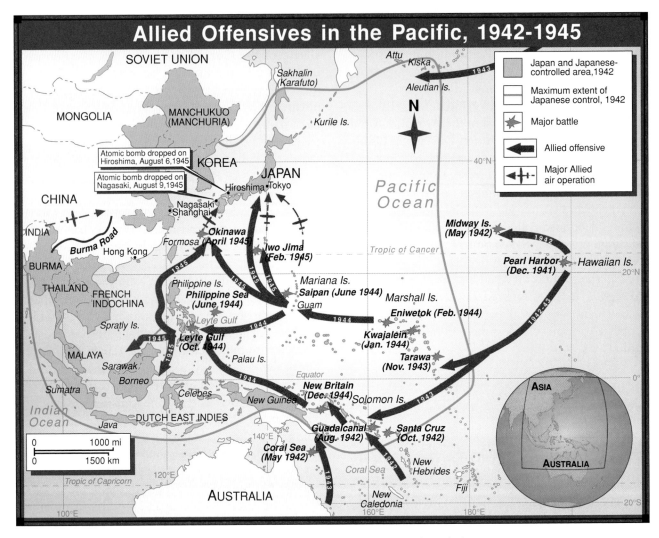

Allied Offensives in the Pacific, 1942-1945

Legend:
- Japan and Japanese-controlled area, 1942
- Maximum extent of Japanese control, 1942
- Major battle
- Allied offensive
- Major Allied air operation

Atomic bomb dropped on Hiroshima, August 6, 1945
Atomic bomb dropped on Nagasaki, August 9, 1945

SOVIET UNION • Sakhalin (Karafuto) • Attu • Kiska • 1943 • Aleutian Is. • MONGOLIA • MANCHUKUO (MANCHURIA) • Kurile Is. • KOREA • JAPAN • Tokyo • Pacific Ocean • 40°N • CHINA • Hiroshima • Nagasaki • Shanghai • Okinawa (April 1945) • Iwo Jima (Feb. 1945) • Midway Is. (May 1942) • 1942 • INDIA • Burma Road • Formosa • Hong Kong • Tropic of Cancer • Pearl Harbor (Dec. 1941) • Hawaiian Is. • 20°N • BURMA • THAILAND • FRENCH INDOCHINA • Philippine Is. • Philippine Sea (June 1944) • Mariana Is. • Saipan (June 1944) • Guam • Marshall Is. • Eniwetok (Feb. 1944) • 1942-43 • Spratly Is. • Leyte Gulf • 1944 • Kwajalein (Jan. 1944) • MALAYA • Leyte Gulf (Oct. 1944) • Palau Is. • Tarawa (Nov. 1943) • Sarawak • Equator • 0° • Sumatra • Borneo • Celebes • New Britain (Dec. 1944) • New Guinea • Solomon Is. • ASIA • Indian Ocean • Java • DUTCH EAST INDIES • 140°E • Guadalcanal (Aug. 1942) • Santa Cruz (Oct. 1942) • 1943 • Coral Sea (May 1942) • New Hebrides • AUSTRALIA • Tropic of Capricorn • 120°E • Coral Sea • New Caledonia • Fiji • 100°E • 160°E • 180°E • 20°S

Scale: 0–1000 mi / 0–1500 km

▲ *Were there any reasonable alternatives to the U.S. strategy of island-hopping through the Central and South Pacific regions?*

After Tarawa, Nimitz's forces advanced rapidly. They captured Kwajalein, a major harbor in the Marshall islands. In summer 1944, American marines captured Saipan, Tinian, and Guam in the Marianas. Naval forces also virtually destroyed Japanese naval airpower in the Battle of the Philippine Sea. These victories marked another turning point in the Pacific war. American B-29 bombers, which carried heavy loads of bombs and flew long distances, could now strike Japan itself.

While Nimitz's forces were advancing toward Japan, MacArthur's troops moved up the northern coast of New Guinea. From April to September 1944, MacArthur struck at successive targets, sometimes leapfrogging over strongly fortified Japanese positions. In October, MacArthur's forces invaded Leyte in the Philippines. Naval forces crippled the Japanese fleet in the **Battle of Leyte Gulf**. This was the largest naval battle of all time, employing 282 warships and hundreds of aircraft. In just three days, Japan lost four carriers, three battleships, and many smaller craft. By the end of 1944, American forces had severely weakened Japan's military strength and were moving ever closer to Japan itself.

1. **Explain** why the Casablanca Conference was important.
2. **State** why the strategic bombing campaign against Germany may have prolonged the war.
3. **Identify** the major obstacle the Allies needed to overcome before invading France.
4. **Describe** the Allied strategy for fighting Japan.
5. **Identify** Chester Nimitz and Douglas MacArthur.

SECTION 5

Onward to Victory

In February 1945, with the defeat of Hitler clearly in sight, Roosevelt, Churchill, and Stalin met at Yalta, a Soviet resort on the Black Sea. Since they were meeting as almost certain victors, their discussions focused on postwar arrangements. Stalin had an especially strong hand to play at the conference. This was so because the Soviet army occupied all the territory in Eastern and Central Europe that would be points of contention with the West. In addition, Roosevelt and Churchill believed that the Soviet army would be needed in the war against Japan. The three Allies resolved several issues, but others, such as the future of Poland, proved much more difficult. These they postponed or papered over with vague agreements. Roosevelt's top military aide, William Leahy, noted that the provision concerning Poland was "so elastic that the Russians can stretch it all the way from Yalta to Washington without technically breaking it."

"I know, Bill—I know it," Roosevelt replied. "But it's the best I can do for Poland at the time." Roosevelt's remark could have applied equally well to most issues the Allies faced as victory neared.

What issues did the Allies discuss at Yalta?
What was the Holocaust?
Were the Allies justified in using atomic bombs to end the war with Japan?

The Yalta Conference

The Allies discussed four principal issues at Yalta. These were:

- the United Nations
- Soviet involvement in the war against Japan
- the future of Poland
- the future of Germany.

The Allies agreed to establish the United Nations (UN) organization. Roosevelt hoped that the UN would encourage cooperation among the great world powers after the war and that it would settle issues not already solved. All member nations would have equal representation in the General Assembly. The major Allies—the United States, Great Britain, the Soviet Union, France, and China—would have special influence through permanent membership in the Security Council. Seven other nations (later increased to ten), elected periodically from the General Assembly, also would sit on the council. The Big Three scheduled the first UN meeting in San Francisco on April 25, 1945.

▼ *British Prime Minister Winston Churchill, President Franklin Roosevelt, and Soviet Premier Joseph Stalin attended the Yalta Conference in February 1945. What sort of relations did the three countries have at that time?*

Stalin agreed to enter the war against Japan after Hitler's defeat. Roosevelt had always wanted Stalin to declare war on Japan, but Stalin had continued to observe the 1941 Russo-Japanese Nonaggression Pact. Roosevelt and Churchill agreed to Soviet claims to Sakhalin Island and the Kuril Islands, to special Soviet interests in Manchuria, and to recognition of a Soviet puppet regime in Outer Mongolia in return for Soviet participation.

Postwar Poland got more attention at Yalta than any other issue. Indeed, each of the Big Three viewed the settlement of Polish issues as an important test case for postwar relations among them. Stalin wanted revisions of the Soviet-Polish border, with Poland to receive German territory as compensation. Second, he wanted to establish a Polish government friendly to Soviet interests. Stalin justified his demands by claiming it was needed for Soviet security. Moreover, since Roosevelt and Churchill had recognized the pro-Western government in Italy in 1943, Stalin felt justified in imposing a pro-Soviet Communist government on Poland. At his allies' insistence, Stalin promised to include non-Communist Poles in the new government and to hold free elections. In fact, Stalin's promises mattered little, since his armies now occupied Poland.

Postwar Germany was the fourth principal issue discussed at Yalta. The three leaders agreed to rid Germany of Nazi and military influences. The Allies would jointly occupy the capital city of Berlin. They then divided Germany into occupation zones and created a joint commission to establish occupation policies. Since Churchill was unsure of American involvement in Europe after the war, he insisted that France get an occupation zone carved from the British and American zones.

With these matters settled, the Allies turned to the issue of reparations. Stalin favored a harsh policy toward Germany. He wanted heavy reparations in factory equipment, goods, and labor to rebuild his country. He thought $20 billion, half for the Soviet Union, was reasonable. Roosevelt and Churchill agreed to reparations, but thought $20 billion was beyond Germany's ability to pay. The Allies agreed to refer this matter to a reparations commission.

▲ *These German-language booklets on how to pick oranges and lemons were intended for German prisoners of war.*

Allied Forces Overrun Germany

Roosevelt returned from Yalta visibly exhausted and very sick. He went to his vacation home in Warm Springs, Georgia, to rest. He died on

▼ *Americans from all classes and races deeply mourned FDR's death in April 1945. For some, he was the only president they remembered.*

◄ It would be many years before Russian and American soldiers would meet again in friendship as they did at Torgau.

▼ Letters home, such as this one from a soldier to his sister, kept family and friends informed of the progress of the war and conditions overseas. How are people kept informed of what is happening during wars today? What technology used by today's military men and women may soon replace letter writing?

April 12, 1945, and Harry S Truman became president.

Meanwhile, Allied forces moved closer to victory. After the Battle of the Bulge ended in January, the Allies amassed troops for an assault on the Rhine River. In February 1945, U.S. casualties amounted to 137,000 and were over 100,000 in March. In early April, Germany's Western Front collapsed. On April 11, American forces reached the Elbe River near Berlin, where Eisenhower ordered them to halt. Two weeks later, the Soviets arrived and laid siege to Berlin. Soviet and American troops met at Torgau, a town on the Elbe.

Hitler committed suicide on April 30 in a bunker deep beneath Berlin. On May 8, all German armed forces officially surrendered. Although the war continued in Asia, people the world over rejoiced in "V-E [Victory in Europe] Day."

The Holocaust Emerging evidence of German wartime atrocities, however, soon dampened the celebration. As early as 1942, word of Nazi death camps had filtered out to the Allies. Jewish leaders lobbied FDR, the State Department, and the War Department to do something about the rumored mass killing of Jews by the Nazis. Suggestions ranged from taking a public stand against the Nazis' anti-Jewish policies to bombing the railroads that carried victims to their death. The Allies did nothing, however, using military priorities as their excuse. As Allied troops liberated the camps, the full horrors of the **Holocaust** became clear.

◀ Under Nazi rule, Jews were forced to wear identifying badges whenever they appeared in public. The star with Jude was worn in Germany, the star with "J" in Belgium, and the others were worn in Hungary.

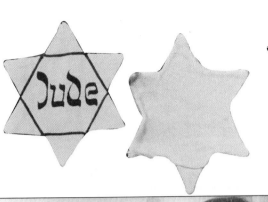

◀ As many as 50,000 Polish children whose physical appearance fit the Nazi notion of a "master race" were kidnapped and taken to Germany to be adopted by German families. The children at left were imprisoned in Auschwitz before being deported to Germany.

◀ This doll was made in a concentration camp.

▼ Concentration camp inmates wore badges identifying their "crimes." Political prisoners wore red triangles, like the one on the uniform below.

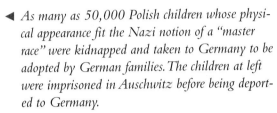

◀ Slave laborers in this concentration camp at Buchenwald lay on bunks several days after their liberation by U.S. troops. Elie Wiesel, future author and Nobel Peace Prize winner, appears at the far right on the top tier.

▼A.15047

Hitler had risen to power in part by espousing hatred of the Jews and making them the scapegoats for many of Germany's problems. He ordered Jews, political opponents, and other "enemies of the German Reich," including homosexuals and the mentally and physically disabled, imprisoned. Then, in 1942, the Nazis began building camps designed for what Hitler termed "the Final Solution"—the systematic extermination of European Jews. The

Nazis rounded up Jews from all over Europe and shipped them to these concentration camps. The able-bodied worked as slave laborers in the camps and in war-related factories. The Nazis murdered men, women, and children in specially built gas chambers disguised as showers. Over two-thirds of Europe's Jewish people—6 million in all—were murdered. Another 6 million people, including Gypsies, Jehovah's Witnesses, and political opponents, were also killed.

Victory in the Pacific

Meanwhile, Allied forces continued to attack Japanese forces in the western Pacific. Nimitz's forces attacked **Iwo Jima** in February 1945. After a month of bloody fighting, three marine divisions overcame fierce Japanese resistance. On April 1, Nimitz attacked **Okinawa.** The island's defenders, fighting from carefully prepared caves and tunnels, fought off the Allies until June. Only 11,000 of the 110,000 Japanese defenders survived. In both battles, Japanese pilots deliberately crashed their bomb-laden planes onto American warships. During the Battle of Okinawa, these suicidal **kamikaze** attacks sank 24 American ships and damaged 66 others.

By capturing Iwo Jima and Okinawa, the Allies could move their air bases even closer to Japan. Many of Japan's cities were reduced to rubble and ashes after General Curtis Le May ordered low-altitude night raids and the use of incendiary bombs (made of flammable jellied gas, or napalm). With

▼ *The Iwo Jima Memorial in Washington, D.C., symbolizes the sacrifices and victorious spirit of the U.S. forces in the Pacific.*

▲ *By 1945, very few observers of the Aircraft Warning System worried that Japanese aircraft would reach the West Coast. How effective would a similar organization be today?*

virtually no navy and a limited number of planes and trained pilots left, the Japanese were nearly defenseless against these assaults. Even so, they seemed determined to fight on.

Military planners estimated that there would be as many as half a million Allied casualties—and many more Japanese—if the Allies invaded Japan. With eventual Japanese defeat now a certainty, these costs seemed very high. Allied leaders surely shared the concern expressed in a letter written to the Navy Department: "Please, for God's sake, stop sending our finest youth to be murdered in places like Iwo Jima. . . . Why can't objectives be accomplished some other way?"

The Age of Atomic Warfare Another way was soon available. In July, while President Truman attended the last wartime conference with his Allies in Potsdam, Germany, he received word of the successful test of an atomic bomb. Truman secured British approval to issue the Potsdam Declaration, an ultimatum for Japan to surrender immediately or face "prompt and utter destruction." The Soviets did not sign the declaration because they were still at peace with Japan. Truman confided to his diary that he was "sure they will not do that [surrender], but we will have given them the chance." The Japanese government rejected the declaration.

On August 6, an American B-29 named the *Enola Gay* dropped an atomic bomb on Hiroshima. Three days later, an atomic bomb destroyed Nagasaki. The casualty toll at Hiroshima was staggering: 68,000 dead, 37,000 injured, and 10,000

The Atomic Bomb

At dawn on July 16, 1945, the first atomic device was detonated near Alamogordo Air Base, in a remote New Mexican desert. "It was a sunrise such as the world had never seen," wrote *New York Times* journalist William Lawrence, "a great green supersun . . . lighting up earth and sky with a dazzling [brilliance]." The assembled military officers and scientists looked through their dark glasses at the incredible burst of flame. (The blast was equivalent to 20,000 tons of high explosives.) Physicist J. Robert Oppenheimer, director of the Manhattan Project that produced the bomb, recalled two passages from the ancient sacred Hindu text *Bhagavad Gita*: "If the radiance of a thousand suns were to burst at once into the sky, that would be like the splendor of the Mighty One. . . . I am become Death, the Shatterer of Worlds."

▼ *"Fat Man" was the code name for the atomic bomb dropped on Nagasaki, Japan.*

The potential of atomic energy had been known for decades, but in 1939 two scientists working in Nazi Germany—Otto Hahn and Fritz Strassman—were the first to split uranium atoms successfully. Physicists everywhere understood the implications: if a chain reaction (split atoms in turn splitting others) could be obtained in a sufficiently large amount of uranium (called a critical mass), a huge amount of energy in the form of an explosion would result. In 1939, several leading scientists—including Hungarian Leo Szilard and Albert Einstein, who had fled Nazi Germany—alerted President Roosevelt to the possibility that Hitler might produce such a weapon first.

By 1942, the top-secret Manhattan Project was moving rapidly to produce an atomic bomb. By the end of the war, it had involved 120,000 people at 37 separate facilities, and had cost $2 billion. Many of the world's leading physicists participated in the project, including Niels Bohr from Denmark and Enrico Fermi from Italy (the first scientist to produce a chain reaction).

By the time Manhattan Project scientists succeeded in making an atomic bomb, many had begun to have second thoughts about producing such an awesome weapon. One group wrote a report, intended for Secretary of War Stimson, stating that "the military advantages and the saving of Amer-

▲ *This color-enhanced photograph shows the mushroom cloud that resulted from the atomic blast at Nagasaki on August 9, 1945. It rose upwards of 60,000 feet.*

ican lives achieved by the sudden use of atomic bombs against Japan may be outweighed by the ensuing loss of confidence and by a wave of horror. . . . A demonstration of the new weapon might best be made . . . on the desert or a barren island." The report had no effect. But this decision was not for the scientists to make.

1. Was the United States justified in developing atomic bombs during World War II?
2. Do you think a demonstration of the bomb's power on a barren island would have caused Japan to surrender?

◄ *The incredible devastation of Hiroshima, Japan, is shown by this photograph taken two months after the atomic bomb was dropped. Why has the decision to use the bomb more than half a century ago remained controversial?*

missing. Another 35,000 perished at Nagasaki. Thousands more Japanese died later of illnesses caused by atomic radiation. Yet thousands of American soldiers, preparing to invade Japan, applauded the bomb's use. As one marine later remarked, "You think of the lives which would have been lost in an invasion of Japan's main islands—a staggering number of Americans, but millions more of Japanese— and you thank God for the atomic bomb."

Historians continue to debate whether using the atomic bombs really hastened Japan's surrender. Even after the atomic bomb drops, many of Japan's military leaders advocated fighting to the bitter end rather than admitting defeat. When informed about Hiroshima, however, Emperor Hirohito said, "We must put an end to the war as speedily as possible so that this tragedy will not be repeated." A handful of

military diehards attempted a coup to prevent surrender. In the end, Hirohito's influence proved decisive. His supporters foiled the coup, and Hirohito himself publicly ordered his people to stop fighting. The war effectively ended on August 15, 1945. On September 2, Japan formally surrendered. The most devastating war in history was finally over.

SECTION 5 REVIEW

1. **Outline** the major agreements reached at Yalta.
2. **Identify** the Holocaust.
3. **Define** kamikaze.
4. **Explain** why Truman issued the Potsdam Declaration.
5. **State** reasons used to justify using atomic weapons against Japan.

Summary

The threat of the Axis powers provided the glue that bound the Allied coalition together through the war. Until mid-1942, Axis armies seemed unstoppable on every battlefront. But the Allies held off defeat, and by 1943 they began to take the offensive against their enemies. Serious issues plagued the Allies throughout the war, especially Stalin's desire for a second front in France. Meanwhile, the Allies' efforts bought time for the American economy to win the battle of industrial production.

World War II caused many changes in American society. Mobilizing American society for war increased the power and influence of the federal government. Orders for war goods stimulated the economy to unprecedented activity. Millions of Americans took advantage of new job opportunities, workers made more money than ever before, and many women and African Americans got good jobs for the first time. Farmers and labor unions also prospered during the war. The war had many side effects. These included greater mobility, more job competition, housing shortages, urban problems, heightened racial antagonisms, and less emphasis on domestic reforms.

As the Axis threat diminished, cooperation among the Allies was more difficult to sustain. Historical antagonisms and differing national interests continually strained Allied relations. As victory neared, these differences led to ever-increasing conflicts among the Allies. Not until after the defeat of Germany did the horrors of the Holocaust become known to the outside world. These conflicts and the worldwide effects of the war were indications of troubles to come.

Vocabulary

Big Three
Holocaust
internment camps
kamikaze

puppet regime
rationing
wildcat strikes

The vocabulary terms are associated with the proper nouns listed below. Match each term to the correct name or names. Then write a sentence explaining the relationships.

1. Gordon Hirabayashi
2. United Mine Workers
3. Churchill, Stalin, Roosevelt
4. Office of Price Administration
5. Outer Mongolia
6. Auschwitz
7. Battle of Okinawa

Review Questions

1. List the advantages of the Axis powers over the Allies in 1942.
2. What effects did defense mobilization have on American politics?
3. How did World War II affect the American economy?
4. Describe briefly the Allied military strategy in Europe and Asia in 1943–1944.
5. Name three patterns in U.S. society that were severely upset by the war.
6. How did the course of the war affect relations among the Allies?
7. List the major decisions made at Yalta.
8. Why did the Allies ignore rumors of the Holocaust?
9. Why did the Allied strategy for fighting Japan focus on the Pacific rather than on the mainland of Asia ?
10. How did Truman justify using atomic bombs on Japan in 1945?

Critical Historical Thinking

Writing Answer each of the following by writing one or more complete paragraphs:

1. Lives of Americans changed dramatically during the Great Depression. The economic calamity ended under the leadership of President Roosevelt. Which do you feel had more effect in ending the depression—the New Deal or World War II? Explain why you think as you do.

2. What do you think were the major mistakes made by the Axis powers leading to their defeat?

3. The atomic bomb was the most terrible weapon ever used in warfare. Weapons today have thousands of times the power of bombs dropped on Hiroshima and Nagasaki. Would any circumstances today necessitate the use of U.S. nuclear weapons? Explain your answer.

4. Read the selection "We Needed Pearl Harbor" in the Unit 8 Archives. Explain why the author felt that the attack had actually been good for America.

Making Connections with Diplomacy

Ever since the American colonists boycotted British goods, economics has been used as a diplomatic weapon by the United States. While sanctions are intended to punish belligerent nations or nations with which we have profound political differences it is not clear whether boycotts accomplish their goals, especially if the targeted country has sufficient resources that other nations want. A case in point is the imposing of sanctions against Germany and Japan in the decade before World War II. The Versailles Treaty (1919) imposed impossibly high reparation payments on Germany to prevent that nation from becoming a threat to world peace again. The League of Nations required the use of economic sanctions against nations which resorted to war.

Numerous boycotts and embargoes were enacted by the United States against Germany, Italy, and Japan. Still, Germany used trade as a means to establish ties to other countries. Japan, which had fewer domestic resources than Germany, was more influenced by the embargoes. In September 1940, Roosevelt placed an embargo on scrap iron and steel, and in July 1941 the President froze all Japanese credits in the United States, bringing all trade between the United States and Japan to a halt. When Roosevelt also cut off oil shipments to Japan, the Tokyo government felt that it had no choice but to go to war with the United States or face economic strangulation.

Writing Conduct research and write a brief report on a recent American boycott or threat of economic sanctions or tariffs of such countries as Cuba, Nicaragua, Iraq, and South Africa. List the factors that made the actions successful or unsuccessful. Then write a policy statement with the premise, "The United States should/should not use boycotts and embargoes as a diplomatic weapon."

Additional Skills Practice

Reading tables is a necessary skill for anyone using public transport systems, such as the city bus or subway. Stop at the city hall or information center for your community and pick up copies of the local bus schedule or mass transit routes. Working with one or two classmates, practice reading schedules by asking each other questions based on the information presented in the table.

Harry S Truman and the Cold War

When told of FDR's death in April 1945, Harry Truman asked Eleanor Roosevelt if there was anything he could do for her. Mrs. Roosevelt replied, "Harry, is there anything we can do for you, for you are the one in trouble now." Her words were prophetic, for Truman soon faced staggering problems. Moreover, the New Deal and World War II had changed the federal government into the single most important force in American life. As manager of a vast military establishment and a growing federal bureaucracy, the president was now the most powerful policymaker in the U.S. government. How would Truman use this vastly increased power? Would the New Deal be extended or cut back? How would the nation meet new challenges in foreign affairs, especially those created by increasingly hostile relations between the United States and the Soviet Union? Was Truman up to these new challenges and the standards of leadership set by FDR? Answers to these questions would emerge slowly, as Truman and the nation dealt with a complicated—and sometimes dangerous—postwar world.

▲ *The Korean War Memorial, located on "The Mall" in Washington, D.C., shows U.S. soldiers dressed for the cold, harsh conditions they encountered during that conflict.*

Truman and the Postwar World

In late 1945, General George Patton told the eight-year-olds in a Sunday school class, "You are the soldiers and nurses of the next war.... There will be another war," the general assured the children. "There always has been." There was, in fact, little peace after the war, for World War II had changed the entire political, economic, and social landscape by creating two superpowers—the United States and the Soviet Union. Given the vast changes brought about by the war, conflicts, especially between the two superpowers, were all but inevitable.

How did World War II shape postwar conditions?

How were United States and Soviet postwar policies different?

What issues caused conflict between the two superpowers?

The Ashes of War

The destruction caused by World War II can barely be imagined. Estimates of wartime deaths range from 40 to 50 million people. Many more were injured or maimed. Moreover, the suffering and sorrow caused by the war lingered long after the last bomb had fallen. Millions faced starvation, and in Europe and Asia 30 to 40 million people were now homeless refugees.

Much of Europe and East Asia was reduced to ashes. Physical damage was estimated at $2 trillion. Farms, villages, cities, factories, roads, railways, and harbor facilities lay in ruins. The economic structures of Europe and Asia were ruined.

The war fundamentally altered international politics. Germany and Japan had been great military and economic powers during the first half of the twentieth century. Now they were devastated. The victorious powers—especially Britain and France—

were little better off. Britain was nearly bankrupt. German occupation and the weeding out of Nazi **collaborators** (supporters) after the war severely weakened France. Although China had not been a major power in the twentieth century, it was even weaker now because of the continued civil war between Nationalist and Communist forces.

The war also had profound effects elsewhere, particularly in the less developed world. Europe's hold on its colonies had weakened during the war. Over the next 15 years, nationalists sought political and economic independence while the Europeans tried to regain their control.

Only two major powers—the United States and the Soviet Union—remained. As one American military planning document predicted, "After the defeat of Japan, the United States and the Soviet Union will be the only military powers of the first magnitude. This is due in each case to a combination of geographical position and extent, and vast [weapons] potential." For a great power, the Soviet Union was in a sorry state. Estimates of Soviet deaths during World War II range from 20 million to 30 million people, nearly half of all wartime deaths. The war destroyed a quarter of the nation's property, 70 percent of its industries, and 60 percent of its transportation facilities. To recover, the Soviet Union sorely needed economic aid.

On the other hand, territory under Soviet control had greatly expanded. By 1945, the Soviets had retaken all the land lost after World War I, including portions of Poland, Finland, and the Baltic states. Three hundred Soviet divisions occupied much of Eastern and Central Europe. Soviet troops were on the borders of Greece and in Iran. They held positions in China, Mongolia, Manchuria, North Korea, and several islands north of Japan.

The United States alone possessed great economic power along with the capacity to expand. It had escaped invasion, bombing, and bloody battles fought within its borders. Military deaths had been about 330,000. While Soviet industrial output had fallen by 40 percent as a result of the war, American output had more than doubled.

Just as the Soviets occupied vast stretches of territory outside their national boundaries, the war had also carried American armed forces around the globe. In 1945, U.S. Army divisions occupied

▶ The devastation in post-World War II Europe was widespread. This photograph was taken after the capture of Saarbrucken, Germany, by American forces. What serious problem resulting from war is illustrated here?

▶ One of Berlin's largest railroad stations, near Potsdamer Platz, was destroyed by Allied bombing. What was the long-term effect of this destruction on the economies of Europe?

portions of Europe, North Africa, Asia, and the Pacific. No one knew how long American forces would remain in those countries.

Friction Between the Superpowers

Political friction between the superpowers began immediately. Stalin's postwar goals included:

- establishing Soviet-dominated spheres of influence in Eastern Europe and parts of Asia

- creating pro-Soviet governments in both regions
- reducing the size of the Soviet military
- rebuilding its war-torn economy
- keeping the nations located on Soviet borders as weak as possible
- extending Soviet influence in these nations by controlling local Communist parties
- keeping potential rivals weak, such as Germany, Japan, and China.

These goals were very different from those pursued by the United States. American postwar for-

Like Germany, Austria and its capital were divided into four occupation zones. Do you think the ten-year occupation of Germany and Austria by the Allies was justified?

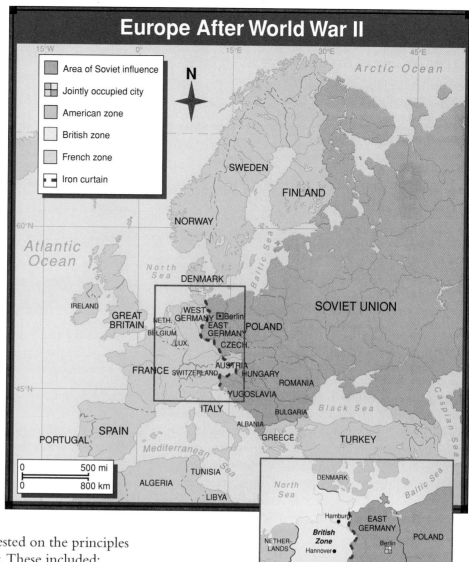

Europe After World War II

Area of Soviet influence
Jointly occupied city
American zone
British zone
French zone
Iron curtain

Allied Occupation of Berlin

Allied Occupation of Germany and Austria

eign policy goals generally rested on the principles of the 1941 Atlantic Charter. These included:

- reliance on collective security through the United Nations
- the elimination of national spheres of influence
- national self-determination for European colonies as well as for the countries of Eastern Europe
- freedom of the seas
- free trade.

U.S. policymakers also wanted to demobilize the armed forces as quickly as possible. The difficulty of pursuing these goals was increased by Roosevelt's death and his replacement as president by Harry S Truman.

Truman had little executive or foreign policy experience when he became president. He had been a little-known Missouri politician, a county judge, a senator, and a solid supporter of the New Deal. As vice president, Truman had not been among FDR's inner circle of advisers. (FDR had not even told Truman about the atomic bomb project.) Despite his inexperience, Truman possessed brash confidence about his ability to handle problems. He took pride in his blunt, salty language, and in his ability to make decisions firmly and quickly. He took seriously the sign he posted on his desk, "The Buck Stops Here."

▲ *This photograph of Senator Harry S Truman, was taken in July 1944, before he secured the Democratic nomination as vice president.*

After Truman became president, Soviet-American relations cooled, sliding eventually into what journalist Walter Lippmann labeled the **Cold War**. The term referred to the tenseness of the relationship between the two superpowers in which hostilities stopped just short of actual military conflict. Before he had been briefed on the complicated issues he would face, Truman told his secretary of state, "We must stand up to the Russians at this point and not be easy with them." In April of 1945, Truman accused the Soviets of violating the Yalta agreements concerning Poland. In May, Truman abruptly stopped lend-lease shipments to Russia. Meanwhile, Stalin's suspicions about his allies' postwar intentions increased when he discovered that he had not been informed about the atomic bomb project. Distrust was growing, and it made cooperation increasingly difficult.

In February, Stalin spoke publicly about the "inevitable conflict between communism and capitalism." Capitalism, he declared, caused war because it needed raw materials and new markets. Conflicts like World War II would continue until communism displaced capitalism throughout the world. While many historians now think Stalin's speech was intended to justify more rigid control at home, at the time it disturbed many Western observers.

Time magazine called Stalin's speech "the most warlike pronouncement uttered by any top-rank statesman since V-J [Victory in Japan] Day." Others thought the speech was a "declaration of World War III." Winston Churchill responded to Stalin's speech with his **iron curtain** speech made at Fulton, Missouri. "From Stetin on the Baltic to Trieste on the Adriatic, an iron curtain has descended across the [European] continent." Countries under Soviet control or influence were said to be behind the iron curtain. Churchill proposed a British-American alliance based on atomic weapons to counter further Soviet penetration into Europe. Truman's presence at Fulton was taken by the Soviets to mean he agreed with Churchill.

Meanwhile, Soviet actions seemed even more threatening than Stalin's words. The Soviets appeared to be aiding Communist rebels in a civil war in Greece. (The aid was actually coming from Yugoslavia.) Since Britain supported the non-Communist Greek government, Communist interference, whether Soviet or Yugoslavian, was unwelcome.

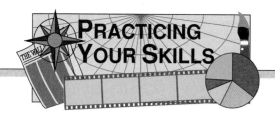

PRACTICING YOUR SKILLS

Using Photographs to Create Images

Paintings and photographs can be used for persuasion purposes. One special type of persuasion is *image-making*. In image-making, the artist or photographer associates the product—whether a person or thing—with places or activities that arouse strong emotions. For instance, an image of a man pushing a child on a swing would immediately suggest "loving father, or strong supporter of family values." A woman dressed in a strong color, such as red, may be seen as aggressive, powerful, or threatening—depending upon your personal viewpoint.

Today, public relations is a multimillion dollar industry and large firms are devoted to creating the right images for politicians, celebrities, and even corporations. Agents and public relations personnel arrange for "photo shoots" that capture images of their clients in activities that will make people relate positively to them. These same public relations experts also make sure the wrong image is not presented to the public by advising their clients on the correct way to dress, speak, and behave.

When looking at photographs of famous people, ask yourself whether the images are set up in advance (posed) or candid (real-life). The following questions may help you to make up your mind:

- **Is it obvious where the photo was taken, and, if so, is there an emotional response to that location?** Some locations, such as parks and kitchens, remind people of home or family; other locations, such as beaches and casinos, are exotic, exciting, or a little bit dangerous; some locations, like offices and government buildings, are powerful or dignified.
- **What activities are taking place?** Like loca-

tions, some activities cause emotional responses. Examples are kissing babies, marching in parades, or working with your hands.

- **What other details are image-makers?** Notice the style of dress. Are the short sleeves rolled-up to suggest hard work? What is the person holding? What pictures are in the background?

Examine the photograph on page 774 and answer the following questions:

1. What is Senator Truman doing? What is his wife Bess doing? How would you describe the setting?
2. (a) Describe the expression on Mrs. Truman's face. What do you think she is about to say? (b) Do you think this scene looks natural? Why, or why not?
3. What evidence can you give from your text and class discussion that would support or deny the image created in this photograph?
4. Why do you think this image was created for Truman as the vice presidential candidate with Roosevelt in 1944? Do you think this image might have been an advantage or a disadvantage when he became president? Why?
5. Describe some of the images created for these presidents: Andrew Jackson, Abraham Lincoln, Teddy Roosevelt, and Franklin Delano Roosevelt.

Stalin had also refused to withdraw Soviet troops from northern Iran, violating wartime Allied agreements. Truman successfully pressured Stalin to withdraw his troops. Then, in August, Stalin demanded that Turkey cede joint control of the Dardanelles, the waterway between the Black and Mediterranean Seas, to the Soviets.

American officials thought these actions showed Stalin's desire for world conquest. They worried that Soviet meddling in Greece, Turkey, and Iran could lead to the entire Middle East and Greece falling under Communist control. This area, with its important oil resources and the Suez Canal, was of vital importance to Western Europe and the United States.

Soviet-American relations slid further into the Cold War as a result of friction over Germany. At first, the Allies had agreed that Germany should be kept weak. The Soviets demanded large reparations from Germany to help rebuild the Soviet economy. Soon, however, American and British officials feared that Germany might become too weak and costly to support. They began to see the rebuilding of Germany as a way to stop further Soviet influence in Central Europe. They stopped the delivery of reparations to the Soviets and proposed a plan to unify all Germany into a single economic entity. Both France and the Soviet Union rejected the plan, so Britain and the United States merged their occupation zones to permit common economic policies. The threat of a revived Germany deepened the fears of the Soviets and heightened their distrust of the West.

SECTION 1 REVIEW

1. **Define** the term *Cold War*.
2. **Describe** briefly the effects of World War II on the postwar world.
3. **Compare** the physical damages suffered by the United States and by the Soviet Union.
4. **List** the primary issues about which the Soviets and the Americans disagreed.
5. **Describe** the circumstances that prompted Winston Churchill to deliver the "iron curtain" speech.

SECTION 2

From War to Peace on the Home Front

As soon as Americans heard that Japan had surrendered, crowds of people took to the streets throughout the United States to celebrate their relief and joy. In New York City, nearly 2 million people descended on Times Square for a two-day celebration. Celebrants threw 5,000 tons of litter from downtown windows onto the streets below. Despite the happy clamor, many Americans were privately worried about the future. When asked about her postwar expectations, a young St. Louis woman said, "Oh, things are going along just wonderfully." Then, frowning, she asked, "Do you think it's really going to last?"

What problems did Americans confront as they demobilized after World War II?

What were the causes and consequences of postwar labor union activity?

What effects did the elections of 1946 have on the nation's domestic policies?

The Problems of Reconversion

Reconversion, changing the economy and the military from wartime to peacetime operations, was the primary task of Truman's first 18 months as president. Reconversion presented Truman with a wide range of difficult problems. After years of depression and war, the nation had a critical shortage of low- and middle-income housing. Returning veterans and other young people had to pay high rents for poor housing or live with their parents or other family members. African Americans and women, severely affected by layoffs at defense plants, wished to keep the gains in employment opportunities they had won during the war. Labor unions wanted to end wartime wage ceilings, while businesses wanted to end controls on prices and raw

▲ *A veteran of the North African, Italian, and French campaigns was greeted by his wife and daughters. What problems faced returning veterans?*

▲ *The GI Bill of Rights provided funds for tuition, fees, and books. What other benefits were allowed under this bill?*

materials. People resented the shortages of consumer goods. Few Americans were willing to continue making patriotic sacrifices after the war.

Truman knew he had to prevent a return to economic depression and high levels of unemployment. He feared that veterans would have difficulty finding jobs if they returned home too quickly, and that they would swell the ranks of the unemployed. As a result, Truman initially delayed **demobilization**, reducing the size of the armed forces. In early 1946, impatient GIs staged protests in Japan, France, India, Germany, and the Philippines. Civilians began extensive letter-writing campaigns to force government leaders to "bring Daddy home." By April of 1946, nearly 7 million soldiers had returned to civilian life.

The GI Bill of Rights, enacted in 1944, eased the transition for veterans from wartime to peacetime. During its 12-year existence, the Veterans' Benefits Program provided money for veterans' education and training, for starting new businesses and farms, and for buying homes. By paying for schooling, the GI Bill kept many returning soldiers out of the job market, while it increased their skills and earning potential.

Concern about depression and unemployment also led to the Employment Act in 1946. The act's basic idea was to use fiscal and monetary policies to avoid the radical swings between economic boom and bust that occurred naturally in the business cycle. The act required the president to watch the economy closely and to submit annual reports to Congress. It established the three-person Council of Economic Advisers to help him.

Inflation was another problem facing Truman. As long as the demand for goods was greater than the supply, inflation was a constant threat. For more than two years, while Truman and Congress battled over whether wartime wage and price controls should be continued, prices rose around fifteen percent annually. Eventually wage and price controls were removed, except for those on rents, sugar, and rice. Production began to catch up with consumer demand and inflation slowed.

The federal government encouraged reconversion by selling war plants to private industries at very reasonable prices. Accustomed to years of economic depression and war, Americans were eager to purchase houses, cars, and such durable consumer goods as washing machines and refrigerators. People had saved nearly $140 billion during the war. Business leaders were confident the time had come to expand their factories as rapidly as possible.

These veterans marched from Philadelphia, Pennsylvania, to the state capital at Harrisburg in 1946. They wanted the state to give unemployment benefits for striking veterans. Does this photograph support the results of the Most Important Problem *poll on this page?*

Labor Union Strikes

Concerns about the economy led labor unions to increase their demands for higher wages and fringe benefits. By 1945, many unions had succeeded in getting higher wages. Yet when prices shot up in 1946, workers discovered those wage increases had been wiped out, and they sought more money. As a result, 5,000 strikes, involving 4.6 million workers, took place in 1946 alone. Most worrisome were strikes in such essential industries as coal, steel, and the railroads, which threatened to bring the whole economy to a halt.

Many people thought the strikers' demands were outrageous. Millions of unorganized workers, farmers, and small-business proprietors resented the unions' power and generally identified with the employers. Moreover, strikes appeared to prevent the rapid return to normal economic activity. Although Truman was generally sympathetic to labor, he took strong anti-union actions in several labor disputes. He seized the coal mines in order to end the coal strike and threatened to draft striking railroad workers into the military. Once drafted, Truman, as

commander in chief, could order them back to work. Truman asked Congress for additional powers to deal with union turmoil. By late 1946, union leaders were calling Truman the "nation's number one strikebreaker."

▼ *The poll below shows the concerns of Americans following the war.*

Most Important Problem, 1945

Question: What do you think will be the most important problem facing this country during the next year?

Jobs/unemployment	62%
Reconversion/demobilization	17%
Peace	5%
Labor trouble/strikes	4%

Source: Gallup, August 24-29, 1945.

©The Public Perspective, a publication of the Roper Center for Public Opinion Research, University of CT, Storrs. Reprinted by permission.

Truman and Congress

Labor unrest was one important factor affecting the public mood as the congressional elections approached in 1946. People were also affected by growing rumors about Communist spies, disloyalty, and subversion. Truman's own attorney general, Thomas C. Clark, saw a connection between the two issues. He stated that "a sinister and deep-seated plot on the part of Communists, ideologists, and small groups of radicals" aimed to take over labor unions, cause strikes, and disrupt the social order in the United States.

Although well liked personally, Truman was considered a second-rate president by most Americans in 1946. The nation's needs appeared to be beyond Truman's control. To no one's surprise Republicans won a decisive victory in the congressional elections of that year. They carried both houses of Congress for the first time since 1928 and won 25 state governorships as well.

The Republican leaders of the Eightieth Congress were extremely conservative, and they were bitter opponents of the New Deal. Although the Eightieth Congress supported Truman's foreign policy, it fought him on his domestic program. That domestic program was clearly in the New Deal tradition. He wanted legislation for public housing, expanded Social Security, national health insurance, increases in the minimum wage and in unemployment benefits, public works projects, and federal aid to education, among other items.

The Eightieth Congress, however, had a legislative agenda of its own. It enacted the **Twenty-second Amendment** to the Constitution, which limited future presidents to two terms—a bit of vengeance aimed at the late Franklin D. Roosevelt's four terms. The necessary three-fourths of the states ratified the amendment in 1951. The Congress reduced federal taxes, especially for Americans in higher tax brackets. To make up the resulting shortfall in federal revenues, the Congress reduced spending on public power projects, school lunches, and agricultural price supports. It also refused to pass most of Truman's liberal domestic program.

The Eightieth Congress also restricted labor unions. Conservatives in Congress thought the National Labor Relations Act of 1935 had given unions too much power. They proposed legislation to decrease union power and stop what they called "unfair" labor practices. The **Taft-Hartley Act (1947)** forbade such practices as **secondary boycotts**, that is, one union's refusal to buy an employer's goods or services in order to help another union in a dispute. State **right-to-work laws**, allowing non-union employees to work in a union-organized shop, and providing for cooling-off periods for further negotiations if strikes threatened the public interest, were permitted. To reduce corruption, the act required unions to file annual financial reports with the secretary of labor. Union leaders also had to sign oaths denying Communist affiliations.

Union leaders bitterly denounced the Taft-Hartley Act, calling it the Slave Labor Act. Truman vetoed the Taft-Hartley bill, but Congress easily overrode his veto. Despite the act, union membership continued to grow and Truman emerged from this episode as the defender of union workers. Indeed, from mid-1947 until the election of 1948, Truman presented himself as the defender of New

▼ *Explain the fact that between 1950 and 1970 the total number of union members grew but the percentage of union members in the labor force declined.*

Labor Union Membership, 1930-1990

Percent of Total Labor Force

Year	Membership (thousands)	Percent
1930	3,401	11.6%
1950	14,267	31.5%
1970	19,381	27.3%
1990	16,740	16.1%

Labor union membership is given in thousands.

Source: Bureau of Labor Statistics, U.S. Department of Labor.

Jackie Robinson

On April 10, 1947, Brooklyn Dodgers' president Branch Rickey announced that Jackie Robinson, an African American, would play first base for the Dodgers that season. In retrospect, breaking down major-league baseball's Jim Crow barriers seemed almost inevitable. Even so, it took courage for Rickey and Robinson to challenge accepted prejudices and practices.

There were other minor league African American ballplayers at that time, such as Satchel Paige, Monte Irvin, Roy Campanella, and Larry Doby. But Rickey sensed that the first African American in the major leagues would face terrible difficulties and he saw in Robinson the sort of person who could succeed in this situation.

Jackie Robinson was born in Cairo, Georgia, on January 31, 1919, but Robinson's mother soon moved her family to Pasadena, California. Faced daily with racial prejudices, Jackie became "an angry, seething, highly competitive athlete with a razor-sharp resentment of ingrained, infuriating injustices," as baseball historian Donald Honig put it. At the University of California, Los Angeles, Robinson demonstrated his athleticism by lettering in baseball, football, basketball, and track. In

▲ *Jackie Robinson "steals home" against the Boston Braves in 1948.*

the army, Second Lieutenant Robinson resisted the military's Jim Crow practices. At Fort Hood, Texas, for example, Robinson faced a court-martial for refusing to sit in the back of the bus. The judges found Robinson not guilty, but handed him an honorable discharge.

When Rickey and Robinson first met in 1945, Rickey lectured Robinson on what to expect in the major leagues. The player would face hostility—from fans, opponents, teammates, and the press. Pitchers would try to knock him down with pitches, and base runners would try to spike him. Rickey told Robinson he could not fight back. "Mr. Rickey," Robinson asked, "do you want a ballplayer who's afraid to fight

back?" Rickey responded, "I want a ballplayer with guts enough not to fight back!" Robinson promised he would cause no incident. Through that lonely first season, he kept his promise and courageously endured every provocation. He played his game, helped the Dodgers win the National League pennant, and became Rookie of the Year.

1. Why did Rickey think Robinson was the man to break the baseball color barrier?
2. Do you think it was important that Robinson not react violently to the taunts of his fellow players? Why, or why not?

Deal liberalism against a conservative Republican Congress. He vetoed many bills, not caring if his vetoes were overridden. He also proposed his own programs, even when their chances for passage were hopeless. While congressional leaders rejoiced in their victories, Truman was building a case against Congress that he would soon take to the people.

For personal as well as political reasons, Truman acted to gain the support of African Americans. In his public speeches, he voiced a stronger commitment to civil rights than any president before him. In 1947, Truman instructed the Justice Department to submit **friend-of-the-court** briefs in civil rights cases. These briefs are legal arguments supporting one side in a law case. In cases involving racial segregation, such as interstate transportation (*Henderson v. United States*) and higher education (*Sweatt v. Painter*) among others, Justice Department attorneys attacked segregation and the separate-but-equal doctrine established in *Plessy v. Ferguson* (1896).

In late 1947, Truman's Civil Rights Committee issued a report entitled *To Secure These Rights*. Truman unsuccessfully proposed to Congress several of the committee's most important recommendations, including a permanent Fair Employment Practices Commission, an anti-lynching act, and a voting-rights act. In July 1948, Truman issued executive orders to end racial discrimination in the federal civil service and to desegregate the armed forces. Many military leaders resisted the desegregation order, but the U.S. Army was almost totally desegregated by the end of Truman's presidency. Truman put the force of his office behind civil rights.

SECTION 3

Into the Depths of Cold War

On February 21, 1947, the British government informed Truman that it would discontinue financial and military aid to Greece and Turkey. Truman invited congressional leaders to the White House to convince them that the United States should replace Britain as protector of Greece and Turkey. The legislators, however, remained unmoved by problems in Greece and Turkey. Undersecretary of State Dean Acheson then took the floor, saying, "Like apples in a barrel infected by one rotten one, the corruption of Greece would infect Iran and all to the east." The effect of Soviet penetration in Greece would eventually endanger Europe. "We and we alone," he continued, "are in a position to break up the play." The legislators sat in stunned silence. Then Senate Foreign Relations Committee Chair Arthur Vandenberg finally said, "If you say that to the Congress and the country, I will support you."

What were the primary features of Truman's containment policy?

What effects did containment have on the Soviet Union?

How did foreign policy influence domestic politics?

Truman and Containment

By early 1947, friction between the United States and the Soviet Union led to a major shift in U.S. foreign policy. Relying on advice from his foreign policy experts, Truman sought to establish U.S. leadership in the world by containing the Soviet Union within its post–World War II boundaries. George F. Kennan, a State Department expert on the Soviet Union, argued that the Soviets would be aggressive and look for weak spots in the non-Communist world. Negotiations with the Soviets

▲ *What major point do you think cartoonist Fred O. Seibel was trying to convey in this editorial cartoon?*

▲ *For many people, the Pentagon came to symbolize the military-industrial complex.*

would gain very little. Rather, America should build "situations of strength" around the Soviet Union. "The main element of any United States policy toward the Soviet Union must be . . . containment of Russian expansive tendencies."

The first element in Truman's evolving **containment policy** was providing military aid. In mid-March 1947, Truman presented a bill to Congress that would provide $400 million in military aid to Greece and Turkey. In urging passage of this bill, the president outlined the **Truman Doctrine**, justifying the military side of containment. Truman persuaded Congress and the American public of the seriousness of the Soviet threat. "I believe that it must be the policy of the United States to support free peoples who are resisting armed subjugation by armed minorities or by outside pressures. The free people of the world look to us for support in maintaining their freedom." Congress passed the aid bill on May 22, 1947. Walter Lippmann called the Truman Doctrine a "vague global policy [that] has no limits." Few heeded the journalist's warning about the costs of military containment.

The National Security Act, passed by Congress in July 1947, expanded the president's defense and foreign policy powers. The National Security Act:

- provided for a single Department of Defense to run the formerly independent military services
- established the Joint Chiefs of Staff to advise the secretary of defense
- created the National Security Council (NSC) to advise the president on foreign and military policy
- established the Central Intelligence Agency (CIA) to coordinate all spying and intelligence-gathering activities. (Unstated in the act, but clear to its framers, the CIA would also be responsible for covert operations against other governments.)

The Marshall Plan

Foreign aid was the second major pillar, after military aid, of Truman's containment policy. Europe's economic recovery had been much slower than expected after World War II. Over 125 million Europeans were starving and the widespread misery shocked visiting Americans. Communist parties throughout Europe used these dismal conditions for

▲ *Secretary of Defense George C. Marshall (right) is seen here with Secretary of State Dean Acheson (left) and President Truman.*

propaganda purposes. Secretary of State George C. Marshall therefore promised large amounts of aid to get Europe's economy restarted. The **Marshall Plan** offered aid to every European country, but required all of them to cooperate in planning a European recovery program.

Europeans responded enthusiastically to Marshall's proposal. Delegates from 17 countries, including the Soviet Union, soon met in Paris. Soviet Foreign Minister Molotov, however, angrily left the meeting after the others rejected his proposal that each nation develop its own recovery program. The remaining nations sent their request for aid to the United States in September 1947. Truman then asked Congress to appropriate $17 billion over four years for European recovery. The Republican-controlled Congress, often skeptical about foreign spending programs and confident that they would defeat Truman in the presidential election of 1948, delayed action on the Marshall Plan.

Soviet Resistance   Soviet actions soon saved the Marshall Plan. Stalin refused to let the Iron Curtain countries participate and announced the Molotov Plan of economic aid to Eastern Europe. In late 1947, Stalin also began to tighten Soviet control in Eastern Europe. Rumania fell under complete Communist control in February 1948, and non-Communist leaders fled Bulgaria, Hungary, and Poland. Communist parties in France and Italy

staged strikes to prevent their governments' acceptance of Marshall Plan aid.

Even more shocking were Soviet actions in Czechoslovakia. Since World War II, the Czech government had included both Communist and non-Communist parties and had tried to steer a middle course in the developing Cold War. In February 1948, Stalin moved Soviet troops to the Czech border and demanded the formation of a new all-Communist government. **Purges** (arrests, removals, or executions of those suspected of disloyalty) completed Moscow's control of Czechoslovakia.

The Czech takeover, President Truman said, "sent a shock wave throughout the civilized world." General Lucius Clay, American military commander in Germany, informed Washington that hostilities with the Soviets "may come with dramatic suddenness." Secretary of State Marshall described the world situation as "very, very serious." On March 17, Truman delivered a blistering speech to Congress urging immediate passage of the Marshall Plan. As a result of these events, Congress acted rapidly on the Marshall Plan and Truman signed the bill in April 1948. Over the next three years, the plan channeled nearly $13 billion into Europe, sparking major economic recovery. Between 1948 and 1952, industrial production in Western Europe rose nearly 200 percent. Meanwhile, Communist influence in these nations declined and American trading opportunities expanded rapidly.

The Cold War Grows Colder

With evidence of Soviet aggression mounting, Truman moved to solve the German problem. France had joined Britain and America in uniting their occupation zones into an independent German state. Truman also said that American military forces would remain in Germany indefinitely.

These actions were severe blows to Soviet foreign policy. On June 24, 1948, Stalin cut overland and rail links between Berlin (located in the Soviet Zone) and the Western occupation zones. The **Berlin blockade** was an attempt to force the Western powers out of West Berlin.

The Berlin Airlift, 1948-1949

Allied occupation zone (West Germany)

Soviet occupation zone (East Germany)

Routes of the Berlin Airlift

Iron curtain

0 200 mi

0 300 km

▲ *More than 277,000 flights of cargo planes kept West Berliners supplied during the blockade of Berlin. What organization was formed shortly after the Berlin Airlift?*

◄ *In June 1948, the Soviets cut vital overland supply routes from West Germany to West Berlin. How did the Allies respond to this blockade?*

Truman's response to the blockade was: "We're going to stay, period!" He ordered three combat wings of B-29 bombers—known as the "atomic bombers"—to England, an obvious warning to the Soviets. He then began to airlift supplies to West Berlin. By late 1948, supply planes were landing in West Berlin every 90 seconds around the clock, delivering 5,000 tons of goods every day. When Stalin lifted the blockade on May 12, 1949, over 277,000 flights and 2.5 million tons of supplies had arrived.

The blockade hastened the formation of the **North Atlantic Treaty Organization (NATO)**, a 12-nation mutual-defense treaty aimed at the Soviet Union. The NATO treaty pledged that "an armed attack against one or more of them in Europe or North America shall be considered an attack against them all." The members further agreed to plan for their common defense and to create a unified military command. NATO was a revolutionary step for the United States, as it was the first formal American military alliance with Europe since the colonies' alliance with France during the Revolutionary War. The United States Senate ratified the treaty in July 1949. The Soviets responded to NATO with a new defense alliance of their own called the Warsaw Pact.

The blockade also sped the division of Germany into two countries. In August 1949, free elections in West Germany resulted in the creation of the Federal Republic of Germany. In October, the Soviets responded by creating the German Democratic Republic in their occupation zone.

Foreign Affairs and Domestic Politics

Truman's responses to the Greek, Czech, and Berlin crises won him some political support at

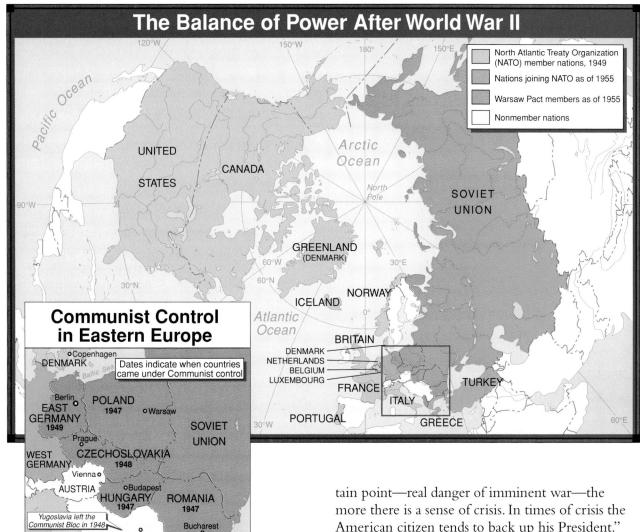

The Balance of Power After World War II

North Atlantic Treaty Organization (NATO) member nations, 1949

Nations joining NATO as of 1955

Warsaw Pact members as of 1955

Nonmember nations

UNITED STATES

CANADA

Pacific Ocean

Arctic Ocean

North Pole

SOVIET UNION

GREENLAND (DENMARK)

ICELAND

NORWAY

Atlantic Ocean

BRITAIN

DENMARK
NETHERLANDS
BELGIUM
LUXEMBOURG
FRANCE

ITALY

TURKEY

PORTUGAL

GREECE

Communist Control in Eastern Europe

Dates indicate when countries came under Communist control

Copenhagen

DENMARK

Baltic Sea

Berlin

EAST GERMANY 1949

POLAND 1947

Warsaw

SOVIET UNION

WEST GERMANY

Prague

CZECHOSLOVAKIA 1948

Vienna

AUSTRIA

Budapest

HUNGARY 1947

ROMANIA 1947

Bucharest

Yugoslavia left the Communist Bloc in 1948

ITALY

Rome

Belgrade

YUGOSLAVIA 1945

BULGARIA 1946

Sofia

Black Sea

Adriatic Sea

Tirane

ALBANIA 1946

GREECE

TURKEY

0   100 mi
0   100 km

▲ *During the Cold War, Europe divided into the North American Treaty Organization (NATO) and the Communist Bloc. (Most countries of the Communist Bloc joined the Warsaw Pact in 1955.) What map changes led people in the West to see the Soviet Union as a threat to their security?*

home. Clark Clifford, Truman's closest political adviser, told him there is "considerable political advantage to the Administration in its battle with the Kremlin.... The worse things get, up to a fairly cer-

tain point—real danger of imminent war—the more there is a sense of crisis. In times of crisis the American citizen tends to back up his President."

Truman also gained popularity from his Middle East policies. Since 1945, hundreds of thousands of Jewish refugees, many survivors of the Holocaust, had flooded into Palestine. They met bitter resistance from Arabs already living there. The problem soon exceeded the control of British authorities, who, along with the French, had governed much of the Middle East under the provisions of the League of Nations. In 1948, the British decided to leave Palestine and on May 14 of that year the Jews proclaimed the new state of Israel. Within minutes, Truman extended official United States recognition. The Palestinian Arabs refused to recognize the new state and the first of many wars erupted.

Not everyone agreed with Truman. Some of his advisers and several of America's allies worried about turning Arabs against the United States.

Control of Middle East oil supplies was their major concern. Truman, however, listened to his political rather than his military and diplomatic advisers. As British Prime Minister Clement Atlee noted, "There's no Arab vote in America, but there's a very heavy Jewish vote and the Americans are always having elections." Truman's handling of foreign crises played a significant role in his upset election in 1948.

SECTION 3 REVIEW

1. **State** briefly the intent of the Truman Doctrine.
2. **Define** the term *purge* as used in this section.
3. **Describe** Stalin's immediate response to the Marshall Plan.
4. **Describe** Truman's response to the Berlin blockade.
5. **Explain** how Truman's foreign policy benefited his domestic policy.

SECTION 4

The Election of 1948 and the Fair Deal

If anything seemed certain in 1948, it was that Harry Truman, now completing FDR's fourth term, would not be elected president in his own right. Truman appeared to be in trouble on all fronts. When the Democrats grudgingly nominated Truman as their candidate in 1948, Republicans rejoiced. "Let us waste no time measuring the unfortunate man in the White House against our specifications," asserted Republican Congresswoman Claire Boothe Luce. "Mr. Truman's time is short; his situation is hopeless. Frankly, he is a gone goose." The 1948 elections appeared very promising for Republicans and disastrous for Democrats.

How did Truman succeed in gaining election in 1948?
What were the major elements of Truman's Fair Deal program?
What effects did the disloyalty controversy have on Truman's presidency?

Upset Victory

Well led and unified, the Republicans had the loyal support of most middle- and upper-class Protestants outside the South, and many farmers and skilled workers. Since this coalition was too small to ensure victory in 1948, Republicans eagerly sought traditional Democratic and independent voters. They chose Thomas E. Dewey, moderate Republican governor of New York, as their candidate for president. Dewey had demonstrated his political popularity in his 1944 campaign against FDR and in his reelection as governor in 1946. Republicans selected California governor Earl Warren as their vice presidential nominee and wrote a moderate platform promising to retain most New Deal programs. Dewey was so certain of victory that he acted "like a man who has already been elected and is merely marking time, waiting to take office."

In contrast, Truman led a party in disarray. Truman's stand on African American civil rights had alienated southern Democrats, traditionally crucial in presidential elections. While Truman wished to soft-pedal civil rights at the Democratic convention, liberals—led by Minneapolis mayor Hubert Humphrey—won adoption of a strong civil rights plank. Southern Democrats bolted the convention. Several days later, those delegates met at Birmingham, Alabama, and formed the States' Rights Democratic Party, nicknamed the Dixiecrats. They nominated South Carolina governor Strom Thurmond as their presidential candidate.

A second split occurred in the Democratic Party. In 1947, Truman had fired Secretary of Commerce Henry Wallace for making a speech critical of Truman's increasingly hard-line approach toward the Soviet Union. In 1948, Wallace supporters formed a new Progressive Party, which nominated him as their presidential candidate. Wallace continued to attack Truman for his "great betrayal" of FDR's foreign policies and for "slamming the door" on peaceful relations with the Soviets.

Despite these splits in the Democratic Party, Truman believed he could win, and he campaigned accordingly. His strategy was to run against the Republican-controlled Eightieth Congress rather than against Dewey. He aimed his campaign at people who had benefited most from New Deal programs—laborers, farmers, African Americans, and liberals. To underscore his differences with the Eightieth Congress, Truman called it into special session in late July and challenged the Republicans to enact their campaign platform. When Congress refused to enact anything, Truman charged that "the do-nothing, Republican Congress . . . never did anything the whole time it was in session." Although false, this charge became the dominant theme in Truman's campaign.

Since most newspapers supported Dewey, Truman embarked on a 31,000-mile "whistle-stop" campaign by train to take his message to the people. As he set out, his running mate, Senator Alben Barkley, told the president "to mow 'em down." Truman replied, "I'll mow 'em down, Alben, and I'll give 'em hell." After a journalist reported this exchange, crowds attending his campaign rallies began to yell, "Give 'em hell, Harry!" and this he did with great relish. During the tour, he made over 350 speeches to an estimated 6 million people. As Truman crisscrossed the nation, he was relentlessly on the attack. "If you send another Republican Congress to Washington," he told one crowd,

▼ *What term is used to describe President Truman's style of campaigning?*

"you're a bigger bunch of suckers than I think you are." Dewey, thinking his election certain, ignored Truman's attacks.

To almost everyone's surprise, Truman won the election. With barely half the eligible voters casting ballots, Truman received 24 million popular votes, to 22 million for Dewey and 2.4 million for Thurmond and Wallace combined. Truman wrote Winston Churchill that his election resulted from

▼ *What factors account for Truman's failure to win a majority of the popular vote?*

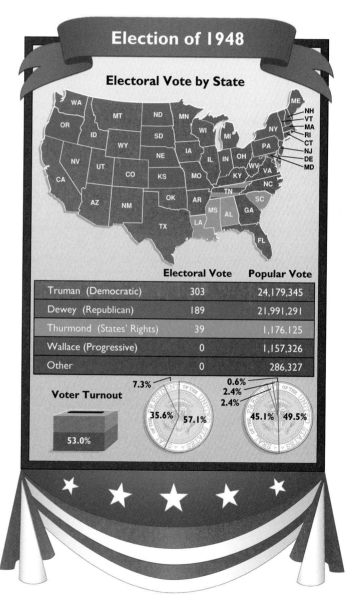

Election of 1948

Electoral Vote by State

	Electoral Vote	Popular Vote
Truman (Democratic)	303	24,179,345
Dewey (Republican)	189	21,991,291
Thurmond (States' Rights)	39	1,176,125
Wallace (Progressive)	0	1,157,326
Other	0	286,327

Voter Turnout

53.0%

7.3%
35.6%   57.1%

0.6%
2.4%
2.4%
45.1%   49.5%

▲ *Based on early voting returns, the* Chicago Daily Tribune *predicted that Truman had lost the 1948 presidential election.*

people wanting "a continuation of the policies which had been in effect for the last sixteen years." Indeed, Truman won by retaining the support of the New Deal coalition, including labor, farmers, Jewish and Catholic voters in the big cities, and African Americans.

A Fair Deal

In his 1949 State of the Union address, Truman pledged himself to the **Fair Deal**, which was basically the domestic program he had supported since 1945. Although Democrats regained control of Congress in 1948, they passed little of the legislation Truman desired. Congress increased the minimum wage from 40 cents to 75 cents an hour, expanded Social Security coverage, and passed the Housing Act of 1949. The latter especially pleased Truman, who said it "opens up the prospect of decent homes in wholesome surroundings for low-income families now living in the squalor of the slums." Although the Housing Act authorized 810,000

housing units, Congress provided funds for only half that number over the next 15 years.

The Fair Deal's more daring and controversial proposals all failed in Congress. Southern Democrats and conservative Republicans continued to prevent enactment of civil rights legislation. In 1949, Truman again proposed legislation to establish a permanent Fair Employment Practices Committee, to outlaw the poll tax, and to make lynching a federal crime. Southern senators prevented votes on these measures by making extremely long speeches, a practice known as **filibustering**. Federal aid to education failed because Congress could not agree on aiding either racially segregated or church-sponsored schools. Truman also failed to persuade Congress to reform federal farm policy.

Truman's failure to secure more Fair Deal legislation was due to a variety of circumstances. Conservatives in Congress continued to block bills. Second, Truman had received less than 50 percent of the popular vote in 1948. Third, the Cold War created a climate of anti-Communist hysteria that diverted attention from other concerns and made change of any sort seem suspect.

The Red Scare

The loyalty issue had first emerged in the elections of 1946 and gained momentum during Truman's administration. Conservatives in general and Republicans in particular found in this issue a powerful new source of political strength and vitality. The **House Un-American Activities Committee (HUAC)**, established in 1938, became a permanent committee in 1945. It was largely responsible for keeping the loyalty issue in front of the American people. HUAC investigations alleged that Communists and Communist sympathizers had been active in the movie industry, in labor unions, and in executive government departments. One of the more sensational HUAC probes concerned a former State Department official, **Alger Hiss**.

In August 1948, Whittaker Chambers, a senior editor for *Time* magazine and a confessed former Communist, testified in HUAC hearings that Hiss

Enduring Constitution

Bad Tendency and Probable Danger

What factors determine the constitutionality of a law? Legal scholars identify such things as strict or loose interpretation of the Constitution, case histories of past decisions, and personal and political convictions of Supreme Court justices. Many historians believe the Court is also strongly influenced by prevailing conditions.

In upholding Schenck's conviction under the Espionage Act of 1917, the Supreme Court set forth the clear-and-present-danger test to determine when free speech could legally be stifled.

Years of unrest followed World War I in the United States. Labor unions went on strike over wages, and often the strikes turned violent. Racial tensions erupted into riots in major cities. There was lingering fear of violent revolution like that which turned Russia into a Communist state.

In this climate of suspicion—and following the example set by the Court—states rushed to put laws against subversive activities on the statute books. These laws made it a crime to use speech and to form groups to urge or conspire to urge illegal actions against the government. Some of the laws forbade using pamphlets, writing, or speech to spread ideas that would incite people. The original Supreme Court standard of clear and present danger began to be replaced by a more restrictive test: that of bad tendency. If a speech or pamphlet urged people to perform illegal acts, it could be restricted. The standard of bad tendency was designed "to kill the serpent in the egg" before producing harm. Dissenting justices Oliver Wendell Holmes Jr. and Luis Brandeis argued that bad tendency was a poor precedent and that a return to the clear-and-present-danger rule would be better. Still, the Court continued to reason that laws are presumed constitutional when passed by a legislative body.

Then, in the midst of the Red Scare in 1948, twelve Communist leaders were indicted under the Smith Act (1940), a law originally passed to prevent agents of Nazi Germany from carrying out espionage activities in the United States. They were convicted of "willfully and knowingly conspiring to teach and advocate the overthrow of the government by force and violence." Although not guilty of any overt activity, the Supreme Court upheld their conviction, agreeing with a lower court that there was a probable danger of such activities taking place, since the Communist Party already existed. No longer did there have to be an immediate danger from subversion, only a likelihood of future risk.

Eventually, the Court began to work its way back from bad tendency and probable danger to the clear-and-present-danger standard. By 1957, the Court ruled that merely talking about taking action in the vague future was not proof of probable danger. In 1969 it declared that the First Amendment was protected in all cases except where speech is inciting to imminent lawlessness. Today, under the First Amendment, people are free to argue, exhort, and persuade regardless of how they appear to others. The freedom of speech guaranteed by our enduring Constitution has become stronger than ever.

1. What was the main difference between the *clear-and-present-danger* test and the *clear-and-probable-danger* test?
2. Identify two political or social attitudes that might affect current rulings of the Supreme Court.

In 1948, Whittaker Chambers, an editor for Time magazine, testified that former State Department official Alger Hiss was a member of the Communist Party in the 1930s. (Hiss is seen in the background at the far left, straining to hear the accusations made by Chambers.) For what crime was Hiss convicted?

◀ Joseph McCarthy, Republican senator from Wisconsin, led a campaign to oust Communists from the government. The methods he used eventually caused his disgrace and withdrawal from public life. What were they?

had been a Communist in the 1930s. He claimed that Hiss had passed classified government documents to him, which he had forwarded to Soviet agents. Hiss denied the charges leveled by Chambers, and Secretary of State Dean Acheson and other Truman administration officials publicly championed Hiss. Chambers, however, soon supplied evidence consisting of classified documents retyped on Hiss's typewriter that showed Hiss had lied under oath. Since the statute of limitations prevented Hiss's indictment for espionage, a court indicted Hiss for perjury. In January 1950, the court found him guilty and sentenced him to four years in prison. In the public's mind, Hiss's conviction forged the link between high government officials and Communist subversion.

In September 1949, Truman announced that the Soviets had exploded an atomic device, a shocking event because it came much sooner than most of the American public had hoped or expected. In February 1950, English police arrested Klaus Fuchs, a British nuclear scientist, for espionage. Fuchs confessed to passing classified documents containing information about building an atomic bomb to Soviet agents during World War II. The capture of Fuchs led to the arrest in the United States of his alleged accomplices, **Ethel and Julius Rosenberg**. The Rosenbergs were tried, convicted, and, in 1953, executed for treason. For many Americans, these events seemed to prove that the nation's problems resulted from disloyalty, subversion, and espionage.

In the midst of this highly charged atmosphere, **Joseph McCarthy**, Republican senator from Wisconsin, captured the nation's attention. On February 9, 1950, McCarthy delivered a speech at Wheeling, West Virginia. He claimed he had in his hands a list of 205 known Communists currently "working and shaping policy in the State Department." None of McCarthy's charges was ever proven, but many Americans believed him anyway. News reporters knew a good story when they heard one, and they began asking for more stories. McCarthy was happy to oblige, and his accusations became even more sensational and increasingly reckless. Over the next four years, McCarthy painted a fearful picture of government conspiracies in high places, and of wicked men and women who were subverting the nation. The term **McCarthyism** was coined to describe the process of accusing people of disloyalty without proving the charges. It had a devastating effect on the nation's political atmosphere.

SECTION 4 REVIEW

1. **Identify** the groups targeted by Truman for the most attention during the campaign.
2. **Explain** why Truman went on a whistle-stop campaign in 1948.
3. **State** the main reason that Truman was unable to get most of the Fair Deal policies passed.
4. **Name** the two events described in this section that triggered increased fears of Communist subversion.
5. **Identify** Joseph McCarthy.

SECTION 5

A Different World

The Marshall Plan, the NATO alliance, victory in the Berlin blockade, and the 1948 election were the high points of Truman's presidency. Within six months of that election, two events rocked Truman's administration, ended bipartisan support of his foreign policies, and set the Cold War on a new course. In 1949, the Soviets detonated an atomic bomb and Mao Zedong's Communist forces were victorious in the Chinese civil war. As Senator Arthur Vandenberg said, "This is now a different world."

What were the major effects of the detonation of the Soviet atomic bomb and of the fall of China?
How did Truman deal with the Korean War?
What effects did the Korean War have on American foreign policies?

China and Japan

During World War II, Roosevelt and his advisers had hoped that Nationalist China would provide stability in postwar Asia. Chiang Kai-shek's regime, however, was corrupt and weaker than Mao Zedong's Communist forces. As late as 1948, Chiang's soldiers outnumbered Mao's by three to one, but they deserted and surrendered in large numbers. One by one, Nationalist-controlled areas fell. The pace of the Communist successes surprised even Mao. By the end of 1949, Communist forces controlled all of the mainland of China and announced the creation of the People's Republic of China (PRC). Chiang fled to the offshore island of Formosa (now Taiwan).

The United States had sent $2 billion to the Nationalists since World War II, but in the final stages of the Chinese civil war, Truman ended almost all aid. In August 1949, the State Department explained that the fall of China had occurred because of problems within the Nationalist government. American assistance could not have overcome the widespread corruption, the absence of needed reforms, or the peasants' distrust of the Nationalists. Only massive United States military intervention would have prevented China from falling to the Communists, and few Americans would have supported that move.

Still, the Communist victory in China surprised and disappointed many Americans. Pro-Nationalist Senators William Knowland and Patrick McCarran criticized the State Department report as a "whitewash of wishful, do-nothing policy which has succeeded only in placing Asia in danger of Soviet conquest." Former American ambassador to China Patrick Hurley called the report "a smooth alibi for the pro-Communists in the State Department who had engineered the overthrow of our ally." The lesson for many Americans was simple and clear: American reverses in the Cold War resulted from officials consciously or unwittingly undermining American policy.

The worsening situation in China had profound effects on American policy toward Japan. After World War II, the United States alone had occupied and governed Japan. Aside from punishing war criminals and outlawing the Shinto religion because of its extreme nationalism, American occupation policy was aimed at rebuilding. It provided a new democratic Japanese constitution, encouraged economic reforms, and allowed Japan to retain its emperor, although he was no longer to be considered a god. As American hopes for Nationalist China faded, Japan's importance in providing Asian stability and prosperity grew. By late 1947, American occupation authorities had begun to rebuild Japan more rapidly than they had previously planned, lifting controls on Japanese industry. American investment in Japan grew from $96 million in 1946 to over $500 million in 1949.

To ensure that Japan stayed in the American sphere of influence, a new treaty signed in 1951 ended American occupation but allowed U.S. military bases to remain. Japan would become an American outpost on the Soviet's Asian rim—an idea that scarcely pleased Stalin. The United States also encouraged Japan to arm itself again, but the Japanese resisted American pressure. American policy makers wished to prevent Japan from establishing close relations with the People's Republic of China. Instead, the United States wanted Southeast Asia to provide raw materials and markets for Japanese industry. To U.S. thinking, this increased the importance of Southeast Asian countries.

Because of Mao's victory in China and because the Soviets now possessed atomic weapons, Truman ordered a thorough review of American defense policies. Completed in April 1950, **National Security Council Document 68 (NSC-68)** changed the course of U.S. Cold War policy. NSC-68 assumed that only the United States could take the lead in defending the free world against communism. A major part of this reorganization would be based on increasing America's military forces. NSC-68 called for greatly increased defense spending. While some people in the Defense Department disagreed with this analysis, the Korean War soon changed their minds.

Korea

In the last stages of World War II, both the United States and the Soviet Union had sent troops to occupy portions of Korea. After the war, neither nation was willing to leave. They temporarily divided Korea at the 38th parallel; Soviet forces occupied North Korea, and American forces stayed in South Korea. When the Soviets finally left in 1949, they left behind a Communist government and a strong Soviet-trained army. U.S. troops left a few months later, leaving behind the pro-Western government of Syngman Rhee, a strident anti-Communist. Rhee had a relatively weak army, which proved a temptation to North Korean nationalists who wanted to reunite the country.

On June 25, 1950, North Korean troops attacked across the 38th parallel. The South Korean army disintegrated in the face of the onslaught. Although no Soviet troops participated in the attack, Truman warned that "the Communists in the Kremlin are engaged in a monstrous conspiracy to stamp out freedom all over the world. The aggression against Korea is the boldest and most dangerous

Civil Defense

On December 6, 1950, the Pentagon message center received a report that radar had picked up 40 unidentified planes approaching the northeast coast of the United States. Because the United States was in the midst of the Korean War, Pentagon analysts assumed that the planes were Soviet atomic bombers about to start World War III. A preliminary "CONDITION RED" signal went out to key defense installations. At the White House, preparations began for atomic attack. Secret Service agents went down to the underground bomb shelter to make certain everything was ready for President Truman. They discovered, to their dismay, that the shelter's heavy door was jammed shut. They were still trying frantically to open the door when word came from the Pentagon that the first message had been a mistake. Rather than 40 planes, there was only one, a U.S. Army C-47 transport on an unscheduled flight.

As columnist Stewart Alsop and nuclear physicist Ralph Lapp reported in *The Saturday Evening Post*, the jammed door to the White House bomb shelter was symbolic. "From President Truman on down," wrote Alsop and Lapp, "our minds have been closed to the real meaning of the Soviet 'atomic explosion' which Truman announced in September 1949. . . .

This meaning is simple enough. From now on, any day in any week in any year may bring a real CONDITION RED signal, and real Soviet bombers flying in over the border. The future course of history . . . [will] depend very largely on a realistically and intelligently organized civil defense."

Indeed, since the Soviets now possessed atomic weapons, civil defense, or protection of the civilian population, became an increasing concern. Communities conducted air-raid drills. Students practiced diving under their desks. People began building personal bomb shelters in their backyards. Yet when the civil defense head Millard Caldwell requested $525 million from Congress for civil defense, he received a cool reception. Missouri Representative Clarence Cannon claimed that "the greatest asset in civil defense is that the nation be so strong from a military point of view that no nation dare attack us." Mississippi Democrat Jamie Whitten added, "We are not trying to neglect civil defense . . . [but] you cannot build enough holes in the ground with all the money in the federal Treasury . . . to be per-

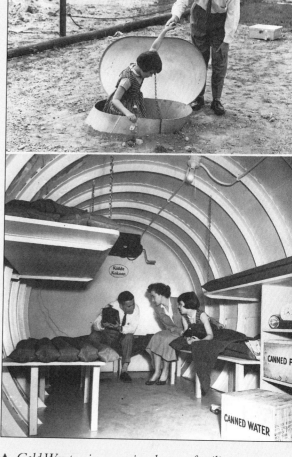

▲ *Cold War tensions convinced many families to buy "H-bomb radiation and blast shelters" such as this one.*

fectly safe from the atomic bomb." Although many Americans now feared nuclear holocaust, Congress trimmed Caldwell's request to $65 million.

1. Describe measures taken by American citizens to minimize the damage done by an atomic bomb.
2. Explain why Congress turned down Caldwell's request for civil defense funds.

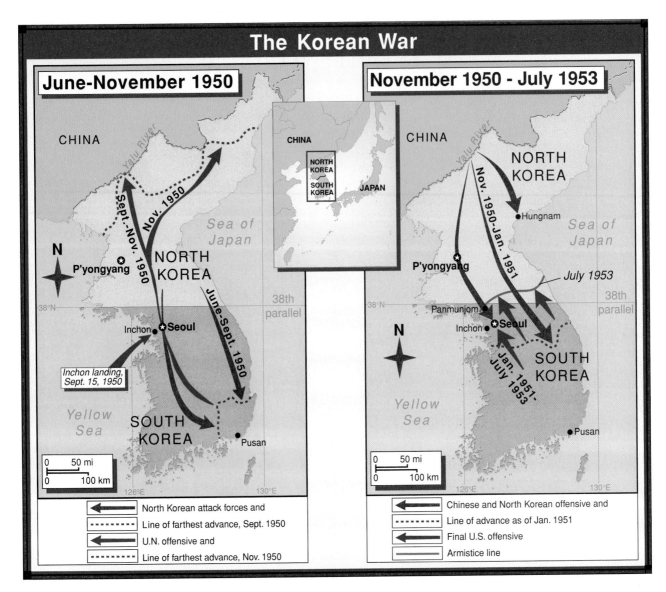

The Korean War

June–November 1950

CHINA

Yalu River

Sept.–Nov. 1950

Nov. 1950

NORTH KOREA

P'yongyang

Sea of Japan

38°N · 38th parallel

June–Sept. 1950

Inchon · Seoul

Inchon landing, Sept. 15, 1950

Yellow Sea

SOUTH KOREA

Pusan

N

| 0 | 50 mi |
| 0 | 100 km |

126°E · 130°E

← North Korean attack forces and
----- Line of farthest advance, Sept. 1950
← U.N. offensive and
----- Line of farthest advance, Nov. 1950

Inset map: CHINA · NORTH KOREA · SOUTH KOREA · JAPAN

November 1950 – July 1953

CHINA

Yalu River

NORTH KOREA

Nov. 1950–Jan. 1951

Hungnam

Sea of Japan

P'yongyang

July 1953

Panmunjom

38°N · 38th parallel

Inchon · Seoul

Jan. 1951–July 1953

SOUTH KOREA

Yellow Sea

Pusan

N

| 0 | 50 mi |
| 0 | 100 km |

126°E · 130°E

← Chinese and North Korean offensive and
----- Line of advance as of Jan. 1951
← Final U.S. offensive
— Armistice line

▲ *Was the United States justified in believing that the North Korean attack on the South was a threat to U.S. national security?*

move the Communists have yet made." On June 27, Truman committed U.S. air and naval units to the conflict.

The same day, Truman asked the United Nations Security Council for a resolution condemning the North Korean attack. The Security Council promptly passed the resolution. This was easy to do because the Soviets were boycotting the UN for its failure to seat the People's Republic of China as the actual government of China. The Security Council demanded that North Korea withdraw from South Korea, but it refused. On June 28, Truman met with congressional leaders to inform them about his actions. While they approved of his military response, they disliked the fact that Truman had not consulted them in advance. Truman never asked Congress for a declaration of war nor for a resolution of support. Instead, Truman called U.S. involvement in the **Korean War** a "police action" under UN auspices.

On June 30, Truman committed U.S. ground forces to the fighting in Korea. He stated that this action was "to restore peace and . . . restore the bor-

▲ *South Korean refugees fled the combat zone while U.S. Army troops moved forward to engage the North Koreans.*

▲ *Truman met with General MacArthur on October 14, 1950, to discuss the military situation in Korea.*

der." On July 7, the United Nations approved U.S. General Douglas MacArthur to lead UN forces in Korea. By early September, MacArthur's forces had secured the area around Pusan, a port in southeast Korea. On September 15, MacArthur took the offensive, launching a surprise sea-to-land attack at Inchon, a town west of Seoul and near the 38th parallel. By late September, his troops had cut off or killed over half the North Korean invaders.

In late September, Truman broadened his goals in Korea. He now wanted to unify Korea with a non-Communist government. Truman granted MacArthur permission to attack north of the 38th parallel even if "there was no indication or threat of entry of Soviet or Chinese Communist elements in force." MacArthur's forces crossed the 38th parallel and began pushing North Korean troops back toward the Yalu River, the border between the People's Republic of China and North Korea. Chinese Foreign Minister Chou En-lai warned that China would not accept an American army on its borders. Meanwhile, Truman met with MacArthur on Wake Island to discuss the war's progress. MacArthur told Truman, "We are no longer fearful

of Chinese intervention. . . . If they attack there would be the greatest slaughter."

MacArthur miscalculated badly. When his forces neared the Yalu in late November, nearly 400,000 Chinese soldiers attacked. Chinese forces inflicted terrible losses on MacArthur's troops. By December 25, the Chinese had driven UN forces south of the 38th parallel again. In early 1951, MacArthur counterattacked, and the fighting then turned into a stalemate along the 38th parallel.

Now Truman and the Joint Chiefs of Staff decided to fight a **limited war** and seek armistice talks with North Korea. When General MacArthur publicly disagreed with this strategy, saying that there was no substitute for victory, Truman fired him for insubordination. Republicans savagely attacked Truman, while MacArthur returned from Korea a hero. Senator Richard Nixon denounced Truman for giving in to the Communists. Congressman Joseph Martin urged impeachment proceedings against Truman.

When General Douglas MacArthur returned to the U.S. in 1951, he received a hero's welcome, as seen by this New York City ticker-tape parade.

MacArthur appeared before a joint session of Congress, where he asked for an all-out effort to defeat communism in Asia. In public Senate hearings, General Omar Bradley defended the limited-war strategy and said that MacArthur's strategy would "involve us in the wrong war, at the wrong place, at the wrong time and with the wrong enemy." Meanwhile, peace negotiations began at Panmunjom, even though the fighting was far from over.

Worldwide Effects of the Korean War

The Korean War was an event of global significance. It convinced Truman and his advisers that the Soviets and their allies were aggressively expanding throughout the world. Communist China had to be contained, so the United States increased its economic and military aid to Chiang Kai-shek's Nationalist regime on Formosa (Taiwan). Truman stepped up military aid to France in the latter's attempt to regain control in Indochina (Southeast Asia). Truman also hastened to sign a security treaty with Japan, over Stalin's objections as well as those of America's allies.

The Korean War and Soviet possession of the atomic bomb also affected American policy elsewhere. Truman moved to increase America's defense spending, doubled the size of the armed forces, and sped the development of the hydrogen bomb. He stationed conventional forces in Europe. Truman also moved to integrate West German armed forces into NATO over the strong objections

Total Cost of U.S. Wars (in Millions of Dollars)

War	Original War Costs	Veterans' Benefits	Interest Payments on War Loans	Total War Costs
Civil War (Union only)	3,200	8,580	1,172	12,952
Spanish-American War	400	6,000	60	6,460
World War I	26,000	75,000	11,000	112,000
World War II	288,000	290,000	86,000	664,000
Korean Conflict	54,000	99,000	11,000	164,000

Source: U.S. Department of Commerce, Bureau of the Census.

▲ *Costs of waging war do not end with the actual fighting. According to the table above, what is the most expensive factor in the total war costs?*

of both France and Britain. Appeasing French objections on this issue was another reason Truman aided France in Indochina.

Finally, the Korean War destroyed the Truman administration politically. The frustrations of conducting a stalemated war and of suffering heavy combat losses in Korea, in addition to the fears of internal subversion discussed earlier, eroded public confidence in Truman. His public approval rating had fallen to less than 25 percent. Truman chose not to run for reelection in 1952. As he told reporters in April 1952, "there are a great many people . . . who could have done the job better than I did. . . . But I had the job and I had to do it." In time, most Americans would agree with his epitaph: "He done his damnedest."

SECTION 5 REVIEW

1. **State** two reasons Communist forces in China defeated Nationalist forces.
2. **Describe** the major effect of the defeat of Nationalist forces on American foreign policy.
3. **Relate** the significance of NSC–68.
4. **Identify** the main area of disagreement between Truman and General MacArthur.
5. **State** the rationale used by Truman to increase military spending in Formosa and Indochina.

Summary

When Roosevelt died, Truman succeeded to an office for which he had little preparation. World War II had largely destroyed the world that people had known before the war. The defeat of Germany and Japan left vacuums of power in both Europe and Asia. The war also severely weakened the other major powers and loosened their grip on their colonies. Only the United States and the Soviet Union remained great powers. In this context, new conflicts soon arose, especially between the Soviet Union and the United States, heightening mutual distrust and creating the Cold War.

In domestic affairs, Truman protected New Deal programs from the conservative coalition that controlled Congress. But he was unable to get Congress to pass most of his own Fair Deal program. Still, the Fair Deal broadened the nation's reform agenda by asserting federal responsibility for health care and education. Truman brought African American civil rights into the political arena and did more to advance them than any earlier president. Ultimately, postwar fears of communism and of internal subversion prevented Truman from getting more of his reform agenda passed. Indeed, scare of communism took attention away from reform and crippled Truman's presidency.

Truman's legacy was the Cold War on the international front and an unrealized reform program at home. He had shown amazing fortitude after stepping into a most difficult job. He guided the nation through the difficult reconversion process after the war, prevented another economic depression, and kept inflation within reasonable bounds. A variety of issues, including the inability to gain a quick victory in Korea, caused Truman to lose popularity toward the end of his administration, and he chose not to run for reelection.

Vocabulary

Cold War
collaborator
containment policy
demobilization
filibustering
friend-of-the-court
iron curtain

limited war
McCarthyism
purge
reconversion
right-to-work laws
secondary boycott

Locate the vocabulary terms in the chapter and write a definition for each term. Write the definition in the form of a complete sentence.

Review Questions

1. What conflicts emerged between the United States and the Soviet Union after the war?
2. What problems did Americans encounter as they demobilized and reconverted from war to peace?
3. Describe the main features of Truman's containment policy.
4. Explain how Soviet actions saved the Marshall Plan.
5. How did Truman's successes in foreign affairs affect domestic politics?
6. What were the major elements of Truman's Fair Deal?
7. What circumstances led to the failure to get most of the Fair Deal measures passed?
8. What was the purpose of the House Un-American Activities Committee?
9. How did Truman and MacArthur disagree over pursuing the Korean War?
10. How did the American public view Truman's administration after the Korean War?

Chapter 24 Review

Critical Historical Thinking

✎ Writing Answer each of the following by writing one or more complete paragraphs:

1. Speculate on what might have been the course of the Korean War if Truman had not fired MacArthur.
2. Explain why the United States could not have returned to a policy of isolationism after World War II.
3. President Truman's whistle stop campaign helped him win an upset victory in 1948. Do you think candidates could accomplish the same result today by taking their messages to the people personally? Explain your answer.
4. Read the selection entitled "There is a Deeper Reason" found in the Unit 8 Archives. Explain what Senator McCarthy is referring to when he says that there is little fear of Communists dropping atomic bombs on Washington D.C., because "they would kill too many of their friends that way."

Making Connections with Sports

Many Americans think of baseball as an ageless sport in which "time is seamless and invisible, a bubble within which players move at exactly the same pace and rhythm as their ancestors." The baseball strike of 1994 over high player salaries and owner profits tells us that baseball is also part of the times in which it is played. This was no less true at the height of the Cold War. As a wave of conformity rolled over American culture, Branch Rickey of the Brooklyn Dodgers, together with the presidents of the American and National Leagues, stressed dress codes for players and forbade foul language on the field. Ohio Senator John W. Bricker held that the sport was essential to the American way of life:

"While the marching hordes in China are spreading the doctrine of communism, officials of the national pastime are helping to make democracy work in this country by giving every youth a chance to carve out his own career."

Baseball was also viewed as an important weapon in the fight against communism in the less developed nations of the world. U.S. Ambassador Walter J. Donnelly was praised for introducing the game to Venezuela: "If more ambassadors," insisted Don Parker of the *New York Mirror*, "used sports instead of double talk as their medium of expression, I'm sure the world would be much better off, and to test the theory, I'd like to see the new envoy to Moscow introduce himself in the Kremlin by fetching Uncle Joe Stalin a resounding whack on the noggin with one of Joe DiMaggio's castoff bats." In 1950, the San Francisco Seals, made a goodwill tour of Japan, allegedly to prevent the spread of communism in that country: "When we got there," announced Seals coach Del Young, "the Communists were on the soap boxes on almost every street corner. But we hadn't been there long before they disappeared in the crowds. I don't think they'll get far now."

▪ Examine back issues of sports magazines such as *Sports Illustrated* to find articles about the 1994 baseball strike. Make a list of statements by players and managers that you think reflect the times. Write a short statement about each entry on the list explaining why you consider it a timely quote.

Additional Skills Practice

Look through current newsmagazines and bring to class an example of a photograph that illustrates image-making. Make a list of the features (location, symbols, activities, dress, etc.) that help to create the image. Describe the effect that the photograph has on your opinion of that person, business, or event.

The Eisenhower Era

As the 1952 presidential election approached, President Truman no longer had sufficient public approval to lead the nation. He was the first (but not the last) president to learn the political costs of fighting a limited war to contain communism. Republicans relentlessly attacked Truman's handling of the Korean War and domestic security. Truman chose not to seek reelection. The Republicans ensured victory in 1952 by nominating the very popular

General Dwight D. Eisenhower as their presidential candidate. Because of his style of leadership, scholars would later call his the "hidden-hand" presidency. Eisenhower's public image often made him appear uninformed, out of touch, or bumbling. We now know that this was a deliberate, but false, impression that Eisenhower created. In fact, Eisenhower was one of the most popular presidents in U.S. history.

▲ *Dwight D. Eisenhower had been nicknamed "Ike" since he was a small boy. Republicans used this nickname on scores of election campaign items, including the campaign button shown here.*

The Return of the Republicans

"Ike," as Americans fondly called Eisenhower, emerged from World War II as the nation's most visible hero. Both Republican and Democratic Party leaders wanted him as their presidential candidate. Eisenhower's diary recorded a visit from New York Governor Thomas Dewey in July 1949. "He stayed at my house for two hours. He says he's worried about the country's future, . . . that only I . . . can save this country from going to Hades in the handbasket of paternalism—socialism—dictatorship. . . . So he dwelt at length on the preservation of freedom—my favorite subject!" But Eisenhower denied interest in the presidency. "I do not want to be president of the United States," Eisenhower declared in 1951, "and I want no other political office or political connection of any kind." By early 1952, however, Eisenhower had changed his mind and decided to seek the Republican presidential nomination.

Why did Eisenhower seek the Republican presidential nomination in 1952?

What were Eisenhower's primary goals as president?

What important problems did Eisenhower first face after becoming president?

President Dwight D. Eisenhower

Eisenhower grew up in the small midwestern town of Abilene, Kansas. His father was an engineer in a creamery. His mother, a religious pacifist, stayed home to raise six sons. Ike loved hunting, fishing, and competitive athletics and was a good enough student to win an appointment to the U.S. Military Academy at West Point. His mother did not object, despite her pacifist convictions. Eisenhower was not a model cadet; his stubbornness, terrible temper, and fun-loving pranks frequently got him into trouble. He graduated in 1915 with a commendable, but not outstanding, academic record. As a career soldier, Eisenhower rose through the ranks, finally becoming supreme commander of the Allied forces in Europe during World War II. His leading role in the defeat of Nazi Germany made Eisenhower an instant hero. After 1945, he served as army chief of staff, president of Columbia University, and commander of NATO forces in Europe.

Eisenhower's decision to seek the Republican nomination for president stemmed from three primary concerns. First, he did not respect Truman's conduct as president, and he believed he could restore dignity to the White House. Second, he was concerned about Truman's Fair Deal and the Democrats' handling of federal budget matters. Finally, Eisenhower was an internationalist who believed in collective security through such organizations as the United Nations and NATO. If Eisenhower did not seek the Republican nomination, the party would surely nominate Senator **Robert Taft**, a midwestern conservative and long-time opponent of foreign aid and of U.S. involvement in NATO and the UN.

Eisenhower beat Taft for the Republican presidential nomination. To appeal to the party's conservative wing, Eisenhower chose California Senator Richard Nixon as his running mate. The party platform promised to "clean up the mess in Washington," a reference to the Truman administration's lagging efforts in weeding Communists out of government. The platform also called for a balanced budget, maintenance of U.S. foreign commitments, and an end to the Democrats' "negative, immoral, and futile" containment policy.

During his campaign, Eisenhower focused on three general themes. First, to check the growth of centralized federal power he urged restoring political power to state and local governments. Second, to reduce federal domination of the economy he emphasized balancing the federal budget and spending only for the nation's essential needs. Third, to correct Truman's approach to containing Communist threats around the world he urged action, but only by carefully balancing the nation's commitments with its financial resources. Despite Eisenhower's determination to balance the budget, he promised to retain such essential New Deal programs as Social Security.

▲ *Eisenhower easily won the Republican nomination in 1952. Why was Eisenhower such a popular candidate?*

▲ *During the 1952 campaign, vice presidential candidate Richard Nixon was accused of having a secret campaign fund. He defended himself on television in his famous "Checkers speech." Who was Checkers?*

Democrats chose Illinois Governor Adlai Stevenson and Alabama Senator John Sparkman to run in 1952. Stevenson was reluctant, recognizing that any Democrat would have difficulty winning in 1952. He also disagreed with much of Truman's Fair Deal, including public housing, civil rights, and deficit spending. As an ardent New Dealer, he campaigned on its principles and programs, the strength of the Democratic Party. Stevenson proved an eloquent and courageous campaigner, earning the respect of many voters.

The Republicans won the presidency for the first time in 20 years. Eisenhower beat Stevenson by 34 million to 27 million in the popular vote, and by 442 to 89 in electoral votes. The Republicans also gained control of both houses of Congress. The elections, however, reflected Eisenhower's personal appeal more than Republican Party popularity. Republicans controlled the Senate by only one vote and the House of Representatives by eight. Indeed, the Democrats regained control of Congress in the 1954 congressional elections and maintained or increased their majorities in the next three elections.

Eisenhower's Cabinet Choices

Eisenhower saw leadership as "the ability to decide what is to be done and then get others to want to do it." Consequently, he relied heavily on aides to run the day-to-day operations of the executive branch. He chose Sherman Adams, former governor of New Hampshire, as his chief of staff. Adams made staff assignments and decided who and what would appear on Eisenhower's daily agenda. Soon Adams appeared so powerful that observers joked, "What if Ike died and Nixon became president?" The punch line was "What if Adams died and Ike became president?"

Eisenhower believed the complexities of governing demanded teamwork. "Now, look," Ike told his cabinet, "this idea that all wisdom is in the president, in me, that's baloney." He therefore chose cabinet officers who had wide management experience. Few professional politicians were chosen for staff or cabinet positions. The result was a cabinet drawn

◄ *John Foster Dulles (right) was secretary of state in the Eisenhower administration. He is shown here with his brother Allen, who was a director of the Central Intelligence Agency.*

from corporate boardrooms, and composed, as the liberal *New Republic* stated, "of eight millionaires and a plumber." Two cabinet members—John Foster Dulles and George M. Humphrey—had special influence with Eisenhower because they shared his priorities.

Eisenhower selected Dulles as secretary of state. After World War II, Dulles had emerged as the leading Republican expert on foreign affairs. Like Eisenhower, Dulles was an internationalist who believed in collective security. Although he had consulted and worked with Truman, Dulles now condemned Truman's containment policy as too "soft on communism." Eisenhower deeply respected Dulles's knowledge of foreign affairs and agreed with his hard-line views about communism.

Ohio businessman George Humphrey became treasury secretary. Humphrey thought that what was good for business was usually good for the economy in general. He also firmly believed in traditional Republican economic policies—reducing federal spending, balancing the federal budget, curbing inflation, and minimizing corporate and business taxes.

Eisenhower sought the advice of Dulles and Humphrey on nearly every matter of importance. Ike also asked Vice President Nixon to participate in cabinet meetings. Although Nixon often served as a public spokesperson for Eisenhower, his influence with the president was small.

Immediate Concerns

When Eisenhower took office, ending the Korean War was his top priority. The fighting in Korea had deadlocked around the 38th parallel. The peace talks begun by Truman had stalled. One difficult issue in the talks concerned the exchange of prisoners of war (POWs). Many of the 27,000 Chinese and North Korean POWs did not want to return home after the war, a position the U.S. supported. China and North Korea, however, insisted upon their return. Like Truman, Eisenhower was willing to settle for returning to the prewar borders between North and South Korea. Eisenhower increased pressure on North Korea and China by implying he would use atomic weapons if a

▼ *How far did Eisenhower's domestic and foreign policies reflect American concerns in this 1953 public opinion poll?*

Most Important Problem, 1953

Question: In your opinion, what are the main problems facing the country today that the new administration should tackle?

Settling the Korean War	60%
The economy/preventing a depression	41%
Reducing taxes	29%
Foreign affairs	16%
Keeping the peace	12%
Communism	8%
Efficiency and economy in government	7%

Source: Survey by the Opinion Research Corporation, February 9-18, 1953.

©The Public Perspective, a publication of the Roper Center for Public Opinion Research, University of CT, Storrs. Reprinted by permission.

settlement was not soon reached. On July 26, 1953, the two sides finally signed a truce. The POWs from both sides were allowed to choose whether or not to return home. The Korean War contained Communist expansion in Korea, but at a great cost in human lives and physical damage to the land.

With the Korean War over, Eisenhower turned his attention to other priorities. Throughout his presidency, Ike's chief concern was balancing the federal budget. This goal required slashing defense spending. On April 16, 1953, Eisenhower stated his position: "Every gun that is made, every warship launched, every rocket fired signifies . . . a theft from those who hunger and are not fed, those who are cold and not clothed."

To meet the threat of communism without endangering the health of the economy, Eisenhower developed a new defense doctrine. Secretary of Defense Charles Wilson called it "more bang for a buck." Eisenhower believed that the nation's defense should rest not on an ability to fight limited wars like the one in Korea, but on "a massive capability to strike back" against Communist aggressors. So Eisenhower began dismantling the nation's conventional forces, replacing them with a huge arsenal of nuclear weapons, B-52 bombers, and an expanded Intercontinental Ballistic Missile (ICBM) program. Pentagon officials frequently opposed Eisenhower's defense cuts and appealed directly to Congress for more money. But Eisenhower drew on his own military prestige and successfully fought excessive defense spending throughout his two terms in office.

SECTION 1 REVIEW

1. **List** three reasons why Eisenhower decided to seek the Republican presidential nomination in 1952.
2. **Identify** Adlai Stevenson.
3. **Describe** the background of Eisenhower's cabinet members.
4. **Summarize** the three chief priorities of Eisenhower as president.
5. **Discuss** Eisenhower's proposal to balance economic and defense needs.

SECTION 2

Domestic Politics and Policies

As president, Eisenhower appeared to spend as much time playing golf and bridge as he did dealing with the papers on his desk. The net result, said newspaper columnist Joseph Harsch during the first hundred days of Eisenhower's presidency, "seems to be a man whanging golf balls at the White House back fence while history flows around him." Harsch warned, however, that the public misjudged Eisenhower if they believed he was not leading the nation. The public did not yet recognize that "leadership . . . might take the form of merely operating with existing laws. . . . Mr. Eisenhower is consciously and actually going in an Eisenhower direction and . . . all of us, whether we know it or not, are following him."

How did Eisenhower handle McCarthyism?
In what ways was Eisenhower's domestic program moderate?
How did Eisenhower try to reduce the federal government's role in the U.S. economy?

McCarthyism and the Hidden-Hand President

Eisenhower's hidden-hand style of governing, in which he appeared not to be directly involved, had many virtues. By deflecting criticism onto his cabinet and other associates, he could appear to be above politics and thus preserve both his popularity and his freedom to operate. Moreover, it proved difficult to bring Republican conservatives and moderates together. These factions disagreed over foreign policy, economic policy, and the extent to which they accepted New Deal welfare programs. By working quietly behind the scenes, Eisenhower was often able to smooth over differences.

By the time Eisenhower became president, Joseph McCarthy's political influence had been growing for three years. Eisenhower's desire to appear removed from the daily operation of politics affected his behavior toward McCarthy. McCarthy's political genius had been his ability to make his name synonymous with rooting out the alleged influence of communism in American society. Events such as the discovery that spies had given the Soviets atomic secrets, the fall of Chiang Kai-shek in China, and the Korean War helped McCarthy to continue his anti-Communist crusade. Anyone who opposed McCarthy risked charges of being "soft on communism." (Despite McCarthy's wild accusations and almost daily headlines about his investigations into possible disloyalty or treason, he failed to identify a single Communist in government.)

Eisenhower had little quarrel with McCarthy's desire to keep Communists and Communist sympathizers out of government. In April 1953, he issued an executive order that toughened the government's loyalty program. The government had once needed reasonable grounds for suspecting the loyalty of an employee. The new program allowed for the dismissal of government workers for "any behavior, activities, or

"We Have Documentary Evidence That This Man Is Planning A Trip To Moscow"

▲ *Herbert Block was a well-known editorial cartoonist who signed his work "Herblock." Whom did he criticize in this cartoon?* [Herblock's Here and Now *(Simon and Schuster, 1955).*]

associations which tend to show that the individual is not reliable or trustworthy." The program uncovered few Communist Party members, yet the administration dismissed over 1500 persons from federal service and another 6000 resigned during Eisenhower's presidency. Eisenhower also supported the 1954 Communist Control Act, which defined the Communist Party as an "agency of a hostile foreign power." The act required all organizations with ties to communism to register with the attorney general.

McCarthy's behavior and tactics, however, disgusted Eisenhower. Even so, on numerous occasions, Ike avoided a public confrontation with McCarthy. Eisenhower did not want, as he said, "to get in the gutter with that guy." He was also concerned about alienating the Republican right wing and further splitting the party. He believed that McCarthy would eventually "hang himself" if given enough rope. Many people mistakenly took Eisenhower's unwillingness to denounce McCarthy as either timidity or actual approval. This helped to increase McCarthy's power.

In 1954, McCarthy accused the army of being soft on communism, and he questioned the loyalty

◄ *During the month-long Army-McCarthy hearings, army attorney Joseph Welch (shown at left, hand to his head) denounced the senator as a "cruelly reckless character assassin." How did McCarthy contribute to his own political downfall?*

and integrity of several generals. The army, in turn, accused McCarthy of seeking favored treatment for a trusted McCarthy aide, whom the army had drafted in 1954. The televised congressional hearings proved to be McCarthy's undoing. Hurling wild accusations and savagely attacking individuals, McCarthy offended many television viewers, as well as his colleagues in the Senate. In December, by a vote of 64 to 23, the Senate officially condemned McCarthy for conduct "unbecoming a member of the United States Senate." McCarthy's power and popularity declined until his death from alcoholism three years later.

largest corporations absorbed 3,404 smaller companies. The Justice Department generally avoided applying antitrust laws in these mergers.

The president sought to promote business interests. The 1953 Tidelands Act gave Texas and Louisiana title to the oil-rich underwater lands in the Gulf of Mexico off the coasts of these states. These lands had been owned by the federal government up to that time. Estimates of their value ranged from $10 billion to $60 billion. Conservationists denounced the act as a giveaway to those oil companies that expected to lease the tidelands from the states at discount prices.

The Economy Takes Precedence

Eisenhower's economic policies closely followed traditional Republican lines. These included:

- cutting taxes and federal spending
- balancing the federal budget
- controlling inflation
- limiting the role the federal government in the economy as much as possible.

The effect of these policies, according to Republican economic theory, would boost business confidence, which, in turn, would lead to investments, economic growth, and general prosperity. In fact, the Eisenhower years were prosperous ones for many Americans.

The economic environment of the 1950s was especially good for businesses. Large corporations continued to grow larger. In the United States, 95 percent of business firms employed fewer than 20 workers. This statistic appears to show that small firms dominated the economy, but this was not so. The other 5 percent, the corporate giants, employed 75 percent of all workers.

In many industries, a few firms controlled most of the market, a situation called **oligopoly**. For example, three giant firms—General Motors, Ford, and Chrysler—dominated automobile manufacturing. The aluminum, meat, copper, liquor, tin can, and office equipment markets were all dominated by a few businesses. During the fifties, the 500

A Moderate Domestic Program

Eisenhower's hidden-hand leadership usually worked well in securing support for his domestic programs. He worked closely—often behind the scenes—with the Republican leadership and with the Democrat-controlled Congresses after 1954. Charting a moderate course probably also helped. "The great political problem," Eisenhower once said, "is to take the straight road down the middle." He was certain that the New Deal and the Fair Deal had strayed too far toward federal intervention in the nation's economy and society. But he also disagreed with conservatives who wanted to cut all federal welfare programs back to the level of the 1920s. **Modern Republicanism** was the label Eisenhower gave to his domestic program—"conservative when it comes to money and liberal when it comes to human beings." Although balancing the federal budget was his first priority, he did not strive to achieve this goal entirely at the expense of social welfare programs.

In fact, Eisenhower modestly extended the welfare programs of the New Deal. In 1953, he secured congressional consent to create a cabinet-level Department of Health, Education, and Welfare to oversee federal programs in these areas. Encouraged by Eisenhower, Congress expanded Social Security coverage to an additional 11 million people, including farmers, household employees, government employees, and the self-employed. Four million more

▲ *Robert Taft, Eisenhower's rival for the 1952 Republican presidential nomination, became Ike's greatest ally in the Senate.*

persons became eligible for unemployment compensation. Congress raised the minimum wage from 75 cents to a dollar an hour and passed two housing bills during Ike's first term in office. One bill provided $500 million for **urban renewal**, the rebuilding of inner cities. The second financed 35,000 units of public housing for low-income people. Eisenhower even gave cautious support to federal aid to education. He encouraged increased federal spending for some public works projects, also in the New Deal tradition. These included the St. Lawrence Seaway project (1953) and the Federal Aid Highway Act (1956), the largest peacetime spending bill in U.S. history up to that time.

SECTION 2 REVIEW

1. **Describe** Eisenhower's hidden hand style of governing.
2. **Evaluate** the effectiveness of Eisenhower's way of dealing with Senator McCarthy.
3. **List** the major elements of Eisenhower's economic policies.
4. **Define** oligopoly.
5. **Explain** how Eisenhower's domestic program could be called moderate.

Eisenhower's Second Administration

On Friday, September 23, 1955, President Eisenhower worked several hours, then relaxed and played a round of golf. That evening, he retired after dining with family and close friends. At 1:30 the next morning, he complained of indigestion. Ike's doctor discovered he had had a heart attack. By January, Ike had returned to a full schedule, but his health and age (he was then 65) concerned many Americans. As Ike wrote to a friend, "no one has the faintest right to consider acceptance of a nomination [for president] unless he honestly believes that his physical and mental reserves will stand the strain of four years of intensive work." Ike believed he was fit, so he stood for reelection in 1956.

What were the major issues in the 1956 presidential campaign?

What events pushed African American civil rights into national prominence?

In what ways did Eisenhower's attitudes and actions affect the civil rights movement?

A Second Term

Republicans believed that without Eisenhower a defeat in 1956 was likely. Eisenhower's rapid recovery from the heart attack and from surgery in early 1956 removed most doubts about his ability to serve a second term. Republicans also regarded Vice President Richard Nixon as an important link between the moderate and conservative wings of the party. So, in August 1956, the Republican national convention jubilantly renominated the Eisenhower-Nixon ticket. The Democrats renominated Adlai Stevenson as their presidential candidate and Tennessee Senator Estes Kefauver as his running mate.

The 1956 presidential campaign was a relatively dull affair, largely because few issues separated the

Integrating Central High School

In September 1957, Little Rock, Arkansas, began racial integration of its high schools to comply with a federal court order. The night before classes started, Governor Orville Faubus ordered the Arkansas National Guard to surround Central High School to prevent nine African American students from enrolling. Several days later, a federal judge forbade Faubus from using the Guard to prevent integration. Faubus withdrew the Guard and said he would appeal the judge's ruling.

On September 23, a howling mob formed outside Central High to prevent the African American students from entering. The nine African American students entered the school through a side door. Later, Melba Beals, one of the African American students, recalled her feelings about that day:

The first day I was able to enter Central High School, what I felt inside was terrible, wrenching, awful fear. On the car radio I could hear that there was a mob. I knew what a mob meant and I knew that the sounds that came from the crowd were very angry . . . There has never been in my life any stark terror or any fear akin to that.

Craig Rains, a white student at Central High, also remembers that day:

You could cut it with a knife, the tension outside the school, with these people who had come in from other parts of the state, other states. There were license plates from out of state. Very few people from Little Rock were there causing these problems, that I could see. But it was an ugly attitude. Especially when Elizabeth Eckford came to try to get into school. And the crowd began to heckle her, and cheer and shout, as she walked along. I was just dumbfounded. . . Well, I can't believe people would actually be this way to other people.

Police removed the nine children—integration had lasted three hours. The next day, Little Rock Mayor Woodrow Wilson Mann telegraphed Eisenhower: "The immediate need for federal troops is urgent. . . . Situation is out of control and police cannot disperse the mob." Eisenhower was forced to use federal power to protect civil rights. He immediately dispatched 1,000 paratroopers of the 101st Airborne Division and put the Arkansas National Guard under his direct order. The next day, the troops dispersed the crowd, and the nine children spent the full day at school.

The crisis slowly faded and by the end of October the African American students were going to Central High without armed guard.

◀ *Elizabeth Eckford was one of nine African American students who first integrated Central High School. Would you describe the behavior of these students as heroic?*

1. Explain why Governor Faubus ordered out the Arkansas National Guard.
2. Do you think the African American students were heroic? Why, or why not?

two candidates or their parties. Generally, the differences between them were matters of emphasis and degree. The Republican platform supported federal aid to schools, revision of the Taft-Hartley labor law, and tax reductions, if possible. Its civil rights plank supported desegregation but opposed the use of force to implement it. The Democratic platform included conservation of natural resources, repeal of the Taft-Hartley Act, and tax cuts for low-income groups. Its civil rights plank, supporting desegregation but with no pledge to implement it, was weaker than the Republicans' cautious endorsement.

Until the very end of the campaign, Stevenson chose not to use the only issue that might have made a difference—Eisenhower's health. It is doubtful, however, that anything Stevenson might have said or done would have affected the outcome. On November 6, voters gave Eisenhower a landslide victory. Eisenhower won 35.6 million popular votes and 457 electoral votes to Stevenson's 26 million popular and 73 electoral votes. Despite Eisenhower's personal popularity, he was the first president-elect since 1848 whose party failed to win a majority in either house of Congress. The Democrats won majorities of 234 to 201 in the House of Representatives and of 49 to 47 in the Senate. These majorities would grow in the 1958 midterm elections.

The Economy and Labor

In his economic policies, Eisenhower tried to plot a middle course between laissez-faire and extensive government responsibility and intervention. Laissez-faire (literally "let them do") was a way of saying no government intervention at all. In practice, he discovered that a middle course was hard to find, despite the fact that almost everyone agreed on the primary goals of economic policy—full employment, high economic growth, and price stability. While Eisenhower avoided deep and enduring economic depressions, he could not prevent the periodic booms and recessions of the business cycle.

Eisenhower's conservative economic policies were most effective in keeping prices stable. Annual inflation rates dropped from 7 percent in the 1940s to between 2 and 3 percent in the 1950s. He was less successful in meeting the goals of high employment and economic growth. Recessions occurred in 1957–1958 and in 1960–1961. In both cases, unemployment rose to about 7 percent of the labor force, and economic output declined.

Each of these recessions showed how the economy had become dependent on government spending. Substantial federal budget cuts—largely in defense spending—preceded both recessions. The lesson most politicians drew from this experience was to not cut government spending. This situation, in turn, made it difficult for Eisenhower to balance the annual federal budget. Still, he was able to do so three out of his eight years in office. Eisenhower's overall budget deficits amounted to only $18 billion, much smaller than those of his successors.

Despite fears about the Taft-Hartley Act, union membership continued to grow in the next decade. Membership reached its peak in the late 1950s. In 1955, the two large rival union federations, the American Federation of Labor and Congress of Industrial Organizations, merged and became the AFL-CIO.

Meanwhile, congressional investigations revealed corruption and racketeering (obtaining money through fraud or threats of violence) in several large unions. In response, Congress passed the Landrum-Griffin Act in 1959. This act was designed to curb labor union racketeering by banning ex-convicts from union leadership and by requiring secret union elections and better financial reporting. Landrum-Griffin also tightened Taft-Hartley rules concerning picketing and secondary boycotts. The percentage of the labor force represented by unions began its steady decline from this point on. But the decline was due less to public opinion than to basic changes in the economy.

Civil Rights for African Americans

On May 17, 1954, the Supreme Court delivered its opinion in the landmark case of *Brown v. Topeka Board of Education*. The central question was, "Does segregation of children in public schools solely on

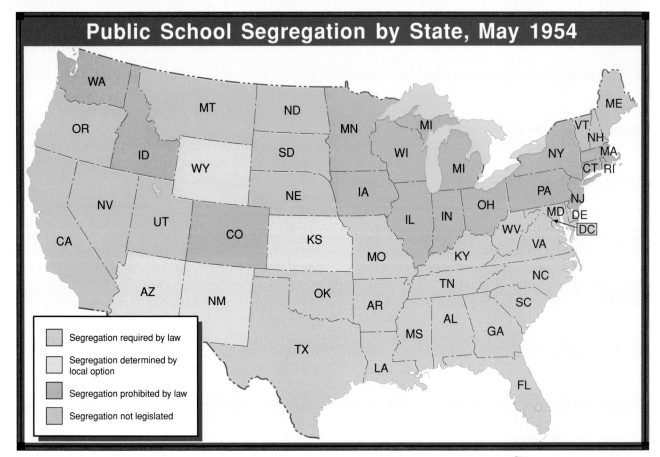

Public School Segregation by State, May 1954

- Segregation required by law
- Segregation determined by local option
- Segregation prohibited by law
- Segregation not legislated

▲ *When the Supreme Court handed down the* Brown *decision, segregation in public schools was a national problem. The Court's ruling specifically exempted schools (mostly in the North) that were segregated due to local residence patterns. What regional generalizations can you make about segregated schools?*

▶ *President Eisenhower appointed California Governor Earl Warren chief justice in 1953. Why did Eisenhower deeply regret this appointment?*

the basis of race, even though the physical facilities and other 'tangible' factors may be equal, deprive the children of the minority group of equal educational opportunities?" The justices answered unanimously, "We believe it does. . . . Separate educational facilities are inherently unequal." The *Brown* decision overturned the 1896 *Plessy v. Ferguson* ruling that had established the separate-but-equal justification for legal racial segregation.

At this time, segregation prevailed throughout American society, and few, if any, aspects were without racial prejudice. The primary difference between segregation in the South and in other regions was that the South had passed an elaborate series of laws to maintain segregation. In most places outside

the South, few laws actually prevented African Americans from voting or from participating in other areas of civic and social life. Even so, **de jure** (legal) segregation in the South differed only slightly in its effects from the **de facto** (a matter of practice, not law) segregation found in other regions.

In the South, the border states, and the District of Columbia, local Jim Crow laws forced African Americans to use separate restaurants, hotels, bus terminals, movie theaters, washroom facilities, and drinking fountains. Local authorities prevented

African Americans from voting through such devices as poll taxes and literacy tests. In Mississippi, a young white law student flunked the bar exam twice. His father asked to see the questions and discovered "you have given him the Negro examination!" If these tactics failed to work, intimidation and violence usually did.

In May 1955, the Supreme Court ordered local boards of education to move toward integrating schools "with all deliberate speed." The Court hoped segregated school districts, North and South, would show good faith by integrating quickly. In fact, white citizens' councils and other organizations opposed to integration sprang up throughout the South. The councils officially renounced violence and terrorism. Instead, they used propaganda, persuasion, and pressure to unify white opinion. They also organized boycotts, established their own schools, and used the courts to delay integration.

Eisenhower avoided getting involved in civil rights issues for as long as he could. He strongly believed that states and local communities, not the federal government, should resolve social problems. Furthermore, Republicans had made inroads in the traditionally Democratic South in recent elections. If Eisenhower took a strong civil rights position, the party might lose those gains. When questioned about his opinion of the *Brown* ruling, Eisenhower replied, "I think it makes no difference whether or not I endorse it.... The Constitution is as the Supreme Court interprets it; and I must conform to that." Many civil rights leaders thought Eisenhower's endorsement would make a difference, and they severely criticized him for remaining silent.

Eisenhower did support voting-rights legislation and signed two acts into law. Both the 1957 and 1960 Civil Rights Acts attempted to remove restrictions on African American voters. Both acts were largely ineffective because responsibility for voter registration remained in the hands of local officials, and the penalties for violations were small. Baseball player Jackie Robinson, with witty understatement, wired Eisenhower in 1957: "Have waited this long for bill with meaning—can wait a little longer."

Civil Rights Leaders Some of the most important civil rights gains of the 1950s occurred because African Americans asserted their rights locally at the

▲ *Rosa Parks, fingerprinted by a deputy sheriff in Montgomery, Alabama, was indicted for violating local laws against boycotting. What was her first "crime?"*

grassroots level of politics. Grassroots movements start locally, with widespread support among ordinary people. In 1955, in Montgomery, Alabama, an African American seamstress, **Rosa Parks**, quietly refused to give up her bus seat to a white person. She was arrested for defying a local law that required African Americans to take seats in the back of the bus and to surrender any seat requested by white patrons. Inspired by this courageous act of protest, African Americans in Montgomery boycotted the local bus company. As many as 95 percent of Montgomery's African Americans participated, and the boycott proved successful. In November 1958, the Supreme Court forbade segregation on Montgomery buses. When asked how the bus boycott had affected her, one elderly African American woman observed that "my feets is sore, but my soul is rested."

Besides pursuing civil rights through grassroots movements, African Americans were fighting for equality in the courtrooms of the nation. One of the best known of these dedicated lawyers was **Thurgood Marshall.** Marshall was chief counsel for the NAACP for more than twenty years. It was his brilliant prosecution of the *Brown v. Topeka Board*

Thurgood Marshall, then an attorney for the NAACP, posed with the president of the Little Rock NAACP and six of the African American students who integrated Central High School. What is the building behind them?

of Education case that began the federally backed process of desegregation of schools. Marshall won a total of 28 Supreme Court cases (losing 5 others) before becoming, in 1967, the first African American appointed to that supreme judicial body.

During the Montgomery bus boycott, an important civil rights leader emerged. A young minister, the Reverend **Dr. Martin Luther King Jr.**, had recently arrived in Montgomery to accept his first position at the Dexter Avenue Baptist Church.

It was there that King asserted a doctrine of nonviolence based on the teachings of Mohandas K. Gandhi. King described his belief in nonviolence to his congregation: "Blood may flow in the streets of Montgomery before we receive our freedom, but it must be our blood that flows and not that of the white man. We must not harm a single hair on the

This group of student protestors received no service at a lunch counter in Charlotte, North Carolina, during the first day of a sit-in demonstration in 1960. Why would the protestors have brought their school books with them?

head of our white brothers." King's creed of nonviolence would have a powerful impact on the civil rights movement in the next decade.

Student Protests   Grassroots protests against racial injustice soon spread throughout the South. In 1960, African American college students in North Carolina asserted their right to eat at public lunch counters that had been designated "whites only." The black students sat at the forbidden lunch counters and refused to leave when they were not served. In retaliation, the store owners often closed down the lunch counters. As these "sit-ins" spread, local authorities arrested the participants. White mobs, fearing the students' challenge to existing race relations, taunted and physically abused them. Because the students refused to respond to the provocations, violence rarely occurred.

The behavior of the black students showed discipline and high moral purpose. As a result, northern public opinion sympathized with them. Even some southern newspapers admired the courage and nonviolence displayed by the African American students. At the same time, they could find little to praise about the white mobs who bullied them. Although consciously disobeying the law, they were willing to accept the consequences because a higher moral principle was at stake. **Civil disobedience**, the intentional breaking of a law believed to be unjust, and nonviolence proved effective in changing American public opinion. African American grassroots action kept the issue of racial injustice before the public, and created political support and public pressure for stronger civil rights laws.

SECTION 3 REVIEW

1. Identify the major issues in the 1956 presidential campaign.
2. Evaluate the success of Eisenhower's economic policies during his second term.
3. Explain what is meant by a grassroots movement.
4. Describe ways African Americans began to secure their civil rights in the 1950s.
5. Name the method of protesting used by followers of Martin Luther King Jr.

SECTION 4

Eisenhower's Foreign Policy

Despite the Republican promise to take a more active stand against communism, containment was still the basis of Eisenhower's foreign policies. At a press conference in early 1954, Eisenhower discussed the threat in the following terms: If communism took root in one area, it would inevitably spread to neighboring regions. He compared the process to the chain reaction of a row of falling dominoes. "You knock one over," he warned, "and what will happen to the last one is certainly that it will go over very quickly." This **domino theory** was soon used to justify not only containment but also opposition to almost any change anywhere in the world.

What effect did anti-Communist feeling have on Eisenhower's foreign policies?
Why did Eisenhower use the CIA to topple regimes in Iran and Guatemala?
How did Eisenhower deal with foreign policy problems in Asia and the Middle East?

Soviet-American Relations

In 1952, Republicans stressed the need for a new look in foreign and defense policies. Rather than just containing the Soviet Union (and eventually Communist China), Republicans wanted to "roll back the Communist tide." Secretary of State Dulles talked of "liberating the captive peoples" of Eastern Europe and "unleashing" National Chinese leader Chiang Kai-shek for attacks on mainland China. Radio Free Europe was an American propaganda broadcast campaign that received most of its funding from the Central Intelligence Agency (CIA). It began broadcasting anti-Communist messages into Eastern Europe. But the actions of the Eisenhower administration did not match these messages.

▶ In 1956, Soviet tanks patrolled the streets of Budapest, Hungary, during an anti-Soviet uprising. How did the U.S. respond?

▼ What is Herblock's view of Dulles's "brinkmanship" policies? [Herblock's Special for Today (Simon and Schuster, 1958).]

"Don't Be Afraid—I Can Always Pull You Back"

In early 1953, for example, workers in East Berlin rioted to protest work speedups and food shortages. Soviet tanks rumbled into Berlin and put down the uprising. Although the U.S. government objected to the Soviet action and praised the heroism of the workers, it could do little else without risking war. In 1956, a similar uprising occurred in Hungary and again the United States did little.

Meanwhile, John Foster Dulles warned Moscow and Peking (Beijing) that Communist aggression would result in massive retaliation by the United States. He was suggesting that the U.S. might attack the major Communist powers with nuclear weapons rather than conventional arms. Dulles described his strategy as **brinkmanship**—pushing a dangerous situation to the brink of war in order to get what he wanted. This was a risky strategy to follow. Dulles's tactics horrified the world, partly because by now both the Americans in 1952 and the

Soviets in 1953 had successfully tested hydrogen bombs. Massive retaliation could actually result in the extinction of human life on Earth.

Moreover, Dulles's threatening tactics may have been badly timed. Soviet Premier Joseph Stalin had died in early 1953. After a period of internal party conflict, Nikita Khrushchev emerged as the new Soviet leader. Khrushchev's approach was quite different from Stalin's. He talked of **peaceful coexistence**—of living in peace while respecting each other's differences. To Dulles, however, communism was evil and any negotiating would be like dealing with the devil.

Despite Dulles's opposition, Eisenhower finally agreed to attend a diplomatic **summit conference** (a meeting between highest ranking officials) with the Soviets. In July 1955, Eisenhower met with Khrushchev and other European leaders in Geneva, Switzerland. Major topics for discussion included disarmament, the future of East and West Germany, and the open skies proposal. Eisenhower wanted one country's airplanes to be free to fly over the other country in order to gather defense-related information. The conference produced no specific agreements, but journalists noted a slight thaw in the Cold War. They called this development "the spirit of Geneva."

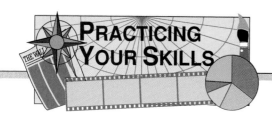

"Don't Be Afraid—I Can Always Pull You Back"

More Practice Analyzing Editorial Cartoons

In Chapter 12, you looked at how editorial cartoons are used to support or attack a particular issue or viewpoint. Unlike straight newspaper reporting, cartoons do not present an impartial, or unbiased, viewpoint. That is why political cartoons are often found on the editorial pages of newspapers. Often, cartoonists intentionally exaggerate situations or conditions to ensure that no one misses the point.

Review the guidelines on page 697 to analyzing an editorial cartoon and then answer the questions below about the editorial cartoon on page 814.

1. Is there a title or caption for this cartoon? What does the title or caption tell you about the characters or the time period?
2. Who, or what, do each of the following symbols represent? (a) Uncle Sam (b) Superman (c) the cliff.

3. Why do you think Block characterized Dulles as Superman? Why do you think he gave Superman the short, squat figure?
4. What do you think Uncle Sam is feeling in this cartoon?
5. What is Block saying about the policy of brinkmanship? About the leadership of Dulles? What specifics in the drawing make you think the United States is on the brink of disaster?
6. Why do you think Block did not draw Eisenhower as Superman instead of Dulles?

Nationalism in the Third World

Eisenhower told Treasury Secretary George Humphrey that "few individuals understand the intensity and force of the spirit of nationalism that is gripping all the peoples of the world today . . . It is my personal conviction that almost any one of the newborn states of the world would far rather embrace communism" than submit to another power. Still, Eisenhower was determined to fight communism, although he wanted to do it as cheaply as possible. Thus, the CIA, rather than the army, became the main way to fight communism in the Third World. The Third World was the name given to de-veloping countries during the Cold War period. (The U.S. and its allies were referred to as the free world, or first world; the Soviet Union, China, and other Communist countries were the Communist world, or second world.)

Eisenhower did not hesitate to use the CIA to help overthrow foreign governments he was against. In early 1953, for example, Eisenhower approved a CIA plan to topple Iranian Prime Minister Mohammed Mossadegh (Moh-suh-DAYGH). The president believed that Mossadegh was leaning toward communism, since he had accepted Soviet financial aid. The CIA aided supporters of the Shah (supreme ruler) of Iran, whom Mossadegh had overthrown. Together, they successfully ousted Mossadegh and restored the Shah to power. As a

This map shows the years in which former European colonies gained (or regained) their independence as self-governing nations. On what continents did most newly independent states emerge between 1951 and 1960?

reward, Iran allowed U.S. oil companies to handle 40 percent of its oil production.

A year later, Eisenhower authorized another CIA operation against alleged Communists in Guatemala. Guatemala's democratically elected president, Jacobo Arbenz, was the target. He had legalized the Guatemalan Communist Party, had accepted arms from the Soviets, and had begun a moderate program of land reform. This program

▼ *The 1954 Geneva Accords created the independent neutral states of Laos and Cambodia, and divided Vietnam at the 17th parallel. Approximately how much of Vietnam did the Communists control between 1946 and 1954?*

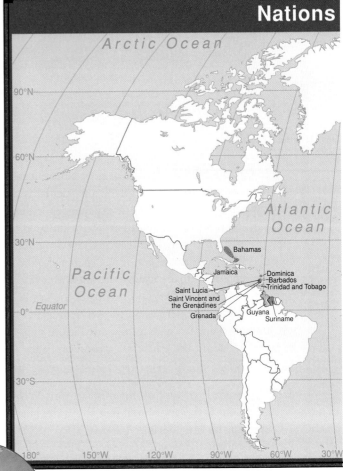

Southeast Asia (Indochina), 1954

Boundary of Indochina, 1954

Extent of Communist control, 1946-1954

0   50 mi
0   100 km

included seizing property belonging to the American-owned United Fruit Company. The CIA provided Colonel Carlos Castillo Armas with arms, equipment and other aid, and helped force Arbenz from power.

Southeast Asia   The situation in Southeast Asia (Indochina), especially in Vietnam, also concerned Eisenhower. France had been the dominant colonial power there prior to World War II. The war had weakened French control and strengthened Vietnamese nationalism. In 1945, **Ho Chi Minh**, a Communist-trained Vietnamese leader, had declared Vietnam independent. France soon went to war to regain its control. The United States supported France in this war. By 1954, the United States had paid 78 percent of the war's costs.

Achieving Independence, 1943-1980

Gained independence
1943-1950

Gained independence
1951-1960

Gained independence
1961-1970

Gained independence
1971-1980

0   1000 mi
0   1500 km

*at the
Equator

cism. As Eisenhower knew it would, Congress refused to grant approval.

Without U.S. intervention, the French at Dien Bien Phu were forced to surrender on May 8, 1954. The next day, a previously scheduled conference opened in Geneva, Switzerland, to deal with Southeast Asia. Nineteen nations, including Communist China, the Soviet Union, France, Vietnam (represented by the Vietminh), and the United States, attended. The conference produced the **Geneva Accords**. These agreements ended all fighting in Indochina and temporarily divided Vietnam at the 17th parallel. They required French troops to move south and Vietminh troops to move north of that line. Vietnamese who desired to move could also do so. One million moved south; 100,000 moved north. The settlement scheduled nationwide elections to reunify Vietnam and it recognized Laos and Cambodia as independent, neutral nations.

Despite increased U.S. aid, France's position in Vietnam worsened. In 1954, Ho Chi Minh's troops, the Vietminh, laid siege to a French stronghold at Dien Bien Phu, located at a crossroads in the northwestern part of Vietnam. As the Vietminh tightened their stranglehold on the French positions there, the political right wing and the press in the United States increased their calls for U.S. intervention. Eisenhower adamantly opposed the introduction of U.S. combat troops to relieve the French garrison. He recognized that "the jungles of Indochina . . . would have swallowed up division after division of United States troops . . . ." Eisenhower did seek congressional approval for U.S. air strikes against Vietminh positions at Dien Bien Phu. But he did so largely to protect himself against right-wing criti-

Eisenhower did not sign the Geneva Accords, deciding he did not want to abandon Vietnam to Ho Chi Minh. Eisenhower believed that Communist China was behind the conflict in Vietnam. The United States announced that it would oppose further Communist advances in Southeast Asia. It also immediately began negotiations to form the **Southeast Asia Treaty Organization (SEATO)**, which would defend the region from Communist aggression. More importantly, the United States decided to support the newly established regime of Ngo Dinh Diem [NOH DIN dee-EM] in South Vietnam.

A devout Roman Catholic in a primarily Buddhist country, Diem was viewed by American officials as the only hope to prevent Ho Chi Minh's election as president of all Vietnam. The Geneva Accords required that elections take place throughout Vietnam in 1956, but Diem refused to hold them in the South. Rather, he sought to create an independent, non-Communist South Vietnam, based largely on vast American support.

To stabilize Diem's regime, the United States sent military advisers to help train his army. Between 1955 and 1961, American aid, which was mostly military, amounted to over one billion dollars. But American aid could not overcome problems within South Vietnam. Diem personally controlled South Vietnamese military operations and promoted undeserving friends to high rank in the army. These practices hampered the development of an effective army and competent officer corps. Furthermore, American aid found its way to corrupt officials rather than to villages where 90 percent of the South Vietnamese lived. Diem's regime was to prove very unpopular.

The Suez Crisis

In 1952, Egyptian nationalist Gamal Abdel Nasser led a successful revolt against the corrupt government of King Farouk. An Arab nationalist, Nasser strongly resented Jewish Israel and the Israeli military victories in 1948 and 1953. Determined to strengthen his army, Nasser bought arms from Czechoslovakia when Western powers seemed reluctant to supply them. This deal worried Eisenhower and Dulles. They feared that it might mean greater Communist influence in the Middle East.

Earlier, Secretary of State Dulles, hoping to establish friendly relations with Nasser, had hinted that the United States might supply money for the Aswân High Dam project. This project would dam the waters of the lower Nile River, produce electricity for all Egypt, and irrigate desert wastelands. But Dulles soured on the idea of sending aid after Nasser's arms deal with Czechoslovakia. Dulles also disliked the formation of an anti-Israel alliance involving Egypt, Saudi Arabia, and Syria. Egyptian recognition of Communist China raised suspicions, too. So, on July 19, 1956, Dulles announced that the United States would not help finance the Aswân High Dam project.

Dulles's decision backfired in several ways. First, Nasser turned to the Soviet Union to help finance the project. Second, he took over the British-controlled Suez Canal, partly to help finance the Aswân Dam project but also to end British domination of the canal which went through Egyptian territory. Nasser promised to keep the canal open to all users, but Britain and France were concerned about the strategically important oil supplies that went through the canal. Third, Eisenhower refused British and French requests for help in seizing the Suez Canal and returning it to the British. In October 1956, British, French, and Israeli forces attacked Egypt anyway. As a result, Eisenhower sponsored a United Nations resolution calling for a cease-fire and the withdrawal of all foreign forces from Egypt. By December, all three nations yielded to U.S. pressure and withdrew. The result was a major diplomatic victory for Eisenhower, but Eisenhower's allies resented his actions.

▲ *Egypt's Colonel Gamal Nasser was a strong leader who received foreign aid from both the U.S. and the Soviet Union. What event soured relations between the U.S. and Egypt?*

SECTION 4 REVIEW

1. **Describe** brinkmanship.
2. **Define** the term *peaceful coexistence.*
3. **Describe** how Eisenhower's determination to fight communism affected foreign policies.
4. **Explain** how Eisenhower used the CIA in Iran and Guatemala.
5. **Summarize** the result of Dulles's decision not to finance the Aswân High Dam project.

The End of the Eisenhower Era

By many accounts, the most shocking event of Eisenhower's presidency occurred on October 4, 1957. A Soviet missile launched the first satellite, *Sputnik I*, into orbit around Earth. A month later, the Soviets launched *Sputnik II*, a 1,300-pound satellite that carried a live dog into orbit for three days. People throughout the U.S. were shocked by the Russian achievement. *Sputnik* shook public confidence in the superiority of American science and technology, the basis of our national security. Since the beginning of the Cold War, Americans had thought the Soviet Union too technologically backward to compete seriously with the United States. *Sputnik* created near panic and new fears of U.S. vulnerability.

What effects did Sputnik have on the United States?
What foreign policy problems did Eisenhower encounter in his second term?
What was the meaning of Eisenhower's warning about the military-industrial complex?

American Confidence Shaken

Eisenhower was aware of the Soviet satellite program, but had not considered it a threat to national security. He did not much care about beating the Soviets into space. His first priority was to give the U.S. satellite project, already well under way, a clearly civilian and scientific image. Even after *Sputnik*, Eisenhower saw no need to speed up the missile or satellite programs. Public anxiety, however, simply would not go away. While Eisenhower tried to reassure the public, the contents of the top-secret Gaither Report were leaked to the press. The Gaither Report concluded that the United States stood on the brink of disaster and that the nation's defenses were inadequate to withstand a Soviet mis-sile attack. It recommended that an additional $10 billion be allocated immediately for bombers, missiles, submarines, nuclear weapons, and conventional forces. "The still top-secret Gaither Report," the *Washington Post* reported, "portrays a United States in the gravest danger in its history . . . [and] exposed to an almost immediate threat from the missile-bristling Soviet Union."

Democrats wanted copies of the Gaither Report, since it suggested that Eisenhower's defense policies had been dangerously inadequate. When Senate Majority Leader Lyndon Johnson called for the release of the document, Eisenhower claimed **executive privilege**. Executive privilege is the principle, founded on the separation of powers, that prevents forcing a president or a president's confidential advisers to testify before congressional committees or to make public secret documents. Even after the United States launched its first satellite, *Explorer I*, in January 1958, concern about a "missile gap" between the U.S. and the Soviet Union mounted. Defense spending in general, and the missile gap in particular, would be important campaign issues in the 1960 presidential election.

Because of *Sputnik*, Eisenhower's public approval rating dropped from 79 percent in February 1957 to 57 percent in December. At that point, Eisenhower recognized *Sputnik's* negative effects on public opinion and called for several new programs. Congress moved quickly. First, it passed the National Defense Education Act. This bill sought to improve high school and university education, especially in science, math, engineering, and foreign languages. It allocated one billion dollars over seven years to support low-interest loans to college students and to improve curriculum and instruction. It also provided $60 million to support vocational education. Second, Congress created the National Aeronautics and Space Administration (NASA) to coordinate the nation's space program.

Foreign Events Plague Eisenhower

Throughout his administration, Eisenhower worked to reduce Soviet influence in the Middle

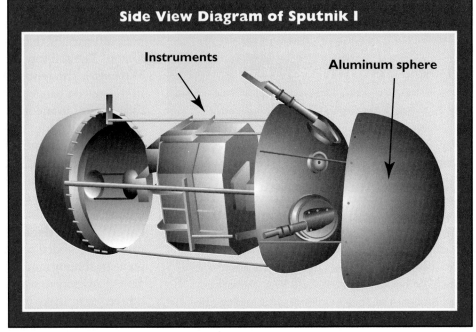

Side View Diagram of Sputnik I

Instruments

Aluminum sphere

▶ Sputnik I *made a full orbit of Earth every hour and a half, staying aloft for 57 days, and relaying scientific data.*

▼ *Why did the Soviet launch of* Sputnik *nearly create a panic in America?*

East. After the Suez crisis in 1956, he asked Congress for authority to protect the region against Communist advances. He wanted blanket permission to use U.S. armed forces "to secure and protect the territorial integrity and independence of such nations . . . against overt armed aggression from any nation controlled by International Communism." This became known as the **Eisenhower Doctrine**. The president hoped that this policy would serve as a warning to the Soviets that the United States would tolerate no interference in the Middle East. Congress approved the doctrine in a resolution in March 1958, even though such broad authority was without parallel in U.S. history. In July 1958, Eisenhower applied the doctrine by sending 14,000 marines into Lebanon to prevent Iraq and Egypt from taking over that nation.

Unsettling events occurred in Latin America as well. Latin America was different from other emerging Third World regions. Nationalists in Latin America did not have to cast off old colonial powers. Rather, they had to try to loosen the economic grip of U.S. companies. By 1955, U.S. companies produced 10 percent of Latin America's products and controlled most of the region's oil and mineral resources. The region had few industries and depended heavily on the production of raw materials. Unfortunately, prices for these raw materials declined steadily through the 1950s. This dismal economic situation was worsened by a rapidly expanding population.

Throughout his presidency, Eisenhower had argued for vastly increased foreign aid to less developed countries. He failed to convince taxpayers or Congress that foreign aid was important, thus U.S. aid to Latin America was small. U.S. aid to Belgium and Luxembourg was three times larger than the aid sent to all 20 Latin American nations combined. Two-thirds of this aid took the form of military assistance. Latin American countries were often unstable. Military dictatorships and demonstrations against American imperialism were common.

In Cuba, **Fidel Castro's** revolutionary movement brought down the dictatorship of Fulgencio Batista in 1959. Batista had become the military dictator after a coup in 1952, and he had allowed the United States to dominate the Cuban economy. U.S. firms had almost complete control of Cuba, including ownership of 50 percent of its sugar crop, 80 percent of its utilities, and 90 percent of its mines and ranches. Although Cuba had the highest per capita income of any country in Latin America, most Cubans lived in poverty. Castro used the discontent this situation produced to spark a revolution.

Eisenhower officially recognized Castro's regime only a week after Batista left Cuba. However, relations between the United States and Cuba soured. Castro's anti-American propaganda alienated many Americans. In 1960, Castro seized over one billion dollars in American-owned property. Eisenhower responded by cutting down on Cuban sugar imports. This was more than just a gesture as the United States was Cuba's largest customer. This action pushed Castro farther toward the Soviet Union, which came to Cuba's political and economic aid. Many of Batista's supporters had already fled the island, but as Castro's regime became increasingly Communist, more and more Cubans immigrated to the United States.

Hoping to provoke Castro, Eisenhower began to act more forcefully. He hoped to build support in the United States for even stronger measures against Castro's regime. Eisenhower cut off relations with Cuba on January 3, 1961. Meanwhile, the CIA had already begun planning Castro's assassination. In addition, the CIA had begun training Cuban exiles for an invasion of Cuba to topple Castro from power. The Bay of Pigs fiasco would occur after Eisenhower left office.

Khrushchev and Eisenhower

Meanwhile, both Eisenhower and Soviet Premier Nikita Khrushchev had decided to pursue better relations, each for his own reasons. Khrushchev wanted peace with the West. He realized that the arms race was a burden on the Soviet economy, and he believed, as Eisenhower did, that nuclear war would be insane. The relations between Soviet and Chinese Communists were also worsening. Yet, Khrushchev feared that the United States would interpret signs of friendship as weakness. He therefore boasted of Soviet power and seemed determined to assert Soviet interests in the Third World. Most Americans took these mixed messages as more reasons to distrust the Soviets.

In September 1959, Khrushchev toured the United States, and many Americans hoped that U.S.-Soviet relations would improve. Khrushchev and Eisenhower met at Camp David, the presidential retreat in Maryland. There they agreed only to meet again at another summit conference in Paris in May 1960. Khrushchev invited Eisenhower to visit the Soviet Union after the conference.

Eisenhower agreed to the Paris summit meeting because he wanted above all to obtain a nuclear test-ban treaty with the Soviets. Reports of radioactive fallout from nuclear weapons tests by both countries alarmed him, and he wanted to ban testing before the atmosphere was completely poisoned. Disaster struck, however, before the summit opened. The Soviets shot down an American U-2 spy plane over Soviet territory just days before the conference was to begin.

The CIA had used U-2 spy flights to gather important military intelligence for years. Eisenhower knew from data gathered by U-2 spy missions, for example, that the Soviets were not ahead in their missile or nuclear technology. Since the CIA assured him that neither the plane nor pilot could survive a crash, Eisenhower denied that spy flights had ever occurred. After the Soviets produced the captured pilot, Francis Gary Powers, Eisenhower accepted full responsibility and promised to end U-2 flights in Soviet airspace. But the damage could not be undone. As the summit conference was about to

The Mercury Astronauts

After *Sputnik*, NASA began Project Mercury with the goal of putting a human being in space as soon as possible. The selection process for the nation's first astronauts was rigorous. NASA wanted jet pilots who were graduates of military test-pilot schools and who had logged at least 1,500 test-flight hours. No women could meet these criteria because only men were allowed to be test pilots at that time. One female applicant, Gerry Cobb, could perform all the physical and mental tests as well as the men. But since Cobb had no test-flight hours, NASA would not consider her for Project Mercury.

When NASA first introduced the astronauts to the nation in April 1959, *Time* magazine hailed them as "seven men cut out of the same stone as Columbus, Magellan, Daniel Boone, Orville and Wilbur Wright." Each of the astronauts was young, bright, educated in engineering, and trained in the military. The American public was immensely interested in the astronauts and in the danger and drama that surrounded their early missions in space. The astronauts seemed to embody the virtues of an earlier, simpler America—courage, individual daring, hard work, and self-sacrifice. They became modern heroes.

▲ *The seven astronauts who would become the first Americans in space were introduced at a press conference on April 9, 1959. They were (from left to right) Wally Shirra, Alan Shepard, Gus Grissom, Deke Slayton, John Glenn, Scott Carpenter, and Gordon Cooper.*

On May 5, 1961, Alan Shepard became the first American in space. His flight was short (300 miles) and brief (15 minutes), but Americans celebrated it enthusiastically. Virgil "Gus" Grissom duplicated Shepard's feat in July. NASA had scheduled six similar flights, but after Soviet Cosmonaut Yuri Gagarin orbited the earth, NASA rushed to put an astronaut into orbit. On February 20, 1962, John Glenn was the first American to orbit the earth, followed the next year by Scott Carpenter, Wally Schirra, and Gordon Cooper. Of the original seven, only "Deke" Slayton never flew in space, grounded because of a heart murmur.

1. Why did *Time* magazine equate the astronauts with such explorers as Columbus and Daniel Boone?

2. In what ways were the astronauts different from early pioneers?

begin, Khrushchev denounced Eisenhower and the U-2 flights. The U-2 incident was a serious stumbling block to Eisenhower's plans for disarmament.

The Military-Industrial Complex

Three days before leaving office, Eisenhower delivered his farewell address. Among other issues, he discussed what he considered to be a dangerous collaboration between the nation's armed forces and its defense industries (corporations making weapons and military supplies). Eisenhower warned that the nation must be on guard against the "influence [by this] **military–industrial complex**."

His warning took many by surprise, although it should not have. Eisenhower had fought against excessive defense spending for eight years. He always thought that American security rested on sufficient weapons and defense spending, but not a dime more. It also rested on a healthy economy that operated without federal intervention. Unchecked defense spending could undermine both these principles. Eisenhower's speech may have been aimed at the Democrats, who, in the 1960 elections, had severely attacked his defense policies.

SECTION 5 REVIEW

1. **Define** the term *executive privilege*.
2. **Describe** the impact of *Sputnik* on American public opinion.
3. **Identify** new programs started by the Eisenhower administration to combat the negative effects of the launching of *Sputnik*.
4. **Discuss** changing relations between the United States and Cuba after Castro's takeover of that country.
5. **Explain** why Eisenhower warned against the military-industrial complex.

Chapter 25 Review

Summary

In domestic affairs, Eisenhower tried to chart a moderate course. He believed Roosevelt and Truman had allowed too much government interference in the nation's economy. Eisenhower wanted to limit the role of government and cut taxes and spending. Yet he did not attempt to dismantle many of the New Deal and Fair Deal programs that he had inherited from Roosevelt and Truman. Instead, Eisenhower expanded Social Security, increased the minimum wage, and agreed to public-housing and massive public works projects.

Many Americans hailed the Supreme Court's *Brown v. Topeka Board of Education* decision in 1954 as a breakthrough for civil rights. The actual results of the ruling were disappointing. Congress made two feeble attempts at voting-rights legislation, but the acts proved ineffective. Grassroots movements among African Americans, inspired by the Reverend Martin Luther King Jr., were more effective in removing some of the laws and customs that had diminished their rights.

In foreign affairs, Secretary of State Dulles had blustered about massive retaliation and brinkmanship even as the Soviets appeared to mellow after Stalin's death. Meanwhile, Eisenhower pursued better relations with the Soviets when opportunities arose. Much of Eisenhower's attention focused on the lesser developed nations where nationalism had become a powerful force. When Communist aggression occurred, he used every means available to him—including the CIA—to stop it. Above all, Eisenhower's defense policies rested on the firm commitment to spending as little on weapons as possible. This commitment explains his warning about the growing influence of the military-industrial complex in American society.

Vocabulary

brinkmanship
civil disobedience
de facto
de jure
domino theory
executive privilege
grassroots
military-industrial complex
oligopoly
peaceful coexistence
summit conference
urban renewal

Write the vocabulary term with the correct definition provided below. Not all terms will be used.

1. strategy that pushes situations to the edge of conflict
2. close association of weapon makers and users
3. a few major corporations controlling the market
4. projects aimed at revitalizing inner cities
5. countries agreeing to respect each other's political differences
6. meeting involving representatives of the highest levels of government
7. starting at a local level and spreading out
8. principle that allows the president or his agents to refrain from testifying before Congress

Review Questions

1. Explain the major domestic and foreign policy priorities of President Eisenhower.
2. What was the effect of Eisenhower's economic policies on his defense and foreign policies?
3. Why did President Eisenhower handle Senator McCarthy in the way he did?
4. Discuss reasons for important gains in civil rights for African Americans during the 1950s.
5. Evaluate the influence of Eisenhower's anti-Communist views on his actions and policies toward the Third World.
6. Compare the domestic policies of Truman and Eisenhower.
7. Compare the containment policies of Truman and Eisenhower.

8. Explain how Secretary of State Dulles's decision not to fund the Aswân High Dam project in Egypt backfired.

9. Why were Americans so devastated by the Soviet launching of *Sputnik*?

10. Why did Eisenhower and Khrushchev explore better relations between the U.S. and the Soviet Union in the late 1950s?

Critical Historical Thinking

Writing Answer each of the following by writing one or more complete paragraphs:

1. Discuss Eisenhower's statement regarding the *Brown* decision: "... The Constitution is as the Supreme Court interprets it; and I must conform to that."

2. Explain why President Eisenhower's use of federal troops to integrate Central High School in Arkansas raised the issue of states' rights versus individual constitutional rights.

3. The excesses of Senator McCarthy put a tremendous strain on American society. Did the position taken by the president help or hurt the situation? Give reasons for your answer.

4. Read the selection entitled "Segregation is a National Problem" in the Unit 8 Archives. Identify the national problem described by Robert Carter and Thurgood Marshall over 40 years ago. Do you think America has solved this problem? Why, or why not?

Making Connections with the Media

Perhaps no twentieth century invention, save the automobile, has influenced our lives more than television.

Producers learned the power of television to persuade the public almost by accident. When Senator Estes Kefauver's Subcommittee on Organized Crime held its hearings in 1950, television was permitted to carry the hearings live. When New York crime boss Frank Costello was called to testify, he refused to allow his face to be televised. The cameras focused instead on his hands which the audience interpreted as proof of his guilt.

In 1952, Eisenhower's campaign began to falter when Nixon was accused of accepting political contributions and putting the money in a private account. Party leaders urged him to dump Nixon. But Nixon went on television and in an emotional speech declared himself innocent. He ended the speech by stating that he had accepted only one gift and that was Checkers, his cocker spaniel. Nixon's "Checkers" speech saved his candidacy, as letters of support poured in.

In the 1960 campaign between Nixon and John F. Kennedy, the two candidates staged a televised debate. Nixon had been ill and had just gotten out of the hospital, but Kennedy was fresh and tanned from a Florida vacation. The public perceived Nixon, with his pale skin, shadow of a beard and darting eyes as shifty and untrustworthy. Kennedy won the presidency in a close election.

■ Study a televised interview. Make notes on the appearance of the guests. What actions make the person appear confident? What actions make the person seem nervous? Create a set of "do's" and "don'ts" for people to follow when speaking in public.

Additional Skills Practice

Sketch a political cartoon based on the opposite premise of Herbert Block's cartoon analyzed in this chapter's Practicing Your Skills. You will be trying to convince your readers that Secretary of State Dulles's policy of brinkmanship is sound and justified as the only way to contain communism. Use symbols and caricature to convey your point of view.

The Affluent Society

The 1950s seemed to many people to be a time of almost unlimited possibilities. The decade offered economic prosperity and material comforts to many Americans accustomed to the harder times of the Great Depression and World War II. On the other hand, contemporary observers like journalist William Shannon judged this period to be "years of flabbiness and self-satisfaction and gross materialism. . . . The loudest sound in the land has been the oink-and-grunt of private hoggishness. . . . It has been the age of the slob." These diverse and conflicting images may be the keys to understanding the social and cultural history of the fifties. The decade brought enormous changes in American life.

▲ *A fad on college campuses during the 1950s was to see how many people could fit into one telephone booth. At a college in Alabama, 24 students (shown above) broke the unofficial record.*

Dimensions of Prosperity

In 1960, an editor of *U.S. News and World Report* returned to the United States after living for 12 years in Paris. Astonishing changes had occurred in his absence. Everywhere he saw signs of affluence—small boats rigged with depth finders and automatic pilots, plastic envelopes containing premixed cocktails, and even striped toothpaste. In France, only one family in ten had a bathtub with hot running water. In contrast, the editor found that in some areas of California, one family in ten owned a backyard swimming pool. Widespread prosperity seemed to characterize much of American society in the 1950s.

What were the major features of economic prosperity during the fifties?

In what ways did work change in the fifties?

Why were some Americans excluded from the prosperity of the fifties?

Widespread Economic Prosperity

Between 1948 and 1960, the gross national product almost doubled, rising to $503 billion. In 1955, the United States had 6 percent of the world's population, but consumed more than a third of the world's goods and services. The steady growth of the economy raised the standard of living for many. Because incomes were rising and people were buying on credit, more people than ever before could purchase a widening array of consumer goods.

Short-term consumer debt—such as the purchase of cars on installment and the use of credit cards—also expanded enormously. The Diners Club introduced the first credit card in 1950. Ten years later, Diners Club and American Express each had over a million cards in circulation.

In the decade after 1950, the annual amount businesses spent on advertising doubled. NBC President Robert Sarnoff claimed that "the reason we have such a high standard of living is because advertising has created an American frame of mind that makes people want more things, better things, and newer things." Consultant Dr. Ernest Dichter advised businesspeople, "We are now confronted with the problem of permitting the average American to feel moral . . . even when he is spending, even when he is not saving, even when he is taking two vacations a year." The **consumer culture** undermined the value that had been placed on thrift and saving.

▼ *Expanding consumer credit was one reason for the economic prosperity of the period. How much did consumer credit increase between 1945 and 1960?*

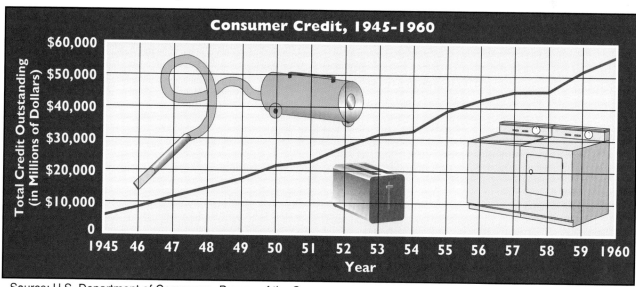

Consumer Credit, 1945–1960

Total Credit Outstanding (in Millions of Dollars)

$60,000 / $50,000 / $40,000 / $30,000 / $20,000 / $10,000 / 0

1945 46 47 48 49 50 51 52 53 54 55 56 57 58 59 1960

Year

Source: U.S. Department of Commerce, Bureau of the Census.

▶ In 1954, Ford Motor Company introduced the Thunderbird, a high-performance sports car. Why would the manufacturer want to make frequent design and style changes in newer models?

Consumption was helped by designing consumer goods so that they quickly wore out. This **planned obsolescence** guaranteed that people would have to replace these goods. Frequent style changes in cars and clothing had the same result. Manufacturers also tried to make their products desirable by improving them. The electric blender, for example, had two speeds (on and off) when introduced in the 1920s. In the 1950s, however, as one executive explained, "it was crazy. . . . The more buttons, the better they sold. We got as high as 16 [speeds], and the things still couldn't do much more than whip cream."

Americans consumed in the fifties. The majority of Americans owned their own homes. By 1956, nearly every family owned a refrigerator, and eight out of every ten families owned a television set. Automatic washing machines, clothes dryers, home freezers, and vacuum cleaners had once been luxuries. Now they were necessities. These and other goods seemed to make life more enjoyable by making housework easier.

Businesses also discovered the teenage market in the fifties. As *Life* magazine reported in 1959,

To a growing number of businessmen . . . teenagers have emerged as a big-time consumer in

▼ In 1951, the General Electric Company used the slogan "G.E. makes you feel it's real!"

the U.S. economy. They are multiplying in numbers. They spend more and have more spent on them. . . . Today teenagers surround themselves with a fantastic array of garish and often expensive baubles and amusements.

Life magazine estimated that teenagers owned 10 million record players, 1 million TV sets, and 13 million cameras.

▶

The wool and felt Romeo-and-Juliet skirt with an angora sweater was a typical outfit worn by "bobby soxers" to Saturday night dances. What was the slang term for teenage dances of the fifties?

Recreation and leisure also became major growth industries, because people had more money to spend and more leisure time. In the 1920s, workers toiled six days a week and typically earned no vacation. By 1960, the average employee worked a five-day week with eight paid holidays and a two-week paid annual vacation. Purchases of boats, swimming pools, and sporting and camping equipment increased, as did tickets for spectator sports, symphony concerts, and live theater. Americans took more vacations, often traveling overseas. Many more took vacations within the United States, to national parks, seaside beaches, resorts, and amusement parks like Disneyland. Consequently, the fifties saw a dramatic growth in travel-related services, such as restaurants, fast-food chains, gas stations, and motel chains. Motel income leaped by 2,300 percent between 1939 and 1958.

The Nature of Work Changes

As late as 1940, nearly 60 percent of all workers held farm jobs or blue-collar jobs that produced actual products. Between 1950 and 1960, the number of clerical workers increased by 35 percent, while the number of professional workers jumped by 47

▶

A fad that spread across the nation during the 1950s was the "hula hoop" craze. Hula hoop contests, such as the one held during this Sunday school picnic, were popular events.

Women who worked outside the home in the 1950s often found themselves employed as secretaries or clerks. How are the men in this photograph portrayed?

percent. By 1956, white-collar jobs outnumbered blue-collar jobs for the first time. The new **postindustrial economy** was focused on providing services—in health, education, accounting, and government—rather than on producing goods. This transition was made possible by automation and technology.

Automation, *Business Week* noted, "is the art and science of going through as many stages of production as possible with as little human help as possible." The auto and steel industries spent a fifth of their budgets on machinery designed to automate production. Altogether, worker productivity increased 50 percent between 1947 and 1956. Automation and increased productivity reduced or eliminated some jobs, including those of factory workers and farm laborers. At the same time, hundreds of thousands of new jobs were created in brand new industries.

The revolution in scientific and technological knowledge also affected the economy. The major growth industries of the fifties—electronics, plastics, and chemicals—relied heavily on research and de-

velopment (R & D). R & D itself became a major industry. Spending on R & D increased 400 percent during this decade.

As a result, colleges and universities experienced rapid growth. They performed basic research and supplied the engineers, mathematicians, and scientists for corporate R & D programs. Many of the jobs, such as business management and accounting, required increasingly higher levels of education.

After reaching its peak in the middle of the decade, labor union membership steadily declined. Part of the cause was the shift from blue-collar to white-collar work. Unionizing white-collar and service workers proved difficult. By 1960, for example, unions had organized less than 4 percent of government workers, office workers, and engineers.

A revolution in agriculture paralleled the revolution in industry. Before World War II, the typical farm was small, family-run, and modestly equipped with machinery. Horses and mules still outnumbered tractors. After the war, new and better machinery, hybrid seeds, fertilizers, and pesticides revolutionized farm productivity. These technologies had several unexpected consequences. In the two decades after 1940, the average size of farms nearly doubled and required more machinery and capital to operate. Small family farms often lacked the financial resources to compete with larger farms, and 600,000 small farms disappeared between 1950 and 1954 alone. **Agribusiness**, an industry consisting of large corporate-run farms, grew increasingly powerful.

Prosperity Eludes Some Americans

Not all Americans took part in the consumer society. Prosperity passed by African Americans living in the central cities, white workers in the depressed coal-mining towns of Appalachia, and many rural Americans, especially migrant workers and small farmers. Factory workers in the declining industrial towns of New England also experienced hardship. Many of the elderly struggled on fixed incomes to maintain a decent standard of living.

While economic prosperity helped everyone to some degree, the gap between the wealthy and the majority of Americans continued. In 1960, one out of five Americans lived below the poverty level (then defined as 4-person families with annual incomes below $3,000).

The change to a postindustrial economy made it increasingly difficult for some workers, especially people from minority groups and those with little formal education, to find steady jobs that paid well. The unemployment rate for minorities was often nearly double the rate for white males.

SECTION 1 REVIEW

1. **Define** the term *consumer culture*.
2. **Describe** how economic prosperity affected middle-class American society in the fifties.
3. **Explain** why recreation and leisure became major economic growth industries in the fifties.
4. **Discuss** changes in the nature of work in the fifties.
5. **Name** groups that did not share in the general prosperity.

SECTION 2

Changes in Population Patterns

Reflecting on his own experience in the 1950s, writer John Cheever observed, "I don't suppose there was a day, an hour, when the middle class got their marching orders, but toward the end of the 1940s the middle class began to move. It was more of a push than a move, and the energy behind the push was the changing economic character of the city. . . . The ranks were thinning and we watched them go with [sorrow] and some scorn. . . . My God, the suburbs." Despite Cheever's attachment to the city and his fear of living a suburban "life of indescribable dreariness," he eventually joined in the rush to the suburbs. This migration to the suburbs was only one of several trends that changed the social geography of the United States during the fifties.

What caused the baby boom after World War II?
What major migration patterns occurred during the 1950s?
How did government policies accelerate the growth of the suburbs?

The Baby Boom

In the 1950s, an astonishing increase in birthrates—called the **baby boom**—affected American society in almost every way. From 1944 to 1948, the United States had one of the highest marriage rates in the world. This resulted in an enormous increase in birthrates. At the same time, fewer babies were dying because of advances in obstetrics, hospital care, and new medicines such as penicillin and streptomycin.

During the 1950s, the number of families with three children doubled, while those with four children tripled. Even traditionally smaller middle-class

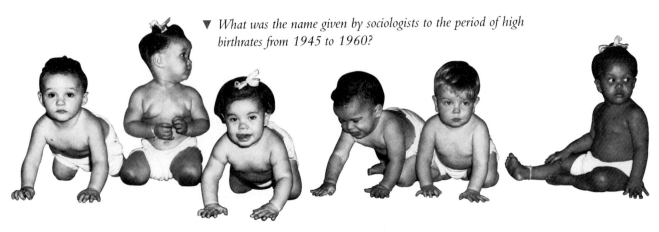

▼ *What was the name given by sociologists to the period of high birthrates from 1945 to 1960?*

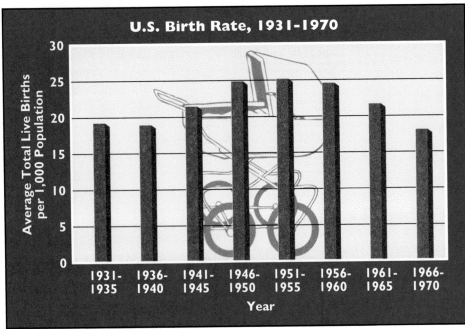

U.S. Birth Rate, 1931-1970

Average Total Live Births per 1,000 Population

Year	
1931-1935	19
1936-1940	19
1941-1945	21
1946-1950	25
1951-1955	25
1956-1960	25
1961-1965	22
1966-1970	18

Source: U.S. Department of Commerce, Bureau of the Census.

▲ *This graph shows the substantial increase in U.S. birthrates during the late 1940s through the 1950s. What implications does the lower birthrate in the 1960s have on the ability to pay for government services?*

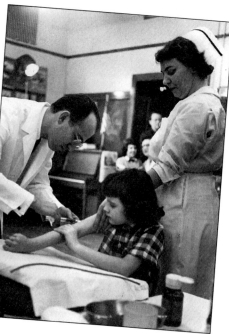

▲ *Dr. Jonas Salk, shown above, pioneered the development of a vaccine to prevent polio. Nearly two million children participated in a field test of the drug in 1954.*

families were having more children. The enormous population growth caused by the baby boom spurred the economic prosperity of the decade. More people required food, clothing, housing, and other consumer goods. Meanwhile, the baby boom put strains on virtually every social institution. School enrollments, for example, increased by 13 million students during the fifties, straining the capacity of local governments to build and staff new schools.

Americans on the Move

Historically, Americans haved moved in three directions—as immigrants into the country, from one region to another within the country, and from the farms to the cities. These population flows continued in the fifties, but there were significant differences. The 1952 McCarren Immigration Act

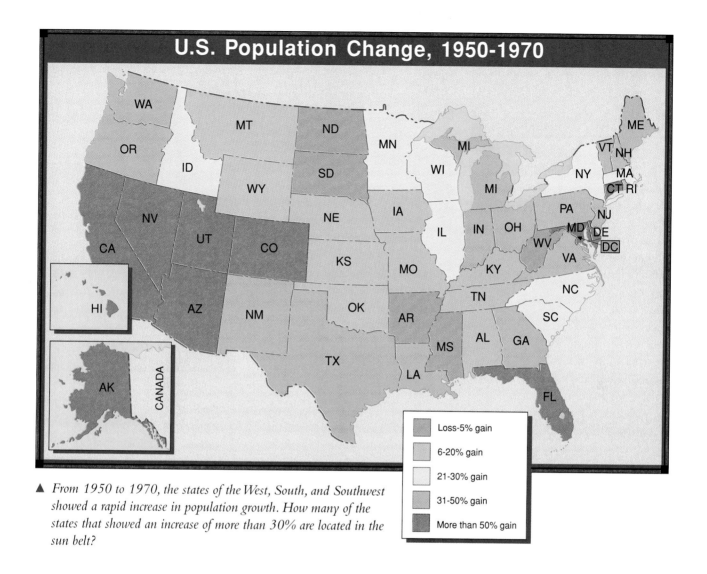

U.S. Population Change, 1950-1970

Legend:
- Loss-5% gain
- 6-20% gain
- 21-30% gain
- 31-50% gain
- More than 50% gain

▲ *From 1950 to 1970, the states of the West, South, and Southwest showed a rapid increase in population growth. How many of the states that showed an increase of more than 30% are located in the sun belt?*

retained the national quotas established by the 1924 National Origins Act, but it removed the restriction on the immigration of Asian people. Immigration increased during the decade as Hispanic and Asian immigrants entered the U.S. in increasing numbers.

Regional migration was the second major pattern of population movement during the 1950s. Native-born white migrants tended to move from midwestern, middle Atlantic, and some states in the Deep South to the **sun belt**. The sun belt is the region of generally sunny states of the South and Southwest. California and Florida were the largest receivers of native-born white migrants. This flow of people to the sun belt would continue in the 1960s and 1970s.

Rural-to-urban migration was the third major pattern of population movement. Fourteen million people left rural America between 1946 and 1960. A higher percentage of African Americans, however, left rural America than did their white counterparts. African Americans had migrated from the South since Reconstruction. Yet as late as 1940, over three-quarters still lived in the South, especially in rural areas. Farm mechanization helped to create a job shortage. Unemployment and continuing segregation and racial hostility led many African Americans to seek better jobs and social opportunities in northern cities. By 1960, 40 percent of African Americans (7.5 million people) lived outside of the southern states.

American Landscape

The Move to the Suburbs

After World War II, Americans began to settle in suburbs, housing areas that spread in widening circles around the nation's largest cities. Veterans returning from the war married, had children (the baby boomers), and sought larger houses and a more attractive environment in which to live and raise their children. Government housing grants, the availability of land on the outskirts of cities, and the mobility afforded by automobiles rapidly expanded the urban landscape. Networks of freeways and beltways were built to knit these suburbs into a single fabric.

By 1950, suburban populations were expanding dramatically. Fully two-thirds of the total population growth in the United States was occurring on the outskirts of central cities. By the 1990s, suburbs housed more than 100 million Americans, and the population in suburbs outnumbered that in central cities by three to two.

City centers still attracted the rural poor and minority groups, because older housing in urban centers was less costly than newer houses in the suburbs and public transport was available. But the middle and upper classes abandoned older urban centers and relocated in suburbs. Here they enjoyed more open environments, larger houses, better schools, greater recreational opportunities, and more privacy. Automobiles had extended what the English historian H.G. Wells called "the magic radius" of the city, and Americans were willing to commute long distances between home and job.

Los Angeles, the archetype of the automobile-oriented urban area, is a metropolitan center where 8.1 million people live in 64 separate municipalities spread over 455 square miles of territory. Between a quarter and a third of the land area in Los Angeles is devoted to the needs of the automobile. Suburban Los Angeles is nearly four times larger than the area enclosed by the city's official incorporated boundaries.

Most city centers are clusters of skyscrapers and high-rise office buildings filled with thousands of workers during the daytime and deserted at night. Mid-city districts were once convenient, pleasant, and busy neighborhoods. Now most of them are places where poor Americans, unable to afford houses in the suburbs, must deal with high crime rates, crowded living conditions, and aging apartment buildings and schools. Incomes are low among most people who live in central cities; incomes are much higher in the suburbs.

The growth of suburbs and the decline of city centers completely transformed America's urban landscapes in the second half

▲ *William Levitt used mass-production techniques to build homes such as these, turning agricultural fields, where land was relatively inexpensive, into suburbs.*

of the twentieth century. It created social and economic divisions within urban populations. It left city centers without enough resources to provide adequate funds to support city school systems, police and fire departments, and other social agencies. Although many efforts at urban renewal have been attempted, few have been able to overcome the economic and social decline generated by the flight to the suburbs.

1. What is a suburb? How does it differ from a city center?
2. If your parents work, describe their daily journey to and from work. Would you be willing to be a commuter?

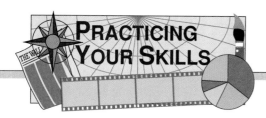

PRACTICING YOUR SKILLS

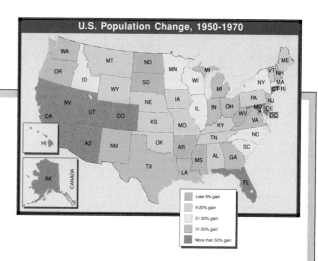

U.S. Population Change, 1950-1970

Loss-5% gain
6-20% gain
21-30% gain
31-50% gain
More than 50% gain

Relating Region and Movement

If you have ever seen the advertisements for Disneyland in California or Disney World in Florida, Sea World in Texas, or the Orange Bowl in Miami, you have seen some results of the sun belt migration.

Although migration is not a new theme in the twentieth century, most previous migration had been from south to north, or from rural areas to urban centers. During World War II and immediately afterward, families followed servicemen around the country. But the nearly 35 percent national gain in population in the three decades following the war was unevenly distributed around the country. The sun belt states gained more than the national average increase in population.

Review the guidelines for reading maps presented in the Practicing Your Skills on page 81. Then answer the following questions about the map on page 833:

1. (a) What is the purpose of this map? (b) What time period does the map cover?
2. (a) According to the map, how many states lost population or showed less than 6% gain in this period? (b) Why does a loss of population mean there must have been very heavy emigration? (c) What might be one explanation for this migration?

3. (a) How many states showed a modest gain in population (6 to 20%)? (b) Why do you think these states also experienced some emigration?
4. List the 11 states that experienced the greatest percentage of growth. In what region(s) are these states located?
5. If you compare the regional location of the states in the three highest categories to the regional location of the states in the three lowest categories, what generalization about population movement or growth can you make?
6. Use the information in the chapter to answer these questions. You may have to make assumptions or inferences, but you should have some facts to support your assumptions.
   (a) What characteristics do the sun belt states have in common? (b) What technological innovations made life in the sun belt more comfortable? (c) Why would the sun belt states have encouraged immigration? (d) How would sun belt immigration affect the balance of political power in the country?

Other minority groups were also moving to the cities. Before World War II, most Mexican Americans had lived in rural areas, but by 1960, 80 percent lived in cities. Los Angeles, Long Beach, El Paso, and Phoenix had major concentrations of Mexican Americans. Chicago, Detroit, Kansas City, and Denver also had large Mexican American communities.

Most newly arrived Puerto Ricans settled in New York City's Spanish Harlem. By 1960, 613,000 Puerto Ricans lived in New York City, more than lived in San Juan, the largest city in Puerto Rico. Puerto Rican immigrants established communities in Chicago, Miami, and other major cities, too.

The proportion of the minority population in the nation's cities increased significantly in the fifties, a pattern continuing into the sixties.

Suburban America

In spite of this movement into the central cities, a far larger population movement actually took place on the suburban fringe between 1950 and 1960. New York City, for example, netted a loss of 2 percent of its population, while the city's suburbs grew by 58 percent. The population of Orange County, California (outside Los Angeles), doubled in the 1940s and tripled again in the 1950s. Similar growth occurred in San Mateo (outside San Francisco), Cook and Du Page counties (outside Chicago), and Prince Georges County (outside Washington, D.C.). During the 1950s, suburbs in general grew six times faster than cities.

While suburbs were not a new phenomenon, the pace and extent of their growth in the 1950s were remarkable.

Federal policies promoted this astonishing suburban growth. The Federal Housing Administration (FHA) begun during the New Deal made it easier for first time buyers to get mortgages. The Veterans Administration (VA) also helped millions of Americans buy homes. Government-backed home mortgages ensured building contractors a stable market. Contractors like William Levitt began to build homes in huge numbers, using mass-production techniques. In New York, New Jersey, and Pennsylvania, Levitt built entire residential suburbs, nicknamed **Levittowns**, almost overnight. He offered home buyers small Cape Cod houses with shuttered windows and steeply pitched roofs. As families of Levitt house buyers grew, these homes were enlarged with additions. The basic Levitt house had only four rooms, but an unfinished second level was designed to be easily made into two more bedrooms. The lots were large by city standards so that adding on first floor rooms and porches was also possible. Moreover, Levitt houses kept their value, a fact doubted by critics at the time.

To keep building costs down, Levitt used ready-made frames and walls, which could be assembled on site by crews of unskilled workers. The new

▼ *Levittown became a model for producing affordable homes quickly. By using precut and preassembled materials, the architect brought down costs. What is one disadvantage of mass-produced housing?*

houses were affordable for the times—$65-a-month payments for a $7,000 house, with stove and refrigerator included. While most building contractors did not produce homes at Levitt's rate, many adopted his techniques. Soon, suburban communities sprang up around cities throughout the nation.

Dependence on Automobiles   In the 1950s, with cheap gasoline and wide open highways, most Americans saw the car as a solution, not a problem. Growing reliance on automobiles had far-reaching effects. Automobiles and highway construction spurred rapid suburban growth. In 1947, Congress authorized 37,000 miles of new roads. In 1956, it funded 90 percent of a new 42,500-mile interstate highway system. (The remaining 10 percent was paid by the various states.) While the federal government encouraged road construction, it largely

▲ *Suburbs often caused congested traffic, as this view of Grand Central Parkway on Long Island suggests.*

▼ *The U.S. interstate highway system changed the landscape of both rural and urban areas. What effects has the interstate system had on your own community?*

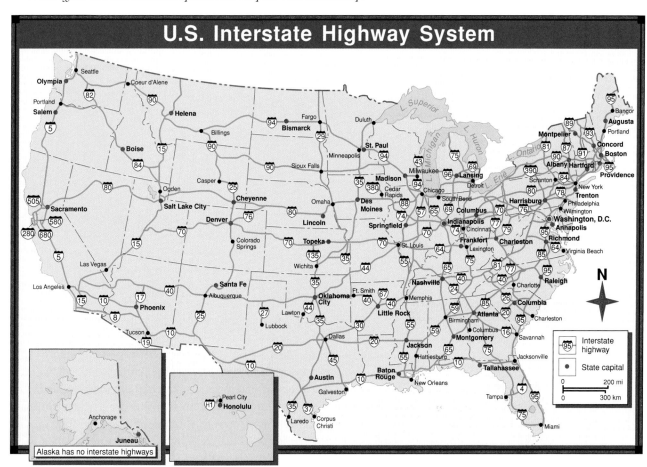

ignored urban public transportation systems. Congress forbade the use of the highway trust funds for improving mass transit. Suburban dwellers soon had few options—they simply had to own a car. Los Angeles, which had had a good mass transit system into the 1940s, became a city of people entirely dependent on the automobile. With two-thirds of all Americans driving to work each day by 1960, it is not surprising that air pollution and traffic congestion began to worsen in metropolitan areas.

Businesses, following potential customers, moved out to the suburbs, too. Plazas and malls, filled with small shops and large chain department stores, became major retail outlets. Suburban consumers were able to find everything they needed close to home, and downtown business districts began to suffer. Access to housing and highways in the suburbs attracted residents, and they, in turn, lured more businesses. Businesses created jobs, and this spurred even more residential development outside the cities.

Many manufacturing industries followed the same pattern. In contrast to such heavy industries as steel and iron production, the new and rapidly growing light industries—electronics, aerospace, chemicals, and R&D firms—did not have to locate near raw materials or rail hubs. These industries could build plants near the suburbs because the expanding highway systems and the growing trucking industry brought raw materials right to their doors. Many suburban communities developed industrial parks—special tracts of land zoned for light industry. As a result, millions of light industrial jobs migrated out of the central cities during the fifties.

SECTION 2 REVIEW

1. **Define** the term *baby boom.*
2. **List** the major causes of the baby boom in the 1950s.
3. **Name** two effects of the baby boom.
4. **Describe** the major trends in migration affecting American society in the 1950s.
5. **Explain** how federal government policy influenced the growth of suburban areas.

SECTION 3

American Social Life

Fortune magazine described the students in the college class of 1949 as "somehow curiously old before their time. Above everything else, security has become their goal. . . . [The class] wants to work for somebody else—preferably somebody big." These were the young adults of the 1950s. Other traits, including political apathy and conformity, distinguished people in the fifties from previous generations. Thornton Wilder, author of the play *Our Town,* called this the "silent generation." There were many reasons for this change in the American character.

What major changes in the American character seemed to occur in the 1950s?

How did the lives of women change during the fifties?

How did the lives of inner-city residents compare to the lives of people in the suburbs?

Two Views of the American Character

Conformity and Consumption Sociologist David Riesman, in *The Lonely Crowd* (1950), argued that the United States had once been a haven for the dissenter, the adventurer, and the free individual. America had promoted new beginnings and diverse ways of life. Americans were the products of hard work, self-denial, and thrift. The inner-directed person had his or her own set of values, and was self-sufficient, individualistic, independent-minded, and nonconformist.

Riesman worried that this American had steadily given way to the "other-directed" person of the modern, urbanized, consumer society. Instead of following their own internal set of values, modern Americans adapted their personality and behavior to match the ideas and lifestyles of their peer group, no matter how often those ideas changed. According to sociologist William Whyte, in *The Organization Man* (1956), "one had to go along to get along." The

▶ *What signs of community life can you identify in this 1949 photograph of a Levittown shopping center?*

worry was that people now succeeded only by conforming to the wishes of others, by avoiding conflict, and by not asserting themselves as individuals.

Critics felt that these "organization men" were the products of the suburbs. Riesman described the impact of the suburbs on American social life: "Today, the worry . . . is conformity: writers point to the uniformity of the ranch style, the ever-present television antennae, the lamp in the picture-window (which usually provides a view of the nearly treeless street, the cars, and someone else's picture-window)." Mass-produced suburbs like Levittown, Pennsylvania, received special criticism. Sociologist Lewis Mumford described the new suburbs as "a multitude of uniform, unidentifiable houses, lined up inflexibly, at uniform distances, on uniform roads, in a treeless communal wasteland, inhabited by people of the same class, the same income, the same age group."

John Keats, author of *Crack in the Picture Window* (1961), complained that the suburbs were "developments conceived in error, nurtured by greed, corroding everything they touch." Keats thought it nearly criminal that picturesque countrysides should be bulldozed for houses or apartments. Sloan Wilson, author of *The Man in the Gray Flannel Suit* (1961), pictured the suburbs as architecturally monotonous, chock-full of children, and settled by rootless, driven adults.

The impact of affluence and growth in advertising also affected the American character. These de-velopments created the compelling desire to "keep up with the Joneses," a phrase that means people felt a need to own the same kind of house, car, and other consumer items as the next person.

McCarthy's anti-Communist crusades also seemed to promote conformity. McCarthyism no doubt increased political apathy and decreased dissent, both characteristic of this generation. Critics bemoaned the level of conformity in American society in the fifties.

Strengthening Family and Community

Other sociologists, such as Herbert Gans and William Dorbriner, believed significant cultural and class diversity could be found in the suburbs. There were wealthy suburbs, such as Winnetka, Illinois; Scarsdale, New York; and Shaker Heights, Ohio. Less affluent people like firefighters, plasterers, and sales clerks moved to suburbs like Levittown. Even the working class had suburbs of its own— Hamtramck, Michigan, or Cicero, Illinois. African Americans also developed suburbs in Lincoln Heights, Ohio; Robbins, Illinois; and Kinlock, Missouri. Life in such places was usually better than in flats or small apartments in the inner city, or in farmhouses in rural America.

Gans believed that the suburbs actually helped to strengthen family life by focusing the family's attention on the home and yard. Moreover, despite

In 1951, Tupperware, a manufacturer of plastic containers and other household items, began marketing its wares in people's homes through Tupperware parties. Would this marketing strategy be as successful today?

the move out of the old neighborhood, family loyalties remained intact, especially among ethnic groups. Visiting patterns showed that family bonds did not break or even show much strain as the younger generation left old inner-city neighborhoods for homes in the suburbs. There was also evidence that traditional political loyalties survived the move to the suburbs, at least at first.

The deep-seated needs of living in a highly mobile society where job transfers were common explain a good deal about the suburbs. In the suburbs, friendship with one's next-door neighbor might only last for two or three years before someone was transferred and had to move away. The suburbs were in constant flux. The average Levittowner moved once every two and one-half years after marriage. In Park Forest, Illinois, one-third of the apartments and one-fifth of the houses had new residents every year.

Voluntary associations and close, if brief, friendships with neighbors provided a way of building a sense of community. The very nature of **suburbia** (all aspects of suburban life) encouraged cooperation. Young families joined together to form car-pools and baby-sitting cooperatives. Parent

organizations made improvements in neighborhood schools and parks. Community-sponsored chili suppers, car washes, and bake sales supported such institutions as Little League, Brownies and Girl Scouts, Cub and Boy Scouts, and many others.

The religious revival that took place in the 1950s can also be explained, in part, by the need to belong. During the 1950s, church membership grew rapidly. By 1960, 64 percent of Americans were church members. Churches in the suburbs became focal points for social activities. Church-sponsored bowling leagues, arts and crafts circles, potluck suppers, choir practices, and other group activities served important social purposes. They supplied many individuals with social outlets and a sense of belonging. Churches provided a source of stability in a mobile and rapidly changing world.

Women in the Suburbs

As women moved to the suburbs in the 1950s, their roles in the family narrowed. Commuter husbands typically left home at daybreak, returning

home in the evening in time to play briefly with the kids. With more husbands commuting long distances to work, time together as a family was short. During the week, the majority of wives focused on cleaning house, driving kids to daily activities, participating in Parent-Teacher Associations (PTAs) and church groups, and passing time with the neighbors. Much of their attention was focused on their families.

Moreover, child rearing became more demanding, even as parents came to rely on experts for advice. Dr. Benjamin Spock's best-selling book, *Baby and Child Care* (1946), sold a million copies a year in the fifties. Spock urged mothers to abandon rigid feeding and baby-care schedules. He recommended that the family be child centered, or focused on the child's needs rather than the parents' needs. While this advice was liberating in one sense, it made child care more demanding than ever before. If mothers needed or wanted to work outside the home, they often felt guilty about "neglecting their maternal responsibilities."

A steady stream of magazine articles, polls, newspaper features, and books promoted the idea that women were, or should be, content with their roles as mothers and housewives. A popular bestseller, *Modern Woman: The Lost Sex* (1947), noted that the *independent woman* was a contradiction in terms. Women could be fulfilled, it claimed, only by devoting themselves to homemaking, pursuing the old arts of canning, preserving, and interior decorating, and making household work an adventure. "Women," another author wrote, "must boldly announce that no job is more exacting, more necessary, or more rewarding than that of housewife and mother."

By the end of the fifties, however, evidence of a variety of issues and problems affecting women was beginning to appear. Statistics show an increase in alcoholism, the use of tranquilizers, and a rise in divorce rates. Popular magazines began to question the wisdom of women who devoted themselves totally to the home. "Once their children have grown," *Life* magazine noted, "a housewife . . . lacking outside interests and training, is faced with vacant years . . . bored stiff with numbing rounds of club meetings and card playing."

Women began to seek jobs outside the home, contradicting the image of women as happy homemakers and housewives. Twice the number of women worked outside the home in 1960 as in 1940. The number of working women with children at home leaped 400 percent—39 percent of mothers with children ages 6 to 17 held jobs by the end of the decade.

Most working women were not pursuing careers or achieving equality in the workplace. Ninety-five percent of all women worked in four job categories: light manufacturing (mostly in home appliances and clothing), retail sales, clerical work, and health and education. High status work within these categories was usually male, and low status work was female. In education in 1960, for example, 90 percent of school principals were male, in spite of the fact that 85 percent of elementary teachers were female. Women's jobs were lower paying, and few offered chances of promotion.

Typically, women were not competing with men for jobs or seeking long careers. The greatest increase in women's employment came among women over 35, who had completed their primary child-rearing responsibilities. Because they were helping the family by earning extra income, their activities were consistent with traditional family norms. Yet these women also enjoyed working outside the home. In one survey, almost two thirds of married women workers referred to their jobs as the basis for feeling important and useful. Only one-third said the same about housekeeping.

In the past, women from lower-income families had made up most of the female workforce. The increase of working women in the 1950s, however, came primarily from married middle-class women or those wanting to be middle-class. By 1960, in over 10 million homes, both the husbands and wives worked. Many families could buy a house, take a vacation, or enjoy other benefits of middle-class status only because of the wife's income.

Problems of the Inner Cities

While many Americans left the inner cities for the suburbs, others did not or could not join this migration. Left behind were working-class white people who could not afford the move, as well as large numbers of minorities. Between 1950 and 1960, 70 percent of the increase in the metropolitan white population occurred in the suburbs. Meanwhile, 81 percent of metropolitan African American population growth took place in the central cities.

Central cities had long provided economic and social opportunities for immigrants and rural migrants. By the time African Americans, Mexican Americans, and Puerto Ricans moved to the cities, however, those places were experiencing rapid

▶ This painting suggested an alienated side of post–World War II city life. (Tooker, George, The Subway, 1950, Egg Tempera on composition board, 18⅛ x 36⅛ in. Collection of Whitney Museum of American Art. Purchase, with funds from the Juliana Force Purchase Award. 50.23. © 1995: Whitney Museum of American Art.)

Expressions of Black Consciousness

During the 1940s and 1950s, African American writers drew on the works of such important writers as W. E. B. DuBois and Harlem Renaissance author Langston

▲ *Richard Wright*

Hughes to define aspects of the black experience and to help develop racial pride. They wrote from the black perspective, exposing the injustices suffered by their race. Along with many others, they have created a body of literature that is unique.

Richard Wright, the "father of the American black novel," inspired a generation of African American writers. His writing focused on the theme of alienation from a dominant culture, and showed how feelings of violence and frustration take hold when a person is forced to act as an inferi-

or being. In *Native Son* (1940), the protagonist, Bigger Thomas, exposes the fear African Americans felt about white justice and the brutal social and economic conditions of life in America's cities.

The experiences of African American women living in urban ghettos were imaginatively depicted in the rhythmic poetry of Gwendolyn Brooks. Brooks was awarded the Pulitzer Prize for *Annie Allen* (1949), a collection of poems about northern urban ghetto living illustrating the concept of "black family" and "community oneness." As time passed, Brooks became increasingly committed to Black Power movements and political empowerment. Through her soul-baring verse, she celebrated the sacrifices of black people from Martin Luther King Jr. to unnamed South African freedom fighters. Her writings inspired a generation of black nationalists.

James Baldwin attempted to

▲ *James Baldwin*

▲ *Gwendolyn Brooks*

"remove all the masks that Americans wear, to strip the country of its self-created illusions, and to speak the simple, often painful truth." Baldwin condemned racism in America on moral grounds. "One cannot deny the humanity of another without diminishing one's own," he wrote. "In the face of one's victim, one sees oneself. Walk through the streets of Harlem and see what we, this nation, have become." This view of the black man as a victim of racism would be further developed in the 1960s by political activists and writers such as Malcolm X and Stokely Carmichael.

———◦◦◦———

1. Name several themes that dominate African American writing in this period.
2. How did Baldwin influence the writings of later political activists?

changes. Good jobs were increasingly difficult to find. Lured to the cities by the prospect of well-paid factory or construction jobs, the new migrants discovered that many of those jobs had moved to the suburbs. Instead of good jobs and economic opportunity, they often faced low-paying, dead-end jobs or unemployment.

Inner-city dwellers also coped with inadequate services. The suburbs drew people and jobs away from the inner cities, and the cities collected less money in taxes. Urban schools did not attract the better teachers, nor could they afford the best materials. Poorly educated inner-city residents found it difficult to compete in the job market, especially for white-collar jobs.

▲ *Many public housing projects were constructed in the 1940s and 1950s. Why did these projects prove to be poor places in which to live?*

Housing had always been a problem for recent arrivals, but the problem worsened in the fifties. Much of the tenement housing built before the fifties had become slums. Only 15 percent of new home construction occurred in inner cities. The federal government's efforts to provide low-cost public housing often hurt as much as helped. When the government built low-cost public housing, it often chose locations far from white neighborhoods. High-rise office buildings, expensive apartments, and some low-income housing projects replaced residences that had formerly housed the poor. As a result, the new immigrants found housing conditions to be even worse than those experienced by earlier immigrant groups.

While a lack of money kept the poor trapped in the inner city, prejudices prevented members of minority groups from moving into the suburbs. Even minorities who held professional jobs had difficulty buying homes in the suburbs. Until the Supreme Court outlawed this practice in *Shelley v. Kramer* (1948), minorities were kept out of many suburban housing developments. Legal housing agreements allowed deeds to contain clauses prohibiting the sale of properties to buyers of certain specified races. Even after the Supreme Court's ruling, many suburbs continued to exclude minorities. In Levittown, for example, homeowners had to sign an agreement that "no dwelling shall be used or occupied by members of other than a Caucasian Race," although the agreement permitted "the employment and maintenance of other than Caucasian domestic servants." Levitt did not sell directly to African Americans until 1960. Even then, he carefully screened minorities so that different races would not live next door to each other. When informal agreements did not keep minorities out, white hostility often did.

SECTION 3 REVIEW

1. **Define** the term *organization man*.
2. **Explain** briefly the changes critics perceived in the American character.
3. **State** two reasons why some sociologists defended the new urban society.
4. **Describe** the major changes experienced by suburban women in the fifties.
5. **Explain** how low-cost housing and urban renewal projects often hurt inner-city residents.

Culture in the Fifties

Americans consumed culture in the fifties much as they consumed other products. In the 15 years after World War II, the number of symphony orchestras in the United States doubled, book sales increased by 250 percent, and art museums appeared in every moderately sized city. Americans spent more of their entertainment dollars going to the theater, museums, and classical concerts than to spectator sporting events. Even so, many intellectuals complained about the popular culture of the fifties. Dwight MacDonald, for example, thought that American culture was bad, and it was getting worse. "[B]ad stuff drives out good, since it is more easily understood and enjoyed." In terms of culture, the fifties had something for everyone.

How did television evolve as an art and entertainment form during the 1950s?

What impact did television have on other forms of entertainment and on popular culture?

How did themes in literature and art reflect concerns about conformity in American society?

Television Captures America's Interest

The 1950s witnessed an astonishing growth in the television industry. Invented in the 1920s, TV did not gain commercial success until after World War II, when advertisers discovered the power of TV. When Hazel Bishop, a lipstick maker, first began TV advertising, the company's annual revenue was $50,000. Two years later, Hazel Bishop's sales had soared to $4.5 million yearly. In 1950, Proctor and Gamble spent only 1.7 percent of its advertising budget on television. A decade later, the company spent 92.6 percent (over $100 million) of its advertising budget on TV. Total TV advertising expenditures increased from $58 million in 1948 to over $1.6 billion in 1960.

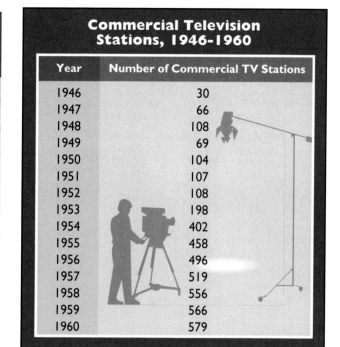

Commercial Television Stations, 1946-1960

Year	Number of Commercial TV Stations
1946	30
1947	66
1948	108
1949	69
1950	104
1951	107
1952	108
1953	198
1954	402
1955	458
1956	496
1957	519
1958	556
1959	566
1960	579

Source: U.S. Department of Commerce, Bureau of the Census.

▲ *The number of commercial television stations grew dramatically between 1946 and 1960.*

To sponsors and network executives larger audiences meant larger profits. To get large audiences, producers generally avoided controversy and appealed to the most common tastes. In fear of offending white southerners the sponsors of *Riverboat*, a TV series based on Mark Twain's *Life on the Mississippi*, imposed a rule forbidding the appearance of African Americans. The fact that African Americans might be offended by the ruling apparently never occurred to the sponsors. Network executives deleted all references to gas in "Judgment at Nuremberg"—a program about the Holocaust and the trials of Nazi war criminals—in order to spare the feelings of the natural gas industry.

Nevertheless, TV offered a wide variety of programming in the 1950s. *Omnibus* was a popular series that carried opera, symphony, ballet, dramatic plays, and real-life adventure films. Financed by the Ford Foundation, *Omnibus* was one of the few programs on commercial TV to have no advertising. *See It Now*, a news program hosted by Edward R. Murrow, was one program that did deal with controversial public issues. *See It Now* was the model for

▲ *Many plots of* The Honeymooners *centered on the "get rich quick" schemes of bus driver Ralph Kramden (Jackie Gleason, left).*

future in-depth television news documentaries. By the end of the decade, variety shows, situation comedies, quiz shows, and drama and Western series dominated TV programming. The *Ed Sullivan Show*, a live variety show, became one of the longest-running prime-time programs in TV history.

From the very beginning, TV programming was criticized. Popular TV host Arthur Godfrey confessed that he almost never watched television. Newton Minnow, future chair of the Federal Communications Commission, called television a "vast wasteland." Even those who watched TV regularly referred to it as "the boob tube."

TV profoundly influenced spectator sports; it transformed athletics into big business. TV favored some sports at the expense of others. Football, for example, was the perfect sport for television, since the games are full of constant movement and suspense. Moreover, the action takes place in a small area, so TV cameras can easily capture it. With an increasing number of viewers and increased revenues, professional football and other sports profited enormously.

Whatever its relative merits, TV altered the shape of American culture. The first frozen dinners, marketed as "TV dinners" in 1954, were designed for families who wanted to gather around the TV set at mealtime. Conversation was hushed as the medium held nearly everyone spellbound. In 1951, high school students were watching an average of 14 hours of television a week. By 1959, they were watching 21 hours. TV helped to foster a national culture, reduced regional differences, and gave people from dissimilar backgrounds a common experience.

Other Forms of Entertainment and Culture

The Movie Industry   As people stayed home to watch TV, no form of entertainment suffered more than motion pictures. Weekly movie attendance plummeted from nearly 100 million in 1946 to 43 million ten years later. The major studios experienced massive financial losses. Hollywood, however, fought back. First, Hollywood increased its efforts to win audiences overseas. This drive was successful, and by 1958, 54 percent of Hollywood's gross revenue came from overseas. Second, the major studios tried to lure customers back with more lavish productions and such innovations as 3-D projection, wide screens, and stereophonic sound. Even so, Hollywood's output of films declined from about 500 to 200 annually between 1946 and 1960.

After some resistance, filmmakers granted television the right to show their recent movies, and they began producing material specially for TV. This fit in with the trend away from live TV programming toward film-based productions. Warner Brothers made TV westerns such as *Cheyenne* and *Maverick*. Desilu, Inc., founded by Lucille Ball and Desi Arnaz, bought an old movie lot and began making *I Love Lucy* and many other filmed TV shows. By 1960, live TV shows were scarce, and a mass exodus of TV industry people from New York City to Hollywood was well under way.

Other outside pressures affected the movie industry. The Justice Department forced the major studios to sell the theater chains they owned to avoid antitrust prosecution. It also ended the practice of "block booking," forcing theaters to take entire packages of films—good, bad, and mediocre. These decisions decreased major studios' profits significantly.

In 1952, the Supreme Court decided that "moving pictures, like newspapers and radio, are included in the press whose freedom is guaranteed by the First Amendment." The Court decreed that "the line between the informing and the entertaining is too elusive for that basic right" to be withheld from movies. The film industry was liberated from the censorship that had existed since the introduction of talking films in the 1920s.

Yet pressures to control movie content continued. Congressional investigations of alleged Communist influence in Hollywood by the House Un-American Activities Committee (HUAC) sent shock waves through the movie industry. Actors and writers accused of "leftist sympathies" were blackballed by nervous studio heads. Self-appointed vigilance groups also carefully scrutinized movie content. As a result, movie content in the late forties and early fifties tended to avoid social issues and political content. At the same time, motion picture content became more sexually explicit and violent.

The Music Industry Music became more widely accessible in the 1950s than ever before. New consumer products, like high-fidelity phonographs and long-playing records, improved the quality of recorded music. The wide variety of musical forms available on records reflected widely different tastes. Indeed, musical tastes were often perceived as being related to social class. It was assumed that the educated elite preferred classical music; lower-class rural dwellers, country and Western; African Americans, rhythm and blues (R & B); the white middle class, Broadway show tunes and big-band swing. Jazz, especially, attracted the musically spirited and daring. Each musical form had separate charts that rated

◄ *James Dean, star of* Rebel Without a Cause, *was one of Hollywood's first antiheroes. What is an antihero?*

record sales and popularity. Rarely did records cross over between different musical categories.

A new musical form revolutionized the music scene in the fifties. In 1951, Cleveland disk jockey Alan Freed observed that white teenagers were buying rhythm and blues records. Freed thought this was notable because most white audiences had previously snubbed R & B, since they associated it with African American musicians. He nevertheless convinced his station manager to air a program called "Moondog's Rock and Roll Party." By renaming R & B "rock and roll" and broadcasting the music in a new format, Freed proved that the music appealed to white audiences. In the next several years, rock and roll grew, as both African American and white groups recorded hits. While African American artists wrote and recorded many popular songs, white musicians scored the best-sellers, often

▲ *African American blues singer Billie Holiday captivated audiences with her love ballads.*

Abstract Expressionism

The effects of war on society are always devastating. When we look at art history, we find that new approaches to making works of art often come about through artists' responses to conflict. This was the case at the end of World War II when European artists fled their war-ravaged homelands. Up to this time, Paris had been the art center of the world. By the late 1940s and 1950s, a style of painting called abstract expressionism emerged, largely in New York City, the destination for most defecting European artists.

Both American-born and European-immigrant artists experimented at this time with media and technique. They tried to simplify images and forms in order to express moods and feelings.

One of the most famous abstract expressionists was Jackson Pollock. Pollock was born in Wyoming and served his artistic apprenticeship with Thomas Hart Benton, a noted landscape artist.

Pollock developed his own style as an abstract expressionist. Rather than using a canvas positioned on a traditional easel, Pollock placed large sheets of canvas on the floor of his studio. He then walked around the perimeter of the canvas, dripping, pouring, and throwing paint on its surface. He believed that traditional strokes of a brush inhibited the artists. The oil and enamel paint would fall at

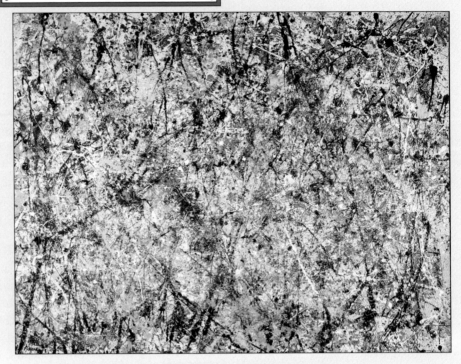

▲ *This painting by Jackson Pollock provides a good example of the artist's use of color and "action painting" style. [* Number 1, 1950 (Lavender Mist) *by Jackson Pollock, Ailsa Mellon Bruce Fund, ©1995 Board of Trustees, National Gallery of Art, Washington.]*

random as it dripped from brushes, sticks, and cans punctured with holes. Pollock "controlled" the paint through the force and direction with which his body moved.

The artist explained how important his physical movements were to the process of painting: "When I am *in* my painting, I'm not aware of what I am doing. It is only after a sort of 'get acquainted' period that I see what I have been about. I have no fears about making changes, destroying the image, etc., because the painting has a life of its own. I try to let it come through. It is only when I lose contact with the painting that the

result is a mess. Otherwise there is pure harmony, an easy give and take, and the painting comes out well."

1. Can throwing or dripping paint on a canvas be considered a technical skill? Why, or why not?
2. List the ways in which Pollock could control the paint with his arms and body.

covering (remaking) songs initially written and recorded by African American artists.

One of the most important figures on the emerging rock scene was Elvis Presley. In late 1955, Elvis signed a recording contract with RCA. Within weeks of recording "Heartbreak Hotel," the song ascended to the top of both the pop and country charts and was in the top five on the R&B chart. Elvis achieved instant popularity, especially with teenagers. He burst onto the scene as a superstar. The repetition of his success with a series of singles and albums made his rise as a star unique.

Elvis demonstrated, perhaps above all else, that teenagers had their own musical tastes. To many adults Elvis looked like a delinquent. He was tough, pouty, and confidently sensual. Most middle-class adults thought his music and stage performances outrageous. Nevertheless, no performer had ever achieved such consistent and gigantic success.

▲ *The legendary Elvis Presley was dubbed "the King" of rock and roll.*

Literature and Art   Rebelling against conformity and yearnings for self-expression were among the major trends in literature and art during the fifties. These themes tied together such otherwise diverse novels as J. D. Salinger's *The Catcher in the Rye* (1951), Saul Bellow's *The Adventures of Augie March* (1949), and Ralph Ellison's *Invisible Man* (1952).

Salinger's protagonist, Holden Caulfield, was a sensitive adolescent bent on preserving his innocence in a world of perverts and phonies who wanted him to conform to their values. Bellow's Augie March revolted against purposelessness and tried to be true to himself. As Augie said, "If you make a move you may lose, but if you sit still you will decay." Everywhere Ellison's nameless hero went, he confronted institutions trying to control his life. A black college president told him that "this is a power set up son, and I'm at the controls." Each of these characters was fearful and confused, buffeted by larger forces beyond his control. Even so, each hero-

ically refused to surrender, and this was the key to his survival.

"Beat" poets like Allen Ginsberg and Lawrence Ferlinghetti attacked the materialism and phoniness of 1950s middle-class life. In *On the Road* (1957), novelist Jack Kerouac portrayed hobos, prostitutes, drug addicts, alcoholics, and minority group members as heroic. For Kerouac, these were "real people," because they had escaped the drabness of middle-class life. The seeming hollowness and injustice of American life offended the Beats. Yet they proposed no remedies and despaired at the prospect of social reform. Instead, they dropped out of society and drifted about the country, seeking their own inner peace.

Great diversity and individualism also characterized American visual art in the fifties. World War II had brought new influences to American painting, as dozens of European artists had emigrated in the thirties and forties to escape fascism. These artists represented every major modern movement in art. In the United States, they painted, exhibited, and taught, and thus they touched off a movement among their American disciples called **abstract expressionism**. In abstract expressionism, the artists sought to convey their innermost feelings without reference to physical objects or common forms. Rather, they used the canvas to express themselves, often as abstractly as possible.

SECTION 4 REVIEW

1. **Explain** why television came to dominate entertainment in the United States.
2. **Describe** the effect of television on other forms of entertainment.
3. **List** conditions that spurred growth in the music industry.
4. **Identify** Jack Kerouac.
5. **Characterize** the major trend in abstract art.

Summary

For many Americans, the fifties was a time of almost unlimited possibilities. Economic prosperity reached more people than ever before in U.S. history. Many Americans could purchase homes, cars, and other consumer items. They could also afford more travel, recreation, entertainment, and culture. By the end of the decade, over 60 percent of Americans enjoyed a middle-class standard of living. In 10 million families, working mothers made this middle-class lifestyle possible.

The booming economy was both the cause and the effect of astonishing changes in the population. The baby boom and improved health care resulted in rapid population growth, and this, in turn, promoted prosperity. Affluence encouraged millions to migrate from region to region in search of a better life. Affluence also attracted a growing number of immigrants to the United States.

Behind this rosy picture, however, the harsh truth remained that a better job and life eluded some Americans. Members of minority groups, women, or those left behind in the inner cities had less chance of finding good jobs than most white males. The best-paying jobs were increasingly in professional, technical, and white-collar professions. The education and training required for such jobs was often not available to those living in inner cities or rural areas. Many Americans lacked opportunities available to members of the white middle class. Growing awareness of these and other problems would usher in a new era of social reform in the 1960s.

Television changed forever the way Americans spent time and money. Motion pictures tended to avoid dealing with social and political issues. With the widespread popularity of record players and radios, music was accessible to more people than ever before. Literature and art reflected the dissatisfaction of many with the materialism and conformity of the decade.

Vocabulary

abstract expressionism
agribusiness
baby boom
consumer culture

planned obsolescence
postindustrial economy
suburbia
sun belt

On your paper, write each vocabulary term followed by the name or phrase found below that correctly identifies or explains it.

1. Jackson Pollock
2. population explosion following World War II
3. key states of the South and Southwest
4. designing items to wear out quickly
5. service-oriented economy
6. the culture involved in living on the outskirts of major cities
7. society that values buying more than saving
8. large corporate-run farms

Review Questions

1. How did the Great Depression influence American society in the postwar years?
2. Describe the changes in the nature of work during the fifties.
3. How did agriculture change during this period?
4. Why did minorities find it difficult to share in the economic prosperity of the fifties?
5. What were the major reasons for the rapid movement to the suburbs in the fifties?
6. What was Riesman's view of the American character during the 1950s?
7. Explain how the constant movement and flux in the suburbs changed American life.
8. What were two ways that social changes in the fifties affected the lives of women?
9. Name two ways television changed American patterns of behavior.
10. How was rock and roll different from most earlier forms of popular music?

Critical Historical Thinking

Writing Answer each of the following by writing one or more complete paragraphs:

1. Does your view of the American character of the fifties more closely match Riesman's or Gans's view? In what specific ways do you support this view?

2. The fifties are often referred to as "the good old days." Were they really that good, or is America better off today? Justify your answer.

3. Is television today still a force for creating a common culture? Or does television act to fragment society? Explain your answer.

4. Read the selection entitled "In the Cities, People Were Doing Things" in the Unit 8 Archives. Describe the change that had taken place in the author's life since he had moved to Long Island.

Making Connections with Art

The Great Depression and World War II left lasting marks on the generations that lived through them. For middle-class Americans, the 1950s became a celebration of affluence and conformity.

But for American artists, the 1950s marked the emergence of New York City as the Western world's capital of experimental art, replacing Paris. At the center of this shift from Europe to America were the abstract expressionists—artists such as Jackson Pollock, Mark Rothko, Robert Motherwell, Willem De Kooning, Barnett Newman, Adolph Gottlieb, and Franz Kline. They expressed their individual feelings and state of mind with their art.

Abstract expressionists did not share a common style of painting. They did share a mutual belief in art as the expression of individual emotional experience. They stopped painting natural images and forms, such as the human body, in favor of creating a visual environment in which the viewer could participate.

Writing Locate books on modern art in your library. Look up the works of the artists mentioned above, as well as Marc Chagall, or Piet Mondrian. Choose either expressionism, cubism, surrealism, or abstract expressionism. Select your favorite artist, and write a report on his or her work or school of painting.

Additional Skills Practice

Use the following data to create a map that updates regional population movement from 1980 to 1990. Remember to give your map a title and a key. Based on your map, what generalization can you make about the trend begun in the early 1950s of migration to the sun belt states?

State	% Change 1980–90	State	% Change 1980–90
AK	+36.9	NV	+50.1
AZ	+34.8	NH	+20.5
CA	+25.7	NJ	+5.0
CO	+14.0	NM	+16.3
CT	+5.8	NC	+12.7
DE	+12.1	OR	+7.9
FL	+32.7	RI	+5.9
GA	+18.6	SC	+11.7
HI	+14.9	TN	+6.2
ID	+6.7	TX	+19.4
ME	+9.2	UT	+17.9
MD	+13.4	VT	+10.0
MN	+7.3	VA	+15.7
		WA	+17.8
		WV	-8.0

Less than 5% change: AL, AR, IL, IN, IA, KS, KY, LA, MA, MI, MS, MO, MT, NE, NY, ND, OH, OK, PA, SD, WI, WY.

Unit 8 Review

Unit Review Questions

1. Explain why the attack on Pearl Harbor was a major strategic error made by Japan.
2. How did Hitler's decision to attack Russia help lead to Germany's defeat in World War II?
3. What caused the lack of cooperation among the Allies as the war drew to a close?
4. How were some women and minorities in the U.S. penalized after the end of the war?
5. Briefly describe the rise of the Cold War during the 1950s.
6. What key Supreme Court decision seemed to kick off many grassroots civil rights movements?
7. Why did Eisenhower fail in his goals to limit the role of government and cut taxes?
8. Describe the effect of the 1950s economy on the typical white, middle-class American family.
9. What specific Soviet actions after World War II worried the United States?
10. Describe the military organization formed by the U.S. and its allies after World War II to combat Soviet aggression.

Personalizing History

The Great Appliance Sacrifice   The American economy prospered after World War II, and American families were able to purchase goods that were once available only to the wealthy. Middle-class homes now had refrigerators, electric toasters, clothes washers and dryers, as well as irons and televisions. Make a list of the appliances used every day at your house.

■ Rank the appliances according to their importance to you. Could you live without them? Try

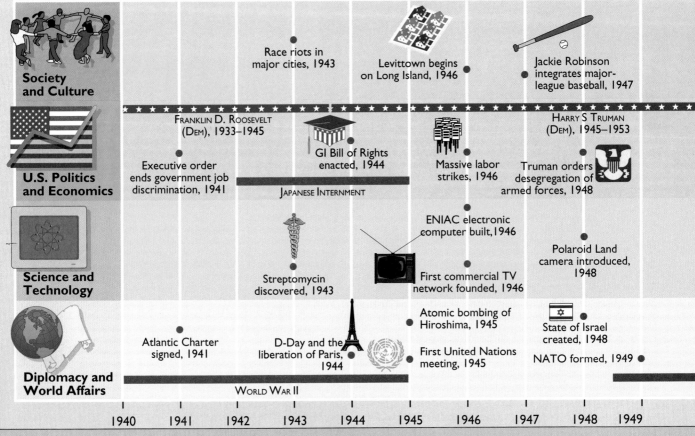

Society and Culture

Race riots in major cities, 1943

Levittown begins on Long Island, 1946

Jackie Robinson integrates major-league baseball, 1947

U.S. Politics and Economics

FRANKLIN D. ROOSEVELT (DEM), 1933–1945

HARRY S TRUMAN (DEM), 1945–1953

Executive order ends government job discrimination, 1941

GI Bill of Rights enacted, 1944

JAPANESE INTERNMENT

Massive labor strikes, 1946

Truman orders desegregation of armed forces, 1948

Science and Technology

ENIAC electronic computer built, 1946

Polaroid Land camera introduced, 1948

Streptomycin discovered, 1943

First commercial TV network founded, 1946

Diplomacy and World Affairs

Atomic bombing of Hiroshima, 1945

State of Israel created, 1948

Atlantic Charter signed, 1941

D-Day and the liberation of Paris, 1944

First United Nations meeting, 1945

NATO formed, 1949

WORLD WAR II

1940 1941 1942 1943 1944 1945 1946 1947 1948 1949

an experiment. Spend one 24-hour day without using any of the appliances on your list. See if your family will participate. Report back to the class on your success. Which appliance was the hardest to live without? Was it the television, microwave, or was it your hair dryer? What did you do with your time without the telephone or television? Were some students not willing to give up an appliance? Why?

Linking Past and Present

Advice from a First Lady   First Lady Hillary Clinton has become an active participant in her husband's administration. She has spoken of her ad-miration for First Lady Eleanor Roosevelt, the first wife of a president to take an active role in shaping public policy. Eleanor Roosevelt offered advice on social issues and sometimes represented the presi-

dent. The first lady also had a career of her own. She wrote a newspaper column and spoke on the radio. If Eleanor Roosevelt were alive today, what advice would she have for the current first lady?

■ Find out more about Eleanor Roosevelt, then write a letter to the current first lady. Pretend you are Mrs. Roosevelt, and share your insights into the responsibilities of the job of serving as first lady. What do you think are the advantages and disad-vantages of your role as an unofficial adviser to the president?

Time Line Activity

Use the time line to trace the roots and growth of the civil rights movement between 1940 and 1960. List at least five items in chronological order and explain the significance of each one.

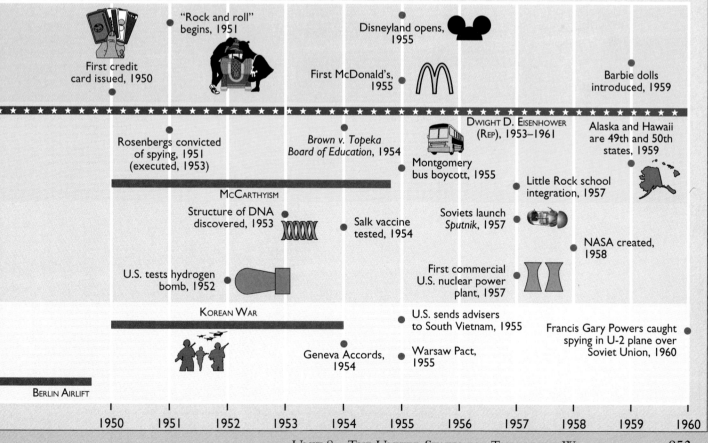

First credit card issued, 1950

"Rock and roll" begins, 1951

Disneyland opens, 1955

First McDonald's, 1955

Barbie dolls introduced, 1959

Rosenbergs convicted of spying, 1951 (executed, 1953)

Brown v. Topeka Board of Education, 1954

DWIGHT D. EISENHOWER (REP), 1953–1961

Alaska and Hawaii are 49th and 50th states, 1959

Montgomery bus boycott, 1955

Little Rock school integration, 1957

McCARTHYISM

Structure of DNA discovered, 1953

Salk vaccine tested, 1954

Soviets launch Sputnik, 1957

NASA created, 1958

U.S. tests hydrogen bomb, 1952

First commercial U.S. nuclear power plant, 1957

KOREAN WAR

U.S. sends advisers to South Vietnam, 1955

Geneva Accords, 1954

Warsaw Pact, 1955

Francis Gary Powers caught spying in U-2 plane over Soviet Union, 1960

BERLIN AIRLIFT

1950 1951 1952 1953 1954 1955 1956 1957 1958 1959 1960

UNIT 9

A Nation in Torment

As the 1960s began, a young president noted that leadership in the United States had passed to a new generation, born in the twentieth century. He called upon his fellow citizens to bear any burden in order to help explore new frontiers and to achieve the nation's highest ideals. By the end of the decade, however, the nation appeared to many Americans to be "coming apart at the seams." The idealism tapped and nurtured by President Kennedy seemed all but dead by 1968. The nation was beset with problems: political assassinations, war in Vietnam, ghetto riots, and a fragmented civil rights movement. Lyndon Johnson's War on Poverty and Great Society became victims of their own excesses and of the Vietnam War.

Chapter 27	Chapter 28	Chapter 29
John F. Kennedy and the New Frontier	The Great Society and Vietnam	Coming Apart

◀ *Jasper Johns, whose painting* Device *(1961–62) is shown here, and Robert Rauschenberg were probably the most important American artists of the generation after the abstract expressionists.* (Device, *by Jasper Johns, 1961–1962, oil on canvas with wood, H:72″ x W:48⅓″ x D:4½″, Dallas Museum of Art/©1995 Jasper Johns/Licensed by VAGA, New York, New York.*)

Themes

- **Democracy and Citizenship** The political consensus of the 1950s splintered in the 1960s as the Vietnam War divided America. Minority groups, women, and youth challenged authority and demanded full and equal participation in the American dream.
- **Multicultural Society** The grassroots civil rights movement, begun in earnest in the 1950s, reached its peak in the 1960s. It began to break down as younger, more militant activists began demanding even more rapid changes.
- **Global Interactions** The decade of the 1960s began with a president's calling on his people to bear any burden in the pursuit of freedom around the world. By the end of the decade, in the wake of a frustrating war in Vietnam, Americans had tired of bearing that burden.

Letter from Birmingham Jail

In the spring of 1963, the Reverend Martin Luther King Jr. went to Birmingham, Alabama, to join in massive demonstrations to secure African American civil rights. King was jailed, along with many others, for his actions. There he wrote a letter to eight clergymen who had criticized his activities.

I am in Birmingham because injustice is here. . . . Injustice anywhere is a threat to justice everywhere. We are caught in an inescapable network of mutuality, tied in a single garment of destiny. Whatever affects one directly, affects all indirectly. Never again can we afford to live with the narrow, provincial 'outside agitator' idea. Anyone who lives inside the United States can never be considered an outsider anywhere within its bounds.

You deplore the demonstrations taking place in Birmingham. But your statement, I am sorry to say, fails to express a similar concern for the conditions that brought about the demonstrations. . . . It is unfortunate that demonstrations are taking place in Birmingham, but it is even more unfortunate that the city's white power structure left the Negro community with no alternative. . . . We know from painful experience that freedom is never voluntarily given by the oppressor, it must be demanded by the oppressed. . . . For years now I have heard the word 'wait!' It rings in the ear of every Negro with piercing familiarity. This 'Wait!' has almost always meant 'Never.'

You express a great deal of anxiety over our willingness to break laws. . . . One may well ask: 'How can you advocate breaking some laws and obeying others?' The answer lies in the fact that there are two types of laws; just and unjust. I would be the first to advocate obeying just laws. One has not only a legal but a moral responsibility to obey just laws. Conversely, one has a moral responsibility to disobey unjust laws. I would agree with St. Augustine that 'an unjust law is no law at all.'

You speak of our activity in Birmingham as extreme. At first I was rather disappointed that fellow clergymen would see my nonviolent efforts as those of an extremist. . . . I have tried to stand between these two forces, saying that we need emulate neither the 'do-nothingism' of the complacent nor the hatred and despair of the black nationalist. For there is the more excellent way of love and nonviolent protest.

 Martin Luther King, "Letter from Birmingham Jail," *Why We Can't Wait* (New York: Harper and Row, 1963).

◄ *Birmingham, Alabama, May 1963*

Kennedy Without Tears

Following John Kennedy's death in 1963, journalist Tom Wicker reviewed the slain president's accomplishments through two of Kennedy's own self-assessments.

There is a limitation upon the ability of the United States to solve these problems . . . there is a limitation, in other words, upon the power of the United

States to bring about solutions. . . . The responsibilities placed on the United States are greater than I imagined them to be and there are greater limitations upon our ability to bring about a favorable result than I had imagined them to be. . . . It is much easier to make the speeches than it is finally to make the judgments. . . .

There is no sense in raising hell and then not being successful. There is no sense in putting the office of the presidency on the line on an issue and then being defeated.

Tom Wicker, "Kennedy Without Tears," *Esquire* (June 1964), pp. 108 ff.

Johnson's Public Honeymoon

Lyndon Johnson realized that the mandate he received in the 1964 election would not last very long. At the end of January 1965, shortly after he'd been inaugurated, he called a meeting of various department heads.

Look, I've just been elected and right now we'll have a honeymoon with Congress. With the additional congressmen that have been elected, I'll have a good chance to get my program through. . . . But after I make my recommendations, I'm going to start to lose the power and authority I have, because that's what happened to President Woodrow Wilson, to President Roosevelt, and to Truman and to Kennedy. . . . Every day that I'm in office and every day that I push my program, I'll be losing part of my ability to be influential, because that's in the nature of what the president does. He uses up his capital. Something is going to come up, either something like the Vietnam War or something else where I will begin to lose all that I have now.

So I want you guys to do everything possible to get everything in my program passed as soon as possible, before the aura and the halo that surround me disappear . . . don't waste a second.

Merle Miller, *Lyndon: An Oral Biography* (New York: G.P. Putnam Sons, 1980).

General Westmoreland Asks for More Troops, 1965

General William Westmoreland discussed the declining military situation in South Vietnam.

The South Vietnamese battlefield strength is declining in the face of North Vietnamese reinforcements and a Viet Cong offensive. It is my considered opinion that the South Vietnamese Armed Forces cannot stand up to this pressure without substantial U.S. combat support on the ground.

Thus, we are approaching the kind of warfare faced by the French in the latter stages of their efforts here. It is entirely possible that the North Vietnamese can and will deploy three or more divisions into South Vietnam by infiltration. It is highly likely that one is already here.

A top secret cable from General William Westmoreland (June 14, 1965).

Three Views on Vietnam

Vice President Humphrey Urges Caution

As President Johnson considered his options in Vietnam, Vice President Hubert Humphrey urged caution.

Some things are beyond our power to prevent. . . . American wars have to be politically understandable by the American people. There has to be a cogent, convincing case if we are to enjoy sustained public support. . . . The public is worried and confused. Our rationale for action has shifted away now even from the notion that we are there as advisers on request of a free government, to the simple and politically barren argument of our 'national interest.' We have not succeeded in making this national interest interesting enough at home or abroad to generate support. The arguments in fact are probably too complicated (or too weak) to be politically useful or effective. . . . People can't understand why we would run grave risks to support a country which is totally unable to put its own house in order. The chronic instability in Saigon directly undermines American political support for our policy.

Hubert H. Humphrey, *The Education of a Public Man* (New York: Doubleday and Company, 1976) pp. 322–323.

▲ *Ground troops in Vietnam*

Clark Clifford Opposes Sending U.S. Ground Forces to Vietnam

In 1965, Clifford offered Johnson this advice. Three years later, he replaced Robert McNamara as secretary of defense.

I wish to make one major point. I believe our ground forces in South Vietnam should be kept to a minimum. . . . My concern is that a substantial buildup of U.S. ground troops would be construed by the Communists, and by the world, as a determination on our part to win the war on the ground. This could be a quagmire. . . . I do not think the situation is comparable to Korea. The political posture of the parties involved, and the physical conditions, including terrain, are entirely different. I continue to believe that the constant probing of every avenue leading to a possible settlement will ultimately be fruitful. It won't be what we want, but we can learn to live with it.

A letter from Clark Clifford to President Johnson (May 17, 1965), Lyndon Baines Johnson Library.

Johnson Asserts His War Aims in Vietnam

On April 7, 1965, President Johnson gave a speech detailing his reasons for increasing U.S. involvement in Vietnam.

Why are we in South Vietnam?

We are there because we have a promise to keep. Since 1954 every American president has offered support to the people of South Vietnam. . . . Thus, over many years, we have made a national pledge to help South Vietnam defend its independence.

And I intend to keep that promise.

To dishonor that pledge, to abandon this small and brave nation to its enemies, and to the terror that must follow, would be an unforgivable wrong.

We are also there to strengthen world order. . . . To leave Vietnam to its fate would shake the confidence of all these people [in nations with defense alliances with the U.S.] in the value of an American commitment and in the value of America's word. The result would be increased unrest and instability, and even wider war.

We are also there because there are great stakes in the balance. Let no one think for a moment that retreat from Vietnam would bring an end to conflict. The battle would be renewed in one country and then another. The central lesson of our time is that the appetite of aggression is never satisfied.

Public Papers of the Presidents of the United States: Lyndon B. Johnson (Washington, D.C.: Archives and Records).

I Was Bound to Be Crucified

After President Johnson retired from office, he consented to extended interviews with Doris Kearns about his life.

I knew from the start that I was bound to be crucified either way I moved. If I left . . . the Great Society in order to get involved with that . . . war on the other side of the world, then I would lose everything at home. But if I left that war and let the Communists take over South Vietnam, then I would be seen as a coward and my nation would be seen as an appeaser.

▲ *President Lyndon B. Johnson*

Once the war began, then all those conservatives in the Congress would use it as a weapon against the Great Society . . . Yet everything I knew about history told me that if I got out of Vietnam . . . then I'd be doing exactly what [British Prime Minister] Chamberlain did in World War II. I'd be giving a big fat reward to aggression. And I knew that if we let Communist aggression succeed in taking over South Vietnam, there would follow in this country an endless national debate—a mean and destructive debate—that would shatter my presidency, kill my administration, and damage our democracy.

Doris Kearns, *Lyndon Johnson and the American Dream* (New York: Signet, New American Library, 1976), pp. 263–264.

The Kerner Commission Reports on Civil Disorders

President Johnson established the Kerner Commission to study the circumstances and causes of race riots in American cities.

White racism is essentially responsible for the explosive mixture which has been accumulating in our cities since the end of World War II. Among the ingredients of this mixture are: *Pervasive discrimination and segregation* in employment, education, and housing, which have resulted in the continuing exclusion of great numbers of Negroes from the benefits of economic progress. *Black in-migration and white exodus*, which have produced the massive and growing concentrations of impoverished Negroes in our major cities, creating a growing crisis of deteriorating facilities and services and unmet human needs. *The Black ghettos*, where segregation and poverty converge on the young to destroy opportunity and enforce failure. Crime, drug addiction, dependency on welfare, and bitterness and resentment against society in general and white society in particular are the result.

Report of the National Advisory Commission on Civil Disorders (Washington, D.C.: GPO, 1968), pp. 3–5, 7, 10–11.

▼ *Watts riot, 1965*

Malcolm X Advocates Bolder Action

Malcolm X urged young African American activists to take bold action to secure their freedom.

I myself would go for nonviolence if it was consistent, if everybody was going to be nonviolent all the time. I'd say, okay, let's get with it, we'll all be nonviolent . . . But as long as you've got somebody else not being nonviolent, I don't want anybody coming to me

◄ *Malcolm X*

talking any nonviolent talk. . . . You get your freedom by letting your enemy know that you'll do anything; then you'll get it. It's the only way you'll get it. When you get that attitude, they'll label you a 'crazy Negro' . . . or they'll call you an extremist or a subversive . . . But when you stay radical long enough, and get enough people to be like you, you'll get your freedom. . . . So don't you run around here trying to make friends with somebody who's depriving you of your rights. They're not your friends, no, they're your enemies. Treat them like that and fight them, and you'll get your freedom.

George Breitman, ed., *Malcolm X Speaks* (1966).

We Are a Proud People

In November 1969, American Indian activists occupied Alcatraz Island to call attention to Indian problems.

We are a proud people! We are Indians! We have observed and rejected much of what so-called civilization offers. We are Indians! We will preserve our traditions and ways of life by educating our own children. We are Indians! We will join hands in a unity never before put into practice. Our Earth Mother awaits our voices. We are Indians of all Tribes!!!

We came to Alcatraz because we were sick and tired of being pushed around, exploited, and degraded everywhere we turned in our own country. . . . Before we took Alcatraz . . . people across the nation . . . never even knew that Indians were alive or ever even knew our problems. They never knew anything about our suicide rate that is ten times the national average, or our education level that is to the fifth grade. Alcatraz focused on the Indian people. Now the Indian people

▼ *Occupation of Alcatraz, 1969*

have a chance for the first time to say what they have to say and to make decisions about themselves, which has never happened before.

...We feel that the island is the only bargaining power that we have with the federal government. It is the only way we have to get them to notice us or even want to deal with us. We are going to maintain our occupation ... Otherwise, they will forget us, the way they always have, but we will not be forgotten.

Congressional Record, 91st Cong. 2nd Sess.

A Full Tribalizing Process

Vine Deloria, a Standing Rock Sioux, made the following observations about Indians in the late 1960s.

The message of the traditionalists is simple. They demand a return to basic Indian philosophy, establishment of ancient methods of government by open councils instead of elected officials, a revival of Indian religions and replacement of white laws with Indian customs; in short, a complete return to the ways of the old people. In an age dominated by tribalizing communications media, their message makes a great deal of sense.

Knowing the importance of tribal survival, Indian people are speaking more and more of sovereignty, of the great political technique of the open council, and of the need for gaining the community's consensus on all programs before putting them into effect.

Indian people have managed to maintain a viable and cohesive social order in spite of everything the non-Indian society has thrown at them in an effort to break the tribal structure. At the same time, non-Indian society has created a monstrosity of a culture where people starve while the granaries are filled and the sun can never break through the smog. ... It just seems to a lot of Indians that this continent was a lot better off when we were running it.

Vine Deloria Jr., "This Country Was a Lot Better Off When the Indians Were Running It," *New York Times Magazine* (Mar. 3, 1970).

A New Kind of Woman

Journalist Caroline Bird discovered that between 1966 and 1970 "a new kind of woman" had appeared on the American scene.

But the most startling innovation since 1966 was the appearance of a new kind of woman, more alien to American tradition than the flapper of the 1920s, the man-suited career spinster of the 1930s, or the Rosie who riveted the bombers in World War II. Virtually nonexistent in 1966, the new, liberated women could be found on every college campus and in every sizable American city in 1970.

The American women she most resembles is the politically alert, fiercely autonomous, and sometimes man-hating suffragette who had won the vote for women at the end of World War I by militant hunger strikes and street demonstrations. ... Well-educated, privileged, ... she is, in addition, idealistic, intense but soft-spoken, and she is furious. ... They want what

▼ *Women's liberation demonstration, 1970*

every feminist of history with a grain of political sense has always denied wanting. 'If we draft women, who will do the housework?' a World War I congressman asked, and none of the fire breathing suffragettes dared to say, 'Why not you, sir?'

Caroline Bird, *Born Female: The High Cost of Keeping Women Down* (New York: David McKay Company, 1968, 1970).

black family's stability problem will disappear and more black women will be able to give first priority to the elimination of oppression because of sex.

Renee Ferguson, "Women's Liberation Has a Different Meaning for Blacks," *The Washington Post* (Oct. 3, 1970).

Women's Liberation Has a Different Meaning for Blacks

Women's movements created dilemmas for women of all races.

The women's liberation movement touches some sensitive nerves among black women—but they are not always the nerves the movement seems to touch among so many whites. . . . Vastly differing attitudes raise a real question about the extent to which the women's liberation movement means very much to black women. . . . Perhaps the lack of involvement of black women in the women's liberation movement can best be explained in terms of priorities. . . . Obviously the first priority of virtually all black people is the elimination of racial prejudice in America—in effect the liberation of black people. Second in importance is the black family problem of establishing a decent way of life in America as it exists today. When racism in America is eliminated, then perhaps the

The New American Revolution Has Begun

A French journalist observed that the United States had produced a revolutionary invention—dissent.

The 'hot' issues in America's insurrection against itself, numerous as they are, form a cohesive and coherent whole within which no one issue can be separated from the others. . . . None of the groups concerned with any one of these points, and none of the points themselves, would have been able to gain as much strength and attention as they have if they had been isolated from other groups and other points. The blacks and the feminists . . . (along with students, of course) have always been most strongly opposed to the Vietnam War.

Jean-Francois Revel, *Without Marx or Jesus: The New American Revolution Has Begun* (New York: Doubleday, 1971).

WORKING WITH THE ARCHIVES

Using a Matrix to Analyze Primary Source Materials

Generally, it is not enough for historians just to know what individuals believed or what actions they took. Historians also need to know the reasoning, motivation, or logic behind the opinions and actions. Often, it is necessary to look carefully in primary source materials for clues that will help identify those attitudes.

A special type of chart known as a *matrix* is a very useful tool for analyzing documents. A matrix is simply a rectangular arrangement of elements into rows and columns. This arrangement allows for the systematic recording and comparison of data. An example is shown below.

Matrix			
	Issue Statement	**Beliefs and Actions**	**Reasons for Beliefs or Actions**
Johnson			
Humphrey			
Clifford			

Directions:

1. Read the archive selections entitled "Vice President Humphrey Urges Caution," "Clark Clifford Opposes Sending U.S. Ground Forces to Vietnam," and "Johnson Asserts His War Aims in Vietnam."

2. On a separate sheet of paper, create a matrix that will help you complete the steps below:

   a. Identify in one concise statement the general position of Johnson, Humphrey, and Clifford on the issue of escalating the Vietnam War.

   b. List the various beliefs and opinions for Johnson, Humphrey, and Clifford that support the position taken above.

   c. Explain briefly why Johnson, Humphrey, and Clifford took the positions they did on escalation. What was the reasoning or logic behind their beliefs?

3. Use the completed matrix to write a brief essay that summarizes the reasons why Johnson, Humphrey, and Clifford held the opinions they did.

John F. Kennedy and the New Frontier

The return of the Democrats to the White House in 1961 marked the beginning of a new era in American politics. John Fitzgerald Kennedy's election symbolized the rise to power of a new generation of leaders born in the twentieth century. One of Kennedy's main goals was "to get the country moving again" after the presumed inaction of President Eisenhower. In foreign affairs, Kennedy shared Eisenhower's desire to limit Communist influence in the Third World. But his approach would be more aggressive than Eisenhower's had been. For example, Kennedy called for increases in defense spending and wanted more combat troops

▲ *Many people believe that John F. Kennedy was elected president, at least in part, because of his youth and charm. This campaign badge illustrates both traits.*

to fight wars against Communist revolutionaries. Kennedy also wanted to promote Third World economic development through such new programs as the Peace Corps and the Alliance for Progress. Kennedy's record in foreign affairs was a mixture of successes and failures. This was also true of his domestic programs. He promised bold action to promote African American civil rights and to solve the nation's poverty, but Congress proved unwilling to pass many of his proposals. Nevertheless, by the time of his assassination in late 1963, Kennedy had given many Americans a sense that the nation was, in fact, moving again.

A New Generation in Charge

"Let the word go forth," John F. Kennedy (JFK) announced in his inaugural address, "that the torch has been passed to a new generation of Americans—born in this century, tempered by war, disciplined by a hard and bitter peace, proud of our ancient heritage." Much as Theodore Roosevelt had in his era, JFK appealed strongly to Americans who believed they could solve the problems they saw around them. These people had renewed hope that they could help create a better world. Young people especially had a sense of urgency about pursuing these ideals. In John Kennedy, they felt they had found an inspiring leader.

What were the major issues in the election of 1960?
What effects did the first televised presidential debates have on the election's outcome?
How did Eisenhower's and Kennedy's cabinets and leadership styles compare?

The Election of 1960

Few fathers groom their sons to be president of the United States. Joseph Kennedy was one of those few. He was determined to make one of his sons president. After his oldest son, Joseph Jr., died in World War II, Joseph Sr.'s attention turned to John. John had attended an elite prep school and then Harvard University. During World War II, he became a war hero as the commander of a PT (patrol torpedo) boat in the Pacific. In 1946, he was elected to the House of Representatives, and six years later, became a senator from Massachusetts. During his years in Congress he wrote *Profiles in Courage* (1956), a Pulitzer Prize–winning book on American political leadership. In 1960, he won the Democratic Party's nomination for president.

In his speech accepting the nomination, Kennedy declared that "we stand today on the edge of a New Frontier—the frontier of the 1960s—a frontier of unknown opportunities and perils—a frontier of unfulfilled hopes and threats." Kennedy's **New Frontier** program promised a strong stand on behalf of civil rights, medical insurance for the elderly, conservation of natural resources and environmental protection, and the expansion of federal programs for urban areas, among other items.

In his campaign, Kennedy hit the Eisenhower administration hard on the issues of defense, foreign policy, and the sluggish economy. Kennedy charged that America's superior military strength had been lost during Eisenhower's two terms. He claimed that the Soviets had surged ahead in the production of long-range missiles, creating what he called a **missile gap** between the two superpowers. The Soviet advantage in missile strength, he claimed, helped explain their increased boldness in supporting Communist revolutionaries in the Third World (commonly referred to as less developed countries). Kennedy pledged to restore America's military lead and to use greater force in resisting Communist expansion throughout the world. Kennedy also criticized Eisenhower's economic record, pointing out that three severe recessions had occurred during Eisenhower's two terms. Kennedy promised to get the economy moving again.

Religion was an important issue in the 1960 election. Because the United States was a predominantly Protestant country, many people assumed that a Roman Catholic like Kennedy could not be elected president. Kennedy decided to meet the issue head on. In September, he traveled to Houston to address a national group of Protestant ministers. He assured his listeners that he believed in the strict separation of church and state, opposed federal aid to parochial schools, and denounced religious intolerance of all kinds. Most people opposed to Kennedy on religious grounds were persuaded to drop their opposition to his candidacy.

Richard Nixon, Eisenhower's vice president, earned the Republican Party's nomination. As the campaign unfolded, there was really little difference between the candidates on most issues. Personalities probably played a greater role than issues in the election. Because of his visibility as vice president,

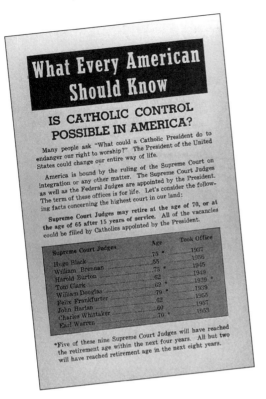

What Every American Should Know

IS CATHOLIC CONTROL POSSIBLE IN AMERICA?

Many people ask "What could a Catholic President do to endanger our right to worship?" The President of the United States could change our entire way of life.

America is bound by the ruling of the Supreme Court on integration or any other matter. The Supreme Court Judges as well as the Federal Judges are appointed by the President. The term of these offices is for life. Let's consider the following facts concerning the highest court in our land:

Supreme Court Judges may retire at the age of 70, or at the age of 65 after 15 years of service. All of the vacancies could be filled by Catholics appointed by the President.

Supreme Court Judges	Age	Took Office
Hugo Black	75 *	1937
William Brennan	55	1956
Harold Burton	73 *	1945
Tom Clark	62	1949
William Douglas	62 *	1939 *
Felix Frankfurter	79 *	1939
John Harlan	62	1955
Charles Whittaker	60	1957
Earl Warren	70 *	1953

*Five of these nine Supreme Court Judges will have reached the retirement age within the next four years. All but two will have reached retirement age in the next eight years.

▲ *This pamphlet claimed that, if elected to two terms, Kennedy could possibly appoint five Supreme Court justices. What fact is not mentioned?*

Nixon took an early lead in public opinion polls. He stressed that his vast experience in government set him apart from the relatively inexperienced Kennedy. Yet when reporters asked Eisenhower about Nixon's participation in administration decisions, Ike replied, "If you give me a week, I might think of one." By fall, Nixon had dropped behind in the public opinion polls, in part because he was in the hospital and could not campaign in late August and early September.

Another factor in Kennedy's popularity was a series of televised debates between the two presidential candidates, which took place in September and October 1960. For the first time in U.S. history, presidential candidates met face-to-face on television. Over 70 million Americans watched. Although radio listeners thought Nixon won the debates, three-fourths of the TV viewers believed that Kennedy had won. As many as 4 million viewers said the debates changed their voting preference. Kennedy's wit and ease in responding to questions contradicted the Republican charges that he was immature. While Kennedy appeared tan, physically fit, and composed, Nixon, who had lost weight in the hospital and refused to wear television makeup, appeared pale, thin, and menacing. Television was proving to be important in American politics, largely because of its power to create images.

Kennedy won the election by the slimmest of margins. He was only 118,000 votes ahead of Nixon, out of the 69 million votes cast. In the end, voting analysts felt that Kennedy's religion probably helped as much as it hurt him. He did lose some Protestant votes in southern states, but he did not need them to win. On the other hand, he gained 78 percent of the Catholic vote in the northern industrial states, and this was essential to his election. Equally important to Kennedy's victory was winning 68 percent of the African American vote, and

▼ *The use of television revolutionized U.S. election campaigning. What did politicians learn from the first televised debates between Kennedy and Nixon in 1960?*

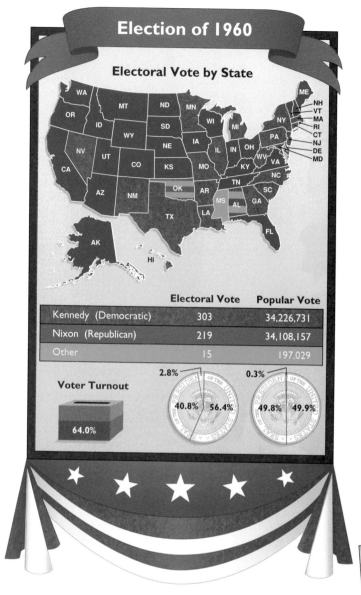

Election of 1960

Electoral Vote by State

	Electoral Vote	Popular Vote
Kennedy (Democratic)	303	34,226,731
Nixon (Republican)	219	34,108,157
Other	15	197,029

Voter Turnout 64.0%

2.8% 40.8% 56.4%

0.3% 49.8% 49.9%

▲ *What is the difference in percentage points of the popular vote received by Kennedy and Nixon in the 1960 election?*

the large majorities he captured in the big cities. Kennedy won by reviving the New Deal voting coalition of labor, African Americans, and other ethnic groups.

The Kennedy White House

JFK wasted little time in the months between his election and his inauguration. During the campaign, Kennedy had appointed a number of task forces to study and prepare reports on the major issues he would confront as president. In December, he organized 11 more task forces on foreign policy and 8 more on domestic issues. By January, Kennedy had hundreds of experts submitting reports on the problems he hoped to solve.

Kennedy spent a great deal of time on cabinet appointments. For key posts, he chose well-established leaders from business and industry. **Robert McNamara**, president of Ford Motor Company, became secretary of defense. Dean Rusk, president of the Rockefeller Foundation, became secretary of state. For secretary of the treasury, Kennedy chose Republican banker Douglas Dillon. Kennedy filled other cabinet positions with able people whose appointments were aimed at satisfying various Democratic Party factions. His most controversial action was to name his brother **Robert Kennedy** as attorney general. He retained **J. Edgar Hoover** as director of the FBI and Allen Dulles as director of the CIA.

Unlike Eisenhower, Kennedy rarely met with the entire cabinet. Instead, he met directly with each

▼ *Kennedy's inaugural address made a plea to his fellow Americans: "Ask not what your country can do for you—ask what you can do for your country."*

▲ The presence of Caroline and John-John Kennedy romping in the Oval Office reinforced the Kennedy image of vigor and youthfulness.

▲ Jacqueline Kennedy was much admired. The "Jackie look" included the three-piece Chanel suit.

► In 1963, President Kennedy met with General Maxwell Taylor and Robert S. McNamara before their fact-finding trip to South Vietnam.

department head concerning each special area. Kennedy made it clear that leadership would come from the White House. As president, he relied heavily on his White House staff, especially his national security adviser, McGeorge Bundy, and his chief economic adviser, Walter Heller.

The "New Frontiersmen," as the press called Kennedy's advisers, soon established a reputation based on their youth, intellect, and, above all, decisiveness. In contrast to the cautious and deliberate Eisenhower administration, Kennedy's advisers believed that quick, bold action was necessary to restore America's self-confidence. Few of them had much political experience. Vice President **Lyndon Johnson** left the first cabinet meeting dazzled by the intellect of the team Kennedy had assembled. When Johnson told Speaker of the House Sam Rayburn of his experience, Rayburn replied, "Well, Lyndon, you may be right and they may be every bit as intelligent as you say, but I'd feel a whole lot better about them if just one of them had run for sheriff once."

Kennedy personified the New Frontier's activist spirit. Long meetings bored him, and he disliked bureaucracies. Kennedy placed many of his own associates within various departments to monitor their activities and report directly to the president outside formal channels. He wanted to make the sluggish federal bureaucracy hum with activity.

SECTION 1 REVIEW

1. **Identify** the term *New Frontier*.
2. **List** the major issues that emerged during the 1960 presidential campaign.
3. **Describe** the effects of the first televised presidential debates on the 1960 election.
4. **Explain** why Kennedy's religion helped him as much as it hurt him.
5. **State** how Kennedy's and Eisenhower's use of their cabinets differed.

SECTION 2

Focus on Foreign Policy

In his inaugural address, Kennedy spoke exclusively of foreign affairs. He said that the United States was at a crossroads, and that Americans were "defending freedom in its hour of maximum danger." In part, JFK's inaugural address was a response to Soviet Premier Khrushchev's boasting of Soviet technological superiority and his country's rate of economic growth. Khrushchev said that a world war would be too destructive in the nuclear age. Yet he approved of wars of national liberation by which people in developing nations would gain their freedom from their colonial overlords. What Khrushchev saw as liberation from colonialism Kennedy saw as Communist "ambitions for world domination." "Our task," Kennedy affirmed, "is to convince them that aggression and subversion will not be profitable routes to pursue these ends."

What changes in foreign policy did Kennedy make?
To what extent did U.S.-Soviet relations dominate Kennedy's thinking about foreign affairs?
How did the Cuban missile crisis threaten world peace?

The Bay of Pigs

Cuban dictator Fidel Castro immediately presented Kennedy with his first international crisis. Ike had broken off diplomatic relations with Cuba as Castro established closer ties to the Soviet Union. During the election campaign, Kennedy severely criticized Eisenhower's handling of Castro and committed himself to strong action. Soon after the election, JFK learned that the CIA was training 1,500 Cuban exiles in Guatemala for an invasion of Cuba. After a favorable review by the Joint Chiefs of Staff, JFK authorized the CIA to proceed with this plan.

Kennedy was warned about the dangers of this plan. J. William Fulbright spoke out bluntly: "The Castro regime is a thorn in the flesh; but it is not a dagger in the heart." Even Dean Acheson thought the scheme a "wild idea." Nevertheless, on April 17, 1961, the troop of Cuban exiles landed at the **Bay of Pigs**, on Cuba's southern coast. The would-be invasion was a disaster from the start. It did not surprise the Cubans, since the preparation for the invasion had been common knowledge. The *New York Times* had even carried news features about the exiles' training. Moreover, the hoped-for spontaneous uprising of the Cuban people to support the

▼ *Cuban leader Fidel Castro and Soviet Premier Nikita Khrushchev visited the United Nations in September 1960.*

invasion never occurred. Castro's troops pinned down the invasion force on the beaches. In a matter of a few days, Castro's soldiers had taken about 1,000 prisoners. The Kennedy administration faced humiliation.

The Bay of Pigs fiasco seriously damaged Kennedy's international prestige. Latin American countries saw the U.S.-sponsored invasion as yet an-other example of Yankee (U.S.) imperialism. The incident also affected American relations with Europe. Veteran diplomat Dean Acheson, in Europe when the invasion occurred, said it "shattered the Europeans . . . [who] had tremendously high expectations of the new administration, and . . . they just fell miles down with a crash." It was not a promising beginning for the Kennedy administration.

People Who Made a Difference

Peace Corps Volunteers

In August 1961, the first Peace Corps volunteers set foot on foreign soil. The Peace Corps sent volunteers only to nations which requested them. By September 1964, more than 10,000 volunteers had served in 46 different countries. Twenty-four other countries were on a waiting list, and their requests for volunteers exceeded 50,000.

"Peace Corps volunteers have all given up opportunities to live comfortably at home," wrote Peace Corps Director Sargent Shriver. "They go into distant countries to work for mere subsistence pay under difficult, sometimes hazardous, conditions. They [have] found more meaning in service than in the easy life. . . . Nothing is more astonishing to people abroad," Shriver continued, "than to see young Americans choosing to leave America—especially the America foreigners know from the movies—to share their lives. There is nothing complicated about what the Peace Corps is trying to accomplish. The Volunteer is a catalyst for self-help projects that will

▲ Here, a Peace Corps volunteer modeled the traditional way Nigerian mothers carry their small children. Do you think the Peace Corps experience is more beneficial to the volunteers or to the host country?

produce something of value that was not there before he [or she] arrived."

In 1962, in the mountains of Colombia, for example, Ron Atwater, a 24-year-old graduate of the Massachusetts Institute of Technology (MIT), helped establish a community newspaper, organized the construction of five schools, and planned for a community center. Atwater also significantly changed the way the residents made and marketed handwoven ponchos, an important source of income. Despite Atwater's successes in helping his assigned village, Peace Corps administrators in Bogotá (Colombia's capital) nearly sent him home because he was "uncombed, unwashed, unshaven, with mud on his shoes." Perhaps for these very reasons, the villagers felt differently: "We all love Señor Ron," said one man. "He is a good Yankee." When asked about his experience, Atwater said, "I guess we help. I know I'm having a ball. This is the best time of my life."

1. Why do you think volunteers would be attracted to a program like the Peace Corps?
2. How did Director Shriver describe the volunteers?

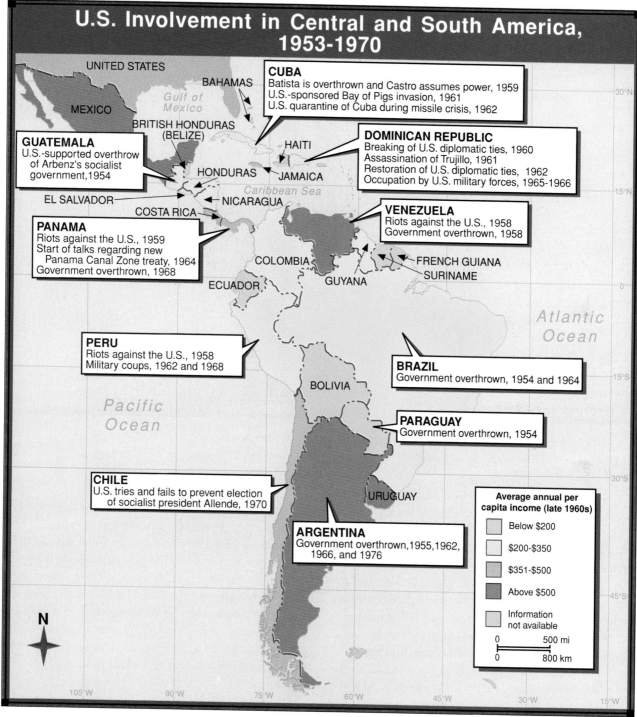

U.S. Involvement in Central and South America, 1953-1970

CUBA
Batista is overthrown and Castro assumes power, 1959
U.S.-sponsored Bay of Pigs invasion, 1961
U.S. quarantine of Cuba during missile crisis, 1962

GUATEMALA
U.S.-supported overthrow of Arbenz's socialist government, 1954

DOMINICAN REPUBLIC
Breaking of U.S. diplomatic ties, 1960
Assassination of Trujillo, 1961
Restoration of U.S. diplomatic ties, 1962
Occupation by U.S. military forces, 1965-1966

VENEZUELA
Riots against the U.S., 1958
Government overthrown, 1958

PANAMA
Riots against the U.S., 1959
Start of talks regarding new Panama Canal Zone treaty, 1964
Government overthrown, 1968

PERU
Riots against the U.S., 1958
Military coups, 1962 and 1968

BRAZIL
Government overthrown, 1954 and 1964

PARAGUAY
Government overthrown, 1954

CHILE
U.S. tries and fails to prevent election of socialist president Allende, 1970

ARGENTINA
Government overthrown, 1955, 1962, 1966, and 1976

Average annual per capita income (late 1960s)

Below $200
$200-$350
$351-$500
Above $500
Information not available

0   500 mi
0   800 km

UNITED STATES
MEXICO
BAHAMAS
Gulf of Mexico
BRITISH HONDURAS (BELIZE)
HAITI
HONDURAS
JAMAICA
Caribbean Sea
EL SALVADOR
NICARAGUA
COSTA RICA
COLOMBIA
ECUADOR
GUYANA
FRENCH GUIANA
SURINAME
BOLIVIA
URUGUAY
Pacific Ocean
Atlantic Ocean

N

▲ *The United States helped maintain regimes friendly to its interests. What generalizations can you make about the overall stability of Latin America in the 1960s?*

Kennedy immediately accepted complete responsibility. He assured Khrushchev that the U.S. had no intention of invading Cuba, but he warned that Soviet moves in the Western Hemisphere would be met with swift American responses. The failure of the Bay of Pigs invasion reinforced

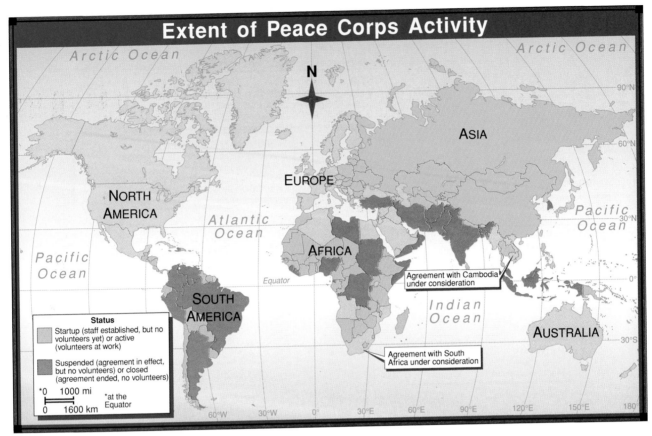

Extent of Peace Corps Activity

Status

Startup (staff established, but no volunteers yet) or active (volunteers at work)

Suspended (agreement in effect, but no volunteers) or closed (agreement ended, no volunteers)

*0   1000 mi   *at the
0   1600 km   Equator

Agreement with Cambodia under consideration

Agreement with South Africa under consideration

▲ *Peace Corps volunteers have served in foreign countries since the program's beginning in 1964. Which continent appears to have the greatest number of host countries?*

Kennedy's conviction that the United States must oppose communism throughout the world.

The affair also reinforced Kennedy's desire to reform the nation's defenses. When he took office, JFK discovered that the missile gap issue he emphasized during the 1960 election campaign did not actually exist. The U.S. had not, in fact, fallen behind the Soviets in nuclear striking power. Even so, Kennedy expanded the Polaris (submarine-based) and Minuteman (land-based) missile programs to offset superior Soviet conventional forces. Under Kennedy, the defense budget increased from $43 billion in 1960 to $56 billion in 1962. By the mid-1960s, the United States had a decisive nuclear advantage over the Soviets. In turn, the Soviets viewed these increases as a threat, and they rapidly expanded their own supply of nuclear arms.

Kennedy made other changes that affected foreign relations. He began the Peace Corps and the Alliance for Progress. The Peace Corps mobilized Americans of all ages to serve in less developed countries. Peace Corps volunteers lived among the people and taught basic literacy, sanitation, infant care, and agricultural techniques, among other things. The Alliance for Progress sought to uplift the nations of Latin America by pledging $10 billion in U.S. economic aid. The purpose was to promote the general economic prosperity, to raise Latin American living standards, and to reduce the appeal of communism.

U.S.-Soviet Relations

U.S.-Soviet relations dominated Kennedy's foreign policy thinking. In 1961, JFK faced a dangerous potential conflict with the Soviets over Berlin.

▶ *After the East Germans constructed the Berlin Wall in August 1961, President Kennedy visited West Berlin to affirm America's commitment to staying in the city. What was the eventual fate of the Berlin Wall?*

Since Truman's administration, Allied occupation of Berlin had been a symbolic issue for both sides. Khrushchev wanted the former Allies out of West Berlin. The Western nations used Berlin as an important base for spying and anti-Communist propaganda activity. Also, nearly 4,000 refugees, many of them skilled workers, escaped from East Germany every week through West Berlin.

Soon after JFK's election, Khrushchev indicated that settlement of the Berlin issue was one of his highest priorities. JFK wanted to delay dealing with the Soviets because he wanted to negotiate from a position of military strength. Even so, Kennedy agreed to Khrushchev's suggestion for an informal summit meeting in Vienna, Austria, in June.

They discussed a wide range of issues, including Berlin. At the summit, Khrushchev was very aggressive and accused the West of avoiding a settlement on Berlin. Kennedy responded by reasserting the West's right to be in Berlin. Since neither leader would compromise his position, the summit ended in deadlock.

Determined to stay in West Berlin, Kennedy called for an additional $3.2 billion in military funding, expanded the army's size by 125,000 soldiers, and called up reserve units. He outlined a civil defense program that included public fallout shelters stocked with food and water. Kennedy warned the Soviets that in an age of nuclear weapons, "any misjudgment on either side about the intentions of the other could rain more devastation in several hours

than has been wrought in all the wars of human history."

In August 1961, the Soviets responded by building the **Berlin Wall** to seal off their sector from the Western zones in the city and stop the embarrassing exodus of people to West Berlin. Kennedy could do nothing about the wall without risking war. The Berlin Wall stood for nearly 30 years, a tragic symbol of the Cold War.

The Cuban Missile Crisis   An even more dangerous situation arose in October 1962. U.S. intelligence agencies learned that Khrushchev had placed missiles with nuclear warheads in Cuba. The Republicans used this issue to attack Kennedy in the approaching 1962 midterm elections.

Kennedy sent both public and private warnings to Khrushchev. Kennedy cautioned that the United States would tolerate defensive weapons in Cuba, but would not allow offensive missiles to be placed so close to the United States. Khrushchev chose to ignore Kennedy's clear warnings and proceeded to construct missile sites in western Cuba. On October 14, an American U-2 spy plane discovered the missile sites still under construction.

Kennedy immediately summoned his most trusted advisers. At first, most of the advisers favored an immediate strike to destroy the missile sites. When the air force could not guarantee complete success, however, Kennedy's advisers discussed

The Soviet ship Kasimov had open crates on its decks so that U.S. aircraft could inspect them from the air. The crates contained offensive missiles that the Soviets agreed to remove from Cuba during the Cuban missile crisis.

several alternatives. Some favored invading Cuba. Others, including UN ambassador Adlai Stevenson, urged diplomatic negotiations that would take U.S. missiles out of Turkey if the Soviets removed their missiles from Cuba. Since the U.S. had already started to remove these missiles from Turkey, giving them up through negotiations would cost nothing.

In the end, President Kennedy listened to his brother Robert, who was attorney general, and Undersecretary of State George Ball. They recommended a naval blockade of Cuba and argued that if the blockade failed, the U.S. would still have several options, including air strikes or invasion.

In a televised speech on October 22, Kennedy told the nation of the grave crisis it faced. He then announced that U.S. ships would quarantine Cuba. Kennedy did not call this a blockade, since a blockade could be interpreted as an act of war. The president warned the Soviets that he would not tolerate nuclear missiles in Cuba and was prepared to use force—including nuclear arms—to get them removed. Kennedy added that American military forces were on full alert.

The next day, nearly 100 U.S. warships took their stations around Cuba. The navy would not allow additional missiles, or the materials needed to complete the missile sites, to be delivered. Khrushchev called the quarantine "outright banditry," and work continued day and night on the Cuban missile sites. At the same time, the largest invasion force ever assembled in the United States began to gather in Florida.

On October 24, several Soviet ships, believed to be transporting missile parts, approached Cuba. The U.S. fleet was fully prepared to stop them, regardless of the military consequences, but the Soviet ships suddenly changed course and headed for home. Secretary of State Dean Rusk said, "We were eyeball to eyeball, and I think the other fellow just blinked." On October 26, Khrushchev sent Kennedy a note that pledged to remove the missiles if the United States guaranteed no future invasion of Cuba. Kennedy accepted Khrushchev's offer, and the **Cuban missile crisis**, which had brought the world to within a breath of nuclear holocaust, faded.

The crisis had far-reaching effects on the U.S. and Soviet governments. Students of the missile crisis have given John Kennedy high marks for listening to his advisers and having the various options aired. Nevertheless, Kennedy's decision to blockade Cuba was dangerous in that it could have caused a nuclear war with the Soviets.

The missile crisis led to a limited thaw, or a period of slightly better relations, in the Cold War between the United States and the Soviet Union. The two nations installed a direct "hot line" telephone link between Moscow and Washington to make communications between the nations' leaders easier. Negotiations began on the **Nuclear Test Ban Treaty** (signed in 1963) that would limit atomic testing in the atmosphere, in the oceans, and in outer space. Relations were still not friendly. Vasily Kuznetsov, the Soviet deputy foreign minister, warned an American official, "Never will we be caught like this again." Accordingly, the Soviets dramatically increased the size of their military forces.

| **SECTION 2 REVIEW** |

1. **State** reasons for the failure of the Bay of Pigs invasion.
2. **Explain** how the Bay of Pigs invasion damaged Kennedy's international prestige.
3. **Describe** changes President Kennedy made in foreign policy.
4. **Discuss** the far-reaching effects of the Cuban missile crisis on the Soviet and U.S. governments.
5. **Identify** the purpose of the Nuclear Test Ban Treaty.

SECTION 3

The Domestic Agenda of the New Frontier

During the election campaign of 1960, Kennedy said, "I believe the American people elect a president to act." One of the ways Kennedy promised "to get the country moving again" was by increasing the rate of economic growth and by putting into action a variety of social programs. Kennedy's slim margin of victory in 1960, however, limited his ability to act boldly. McGeorge Bundy, Kennedy's national security adviser, summed up administration accomplishments in the first hundred days of Kennedy's presidency in this way: "At this point, we are like the Harlem Globetrotters, passing forward, behind, sideways, and underneath. But nobody has made a basket yet." The Kennedy administration made several baskets (largely national security legislation) during the following thousand days. But Congress had enacted less than a third of Kennedy's domestic agenda by November 1963.

What were Kennedy's priorities in domestic affairs?

What kept Kennedy from vigorously pursuing his domestic agenda?

Why did many Americans oppose Kennedy's proposed manned space program?

The New Frontier Falters

The roots of much of Kennedy's domestic program lay in Truman's Fair Deal. The reforms Kennedy wanted included federal aid to education, civil and voting rights for minorities, and health insurance for the elderly. Many Americans thought that these reforms were long overdue. On the surface, the outlook for reform seemed bright, since Democrats held majorities in Congress—261 to 174 in the House and 65 to 35 in the Senate. Actually, the chances for passing reform legislation were slim. In the 1960 election, the Democrats had actually lost 22 seats in the House (mostly seats held by northern liberals) and one seat in the Senate. However, because of the narrowness of his victory in 1960, Kennedy lacked a clear **mandate**, or authorization from the people to act.

The House posed particular difficulties since its members were split three ways. There were 174 Republicans, 160 northern Democrats, and 101 southern Democrats. This last group often voted with the Republicans to block Kennedy's domestic

▼ *Do you see any duplication or overlap in the responses to this opinion poll?*

Most Important Problem, 1961

Question: What do you think is the most important problem facing this country today?

Unemployment	25%
Threat of war	19%
Threat of communism	14%
Foreign relations/getting along with other peoples and nations	10%
Relations with Russia (no mention of war threat)	8%
Domestic economic problems - general	8%
Racial problems	6%

Source: Gallup, February 10-15, 1961.

©The Public Perspective, a publication of the Roper Center for Public Opinion Research, University of CT, Storrs. Reprinted by permission.

programs. In fact, this conservative coalition of Republicans and southern Democrats had blocked most reform legislation since 1938.

To secure enactment of any of his programs, JFK needed 60 to 70 votes in the House of Representatives from southern states. In an effort to gain southern support, he appointed a number of pro-segregation judges to federal courts in the South. He also raised federal subsidies to cotton farmers and channeled as much patronage and federal construction to the South as he could.

Nevertheless, Kennedy could not pull together sufficient support in Congress to get his social reform measures enacted. Federal aid to education, for example, could not be passed for several reasons. Republicans opposed it because of the costs. Church groups opposed it because parochial schools would not receive aid. Southern Democrats opposed it because they feared federal interference in racially segregated schools.

Strong lobbying by the American Medical Association defeated a national health insurance program for the elderly. Kennedy could find little support for his mass transportation bill, again because of the coalition of conservative Republicans and southern Democrats. Kennedy's more innovative ideas, such as a war on poverty, had no chance of success in Congress.

Focus on the Economy

The economy was the primary focus of Kennedy's domestic program. Kennedy and his advisers grappled with several related economic problems—unemployment, inflation, and slow economic growth. Throughout the 1950s, the rate of economic growth had not exceeded 2.5 percent a year. Unemployment had hovered around 4.6 percent of the labor force, and it reached nearly 7 percent in 1961. The inflation rate was low, as consumer prices rose from 1 to 2 percent a year. Although these figures look very good by today's standards, Kennedy thought the nation could do better.

To lift the country from these economic doldrums and raise the rate of growth to 5 percent a year, Kennedy asked Congress to enact a series of

▲ *Nine people lived in this Appalachian shanty in 1963. What was the Kennedy administration's response to the problem of poverty?*

proposals. These included increased unemployment benefits, higher Social Security benefits, a higher minimum wage, more money for public works in areas with high unemployment rates, and a housing act to stimulate the construction industry. Congress, equally concerned about the economy, enacted these proposals. Kennedy also asked for increased defense expenditures and funds for the new space program. The recession that had begun in 1960 ended by mid-1961. Yet unemployment remained between 6 and 7 percent, and the rate of economic growth was not much better than in the fifties. It would take time for Kennedy's proposals to work.

Further reducing the rate of inflation was also high on Kennedy's domestic agenda. He established voluntary guidelines that would permit small wage and price increases. Kennedy wanted all large industries and unions to observe these guidelines, but several industries were especially important if his inflation-control policy was to succeed. Steel was one of those industries.

In March 1962, the United Steelworkers of America negotiated a new contract with the steel industry. Kennedy pressured the union and the steel companies to keep both wages and prices down. As

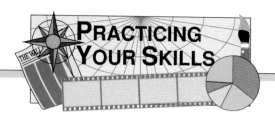

Analyzing Public Opinion Polls

The public opinion poll is used to determine how the public feels about a particular issue. Elmo Roper and George Gallup were pioneers in the opinion poll business, developing methods of market research that improved the reliability of the polls. Polls sometimes gave misleading results. One famous example of a misleading opinion poll was a newspaper's telephone poll of their subscribers on the eve of the 1948 election between Dewey and Truman. The results of the poll indicated that Dewey would win by a landslide. Having printed the headline, the pollsters were embarrassed the next day when the election results were tallied. The poll had failed to take into consideration the fact that the majority of people with private telephones taking their paper belonged to the Republican Party and were members of the middle class. The poll failed to sample enough working-class Democrats, who heavily favored Truman.

Following are some guidelines to consider when analyzing public opinion polls:

- **How large was the sample?** Were enough people included in the poll to get a statistically significant result? A sample which is too small will not be reliable.

- **Were the questions without bias?** Leading questions that point to a desired answer can influence the way people answer. Questions should be free of bias.

- **Was the sample truly random?** What efforts were made to ensure that the poll was not lim-

---

Most Important Problem, 1953

Question: In your opinion, what are the main problems facing the country today that the new administration should tackle?

Settling the Korean War	60%
The economy/preventing a depression	41%
Reducing taxes	29%
Foreign affairs	16%
Keeping the peace	12%
Communism	8%
Efficiency and economy in government	7%

Source: Survey by the Opinion Research Corporation, February 9-18, 1953.

Most Important Problem, 1961

Question: What do you think is the most important problem facing this country today?

Unemployment	25%
Threat of war	19%
Threat of communism	14%
Foreign relations/getting along with other peoples and nations	10%
Relations with Russia (no mention of war threat)	8%
Domestic economic problems - general	8%
Racial problems	6%

Source: Gallup, February 10-15, 1961.

---

ited to particular classes, races, ethnic groups, educational levels, geographic regions, or occupations?

- **How was the survey interpreted?** Was the data resulting from the survey interpreted fairly? Often, the results of surveys influence people to change their beliefs, or help them to make up their minds. It is important that opinion polls analyze people's behaviors and beliefs based on a sufficient amount of data.

Examine the opinion polls on pages 803 and 875 and answer the following questions:

1. According to the poll, what was the most important problem facing the nation in 1953? What was the most important problem in 1961?
2. Read the survey question asked by each poll. How do the survey questions differ on the opinion poll?
3. What events influenced the results of the 1953 poll? What events influenced the 1961 poll?
4. Make a list of the domestic issues identified in the 1953 Eisenhower poll and a list of the domestic issues in the 1961 Kennedy poll. Based on your analysis of the two lists, make a statement comparing and contrasting what Americans were most concerned about in 1953 and 1961.
5. How do you think Americans might answer these questions today?

a result, the union settled for only a modest increase in benefits. Then on April 10, Roger Blough, president of United States Steel, went to the White House to inform Kennedy that his company was raising the price of steel by $6 a ton. Kennedy was furious, since the increase violated the price guidelines. Because he had pressured the union to settle for a modest contract, Kennedy's integrity was at stake. The president put great pressure on the steel companies to remove the price increase. The Justice Department threatened to investigate price fixing and to take antitrust action. Kennedy told McNamara to give defense contracts to the companies that were not raising their prices. The major companies eventually removed the price increase.

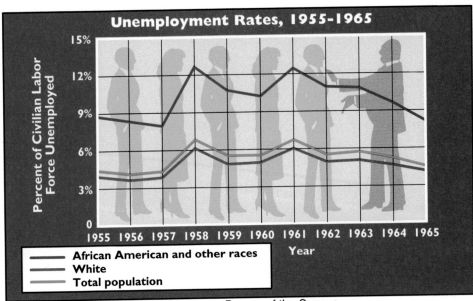

Source: U.S. Department of Commerce, Bureau of the Census.

▲ *Which single event was probably most responsible for the declining unemployment rates after 1963?*

Although Kennedy had forced the steel industry to back down, he was by no means antibusiness. To increase foreign markets for American industries, the administration required that 80 percent of all foreign aid be used to purchase American-made goods transported by American ships. In this way, money leaving the country found its way back through trade. The Trade Expansion Act of 1962 was also intended to increase American foreign trade and to stimulate business activity by negotiating mutual tariff reductions with other nations. In 1962, Kennedy asked Congress for a tax revision that resulted in corporate tax savings worth over $1 billion. In the years from 1961 to 1965, corporate profits rose 76.5 percent. Meanwhile wages rose by 18 percent.

To stimulate higher levels of economic growth, some of Kennedy's advisers urged him to increase government spending on public works, including public transportation and cleaning up the environment. Another group, led by the Council of Eco-

nomic Advisers, urged Kennedy to cut taxes. A tax cut would be popular and would stimulate the economy faster than would spending money on public works. The House of Representatives passed Kennedy's tax bill in September 1963, but the Senate did not act until January of 1964, after Kennedy's death.

Kennedy and the Moon Landing

On April 12, 1961, less than four years after the historic *Sputnik* satellite program, the Soviets achieved another dramatic victory in space. Cosmonaut **Yuri Gagarin** became the first person to orbit Earth. This event reinforced the view that the U.S. space program lagged behind that of the Soviets. Kennedy asked Vice President Lyndon Johnson to explore the possibility of sending an astronaut to the Moon. JFK wanted to know: "Is there any other space program which promises dramatic results in which we could win? Are we working 24 hours a day on existing programs? Are we making maximum effort? Are we achieving results?"

▲ *Astronaut Neil A. Armstrong took this photograph of Edwin ("Buzz") Aldrin descending from the Apollo 11 lunar module.*

space race was worth the cost. Eight years later, on July 20, 1969, U.S. astronaut Neil Armstrong became the first person to walk upon the surface of the moon.

SECTION 3 REVIEW

1. **Name** the major parts of Kennedy's domestic program.
2. **Define** the term *mandate* as used in this section.
3. **Explain** what prevented enactment of most of Kennedy's domestic programs.
4. **Recount** the moves made by the president to help build American business in foreign markets.
5. **Explain** why many Americans opposed the Apollo moon program.

Johnson, who had long been a space enthusiast, soon came back with an answer. Yes, a rush program could put an American on the Moon before the Soviets. On May 25, 1961, JFK announced the creation of the Apollo moon program. He declared it was "time for this nation to take a clearly leading role in space achievement, which in many ways may hold the key to our future on earth." He also said the costs would be staggering, as much as $30 to $40 billion in the next ten years. Even so, Kennedy argued that it was necessary to beat the Soviets to the moon, because "whatever mankind must undertake, free men must fully share."

Some Americans were less enthusiastic about putting an astronaut on the Moon. Many U.S. scientists, including Jerome Weisner, JFK's science adviser, questioned the scientific value of this goal. Weisner finally—and reluctantly—supported the moon program, for diplomatic and military, but not scientific, reasons. Opinion polls showed 58 percent of Americans opposed the Apollo program. Former President Eisenhower commented bluntly, "Anybody who would spend $40 billion in a race to the moon for national prestige is nuts."

The heavy expenditures for putting an astronaut on the Moon would help stimulate the economy, something Kennedy counted on in making his decision. Kennedy and his successor, Lyndon Johnson, both believed the prestige attached to winning the

SECTION 4

The Expansion of Civil Rights

African Americans looked to the Kennedy administration for bold leadership in civil rights. African Americans were the key to Kennedy's victory in several states in 1960. Yet the very closeness of the election made him cautious. Kennedy needed the support of southern members of Congress for other legislative priorities, so he did not ask for civil rights legislation in 1961 or 1962. African American leaders were sorely disappointed. As the Reverend Martin Luther King Jr. said, "For years now I have heard the word 'Wait.' It rings in the ears of every Negro with piercing familiarity. The 'Wait' has always meant 'Never.' " Like King, most African Americans were no longer willing to wait. They soon forced Kennedy to take action.

What did Kennedy believe was the key to advancing African American civil rights?

In what ways did grassroots civil rights activities force Kennedy to act?

What significant decisions did the Supreme Court make regarding equality in American society in the early 1960s?

Kennedy and Civil Rights

Kennedy was convinced that the right to vote held the key to all other civil rights. With the help of his brother Robert, Kennedy appointed extremely able civil rights advocates to important posts in government, especially in the Justice Department. These included Robert Weaver as head of the Housing and Home Finance Agency, Carl Rowan as deputy assistant secretary of state for public affairs, and Louis Martin as deputy chairman of the Democratic National Committee, among many others. The Kennedys also asked FBI Director J. Edgar Hoover to gather information on how African Americans had been denied their voting rights. In the next three years, the Justice Department filed 37 suits, and scores of federal officials appeared in the South to help African Americans exercise the right to vote.

In 1962, Kennedy issued an executive order aimed at ending discrimination in the hiring practices of companies that did business with the federal government. Kennedy appointed Lyndon Johnson to head the Committee on Equal Employment Opportunity to make sure the executive order was obeyed. Yet despite Kennedy's actions, by 1961 the White House controlled neither the agenda nor the pace of civil rights activities.

Freedom Rides Aggressive civil rights organizations such as the Congress of Racial Equality (CORE), the Southern Christian Leadership Conference (SCLC) of Dr. Martin Luther King Jr., and the Student Nonviolent Coordinating Committee (SNCC, pro-

nounced "Snick") began to take direct action to secure African American rights. In May 1961, CORE decided to force the federal government to comply with *Boynton v. Virginia* (1960). This case extended the prohibition of segregation on interstate buses to include terminal facilities. CORE organized African American volunteers to ride on buses that traveled into the deep South to challenge segregation of facilities that had continued despite the Supreme Court's ruling. James Farmer and other CORE leaders believed that the expected confrontations would force federal officials to intervene to uphold the law of the land.

Many confrontations did occur. The most violent ones took place in Alabama. In Anniston, Alabama, a white mob burned a bus. In Birmingham, an angry white crowd pulled the riders off a bus and beat them. Another mob seized the terminal in Montgomery. In an effort to restore order, Attorney General Robert Kennedy sent 400 United States marshals to Montgomery. President Kennedy asked CORE to end the freedom rides, but they continued. In all, over 1,000 people participated. In response, local authorities arrested freedom riders by the hundreds. In November, the federal government

▼ *Freedom riders sit outside Anniston, Alabama, after the fire-bombing of their bus in May 1961. What was their goal?*

officially banned segregation in facilities servicing all interstate buses and trains.

Kennedy Supports the Activists These successes served to raise the hopes and expectations of African American activists. They soon turned their attention to segregated universities. In 1962, the University of Mississippi denied James Meredith, an African American air force veteran, admission to the law school there. A United States appeals court ordered that he be admitted, ruling that Meredith had been turned away solely on the basis of race. In September, federal marshals escorted Meredith onto campus. White segregationists, both students and nonstudents, attacked the marshals, and two people died in the riot that followed. President Kennedy sent several thousand federal troops to restore order and to protect Meredith's civil rights. Kennedy acted to uphold the principle of the supremacy of federal over state law, as Eisenhower had in 1957 at Central High School in Little Rock.

Time after time, nonviolent protests led by civil rights workers pressured the Kennedy administration to act on behalf of civil rights. In April 1963, African Americans in Birmingham began a massive protest against segregated restaurants, washrooms, and drinking fountains. They staged sit-ins and organized huge marches that attracted the attention of the national news media. After arresting hundreds of demonstrators, Sheriff Eugene "Bull" Connor lost his temper and ordered the police to attack the nonviolent demonstrators with clubs, police dogs, and high-pressure fire hoses. These actions contrasted sharply with the nonviolence of the civil rights activists. Millions of Americans across the nation watched these events on TV and were outraged. "The civil rights movement should thank God for

▲ *Why were federal marshals needed to protect James Meredith as he enrolled at the University of Mississippi in 1962?*

Bull Connor," President Kennedy later remarked to an aide. "He helped as much as Abraham Lincoln."

In response to events in Birmingham, Kennedy sent a civil rights bill to Congress that went far beyond any legislation ever proposed to ensure equal rights for African Americans. The bill would

▼ *In Birmingham, Alabama, police used dogs to break up a demonstration in May 1963.*

- guarantee citizens equal access to hotels, restaurants, places of amusement, and retail businesses
- contain stronger provisions to ensure African American voting rights
- give the attorney general more power in desegregating public schools
- improve economic opportunities for African Americans through training programs and end racial discrimination in the workplace.

On August 28, 1963, nearly 200,000 people marched on Washington to show support for this civil rights bill. Gathered before the Lincoln Memorial, they heard Martin Luther King Jr. give what many said was the most moving and magnificent public address they had ever heard. "I say to you today, my friends," King said, "that in spite of the difficulties and frustrations of the moment, I still have a dream. It is a dream deeply rooted in the American dream. I have a dream that one day this nation will rise up and live out the true meaning of its creed: 'We hold these truths to be self-evident— that all men are created equal.'" Still Congress delayed action on the civil rights bill.

▲ *Martin Luther King Jr. spoke at the Lincoln Memorial in August 1963. What is the popular name of this speech?*

The Warren Court

In extending the principles of equal protection of the law and individual rights on behalf of African Americans, the Supreme Court helped promote revolutionary changes in race relations in the United States. Throughout Earl Warren's tenure as chief justice (1953–1969), the Supreme Court extended its commitment to both principles, not only in cases affecting African Americans, but also in cases that touched the lives of all citizens. The Court insisted that state and local governments observe the individual rights and protections guaranteed by the U.S. Bill of Rights and the Fourteenth Amendment.

In *Brown v. Board of Education of Topeka* (1954) the Court outlawed racial segregation in public schools. In *Baker v. Carr* (1962) and *Reynolds v. Sims* (1964), the Court discovered that **gerrymandering** (setting election district boundaries to favor some groups at the expense of others) could be used to deprive voters of equal representation. The Court

ruled that states had to redraw election districts so that rural representatives could not dominate state legislatures and so that the districts reflected the vast growth that had occurred in cities and suburbs since World War II. Eventually, the Court made similar rulings about U.S. congressional districts.

Extending due process protections to state and local courts and police officers was another result of Warren Court decisions. The extent to which state and local governments had previously guaranteed due process to their residents had been left up to local authorities. In the 1960s, however, the Supreme Court extended the guarantees of due process contained in the Bill of Rights and Fourteenth Amendment to the states. In *Mapp v. Ohio* (1961), the Court ruled that material found in unlawful searches and seizures by police officers could not be used as evidence in trials. The Court guaranteed the right to legal counsel, even if the accused could not afford a lawyer, in *Gideon v. Wainwright* (1963). The Court forbade the use of confessions

Judicial Activism and the Warren Court

Earl Warren was Chief Justice of the Supreme Court from 1953 to 1969. Few justices have been as widely admired or condemned. He set the tone for a Supreme Court that his critics claimed went beyond interpreting law and into the realm of making law. In *Brown v. Topeka Board of Education,* Warren wrote: "In approaching this problem, we cannot turn the clock back to 1868 when the Amendment was adopted, or even to 1896 when *Plessy v. Ferguson* was written. We must consider public education in the light of its full development and its present place in American life throughout the nation." Warren based this important decision on psychological and sociological evidence, as well as legal principles.

Throughout his career, Warren used fairness as a standard of judgment in Court cases. The Warren Court is noted for its "breathtaking extension of defendants' rights." It held that even the guilty—especially the guilty—are in need of constitutional rights.

In *Griffin v. Illinois* (1956), a convicted felon was denied an appeal by the state. Griffin could not afford to pay the fee to have a written transcript of the trial sent to the appeals court. The Warren Court ordered the appeal, holding that "We cannot have one rule for the rich and one for the poor." In *Gideon v. Wainwright* (1963), the Court determined that any person who is too poor to hire a lawyer must have an attorney provided by the state.

Another important case that defined the rights of the accused was *Mapp v. Ohio* (1961). In this case the Warren Court established the *exclusionary rule.* The rule forbids the admission into court of evidence obtained in an illegal manner such as evidence gathered by police without a warrant or with an error in the process of obtaining a warrant. The rule protects against unreasonable searches and seizures as stated in the Fourth Amendment.

In one of its most famous cases, the Warren Court ruled on the rights of suspects upon arrest. Miranda, a suspect, was questioned without a lawyer present. His confession was later used to convict him. In *Miranda v. Arizona* (1966), the Court ordered that suspects in police custody must be told that they have the right to remain silent; that they may consult with an attorney before answering any questions; that they may have an attorney appointed if they cannot afford one; and that anything they say can be used against them in court.

Some segments of society have protested these restrictions to law enforcement. They believe that the rights of victims have not been given due consideration under the Court's interpretation of the Constitution. Some subsequent Supreme Court decisions have interpreted the Constitution to favor law enforcement and the state. Each Supreme Court interprets the Constitution based not only on legal precedents and the intent of the framers of the Constitution, but also on the current attitudes and needs of the citizenry. The ability of the Constitution to respond to changes in generally accepted values is one reason it has endured.

1. What is meant by the term *judicial activism?*
2. Do you believe the Supreme Court should be able to reverse earlier rulings?

▲ *In 1812, Elbridge Gerry drew the boundaries of this voting district in Massachusetts to ensure the election for his party. What term is used to describe the drawing of electoral boundaries to the advantage of one political party?*

obtained by force in *Escobedo v. Illinois* (1964). In *Miranda v. Arizona* (1966), the Court required law enforcement officers to clearly inform accused persons of their rights.

Warren Court decisions also extended the protections of the First Amendment. One area concerned freedom of speech. In a series of cases, including *Roth v. United States* (1957), the Court ruled that local authorities could not censor obscene material—books, films, magazines—unless it was "utterly without redeeming social importance." This standard of defining obscenity made it more difficult for local authorities to control pornography. Many citizens condemned the Court's stand because they believed that pornography helped undermine the nation's moral fiber. In another landmark case, *The New York Times Co. v. Sullivan* (1964), the Court ruled that public criticism of public officials was fully protected by the First Amendment. The Court held "that debate on public issues should be uninhibited, robust, and wide open." As a result, public officials could not sue for libel or take other legal actions against critics.

A second set of First Amendment cases concerned the principle of the separation of church and state. In *Engel v. Vitale* (1962), the Court ruled that the prayer required at the start of each day in New York State public schools violated this principle. The public reaction to the ruling was strong and

▶ *Under the guidance of Earl Warren, the Supreme Court extended the principle of equal protection under the law. What landmark case set aside the separate-but-equal doctrine established in* Plessy v. Ferguson?

largely unfavorable. Many people feared that it would promote antireligious beliefs and undermine morality in American society. Some members of Congress began efforts to pass legislation that would overturn the Court's ruling. Undaunted, the Court subsequently ruled that it was unconstitutional to conduct Bible readings or recite the Lord's Prayer as part of public school programs.

Finally, the Warren Court ventured into the area of privacy. This word is not explicitly mentioned in the Constitution or the Bill of Rights. But in *Griswold v. Connecticut* (1965), Justice William O. Douglas argued that a number of "modern rights," including privacy, were implied by the Bill of Rights. The specific issue in the *Griswold* case concerned whether a constitutional right to privacy prohibited a state from making the use of birth control devices by a married couple a crime. The Court held that a right of privacy ought to be protected, especially in marriages, and thus the state statute was void. The Court later extended this protection to single as well as married persons (in *Eisenstadt v. Baird*, 1972). As you will see, the privacy right also played an important role in the *Roe v. Wade* (1973) abortion case.

By extending federal Bill of Rights guarantees to the states, the Court significantly changed the way in which state and local governments acted toward their citizens. Such extensions of the Bill of Rights had begun in the early twentieth century, but the decisions of the Warren Court pushed this process forward significantly. Indeed, the Warren Court had a revolutionary impact on the United States, an impact that disturbed as many Americans as it pleased.

SECTION 4 REVIEW

1. **Describe** some tactics used early in the Kennedy administration to advance the civil rights of African Americans.
2. **Explain** how grassroots civil rights activists forced Kennedy to act more vigorously.
3. **Explain** why nearly 200,000 people marched on Washington in August of 1963.
4. **Define** gerrymandering.
5. **Discuss** the extension of due process protection under the Warren Court.

SECTION 5

Vietnam and Kennedy's Assassination

Neither Kennedy nor his advisers regarded Vietnam as a major trouble spot early in JFK's administration. In briefing Kennedy during the presidential transition, President Eisenhower had been much more concerned about Laos than Vietnam. In May 1961, however, Kennedy received sobering advice from General Douglas MacArthur and President Charles de Gaulle of France. MacArthur said, "We couldn't win a fight in Asia." De Gaulle was even more pointed: "For you intervention in this region [Vietnam] will be an entanglement without end. I predict to you that you will, step by step, be sucked into a bottomless military and political quagmire." By this time, however, setbacks in other areas of foreign policy—the Bay of Pigs, the Vienna summit—had led Kennedy to think of U.S. involvement in Vietnam as an important way to make a stand against communism. By the time of Kennedy's assassination in late 1963, he had clearly committed the United States to saving South Vietnam from Communist forces.

Why did Kennedy commit the United States to supporting South Vietnam?
How did Americans react to Kennedy's assassination?
Why were the Warren Commission's findings concerning Kennedy's assassination disputed?

America's Commitment to Vietnam

While Kennedy's attention had initially focused on Soviet and Latin American affairs, events in Southeast Asia soon called for his attention. A civil war erupted in Laos, as a result of the attempt by Communist Pathet Lao forces to gain control. The outcome was of vital concern to South Vietnam, since the **Ho Chi Minh Trail**—the primary route by which North Vietnam supplied its allies in the south—ran through Laos. Seeking to neutralize Laos in 1962, Kennedy encouraged the formation of a coalition government headed by Prince Souvanna Phouma (soo-VAH-nah FOO-mah) that included the Pathet Lao.

Kennedy was unwilling to settle the situation in South Vietnam in a similar way. He viewed the civil war in Vietnam as a crucial test of Khrushchev's support of wars of national liberation. Kennedy believed that if Communist forces won in South Vietnam, the West would face similar challenges in many less developed countries. He also realized that dealing with South Vietnam would not be easy.

Kennedy nevertheless decided he could not abandon Ngo Dinh Diem, president of South Vietnam. He sent Vice President Johnson to South Vietnam as a gesture of U.S. support. On his return, Johnson urged JFK to continue to support Diem. In May 1961, Kennedy dispatched additional U.S. advisers to train the army of South Vietnam (ARVN) in **counterinsurgency tactics** such as infiltration, sabotage, and commando raids against rebel forces. For the first time the United States exceeded the 687 advisers allowed by the 1954 Geneva Accords. The North Vietnamese organized the National Liberation Front (NLF) in South Vietnam in late 1960. The idea was to bring together all groups opposed to Diem's regime, but clearly the North was in control. As a supposedly southern movement, the NLF gave cover to Hanoi's claim that it was not violating the Geneva Accords by sending forces into the South. Diem's public relations advisers gave the NLF the name **Vietcong**—or Vietnamese Communists—and it stuck. By September, however, the situation had become critical. The South Vietnamese army had failed to halt the Vietcong, and Diem appealed for additional American aid.

Kennedy sent his trusted advisers Walt Rostow and General Maxwell Taylor to Vietnam in October 1961 to assess Diem's worsening situation. They reported privately to Kennedy that the ARVN was weak, ineffective, and without capable officers. Diem's government was disorganized, inefficient, and unpopular. The situation was "serious" and demanded "urgent measures."

Yet Rostow and Taylor believed that South Vietnam could survive as an independent, democratic nation. To reverse the tide, however, they recommended that Kennedy order extensive bombing operations and send over 8,000 U.S. combat troops. As Taylor stated it,

> The risks of backing into a major Asian war by way of South Vietnam are present but are not impressive. . . . North Vietnam is extremely vulnerable to conventional bombing, a weakness which should be exploited diplomatically in convincing Hanoi [North Vietnam] to lay off South Vietnam.

The president received the Rostow-Taylor report skeptically. He realized that sending a few troops would lead almost inevitably to sending more. As he said, "The troops will march in; the bands will play; the crowds will cheer; and in four days everyone will have forgotten. Then we will be told we have to send in more troops. It's like taking a drink. The effect wears off, and you have to take another." Dean Rusk and Robert McNamara, however, supported the Rostow-Taylor recommendations. "The loss of South Vietnam to communism would not only destroy the Southeast Asia Treaty Organization (SEATO) but would undermine the credibility of American commitments elsewhere." In addition, they believed that Vietnam's loss "would stimulate bitter domestic controversies in the United States and would be seized upon by extreme elements to divide the country and harass the administration." This reasoning struck a chord with Kennedy, who recalled the extreme criticism that Truman had faced after the loss of China to communism in 1949.

Kennedy decided not to send combat troops, but he did increase economic aid and the number of U.S. military advisers to South Vietnam from 700 to nearly 16,500. ARVN units soon took the offensive against the Vietcong. But, by late 1962, the Vietcong were inflicting heavy losses on ARVN units. Because the Vietcong dressed and looked just like the peasants, ARVN troops made no distinction between Vietcong and civilians. The peasants themselves were angered by the use of napalm and chemical defoliants on their land. In addition, a campaign to relocate the peasants helped fuel their discontent with Diem's regime.

► *According to the chart, what years saw the biggest escalation in American personnel stationed in Vietnam?*

U.S. Troops Stationed in Vietnam, 1960-1968

Role	Administration	Year	Troops Added During Year	Year-End Total
Advisory	Dwight D. Eisenhower	1960	327	700
Advisory	John F. Kennedy	1961	2,500	3,200
Advisory	John F. Kennedy	1962	8,800	12,000
Advisory	John F. Kennedy	1963	4,500	16,500
Combat	Lyndon B. Johnson	1964	6,500	23,000
Combat	Lyndon B. Johnson	1965	158,000	181,000
Combat	Lyndon B. Johnson	1966	204,000	385,000
Combat	Lyndon B. Johnson	1967	101,000	486,000
Combat	Lyndon B. Johnson	1968	50,100	536,100

◄ *Flames erupt around the Rev. Quang Duc, a Buddhist monk, as he burned himself to death in Saigon, South Vietnam, on June 14, 1963. Why did the monk self-immolate?*

In 1963, a Buddhist upheaval in South Vietnam added strength to to Diem's opposition. Diem, a Catholic, had rarely tried to compromise with Buddhists, who made up the majority of South Vietnam's population. The situation reached a climax in May 1963, when Diem's soldiers fired into a crowd of Buddhists who were protesting a ban on the display of religious symbols. The shootings stirred even more vigorous protests. On June 11, a Buddhist monk, drenched in gasoline, set himself on fire. This self-immolation was only the first of seven. Protests spread to students, and discontent engulfed the army. Diem responded with raids in which the police ransacked Buddhist temples and arrested more than 1,400 people.

Just days after these raids, with the majority of the South Vietnamese united against Diem, a group of ARVN generals secretly informed the American ambassador, Henry Cabot Lodge, that they were planning to overthrow Diem. On instructions from Washington, Lodge did nothing to discourage the coup. On November 1, 1963, the conspirators abducted and killed Diem, opening a new era in relations between the U.S. and South Vietnam.

Kennedy Assassinated

In preparation for the 1964 presidential elections, Kennedy went to Dallas, Texas, in late November 1963. He considered his first term a time of preparation; now he wanted a clear election mandate for his domestic programs. Kennedy went to

The Assassination of John F. Kennedy

Few events in American history have had such an impact on the American people as Kennedy's assassination. Most Americans who lived through that time can recall exactly what they were doing when they first heard the news that Kennedy had been shot. Radio and television news coverage made the assassination even more immediate and shocking. People throughout the world shared the experience simultaneously.

Many of the nation's normal activities came to a standstill in the shock that followed this national tragedy. Schools and businesses closed on the day of the president's funeral. Millions of people, watching the funeral on television, were moved by the overwhelming display of symbols of a fallen hero: the riderless horse; the bugler playing taps; Kennedy's burial at Arlington National Cemetery; the eternal flame lit on Kennedy's grave. These symbols brought most Americans—whatever their politics—together emotionally and gave them a shared sense of loss.

To many Americans, John Kennedy's death marked a dividing line in American history. On one side was an age of youthfulness, excellence, hope, idealism, and faith in government. On the other side was violent social conflict, disillusionment, the unending Vietnam War, and the assassinations of Malcolm X, Martin Luther King Jr., and Robert Kennedy. It was, as

▲ *As Kennedy's bier was carried from St. Matthew's Cathedral, his young son gave a touching salute.*

Lance Morrow observed 20 years later, as though JFK's murder "opened some malign trap door in American culture, and the wild bats flapped out." In 1983, a Gallup poll showed that Kennedy had been, by far, America's most popular president. Because of Kennedy's commitment to the downtrodden, to racial justice, and to infusing the nation with a new spirit, two-thirds of those polled thought that the United States would have been "much different" had Kennedy lived.

1. Why did Kennedy's assassination touch people so deeply?
2. Explain why many view the assassination as a critical turning point in American history.

▼ *President John F. Kennedy lay in state in the U.S. Capitol Building.*

◄ *This photograph was taken just moments before Kennedy's assassination in Dallas, Texas. Why do you think there is still controversy over the results of the assassination investigation?*

Texas to help unify the liberal and conservative factions within the state's Democratic Party. He arrived in Dallas on November 22. At 12:30 P.M., as his motorcade drove toward downtown Dallas, Kennedy was struck by an assassin's bullets. Dallas police captured Kennedy's apparent assassin, Lee Harvey Oswald. Two days later, Jack Ruby fatally shot Oswald while Oswald was in police custody.

Americans were stunned that Kennedy was murdered in his prime, before he could fulfill the

▼ *Vice President Lyndon B. Johnson was sworn in as president aboard Air Force One with his wife, "Lady Bird Johnson," on his right and Mrs. Kennedy on his left. Why did this happen so quickly?*

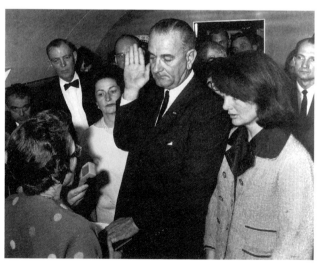

promise he showed. They wanted to know why the assassination had happened and who was responsible. Many believed the assassination was the result of a conspiracy. Some thought organized crime was responsible; others thought Castro was behind it. The new president, Lyndon B. Johnson, appointed a commission, chaired by Chief Justice Earl Warren, to sift through the evidence of the assassination. The Warren Commission concluded that a lone assassin, Lee Harvey Oswald, acting on his own, had shot Kennedy. Jack Ruby, also acting alone, had killed Oswald. The Warren Commission Report found no reliable evidence of a conspiracy.

As soon as the Warren Commission Report was published, it came under severe criticism. Careful students of the Warren Commission's investigation criticized its rather hurried and sloppy procedures. Several issues—whether Oswald could have accurately fired his rifle three times in the brief time it took for the bullets to strike their targets; whether one bullet or two hit both Kennedy and fellow passenger Texas Governor John Connally; whether shots struck Kennedy from both the rear and front—caused many arguments. In 1976, the House of Representatives formed a Select Committee on Assassination to reexamine the Warren Commission's evidence. It concluded that it was possible, if not probable, that two people had fired on the presidential motorcade. These issues continue to be disputed, fueled in part by numerous books and articles and such films as Oliver Stone's *JFK*.

SECTION 5 REVIEW

1. **Describe** how the outcome of the civil war in Laos affected South Vietnam.
2. **Identify** the ARVN.
3. **Define** counterinsurgency.
4. **Explain** why Kennedy decided to commit more troops to Vietnam.
5. **Explain** why the Warren Commission's findings were disputed.

Summary

The return of the Democrats to the White House in 1961 marked the beginning of a new era in American history. John Kennedy's election signified the coming of age of a new generation of leaders. Kennedy promised to get the country moving again in both foreign and domestic affairs.

In foreign affairs, Kennedy was especially concerned about Communist aggressiveness, particularly Communist support of wars of national liberation. Kennedy made a number of changes in foreign affairs. These changes included increasing expenditures on defense and strengthening conventional combat forces. They also included establishing the Peace Corps and the Alliance for Progress, increasing foreign trade, and other activities designed to stem the Communist tide around the world. At the same time, Kennedy experienced a number of reverses in foreign affairs. These included the Bay of Pigs fiasco, the Vienna summit conference with Khrushchev, and increased involvement in Vietnam.

In domestic affairs, Kennedy promised action, but much of his domestic program was stalled in Congress. Kennedy's election victory in 1960 had been slim, and a coalition of conservative Republicans and southern Democrats in Congress blocked many of his welfare and civil rights programs. Events outside of the White House sometimes moved faster than JFK's administration. The Supreme Court, for example, virtually revolutionized American constitutional law by strongly asserting equal protection for all citizens. In the area of African American civil rights, Kennedy failed to lead the way until early 1963, when grassroots activities finally forced him to take action. What additional action Kennedy may have taken in either foreign or domestic affairs will never be known because of his assassination in Dallas in late 1963.

Vocabulary

counterinsurgency tactics
gerrymandering
Ho Chi Minh Trail
mandate
missile gap
New Frontier

For each of the above terms, write one or two sentences that explain its relationship to the Kennedy administration.

Review Questions

1. What criticisms did Kennedy make of the Eisenhower administration?
2. Name two decisive factors that influenced the election of 1960.
3. Describe the steps taken by Kennedy to build up U.S. defenses after the Vienna summit.
4. Describe Kennedy's response to reports of Soviet missile sites in Cuba and the risk he took with his decisions.
5. Identify Kennedy's New Frontier and explain why much of it failed.
6. What prompted Kennedy to promote the program to send an astronaut to the moon?
7. Explain why African Americans looked to the Kennedy administration for expansion of their civil rights and why they were disappointed.
8. What were three ways that the Warren Court expanded the principles of individual rights and equal protection of the law?
9. Explain the problems Kennedy faced in deciding whether or not to send American troops into Vietnam.
10. Why did Kennedy travel to Dallas in late 1963?

Critical Historical Thinking

Writing Answer each of the following by writing one or more complete paragraphs:

1. Explain why you think President Kennedy chose the New Frontier as the name for his domestic program.
2. Television played an extremely important part in the 1960 election. How does it compare with the role television plays in presidential elections today?
3. General MacArthur warned that a western power could not win a conventional ground war in Asia. What do you think he meant?
4. Read the selection entitled "Kennedy Without Tears" in the Unit 9 Archives. What did Kennedy's self-assessment tell you about making decisions as president?

Making Connections with Media

Edward R. Murrow's broadcasts from World War II battlefields brought the drama of battle home to his audience. His broadcasts and the dispatches of newspaper reporters such as Ernie Pyle served to confirm American opinion that the "Crusade in Europe" was a necessary war to resist dictatorship and aggression. Twenty years later, correspondents reported the war in Vietnam to television audiences. American viewers saw graphic scenes of war and death in a far-off Asian country. America's "Living Room War" helped many come to the conclusion Americans should get out of Vietnam.

Depending upon one's position for or against the war, the media were praised or blamed for fueling the debate at home over the purpose and morality of the war. Those who supported the war claimed that television reporters were biased and selective in their coverage of the war. Those who opposed the war praised television networks. The debate over television's role served to convince the Pentagon to severely restrict television's access to subsequent military actions. During the 1991 Desert Storm operation, reporters were kept out of the combat zone until it was deemed safe by the military, and then only pools of reporters escorted by military personnel were allowed into the area. All other information came from Pentagon officials who regularly briefed television reporters on the war.

▪ Do you think that television has a greater power to persuade than other forms of media (such as radio, newspapers, news magazines, and film), or does television simply reinforce positions that people already hold? To help you decide, complete this simple exercise. List all the products, including candy and fast foods, that you have purchased in the last week or month. List your ten favorite television commercials, stating the product advertised and the method of advertising. Place a check mark beside each product that corresponds with a commercial on your list. Finally, circle any other product you have both purchased and seen in a television commercial. Compile your findings and be prepared to report them to the class.

Additional Skills Practice

Design a simple questionnaire to be used as the basis for a public opinion poll for use in your school. As a class, identify an issue of great interest to the students such as homework, dress codes, or curriculum. Each person should then write three questions that can be answered *quantitatively*, with a number value or with a "yes" or "no." Compare your questionnaire with those of your classmates. Correct vague or leading questions. Discuss the advantages and disadvantages of the different ways the questions were phrased. Select the best questions for the final poll. Tabulate the results and present them to the entire class.

The Great Society and Vietnam

When Lyndon Baines Johnson (LBJ) became president after John Kennedy's assassination, he vowed to fulfill Kennedy's reform promises. Johnson was remarkably successful. After he was elected in his own right in 1964, Johnson went far beyond Kennedy's New Frontier agenda. Johnson offered the American people a blueprint for a "Great Society." The phrase *Great Society*, compared to the more modest phrases *New Deal* or *Fair Deal*, provides an important insight into Lyndon Johnson. He longed for the American people to like,

even love, him. He wanted to outperform all earlier Democratic presidents in terms of reform legislation. These reasons, plus Johnson's genuine concern for those Americans outside the mainstream of society, led him to promote programs designed to give all Americans greater economic, social, and political opportunities. Johnson made great strides toward his goals. But even as the Great Society was starting to take shape, the Vietnam War began to undermine LBJ's cherished reform program.

▲ *President Lyndon B. Johnson is relaxed in this photograph. He was more often captured on film as a man of great energy and action.*

President Lyndon Johnson

Only hours after John Kennedy's death, Lyndon B. Johnson was sworn in as president of the United States. Johnson seemed to set just the right tone after Kennedy's assassination. In Johnson's first State of the Union Address in January 1964, he said, "All I have, I would have given gladly not to be standing here today." Intending to pressure Congress to enact Kennedy's domestic legislative program, Johnson continued, "Let us here highly resolve that John Fitzgerald Kennedy did not live—or die—in vain." Johnson immediately devoted himself to the task of completing Kennedy's work, and much more.

What were Johnson's legislative priorities in 1964?

Why did Congress grant Johnson such great authority in the Tonkin Gulf Resolution?

Why did Johnson defeat Barry Goldwater by such a wide margin in the 1964 presidential election?

▲ *What was Hubenthal suggesting in this editorial cartoon about President Johnson's relationship with the 88th Congress?*

Lyndon Johnson Takes Office

Few presidents have assumed the Oval Office with as much government experience and skill in politics as Lyndon Johnson. Born on a farm in south central Texas in 1908, Johnson first went to Washington in 1932 as an assistant to a Texas congressman. In 1936, Franklin Roosevelt appointed Johnson head of the National Youth Administration in Texas. Two years later, Johnson won election to the House of Representatives. In 1948, Texans elected him senator, and before his first term ended Johnson had become minority leader. When the Democrats became the majority party in 1954, he became majority leader. Johnson understood how to negotiate and compromise with people to get legislation through the Senate. This knowledge and talent became legendary.

Following Kennedy's death, Johnson used all his political skills to get Kennedy's legislative program passed. Johnson gave three bills priority. In February 1964, the Senate completed action on a tax bill. Designed to stimulate the economy by putting more money in consumers' hands, the Tax Reduction Act cut taxes by $11.5 billion. The tax cut was a great success. In the following 18 months, consumer spending rose by $45 billion, and this, in turn, stimulated general economic activity. By 1965, the economy was growing at 5 percent annually, and unemployment fell to under 4 percent, its lowest level in eight years. As a result of rapid economic growth, the government collected more revenue even with lower tax rates.

Civil rights legislation was Johnson's second priority. Soon after Kennedy's assassination, Johnson declared, "We have talked long enough about equal rights in this country. We have talked for 100 years or more. It is time now to write the next chapter

Civil Rights Act of 1964

Title I	Banned arbitrary registration standards for African American voters. If literacy tests are given, the same tests must be given to all potential voters.
Title II	Outlawed discrimination in public facilities, such as hotels, restaurants, movie theaters, public transportation, and snack bars, on the basis of race, color, religion, or national origin. Empowered the Attorney General to bring civil action against any business that did not comply.
Title III	Ensured equal entry into and behavior toward whites and minorities in all publicly owned and operated facilities.
Title IV	Called for school desegregation and empowered the federal government to provide technical and financial aid to any school district which was in the act of desegregating.
Title V	Extended the life of the Civil Rights Commission until January 31, 1968.
Title VI	Ensured that no person should be subjected to racial discrimination in any program financed with federal funds. Authorized ending federal funds if program did not comply.
Title VII	Forbade discrimination from employers or labor unions on the grounds of race, color, religion, sex, physical disability, or age.
Title VIII	Instructed the Census Bureau to collect voting statistics by race in those geographic areas listed by the Civil Rights Commission.
Title IX	Enabled higher federal courts to prohibit lower federal courts from sending civil rights cases back to state or local courts.
Title X	Organized a Community Relations Service within the Commerce Department to intercede and negotiate in local-level racial disputes.
Title XI	Upheld the right to trial by jury in criminal contempt cases which come out of any part of the Civil Rights Act, except for Title I. Ensured that this Civil Rights Act cannot be nullified in its entirety, even if a single part of it should be nullified.

▲ *The Civil Rights Act of 1964 was a remarkable piece of legislation in terms of its efforts to end discrimination. Name three of the many areas that were affected by this act.*

and to write it in the books of law." The **Civil Rights Act of 1964**:

- outlawed discrimination in public facilities
- authorized the attorney general to sue to desegregate public facilities and schools
- stopped federal funds to states and localities that failed to integrate
- forbade the unequal application of voter registration standards.

The act, however, did not outlaw literacy tests for voting. Critics thought this was a major flaw, since literacy tests had long been used to prevent African Americans from registering and voting.

Johnson's third priority was the "war on poverty." Although the tax cut greatly stimulated the economy, it offered little relief to the 35 million Americans trapped in poverty. These people lived in an environment characterized by disease, helplessness, a hand-to-mouth existence, and a sense of hopelessness. Among the poor were children, the elderly, and female heads of households. The poor lived in urban slums and economically depressed rural areas. They remained in poverty partly because they were invisible to the majority of Americans. Lacking work skills and training, these people were largely unemployable. They could only be helped by special programs designed to meet their needs.

Kennedy had begun planning a program to fight poverty before his death, but Johnson now adopted the idea as his own. In January 1964, he said, "This administration today, here and now, declares unconditional war on poverty in America. . . . We shall not rest until that war is won." In August, Congress passed the Economic Opportunity Act. Administered by the Office of Economic Opportunity, the act provided nearly $1 billion for a variety of programs. These included the Job Corps (which provided employment for youths aged 16 to 21); job training for unemployed adults; work-study funds for college students; and loans for employers to hire unemployed workers who had few job skills. The Head Start program sought to improve the early education of deprived youngsters. VISTA (Volunteers in Service to America) was established as the domestic equivalent of the Peace Corps. The Community Action Program was set up to help give the poor a larger voice in making the decisions that affected their own communities.

Vietnam Presses for Johnson's Attention

While Johnson pushed his legislative priorities through Congress, the situation in Vietnam worsened. After Ngo Dinh Diem's assassination, South Vietnam was plagued by political instability. A series of ineffective military governments came and went in Saigon, the country's capital. Meanwhile, the Vietcong gradually strengthened their grip on the countryside. In March 1964, Secretary of Defense Robert McNamara reported that the Vietcong controlled 40 percent of South Vietnam. Moreover, "large groups of the population," McNamara said,

"are now showing signs of apathy and indifference. . . . In the last 90 days the weakening of the government's position has been particularly noticeable." The Joint Chiefs of Staff recommended bombing North Vietnam to turn the tide.

Johnson refused at that time to increase U.S. participation in the war. First, he wanted to focus on getting his legislation through Congress. Second, Johnson was afraid of the impact that **escalation**, or increasing involvement in Vietnam, would have in an election year. Still, believing he had to do something, he authorized covert operations against North Vietnam. These included air strikes in Laos, South Vietnamese raids against North Vietnam, and U.S. warship patrols along North Vietnam's coast. Johnson also ordered the State Department to prepare a resolution that he could present to Congress that would give him broad, emergency authority to wage war in Vietnam.

In early August 1964, two U.S. destroyers, the *Maddox* and *C. Turner Joy*, were conducting operations off the coast of North Vietnam in the Gulf of Tonkin. At the same time, South Vietnamese forces were raiding two islands north of the 17th parallel (the dividing line between North and South Vietnam). The U.S. ships reported that North Vietnamese patrol boats had attacked them. Soon, however, the task force commander cabled Washington, "Review of action [suggests that] freak weather effects and over-eager sonarman may have accounted for many reports [of hostile actions]. No actual visual sighting by *Maddox*. Suggest complete evaluation before any further action." Johnson ignored this advice and ordered air raids against North Vietnamese torpedo boat bases and oil storage facilities. He also requested congressional action on the State Department's Vietnam resolution.

Congress promptly passed the **Gulf of Tonkin Resolution**—unanimously in the House and with only two dissenting votes in the Senate. The resolution granted Johnson vast authority to "take all necessary measures to repel any armed attack against forces of the United States and to prevent further aggression." Although the resolution gave enormous power to the president, few in the press or Congress questioned its wisdom. The Gulf of Tonkin Resolution became the basis of Johnson's later escalation of American fighting in Vietnam.

Arkansas Senator J. William Fulbright was chairman of the Senate Foreign Relations Committee. Fulbright became an early and eloquent critic of U.S. involvement in South Vietnam.

President Johnson was quite cautious initially in using the power the resolution gave him. He played down the war as he campaigned for reelection in 1964. He promised not to send U.S. troops to fight in Southeast Asia, saying, "We don't want our boys to do the fighting for Asian boys." He constantly emphasized his hopes for peace and American restraint in Vietnam. At this point, he also chose to ignore continued North Vietnamese and Vietcong actions against South Vietnam.

Johnson Wins in a Landslide

The Democrats entered the election campaign of 1964 in their strongest position in years. Johnson,

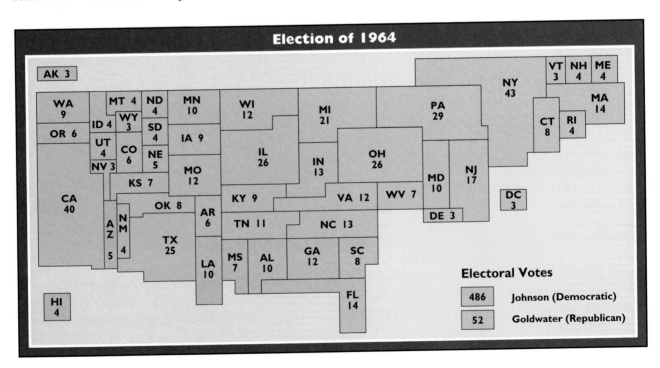

Election of 1964

Electoral Votes

| 486 | Johnson (Democratic) |
| 52 | Goldwater (Republican) |

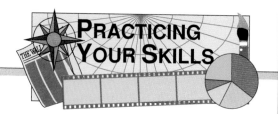

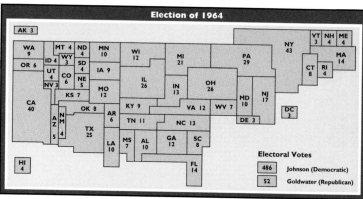

Election of 1964

| AK 3 | | | | | | | | | | VT 3 | NH 4 | ME 4 |

WA 9 | MT 4 | ND 4 | MN 10 | WI 12 | MI 21 | PA 29 | NY 43

OR 6 | ID 4 | WY 3 | SD 4 | IA 9

UT 4 | CO 6 | NE 5 | IL 26 | IN 13 | OH 26 | CT 8 | RI 4

NV 3 | KS 7 | MO 12 | MD 10 | NJ 17 | MA 14

CA 40 | OK 8 | AR 6 | KY 9 | VA 12 | WV 7 | DC 3 | DE 3

AZ 5 | NM 4 | TX 25 | TN 11 | NC 13

LA 10 | MS 7 | AL 10 | GA 12 | SC 8

HI 4 | FL 14

Electoral Votes
486 Johnson (Democratic)
52 Goldwater (Republican)

Map Skills: Understanding Cartograms

Somebody once quipped that a cartogram is an example of a map produced by an abstract expressionist. In a cartogram, the size and shape of each country or state is determined by its relative share of the map's theme. For instance, a population map would show California, New York, Texas, and Florida much larger than states with small populations. Wyoming, Utah, and Alaska would appear as very small states to match their small populations.

A cartogram assigns to a particular region an area based on some value other than land-surface area. Common subjects for cartograms are population, income, distribution of major industries and natural resources, and political affiliations. For example, a world cartogram that depicts natural oil reserves would show the country of Kuwait many times larger than China.

The cartogram on page 896 examines the results of the 1964 presidential election. Since the number of electoral votes cast by each state is a function of its population (the number of representatives plus two senators), this cartogram is also a relative population map.

Study the cartogram on page 896 and answer the following questions:

1. Which states appear most distorted by this cartogram?
2. (a) According to the cartogram, what are the six states with the greatest number of electoral votes? (b) Which six states have the fewest votes?
3. (a) What was the total number of electoral votes received by Goldwater? (b) How many electoral votes did Johnson receive?
4. How does the electoral college give extra power in election years to states with large populations? (Hint: As a presidential candidate, in what states would you concentrate your campaign efforts?)
5. What effect do you think Johnson's speech on civil rights had on the election of 1964? Do you think the results would have been different if Johnson had delayed his speech until after the election? Give reasons for your answer.

their presidential candidate, had an impressive record and was at the height of his popularity. His running mate, Hubert Humphrey, was a popular liberal senator from Minnesota. They appealed to the

◀ *In this cartogram, states are sized in proportion to the number of their electoral votes. How small can this number be?*

New Deal coalition of voters—the poor, organized labor, southern moderates, African Americans and civil rights groups, and liberals. All of these groups had been aided by Johnson's programs.

The Republicans, on the other hand, were weak and divided. The conservative faction of the party took control of the Republican National

Convention held in July 1964. The Republicans nominated Arizona Senator Barry Goldwater on the first ballot. Goldwater had emerged as the party's most prominent conservative in 1960. In his acceptance speech at the Republican National Convention Goldwater declared, "Extremism in the defense of liberty is no vice . . . moderation in the pursuit of justice is no virtue." Goldwater reflected the frustrations many Republicans felt about the direction the nation was taking under the Democrats. He spoke out against big government, Social Security, and civil rights. He advocated selling the Tennessee Valley Authority and ending federal farm subsidies. He also opposed arms reductions. Goldwater had limited appeal. Democrats painted Goldwater as an irresponsible, insensitive **reactionary**, or ultraconservative, whose election would lead to economic depression and nuclear war.

Even though political pollsters predicted a Democratic victory, Johnson campaigned as though the election were very much in doubt. He traveled extensively around the country and attacked Goldwater relentlessly. Johnson and the Democrats won by a landslide. Forty-three million people—61 percent of those casting ballots—voted for Johnson's brand of moderate politics. The landslide victory gave Johnson better than two-to-one majorities in both houses of Congress. Goldwater carried only Arizona and five states in the deep South. Johnson was now president in his own right and possessed a convincing electoral mandate for his programs.

SECTION 1 REVIEW

1. **List** President Johnson's legislative priorities in 1964.
2. **Outline** the major terms of the Civil Rights Act of 1964.
3. **Explain** why Johnson refused to escalate the Vietnam War at the beginning of his administration.
4. **Describe** circumstances that prompted Congress to give President Johnson broad powers in the Gulf of Tonkin Resolution.
5. **Explain** the wide margin of victory by Johnson over Goldwater in the election of 1964.

The Great Society

Lyndon Johnson was one of the nation's most effective chief executives in terms of the amount of legislation enacted during his tenure. Johnson had an extraordinary ability to persuade Congress to vote his way. The press dubbed such skills "the Johnson Treatment." As described by journalists Rowland Evans and Robert Novak, the Treatment began with "his face a scant millimeter from his target, his eyes widening and narrowing, his eyebrows rising and falling. From his pockets poured clippings, memos, statistics, mimicry, humor, and the genius of analogy [which] made the Treatment an almost hypnotic experience and rendered the target stunned and helpless." Johnson would "twist arms," appeal to patriotism, offer patronage, and use his vast store of political knowledge to win support for his legislative proposals. He was a masterful legislator.

What traditional Democratic reforms did Johnson include in his Great Society programs?

What new areas of concern did Great Society legislation include?

What made the vast outpouring of Great Society legislation possible?

Major Features of the Great Society

Johnson began preparations for his Great Society legislative program soon after his election in 1964. He realized that time was short to enact the legislation he wanted. As he told his aides, "Now look, I've just been reelected by an overwhelming majority . . . [but] every day while I'm in office, I'm going to lose votes. I'm going to alienate somebody. . . . We've got to get this legislation fast."

The major features of the Great Society—aid to education, medical care for the elderly, and civil rights—dated back to Harry Truman's Fair Deal. Thanks to Johnson's landslide victory over Barry Goldwater, the time seemed ripe to enact programs for these long-delayed goals. The Congress elected in 1964 had its largest Democratic majorities since the New Deal in 1937. They would prove strong supporters of Great Society legislation. The election of 1964 shattered the old coalition of Republicans and conservative Democrats that had blocked these reforms since 1938.

Improving education was a cause dear to Johnson's heart since he had taught school in

▲ *Lyndon Johnson honed his political skills in the Senate. What was "the Johnson Treatment?"*

Texas as a young man. He hoped, in fact, to be known as "the education president." The Elementary and Secondary Education Act, passed in April 1965, provided $1 billion to improve education. The act aided pupils rather than schools and thus sidestepped the objections of some religious groups to federal aid. It allocated funds based on the number of impoverished children in each state. Nearly 90 percent of the nation's schools benefited from the program. The act provided funds for library books, experimental learning centers, educational research, and state departments of education.

▼ *Great Society legislation initiated federal programs in many areas. Do you think the term* Great Society *was an accurate name for Johnson's legislative agenda?*

Major Great Society Legislation

Date	Act	Purpose
February 1964	Tax Reduction Act	Cut personal taxes by $11.5 billion
July 1964	Civil Rights Act	Banned discrimination in public facilities and in employment practices
August 1964	Equal Opportunity Act	Ten programs to aid urban and rural poor, including Job Corps, Head Start, and Vista
April 1965	Elementary and Secondary Education Act	Provided $1 billion in aid to improve public education
July 1965	Medicare and Medicaid	Provided health care for the aged and needy
August 1965	Voting Rights Act	Banned literacy tests; authorized federal supervision of voting registration in some districts
September 1965	National Endowments for the Arts and Humanities	Supported the work of artists and scholars
October 1965	Higher Education Act	Provided funds for college student loans and scholarships
September 1966	National Traffic and Motor Vehicle Safety Act	Established federal safety standards
September 1966	Highway Safety Act	Established federally mandated state-run safety programs

Johnson's concern for education went even further. The Higher Education Act (1965) earmarked federal funds for college student loans and scholarships and for the improvement of college libraries. Upward Bound helped talented but disadvantaged students attend college. The Teacher Corps program sought to improve the educational opportunities of the inner-city poor by sending experienced teachers into urban slum schools. Congress also created the National Endowment for the Arts and the National Endowment for the Humanities. Each endowment was authorized to give grants to scholars and artists to support their work and education.

▲ *President Johnson signed the Medicare bill in 1965. Why did Johnson invite former President Truman to the ceremony?*

Federally funded medical aid to the elderly had been stalled in Congress for 20 years. The American Medical Association had been a primary opponent of federal involvement in providing medical services. In 1965, Congress enacted Medicare, a national health insurance program for the aged under the Social Security system. The Medicare Act provided hospitalization and other medical benefits for nearly 19 million elderly persons. Medicaid, a part of Medicare, paid doctors' fees and other health services for nearly 8 million elderly poor people. Medicaid also helped other needy people who were not among the elderly. Johnson prodded Congress to increase federal aid to other medical and health services. The titles of these programs give a sense of their scope: Community Health Services, Child Health, Medical Libraries, Health Professions, and Mental Health Facilities.

Johnson had not originally planned to seek civil rights legislation in 1965. Dramatic events in the South, however, forced him to take action. In January, Martin Luther King Jr. began a drive to register over three million African Americans previously not registered to vote. On March 7, King staged a march in Alabama from Selma to Montgomery, to draw at-

▼ *What does this poll indicate about the economy of the time?*

Most Important Problem, 1964

Question: What do you think is the most important problem facing this country today?

Racial discrimination/civil rights	34%
Threat of communism/Russia/Cuba	20%
International problems	10%
Peace/war	8%
Unemployment	8%
High cost of living/inflation	6%

Source: Gallup, March 27 - April 2, 1964.

©The Public Perspective, a publication of the Roper Center for Public Opinion Research, University of CT, Storrs. Reprinted by permission.

tention to the voting-rights issue. Along the way, an armed posse led by Sheriff Jim Clark brutally attacked the peaceful marchers. A few days later, a white mob killed James Reeb, a white Boston minister. The entire nation watched these horrifying events unfold on television. This coverage influenced public opinion in support of civil rights legislation.

Rachel Carson's Silent Spring

In 1939, Paul Müller, a Swiss chemist, discovered that the compound DDT (a mixture of fuel oil and chemicals) was extremely toxic to insects. At the same time, DDT appeared harmless to humans and other mammals. Scientists in the United States learned of Müller's discovery during World War II, just as the U.S. military was trying to solve several problems associated with warfare in the tropics. Of particular concern were mosquitoes, which carried malaria, and lice, which carried typhus. Unless these pests could be controlled, thousands of U.S. troops might die from disease. In this situation, DDT seemed an ideal solution, and the U.S. military used the compound extensively. DDT proved so effective—and apparently safe—that Müller was awarded a Nobel Prize in medicine in 1948.

In 1945, the Food and Drug Administration allowed public sale of DDT. FDA scientists noted, however, that the pesticide accumulated in the fatty tissues of mammals and was passed on

▲ *Rachel Carson, marine biologist and best-selling author of* Silent Spring.

through milk. In large doses, DDT also damaged the central nervous systems of mammals. There was little scientific data concerning the possible long-term effects of the compound, however, and the FDA did not wait for additional research because of the great demand for the product. Over the next decade, the use of DDT rapidly increased.

Rachel Carson, a marine biologist, documented the effects of pesticides for many years. In 1957, she decided to act. She began assembling the available research. In

1962, Carson was ready to publish the results in *Silent Spring*. Writing eloquently, she warned that pesticides were threatening wildlife, the environment, and human health. The book was based on observations of the negative effect of DDT in urban areas where spraying attempted to protect Dutch elm trees from insect pests.

The chemical industry threatened lawsuits against Carson and her publisher in an attempt to stop the publication of *Silent Spring*. When these threats failed, the industry tried to discredit Carson's research, claiming, in part, that she was simply against technological progress. In spite of these efforts, the book sold nearly 500,000 copies in its first six months. It became one of the most controversial books of the decade. Although Carson died of cancer in 1964, *Silent Spring* continued to play a significant role in shaping the nation's environmental policies. In 1972, the United States banned the domestic sale of DDT.

1. Why did the U.S. military make extensive use of DDT during World War II?
2. Name one impact of Carson's *Silent Spring* study.

▲ *What was the main goal of this march to the state capitol in Montgomery, on March 7, 1965?*

▲ *This young man worked at the grassroots level to help secure rights. Why are grassroots movements usually effective?*

To underscore the importance of new civil rights legislation, Johnson appeared in person before Congress. Johnson eloquently stated his case:

> It is wrong—deadly wrong—to deny any of your fellow Americans the right to vote in this country.... Their cause must be our cause, too, because it is not just Negroes, but really it is all of us who must overcome the crippling legacy of bigotry and injustice. And we shall overcome.

In August 1965, Johnson signed the Voting Rights Act which did the following:

- authorized federal voting registrars to go into counties where less than half the eligible voters had gone to the polls in 1964

- forbade literacy tests as a means of discriminating against racial minorities
- gave the attorney general the right to assign federal observers to ensure fair elections.

As a result of the new legislation, large numbers of African Americans registered to vote. These new voters eventually became an important political force in the South. The number of registered white voters increased as well.

A Response to New Concerns

The Great Society continued the war on poverty begun in 1964, attacking the problem with a variety of new programs. Much of this Great Society legislation focused on specific urban problems. These included the creation of the cabinet-level Department of Housing and Urban Development (1965), whose first administrator was Robert Weaver, an African American.

Great Society programs also dealt with environmental issues. Since the mid-1950s, Americans had grown increasingly concerned about water and air pollution and other ecological problems. As people's knowledge increased, the demand for federal action grew. During the outpouring of Great Society legislation, Congress enacted several bills to set standards for clean air and water.

Consumer protection was also a part of the Great Society reform agenda. Ralph Nader, a young Connecticut attorney, raised concerns about automobile safety in his book *Unsafe at Any Speed*. Nader demanded that American auto manufacturers produce safer cars. This publicity led to the passage of federal safety standards for American-made motor vehicles and required the states to improve driver education, testing, and licensing. Another consumer protection law required manufacturers to provide accurate information on package labels. Growing concern about violence and crime led to several major crime bills that aided local law enforcement agencies. By late 1965, Johnson had prodded Congress to enact nearly 90 different bills. This was its largest burst of legislative activity since Franklin Roosevelt's first Hundred Days in 1933. All this activity resulted partly from the public's continued remorse over Kennedy's murder and from the Democrats' overwhelming victory in 1964.

By the late 1960s, however, many Americans were saying that Great Society reforms "threw money at problems" but didn't actually solve them. Certainly Johnson was not able to end racial inequality or poverty, nor did his programs secure full employment. But those programs did substantially improve the lives of many Americans. The improvements made to Social Security, along with unemployment benefits, public assistance to the aged and disabled, and such programs as Aid to Families with Dependent Children, worked reasonably well.

Medicare and Medicaid provided better medical care for groups formerly without such care. Housing programs made it possible for low-income minority families to escape the ghetto. Retraining programs helped these people improve their jobs and wages. Civil rights laws greatly improved the political and social standing of many minorities. Johnson may not have achieved a "Great Society," but American society in general was much improved for his efforts.

SECTION 2 REVIEW

1. List traditional Democratic reforms Johnson included in the Great Society agenda.
2. Describe features of the Voting Rights Act of 1965, and explain its immediate results.
3. List new concerns addressed by Great Society legislation.
4. Identify Ralph Nader.
5. Explain why Johnson was able to get so much Great Society legislation passed.

SECTION 3

The Vietnam War, 1965–1967

The Great Society peaked in 1965. After that, support for President Johnson's legislative programs began to falter. The very boldness of Johnson's legislative goals aroused opposition. Conservatives especially were unhappy about the government spending the huge sums that Great Society programs required. As Republican Senate leader Everett Dirksen said, "a billion dollars here, a billion dollars there, and pretty soon you're talking real money."

Even more staggering were the billions of dollars being spent on the Vietnam War. In May 1966, the president said, "We do not seek to enlarge this war, but we shall not run out on it." That year the Vietnam War cost $8 billion. It cost nearly $21 billion in 1967. To pay these huge military bills, Congress began to pare down Great Society programs or to end them altogether. The Vietnam War eventually crippled Johnson's Great Society, and caused him not to seek another term.

What policy alternatives concerning Vietnam did Johnson and his advisers consider in 1965?

What was the nature of the United States' combat role in Vietnam?

On what diplomatic issues did North Vietnam and the United States disagree?

Worsening Situation in Vietnam

Foreign policy proved to be Johnson's undoing. During most of his public service, Johnson had dealt almost exclusively with domestic issues. Before becoming vice president, he had traveled little outside the United States, and he knew few foreign leaders personally. Like many Americans of his generation, however, Johnson believed he had learned several lessons from World War II and the Korean War.

The first lesson was that the United States should stop foreign aggression as soon as it appeared. He had learned from Europe's experience with Hitler that appeasement did not work. A second lesson was that U.S. leaders should strongly assert America's interests throughout the world. For Johnson, U.S. foreign policy setbacks, such as the stalemate of the Korean War and Castro's rise to power in Cuba, were examples of the nation's not being tough enough in protecting its vital interests.

Johnson also recognized that foreign policy failures could have drastic political consequences for a president. He recalled how the Communist takeover of China and the Korean War had crippled Truman's presidency. Johnson wanted to avoid Truman's mistakes. These beliefs guided Johnson's choices as he dealt with the situation in Vietnam.

By January 1965, Johnson and his advisers thought that South Vietnam was on the verge of collapse. Continued political chaos in Saigon, as well as Vietcong successes on the battlefield, had nearly convinced National Security Adviser McGeorge Bundy and Secretary of Defense Robert McNamara "that our current policy can lead only to disastrous defeat." Bundy and McNamara saw only two alternatives—"to use our military power in the Far East and to force a change of Communist policy [or] deploy all our resources along a track of negotiation." Secretary of State Dean Rusk disagreed, saying "the consequences of both escalation and withdrawal are so bad that we simply must find a way of making our present policy work."

Johnson sent Bundy to Saigon in February to study the situation firsthand. When Bundy returned to Washington, he reported that "the situation in Vietnam is deteriorating and without new U.S. action defeat appears inevitable." For Bundy, the stakes for the United States were high. "The international prestige of the United States, and a substantial part of our influence," Bundy asserted, "are directly at risk in Vietnam." He therefore recommended "sustained reprisal against North Vietnam." A week later, Johnson approved Operation Rolling Thunder—the systematic bombing of North Vietnam. Rolling Thunder would continue for the next three years.

U.S. air strikes against North Vietnam led to the buildup of American ground forces in South Vietnam. The daily air raids required new air bases in South Vietnam, and these, in turn, needed protection. In April 1965, 33,500 U.S. soldiers served in South Vietnam. By June, that number had more than doubled. Johnson also expanded the troops' role beyond simply the defense of U.S. military installations. By summer, U.S. ground forces had begun offensive operations north of Saigon against the Vietcong.

Deciding on Policy   In July, McNamara visited South Vietnam. His assessment was gloomy. "The situation in South Vietnam," he reported, "is worse than a year ago." McNamara outlined three alternatives: "(a) Cut our losses and withdraw. . . . (b) Continue at about the present level, with U.S. forces limited to say 75,000 . . . (c) Expand promptly and substantially the U.S. military pressure against the Viet Cong in the South and maintain the military pressure against the North Vietnamese." McNamara favored the third option, saying it offered "the best odds of the best outcome with the most acceptable cost to the United States." He proposed increasing U.S. ground forces to 200,000 by the end of 1965, with an additional 100,000 to be sent over in 1966.

Most of Johnson's advisers agreed with McNamara's reasoning. George Ball, undersecretary of state, and Clark Clifford, a trusted personal adviser, were among the few who opposed McNamara's suggested course of action. Ball insisted that France's experience in Vietnam was directly relevant. France had sent 250,000 troops only to suffer humiliation. Clifford told Johnson, "I don't believe we can win in South Vietnam. If we send in 100,000 more men, the North Vietnamese will meet us. If North Vietnam runs out of men, the Chinese will send in volunteers. . . . I can't see anything but catastrophe for my country." Despite this advice, Johnson decided to escalate the conflict.

Escalating the War

The sustained air war against North Vietnam and the steady increase in U.S. ground troops changed the nature of the Vietnam War. What had been essentially a civil war between factions within South Vietnam now changed to a struggle between the United States and North Vietnam. As Clark Clifford had predicted, North Vietnam responded to U.S. escalation by sending more of its own troops south down the Ho Chi Minh Trail.

By any measure, the air war was unsuccessful. Between 1965 and 1968, U.S. bombers inflicted $600 million damage on North Vietnam. They leveled North Vietnamese cities and knocked out many military and industrial installations. Yet, despite a fourfold increase in bombing between 1965 and 1967, the bombing had little effect on the war.

One reason was that as the bombing escalated, the North Vietnamese quickly developed various countermeasures. They relocated industries and storage facilities, and they relied on carts, bicycles, and foot transportation to move supplies. Their losses in military equipment and raw materials were offset by imports from China and the Soviet Union. North Vietnam also relocated its civilians away from urban areas and built underground cities. They dug 30,000 miles of tunnels in which many civilians lived and worked during the height of the bombing campaign. The bombing failed to weaken North Vietnam's will to fight and may even have increased civilian support for the war.

Meanwhile, the United States was paying a heavy price for small gains. Each B-52 sortie, or bombing mission, cost $30,000 in bombs alone. Between 1965 and 1968, the United States lost 650 aircraft. In addition, the North Vietnamese captured and imprisoned the U.S. airmen they shot down. These prisoners of war (POWs) would become a critical issue as the war reached a stalemate.

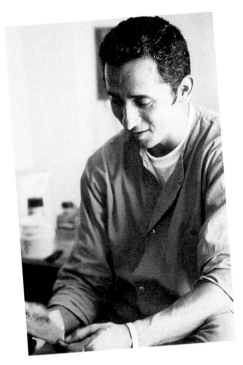

▲ *Lt. Commander Everett Alvarez was captured early in the Vietnam conflict.*

U.S. Ground Operations The ground war in South Vietnam also escalated dramatically between 1965 and 1967. General William Westmoreland had taken command of U.S. forces in Vietnam in the middle of 1964. Westmoreland used a strategy of **attrition**—wearing down the enemy by inflicting as many casualties as possible. The war in South Vietnam had no set battle lines or permanent fronts. The Vietcong and North Vietnamese regular army units used guerrilla tactics, hiding among the civilian population and fighting wherever and whenever they chose. To counter these tactics, Westmoreland sent his troops out into the countryside on "search-and-destroy" missions. These aggressive tactics required vast increases in military personnel.

The United States sought to exploit American technological superiority. Chemical sprays, such as Agent Orange (a defoliant that caused trees to lose their leaves), and huge bulldozers removed the dense jungle cover that made guerrillas difficult to find. Electronic sensors picked up enemy movements in jungle areas. The army employed helicopters to move troops more easily. Cobra helicopters and C-47 airplanes (called "Spooky" and "Puff the Magic Dragon" because they were equipped with mini-

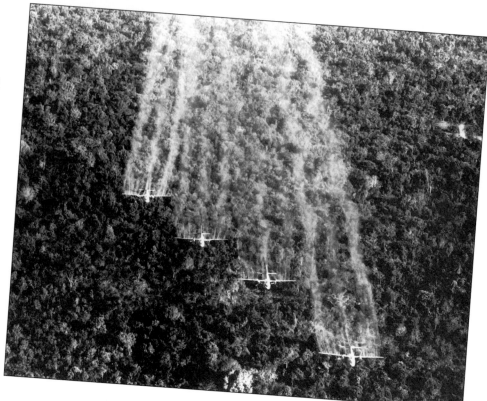

Taken in September 1965, this photograph shows four American C-123 airplanes spraying a liquid defoliant on a jungle in South Vietnam. What military strategy was served by widespread defoliation? What were the governmental consequences of using these chemicals?

guns capable of firing 6,000 rounds a minute) gave U.S. troops vast firepower. Artillery bases located throughout the countryside supported American ground operations. American fighter planes dropped napalm and other bombs to support combat units on the ground. Between 1965 and 1967, the U.S. dropped over a million tons of bombs in South Vietnam, more than double the bombs dropped on North Vietnam.

U.S. bombing and the use of chemicals to kill the dense jungle-vegetation in rural areas of Vietnam drove peasants from their villages. Nearly four million people, roughly a quarter of South Vietnam's population, became refugees. Living in refugee camps or on the fringes of towns and cities, many suffered great hardships from starvation, diseases, and inadequate shelter.

It is difficult to assess the effects of U.S. ground operations. Despite miserable conditions—dense jungle, monsoon rains, and a deadly and elusive enemy—U.S. troops fought well in this period. When they engaged the enemy, they usually won, largely because of their vastly superior firepower. The increase in their numbers between 1965 and 1967 no doubt prevented South Vietnam's defeat.

◀ *This rifle attachment chemically detected the presence of hidden troops. In spite of superior technology, the U.S. was only able to achieve a stalemate. Why?*

By any estimate, U.S. forces inflicted horrible losses on the enemy, perhaps as many as 220,000 casualties by 1967.

On the other hand, Westmoreland's strategy of attrition had serious limitations. First, it assumed that U.S. forces could inflict enough losses on the enemy to make them stop the war, while keeping U.S. losses "within acceptable bounds." Nearly 200,000 North Vietnamese reached draft age each year, however, and Hanoi matched every U.S. increase in manpower with its own. In addition, because North Vietnam and the Vietcong could choose when and where to fight, they could withdraw, melt into the civilian population, and resume guerrilla tactics if their losses became too high in any one place. Finally, in assuming the major responsibility for the fighting, U.S. forces undermined the morale of South Vietnam's army, and South Vietnam became increasingly dependent on the United States. By 1967, the U.S. had achieved no better than a stalemate.

Peace Negotiations Prove Impossible

The escalation of the Vietnam War brought demands from countries around the world for the United States and North Vietnam to begin peace negotiations. As a result of this pressure, between 1965 and 1967 American officials made nearly 2,000 diplomatic contacts to bring the United States and North Vietnam together to talk. But peace talks depended on the willingness of both sides to compromise, and the political position of each side left little room for negotiation.

For several years, North Vietnam had insisted that the United States meet three conditions before negotiations could begin:

- The United States had to stop the bombing and withdraw its ground forces.
- The United States had to replace the government in South Vietnam with a representative government that included the Vietcong.
- North and South Vietnam had to be reunified under a single government.

The diplomatic goals of the United States were also firm. The United States would stop the bombing only if North Vietnam withdrew its forces from South Vietnam. The U.S. was willing to withdraw its troops *after* a satisfactory political settlement had been arranged. President Johnson accepted the principle that the South Vietnamese should solve their own political problems, but he was determined to have a non-Communist government. To allow the Vietcong into a coalition government in South Vietnam would be, as Vice President Humphrey said, like putting a "fox in the chicken coop."

As the war intensified and the prospect of a peaceful settlement dimmed, criticism of the war grew. More and more Americans saw that the war would not end without even greater escalation, and they objected to the growing losses of American lives. Sensitive to such criticism, Johnson began a campaign to convince the critics that the United States was winning the war. And in fact, in September 1967, Johnson had reasons for optimism. General Nguyen Van Thieu (nuh-WIN vahn tee-oo) had recently become president of South Vietnam. Nearly 83 percent of eligible South Vietnamese voted, and political stability finally seemed assured. Johnson administration officials made scores of speeches around the United States to convince skeptics that the U.S. was winning the Vietnam War. General Westmoreland came home to reassure the nation that all was well. Westmoreland told reporters, "I am very encouraged. . . . We are making real progress." McNamara said he "could see light at the end of the tunnel."

SECTION 3 REVIEW

1. **State** reasons for the lack of support for Great Society programs after 1965.
2. **Identify** McGeorge Bundy.
3. **List** policy alternatives Johnson and his advisers considered toward Vietnam in July 1965.
4. **Describe** the serious limitations of attrition strategy.
5. **Explain** why early attempts at a peace negotiation in Vietnam failed.

The Impact of the Vietnam War

On Friday, October 16, 1965, David J. Miller, a 22-year-old pacifist, climbed atop a sound truck parked outside the Whitehall Street Army Induction Center in lower Manhattan, New York City. Miller tried to ignite his draft card with a match, but the match kept blowing out. Finally, someone in the crowd gave him a cigarette lighter. Miller hunched over the card to light it, and then he held it above his head for all to see. This image—the small flame, with Miller and a silent crowd watching—was broadcast by television across the country. Miller's gesture, for which he would serve two years in prison, symbolized the growing opposition of many Americans to the war in Vietnam.

Why did public support for the Vietnam War decline?
How did the Vietnam War divide U.S. public opinion?
What impact did television coverage have on U.S. public opinion toward the Vietnam War?

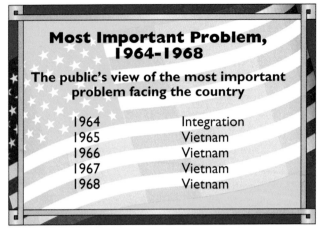

Most Important Problem, 1964–1968

The public's view of the most important problem facing the country

1964	Integration
1965	Vietnam
1966	Vietnam
1967	Vietnam
1968	Vietnam

©The Public Perspective, a publication of the Roper Center for Public Opinion Research, University of CT, Storrs. Reprinted by permission.

▲ *During President Johnson's second term in office the war in Vietnam was an overriding concern.*

Growing Opposition to the War

When Johnson escalated involvement in the Vietnam War in 1965, most Americans supported his decision. Public opinion changed when escalation failed to produce the desired results. Increasing the number of U.S. troops in Vietnam only increased the number of deaths and injuries.

The war affected growing numbers of Americans whose relatives and friends were drafted. Monthly draft calls of 5,000 in 1965 were increased to 50,000 a month by 1967. Most of the draftees were young men aged 19 to 26. Two million young men served a one-year tour of duty in Vietnam. Women were not eligible for the draft, although 6,431 women served in Vietnam voluntarily.

Initially, the draft worked unfairly. Each local draft board took in men according to its own selection criteria. Until 1969, the draft system allowed many deferments, exemptions, and noncombat military alternatives. Middle-class youths and college students received exemptions more often than minorities or white youths from blue-collar classes. By 1966, the inequalities of the draft had become increasingly apparent. Army historian S. L. A. Marshal observed:

> In the average rifle company, the strength was 50 percent composed of [African Americans], southwestern Mexicans, Puerto Ricans, Guamanians, Nisei [third-generation Japanese Americans], and so on. But a real cross section of American youth? Almost never.

Once these inequalities came to light, the army moved to correct them.

By 1967, public opinion at home and abroad was growing critical of U.S. bombing. As many people saw it, bombing North Vietnam was ineffective at best, immoral at worst. Even some of Johnson's closest advisers began to question the wisdom of continuing the bombing. Defense Secretary McNamara said, "The picture of the world's greatest superpower killing or seriously injuring 1,000 non-combatants a week, while trying to pound a tiny, backward nation into submission . . . is not a pretty one." Johnson himself conceded that the bombing had accomplished little. Even so, Johnson felt he could not stop bombing as long as U.S. ground troops were in South Vietnam.

Johnson avoided putting the nation in an official state of war, even though the Joint Chiefs of Staff had recommended it. He feared that calling attention to Vietnam would sabotage the passage of Great Society legislation in Congress. As a result, by 1967 the cost of the war was beginning to damage the economy. As the war's costs began to grow Johnson's economic advisers urged him to ask for a sharp increase in taxes in 1966 to head off potentially severe inflation. He refused, and the next year the federal budget deficit jumped to nearly $10 billion. In late 1967, Johnson finally asked Congress for additional taxes to help pay for the war. Congress consented only after Johnson agreed to cuts in domestic spending. But it was too little, too late. The federal budget deficit was $28 billion in 1968, and rapid inflation began to wipe out economic gains that had been made during the decade.

Divided Americans

Among the American people there were significant differences of opinion about the Vietnam War from the very beginning. At one extreme were the **hawks**, nationalists who viewed the conflict in Vietnam as part of a global struggle against Communism. If the United States did not hold the line in South Vietnam, they argued, other countries would fall to Communist aggression like a row of dominoes. Moreover, if the United States did not stand by its South Vietnamese allies, other American allies—and neutral nations, too—would lose faith in the word of the United States and thus be more open to Communist pressure. Eventually, the United States would stand alone against a powerful enemy. Hawks believed that the United States could win the war if the U.S. military were given a free hand.

Lower-middle-class and working-class people tended to support the war. Because working-class youths were more often drafted than college students (and than middle-class youths in general), the working classes bitterly resented the college students who led antiwar protests, burned their draft cards or the U.S. flag, or who flew the Vietcong flag. They also resented that poorer kids did not get the same breaks as college kids. Working-class youth tended to conform rather than rebel, and tended to volunteer for service or accept being drafted.

At the other extreme were the **doves**, people who were opposed to war on moral grounds or who wanted peace in Vietnam at almost any price. In April 1965, 12,000 protesters marched on Washington, D.C., in the first large demonstration against the war. In May, the first national teach-in, an extended series of antiwar lectures, debates, and discussions, took place at the University of Michigan. In October, thousands marched in New York City to protest the war, and antiwar demonstrations began to take place in many other cities as well.

Antiwar protests increased in November 1965. On November 2, Norman Morrison, a Quaker

▼ *This photograph represents the intensity of feelings in support of the war beginning to surface during the Nixon administration.*

pacifist, burned himself to death in front of the Pentagon. A week later, Roger La Porte, also a pacifist, did the same thing before the United Nations building in New York City. At the end of November, 35,000 people marched on Washington. In 1966, antiwar demonstrations became even more militant. Activists staged sit-ins at army draft centers, young men publicly burned their draft cards, and students tried to prevent companies involved in the war from recruiting on college campuses. Some young men left the country to avoid being drafted.

▲ *What does this photograph of an antiwar demonstration tell you about the people who opposed U.S. involvement in Vietnam?*

In April 1967, the inequalities of the draft and the barbarity of the war led Martin Luther King Jr. to take a forceful antiwar stand. King believed the war was devastating the hopes of the poor by undermining Great Society programs.

> So we have been repeatedly faced with the cruel irony of watching black and white boys on TV screens as they kill and die together for a nation that has been unable to seat them together in the same schools. . . . I could not be silent in the face of such cruel manipulation of the poor.

By 1967, the antiwar movement was a broad-based movement composed of draft-age students, pacifists, political liberals, and civil rights activists. It also included a number of visible politicians, including Senator J. William Fulbright from Arkansas, Senator Frank Church from Idaho, and Senator George McGovern from South Dakota. Some middle-class parents, afraid that their sons would be drafted and sent to Vietnam, also joined the antiwar movement. By this time, Johnson had become a virtual prisoner in the White House. The president

and his administration officials were afraid to make public appearances because such appearances usually involved confrontations with antiwar protesters.

As the war dragged on, more and more people became frustrated and impatient. Public opinion analyst Sam Lubbell commented that most Americans now had a "fervent desire to shake free of an unwanted burden." One housewife told Lubbell, "I want to get out but I don't want to give up." By August 1967, polls indicated for the first time that the majority of Americans thought U.S. intervention in Vietnam had been a mistake.

SECTION 4 REVIEW

1. **State** reasons public support for the Vietnam War declined.
2. **Describe** the inequities of the draft system.
3. **Explain** Johnson's reluctance to ask Congress to put the country in an official state of war.
4. **Contrast** the beliefs of the hawks and those of the doves on the war.
5. **Explain** why Johnson avoided public appearances after 1967.

The Tet Offensive and Its Aftermath

In the early morning hours of January 30, 1968, the beginning of the Vietnamese Lunar New Year, or Tet, Vietcong and North Vietnamese regular troops began a new offensive operation. They attacked nearly every principal city in South Vietnam. A team of 19 Vietcong sappers (armed infiltrators) blew a hole in the wall surrounding the American embassy in Saigon. They entered the embassy grounds and attacked it for nearly seven hours. Although all 19 Vietcong sappers died before they could penetrate the embassy building, the attack—carried on television—symbolized American vulnerability and the frustrating lack of progress the U.S. had made in South Vietnam. The Tet Offensive was a tactical disaster for the Vietcong and North Vietnam. At the same time, it was a great psychological victory. The **Tet Offensive** marked the beginning of the end of U.S. involvement in Vietnam.

What was the Tet Offensive?

How could the Tet Offensive be a tactical defeat and yet also a strategic victory for North Vietnam?

How did the Tet Offensive change U.S. policy toward Vietnam?

The Tet Offensive

North Vietnam began preparing for the Tet Offensive in late 1967. Hanoi's plan was first to lure American and South Vietnamese regular units away from the large population centers by conducting North Vietnamese Army (NVA) operations in outlying areas. The cities would then be vulnerable to Vietcong attack. Westmoreland dispatched reinforcements to all the trouble spots. U.S. troops inflicted heavy losses on the North Vietnamese, but this scattered U.S. forces and left the population centers vulnerable to attack.

On January 30, Vietcong and NVA forces began a series of attacks that coincided with the most festive of Vietnamese holidays, the Lunar New Year celebration of Tet. Both sides had traditionally observed cease-fires during Tet holidays, and Hanoi hoped that ARVN and U.S. soldiers would be relaxing and would be unprepared for military action. And, in fact, the attacks initially succeeded by catching both the South Vietnamese and the Americans off guard.

But the U.S. forces were able to spring into action. The Tet Offensive was exactly what General Westmoreland had hoped for—frontal assaults, made out in the open by an enemy whose usual strategy was based on guerrilla tactics. In Saigon, ARVN and American units cleared the city of Vietcong within several days. In much of South Vietnam, U.S. and ARVN troops used their superior mobility and firepower to recapture places that the NVA and Vietcong had taken during the Tet Offensive. The ancient imperial capital of Hue, however, took three weeks of vicious house-to-house fighting and devastating bombing raids before it was retaken. By the end of February, U.S. and South Vietnamese forces had crushed the Tet Offensive.

The Tet Offensive was a devastating defeat for the Vietcong and Hanoi in a strictly tactical sense. The enemy failed to hold a single capital they had captured, and they sustained terrible losses. Westmoreland estimated that 37,000 of the enemy had been killed, compared to 2,500 Americans. On the other hand, the Tet Offensive shattered many Americans' confidence that the Vietnam War could ever be won.

Changes in American Policy

The Tet Offensive occurred at a time when President Johnson was already feeling the strains of divided opinion among his advisers and the American public over continued American involvement in Vietnam. The military and other hawks were urging him to escalate the war further. Westmoreland and the Joint Chiefs of Staff wanted to commit the nation to an all-out effort for military victory. They

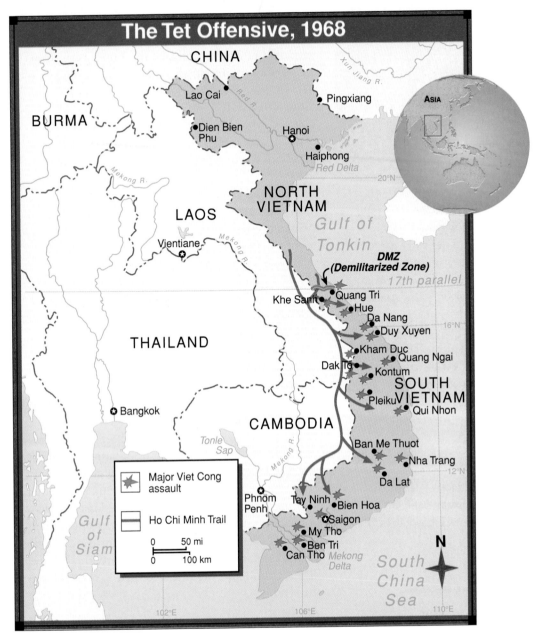

The Tet Offensive, 1968

▲ *Why would General William Westmoreland have wanted to expand U.S. military operations into Laos and Cambodia?*

asked for yet another increase of 206,000 troops, which would require calling up reserve units for active duty, enlarging draft calls, and possibly extending the length of combat tours. Hawks also pressed for extensive ground and air operations against enemy camps in Cambodia and Laos. Johnson had chosen not to attack these areas because Laos and Cambodia were neutral. The military urged even more bombing, especially of the Hanoi-Haiphong area, and laying mines in Haiphong harbor.

At the same time, Johnson felt great pressure to de-escalate the conflict and to begin earnest negoti-

► In a scene caught in one of the most famous photographs of the Vietnam War, a South Vietnamese police officer executed a Vietcong suspect on a Saigon street in 1968. How do you think this image affected efforts to end the war?

ations to end the war. By the end of 1967, antiwar protests had grown in number and harshness. On October 21, in Washington, D.C., a protest march of 50,000 people began peacefully, but ended in violence. Police arrested over 1,000 when demonstrators attempted to disrupt operations at the Pentagon. America's allies and such third parties as U Thant, the secretary-general of the United Nations, pressed Johnson to negotiate for peace.

On March 1, 1968, Clark Clifford succeeded Robert McNamara as secretary of defense. President Johnson instructed Clifford to reassess America's Vietnam policy "from A to Z." The Clifford task force looked closely at Westmoreland's request for 206,000 additional troops. To Clifford's astonishment, he could find "no military plan to win the war," except to wear the enemy down by attrition. Clifford reported to Johnson on March 4 that he was not optimistic that additional troops would bring eventual military success. On March 13, Johnson announced he would send 10,500 reinforcements and call up 20,000 more reservists. He told the military that he would not extend the troop commitment beyond this level.

March 1968 saw a reversal of Johnson's escalation policy in Vietnam. Johnson was losing his health and was steadily losing his popularity. On March 10, the *New York Times* published the story

about Westmoreland's request for 206,000 more troops. The revelation shocked the nation. On March 12, Senator Eugene McCarthy, campaigning as an opponent of the war, nearly tied Johnson in the New Hampshire presidential primary, opening the door for a bitter fight over war policy within the Democratic Party. On March 17, the *New York Times* reported Johnson's recent approval of sending another 30,000 soldiers to Vietnam. This created a thunderous negative response. On March 18, Senator Robert Kennedy announced his candidacy for the Democratic Party's presidential nomination, in opposition to the war. On March 25, a Harris opinion poll showed that 60 percent of the American public regarded the Tet Offensive as a defeat of American objectives in Vietnam. A Gallup poll reported that only 36 percent of Americans approved Johnson's handling of the Vietnam War and that a majority favored withdrawal. On March 26, a group of Johnson's senior advisers shocked him by recommending against further troop increases and by advocating a negotiated settlement.

On March 31, 1968, Johnson went on television to speak to the nation. He began, "Tonight, I want to speak to you of peace in Vietnam, and Southeast Asia. No other question so preoccupies our people." Johnson announced a halt to bombing except in the area between the 17th and 20th

The Living Room War

"**N**ever in the history of warfare," *Newsweek* magazine reported in July 1967, "has so much information [about a war] been inflicted upon so many. . . . [The output] of more than 400 reporters [assigned to cover] General Westmoreland's command . . . bursts into the home in living—or dying—color." By this time, there was little question that television coverage of the Vietnam War far surpassed that of any previous war. There were, however, different claims about what effects the "living room war" was having on viewers.

Some evidence suggested that television coverage of the war increased opposition to it. When asked by reporter Dan Wakefield in late 1967 why there was so much opposition to the Vietnam War, Vice President Hubert Humphrey said that this was "the first time people have seen a real war, live, in their living rooms." Several months later, Humphrey reasserted this idea: "In the quiet of your living room . . . this cruel, ugly, dirty fact of life and death and war and pain and suffering comes right to you." After the war, General William Westmoreland accused the press generally, and television particularly, of creating negative public opinion. Westmoreland claimed that news coverage had transformed a costly Communist military defeat during the 1968 Tet Offensive into a psychological de-

▲ *A Vietnamese mother and children attempt to escape by a dangerous river crossing. What were the extreme hardships suffered by the Vietnamese civilian population?*

feat for the United States. Other evidence indicated that television coverage of the war actually increased support for it. A *Newsweek* Harris public opinion poll in July 1967 discovered "that TV has encouraged a decisive majority of viewers to support the war."

Finally, there was evidence that television usually reinforced attitudes that people already held. A *U.S. News and World Report* article suggested that "few people say that their attitudes toward the war have been changed by the nightly fare of violence on TV." A *Newsweek* article concluded: "television creates neither hawks nor doves but merely reinforces existing opinions." The article included several interviews. A labor-relations expert in New York said, "TV coverage we see causes me to want to

become more 'hawklike.' It causes me to step up to the point of wanting to use nuclear bombs to put an end to this [war] fast." In contrast, a Houston housewife admitted that television coverage had reinforced her dovish views: "After what I've seen in the last few weeks on the news shows, it makes me wonder how much longer this thing is going to go on."

1. What impact do you think television had on American public opinion concerning the Vietnam War?
2. Talk to people who saw the Persian Gulf War on television. How did their attitudes toward the television coverage compare with attitudes toward coverage of the Vietnam War?

▲ A visibly exhausted Lyndon Johnson was photographed on March 30, 1968, working on a television speech. The next day it turned out to be a political bombshell.

▲ This headline indicated the substance of Johnson's March 31 televised speech. How did this speech mark a turning point in peace negotiations?

parallels. This would spare virtually 90 percent of North Vietnam from bombing attack. A bombing halt was North Vietnam's condition for peace negotiations to begin. Johnson then said he was prepared to meet with the North Vietnamese "any time, any place" to begin peace negotiations. His speech marked a turning point in the Vietnam War. At the end of his remarks, he said, "I have concluded that I should not permit the presidency to become involved in the partisan divisions that are developing in this political year. . . . Accordingly, I shall not seek, and I will not accept, the nomination of my party for another term as your president."

A major reassessment of American Vietnam policy had begun. It had become obvious that current policies were simply not working. American officials decided to limit the resources sent to Vietnam and to seek a negotiated settlement with the North Vietnamese. Preliminary peace talks between the United States and North Vietnam opened in Paris on May 10, 1968. They would continue for the next five years.

SECTION 5 REVIEW

1. **Identify** the Tet Offensive.
2. **Explain** how the Tet Offensive was a tactical defeat and yet a strategic victory for North Vietnam.
3. **Summarize** the aims of the hawks toward Vietnam.
4. **Describe** pressures on the president to scale back the conflict and negotiate to end the war.
5. **Explain** circumstances that forced Johnson to change his policy toward Vietnam.

Summary

After John Kennedy's assassination, Lyndon Johnson pledged to try to fulfill Kennedy's promises. By June 1964, Johnson had prodded Congress to enact major pieces of Kennedy's legislative program —a tax cut, a war on poverty, and a civil rights act. LBJ was also planning for election in his own right. Emphasizing his legislative accomplishments and promising many more, LBJ overwhelmed Republican conservative Barry Goldwater in 1964. During the campaign, LBJ played down the Vietnam issue, although events in Vietnam after Diem's death were reaching a crisis. Just after Johnson's resounding election victory as a peace candidate, the nation's military involvement in Vietnam escalated.

When elected president in 1964, Lyndon Johnson set out to create a "Great Society" in the United States. With his leadership, Congress enacted a substantial amount of reform legislation, affecting almost every area of American life. Great Society legislation dealt with education, health care, law enforcement, pollution control, veterans' benefits, voting, and care of the elderly. Before the Great Society's promise could be realized, however, the Vietnam War began to take attention and funds away from domestic programs.

Johnson's escalation of U.S. military involvement in Vietnam began with the strategic bombing of North Vietnam. Increasing the number of U.S. ground troops in South Vietnam followed soon after. Bombing and ground combat did not solve the Vietnam problem. Bombing North Vietnam was ineffective. American search-and-destroy missions in South Vietnam required more and more draftees and led to staggering increases in American casualties. Both the air war against North Vietnam and combat in South Vietnam brought growing opposition to the war in the United States. In 1965, antiwar activity took the form of peaceful protest marches and teach-ins. By late 1967, frustrated antiwar activists employed tactics that led to violent confrontations. The number of Americans opposing the war grew steadily. The Tet Offensive in February 1968 sealed LBJ's political fate and symbolized the beginning of the end of U.S. military involvement in Vietnam.

Vocabulary

attrition   hawks

doves   reactionary

escalation

Define each of the vocabulary terms by writing one or more sentences using the term. Be sure your sentences provide context for each term.

Review Questions

1. Describe the top three priorities of Lyndon Johnson's legislative program in 1964.
2. Why did the Gulf of Tonkin Resolution have such far-reaching effects on the war in Vietnam?
3. What accounted for Johnson's landslide victory over Goldwater in 1964?
4. Name some significant areas dealt with by Johnson's Great Society reforms.
5. Why did support for Johnson's Great Society begin to falter after 1965?
6. List the three policy alternatives outlined by McNamara for Vietnam in 1965.
7. Was the attrition strategy used by General Westmoreland in the Vietnam War successful? Why, or why not?
8. Contrast conditions demanded by North Vietnam and the United States before starting peace negotiations.
9. Name the factors that led to the increasing opposition to the Vietnam War.
10. Explain why President Johnson's televised talk in March 1968 was a turning point in the Vietnam War.

Critical Historical Thinking

Writing Answer each of the following by writing one or more complete paragraphs:

1. The United States did not commit substantial forces in Vietnam until 1965. Why do you think Johnson believed the U.S. could succeed where France had failed?
2. Americans who opposed the war took part in demonstrations, burned draft cards in protest, and fled the country to avoid military service. Should these people have been considered traitors to America? Explain your answer.
3. Compare and contrast the Great Society reforms with those of the Progressive Era.
4. Read the selection from the Unit 9 Archives entitled "General Westmoreland Asks for More Troops, 1965." Did the government have a duty to keep Americans informed of the important request that would affect many citizens? Explain your answer.

Making Connections with Literature

In his inaugural speech, President Kennedy advised Americans to "Ask not what your country can do for you, but ask what you can do for your country." College students discovered untapped reserves of idealism for public service. The civil rights movement laid the groundwork for this resurgence of commitment to improving American society. The war on poverty and the environmental movements were also born out of this idealism.

Two books that greatly influenced college students in these areas were Michael Harrington's *The Other America* (1962) and Rachel Carson's *Silent Spring* (1962). "The other America," Harrington wrote, " . . . is populated by failures, by those driven from the land and bewildered by the city, by old people suddenly confronted with the torments of loneliness and poverty, and by minorities facing a wall of prejudice." Scholars began to study seriously poverty and welfare. Many groups became involved in the debate: political leaders, scholars, students, and the general public.

Following the publication of Carson's *Silent Spring*, a strong environmental protection movement began to appear. After large Earth Day rallies in 1970, environmentalists focused on the threats to health posed by food additives, cancer-causing pollutants, and toxic wastes. Congress passed the Environmental Protection Act and the Environmental Protection Agency was created. Conservation groups served to further raise people's awareness of environmental issues and industries began to change the way they handled toxic wastes and other pollutants.

Writing Research an ongoing or recent environmental problem in your community. How did the public become aware of it? Was anyone found responsible for the problem? What agencies are concerned with solving it? Interview the people involved. Write a report that summarizes your findings.

Additional Skills Practice

Write a paragraph explaining why cartographers (map makers) would find it useful to present information in the form of a cartogram. Identify three graphs or charts in the text that could be presented in the form of a cartogram.

Coming Apart

By the late 1960s, many Americans feared that their society was fragmenting beyond repair. Feelings about the Vietnam War caused a great deal of divisiveness, and sometimes this led to violent confrontations at home. But Vietnam was only one source of social tension in the United States. After 1963, movements advocating "black power" began to compete with the non-violent civil rights movement that had embraced both black and white participants. Between 1965 and 1968, race riots occurred in many of the nation's urban ghettos. Other minority groups began to adopt the tactics of African Americans—both non-violent civil rights activities as well as more militant methods. There were calls for "brown

▲ *What were some of the traditional values challenged by youthful members of the 1960s counterculture, the so-called hippies?*

power," "red power," and "women's liberation." The actions of youth, as a whole probably the most privileged in American history, were of great concern to adults. Student protests against the Vietnam War, often targeting colleges and universities, bewildered many Americans who had not had so many opportunities and advantages. Adults were equally dismayed by members of the youth counterculture, so-called hippies who dropped out of society, assumed unconventional lifestyles, and "turned on" to drugs. Given the idealism and sense of hope so prevalent in the early sixties, it now seemed, in the words of historian William O'Neill, that American society was coming apart at the seams.

From Civil Rights to Black Power

In August 1965, five days after President Johnson signed the Voting Rights Act, riots exploded in Watts, a black ghetto in Los Angeles. In one devastating week, 34 people died, and fires gutted over 1,000 buildings. Rioters smashed cars and looted local stores. The Watts riot bewildered many Americans, including civil rights leader Martin Luther King Jr., who visited Watts just after the riot. A 20-year-old rioter said to King, "We won!" King asked the young man how they had won with so many people dead, homes destroyed, and the community in ruins. The rioter replied, "We won because we made the whole world pay attention to us."

What caused the ghetto riots in U.S. cities in the 1960s?

What impact did rising expectations have on African Americans in the 1960s?

What did the term black power mean to various groups?

"Help!"

▲ *To what major urban problems did Herblock call attention in this cartoon? (The Herblock Gallery,* Simon & Schuster, *1968.)*

Ghetto Conditions

Following the Detroit riot in 1967, President Johnson appointed the National Advisory Commission on Civil Disorders, chaired by Illinois Governor Otto Kerner. The Kerner Commission investigated the causes of the riots. In early 1968 it issued its report. "What white Americans have never fully understood—but what the Negro can never forget—is that white society is deeply implicated in the ghetto. White institutions created it, white institutions maintain it, and white society condones it." The commission concluded that the outbreaks were spontaneous events resulting from intolerable conditions in the ghetto. Foul, rat-infested slum housing was rented at high prices. A declining inner-city tax base resulted in poor services, educational institu-

tions, and job training. All this was aggravated by intolerably high levels of unemployment.

The Kerner Commission recommended an all-out effort to improve slum conditions; otherwise, America would continue along a well-trodden path toward "two societies, one black, one white—separate and unequal." Congress felt compelled to act on these findings. The Civil Rights Act of 1968 extended the protections against discrimination in real estate and housing stated in the 1964 Civil Rights Act.

By the 1960s, most of the best-paying jobs were found in the suburbs. Unemployment rates among people in the ghetto were nearly double those of white suburbanites, with those of African American youths even higher. Those who had work typically had low-paying jobs, especially unskilled, service, and menial jobs. Consequently, a wide gap existed between black and white incomes.

African Americans also faced serious housing problems. Poor job opportunities and discrimination kept many African Americans too poor to be able to move away from the inner-city slums. In

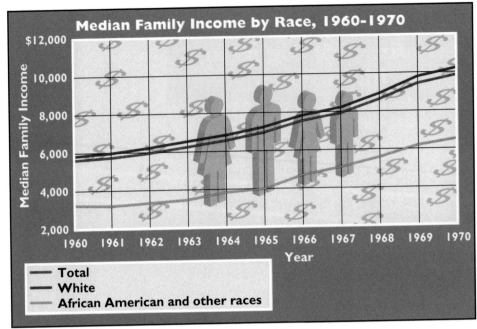

Did the income of minorities keep pace with the general increase in median family income from 1960 to 1970?

Median Family Income by Race, 1960–1970

Median Family Income: $12,000 / 10,000 / 8,000 / 6,000 / 4,000 / 2,000

Year: 1960 1961 1962 1963 1964 1965 1966 1967 1968 1969 1970

— Total
— White
— African American and other races

Source: U.S. Department of Commerce, Bureau of the Census.

addition, inner-city schools were as segregated as the surrounding housing, and they were often run-down and offered an inferior education.

Lack of jobs, income, housing, and education caused frustration, and this frustration intensified as African Americans' expectations grew. When questioned about his participation in the 1967 Detroit riot, one rioter explained why ghetto dwellers had taken to the streets. "The rebellion—it was all caused by the commercials. I mean, you saw all those things you'd never be able to get—go out and get 'em . . . men's clothing, furniture, appliances, color TV." The promise of better opportunities had brought African Americans to the cities. The gulf between that promise and the reality of urban America caused widespread frustration and led to America's urban riots.

The civil rights victories of the 1960s and government programs that promised to uplift the poor had also raised African Americans' expectations. Such programs as the war on poverty and the development of public housing, however, often delivered less than expected. This was partly because the costs of the Vietnam War led to cutbacks in social programs. As civil rights leader Bayard Rustin wrote in 1966, "[African Americans] today are in worse eco-

nomic shape, live in worse slums, and attend more highly segregated schools than in 1954." In short, Rustin continued, "The day-to-day life of the ghetto has not been improved by the various judicial and legislative measures of the past decade."

On the other hand, those African Americans who lived outside urban ghettos made significant gains after World War II. Larger percentages of African American children were completing high school. Their college attendance doubled between 1940 and 1960 and nearly doubled again between

▼ *Throughout her career and until her death in 1996, Barbara Jordan worked hard to end racism and intolerance among all people.*

1960 and 1970. African American employment opportunities also increased. Evidence of a significant and growing African American middle class appeared.

In 1966, Barbara Jordan became the first black woman to win a seat in the Texas State Senate. She authored minimum-wage bills and pushed for civil rights legislation in her home state before being elected to the U.S. House of Representatives in 1972. The very success of some African Americans, however, made the gap between expectations and achievement for others all the more frustrating.

Riots in the Nation's Cities

The Watts riot did catch the attention of Americans throughout the nation. Many could not understand why a riot had occurred there. The National Urban League had rated Watts as the best place, among 68 cities, for African Americans to live. Watts, with palm-lined streets, single-family houses, and parks and other public amenities, bore little physical resemblance to typical big-city ghettos. Recent civil rights victories and Great Society programs aimed at urban areas offered the promise of even better living conditions. Moreover, Watts residents were gaining political power. They had elected African Americans to Congress, the state assembly, and the Los Angeles city council. African Americans held one-quarter of all Los Angeles County government jobs. But the Watts riot revealed a startling antiwhite bitterness among the people living in the ghetto.

The immediate cause of the Watts riot was the issue of police brutality in the African American community. Other issues, however, contributed to bitterness. These included white control of business and real estate. Many businesses charged people in the ghetto higher prices for often inferior goods. African Americans suffered higher unemployment and poverty levels than the white population. The McCone Commission, formed to investigate the Watts riot, concluded: "The existing breach [between the black and white communities], if allowed to persist, could in time split our society irretrievably.... Unless it is checked, the August riots may

▲ *One of the great tragedies of urban riots, such as the Watts riot of 1965, is that when ghetto neighborhoods are destroyed, the people hurt most are those who are most needy.*

seem by comparison to be only a curtain-raiser for what could blow up one day in the future."

During the next summer, in 1966, racial upheavals became more widespread and increasingly violent. Riots had begun early in the year in several southern cities. In July and August, racial conflicts engulfed 22 cities, including Toledo, Ohio; Grand Rapids, Michigan; and Milwaukee, Wisconsin. In 1967, eight riots were so severe that the military was called in to restore order.

During a five-day riot in Newark, New Jersey, 26 people died, and over 1,200 suffered injuries. Ironically, the federal government had spent more per capita on antipoverty programs in Newark than in any other northern city. An even worse riot occurred in Detroit in late July 1967. In five days of violence, 43 people died, and more than 2,000 were injured. Four thousand fires gutted a quarter of downtown Detroit, causing at least $50 million in damage. The Detroit riot was even more shocking to white America than the one in Watts. The city boasted antipoverty and urban renewal programs, African Americans held public office, industries paid high wages, many blacks owned their own homes, and the mayor was sensitive to ghetto problems. "There was probably more widespread affluence

Splinters in the Civil Rights Movement

While the militant wing of the civil rights movement became much stronger in the 1960s, its roots went back to a much earlier time. In 1933, **Elijah Muhammad** had founded the Nation of Islam, a separatist movement also known as the Black Muslims. Elijah Muhammad preached that by following the teachings of the prophet Muhammad and by working hard for economic independence, African Americans would be freed by Allah (God) from "white oppressors." Then, by the early 1960s, one of Elijah Muhammad's followers, who had assumed the name of **Malcolm X**, gained national

▼ *U.S. Olympic athletes Tommie Smith and Juan Carlos gave "black power" salutes during the 1968 Mexico City award ceremonies.*

▲ *The "X" in Malcolm X's name symbolized the "stolen" identity of enslaved African Americans. This militant leader addressed many rallies on black separatism.*

among Negroes in Detroit," noted one observer, "than in any other American city."

On April 4, 1968, another round of urban rioting began after the assassination of Martin Luther King Jr. in Memphis, Tennessee. In response to King's murder, violent riots broke out in more than 40 cities. In Washington, D.C., National Guardsmen carrying machine guns stood guard around the Capitol while the city's African American neighborhoods burned. Rioting and looting engulfed most of Chicago's West Side ghetto. One of the enduring tragedies of all these outbreaks was that the ghetto neighborhoods in which the riots occurred never recovered. The riots hastened urban decay and made these neighborhoods even worse places in which to live.

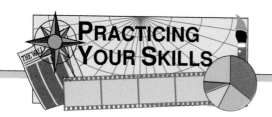

Interpreting Symbolic Speech

One of our most cherished freedoms is the one that allows free speech. Speech and writing are the usual ways that people express point of view. But there are many nonverbal ways of expressing opinion, as well. Dress style, body language, demonstrations such as flag burning, wearing red ribbons, or tying yellow ribbons are all forms of *symbolic speech*. Symbolic speech may be thought of as conduct or actions that express ideas, such as political beliefs. The ideas expressed may be popular or unpopular. It is important to remember that learning how to deal peacefully with viewpoints and ideas that you may not agree with is a fundamental skill for living in a democratic society.

Historians identify the common viewpoints of groups to help them understand the decisions and behaviors of these groups. Understanding symbolic speech helps identify common viewpoints. Here are some guidelines to follow when looking at photographs that represent symbolic speech:

- **Identify the people, important objects, and location of the photograph.** What event is being recorded? What are the individuals doing? Are the people truly representative of the group or movement depicted?
- **Determine what point of view is being expressed.** What outside factors may have influenced the subjects of the photo? Did the people know they were being photographed?
- **Try to discover competing points of view on the issue.** What are other valid interpretations about the issue? Are the other points of view supported by facts?

Examine the photograph on the bottom of page 922 and answer the following questions:

1. Identify the people and location of this photograph. What is the event? What are the individuals doing?
2. What point of view is being expressed by the athletes? What specific action represents symbolic speech in this photograph?
3. Do you think the photograph was posed or candid?
4. Do you feel the athletes had a right to use the Olympic Games as a forum for protest?
5. Do you think the Olympic Committee had a right to eject the athletes from the games?

attention by urging African Americans to pursue a more militant path, including the use of violence, to obtain their goals. Malcolm X suggested that bullets might work faster than ballots to achieve African American demands. Eventually, he and his followers broke with the Nation of Islam. In 1965, Malcolm X was assassinated, and three members of the Nation of Islam were charged with the crime and convicted. Still, many young African Americans continued to search for alternatives to the integrated nonviolent civil rights movement. They began to talk of "freedom now" and "black power."

Stokely Carmichael, an experienced civil rights activist, coined the term **black power** at a civil rights rally in mid-1966. "The only way we gonna stop them from whuppin' us is to take over," Carmichael told his audience. "We been saying freedom for six years, and we ain't got nothin'. What we gonna start saying now is black power." In unison, the excited crowd chanted, "Black power! Black power!" The term, however, meant different things to different people. As one observer noted, "black power was nothing but a cry of rage."

In 1966, Floyd McKissick, national director of the Congress for Racial Equality (CORE), testified before a Senate committee that

> for many weeks …you gentlemen have seen in exquisite detail, the frustration, the hopelessness, and the powerlessness of the American urban Negro. There is no better argument for black power—for the mobilization of the black community as a political, social, and economic bloc. Moreover [black power] is a rational, militant call for a whole segment of this nation's population to do what you have not been able to do—destroy racism in this country, create full employment in the American ghetto, revise the educational system to cope with the twentieth century, and make the American ghetto a place in which it is possible to live with hope.

Some African Americans believed that black power meant ousting white supporters from the civil rights movement. For others, black power meant preserving an integrated civil rights movement, but with an all-black leadership. More radical advocates of black power talked of a violent revolu-tion that would overturn the white power structure. The Black Panthers, an urban revolutionary group, began arming themselves and clashing with police in many cities.

By the late 1960s, black power had become an important cultural as well as political force. The movement sought to instill a sense of identity and pride in being black. African Americans began to wear "afro" hairdos and dashikis (native African garments), eat traditional African American foods, and research their own distinctive history. To many, black power simply meant "black is beautiful."

The strategies and language used by members of the black-power movement turned off many whites. White people could not easily distinguish one form of black power from another. A **backlash**, a strong, adverse reaction to a social or political movement, grew in the late 1960s. The sympathy and support that many white groups and white politicians had given the civil rights movement declined.

Whether the influence of Martin Luther King Jr. could have prevented fragmentation of the civil rights movement is a matter of speculation. He never got the chance. Convinced that the African American civil rights movement had to demand economic as well as political justice, King went to Memphis, Tennessee, in April to help organize support for striking city garbage workers. The strike had lasted for two months and marches, demonstrations, and arrests gave it the flavor of the early civil rights movement. On April 4, just hours before King was to lead another peaceful march on city hall, James Earl Ray, a white ex-convict, shot him from ambush. Ghettos across the country exploded in riots in the wake of King's assassination, and his death marked the end of the integrated nonviolent civil rights movement.

SECTION 1 REVIEW

1. **Discuss** findings of the Kerner Commission.
2. **Describe** the impact of rising expectations on African Americans in the 1960s.
3. **List** reasons for the Watts riot in 1966.
4. **Identify** Elijah Muhammad.
5. **Explain** some of the aims of the black power movement.

American Landscape

Environmental Concerns

Many American environmentalists believe that unplanned economic growth and the exploitation of resources have damaged our environment beyond repair.

Some of the worst early environmental abuses, such as soil exhaustion and timber stripping, were curbed by federal regulation in the early 1900s. Programs of soil conservation, the national park system established by President Theodore Roosevelt, and the Tennessee Valley Authority (TVA) preserved and renewed substantial areas of the United States. But today, scientists are uncovering new disruptions in natural ecosystems.

Air Pollution. Some 156 million registered vehicles pour hydrocarbons, sulfur dioxide, and nitrogen oxide into our atmosphere. Industries further contribute to the pollution. Electricity generated in power plants by burning coal and petroleum adds to the total. Despite the passage of a series of clean air acts, the amount of pollutants remains stubbornly high.

Smog, the most obvious indicator of atmospheric pollution, is greatest near Los Angeles where an estimated 16 million vehicles are driven in a mountain-ringed basin. At least two-thirds of health-threatening pollutants have been removed from the air in two decades of stringent emission controls on vehicles and industry. In

1970, the pollution level in the Los Angeles basin exceeded safety standards on four days out of every five. Today this occurs on less than two days of every five. Although pollution is severe in Los Angeles, few U.S. cities can match this progress.

Automobile emissions are also partially responsible for creating acid rain. The impact of acid rain on plant and animal life in the Northeast has been dramatic. A four-year study of the Adirondack Mountains identified 212 high-altitude lakes and ponds with no fish. Other damage is more difficult to estimate, but experts suggest that timber yields may decrease by 15 percent over the next 20 years.

Water Pollution. Sources of water pollution include sewage disposal; industrial wastes; pesticides, herbicides, and fertilizers from America's farms; and coastal oil refineries and offshore drilling rigs. The elements that produce the wealth of American society also produce its pollution.

The deterioration of water quality in the great watersheds of the continent is a serious problem. They include the Hudson, the Mississippi, the rivers of the Central Valley of California, the Columbia, and the greatest reservoir of freshwater on earth, the 94,710-square-mile Great Lakes system. In Lake Erie, particularly, pollutants have reduced the water's oxygen content, leading to the growth of algae.

▶ *Earth Day celebrations on college campuses drew attention to the environmental movement.*

Other areas are improving. Water in New York's Hudson River is gradually becoming cleaner. A determined environmental action group forced the paper industry to clean up the Willamette River in Oregon, demonstrating that environmental issues are as much a matter of public concern as of legislative enactment.

Environment and Economy. Americans consume energy per capita at double the rate of other technological nations and six times faster than the rest of the world.

Environmentalists argue that pollution derived from coal, oil, or nuclear power must be decreased. Private and class-action lawsuits are filed to preserve and protect the environment. But the proponents of cleaner air and water often lose ground to those who champion greater economic growth. In the end, it is a matter of priorities.

1. Identify examples of pollution that exist in your community. In your opinion, do the benefits outweigh the damage? Is there a way both interests can be served?

2. Do you believe that "In the end, it is a matter of priorities?"

Hispanic Americans

The successes that African Americans had in asserting their civil rights through direct action made an impression on other groups. As *Business Week* reported in May 1971, "After generations of [passive silence] . . . the Mexican American community is beginning to stir. Moved by the success achieved by militant blacks, it is claiming its ancestral lands in New Mexico, striking for a living wage in the San Joaquin Valley, charging police brutality in the **barrios** [Hispanic urban neighborhoods] of Denver, demonstrating for bilingual schools in Los Angeles, playing politics in Texas, and creating community organizations across the map of the Southwest and in parts of the Midwest. . . . Tentative and scattered, the ferment is not yet a movement."

What groups comprised the Hispanic Americans, and where did they live in the 1960s?

What impact did continual migration from Mexico have on the United States between World War II and 1970?

How did Hispanic American political activity change between World War II and the early 1970s?

Increases in the Hispanic American Population

By far the largest Hispanic group in the United States was made up of people of Mexican descent. In 1970, the average Mexican American family made about one-third less money per year than the general population. Mexican Americans tended to be less educated, and their unemployment rate was double the U.S. average. The overwhelming majority worked in unskilled jobs. The Mexican American middle class and professional class were small.

Geography has complicated the Mexican American experience in the United States. Many Mexican Americans were native inhabitants of the

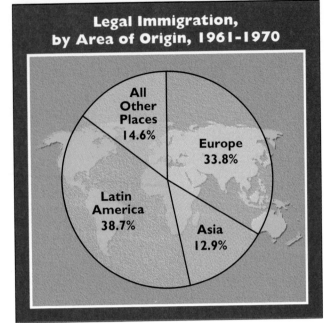

Legal Immigration, by Area of Origin, 1961–1970

All Other Places 14.6%

Europe 33.8%

Latin America 38.7%

Asia 12.9%

Source: U.S. Department of Justice, Immigration and Naturalization Service.

▲ *This pie graph shows which regions the immigrants came from in the period 1961 to 1970.*

Southwest, territories that had been absorbed by the United States. Many more Mexican nationals, however, had migrated to the United States—both legally and illegally—over time. Poorly supervised borders, Mexico's economic stagnation and explosive population growth, and the huge demand for farm laborers in the Southwest encouraged large-scale migration from Mexico.

During World War II, a shortage of farm labor in the Southwest led to the **bracero** program. The U.S. and Mexican governments recruited Mexican nationals to work temporarily in the United States. About 250,000 braceros worked on farms in the Southwest from 1942 to 1947. Each bracero worked for a year in the States, and most then returned home. The program began again in 1948, and by the time the program ended in 1965, nearly 4.5 million Mexican nationals had worked temporarily on U.S. farms.

Most of the Mexicans who participated in the bracero program did so eagerly, since they could earn far more in the United States than at home. Work and living conditions for braceros, however, were often grim. Moreover, these laborers, because they would work for low wages, brought down

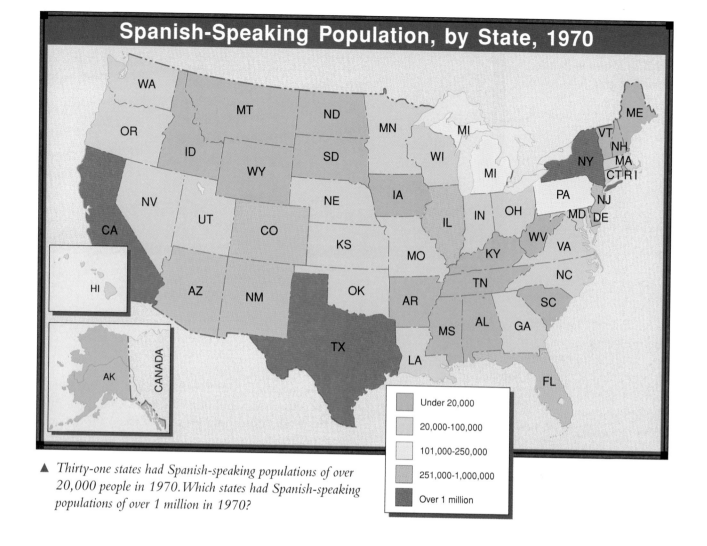

Spanish-Speaking Population, by State, 1970

Legend:
- Under 20,000
- 20,000–100,000
- 101,000–250,000
- 251,000–1,000,000
- Over 1 million

▲ *Thirty-one states had Spanish-speaking populations of over 20,000 people in 1970. Which states had Spanish-speaking populations of over 1 million in 1970?*

farm wages throughout the region. As one labor organizer put it, "The growers are using the poorest of the poor of another country to defeat the poorest of the poor in this country."

The situation was far worse for another group of migrant Mexican laborers. These were the Mexicans who entered the United States illegally. They got the lowest wages, lived in the worst conditions, and could easily be exploited. They could not appeal to the authorities if they were mistreated by employers or landlords. Despite these terrible conditions, they made a significant contribution to the explosive growth of agriculture in the Southwest during the 1950s and 1960s.

Periodically, the federal government attempted to send large numbers of illegal migrant workers back to Mexico. The vast majority of the deporta-

tions were carried out without benefit of formal legal proceedings. The process disrupted many families, deported individuals who had been living in the States for more than ten years, and caused increasing bitterness among Mexican Americans. Many of those left behind noticed, however, that wage rates increased by one-third after the deportations.

Other Hispanic Groups

Puerto Ricans formed the second largest group of Hispanic Americans. They moved to the mainland, especially in and around New York City, in

► What correlation in the table is made between poverty level and percent of high school graduates?

Poverty and Education Levels of Hispanic Americans, 1970

	Hispanic American Population	General U.S. Population
Percent living below the poverty level	23.0%	13.7%
Mexican	27.0%	
Puerto Rican	31.0%	
Cuban	14.0%	
Percent high school graduates or higher	30.0%	58.0%

Source: *Current Population Reports.*

increasing numbers after World War II. By 1970, 1.5 million Puerto Ricans lived in the States. Nearly 900,000 lived in New York City alone, about twice the number who lived in San Juan, Puerto Rico's capital.

Cuban Americans comprised the third largest group of Hispanics. When Fidel Castro came to power in Cuba in 1959, nearly half a million Cuban refugees fled to the United States. So large and active was their community in southern Florida that they rapidly changed Miami into a bilingual city. At first, most Cuban refugees were dedicated to Castro's overthrow and to their eventual return to the island. But as Castro solidified his position, their prospects of returning home diminished. As a result, most turned their attention to improving themselves economically, and they became more active in U.S. politics. Cuban Americans were predominantly middle-class business people and professionals. Politically, they tended to be conservative and militantly anti-Communist.

On average, Hispanic Americans ranked low in terms of education, social and occupational status, and income. In 1971, only 16 percent of Hispanic Americans had completed four years of high school, compared to 60 percent for the general population. Hispanic Americans attended college less than half as often as the general population. Thus, Hispanic Americans were at a disadvantage in the job market. As Senator Joseph Montoya from New Mexico said, "We are first in janitors . . . last in equal opportunity."

Rights for Mexican Americans

Traditionally Mexican Americans did not fully participate in U.S. politics. Few had U.S. citizenship. Many were poor, and poor people often are not active politically. Since many Mexican Americans were migrant farm laborers, they could rarely establish residency in order to register and vote. Moreover, local governments, dominated by white Americans, rarely helped Mexican Americans. Because of the heavy Mexican migration after 1945, only one-fourth of Mexican Americans regarded English as their first language, and this was a significant barrier to their full social, economic, and political participation in this country.

Despite all of this, Mexican American political activity increased after World War II. During that war, 300,000 Mexican Americans served in U.S. armed forces. The proportion of Mexican Americans serving in combat forces (compared to their number in the population) was higher than that of any other group, except perhaps for Japanese Americans. Mexican American participation in World War II was partly a symbol of their desire for equal status in U.S. society. Many on the home front found better-paying jobs. Overall, these wartime experiences energized the Mexican American community. When Mexican American veterans returned after the war, the G.I. Bill of Rights helped them go to college and begin businesses.

César Chávez

In the early 1960s, **César Chávez** emerged as a significant leader among Hispanic Americans. In his philosophy and tactics, Chávez was similar to African American civil rights leader Martin Luther King Jr. Chávez explained what prompted him to work for the rights of migrant workers in this way: "If you're outraged at conditions, then you can't possibly be free or happy until you devote all your time to changing them. . . . We can't change anything if we want to hold on to a good job, a good way of life, and avoid sacrifice."

Chávez was born near Yuma, Arizona, in 1927. During the Great Depression, Chávez's migrant-farmworker family moved to California. From early childhood, Chávez worked in the fields and orchards and received little formal education. During World War II, he served in the navy and then returned to farmwork once more. In 1952, he began organizing migrant farm families, and he campaigned to increase Mexican American voter registration. Four years later, Chávez established the National Farm Workers Association (NFWA). This organization soon evolved into the United Farm Workers (UFW), an affiliate of the AFL-CIO.

▲ *César Chávez (front left) organized migrant workers into unions and worked to register farm laborers to vote. He made many speeches on behalf of the United Farm Workers.*

Under Chávez's influence, the United Farm Workers used the nonviolent, direct-action techniques of the civil rights movement—boycotts, church meetings, and marches—to publicize its cause. In 1970, a UFW-sponsored boycott forced the growers of table grapes to improve conditions for the grape pickers and to recognize the UFW as the bargaining agent in labor contracts for migrant laborers. The boycott of lettuce and the attempts to organize citrus workers in California and Florida proved less successful. Although Chávez was able to organize less than 10 percent of migrant workers, he and the UFW symbolized, for many, Mexican American aspirations, identity, and power.

1. What was Chávez's philosophy concerning change?
2. Compare the tactics of César Chávez to those of Martin Luther King Jr.

▲ *In this 1954 photograph a Mexican border official is seen trying to prevent a migrant laborer from crossing over into the United States.*

After 1945, Mexican American veterans started such political organizations as the G.I. Forum and the Mexican American Political Association (MAPA). These organizations reflected the rise of many Mexican Americans to middle-class status in income and occupation. They also signified that Mexican Americans were unwilling to accept an inferior status or role in U.S. society. In the presidential election of 1960, MAPA and the League of United Latin American Citizens (LULAC) became much more active. John Kennedy and his brother Robert recognized the political significance of these groups, and they encouraged them to form "Viva Kennedy" clubs throughout the Southwest to register and mobilize voters of Mexican descent. Hispanic American voters provided Kennedy's margin of victory in New Mexico and in the key states of Texas and Illinois in 1960.

Hispanic Americans helped win enactment of the Bilingual Education Act of 1968, which created special bilingual programs in the nation's schools. In 1970, the California Supreme Court recognized literacy in Spanish as meeting the requirement for voting in state elections. In southwestern Texas, José Angel Gutiérrez created a political party, *La Raza Unida,* which sought political power. *La Raza* called for bilingual education, an end to job discrimination, and increased public services in Hispanic neighborhoods. Hispanic Americans also became more successful in electing members of their groups to national, state, and local government offices.

Just as the African American civil rights movement became more militant, some Hispanic American political activists became more radical. Many young Mexican Americans adopted the label "Chicano," a term originally meaning rebel or outsider. In 1965, in Denver, Colorado, Rudolfo "Corky" Gonzales established the Crusade for Justice. This group intervened in disputes between the police and the Hispanic community, won parks and playgrounds for the West Denver barrio, and fought public and private discrimination against Hispanics. In New Mexico, Reies López Tijerina unsuccessfully sued the state for the return of the old Spanish land grants, sold off years earlier to non-Mexicans, to their rightful Mexican American owners. The Brown Berets, a youthful organization patterned on the Black Panthers, emerged in such southwestern cities as Los Angeles. *La Comunidad Latina* was a similar radical group founded in Chicago. Besides teaching about self-defense, these groups also set up community health clinics and established breakfast programs for young children. Although they pursued many conventional political, economic, and social goals, the radical messages these groups conveyed often alarmed non-Hispanic Americans.

SECTION 2 REVIEW

1. Identify the three largest groups of Hispanic Americans in the United States in the 1960s.
2. List four reasons for the large-scale migration from Mexico during and after World War II.
3. Explain what impact the bracero program had on the United States.
4. Describe the political activity of Hispanic Americans after World War II.
5. Identify the goal of the Bilingual Education Act of 1968.

American Indians

On July 8, 1970, President Richard Nixon sent a message to Congress in which he described the problems faced by American Indians in U.S. society. "The first Americans—the Indians—are the most deprived and most isolated minority group in the Nation. On virtually every scale of measurement—employment, income, education, health—the condition of the Indian people ranks at the bottom." Nixon said these conditions were the "heritage of centuries of injustice." He said that the time had come "to break decisively with the past and to create the conditions for a new era in which the Indian future is determined by Indian acts and Indian decisions." In fact, Nixon was only one of a long line of American political leaders who had called for a "new era" for American Indians.

How did federal policies toward American Indians change between the 1880s and 1960s?

How did Presidents Kennedy and Johnson respond to American Indians' problems in the 1960s?

How did American Indians seek to improve their condition in the late 1960s?

Failure of Federal Policy

The desperate plight of the American Indians was largely the result of the repeated failure of federal policy toward the Indians. Some of these policies dated back to the late nineteenth century. The federal government had gone back and forth, first putting the Indians onto reservations, then encouraging them to take up small individual homesteads, and then back again to reservations. At times, the government also wanted to educate young Indians in the ways of European American culture and to assimilate them into society. The result of these policies was to take nearly 70 million acres of land away from the Indians. Many American Indians faced a wretched future. They were illiterate, lived in shacks and huts, suffered from malnutrition, and felt hopeless about improving the quality of their lives.

Federal policies toward American Indians became somewhat more humanitarian in the 1930s and 1940s under Presidents Herbert Hoover and Franklin Roosevelt. But after World War II, Indian lands were once again the target of white farmers, ranchers, and lumbermen. In 1950, the commissioner of the Bureau of Indian Affairs (BIA) began the process of "termination"—ending all federal services to Indians and placing them under state government supervision. In 1953, House Concurrent Resolution 108 made this policy official. The resolution stated the new federal policy was "to make the Indian . . . subject to the same laws and entitled to the same privileges and responsibilities as . . . other citizens . . . and to end their status as wards of the United States."

The real intent of this policy was to allow white developers access to Indian land. From 1952 to 1956, the government sold 1.6 million acres of Indian land. Thinking that the ultimate solution to the Indian problem was to relocate them to urban areas, the Bureau of Indian Affairs provided moving costs and helped American Indians find housing and jobs in the city. By the 1960s, about 250,000 of the nation's Indian population had become city dwellers, while 370,000 continued to live on reservations.

Lack of Opportunities

During the 1960s, American Indians suffered perhaps more than any other minority group. American Indian life expectancy was much lower, and infant mortality rates were much higher than those in other groups. The suicide rate in this group was double the national average. American Indians faced bleak prospects wherever they turned. Their reservations lacked jobs and decent schools. Their unemployment rate was nearly three times the national average, worse than that of African Americans. Nearly 40 percent lived below the poverty line. They had the worst housing, the highest disease rates, and the least access to education of any ethnic group in the United States.

What conclusion can you draw from the figures in this table?

Social and Economic Condition of American Indians, 1970

	American Indian Population	General U.S. Population
Median age	20.4 years	28.1 years
Median years of schooling	9.8 years	12.2 years
Percent living below the poverty level	40.0%	13.7%
Annual median family income	$5,832	$9,867
Unemployment rate	15.0%	4.9%

Source: U.S. Department of Commerce, Bureau of the Census.

Federal Indian policy flip-flopped yet again in the 1960s. In the presidential election of 1960, both John Kennedy and Richard Nixon vowed to end federal policies that tended to break down the Indians' culture and to "Americanize" them. The Federal Housing Authority actively helped Indians build their own homes. Kennedy and Johnson also encouraged businesses to build factories on Indian lands in order to provide Indians with good job opportunities. By 1968, businesses had invested almost $100 million on Indian lands.

In 1968, Lyndon Johnson sent a special message to Congress asking for aid to American Indians. Johnson wanted them to have "an opportunity to remain in their homeland, if they choose, without surrendering their dignity; an opportunity to move to the towns and cities of America, if they choose, equipped with the skills to live in equality and dignity." Johnson also created the National Council on Indian Opportunity, chaired by Vice President Hubert Humphrey. The council provided funds for community improvement, job training, youth activities, and health services for Indians. Under President Nixon, the Bureau of Indian Affairs began issuing grants to Indian tribes so they could develop the natural resources on and under their land.

Red Power

In the late 1960s and early 1970s, American Indian authors published a number of books to publicize their cause. Among the most popular were Vine Deloria Jr.'s *Custer Died for Your Sins* (1969),

N. Scott Momaday's *House Made of Dawn* (1968), which won a Pulitzer prize, and Dee Brown's *Bury My Heart at Wounded Knee* (1971). These books increased public awareness and empathy for American Indian issues. In a more far-reaching and directly effective tactic, American Indians sued to reclaim Indian lands that had been taken away in violation of various federal laws and treaties. American Indians brought suit against the current owners of former Indian lands from Alaska to Maine. Although the American Indians did not win all these suits, court battles increased public awareness of the injustices that had been suffered for many years.

Some American Indians—usually the younger and more militant ones—used more radical tactics. Much like other groups in American society, American Indians began to organize pressure groups to win better treatment for themselves. In 1968, in an effort to publicize the special plight of American Indians, young militants formed the American Indian Movement (AIM). AIM drew many of its members from American Indians living in the "red ghettos" of western cities. AIM modeled itself on the black power movement. For a few years, AIM and other American Indian radical groups attracted considerable public attention. The results were sometimes positive and sometimes not.

In November 1969, 78 AIM members captured national attention by occupying Alcatraz. Alcatraz is an island located in San Francisco Bay, and it was once the site of a federal maximum-security prison. The government did not confront the Indians on Alcatraz and the occupation ended in June 1971, when 15 Indians surrendered peacefully to federal marshals. Because of the publicity generated by this

◀ *In 1969, members of the American Indian Movement occupied the former island-prison of Alcatraz.*

▶

Members of the American Indian Movement (AIM) flew a U.S. flag upside down near the site of the 1890 massacre at Wounded Knee, South Dakota.

action, the federal government allocated more money for urban Indian problems and for the Bureau of Indian Affairs.

In late 1972, several thousand American Indians drove in a car caravan called "The Trail of Broken Treaties" to Washington, D.C. They hoped to convince the BIA to accept a document called *The Twenty Points*, authored by American Indians, as the basis for their relationship with the federal government. *The Twenty Points* asked not for more social programs or integration, but a return to the treaties that had been negotiated between the Indians and the government. One thousand AIM members occupied the BIA headquarters. They sealed off the building and remained there for a week. AIM members rifled through, carted off, and destroyed bureau files. Two million dollars in damage was done. This occupation failed to convince government officials to recognize *The Twenty Points*.

Several months later, American Indian Movement members occupied Wounded Knee, a village on the Pine Ridge Indian reservation in South Dakota. "We believe we are still a sovereign nation," reported Frank Fools Crow, "and the government has no right to . . . tell us what we can and can't do in the way of governing ourselves." The protesters

took 11 hostages and occupied several buildings at the site. This time federal officials responded to the occupation and surrounded the village with federal law officials. After a brief gun battle left one protester dead and another wounded, the siege at Wounded Knee collapsed. While the media covering Wounded Knee suggested that this episode was simply another 1960s-style battle between angry Indians and federal authorities, there was a deeper and more subtle conflict. That conflict was between Indians who believed in working outside the system and those who were increasingly successful working within that system. Such groups as the Native American Rights Fund, the American Indian Law Center, and the Indian Law Resource Center, among others, pursued legal remedies for various alleged federal violations of Indian treaties.

In the mid-1970s, for example, the federal government agreed to a settlement—in both land and money—of a suit brought by several Indian tribes which asserted their legal ownership of the majority of land in Maine. In South Dakota, the U.S. Supreme Court awarded the Lakota tribe $105 million to settle their claims to the Black Hills. The Lakotas, however, wanted their land back and refused to accept the cash offer. In several states, the courts upheld the treaty rights of tribes to regulate their own hunting and fishing. By the 1980s, both federal and state governments had recognized tribal sovereignty and Indian self-determination in many ways, including the right to open high-stakes bingo and gambling casinos on Indian lands.

SECTION 3 REVIEW

1. **Explain** why humanitarian moves to help American Indians were abandoned after World War II.
2. **Describe** the standard of living of Indians during the 1960s.
3. **Describe** the actions taken by Kennedy and Johnson to help Indians after the election of 1960.
4. **Identify** AIM.
5. **Discuss** reasons for increased awareness of the plight of American Indians in the late sixties and early seventies.

SECTION 4

Youth Movements

On January 14, 1967, San Francisco's Golden Gate Park was the scene of the first "Human Be-In," a celebration of America's youth movement. Hippies mingled with political activists from nearby college campuses. The music was acid rock, played by such groups as the Jefferson Airplane, the Grateful Dead, and Quicksilver Messenger Service. Former Beat poet Allen Ginsburg read poetry. Drug guru Timothy Leary urged the crowd to "turn onto the scene, tune in to what is happening, and drop out—of high school, college, grad school, junior executive—and follow me, the hard way." Journalists on hand reported, "It was a love fest, a psychedelic picnic, a hippie happening." Older Americans found it difficult to understand.

How did the baby-boom generation influence American society in the 1960s?

What caused student radicalism in the 1960s?

How did the counterculture challenge traditional American values?

Effects of the Baby Boom

In the 1960s, young people and their activities were a major focus for the entire country. This was primarily because young people made up such a large proportion of the population. In 1964 the largest population group by age consisted of people in their late teens. Roughly 40 percent of living Americans had been born within the previous 15 years. The baby boom of the late 1940s and early 1950s created a population that was much younger than that of the generation before.

According to sociologists, the period between ages 18 and 22 is always a time of great change for young people. They usually establish their own lives outside their families for the first time, they try new lifestyles, and they continue to shape their own identities, often by rebelling against authority. In earlier eras, most of these youths would have gone right to work and started families. In the middle of the twentieth century, however, fewer and fewer went directly into the job market. By the early sixties, nearly half went to college, and this stretched out the period of freedom from work and family responsibilities. The increasing demand for professionals and persons with graduate training extended the years spent in school even further.

Student Campaigns to Change America

John Kennedy's talk of the New Frontier sparked students' idealism and raised their expectations of what they and their society could accomplish. The civil rights movement influenced many students, especially those who went south to help in voter registration drives. It also exposed white youths to the brutality that was often characteristic of racial confrontations. The movement taught them new protest tactics—marches, sit-ins, and planned confrontations with the "establishment," or controlling authorities. Finally, the escalation of the Vietnam War in 1965 offered a compelling political cause around which many college students rallied.

Because college campuses and enrollments were growing larger, students often felt as though they were nameless, faceless cogs in a large machine. This sense of alienation was another reason that students began to stage protests. In mid-1962, students from several eastern and midwestern universities met in Port Huron, Michigan, to form Students for a Democratic Society (SDS). Tom Hayden, a student at Michigan University, wrote their platform. Hayden spoke out against bureaucracy and the Cold War, and he encouraged grassroots participation in politics. He felt that students could be a major force in changing society. SDS modeled itself on the Student Nonviolent Coordinating Committee (SNCC), a youthful African American civil rights organization. SDS members called themselves the "New Left," to distinguish themselves from the Communist-dominated "old left" of the 1930s.

As President Johnson's escalation of the war in Vietnam increased, so did many students' moral outrage about the war. At the University of Michigan, faculty and student activists organized a "teach-in" against the war. Similar forums quickly sprang up at other colleges and universities. As the policy allowing student deferments from the draft ended, many students had a very practical reason to protest.

Students also protested the role of universities in the war. In some cases, 60 percent of a university's research budget came from government grants and contracts, many from the Defense Department. Students organized to block campus recruiting by the armed services, the CIA, and many corporations, especially Dow Chemical Company, producer of the napalm jelly used in Vietnam. Student antiwar activities became increasingly strident, confrontational, and violent.

The Counterculture

A **counterculture** is a large group of people within a culture who hold values that oppose the mainstream, or norm. The counterculture of the 1960s had had forerunners in other generations, such as the "flaming youth" of the 1920s and the Beat generation of the 1950s. The impact of the baby boom, however, produced a youth movement

▲ *Mario Savio (standing with bull horn) was one of the leaders of a 1964 free speech movement at the University of California at Berkeley.*

of unusual proportions. Many youths had a keen sense of belonging to their own subculture. They questioned the values and attitudes held by older, middle-class Americans. Among these values were the work ethic, the emphasis on competition, conventional modes of dress and manners, rational or science-based knowledge, and self-discipline. Hippies and other members of the emerging counterculture felt that these values had led Americans to "make things nobody needs so they can afford to buy things nobody needs."

As part of their rebellion against traditional middle-class values, hippies left their families and the suburbs to move to urban "crash pads" and rural or mountain communes. Their clothing was looser and more relaxed and their hair was longer and less well groomed than the clean-cut styles of the middle class. The use of such drugs as marijuana, hashish, and LSD (or acid) became increasingly commonplace in the counterculture. Jerry Rubin, one of the counterculture's leaders, explained that drug use "signifies the total end of the Protestant ethic: [forget] work, we want to know ourselves." Over time, as research showed that LSD caused genetic damage, its use declined. Since the long-term

The Woodstock Music Festival

The Woodstock Music and Art Fair of 1969, *Time* magazine noted, "turned out to be history's largest 'happening.' As the moment when the special culture of U.S. youth of the '60s openly displayed its strength, appeal, and power, it may well rank as one of the significant political and sociological events of the age."

On August 15, 1969, 400,000 people, mostly between 16 and 30 years old, showed up at Max Yasgur's 600-acre dairy farm near Bethel, New York. Enduring rain, mud, and shortages of food, water, and toilets, they listened to 24 rock and roll performers and bands, including Janis Joplin, Jimi Hendrix, the Jefferson Airplane, and Country Joe and the Fish.

Newsweek magazine reported that Woodstock "was different from the usual pop festival from the outset. It was not just a concert but a tribal gathering, expressing all the ideas of the new generation: communal living, . . . getting high, digging arts, clothes and crafts exhibits, and listening to the songs of revolution." Blues singer Janis Joplin agreed: "There's lots and lots and lots of us, more than anybody ever thought before. We used to think of ourselves as little clumps of weirdos. But now we're a whole new minority."

No one was quite certain what to make of the happening at

▲ *The turnout of people for Woodstock far exceeded the planners' expectations and exhausted available facilities, food, and water.*

Woodstock. Psychoanalyst Rollo May thought Woodstock "showed the tremendous hunger, need and yearning for community on the part of youth." The *New York Times*, however, called it "a nightmare of mud and stagnation," and compared the gathering to the march of lemmings to the sea. "What kind of culture is it that can produce so colossal a mess?" Reporter John Garabedian noted that "the lesson of Woodstock is that the hippie population of the U.S. has grown incredibly (and invisibly) and that, today, far more kids than anyone thought have a more radical vision about the American way of life than most of us imagined." *Time* magazine agreed: "Adults were made more aware then ever before that the children of the welfare state and the atom

▶ *In the summer of 1969, brochures such as this one advertised tickets to the Woodstock Music Festival.*

bomb do indeed march to the beat of a different drummer, as well as to the tune of an electric guitar."

1. Explain why *Newsweek* reported that Woodstock was different from other pop music festivals.
2. Why did both youths and adults attach such significance to Woodstock?

▲ *These two hippie outfits were typical of the costumes worn by young people embracing the counterculture of the 1960s. Can you name other groups that have been identified by a particular style of dress?*

▲ *The Beatles were at the forefront of the so-called "British invasion" in the mid-1960s. Their music and philosophy profoundly influenced the emerging counterculture.*

effects of marijuana, or pot, were hard to determine, its use increased. Sometimes users went on to harder drugs, including amphetamines, or speed, and even heroin, resulting in the ruin of many people's lives.

Music was another way in which youths set themselves apart from the adult world. In the early 1960s, folk music by such writers as Pete Seeger ("Where Have All the Flowers Gone?"), Bob Dylan ("Blowin' in the Wind"), and Joan Baez ("Where Are You Now, My Son?") expressed youthful idealism. Rock and roll mocked traditional values, beliefs, and behavior. The lyrics of acid rock increasingly set young people off from their elders. Steppenwolf's "Magic Carpet Ride," the Beatles' "Lucy in the Sky with Diamonds," and Jefferson Airplane's "White Rabbit" all spoke of drug-induced euphoria. In addition, rock and roll performers' lifestyles and stage performances often outraged middle-class "straights." A host of musicians sang of revolution, peace, love, and drugs. The music not only reflected young people's values, but also helped to shape them.

The counterculture questioned American self-satisfaction and materialism. Hippies thought adults were caught up in the rat race and were afraid to let their natural instincts emerge. They believed that

science was the tool of the military-industrial complex and had made modern life less humane. They felt that life was more dangerous than ever before and that atom bombs, pesticides, and a soiled environment were the results of science. Hippies rejected reason and systematic knowledge in favor of sensitivity, intuition, mysticism, and the occult. The counterculture saw humans as more than rational beings; it emphasized their spiritual side.

There were, however, divisions within the younger generation. While half of the nation's youths went to college in the early 1960s, the other half did not. These young people followed more traditional patterns of job hunting and family formation. After the recession of 1960–1961, employment opportunities were good. Rapid economic growth created many new jobs and generally reduced unemployment. After President Johnson escalated the Vietnam War in 1965, many of these youths volunteered or chose to be drafted into military service. For these young people, there wasn't such a big gap between their values and those of their parents. For them, actor John Wayne, football coach Vince Lombardi, and evangelist Billy Graham remained cultural heroes.

▲ *The Hare Krishnas is the popular name of a sect, founded in 1965, whose members chanted and prayed in such busy locations as New York's Central Park.*

While the counterculture scoffed at middle-class values, middle-class and lower-middle-class workers defended the value they placed on hard work and achievement. To get even a small share of the material rewards available in American society, they worked hard and saved their money. They tended to view members of the counterculture as lazy, filthy, and ungrateful. Appalled by campus protests and radical politics, millions of Americans rejected the social and cultural revolution of the sixties. Yet even the most traditional Americans were exposed to its impact, through the media and through the selling of new clothes, hairstyles, and lifestyles.

SECTION 4 REVIEW

1. **Explain** the increase of student political activism in the 1960s.
2. **Identify** the SDS.
3. **Describe** the connection made by students between the Vietnam War and the universities.
4. **Explain** how the counterculture challenged traditional American values.
5. **Discuss** the reaction of the middle class to the counterculture ideals.

SECTION 5

Women's Movements

Betty Friedan published her book, *The Feminine Mystique*, in 1963. Growing out of Friedan's own experiences as a housewife and mother in the 1950s, the book condemned the "domestic captivity" that women felt living in middle-class suburbs. Friedan wrote, "As she made the beds, shopped for groceries, matched slipcover material, ate peanut butter sandwiches with her children, chauffeured Cub Scouts and Brownies, lay beside her husband at night—she was afraid to ask even to herself the silent question—'Is this all?' " By the early 1960s, many women had begun to question their status in American culture.

Why did women's movements reemerge in the 1960s?
What did women's movements seek to achieve?
What had women's movements accomplished by the early 1970s?

The Pursuit of Women's Rights

In 1900, the average woman married at age 22, bore three to four children, and had a life expectancy of just over 60 years. These women could expect to devote most of their adult lives to childrearing. By the 1960s, women continued to marry at 22, but had, on the average, less than two children. A woman in the 1960s who survived to marrying age had a life expectancy of 80 years. For the last half of those 80 years, childrearing would not be the primary activity.

Rising divorce rates were another factor reshaping women's lives by the 1960s. In 1900, 8 percent of married couples divorced. This percentage rose quite slowly until the 1960s. In 1965, the divorce rate had reached 27 percent and was increasing rapidly. Women could no longer assume that their marriages would last.

Divorce hurt women economically far more than it did men. Only one in ten women received alimony, and only half received child support from their former husbands. Child-support agreements were hard to enforce. Most divorced women lacked work experience outside the home, and this generally forced them into low-paying service jobs. They consequently earned considerably less than men.

Many women noted that equality of opportunity was passing them by in other ways. They pointed out that women comprised a smaller percentage of college students in the 1950s than in the 1920s. Women graduates earned about half the salary of men with similar training. While most women graduates found employment if they sought it, they were often hired for typically female jobs. Women discovered they had difficulty getting promotions. These social realities fostered the revival of various women's movements in the 1960s.

Activists for women's rights tended to split into two distinct groups. The first movement stressed working through the political system using traditional pressure-group tactics to achieve equality. Although women had full political rights and many had good jobs outside the home, women's rights activists saw that there was still discrimination. In 1961, President Kennedy formed the Commission on the Status of Women, chaired by Eleanor Roosevelt. The commission reported in 1963 that women did face discrimination in employment and education. Equally important, commission activities established a network of people concerned about women's issues.

Women in this network began to pressure Congress for legislation favorable to women. In 1963, Congress passed the Equal Pay Act, which stated that men and women should receive equal pay for comparable work. More important was the 1964 Civil Rights Act. Title VII barred employment discrimination based on race, color, religion, national origin, or sex. Ironically, House member Howard Smith, a Virginia conservative, had added the term *sex* to the bill to make the entire act so controversial that it would not pass Congress. Smith's strategy backfired, and Title VII became a powerful legal tool in the fight against sex discrimination.

Despite these legislative victories, many women were dissatisfied with how slowly Title VII was implemented. In 1966, this dissatisfaction led to the formation of the **National Organization for**

Comparing Male and Female Earning Power, 1970

Occupation	For every $1.00 a man earned in 1970, a woman earned . . .
Overall	$0.59
Teacher	$0.79
Clerical worker	$0.64
Professional	$0.64
Manufacturing worker	$0.60
Manager	$0.55
Skilled craftworker	$0.54
Retail salesperson	$0.51

Source: U.S. Department of Commerce, Bureau of the Census.

▲ *Women's income continued to lag behind men's income in every occupation category during this period. What is especially significant about this difference in a field such as teaching?*

Women (NOW). "The purpose of NOW," its organizing document declared, "is to take action to bring women into full participation in the mainstream of American society now, exercising all the privileges and responsibilities thereof in truly equal partnership with men." Betty Friedan served as NOW's first president. Its membership grew rapidly, from nearly 1,000 in 1967 to 15,000 four years later. Nearly one-fourth of its members were men.

Women's Liberation

The second women's movement viewed women's issues from a more radical perspective. Many of the leaders of the emerging women's liberation movement had participated in grassroots civil rights activities. When these young college women went south in voter registration drives and other civil rights activities, they received conflicting messages. They developed self-confidence and organizational skills through their work. They also met southern women (both white and African American) whose involvement in the civil rights move-

▲ *This women's liberation demonstration in Washington, D.C., occurred in 1970, the fiftieth anniversary of the Nineteenth Amendment.*

media attention publicized women's issues widely, and this attracted new converts and brought the two branches of the women's movement closer together. On August 26, 1970, thousands of women across the nation marched to celebrate the fiftieth anniversary of the Nineteenth Amendment, which gave women the vote.

Certainly, the women's lib movement made many Americans more aware and sympathetic to women's issues. The Future Homemakers of America, for example, declared that women's lib had had a "definite influence" on its 600,000-person membership. Baptist women threatened a floor fight at a national convention if a woman was not included in the hierarchy of the church. Catholic nuns protested their supervision by priests. Many universities established women's studies programs, and formerly all-male colleges, including Yale, Princeton, and West Point, began to admit women undergraduates. The number of women in professional and graduate schools rose, as did the number of women in public office.

Other Americans viewed women's liberation as a threat to traditional roles and values. Just as the militant civil rights and antiwar movements sparked a backlash, so did the feminist movement. Individuals such as Phyllis Schlafly emphasized the important role of women as mothers and homemakers, a role they felt was belittled by the proponents of women's liberation. Women's organizations continued to lobby for legislation favorable to women. In 1972, Congress enacted legislation broadening the coverage of the 1964 Civil Rights Act. This legislation banned sex discrimination in colleges that received federal financial aid.

The Equal Rights Amendment (ERA) was originally introduced to Congress in 1923 and reads: "Equality of rights under the law shall not be abridged by the United States or any state on the basis of sex." Intended to do away with legal discrimination against women forever, it became a focal point of controversy during the seventies. Critics argued that the ERA might be used to deprive women of such protections as noncombatant status in the military and maternity benefits in the workplace. The Equal Rights Amendment passed Congress in 1972, but has not been ratified by the required number of states.

ment provided an inspiring role model for them. At the same time, male civil rights workers expected the women to do all the cleaning and cooking. Many of these women came to believe, as one said, that "assumptions of male superiority are as widespread and deeply rooted and every much as crippling to the woman as the assumptions of white superiority are to the Negro." When the black power movement made white women feel less welcome in the African American civil rights ranks, many turned to antiwar activities. Once again, male leaders expected them to do the menial tasks and not involve themselves in leadership roles.

By 1968, many of these women realized they needed their own movement. That year, women's liberationists staged a protest at the Miss America pageant. The demonstration included a "freedom trash can" into which protesters threw false eyelashes, hair curlers, bras, and girdles—all symbols, they argued, of their oppression. The media labeled the protesters "bra burners," a name that stuck. In fact,

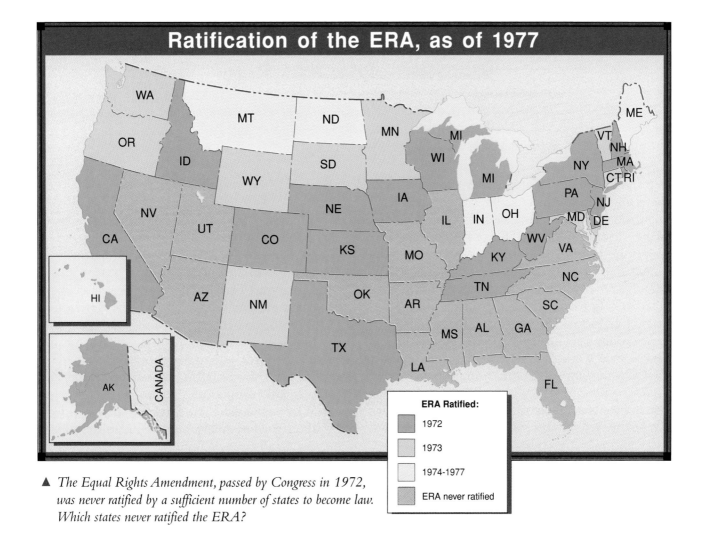

Ratification of the ERA, as of 1977

ERA Ratified:
- 1972
- 1973
- 1974-1977
- ERA never ratified

▲ *The Equal Rights Amendment, passed by Congress in 1972, was never ratified by a sufficient number of states to become law. Which states never ratified the ERA?*

The Equal Credit Opportunity Act (1974) prohibited lenders from discriminating against women. Congress authorized income tax deductions for child care and increased the benefits received by female federal employees.

Women brought suits in the courts to challenge unfavorable laws. The Supreme Court handed down a series of decisions important to the women's movement. In *Phillips v. Martin-Marietta Corp.* (1971), the Court ruled that employers could not set different rules for male and female employees. In *Roe v. Wade* (1973), the Court ruled that a state could not prevent women from having abortions during the first trimester (three months) of pregnancy. The Court made this decision in *Roe v. Wade* in order to maintain the confidentiality of the doctor-patient relationship—not to affirm women's right to control their own bodies, as feminists wanted. Nevertheless, this decision undermined anti-abortion laws in 46 states.

SECTION 5 REVIEW

1. Relate causes for the reemergence of the women's movement in the sixties.
2. Identify NOW.
3. Name three goals of the women's movement.
4. Describe how Phyllis Schlafly and her followers felt about women's liberation.
5. List the major pieces of legislation in the early seventies that were the results of pressure from women's groups.

Summary

Before new social and political movements begin, groups of people must be ready for leadership and mobilization. In the 1960s, those left out of the mainstream of American life were ready and willing to seek their rights and better opportunities. Many African Americans, Hispanic Americans, American Indians, and women had experienced discrimination, limiting their access to jobs, good schools, and decent housing. They had therefore failed to keep pace with white males in income, education, and social standing. Many individuals in these groups had also experienced significant advances since World War II, and these advances raised their expectations of even more improvement.

Using pressure-group tactics within the existing system had secured victories for many of those left out before. Yet voting, civil rights, and court victories began to seem too few, too little, and too slow for many, especially younger, members of these groups. African Americans rioted in every major city and began to speak of black power. Other groups used similar language: Hispanic and Native Americans now pursued brown power and red power. Women's movements sought not only their rights but also liberation. Student radicals talked of tearing down the establishment, while hippies wanted to drop out of society altogether.

These challenges to traditional values and existing power relationships created a backlash among the white working and middle classes. The backlash would help elect Richard Nixon to the presidency in 1968 and would continue to flavor American politics and policies for years to come.

Vocabulary

backlash	bracero
barrios	counterculture
black power	

Look up the vocabulary terms in an encyclopedia or other reference book. Write a brief paragraph on each topic.

Review Questions

1. What were the major causes of the ghetto riots in the 1960s?
2. Explain what black power was and why it emerged in the mid-1960s.
3. Name ways that the African American civil rights movement affected Hispanic Americans.
4. Describe one effect of the continuous migration from Mexico on the Mexican-American community.
5. Identify the effects of changing federal Indian policies on American Indians.
6. Why would older Americans in the sixties feel threatened by college student radicalism and the youth counterculture?
7. How did increased life expectancy affect women's movements in the 1960s?
8. Describe the two major types of women's movements resulting from the attempt to achieve equality and civil rights.
9. Why did the dramatic increase in divorce rates have more effect on women than on men during the sixties?
10. What were the major legislation and Supreme Court decisions in the sixties and seventies resulting from the women's movement?

Critical Historical Thinking

Writing Answer each of the following by writing one or more complete paragraphs:

1. Many African Americans were frustrated in the 1960s with the slow pace of civil rights progress. Do you think the emergence of radical civil rights groups that embraced violence helped or hindered African Americans' equality? Why?

2. Do you think women today should be considered a minority group under the law? Explain why you think as you do.

3. Vietnam and the countercultural revolution preoccupied American youth in the sixties. What are some of the issues that concern the youth of America today? How are they similar to or different from the youth concerns of the 1960s?

4. Read the Unit 9 Archives selection entitled "We Are a Proud People." What led American Indian activists to occupy Alcatraz Island? In your own words, explain what they hoped to accomplish.

Making Connections with Music

Every war has produced songs that capture the sentiments of the time. "Yankee Doodle Dandy," "Battle Hymn of the Republic," "Over There," and "When Johnny Comes Marching Home Again" provide some understanding of these periods. The Vietnam War was no exception. However, songs about the Vietnam War joined the debate over the war itself. Those who opposed the war and those who supported the war wrote and sang songs that expressed their convictions.

For the most part, folk music and rock and roll songs protested the war, and country and western music supported the war. A complete list of songs on both sides of the issue would be quite long. But Phil Ochs's "I Ain't Marchin' Any More" is a representative antiwar folk song, and Barry Sadler's "Ballad of the Green Berets" is a representative country and western song supporting the war. The draft also was debated in many songs. Arlo Guthrie's "Alice's Restaurant" and Phil Ochs's "Draft Dodger Rag" protested the draft, while Keith Everett's "Conscientious Objector" and Merle Haggard's "Okie from Muskogee" spoke for the supporters of the war. An interesting exchange was Victor Lundberg's "An Open Letter to a Teenage Son" and Brandon Wade's "Letter from a Teenage Son."

Many young people who protested the Vietnam War saw the war as part of larger social problems such as racism and materialism. Thus folk and rock music reflected these concerns as well, and country and western music replied with appeals to patriotism and standard American values. Steppenwolf's "Monster" and Credence Clearwater Revival's "Who'll Stop the Rain?" protested society's values, while Ernest Tubbs's "It's America (Love It or Leave It)" and Merle Haggard's "Fightin' Side of Me" defended traditional American lifestyles.

▪ Popular music often expresses the social or political concerns of the people. Select a popular group or singer and list some of the major issues that are addressed in the music. Are they issues that concern you and your friends? Compare your lists. What issues appear frequently? Are they issues that also concern your parents' generation?

Additional Skills Practice

Search the newspapers and news magazines for examples of photographs that represent symbolic speech. Cut out the two best examples and mount them on a sheet of paper. Identify the figures and the point of view that is being expressed. Then write why you agree or disagree with the expressed viewpoint.

Unit Review Questions

1. How did Kennedy's attitude toward communism lead to his greatest foreign affairs triumph and failure?
2. Explain why most of Kennedy's proposed domestic legislation did not pass until after his death.
3. How did America's shift to the suburbs affect the use of natural resources?
4. Characterize most of the civil rights movements begun by young African American students.
5. How did Lyndon Johnson achieve his early success as president?
6. How did the Vietnam War affect the Great Society legislation?
7. Why was the Tet Offensive so pivotal in deciding future American involvement in the Vietnam War?

8. List some of the arguments favoring and opposing efforts of the federal government to solve problems.
9. Draw a comparison between the Great Society and Reconstruction.
10. How did the conservative backlash of the late 1960s aid Republican Richard Nixon in his presidential election?

Personalizing History

Saying Goodbye to Woodstock Did your parents ever begin a story by saying "I remember when . . . ?" Your parents may have been part of a generation of youth that created many memories for the nation. The Woodstock generation made some strong demands on American culture during the 1960s and 70s. Antiwar marches on Washington, protests for civil rights reform, and the deter-

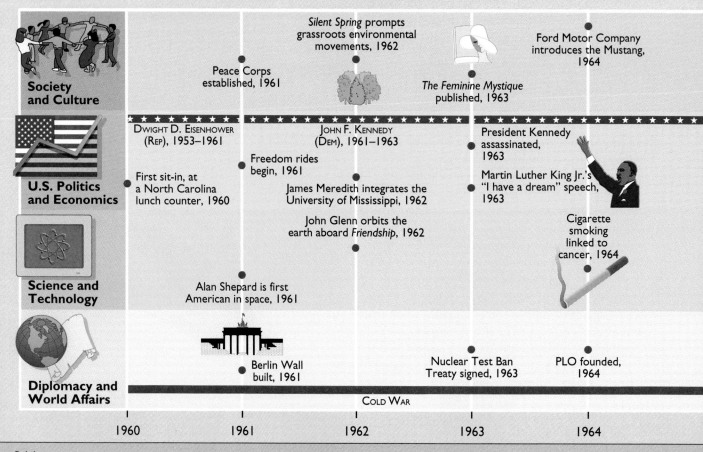

Society and Culture

Peace Corps established, 1961

Silent Spring prompts grassroots environmental movements, 1962

The Feminine Mystique published, 1963

Ford Motor Company introduces the Mustang, 1964

U.S. Politics and Economics

DWIGHT D. EISENHOWER (REP), 1953–1961

JOHN F. KENNEDY (DEM), 1961–1963

First sit-in, at a North Carolina lunch counter, 1960

Freedom rides begin, 1961

James Meredith integrates the University of Mississippi, 1962

President Kennedy assassinated, 1963

Martin Luther King Jr.'s "I have a dream" speech, 1963

Science and Technology

John Glenn orbits the earth aboard *Friendship*, 1962

Cigarette smoking linked to cancer, 1964

Alan Shepard is first American in space, 1961

Diplomacy and World Affairs

Berlin Wall built, 1961

Nuclear Test Ban Treaty signed, 1963

PLO founded, 1964

COLD WAR

1960 1961 1962 1963 1964

mination of America's youth to speak out brought serious upheaval to the nation. The times were reflected in ethnic pride, music, and a change in the way we look at our leaders. The youth of the 1960s are now gradually moving into retirement, and your generation will become voting policy makers in just a few years.

■ Say goodbye to the Woodstock youth by writing an epitaph to that generation. Highlight the areas that have most affected you. An epitaph could be a poem, short paragraph, or even a song lyric. Include what you see as the future for your generation.

sticker to the back of their car. Stickers support candidates, environmental issues, and personal philosophy. As we drive around town, we inform and entertain others with bumper stickers. The space ships that venture out into the solar system could be ready to carry our ideas as well.

■ Design a bumper sticker for the space shuttle that carries a message you believe important enough to share with the whole planet—or universe! Your teacher may wish to design a bulletin board with space exploration as a theme and display the bumper stickers, so be creative.

Linking Past and Present

Express Your Idea   Americans often express their ideas and ambitions by posting a bumper

Time Line Activity

Choose three events from the time line that illustrate the divisiveness in American society during the 1960s. What issue(s) prompted each event?

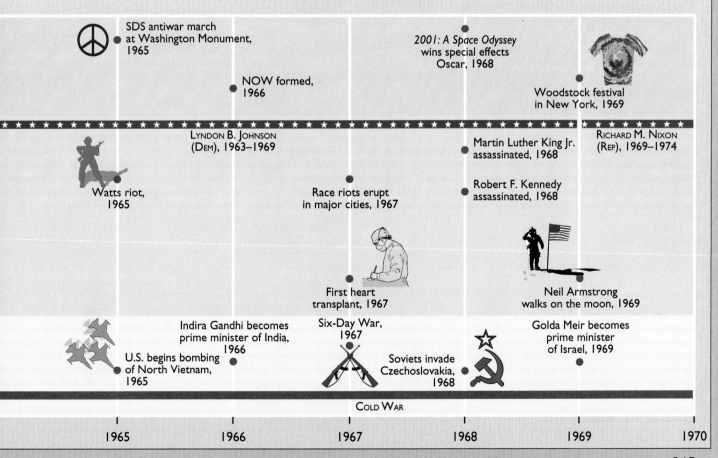

SDS antiwar march at Washington Monument, 1965

NOW formed, 1966

2001: A Space Odyssey wins special effects Oscar, 1968

Woodstock festival in New York, 1969

LYNDON B. JOHNSON (DEM), 1963–1969

RICHARD M. NIXON (REP), 1969–1974

Martin Luther King Jr. assassinated, 1968

Watts riot, 1965

Race riots erupt in major cities, 1967

Robert F. Kennedy assassinated, 1968

First heart transplant, 1967

Neil Armstrong walks on the moon, 1969

Indira Gandhi becomes prime minister of India, 1966

Six-Day War, 1967

U.S. begins bombing of North Vietnam, 1965

Soviets invade Czechoslovakia, 1968

Golda Meir becomes prime minister of Israel, 1969

COLD WAR

1965   1966   1967   1968   1969   1970

946

UNIT 10

Searching for Stability

The Vietnam War and the apparent excesses of the Great Society fragmented American society and politics in almost every imaginable way. Richard Nixon, backed by the silent majority, appealed to people who were tired of challenges to traditional authorities, and who wanted an honorable end to the Vietnam War. Nixon accomplished much in both foreign affairs and in domestic policies. But Nixon's attempt to "bring the nation together again" proved difficult. Not only did the Watergate crisis force Nixon's resignation, but it also led many to question more than ever American social and political institutions. Watergate undermined Americans' faith in their government and in themselves. The failure of Gerald Ford and Jimmy Carter to exert leadership supplied the context for the presidency of Ronald Reagan.

Chapter 30 The Nixon Years	**Chapter 31** The Ford and Carter Years	**Chapter 32** The Reagan Era

◀ This Washington, D.C., memorial for Vietnam veterans was designed by a Chinese American woman named Maya Ying Lin. Born in 1960, she studied architecture as an undergraduate student at Yale University. The Vietnam Veterans Memorial was dedicated on Veterans Day, 1982.

Themes

- **Democracy and Citizenship** The political fragmentation of the 1960s worsened in the 1970s. Antiwar activism, the pervasive challenge of authority, and accelerated demands for minority and civil rights created a strong political backlash.
- **Geography and Environment** Environmental concerns had been gradually increasing in the United States. In the 1970s, some of these concerns resulted in significant new legislation to protect and clean up the environment. Environmental laws and activism created their own backlash.
- **Economics** Blessed with huge stores of natural resources, Americans were forced in the 1970s to confront a variety of issues, such as energy and stagflation, focusing on the economy.
- **Global Interactions** Partially as a result of the failure of the Vietnam War and the energy crisis, Americans and their leaders seemed to lose confidence in their ability to shape world affairs, at least until President Reagan urged them again to take up the burdens of a great power.

The Forgotten American

A journalist described some of the people who felt threatened by the demands of minorities, students, and women for recognition and power.

Stability is what counts, stability in the job and home and neighborhood, stability in the church and in friends. . . . Law and order is the stability and predictability of established ways. Law and order is equal treatment—in school, in jobs, in the courts. . . . Somewhere in his gut the man in those communities knows that mobility and choice in this society are limited. He cannot imagine any major change for the better; but he can imagine change for the worse. And yet for a decade he is the one who has been asked to carry the burden of social reform, to integrate his schools and neighborhoods, has been asked by comfortable people to pay the social debts due to the poor and the black. . . .

The frustrated middle. The liberal wisdom about welfare, ghettos, student revolt, and Vietnam has only a marginal place, if any, for the values and life of the working man. It flies in the face of most of what he was taught to cherish and respect: hard work, order, authority, self-reliance. . . . Marijuana, sexual liberation, dress styles, draft resistance, even the rhetoric of change become monsters and demons in a world that appears to turn old virtues upside down. . . . Perhaps none of this is new. And perhaps it is also true that the American lower middle has never had it so good. And yet surely there is a difference, and that is that the common man has lost his visibility and, somehow, his claim on public attention.

Peter Schrag, "The Forgotten American," *Harper's Magazine* (Aug. 1969).

A Vietnam Veteran Comes Home

This is not the World. Lord, how can they do this to me? How can they bring me back to a World where I don't know what they're talking about? The United States is saying one thing. The people are saying something else. President Nixon is talking about the silent majority. The people are in the streets protesting. Who are these people out here protesting while there are guys in the Nam going through psychological and physical hell? Walking in monsoon when it rains for months at a time. Being sniped at. Being killed. Stepping in booby traps. Catching jungle rot. Getting eaten up by leeches. How can they say the war is unjust? How can you walk out of Nam and leave guys out in the field or missing in action?

◄ *Vietnam veterans*

I wasn't thinking they were un-American, but man, somebody pulled the rug out from under us. Somebody stabbed us in the back. The average person in the peace struggle didn't understand. We got stabbed in the back when we got back to the United States by the Peace people. We got stabbed in the back by President Nixon. He's talking nonsense. Henry Kissinger is talking about peace and ending the war. All this is garbage.

I felt a guilt trip. I said to myself, 'I can't let people know that I've been to Vietnam.'

Mark Baker, *NAM* (New York: Quill, 1982), pp. 288–289.

Nixon's Ideological War

Political journalist Theodore White explained his view of why the Watergate scandals occurred.

Another set of questions presses on—not how the criminals were caught, but why Nixon did what he was caught doing.

To trace the answers to the question of "Why?" one must accept the political reality that Richard Nixon and his aides were, for the first time in American politics since 1860, carrying on an ideological war. Because they felt their purpose was high and necessary and the purpose of their enemies dangerous or immoral, he and his aides believed that the laws did not bind them—or that the laws could legitimately be bent. . . .

By the time Nixon came to power, that realization [losing the war in Vietnam] had split the country at every level. Resentment at the waste and killing in Vietnam had spilled out into the streets in sputtering violence and frightening bloodshed. . . . If the end was good then the means, however brutal, must also be good. And from this idea of the President's authority came most of the early illegalities, the buggings, the wire-taps, the surveillances, the minor crimes. Until finally the President's aides saw no distinction between ends and means. They were making war not just in Vietnam but all across the home front, too. All the disputes over home issues, as

well as foreign issues, became part of the ideological war. . . .

To explain the spite and hatred of their struggle, one must add one more condition—the change of culture that was taking place all over America in the 1960s. The Nixon aides were people of the embattled old culture. As such, they believed the new culture was not only undermining the authority of their President to make war-and-peace, but striking into their homes, families, and schools, too. It was undermining the values with which they had grown up and still held dear. . . .

The two cultures clashed in every form of expression—in language, in costume, in slogans. They clashed over important matters—civil rights, 'law-and-order,' safety in the streets, drug abuse, the dignity of women.

Theodore White, *Breach of Faith* (New York: Dell Publishing Company, 1975), p. 416 ff.

Affirmative Action

The following three documents offered differing perspectives on affirmative action.

Have We Overcome?

The question is have we [African-Americans] overcome? . . . Have we done it? No, a thousand times no. . . . It is true, and important, that blacks are going places today they couldn't go twenty-four years ago [the year of the *Brown* decision]. Everything, in fact, has changed in Mississippi and America, and yet, paradoxically, nothing has changed.

Despite court orders and civil rights laws, blacks are still the last hired and the first fired. They are still systematically exploited as consumers and citizens. To come right out with it, the full privileges and immunities of the U.S. Constitution do not apply to blacks tonight, in Mississippi or in Massachusetts, and they never have. . . . Contrary to popular belief, the economic gap between blacks and whites is widening. Between 1975 and 1976, the black to white family income ratio fell sharply from 62 to 59 percent.

 To Listen, *a stainless steel sculpture by African American Melvin Edwards*

Not only is black unemployment at its highest level today, but the jobless gap between blacks and whites is the widest it has ever been. . . . The proportion of middle-income black families has not significantly increased. The proportion of upper-income black families has steadily declined. White high school drop-outs have lower unemployment rates than black youth with college education.

These figures are terrible, and the reality is worse. How did this happen? How is it possible for black America to be in so much trouble after all the demonstrations, and marches, and court orders? What is the meaning of this terrible indictment?

Lerone Bennett Jr., *Have We Overcome? Race Relations Since Brown* (1978).

Justice Thurgood Marshall's Opinion in the *Bakke* Case

I agree with the judgment of the Court only insofar as it permits a university to consider the race of an applicant in making admissions decisions. I do not agree that the [U of C] admissions program violated the Constitution. . . . The position of the Negro today in America is the tragic but inevitable consequence of centuries of unequal treatment. Measured by any benchmark of conduct or achievement, meaningful equality remains a distant dream for the Negro.

It is because of a legacy of unequal treatment that we now must permit the institutions of this society to give consideration to race in making decisions about who will hold the position of influence, affluence and prestige in America. For far too long, the doors to those positions have been shut to Negroes. If we are ever to become a fully integrated society, one in which the color of a person's skin will not determine the opportunities available to him or her, we must be willing to take steps to open those doors. I do not believe that anyone can truly look into America's past and still find that a remedy for the effects of the past is impermissible. . . .

I fear that we have come full circle. After the Civil War our government started several 'affirmative action' programs. This Court in the Civil Rights cases and *Plessy v. Ferguson* destroyed the movement toward complete equality. For almost a century no action was taken and this nonaction was with the tacit approval of the Courts. Then we had *Brown v. Board of Education* and the Civil Rights Acts of Congress followed by numerous affirmative action programs. Now, we have this Court again stepping in, this time to stop affirmative action programs of the types used by the University of California.

 Regents of the University of California v. Bakke, 438 U.S. 265, 95 S. Ct. 2733 (1978).

Are Quotas Good for Blacks?

Black economist Thomas Sowell examined the quota system in 1978.

The growth of special minority programs in recent times has meant both a greater availability of money and lower admissions standards for black and other designated students. It is as ridiculous to ignore the role of money in increasing the numbers of minority students in the system as a whole as it is to ignore the effect of double standards on their maldistribution among institutions. It is the double standards that are the problem, and they can be ended without driving minority students out of the system. Of course, many academic hustlers who administer special programs might lose their jobs, but that would hardly be a loss to anyone else.

As long as admission to colleges and universities is not unlimited, someone's opportunity to attend has to be sacrificed as the price of preferential admission for others. No amount of verbal sleight-of-hand can get around this fact. None of those sacrificed is old enough to have had anything to do with historic injustices that are supposedly being compensated. Moreover, it is not the offspring of the privileged who are likely to pay the price. It is not a Rockefeller or a Kennedy who will be dropped to make room for quotas; it is a DeFunis or a Bakke. Even aside from personal influence on admissions decisions, the rich can give their children the kind of private schooling that will virtually assure them test scores far above the cut-off level at which sacrifices are made.

Just as the students who are sacrificed are likely to come from the bottom of the white distribution, so the minority students chosen are likely to be from the top of the minority distribution. In short, it is a forced transfer of benefits from those least able to afford it to those least in need of it.

Thomas Sowell, "Are Quotas Good for Blacks?" Reprinted from *Commentary* (June 1978), pp. 39–43.

President Carter Speaks of Spiritual Crisis

Jimmy Carter delivered this speech on July 15, 1979, after two weeks of consultation and soul-searching.

I want to talk to you right now about a fundamental threat to American democracy. . . . The threat is nearly invisible in ordinary ways. It is a crisis of confidence. It is a crisis that strikes at the very heart and soul and spirit of our national will. We can see this crisis in the growing doubt about the meaning of our own lives and in the loss of a unity of purpose for our nation.

The erosion of our confidence in the future is threatening to destroy the social and the political fabric of America. . . . Our people are losing that faith, not only in government itself but in the ability as citizens to serve as the ultimate rulers and shapers of our democracy. As a people we know our past and we are proud of it. Our progress has been part of the living history of America, even the world. . . . But just as we are losing our confidence in the future, we are also beginning to close the door on our past.

In a nation that was proud of hard work, strong families, close-knit communities, and our faith in God, too many of us now tend to worship self-indulgence and consumption. Human identity is no longer defined by what one does, but by what one owns. But we've discovered that owning things and consuming things does not satisfy our longing for meaning. We've learned that piling up material goods cannot fill the emptiness of lives which have no confidence or purpose.

The symptoms of this crisis of the American spirit are all around us. For the first time in the history of our country a majority of our people believe that the next 5 years will be worse than the past 5 years. Two-thirds of our people do not even vote. The productivity of American workers is actually dropping, and the willingness of Americans to save for the future has fallen below that of all other people in the Western world.

As you know, there is a growing disrespect for government and for churches and for schools, the news media, and other institutions. This is not a message of happiness or reassurance, but it is the truth and it is a warning.

Televised speech by Jimmy Carter (July 15, 1979).

The Duke: More Than Just a Hero

John Wayne was a film actor who died of cancer in 1979. The following document suggested what Wayne meant to those who flocked to his movies.

John Wayne was an American folk hero by reason of countless films in which he lived bigger, shot straighter and loomed larger than any man in real life ever could. . . . In more than 200 features in which he appeared in a career that spanned half a century, 'Duke' Wayne projected an image of rugged, sometimes muleheaded and always formidable masculinity.

His name was synonymous with the Western and, beyond that, with Hollywood and with what many Americans would like to believe about themselves and their country. He became a figure whose magnitude and emotional conviction took on an enduring symbolic importance.

▲ *John Wayne, film star*

In a statement issued by the White House, President Carter said that 'in an age of few heroes' Mr. Wayne was 'the genuine article. But he was more than just a hero,' the president said. 'He was a symbol of many of the most basic qualities that made America great. The ruggedness, the tough independence, the sense of personal conviction and courage—on and off the screen—reflected the best of our national character. It was because of what John Wayne said about what we are and what we can be that his great and deep love of America was returned in full measure.'

Gary Arnold and Kenneth Turan, "The Duke: 'More Than Just a Hero,' " *The Washington Post* (June 13, 1979).

A New Right Activist Explains His Movement

Richard Viguerie became an expert at using direct mail to organize conservative single issue groups.

Conservative single issue groups have been accused of not only fragmenting American politics but threatening the very existence of our two-party system. Congressman David Obey of Wisconsin, a liberal Democrat, has even charged that government has nearly been brought to a standstill by single issue organizations. . . .

Single issue groups naturally emerge because the political parties run away from issues. Single issue groups are the result *of* not the reason *for* the decline of political parties.

If one of the two major political parties had concerned itself more with issues like right to life, high taxes, the growth of the federal government, the right to keep and bear arms, a strong national defense, prayer in the schools, strengthening the family, sex on TV and in the movies, there probably would not have been an explosion of conservative single issue groups. . . .

Frankly, the conservative movement is where it is today because of direct mail. Without direct mail, there would be no effective counterforce to liberalism, and certainly there would be no New Right. . . .

We sell our magazines, our books, and our candidates through the mail. We fight our legislative battles through the mails. We alert our supporters to upcoming battles through the mail. We find new recruits for the conservative movement through the mail. Without the mail, most conservative activity would wither and die.

Most political observers agree that liberals have effective control of the mass media—a virtual monopoly on TV, radio, newspapers and magazines.

Richard A. Viguerie, *The New Right: We're Ready to Lead* (The Viguerie Co., 1981).

The Zero-Sum Society

Economist Lester Thurow discussed the difficulties of dealing with domestic problems in the United States.

But our problems are not limited to slow growth. Throughout our society there are painful, persistent problems that are not being solved. Energy, inflation, unemployment, environmental decay, ever-spreading waves of regulations, sharp income gaps between minorities and majorities—the list is almost endless. Because of our inability to solve these problems, the lament is often heard that the U.S. economy and political system have lost their ability to get things done.

Domestic problems are much more difficult. When policies are adopted to solve domestic problems, there are American winners and American losers. Some incomes go up as a result of the solution, but others go down. Individuals do not sacrifice equally. Some gain, some lose. A program to raise the occupations position of women and minorities automatically lowers the occupations position of white men. . . .

Secondly, the solutions to our problems have a common characteristic. Each requires that some large group—sometimes a minority and sometimes the majority—be willing to tolerate a large reduction in their real standard of living . . . there are large economic losses. These have to be allocated to someone, and no group wants to be the group that must suffer economic losses for the general good.

This is the heart of our fundamental problem. Our political and economic structure simply isn't able to cope with an economy that has a substantial zero-sum element. A zero-sum game is any game where the losses exactly equal the winnings. All sporting events are zero-sum games. . . . The problem with zero-sum games is that the essence of problem solving is loss allocation. But this is precisely what our political process is least capable of doing. . . . Lacking a consensus on whose income ought to go down, or even the recognition that this is at the heart of the problem, we are paralyzed.

Lester Thurow, *The Zero-Sum Society* (New York: Basic Books, 1980).

Wrong, Rambo!

A Vietnam veteran reflected on the meaning of the Vietnam War for the United States in 1985.

More than anything else, though, I no longer felt, as I had 16 years before, that my friends had died for nothing. For in their dying, we, as a nation, became wiser about ourselves, about the world and our role in it.

The members of India Company, and millions of other Americans, fought to change Vietnam. But, in the end, Vietnam changed little. What changed was America. Most Americans no longer accept the illusion that we can defy history, as we tried to in Vietnam. We should mourn the loss of American lives in Vietnam. We needn't mourn the loss of the illusions that brought us there.

Today, as a veteran, I am bothered that some would dishonor the memory of those who died in Vietnam by reviving Americans' shattered illusions. 'Are you gonna let us win this time?' Rambo demands to know as impressionable kids watch in air-conditioned awe. As the Rambo illusion would have it, our gallant soldiers would've won in Vietnam if only they'd been turned loose by the bureaucratic wimps on the home front.

Wrong Rambo, dead wrong. The bureaucrats didn't put us into a winnable war and then tie our hands. What they did was actually far worse. They put us into a war that was as unwinnable as it was immoral. They put us into a war that even they could not explain, and, so, young men died for old men's pride. . . .

The illusion of American invincibility should have been left behind in Vietnam. But, then, there's Rambo, whose appeal, unfortunately, is not limited to youthful moviegoers alone. The Rambo mystique even invades Washington: While policy makers fall over themselves to flex American muscle in the world, macho journalists, from the safety of their typewriters, lob verbal grenades at tiny Third World countries. . . .

We should learn from Vietnam that history can't be beaten.

But neither can history be ignored. We cannot allow the need to avoid another Vietnam let us selfishly retreat from the realistic problems of the world. America *does* have a role to play in the world, as a moral force, a beacon of hope, a model of democratic idealism. We cannot turn our backs to injustice, whatever its form, be it terrorism, tyranny, poverty, hunger, or torture.

Thomas J. Vallely, "Dishonoring the Vietnam Tragedy," *Boston Globe* (Nov. 10, 1985).

The Landslide of 1984

Journalist Theodore White discussed the implications of Ronald Reagan's reelection in 1984.

Yet, in the end, politics is the entry way to power, and in our system, politics delivers power into the hands of the most potent constitutional leader in the world. It is into Ronald Reagan's hands, instincts, purposes that this election has delivered us.

Much will depend on how Ronald Reagan interprets the vote. Landslides give presidents enormous authority, but they can lead either to disasters, as did the landslides of Herbert Hoover, Lyndon Johnson and Richard Nixon, or to profound redefinitions of American life, as Franklin Roosevelt engineered. Of course, squeakers, too, can change American life, as Lincoln and Kennedy proved. What is critical in both landslides and squeakers is the ability of a president to read the tides, the yearnings that went into his victory, to distinguish between his own campaign rhetoric and the reality he must force his people to face.

With reelection, Reagan has been handed enormous authority to make the Soviets face U.S. strength and truly negotiate, with some hope of realism on both sides. What is less sure is whether his victory will give him sufficient new vigor to reorganize his discordant White House staff, his cabinet and his Pentagon.

Theodore White, "The Shaping of the Presidency 1984," *Time* (Nov. 19, 1984).

WORKING WITH THE ARCHIVES

Comparing Perspectives Using Primary Sources

This activity will help you examine the opinions expressed by three individuals on the subject of preferential treatment for minority groups.

Directions:

- Read "Have We Overcome?", "Justice Thurgood Marshall's Opinion in the *Bakke* Case," and "Are Quotas Good for Blacks?"

- Design a graphic organizer that will help you gather information about how Bennett, Marshall, and Sowell viewed (a) the purpose of affirmative action programs, (b) the effects of affirmative action programs, and (c) affirmative action.

- Summarize the information in your organizer and write as complete an answer as possible (based on the information provided in the excerpts) to each of the following questions:

1. When were these excerpts written? Does the fact that they were written in the same year make your comparison more valid or less valid? Why?
2. What does each of the writers believe is the purpose of affirmative action programs? How are their beliefs similar? How are they different?
3. What does each of the writers believe is the effect of affirmative action programs? How are their beliefs similar? How are they different?
4. What is Justice Marshall's opinion of affirmative action programs?
5. What is Thomas Sowell's opinion of affirmative action programs?
6. In what ways do the writers disagree on the economic and social progress made by African Americans?
7. With which writer are you most sympathetic? Why?

The Nixon Years

By 1968, student radicals, the counterculture, antiwar protests, militant minority and women's groups, and increasing crime rates and violence had created a conservative political backlash among many Americans from both the middle and working classes. The 1968 presidential election took place in the midst of this conservative reaction. Richard Nixon narrowly won that election. As president, Nixon continued to appeal to those Americans tired of reform policies and domestic turmoil. This strategy, along with his bold foreign policy initiatives, resulted in his reelection in 1972 by an overwhelming margin. Even as President Nixon reached the pinnacle of power, the press and congressional investigators looking into his reelection campaign uncovered a variety of "dirty" campaign tricks and executive abuses. This Watergate political scandal shattered many Americans' confidence in their elected leaders and drove Nixon from office.

▲ *Richard M. Nixon struck a familiar pose as he responded to the applause of the delegates at the Republican National Convention in Miami in 1968.*

Richard Nixon's Election

During the 1968 presidential campaign, Nixon's strategy focused on those he called the "forgotten and silent majority" of Americans—the working class, white southerners, and the suburban middle class. His speeches were designed to appeal directly to many of their concerns. "We live in a deeply troubled and profoundly unsettled time," Nixon said in a campaign speech. "Drugs, crimes, campus revolts, racial discord, draft resistance—on every hand we find old standards violated, old values discarded." On the day after his election, he recalled that during the campaign a Deshler, Ohio, teenager had carried a sign that read, "Bring Us Together." "That will be the great objective of this administration . . .," Nixon declared, "to bring the American people together."

How did domestic conflicts in the 1960s influence the political climate in 1968?

How did the 1968 presidential campaign reflect political divisions in American society?

Why did President Nixon organize his administration as he did?

A Swing to the Right

Throughout history, spurts of reform have often been followed by a more conservative political climate. But the turn to the right in 1968 was of unusual proportions. The very scope of the Great Society reforms partly explains the conservative atmosphere that followed. Many Americans who had recently moved into the economic and social mainstream of American life resented the Great Society programs that seemed to favor minority groups. They believed that they had pulled themselves up in society by their own hard work and without government aid, and they resented paying the costs of the new programs aimed at poor minorities.

Calls for black, red, brown, and women's power alienated many middle- and lower-class white

Americans. To them, these movements, along with the drug scene and the alternative lifestyles of the 1960s, showed an unacceptable level of permissiveness and represented the breakdown of discipline and authority. In addition, ghetto riots and rising crime rates fueled demands for law and order. These political tensions would unify the Republicans and fragment the Democratic Party.

The Election of 1968

Lyndon Johnson's announcement in late March 1968 that he would not seek reelection threw the Democrats into turmoil. Many conservative Democrats leaned toward Alabama Governor George C. Wallace. Wallace had won election as governor in Alabama by advocating "segregation now . . . segregation tomorrow . . . segregation forever." His national campaign in 1968 denounced student radicals, the counterculture, school busing for racial integration, and the urban riots. Conservatives also liked Wallace because he was a hawk on the Vietnam War. Wallace appealed to many white southerners, and support for him was growing among many northern blue-collar white ethnic groups.

Minnesota Senator Eugene McCarthy and New York Senator Robert F. Kennedy (brother of JFK) drew support from the left wing of the Democratic Party, from student groups, and from antiwar activists. Despite early successes in the New Hampshire and Wisconsin presidential primary elections, McCarthy had limited appeal among many traditional Democratic voting groups. Although McCarthy was Catholic, he had few followers among the Catholic blue-collar working class. He also had little support from minority groups, especially African and Hispanic Americans. This may have been due to McCarthy's being too intellectual and too closely identified with his student supporters.

Robert Kennedy, on the other hand, aroused passionate support among African and Hispanic Americans, Catholics, and many blue-collar workers. It appeared he might be able to overcome his party's many divisions. Kennedy's popularity peaked

Robert F. Kennedy is shown here campaigning for the Democratic presidential nomination in 1968. In what ways did "Bobby" appear to resemble his famous older brother?

in June when he decisively won California's presidential primary election. He never got the chance to win the Democratic nomination. A Jordanian immigrant, Sirhan Sirhan, assassinated Kennedy as he was leaving the primary victory party. Kennedy's death stunned an already troubled nation and threw the Democratic Party into further disarray.

Vice President Hubert Humphrey controlled the center of the Democratic Party. Humphrey had strong liberal credentials as a longtime supporter of civil rights and social reform. On the other hand, as vice president he had fully supported Johnson's Vietnam policy and had condemned antiwar activists as un-American and cowardly. Consequently, only labor unions, city political machines (those controlled by political bosses like Chicago Mayor Richard Daley), and some African American leaders supported his nomination. At the Democratic National Convention in Chicago, the various party factions could not pull together. On the streets outside the convention, Chicago police battled with antiwar protesters, causing even more disagreement within the Democratic Party. Humphrey's eventual nomination as the Democratic presidential candidate did not heal these divisions.

The Republicans rallying around former Vice President Richard Nixon were much more unified than the Democrats. Nixon had appeared politically

dead after losing to John Kennedy in the 1960 presidential election and losing the California governor's race in 1962. But Nixon worked hard for other Republican candidates over the next six years, and he received much of the credit for the party's recovery after the Goldwater defeat in 1964. By the

▼ In August 1968, the Chicago police clashed with demonstrators outside the Democratic National Convention.

▲ *On which party's ticket did Alabama Governor George C. Wallace run for president in 1968?*

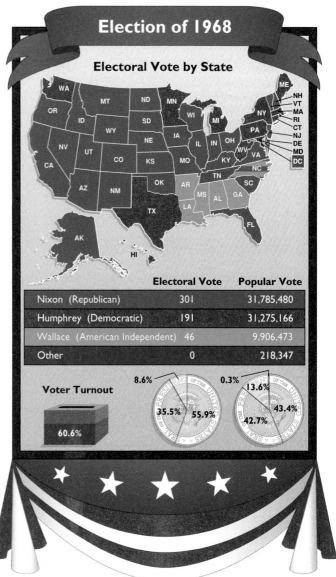

Election of 1968

Electoral Vote by State

	Electoral Vote	Popular Vote
Nixon (Republican)	301	31,785,480
Humphrey (Democratic)	191	31,275,166
Wallace (American Independent)	46	9,906,473
Other	0	218,347

Voter Turnout 60.6%

8.6% 35.5% 55.9%

0.3% 13.6% 43.4% 42.7%

▲ *Which figure gives a more accurate representation of the closeness of this election: the electoral vote or the popular vote?*

time of the Republican National Convention in 1968, Nixon was the front-runner among potential Republican presidential candidates. He won the party's nomination and chose Maryland Governor Spiro Agnew as his running mate.

The election of 1968 was a three-way race. George Wallace ran as a third-party candidate on the American Independent Party ticket. As the campaign unfolded, Nixon's call for law and order and his vague stand on the Vietnam War failed to attract Wallace supporters. Humphrey's campaign started slowly, but caught fire as he distanced himself from Johnson's Vietnam policy. When Johnson announced a bombing halt on October 31, it appeared that Humphrey might win.

The election was close. Nixon won 43 percent of the popular vote, the smallest share for a winning candidate since 1912. His victory margin over Humphrey was less than 1 percent of the popular vote. Nixon, however, won 301 electoral votes compared to Humphrey's 191 and Wallace's 46. Nixon's margin of victory gave him little reason to rejoice. He was the first president elected in the twentieth century not to have at least one house of Congress under his party's control.

The Nixon Presidency

Richard Nixon was born in Whittier, California, in 1913. His family was lower middle class and staunchly Republican. His mother was a devout Quaker. Nixon worked hard to pull himself up from his humble origins to become a lawyer and national political figure. He believed that America offered great opportunities to all who would work hard to succeed. He also thought that people should not rely on the government. Rather, the American free-enterprise system, if kept free from government interference, would solve the nation's problems.

Despite his visibility and success as a politician, Nixon was actually a shy, retiring, and very private man. Nixon surrounded himself with White House aides who insulated him from the daily hurly-burly

▲ *To what extent did Nixon's priorities agree with the priorities expressed in this opinion poll?*

of party politics. Nixon went months without holding a press conference. Presidential aides John Ehrlichman and H. R. Haldeman refused to let congressional leaders or even cabinet appointees meet with Nixon without their approval, thus isolating the president even further.

Nixon gave vast authority and power to the White House staff. His staff was the largest in U.S. history up to that time. Rather than relying on his cabinet or the executive departments, Nixon and his White House aides set both domestic and foreign policies. So elaborate was Nixon's control and so secretive was his style that some people felt that he had created a "shadow" or "parallel" government. This shadow government, they complained, upset the balance of power set up by the Constitution among the executive branch, Congress, and the courts.

SECTION 1 REVIEW

1. **Describe** the political tensions that helped unify the Republicans in 1968.
2. **Name** the basis for George Wallace's support as a third-party candidate in the election.
3. **Identify** Robert Kennedy.
4. **Explain** why Nixon's election in 1968 did not indicate widespread support.
5. **Discuss** Nixon's leadership style.

SECTION 2

Winding Down the War in Vietnam

During the election campaign of 1968, Nixon promised to bring "peace with honor" to Vietnam. But he refused to discuss his plan in detail. Nixon knew that the majority of Americans favored ending the war. As he confided to aide H. R. Haldeman, "I'm not going to end up like LBJ, holed up in the White House afraid to show my face on the street. I'm going to stop that war. Fast." Despite Nixon's desire to end U.S. involvement in Vietnam quickly, the war dragged on for another four years.

What were the major elements of Nixon's Vietnamization policy?

What events most influenced American public opinion about Vietnam between 1969 and 1972?

What were the major provisions of the final peace settlement in Vietnam?

Vietnamization

Nixon's primary goal in Vietnam was not very different from Lyndon Johnson's. Nixon's definition of "peace with honor" included an independent, non-Communist government in South Vietnam. In June 1969, Nixon unveiled his comprehensive peace plan. He proposed that both the United States and North Vietnam gradually withdraw their forces from South Vietnam. Eventually, the United Nations would supervise free elections there. The North Vietnamese government in Hanoi called Nixon's peace plan a farce and said they would sit in Paris for peace talks "until the chairs rot." Even after Ho Chi Minh's death in September 1969, North Vietnamese leaders continued to insist on complete American withdrawal from South Vietnam before serious peace negotiations could begin. They believed they could outlast Nixon, because American public opinion would force him to withdraw.

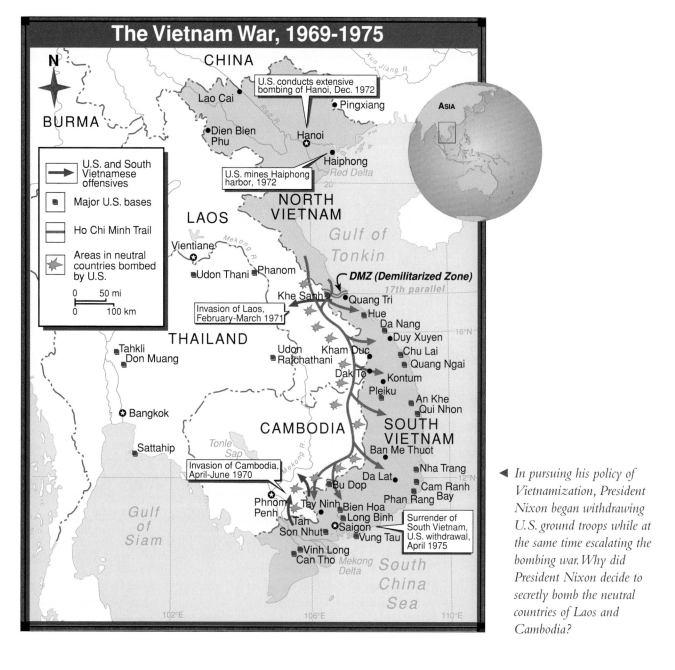

The Vietnam War, 1969-1975

N

BURMA

CHINA

Lao Cai

U.S. conducts extensive bombing of Hanoi, Dec. 1972

Pingxiang

Dien Bien Phu

Hanoi

Haiphong

U.S. mines Haiphong harbor, 1972

Red Delta

NORTH VIETNAM

Gulf of Tonkin

LAOS

Vientiane

Mekong R.

Udon Thani

Phanom

DMZ (Demilitarized Zone)

17th parallel

Khe Sanh

Quang Tri

Invasion of Laos, February-March 1971

Hue

Da Nang

THAILAND

Duy Xuyen

16°N

Tahkli

Don Muang

Udon Ratchathani

Kham Duc

Chu Lai

Quang Ngai

Dak To

Kontum

Pleiku

Bangkok

An Khe

Qui Nhon

CAMBODIA

SOUTH VIETNAM

Ban Me Thuot

Tonle Sap

Sattahip

Nha Trang

12°N

Invasion of Cambodia, April-June 1970

Da Lat

Cam Ranh Bay

Bu Dop

Phan Rang

Mekong R.

Phnom Penh

Tay Ninh

Bien Hoa

Tan Son Nhut

Long Binh

Saigon

Surrender of South Vietnam, U.S. withdrawal, April 1975

Gulf of Siam

Vung Tau

Vinh Long

Can Tho

Mekong Delta

South China Sea

102°E

106°E

110°E

ASIA

Legend

→ U.S. and South Vietnamese offensives

■ Major U.S. bases

▬ Ho Chi Minh Trail

✦ Areas in neutral countries bombed by U.S.

0   50 mi
0   100 km

◄ *In pursuing his policy of Vietnamization, President Nixon began withdrawing U.S. ground troops while at the same time escalating the bombing war. Why did President Nixon decide to secretly bomb the neutral countries of Laos and Cambodia?*

Despite Hanoi's refusal to negotiate on Nixon's terms, Nixon began to withdraw combat troops from Vietnam in order to placate antiwar opinion at home. Nixon's policy of **Vietnamization** was designed to turn over the responsibility for the war to the South Vietnamese. One aspect of this policy was to bring U.S. troops home. Nixon began troop withdrawals in June 1969. As troops came home, U.S. combat deaths declined—from 8,250 in 1969, to 5,000 in 1970, to fewer than 2,000 in 1971.

A second goal of Vietnamization was to strengthen South Vietnamese armed forces so they could fight without direct U.S. involvement. But a strong, self-sufficient South Vietnam had been the focus of U.S. policy for 15 years. There was little reason to believe that Nixon's policy would succeed when previous efforts had failed.

The third major aspect of Vietnamization was increased bombing. Nixon took several bold steps urged by the Joint Chiefs of Staff. In the mid-1960s,

The Pentagon Papers Case

On Sunday morning, June 13, 1971, the *New York Times* ran a small headline on its front page: *Vietnam Archive: Pentagon Study Traces 3 Decades of Growing U.S. Involvement.* This was the way the famous "Pentagon Papers" case began. A Pentagon employee named Daniel Ellsberg had turned over a secret study to the *Times* as a protest against the Vietnam War. Two sections of the 7,000-page study were printed in the next several issues of the *Times*.

The United States Justice Department asked the *Times* not to print any more of the document on the grounds that its publication violated the United States Espionage Act of 1917. When the editors refused, the United States attorney general filed a motion for an injunction in the district court in New York. Legal scholars believe this was the first time a federal judge had issued an injunction against a newspaper in the history of the nation. When additional injunctions were requested by the government against other newspapers planning to print parts of the study, the judge who

first issued the injunction changed his mind and lifted the order against the *Times*.

The United States Department of Justice appealed the judge's decision. The United States Court of Appeals for New York agreed with the government and issued a restraining order directing the newspapers to stop publishing the study. The *Times* appealed to the United States Supreme Court. The case became known as *New York Times Co. v. United States* (1971), or the Pentagon Papers.

In their brief before the Supreme Court, the government lawyers argued that the president, as the executive authority under the Constitution, had the power to protect the nation against publication of information whose disclosure would endanger the national security. The lawyers argued this power comes from two sources — first, the president has exclusive conduct over foreign affairs, and second, the president is commander in chief. The national security might be threatened if the details of the war and associated matters were published. The nation and its armed forces might be in danger. The president was responsible for both.

The arguments used by lawyers for the *Times* focused on

the First Amendment. Censoring information already obtained by newspapers had been called *prior restraint* by the court in an injunction case in 1931. At that time, the Court had said the First Amendment did not allow for prior restraint, or censorship. Additionally, they pointed out that there had to be a clear and present danger before any action could be taken by government to restrict freedom of the press. No specific law, they noted, had ever been passed to give the president broad authority to stop publication of items dangerous to the national interest.

Several issues were raised by this case. Was prior restraint (government censorship) ever justified? Would continued publication of this document really endanger national security? Would publication affect national security in the future?

In an unusually speedy decision — reached after only four days in conference — the Supreme Court responded to these questions. The *per curiam,* or short, decision simply said that the government had failed to meet its "heavy burden" of proving a clear and present danger. Six of the justices were not convinced that the publication of a report about events or decisions several years after they occurred

(continued)

was a significant threat to national security.

Some of the judges felt that censorship and secrecy are not appropriate to a democracy and could lead to government corruption. The best check on government policy lies in having enlightened citizens who, in turn, depend on an informed and free press. They said that the government should now pursue the case in criminal court. It should have prevented the disclosure of secret information by preventing the theft of the papers.

The dissenting justices argued that it may be necessary for a president to operate in absolute secrecy in dealing with foreign affairs as he was responsible for the safety of his country.

The dissenters wrote that the court had been rushed, that not all of the facts were known, and that more time was necessary to write a major decision. They asked why the *Times* had not returned the classified documents to the government, a duty of every citizen regarding stolen government property. One judge mentioned that even the Supreme Court has an inherent need to keep its proceedings secret and out of the public eye. Why would the president not have the same power relating to activities of the executive?

▲ *This headline began a series of legal battles that led all the way to the Supreme Court.*

Many newspapers subsequently published Ellsberg's study. A paperback version was printed and sold by the *New York Times* in July, 1971. The Pentagon Papers case prevented the executive department from forcing the judicial department to issue injunctions in national security cases. It required the executive department to follow the laws that Congress had already passed, which imposed criminal penalties on those that stole secret documents or harmed national security in other ways. It

returned a balance to the three departments and required each one to attend to its own job. This separation of powers of the three departments characterizes our enduring Constitution.

1. What arguments did the government present in its effort to stop the *Times* from publishing the secret report?
2. According to some of the justices, what should have been the government's course of action regarding Ellsberg?

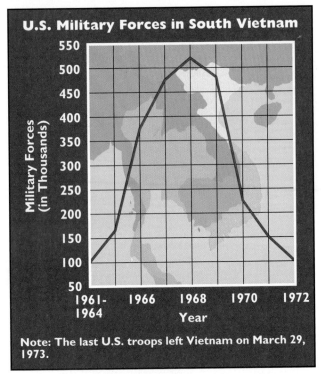

U.S. Military Forces in South Vietnam

Military Forces (in Thousands) vs **Year**

Note: The last U.S. troops left Vietnam on March 29, 1973.

Source: U.S. Department of Defense, *Selected Manpower Statistics.*

▲ *The number of U.S. troops in South Vietnam grew slowly from 700 to over half a million.*

North Vietnam had set up areas in neutral Laos and Cambodia from which they attacked South Vietnam. Early in 1969, Nixon ordered these areas bombed. During the next year, the U.S. launched nearly 3,500 B-52 bombing raids on Cambodia alone. Nixon hid these actions from both the public and Congress. Although news of the secret bombing campaign leaked to the press, the published stories went almost unnoticed by the public. The leaks of sensitive information, however, prompted Nixon to order FBI phone taps of several administration officials. These illegal actions would come to light during the Watergate investigations.

Nixon's gradual withdrawal of U.S. troops reinforced Hanoi's decision to delay a negotiated settlement. Nixon therefore decided to "show the enemy we are still serious about our commitment in Vietnam." In May 1970, without consulting Congress, Nixon ordered U.S. forces to attack North Vietnamese positions in neutral Cambodia. "If the world's most powerful nation . . . acts like a pitiful, helpless giant," Nixon said, the United States would lose its credibility with both its allies and foes, despite its overwhelming power.

The attack into Cambodia set off a political uproar at home. Massive demonstrations occurred across the nation. They were larger and more widespread than Nixon's worst fears. Over 100,000 antiwar protesters marched on Washington. Strikes involving 1.5 million students shut down hundreds of colleges. At Kent State University, members of the Ohio National Guard killed four students and wounded 22 others during an antiwar demonstration. Another antiwar protest at Jackson State College in Mississippi resulted in the deaths of two African American students. These tragic events shocked many Americans. Antiwar feelings increased among members of Congress. By the end of the year, Congress had repealed the Gulf of Tonkin Resolution, and was considering numerous bills to limit the war. American public opinion pressured Nixon to withdraw U.S. troops even more rapidly.

Peace Talks Flounder

Nixon clung to his Vietnamization policy in the face of deepening divisions at home and continuing

▼ *What were the tragic results of summoning troops to Kent State University in May 1970?*

failures at the Paris peace talks. In February 1971, South Vietnamese army units failed miserably in an attack on the Ho Chi Minh Trail in Laos. Despite this setback, Nixon sped up American troop withdrawals, bringing home 100,000 more by the end of the year. To keep pressure on Hanoi, Nixon also continued bombing North Vietnamese troops and their installations in Laos and Cambodia. But no progress occurred in either the formal Paris peace talks or in the secret discussions begun in 1970 between Henry Kissinger, Nixon's national security adviser, and the North Vietnamese.

The increasingly unmanageable and vocal antiwar movement in the United States encouraged Hanoi to resist serious negotiation. In April, Vietnam combat veterans staged a protest in front of the United States Capitol. There, the Vietnam veterans confessed to what they termed war crimes and threw away their combat medals. Several days later, 30,000 protesters went to Washington intent on shutting down the city with "lie-ins" on bridges and streets. Washington police arrested thousands of protesters. More importantly, antiwar feeling was spreading among middle-class Americans.

The My Lai Massacre   In mid-1971, a military court convicted Lieutenant William Calley of "at least 22 murders" of Vietnamese civilians in the 1968 My Lai massacre. My Lai was a village in South Vietnam which U.S. troops believed hid and protected Vietcong guerrillas. Calley's troops attacked the village and killed between 175 and 400 unarmed civilians, many of them women and children. The court sentenced Calley to life imprisonment at hard labor for his role at My Lai. Nixon ordered Calley released while he personally reviewed his case. Calley's sentence was eventually reduced to ten years; he was later released after serving three years.

One veteran noted that "My Lai was not an isolated incident [but] only a minor step beyond the standard official United States policy in Indochina." Such stories horrified many Americans and underscored the brutality of guerrilla warfare in Vietnam.

The Pentagon Papers   Meanwhile, the *New York Times* published the *Pentagon Papers*, a classified Defense Department history of U.S. involvement in

▲ *For what action was former Defense Department official Daniel Ellsberg taken into custody on June 28, 1971?*

Vietnam. Leaked to the *Times* by former Pentagon official Daniel Ellsberg, the documents showed that Kennedy and Johnson had consistently misled the American public about their intentions in Vietnam.

By mid-1971, after the revelations of the My Lai massacre and the *Pentagon Papers*, 71 percent of Americans thought that sending U.S. combat troops to Vietnam had been a mistake. Nearly 65 percent believed the war was immoral, and a substantial majority favored withdrawal of all troops, even if that meant a Communist victory in Vietnam.

Despite widespread antiwar sentiment, administration officials continued to attack the patriotism of antiwar protesters. Nixon also moved to prevent leaks of administration secrets to the press. He approved the creation of the "plumbers," a secret group assigned to plug leaks to the press and to discredit Ellsberg. The plumbers engaged in various activities, many of them illegal, including putting wiretaps on the phones of administration officials and reporters, breaking into Ellsberg's psychiatrist's office, and bugging the headquarters of the National Democratic Party.

Withdrawal from the War

Increasing antiwar sentiment put great pressure on Nixon to make headway in the peace talks. Hanoi was not yet willing to compromise. In March

▲ *What agreement was reached between Henry Kissinger and Le Duc Tho in January 1973?*

1972, the North Vietnamese mounted a major offensive into South Vietnam. This was successful in its early stages, since it caught U.S. and South Vietnamese forces off guard. Nixon responded with massive air attacks on Hanoi and Haiphong. In a drastic escalation of the war, Nixon ordered the mining of Haiphong harbor. China and the Soviet Union pressured North Vietnam to suspend military operations and to begin negotiations in earnest.

On October 11, 1972, Kissinger and North Vietnam's chief negotiator, Le Duc Tho [Lay DUK TOH], announced they had reached a provisional peace agreement. Since no one had consulted him, South Vietnamese President Nguyen Van Thieu [nuh–WIN vahn tee-OO] balked. Nixon agreed to a temporary delay in the peace settlement, and sent an additional billion dollars in military equipment to South Vietnam. Nixon also gave Thieu "absolute assurances" that the United States would intervene should Hanoi violate the peace. Because of these actions, Hanoi now refused to sign the agreement. After his reelection in November 1972, Nixon unleashed the most devastating bombing of the war, trying to force Hanoi to agree to the initial settlement. In early January, peace talks resumed.

In January, Kissinger and Le Duc Tho again reached an agreement, with few changes from the October version. This time, however, Nixon forced Thieu to accept it. The **Paris Peace Accords** called for complete withdrawal of U.S. troops. (The last troops left on March 29, 1973.) The settlement promised American prisoners of war would be returned, and it left the Thieu government intact. North Vietnamese troops, however, would remain in South Vietnam. The agreement also recognized the Provisional Revolutionary Government (the Vietcong) as a legitimate political force in South Vietnam. Thus, America's major goal in the war—South Vietnam's independence—remained in doubt.

SECTION 2 REVIEW

1. **List** three aspects of Vietnamization.
2. **Explain** why Nixon decided to bomb Cambodia and what the results were.
3. **Name** the three events in Nixon's first administration that had the most influence on American attitudes toward the war.
4. **Identify** My Lai.
5. **State** provisions of the agreement signed by the United States and Hanoi in January 1973.

SECTION 3

Nixon's Domestic Programs

For Richard Nixon, domestic policies were always secondary to foreign policies. "I've always thought this country could run itself domestically without a president," Nixon said in 1968. "All you need is a competent cabinet to run the country at home." Still, Nixon and his close advisers were actively involved in his administration's domestic policies. Two basic goals underlay their approach to domestic issues. First, Nixon wanted to strengthen the power of state and local governments. Second was Nixon's nearly obsessive desire to be reelected in 1972.

What were Nixon's major domestic policy initiatives?
How did Nixon handle the economy and relations between the federal and state governments?
What impact did energy and environmental issues have on the United States during this period?

New Federalism

Many of Nixon's domestic policies were driven by what he perceived to be the needs and demands of the "silent majority." Nixon pinned his hopes for reelection in 1972 on this group. He described **New Federalism** as a means "to reverse the flow of power and resources from the states and communities to Washington and start power and resources flowing back . . . to the people." Nixon's New Federalism took many forms.

Nixon cut many federal grants for programs such as urban renewal, job training, education, and social welfare. In 1973, Nixon abolished the Office of Economic Opportunity, the centerpiece of Lyndon Johnson's antipoverty program. Congress, controlled by Democrats, blocked his efforts to cut dozens of other federal programs. Occasionally, Nixon responded by **impounding** (refusing to release) funds Congress had appropriated for certain programs. Many in Congress believed this practice to be an abuse of executive power.

Nixon wanted to reduce the role of the federal government in other ways. "We have made the federal government so strong," Nixon argued, "that it grows muscle-bound and the states and localities so weak they approach impotence." His answer to this problem was **revenue sharing**, by which federal tax money would be given to state and local governments through various grants. In October 1972, Congress passed the State and Local Fiscal Assistance Act. The act provided $32 billion in grants to be divided among local and state governments over five years. Many state and local officials thought revenue sharing was the solution to their growing financial problems. Others thought Nixon would soon cut other government programs, and this would leave state and local governments with fewer funds than before revenue sharing.

Nixon also called for a sweeping overhaul of the nation's welfare system. Welfare, especially Aid to Families with Dependent Children (AFDC), had expanded dramatically during the 1960s. The number of people on welfare had doubled between 1961 and 1972, to nearly 15 million people. The amount of money spent on welfare had increased even more rapidly, from $2.1 billion to nearly $18 billion. The existing system struggled under these growing burdens. Democrats and Republicans condemned the welfare system. Nixon proposed the Family Assistance Plan, which would have established a guaranteed income level for the poor and would have required welfare recipients to work or to train for work. Liberals opposed Nixon's welfare reform plan because its income level was too low and its work requirements were too harsh. Conservatives thought the plan's payments were too generous, and together they defeated the measure.

The Burger Court Consistent with New Federalism, Nixon vowed to change the liberal slant of the Supreme Court by appointing conservative judges to federal courts. When Chief Justice Earl Warren retired in 1969, Nixon appointed a conservative Minnesotan, **Warren Burger**, to replace him. Nixon had more difficulty filling other Supreme Court vacancies. The Senate rejected South Carolina judge Clement Haynesworth because he believed in segregation and because there was some evidence that he had ruled on a case in which he had a personal interest. It refused to confirm Harrold Carswell of Florida because of his dismal judicial record (many of his decisions had been reversed by higher courts on appeal). Nixon eventually gained Senate approval of a southern appointee, Virginian Lewis F. Powell (1972). Two additional vacancies, which Nixon filled with Harry F. Blackmun and **William Rehnquist**, enabled him to strengthen the conservative element on the Supreme Court.

The Burger Court was more conservative than the Warren Court, especially in the area of criminal rights. Yet many of its rulings displeased Nixon and other conservatives. Nixon opposed court-ordered busing of students to achieve racial integration. He hoped the Supreme Court would support his position. In *Alexander v. Holmes Board of Education* (1969), however, the Burger Court unanimously ordered the end of school segregation "at once." In *Swann v. Charlotte-Mecklenburg County Board of Education* (1971), the Court ruled that integration would proceed even if it required "administratively awkward, inconvenient, and even bizarre" methods, including busing.

▲ *Abortion-rights supporters (shown at left) were demonstrating on the west steps of the U.S. Capitol on November 20, 1971. Demonstrators against abortion (shown at right) were rallying at the same time on the east steps. Which controversial Supreme Court ruling decided that the "right of privacy" covers abortion in the first trimester?*

The Burger Court's most controversial decision was *Roe v. Wade* (1973) concerning abortions. The Court held that "the right of privacy, however based, is broad enough to cover the abortion decision." The ruling distinguished among the three trimesters of pregnancy. During the first trimester, or three months, the decision to have an abortion may be left entirely to a woman and her physician. During the second trimester, the state may regulate abortion in relation to maternal health. In the third trimester, however, the state may forbid all abortions except those necessary to save the mother's life.

When fundamental rights were involved, regulations limiting these rights could be justified only by "a compelling state interest." *Roe v. Wade* therefore invalidated state laws, many over a century old, that restricted the "fundamental right" to abortion.

No Burger Court decision was more bitterly attacked than *Roe v. Wade*. On the one hand, many people believed that abortion was morally wrong in all situations because life begins at conception and must be protected from that point on. On the other hand, many others believed that women's privacy rights included the personal control of their own bodies and that abortion was a personal matter to be decided by the individual.

The Economy and the Energy Crisis

When Nixon took office, inflation was the biggest economic problem facing his administration. At first, Nixon tried to slow inflation by adopting a tight monetary policy—decreasing the supply of money and raising interest rates. The immediate effect of this policy was economic recession, the first in a decade. Yet inflation would not stop, rising 14.5 percent in the 18 months after January 1969. The result was **stagflation**, a new economic phenomenon. Stagflation is the result of a stagnant, slow-growing economy—typical of a recession—that also has a high rate of inflation. By 1970, the cost of consumer goods was 16 percent higher than three years before, due largely to the continuing huge costs of the Vietnam War.

Initially Nixon rejected wage and price controls as a way to control inflation. "I will not take this nation down the road of wage and price controls however politically expedient that may seem," he said in June 1970. Within a year, however, Nixon had chosen the "politically expedient" course and announced wage and price controls. For a while,

The Energy Crisis

The energy crisis of 1973 pushed the United States to the very edge of economic disaster. The sudden shortage of oil caused by the embargo and the OPEC price increases immediately drove up the price of all petroleum products. By January 1974, for example, the price of diesel truck fuel had risen from 27 cents per gallon to as high as 80 cents. Gasoline prices rose by over 25 percent, up to 54 cents per gallon. They continued to increase steadily throughout the 1970s and 1980s. The price of home heating oil nearly doubled, rising to 39 cents per gallon. Soaring oil prices sent shock waves throughout an economy that was heavily dependent on fossil fuel (petroleum) energy.

The American people found it very difficult to adjust to the energy crisis. Since the end of World War II, Americans had settled into lifestyles and technologies that depended on the availability of cheap energy. Americans heated their homes to much higher temperatures than anyone else in the world. By far the greatest consumer of petroleum was the automobile. Detroit auto manufacturers had long built powerful, heavy cars that guzzled gasoline, and Americans happily bought them so long as gas was cheap. Americans relied on their own cars for commuting to work rather than mass transit.

▲ *Scenes similar to the one above were repeated all over the country as the OPEC oil embargo and price increases drove up the cost of gasoline to consumers.*

When the energy crisis struck, Americans found themselves waiting hours in long lines at gas stations to buy an increasingly precious commodity.

The energy crisis taught Americans several lessons. This crisis showed the United States' increasing interdependence with other nations and the impact that had on daily life at home. It underscored the great dependence of Americans on fossil fuels. It showed how difficult it was for a complex society to establish public policy that spread sacrifices evenly among its people. It stimulated the search for alternative energy sources and technologies. Finally, it made energy conservation, rather than consumerism, a patriotic act.

1. Why did the sudden shortage of oil, due to the OPEC embargo, cause an energy crisis in the United States?
2. What lessons did Americans learn from the energy crisis?

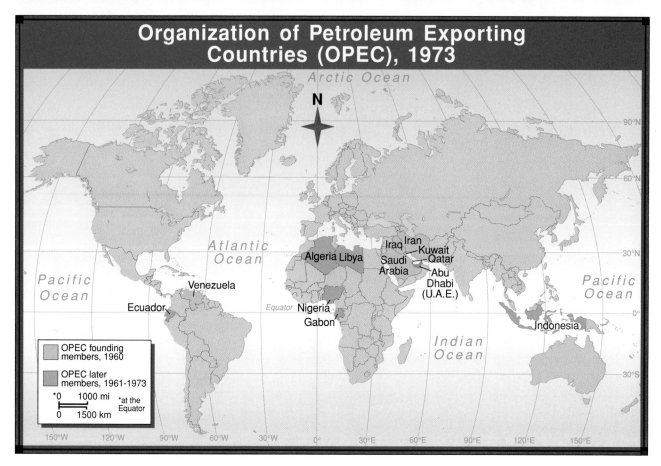

Organization of Petroleum Exporting Countries (OPEC), 1973

Arctic Ocean

N

Atlantic Ocean

Pacific Ocean

Pacific Ocean

Venezuela

Ecuador

Equator

Algeria Libya

Iraq Iran
Kuwait
Saudi Qatar
Arabia
Abu
Dhabi
(U.A.E.)

Nigeria
Gabon

Indian Ocean

Indonesia

OPEC founding members, 1960

OPEC later members, 1961-1973

*0   1000 mi   *at the Equator
0   1500 km

▲ *In the 1950s, the U. S. produced almost all the oil it used. By 1973, however, it purchased one-third of its oil from OPEC countries, especially Venezuela and those in the Middle East. Using the map and other information you have, what generalizations can you make about OPEC?*

these controls helped reduce inflation. But when they ended in 1973, inflation became worse.

Nixon's economic policies received a severe blow in late 1973 when a consortium of Middle Eastern oil producers stopped oil shipments to the United States. This action was to punish the U.S. for supporting Israel in the October 1973 Yom Kippur War between Israel and Egypt. The embargo set off an energy crisis in the United States. The crisis worsened when the **Organization of Petroleum Exporting Countries (OPEC)** raised the price of oil 300 percent, from $2 to $8 a barrel.

The energy crisis produced a cry to save energy and to take advantage of every energy source. Practices that damaged the environment such as strip-mining coal and relaxing air pollution standards, became more acceptable. Congress approved construction of the Alaska oil pipeline despite environ-

mentalists' concerns that the pipeline would cause pollution and damage local wildlife. The Interior Department ruled that national energy needs outweighed ecological considerations, and it allowed the development of federal lands in Colorado and Utah that contained only small deposits of oil.

Congress debated a variety of ways to deal with the energy crisis, including gasoline rationing, higher fuel taxes to discourage waste, new taxes on the oil companies (which were making large profits because of OPEC price increases), nuclear energy, and alternative energy sources. Congress passed the 55-mile-per-hour speed-limit law for highway travel, but it could not agree on a comprehensive energy policy. When OPEC ended its embargo on March 18, 1974, some of the incentive for seeking such a policy vanished. But energy issues would continue to plague the United States.

▲ *Why did environmentalists protest the development of the Concorde jet?*

Increasing Awareness of Environmental Issues

Environmental issues entered the mainstream of American consciousness during the early 1970s. A growing number of environmental activists protested against threats to the environment. Development of the supersonic transport (SST) aircraft known as the Concorde, for example, was opposed because it was very fuel inefficient and caused air pollution. In 1969, Congress responded to increasing public concern by passing the National Environmental Policy Act. The act required federal agencies to file environmental impact statements that would assess ahead of time how much environmental damage might be caused by federal projects. It also required agencies to make plans that would minimize any

negative effects. This landmark legislation was quickly followed by other acts designed to clean up the land, air, and water.

Despite the public call for environmental legislation, many special interest groups opposed these regulations. Reducing pollution was quite costly. The Council on Environmental Quality estimated that it would cost $121 billion to clean up the nation's entire water supply. If industries had to pay these costs, they might close factories rather than comply. Thus, business and industrial groups lobbied for government subsidies to offset pollution control costs. They sought exemptions from meeting federal standards, and they were granted delays in meeting these standards. At the same time, workers who believed they would lose their jobs adopted slogans like "Hungry? Eat an environmentalist."

Concerned about reelection and always sensitive to shifts in public opinion, Nixon by 1972 was beginning to attack the environmental lobby. "We are not going to allow the environmental issue to be used to destroy the system," he declared. In 1973, Nixon impounded $6 billion that Congress had allocated for water pollution control. (The bill had passed over Nixon's veto.) Congress sued the president to force him to spend the impounded funds. One federal judge described Nixon's action as a "flagrant abuse of executive discretion and in violation of the spirit, intent, and letter of the congressional act providing the funding."

▼ *The growing concern of many Americans about environmental issues was reflected in the environmental regulatory legislation passed during the 1970s. Why would some businesses be opposed to this type of legislation?*

| Important Environmental Legislation, 1970-1976 |||
Year	Act, Agency, or Agreement	Description
1970	Environmental Protection Agency	Combined existing government agencies concerned with pollution and environmental controls
1970	Clean Air Act of 1970	Required automakers to reduce emissions of hydrocarbons, the major exhaust pollutants
1972	Great Lakes Water Quality Agreement	Sought to clean up the badly polluted waterways between the United States and Canada
1972	Clean Water Acts	Authorized funds for sewage treatment plants
1976	Resource Conservation and Recovery Act	Concerned methods of recycling and disposing of solid wastes

SECTION 3 REVIEW

1. **List** the major goals of New Federalism.
2. **Define** the term *revenue sharing*.
3. **Explain** how President Nixon fought inflation in the United States.
4. **Describe** briefly the cause and effect of the OPEC oil embargo in 1973.
5. **Discuss** the major effect of the energy crisis during the early seventies.

SECTION 4

Nixon's Foreign Policies

Few people in American politics knew more about foreign policy, had greater experience in international relations, or been as fascinated with foreign affairs as Richard Nixon. He and his National Security Adviser, Harvard professor Henry Kissinger, decisively changed U.S. foreign policies. In February 1970, Nixon admitted that the United States could not "conceive all the plans, design all the programs, execute all the decisions and undertake all the defense of the free nations of the world." He wished to pull back from the old Cold War system of rigid interlocking commitments that had existed since World War II. Above all, Nixon wanted to be free to pursue the nation's vital interests, as he defined them.

What approach did Nixon take toward U.S.-Soviet relations?

Why did Nixon seek better relations with the People's Republic of China?

What was Nixon's policy toward developing countries?

Revolutionizing U.S. Foreign Policy

Nixon's foreign policy was a throwback in many ways to Theodore Roosevelt's approach in the early twentieth century—realistic, nationalistic, and uni-

lateral. He believed that international tensions would never entirely disappear. Therefore, the role of a great power was to stay well armed, promote its vital interests, and remain flexible. A friendly power today could become an enemy power tomorrow, and vice versa. Only through diplomacy based on maintaining the world balance of power could a nation protect its vital interests.

Just as importantly, Nixon recognized that the world was not simply divided between the free world and the Communist states. From his perspective, the world contained several centers of economic power—Europe, Japan, China, the Soviet Union, and the United States. It was in America's interest to create a balance among these centers. U.S. foreign policy should avoid being rigidly tied to any one of these areas, whether currently friendly or hostile.

In part to ensure U.S. military strength and in part to have an important bargaining chip in his negotiations with the Soviet Union, Nixon began a vast military buildup. He authorized the development of multiple independently targeted reentry vehicle (MIRV) technology for nuclear missiles. With this technology, each rocket could carry several nuclear warheads, which could be launched in midflight toward different targets. MIRV technology vastly increased the destructive capacity of U.S. nuclear missiles.

At the same time, Nixon authorized development of defensive antiballistic missiles (ABMs). In theory, ABMs could knock enemy missiles out of the air before they could do any harm, thus protecting U.S. targets from nuclear missile attack. The Soviets also began building their own versions of these technologies, escalating the nuclear arms race.

Pursuing Détente

Nixon believed that the cornerstone of U.S. foreign policy was Soviet-American relations. Nixon's approach toward the Soviet Union came to be called **détente**, an attempt to relax tensions between the two superpowers. He wanted to curb revolution in the less developed countries. Opposing "wars of national liberation" by force, as in Vietnam, had proved entirely too costly for the United States. Nixon assumed that Soviet actions were creating instability in developing nations. He therefore hoped that U.S.-Soviet détente would lessen Soviet interference in these nations. Nixon failed to realize that Soviet agents were usually only taking advantage of problems that already existed in the developing nations.

The first positive step toward détente was the Four Power Agreement on Berlin, signed in 1971. In this treaty, the Soviet Union guaranteed the Western powers would always have access to West Berlin. The treaty removed a dangerous source of U.S.-Soviet conflict that had existed since 1946. East and West Germany also recognized their "permanent" division and established rules under which German civilians could cross into the other's territory.

In 1972, the Soviets and Americans negotiated a trade agreement that sold grain worth $1 billion to the Soviet Union at bargain prices. Although American farmers and the Soviets liked the deal, the sale caused a shortage of grain in U.S. markets and a steep rise in food prices. Thus, it contributed to inflation in the United States.

More important, perhaps, was Nixon's historic May 1972 visit to Moscow. During their meeting, he and Soviet Premier Leonid Brezhnev signed several agreements in a very friendly atmosphere. The most important of these agreements was the Strategic Arms Limitation Treaty (SALT). The SALT I agreement limited the number of ABMs either nation could set up. If both sides limited their ABMs, then they could reduce their offensive missiles as well. SALT thus placed a five-year freeze on each nation's production of offensive missiles. The two countries were roughly equal in the size of their nuclear arsenals. Although the Soviets had a larger number of missiles, the United States had twice as many nuclear warheads (a two-to-one advantage) because of its MIRV technology. Since the SALT agreement did not cover MIRVs, the arms race slowed only slightly, as the Soviets scrambled to catch up to the United States in MIRV technology. Nixon and Brezhnev also agreed to increase trade between the two nations and to encourage cooperative projects in space, science, and technology.

▲ *President Nixon met with Soviet Premier Leonid Brezhnev in Moscow on May 26, 1972.*

The People's Republic of China

Part of the genius of Nixon's foreign policy was that he established closer ties with the People's Republic of China (PRC) at the same time that he was pursuing détente with the Soviet Union. Since the defeat of Chiang Kai-shek's Nationalist forces by Mao Zedong's Communist forces in 1949, the United States had refused to recognize the existence of Mao's government on the mainland of China.

Relations between the two countries had indeed been poor. The United States had intervened in Vietnam, for example, in order to contain Chinese Communist expansion into Indochina. Nixon hoped to establish normal relations between the two countries and to open the Chinese market to American businesses. He wanted Chinese leaders to sign the **Nuclear Nonproliferation Treaty**, originally signed by other nuclear powers in 1968. The intent of this treaty was to stop the spread of nuclear weapons to powers that did not already have them.

▲ *President Nixon visited Chinese Communist Party leaders Mao Zedong (center) and Chou En-lai (far left) in Beijing, China, in 1972. Why has Nixon's trip to China been viewed as one of his most significant contributions in U.S. foreign affairs?*

Nixon's quest for better relations with the People's Republic of China was ironic. Nixon had been a vehement anti-Communist throughout his political career. In spite of this, he now wanted to achieve a diplomatic breakthrough with this major Communist power. In July 1971, Nixon secretly sent Kissinger to China to arrange a presidential visit.

Chinese leaders also wanted better relations with the United States. Mao and Foreign Minister Chou En-lai viewed Soviet troops on their common border as a constant threat. In addition, the Soviets supported India in the Pakistan-Indian conflict in 1971 and backed India in border disputes with China. Chinese leaders hoped to use the United States to balance the power of the Soviets in Asia.

Nixon went to China in February 1972. Although little of substance occurred, it was a symbolic act of vast importance. The two nations issued a joint statement in which they accepted the idea of peaceful coexistence and agreed to settle disputes through negotiation. The two nations agreed to cultural and scientific exchanges and opened the way

for possible future trading agreements. Within a year of Nixon's visit, each nation had established diplomatic offices in the other nation's capital. Exchanging ambassadors and establishing full diplomatic relations between the two superpowers would begin later, during Jimmy Carter's presidency.

Latin America and the Middle East

Nixon's approach to Latin America was to continue the long-standing U.S. tradition of supporting non-Communist governments. Many of Nixon's actions in Latin America were consistent with those of Presidents Eisenhower, Kennedy, and Johnson. Most recently, Lyndon Johnson had announced the Johnson Doctrine, which stated that the United States would intervene in Western Hemisphere countries to prevent Communists from taking power there, whether by elections or force.

In 1970, Chile elected Salvador Allende as president. Since Allende was a Marxist, Nixon saw his election as a possible threat to Latin American stability. He decided to intervene secretly to topple Allende's constitutionally elected government. Nixon suspended foreign aid to Chile and ordered the Central Intelligence Agency (CIA) to begin secret operations to destabilize the Chilean government. The CIA sent money to anti-Allende newspapers and encouraged Chilean army elements to stage a coup. In 1974, the Chilean army ousted the Allende government. In the process, nearly 27,000 Chileans lost their lives, including Allende. Despite the fact that Allende's successor, General Augusto Pinochet, was a dictator, Nixon believed his policy had achieved its objective of ending the Communist government.

Solving conflict in the Middle East proved to be beyond the capacity of U.S. policy. A series of wars between the Arabs and Israelis had resulted in stunning Israeli military victories. During the Six-Day War of June 1967, the Israelis had seized Jerusalem and the West Bank of the Jordan River from Jordan, the Golan Heights from Syria, and the Sinai peninsula from Egypt. Palestinian Arabs, originally residents of territory now held by Israel, formed the Palestinian Liberation Organization (PLO) and pledged to destroy Israel. The PLO increased tensions in the Middle East through their terrorist activities, which included hit-and-run attacks from bordering countries on Jewish settlements. Soviet support for several Arab nations and U.S. support for Israel further complicated the situation.

Then, in October 1973, Egyptian and Syrian armies attacked Israel. The attack caught the Israelis, celebrating the Yom Kippur holidays, completely by surprise. Israel soon rallied to halt the Arab offensive and inflicted heavy losses on its attackers. United States support of Israel was a major reason that Arab oil producers halted all oil shipments to this country. These events encouraged Nixon to seek a solution to Middle Eastern hostilities. By the end of October, Kissinger had arranged a cease-fire, and in December he began negotiations with Israel and several Arab states. In March 1974, OPEC lifted its oil embargo, although oil prices remained much higher than before. In 1975, Kissinger convinced Egypt and Israel to agree to a United Nations peacekeeping force on the Sinai peninsula. But the basic conflicts in the Middle East remained.

SECTION 4 REVIEW

1. Compare Nixon's general approach to foreign policy to Theodore Roosevelt's.
2. Define détente.
3. Identify SALT.
4. State reasons why Nixon attempted to seek better relations with the People's Republic of China.
5. Summarize briefly Nixon's guidelines for foreign policy in Latin America.

SECTION 5

The Watergate Scandal

In the early morning hours of June 17, 1972, security guard Frank Wills made his rounds at the Watergate office complex in Washington, D.C. Wills noticed some suspicious activity and called the police. They arrested five men who had broken into the headquarters of the Democratic National Committee. The five were not typical burglars—they wore business suits and carried sophisticated tools and electronic devices. One of the burglars, James McCord, a former employee of the Central Intelligence Agency, was a security adviser to the Republican Committee to Reelect the President (popularly known as CREEP). Furthermore, the burglars possessed an address book that contained the name of White House employee E. Howard Hunt, also a former CIA agent. When questioned about this apparent link to the White House, Nixon's press secretary, Ron Ziegler, dismissed its significance, calling the break-in "a third-rate burglary." Though little noticed at the time, this third-rate burglary would eventually force Richard Nixon to resign from the presidency.

How did Nixon's concern for reelection lead to the Watergate scandal?

What evidence of wrongdoing did Watergate investigators uncover?

What evidence in the Watergate scandal caused Nixon to resign?

As read by this delegate at the 1972 Democratic National Convention, Hubert Humphrey and Edmund Muskie dropped out of the race for the nomination, allowing George McGovern to win on the first ballot.

Reelection Concerns

Watergate might never have happened had it not been for Richard Nixon's overriding concern about reelection. Elected by a slim margin in 1968, Nixon worried about reelection from the start of his first administration. Public opinion polls gave him little encouragement. In December 1971, only 49 percent of Americans approved of the way Nixon was handling his job as president. A May 1972 poll showed voters preferred Democratic Senator Edmund Muskie from Maine over Nixon as president by 47 to 39 percent. It seemed to many, including Nixon, that he might be a one-term president.

Through the summer, however, Nixon's re-election campaign gained momentum. One reason was his stunning success in foreign policy matters, especially his visits to Beijing and Moscow. Another reason was that Nixon campaign aides used a variety of political dirty tricks to wreck the campaign of Senator Muskie. When Muskie's campaign was derailed, the Democrats nominated Senator George McGovern from South Dakota as their candidate.

McGovern's nomination practically assured Nixon a decisive victory in the November election.

McGovern's campaign was filled with problems from the start. McGovern chose Senator Thomas Eagleton from Missouri as his running mate. Then he discovered that Eagleton had undergone treatments for emotional illness. After pledging "1,000 percent support" for Eagleton, McGovern soon abandoned him in favor of Sargent Shriver, John Kennedy's brother-in-law and former director of the Peace Corps. More importantly, McGovern's main support came from the young and from anti-war activists. He had little appeal among labor, white ethnic groups, and other traditional Democratic Party supporters.

Despite these advantages, Nixon and his aides sought to ensure a massive reelection victory. As subsequent investigations would prove, the Watergate break-in was only one of many illegal activities and dirty tricks that Nixon and his aides used against the Democrats and other political opponents. They sent fake letters and made false announcements on Democratic Party stationery. They attempted to use the CIA and FBI to gather information on student radicals, prominent Democrats, and other alleged enemies. They demanded massive

▲ *The Senate Watergate Committee questioned two of Nixon's advisors, H.R. Haldeman (left) and John Ehrlichman. What did their nickname, "Berlin Wall," imply?*

"He says he's from the phone company..."

▲ *This cartoonist's view of the Watergate break-in focuses on what abuse?*

"campaign contributions" from various interest groups in exchange for favorable treatment.

All of these activities were hidden from public view. Although McGovern warned Americans that Nixon's administration was thoroughly corrupt, his message went unheeded. At first, most newspapers carried the Watergate break-in story in the back pages, and few readers paid much attention to it. An October poll showed that only half the public had even heard of the break-in. Nixon thus won reelection in a landslide. McGovern carried Massachusetts and the District of Columbia, and received only 17 electoral votes. Nixon won nearly 61 percent of the popular vote.

The Scandal Unfolds

Just after Nixon's reelection, startling revelations began to surface in the Watergate scandal. In late 1972, the five Watergate burglars, White House adviser E. Howard Hunt, and campaign advisor G. Gordon Liddy went on trial. The court found them guilty in January 1973. When Judge John Sirica sentenced the defendants to prison terms, he made public a letter written by James McCord, one of the five burglars. McCord wrote that the defendants had perjured themselves during their trial. He said that high Nixon administration officials, wanting to hide the truth about the break-in, had pressured the defendants to plead guilty in return for payoffs.

By April 1973, investigations revealed that John Mitchell (former attorney general and Nixon's campaign manager) and Maurice Stans had misused campaign funds and had covered up illegal activities. Meanwhile, L. Patrick Gray, the FBI director, resigned when investigators discovered he had burned documents related to Watergate. On April 30, two of Nixon's closest aides, H. R. Haldeman and John Ehrlichman, resigned because of mounting evidence of their involvement in the Watergate scandal. Nixon appeared on television and said it would be easy to blame those who had worked for him. "But," Nixon suggested, "that would be a cowardly thing to do. . . . The man at the top must bear the responsibility . . . [and] I accept it." At the same time, Nixon appointed Elliot Richardson as

The Watergate Hearings

In May 1973, the Senate Select Committee on Presidential Campaign Activities, chaired by Senator Sam Ervin from North Carolina, began public, televised hearings on Watergate. From the beginning, Nixon invoked executive privilege, arguing that requiring senior administration officials to testify before Congress was a violation of the separation of powers principle. Nixon's tactic failed because Congress could subpoena (legally compel) people to testify and because many of Nixon's aides wanted to testify in the hope of saving themselves.

▲ Former White House attorney John Dean electrified the American public with his testimony to the Senate Watergate Committee about President Nixon's involvement in the Watergate scandals.

The committee's televised hearings held the attention of millions of American viewers. As the nation watched, they saw high Nixon administration and campaign officials describe such activities as illegal wiretapping, perjury, blackmail, and dirty campaign tricks. During the proceedings, Chairman Sam Ervin's "good old country lawyer" manner and wit charmed many viewers. Senator Howard Baker from Tennessee, the senior Republican on the committee, earned viewers' respect by constantly asking witnesses, "What did the president know, and when did he know it?" As the hearings progressed, both the senators and the witnesses became national celebrities.

In June, former White House Counsel John Dean testified before the Ervin committee. Dean's testimony stunned the nation. He revealed that Mitchell, Haldeman, Ehrlichman, and even Nixon had tried to hide the truth and had suppressed evidence concerning the burglary. He also provided evidence that Nixon and his aides had illegally used the Internal Revenue Service and intelligence agencies. Dean's testimony implicated Nixon in abuses of executive powers and the crime of obstructing justice. Still, there was no other evidence yet to support Dean's testimony. For now, it was Dean's word against that of the president.

Then, in July, Nixon aide Alexander Butterfield testified that Nixon had installed an elaborate system of tape recorders in the Oval Office. Voice activated, the tapes recorded every conversation that took place there. Obviously, the tapes could prove who was lying and who was telling the truth about the Watergate scandals. Moreover, the tapes would provide the best evidence in possible criminal trials of Nixon's aides. The battle over the tapes and the evidence they contained would continue for a year.

1. How effective was Nixon's claim of executive privilege?
2. Explain why Alexander Butterfield's testimony was so damaging to Nixon.

► *What was responsible for President Nixon's plummeting approval rating in 1973?*

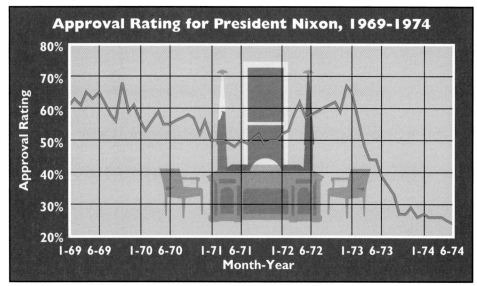

Approval Rating for President Nixon, 1969–1974

©The Public Perspective, a publication of the Roper Center for Public Opinion Research, University of CT, Storrs. Reprinted by permission.

attorney general. Richardson, in turn, appointed Archibald Cox as special prosecutor in charge of the Watergate investigation.

On July 23, Cox sought a court order directing Nixon to turn over tapes containing conversations between Nixon and his aides. Judge Sirica ordered the release of the tapes, but Nixon appealed the decision on grounds of executive privilege and separation of powers. He argued that if advisers could not discuss matters confidentially, a president would not get frank advice. In addition, some matters involved national security and therefore needed to be kept secret. In October, a federal appeals court ruled against Nixon. Hoping to prevent release of the tapes, Nixon ordered Richardson to fire Cox. Richardson and his deputy William Ruckelshaus resigned rather than execute Nixon's order. Another Justice Department official, Robert Bork, fired Cox. The "Saturday Night Massacre," as this episode was called, suggested that Nixon was deeply involved in the scandal and that he would not allow a truly impartial investigation to proceed.

Calls for Impeachment

Public reaction to these events ran strongly against Nixon, and many people began calling for Nixon's impeachment. If a president is accused of "high crimes" by the House of Representatives, the Senate is required to conduct a trial to discover guilt or innocence of the accused. Hoping to avoid this, Nixon appointed Leon Jaworski as special prosecutor and released some of the tapes. These tapes showed that Nixon seemed obsessed by trivial matters and spoke in remarkably offensive terms about many people, including racial and ethnic groups and even supposed friends. Moreover, some tapes were mysteriously missing, and one important tape had an 18½-minute gap—the result, experts said, of deliberate tampering.

Meanwhile, another scandal beset the White House. While governor of Maryland and then as vice president, Spiro Agnew had received illegal payments from construction contractors and had lied on his income-tax returns. Agnew resigned, pled "no contest" to one count of income-tax evasion, and paid a fine of $10,000. Agnew received three years unsupervised probation. The Twenty-fifth Amendment, which had been ratified in 1967, determined the presidential succession. Under this amendment, Nixon appointed **Gerald Ford** as vice president. Nixon hoped Ford's reputation for integrity would bolster his own public standing.

In March 1974, a federal grand jury returned indictments against Mitchell, Haldeman, Ehrlichman, and several other Nixon aides. They

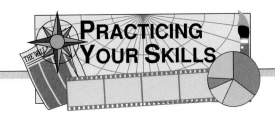
Using Text to Interpret Graphs

In the Practicing Your Skills for Chapter 27, you were given practice in evaluating and analyzing opinion polls. The graph entitled "Approval Rating for President Nixon, 1969–1974" on page 979 is also a type of opinion poll. The results are from a Gallup survey that asked the question "Do you approve or disapprove of the way President Nixon is handling his job as president?"

The graph tracks the changes in the president's approval rating over a period of years. From the graph, you learn *what* and *when*. The reason *why* the rating changed is found in the text. For a complete understanding of the information in the graph, it is necessary to relate the time on the graph to the dates given in the narrative in the text. When this has been done, you should be able to supply plausible explanations for the changes in Nixon's approval rating.

Read the rest of Section 5, and then answer the questions below. You may need to look back in the chapter to check your answers.

1. What probably accounted for Nixon's 60-plus percentage rating in the first half of 1969?
2. What process or policy might have been responsible for the surge of favorable opinion (68%) around October 1969?

©The Public Perspective, a publication of the Roper Center for Public Opinion Research, University of CT, Storrs. Reprinted by permission.

3. What tragic events were probably responsible for Nixon's declining ratings in the polls toward the end of 1970?
4. Two well-publicized events in mid–1971 tarnished the military image and lowered the credibility of the administration. What were they, and how did they affect Nixon's approval rating in 1971?
5. During 1972, Nixon's approval ratings climbed rapidly. What was the rating in November 1972? What event was probably responsible for this rating?
6. According to the graph, was Nixon justified in believing that his reelection campaign was in trouble?

were officially charged with crimes and would go to trial. The grand jury named Nixon an unindicted co-conspirator. This meant that they believed Nixon was involved, but the grand jury was not certain it had the power to indict a sitting president. In April, Jaworski requested 64 more tapes. Nixon responded by providing transcripts of the requested tapes. Not satisfied, Jaworski asked Sirica to order Nixon to turn over the actual tapes. Sirica complied, but Nixon appealed to the Supreme Court.

Again, Nixon claimed executive privilege and argued that the tapes contained sensitive national security material. In *United States v. Nixon*, a unanimous Supreme Court ordered Nixon to release the tapes because they believed evidence in a criminal case was more important than executive privilege.

The tapes confirmed Nixon's guilt. A conversation between Haldeman and Nixon on June 23, 1972, just days after the Watergate burglary, revealed Nixon had participated in the Watergate cover-up from the beginning. He had tried to limit the FBI's investigation of Watergate. The House Judiciary Committee soon approved three articles of impeachment: obstruction of justice; abuse of presidential powers (such as the illegal wiretaps and the use of the FBI, the CIA, and the Internal Revenue Service against his enemies); and contempt of Congress for not responding to congressional subpoenas.

It was now certain that the House would vote to impeach Nixon. On August 8, 1974, Nixon announced his resignation. He was the first president ever to resign. Under the terms of the Twenty-fifth Amendment, Gerald Ford became the first unelected person to gain the office of president.

SECTION 5 REVIEW

1. **Identify** the concern that led Nixon to authorize actions such as the Watergate burglary.
2. **Describe** tactics used by Nixon and his aides to ensure reelection.
3. **Define** the term *executive privilege*.
4. **Explain** the events that led to Gerald Ford becoming the first unelected person to become president.
5. **Name** the pieces of evidence in the Watergate scandals that eventually caused Nixon to resign.

Summary

In 1968, Richard Nixon narrowly won the presidential election. His strategy during his first term emphasized law-and-order issues, the appointment of conservative justices to the Supreme Court, the delay of racial desegregation, and the removal of at least some Great Society programs. Nixon also initiated such innovations as revenue sharing in an attempt to decrease the role of the federal government in the economy.

President Nixon was much more interested in the conduct of foreign affairs than in domestic affairs. Chief among his foreign policy goals was détente with the Soviet Union and the People's Republic of China. Nixon believed that improved relations between the United States and the Communist superpowers would not only result in such successes as the Strategic Arms Limitations Agreement (SALT) and better trading relations, but it would also reduce Soviet meddling in less developed countries. Other foreign problems such as ending the Vietnam War proved more difficult.

As economic and energy problems rocked the Nixon administration, the Watergate scandal began to unfold. Watergate investigators eventually discovered the existence of tapes of White House conversations. When the Supreme Court ordered the release of the tapes, they proved that Nixon had known about the Watergate break-in and had attempted to obstruct the investigation. When Nixon resigned his office, most Americans breathed a sigh of relief. They thought this grave constitutional crisis was over at last. What they could not foresee was how the Watergate crisis would continue to affect Americans' faith in their government and political leaders far into the future.

Vocabulary Skills

détente	stagflation
impounding	Vietnamization
revenue sharing	

Write the vocabulary term followed by the phrase found below that defines or describes it.

1. turning over responsibility for conducting the war to South Vietnam
2. refusing to release funds that have been allocated by Congress for a program or project
3. returning tax money to state and local governments through grants from the federal government
4. relaxation of relations between the United States and Soviet Union
5. when inflation and rising unemployment occur at the same time

Review Questions

1. How did the domestic turmoil in the 1960s influence the 1968 campaign for the presidency?
2. What were reasons for the split in the Democratic Party and what factions were created in the election of 1968?
3. List Nixon's terms for ending the Vietnam War.
4. Outline Nixon's plan of New Federalism.
5. Explain why energy became such an important issue during Nixon's administration.
6. What did Nixon believe were the two ways the United States should promote its vital interests?
7. Explain the major objectives of Nixon's policy of détente with the Soviet Union.
8. Describe the change in United States policy toward the People's Republic of China during the Nixon presidency.
9. How did Nixon's concern for reelection in 1972 lead to the Watergate scandal?
10. Describe the major constitutional issue involved in the Watergate scandal.

Critical Historical Thinking

Writing Answer each of the following by writing one or more complete paragraphs:

1. Do you think the president should have the right to call for a freeze on prices and wages, as President Nixon did? Give reasons to support your answer.
2. Explain why many Americans found it alarming when the covert and illegal actions of the CIA and the FBI came to light concerning the 1972 election campaign.
3. Many people think that Nixon's actions threatened the constitutional principle of separation of powers. Explain why you believe this is, or is not, true.
4. Read the selection entitled "Nixon's Ideological War" in the Unit 10 Archives. According to the author, what were the underlying causes of the Watergate scandal?

Making Connections with Journalism

You have learned earlier how colonial writers like Thomas Paine and Samuel Adams used newspapers and pamphlets to influence the course of politics. By 1800, the *penny press*, written for the ordinary person, was fully developed. These articles were often highly sensational, attracting readers with stories of crime, sex, and violence. *Yellow journalism* flourished during the time of the Spanish-American War when exaggeration and biased reporting were commonplace. Finally, in 1903, in an effort to upgrade journalism to a profession, Joseph Pulitzer gave Columbia University $2 million to start a program for teaching responsible journalism. *Investigative journalism*, with the emphasis on uncovering abuses of power and misplaced trust, became especially popular during the Watergate affair. More recently, *New Journalism* describes the style of "nonfiction reporting" employed by authors who com-bine reporting with literature. Truman Capote's *In Cold Blood*, a semi-fictionalized account of a serial killer known as the Boston Strangler, is an example of New Journalism. *Television journalism* focuses on round-the-clock reporting and late-breaking news. Many people believe that the emphasis on sensationalism and the race for TV ratings distort news coverage.

Writing Write at least one page that considers one of the following questions: What should be the primary goal of a professional journalist? Should journalists be investigators as well as reporters? Must a free press be responsible for the consequences of the news it reports? When, if ever, is it ethical to present fictional information as factual reporting? Does the public always have a "right to know"?

Additional Skills Practice

Examine the graph on page 964 that shows the number of U.S. troops in South Vietnam. For each number below, write "yes" if the information asked for can be determined from the graph, and "no" if the information asked for cannot be determined from the graph.

1. the number of years the war lasted
2. the greatest number of troops in South Vietnam at any one time
3. the number of medical vs. combat troops
4. the year the peace talks began
5. the year the peace treaty was signed
6. the average length of a tour of duty
7. the overall pattern of troop buildup
8. the period of heaviest troop commitment
9. the total number of troops in South Vietnam between 1965 and 1972

The Ford and Carter Years

Many Americans found that the Vietnam War and the Watergate scandal had destroyed their confidence in their political leaders. One 1975 public opinion poll revealed that 69 percent of Americans believed "this country's leaders have consistently lied to the people." This lack of confidence spread to other areas of American life

as well. Less than half the people interviewed in a 1976 poll said they trusted those in the medical profession, and even fewer expressed confidence in large corporations and attorneys. For Presidents Gerald Ford and Jimmy Carter, these attitudes made political leadership extremely difficult.

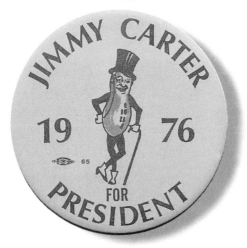

▲ *What does the car in the top campaign button represent? Why was Jimmy Carter associated with peanuts?*

The Ford Transition

To many Americans in 1974, Gerald Ford seemed to be just the person the nation needed as president after Watergate. Born in 1913, Ford grew up in a conservative Republican family in Grand Rapids, Michigan. He played football at the University of Michigan and earned a law degree from Yale University. He served as a naval officer during World War II and came home to practice law. In 1948, Ford won a seat in the U.S. House of Representatives. During his 25 years of service in the House, Ford earned a reputation as a staunch Republican. Democrats and Republicans alike gave him high marks for honesty and integrity. When Ford became president, many Americans breathed a sigh of relief.

What effects did Nixon's pardon have on Ford's presidency?

What economic and energy issues did Ford face?

In what ways did economic and demographic changes affect U.S. cities?

The Nixon Pardon and Watergate Backlash

As Ford took office, he said, referring to Watergate, "Our long national nightmare is over." Ford continued, "Our Constitution works. Our great Republic is a government of laws and not of men." Despite Ford's hopes, however, the effects of Watergate were far from over. Since Nixon was no longer president, he could now be prosecuted for his alleged Watergate crimes. Special Watergate Prosecutor Leon Jaworski informed Ford that his office was preparing to prosecute Nixon. Nixon's trial, however, was a year away. And, with appeals, it was expected that the whole affair could take several years. Therefore, on September 8, 1974, Ford granted Nixon "a full, free, and absolute pardon" to avoid the "ugly passions" and polarized opinions that an extended trial might arouse.

While some Americans agreed that the pardon was necessary to put Watergate to rest, most reacted negatively. Ford's standing in public opinion polls fell from 72 to 49 percent virtually overnight. The *Chicago Tribune* reported "a sour smell" in the White House, and many suspected that Ford had agreed to pardon Nixon before Nixon resigned. Ford personally testified before the House Judiciary Committee, denying any agreement between himself and Nixon, saying, "There was no deal, period!" Even so, the majority of Americans believed that Nixon should be prosecuted for his crimes.

Ford's nomination of Nelson Rockefeller as vice president did not help Ford's public standing. The Twenty-fifth Amendment to the Constitution empowered the president to appoint a vice president when there was a vacancy in that office. Rockefeller was one of the world's richest men. His family fortune was worth around a billion dollars. During Senate confirmation hearings, investigators discovered he had underpaid his income taxes and had given large gifts of money to friends and associates, including Secretary of State Henry Kissinger. This raised the possibility of a conflict of interest. In spite of this, the Senate confirmed Rockefeller's appointment in December. But the public hearings had done little to improve his, or Ford's, public image.

Meanwhile, Congress reacted to Watergate by enacting a series of laws aimed at curbing "the imperial presidency" and reforming federal election laws. In late 1973, Congress had passed the War Powers Act (over Nixon's veto) to limit the president's authority to send troops overseas. In 1974, it moved to prevent a president from impounding funds appropriated by Congress, as Nixon had done. In 1974 and again in 1976, Congress passed campaign reform acts designed to prevent corruption and to limit the influence of wealthy people over public officials. Congress also authorized federal funding of presidential campaigns within certain spending limits.

Despite these reforms, voter disgust with the state of American politics was evident in the midterm elections of 1974. Only 38 percent of eligible voters went to the polls, the lowest turnout in a midterm election since World War II. Although

After Ford issued the pardon, Nixon said, "No words can describe the depths of my regret and pain at the anguish my mistakes over Watergate have caused the nation and the presidency, a nation I so deeply love and an institution I so greatly respect."

◀ *What did the letters "WIN" on Ford's lapel button represent?*

Ford campaigned strenuously for Republican candidates, the Democrats gained 52 seats in the House, giving them a 291-to-144 majority. Democrats also gained four seats in the Senate and held a 60-to-37 majority. (Three senators had other party affiliations.) Despite these majorities, the Democrats were hampered because they could not agree among themselves.

Economic and Energy Problems

Ford inherited a variety of difficult problems ignored by Nixon in his last troubled months in office. The economy was in shambles. The country was facing the worst inflation ever in peacetime and the highest interest rates in over a century. As a re-

sult, the economy was stagnant and unemployment was growing. In January 1975, Ford admitted "the state of the Union is not good."

Ford called inflation "public enemy number one" and proposed to combat it with typical Republican remedies—tight monetary policies. Ford rejected federal action to freeze wages and prices, saying "wage and price controls are out, period!" He pleaded for voluntary restraint and asked each person to "make a list of some ten ways you can save energy and you can fight inflation." He soon donned lapel buttons printed with WIN: "Whip Inflation Now!" Many Americans ridiculed the "WIN" campaign because it seemed to be Ford's substitute for establishing a clear policy and taking decisive action.

President Ford and the Democrat-controlled Congress had difficulty working together. Seeing inflation as the major economic problem, Ford wanted to cut federal spending drastically, especially on social welfare programs. Congressional Democrats, however, were more concerned about economic recession, and they introduced legislation aimed at curing it. To keep government spending

American Resources and the World Economy

The United States imports half of its oil and gas and many of the minerals and metal ores that it needs to maintain its economy in the 1990s. Today, we are more dependent on foreign trade than at any other time in our history, in spite of having an extensive natural resource base.

In the last few years, the United States has become the world's largest consumer and importer of energy resources. During this period, U.S. energy production has remained steady, but energy consumption has increased dramatically. The high cost of importing oil is a major factor in our trade deficit.

It is extremely expensive to bring oil and natural gas to the surface. That is why America is increasing its imports of less expensive foreign oil from places like Canada, Mexico, Venezuela, and the Persian Gulf.

Our greatest undeveloped oil deposits lie 200 miles north of the Arctic Circle in Alaska. Here, on the north slope of the Brooks Range, an estimated 10 billion barrels of oil lie 10,000 feet below the surface. In a remarkable feat of engineering, this oil field has been drilled and a 799-mile pipeline has been built across Alaska to the port of Valdez on Prince William Sound. It began transporting oil

from the north slope in 1975. If demand for energy increases, this relatively expensive north slope oil may be further developed in spite of the ecological damage inflicted on the wildlife of Prince William Sound by a massive oil spill in 1989.

Development of other potential energy resources faces stiff opposition from environmentalists who fear that local environments might sustain severe ecological damage.

The United States is well endowed in minerals and metals, but our complicated industries require large quantities of many different types of raw materials. We now import minerals and metals from neighboring countries like Canada and Mexico, and from faraway places like Zaire and Australia.

The United States is an important producer of metals like iron, copper, lead, and zinc, which are used in heavy industry. Along with Minnesota, Arizona and Utah are our most important mining areas. These three states produce half of the country's minerals and metals. Recently, however, rising demand for these metals has outstripped domestic production so that we are now dependent on foreign imports. The United States now imports more than half of its

▲ *This photo shows caribou feeding underneath the pipeline that transports oil from Alaska's north slope.*

supply of two dozen important minerals and metals.

Because the United States must now import oil and gas, as well as many minerals and metals, wise management, conservation, and recycling of our natural resources are of growing importance.

———※———

1. What is the major reason why the United States must import oil and natural gas? How much is imported?
2. How can Americans reduce their dependence on foreign imports of energy, minerals, and metals?

Congressional Bills Vetoed, 1961-1990

Years	President	Total Vetoes	Vetoes Overridden by Congress
1961-1963	Kennedy	21	0
1963-1969	Johnson	30	0
1969-1974	Nixon	43	7
1974-1977	Ford	66	12
1977-1981	Carter	31	2
1981-1989	Reagan	67	9
1989-1990	Bush	13	0

Source: *Congressional Quarterly Weekly Report*, 1990.

▶ *What factor was primarily responsible for the large number of vetoes during Ford's term and the relatively large number of congressional overrides?*

down, Ford vetoed 66 bills, although Congress overrode his vetoes 12 times. By late spring 1975, Ford's spending cuts and high interest rates had halved the rate of inflation, but unemployment had reached 9 percent and the economy remained sluggish. Because federal tax revenues were short of expected income, the federal government faced a staggering $60 billion budget deficit.

President Ford and the Democratic Congress could not agree on an energy policy either. Under-lying America's economic troubles was the continuing rise in the costs of energy. Ford warned that "Americans are no longer in full control of their own national destiny when that destiny depends on uncertain foreign fuel." He wanted to develop nuclear power and to rely more heavily on coal. Many in Congress disagreed with Ford's proposals, fearing worse air pollution from burning coal and the problem of waste disposal if nuclear power was used. Passing a comprehensive energy program proved impossible.

▼ *This Draper Hill cartoon suggests Americans faced hard choices because of the OPEC oil embargo.*

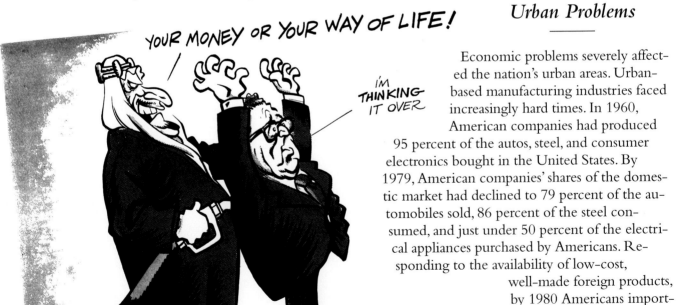

YOUR MONEY OR YOUR WAY OF LIFE!

I'M THINKING IT OVER

ARAB OIL

Urban Problems

Economic problems severely affected the nation's urban areas. Urban-based manufacturing industries faced increasingly hard times. In 1960, American companies had produced 95 percent of the autos, steel, and consumer electronics bought in the United States. By 1979, American companies' shares of the domestic market had declined to 79 percent of the automobiles sold, 86 percent of the steel consumed, and just under 50 percent of the electrical appliances purchased by Americans. Responding to the availability of low-cost, well-made foreign products, by 1980 Americans imported 22 percent of all the goods they consumed (up from 9.3 percent ten years earlier).

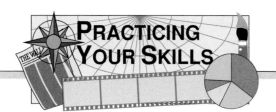

More Practice Analyzing Editorial Cartoons

In the mid-1970s, people in industrialized nations were feeling the effects of the oil embargo and OPEC's price increases. Many Americans were asking themselves how a nation as rich and powerful as the United States could find itself in such a predicament. There was an increasing perception that our social and economic life was dependent on the goodwill of a few foreign nations.

Review the guidelines for analyzing editorial cartoons on page 697 and answer the following questions about the cartoon on page 988:

1. (a) What is the title of the cartoon? (b) Describe the action taking place in this cartoon.
2. Make a list of the symbols and characterizations and what they represent. (Consider facial expressions as well.) Can you identify any of the figures?
3. What do you think is the cartoonist's opinion of the Middle Eastern positions? What does the cartoonist feel is the American attitude toward the oil crisis?
4. Might Americans of Middle Eastern background find this cartoon offensive? If so, in what way?

Changing manufacturing and trading patterns led to increasing distress in the industrial cities of the Northeast. Large numbers of factory workers lost their jobs. Job losses were due to the relocation of factories to the sun belt, the suburbs, overseas, or simply to plant closings. As one observer noted, "the urban landscape across the northern tier of states from Massachusetts to Minnesota is marred by vacant factories, warehouses and great open spaces where such buildings once stood, visual testimony to a great migration whose impact on the nation is becoming increasingly clear." Industrial cities like Buffalo, Cleveland, and St. Louis lost nearly one-quarter of their populations in the 1970s.

The overall loss of jobs was the primary reason for the migration away from urban centers, and this, in turn, created more problems. As people left the central cities for the suburbs, cities' tax bases were eroded. Unemployment rates among nonwhite city residents remained nearly twice the national average. In October 1975, New York City asked the federal government to provide $2.3 billion in loan guarantees to avoid bankruptcy.

As white people fled the city, many neighborhoods became almost totally nonwhite. This strained the nation's commitment to racial desegregation. It was one thing to enact laws to end legal segregation. It was quite another to end actual segregation based on informal residential patterns. Ending segregation, especially in neighborhood schools, severely tested public policymakers.

In the *Swann v. Charlotte-Mecklenburg County Board of Education* (1971) decision, the Supreme Court upheld busing of schoolchildren as a remedy

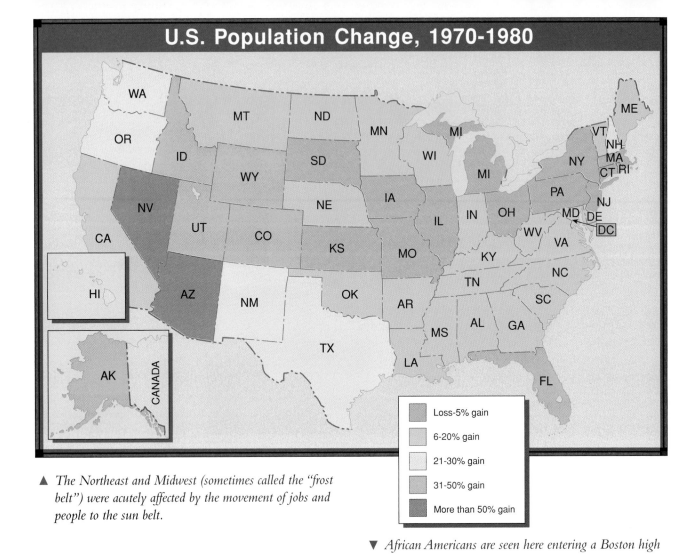

U.S. Population Change, 1970-1980

Legend:
- Loss-5% gain
- 6-20% gain
- 21-30% gain
- 31-50% gain
- More than 50% gain

▲ *The Northeast and Midwest (sometimes called the "frost belt") were acutely affected by the movement of jobs and people to the sun belt.*

▼ *African Americans are seen here entering a Boston high school. What does the police presence indicate about this court-ordered move?*

to racial segregation in the schools caused by segregated neighborhoods. Over the next several years, federal courts ordered busing to achieve school integration in many localities throughout the nation. Violent confrontations occurred in Boston, Massachusetts, when a court-ordered busing plan went into operation. In Louisville, Kentucky, the National Guard had to restore order after antibusing mobs rioted and destroyed city property. In Denver and Grand Rapids, antibusing fanatics bombed empty school buses parked on district lots. In the face of such opposition, federal judges hesitated to order more busing plans to achieve desegregation. The Supreme Court, too, backed away from its earlier commitment to busing. In 1976, it ruled that school officials had no obligation to maintain racial balance in the schools if segregation was caused by random residential patterns.

In all, Ford faced an extremely difficult situation during his brief tenure as president. The Watergate scandal and the Vietnam War had undermined many Americans' faith in their government and political leaders. Matters were made worse because the nation continued to face a variety of problems that required strong leadership.

SECTION 1 REVIEW

1. Evaluate the effect on public opinion of Ford's pardon of Nixon.
2. Explain why Ford's nomination of Nelson Rockefeller as vice president hurt the president's public standing.
3. Describe actions taken by Congress in 1973 and 1974 aimed at curbing presidential power.
4. Describe economic and energy issues faced by Ford.
5. Explain the problems that were created when white residents fled the cities for the suburbs.

SECTION 2

Ford's Foreign Policies

Although Ford had served in the House of Representatives for 25 years, he had little firsthand knowledge of foreign affairs. At one press conference, for example, Ford made a serious error in discussing the Middle Eastern policy of the United States. One journalist passed the incident off, saying, "It was just Gerry talking about things he doesn't understand." Similar public mistakes concerning U.S. foreign policy diminished Ford's credibility as an effective leader. Over time, Ford's foreign policies drew withering criticisms, especially from the conservative wing of his own party.

Why did U.S.-Soviet détente become more difficult to sustain during Ford's presidency?

How did Ford approach issues in the less developed countries?

How did Congress try to reassert its authority in foreign affairs?

Ford Continues Détente

Ford tried to continue Nixon's policy of détente with the Soviet Union. In November 1974, Ford traveled to Vladivostok, a city on the Pacific coast of the Soviet Union, for meetings with Premier Leonid Brezhnev. There they discussed further reductions in strategic arms. In 1975, Ford went to Finland to sign the Helsinki Accords with the Soviet Union and 33 other nations. These agreements ratified the post–World War II national boundaries in Europe. Since the accords implicitly recognized Soviet "special foreign policy interests" in Eastern Europe, many Eastern Europeans living in the United States severely criticized the agreement.

The détente policy was becoming increasingly difficult to sustain for other reasons as well. Conservatives in both parties had been critical of détente because they believed that the Soviets could not be trusted. Claiming that the Soviets had violated the first SALT agreements, these conservative voices warned that the Soviets should not be trusted in further arms reduction talks. The Soviets had already upset détente by aiding Portugal's Communist Party and supplying arms to Angola, a former Portugese colony in southwestern Africa. They had also involved Cuban soldiers in the civil war in Angola.

▼ *This U.S.-Soviet meeting in Finland in 1975 led to the Helsinki Accords. Why was this agreement criticized?*

There was constant concern about Soviet influence in the oil-rich Middle East. When the Soviets installed a pro-Soviet government in Afganistan in 1976, fears increased.

Ford and Southeast Asia

Despite the complete withdrawal of U.S. troops following the 1973 Paris Peace Accords, Vietnam remained a troubling issue during Ford's presidency. The fighting had continued there after U.S. troops withdrew. In 1975, the South Vietnamese army disintegrated in the face of a massive North Vietnamese offensive. President Nguyen Van Thieu of South Vietnam asked Ford to provide the "full-force" aid that Nixon had promised to encourage him to accept the Paris Peace Accords.

Ford asked Congress to give emergency aid to South Vietnam. The United States should, he said, "put an end to self-inflicted wounds [and reassert] our strength, our authority, and our leadership." Congress refused to send U.S. combat troops back to Vietnam, and South Vietnam fell to the North Vietnamese in April 1975. Television captured the chaotic scenes of helicopters carrying away the last Americans. A flood of South Vietnamese fled their country, afraid of what the North Vietnamese might do to them. Many became homeless refugees scattered throughout Southeast Asia.

Meanwhile, Vietnam remained a vexing problem for Americans at home. In September 1974, President Ford offered **clemency** (an official pardon) to tens of thousands of draft evaders. To receive clemency, evaders had to swear allegiance to the United States and perform two years of public service. Deserters from the military would receive pardons if they served two years in the military service from which they had fled. Veterans' organizations condemned Ford's plan as being too lenient. Many draft evaders refused Ford's offer of clemency because acceptance would appear to be an admission that they had done something wrong. Only 6 percent of the 350,000 persons eligible for Ford's program ever applied for clemency.

The full costs of the Vietnam War will probably never be known. Millions of Vietnamese died. The war devastated South Vietnam, caused permanent ecological damage, and left millions homeless. More than 55,000 U.S. soldiers lost their lives in the fighting. Over four times that number suffered battle wounds, and thousands more came home with deep psychological problems as a result of combat experiences. Spending billions of dollars on the war caused the worst inflation in U.S. history.

▶

In the last terrifying moments of U.S. presence in South Vietnam, Americans and their South Vietnamese allies were desperate to leave the country before it fell to North Vietnam.

Dealing with Vietnam

By the mid-1970s, opinion polls showed that the majority of Americans had come to think of the Vietnam War as a senseless tragedy that the United States should have avoided. Reverend Theodore Hesburgh, president of Notre Dame University, suggested in 1977 that "the American people tend to put unpleasant and unsuccessful events far behind them as quickly as possible. Now one rarely speaks about the war or hears about it." Former U.S. Marine lieutenant Robert Miller noted, "Going to war is a landmark experience in the life of an individual, but in the case of Vietnam you learned very quickly to repress it, keep it secret, shut up about it, because people either considered you a sucker or some kind of psychopath who killed women and children." According to much-decorated combat veteran Dave Christian, this feeling that it was necessary to remain silent, to deny involvement, "twisted a lot of guys" who were Vietnam veterans.

By 1980, however, books and movies had begun to deal with the meaning of the Vietnam experience. Such films as *The Boys in Company C, Coming Home, Go Tell the Spartans, The Deer Hunter,* and *Apocalypse Now* dealt with the experience of war, the difficulties that veterans faced on returning home, or both. Memoirs such as Philip Caputo's *A Rumor of War*

▲ Born on the Fourth of July, *starring actor Tom Cruise, was a major motion picture about Vietnam.*

and Ron Kovic's *Born on the Fourth of July* and such fiction as Tim O'Brien's *Going After Cacciato* and *If I Die in the Combat Zone* developed similar themes. Journalists such as Michael Herr *(Dispatches),* Gloria Emerson *(Winners and Losers),* and C. D. B. Bryan *(Friendly Fire)* gave additional insights into the Vietnam experience, often through the voices of participants.

Film, literature, and other art forms have perhaps helped to heal the wounds of Vietnam. Filmmakers and writers in the 1980s and 1990s have continued to tell important stories about Americans'

experiences during the Vietnam era. Feature films such as *Full Metal Jacket, Platoon,* and *Casualties of War* dealt not only with the horrors and absurdities of war, but with heroism as well. Films like *Jackknife* showed some of the delayed emotional effects that combat could have on returning veterans. Documentaries such as *Hearts and Minds* and *Letters Home* (based on the book of the same title) presented more comprehensive views of the war. All were aimed, in one way or another, at what veteran Stephen Smith suggested: "The only dignity left is in telling the truth and hoping other generations will learn from it."

One of the chief architects of the Vietnam War was former Secretary of Defense Robert McNamara. In this same spirit of soul-searching, McNamara wrote in 1995 that it is apparent the threat to the U.S. posed by communism was greatly overestimated by American presidents and policymakers.

―――――◆―――――

1. According to Marine Robert Miller, why did veterans not speak of their Vietnam experiences?
2. How do you think movies about World War II were generally different from the Vietnam era films mentioned in the feature?

The Vietnam War caused a huge change in public attitudes about foreign affairs and U.S. military involvement overseas. In the two decades after World War II, Americans had consistently ranked foreign policy near the top of national priorities. By the mid-1970s, however, the majority of Americans thought that foreign policy issues were much less important. Polls taken in 1975 showed that less than a third of the public thought it important to make and keep commitments to other nations. As *Washington Post* columnist David Broder observed in early 1975, "Vietnam has left a rancid aftertaste that clings to almost every mention of direct [overseas] military intervention."

Given this atmosphere, the outpouring of public support for Ford's 1975 intervention in Cambodia was surprising. In May 1975, Cambodian patrol boats seized an American cargo ship, the *Mayaguez*. Ford feared a repetition of the 1968 *Pueblo* incident, when North Korea captured an American spy vessel and held its crew captive for over a year. To show he was decisive and tough with Communists, Ford ordered a military raid into Cambodia to free the crew of the *Mayaguez*. When Ford ordered the raid, he was unaware that Cambodia had released the ship's 38-man crew before U.S. forces attacked. In the ensuing raid, 40 U.S. soldiers died. Even so, public opinion strongly supported Ford's action.

Congress and Foreign Affairs

Throughout most of the twentieth century, presidents had controlled foreign policy with relatively little interference from Congress. Because of Watergate and Vietnam, however, Congress began to reassert its authority in foreign affairs. The War Powers Act of 1973 was one general way in which it did this. Congress also passed a series of initiatives in 1975 and 1976 that affected American foreign policy in specific areas of the world. As already described, it denied Ford's request for emergency military aid to South Vietnam. Congress threatened to prevent a new U.S.-Soviet trade agreement unless the Soviets relaxed restrictions on Jewish emigration from the USSR. It blocked military aid and CIA involvement in the civil war in Angola.

In general, Congress was trying to assert more control over the nation's intelligence establishment, especially the CIA and FBI. In 1975, the Senate formed the Select Committee on Intelligence Activities, chaired by Idaho Democrat Frank Church. The Church committee discovered that the CIA had been responsible for many shocking espionage activities in the United States, including wiretapping, burglary, and intercepting mail. These activities violated both Americans' civil rights and the CIA's legal authority. By law, the agency was limited to activities overseas. Investigators also discovered that government agents had conducted mind-altering drug experiments with unsuspecting subjects. Perhaps most shocking was the discovery of CIA secret operations to overthrow "unfriendly" foreign governments and to assassinate foreign leaders, including Patrice Lumumba (the Congo), Fidel Castro (Cuba), and Ngo Dinh Diem (South Vietnam), among others.

Meanwhile, investigators discovered that for 30 years the FBI had gathered information and kept files on many Americans without sufficient legal cause. Those the FBI investigated included journalists, critics of national policy, political opponents of presidents, and various radical groups. During the Vietnam War, the FBI had allowed administration officials to leak information to the media to discredit critics of the war. As a partial remedy, Congress passed the Freedom of Information Act (1976), which allowed Americans to see what information government agencies had collected about them. And Congress established much tighter control over the CIA's and FBI's intelligence-gathering operations.

SECTION 2 REVIEW

1. **Explain** problems faced by Ford in attempting to sustain détente.
2. **Describe** the results of Ford's attempt to pardon Vietnam War draft evaders.
3. **Summarize** the change in public attitudes about foreign affairs due to the Vietnam War.
4. **Identify** the *Mayaguez*.
5. **Name** two organizations that Congress reasserted its control over in the 1970s.

The Political Landscape in 1976

In 1973, the governor of Georgia appeared on the popular television quiz show "What's My Line?" in which celebrity panelists tried to guess contestants' occupations. He was so little known that none of the panelists that night could guess who **Jimmy Carter** was or what he did. Carter took advantage of this anonymity in his quest for the presidency. He ran for president as someone from outside Washington politics, and therefore untainted by them. Popular bumper stickers in the mid-seventies, such as "Don't Vote, It Only Encourages Them" and "The Lesser of Two Evils Is Still Evil," expressed many Americans' sense of alienation from politics and their distrust of politicians. Carter's campaign as a political outsider found support among these people.

How did Watergate affect the political climate in 1976?

Why did Carter defeat Ford in the election of 1976?

How did Carter's actions immediately after taking office affect his presidency?

▲ *During his campaign, Jimmy Carter projected a "common man" image. Why was he later criticized for this image?*

A New Political Landscape

With the Republicans saddled with the Watergate scandal, the Democrats looked forward to the elections of 1976. The prospect of victory in 1976 brought out many contenders for the Democratic nomination for president. The Democrats had recently reformed the party's presidential nominating process. In states that held primary elections, each candidate would collect delegates to the nominating convention based on his or her proportion of the primary election vote. The Democrats held primary elections in 31 states in 1976—more than ever before. This meant that nearly three-fourths of Democratic delegates would be elected by popular vote rather than through party caucuses. These reforms helped Carter, who was not well known outside his home state of Georgia.

During the primary campaign, Carter spoke about the widespread mistrust of government. He emphasized his integrity and moral uprightness as a born-again Christian. He stressed that he was untainted by the scandals of Washington politics. "I have been accused of being an outsider," Carter said, "and I plead guilty." Carter reminded Americans that "we know from bitter experience that we're not going to get the changes we need simply by shifting around the same group of Washington insiders." This approach appealed to voters.

The Republicans feared disaster in the 1976 elections. The 1974 midterm elections had demonstrated the stigma that Watergate attached to the party. Ford had several political liabilities. Most Americans still remembered his pardon of Richard Nixon. Moreover, Republican conservatives judged his economic policies a disaster, largely because of vast budget deficits, and they detested détente with the Soviet Union. As a consequence, Ford faced a major challenge from conservative Republicans during the primary elections. His principal conservative rival was Ronald Reagan, former governor of California. Ford managed to capture the Republican nomination for president, even though the party platform was critical of his foreign policies.

Carter Defeats Ford

During the campaign, few significant differences emerged to distinguish Ford from Carter. Their disagreements over handling the economy ran along traditional party lines. Carter charged that Ford was insensitive to high unemployment rates. Ford warned of the economic dangers of "tax-and-spend Democrats." Their foreign policy differences were based on Carter's moralism and concern for human rights, compared to Ford's emphasis on the "realism" of balance-of-power diplomacy. As one observer noted, "In 1976, issues were no more important than the price of hoopskirts."

Ford's major problem in the campaign was a poor public image. Ford was not an effective public speaker, often making mistakes and misquoting facts. TV cameras captured Ford stumbling as he left his plane and bumping his head. Episodes such as these detracted from Ford's presidential image. As journalist Richard Reeves noted, "One of the incumbent's problems has always been to 'appear presidential,' which, in his case, has come down to first proving he is not a dummy, that he can read and write."

Carter's major problem seemed to be his waffling on issues. In one campaign speech, he might support affirmative action or higher taxes. In another, he might support the opposite stand. Carter led Ford by 33 percentage points just after the Democratic convention, but by election day political forecasters thought the election was too close to call.

The voting was extremely close. Carter won by 2 percent of the popular vote (about 2 million votes) and by 297 to 241 electoral votes. Carter carried 23 states, including every southern state but

Virginia. Over 90 percent of African American voters cast ballots for Carter, and they gave him his margin of victory in many states. Hispanic Americans also voted heavily for Carter, and he did well with low-income rural white voters. Ford carried every state west of the Mississippi, and the majority of white voters cast ballots for him.

In the 1976 congressional elections, results were similar to those of the 1974 midterm-elections. The Democrats enjoyed majorities of 61 to 38 (with one

▼ *By how many percentage points did Carter win the popular vote?*

On January 20, 1977, President and Mrs. Carter walked from the Capitol to the White House after his inauguration. No president had done this since Thomas Jefferson. Why would Carter seek to be identified with Jefferson?

independent) in the Senate and 292 to 143 in the House of Representatives. With Congress in his party's control, it appeared Carter would have little trouble. But many of the Democratic congressional winners received a higher proportion of votes than Carter and felt little obligation to him. The newly elected Democrats felt a greater obligation to the voters back home.

The Carter Presidency

With a very thin margin of victory and immense public distrust of government and public officials, Carter faced a difficult political situation. "One result was certain," journalist Haynes Johnson wrote. "The [new] president would be watched more critically than ever before." Carter acted quickly to make government appear closer to the people. He wore a plain business suit, rather than formal attire, to his inauguration. He and his wife Rosalynn walked from the Capitol to the White House, rather than driving in the inaugural parade.

Carter reduced the size of the White House staff, which had grown immensely under Nixon. He ordered his cabinet secretaries to cease taking government limousines to work. The new president established new ethical guidelines for executive appointees. They now had to disclose all financial

holdings and get rid of any potential conflicts of interest. In addition, Carter wanted to reduce possible unethical or corrupt links between former government officials and businesses that were regulated by, or that received contracts from, government agencies. He therefore increased the time that former government officials had to wait before they could take jobs with corporations, law firms, or lobbying firms that did business with the federal government.

As Carter formed his administration, he tried to keep his distance from Washington political insiders. He chose as his closest domestic advisers many who had served him during his campaign or his tenure as governor of Georgia. Most of them lacked Washington experience, which led to many early mistakes and clashes with Congress.

Moreover, Carter was not the only political candidate who ran for office as an outsider in 1976. In the House of Representatives in 1977, 41 percent of the Democrats were new representatives, first elected in the previous two elections. "Like Carter," journalist Theodore White remarked, "they had run against Washington and the establishment, both local and national." Carter might have reached out to these representatives for support for his programs. Instead, he mistook them for Washington insiders and failed to cultivate their support.

In part because of recent campaign reforms, legislators now gained and held office by building political organizations devoted to them personally rather than by being loyal party members. In addition, changes in congressional rules and procedures reduced the powers once enjoyed by committee chairpersons and spread them out among subcommittee heads. In these ways, Carter faced a more fragmented legislative process and found it more difficult to build support for his proposals.

SECTION 3 REVIEW

1. Describe the campaign methods used by Carter to distance himself from other candidates in the presidential election of 1976.
2. List the problems faced by Ford in his attempt to be reelected.
3. Describe the image problems faced by Carter.
4. Identify steps taken by Carter to reinstall trust in the presidency.
5. Explain how Carter failed to take advantage of the 1976 congressional elections.

SECTION 4

Carter's Domestic Troubles

After less than a month in office, Carter confided to his diary, "Everyone has warned me not to take on too many projects so early in the administration, but it's almost impossible for me to delay something that I see needs to be done." Carter wanted to act, but he had established no clear priorities to guide his actions. He had a jumbled list of program ideas, but no coherent political philosophy or clear mandate from the voters. The Carter team introduced legislation to Congress in an uncoordinated rush. As Carter speechwriter James Fallows later reflected, "You can't inspire people with a jigsaw puzzle."

Why did the energy crisis prove so difficult to solve?
What economic problems did Carter face?
Why were federal affirmative action policies so controversial?

A Mixed-Success Presidency

After graduating from the U.S. Naval Academy, Jimmy Carter became an engineer in the new nuclear submarine program. After his father's death, he returned to his hometown, Plains, Georgia, and became a successful peanut farmer and businessperson. As president, Carter proved capable of mastering the details of issues that faced his administration. He rose early and worked hard. He even took a speed-reading course to improve his ability to take in information. Yet in spite of all Carter's strengths, he seemed incapable of providing a clear vision and direction for the nation. Consequently, the public began to lose confidence in him. After three months, 72 percent of Americans approved of Carter's performance. After one year, that rating dropped to 50 percent.

Despite differences with Carter, Congress did enact many of his legislative requests. Carter created the cabinet-level Department of Energy and the Department of Education. He oversaw the deregulation of the airline, railroad, and trucking industries. He designed a package to stimulate the economy that included a tax cut and a major public works measure. Even so, Carter could not persuade Congress to enact his highest priorities. These included tax reform, national health insurance, welfare revision, labor legislation, instant voter registration, and the Consumer Protection Agency.

The Energy Crisis

Carter saw the energy crisis as the most pressing issue of his presidency. In April 1977, Carter sent Congress a comprehensive energy package. "Many of these proposals," he informed the nation, "will be unpopular. Some will cause you to put up with inconveniences and to make sacrifices. . . . This difficult effort will be the 'moral equivalent of war.' " Carter's plan sought to reduce the nation's appetite for oil through such methods as encouraging energy conservation, setting up standards of energy efficiency, and placing new taxes on gas-guzzling cars.

This United Press International photograph of the nuclear power plant at Three Mile Island (near Harrisburg, Pennsylvania) was taken just after the danger of nuclear meltdown had passed. What was the long-term effect of the near disaster at Three Mile Island?

For the next three years, Carter's comprehensive energy plan languished in Congress. It was nearly impossible to create a consensus on energy policy. Every proposed tax and regulation threatened the interests of one group or another. Thus, Congress enacted legislation only in bits and pieces. Congress removed controls on natural gas prices, allowed power plants and factories to reconvert to coal, and encouraged conservation. This was much less than Carter hoped to accomplish.

Many people thought that available technologies, such as nuclear power or solar power, would soon solve the energy crisis. Their optimism received a severe blow in March 1979, when an accident occurred at a nuclear power plant at **Three Mile Island**, Pennsylvania. A cooling system malfunction nearly caused dangerous levels of radioactive pollution to be released into the surrounding countryside. Accidents had occurred at other nuclear power plants before, but the one at Three Mile Island was far more dangerous. Walter Cronkite, the anchor for CBS television news, said, "The world has never known a day quite like today. It faced the considerable uncertainties and dangers of the worst nuclear power plant accident of the atomic age." Though some scientists, engineers, and politicians continued to minimize the risks of nuclear power, others were less certain that nuclear energy was a safe alternative energy source.

In June 1979, energy shortages led drivers to vent their frustration and rage. On June 7, truck drivers began a strike to protest the rising costs of diesel fuel and scarce supplies. Within a week, nearly 60 percent of the country's truckers were on strike. Violence broke out against nonstriking truckers. In Levittown, Pennsylvania, two nights of violent riots injured more than 100 people and led to 170 arrests. Governors of several states called out the National Guard to restore order. Meanwhile, OPEC announced another 50 percent hike in oil prices.

Carter tried again to secure enactment of a comprehensive energy program, this time with a bit more success. By executive order, he placed limits on the amount of oil that could be imported. He urged Congress to allocate funds to explore alternative energy sources. The Crude Oil Windfall Profits Tax Act (1980) taxed the "excess" profits that American oil companies received from the recent steep increases in oil prices. At the same time, Congress removed price controls on oil produced in the United States in order to encourage domestic production. Congress also passed the Energy Security Act in 1980, which allocated $88 billion for research and production of alternative energy sources. The act authorized the Strategic Petroleum Reserve, whose initial goal was to store and maintain a six-months' supply of oil for the entire nation.

Carter's "Malaise" Speech

With the beginning of another energy crisis in June 1979 and his public approval ratings dropping to an all-time low, President Carter retreated to Camp David, the presidential compound in the Maryland mountains. There, Carter summoned 135 people—mayors, governors, members of Congress, and academics—to advise him on the sorry state of the nation and of his presidency. After a week of seclusion and candid advice, Carter returned from Camp David to address the nation on July 15. Widespread rumors about Carter's physical and mental health ensured a large television audience for his speech.

"All the legislation in the world can't fix what's wrong with America," a solemn Carter told his television audience. "It is a crisis of confidence. It is a crisis that strikes at the very heart and soul and spirit of our nation . . . [and] is threatening to destroy the social and political fabric of America." Carter lamented Americans' loss of confidence in their future and the decline of traditional values, such as "hard work, strong families, close-knit communities, and our faith in God." Carter concluded, "This is not a message of happiness or reassurance, but it is the truth. And it is a warning."

▲ *President Carter delivered a televised address on the energy crisis from the White House on July 15, 1979.*

Although he did not use the term malaise, journalists used it later to capture the essence of Carter's message. It means "a sense of uneasiness." Americans initially received Carter's speech positively. Speaking in short, crisp sentences, he had appeared strong and decisive. Opinion polls suggested that the president's public standing had improved. Within two weeks, however, in a seeming lack of confidence, Carter dismissed five cabinet secretaries and reorganized his White House staff. Opinion polls, taken after the dismissals, showed that his approval rating—23 percent—was now lower than before his July 15 address to the nation. Whether fair or not, the dismissals seemed to be yet another example of Carter saying one thing and then doing another.

---

1. What did Carter describe as the problem with America?
2. How did Carter "say one thing and then do another?"

Carter and the Economy

Even more than the energy crisis, economic problems proved to be Carter's downfall. When he took office, Carter moved to reduce unemployment. He sent Congress a spending program designed to stimulate industry and create thousands of new jobs. As a result, the economy picked up, and unemployment dropped below 6 percent. At the same time, Carter virtually ignored inflation, the nation's other severe economic problem. Stimulated by Vietnam War spending and worsened by rising energy prices, the rate of inflation rapidly increased.

In 1978, Carter finally acted to curb inflation. His primary weapon was tightening the money supply by raising the **prime interest rate** (the rate at which central banks lend money to other banks). In 1976, the prime interest rate was under 7 percent. By 1979, the rate was nearly 16 percent, and by 1980 it was over 20 percent. The impact of Carter's remedy for inflation was devastating to the U.S. economy. High interest rates caused retail sales to

LOVE AT FIRST SIGHT

WATCH THE WHIP, FELLA

NEW BUSINESS

95TH CONGRESS

▲ *Draper Hill's editorial cartoon suggested that all was not well between the new Democratic president and the 95th Congress.*

▼ *How did the Carter administration combat the problems identified in this poll?*

Most Important Problem, 1977

Question: What do you think is the most important problem facing this country today?

Inflation/high cost of living	58%
Unemployment/recession	39%
Energy shortage	23%
International problems/national defense	18%
Crime/courts	18%
Dissatisfaction with gov't./corruption	7%
Moral decline	6%

Note: Multiple responses allowed.

Source: Survey by Gallup, March 18-21, 1977.

©The Public Perspective, a publication of the Roper Center for Public Opinion Research, University of CT, Storrs. Reprinted by permission.

drop dramatically. They reduced home construction, sent the prices of homes soaring, and made home purchases extremely difficult. Inflation and tight money hurt many other industries and caused a sharp increase in the U.S. trade deficit. (In a trade deficit, imports exceed exports.)

The automobile industry was especially hurt by these policies. In 1979, Chrysler Motor Company, the third largest U.S. automobile manufacturer, appealed to the federal government for help. Its sales were sagging because of foreign competition, and the company was losing money. Senator William Proxmire, a Democrat, opposed bailing out Chrysler, arguing that "you just can't have a free enterprise system without failures." Chrysler's president, Lee Iacocca, countered by saying that not only would thousands of Chrysler workers lose their jobs if the government failed to help, but many other firms would fail, too, like falling dominoes. Congress agreed to stand behind $1.5 billion in loans to Chrysler. By the 1980s, Chrysler had paid off its loans and had begun to earn a profit once more.

Affirmative Action

By the late 1970s, the discussion about how to end discrimination and ensure the equality of

African Americans, other minorities, and women focused on **affirmative action** policies. Since the mid-1960s, affirmative action laws had been passed to provide minorities and women with greater opportunities in employment, business, and education. Government and business had created programs that ensured minority hiring and job promotion and set aside contracts for minority-owned businesses. Colleges and universities had set aside places for, and actively recruited, minority students. Supporters argued affirmative action was necessary to make up for past discrimination in education and employment. Opponents argued affirmative action actually discriminated against white people, especially white males. They claimed that the policy was little more than **reverse discrimination,** actions that penalized members of the majority class.

Allan Bakke decided to test the legality of affirmative action after the medical school at the University of California, Davis, rejected his application for admission. The Davis medical school admitted only 100 applicants every year, reserving 16 of those places for minority applicants. Bakke, a Norwegian American, had scored higher on admissions tests than had several minority candidates who were admitted. In *University of California Regents v. Bakke* (1978), a closely divided Supreme Court ruled that the medical school's affirmative action policy was too inflexible and violated the 1964 Civil Rights Act. In effect, the school had discriminated against Bakke because he was white. Still, the Court de-

clared that carefully drawn affirmative action programs were permissible under the Constitution as a remedy to past discrimination.

SECTION 5

Carter's Foreign Policies

Carter, like other modern presidents, found foreign affairs and diplomacy more attractive than the details and tangles of domestic politics. "Under our Constitution, the president has much more authority in foreign affairs [than in domestic affairs]," Carter wrote later, "and therefore decisions can be made more quickly, more incisively, and usually with more immediate results." Although Carter had several notable successes in foreign affairs, this was also the area of his most conspicuous failure.

What did Carter do on behalf of human rights?
How did Carter approach U.S. relations with the Soviets?
How did events in the Middle East affect Carter's presidency?

▶ *Allan Bakke sued the regents of the University of California for reverse discrimination after being denied entry to the medical school at Davis. Did the Supreme Court overturn the doctrine of affirmative action as a result of this case?*

A New Direction in Foreign Policy

In his campaign for president, Carter had outlined a new approach to foreign policy. He suggested that "we replace balance-of-power politics with world-order politics." From Carter's point of view, most important foreign policy issues were no longer military problems but social and economic problems. To cope with this changing international environment, Carter wanted to end America's excessive "fear of communism," to advocate human rights in all nations, and to eliminate nuclear weapons.

The most distinctive aspect of Carter's foreign policy was his advocacy of human rights in other countries. Carter created the Bureau of Human Rights within the Department of State. Each year, the bureau published a report on the state of political and civil liberties around the world. Among the nations denounced for their human rights violations were the Philippines, South Korea, Chile, Brazil, and Argentina. Carter cut U.S. economic aid and pressured the World Bank and other sources of funds to stop loans to these countries. Yet Carter was not always consistent in applying such pressure to nations that had repeatedly violated human rights.

Carter supported several rulers whose regimes were notorious for violating human rights. Among them was the Shah of Iran. Carter's secretary of state, Cyrus Vance, later described Iran's importance to the United States: "Iran was seen as the major force for stability in the oil-rich Persian Gulf. Its military strength ensured Western access to [Persian] Gulf oil and served as a barrier to Soviet expansion. Its influence in OPEC made it important to the American economy." As a result, Carter ignored the Shah's dismal record on human rights, particularly the activities of the secret police. This group imprisoned and tortured the Shah's political opponents. In 1977, the United States sold Iran weapons worth $5.7 billion. Carter's continued support for the Shah blinded him to the growing political opposition to the Shah's regime in Iran.

A New Latin American Policy

Early in his administration, Carter turned his attention to the future of the Panama Canal. Carter, like Ford, wanted to reduce Latin American resentment over U.S. control of the Canal Zone. U.S. citizens operated the locks and piloted ships through the canal, while Panamanians worked only in unskilled jobs. Moreover, Panamanian children could not attend school in the Canal Zone, but natives could be arrested and tried in U.S. courts. Panamanians saw U.S. control of the Canal Zone as a leftover of "yanqui imperialism."

Within months of taking office, Carter signed two treaties with Panama. The first would return legal jurisdiction of the Canal Zone to Panama. The United States would agree to operate and defend the zone until the end of 1999. After that time, Panama would operate the canal. The second treaty gave the United States the right to defend the canal. The treaties faced considerable opposition from conservative Republicans and Democrats. Ronald Reagan declared, "We built it, we paid for it, it's ours, and we should tell [President] Torrijos and company that we are going to keep it." In response, Senator S. I. Hayakawa of California quipped, "It's ours, we stole it fair and square." Despite the opposition, Carter secured just enough votes in March 1978 to ratify the treaties.

Carter's handling of the Sandinista revolution in Nicaragua also reflected his desire to overcome historic Latin American hatred of the United States. Earlier, the U.S. government had intervened in Nicaragua to help the Somoza military regime put down a popular rebellion led by Augusto Sandino. When the marines left in 1933, the Somoza family virtually owned the country. By the mid-1970s, Anastasio Somoza's corruption and brutality had alienated the Catholic church, the middle classes, and the peasantry. In 1976, rebel Sandinistas (named after murdered rebel leader Sandino) began battling Somoza's national guard. As the civil war raged on, the United States ended support to Somoza. In June 1979, Somoza fled Nicaragua, and the Sandinistas took over. Carter soon provided $80 million in aid to help improve U.S. relations with the Sandinista government. The Nicaraguan revolutionaries, however, distrusted the United States and aligned themselves more closely with Cuba. Political unrest in Central America would continue to create problems for U.S. policymakers throughout the next decade.

Soviet-American Relations

In January 1979, the United States and the People's Republic of China exchanged ambassadors. This completed the process begun by Richard Nixon of establishing normal relations between the two nations. Carter's diplomatic recognition of Communist China increased tensions with the Soviet Union. In part, this resulted from anti-Soviet statements made by Red Chinese leaders. Deng Xiaoping (duhng shee-OW-ping), vice chairman of the Chinese Communist Party, visited the United States in January 1979. Deng warned of a new world war if the West did not stand up to the Soviets. Two weeks after his U.S. tour, Deng ordered an invasion of Vietnam (a Soviet ally), which had just invaded China's ally, Cambodia. The timing of Deng's anti-Soviet words and actions made it appear that the United States had approved them in advance. Thus, cordial Chinese-American relations served to poison Soviet-American diplomacy.

The signing of the second strategic arms limitations agreement (SALT II) in June 1979 did not stop relations from worsening. Carter had come to office hoping to reduce the two superpowers' nuclear arsenals. After two years of hard negotiations, the Soviets and Americans agreed to parity (equality) in their nuclear forces. Soon after Carter and Brezhnev signed the SALT II agreement in Vienna, however, opposition to the treaty arose in the United States. Democrats as well as Republicans opposed it. Senator Henry Jackson, a Democrat who was a longtime hawk on defense issues, called SALT II "appeasement in its purest form." Paul Nitze, former head of the Arms Control and Disarmament Agency, called the treaty's provisions "screwball."

The Soviet invasion of Afghanistan in December 1979 doomed the SALT II agreement. The Soviets wanted to prop up the government they had installed in Afghanistan in 1976. The invasion, Carter warned, was "the gravest threat to peace since the Second World War." In January 1980, Carter withdrew SALT II from Senate consideration. Carter also promised to raise defense spending by 5 percent per year for the next five years, forbade U.S. participation in the 1980 Olympic Games held in Moscow, and stopped U.S. grain and electronics sales to the Soviet Union. Finally, he issued the **Carter Doctrine**, which warned the Soviets that the United States would fight to protect its vital interests in the Persian Gulf region. Despite Carter's increasingly tough stands, many Americans continued to think that Carter was both indecisive and inept in foreign affairs. The president's public support continued to erode.

Carter and the Middle East

In September 1978, Carter mediated a peace settlement between Israel and Egypt at Camp David, Maryland. The agreement, which became known as the **Camp David Accords**, was a remarkable diplomatic success for Carter. Not only had Arab states not recognized Israel diplomatically, but also most of them wanted Israel destroyed. Israeli occupation of large areas of Arab territory, the issue of homeless Palestinian refugees, and the activities of the Palestinian Liberation Organization (PLO) further complicated the situation.

Carter's call in September 1977 for the creation of a Palestinian homeland spurred Israeli and Egyptian leaders to action. President Anwar Sadat of Egypt initiated the peace process by making a historic visit to Israel. After months of diplomatic groundwork, Sadat and Prime Minister Menachem Begin of Israel met with Carter at Camp David, Maryland. For two weeks in September 1978, Carter mediated between the two national leaders. Finally, the two leaders agreed to a "framework for peace in the Middle East." Israel agreed to evacuate its military positions and settlements in the Sinai peninsula in exchange for peace and diplomatic recognition from Egypt. The two leaders agreed to continue discussions about the Palestinian and West Bank problems. The United States agreed to provide financial aid to both nations and to organize an international peacekeeping force in the Sinai.

Jimmy Carter received widespread praise for his efforts on behalf of peace in the Middle East. Yet Carter's acclaim was short-lived, for no other Arab nation—not even Jordan or Saudi Arabia, with whom the United States enjoyed good relations—

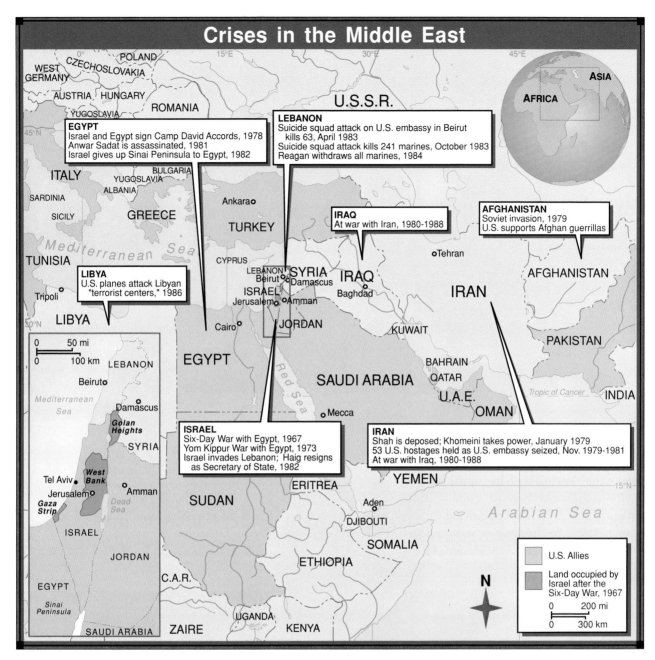

Crises in the Middle East

EGYPT
Israel and Egypt sign Camp David Accords, 1978
Anwar Sadat is assassinated, 1981
Israel gives up Sinai Peninsula to Egypt, 1982

LEBANON
Suicide squad attack on U.S. embassy in Beirut kills 63, April 1983
Suicide squad attack kills 241 marines, October 1983
Reagan withdraws all marines, 1984

IRAQ
At war with Iran, 1980–1988

AFGHANISTAN
Soviet invasion, 1979
U.S. supports Afghan guerrillas

LIBYA
U.S. planes attack Libyan "terrorist centers," 1986

ISRAEL
Six-Day War with Egypt, 1967
Yom Kippur War with Egypt, 1973
Israel invades Lebanon; Haig resigns as Secretary of State, 1982

IRAN
Shah is deposed; Khomeini takes power, January 1979
53 U.S. hostages held as U.S. embassy seized, Nov. 1979–1981
At war with Iraq, 1980–1988

U.S. Allies

Land occupied by Israel after the Six-Day War, 1967

▲ *As the United States became increasingly dependent on imported oil, its vital national interests involved maintaining political stability in the Middle East.*

would join the peace process. The PLO denounced the agreement and warned other Arab nations not to participate. Virtually every Arab nation broke off relations with Egypt.

Revolution in Iran   Subsequent events in the Middle East soon eclipsed the peace settlement. In

November 1979, Iranian nationalists seized the U.S. embassy in Tehran and held 53 U.S. citizens hostage. The seizure of the American hostages took place following a successful revolution, led by Islamic fundamentalists, against the Shah of Iran. The Shah's regime, a firm ally of the United States, had faced growing internal opposition over the years. In mid-

In early September 1978, Egyptian President Anwar Sadat (left), President Carter, and Israeli Prime Minister Menachem Begin (right) met at Camp David, Maryland, to negotiate a peace settlement between the two Middle Eastern nations. What was Carter's role in the negotiations?

January 1979, the Shah fled to Egypt. Within two weeks, the **Ayatollah Khomeini** [kho-MAY-nee], leader of the revolution, returned in triumph from exile in Paris. After Carter allowed the deposed Shah to travel to the United States for cancer treatments, Iranians stormed the American embassy and threatened to execute the hostages if Carter did not return the Shah to Iran.

Carter froze $8 billion in Iranian assets in the United States, and the Shah soon departed for Panama. With the monarch gone, Carter hoped he could exchange the hostages for the Iranian assets.

Angered by Carter's decision to allow the deposed Shah to enter the United States for medical treatment, Iranian fundamentalists stormed the American embassy in Tehran in early November 1979 and took hostages. How long was it before the hostages were finally released?

In December, Carter's public approval rating rose to 66 percent, but the hostage crisis seemed to defy solution. In April 1980, a frustrated Carter ordered the military to try to rescue the hostages. The plan failed dismally when two of the eight helicopters assigned to the rescue mission collided in the Iranian desert. Americans severely criticized his apparent bungling. In late July, the Shah died in Egypt, and earnest negotiations to exchange the American hostages for Iranian assets began. The negotiations continued through the fall but broke down the week before the 1980 presidential election. Carter worked tirelessly for the release of the hostages. But, in a final humiliation, the Iranians released the hostages moments after Carter left office.

SECTION 5 REVIEW

1. Name the two areas of foreign policy concerns that Carter thought more important than military concerns.
2. Explain why Carter continued to support the Shah of Iran despite human rights violations in that country.
3. List the purposes of the Bureau of Human Rights.
4. Describe ways Carter tried to overcome Latin American hostility toward the United States.
5. Identify the intent of the Carter Doctrine.

Summary

Presidents Ford and Carter inherited the political uproar caused by Watergate. The scandal had resulted in widespread distrust of political authority and leadership. This, in turn, made dealing with the nation's many domestic and foreign problems especially difficult. Both presidents faced an energy crisis that was largely beyond their control. Similarly, the economy plagued both Ford and Carter.

Just as Watergate undermined political authority in domestic affairs, Vietnam made Americans wary of foreign affairs. Between 1974 and 1981, events seemed to show how vulnerable the United States was to developments beyond its leaders' control. Poverty and political instability inspired revolutionary forces—in Iran, Central America, and other less developed countries. Those forces were now apparently beyond the ability of U.S. leaders to control. In addition, Soviet arms increases and meddling in many trouble spots around the world undermined détente. Many Americans interpreted these events as indications of the incompetency of U.S. leaders.

Vocabulary Skills

affirmative action   prime interest rate
clemency   reverse discrimination

Write a brief paragraph of three or four sentences explaining the meaning of each of the vocabulary terms.

Review Questions

1. What reason did President Ford give for pardoning former President Nixon?

2. Explain what caused inflation during the Ford and Carter administrations.
3. Discuss reasons that made the energy issue so hard for Ford and Carter to handle.
4. How did Congress attempt to reassert its authority in foreign affairs in the mid-1970s?
5. How did the Vietnam War affect Americans' attitudes toward foreign affairs?
6. Discuss briefly the effect of Watergate on American politics.
7. List occurrences from 1974 to 1980 that undermined détente with the Soviet Union.
8. Explain why Carter had so much trouble in spite of a Democratic majority in both houses.
9. Why did affirmative action meet with opposition in the 1970s?
10. What was Carter's new direction in foreign policy?

Critical Historical Thinking

Writing Answer each of the following by writing one or more complete paragraphs:

1. Do you think President Ford was justified in granting a full pardon to Richard Nixon? Explain why, or why not.
2. What two seemingly contradictory goals did Carter have to choose between in the face of Soviet aggression in Afghanistan? Do you think he made the right decision? Why, or why not?
3. Explain why Congress felt it was necessary to pass laws in the early 1970s that limited presidential power.
4. Read the selection entitled "Justice Thurgood Marshall's Opinion in the Bakke Case" in the Unit 10 Archives. Was Marshall in favor of affirmative action? Support your answer with historical evidence.

Making Connections with Human Rights

Although many historians have rated Jimmy Carter as an ineffective president, he showed a commitment to human rights that was unmatched by earlier presidents. Carter's human rights policy annoyed many political leaders, especially in the USSR, who felt it was unwarranted American interference in the way they ran their own countries.

Human rights are basic rights that all persons enjoy as a protection against such government abuses as summary execution, kidnapping, torture, exile, and slavery. Some people consider certain political rights to be human rights. These include the right to assemble peacefully, the right of due process, freedom of expression, and freedom from discrimination on the basis of race, religion, sex, or ethnicity. Recently, emphasis has also been put on human rights for women and children, including political and social equality for women and a child's right to decent food, health care, and education.

Your individual perception, or opinion, on what human rights are will depend upon your particular culture and upbringing. The goal of people who work in international relations is to identify human rights that all countries of the world will accept as basic and agree to guarantee for their citizens.

▪ Research such human rights organizations as Human Rights Watch, the International Commission of Jurists, Amnesty International, and Helsinki Watch. The following documents will also provide information on human rights: the Universal Declaration of Human Rights, (1948), The International Covenant of Civil and Political Rights (1966), and the UN Convention on the Rights of the Child. Imagine that you have been assigned by the United Nations the task of presenting a list of basic human rights to the UN General Assembly for ratification. Prepare a report that you could present. Be prepared to defend all the items on your list.

Additional Skills Practice

Look through magazines, such as *Time* and *Newsweek*, from the mid-1970s for cartoons on the oil embargo or the energy crisis. If you can get permission, bring the magazine to class. Write an analysis of the cartoon to share with your classmates.

The Reagan Era

At 69, Ronald Reagan was the oldest elected president of the United States. A genial, tall, strongly built man with ruddy good looks, Reagan had been a movie star in the 1940s and 1950s. He could not escape his Hollywood image in the public's mind; instead, he consciously played it up. For example, he used a Western movie metaphor to explain his election. The voters, he said, "rounded up a posse, swore in this old sheriff, and sent us riding into town." The Secret Service gave Reagan the code name "Rawhide."

While many people scoffed at his acting background, President Reagan once reflected that "there have been times in this office when I've wondered how you could do the job if you hadn't been an actor." Most Americans, whatever their political persuasion, liked Reagan. When he left office in 1989, 53 percent continued to approve of his handling of the presidency. This was no small accomplishment, considering the ratings of his four immediate predecessors.

▲ *Ronald Reagan's ready smile and positive outlook endeared him to many Americans. How did Reagan's background help prepare him for public life?*

Ronald Reagan's Election

In 1980, runaway inflation, the unresolved fate of American hostages in Iran, and the collapse of détente with the Soviet Union doomed Jimmy Carter's bid for reelection and energized the candidacy of **Ronald Reagan**. While Carter spoke of the need to accept limits, Reagan spoke of restoring national pride and strength. "This is the greatest country in the world," Reagan said. "We have the talent, we have the drive, we have the imagination. Now all we need is the leadership." Many Americans shared Reagan's belief that it was "time for us to realize that we are too great a nation to limit ourselves to small dreams."

What were Ronald Reagan's political beliefs?

What issues were important in the presidential election of 1980?

How did Reagan's treatment of striking air traffic controllers affect his popularity?

▲ *President and Mrs. Reagan posed for this photograph at the "Western White House," their ranch near Santa Barbara, California.*

Ronald Reagan Enters Politics

Ronald Reagan's long career in radio and films began during the Great Depression. In the late 1940s, after he had made 54 movies, Reagan became president of the Screen Actors Guild, a labor union for actors. There he battled corporate Hollywood to secure better wages, benefits, and working conditions for film workers. At the same time he fought Communist influence in the film industry. In the early 1950s, Reagan often spoke publicly about the "Communist conspiracy" in the United States. Meanwhile, he actively campaigned for Democratic candidates. Reagan then turned to television, hosting such programs as the "G. E. Theater" and "Death Valley Days." He became General Electric's national spokesman and, in countless speeches to civic and business groups, pronounced, "Progress is our most important product," G. E.'s corporate slogan.

By the early 1960s, Reagan's involvement with General Electric had changed many of his views. As journalist and Reagan biographer Lou Cannon wrote, "More than anything, it is his G. E. experience that changed Reagan from an adversary of big business into one of its most ardent spokesmen." By 1964, Reagan had become a passionate conservative and an enthusiastic supporter of conservative Republican presidential candidate Barry Goldwater. Late in the 1964 campaign, Reagan made a televised fund-raising speech for Goldwater. Reagan stressed that "outside of its legitimate functions, government does nothing as well or as economically as the private sector of the economy." Overnight, viewers contributed $1 million to Goldwater's struggling campaign.

In 1966, Reagan became governor of California. In his eight years as governor, Reagan cut the size and cost of state government and balanced the state's budget. Again and again, Reagan condemned big government, high taxes, social welfare programs, and communism. Despite his conservative record, California liberals applauded Reagan for signing such legislation as a more liberal abortion law and environmental protection laws.

After Reagan stepped down as governor, he continued to comment on current events in syndicated radio broadcasts and newspaper columns and in speeches. Since President Calvin Coolidge in the 1920s, few politicians had expressed a purer faith in traditional America—in self-reliance, unregulated free enterprise, and getting ahead—than Ronald Reagan. Reagan's view of traditional values attracted many people, especially conservatives who felt abandoned by the Republican Party and by President Eisenhower in the 1950s. Eisenhower's brand of modern republicanism—which included acceptance of many federal programs and regulations—had alienated many conservatives.

The Election of 1980

Since the 1950s, some conservatives had worked to get rid of New Deal social welfare programs and business regulations and had denounced the "Communist menace." **New Right** activists of the 1970s and 1980s believed that liberal programs and policies had encouraged permissiveness that had undermined the church, the family, and incentives for hard work. They condemned welfare, the women's liberation movement, abortion rights, gay and lesbian rights, affirmative action, pornography, gun control, and détente with the Soviet Union. The New Right wished to reduce big government, to challenge liberal politics, and to restore a traditional moral order in the United States.

New Right activists made use of computerized fund-raising techniques and relationships with powerful political action committees (PACs) to create an effective network that supported conservative causes and candidates.

◄ *What campaign themes are suggested by the buttons on this hat?*

They also established conservative "think tanks," organizations dedicated to finding new conservative solutions to problems that were part of the public agenda. By the late 1970s, the New Right began to use their resources to elect political candidates who supported their agenda. With their help, Reagan nearly took the Republican presidential nomination away from Gerald Ford in 1976.

Undaunted by this near miss, Reagan geared up for the 1980 presidential election almost as soon as Jimmy Carter took office in 1977. The Democrats renominated Carter and Walter Mondale as their presidential ticket in 1980. The Republicans nominated Reagan as their presidential candidate and **George Bush** as his running mate.

In the elections of 1980, Ronald Reagan beat Jimmy Carter by a margin of 51 percent to 41 percent. (Independent candidate John Anderson received nearly 7 percent of the popular vote.) Reagan's margin of victory in the electoral college was 489 to 49, a landslide in which he carried 44 of the 50 states. Republicans also made impressive gains in the House of Representatives and in state legislatures. In the U.S. Senate, Democrats had a 58 to 41 majority before the elections. Afterward, Republicans controlled the Senate for the first time in 26 years by a seven-vote margin. This startling turnaround in the Senate resulted from the New Right's effective campaigns against liberal incumbents.

Reagan's Administration

Reagan often said publicly that he relied heavily on his cabinet to form and implement administration policies. In fact, the cabinet generally played a minor role. Advisers gained influence in Reagan's administration because of their personal relationships with the president rather than their official positions. Caspar Weinberger, an adviser during Reagan's terms as governor of California, became a powerful secretary of defense. Reagan gave CIA Director William Casey, a close personal friend, great authority to reinvigorate the agency's secret operations. Reagan's first secretary of state, Alexander Haig, did not serve long enough to be influential. Haig's replacement, George Schultz,

Sound Bites and Photo Ops

With the help of his advisers, Reagan perfected the "ceremonial presidency." With his actor's good looks, strong speaking voice, charming smile, and twinkling eyes, Reagan fit many Americans' image of the ideal president. His soothing words and use of symbolic images were perfect for the television medium. His speechwriters wrote phrases—often called sound bites because they were short and easily captured in brief news stories—that appealed to the heart rather than to the head. Reagan's managers also recognized the importance of photographic images and made certain the press had many photo opportunities (or "photo ops") to capture Reagan at work. In fact, the White House released 4,000 to 6,000 photos of Reagan every month. Through such public relations work, Reagan built a strong bond with the American public.

Television is the main source of news for many Americans. The number of Americans who read daily newspapers declined in the 1980s from 73 to 50 percent. Images had a deeper effect on television audiences than words. In 1984, CBS television journalist Leslie Stahl narrated a feature on the "Nightly News" that contrasted Reagan's attendance at the Handicapped Olympics with his

▲ *President Reagan prepared his last State of the Union address at his desk in the Oval Office.*

pressuring Congress to cut federal funding for people with disabilities. White House staffer Richard Darman thanked Stahl for the "five-minute commercial." Stahl replied, "Didn't you hear what I said?" Darman responded, "Nobody heard what you said. They just saw five minutes of beautiful pictures of Ronald Reagan. . . . Haven't you people figured out yet that the picture always overrides what you say?"

On the other hand, the White House also recognized the importance of words. Reagan's pollster, Richard Wirthlin, set up test audiences who viewed Reagan speeches to identify "power phrases." Wirthlin noted which words had

the most favorable effect on the audience. These words and phrases were then included in Reagan speeches, while other weaker words and phrases were dropped. Such attention to detail and skillful public relations built up Reagan's public image and his political power.

1. Describe some of the public relations tactics used to build bonds with the American public.
2. How important do you think Reagan's public relations activities were?

became the principal architect of Reagan's foreign policy after 1982.

Reagan's White House staff generally had more influence with him than did his cabinet. Chief of Staff James Baker proved especially skillful at helping to get Reagan's legislative program passed by Congress. Baker persuaded Reagan to set clear legislative priorities and to act on key legislation quickly. He urged Reagan to make the budget and tax package and increased defense spending his top priorities. Baker convinced Reagan not to spend time on such controversial New Right issues as abortion and prayer in public schools.

Besides Baker, two close associates from Reagan's days as governor of California held key White House posts. Edwin Meese served as White House counselor, a loosely defined but important position because Meese met regularly with the president. Meese advised Reagan on most policy and political issues. Michael Deaver, a skilled public relations expert, served as assistant chief of staff. Deaver controlled the media's access to Reagan and prepared the president's daily schedule. Reagan's aides protected him from impromptu meetings with the press and allowed Reagan to hold only six press conferences during his first year, a new low for modern presidents.

Effective staff work and public relations were critical to Reagan's initial success as president. "The most important thing is to have the vision," Reagan once said. "The next is to grasp and hold it. . . . That is the very essence, I believe, of successful leadership." While Reagan supplied the vision, he was often ill informed on the details of policy issues. Nevertheless, supplying the vision and direction while his close staff took care of daily business served Reagan well during his first term.

▼ How heavily did President Reagan depend on advisors (left to right) James Baker, Edwin Meese, and Michael Deaver?

▲ *This 1981 rally in Boston was one of many showing support for PATCO's strike for better wages and working conditions.*

Reagan's decisive actions appealed to voters. In August 1981, for example, nearly 12,000 members of the Professional Air Traffic Controllers Organization (PATCO) walked off the job. PATCO had legitimate complaints about the difficult job performed by the controllers. Since PATCO had supported Reagan's campaign for president, they thought he would support their strike. Reagan, however, had little sympathy for labor unions, and he jumped at this chance to impress Congress and the public with his toughness. He warned the strikers to honor their contract or face dismissal. When Reagan's deadline passed, he fired the strikers and ordered military personnel to take over their jobs. As Reagan hoped, the public supported his tough stand and blamed the controllers for the resulting delays in air travel. Such actions increased Reagan's popularity during his first term.

SECTION 1 REVIEW

1. **Explain** how Ronald Reagan's role as a corporate spokesman helped develop his conservative political beliefs.
2. **List** the major areas criticized by Reagan while governor of California.
3. **Define** the term *New Right*.
4. **Name** the political issues that were significant in the presidential election of 1980.
5. **Describe** the role of Michael Deaver.

SECTION 2

The Reagan Revolution

On March 30, 1981, just nine weeks into Reagan's first term, John Hinckley attempted to assassinate Reagan as he left a Washington, D.C., hotel. Using a cheap handgun and exploding bullets, Hinckley's shots hit Reagan an inch from the heart and severely injured several bystanders, including James Brady, Reagan's press secretary. As Reagan was about to be wheeled into surgery, he joked with the hospital staff, asking them if they were Republicans. They assured him they were "all Republicans today." Reagan's spunkiness under adverse conditions endeared him to most Americans and also created broader support for his programs.

What were President Reagan's legislative priorities during his first term in office?

What did President Reagan do to "get government off people's backs?"

How did the economy pull out of the early 1980s recession?

Reordering America's Priorities

Since the 1950s, Reagan had opposed high taxes and big government. When he became president in 1981, Reagan unveiled his economic program, titled "America's New Beginning: A Program for Economic Recovery." His economic package included:

- big reductions in federal spending
- a huge tax cut
- elimination of many federal regulations.

The plan drew its inspiration from **supply-side economics**. This theory held that high taxes discouraged work, investments, and productivity. Supply-side economists believed that lower taxes would give taxpayers more money to spend, savings to invest, and more incentive to work. The result would be rapid economic growth, prosperity, and eventually more tax revenue and decreased federal budget

This photograph was taken moments after John Hinckley attempted to assassinate President Reagan outside a Washington, D.C., hotel on March 31, 1981. James Brady (foreground), Reagan's press secretary, was seriously wounded. What legislation was eventually passed as a result of this attack?

deficits. Other economists thought these predictions outlandish. The U.S. economy never approached the levels of investment and growth that supply-siders predicted would occur.

Reagan effectively lobbied Congress to pass his economic package. In his first four months in office, he met with congressional leaders nearly 70 times to urge passage of his program. After the assassination attempt, public opinion favored passage of Reagan's economic package by a margin of 2 to 1. Congress passed the Economic Recovery Tax Act in July 1981. It reduced federal income-tax rates by 25 per-

▼ *To what extent did the priorities of Reagan's first administration match up with the opinions reflected in this poll?*

▲ *What view of supply-side economics does this cartoon present?*

cent, which resulted in a cut of nearly $750 billion in federal tax revenues over the next five years.

Reagan's budget adviser David Stockman said that staggering budget deficits would result from the tax cuts if there were not drastic reductions in spending, too. The Budget Reconciliation Act, signed in August 1981, slashed spending on many domestic programs. Hardest hit were such welfare programs as unemployment insurance, aid to dependent children, food stamps, child nutrition, job retraining, student loans, and health services. Since Reagan believed that welfare programs reduced the

Most Important Problem, 1981

Question: What do you think is the most important problem facing this country today?

Inflation/high cost of living	72%
Unemployment/recession	8%
Energy problems/fuel shortages	5%

Source: Gallup, January 30–February 2, 1981.

©The Public Perspective, a publication of the Roper Center for Public Opinion Research, University of CT, Storrs. Reprinted by permission.

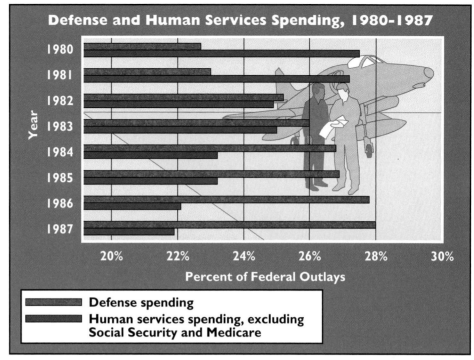

Defense and Human Services Spending, 1980-1987

▶

This bar graph shows the revolutionary changes in federal government spending priorities begun by President Reagan. By what percentage of the federal outlay did defense spending increase from 1980 to 1987?

Percent of Federal Outlays

■ Defense spending
■ Human services spending, excluding Social Security and Medicare

Source: U.S. Department of Commerce, Bureau of the Census, *Statistical Abstract of the United States.*

work incentive among the poor, he wanted even bigger cuts. Although Congress agreed to substantial cuts, it would not go as far as Reagan desired.

The spending cuts Congress made were not enough to avoid large federal budget deficits. By looking at the 1982 federal budget, the reasons for this situation become obvious. First, Reagan intended to vastly increase defense spending to about 25 percent of the federal budget. Second, the government could not avoid paying interest on the existing national debt, which accounted for about 10 percent of the budget. Third, Social Security and Medicare together amounted to about 48 percent of the federal budget. When Reagan suggested cutting Social Security and Medicaid benefits, however, he encountered a storm of political opposition, and he quickly retreated. Finally, the remaining 17 percent of the budget was composed of all other government programs, ranging from veterans' benefits to school lunch programs. Those who benefited from these programs fought hard for their retention. The federal government borrowed to cover the costs.

The budget act also turned the responsibility for many domestic programs over to state and local governments. Reagan called this approach **New Federalism.** The federal government would help fund these programs through a series of block grants that would give state and local governments more choice in the programs they wished to implement. State and local governments, however, had to increase taxes to pay for these programs. In the long run, federal tax reductions were nearly equaled by tax increases at the state and local levels.

Deregulating Business and Industry

Reagan firmly believed in the traditional American virtues of rugged individualism and self-reliance. For years, Reagan fought against federal regulations because he thought they stifled these virtues. Reagan charged that Americans' freedoms were in jeopardy because of the emergence of a "permanent government." According to Reagan, the federal bureaucracy had grown so powerful it could set policy and regulate the economy regardless of the desires of ordinary citizens or elected officials. Reagan spoke about waste, fraud, and gross mismanagement by federal officials.

Reagan acted decisively to cut back federal regulations in such areas as consumer protection, the

▲ *How did James Watt's policies affect such treasures as the Olympic National Park, pictured above?*

environment, and health and safety. Reagan believed that such regulations stifled economic growth by restricting business freedom. Deregulation of the economy had already begun under President Carter. Carter had targeted regulations that limited competition and kept prices high in the trucking, railroad, airline, and telephone industries. Consumers generally applauded these actions, since prices fell and service often improved.

Unlike Carter, the Reagan team made little distinction between those regulations that stifled competition and those that protected consumers, the environment, or workers. Wanting to "get government off the backs of the people," the administration reduced or eliminated hundreds of federal regulations. James Watt, secretary of the Interior Department, thought that economic development was more important than environmental protection. A lawyer and New Right activist from Colorado, Watt, on taking office, said, "We will mine more, drill more, cut more timber." At Watt's direction, the Interior Department stopped acquiring new lands for national parks. He purged the department of career employees whom he considered to be against development or for the environment. He changed the method of leasing offshore federal oil lands so that oil companies, rather than government, would determine which lands to exploit.

Federal agencies vigorously pursued deregulation. The Environmental Protection Agency

rewrote many regulations that previously restricted development. The National Highway Traffic Safety Administration lowered requirements that automobile manufacturers make cars more fuel efficient and install safety air bags. Federal Communications Commission head Mark Fowler resisted regulation of broadcast television, saying, "Television is just another appliance. It's a toaster with pictures." The Reagan administration deregulated the banking industry, the savings and loan industry, and the stock market. These measures encouraged widespread financial speculation and soon led to abuses. The Justice Department took a more relaxed approach to antitrust laws, which fueled a new round of corporate mergers.

The Department of Energy and the Nuclear Regulatory Agency ignored mounting evidence of problems in the nuclear industry. Civilian nuclear power plants were rarely penalized for safety violations. Military facilities often had such severe on-site nuclear pollution that they were shut down. Even so, with Reagan's push to produce more nuclear weapons and save money at the same time, these agencies scrimped on safety measures. As chemical and radioactive pollution seeped outside these plants, alarmed local communities sometimes demanded plant shutdowns.

The Economy Rebounds

President Reagan inherited a dismal economic situation from his predecessor Jimmy Carter. Recession, inflation, and budget deficits shook business confidence, and the recession begun in 1981 deepened in 1982. Unemployment rose to 10.7 percent, the highest since 1941. Interest rates had declined but were still a staggering 16.5 percent. Businesses were failing more than at any time since the Great Depression at a rate nearly three times higher than in 1979.

Then, in the summer of 1982, with the economy a shambles, the Federal Reserve Board cut interest rates to a two-year low of 10 percent. By early 1983, the economy began to respond to lower interest rates, tax cuts, and massive federal defense spending. In 1984, the gross national product (GNP) grew rapidly, and unemployment fell to 7.2 percent. The rate of inflation fell to 5 percent. Wall Street financial analyst Louis Rukeyser observed that Federal Reserve policy and the 1983 tax cut have "now clearly produced a near-boom snapback from last year's severe recession." Rukeyser was right.

SECTION 2 REVIEW

1. **List** three main points of Reagan's 1981 economic program.
2. **Identify** the main premise of supply-side economics.
3. **Define** the term *New Federalism*.
4. **Explain** President Reagan's desire for deregulation and what effects the policy had on environmental protection.
5. **Discuss** reasons for the economic recovery by 1984.

SECTION 3

Domestic Complications

In 1984, no one challenged Ronald Reagan to become the Republican Party's presidential nominee. In his acceptance speech at the Republican National Convention, Reagan blasted the Democrats as the party of high taxes and inflation. He warned that returning Democrats to power under Walter Mondale would mean a return to the economic distress of the 1970s. The Republican platform called for constitutional amendments to ban abortion and to require a balanced federal budget, and it flatly opposed any increase in taxes. In contrast, Walter Mondale surprised many observers by bluntly warning about mounting federal budget deficits and the need to raise taxes: "Mr. Reagan will raise taxes and so will I. He won't tell you. I just did."

What accounted for Reagan's resounding reelection in 1984?

What effects did federal budget deficits have on the economy and politics?

What values guided Reagan's appointments to the Supreme Court?

The Second Term

As President Reagan stood for reelection in 1984, he had accomplished little of significance in foreign affairs, even though he had devoted a lot of energy to this area. But the American people generally liked his nationalistic, assertive, anti-Soviet style. More important for his reelection prospects, the economy was booming. Although Democrats and many economists issued warnings about the nation's growing budget deficits, the GNP had expanded rapidly, unemployment had dropped, businesses and corporations were investing heavily in expanding their plants and equipment, and foreign investment funds were pouring into the country.

Thus, Reagan approached the 1984 elections with confidence, promising the public more of the same. To "stay the course," Reagan again chose George Bush as his vice presidential running mate. The Democrats, on the other hand, were still in disarray. A large number of presidential hopefuls waged

▼ *President Reagan and Walter Mondale debated on television during the 1984 presidential election campaign.*

a brutal primary election battle. Walter Mondale, Jimmy Carter's vice president, eventually secured the Democratic Party nomination. Mondale chose Geraldine Ferraro, a New York congresswoman, as his running mate, the first woman ever to run on a major political party's presidential ticket.

The outcome of the election was never seriously in doubt. According to one Gallup poll, Reagan led Mondale by 64 to 36 percent for his "strong leadership qualities" and by 63 to 37 percent for his "colorful, interesting personality." Mondale did lead Reagan for his concern about the problems of women, blacks, and the average citizen. Even so, this perception branded Mondale as a liberal candidate, a very negative label in the minds of most voters at that time. It was associated with high government spending and high taxes. Mondale's association with the Carter presidency also hurt him.

People Who Made a Difference

Sandra Day O'Connor

In the 1980 campaign, Ronald Reagan pledged not only to appoint conservatives to the Supreme Court, but the first woman as well. Just three months into Reagan's first term, Justice Potter Stewart, after serving 22 years on the Court, decided to resign. Reagan told his advisers he wanted women on the list of candidates to be considered for the nomination. Women with the proper conservative legal qualifications were few, and Sandra Day O'Connor's stock rose quickly. She was a conservative and a Republican. Moreover, her prominence in Arizona politics gave her the backing of Senator Barry Goldwater from Arizona and of Chief Justice William Rehnquist.

Sandra Day was born in El Paso, Texas, in 1930. She grew up on a 300-acre ranch straddling the border between Arizona and New Mexico. There she learned the necessity of hard work. By age ten, she could drive trucks and tractors, brand calves, repair fences, and shoot a rifle. After attending pri-

▲ Sandra Day O'Connor was the first woman to serve on the Supreme Court.

vate school in El Paso, she went to Stanford University, where she earned her undergraduate and law degrees in just five years. Her outstanding academic credentials, however, failed to land her a job with a major law firm in the San Francisco area. These firms usually hired only male lawyers. In 1957, she and her husband John O'Connor settled in Phoenix where she joined a law firm, raised three children, and became active in state Republican politics.

There was little question about O'Connor's qualifications to serve on the Supreme Court. Still, her judicial experience had been limited. To compensate for that inexperience, O'Connor worked relentlessly. Through hard work, she made herself into one of the most respected members of the Court. Probably the most moderate of the conservatives on the Court, by 1987 she held the pivotal vote on the most important and controversial cases coming before the Court—affirmative action, abortion, religion, the death penalty, and criminal justice. The opinions she wrote and the votes she cast were rather unpredictable, since she judged specific cases on their own merits, not according to any one set way of thinking.

1. What prompted Reagan to nominate O'Connor to be the first woman on the Supreme Court?

2. Why has Justice O'Connor been so important to the court?

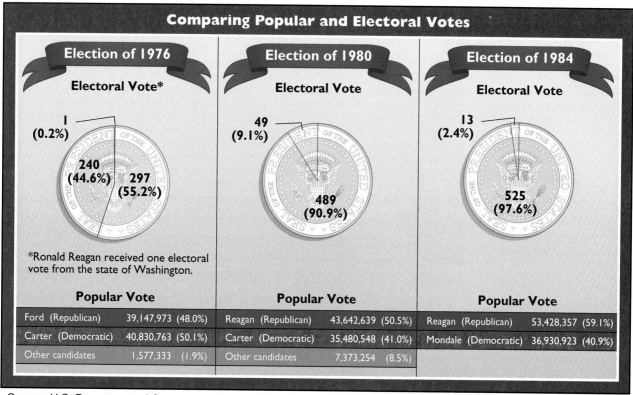

Comparing Popular and Electoral Votes

Election of 1976

Electoral Vote*

1 (0.2%)
240 (44.6%)
297 (55.2%)

*Ronald Reagan received one electoral vote from the state of Washington.

Popular Vote

Ford (Republican)	39,147,973	(48.0%)
Carter (Democratic)	40,830,763	(50.1%)
Other candidates	1,577,333	(1.9%)

Election of 1980

Electoral Vote

49 (9.1%)
489 (90.9%)

Popular Vote

Reagan (Republican)	43,642,639	(50.5%)
Carter (Democratic)	35,480,548	(41.0%)
Other candidates	7,373,254	(8.5%)

Election of 1984

Electoral Vote

13 (2.4%)
525 (97.6%)

Popular Vote

Reagan (Republican)	53,428,357	(59.1%)
Mondale (Democratic)	36,930,923	(40.9%)

Source: U.S. Department of Commerce, Bureau of the Census.

▲ *Ronald Reagan's landslide victories were similar to those of President Eisenhower in 1952 and 1956. How does the percentage of electoral votes received by Mondale compare to the percentage of the popular vote he received?*

Reagan won the 1984 election by a landslide. Mondale carried only his home state, Minnesota, and the District of Columbia. Reagan got 525 electoral votes compared to Mondale's 13, and 59 to 41 percent of the popular vote. The voters had resoundingly ratified Reagan's presidency. Second terms, however, have often proved difficult for reelected presidents, whatever their margin of victory.

Problems with Economic Boom

The economic recovery that began in 1983 continued through much of Reagan's second term. The boom rested on vast defense spending made possible by equally vast borrowing. By the end of Reagan's second term, the federal deficit was nearly three times higher than the deficits of all his presidential predecessors combined.

Many Americans began to worry about these mounting debts. Some supported additional cuts in federal spending, although there was little agreement about what should be cut. In December 1985, Congress passed the **Gramm-Rudman-Hollings Act**. This law required major deficit reductions over five years and automatic budget cuts should the president and Congress not agree on a budget. It also required that Congress specify how new programs would be funded before they could be enacted. Then, in 1986, Congress enacted sweeping tax reform. It simplified the federal tax code, ended many tax shelters, dropped millions of low-income people from the tax rolls, and shifted the tax burden from individuals to corporations. But tax reform did little to reduce the federal deficit.

The growing deficit created many economic problems. Interest payments on the federal debt grew to $151 billion annually. Because prices for U.S.-made goods were relatively high, demand for U.S. exports was low. As a result, the United States

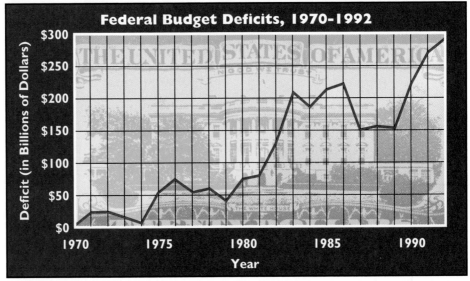

Federal Budget Deficits, 1970-1992

Annual budget deficits tripled between Carter's last budget and Reagan's 1986 budget. Does this graph record the accumulated national debt?

Source: *Economic Report of the President* (Washington, D.C.: U.S. Government Printing Office, 1993).

became a debtor nation for the first time since World War I. In 1980, foreign investors owed the United States an average of $2,500 per family. In 1988, by contrast, the United States owed foreign investors nearly $7,000 per family.

Reagan's economic policies led to other problems. His tax cuts fell unequally on the public, with people in upper income brackets getting much bigger tax benefits. This meant that more money was available for investment purposes. Unfortunately, much of this potential investment went into stock-market speculation. As a result of such speculation, many stocks' prices rose far beyond their actual value or earning power. Eventually, the prices of stocks would have to move toward their real market value. In late 1987, the stock market experienced a severe crash, the worst since 1929. The stock-market crash wiped out many investors and undermined business confidence. Within six months, however, the stock market had recovered fully and business investment had begun to increase.

The New Right's Agenda

Ronald Reagan supported the political and social agenda of the New Right. The federal courts had long been a target of conservatives. Reagan's Justice Department began to screen potential federal judges carefully. Of primary concern were their views on abortion, school prayer, affirmative action, police powers, and criminal rights. During his two terms, Reagan appointed nearly 400 federal judges; these made up the majority of sitting judges when he left office in 1989. In addition, he chose one chief justice and three associate justices for the Supreme Court. The Senate confirmed **Sandra Day O'Connor** (in 1981), and William Rehnquist was promoted from associate to chief justice in 1986. Antonin Scalia was also confirmed in 1986 as an associate justice without much dissent.

▼ *What message was intended by the creator of this editorial cartoon?*

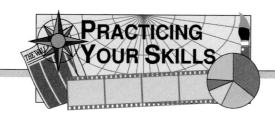

PRACTICING YOUR SKILLS

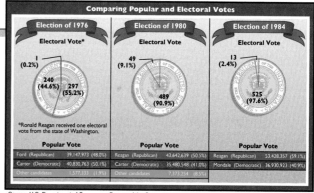

Comparing Popular and Electoral Votes

Election of 1976	Election of 1980	Election of 1984
Electoral Vote*	**Electoral Vote**	**Electoral Vote**
1 (0.2%)	49 (9.1%)	13 (2.4%)
240 (44.6%) 297 (55.2%)	489 (90.9%)	525 (97.6%)

*Ronald Reagan received one electoral vote from the state of Washington.

Popular Vote		
Ford (Republican) 39,147,973 (48.0%)	Reagan (Republican) 43,642,639 (50.5%)	Reagan (Republican) 53,428,357 (59.1%)
Carter (Democratic) 40,830,763 (50.1%)	Carter (Democratic) 35,480,548 (41.0%)	Mondale (Democratic) 36,930,923 (40.9%)
Other candidates 1,577,333 (1.9%)	Other candidates 7,373,254 (8.5%)	

Source: U.S. Department of Commerce, Bureau of the Census.

Analyzing Pie Charts

Every four years on the Tuesday after the first Monday in the month of November, Americans choose their president. When the votes are counted, political analysts make generalizations about the significance of the results, as well as predictions about how the results will affect future elections.

Review the guidelines for comparing multiple graphs in the Practicing Your Skills on page 719. Then, answer the following questions about the graphs on page 1021:

1. What type of graphs are represented here?
2. (a) What theme or topic are the graphs illustrating? (b) What time period is covered by the graphs?
3. (a) How many electoral votes were cast in each of the elections? (b) How many electoral votes would a candidate have to receive to win the election?
4. (a) How many electoral votes did Carter receive in 1976? (b) What percentage of the electoral votes did Carter receive? (c) How many popular votes did Carter receive? (d) What percentage of the popular vote did Carter receive? (e) How would you describe this election in terms of closeness?
5. (a) How many electoral votes did Carter receive in 1980? (b) What percentage of the electoral

votes did Carter receive? (c) How many popular votes did Carter receive? (d) What percentage of the popular vote did Carter receive? (e) Was this a close election?

6. (a) How many electoral votes did Reagan receive in 1984? (b) What percentage of the electoral votes did Reagan receive? (c) How many popular votes did Reagan receive? (d) What percentage of the popular vote did Reagan receive? (e) How would you describe this election in terms of closeness?
7. Why does it appear that the Republican candidate won by a much larger majority in 1984 than in 1980?
8. (a) After examining these graphs, what trend do you see? (b) Could you make a prediction for the 1988 and 1992 elections based on these graphs? Why, or why not? (c) What other factors play a more important role in elections than previous election results or voting trends?

Reagan had more difficulty filling a third vacancy on the Court. In 1987, the Senate, again in Democratic hands, rejected Reagan's nomination of Robert Bork to the Supreme Court. Anthony Kennedy, a federal appeals court judge from California, easily won Senate confirmation in late 1988. Ironically, Kennedy's views were similar to those of Bork, but Kennedy's personal manner was less grating and combative. The Supreme Court

now had a clearly conservative majority, although it remained to be seen what effect this more conservative majority would have on constitutional issues.

The Reagan administration acted in other ways in behalf of the New Right's social agenda. The Justice Department argued in the courts against affirmative action programs. Reagan also urged Congress not to renew the landmark 1965 Voting Rights Act, which had protected African

Americans' rights to register and vote. When Congress renewed the law anyway, the Justice Department often declined to investigate alleged violations of the law. The Department of Education and the Equal Employment Opportunity Commission (EEOC) also failed to process similar complaints about age-, gender-, and race-related discrimination.

SECTION 3 REVIEW

1. **State** two reasons for the overwhelming reelection of Reagan in 1984.
2. **Explain** why federal budget deficits became an important issue during Reagan's second term.
3. **Summarize** the main purpose of the Gramm-Rudman-Hollings Act of 1985.
4. **Identify** causes of the 1987 stock-market crash.
5. **Describe** how President Reagan sought to promote the New Right's agenda through federal courts.

SECTION 4

Reagan's Foreign Policies

In August 1984, as Reagan prepared to deliver one of his frequent Saturday morning radio talks, he spoke into a microphone to test sound levels. A technician mistakenly turned on the microphone, and radio listeners heard some of Reagan's unscripted remarks. "My fellow Americans," Reagan declared, "I'm pleased to tell you today that I've signed legislation that will outlaw the Soviet Union forever. We begin bombing in five minutes." Reagan's offhand remarks were a good indicator of his anti-Communist and anti-Soviet views. These firmly held beliefs underlay most of Reagan's defense and foreign policies.

What were the major elements of Reagan's defense policies?

What happened in U.S.-Soviet relations during Reagan's first term?

Why did Reagan and Gorbachev seek better relations between their countries after 1985?

Worsening U.S.-Soviet Relations

U.S.-Soviet relations, which had steadily deteriorated during Carter's presidency, grew even worse during Reagan's first term. Reagan described the Soviet Union as "the focus of evil in the modern world," led by people who "reserved the right to lie, cheat, and steal" their way to world domination. Further, he charged that a Soviet conspiracy underlay "all the unrest that is going on. If they weren't engaged in this game of dominoes, there wouldn't be any trouble spots in the world."

A number of events reinforced these beliefs. In December 1981, the activities of Solidarity, an independent labor union in Poland, undermined the Soviet-supported Communist government there. Moscow forced the Polish government to impose martial law in order to stop Solidarity and quiet the unrest. Reagan accused the Soviets of unleashing the "forces of tyranny" and asked Americans to light "candles of freedom" for Solidarity. Reagan also imposed embargoes on selling U.S.-made computers to the Soviets and on materials for a natural-gas pipeline between the Soviet Union and Western Europe. The latter provoked considerable opposition among America's European allies, who needed Soviet natural gas to decrease their dependency on Middle Eastern oil. Reagan soon lifted the embargo.

In 1983, the Soviets shot down South Korean Airline flight 007, a civilian plane flying from Alaska to Seoul. The plane had strayed off course and flown over Soviet territory where a secret missile test site was located. A Soviet fighter shot the plane down, killing 269 passengers, including 69 Americans. Reagan denounced the attack as "an act of barbarism" and a "massacre" and moved to cut back cultural, scientific, and diplomatic exchanges between the U.S. and the Soviets. Reagan also used the episode to pressure Congress to enact his defense requests.

Meanwhile, anti-Communism led Reagan to revise Carter's human rights initiatives. The Carter administration had criticized human rights violations by a number of authoritarian regimes. Reagan, however, wanted the support of these regimes in opposing Communism. Consequently, he established closer diplomatic ties with Brazil, Haiti, Panama, Pakistan, and the Philippines, and increased economic and military aid to these countries. For Reagan and his foreign policy advisers, relations with any regime were justifiable so long as the regime was anti-Communist.

Against this backdrop, Reagan initially avoided any negotiations with the "evil empire." When a reporter asked about his reluctance to hold a summit meeting with the Soviets, Reagan quipped that the Soviet leaders "keep dying on me." Indeed, Soviet leadership was unstable after Leonid Brezhnev, the Soviet leader since 1964, died in 1982. Brezhnev's successors, Yuri Andropov and Konstantin Chernenko, both suffered chronic illnesses and died in office. Only in 1985, when **Mikhail Gorbachev** became general secretary of the Soviet Communist Party, did Soviet leadership stabilize.

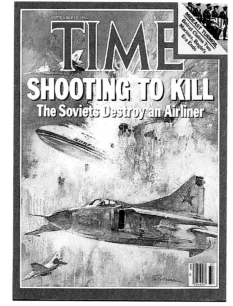

▲ *This lead article concerned Korean Airlines Flight 007.*

trillion. Reagan wanted to increase the number of navy warships from 456 to 600 to counter the recent expansion of the Soviet navy. He also wanted to develop new systems to deliver nuclear weapons, including new types of bombers and new land-based and airplane-launched (cruise) missiles. Perhaps most controversial was Reagan's call for the Strategic Defense Initiative (SDI), a vast research and development program designed to create an antimissile defense system. Its developers hoped to produce high-energy laser beams that could shoot down Soviet missiles in flight. It was this high-tech science fiction aspect of the program that earned it the "Star Wars" nickname.

Reagan's defense program was strongly criticized. First, critics disputed Reagan's assertion that the United States had fallen behind the Soviets militarily in the 1970s. When

▼ *Although "Star Wars" employed laser beams for military purposes, Space Shuttle* Discovery's *experimental laser helped scientists gather information.*

Increases in U.S. Defense Spending

Reagan was sure that the best defense and foreign policies depended on renewed military strength. He also believed that Soviet actions in Afghanistan, Angola, and elsewhere had only been possible because of the recent growth in Soviet military power. Although Reagan conceded that the United States had a nine-to-seven advantage over the Soviets in nuclear warheads, the Soviets had larger missiles, more destructive nuclear warheads, and advantages in conventional forces. Reagan wanted to reestablish a clear U.S. military advantage over the Soviets. "Defense is not a budget item," Reagan told his staff. "You spend what you need."

Reagan proposed the largest, most expensive peacetime military expansion in U.S. history. The increase over eight years would total nearly $1.8

asked whether he would exchange forces with the Soviets, General John Vessey, head of the Joint Chiefs of Staff, replied, "Not on your life." Second, critics questioned the economic wisdom of Reagan's spending on weapons rather than domestic programs. They saw the issue as an example of the classic choice between "guns or butter." Proposed cuts in domestic programs alone would not pay for Reagan's increased defense spending. The result, they argued, would be enormous borrowing and staggering budget deficits.

Third, some critics warned that SDI would stimulate the U.S.-Soviet arms race. The Soviets would respond by producing enough new missiles to overwhelm the SDI defense. Despite such opposition, Reagan got much of what he wanted through Congress.

U.S.-Soviet Relations Improve

In 1985, Mikhail Gorbachev emerged suddenly as a new Soviet leader with a major reform agenda. Gorbachev wanted to transform the internal politics and domestic economy of the Soviet Union, and at the same time improve Soviet relations with the rest of the world. He had to accomplish the second goal in order to achieve the first. While Soviet citizens stood for hours in long lines to purchase scarce food and consumer items, the Soviet government spent billions of rubles (Soviet currency) on tanks and rockets. In 1985, more than 10 percent of the Soviet GNP went to defense. The Soviet economy could not increase productivity or meet growing consumer demands as long as Soviet resources were so heavily committed to military purposes. Thus, Gorbachev announced two new policies. **Glasnost** was the term Gorbachev used to describe the policy of greater openness in Soviet society. **Perestroika** identified the policy of allowing more freedom in the Soviet economy away from total state control toward a market or capitalist system. He also proposed startling cuts in Soviet defense spending and expressed a desire for new cooperation with the U.S. and its allies.

▲ *Reagan visited Mikhail Gorbachev in Moscow in June 1988. What was ironic about this meeting?*

At first, Reagan thought Gorbachev's proposals were yet another Soviet trick to lull the West into a false sense of security. Slowly, contrary evidence accumulated. Glasnost resulted in the release of political opponents from prison. The Soviet people were allowed to criticize the Soviet regime. Scholars experienced a new freedom of expression, and art and theater also flowered. Perestroika led to changes in the Soviet economy, including the establishment of farmers' markets where people sold homegrown produce. To sustain the momentum for change at home, Gorbachev aggressively pursued renewed U.S.-Soviet arms reduction talks. Pressured by U.S. allies in Western Europe, Reagan agreed to meet with the Soviet leader.

Reagan and Gorbachev would hold five summit meetings in the next two and a half years. Not all the summit conferences went well. The two leaders first met in Geneva in November 1985. They were cool to each other, and they accomplished little. They next met in Reykjavík, Iceland, in October 1986. Gorbachev surprised Reagan by proposing that both nations reduce their strategic nuclear weapons by 50 percent in exchange for canceling the Strategic Defense Initiative. In the end, however, neither would compromise on SDI. Still, they established a foundation for further talks.

By 1987, it was Reagan—struggling with scandals and the stock-market crash—who badly needed a foreign policy success. In December 1987, the two leaders met in Washington and signed the Intermediate Nuclear Forces (INF) Treaty. They agreed to withdraw and destroy all the short- and intermediate-range missiles placed in Europe over the past decade. Then, in April 1988, Gorbachev announced the withdrawal of Soviet troops from Afghanistan. This had been a barrier to better U.S.-Soviet relations since 1979.

In June 1988, Reagan traveled to Moscow. Even though the Strategic Arms Reduction Talks begun in 1982 were still stalled because of SDI, the meeting was cordial. Reagan's very presence symbolized better relations. He said, "They've changed," and he called Gorbachev "friend." In December 1988, the two leaders again met, along with President-elect George Bush, in New York City. At the United Nations, Gorbachev announced a reduction of Soviet conventional forces. In a very short period of time, the two leaders, each for his own reasons, had taken giant steps toward more peaceful relations between the two superpowers.

SECTION 4 REVIEW

1. **Explain** why U.S. and Soviet relations cooled during Reagan's first administration.
2. **State** the main reason Reagan first moved U.S. foreign policy away from détente.
3. **Describe** the purpose of the Strategic Defense Initiative.
4. **Define** perestroika and glasnost.
5. **Discuss** reasons that led Gorbachev and Reagan to pursue better relations after 1985.

SECTION 5

Foreign Policy Frustrations

By the 1980s, Libyan dictator Colonel Muammar Gadhafi's plans for expanding his control in Africa, his hatred of Israel, and his growing military ties with the Soviet Union had put him on a collision course with the United States. Gadhafi received huge revenues from oil sales, and he used some of this money to support terrorist groups in the Middle East and Europe. In April 1986, Reagan blamed Gadhafi for the terrorist bombing of a West Berlin nightclub frequented by U.S. soldiers. The bombing resulted in the death of a U.S. soldier. Reagan called Gadhafi "the mad dog of the Middle East" and ordered a bombing raid on Libya. Dozens were injured in the attack, but Gadhafi himself escaped injury. Many Americans thought the attack on Libya was a mistake, a matter of replying to one kind of terrorism with another. Still, the attack succeeded in forcing Gadhafi to be much more cautious in supporting terrorism. Reagan would have few such successes during his second term.

What frustrations did Reagan face concerning U.S. policies in the Middle East and Latin America?
What were the major issues in the Iran-contra scandal?
What did the Iran-contra scandal show about President Reagan's administration?

Vexing Problems in the Middle East

Reagan's opposition to communism influenced his policies in the Middle East. In 1981, Reagan and Secretary of State Alexander Haig attempted to form an anti-Soviet alliance involving Israel, Saudi Arabia, Jordan, and Egypt. All these nations welcomed increased American aid, but each was more concerned about its local rivals than about any Soviet threat. The Arabs continued to see Israel as the primary threat to Middle Eastern peace. Israel continued to distrust its Arab neighbors.

▲ *After a 1983 terrorist bomb attack, rescue crews worked through the wreckage of a U.S. Marine Corps command center near the Beirut airport.*

A major stumbling block to peace in the region was the Palestinian question. **The Palestine Liberation Organization (PLO)** had vowed to continue attacks on Israel and to take back Israeli-controlled lands on the West Bank of the Jordan River for a Palestinian homeland. In June 1982, Israel invaded Lebanon, its northern neighbor, in order to destroy PLO forces and Syrian missiles there. Both had been used in terrorist attacks on Israel. Israel's action angered many of Reagan's closest advisers, and they criticized Haig for having encouraged the Israeli attack. Haig resigned, and Reagan replaced him with George Schultz.

In August 1982, Reagan and Schultz urged Israel to give the PLO land on the West Bank in return for Arab guarantees of peace. Neither the Israelis nor the PLO agreed. Meanwhile, the situation in Lebanon became even more chaotic. In September, Reagan sent U.S. Marines to Lebanon as part of a multinational peacekeeping force. Lebanese Muslims bitterly resented the Western intrusion. In April 1983, a suicide squad attacked the U.S. embassy in Beirut, killing 63 people. Then, in October, another tragedy occurred when a Palestinian suicide squad bombed the U.S. Marine barracks near Beirut, killing 241 marines. Reagan, under criticism for endangering the lives of American military personnel, withdrew the marines in February 1984.

Other conflicts wracked the region. Between 1980 and 1988, Iran and Iraq fought one another in a bloody war for influence in the oil-rich Persian Gulf area. It was difficult for the U.S. government to choose sides. On the one hand, Iranian hostility and memories of the Iranian hostage crisis influenced U.S. policymakers. On the other hand, Iraqi president Saddam Hussein's Soviet ties and his ambitions to expand his control worried Reagan's advisers. A victory by either nation would probably result in its domination of the Persian Gulf. U.S. policy therefore sought to create a stalemate by supporting whichever side appeared to be losing the war at any given time. Between 1981 and 1986, the United States generally—although secretly—supported Iran. When Iran appeared to be near victory in 1987, the U.S. increased its aid to Iraq. In 1988, with a death toll of nearly 2 million people, the two nations agreed to a cease-fire.

Meanwhile, Middle Eastern terrorism continued unabated. Terrorist acts were often committed by powerless splinter groups associated with the Palestinians or with Islamic fundamentalists. The acts were desperate attempts by these groups to force the Western world to pay attention to their grievances. Instead, terrorist acts, such as hijackings or bombings, usually provoked outrage rather than understanding. The Reagan administration spoke out against "state-sponsored terrorism." President Reagan told an American Bar Association audience that "America will never make concessions to terrorists," and called Iran and Libya "outlaw states."

Grenada and Latin America

The perceived threat of Communist expansion greatly influenced Reagan's Latin American policies. Those policies met with some success but more often with frustration. One of Reagan's successes in the public's mind involved Grenada, a small island in the Caribbean Sea. In 1979 Maurice Bishop had established a Marxist government there with close ties to Cuba. Reagan ended all U.S. aid and tried to isolate Grenada from other nations in the Western Hemisphere. In mid-1983, Bishop began to draw away from Cuba and softened his anti-U.S. stand. As a result, a radical faction in Bishop's ruling party staged a coup, killed Bishop, and declared martial

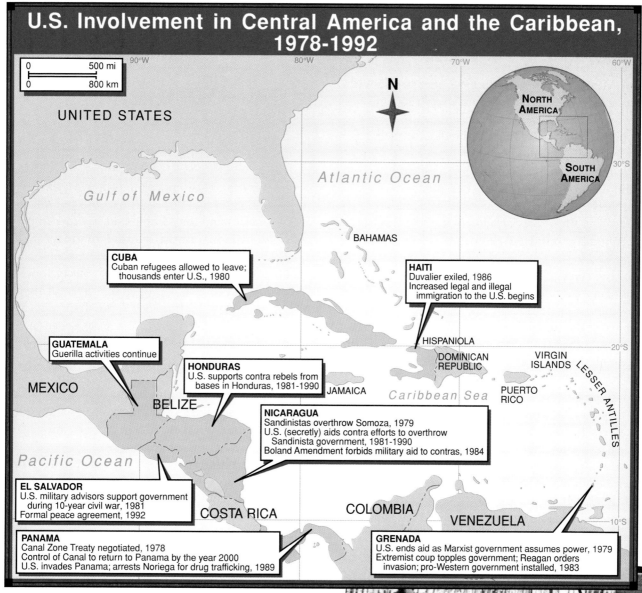

U.S. Involvement in Central America and the Caribbean, 1978-1992

CUBA
Cuban refugees allowed to leave; thousands enter U.S., 1980

HAITI
Duvalier exiled, 1986
Increased legal and illegal immigration to the U.S. begins

GUATEMALA
Guerilla activities continue

HONDURAS
U.S. supports contra rebels from bases in Honduras, 1981-1990

NICARAGUA
Sandinistas overthrow Somoza, 1979
U.S. (secretly) aids contra efforts to overthrow Sandinista government, 1981-1990
Boland Amendment forbids military aid to contras, 1984

EL SALVADOR
U.S. military advisors support government during 10-year civil war, 1981
Formal peace agreement, 1992

PANAMA
Canal Zone Treaty negotiated, 1978
Control of Canal to return to Panama by the year 2000
U.S. invades Panama; arrests Noriega for drug trafficking, 1989

GRENADA
U.S. ends aid as Marxist government assumes power, 1979
Extremist coup topples government; Reagan orders invasion; pro-Western government installed, 1983

▲ *Why was the Reagan administration so concerned about Soviet influences in Central America and the Caribbean?*

law. Reagan called the resulting regime "a brutal gang of leftist thugs." He maintained that U.S. citizens attending medical school on the island were in danger. On October 25, Reagan ordered U.S. forces to invade Grenada. After three days of fighting the

▶

President Reagan authorized the invasion of the island nation of Grenada in October 1983. Why does the president have control over the armed forces?

Grenada army and 600 Cubans, U.S. forces secured the island. Public approval of the military soared in the United States as a result.

Meanwhile, Reagan's policies met largely with frustration in Central America, an area much more important than Grenada to U.S. policy. Reagan sought a military solution to the bloody civil war raging in El Salvador. The U.S. supported a repressive regime there dominated by a few wealthy landowners and the military. U.S. military aid jumped from $6 million in 1980 to $82 million two years later. By 1983, Salvadoran death squads had tortured and murdered thousands of Salvadorans opposed to the regime. Neither U.S. military aid nor the election in 1983 of middle-of-the-roader José Napoleon Duarte as president succeeded in ending the civil war. Some 53,000 Salvadorans, one in every 100 people, lost their lives in the conflict. Six times that many Salvadoran refugees entered the United States—most of them illegally—between 1979 and 1985. The civil war in El Salvador would continue beyond Reagan's presidency.

Nicaragua was equally vexing to Reagan and his advisers. In 1979, President Carter had sent aid to the Sandinistas after they overthrew the cruel dictatorship of Anastasio Somoza in Nicaragua. Reagan believed, however, that the Sandinistas were pawns of the Soviet Union and Cuba. Moreover, Reagan accused the Sandinistas of funneling arms from the Soviets and Cubans to rebels in neighboring El Salvador. Soon, the Reagan administration committed itself to toppling the Sandinistan regime, and it began secret support, through the CIA, of anti-Sandinistan forces known as **contras.**

Congressional opposition to supporting the contras grew as news of the CIA's secret actions—including the mining of Nicaraguan ports—became public. The Boland Amendment, enacted by Congress in 1984, forbade any military aid to the contras from the Defense Department, the CIA, or any other U.S. agency. But several of Reagan's National Security Council (NSC) advisers were unwilling to abandon the contras or abide by the Boland Amendment. They raised funds from private donors in the United States and other countries. Saudi Arabia, for example, contributed $32 million over 18 months to buy weapons for them. Marine Colonel Oliver North, an NSC staffer, gave potential donors impassioned briefings about the contras' bleak situation. North's plea would then be followed by a sales pitch from a nongovernment associate.

The Iran-Contra Scandal

It is important to understand the Reagan administration's foreign policy frustrations in both Latin America and the Middle East in order to understand the **Iran-contra scandal**. In the spring of 1985, U.S. and Israeli intelligence agents proposed a plan that the U.S. should supply weapons to Iran in return for that country's cooperation in securing the release of several U.S. hostages. A pro-Iranian terrorist group was holding these hostages in Lebanon. Israel would serve as a go-between. Although Reagan had insisted that the U.S. would never negotiate with terrorists or ransom the hostages, that was exactly what this scheme proposed to do. The president truly sympathized with the hostages and their families, and he was frustrated because nothing had worked to secure their release.

Reagan authorized the first transfer of weapons in August 1985, over the strenuous objections of both Secretary of Defense Weinberger and Secretary of State Schultz. Only one hostage was released, but the process had been set in motion. Reagan soon considered another weapons-hostage exchange with Iran early in 1986. Again, Weinberger and Schultz adamantly opposed the idea, and they thought they had won the argument. But Reagan sided with his NSC advisers and agreed to exchange more weapons for hostages.

At this point, the link was forged between the Iranian arms deals and funding for Nicaraguan contras. Because the amount Iran paid for the arms was more than it cost to replace these weapons, the sales made a profit. Oliver North spent this money on arms for the Nicaraguan contras, joking that the Iranians were making a "*contra*bution." North believed this action was a legal way around the Boland Amendment, which only barred spending money appropriated by Congress. Consciously or not, North misread the law. Federal statutes required that profits from sales of federal property had to be turned over to the U. S. Treasury. Federal laws also barred the executive branch from spending any funds that Congress had not appropriated.

As the scheme unfolded, it was practically inevitable that word of it would leak to the press. When the story broke, several investigations began. One, the Tower Commission, chaired by former Senator John Tower, a Republican, said that President Reagan did not know about the Iran-contra link before it was publicly disclosed. The commission, however, stunned the nation with its portrait of a chief executive far removed from decision-making responsibilities. Reagan, the commission reported, "did not seem to be aware" of either the specific actions being taken in his name or of the implications and consequences of those actions. It seemed that Reagan's NSC staff could act with almost total freedom simply by phrasing memos and briefings so that the president would not know the full extent of the illegal actions taken in his name.

In congressional hearings on the scandal, even more frightening news surfaced. A few of Reagan's NSC advisers testified that they felt free to create a secret government beyond the reach of the law or the oversight of Congress. Admiral Poindexter testified that he had the right and duty to lie to Congress and to the press. He argued that since he knew what the president wanted and the people had elected the president, he had had the authority to act as he did. Moreover, Poindexter decided not to inform the president of policy details so that Reagan could deny that he had approved the scheme in case it became known. Poindexter thought that protecting the president in this way was more important than giving Reagan the details so he could make an informed decision.

North acknowledged that he had lied repeatedly to Congress and admitted shredding hundreds of documents to cover the trail of responsibility in the scandal. Even more shocking, North testified that he, Poindexter, and CIA director William Casey had planned to finance "an overseas entity capable of conducting activities similar to the ones we had conducted here." In essence, "the enterprise," as North called it, would be a secret CIA operating outside the CIA, the normal system of government, and the rule of law. When asked how he could be confident about the wisdom of such operations,

▲ In 1988, Special Prosecutor Lawrence Walsh indicted Colonel Oliver North (pictured taking oath) and others for Iran-contra arms deals.

North replied that these actions could be trusted because they would be run by patriots like himself.

Together, the Tower Commission report and congressional hearings suggested that Reagan's administration was not really under the control of its chief executive. By late fall 1987, observers of virtually every political persuasion had concluded that the Reagan presidency was finished, a victim of its own excesses and of Reagan's passive management style. *Washington Post* columnist David Broder wrote, "No sadder tale could be spun . . . than the unraveling of yet another presidency." Wyoming Republican Richard Cheney observed, "You have to say it's a pretty fundamental flaw that would allow a lieutenant colonel on the White House staff to operate in defiance of the law."

SECTION 5 REVIEW

1. **Discuss** events that prompted President Reagan to send U.S. Marines to Lebanon in 1982.
2. **State** reasons given for the American invasion of Grenada.
3. **Identify** the Boland amendment.
4. **Describe** how the sale of arms to Iran involved Nicaraguan contras.
5. **Explain** how the Iran-contra scandal pointed out flaws in President Reagan's management style.

Summary

President Ronald Reagan was able to accomplish many of the things he set out to do. He succeeded in reducing federal income taxes, he changed the nation's domestic priorities by slashing spending on a range of federal welfare programs, and he eliminated many business regulations. Reagan also convinced Congress to increase military spending drastically. His many appointments to the federal courts ensured a more conservative judiciary for years to come. Reagan benefited from the willingness of Mikhail Gorbachev to negotiate revolutionary changes in U.S.-Soviet relations. Despite several reversals in his second term, Reagan retired with a 53 percent public approval rating.

On the other hand, Reagan's economic policies created huge federal budget deficits, and these had, and would continue to have, profound negative effects on the economy and government services at all levels. His support for limited government and his antiregulatory philosophy and policies led to financial speculation and increasing problems of environmental cleanup. Finally, the scandals that came to light both during and after his administration cast doubt on Reagan's ethics, and they revealed the weaknesses of his hands-off management style. Reagan's legacies would continue to shape the nation in the years to come.

Vocabulary

contra   New Right
glasnost   perestroika
New Federalism   supply-side economics

Write each of the vocabulary terms on a piece of paper. Under each term write the phrases listed below that best describe or relate to that vocabulary term. Use each phrase only once.

1. Boland Amendment
2. restore traditional morality
3. eliminating federal regulations
4. openness in Soviet society
5. looking toward a market economy
6. rebel guerrilla fighters
7. release of prisoners
8. increased local and state taxes
9. against affirmative action
10. reduce big government
11. local choice over block grants
12. CIA covert actions
13. condemned the welfare state
14. large tax cuts
15. criticism of Soviet leaders

Review Questions

1. Describe briefly the social and political agenda of the New Right.
2. How did Reagan's handling of the PATCO strike help his public image?
3. What were some of the traditional American virtues that guided Reagan's thinking during his administration?
4. Describe areas that Reagan targeted for government deregulation.
5. How was Reagan able to win such an overwhelming victory in the 1984 election?
6. Describe the economic problems caused by the growing federal deficit.
7. Discuss the major elements of Reagan's defense policies.
8. Explain why relations between the United States and the Soviet Union changed so dramatically during Reagan's two terms.
9. What were the major problems faced by President Reagan in dealing with Nicaragua?
10. What role did Oliver North play in the Iran-contra scandal?

Critical Historical Thinking

Writing Answer each of the following by writing one or more complete paragraphs:

1. Compare the Iran-contra scandal during the Reagan administration with the Watergate scandal during the Nixon administration. In what ways were they similar? In what ways were they different?
2. Explain how Gorbachev's policies of glasnost and perestroika improved relations with the Reagan administration.
3. Discuss how the Iran-contra scandal may have raised questions concerning the balance of power.
4. Read the selection entitled "The Duke: More Than Just A Hero" in the Unit 10 Archives. Do you think that John Wayne would have approved of President Reagan's policies? Explain your answer.

Making Connections with Shaping Public Opinion

When Ronald Reagan entered the White House at age 69, he was the oldest person ever to be inaugurated president. Yet, his campaign was the outcome of a new age in political campaigning. Reagan's campaign organization made use of the most up-to-date political techniques: direct mail and telephone campaigns to both solicit contributions and to discover public interest in issues, and the effective use of television. Ronald Reagan, a former movie actor, was an old hand at using electronic media to get his message across to the public.

What is the media's impact on politics? A public figure who finds he or she is the subject of an investigation or scandal is likely to blame the media for blowing the issue out of proportion, or making it a media event. But just what role the media plays in shaping public opinion depends on the viewer's family background, education, work experience, and age.

The media play a powerful role in shaping the public agenda, not by telling the public what to think, but by telling it what issues to think about and by emphasizing particular events and not others. Politicians will focus on these events.

Writing For several days keep a diary that records the topics, and the number of minutes per topic, covered by a 30-minute news broadcast. Also record the topics presented on the front page of a major newspaper for that same day. Write a report (or create a visual display) that compares the range and focus of the news issues covered. Does the television reporting tend to focus on stories with high visual appeal? Is the television coverage as thorough as the print media? For additional insight, compare more than one news broadcast, choosing from a cable news service as well as one of the major network channels.

Additional Skills Practice

Create three pie charts similar to the ones on page 1021 that reflect the popular vote from each of these elections, rather than the electoral vote. The information you will need is provided in the graph. Compare your graph with the graph on page 1021. Make a general statement based on the apparent differences between the graphs.

Unit Review Questions

1. What circumstances made the U.S. policy of détente possible with the Soviet Union?
2. Describe successes achieved by the Nixon administration in foreign affairs.
3. Do you think President Nixon was right to resign as president?
4. What was the major effect of the Watergate scandal on Americans?
5. Give evidence to show that President Carter made his concern for human rights a major part of his foreign policy.
6. What was one major consequence of the Iranian hostage situation?
7. What was one overall effect of Carter's foreign policy on relations with the Soviet Union?
8. Why did Carter continue to support the Shah of Iran even though there were continuous violations of human rights in that country?
9. Do you believe that President Reagan was hurt by the Iran-contra scandal?
10. State reasons why Reagan was such a popular president.

Personalizing History

Design a Poster   Design a poster that reflects the events of your youth. Use pictures, photographs of yourself, drawings, sayings, a time line, or headlines that portray life in America during the 1980s and 1990s. You could include topics such as popular music, dance, fashion, education, television, movies, politics, immigration, drugs, computers, or science.

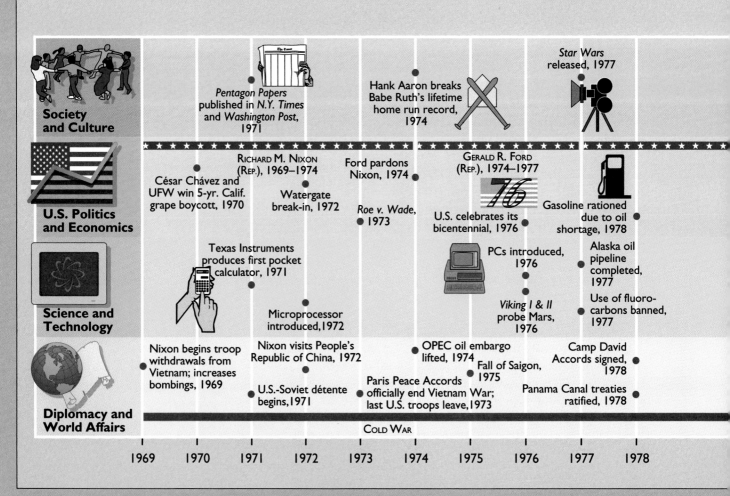

Society and Culture

Pentagon Papers published in *N.Y. Times* and *Washington Post*, 1971

Hank Aaron breaks Babe Ruth's lifetime home run record, 1974

Star Wars released, 1977

U.S. Politics and Economics

RICHARD M. NIXON (REP.), 1969–1974

César Chávez and UFW win 5-yr. Calif. grape boycott, 1970

Watergate break-in, 1972

Ford pardons Nixon, 1974

Roe v. Wade, 1973

GERALD R. FORD (REP.), 1974–1977

U.S. celebrates its bicentennial, 1976

Gasoline rationed due to oil shortage, 1978

Science and Technology

Texas Instruments produces first pocket calculator, 1971

Microprocessor introduced, 1972

PCs introduced, 1976

Viking I & II probe Mars, 1976

Alaska oil pipeline completed, 1977

Use of fluorocarbons banned, 1977

Diplomacy and World Affairs

Nixon begins troop withdrawals from Vietnam; increases bombings, 1969

Nixon visits People's Republic of China, 1972

U.S.-Soviet détente begins, 1971

OPEC oil embargo lifted, 1974

Paris Peace Accords officially end Vietnam War; last U.S. troops leave, 1973

Fall of Saigon, 1975

Camp David Accords signed, 1978

Panama Canal treaties ratified, 1978

COLD WAR

1969   1970   1971   1972   1973   1974   1975   1976   1977   1978

■ Share your poster with the class and explain one event on the poster that has had a lasting effect on you and an event that will have a lasting effect on the world. Display the posters around the classroom.

Linking Past and Present

Media Coverage The events of the 1970s still color the way we look at our leaders. There is so much negative information in the press that we seldom hear a positive end to a news story.

■ Watch the evening news for one week. Keep a record of those stories that concern political figures. How many are positive? How many are critical? How many do a fair job of unbiased reporting? Summarize your data in a short report that also in-

cludes recommendations from you on future media coverage of political issues.

Time Line Activity

Find an example of an event from this time line's "Diplomacy and World Affairs" category that caused or was the result of a specific domestic response. Explain the relationship between the two events.

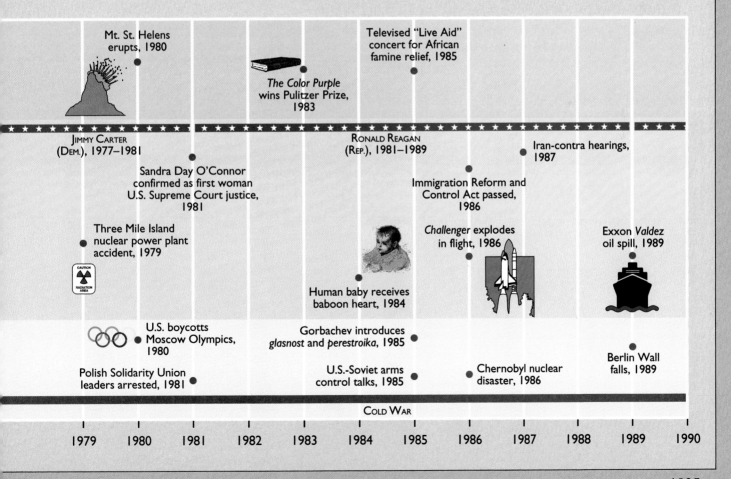

Mt. St. Helens erupts, 1980

The Color Purple wins Pulitzer Prize, 1983

Televised "Live Aid" concert for African famine relief, 1985

JIMMY CARTER (DEM.), 1977–1981

RONALD REAGAN (REP.), 1981–1989

Iran-contra hearings, 1987

Sandra Day O'Connor confirmed as first woman U.S. Supreme Court justice, 1981

Immigration Reform and Control Act passed, 1986

Three Mile Island nuclear power plant accident, 1979

CAUTION RADIATION AREA

Challenger explodes in flight, 1986

Exxon *Valdez* oil spill, 1989

Human baby receives baboon heart, 1984

U.S. boycotts Moscow Olympics, 1980

Gorbachev introduces *glasnost* and *perestroika*, 1985

Berlin Wall falls, 1989

Polish Solidarity Union leaders arrested, 1981

U.S.-Soviet arms control talks, 1985

Chernobyl nuclear disaster, 1986

COLD WAR

| 1979 | 1980 | 1981 | 1982 | 1983 | 1984 | 1985 | 1986 | 1987 | 1988 | 1989 | 1990 |

UNIT 11

A New Era of Turmoil

George Bush reaped the advantages and suffered the fallout of the Reagan administration's policies in foreign and domestic affairs. After the collapse of the Communist bloc, the United States remained the sole superpower in the world. The emerging new world order produced great debate about the role the United States should play in foreign affairs. In domestic affairs, Reagan's legacies included a growing budget deficit, the savings and loan crisis, and a variety of festering social and economic problems. As George Bush and Bill Clinton both discovered, American voters became increasingly angry over their declining real wages and standards of living, over such social policies as welfare and affirmative action, and over political parties that seemed more intent on securing election than on solving the nation's problems.

Chapter 33	**Chapter 34**
The Bush and	America in the
Clinton	Twenty-first
Administrations	Century

◄ *Street art, or wall murals, began to appear in the late 1960s. Traditional symbols, heroes, and villains from minority cultures are often used in these works of art.* Crosswinds *was painted on a wall near Central Square in Cambridge, Massachusetts, in about 1992.*

Themes

■ **Multicultural Society** By the late 1980s, Americans perceived that society was becoming more diverse. U.S. immigration policies, governing both legal and illegal immigrants, were widely debated.

■ **Arts and Humanities** The arts and humanities became a battleground in the search for the very meaning of America. A culture war was waged to determine what was acceptable in art, books, and films.

■ **Technology** Computer advances and new technologies began to raise significant questions concerning medical ethics and the access to information.

■ **Global Interactions** With the demise of the Soviet Union, the United States faced a very different world. Americans debated the roles their nation could and should play in foreign affairs. Multinational corporations and keen foreign competition were creating profound changes in the way the United States did business.

► *George Bush*

President Bush Proclaims a New World Order

These goals [in the Persian Gulf] are not ours alone. They have been endorsed by the UN Security Council five times in as many weeks. Most countries share our concern for principle, and many have a stake in the stability of the Persian Gulf....

We stand today at a unique and extraordinary moment. The crisis in the Persian Gulf, as grave as it is, also offers a rare opportunity to move toward a historic period of cooperation. Out of these troubled times, our fifth objective—a new world order—can emerge; a new era—freer from the threat of terror, stronger in the pursuit of justice, and more secure in the quest for peace, an era in which the nations of the world, East and West, North and South, can prosper and live in harmony....

Today, that new world is struggling to be born, a world quite different from the one we have known, a world where the rule of law supplants the rule of the jungle, a world in which nations recognize the shared responsibility for freedom and justice, a world where the strong respect the rights of the weak....

America and the world must defend common vital interests. And we will. America and the world must support the rule of law. And we will. America and the world must stand up to aggression. And we will. And one thing more; in the pursuit of these goals, America will not be intimidated....

Recent events have surely proven that there is no substitute for American leadership. In the face of tyranny, let no one doubt American credibility and reliability. Let no one doubt our staying power. We will stand by our friends.

 Speech of President George Bush before Congress (Jan. 1990).

So What Do Polls Mean?

The following document discussed public opinion polls and asks what they really mean.

A more curious fact is that while pollsters were finding these high levels of dissatisfaction with 'the way things are going' [in the spring of 1993] they were also finding that 85 percent of our people—both black and white—were quite satisfied with the way things were going in their own lives; nearly 70 percent said things were going well in their own communities. The lobbyists and interest groups, which journalists and politicians often confuse with the voice of God, deny this of course. They are paid to whine, beg and complain. But they have no evidence on their side.

In the United States, from 80 to 95 percent of the labor force—depending on the job classification—reported very high levels of satisfaction with their work. . . . A sizable majority (60 percent) of our citizens were optimistic about their own futures and 90 percent 'if free to do so' would not move to another land.

How, in light of these data, did Clinton's pollster conclude that 'people had lost a sense of possibility'? Their 'bleak' view of things may have referred to nothing more than news headlines and their bleak view of Washington politicians, which is not necessarily a mark of insanity. Journalists constantly take a 'bleak' view of politics and government, the bleaker the story the more prize-worthy it becomes. . . .

So what do these national polls signify? What are they measuring? Whose heads are being explored in any meaningful sense? . . . It would be nice if just one time our poll sponsors would tell us what and who they are measuring out there, what the electorate knows about what is going on and who is paying attention to it all. We would certainly find there is less there than meets the eye; we might find there is no there at all.

Richard Harwood, "So What Do Polls Signify?" *The Washington Post* (June 25, 1994), p. A21.

500 Days of Clinton

Journalist Mark Shields assessed Clinton's presidency after 500 days in office.

What is missing, not only here [Dayton, Ohio] but in more than a dozen states I have visited recently, is any clear idea on people's part of what Bill Clinton is committed to, of what he really stands and for what, if necessary, he would be willing to sacrifice himself politically.

▼ *Campaigning via the Internet, 1996*

► *Bill Clinton*

As Democratic analyst Guy Molyneaux ... puts it, comparing first-term Democrat Clinton in 1994 to first-term Republican Ronald Reagan in 1982, 'People had a sense of where Reagan was going then, of the fixed star by which he was navigating. With Clinton ... that is not now the case.'

What is good news for Clinton is that voters do not see him as an old-fashioned liberal, too close to the party's special-interest constituencies or soft on crime. But while voters have a positive sense of what Clinton is not, those same voters cannot say what Clinton has done, is committed to, does believe in. ...

Bill Clinton has to identify and communicate his personal core beliefs and the goals for the nation he believes in and will fight for. After 500 days, people still don't know.

Mark Shields, "500 Days of Clinton," *The Washington Post* (June 25, 1994), p. A21.

The Third Wave

Alvin Toffler argues that human history may be divided into three periods, or waves. The first wave was the period during which all the world's people depended on agriculture. The second was associated with the Industrial Revolution. The third wave, a postindustrial one, is just emerging.

The Third Wave brings new problems, a new structure of communications, and new actors on the world stage—all of which drastically shrink the power of the individual nation-state.

New [problems] are fast arising that are too large for any nation to cope with alone. ... Tightened economic linkages between nations make it virtually impossible for any individual national government today to manage its own economy independently or to [control] inflation. ...

Oil tankers spills, air pollution, inadvertent weather modification, the destruction of forests, and other activities often involve side effects that sweep across national borders. Frontiers are now porous.

The new global communications system further opens each nation to penetration from the outside ... made possible by Third Wave communications systems based on satellites, computers, teleprinters, interactive cable systems, and dirt-cheap ground stations. All these developments ... are converging to undermine the position of the nation-state in the global scheme of things. What's more, they come together at precisely the moment when potent new actors appear on the world scene to challenge national power.

▲ *Virtual reality*

The best-publicized and most powerful of these new forces is ... the multinational corporation. The size, importance, and political power of this new player in the global game has skyrocketed since the mid-1950s. ... What we are creating is a new multi-layered global game in which not merely nations but corporations and trade unions, political, ethnic, and cultural groupings, transnational associations and supranational agencies are all players.

Alvin Toffler, *The Third Wave* (New York: William Morrow and Co., 1980).

Women in the Nineties

Liberate Us from the Liberators

Teddi Holt helped organize "Mothers on the March," a New Right organization founded to help preserve and strengthen the home.

I am pleased that God blessed me with the privilege of being a woman. I have never been envious of the role of men but have had respect for both sexes. There's no doubt that there has been discrimination against women, but that is past history, just as discrimination against blacks is past history in the U.S.

[The National Organization for Women's] primary goal was to pass the Equal Rights Amendment (ERA) without amendment. Second, it included as a secondary goal—'right to abortion on demand.' And third, it supported 'a woman's right to ... express her own sexuality and to choose her lifestyle....' Such goals were foreign to me. I could not imagine any woman with my background having such goals, because they did not hold to traditional values and/or Judeo-Christian ethics on which the Constitution and our laws are based....

We believe that the mothers of this and other nations must stand up for the protection of our homes and our children. In no way are we extremists, unless we be guilty of extreme devotion to our husbands, our children, and our homes.

 Robyn Rowland, ed., *Women Who Do and Women Who Don't Join the Woman's Movement* (Routledge & Kegan Paul, 1984).

▲ *Woman trying to balance work and family, 1990s*

Can we keep on shrugging all this off as enemy propaganda—'their problem, not ours?' I think we must at least admit and begin openly to discuss feminist denial of the importance of family, of women's own needs to give and get love and nurture, tender loving care....

What worries me today is 'choices' women have supposedly won, which are not real. How can a woman freely 'choose' to have a child when her paycheck is needed for the rent or mortgage, when her job isn't geared to taking care of a child, when there is no national policy for parental leave, and no assurance that her job will be waiting for her if she takes off to have a child?

 Betty Friedan, *The Second Stage* (Summit Books, 1981), pp. 26–29, 47–51.

Betty Friedan Reflects on the Women's Movement

The women's movement is being blamed, above all, for the destruction of the family. Churchmen and sociologists proclaim that the American family, as it has always been defined, is becoming an 'endangered species,' with the rising divorce rate and the enormous increase in single-parent families and people—especially women—living alone. Women's abdication of their age-old responsibility for the family is also being blamed for the apathy and moral delinquency of the 'me generation.'

Women's Generation Gap

The group around the dinner table were women, two generations of them. The topic was relationships and pretty soon we came to the edge of the generation gap.... It became apparent that we were talking from one vantage point and they were listening from another. We were telling tales from the bad old days. They were listening with nostalgia. We were sure that they had much more freedom than we'd had. They were not.

As for young marriages, it is an article of faith among my generation that it is better to wait than to end up, as we often did, divorced. It is an article of faith among mothers that their daughters should start careers first rather than wake up as we did, unskilled.

▲ *Office workers, 1990s*

But the pressure on the women to plan their lives with split-second timing and an eye on the biological clock begins younger and younger. At twentysomething, they look ahead, as we did not, and see their thirtysomething sisters who are often stressed or lonely or in line at the fertility clinic.

From their vantage point, an early marriage may seem less like a risk than a shelter. . . .

Does all this sound too worrisome? If the quartet we dined with are any example, the younger generation of women is more self-confident, stronger, far more introspective than mine. They don't take much for granted. They don't live by a set program.

But it is not an easy time. Not at all.

Ellen Goodman, *Making Sense* (The Washington Post Company, 1989).

Poverty in the South

The Commission on the Future of the South reported on regional poverty.

During the [mid-eighties] poverty in the South and the nation has generally been rising. . . .

As in the past, blacks and children endure the highest rates of poverty. . . . Women now constitute the largest segment of the adult population in poverty—60 percent of all poor over the age of 18. The number of women who are the sole support of poor households has almost doubled over the last twenty years. . . . A family of four with two wage earners at or near the minimum wage, working a combined sixty hours a week and fifty weeks a year, will still be below the poverty line. Of course, most poor people work. When the young, old and disabled are not considered, the nationwide level of working poor among the able-bodied poor in 1984 was 60 percent—a remarkable fact for a population where almost half the poor live in families with one female parent.

The 1986 Commission on the Future of the South, "Equity: The Critical Link in Southern Economic Development" (Research Triangle Park, 1986), pp. 8–10.

Two Views on Immigration

The Unending Dream

Leonel Castillo, a former head of the U.S. Immigration and Naturalization Service, comments on immigration.

New immigrants are trying all over again to integrate themselves into the system. They have the same hunger. On any given day, there are about three million [people] throughout the world who are applying to come to the United States and share the American Dream. . . .

Half the people here without papers are not Mexicans. They're from all over the world. They came legally, with papers, as tourists then years ago. . . . All too often, the public gets the impression that all immigrants are on welfare. It's the exact opposite. Very few go on welfare. . . .

▲ *Naturalization ceremony*

The only thing that helps me is remembering the history of this country. We've always managed . . . to rejuvenate ourselves, to bring in new people. Every new group comes in believing more firmly in the American Dream than the one that came a few years before. Every new group is scared of being in the welfare line or in the unemployment office. They go to night school, they learn about America. We'd be lost without them.

The old dream is still dreamt. The old neighborhood Ma-Pa stores are still around. They are not Italian or Jewish or Eastern European any more. Ma and Pa are now Korean, Vietnamese, Iraqi, Jordanian, Latin American. They live in the store. They work seven days a week. Their kids are doing well in school. They're making it. Sound familiar?

 Studs Terkel, *American Dreams: Lost and Found* (New York: Ballantine Books, 1980), pp. 6–12.

Mr. Ji's America

I don't understand America's policy. They let you come. But once you are here, they don't care at all. They don't care if you can get a job or what you do. You are all on your own. It's one thing to let immigrants in. But once they are here, you have to digest them. We get below minimum wages. This is the tenth factory we worked in. It's all the same. Finally we decided to stop shopping around. There is no labor law here. The government is acting like an idiot who doesn't know what's going on. The minimum wages are not for real. . . . In China, I just do desk work, giving people ideas. Now I'm doing this totally meaningless work. America is a world where the strong devours the meek.

I am at the point of no return. If I go back, I'll be looked down on by everybody. They'll think I'm such a failure. . . . I can't go back empty-handed. It'll be so embarrassing. . . . I want to learn English, I felt handicapped. I feel I'm without my limbs. I don't want to be dependent on other people. But I don't have any time at all. . . . We have to work so hard for so little money. Last Saturday we worked from 9 [a.m.] to 10:30 p.m. Between us we made eighty dollars. It's the best day since I came to the U.S. . . . I am tied down to my job. I feel like a slave. I can't go anywhere. Even if there is gold out there, I won't have time to pick them up. . . . There is blood in every dollar I make. . . . We all thought U.S. is such an advanced country. I don't see too much personal freedom here. You are free if you have money.

Interview by Ying Chan, New York City (1990), from American Social History Project, *Who Built America?* (New York: Pantheon, 1992), p. 643.

▲ *Biotechnology lab scientist*

A Technology Bill of Rights

This excerpt is from a manifesto written in 1984 by the International Association of Machinists and Aerospace Workers.

In the face of [shortsighted and dangerous implementation of technology] labor must act forcefully and quickly to safeguard the rights of workers and develop technology in a way that benefits the entire society. Key to this is proclaiming and implementing a Technology Bill of Rights. . . . This approach is based on the following assumptions:

1. A community has to produce in order to live. As a result, it is the obligation of an economy to organize people to work.
2. The well-being of people and their communities must be given the highest priority in determining the way in which production is carried out.
3. Basing technological and production decisions on narrow economic grounds of profitability has made working people and communities the victims rather than the beneficiaries of change.
4. Given the widespread scope and rapid rate of introduction of new technologies, society requires a democratically determined institutional, rather than individual, response to changes taking place. Otherwise, the social cost of technological change will be borne by those least able to pay it: unemployed workers and shattered communities.
5. Those that work have a right to participate in the decisions that govern their work and shape their lives.

6. The new automation technologies and the sciences that underlie them are the product of a worldwide, centuries-long accumulation of knowledge. Accordingly, working people and their communities have a right to share in the decisions about, and the gains from, new technology.

The choice should not be new technology or no technology but the development of technology with social responsibility. . . . The following is the foundation of such a program, A Technology Bill of Rights:

1. New technology must be used in a way that creates or maintains jobs. . . .
2. New technology must be used to improve the conditions of work. . . .
3. New technology must be used to develop the industrial base and improve the environment. . . .

International Association of Machinists and and Aerospace Workers, Eileen Boris and Nelson Lichtenstein, eds., *Major Problems in the History of American Workers* (Lexington, MA: D. C. Heath, 1991), pp. 651–653.

Using Primary Sources to Examine Stereotypes

This activity asks you to record details from two representative excerpts about attitudes and characteristics of immigrants coming to the United States toward the end of the twentieth century. You will then be asked to look for common patterns and draw conclusions from what you have read.

Directions: Read "The Unending Dream" and "Mr. Ji's America" and complete the following steps:

1. In short phrases, without including your own beliefs, record characteristics that describe recent immigrants to America. For example, you may write "Purpose for coming: to share in the American Dream" or "Misconceptions about immigrants: all immigrants are on welfare."

2. Interpret the information from Step 1 by looking for patterns or clues that relate the characteristics and allow you to make your own conclusions. For instance, you might note in Step 1 that the goal of many immigrants is a share in the "American Dream." You may also note the difficulty many immigrants face in finding good jobs. From these two facts you might conclude that many immigrants realize attaining the dream is difficult and far off in the future.

3. Use the conclusions you reached in Step 2 to write an informed essay about the immigrant experience.

The Bush and Clinton Administrations

isenchanted with the presidential election campaigns—and politics generally—only 50 percent of eligible voters bothered to go to the polls in 1988. This was the smallest proportion of voters to cast ballots in any presidential election in U.S. history. With no voter mandate, facing staggering budget deficits, and saddled with a Democrat-controlled Congress, President George Bush was perceived as "clumsy and irresolute" at home. In international affairs the reverse was true. Bush was viewed as "shrewd and energetic" as his dealings with Russia, China, and the Middle East demonstrated. In the end, however, problems with the

▲ *This 1988 campaign button shows candidate George Bush in the company of some previous Republican presidents. Why were these particular presidents selected?*

domestic economy brought an end to Republican control of the White House.

In 1992, a "new kind of Democrat" and a pivotal third-party candidate revived flagging voter interest in presidential elections. New to Washington politics, Bill Clinton and his inexperienced staff made mistakes that cost the Democrats precious legislative momentum. When the 1994 midterm congressional election sent a Republican majority to both houses of Congress, the legislative initiative was taken away from the Democrats. The Democratic president was put on the defensive.

The Bush Administration

George Bush was from a wealthy family. His father had been a powerful senator from Connecticut. After graduating from prep school in 1942, George became the youngest pilot in the U.S. Navy during World War II. When he returned from the war, he attended Yale University where he completed his degree. After graduation, Bush set out to make his fortune in the Texas oil business. Later he turned to public service. He served as a Texas congressman, as chair of the Republican National Committee and as director of the CIA under President Ford, among other important offices. During the Reagan administration, Bush served two terms as vice president. As the Reagan presidency came to a close, Bush seemed the likely candidate for the Republican nomination.

Why did some observers call the 1988 presidential campaign a "junk food" campaign?

What is meant by the concept of "government gridlock?"

What effect did conservative appointments have on Supreme Court decisions?

A Republican White House

Bush used the vice presidency as his launching pad for election as president as he campaigned actively for his party's nomination. Senator Robert Dole from Kansas became Bush's chief rival for the Republican nomination, but Dole's campaign lost momentum in the primary elections. Bush's successes in the primaries soon gave him sufficient support for nomination. To virtually everyone's surprise, Bush chose a young Indiana senator, Dan Quayle, as his running-mate.

The race for the Democratic nomination narrowed from a large group to two candidates. Jesse Jackson, an influential African American minister and a friend of the late Martin Luther King Jr., ran well in early primary elections. Governor Michael Dukakis of Massachusetts, however, won primary election victories in such large states as New York and California, which assured his nomination. Dukakis chose Senator Lloyd Bentsen of Texas as his running-mate.

The candidates seemed determined to avoid discussing serious issues during the campaign. Instead, they typically offered sound bites, catch phrases that meant little but sounded good in short

▼ *What percentage of the popular vote did George Bush receive in this election?*

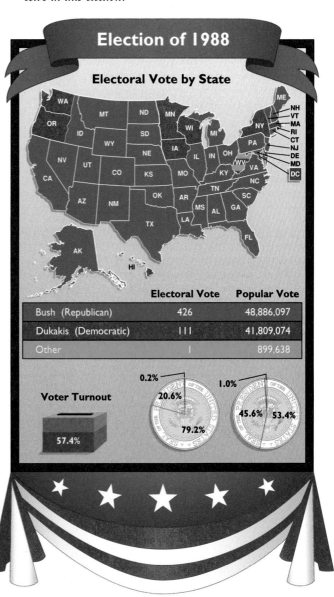

Election of 1988

Electoral Vote by State

	Electoral Vote	Popular Vote
Bush (Republican)	426	48,886,097
Dukakis (Democratic)	111	41,809,074
Other	1	899,638

Voter Turnout
57.4%

0.2%
20.6%
79.2%

1.0%
45.6% 53.4%

Enduring Constitution

The Presidency and the Constitution

When George Washington became the nation's first president, he offered to serve for free if Congress would cover his expenses. Instead, Congress voted him a salary of $25,000 per year plus a handful of personal assistants. Today, the president's salary is $200,000 plus $50,000 for expenses. Cost estimates to taxpayers for operating the White House with its 500 staff members run to more than $100 million per year.

These numbers give an indication of the extent of growth in the executive department since the time of the founding fathers. To keep busy, Washington had open houses for the general public, weekly tea parties, and regular dinners for the families of his staff. When President Adams moved to the White House in 1800, all his papers were packed in only seven boxes.

Today, it is virtually impossible for ordinary citizens to visit the president. His schedule is controlled to the minute. He commands a military force of several million men and women, and controls an even larger civil-

ian workforce. As the most powerful leader in the world, Americans look to him to solve all the nation's problems and lead the country through crisis periods.

What is the source of this immense power? Unlike the British parliamentary system, in which the prime minister is the leader of the majority party in the House of Commons and must first be elected to the Commons, the president is elected separately from Congress and has a different base of political power. He is answerable to the people, but not directly to Congress. In fact, the Constitution expressly bars any member of Congress from holding an executive office.

Article II of the Constitution describes the powers of the presidency. The executive power is vested in the president. He is commander in chief of the armed forces. He may grant pardons to those involved in federal crimes. He can make treaties and appointments (both subject to Senate ratification). The president may demand accounts of department heads. He is commanded "from time to time" to give Congress "information of the State of the Union and recommend to their consideration such measures as he shall judge necessary and expedient."

Over the years, by custom, by presidential claim, by congressional agreement, and by the courts, presidents have expanded the scope of these powers.

The greatest power of the president lies in the power of executive authority. The executive power has been used to proclaim neutrality, emancipate slaves, seize railroads, call up state militias, create the Peace Corps, and suspend claims of private citizens in U.S. courts against Iran.

The power of the president is not unlimited, however. The framers of the Constitution had no intention of establishing a monarchy, and they created a system of checks and balances in the Constitution to prevent any one branch becoming too strong. Congressional and presidential powers overlap in many areas. The president may command the troops in time of war, but only Congress can declare war. The president nominates people to office, but the Senate must confirm the appointments. The president may create extensive programs, but only Congress can authorize funding for them.

In addition to Congress acting as a check on the powers of the president, the Supreme Court watches carefully the actions of the chief executive. It denied President Truman the

(continued)

power to seize the steel mills to prevent a steel strike, even in the midst of the Korean War. It took a near constitutional crisis during the presidency of Richard Nixon to define the limits of presidential power. Nixon's attempt to put the president "beyond the power of the law" was blocked by the Supreme Court. "The president, like everyone else, must yield to the courts when he is reasonably believed to have participated in a crime."

Although the power of the executive branch has expanded over the years, congressional overlap and judicial review comprise the system of checks and balances that has so well preserved our form of government. The writers of the Constitution crafted a document that continues to function and endure even in the face of remarkable change.

1. Besides the ways described in the text, in what way have some presidents increased their power?
2. What do you consider to be the Constitution's greatest weakness and its greatest strength?

---

television news stories and political advertisements. The candidates also engaged in negative campaigning by attacking each other on personal grounds. Many observers called the 1988 campaign a "junk food" campaign and the worst in recent memory because the candidates seemed to avoid substantive discussion of basic issues.

In the end, Bush carried 40 states and received 54 percent of the popular vote. Bush's electoral vote majority was 426 to 112. The Democrats maintained their control of both houses of Congress and of many state legislatures and governorships.

Government Gridlock

As president, Bush showed greater interest than Reagan in such domestic issues as education, environmental protection, and homelessness. Even so, he had difficulty in creating and promoting a clear domestic agenda.

First, Bush had inherited a staggering burden of federal debt and federal budget deficits. Bush's commitment to fiscal restraint and no new taxes prevented him from seeking significant funding from Congress for domestic programs. Second, President Bush faced a Democrat-controlled Congress that was not disposed to cooperate with him. Because

▼ *President Bush wanted to be remembered for caring about education and the environment.*

Most Important Problem, 1989

Question: What do you think is the most important problem facing the country today?

Economy	35%
Drug abuse	27%
Poverty	10%
Crime	6%
Moral decline	5%

Note: Multiple responses allowed.

Source: Gallup, May 4-7, 1989.

▲ *Judging from the results of the 1992 election, how successfully did President Bush handle the problems identified here as most important?*

▲ *This Draper Hill cartoon depicts President Bush surrounded by Senate and House sharks. How is the concept of gridlock illustrated here?*

Bush was eager to please conservative Republicans, he fought bitter and often unproductive battles with congressional Democrats over such issues as crime, abortion, child care, school prayer, and family leave. The result was **gridlock**, a situation in which neither the president nor Congress had sufficient political clout to produce positive action. In fact, this term saw fewer bills proposed and fewer acts passed by Congress than during any administration over the previous two decades.

The framers of the U.S. Constitution had built the potential for gridlock into the federal system through the separation of powers and checks and balances. To prevent political tyranny, the framers had made federal action a slow and deliberate process. Federal action is even more difficult when the executive and legislative branches are controlled by different political parties, as they were during Bush's presidency. In addition, special interest groups had become more influential in the 1980s than ever before. Such groups as the National Rifle Association (NRA) and the American Association of Retired Persons (AARP) could exert great pressure for or against specific pieces of legislation. Still, President Bush was criticized for the situation.

A Conservative Supreme Court

Liberal Supreme Court Justice William Brennan used to tell his clerks, "Five votes can do anything around here." President Bush continued Reagan's effort to ensure that those five votes would be cast by conservative justices. When Justice Brennan retired in 1989, Bush nominated Judge David Souter of the New Hampshire federal appeals court to replace him. Souter won Senate approval by a vote of 90 to 9. Bush's nomination of Clarence Thomas to replace retiring Justice Thurgood Marshall in 1991, however, ran into difficulty in the Senate.

During his tenure, the liberal Marshall, an African American, had staunchly supported civil rights, rights of those accused of crimes, and affirmative action. Thomas, also an African American, was a conservative who opposed many federal programs, including affirmative action. Reagan appointed Thomas to head the Equal Employment Opportunity Commission (EEOC) where he often declined to investigate cases of alleged race, gender, and age discrimination. Bush appointed Thomas as a federal appeals court judge at the start of his administration.

A graduate of Yale Law School, Thomas's lack of judicial experience concerned some senators.

Clarence Thomas was sworn in by the Senate Judiciary Committee during confirmation hearings concerning Thomas's nomination to the Supreme Court. A month later, Anita Hill, a University of Oklahoma Law School professor, was sworn in by the same committee. Hill testified that Thomas had sexually harassed her during the time she worked as his aide. What was the result of the investigation?

Others disagreed with his conservative views. His Senate confirmation became even more difficult when a former associate at EEOC, Anita Hill, charged him with sexual harassment. A law professor at Oklahoma University, Hill riveted the Senate Judiciary Committee—and the television public—for several days with her accusations. The Senate nevertheless confirmed Thomas's appointment by a vote of 52 to 48. With the Souter and Thomas appointments, the Supreme Court seemed likely to be more conservative on a range of issues.

Decisions made by the Rehnquist Court chipped away at legal precedents of the Warren (1953–1969) and Burger (1969–1986) Courts, often by votes of 5–4. In *City of Richmond v. J. A. Croson Co.* (1989), the Court made it easier for people to challenge government affirmative action policies. In this case, a white-owned business challenged the policy of Richmond, Virginia, which set aside 30 percent of the city's construction contracts for minority-owned businesses. The Court ruled that states and cities should not use race alone as a standard for awarding contracts or other benefits (including college scholarships) except as a remedy for past discrimination. Then, in 1995, in a landmark case that was viewed as a "potentially fatal blow to most federal affirmative action programs," the Court ruled that race-based preferential treatment is almost always unconstitutional.

In another controversial decision in June of 1995, the Supreme Court ruled to allow random drug testing on high school students involved in school-sponsored activities.

The Court also tackled the abortion issue. In *Webster v. Reproductive Health Services* (1989), the Court permitted states to restrict abortion and, in *Rust v. Sullivan* (1991), it upheld a rule forbidding personnel at federally funded health clinics from discussing abortion with clients. In *Planned Parenthood of Southeastern Pennsylvania v. Casey* (1992), a 5–4 decision upheld a Pennsylvania law requiring a 24-hour waiting period and informed consent before abortions could be performed. Despite allowing such new restrictions, the majority reaffirmed the "essential holding" of *Roe v. Wade* that the constitution protected a woman's right to abortion.

SECTION 1 REVIEW

1. State reasons why political observers labeled the 1988 presidential election campaign a "junk food" campaign.
2. Define gridlock.
3. Explain why the framers of the U.S. Constitution allowed for gridlock in the federal system.
4. Identify Clarence Thomas.
5. Discuss the significance of *Richmond v. Croson*.

Bush's Foreign Policies

For three decades the Berlin Wall symbolized the tensions of the Cold War. In November 1989, in the wake of revolutionary changes in Eastern Europe, the East Germans finally ordered the dismantling of the Wall. Just as it had previously symbolized the Cold War, the tearing down of the Wall by both East and West Germans signified the Cold War's end. This episode was only one of many that fundamentally changed the international scene in the late 1980s.

What were the major causes and effects of the collapse of Soviet and Eastern European communism?

How did the collapse of the Soviet Union affect U.S. foreign policies toward other areas of the world?

What effects did war in the Persian Gulf War have on its participants?

▲ *These two young people chipped away pieces of the Berlin Wall in January 1990. Many other memento-seekers did the same. For how many years did this wall divide the city of Berlin?*

The Collapse of Communism

Premier Mikhail Gorbachev had set momentous changes in motion in the Soviet Union in 1985. Gorbachev and his advisors encouraged more open and critical discussion of Soviet politics and the economy. Glasnost exposed glaring problems in Soviet society. The Soviet standard of living was poor; food, consumer goods, and housing were in short supply. Despite Gorbachev's policy of perestroika, the Soviet economy continued to stagnate. As a result, Gorbachev ran into trouble with Communist Party conservatives who opposed a free-market economy and reformers who wanted to move even faster toward a free-market system.

In addition, Gorbachev recognized the enormous drain on the Soviet economy caused by vast military spending. He wished to begin serious arms control negotiations with the United States. In July 1989, Gorbachev announced he would withdraw troops and reduce Soviet control of its satellites in Eastern Europe. Within the next 18 months, largely bloodless revolutions toppled Communist regimes throughout the region.

The transition from socialism to capitalism proved difficult. Lack of capital, shortages of goods, high prices, and high rates of unemployment prevented quick economic prosperity. By 1992, citizens in many former Communist countries were restless and dissatisfied. Internal social and ethnic tensions, stifled by the presence of Soviet troops, soon surfaced in most of these countries and made matters even worse. In Czechoslovakia, for example, resentments between the Czechs and Slovaks led to the peaceful division of the country into separate republics: the Czech Republic and Slovakia. Yugoslavia disintegrated into four separate nations, and a brutal civil war soon erupted.

▲ *A Soviet woman unsuccessfully shopped at a nearly empty general food store in Moscow in October 1990.*

Similar tensions and conflicts appeared within the Soviet Union itself. In 1990, the Baltic Republics of Estonia, Latvia, and Lithuania declared their independence from the Soviet Union, but Gorbachev refused to recognize their new status. The remaining 12 Soviet republics also wanted greater freedom. In 1990 and 1991, noncommunist politicians came to power in local elections throughout the Soviet Union. In March 1991, citizens of Russia, by far the largest and most powerful of the Soviet republics, elected a noncommunist majority to their parliament. **Boris Yeltsin**, President of the Russian Republic, soon resigned from the Communist Party.

By the summer of 1991, Gorbachev asked the West for $13 billion to help jump-start the Soviet economy and to prevent total political collapse. Meanwhile, Gorbachev prepared a new Union Treaty that would have given the 15 Soviet republics greater freedom and self-government within the Soviet Union. As a result, a group of conservative Communist Party officials attempted to oust Gorbachev from power on August 19. The attempted coup, however, ran into massive opposition led by Russian President Boris Yeltsin. By August 21, the coup had failed. Yeltsin emerged from this tur-

moil as the most powerful political leader. In December 1991, Russia, Ukraine, and Belarus formed the Commonwealth of Independent States (CIS). They were soon joined by other former Soviet republics. Mikhail Gorbachev recognized the CIS and then resigned as president of the USSR. The Soviet Union had ceased to exist.

New Challenges

The American victory in the Cold War created new problems. First, United States military power had largely been designed for use against the Soviet Union. What level of military spending was adequate to the nation's security in the post-Soviet world? Could some of the money usually spent on defense now be used to solve domestic problems? Second, U.S. foreign and defense policies had been based on containment of Soviet Communism since the end of World War II. What would the central focus of U.S. policies be now? Third, many Americans believed that foreign affairs were less important now that the Soviet threat was gone.

Suggestions started to be heard that the United States should isolate itself from the world and concentrate on domestic problems. Many Americans wondered how U.S. leaders could conduct foreign affairs and how they could assert world leadership without the firm support of American public opinion. How should the United States deal with the many international issues—the environment, the spread of nuclear arms, economic development, and massive movement of people—that had sometimes been delayed or ignored during the Cold War?

For over a decade, deficits in foreign trade generally had concerned many Americans. This was especially true concerning trade with Japan. In 1987, the U.S. trade deficit with Japan was $55 billion. Many Americans began to call for tariffs and other limits on Japanese imports into the United States.

The Republic of China   U.S. policy toward the People's Republic of China also changed. By the end of the 1980s, the People's Republic of China possessed one of the fastest growing economies in

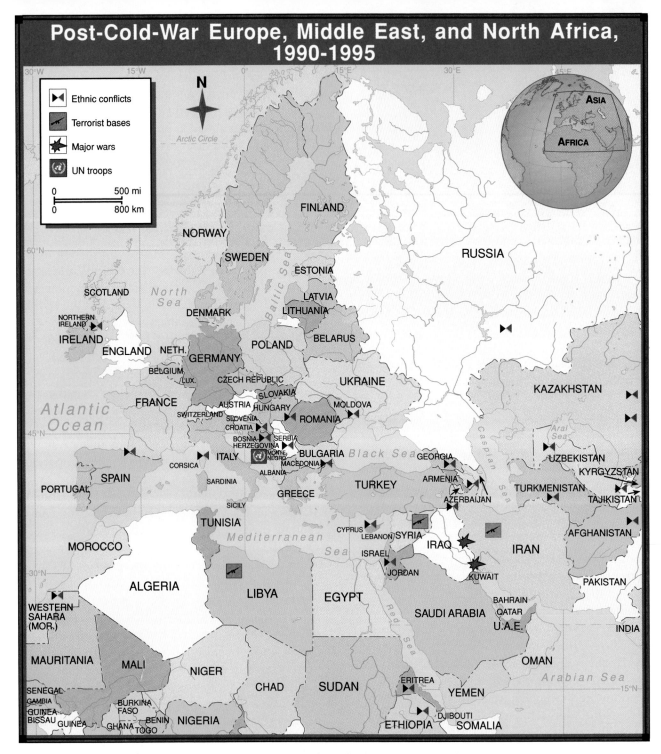

Post-Cold-War Europe, Middle East, and North Africa, 1990–1995

Legend:
- Ethnic conflicts
- Terrorist bases
- Major wars
- UN troops

0   500 mi
0   800 km

▲ *The end of the Cold War left the countries in this region formerly under Soviet control with many difficult problems to solve.*

the world. While China's economy was moving toward free-market capitalism, its Communist government continued its repressive policies. In May 1989,

Chinese students began demonstrating for greater democracy. The unrest became so intense and widespread that the Communist regime seemed ready to

▲ *Thousands of pro-democracy protesters surged into Tiananmen Square in May 1989. Whose portrait appears there?*

fall. Hard-liners took control and sent the military to crush the student uprising. On June 3, a bloody massacre in which hundreds of student demonstrators died occurred in **Tiananmen Square** in Beijing. The massacre solidified the hard-liners' control. The United States was presented with a dilemma. On the one hand, they condemned the Chinese government's brutal repression of the democracy movement. On the other hand, American business interests wanted better trading relations with China.

Latin America   The end of the Cold War had mixed results for U.S. policies toward Latin America. With the exception of Cuba, the United States abandoned anticommunism as the basis for determining U.S. policy in Latin America. In Nicaragua, for example, President Bush ended U.S. aid to the right-wing contras who had fought against the Sandinista regime of Daniel Ortega. In 1989, the contras and Sandinistas agreed to end their civil war, to hold free elections in 1990, and to release all political prisoners. In those elections, Nicaraguans elected an anti-Sandinista, Violetta Chamorro, as president. A similar agreement ended a 12-year civil war in neighboring El Salvador.

President Bush, however, did not completely abandon U.S. intervention in Latin America. In December 1991, as part of Bush's "war on drugs," U.S. combat troops invaded Panama to try to slow the flow of illegal drugs to the United States. Military forces arrested Panamanian President General Manuel Noriega and brought him to Florida to stand trial for drug trafficking. Noriega's arrest and conviction were unprecedented and probably illegal under international law. So unsavory was Noriega's regime, however, that most Americans applauded Bush's actions.

The Collapse of Apartheid   From the 1950s to the 1990s, the guiding principle of the South African government was **apartheid**, a policy that legalized racial separation and discrimination. Opposing this racist regime, the United States, the European Community, and the United Nations had imposed economic and cultural sanctions on South Africa in the mid-1980s. The result was to make South Africa an international outcast.

In 1990, the white South African government began reforms leading to the abolition of apartheid and the scheduling of democratic elections. In February, the South African government released

▼ *What did the release of Nelson Mandela from Vorster Prison on February 11, 1990, symbolize for the people of South Africa?*

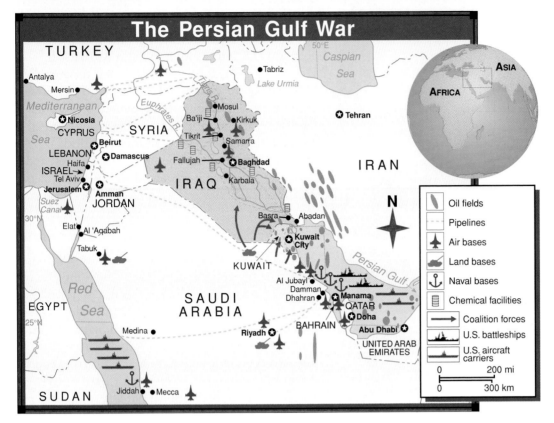

The Persian Gulf War

▲ *Given Iraq's location in the Middle East, do you think President Bush was wise not to press the war further against Saddam Hussein?*

Nelson Mandela, a well-loved symbol of black resistance to white oppression. For 27 years, Mandela had been a political prisoner at Robben Island, one of the worst prisons in South Africa. In 1991, the United States lifted the restrictions it had placed on trade with South Africa and began a policy aimed at helping the country develop democratic institutions and strengthen its free enterprise economy.

Elected president in 1994, Mandela worked tirelessly to unite a country plagued with civil violence resulting from deep racial and tribal divisions. Like the United States, the citizens of South Africa must protect their new freedoms through the writing of a new constitution that fairly addresses the needs of a multiracial and multicultural society.

Operation Desert Storm

Problems in the Middle East continued to plague U.S. policymakers. On August 2, 1990, Iraq invaded neighboring Kuwait, an oil-rich sheikdom. President Bush immediately condemned the invasion and began to build support for action against Iraq in Congress, with the American public, and in the United Nations. Bush's objective was quite clear—Iraq's total withdrawal from Kuwait. At Bush's initiative, the United Nations Security Council passed a resolution that demanded Iraq's withdrawal and that imposed an embargo and trade sanctions on Iraq.

Iraqi dictator Saddam Hussein failed to comply with the UN's deadline for withdrawal. In November, at Bush's urging, the Security Council passed another resolution committing UN military forces against Iraq if it did not withdraw by January 15, 1991. A multinational UN force (eventually 37 nations sent troops) began arriving in the Middle East. As the UN's deadline approached, Congress debated whether to give the economic sanctions more time to work. In a close vote, Congress authorized war. On January 16, Bush announced: "The liberation of Kuwait has begun."

The Persian Gulf War

Although strictly controlled by U.S. military intelligence, television closely covered the Persian Gulf War from beginning to end. Satellite communication news organizations like Cable News Network (CNN) allowed instantaneous round-the-clock coverage. At almost any time of the day or night, Americans could tune into live news broadcasts that showed "smart bombs" falling on their targets and news correspondents fearfully ducking missiles whizzing overhead or reacting to nearby explosions. To a degree, TV coverage gave viewers the impression that the war was like playing a combat video game. The language used by the U.S. military also gave the war an air of unreality. Jargon like *attriting* (killing) the enemy and *collateral damage* (destruction of nonmilitary targets) helped to disguise some of the actual horrors of war.

Global news media carried pictures and stories of the war's devastating effects on the region. Both Kuwait and Iraq suffered many casualties and vast physical damage. The war also created a significant refugee problem. Nearly two million Kurd and Shi'ite refugees fled Iraq to bordering Turkey and Iran. At the same time, Kuwait expelled thousands of Palestinian laborers who had supported Iraq during the war.

▲ *This March 1, 1991, photograph shows several Kuwaiti oil wells burning after being ignited by Iraqi soldiers.*

Television showed that the war had created an environmental catastrophe. Retreating Iraqi soldiers had not only set fire to Kuwait's oil fields, but had also released over 300 million gallons of crude oil into Persian Gulf waters.

The rapid pace of combat victory was stunning. The majority of Americans saw the U.S. military's performance as some vindication of Reagan-era spending on military technology. Many also believed that the effects of Vietnam had finally worn off. "By God," President Bush said, "we've kicked the Vietnam Syndrome once and for all." The war spawned a renewed sense of American patriotism. U.S. military leaders such as General Colin Powell, chairman of the Joint Chiefs of Staff, and General Norman Schwarzkopf, U.S. field commander, enjoyed hero status. Even common soldiers were seen as heroes. President Bush's public approval rating rose to nearly 90 percent.

———⚔———

1. Describe the refugee problem caused by the war.
2. Explain how the rapid victory affected the thinking of Americans toward our military.

Operation Desert Storm, as the war in the Persian Gulf was called by the military, began with a month of air attacks designed to knock out Iraqi command and communications centers and to destroy stockpiled armaments. Iraq was nearly defenseless against the air assault. Iraq did launch Scud missile attacks on Israel and Saudi Arabia, but these attacks were largely ineffective. On February 23, the ground war began. Iraqi military forces were soon in full retreat and Iraqi soldiers surrendered by the thousands. Within days, Bush declared a cease-fire. U.S. combat losses were relatively light, with 148 soldiers killed and nearly 500 wounded.

From the beginning, President Bush had a limited objective in the Persian Gulf War—Iraqi withdrawal from Kuwait. Most foreign policy experts believed Bush's restraint was the best course. They agreed with Bush that U.S. interests in the Persian Gulf would be best protected if no single country dominated the region. If Iraq were further weakened by U.S. military action, Iran might well become such a dominant power. Still, many Americans wondered why Bush did not topple Saddam Hussein's regime. Criticisms of Bush increased in the immediate postwar period for several reasons. These included Iraqi violations of the cease-fire agreement, growing public awareness of Iraq's possession of nuclear and biological weapons, and Hussein's brutal repression of rebellions by Kurd and Shi'ite Moslem minorities after the war. Despite such doubts in the postwar period, the Persian Gulf War showed that Americans would support U.S. policy and even armed intervention if an important objective could be clearly shown.

SECTION 2 REVIEW

1. Name three causes of the collapse of communism in the Soviet Union and Eastern Europe.
2. Identify Boris Yeltsin.
3. Write two questions that the collapse of the Soviet Union raised for the Bush administration.
4. Explain the dilemma facing the U.S. in its relations with China.
5. Explain why Bush was hesitant to completely destroy Iraq as a power in the Gulf region.

SECTION 3

Economic Turmoil and the Election of 1992

Political scientist Walter Dean Burnham explained the results of the 1992 presidential election as "the politics of repudiation." Burnham argued that President Bush's failure to win reelection was an overwhelming vote of no confidence "in an incumbent president and the regime he led." In 1988, Bush received 53.4 percent of the popular vote. In 1992, his popular vote fell to 38 percent, the third largest decline for an incumbent president in U.S. history. What had happened between the end of the Persian Gulf War and the presidential election eighteen months later? The sentiment of one ordinary American perhaps best explains this remarkable turnaround: "The country is feeling good about the [Persian Gulf] war. I'm feeling good about it, but I still can't afford a new car."

With what economic problems did President Bush have to deal?

How did the federal budget deficit affect local and state governments?

How did such issues as character and distrust of government influence the 1992 election?

Economic Problems

Several economic problems plagued Bush during his term as president. The savings and loan (S & L) industry had virtually collapsed by 1989. For decades, S & Ls, also called thrifts, had invested their depositors' savings in home mortgages. Both deposits and loans carried relatively low interest rates. The inflation of the late seventies and early eighties had been disastrous for the S & Ls since they now had to pay high interest rates to attract depositors. Most of their loans, however, continued to be long-term mortgages at low interest rates. The S & L industry wanted Congress to allow them to

▲ *What does this Draper Hill cartoon suggest about the crisis in the savings and loan industry?*

make loans (at higher interest rates) to commercial real estate and other business ventures.

The Reagan administration reduced federal supervision of the industry. As a result, S & Ls loaned money to higher risk ventures during the real estate boom of the 1980s. As long as the real estate market prospered, loans and investments were profitable and potential problems went unnoticed. Between 1988 and 1990, as the economic boom cooled, nearly 600 S & Ls failed, wiping out the savings of thousands of depositors. The crisis was brought on by loose federal supervision and by the greed and corruption of many S & L executives.

Since the federal government insured depositors' accounts, President Bush had to design a program to repay the depositors and to sell millions of dollars' worth of foreclosed office and apartment buildings. Estimates of the cost to taxpayers of the S&L bailout range from $200 to $400 billion.

President Bush also inherited the problem of vast budget deficits from Ronald Reagan. In 1990, after difficult negotiations, the president and Congress reached agreement on a five-year deficit-reduction package that included both drastic spending cuts and tax increases, in spite of Bush's campaign promise not to raise taxes. Deficits continued despite the agreement. In 1991, the annual deficit was $269 billion, and in 1992 nearly $350 billion. The total federal debt rose to over $3 trillion. Interest on the debt was the fastest growing federal budget item.

The underlying problem was that the federal government was locked into huge interest payments on an ever-growing national debt and costly programs ranging from defense spending to Social Security and Medicare. Because many government programs were indexed to inflation (i.e., benefit payments automatically increased at the same rate as inflation), their costs were always rising. To compound these problems, the incomes of nearly 80 percent of Americans had either decreased or stayed about even over the previous two decades. They could not really afford to pay more taxes. It is not surprising that politicians were generally wary of raising taxes or cutting favored programs.

Meanwhile, state and local governments experienced increasing financial difficulties. President Reagan's New Federalism had shifted much of the responsibility for many federal programs to state and local governments. At the same time, the Reagan administration slashed federal funding that had helped pay for these programs. As a result, joint federal-state programs such as Medicaid became increasingly heavy burdens on state budgets.

In the 1990s, many state and local governments turned to lotteries as a major source of new tax revenues. In 1992 Americans legally bet about $330 billion, an amount that surpassed the Department of Defense budget. Lotteries raised funds for such purposes as education and recreation.

People criticized government lotteries for a number of reasons. Some were morally opposed to government sponsored gambling. Others complained that poor people, minorities, and people with less than average education and income played the lotteries far more often than the better-educated middle class. To some observers, state-operated gambling amounted to an unfair tax on those people least able to pay.

To compound these fiscal problems, an economic recession struck the nation in mid-1990. The decline in business activity further eroded local, state, and federal tax revenues. This situation, in turn, forced state and local governments to lay off workers and cut programs even as greater demands for public services were made.

The Run for President

Given the advantages of an incumbent and his 89 percent public approval rating following the Persian Gulf War, President Bush seemed positioned for easy reelection in 1992. But, by December 1991, public opinion polls showed that Bush's public approval rating had declined to 40 percent and that his reelection was in jeopardy. Voters seemed especially concerned about Bush's inaction in the face of the economic recession, the decline of good jobs, the soaring costs of health care, and environmental issues. Even conservatives in his own party opposed his renomination. Patrick Buchanan, a conservative journalist, challenged Bush in early primary elections. But Bush soon won sufficient support for renomination.

▼ *On October 16, 1992, presidential candidates Bush, Perot, and Clinton squared off in an informal debate at the University of Richmond, Virginia. Is this type of public forum effective in educating voters?*

Meanwhile, well-known Democratic politicians—including New York Governor Mario Cuomo, Georgia Senator Sam Nunn, and New Jersey Senator Bill Bradley—chose not to seek their party's nomination when Bush's public approval rating was still high. Lesser-known Arkansas Governor **Bill Clinton**, however, did seek the presidential nomination. Even with negative publicity such as charges of draft dodging, Clinton won enough primary elections to lock up the Democratic nomination.

The 1992 presidential election was also notable for the emergence of independent candidate **Ross Perot**. Perot, a Texas billionaire with no experience in politics, appealed to voters who were dissatisfied with what Perot called "politics as usual." Many voters liked Perot's outspoken style and thought his great wealth would put him above the corrupting influence of special interest groups. In June, Perot led Bush and Clinton in the public opinion polls, but his own erratic behavior hurt his chances. He dropped out of the campaign in July, announcing that his candidacy was unnecessary since Clinton's nomination was a serious challenge to Bush's reelection. Perot then reentered the race just five weeks before the national elections.

Soon after the July Democratic convention, Clinton surged from third to first place in the public opinion polls. Clinton's strategy during the 1992 campaign proclaimed him a "new kind of Democrat." Clinton's campaign staff posted a sign in his Little Rock, Arkansas, headquarters that captured the most emphatic theme of his campaign: "THE ECONOMY, STUPID." Although it was unclear how he would pay for them, Clinton also pledged himself to a number of domestic programs, including welfare reform and health care.

Bush strategists were slow to react to Clinton's momentum. When his campaign finally got going, Bush resorted to the hard negative campaigning that had been so effective in 1988 against Michael Dukakis. Bush tried to brand Clinton as untrustworthy and un-American.

Clinton won 43 percent of the popular vote, compared to Bush's 38 percent and Perot's 19 percent. The results in the electoral college were somewhat more lopsided: Clinton won 370 to Bush's 168 electoral votes. Perot did not win a single state, but

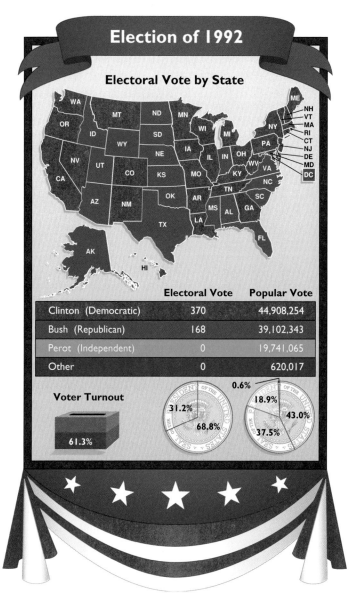

Election of 1992

Electoral Vote by State

	Electoral Vote	Popular Vote
Clinton (Democratic)	370	44,908,254
Bush (Republican)	168	39,102,343
Perot (Independent)	0	19,741,065
Other	0	620,017

Voter Turnout

61.3%

0.6%
31.2%
68.8%

18.9%
43.0%
37.5%

▲ *How did Perot's third-party candidacy affect the outcome of this election?*

ceived more electoral votes than any Democratic presidential candidate since Lyndon Johnson in 1964. On the other hand, Clinton had won only 43 percent of the popular vote, exactly the average share received by Democratic presidential candidates in every election between 1968 and 1988. In five of those elections, Democrats had been soundly defeated. Did 62 percent of the popular vote (combining Clinton's 43 and Perot's 19 percent) against Bush mean a mandate for change or simply a repudiation of Bush? Did 57 percent of the popular vote (combining Bush's 38 and Perot's 19 percent) mean that most voters opposed Clinton and his proposals?

It became apparent that the politically active middle class was discontented with government and distrusted politicians. With Ross Perot helping to focus public opinion, opposition to annual budget deficits and increased spending on federal programs grew. Congress and the president could not afford to ignore this voter trend.

The elections of 1992 had significant outcomes besides the change of presidents. Democrats retained their control of both houses of Congress (by 57 to 43 in the Senate and by 258 to 176 in the House). With both the White House and Congress in Democratic hands, many observers hoped that government gridlock was over. Aside from Bush's defeat, however, the Republicans actually did well in the 1992 elections. They gained ten seats in the House and one in the Senate (following a special election in Texas). Congressional Republicans also demonstrated firm party cohesion and posed an ever-present obstacle to Clinton. Since Clinton received only 43 percent of the popular vote, his influence in Congress remained in doubt.

his popular vote was the largest received by a third-party candidate since Theodore Roosevelt's 1912 Progressive Party candidacy. Partly as a result of Perot's candidacy, a larger share of eligible voters—55.2 percent—cast ballots in 1992 than in any presidential election since 1968.

A Difficult Political Context

The meaning of the 1992 elections was not immediately obvious. On one hand, Clinton had re-

---

SECTION 3 REVIEW

1. **Name** four economic problems that faced President Bush.
2. **Describe** one effect of the federal budget deficit on local and state governments.
3. **State** the major reason for the decline in Bush's popularity after the Persian Gulf War.
4. **Identify** Ross Perot.
5. **Explain** how the third-party vote in 1992 affected Clinton's win.

The Clinton Administration Begins

Clinton administration blunders got the first hundred days off to a rocky start. James Pfiffner, a leading authority on presidential transitions, noted, "Blunders during the early days of an administration may haunt it, while early victories may establish the momentum necessary to accomplish presidential goals." Bill Clinton had routinely promised during the 1992 campaign that the first hundred days of his administration would be similar to Franklin Roosevelt's action-packed first three months. Clinton's promise created false hopes of swiftly accomplished goals. By the end of Clinton's first hundred days, the new president's accomplishments were few and his major initiatives were still works in progress. Indeed, Clinton seemed to struggle and remain off-balance for much of his first two years in office.

What difficulties did Clinton face during the transition between presidential administrations?

What was Clinton's strategy for working with Congress?

What evidence did political observers cite to show that gridlock was over?

Most Important Problem, 1993

Question: What do you think are the two most important issues for the government to address?

Health care	35%
Deficit	26%
Economy (general)	26%
Employment/jobs	20%
Taxes	15%
Crime/drugs	9%
Education	9%
Domestic/social issues	8%

Source: Louis Harris and Associates, March 4-10, 1993.

©The Public Perspective, a publication of the Roper Center for Public Opinion Research, University of CT, Storrs. Reprinted by permission.

▲ *Which of the identified priorities did President Clinton try to address in the first year of his term?*

A Rocky Start

Most of Clinton's difficulties during the transition were due to his own and his advisors' lack of experience in Washington. The *Wall Street Journal's* Albert Hunt, a long-time member of the Washington press corps, judged Clinton's White House staff to be the least competent he had seen in 25 years. Clinton soon recognized that "there's a lot I have to learn about this town [Washington]."

Just eight days after his election, Clinton announced he would keep his campaign promise to end the ban on homosexuals serving in the armed forces. Unfortunately neither Clinton nor his staff consulted with potential opponents in Washington

before the announcement. General **Colin Powell**, chairman of the Joint Chiefs of Staff (JCS), Georgia Senator Sam Nunn, chairman of the powerful Senate Armed Services Committee, and such influential groups as the American Legion and Veterans of Foreign Wars firmly opposed lifting the ban. In the face of widespread opposition, Clinton soon retreated. Eventually, Clinton and the military services reached a compromise aimed at preventing sexual misconduct by all service personnel. One of Clinton's aides judged the episode "a huge mistake."

Clinton's approach to staffing his administration, especially high-level cabinet appointments, also made the transition difficult. During the campaign, Clinton had committed himself to three values in choosing administration officials—diversity, competence, and ethical propriety. Clinton proceeded slowly. By the end of February 1993, Clinton had filled only 30 of 290 administration positions that required Senate confirmation. Clinton's eventual appointments did reflect gender and ethnic diversity, but his delays in staffing his administration left most federal agencies without leadership and made communication with Congress difficult.

President-elect Bill Clinton participates in a sing-along with a number of entertainment celebrities during the inaugural celebrations at the Lincoln Memorial. Can you identify the people on stage?

The Bush-to-Clinton transition proved especially difficult because, like Jimmy Carter, Clinton had trouble identifying his priorities. He also failed to realize how much the public's desire for deficit reduction would affect his many legislative proposals, including health care and welfare reforms.

Health care presented especially vexing issues. Clinton had insisted that he would sign a health care bill only if it provided universal coverage regardless of age, race, or preexisting medical conditions, and if it provided better health care services in inner-city and rural areas. A government task force under the leadership of First Lady **Hillary Rodham Clinton** interviewed hundreds of health care providers and consumers trying to create a comprehensive plan that would provide health care to all needy Americans. In the end, the nation decided it could not afford such an ambitious program.

To achieve his ambitious domestic agenda, Clinton decided to work closely with Congress rather than act as a Washington outsider as Carter and Reagan had. Soon after the election, Clinton began meeting with Democratic and Republican leaders in Congress to gain their support.

For several months, Clinton's strategy produced little fruit. While House Democrats and their leaders strongly supported Clinton's legislative proposals, Senate Democrats were less supportive. To get Democratic senators to vote for some of his proposals, Clinton often seemed too eager to please them

and too willing to compromise. At the same time, the 43 Senate Republicans, by acting together, wielded considerable influence. They could demand changes in administration bills or block their passage entirely.

By the end of April 1993, Congress had acted on few of Clinton's domestic proposals. As a result, Clinton's public approval rating was lower than that

▼ *In 1993, Hillary Rodham Clinton addressed medical students in Los Angeles, California, on health care.*

of any other recent president at a comparable time in his term. When Clinton's public approval ratings dropped to around 40 percent in May 1993, numerous editorials, columns, and articles appeared asking "Can the Clinton Presidency Be Saved?" or "Can Clinton Govern?" The public and the press asked essentially, "What's gone wrong, and can he [Clinton] regain the initiative?"

Momentum Regained

By June 1993, Clinton began to have more success in Congress. Congress confirmed Clinton's first appointment to the Supreme Court with little opposition. Clinton chose Ruth Bader Ginsburg, a federal appeals court judge, to replace retiring Justice Byron White. Clinton's selection of Ginsburg reflected his desire to appoint more women to important offices and to choose a moderate justice who would have little trouble being confirmed in the Senate. Clinton's choice to succeed the retiring Justice Harry Blackmun also reflected his priority of selecting moderates to the Court. That choice was Stephen Breyer, also a federal appeals court judge. These two selections seemed likely to moderate the conservatism of the Rehnquist Court.

Another important success in Congress was Clinton's budget plan in 1993. This proposed budget symbolized a return to the idea that the federal budget could, and should, be balanced. Clinton's budget would cut the federal deficit by $500 billion over the next five years. Republicans and Democrats alike criticized Clinton's budget proposal for too slight a reduction in the deficit. Still, the budget passed Congress with very small majorities. Not one Senate Republican voted for the proposal.

Clinton maintained his momentum in the fall when he persuaded Congress to ratify the **North American Free Trade Agreement (NAFTA)**. This regional trade agreement would give special trade advantages to the U.S., Canada, and Mexico. Representatives from the U.S., Canada, and Mexico had negotiated the terms of the trade agreement under the watchful eye of the Bush administration. Clinton was slow to actively push the agreement because many Democrats in Congress and their constituencies were opposed. Labor unions, for example, opposed NAFTA primarily because they feared that U.S. companies would move their businesses and jobs to Mexico where labor costs were cheaper. Environmental groups also opposed NAFTA because of weak provisions for protecting the environment. On the other hand, most business groups and congressional Republicans supported NAFTA, primarily because they believed it would

▶ *In 1996, the justices of the U.S. Supreme Court included (seated left to right) Antonin Scalia, John Paul Stevens, Chief Justice William Rehnquist, Sandra Day O'Connor, and Anthony Kennedy; (standing, left to right) Ruth Bader Ginsburg, David H. Souter, Clarence Thomas, and Stephen Breyer.*

▲ *James Brady gave the "thumbs-up" sign to photographers prior to his testimony before a 1989 Senate Judiciary subcommittee considering handgun legislation.*

New Problems Emerge

Clinton's legislative victories during his first year were little guarantee that he could repeat those successes. First, Clinton's effectiveness was blunted by questions of past ethical conduct. Both Congress and a special prosecutor investigated Clinton's connection to what was dubbed the Whitewater scandal. Investigators wanted to know if funds from an Arkansas S & L, run by a Clinton business partner, had been illegally diverted to a failed real estate venture and to one of Clinton's election campaigns in Arkansas. In a second event, Paula Jones, a former Arkansas state government worker, filed a civil suit against Clinton alleging sexual harassment. (A court ruling delayed hearing of the case until Clinton would leave the presidency.) Clinton denied wrongdoing in both cases, but these scandals undermined Clinton's political support and diverted his attention from other important matters.

Second, 1994 was a congressional election year which intensified partisan politics. It seemed unlikely that Clinton could persuade Congress to pass either of the two most important items left on his domestic agenda—welfare reform and health care reform. Both of these issues were extremely complicated and split people along party lines.

There was wide agreement that the existing welfare system was largely a failure. There was a growing consensus that the welfare system discouraged people from working, and that it encouraged dependency for generation after generation of welfare recipients. There was, however, much less agreement about possible reforms. Could education and job training programs really break the cycle of welfare dependency? Given the deficit, could enough money be found to pay for such programs? Could people with training find jobs that paid well enough to lift them out of poverty?

Republican Landslide   Clinton's difficulties became even more pronounced as a result of the congressional elections in November 1994. While the Democrats expected to lose seats in both the Senate and the House, they were not prepared for the Republican landslide that actually occurred. In the

stimulate U.S. economic growth. Clinton worked closely with Republicans to secure passage of the agreement in November.

Clinton and Congress also cooperated to secure passage of the Brady bill, overcoming an intense lobbying effort by the National Rifle Association. The Brady Bill established modest regulation of hand guns and some assault weapons. In February 1994, Clinton prodded Congress to pass a comprehensive crime control bill. As eventually enacted, this legislation allocated nearly $30 billion to provide more local police officers, to build more prison cells, and to establish crime prevention programs. It also banned 19 types of assault weapons.

By the end of Clinton's first year in office—despite a slow start—his public approval ratings had improved to 54 percent. As *Newsweek* magazine observed in early 1994, "by most rational standards, this president has had a pretty good first year." *Time* magazine agreed and suggested that government gridlock had at least loosened. "Congress passed the two big measures Clinton fought hard for. . . . Most remarkable of all, perhaps, the lawmaker's work did not draw even one presidential veto—the first time that has happened since 1969."

Beyond the Moon

" That's one small step for a man, one giant leap for mankind." The echo of Neil Armstrong's first words spoken on the Moon had hardly faded when public interest in the U.S. space program declined. Failed projects, the fear of research being used to further aggressive military aims, and disasters such as the *Challenger* space shuttle tragedy have drastically reduced funding for space exploration, especially as legislators face large budget deficits and deep cuts in social programs.

Despite major setbacks and criticisms of the U.S. space program, many benefits have been reaped from space-related research. The use of satellites for communication, earth survey, and navigation has revolutionized the way Americans receive information. Numerous products developed for the space program are now commonly used by industry and the public, including television satellites, miniaturized computer processors (the computer "chip"), advanced cellular telephone technology, disposable diapers, Teflon, and freeze-dried food products.

The *Voyager* spacecraft program that explored the outer planets of the solar system was called "spectacularly successful" in gathering scientific data. After an initial malfunction in the Hubble Telescope, a space shuttle rescue mission fixed the problem. The

▲ *This photograph of the U.S. space shuttle* Atlantis *was taken by Russian cosmonauts aboard Russia's* Mir *space station.*

telescope is now sending back high-resolution images from the far reaches of the universe. This data is helping astronomers gain new understandings about how our universe functions.

The U.S. space program received a welcome "boost" in June 1995 when the space shuttle *Atlantis,* during the 100th manned U.S. space mission, joined with the Russian space lab *Mir*. The Atlantis-Mir craft was large enough to be seen as a bright star moving quickly across the horizon. Millions on Earth watched spellbound as American astronauts exchanged greetings and gifts with welcoming Russian cosmonauts.

The docking mechanism used by the *Atlantis* was originally developed by the Russians and modified by the U.S. at the bargain

price of $400 million. "No one has enough money in their budget to do space exploration alone," explained a NASA director. "If it weren't for the Russians, we wouldn't have an astronaut today with 100 days in space." The heavy burden space exploration places on national budgets, coupled with the success of the historic *Atlantis-Mir* docking, has bolstered support for an international space station. Perhaps this example of international cooperation will encourage other international problem-solving efforts.

1. What have been some practical applications of space research?
2. Do you favor funding for an international space station? Why, or why not?

Senate, Republicans gained nine seats (from 44 to 53 senators) and in the House they gained 49 seats (from 179 to 228 representatives). Republicans were also very successful in elections of state governors and legislatures. Although there had been real increases in economic growth and productivity, and inflation and unemployment had remained relatively low, the Democrats took a beating at the polls in 1994. What had happened?

Because of real wage declines, middle- and working-class Americans had deserted the Democratic Party in droves. It was precisely these Americans who had suffered the largest wage declines over the last two decades. For a substantial number of voters, "politics as usual" was no longer assuring their standard of living.

The victorious party claimed that the 1994 elections were evidence of a growing conservative shift among American voters. Republicans claimed that they had a mandate to enact into law their "Contract with America" campaign pledges. The contract included such ideas as

- a constitutional amendment to require a balanced federal budget
- funding more prisons and police officers
- welfare reform
- tax cuts of several kinds
- government deregulation
- increased spending on national defense
- congressional term limits.

Georgia Representative Newt Gingrich, elected as Speaker of the House, promised to enact the entire contract during the first hundred days of the new Congress.

At Gingrich's prodding, the House worked at a feverish pace to pass bills containing elements of the contract as quickly as possible. The Senate, however, moved much more slowly, so only a small portion of the contract was enacted into law during 1995. The greatest conflict occurred over the federal budget. Republicans wanted to cut taxes, increase defense spending, and cut many social programs, all while balancing the budget. Democrats attacked many of the Republicans' proposals because, they claimed, cutting Medicare, Medicaid, Social Security, and

▲ *Newt Gingrich was elected Speaker of the House of Representatives of the 104th Congress.*

other social programs would hurt the poor, the elderly, and the middle classes. By the end of 1995, public opinion polls indicated that as Americans learned more about the contract and its implications, they liked it less and less.

So sharp was the conflict over the budget that by late 1995, the president and Congress had not yet agreed on the federal budget for 1996. One result was that the federal government had to be shut down for a short period. Clinton and the Republicans then agreed to provide sufficient funding to begin all federal operations again. For some time, the larger goal of a budget agreement remained beyond their grasp.

SECTION 4 REVIEW

1. **State** the reason for Clinton's difficulties during the transition from Bush's presidency.
2. **Explain** the significance of Clinton's failure to consult with military leaders before attempting to end the ban on homosexuals in the armed forces.
3. **Relate** why labor unions and environmental groups were generally opposed to NAFTA.
4. **Identify** the Brady bill.
5. **Name** the two areas in which Clinton promised, and failed, to get legislative reform.

Clinton's Foreign Policies

With the end of the Cold War, public opinion polls showed that most Americans were much more anxious about the economy and other domestic problems than about foreign affairs. Democratic Party pollster Geoffrey Garin echoed this interpretation: "When the voters said in 1992 that they wanted a president to pay attention to the home front, they were perfectly serious about it. . . . it is clearly a skeptical electorate out there on these [foreign policy] questions." The day after his election, Clinton promised "to focus on the economy like a laser. Foreign policy in large measure will come into play as it affects the economy." Indeed, Clinton seemed concerned that the public thought he was spending any time at all on foreign affairs. In a televised town hall meeting at the White House on May 27, 1993, the president even produced statistics to reassure the public that he was indeed concentrating on problems at home.

What did the 1992 elections say about the importance of foreign affairs to Americans?

With what immediate foreign problems did President Clinton have to deal?

How does the emerging global economy affect vital U.S. interests?

Immediate Foreign Problems

Whether or not Clinton wanted to devote time to them, several tricky foreign policy problems confronted him almost immediately after his inauguration. First was the effort to provide relief to famine-plagued Somalia. In late November 1992, President Bush, with the approval of the United Nations, had ordered 28,000 U.S. soldiers to Somalia to protect food shipments to millions of Somalians in the midst of a brutal civil war. Clinton supported two United Nations resolutions which changed the mission of the UN forces in Somalia.

In addition to famine relief, the new mission called for restoring order and removing Somalian warlord General Mohammed Farah Aidid. By early October, 23 U.S. soldiers had been killed in Somalia and many opinion makers and politicians urged Clinton to withdraw U.S. troops. Under mounting pressure in the press and Congress, Clinton withdrew U.S. forces in March 1994.

Haiti presented Clinton with a problem closer to home. The primary issues in that country were chronic poverty and political unrest, leading thousands of Haitian refugees to attempt to immigrate illegally to the United States. When a military coup ousted the democratically elected government of Jean-Bertrand Aristide (ar-is-TEED), President Bush had imposed economic sanctions on Haiti to force the military regime from power. Clinton tightened these sanctions. When the United States tried to land a small force in Haiti to restore order, a Haitian mob resisted the landing. Clinton backed away, provoking sharp criticism in the press. Eventually, with U.S. backing, Aristide returned to power.

Clinton's third problem was a bloody civil war in what was formerly Yugoslavia. Historical ethnic conflicts, kept in check by Soviet control, flared after the end of the Cold War. The Serbians, the majority

▼ *Ethnic fighting flared in Bosnia-Herzegovina after the Soviet Union's dissolution.*

ethnic group in the region, had initiated a policy of "ethnic cleansing" against the Islamic Bosnian minority. Thousands of Bosnian men, women, and children were systematically starved and murdered.

European nations seemed unwilling to intervene to stop the brutal war. Fearful of repeating the mistakes of Vietnam, many congressional leaders opposed sending U.S. troops to fight in a land war. Attacks on UN peacekeeping forces and a continued refusal on both sides to compromise led to public demand for an end to the uneven contest.

Clinton avoided direct U.S. military intervention in Bosnia. Rather, he favored ending an arms embargo—originally imposed on Yugoslavia—so Bosnians could better fight the Serbs. When America's European allies—especially Britain and France—opposed the plan, Clinton retreated. In late 1995, however, Clinton arranged for the warring factions to meet in Dayton, Ohio, to negotiate an end to the civil war. It was agreed that NATO forces, including U. S. ground troops, would be stationed in Bosnia to help secure the peace.

The Global Economy

According to foreign policy "realists," national interests do not shift back and forth from crisis to crisis, from adversary to adversary, or from president to president. Vital U.S. national interests include not only national defense, but economic security and trade—a stable world in which democracy and free markets can expand and flourish. Americans are still debating the best way to attain these goals.

When Americans today seek to buy American products to support U.S. companies and workers, they sometimes encounter perplexing difficulties. If they purchase a Pontiac Le Mans, assuming it is an American-made car, they may discover that West Germans designed the car, South Koreans assembled it, and it includes parts manufactured in the United States, Japan, France, South Korea, Singapore, and Australia. If they purchase a Toyota Camry, presumably a Japanese-made car, it might well have been assembled in Georgetown, Kentucky, from parts made in no fewer than 25 states. This illustrates that

the U.S. economy has become part of an increasingly integrated, interdependent, **global economy**.

More individuals and interest groups in the United States than ever before are dependent on shifts in the global economy. The interests of these groups however, are often not the same. Automobile workers in Japanese-owned factories in Ohio could have different interests at stake in international trade agreements from those of automobile workers in American-owned factories in Michigan.

Many U.S. industries now experience heavy foreign competition. In the automobile industry, for example, better-made and smaller European and Japanese cars drastically cut into the U.S. automobile market. By 1981, the United States was importing 26 percent of its cars, 25 percent of its steel, 35 percent of its textile machinery, 53 percent of its computer-controlled machine tools, and 60 percent of its televisions, radios, and other consumer electronics. In comparison, imports of these items had been less than 10 percent of U.S. consumption only 20 years before.

One great advantage that Japan and Western Europe had over the United States was that, early on, their factories used the most automated and efficient technology available. Computer-controlled manufacturing allowed them to make better

▼ *Foreign-made automobiles rolled out of a transport ship and onto American shores in New Jersey in 1992. What have been the effects on the economy?*

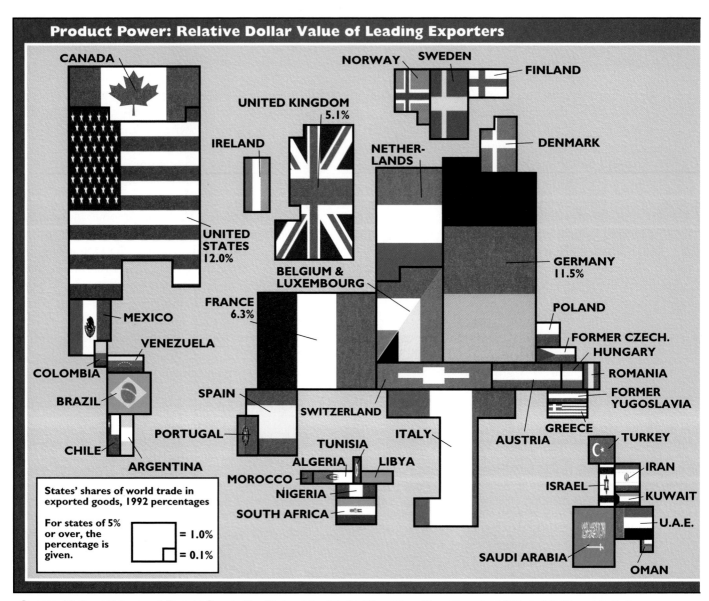

Product Power: Relative Dollar Value of Leading Exporters

CANADA

UNITED STATES 12.0%

MEXICO

VENEZUELA

COLOMBIA

BRAZIL

CHILE

ARGENTINA

IRELAND

UNITED KINGDOM 5.1%

BELGIUM & LUXEMBOURG

FRANCE 6.3%

SPAIN

PORTUGAL

MOROCCO

ALGERIA

TUNISIA

LIBYA

NIGERIA

SOUTH AFRICA

SWITZERLAND

ITALY

NORWAY

SWEDEN

FINLAND

NETHER-LANDS

DENMARK

GERMANY 11.5%

POLAND

FORMER CZECH.

HUNGARY

ROMANIA

FORMER YUGOSLAVIA

GREECE

AUSTRIA

TURKEY

IRAN

ISRAEL

KUWAIT

U.A.E.

SAUDI ARABIA

OMAN

States' shares of world trade in exported goods, 1992 percentages

For states of 5% or over, the percentage is given.

= 1.0%

= 0.1%

Source: Michael Kidron and Ronald Segal, *The State of the World Atlas*, 5th edition. Copyright ©Myriad Editions Limited.

products, in less time, and at much lower prices. In addition, because of an overvalued dollar, imported goods of every kind were relatively cheaper and American goods more expensive.

As a further result, America's **balance of trade** (the difference between the value of imports compared to the value of exports) faced a deficit throughout the 1980s and into the 1990s. In 1990, the U.S. posted a $145 billion trade deficit; Japan showed a $32 billion surplus. It was this negative trade balance that convinced the Clinton administration to threaten vigorous trade sanctions against

Japan with the goal of increasing Japanese imports of U.S. products.

One characteristic of the global economy is the increasing number of **multinational corporations**, or "multinationals." Multinationals are businesses with operations in more than one country. The emergence of a worldwide marketplace for goods and services encouraged multinationals to produce goods and to sell them in every major region of the world. Using revolutionary communication technologies, they compete for shares of the global market. Instantaneous global communication through

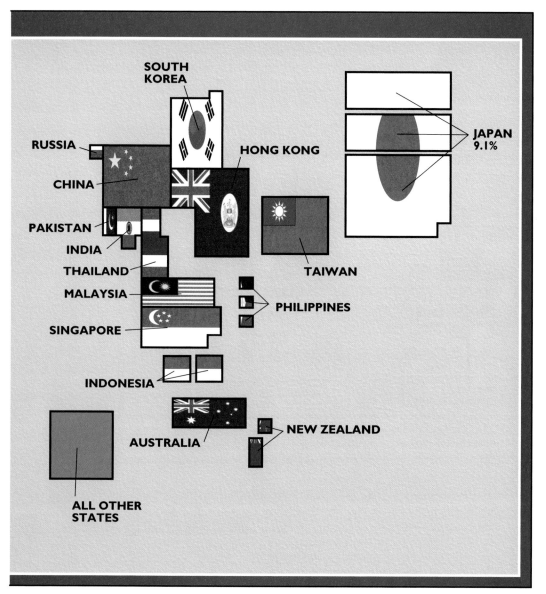

SOUTH KOREA

RUSSIA

CHINA

HONG KONG

PAKISTAN

INDIA

THAILAND

MALAYSIA

SINGAPORE

TAIWAN

PHILIPPINES

INDONESIA

AUSTRALIA

NEW ZEALAND

ALL OTHER STATES

JAPAN
9.1%

◀ *This cartogram shows the relative shares of trade in exported goods of various nations. Note that three economic superpowers—the United States, Germany, and Japan—account for nearly one-third of all world trade in exported goods.*

such technologies as satellites, fax machines, and computers has resulted in the nearly free flow of information, ideas, and news.

Multinationals often locate their factories in developing nations with very low wage rates for local workers. They buy raw materials in such huge quantities that they pay less for the materials and can produce the goods at lower costs. This is called **economy of scale**.

Multinationals can protect themselves against local economic fluctuations. A recession in Asia, for example, is not so troubling to a company that also produces and sells its products in Europe or North America. They can avoid tariffs and other trade barriers when they sell their goods in the countries where they have manufacturing plants. Finally, multinationals avoid the environmental, health, or labor regulations imposed by specific governments by moving elsewhere. For example, a company that produces chemicals may avoid regulations forbidding dumping waste materials into local waterways or requiring workers to observe safety precautions, by moving its plant to a country where no similar regulations apply.

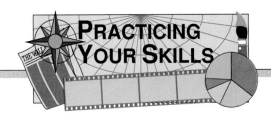
Special Purpose Map: Analyzing an Economic Map

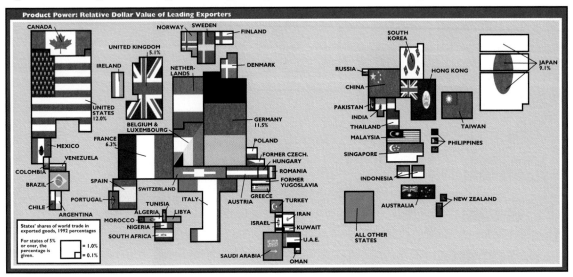

Product Power: Relative Dollar Value of Leading Exporters

States' shares of world trade in exported goods, 1992 percentages

For states of 5% or over, the percentage is given. □ = 1.0% □ = 0.1%

In the Practicing Your Skills on page 897, you analyzed a cartogram of the distribution of the 1964 electoral college vote.

The cartogram on pages 1070 and 1071 shows the relative dollar value of the exports of the leading export countries of the world. The size of each country is determined by the dollar value of its exports, as compared to other countries. Review the steps for reading a map on page 81 and then answer these questions:

1. (a) What information does the title of the map provide? (b) What is the source of the map? (c) Does this seem to be a reliable source?
2. Compare the location of the countries on the cartogram to the world political map in the atlas at the back of this book. Are the countries generally in the same relative location?
3. (a) Which country is the largest exporter in North America? (b) Which country is the largest exporter in Asia? (c) Which country is the largest exporter in Europe?

4. According to the map key, approximately what percentage of world trade is exported by Costa Rica?
5. Which continent shows the smallest amount of exports? What does this suggest about the relationship between value of exports and gross national products?
6. The CIS is a major industrial power, but a relatively small exporter. What factor(s) could account for this?
7. Saudi Arabia produces very few manufactured products for export. What accounts for its presence as a leading exporter?
8. Look at the world political map in the atlas at the back of this book. (a) Which country shows the greatest increase in size? (b) Which country shows the greatest decrease?
9. What additional information would be needed to determine whether a country has a favorable balance of trade?

▲ *McDonald's Corporation, a multinational, opened a hamburger franchise in Moscow. Would you expect this to be a successful venture, or not?*

The globalization of production, finances, and services has had serious consequences. Global competition has led multinational companies to stop being loyal to a particular community or nation. As a result, towns, cities, regions, states, and nations have had to compete for new plants and businesses or for retaining old ones. If the locality is attractive enough—if it has offered favorable labor contracts and tax incentives, for example—it has usually gotten or retained the plant. But if not, the companies have often located the plant elsewhere, taking jobs, families, and economic vitality with them.

SECTION 5 REVIEW

1. **Describe** Clinton's approach to foreign affairs after he was elected.
2. **Identify** three immediate foreign problems facing Clinton.
3. **List** vital national interests, according to foreign policy realists.
4. **Define** the term *global economy*.
5. **Discuss** several advantages of conducting business in more than one country.

Summary

George Bush and Bill Clinton faced difficult legacies. Perhaps the most important concerned the vast federal budget deficit that accumulated during Reagan's two administrations. The deficit clearly became a significant political issue, but it had other far-reaching effects on the economy and on federal, state, and local governments' abilities to deal with enduring and emerging social issues.

During his term in office, President George Bush was very successful in foreign affairs. Bush shrewdly handled the emergence of the new world order and deftly began revising U.S. policies toward many regions of the world. His 89 percent public approval rating following the Persian Gulf War testified to his superior conduct of foreign affairs.

Within eighteen months after the end of that war, however, American voters repudiated Bush's leadership and elected Bill Clinton to replace him as president. The budget deficit, economic recession, and the emergence of a number of social issues along with Ross Perot's third-party candidacy doomed Bush's reelection bid. Voters had become disenchanted with government's and politicians' apparent inability to act positively in solving the nation's most pressing problems. The political system appeared increasingly fragmented and ineffective.

The global economy and spread of multinational corporations made political cooperation between world regions more vital than ever. Future leaders will be affected by all of these factors and forces.

Vocabulary

apartheid	global economy
balance of trade	gridlock
economy of scale	multinational corporations

Complete the following sentences about the chapter vocabulary terms:

1. Apartheid was an unjust and cruel system because ||||||||||.
2. An example of a product that depends on a healthy global economy is ||||||||||.
3. Legislative gridlock is similar to freeway gridlock in that ||||||||||.
4. Economy of scale results in ||||||||||.
5. Countries try to achieve a foreign trade balance that ||||||||||.
6. Two examples of multinational corporations are |||||||||| and ||||||||||.

Review Questions

1. What were the primary issues in the presidential campaign of 1988?
2. Explain the government gridlock that confronted Bush.
3. Describe how glasnost and perestroika hastened the collapse of communism in Eastern Europe and the Soviet Union.
4. How were historic ethnic tensions affected by the collapse of communism?
5. Discuss how the collapse of Soviet communism affected American foreign policy.
6. How did economic problems plague the Bush administration?
7. Identify four issues in the presidential campaign of 1992.
8. Discuss gains that gave Clinton momentum after his lack of success in the first year of his presidency.
9. What did the 1992 election teach Clinton about public opinion on foreign policy?
10. How have technological developments in communications affected international business?

Critical Historical Thinking

Writing Answer each of the following by writing one or more complete paragraphs:

1. Do you believe that President Bush should have pressed an invasion of Iraq after Saddam Hussein had withdrawn his troops during the Persian Gulf War? Give reasons to support your answer.

2. What do you think would have been the outcome of the presidential election of 1992 if Ross Perot had not entered the race? Why?

3. Support or refute this statement: America should move toward a more isolationist policy since the Cold War has ended and concentrate on domestic problems.

4. Read the selection entitled "The Unending Dream" in the Unit 11 Archives. According to the author what has changed about immigration to America and what has remained the same?

Making Connections with Government and Art

What is the government's role in supporting the culture of a society? Does government have a responsibility to pay for art projects and educational programs unable to fund themselves?

In the past, our government has taken an active role in development of the arts. The National Endowment for the Arts (NEA), established by Congress in 1965, uses federal funds to underwrite fine arts and performing arts, such as dance, theater, music, photography, and painting.

In 1967, Congress created the Public Broadcasting System (PBS) to help educational television programming. PBS programs often appeal to special interest groups unable to afford their own programs. Some have achieved tremendous success, such as *The MacNeil/Lehrer News Hour* and *Sesame Street*.

The justification for government's involvement in these areas is how art benefits society. Often, federal grants are bestowed on minority or disadvantaged artists who might otherwise be unable to work. Many of the projects are out of the mainstream of artistic trends. Federal funding gives unknown and experimental artists a chance.

Critics of federal funding for cultural programs claim that these programs are luxuries, and that tax money is better spent on reducing the federal deficit. They also believe that some of these programs threaten traditional American values and are of an offensive nature.

Writing In 1982, federal budget constraints forced major cuts in NEA and PBS funding. By 1995, these agencies faced serious cutbacks. Write a short essay addressing the issue of government sponsorship of culture (as exemplified by the National Endowments for the Arts or the Public Broadcasting System). You may want to consider these questions: Under what circumstances, if any, should taxpayer money be used? If funding is given, what restrictions should government be allowed to place on artists or projects? What might be the effect on current programs of ending government subsidies?

Additional Skills Practice

Use the following data from the 1993 United Nations *Monthly Bulletin of Statistics* to determine which countries have a favorable balance of trade. Assume that the balance of trade is determined by subtracting the value of imports from the value of exports. On a separate sheet of paper, write "F" for favorable or "U" for unfavorable next to the name of each country.

Country	Imports	Exports
	(in millions of U.S. dollars)	
1. Canada	122,477	134,223
2. Japan	233,548	340,483
3. Germany	408,358	430,315
4. Russia	35,000	38,100
5. Saudi Arabia	24,069	44,417
6. United Kingdom	222,655	190,052
7. United States	532,665	448,164

America in the Twenty-first Century

As the United States approaches the twenty-first century, Americans everywhere are confronting issues that define what it means to be an American. While Americans take pride in living in a multicultural society, many people feel that the immigration policies of the last three decades have fragmented society and culture, leading to ethnic, racial, religious, and class conflicts. We are struggling with the meaning of living in a multicultural society. After initial successes in cleaning up the air and water, we are now trying to find an acceptable balance between protecting the environment and creating economic opportunities and jobs. While aware of the need to control the impact of science and technology in our lives, we develop and market increasingly advanced technological products. In the 1990s, Americans find themselves confronted on all sides by the promises and problems of change.

▲ *Young people in the U.S. embrace American popular culture regardless of their race, ethnicity, or national origins.*

The New American Kaleidoscope

In the early twentieth century, Jewish immigrant and playwright Israel Zangwill wrote that "America is God's crucible, the great melting pot." Zangwill's metaphor attempted to describe the immigrant and ethnic mix in the United States. But according to historian Lawrence Fuchs, the melting pot has never been the best metaphor to describe the country's ethnic and racial diversity. For Fuchs, the best metaphor is a kaleidoscope, an instrument with shards of colored glass whose pattern is "complex and varied, changing form, pattern, color . . . continually shifting from one set of relations to another; rapidly changing." The American kaleidoscope continues to shift.

What impact did the 1965 Immigration Act and the 1980 Refugee Act have on the diversity of the U.S. population?

How have Americans responded to the nation's increasing immigration and diversity?

What have recent immigration reforms tried to achieve?

▲ *Cuban refugees hugged one another after being rescued from a makeshift raft in the Straits of Florida.*

Open Immigration

In 1965, Congress enacted the **Immigration and Nationality Act,** the first significant revision of immigration law since the 1924 National Origins Act. The 1965 act ended the quotas that had favored immigrants from northern Europe. Rather, the 1965 law assigned total annual quotas of 170,000 immigrants from the Eastern Hemisphere and 120,000 from the Western Hemisphere. Congress established an annual ceiling of 20,000 immigrants from any single country.

The 1965 legislation exempted immediate family members—defined as spouses and minor children—from the numerical limits. These family exemptions were soon much larger than anyone ex-

pected, running at about 90,000 annually to 1978 and increasing thereafter. The 1965 legislation allowed for the yearly admission of 54,000 additional immigrants who possessed exceptional professional abilities or valuable work skills. The law also allowed more nonimmigrant aliens, mostly foreign students and tourists, to enter the United States each year. In the 1970s, nearly 5 million entered the country annually; by the 1980s, the figure was over 12 million per year. Finally, the 1965 amendments provided for 17,000 refugees to be admitted annually.

Later, Congress passed several additional refugee acts. The Cuban Refugee Act (1966) allowed over 400,000 Cuban refugees to enter the United States. In 1973, Congress passed legislation that allowed more than 900,000 Southeast Asian refugees to enter the U.S. by 1990.

In 1980, Congress passed the Refugee Act in an attempt to treat refugees from all countries equally. After one year any refugee could adjust his or her status to immigrant without regard to the general numerical limits on immigration. But the Reagan administration implemented the law selectively. Nearly anyone fleeing a Communist or otherwise hostile regime (such as Cuba or Nicaragua) received political asylum and could become a resident of the United States. The Reagan administration refused

The Children of Immigrants

In the 1990 census, the U.S. government asked people to identify their ancestry. There were 197 different responses. The largest groups claimed German, Irish, or English descent. African Americans were the fourth-largest group. Among the smallest groups were those from Uganda, Singapore, and Nepal. The government found out in this census what President Franklin D. Roosevelt noted years ago, that "we are all children of immigrants."

Today, new immigrants are attracted to America. According to the 1990 census, one-third of these new immigrants are Asian American from South Korea, Taiwan, China, Vietnam, Laos, and Cambodia, and more than one-third are Hispanic Americans from Mexico, Central America, and South America. If this trend continues, these ethnic groups will soon be named among the leading ancestry groups of people living in the United States.

Always a nation of immigrants, the United States is once again gathering in new ethnic groups from different parts of the world. As these immigrants, our "new pilgrims," recreate the American dream, the benefits to our country could be enormous.

1. What ethnic groups comprise your family background?
2. Why does the author refer to immigrants as the "new pilgrims"?

Thousands of immigrants entered the United States through Ellis Island in New York. Can you identify the famous person in this group? (©1996 Estate of Ben Shahn/Licensed by VAGA, New York, New York.)

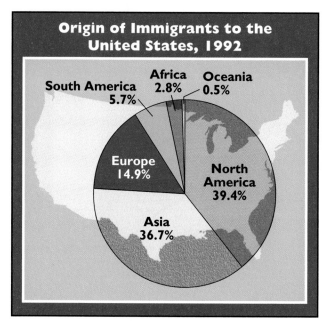

Origin of Immigrants to the United States, 1992

- South America 5.7%
- Africa 2.8%
- Oceania 0.5%
- Europe 14.9%
- North America 39.4%
- Asia 36.7%

Source: U.S. Department of Commerce, Bureau of the Census.

▲ *Between 1965 and the 1990s, Congress enacted changes in U.S. immigration laws, resulting in shifts in the regional origins of legal immigrants.*

to grant refugee status to Salvadorans, Haitians, or Guatemalans, because it considered these regimes friendly. Some Americans saw this practice as a violation of both law and morality, and they organized

a **sanctuary movement** for people seeking refuge or asylum, modeled on the pre–Civil War underground railroad. The sanctuary network smuggled refugees, sheltered them, and found them jobs.

Illegal Immigration

In addition to large numbers of legal immigrants and refugees, substantial numbers of illegal immigrants entered the United States. Official estimates of the numbers of illegal immigrants living in the United States vary widely, from 6 million to 12 million people. Mexico continues to be the source of most illegal migrants (about 55 percent), while 22 percent come from other Western Hemisphere countries, and the remaining 23 percent from throughout the world. Most illegal immigrants cross the Mexican or Canadian borders, arrive by plane with false papers, or stay after their tourist or student visas have expired.

Recently many Americans became concerned about illegal immigration. They thought that illegal immigrants took jobs that rightly belonged to Americans. Others believed that illegal immigrants faced the worst sort of exploitation by their

▼ *What accounted for the dramatic change in patterns of immigration to the U.S. after 1965?*

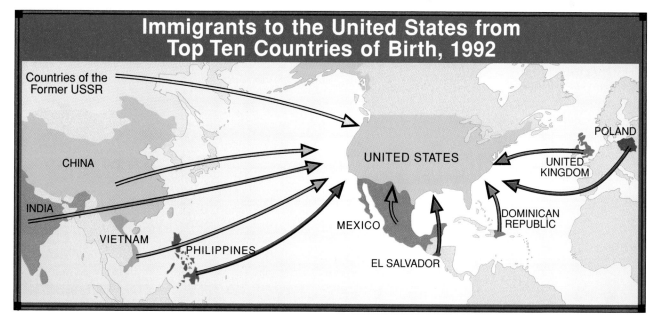

Immigrants to the United States from Top Ten Countries of Birth, 1992

- Countries of the Former USSR
- CHINA
- INDIA
- VIETNAM
- PHILIPPINES
- MEXICO
- EL SALVADOR
- UNITED STATES
- POLAND
- UNITED KINGDOM
- DOMINICAN REPUBLIC

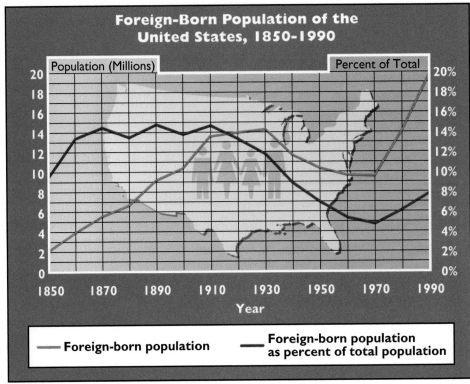

Foreign-Born Population of the United States, 1850–1990

Source: U.S. Department of Commerce, Bureau of the Census.

▶ *This graph provides two measures of the foreign-born population. What are they?*

Legend:
— Foreign-born population
— Foreign-born population as percent of total population

employers. Such concerns led to changes in public policy. First, the Immigration and Naturalization Service (INS) stepped up its efforts to stop the flow of illegals at the border. The INS also conducted roundups of illegal immigrants living in the United States and deported those it caught. Second and more important, Congress passed the Immigration Reform and Control Act in 1986. The primary

▶ *The distribution of various ethnic groups varies widely across the United States. Which state listed has the highest percentage of Asian ethnic groups? Why would you expect that result? Which state has the lowest percentage of minorities? What explanation can you give for these facts?*

Concentrations of Ethnic Groups by Population Percentages in Selected States

State	White	African American	American Indian	Asian	Latino
Alaska	74.0%	3.9%	15.3%	3.6%	3.2%
Arizona	73.7%	2.8%	5.1%	1.4%	17.1%
California	61.2%	6.6%	0.7%	8.5%	22.9%
District of Columbia	28.8%	64.0%	0.2%	1.7%	5.3%
Florida	75.3%	12.3%	0.2%	1.1%	11.0%
Hawaii	31.7%	2.4%	0.4%	58.6%	7.0%
Mississippi	63.1%	35.4%	0.3%	0.5%	0.6%
Nevada	80.0%	6.2%	1.5%	2.9%	9.7%
New York	69.7%	14.9%	0.3%	3.6%	11.5%
Texas	65.4%	10.4%	0.8%	1.6%	22.2%
Vermont	98.0%	0.3%	0.3%	0.5%	0.5%
Virginia	76.2%	18.5%	0.2%	2.5%	2.5%
Wyoming	91.0%	0.8%	1.9%	0.6%	5.5%

Source: U.S. Department of Commerce, Bureau of the Census.

purpose of this law was to keep "the front door open" to legal immigrants while "closing the back door" to illegal ones. The law allowed people who could prove they had lived and worked in the U.S. since 1981 to apply for legal residency. The lawmakers believed that legal immigration was useful but illegal immigration was harmful.

Many considered the 1986 law only a temporary remedy. After further consideration, Congress passed the Immigration Act of 1990. This law increased the number of legal immigrants allowed to enter the U.S. each year by 35 percent. It reserved 140,000 visas annually for immigrants with special skills (up from 54,000) and 10,000 visas for foreigners who would invest at least $1 million dollars and employ ten workers in the United States. The law's "diversity provision" set aside 48,000 visas for individuals from 35 countries that had been virtually shut off from immigration during the prior two decades. The remaining visas favored applicants with family members in the United States.

A Diverse Population

By 1990, the number of foreign-born people in the U.S. was at an all-time high. Nearly 20 million people, about 8 percent of the population, were immigrants. Still, the proportion of immigrants to natives was only half of what it had been a century before. There were, however, more than twice as many different nationalities as there had been in 1920. During the 1980s, immigrants came from 174 nations and colonies. The two largest immigrant groups in the 1980s and early 1990s were Hispanics and Asians. Experts predict that Hispanics will pass African Americans as the nation's largest minority group by the year 2010.

Demographers, scientists who study human population, predict that by the beginning of the twenty-first century, one in every four Americans will have Hispanic, African, Asian, or Middle Eastern ethnic backgrounds. Furthermore, they predict that by the middle of the next century, the majority of Americans will be members of minority groups. In several states and cities, this is already the case.

Americans of European descent are divided about the impact of these new groups on a predominantly Western society.

SECTION 1 REVIEW

1. **Outline** the main terms of the 1965 Immigration and Nationality Act.
2. **Name** the act that was passed to allow aliens from all countries to claim political asylum in the U.S.
3. **Identify** the sanctuary movement.
4. **State** two reasons people are concerned about illegal immigration.
5. **Explain** the main purpose of the 1986 Immigration Reform and Control Act.

SECTION 2

Population Changes and the Family

In the 1950s and 1960s, television programs such as "Father Knows Best" presented what was supposed to be an ideal image of the American family. The husband was an insurance salesman and the only breadwinner in the family. The wife was a mother and homemaker who did not work outside the home. The Anderson family's three children lived in economic security within a stable family. During the program's run, there were certainly some American families who resembled the fictional Andersons. But by 1990, most families functioned quite differently from the way the Andersons did. Now, families are likely to have two or fewer children, the mother is likely to be employed outside the home, and the parents are as likely to divorce before the children are grown as they are to stay together.

What changes affected American families in the 1980s and 1990s?

What impact did economic conditions have on American families?

What are the primary causes and consequences of the increasing numbers of elderly persons in the United States?

▲ *The model of the typical American family has changed considerably since the time of the television show* Father Knows Best *of the 1950s.*

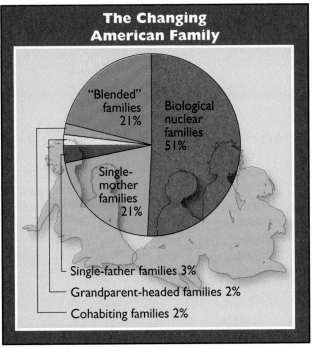

Source: *Current Population Reports*, Series P-20, No. 461, 1994.

▲ *Nuclear families were still a slight majority in 1991. What term refers to the emphasis politicians have recently put on family-related issues?*

The Changing American Family

By the early 1980s, many Americans felt that the family was a social institution in crisis. Since 1970, people had been delaying marriage. The median age at which men and women married increased from 22.8 years for men and 20.3 for women in 1960 to 26.5 years for men and 24.4 years for women in 1992. Changing values, the women's liberation movement, and increases in women's job opportunities help explain the fact that people were getting married at a later age. Young men were finding it more difficult to earn a living, making an early marriage less possible for many. As a result, the marriage rate fell by 30 percent between 1970 and 1990. In a trend that continues today, women were waiting longer before starting a family and having fewer children.

The early 1990s marked a shift from the traditional family system based on the nuclear (two-parent, lifetime partners) family to families created by divorce, remarriage, and births to single women.

Many young people now live in single-parent families and blended families, in which one or both partners have children from previous relationships. Half of all marriages involve at least one person previously married. It is predicted that nearly half of all children born in the 1990s will live in single-parent families sometime during childhood.

The increasing incidence of divorce in U.S. society has been seen by many as the major threat to American family life and values. Between 1960 and 1990 the divorce rate nearly doubled in the United States. In 1992, 2.4 million marriages and 1.2 million divorces occurred.

A number of influences accounts for the rising divorce rate. First, Americans now place a higher value on forming a successful marriage than did earlier generations. People seem to expect more from marriage and may be less tolerant of marital problems. While many Americans believe that marriage

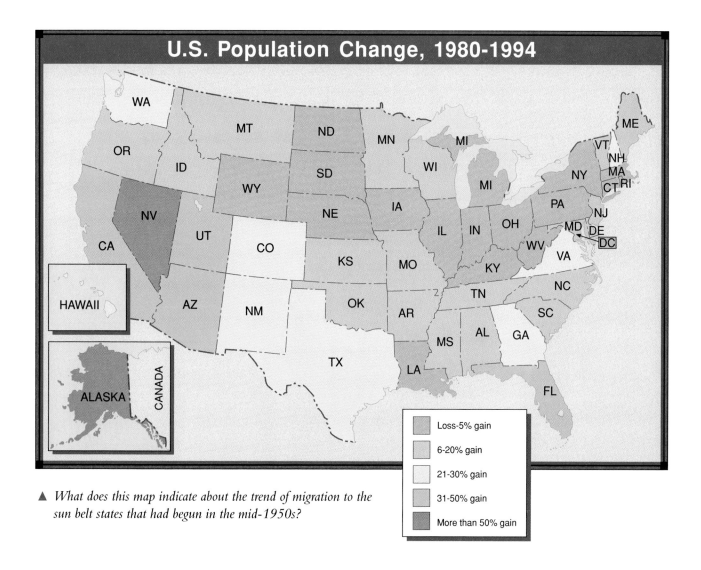

U.S. Population Change, 1980-1994

Legend:
- Loss-5% gain
- 6-20% gain
- 21-30% gain
- 31-50% gain
- More than 50% gain

▲ *What does this map indicate about the trend of migration to the sun belt states that had begun in the mid-1950s?*

is a lifelong commitment, a decreasing number believe that couples should stay together in an unhappy marriage, even if children are involved. Second, society now seems to see divorce as an acceptable alternative to an unhappy marriage. Most states have laws that make divorce easier and that do not assign blame to one party or the other. Third, the entry of married women into the labor force has given them greater financial independence and allows them to leave unhappy marriages.

Whether trends in divorce rates suggest the erosion of the American family and family values is not clear. For example, the number of marriages averaged 2.4 million annually in the early 1990s, an all-time high. Indeed, the U.S. marriage rate was one of the highest in the world, higher even than in many countries with more traditional or religiously fundamental cultures. This suggests that Americans still value the institution of marriage.

American Families and the Economy

In the ever-changing job market, families sustained their relative affluence (if they could) in the 1980s and early 1990s by what social scientists called "family speedup." Family speedup refers to family members having less leisure time, getting second jobs, and to more family members working. In 1990, Americans generally averaged nearly 10 hours

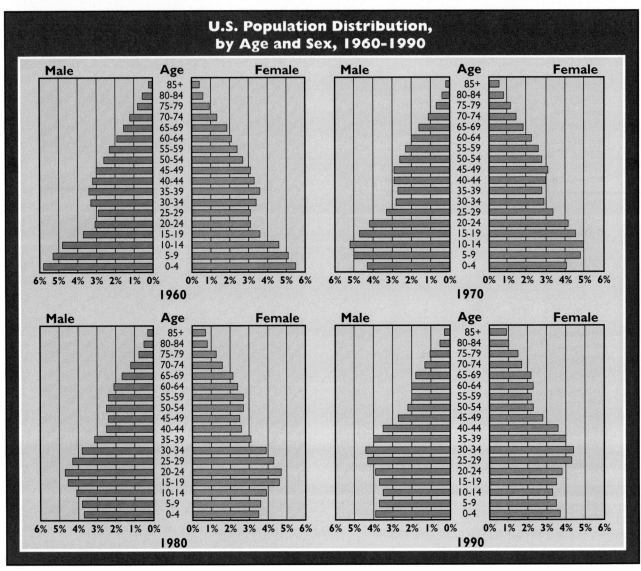

U.S. Population Distribution, by Age and Sex, 1960–1990

1960

1970

1980

1990

Source: U.S. Department of Commerce, Bureau of the Census.

▲ *Population pyramids may illustrate a number of demographic trends. Can you identify one U.S. population trend?*

less leisure time per week than they had a decade earlier. In 1991, nearly 60 percent of women with children under six worked outside the home. Even so, a two-paycheck income did not prevent declining standards of living for many families. For at least two-thirds of the working class, standards of living have fallen since the 1980s. Child care, meal preparation, laundry, and housecleaning increasingly require more teamwork between husbands and wives. Nevertheless, women working outside the home still spend more than twice as many hours as men doing housework.

The trend toward a greater number of women entering the workforce has continued. Women in 1994 constituted 46 percent of the labor force, as opposed to 35 percent in 1964. Nearly 58 percent of all women age 16 and over are now in the labor force. And while women, on the average, earn only 76 percent of what men earn, that figure is up from 68 percent in 1984. In fact, studies show that younger, educated women earn nearly the same as men earn for comparable work. In about half of two-income households, women contribute 50 percent or more of the total income.

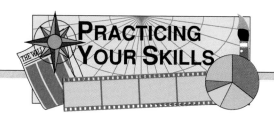

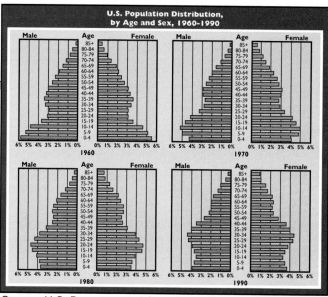

U.S. Population Distribution, by Age and Sex, 1960-1990

Source: U.S. Department of Commerce, Bureau of the Census.

Working with Population Pyramids

The graphs on page 1084 are examples of a special type of graph used by demographers known as a *population pyramid*. They illustrate the age distribution of the U.S. population. Review the steps for analyzing and interpreting graphs found in the Practicing Your Skills on page 123. When you have spent several moments studying these graphs, answer the following questions:

1. (a) What do the numbers on the horizontal axis represent? (b) What do the numbers along the center vertical axis represent? (c) What number should be the sum of the percentages of all age groups?

2. (a) Why do the graphs show a left-right symmetry? (b) At what point does the symmetry clearly begin to break down? (c) What statement can you make regarding this loss of symmetry?

3. In 1990, in what age group did women begin to outnumber men?

4. (a) In 1960, approximately what percentage of the population was 0–4 years old? (b) Approximately what percentage of the population was 0–4 in 1990? (c) What general comparison can you make about the birth rate from 1960 to 1990?

5. (a) In 1960, approximately what percentage of the population was made up of children under 15 years of age? (b) Approximately what percentage of the population was made up of children under 15 years of age in 1990?

6. (a) What age groups comprised the largest percentage of the population in 1960, 1970, 1980, and 1990? (b) What age group would you predict will comprise the largest percentage of the population in the year 2000?

7. What might be some practical applications of this type of graph? (Hint: What groups or businesses would want to know population projections?)

In spite of the fact that women have made advances in the workforce, the **glass ceiling** that has traditionally prevented women from rising above lower managerial levels is still in place. A recent study shows that of the senior managers and above in the *Fortune 500* companies only 3 to 5 percent are women. Many jobs are still defined by traditional stereotypes. Physicians are still 77 percent male, while 92 percent of all nurses are female.

The Aging American Population

By the 1980s, one important characteristic of American society was its aging population. The median age of the population doubled between 1800 and 1990 (from 16 years to 33 years). In general, increases in the U.S. population's median age have resulted from rising **life expectancy** (the average number of years comprising a life span). The use of antibiotics, other medical advances, the drop in infant mortality rates, better nutrition and healthier lifestyles, and greater access to health care have also been responsible. Life expectancy was at its highest point ever in the 1990s. A child born in 1990, for example, can expect to live to be almost 76 years old—20 years longer than a person born in 1920.

After World War II, the baby boom reversed the aging trend and brought the median age down for a short time. As the baby boomers age, however, the median age has again increased. The Census Bureau has projected that by the year 2035 the median age in the U.S. will be 39.1 years. As a result, some observers predict that as the baby-boomers begin to retire, they will place an incredible burden on such programs as Medicare and Social Security. This will happen, observers claim, because the number of people contributing to these programs will decline in comparison to the number of elderly.

Between 1945 and the 1980s, costly programs were passed, such as Medicare and Social Security, that drastically reduced the number of elderly people living in poverty. Because of their numbers, the elderly have the political influence needed to lobby for and to preserve programs benefiting them, although these programs strain the federal budget.

SECTION 2 REVIEW

1. **Compare** the traditional and blended family structures.
2. **State** three reasons for rising divorce rates.
3. **Explain** briefly what sociologists mean by the term *family speedup*.
4. **Define** the term *glass ceiling*.
5. **Name** one of the changing characteristics of the American population.

SECTION 3

Social Issues in the United States

In April 1992, five days of riots and looting—the worst since the urban riots of the late 1960s—erupted in Los Angeles. The riots were sparked by the acquittal of four white police officers charged with beating an African American motorist. The motorist, Rodney King, had tried to elude police cars chasing him for a traffic violation. When the police caught King, they beat him with batons and flashlights. A bystander videotaped this ugly incident, and the video was shown over and over on television. The L.A. riots stemmed from long-term urban problems and underscored the nation's fragile race relations. Race is only one of many social issues that have increased tensions in the last fifteen years.

How has the nature of poverty changed in the United States since the 1960s?

What are the principal causes of homelessness in the United States?

What has been the impact of increased drug use on American society?

▼ *Political activist seniors, such as this group of Gray Panthers, have formed special interest groups to advocate legislation and to demonstrate in support of their causes. Why would senior citizens be especially concerned about budget items in Washington, D.C.?*

A New Underclass

President Reagan once said that the United States had fought a war on poverty for over 20 years "and poverty won." At first glance, statistics seem to confirm Reagan's assessment. After a decline in the number of people living below federal poverty levels in the late 1960s and early 1970s, the rate stalled at about 13 percent of the population until the early 1980s. Then the poverty rate increased. There were several causes, including the changing job market, layoffs, and the Reagan administration's dramatic cuts in welfare spending. In 1992, the income of roughly 35.7 million people, or 14.2 percent of the population, fell below the federal poverty standard, defined as $13,924 per year for a family of four.

More careful analysis indicated that the nature of poverty in the United States was also changing. Three trends were especially important. First, between 1970 and 1992, the percentage of 65-year-olds living in poverty declined by half because of Social Security, Medicare, Medicaid, and other welfare programs. Second, there were significant variations in poverty rates among ethnic and racial groups. The percentage of African Americans living in poverty, for example, was higher than for either Hispanic or white people throughout this period. Third, regardless of ethnic group, the percentage of children living in poverty was greater than for their ethnic group as a whole.

High divorce rates and out-of-wedlock births partly accounted for the third trend. In 1992, one quarter of all children lived with only one parent, but this situation mostly affected minority children. In 1960, two-thirds of African American children lived in two-parent households. By 1980, 42 percent lived with two parents, and by 1992 only 35 percent. The number of Hispanic children living in single-parent families doubled in the decade after 1980. By 1992, one of every four births in the U.S. was to a single mother. These women were least likely to get prenatal child care, to graduate from high school, or to have the job skills necessary to get and hold a well-paying job. These were all long-term disadvantages for the children.

Many single mothers and their children found themselves trapped in urban ghettos or barrios. Fewer entry-level and unskilled jobs were available, and schools and social services in the barrios were

▼ *A minority group member was more likely to live in poverty than a white person. In absolute terms, however, more white persons lived in poverty.*

▼ *Riots erupted in South Central Los Angeles in April 1992. What was the catalyst sparking the violence?*

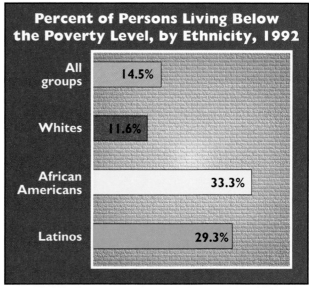

Source: U.S. Dept. of Commerce, Bureau of the Census. *Statisitical Abstract of the United States*, 1994. Washington, D.C.: U.S. Government Printing Office, 1994.

often poor. Young minority men with little education and few job skills were also likely to be impoverished. People in this situation form part of what social scientists term the **underclass**. This expanding group is the hardest hit by economic problems. By the early 1990s, several minority generations had grown up in inner cities where decaying housing, rampant crime, pervasive drug use, joblessness, and inadequate health care had created a culture of despair and a sense being trapped. These conditions can breed violent civil unrest, such as happened in the 1992 Los Angeles riots.

Economic Opportunities and Race

The rise of African American middle and professional classes stands in stark contrast to the plight of the underclass. The civil rights movement increased the social and economic opportunities for those African Americans able to take advantage of them. Between 1960 and 1992, the percentage of African Americans completing high school rose from 28.9 to 69.8 percent. The percentage of

AMERICAN SCENES

The Urban Village

During the 1970s, television viewers across the nation would gather in front of their sets to watch "The Brady Bunch," a sitcom devoted to the problems of a "typical" white middle-class suburban family. There was no crime, no air pollution, and no problem that could not be happily resolved within the allotted 30 minutes.

The image created by television was that the suburbs provided the source for the good life in America. By the 1970s, the number of people living in suburbs exceeded the population of the central cities.

Today, many planners believe suburbs have grown too large to be practical. While sociologists long ago recognized the social costs that people pay to live in the suburbs, experts are now analyzing environmental and economic costs associated with unchecked suburban sprawl. Greater New York is push-

▲ *Suburban sprawl in Orange County, California.*

ing into Pennsylvania. Suburbs surrounding Phoenix, Arizona, consume the desert at the rate of one acre per hour. Many planners now look for alternative and more economical ways to house people.

One environmental cost of living in suburbs is the ever-increasing dependence upon the automobile. The number of miles being driven is increasing at a far greater rate than the population growth—an indication that people are living farther and farther from the workplace. Working spouses and young adults each demand their own cars. In 1994, nearly 20 percent of the total family budget was used in maintaining the fleet of family vehicles.

Another cost of suburban sprawl is the loss of open spaces and recreational areas that are converted into housing developments.

Besides houses, development projects must include basic services such as sewers, roads, water, electricity, and fire and police protection. The economic costs of installing and maintaining these services skyrocket when relatively few people occupy a large area. There is no *economy of scale* in sprawling, or low-density, housing.

Architects are now trying to discover alternatives to suburban sprawl that will still attract buyers.

African Americans having four or more years of college rose from 4.3 to 12 percent.

By 1990, 46 percent of African American workers held white-collar jobs. The differences in earnings between white and black professionals with similar training, however, did not disappear. In 1991, the Census Bureau reported that college-educated white men 25 years and older earned nearly one-third more a year than black men of similar age and education. The gap between what black and white women earned was narrower—college-educated black women earned on average $26,730, while similarly educated white women earned $27,440. Ronald Walters of Howard University said that the Census Bureau report dealt a devastating blow to the idea that race discrimination was declining in the United States.

Homelessness in the United States

Anyone visiting the downtown areas of most major U.S. cities could hardly fail to notice home-

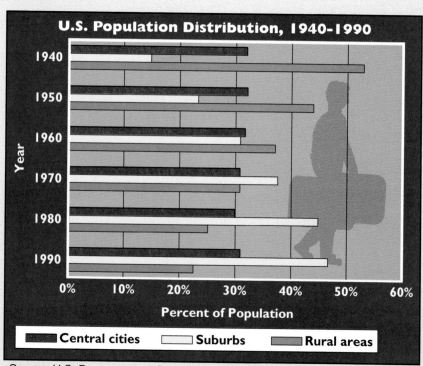

U.S. Population Distribution, 1940–1990

Percent of Population

Central cities • Suburbs • Rural areas

Source: U.S. Department of Commerce, Bureau of the Census.

▲ *Which decade was the first to see more Americans living in suburbs than in central cities?*

acre), and placing a corner store and mass transit stop within walking distance, planners hope to provide services more economically. Replacing large, private lawns with commons (public green areas) and parks where people can interact will save space and water, and provide a place for people to meet and mingle. Offering various housing types, including affordable and low-cost units, will encourage a mixture of social and economic classes. This will provide an alternative for people who believe suburbs are too private and exclusive.

Whatever the living arrangement, it is certain many young people will face lifestyle choices very different from those their parents faced. These choices will most likely determine whether society grows apart or grows together.

How can people enjoy the benefits of suburbia—clean air, safe play areas, and good schools—as well as the economic advantages of city life, such as access to cultural centers, diverse neighborhoods, and mass transit?

One answer being proposed is the "urban village." By increasing density (more housing units per

1. Name two major costs to society of suburban sprawl.
2. Identify three ways your city or suburb could be made more efficient or practical.

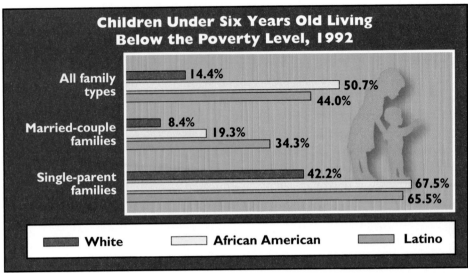

Children Under Six Years Old Living Below the Poverty Level, 1992

	White	African American	Latino
All family types	14.4%	50.7%	44.0%
Married-couple families	8.4%	19.3%	34.3%
Single-parent families	42.2%	67.5%	65.5%

Source: U.S. Department of Commerce, Bureau of the Census. *Statisitical Abstract of the United States*, 1994. Washington, D.C.: U.S. Government Printing Office, 1994.

▲ *According to the graph, which category of family type runs the greatest risk of raising children in poverty?*

less people on the streets. Homelessness is not a new phenomenon, but it has increased dramatically. There are a number of causes.

In the early 1980s, an increased awareness of the rights of mental patients plus severe budget crunches resulted in the release of many people from treatment facilities. Care was put in the hands of their families or of the patients themselves. Often, neither could deal with the patients' problems adequately and the result was that more of these people lived on the streets. For the rest of the homeless, steep cutbacks in social welfare programs and low-income housing played an important role. Today, homeless families represent about a quarter of the homeless population and are its fastest-growing segment.

Meanwhile, many policy analysts began to blame rising homelessness on the changing job market and the resulting sharp decline both in the number of unskilled jobs and in incomes. Even when one or more family members held jobs, families sometimes found themselves without homes.

City governments have had difficulty dealing adequately with homelessness because of the other demands already placed on their overburdened budgets. Homelessness is not a temporary problem, and

pressure has mounted to build more specialized shelters to treat drug addicts and stabilize the mentally ill. Cities have too few resources to respond adequately to these demands. As a result, much of the daily care of the homeless has been undertaken by churches, charities, and volunteers who run shelters, soup kitchens, and other similar projects. Despite the merits of these programs, they have failed to solve the homeless problem because their clients face a nearly impossible job market and an extreme shortage of affordable housing.

AIDS and Drug Use

Acquired immune deficiency syndrome (AIDS) became a significant social issue during the 1980s. First reported in 1981, AIDS is a lethal disease caused by a virus transmitted by such body fluids as blood and semen. The virus destroys the human body's immune system and makes it more susceptible to other health problems like cancer and pneumonia. These problems usually cause the victim's death.

Between 1981 and October 1995, over 500,000 cases of AIDS were reported in the United States. During the same period, nearly 312,000 Americans died as a result of AIDS. Homosexual men were initially the main sufferers of AIDS. By the late 1980s, however, AIDS infection among intravenous drug users—transmitted by sharing hypodermic needles—was increasing rapidly. At first, moral condemnation of these two groups' lifestyles kept funding for public information campaigns and for research relatively low. As the epidemic spread and as heterosexual Americans began to contract the disease through blood transfusions, however, such barriers began to crumble and funds for research increased. Still, medical experts have predicted that the epidemic will grow worse.

Virtually every community in the nation continues in the 1990s to face another serious health crisis—drug use. The use of illegal drugs—whether marijuana, cocaine, a cocaine derivative called "crack," or heroin—has reached almost epidemic proportions. The Reagan and Bush administrations advocated a war on drugs, and national and local campaigns against drugs have continued. Antidrug

▲ *Scenes like this one of a homeless man lying on a park bench have become increasingly common in most of America's large cities. What is ironic about this particular photograph?*

▼ *The NAMES Project was an effort to heighten public awareness of AIDS sufferers. The names embroidered into quilts were those of people who had died from the disease, as seen in the quilt section below.*

programs include stepping up efforts to stop drug smuggling, expanding police forces to stop the drug trade, giving mandatory prison sentences for drug-related crimes, and establishing educational programs. Nevertheless, the war on drugs has failed to stop the multibillion-dollar black market in drugs.

Other drug-related crimes, including possession, selling, and the crimes committed by addicts to pay for their drug habits, filled the nation's newspapers and crowded court schedules. Many state legislatures enacted mandatory prison sentences for drug-related offenses, hoping to reduce drug use and sales. Indeed, the swelling prison population in the United States was directly related to drugs. Since the 1980s, the prison population in the U.S. has grown by more than 200 percent. By 1994, one million Americans—a rate of 350 per 100,000 people—were in jail or prison. The United States led the world in the percentage of the general population imprisoned. Prison construction and maintenance became the fastest-growing item in many states' budgets. Prisons have become so crowded that many felons (those convicted of serious offenses) are being released early, to the dismay of most citizens.

▲ *On April 19, 1995, a car bomb ripped through a federal office building in Oklahoma City, Oklahoma. Is terrorism a new problem?*

SECTION 4

The Growing Influence of Science and Technology

American scientists do more research than anyone else in the world. No fewer than 101 out of 177 Nobel Prizes were awarded to Americans in physics, chemistry, and physiology and medicine between 1965 and 1993. But during the same period, science education and knowledge of science among the general public declined in the United States. In 1983, scientist Stephen Graubard noted, "By even the most elementary standards, instruction in the sciences in most schools for most Americans is minimal. . . . Science is avoided—evaded—by the [majority] of American schoolchildren." The fact that science and technology were becoming increasingly sophisticated while science education among the American public was falling behind created many problems. Science and technology in the 1990s are creating a variety of new choices that Americans have never before had to face.

How have science and technology changed the workplace?

Why did Americans become more concerned about environmental issues in the 1980s and 1990s?

How have science and technology affected lifestyle choices of many Americans?

In 1993, for the first time, the federal government published data on **hate crimes**. Hate crimes are illegal acts against an individual or group solely because of race, gender, religion, or ethnicity. Research has shown that 60 percent of hate crimes are motivated by race, 20 percent by religion, and 10 percent each by gender and ethnic bias. The offenses run from threats and intimidation to assault and murder. Sixty-five percent of hate crimes are committed by white people and 30 percent by African Americans. States have begun to pass legislation that would make people accountable for "hate talk," or speech that incites others to hate crimes. Undoubtedly, the courts in coming years will be occupied with defining the difference between First Amendment freedom-of-speech rights and hate talk.

SECTION 3 REVIEW

1. **List** the major causes of the increase in poverty.
2. **Identify** two major obstacles to solving the problem of homelessness.
3. **Explain** why funding for research on AIDS was delayed.
4. **Evaluate** the success of the war on drugs.
5. **Define** the term *hate crime*.

Changes in the U.S. Workforce

The competitive global economy has stimulated many businesses to make changes in the nature of U.S. jobs. As U.S. manufacturers tried to become more competitive in global markets, they moved their operations to favorable labor markets (in the sun belt or other countries) or replaced high-wage laborers with automated machinery. While most of the jobs lost in this way have been assembly-line or

After examining these 1990s office workers, look back to the photograph on page 571. Has the clerical workplace changed?

and compensation. Only half the jobs created in the 1980s paid $20,000 or more a year. Many of the new jobs were part time only and therefore did not offer medical or other benefits.

In 1989, Marvin Cetron and Owen Davies predicted that "most of the new jobs that appear, not just in the 1990s but from now on, will fall into only two categories: the ones you don't want and

blue-collar jobs, automation has also reduced the need for other jobs as well. Computers have helped managers become more efficient, allowing companies to **downsize**, or reduce the number of middle-management employees. Nearly four million executive and middle-level managerial jobs were lost in the 1980s.

In the long run, automation creates more jobs than it makes obsolete. During the 1980s, the U.S. economy created nearly 17.5 million new jobs. While jobs in mining and manufacturing declined in number, those in transportation, wholesale trade, and construction all increased. By far the greatest number of new jobs, however, occurred in retail trade, finance, insurance, real estate, and services. These new jobs varied a good deal in terms of quality of work

Government experts predict an increase in the availability of some jobs but not others. What would your chances of employment be with the Fish and Game Department in the year 2005?

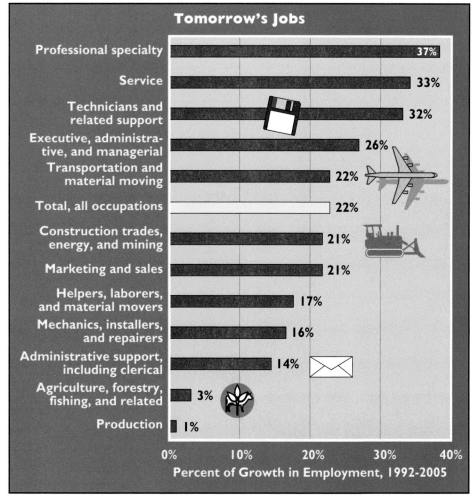

Tomorrow's Jobs

Job Category	Percent of Growth
Professional specialty	37%
Service	33%
Technicians and related support	32%
Executive, administrative, and managerial	26%
Transportation and material moving	22%
Total, all occupations	22%
Construction trades, energy, and mining	21%
Marketing and sales	21%
Helpers, laborers, and material movers	17%
Mechanics, installers, and repairers	16%
Administrative support, including clerical	14%
Agriculture, forestry, fishing, and related	3%
Production	1%

Percent of Growth in Employment, 1992-2005

Source: Bureau of Labor Statistics, April 1994.

the ones you can't get—not, at least, without extensive preparation." By extension, this means that the more years of schooling a person completes, the higher his or her average annual earnings will be. In 1990, a male with five years or more of college, for example, earned almost three times more than a male without a high school diploma.

Information Technology   Since the 1980s, **information technology**, more than any other development, has shaped the American workplace. Devices such as telephone answering machines, facsimile (fax) machines, modems, networked computers, e-mail, and closed-circuit television systems allow people to store, manipulate, and share large amounts of data. This, in turn, has led to **telecommuting**, the practice of working at home or at a remote location using information technology to communicate. An estimated 2 million people telecommute full time and another 6 million part time. Large companies such as American Express, IBM, and MCI have successfully instituted telecommuting programs. Besides saving office space, telecommuting has an enormous potential for reducing traffic and cutting down on air pollution.

▼ *How might new developments in communications technology affect the way people conduct business?*

Many businesses are slow to take advantage of telecommuting because of the outdated management idea that managers need to continually supervise and watch employees. In a number of industries, especially the service-related ones such as retail stores, telecommuting is not a practical option.

Advances in Biotechnology

Researchers in **genetic engineering** have discovered techniques for manufacturing and altering new life forms. In the 1980s, the Supreme Court permitted a patent on a new life form—a genetically engineered bacterium that could "eat" oil spills. When the U.S. Patent Office issued a patent for a genetically altered mouse in 1988, the first patent ever issued for an animal, the biotechnology industry was born.

Genetic engineers have inserted bacteria genes into tomato plants to kill plant viruses and insect pests. They have engineered bacteria that reduce the effects of frost on potatoes and strawberries. Researchers are at work on slowing down the process of aging, manufacturing human organs, and synthesizing life-saving drugs. Livestock breeders hope to use a human growth hormone to produce fast-growing and disease-resistant farm animals. While the possibilities for using biotechnology appear limitless, so do the dangers.

Critics have accused genetic engineers of playing God by creating and altering life. One of the most vocal critics, Jeremy Rifkin, has argued that by changing the genetic structure of life, "we have the potential to do irreparable psychological, environmental, moral, and social harm to ourselves and our world." Religious leaders from many churches and faiths have called for a ban on the patenting of human and animal life forms for profit. Most do not object to patenting processes that result from gene experimentation, but they do not believe in the private ownership of life forms. It also remains unclear what the long-term effects of biological "inventions" might be. Researchers wonder who will finance the experiments, if corporations are not allowed to own or control the end product of their research. By the end of this century, if not sooner,

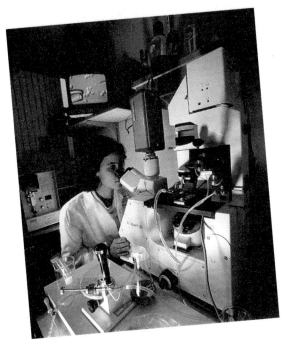

▲ *This woman is injecting cells with DNA. In the 1990s, genetic engineering advances have been both exciting and controversial.*

money problems may limit America's ability to fund high-tech research.

The nation is again faced with difficult policy choices. On one hand, biotechnology promises to be a vital new growth industry that may employ many workers and create revolutionary new products. On the other hand, the potential risks of biotechnology have led to the creation of extensive regulations to govern the operations of biotechnology laboratories and the testing and marketing of their products.

Environmental Concerns

A variety of public opinion polls measured Americans' views about environmental issues in the early 1990s. They showed that 68 percent thought the U.S. government was not involved enough in environmental protection; 85 percent thought that dealing with environmental issues could not wait until the future; and 80 percent thought protecting the environment was so important that requirements and standards could not be too high and that improvements had to be made regardless of cost.

Why this high level of concern? Certainly, dramatic events played a significant role. For example, in Bhopal, India, in 1984, poisonous gases escaped from a plant owned by a U.S. chemical manufacturer. Seventeen hundred local residents were killed. In 1986, an accident at an atomic power plant in Chernobyl, Ukraine, released a 50-ton cloud of radioactive dust into the air. The resulting fallout, 10 times worse than from the Hiroshima bomb, was spread by air and water throughout Europe. Between 1967 and 1991, 14 oil tanker accidents each spilled at least 23 million gallons of crude oil on the high seas. Then, in 1991, Iraq's deliberate release of over 300 million gallons of crude oil during the Persian Gulf War made other oil spills seem small by comparison. These events and many others have kept environmental issues at the forefront of public awareness.

Meanwhile, Americans have become increasingly aware of special environmental issues. In the mid-1980s, scientists became convinced that waste gases (chlorofluorocarbons, or CFCs) from aerosol sprays, air conditioners, and refrigerators were eating holes in the earth's ozone layer. Ozone in the atmosphere protects the earth from the sun's ultraviolet rays. Increased exposure to these rays is potentially dangerous for plant and animal life.

The United States has achieved some success in reducing the number of CFCs it produces. In 1987, 24 major industrial nations signed the **Montreal Protocol**, limiting the use of CFCs. This agreement was a landmark in global environmental diplomacy. In 1992, 87 countries agreed to even more stringent restrictions on the use of CFCs. Unfortunately, once in the atmosphere, these compounds stay active for 70 years or more.

Concerns about global warming and the associated greenhouse effect became common and widespread by the 1980s, although scientists continue to debate the significance of the data they have gathered. The mechanisms that regulate the atmosphere and climate are not yet well understood. Scientists do agree, however, that extensive burning of fossil fuels such as coal and oil releases large amounts of carbon dioxide into the air. Technological countries consume a high rate of oil and gas. Developing countries burn fuels in the form of wood, high-polluting peat, and low-grade coal. Major changes in lifestyles would be required to reduce these dependencies.

▲ *Even very young children have learned the importance of recycling. Are recycling programs offered in your community?*

Another issue that greatly concerns Americans is how to dispose of nuclear waste and toxic chemicals. No one wants a toxic waste dump in his or her community, an attitude characterized as NIMBY (not in my backyard). Some companies are paying developing countries, who need foreign currency to pay for machinery and technology, to act as dumps for toxic wastes. Here, the potential for catastrophes is great, as the storage methods for these dangerous materials are not regulated.

The 1980s also witnessed the spread of the grassroots recycling movement. Historically, the United States has been a nation of consumers, replacing rather than repairing. Americans in the eighties were creating twice as much garbage per person as any other industrialized nation. Public awareness of the need to start controlling the amount of waste was fostered at a local level.

Schools and city governments now support recycling projects of all types. In one elementary school in California, for example, students decided to bring their lunches in completely recyclable packaging. No paper or trash is discarded. The entire school collects less than one barrel of trash per day. In spite of the successes of these types of locally supported programs, the United States still only recycles approximately 15 percent of its trash. By comparison, Western Europe recycles more than one-third of its trash, and Japan more than half.

Environmentalists have taken action to protect species of animals in danger of extinction. They lobby governments throughout the world to pass laws to better control the hunting and fishing of endangered species. They have stopped or delayed logging, strip mining, and other economic activities that are believed to endanger the ecology. There are continuing and widespread movements to create and maintain game preserves and wilderness areas.

Increasing awareness of environmental issues has created difficult public policy choices. In attempts to monitor water quality, federal agents have been accused of trespassing on private property by landowners in many states. Actions taken to protect and preserve the environment have also led to conflicts with businesses and their workers. One important question to address in the 1990s is how to protect the environment without shutting down businesses and costing workers their jobs. An example involved efforts to save the northern spotted owl. Environmentalists claimed that its habitat was threatened by logging practices in the Pacific Northwest. Others felt prohibiting logging of owl habitat areas would put loggers out of work and damage the economy of logging towns.

SECTION 4 REVIEW

1. **Name** three areas that show growth and that generate jobs in the 1990s.
2. **Define** telecommuting.
3. **Explain** why some people are critical of the biotechnology industry.
4. **Describe** the environmental damage done by the Persian Gulf War.
5. **Identify** the nature of the conflict between environmentalists and many businesspeople.

Culture and Change

In June 1995, Robert Dole, Republican Senate Majority Leader from Kansas, accused American filmmakers of flooding the country with such "nightmares of depravity" as the films **Natural Born Killers** and **True Romance**. "We must hold Hollywood and the entire entertainment industry accountable for putting profit ahead of common decency." Dole's speech was aimed at gaining the support of the conservative wing of the Republican Party. Still, his message appealed to many Americans increasingly concerned about the content of the mass communications media.

How is the culture war polarizing American society?
In what ways is the increasing diversity of American society affecting cultural values?
How are developing technologies influencing future opportunities and lifestyles?

▲ *Do you think the 1988 protest of the film* The Last Temptation of Christ *at Universal Studios supported or restricted First Amendment rights?*

The Culture War

By the 1990s, conflict over the content of television programs, the visual arts, school curriculum, books and magazines, films, and even computer networks, could be seen, in the words of James Davison Hunter, as a **culture war**. For Hunter, the culture war is a struggle over national identity, defining what America has been, what it is today, and what it will be in the future. The conflict is about values. Such cultural conflict often occurs when a society is experiencing rapid changes in uncertain times.

Because America's population is so diverse, its people possess quite different ideas concerning authority, the meaning of truth, the limits of free expression, and the nature of community. The culture war affects the lives of all Americans. It involves nearly every part of American life, especially the mass media.

In selecting what stories to cover, what music to play, what films to produce and distribute, what art to sponsor and display, and what books to publish, the mass media define what is important and what issues are worthy of public consideration. The persons and groups who make these decisions have enormous cultural and political power. Controlling and influencing the mass media is therefore a central feature of the culture war.

Conservatives generally believe that the media are unfairly biased against traditional values. They claim that the mass media often censor their books, films, and other forms of expression, by ignoring or ridiculing them. For example, they claim that subjects such as religion are often portrayed in the worst possible light.

Conservatives have developed many strategies to influence the mass media. First, grassroots organizations that hold the media accountable for the content of programs and products have sprung up across the nation. These include Parents' Music Resource Center and the American Family Association, among many others. Second, by the early 1990s, religious evangelicals were operating 1,300 radio stations, 200 television stations, three television networks, 80 publishing houses, over 6,000 independent bookstores, and a number of independent movie studios. Third, conservatives have threatened

Postmodern Art

By the early 1970s, modern abstract art was "dead," largely because it had become commercially successful and widely accepted—although often still misunderstood—in the mainstream of American art. In its place was a jumble of diverse art styles, collectively called postmodern art.

Realism became acceptable once again as an alternative to abstract art. Originality was no longer a quality necessary for an artist to be considered accomplished. Many artists realized that world history provided a wealth of artistic ideas and symbols that could be tapped and applied to present-day circumstances. In the late 1980s, postmodern artists freely borrowed styles and images from art history and adapted them to suit their own styles.

Postmodern artists sometimes work alone, but just as often collaborate with others in the art-making process. The idea of artistic collaboration is influenced by, among other things, quilting bees of eighteenth- and nineteenth-century America, when several women would work together on a single quilt. Such quilts, following traditional patterns, would not have been considered serious art or fine art by modernists. Postmodernism breaks down such barriers and accepts all manner of cultural, creative expression as art.

Several postmodern styles were pursued by minority artists

▼ *Feminist artist Miriam Schapiro's* Presentation *(1982) is composed of cloth, paint, needlework, and embroidery.*

▲ *Romare Bearden often uses collage and photo-montage to illustrate African American life, as in this work,* Dinner Before Revival Meeting *(1978).*

who had been outside the mainstream of American art. The People's Mural Movement, for example, was a national movement of minority group artists. After 1967, these artists painted public murals depicting the aspirations and oppression, heroes and villains in Hispanic and African American communities from Boston to San Diego. African American artist Romare Bearden returned to figurative art and created collages that explored the African American experience.

Similarly, feminist artists became more active and critically acclaimed. For example, Miriam Schapiro began to include clearly feminist content in her work. After 1975, her "femmages" became mural-sized and were composed of paint and needlework.

1. How does postmodern art differ from modern abstract art?
2. Why is postmodern art considered more democratic than other art styles?

consumer boycotts of offending local theaters and bookstores and of sponsors of television programs.

On the other side of the culture war, liberals and media decision makers have argued that all forms of entertainment are driven by market forces. They claim it is the consumers who determine the content of popular culture. As writer Katha Pollitt argued,

> People like pop culture—that's what makes it popular. Movies drenched in sex and gore, gangsta rap, even outright pornography are not some sort of alien interstellar dust malevolently drifting down on us, but products actively sought out and beloved by millions.

Liberals have defended the content of the mass media. Author John Edgar Wideman asked, "Which is more threatening to America—the violence, obscenity, sexism, and racism of movies and records, or the stark reality these movies and music reflect?" Moreover, Wideman relied on the value of freedom of expression—"We can't have the best art unless we are willing to risk living with the rest, the second rate and 15th rate, the stuff that eventually [disappears] because its worthlessness teaches us not to buy or listen."

A 1995 opinion poll discovered that many people were very concerned about the amount of sex and violence depicted in movies, television shows, and popular music. This poll also discovered, however, that most people thought that individuals should take responsibility to correct the problems. The vast majority favored such solutions as tighter parental supervision, warning labels on records, and voluntary self-restraint by entertainment companies. Only 27 percent favored government censorship. At the same time, there was growing concern about the impact of television on children. Research has shown that by the time Americans reach age 18, they have spent more time watching television than in school. The problem, according to Newton Minnow, was that "Our television system is a business attuned to the marketplace. Children are treated as a market to be sold to advertisers at so many dollars per thousand eyeballs."

Diversity in the Mass Media   During the 1980s and 1990s, American films exhibited increasing diversity. In part, the diversity reflected changing technologies. The videocassette recorder (VCR) for playing purchased and rented tapes became commonplace in American homes. By the 1990s, home video rentals outnumbered purchases of movie tickets by four to one. By 1993, over 93 million households contained a television and over 57 million of these had cable hookups. Cable channels provided a range of choices, from all-sports channels to the History Channel and from all-movie channels to Nickelodeon. The cable networks wanted films of all kinds to offer to their viewers.

Minorities and women had more opportunities to direct and produce films which contributed to movie diversity. These included African Americans such as John Singleton, whose film *Boyz N the Hood* (1991) dealt with the aspirations and tragedies of African American teens in the area of Los Angeles known as South Central, and Spike Lee, who studied race relations in *Do the Right Thing* (1989) and African American self-pride in *Malcolm X* (1992). Women directors such as Barbra Streisand (*The Prince of Tides*, 1992), Penny Marshall (*Big*, 1988), and Amy Heckerling (*Look Who's Talking*, 1989) achieved both critical and commercial successes.

New Information Technologies

The power of television had been undeniably demonstrated during the Vietnam War when filmed images of the war became staples of evening news broadcasts. These images showed what had already happened. During the 1980s and 1990s, television was able to show such events as they happened. Television's ability to deliver live coverage has been aided by technological breakthroughs. Mobile satellite uplinks, allowing camera crews in the field to send signals around the world via satellites, are but one of these technological breakthroughs.

Technology, however, has made its biggest impact in other areas of communication. The 1990s saw millions of people in America and around the world take their first "drives" on the **information superhighway**. The term *information superhighway* has been used to describe many different aspects of electronic media. One example is the **Internet**, or "Net," the world's largest computer network.

Actually, the Internet isn't simply a single computer network, but rather a network of networks, joining millions of computer users and thousands of computer networks from all over the world. The networks include large networks from businesses, such as AT&T and Hewlett-Packard, to small networks featuring very few users. There were more than 60 million Net users worldwide as of December 1995. The number of Internet users has been growing so quickly most predictions fall far short of actual use.

On the Internet, people can make use of a wide variety of services. Users can send each other messages via electronic mail or e-mail. They can have on-line conversations, retrieve information, or even play games. Businesses use the Internet to stay abreast of changes in their fields and to link employees electronically in different offices. Businesses also use the Internet to promote their products.

New technologies offer exciting new opportunities even while they pose new challenges. Microsoft's Bill Gates observed,

> [W]ith the revolution in communications, the world becomes a smaller place. The ability to create islands and restrict things goes down dramatically. This has already been true with the phone, video, and the fax. The new interactive technologies take it a step further by allowing people to find common interests with others outside their local community.

The information superhighway makes an enormous variety of information accessible to anyone with a personal computer, raising questions of privacy and of censorship. In June 1995, the Senate voted by a wide margin to impose heavy penalties for transmitting obscene material over the Internet. The culture wars have a new front in cyberspace.

America faces a future that promises new technologies, growing cultural and ethnic diversity, as well as increasing interdependence with other countries of the world. The challenge of each new

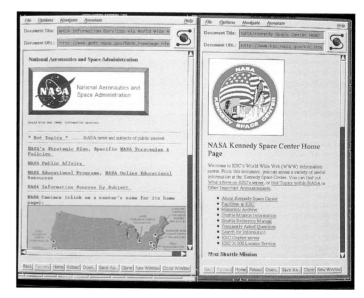

▲ *Both NASA and the Kennedy Space Center have set up home pages on the World Wide Web. The Web is a global network connecting host-site computers for the free exchange of information. Who benefits the most from this system?*

generation is to understand better than earlier generations the history of this country as well as the different societies of the world. The application of the ideas of liberty, equality, and justice on which this democracy is founded are constantly evolving in response to changing times. How these fundamental ideas are applied to emerging domestic circumstances and international relationships will determine the continuing story of this great nation.

SECTION 5 REVIEW

1. **Define** the term *culture war.*
2. **Explain** how the mass media influence what you believe.
3. **State** the charge leveled by many conservatives against the mass media.
4. **Describe** how some liberals defend accusations that they control the mass media.
5. **Explain** how advanced communication technology can interfere with basic rights.

Chapter Summary

Several significant demographic trends affected the U.S. population in the 1980s and 1990s. The population continued to grow, despite decreases in birthrates. At the same time, the population was growing older, and many people claimed this would have severe effects on the allocation of resources, particularly through Social Security and Medicare. Meanwhile, social and economic forces created the widespread perception that the American family was an institution in crisis. Immigration and high birthrates among minority groups created greater ethnic diversity within society. These changes raised a variety of questions and issues about the health of society in the United States.

A new underclass of the poor and undereducated has grown up in ghettos where crime and unemployment may breed violent civil unrest. Homelessness, increasing drug use, and a swelling prison population are social problems demanding attention.

During the 1980s, Americans grew increasingly concerned about the environment around them. A series of nuclear accidents and oil spills riveted the public's attention on the environment. Scientists studied other potentially serious environmental problems, including ozone depletion, the greenhouse effect, and acid rain. Meanwhile, developments in biotechnology and medicine created new, extremely difficult choices for Americans. Technological advances in communications have opened an information superhighway to people of all ages and social and economic backgrounds.

Finally, the cultural conflict in the 1980s and 1990s over values has left many people questioning and searching for a way to achieve national unity without sacrificing ethnic and cultural diversity.

Vocabulary

demographers
downsize
genetic engineering
glass ceiling
hate crimes
information superhighway

information technology
Internet
sanctuary movement
telecommuting
underclass

Use each of the vocabulary terms in sentences that provide contextual definitions. You may relate terms of similar concepts by using two or more terms in the same sentence.

Review Questions

1. What are the largest classifications of nonimmigrant aliens?
2. Explain how U.S. lawmakers responded to immigration issues in 1986 and 1990.
3. State reasons that explain why people today wait longer to marry than they did in previous times.
4. What are some reasons for the rising divorce rate in this country?
5. Explain why the aging of the baby boom generation poses difficult national policy choices.
6. Discuss reasons for the rise in poverty during the 1980s and the changing nature of poverty.
7. What are some reasons for the increase in homelessness during the 1980s and 1990s?
8. What programs have been instituted to fight the use of illegal drugs?
9. Describe the agreement reached at the international level to protect the environment.
10. Explain briefly how television has become an integral part of American society.

Critical Historical Thinking

⟶⊶⌁Writing Answer each of the following by writing one or more complete paragraphs:

1. Do you think the federal government has too large a role in the life of Americans? Give examples and reasons for your answer.
2. The attempt to preserve and protect our environment has become important to most Americans. Give examples of ways individuals can help the environmental conservation movement.
3. Do you believe it is ethical to allow human and other life forms to be patented? What limits, if any, should be placed on genetic research?
4. Discuss what restraints, if any, should be placed on people who use the information superhighway. Should access be controlled? Should contributors be responsible for harmful effects resulting from their actions? Who ought to have ultimate control over information that enters a home?

Making Connections with Citizenship

Thomas Jefferson used the term *office of citizen* in his description of democracy built upon republican principles. He believed that citizens should be informed about their country as if they held public office. The idea that each citizen should put the needs of the community as a whole ahead of each one's personal desires was called civic virtue by the founding fathers.

Studying history is one aspect of this process of continuing education. Today, you know more about the history of the United States than you did before you began this course. You also know more about the history of the United States than most average adult citizens you will meet on any given day. To achieve Jefferson's vision requires that everyone make the most of available opportunities. An under-standing of, and involvement with, the concerns and affairs of the nation, state, and community must continue regardless of career or level of education.

⟶⊶⌁Writing Identify an issue that is prominent in the news. Develop a written background report on the issue, including who is involved, what branch or branches of government are concerned with this issue, and the historical background. For example, for the problem of low farm prices, you could draw on information from the Populist Movement, the Great Depression, and the New Deal. You might also draw upon historical images of rural America and the idea that the independent farmer is the backbone of the nation. After you have written your report, use it as the basis for a letter to the editor of your local newspaper.

Additional Skills Practice

Examine the series of graphs on page 1084. Assuming the trend continues in the same pattern, draw a projected population pyramid for the year 2030. What age group makes up the largest percentage of the population?

Unit Review Questions

1. What major problems from the Reagan administration were faced by Presidents Bush and Clinton?
2. What circumstances combined to end Soviet control of Eastern Europe?
3. What have been some serious consequences of the dissolution of the Soviet Union for the people of Eastern Europe?
4. What was the major cause of the Persian Gulf War?
5. Compare world reaction to the aggression of Iraq in the Middle East with the reaction to Germany's aggression prior to World War II.
6. What circumstances led to the end of the Cold War?
7. What role have special interest groups played in American government since the end of World War II?
8. What has been the impact of affirmative action on job opportunities for minorities?
9. Considering the current level of civil rights legislation and protection of individual rights by the courts and our government, why are political, economic, and social equality continuing problems in America?
10. What effect did the candidacy of Ross Perot have on the 1992 presidential election?

Personalizing History

A Dinner Invitation   During your study of American history you have met some fascinating people. From the time of the Pilgrims to the president today, political leaders have changed the direc-

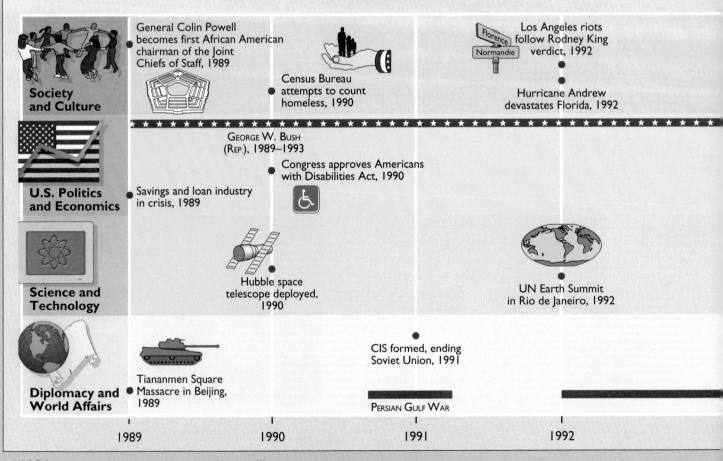

Society and Culture

General Colin Powell becomes first African American chairman of the Joint Chiefs of Staff, 1989

Census Bureau attempts to count homeless, 1990

Los Angeles riots follow Rodney King verdict, 1992

Hurricane Andrew devastates Florida, 1992

U.S. Politics and Economics

GEORGE W. BUSH (REP.), 1989–1993

Savings and loan industry in crisis, 1989

Congress approves Americans with Disabilities Act, 1990

Science and Technology

Hubble space telescope deployed, 1990

UN Earth Summit in Rio de Janeiro, 1992

Diplomacy and World Affairs

Tiananmen Square Massacre in Beijing, 1989

CIS formed, ending Soviet Union, 1991

PERSIAN GULF WAR

1989   1990   1991   1992

tion of our nation. Scientists, poets, athletes, military leaders, authors, reformers and civil rights activists have led heroic battles during the past three centuries. If you could hold a special dinner for your favorite personalities in American history, whom would you invite?

■ Plan a dinner for four American guests from the past. They could be from any time in American history. Design a colorful invitation and include the names of the guests as well as your reasons for honoring them. Share your plan for the evening with the class by exchanging invitations. Be ready to predict how the evening will proceed. Will your guests enjoy each other, or will there be a clash of personalities?

Linking Past and Present

Community Needs   You have learned how people who make up communities, like the one where

you live, have a stake in the future of the country. Where will your town be in the twenty-first century?

■ Conduct some research at the public library and report the answers to the following questions: What business and industries have opened in your town in the past five years? Which ones have closed or moved their operations elsewhere? Which kinds of shops are flourishing, and which kinds appear to be stagnant or doing poorly? What is a special need that faces your community, and how can you help to meet this need?

Time Line Activity

Identify three events from the time line: one that represents the resolution of an old problem, one that offers promise for improved quality of life, and one that presents a new challenge to be overcome. Give reasons for your choices.

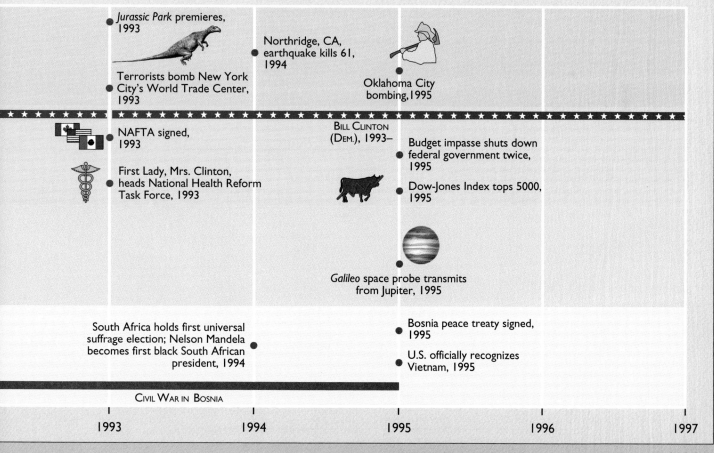

Jurassic Park premieres, 1993

Northridge, CA, earthquake kills 61, 1994

Terrorists bomb New York City's World Trade Center, 1993

Oklahoma City bombing, 1995

NAFTA signed, 1993

BILL CLINTON (DEM.), 1993–

Budget impasse shuts down federal government twice, 1995

First Lady, Mrs. Clinton, heads National Health Reform Task Force, 1993

Dow-Jones Index tops 5000, 1995

Galileo space probe transmits from Jupiter, 1995

South Africa holds first universal suffrage election; Nelson Mandela becomes first black South African president, 1994

Bosnia peace treaty signed, 1995

U.S. officially recognizes Vietnam, 1995

CIVIL WAR IN BOSNIA

1993   1994   1995   1996   1997

Resources

How to Write a History Paper

Beginning the Research

Writing a good history paper can be divided into a series of easily managed tasks. First, determine the purpose for your writing and its audience. In writing a narrative you should arrange your evidence in a chronological order. In expository writing, the task is explanation, using evidence and showing the relevance of your research data to the topic. If your assignment is a comparative essay, compare and contrast facts, opinions, and ideas; begin with the least important and conclude with the most important. The tone and vocabulary of your writing style are determined by the intended audience. A personal letter would naturally be written in a casual style, but the reasoned thesis of a good history paper should demonstrate clear thought and a carefully chosen vocabulary.

If you are assigned a broad topic to research, ask yourself specific questions about that area. Select one question as the basis for your research. This question will narrow down your topic into a manageable research project and serve as a guide for your research. Once you have decided on your research topic, you may want to discuss it with your teacher to make sure it meets the requirement of the assignment.

An excellent start for your research is your school or community librarian. He or she can direct you to relevant sources and show you how to use references, both print and electronic. As soon as you begin your research, record the bibliographical references you use. This will help you later to verify facts, add footnotes, and compile your bibliography.

When your research is complete, determine your position on the topic and state it clearly and simply. This statement is the thesis of your paper. To save time and effort during the writing and revising stages, compose an outline to be followed when you begin your first draft. To create the outline, review and order your research notes. Prepare a paragraph web identifying the controlling thought, main idea, or focal point for a paragraph. To write your outline, arrange the web items in a logical order. Review your outline carefully. Have you included all the arguments and data you need to write a strong paper? Are the topics in your outline listed in a coherent, logical, sequential manner? Will shifting the paragraphs around create a stronger outcome? Think critically, and, if needed, revise your outline.

Writing a First Draft

The introductory paragraph should clearly present the thesis of your essay. The reader should be able to identify the subject and your position on that subject.

Paragraphs are the building blocks of writing. To organize a paragraph, you may wish to create a paragraph map. In the center, write your main idea or thought. In the branches, add supporting arguments, factual documentation, and additional information. Each branch will become one supporting sentence in the paragraph, and your main idea will become the topic sentence. Using the map, write the first draft of your paragraph. The paragraph should be clear, coherent, and logical. Each paragraph should contain only one central topic or focus point. (Not every paragraph must have a topic sentence. Some topics are implied, and some paragraphs are descriptive in nature. However, the reader must be able to recognize the purpose of each paragraph.)

A well-written paragraph has an introduction, a body, and a conclusion. Transitions are made between sentences, linking the paragraph into a whole. The concluding sentence should *not* present new information but should bring the material in the paragraph to a logical end. In an essay, a concluding sentence can also serve as a transition to the next paragraph.

The complete essay has a similar structure. It has an introduction, a body of paragraphs, transitions from one paragraph to the next, and a conclusion which summarizes and restates your position.

Rewriting

After the first draft is written, read and revise. Does the first draft follow the outline you prepared? It is important to verify that each major point has been made and is supported. Generalizations should be supported by specific facts. If they are not, check your research notes to see if you can add supporting data. If you have made comparisons in the essay, are they relevant and supportive of your position? Check your vocabulary and word choice. A thesaurus is helpful for finding alternatives to overused and "tired" words. Check your spelling and language mechanics. You may wish to refer to *Writers Inc: A Guide to Writing, Thinking, and Learning* by Sebranek, Meyer, and Kemper, or Strunk and White's *The Elements of Style* to verify punctuation or bibliographical form. Ask someone to read your revised draft before writing your final essay.

The Mayflower Compact

The Mayflower Compact was entered into by the adult male Pilgrims in the cabin of the Mayflower on November 11, 1620, before they landed at Plymouth. The forty-one men who signed it agreed to establish a preliminary government. The compact bound the signers to a government by majority rule during the time they knew they had to wait for a royal charter. The compact actually remained in force until the colony was absorbed by the Massachusetts Bay Colony in 1691. Many view this compact as the first step in the development of democracy in America.

In the Name of God, Amen. We, whose names are underwritten, the Loyal Subjects of our dread Sovereign Lord King James, by the Grace of God, of Great Britain, France, and Ireland, King, Defender of the Faith, &c. Having undertaken for the Glory of God, and Advancement of the Christian Faith, and the Honour of our King and Country, a Voyage to plant the first colony in the northern Parts of Virginia; Do by these Presents, solemnly and mutually in the Presence of God and one another, covenant and combine ourselves together into a civil Body Politick, for our better Ordering and Preservation, and Furtherance of the Ends aforesaid; And by Virtue hereof do enact, constitute, and frame, such just and equal Laws, Ordinances, Acts, Constitutions, and Offices, from time to time, as shall be thought most meet and convenient for the general Good of the Colony; unto which we promise all due Submission and Obedience. In WITNESS whereof we have hereunto subscribed our names at Cape Cod the eleventh of November, in the Reign of our Sovereign Lord King James of England, France, and Ireland, the eighteenth and of Scotland, the fifty-fourth. Anno Domini, 1620.

The Declaration of Independence

The Declaration of Independence was adopted by the Second Continental Congress on July 4, 1776. It was the formal mechanism by which the thirteen American colonies justified their separation from Britain. The formal signing of the declaration took place on August 2, 1776.

IN CONGRESS, JULY 4, 1776

THE UNANIMOUS DECLARATION OF THE THIRTEEN UNITED STATES OF AMERICA,

When in the Course of human events, it becomes necessary for one people to dissolve the political bands which have connected them with another, and to assume among the Powers of the earth, the separate and equal station to which the Laws of Nature and of Nature's God entitle them, a decent respect to the opinions of mankind requires that they should declare the causes which impel them to the separation.

We hold these truths to be self-evident, that all men are created equal, that they are endowed by their Creator with certain unalienable Rights, that among these are Life, Liberty and the pursuit of Happiness. That to secure these rights, Governments are instituted among Men, deriving their just powers from the consent of the governed, That whenever any Form of Government becomes destructive of these ends, it is the Right of the People to alter or to abolish it, and to institute new Government, laying its foundation on such principles and organizing its powers in such form, as to them shall seem most likely to effect their Safety and Happiness. Prudence, indeed, will dictate that Governments long established should not be changed for light and transient causes; and accordingly all experience hath shown, that mankind are more disposed to suffer, while evils are sufferable, than to right themselves by abolishing the forms to which they are accustomed. But when a long train of abuses and usurpations, pursuing invariably the same Object evinces a design to reduce them under absolute Despotism, it is their right, it is their duty, to throw off such Government, and to provide new Guards for their future security. Such has been the patient sufferance of these Colonies; and such is now the necessity which constrains them to alter their former Systems of Government. The history of the present King of Great Britain is a history of repeated injuries and usurpations, all having in direct object the establishment of an absolute Tyranny over these States. To prove this, let Facts be submitted to a candid world.

He has refused his Assent to Laws, the most wholesome and necessary for the public good.

He has forbidden his Governors to pass Laws of immediate and pressing importance, unless suspended in their operation till his Assent should be obtained; and when so suspended, he has utterly neglected to attend to them.

He has refused to pass other Laws for the accommodation of large districts of people, unless those people would relinquish the right of Representation in the Legislature, a right inestimable to them and formidable to tyrants only.

He has called together legislative bodies at places unusual, uncomfortable, and distant from the depository or their Public Records, for the sole purpose of fatiguing them into compliance with his measures.

He has dissolved Representative Houses repeatedly, for opposing with manly firmness his invasions on the rights of the people.

He has refused for a long time, after such dissolutions, to cause others to be elected; whereby the Legislative powers, incapable of Annihilation, have returned to the People at large for their exercise; the State remaining in the mean time exposed to all the dangers of invasion from without, and convulsions within.

He has endeavored to prevent the population of these States; for that purpose obstructing the Laws for Naturalization of Foreigners; refusing to pass others to encourage their migration hither, and raising the conditions of new Appropriations of Lands.

He has obstructed the Administration of Justice, by refusing his Assent to Laws for establishing Judiciary powers.

He has made Judges dependent on his Will alone for the tenure of their offices, and the amount and payment of their salaries.

He has erected a multitude of New Offices, and sent hither swarms of Officers to harass our People and eat out their substance.

He has kept among us in times of peace, Standing Armies, without the Consent of our legislatures.

He has affected to render the Military independent of and superior to the Civil power.

He has combined with others to subject us to a jurisdiction foreign to our constitution, and unacknowledged by our laws; giving his Assent to their Acts of pretended Legislation:

For Quartering large bodies of armed troops among us:

For protecting them, by a mock Trial, from Punishment for any Murders which they should commit on the Inhabitants of these States:

For cutting off our Trade with all parts of the world:

For imposing taxes on us without our Consent:

For depriving us in many cases, of the benefits of Trial by Jury:

For transporting us beyond Seas to be tried for pretended offenses:

For abolishing the free System of English Laws in a neighbouring Province, establishing therein an Arbitrary government, and enlarging its Boundaries so as to render it at once an example and fit instrument for introducing the same absolute rule into these Colonies:

For taking away our Charters, abolishing our most valuable Laws, and altering fundamentally the Forms of our Governments:

For suspending our own Legislatures, and declaring themselves invested with Power to legislate for us in all cases whatsoever.

He has abdicated Government here, by declaring us out of his Protection, and waging War against us.

He has plundered our seas, ravaged our Coasts, burnt our towns, and destroyed the lives of our people.

He is at this time transporting large Armies of foreign Mercenaries to compleat the works of death, desolation and tyranny, already begun with circumstances of Cruelty and perfidy scarcely paralleled in the most barbarous ages, and totally unworthy the Head of a civilized nation.

He has constrained our fellow Citizens taken Captive on the high Seas to bear Arms against their Country, to become the executioners of their friends and Brethren, or to fall themselves by their Hands.

He has excited domestic insurrections amongst us, and has endeavored to bring on the inhabitants of our frontiers, the merciless Indian Savages, whose known rule of warfare, is an undistinguished destruction of all ages, sexes and conditions.

In every stage of these Oppressions We have Petitioned for Redress in the most humble terms. Our repeated Petitions have been answered only by repeated injury. A Prince, whose character is thus marked by every act which may define a Tyrant, is unfit to be the ruler of a free people.

Nor have We been wanting in attentions to our British brethren. We have warned them from time to time of attempts by their legislature to extend an unwarrantable jurisdiction over us. We have reminded them of the circumstances of our emigration and settlement here. We have appealed to their native justice and magnanimity, and we have conjured them by the ties of our common kindred to disavow these usurpations, which, would inevitably interrupt our connections and correspondence. They too have been deaf to the voice of justice and consanguinity. We must, therefore, acquiesce in the necessity, which denounces our Separation, and hold them, as we hold the rest of mankind, Enemies in War, in Peace Friends.

We, therefore, the Representatives of the united States of America, in General Congress, Assembled, appealing to the Supreme Judge of the world for the rectitude of our intentions, do, in the Name, and by the Authority of the good People of these Colonies, solemnly publish and declare, That these United Colonies are, and of Right ought to be Free and Independent States; that they are Absolved from all Allegiance to the British Crown, and that all political connection between them and the State of Great Britain, is and ought to be totally dissolved, and that as Free and Independent States, they have full Power to levy War, conclude Peace, contract Alliances, establish Commerce, and to do all other Acts and Things which Independent States may of right do. And for the support of this Declaration, with a firm reliance on the protection of Divine Providence, we mutually pledge to each other our Lives, our Fortunes and our sacred Honor.

John Hancock
President of the Continental Congress

NEW HAMPSHIRE
Josiah Bartlett
William Whipple
Matthew Thornton

MASSACHUSETTS
Samuel Adams
John Adams
Robert Treat Paine
Elbridge Gerry

RHODE ISLAND
Stephen Hopkins
William Ellery

CONNECTICUT
Roger Sherman
Samuel Huntington
William Williams
Oliver Wolcott

NEW YORK
William Floyd
Philip Livingston
Francis Lewis
Lewis Morris

NEW JERSEY
Richard Stockton
John Witherspoon
Francis Hopkinson
John Hart
Abraham Clark

PENNSYLVANIA
Robert Morris
Benjamin Rush
Benjamin Franklin
John Morton
George Clymer
James Smith
George Taylor
James Wilson
George Ross

DELAWARE
Caesar Rodney
George Read
Thomas McKean

MARYLAND
Samuel Chase
William Paca
Thomas Stone
Charles Carroll
  of Carrollton

VIRGINIA
George Wythe
Richard Henry Lee
Thomas Jefferson
Benjamin Harrison
Thomas Nelson, Jr.
Francis Lightfoot Lee
Carter Braxton

NORTH CAROLINA
William Hooper
Joseph Hewes
John Penn

SOUTH CAROLINA
Edward Rutledge
Thomas Heyward, Jr.
Thomas Lynch, Jr.
Arthur Middleton

GEORGIA
Button Gwinnett
Lyman Hall
George Walton

Documents

Federalist Paper No. 10 (Excerpts)

During the battle over ratification of the U.S. Constitution in 1787 and 1788, Alexander Hamilton, James Madison, and John Jay wrote a series of eighty-five political essays favoring the adoption of the document. James Madison wrote The Federalist No. 10. *Considered a classic in political theory, Number 10 deals with the nature of groups, or factions, as he called them.*

James Madison
November 22, 1787

To the People of the State of New York.

. . . .

There are two methods of curing the mischiefs of faction: the one, by removing its causes; the other, by controlling its effects.

There are again two methods of removing the causes of faction: the one by destroying the liberty which is essential to its existence; the other, by giving to every citizen the same opinions, the same passions, and the same interests.

It could never be more truly said than of the first remedy, that it is worse than the disease. Liberty is to faction, what air is to fire, an aliment without which it instantly expires. But it could not be a less folly to abolish liberty, which is essential to political life, because it nourishes faction, than it would be to wish the annihilation of air, which is essential to animal life, because it imparts to fire its destructive agency.

The second expedient is as impracticable, as the first would be unwise. As long as the reason of man continues fallible, and he is at liberty to exercise it, different opinions will be formed. As long as the connection subsists between his reason and his self-love, his opinions and his passions will have a reciprocal influence on each other; and the former will be objects to which the latter will attach themselves. The diversity in the faculties of men from which the rights of property originate, is not less an insuperable obstacle to a uniformity of interests. The protection of these faculties is the first object of Government. From the protection of different and unequal faculties of acquiring property, the possession of different degrees and kinds of property immediately results: and from the influence of these on the sentiments and views of the respective proprietors, ensues a division of the society into different interests and parties.

. . . .

From this view of the subject, it may be concluded, that a pure Democracy, by which I mean, a Society, consisting of a small number of citizens, who assemble and administer the Government in person, can admit of no cure for the mischiefs of faction. A common passion or interest will, in almost every case, be felt by a majority of the whole; a communication and concert results from the form of Government itself; and there is nothing to check the inducements to sacrifice the weaker party, or an obnoxious individual. Hence it is, that such Democracies have ever been spectacles of turbulence and contention; have ever been found incompatible with personal security, or the rights of property; and have in general been as short in their lives, as they have been violent in their deaths. Theoretic politicians, who have patronized this species of Government, have erroneously supposed, that by reducing mankind to a perfect equality in their political rights, they would, at the same time, be perfectly equalized and assimilated in their possessions, their opinions, and their passions.

A Republic, by which I mean a Government in which the scheme of representation takes place, opens a different prospect, and promises the cure for which we are seeking. Let us examine the points in which it varies from pure Democracy, and we shall comprehend both the nature of the cure, and the efficacy which it must derive from the Union.

The two great points of difference between a Democracy and a Republic are, first, the delegation of the Government, in the latter, to a small number of citizens elected by the rest: secondly, the greater number of citizens, and greater sphere of country, over which the latter may be extended.

. . . .

Hence it clearly appears, that the same advantage, which a Republic has over a Democracy, in controlling the effects of faction, is enjoyed by a large over a small Republic—is enjoyed by the Union over the States composing it. Does this advantage consist in the substitution of Representatives, whose enlightened views and virtuous sentiments render them superior to local prejudices, and to schemes of injustice? It will not be denied, that the Representation of the Union will be most likely to possess these requisite endowments. Does it consist in the greater security afforded by a greater variety of parties, against the event of any one party being able to outnumber and oppress the rest? In an equal degree does the encreased variety of parties, comprised within the Union, encrease this security. Does it, in fine, consist in the greater obstacles opposed to the concert and accomplishment of the secret wishes of an unjust and interested majority? Here, again, the extent of the Union gives it the most palpable advantage.

The influence of factious leaders may kindle a flame within their particular States, but will be unable to spread a general conflagration through the other States: a religious sect, may degenerate into a political faction in a part of the Confederacy; but the variety of sects dispersed over the entire face of it, must secure the national Councils against any danger from that source: a rage for paper money, for an abolition of debts, for an equal division of property, or for any other improper or wicked project, will be less apt to pervade the whole body of the Union, than a particular member of it; in the same proportion as such a malady is more likely to taint a particular county or district, than an entire State.

In the extent and proper structure of the Union, therefore, we behold a Republican remedy for the diseases most incident to Republican Government. And according to the degree of pleasure and pride, we feel in being Republicans, ought to be our zeal in cherishing the spirit, and supporting the character of Federalists.

PUBLIUS.

Washington's Farewell Address (Excerpts)

In his Farewell Address, printed in newspapers on September 19, 1796, Washington spoke as "a parting friend." He advised Americans to "steer clear of permanent Alliances with any portion of the foreign world," and warned of the "continual mischiefs" of party politics. Washington was keenly aware that the new nation needed time to develop.

Citizens by birth or choice of a common country, that country has a right to concentrate your affections. The name of American, which belongs to you, in your national capacity, must always exalt the just pride of patriotism more than any appellation derived from local discriminations. With slight shades of difference, you have the same religion, manners, habits, and political principles. You have in a common cause fought and triumphed together. . . .

In contemplating the causes which may disturb our Union, it occurs as matter of serious concern that any ground should have been furnished for characterizing parties by geographical discriminations: Northern and Sourthern; Atlantic and Western. . . .

No alliances, however strict between the parts, can be an adequate substitute. They must inevitably experience the infractions and interruptions which all alliances in all times have experienced. . . .

The basis of our political systems is the right of the people to make and to alter their constitutions of government. But the constitution which at any time exists, till changed by an explicit and authentic act of the whole people, is sacredly obligatory upon all. . . .

The great rule of conduct for us, in regard to foreign nations, is in extending our commercial relations to have with them as little political connection as possible. So far as we have already formed engagements, let them be fulfilled with perfect good faith. Here let us stop.

Europe has a set of primary interests which to us have none or a very remote relation. Hence she must be engaged in frequent controversies, the causes of which are essentially foreign to our concerns. Hence, therefore, it must be unwise in us to implicate ourselves by artificial ties in the ordinary vicissitudes of her politics or the ordinary combinations and collisions of her friendships or enmities.

Our detached and distant situation invites and enables us to pursue a different course. If we remain one people, under an efficient government, the period is not far off when we may defy material injury from external annoyance; when we may take such an attitude as will cause the neutrality we may at any time resolve upon to be scrupulously respected; when belligerent nations, under the impossibility of making acquisitions upon us, will not lightly hazard the giving us provocation; when we may choose peace or war, as our interest, guided by justice, shall counsel. . . .

Relying on its kindness in this as in other things, and actuated by that fervent love toward it which is so natural to a man who views in it the native soil of himself and his progenitors for several generations, I anticipate with pleasing expectations the sweet enjoyment of partaking, in the midst of my fellow citizens, the benign influence of good laws under a free government, the ever favorite object of my heart, and the happy reward, as I trust, of our mutual cares, labors, and dangers.

The Seneca Falls Declaration of Sentiments (Excerpts)

In 1848, Elizabeth Cady Stanton, Lucretia Mott, and other advocates of full rights for women met at Seneca Falls, New York, to hold the first women's rights convention. The Seneca Falls Convention marked the beginning of the women's rights movement in the United States. More than 100 people attended the convention where Stanton declared "men and women are created equal." Among the resolutions in her declaration, Cady Stanton included voting rights for women.

When, in the course of human events, it becomes necessary for one portion of the family of man to assume among the people of the earth a position different from that which they have hitherto occupied, but one to which the laws of nature and nature's God entitle them, a decent respect to the opinions of mankind requires that they should declare the causes that impel them to such a course.

We hold these truths to be self-evident: that all men and women are created equal; that they are endowed by their Creator with certain inalienable rights; that among these are life, liberty, and the pursuit of happiness; that to secure these rights governments are instituted, deriving their just powers from the consent of the governed. . . .

The history of mankind is a history of repeated injuries and usurpations on the part of man toward woman, having in direct object the establishment of an absolute tyranny over her. . . .

Now, in view of not allowing one half the people of this country to vote, of their social and religious degradation . . . and because women do feel themselves aggrieved, oppressed, and fraudulently deprived of their most sacred rights, we insist that they have immediate admission to all the rights and privileges which belong to them as citizens of the United States.

In entering upon the great work before us, we anticipate mistaken ideas, misrepresentations, and ridicule; but we shall make every effort within our power to secure our object.

The Emancipation Proclamation

On September 22, 1862, shortly after the Battle of Antietam, President Lincoln issued a preliminary proclamation about emancipation. He declared that on the first day of January 1863 he would emancipate all slaves in states that "shall then be in rebellion against the United States." In a second proclamation on January 1, Lincoln declared that slaves in all the areas still under Confederate control were freed. The Emancipation Proclamation announced to the world that the abolition of slavery had become a major purpose of the Civil War.

Whereas on the 22d day of September, A.D. 1862, a proclamation was issued by the President of the United States, containing, among other things, the following, to wit:

"That on the 1st day of January, A.D. 1863, all persons held as slaves within any State or designated part of a State the people whereof shall then be in rebellion against the United States shall be then, thenceforward, and forever free; and the executive government of the United States, including the military and naval authority thereof, will recognize and maintain the freedom of such persons and will do no act or acts to repress such persons, or any of them, in any efforts they may make for their actual freedom.

"That the executive will on the 1st day of January aforesaid, by proclamation, designate the States and parts of States, if any, in which the people thereof, respectively, shall then be in rebellion against the United States; and the fact that any State or the people thereof shall on that day be in good faith represented in the Congress of the United States by members chosen thereto at elections wherein a majority of the qualified voters of such States shall have participated shall, in the absence of strong countervailing testimony, be deemed conclusive evidence that such State and the people thereof are not then in rebellion against the United States."

Now, therefore, I, Abraham Lincoln, President of the United States, by virtue of the power in me vested as Commander-in-Chief of the Army and Navy of the United States in time of actual armed rebellion against the authority and government of the United States, and as a fit and necessary war measure for suppressing said rebellion, do, on this 1st day of January, A.D. 1863, and in accordance with my purpose so to do, publicly proclaimed for the full period of one hundred days from the first day above mentioned, order and designate as the States and parts of States wherein the people thereof, respectively, are this day in rebellion against the United States the following, to wit:

Arkansas, Texas, Louisiana (except the parishes of St. Bernard, Plaquemines, Jefferson, St. John, St. Charles, St. James, Ascension, Assumption, Terrebonne, Lafourche, St. Mary, St. Martin, and Orleans, including the city of New Orleans), Mississippi, Alabama, Florida, Georgia, South Carolina, North Carolina, and Virginia (except the forty-eight counties designated as West Virginia, and also the counties of Berkeley, Accomac, Northhampton, Elizabeth City, York, Princess Anne, and Norfolk, including the cities of Norfolk and Portsmouth), and which excepted parts are for the present left precisely as if this proclamation were not issued.

And by virtue of the power and for the purpose aforesaid, I do order and declare that all persons held as slaves within said designated States and parts of States are, and henceforward shall be, free; and that the Executive Government of the United States, including the military and naval authorities thereof, will recognize and maintain the freedom of said persons.

And I hereby enjoin upon the people so declared to be free to abstain from all violence, unless in necessary self-defense; and I recommend to them that, in all cases when allowed, they labor faithfully for reasonable wages.

And I further declare and make known that such persons of suitable condition will be received into the armed service of the United States to garrison forts, positions, stations, and other places, and to man vessels of all sorts in said service.

And upon this act, sincerely believed to be an act of justice, warranted by the Constitution upon military necessity, I invoke the considerate judgment of mankind and the gracious favor of Almighty God.

The Gettysburg Address

For three days in early July 1863, one of the most critical battles of the American Civil War was fought outside the village of Gettysburg. When it was over, more than 7,000 soldiers, northern and southern, were buried in temporary graves near where they fell. The site of the battle was purchased for a permanent cemetery, and was formally dedicated on November 19. Lincoln was anxious to pay tribute to the men who gave their lives in this battle. The Gettysburg Address is the memorable speech given by President Abraham Lincoln at the dedication of the Soldiers' National Cemetery at Gettysburg, Pennsylvania.

Four score and seven years ago our fathers brought forth on this continent, a new nation, conceived in Liberty, and dedicated to the proposition that all men are created equal.

Now we are engaged in a great civil war, testing whether that nation, or any nation so conceived and so dedicated, can long endure. We are met on a great battlefield of that war. We have come to dedicate a portion of that field, as a final resting place for those who here gave their lives that that nation might live. It is altogether fitting and proper that we should do this.

But, in a larger sense, we can not dedicate—we can not consecrate—we can not hallow—this ground. The brave men, living and dead, who struggled here, have consecrated it, far above our poor power to add or detract. The world will little note, nor long remember what we say here, but it can never forget what they did here. It is for us the living, rather, to be dedicated here to the unfinished work which they who fought here have thus far so nobly advanced. It is rather for us to be here dedicated to the great task remaining before us—that from these honored dead we take increased devotion to that cause for which they gave the last full measure of devotion—that we here highly resolve that these dead shall not have died in vain—that this nation, under God, shall have a new birth of freedom—and that government of the people, by the people, for the people, shall not perish from the earth.

Documents

Universal Declaration of Human Rights (Abbreviated)

The Universal Declaration of Human Rights was adopted unanimously in December, 1948, by the United Nations General Assembly. The objective of the thirty article declaration is to promote and encourage respect for human rights and fundamental freedoms. Among the rights cited by the declaration are the rights of life and liberty.

Now, therefore, THE GENERAL ASSEMBLY proclaims this Universal Declaration of Human Rights as a common standard of achievement for all peoples and all nations, to the end that every individual and every organ of society, keeping this Declaration constantly in mind, shall strive by teaching and education to promote respect for these rights and freedoms:

Article 1	Right to Equality
Article 2	Freedom from Discrimination
Article 3	Right to Life, Liberty, Personal Security
Article 4	Freedom from Slavery
Article 5	Freedom from Torture, Degrading Treatment
Article 6	Right to Recognition as a Person before the Law
Article 7	Right to Equality before the Law
Article 8	Right to Remedy by Competent Tribunal
Article 9	Freedom from Arbitrary Arrest, and Exile
Article 10	Right to Fair Public Hearing
Article 11	Right to be considered Innocent until proven Guilty
Article 12	Freedom from Interference with Privacy, Family, Home, and Correspondence
Article 13	Right to Free Movement in and out of the Country
Article 14	Right to Asylum in other Countries from Persecution
Article 15	Right to a Nationality and Freedom to Change It
Article 16	Right to Marriage and Family
Article 17	Right to own Property
Article 18	Freedom of Belief and Religion
Article 19	Freedom of Opinion and Information
Article 20	Right of Peaceful Assembly and Association
Article 21	Right to Participate in Government and in Free Elections
Article 22	Right to Social Security
Article 23	Right to Desirable Work and to join Trade Unions
Article 24	Right to Rest and Leisure
Article 25	Right to Adequate Living Standard
Article 26	Right to Education
Article 27	Right to Participate in the Cultural Life of Community
Article 28	Right to Social Order assuming Human Rights
Article 29	Community Duties essential to Free and Full Development
Article 30	Freedom from State or Personal Interference in the above Rights

Plain Language Version*

*The plain language version is only given as a guide. For an exact rendering of each principle, refer students to the original. This version is based in part on the translation of a text, prepared in 1978, for the World Association for the School as an Instrument of Peace, by a Research Group of the University of Geneva, under the responsibility of Prof. I. Massarenu.

Article 1

When children are born, they are free and each should be treated in the same way. They have reason and conscience and should act towards one another in a friendly manner.

Article 2

Everyone can claim the following rights, despite
- a different sex
- a different skin color
- speaking a different language
- thinking different things
- believing in another religion
- owning more or less
- being born in another social group
- coming from another country.

It also makes no difference whether the country you live in is independent or not.

Article 3

You have the right to live, and to live in freedom and safety.

Article 4

Nobody has the right to treat you as his or her slave and you should not make anyone your slave.

Article 5

Nobody has the right to torture you.

Article 6

You should be legally protected in the same way everywhere, and like everyone else.

Article 7

The law is the same for everyone, it should be applied in the same way to all.

Article 8

You should be able to ask for legal help when the rights your country grants you are not respected.

Article 9

Nobody has the right to put you in prison, to keep you there, or to send you away from your country unjustly, or without a good cause.

Article 10

If you must go on trial this should be done in public. The people who try you should not let themselves be influenced by others.

Article 11

You should be considered innocent until it can be proved that you are guilty. If you are accused of a crime, you should always have the right to defend yourself. Nobody has the right to condemn you and punish you for something you have not done.

Article 12

You have the right to ask to be protected if someone tries to harm your good name, enter your house, open your letters, or bother you or your family without a good reason.

Article 13

You have the right to come and go as you wish within your country. You have the right to leave your country to go to another one, and you should be able to return to your country if you want.

Article 14

If someone hurts you, you have the right to go to another country and ask it to protect you.

You lose this right if you have killed someone and if you, yourself, do not respect what is written here.

Article 15

You have the right to belong to a country and nobody can prevent you, without a good reason, from belonging to another country if you wish.

Article 16

As soon as a person is legally entitled, he or she has the right to marry and have a family. In doing this, neither the color of your skin, the country you come from nor your religion should be impediments. Men and women have the same rights when they are married and also when they are separated.

Nobody should force a person to marry.

The government of your country should protect your family and its members.

Article 17

You have the right to own things and nobody has the right to take these from you without a good reason.

Article 18

You have the right to profess your religion freely, to change it, and to practice it either on your own or with other people.

Article 19

You have the right to think what you want, to say what you like, and nobody should forbid you from doing so.

You should be able to share your ideas also—with people from any other country.

Article 20

You have the right to organize peaceful meetings or to take part in meetings in a peaceful way. It is wrong to force someone to belong to a group.

Article 21

You have the right to take part in your country's political affairs either by belonging to the government yourself or by choosing politicians who have the same ideas as you.

Governments should be voted for regularly and voting should be secret. You should get a vote and all votes should be equal. You also have the same right to joint the public service as anyone else.

Article 22

The society in which you live should help you to develop and to make the most of all the advantages (culture, work, social and welfare) which are offered to you and to all the men and women in your country.

Article 23

You have the right to work, to be free to choose your work, to get a salary which allows you to live and support your family. If a man and a woman do the same work, they should get the same pay. All people who work have the right to join together to defend their interests.

Article 24

Each work day should not be too long, since everyone has the right to rest and should be able to take regular paid holidays.

Article 25

You have the right to have whatever you need so that you and your family do not fall ill; go hungry; have clothes and a house; and are helped if you are out of work, if you are ill, if you are old, if your wife or husband is dead, or if you do not earn a living for any other reason you cannot help. The mother who is going to have a baby, and her baby should get special help. All children have the same rights, whether or not the mother is married.

Article 26

You have the right to go to school and everyone should go to school. Primary schooling should be free. You should be able to learn a profession or continue your studies as far as you wish. At school, you should be able to develop all your talents and you should be taught to get on with others, whatever their race, religion or the country they come from. Your parents have the right to choose how and what you will be taught at school.

Article 27

You have the right to share in your community's arts and sciences, and any good they do.

Your works as an artist, a writer, or a scientist should be protected, and you should be able to benefit from them.

Article 28

So that your rights will be respected, there must be an "order" which can protect them. This "order" should be local and worldwide.

Article 29

You have duties towards the community within which your personality can only fully develop. The law should guarantee human rights. It should allow everyone to respect others and to be respected.

Article 30

In all parts of the world, no society, no human being, should take it upon her or himself to act in such a way as to destroy the rights which you have just been reading about.

John F. Kennedy's Inaugural Address (Excerpts)

John Fitzgerald Kennedy's election symbolized the rise to power of a generation of leaders born in the twentieth century. One of Kennedy's main goals was "to get the country moving again." In his inaugural speech delivered on January 6, 1961, JFK appealed strongly to Americans who believed they could solve the problems they saw around them. These people had a renewed hope that they could help create a better world. Young people, especially, had a sense of urgency about pursuing these ideals. In John F. Kennedy, they felt they had found an inspiring leader.

We observe today not a victory of party but a celebration of freedom—symbolizing an end as well as a beginning—signifying renewal as well as change. For I have sworn before you and Almighty God the same solemn oath our forebears prescribed nearly a century and three-quarters ago.

The world is very different now. For man holds in his mortal hands the power to abolish all forms of human poverty and all forms of human life. And yet the same revolutionary beliefs for which our forebears fought are still at issue around the globe—the belief that the rights of man come not from the generosity of the state but from the hand of God.

We dare not forget today that we are the heirs of that first revolution. Let the word go forth from this time and place, to friend and foe alike, that the torch has been passed to a new generation of Americans—born in this century, tempered by war, disciplined by a hard and bitter peace, proud of our ancient heritage—and unwilling to witness or permit the slow undoing of those human rights to which this nation has always been committed, and to which we are committed today at home and around the world.

Let every nation know, whether it wishes us well or ill, that we shall pay any price, bear any burden, meet any hardship, support any friend, oppose any foe to assure the survival and the success of liberty.

This much we pledge—and more.

To those old allies whose cultural and spiritual origins we share, we pledge the loyalty of faithful friends. United, there is little we cannot do in a host of cooperative ventures. Divided, there is little we can do . . .

Let us never negotiate out of fear. But let us never fear to negotiate. . . . Let both sides explore what problems unite us instead of belaboring those problems which divide us. . . . Let both sides seek to invoke the wonders of science instead of its terrors. Together let us explore the stars, conquer the deserts, eradicate disease, tap the ocean depths, and encourage the arts and commerce.

All this will not be finished in the first 100 days. Nor will it be finished in the first 1,000 days, not in the life of this administration, nor even perhaps in our lifetime on this planet. But let us begin.

In your hands, my fellow citizens, more than in mine, will rest the final success or failure of our course. Since this country was founded, each generation of Americans has been summoned to give testimony to its national loyalty. The graves of young Americans who answered the call encircle the globe.

Now the trumpet summons us again—not as a call to bear arms, though arms we need—not as a call to battle, though embattled we are—but a call to bear the burden of a long twilight struggle, year in and year out, "rejoicing in hope, patient in tribulation"—a struggle against the common enemies of man: tyranny, poverty, disease, and war itself.

In the long history of the world, only a few generations have been granted the role of defending freedom in its hour of maximum danger. I do not shrink from this responsibility—I welcome it. I do not believe that any of us would exchange places with any other people or any other generation. The energy, the faith, the devotion which we bring to this endeavor will light our country and all who serve it—and the glow from that fire can truly light the world. And so, my fellow Americans—ask not what your country can do for you—ask what you can do for your country.

My fellow citizens of the world—ask not what America will do for you, but what together we can do for the freedom of man.

Finally, whether you are citizens of America or citizens of the world, ask us here that same high standards of strength and sacrifice which we ask of you. With a good conscience our only sure reward, with history the final judge of our deeds, let us go forth to lead the land we love, asking His blessing and His help, but knowing that here on earth God's work must truly be our own.

United States Political Map

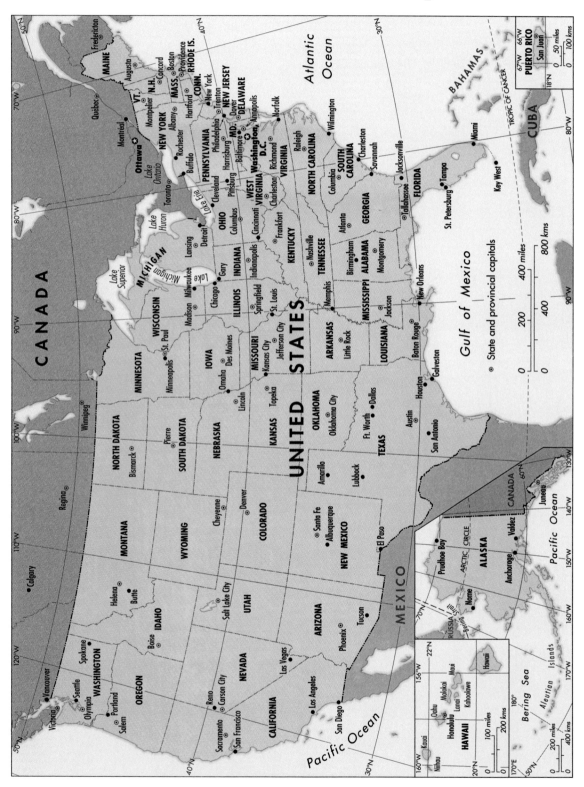

United States Physical Map

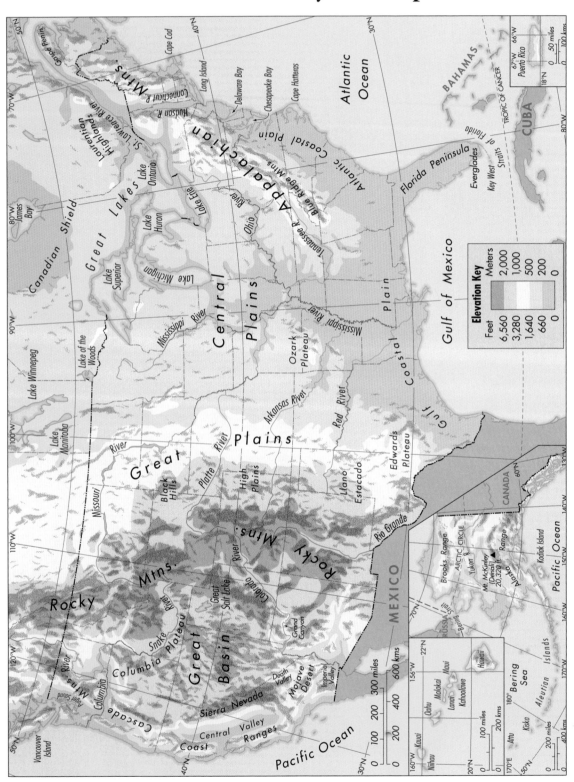

Atlas

The Growth of the United States

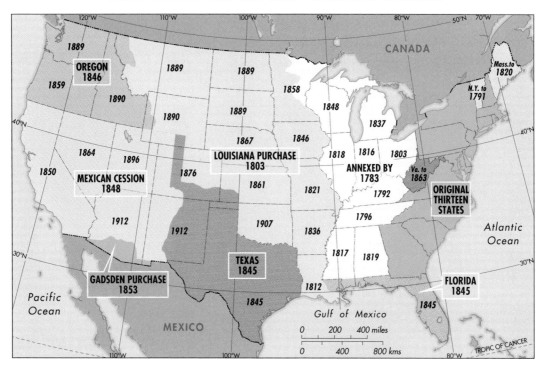

United States Resources and Industrial Areas

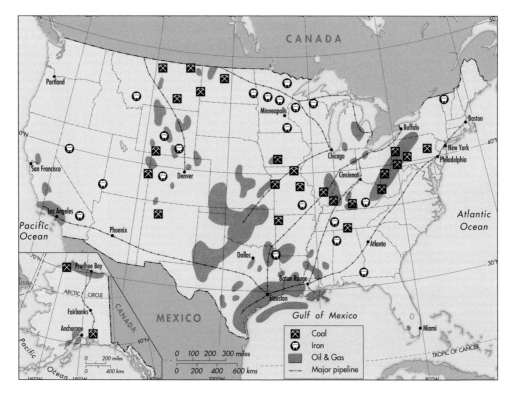

United States Land Use Map (North)

United States Land Use Map (South)

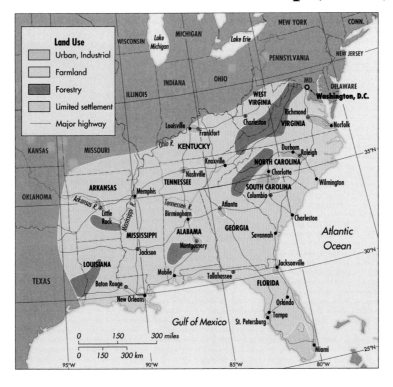

United States Land Use Map (Central Plains)

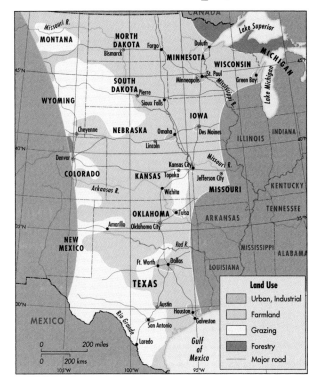

United States Land Use Map (West)

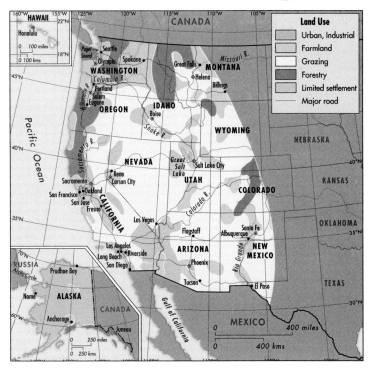

Western Europe Political Map

Microstates
1. ANDORRA
2. GIBRALTAR (U.K.)
3. LIECHTENSTEIN
4. MALTA
5. MONACO
6. SAN MARINO
7. VATICAN CITY

Atlas

C.I.S. Political Map

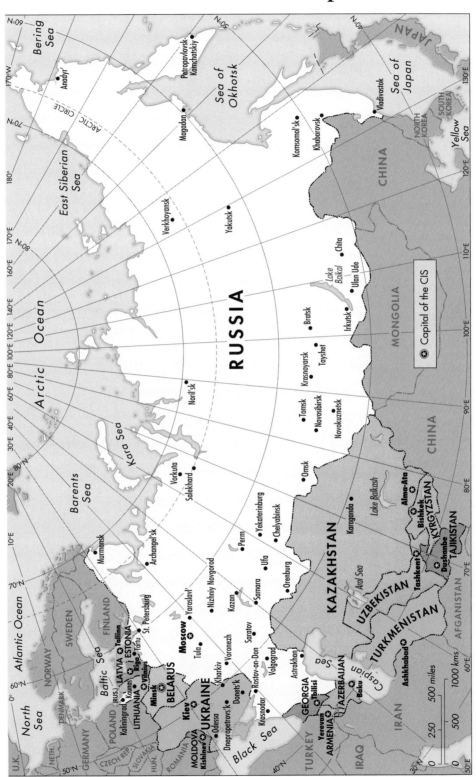

World Political Map

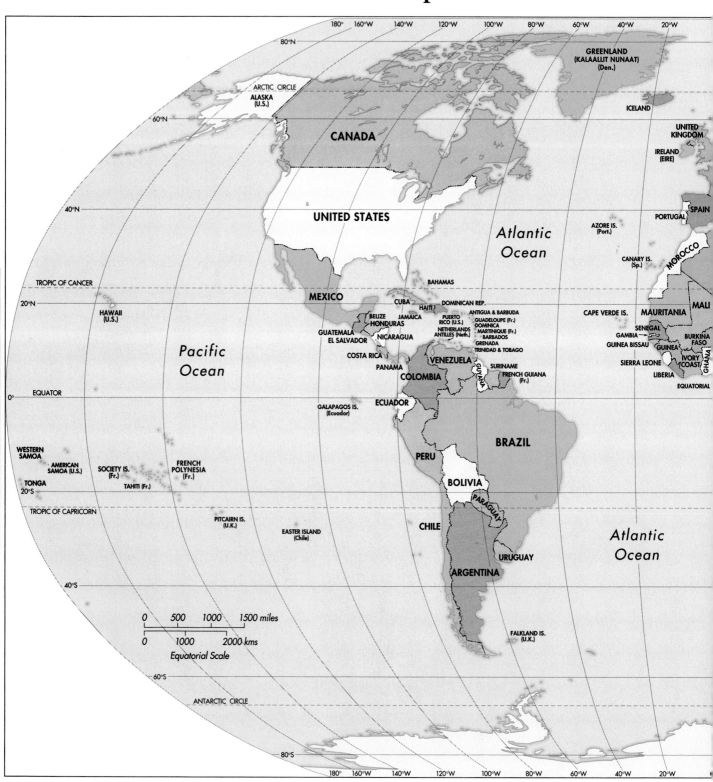

80°N

GREENLAND
(KALAALLIT NUNAAT)
(Den.)

ARCTIC CIRCLE

ALASKA
(U.S.)

ICELAND

60°N

CANADA

UNITED
KINGDOM

IRELAND
(EIRE)

40°N

UNITED STATES

*Atlantic
Ocean*

AZORE IS.
(Port.)

SPAIN

PORTUGAL

CANARY IS.
(Sp.)

MOROCCO

TROPIC OF CANCER

BAHAMAS

20°N

MEXICO

CUBA

MALI

HAITI

DOMINICAN REP.

CAPE VERDE IS.

MAURITANIA

HAWAII
(U.S.)

BELIZE

JAMAICA

PUERTO
RICO (U.S.)

ANTIGUA & BARBUDA

GUADELOUPE (Fr.)

SENEGAL

HONDURAS

DOMINICA

GAMBIA

BURKINA
FASO

GUATEMALA
EL SALVADOR

NICARAGUA

NETHERLANDS
ANTILLES (Neth.)

MARTINIQUE (Fr.)

BARBADOS

GUINEA BISSAU

GUINEA

*Pacific
Ocean*

COSTA RICA

GRENADA

TRINIDAD & TOBAGO

SIERRA LEONE

IVORY
(COAST)

GHANA

PANAMA

VENEZUELA

SURINAME

LIBERIA

GUYANA

FRENCH GUIANA
(Fr.)

EQUATORIAL

COLOMBIA

GALAPAGOS IS.
(Ecuador)

ECUADOR

EQUATOR

0°

WESTERN
SAMOA

BRAZIL

AMERICAN
SAMOA (U.S.)

SOCIETY IS.
(Fr.)

PERU

FRENCH
POLYNESIA
(Fr.)

TONGA

TAHITI (Fr.)

BOLIVIA

20°S

PARAGUAY

TROPIC OF CAPRICORN

PITCAIRN IS.
(U.K.)

EASTER ISLAND
(Chile)

CHILE

*Atlantic
Ocean*

URUGUAY

ARGENTINA

40°S

0   500   1000   1500 miles

FALKLAND IS.
(U.K.)

0   1000   2000 kms

Equatorial Scale

60°S

ANTARCTIC CIRCLE

80°S

180° 160°W 140°W 120°W 100°W 80°W 60°W 40°W 20°W

Atlas

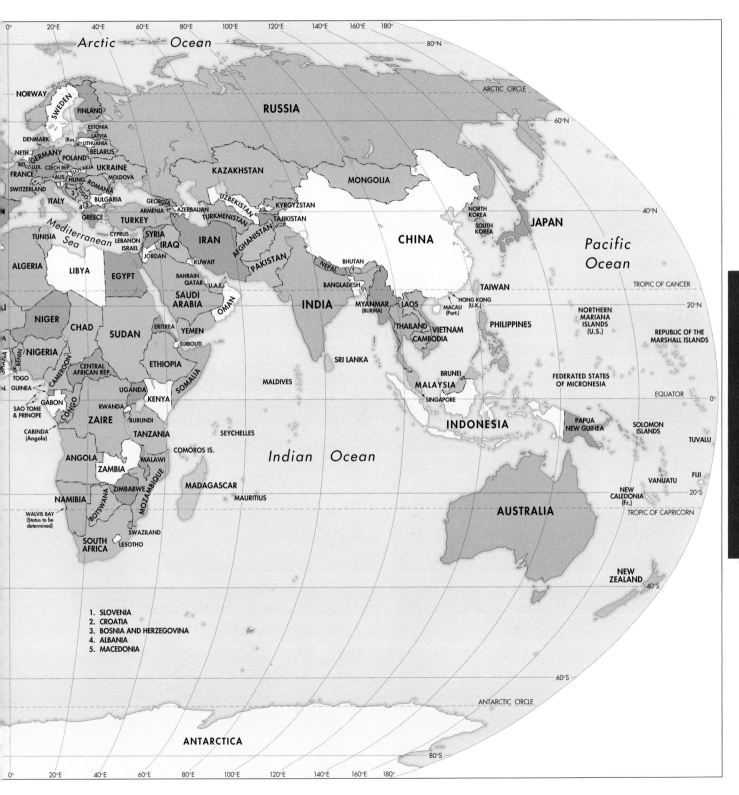

1. SLOVENIA
2. CROATIA
3. BOSNIA AND HERZEGOVINA
4. ALBANIA
5. MACEDONIA

The Presidents of the United States

1   George Washington

Dates in office: 1789–1797
Born: February 22, 1732
Died: December 14, 1799
Profession: Planter
Political party: None
Elected from: Virginia
Vice president: John Adams

2   John Adams

Dates in office: 1797–1801
Born: October 30, 1735
Died: July 4, 1826
Profession: Lawyer
Political party: Federalist
Elected from: Massachusetts
Vice president: Thomas Jefferson

3   Thomas Jefferson

Dates in office: 1801–1809
Born: April 13, 1743
Died: July 4, 1826
Profession: Planter, Lawyer
Political party: Democratic-
  Republican
Elected from: Virginia
Vice president: Aaron Burr,
  George Clinton

4   James Madison

Dates in office: 1809–1817
Born: March 16, 1751
Died: June 28, 1836
Profession: Lawyer
Political party: Democratic-
  Republican
Elected from: Virginia
Vice president: George Clinton,
  Elbridge Gerry

5   James Monroe

Dates in office: 1817–1825
Born: April 28, 1758
Died: July 4, 1831
Profession: Lawyer
Political party: Democratic-
  Republican
Elected from: Virginia
Vice president: Daniel D. Tompkins

6   John Quincy Adams

Dates in office: 1825–1829
Born: July 11, 1767
Died: February 23, 1848
Profession: Lawyer
Political party: Democratic-
  Republican
Elected from: Massachusetts
Vice president: John C. Calhoun

7   Andrew Jackson

Dates in office: 1829–1837
Born: March 15, 1767
Died: June 8, 1845
Profession: Lawyer
Political party: Democratic
Elected from: Tennessee
Vice president: John C. Calhoun,
  Martin Van Buren

8   Martin Van Buren

Dates in office: 1837–1841
Born: December 5, 1782
Died: July 24, 1862
Profession: Lawyer
Political party: Democratic
Elected from: New York
Vice president: Richard M. Johnson

Presidents' Gallery

9　William Henry Harrison

Dates in office: 1841
Born: February 9, 1773
Died: April 4, 1841
Profession: Soldier
Political party: Whig
Elected from: Ohio
Vice president: John Tyler
Harrison died from pneumonia after spending only one month in office.

10　John Tyler

Dates in office: 1841–1845
Born: March 29, 1790
Died: January 18, 1862
Profession: Lawyer
Political party: Whig
Elected from: Virginia
Vice president: None
As vice president, Tyler took the office of president upon Harrison's death.

11　James K. Polk

Dates in office: 1845–1849
Born: November 2, 1795
Died: June 15, 1849
Profession: Lawyer
Political party: Democratic
Elected from: Tennessee
Vice president: George M. Dallas

12　Zachary Taylor

Dates in office: 1849–1850
Born: November 24, 1784
Died: July 9, 1850
Profession: Soldier
Political party: Whig
Elected from: Louisiana
Vice president: Millard Fillmore
Taylor died in the summer of 1850.

13　Millard Fillmore

Dates in office: 1850–1853
Born: January 7, 1800
Died: March 8, 1874
Profession: Lawyer
Political party: Whig
Elected from: New York
Vice president: None
As vice president, Fillmore took the office of president upon Taylor's death.

14　Franklin Pierce

Dates in office: 1853–1857
Born: November 23, 1804
Died: October 8, 1869
Profession: Lawyer
Political party: Democratic
Elected from: New Hampshire
Vice president: William R. King

15　James Buchanan

Dates in office: 1857–1861
Born: April 23, 1791
Died: June 1, 1868
Profession: Lawyer
Political party: Democratic
Elected from: Pennsylvania
Vice president: John C. Breckinridge

16　Abraham Lincoln

Dates in office: 1861–1865
Born: February 12, 1809
Died: April 15, 1865
Profession: Lawyer
Political party: Republican
Elected from: Illinois
Vice president: Hannibal Hamlin, Andrew Johnson
Lincoln was assassinated in 1865.

Presidents' Gallery

17	**Andrew Johnson**

Dates in office: 1865–1869
Born: December 29, 1808
Died: July 31, 1875
Profession: Tailor
Political party: National Union
Elected from: Tennessee
Vice president: None
As vice president, Johnson took the office of president upon Lincoln's death.

18	**Ulysses S. Grant**

Dates in office: 1869–1877
Born: April 27, 1822
Died: July 23, 1885
Profession: Soldier
Political party: Republican
Elected from: Illinois
Vice president: Schuyler Colfax,
   Henry Wilson

19	**Rutherford B. Hayes**

Dates in office: 1877–1881
Born: October 4, 1822
Died: January 17, 1893
Profession: Lawyer
Political party: Republican
Elected from: Ohio
Vice president: William A. Wheeler

20	**James A. Garfield**

Dates in office: 1881
Born: November 19, 1831
Died: September 19, 1881
Profession: Lawyer
Political party: Republican
Elected from: Ohio
Vice president: Chester A. Arthur
Garfield was assassinated in July of 1881 by Charles Guiteau.

21	**Chester A. Arthur**

Dates in office: 1881–1885
Born: October 5, 1829
Died: November 18, 1886
Profession: Lawyer
Political party: Republican
Elected from: New York
Vice president: None
As vice president, Arthur took the office of president upon Garfield's death.

22	**Grover Cleveland**

Dates in office: 1885–1889
Born: March 18, 1837
Died: June 24, 1908
Profession: Lawyer
Political party: Democratic
Elected from: New York
Vice president: Thomas A. Hendricks
Cleveland was reelected in 1893.

23	**Benjamin Harrison**

Dates in office: 1889–1893
Born: August 20, 1833
Died: March 13, 1901
Profession: Lawyer
Political party: Republican
Elected from: Indiana
Vice president: Levi P. Morton

24	**Grover Cleveland**

Dates in office: 1893–1897
Vice president: Adlai E. Stevenson
See statistics under #22.

Presidents' Gallery

25   William McKinley

Dates in office: 1897-1901
Born: January 29, 1843
Died: September 14, 1901
Profession: Lawyer
Political party: Republican
Elected from: Ohio
Vice president: Garret A. Hobart,
    Theodore Roosevelt
McKinley was assassinated in 1901.

26   Theodore Roosevelt

Dates in office: 1901-1909
Born: October 27, 1858
Died: January 6, 1919
Profession: Author
Political party: Republican
Elected from: New York
Vice president: Charles W. Fairbanks
As vice president, Roosevelt took the office of president upon McKinley's death.

27   William Howard Taft

Dates in office: 1909-1913
Born: September 15, 1857
Died: March 8, 1930
Profession: Lawyer
Political party: Republican
Elected from: Ohio
Vice president: James S. Sherman

28   Woodrow Wilson

Dates in office: 1913-1921
Born: December 29, 1856
Died: February 3, 1924
Profession: Educator
Political party: Democratic
Elected from: New Jersey
Vice president: Thomas R. Marshall

29   Warren G. Harding

Dates in office: 1921-1923
Born: November 2, 1865
Died: August 2, 1923
Profession: Editor
Political party: Republican
Elected from: Ohio
Vice president: Calvin Coolidge
Harding died of a heart attack in 1923.

30   Calvin Coolidge

Dates in office: 1923-1929
Born: July 4, 1872
Died: January 5, 1933
Profession: Lawyer
Political party: Republican
Elected from: Massachusetts
Vice president: Charles G. Dawes
As vice president, Coolidge took the office of president upon Harding's death.

31   Herbert C. Hoover

Dates in office: 1929-1933
Born: August 10, 1874
Died: October 20, 1964
Profession: Engineer
Political party: Republican
Elected from: California
Vice president: Charles Curtis

32   Franklin D. Roosevelt

Dates in office: 1933-1945
Born: January 30, 1882
Died: April 12, 1945
Profession: Lawyer
Political party: Democratic
Elected from: New York
Vice president: John N. Garner,
    Henry A. Wallace, Harry S Truman
Roosevelt died during his fourth term.

Presidents' Gallery

33   Harry S Truman

Dates in office: 1945–1953
Born: May 8, 1884
Died: December 26, 1972
Profession: Businessman
Political party: Democratic
Elected from: Missouri
Vice president: Alben W. Barkley
As vice president, Truman took the office of president upon Roosevelt's death.

34   Dwight D. Eisenhower

Dates in office: 1953–1961
Born: October 14, 1890
Died: March 28, 1969
Profession: Soldier
Political party: Republican
Elected from: New York
Vice president: Richard M. Nixon

35   John F. Kennedy

Dates in office: 1961–1963
Born: May 29, 1917
Died: November 22, 1963
Profession: Author
Political party: Democratic
Elected from: Massachusetts
Vice president: Lyndon B. Johnson
Kennedy was assassinated in November, 1963, in Dallas, Texas.

36   Lyndon B. Johnson

Dates in office: 1963–1969
Born: August 27, 1908
Died: January 22, 1973
Profession: Teacher
Political party: Democratic
Elected from: Texas
Vice president: Hubert H. Humphrey
As vice president, Johnson took the office of president upon Kennedy's death.

37   Richard M. Nixon

Dates in office: 1969–1974
Born: January 9, 1913
Died: April 22, 1994
Profession: Lawyer
Political party: Republican
Elected from: New York
Vice president: Spiro T. Agnew,
   Gerald R. Ford
Nixon resigned the presidency in 1974.

38   Gerald R. Ford

Dates in office: 1974–1977
Born: July 14, 1913
Profession: Lawyer
Political party: Republican
Elected from: Michigan
Vice president: Nelson A.
   Rockefeller
As vice president, Ford took the office of president upon Nixon's resignation.

39   James E. Carter, Jr.

Dates in office: 1977–1981
Born: October 1, 1924
Profession: Businessman
Political party: Democratic
Elected from: Georgia
Vice president: Walter F. Mondale

40   Ronald W. Reagan

Dates in office: 1981–1989
Born: February 6, 1911
Profession: Actor
Political party: Republican
Elected from: California
Vice president: George H. W. Bush

41   George H. W. Bush

Dates in office: 1989–1993
Born: June 12, 1924
Profession: Businessman
Political party: Republican
Elected from: Texas
Vice president: J. Danforth Quayle

42   William J. Clinton

Dates in office: 1993–
Born: August 19, 1946
Profession: Lawyer
Political party: Democratic
Elected from: Arkansas
Vice president: Albert Gore, Jr.

About the Fifty States

ALABAMA
"The Yellowhammer State"
Capital: Montgomery

Date Entered Union: Dec. 14, 1819
Ranking in Entering Union: 22
Ranking in Land Area: 29

Population (1990): 4,040,587
Ranking in Population: 22
1997 Electoral Votes: 9

ALASKA
"The Last Frontier"
Capital: Juneau

Date Entered Union: Jan. 3, 1959
Ranking in Entering Union: 49
Ranking in Land Area: 1

Population (1990): 550,043
Ranking in Population: 49
1997 Electoral Votes: 3

ARIZONA
"The Grand Canyon State"
Capital: Phoenix

Date Entered Union: Feb. 14, 1912
Ranking in Entering Union: 48
Ranking in Land Area: 6

Population (1990): 3,665,228
Ranking in Population: 24
1997 Electoral Votes: 8

ARKANSAS
"The Land of Opportunity"
Capital: Little Rock

Date Entered Union: June 15, 1836
Ranking in Entering Union: 25
Ranking in Land Area: 27

Population (1990): 2,350,725
Population Rank: 33
1997 Electoral Votes: 6

CALIFORNIA
"The Golden State"
Capital: Sacramento

Date Entered Union: Sept. 9, 1850
Ranking in Entering Union: 31
Ranking in Land Area: 3

Population (1990): 29,760,021
Population Rank: 1
1997 Electoral Votes: 54

COLORADO
"The Centennial State"
Capital: Denver

Date Entered Union: Aug. 1, 1876
Ranking in Entering Union: 38
Ranking in Land Area: 8

Population (1990): 3,294,394
Population Rank: 26
1997 Electoral Votes: 8

CONNECTICUT
"The Constitution State"
Capital: Hartford

Date Entered Union: Jan. 9, 1788
Ranking in Entering Union: 5
Ranking in Land Area: 48

Population (1990): 3,287,116
Population Rank: 27
1997 Electoral Votes: 8

DELAWARE
"The Diamond State"
Capital: Dover

Date Entered Union: Dec. 7, 1787
Ranking in Entering Union: 1
Ranking in Land Area: 49

Population (1990): 666,168
Population Rank: 46
1997 Electoral Votes: 3

FLORIDA
"The Sunshine State"
Capital: Tallahassee

Date Entered Union: March 3, 1845
Ranking in Entering Union: 27
Ranking in Land Area: 22

Population (1990): 12,937,926
Population Rank: 4
1997 Electoral Votes: 25

GEORGIA
"The Peach State"
Capital: Atlanta

Date Entered Union: Jan. 22, 1788
Ranking in Entering Union: 4
Ranking in Land Area: 21

Population (1990): 6,478,216
Population Rank: 11
1997 Electoral Votes: 13

HAWAII
"The Aloha State"
Capital: Honolulu

Date Entered Union: Aug. 21, 1959
Ranking in Entering Union: 550
Ranking in Land Area: 47

Population (1990): 1,108,229
Population Rank: 41
1997 Electoral Votes: 4

IDAHO
"The Gem State"
Capital: Boise

Date Entered Union: July 3, 1890
Ranking in Entering Union: 43
Ranking in Land Area: 13

Population (1990): 1,006,749
Population Rank: 42
1997 Electoral Votes: 4

ILLINOIS
"The Prairie State"
Capital: Springfield

Date Entered Union: Dec. 3, 1818
Ranking in Entering Union: 21
Ranking in Land Area: 24

Population (1990): 11,430,602
Population Rank: 6
1997 Electoral Votes: 22

INDIANA
"The Hoosier State"
Capital: Indianapolis

Date Entered Union: Dec. 11, 1816
Ranking in Entering Union: 19
Ranking in Land Area: 38

Population (1990): 5,544,159
Population Rank: 14
1997 Electoral Votes: 12

IOWA
"The Hawkeye State"
Capital: Des Moines

Date Entered Union: Dec. 28, 1846
Ranking in Entering Union: 29
Ranking in Land Area: 25

Population (1990): 2,776,755
Population Rank: 30
1997 Electoral Votes: 7

KANSAS
"The Sunflower State"
Capital: Topeka

Date Entered Union: Jan. 29, 1861
Ranking in Entering Union: 34
Ranking in Land Area: 14

Population (1990): 2,477,574
Population Rank: 32
1997 Electoral Votes: 6

KENTUCKY
"The Bluegrass State"
Capital: Frankfort

Date Entered Union: June 1, 1792
Ranking in Entering Union: 15
Ranking in Land Area: 37

Population (1990): 3,685,296
Population Rank: 23
1997 Electoral Votes: 8

LOUISIANA
"The Pelican State"
Capital: Baton Rouge

Date Entered Union: April 30, 1812
Ranking in Entering Union: 18
Ranking in Land Area: 31

Population (1990): 4,219,973
Population Rank: 21
1997 Electoral Votes: 9

MAINE
"The Pine Tree State"
Capital: Augusta

Date Entered Union: March 15, 1820
Ranking in Entering Union: 23
Ranking in Land Area: 39

Population (1990): 1,227,928
Population Rank: 38
1997 Electoral Votes: 4

MARYLAND
"The Old Line State"
Capital: Annapolis

Date Entered Union: April 28, 1788
Ranking in Entering Union: 7
Ranking in Land Area: 42

Population (1990): 4,781,468
Population Rank: 19
1997 Electoral Votes: 10

MASSACHUSETTS
"The Bay State"
Capital: Boston

Date Entered Union: Feb. 6, 1788
Ranking in Entering Union: 6
Ranking in Land Area: 45

Population (1990): 6,016,425
Population Rank: 13
1997 Electoral Votes: 12

MICHIGAN
"The Wolverine State"
Capital: Lansing

Date Entered Union: Jan. 26, 1837
Ranking in Entering Union: 26
Ranking in Land Area: 23

Population (1990): 9,295,297
Population Rank: 8
1997 Electoral Votes: 18

MINNESOTA
"The North Star State"
Capital: St. Paul

Date Entered Union: May 11, 1858
Ranking in Entering Union: 32
Ranking in Land Area: 12

Population (1990): 4,375,099
Population Rank: 20
1997 Electoral Votes: 10

MISSISSIPPI
"The Magnolia State"
Capital: Jackson

Date Entered Union: Dec. 10, 1817
Ranking in Entering Union: 20
Ranking in Land Area: 32

Population (1990): 2,573,216
Population Rank: 31
1997 Electoral Votes: 7

MISSOURI
"The Show-me State"
Capital: Jefferson City

Date Entered Union: Aug. 10, 1821
Ranking in Entering Union: 24
Ranking in Land Area: 19

Population (1990): 5,117,073
Ranking in Population: 15
1997 Electoral Votes: 11

MONTANA
"The Treasure State"
Capital: Helena

Date Entered Union: Nov. 8, 1889
Ranking in Entering Union: 41
Ranking in Land Area: 4

Population (1990): 799,065
Population Rank: 44
1997 Electoral Votes: 3

NEBRASKA
"The Cornhusker State"
Capital: Lincoln

Date Entered Union: March 1, 1867
Ranking in Entering Union: 37
Ranking in Land Area: 15

Population (1990): 1,578,385
Population Rank: 36
1997 Electoral Votes: 5

NEVADA
"The Sagebrush State"
Capital: Carson City

Date Entered Union: Oct. 31, 1864
Ranking in Entering Union: 36
Ranking in Land Area: 7

Population (1990): 1,201,833
Population Rank: 39
1997 Electoral Votes: 4

NEW HAMPSHIRE
"The Granite State"
Capital: Concord

Date Entered Union: June 21, 1788
Ranking in Entering Union: 9
Ranking in Land Area: 44

Population (1990): 1,109,252
Population Rank: 40
1997 Electoral Votes: 4

NEW JERSEY
"The Garden State"
Capital: Trenton

Date Entered Union: Dec. 18, 1787
Ranking in Entering Union: 3
Ranking in Land Area: 46

Population (1990): 7,730,188
Population Rank: 9
1997 Electoral Votes: 15

NEW MEXICO
"The Land of Enchantment"
Capital: Sante Fe

Date Entered Union: Jan. 6, 1912
Ranking in Entering Union: 47
Ranking in Land Area: 5

Population (1990): 1,515,069
Population Rank: 37
1997 Electoral Votes: 5

NEW YORK
"The Empire State"
Capital: Albany

Date Entered Union: July 26, 1788
Ranking in Entering Union: 11
Ranking in Land Area: 30

Population (1990): 17,990,455
Population Rank: 2
1997 Electoral Votes: 33

NORTH CAROLINA
"The Tar Heel State"
Capital: Raleigh

Date Entered Union: Nov. 21, 1789
Ranking in Entering Union: 12
Ranking in Land Area: 28

Population (1990): 6,628,637
Population Rank: 10
1997 Electoral Votes: 14

NORTH DAKOTA
"The Flickertail State"
Capital: Bismark

Date Entered Union: Nov. 2, 1889
Ranking in Entering Union: 39
Ranking in Land Area: 17

Population (1990): 638,800
Population Rank: 47
1997 Electoral Votes: 3

OHIO
"The Buckeye State"
Capital: Columbus

Date Entered Union: March 1, 1803
Ranking in Entering Union: 17
Ranking in Land Area: 35

Population (1990): 10,847,115
Population Rank: 7
1997 Electoral Votes: 21

OKLAHOMA
"The Sooner State"
Capital: Oklahoma City

Date Entered Union: Nov. 16, 1907
Ranking in Entering Union: 46
Ranking in Land Area: 18

Population (1990): 3,145,585
Population Rank: 28
1997 Electoral Votes: 8

OREGON
"The Beaver State"
Capital: Salem

Date Entered Union: Feb. 14, 1859
Ranking in Entering Union: 33
Ranking in Land Area: 10

Population (1990): 2,842,321
Population Rank: 29
1997 Electoral Votes: 7

PENNSYLVANIA
"The Keystone State"
Capital: Harrisburg

Date Entered Union: Dec. 12, 1787
Ranking in Entering Union: 2
Ranking in Land Area: 33

Population (1990): 11,881,643
Population Rank: 5
1997 Electoral Votes: 23

RHODE ISLAND
"The Ocean State"
Capital: Providence

Date Entered Union: May 29, 1790
Ranking in Entering Union: 13
Ranking in Land Area: 50

Population (1990): 1,003,464
Population Rank: 43
1997 Electoral Votes: 4

SOUTH CAROLINA
"The Palmetto State"
Capital: Columbia

Date Entered Union: May 23, 1788
Ranking in Entering Union: 8
Ranking in Land Area: 40

Population (1990): 3,386,703
Population Rank: 25
1997 Electoral Votes: 8

SOUTH DAKOTA
"The Coyote State"
Capital: Pierre

Date Entered Union: Nov. 2, 1889
Ranking in Entering Union: 40
Ranking in Land Area: 16

Population (1990): 696,004
Population Rank: 45
1997 Electoral Votes: 3

TENNESSEE
"The Volunteer State"
Capital: Nashville

Date Entered Union: June 1, 1796
Ranking in Entering Union: 16
Ranking in Land Area: 34

Population (1990): 4,877,185
Population Rank: 17
1997 Electoral Votes: 11

TEXAS
"The Lone Star State"
Capital: Austin

Date Entered Union: Dec. 29, 1845
Ranking in Entering Union: 28
Ranking in Land Area: 2

Population (1990): 16,986,510
Population Rank: 3
1997 Electoral Votes: 32

UTAH
"The Beehive State"
Capital: Salt Lake City

Date Entered Union: Jan. 4, 1896
Ranking in Entering Union: 45
Ranking in Land Area: 11

Population (1990): 1,722,850
Population Rank: 35
1997 Electoral Votes: 5

VERMONT
"The Green Mountain State"
Capital: Montpelier

Date Entered Union: March 4, 1791
Ranking in Entering Union: 14
Ranking in Land Area: 43

Population (1990): 562,758
Population Rank: 48
1997 Electoral Votes: 3

VIRGINIA
"The Old Dominion"
Capital: Richmond

Date Entered Union: June 25, 1788
Ranking in Entering Union: 10
Ranking in Land Area: 36

Population (1990): 6,187,358
Population Rank: 12
1997 Electoral Votes: 13

WASHINGTON
"The Evergreen State"
Capital: Olympia

Date Entered Union: Nov. 11, 1889
Ranking in Entering Union: 42
Ranking in Land Area: 20

Population (1990): 4,866,692
Population Rank: 18
1997 Electoral Votes: 11

WEST VIRGINIA
"The Mountain State"
Capital: Charleston

Date Entered Union: June 20, 1863
Ranking in Entering Union: 35
Ranking in Land Area: 41

Population (1990): 1,793,477
Population Rank: 34
1997 Electoral Votes: 5

WISCONSIN
"The Badger State"
Capital: Madison

Date Entered Union: May 29, 1848
Ranking in Entering Union: 30
Ranking in Land Area: 26

Population (1990): 4,891,769
Population Rank: 16
1997 Electoral Votes: 11

WYOMING
"The Equality State"
Capital: Cheyenne

Date Entered Union: July 10, 1890
Ranking in Entering Union: 44
Ranking in Land Area: 9

Population (1990): 453,588
Population Rank: 50
1997 Electoral Votes: 3

U.S. Database

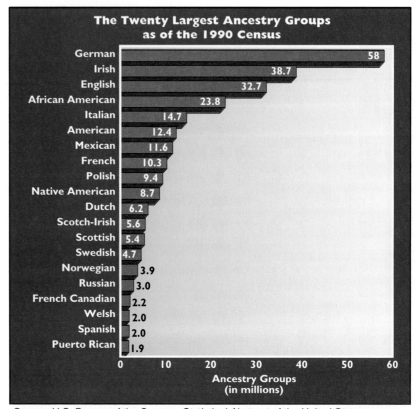

The Twenty Largest Ancestry Groups as of the 1990 Census

Ancestry Group	In millions
German	58
Irish	38.7
English	32.7
African American	23.8
Italian	14.7
American	12.4
Mexican	11.6
French	10.3
Polish	9.4
Native American	8.7
Dutch	6.2
Scotch-Irish	5.6
Scottish	5.4
Swedish	4.7
Norwegian	3.9
Russian	3.0
French Canadian	2.2
Welsh	2.0
Spanish	2.0
Puerto Rican	1.9

Ancestry Groups (in millions)

Source: U.S. Bureau of the Census, *Statistical Abstract of the United States*. Washington, D.C.: U.S. Government Printing Office, 1994.

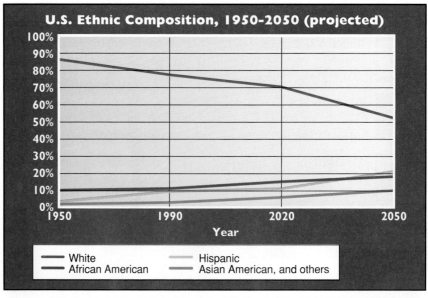

U.S. Ethnic Composition, 1950-2050 (projected)

Year

— White
— African American
⋯ Hispanic
— Asian American, and others

Source: U.S. Bureau of the Census, *Statistical Abstract of the United States*. Washington, D.C.: U.S. Government Printing Office, 1994.

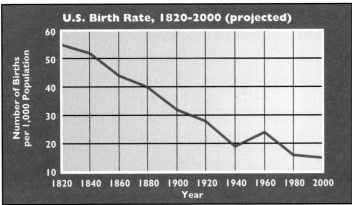

Source: *Historical Statistics of the United States; Statistical Abstract of the United States.*

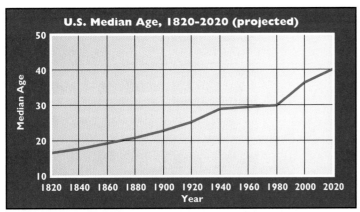

Source: *Historical Statistics of the United States; The Universal Almanac.*

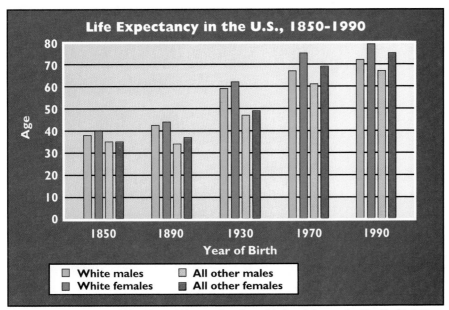

Source: Department of Health and Human Services, National Center for Health Statistics.

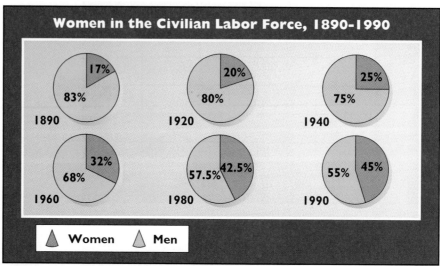

Source: U.S. Department of Commerce, Bureau of the Census.

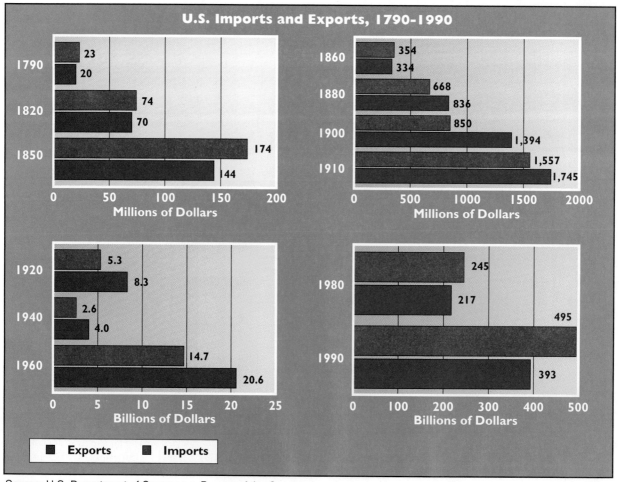

Source: U.S. Department of Commerce, Bureau of the Census.

Biographical Dictionary

This Biographical Dictionary identifies key people listed within each chapter. The year in which each person was born and died is listed in parentheses after his or her name. Doubtful dates are followed by a question mark. Approximate dates are preceded by a "c." which stands for "circa," and means "approximately." When a "d." appears with only a single year, that is the year in which that person died: no accurate records were kept for that person's date of birth.

A

Adams, John (1735–1826) second president of the United States.

Adams, John Quincy (1767–1848) sixth president of the United States; chief framer of the Monroe administration's foreign policy.

Adams, Samuel (1722–1803) publisher and radical leader of the Sons of Liberty.

Addams, Jane (1860–1935) reformer and social worker who founded Hull House in Chicago, Illinois.

Alcott, Louisa May (1832–1888) author of popular novel, *Little Women*.

Allen, Ethan (1738–1789) leader of the Green Mountain Boys, a militia unit from Vermont.

Anthony, Susan Brownell (1820–1906) American suffragist; organized (with Elizabeth Cady Stanton) the National Woman Suffrage Association; died before the Nineteenth Amendment was adopted (1920).

Armstrong, Neil Alden (1930–) U.S. astronaut; first person to walk on the moon (July 20, 1969).

Arthur, Chester A. (1829–1886) twenty-first president of the United States; signed the 1883 Pendleton Civil Service Act requiring that federal jobs be filled by competitive examination.

Austin, Stephen F. (1793–1836) land promoter who brought settlers to Mexican-owned Texas.

B

Banneker, Benjamin (1731–1806) free African American, mathematician, inventor, and designer; published an astronomical almanac.

Barnum, Phineas T. (1810–1891) co-owner of the Barnum and Bailey circus and showman.

Beecher, Henry Ward (1813–1887) New York clergyman; active in the antislavery movement.

Beecher, Lyman (1775–1863) Connecticut minister active during the Second Great Awakening in the 1830s; father of Harriet Beecher Stowe.

Bell, Alexander Graham (1847–1922) American inventor; invented the telephone in 1876.

Booth, John Wilkes (1838–1865) actor and assassin of President Abraham Lincoln, April 14, 1865.

Bradstreet, Anne (c.1612–1672) Puritan poet; author of first book of poetry published in America.

Brandeis, Louis D. (1856–1941) U.S. Supreme Court justice (1916–1939).

Brown, John (1800–1859) strident abolitionist who led a raid against proslavery immigrants and against the Federal Arsenal at Harpers Ferry.

Bryan, William Jennings (1860–1925) American lawyer and politician; leader of the movement for the unlimited coinage of silver.

Buchanan, James (1791–1868) Democrat elected to serve as the fifteenth president of the United States.

Burger, Warren (1907–1995) Chief Justice U.S. Supreme Court (1969–1986).

Burr, Aaron (1756–1836) vice president under Thomas Jefferson; opponent of Alexander Hamilton; inflicted Hamilton with a fatal wound during a duel.

Bush, George (1924–) forty-first president of the United States.

C

Calhoun, Henry (1782–1850) congressman from South Carolina and states' rights proponent; with Henry Clay, a leader of the war hawks.

Calhoun, John Caldwell (1782–1850) American politician from South Carolina; supported slavery, cotton exports, states' rights; vice president of the United States under President John Q. Adams (1825–1832).

Calvert, Sir George (1580?–1632) (Lord Baltimore) founder of Maryland; set up the colony as a haven for English Catholics.

Carmichael, Stokely (1941–) now known as Kwame Toure, civil rights activist who coined the phrase *black power.*

Carnegie, Andrew (1835–1919) Scottish immigrant who built a fortune by building cost-effective and highly productive steel mills.

Carter, James Earl, Jr. (1924–) thirty-ninth president of the United States (1977–1981); greatest accomplishment was the Camp David agreement of 1978 between Egypt and Israel.

Castro, Fidel (1926–) led the Cuban revolt against

dictator Fulgencio Batista and became head of the Cuban Communist government in 1959.

Champlain, Samuel de (c. 1567–1635) French explorer; set up the first settlements in Quebec and Montreal.

Chávez, César (1927–1993) farm labor activist and founder of the United Farm Workers.

Chiang Kai-shek (1887–1975) general who served as head of the Chinese Nationalist government.

Churchill, Winston (1874–1965) noted statesman and British Prime Minister during World War II.

Clark, William (Captain) (1770–1838) American explorer; with his private secretary, Meriwether Lewis, explored the lands West of the Mississippi River to find an overland route to the Pacific ocean.

Clay, Henry (1777–1852) Congressman from Kentucky known as the "Great Compromiser" and Speaker of the House of Representatives for 11 years.

Clemens, Samuel L. (1835–1910) author, under the name of Mark Twain, of classic American novels, including *Huckleberry Finn* and *Tom Sawyer.*

Cleveland, Grover (1837–1908) twenty-second and twenty-fourth presidents of the United States (1885–1889; 1893–1897); supported railroad regulation; favored the repeal of the Sherman Silver Purchase Act.

Clinton, Hillary Rodham (1947–) attorney and wife of President Bill Clinton.

Clinton, William (Bill) (1946–) forty-second president, elected in 1992.

Columbus, Christopher (1451–1512) Italian-born trader and explorer who landed in San Salvadore in 1492 by sailing west to reach the East Indies.

Coolidge, Calvin (1872–1933) vice president under President Harding; assumed presidency upon Harding's death; thirtieth president of the United States (1923–1929); promoted big business and opposed social aid.

Crazy Horse (1842–1877) Sioux Indian chief who resisted government demands that his tribe leave the Black Hills of South Dakota and Montana.

Custer, George A. (1839–1876) colonel in the U.S. Army cavalry; led his troops in a disastrous attack on an Indian village, known as the Battle of the Little Big Horn.

D

Dare, Virginia (1587–?) first English child born in the American colonies.

Davis, Jefferson (1808–1889) president of the Confederate States of America.

Debs, Eugene V. (1855–1926) American socialist; founded the American Railway Union (ARU) in 1893.

Douglas, Stephen A. (1813–1861) Democratic senator from Illinois known for his efforts to gain approval of the Compromise of 1850.

Douglass, Frederick (1817–1895) former slave, writer, and advocate of abolition.

DuBois, William E. B. (1868–1963) African American historian and sociologist; a strong voice for racial equality and a founder of the NAACP.

E

Edison, Thomas Alva (1847–1931) American inventor of the incandescent light bulb, the phonograph, and other electrical devices.

Edwards, Jonathan (1703–1758) Massachusetts minister during the Great Awakening who believed that sinners needed to be brought back to the church.

Einstein, Albert (1879–1955) American physicist; theory of relativity led to harnessing nuclear energy.

Eisenhower, Dwight D. (1890–1969) general who led American forces in Europe during World War II; thirty-fourth president of the United States.

F

Fillmore, Millard (1800–1874) vice president under President Taylor; assumed presidency upon Taylor's death; thirteenth president of the United States (1850–1853); promoted the Compromise of 1850.

Fitzgerald, F. Scott (1896–1940) American novelist and short story writer; depicted the cultural rebellion of the 1920s.

Ford, Gerald (1913–) appointed vice president by Richard M. Nixon; became thirty-eighth president of the United States, the first nonelected president.

Ford, Henry (1863–1947) American automobile manufacturer.

Franklin, Benjamin (1706–1790) noted inventor, author, printer, and American patriot.

Fremont, John C. (1813–1890) American general and explorer.

G

Gagarin, Yuri (1934–1968) Russian cosmonaut; the first person to orbit the Earth (April 12, 1961); prompted President Kennedy's announcement of the creation of the Apollo moon program (May 25, 1961).

Garfield, James A. (1831–1881) twentieth president of the United States; assassinated in 1881 by Charles Guiteau, a disappointed office seeker.

Garrison, William Lloyd (1805–1879) publisher and

advocate for the immediate abolition of slavery.

Garvey, Marcus (1887–1940) Jamaican immigrant; led the Universal Negro Improvement Association, a movement dedicated to self-reliance for African Americans.

George, Henry (1839–1897) American economist; voiced criticism about the gap between the rich and the poor in his book *Progress and Poverty* (1879).

Geronimo (1829–1909) Apache Indian chief who led a band of warriors resisting a move to a reservation.

Gompers, Samuel (1850–1924) president of the American Federation of Labor (AFL) and major spokesperson for labor in the late 1800s.

Gorbachev, Mikhail (1931–) first secretary of the Communist Party in the USSR (1985–1991), and president (1990-1991); proposed the policies of perestroika and glasnost.

Gore, Albert, Jr. (1948–) vice president of the United States under President Clinton (1993–).

Grant, Ulysses S. (1822–1885) eighteenth president of the United States; army general; named commander in chief of the Union army during the Civil War.

H

Hamilton, Alexander (1755–1804) American statesman and author; fought for ratification of the Constitution in New York.

Harding, Warren G. (1865–1923) twenty-ninth president of the United States; died in office in 1923.

Harrison, Benjamin (1833–1901) twenty-third president of the United States.

Harrison, William (1773–1841) ninth president of the United States; army general who defeated Tecumseh's troops at the Battle of Tippecanoe.

Hayes, Rutherford B. (1822–1893) nineteenth president of the United States; elected in 1876 by a majority of one electoral vote.

Hearst, William Randolf (1863–1951) American newspaper publisher and political figure.

Henry the Navigator (1394–1460) Portuguese prince who had great interest in navigation and sponsored voyages to chart unknown waters.

Henry, Patrick (1736–1799) American patriot and orator; denounced the Stamp Act as a conspiracy against the colonies.

Hiss, Alger (1904 –) State Department official; allegedly involved in passing classified documents to Soviet agents.

Hitler, Adolf (1889–1945) German political and government leader; converted Germany into a fully militarized society and launched World War II in 1939.

Ho Chi Minh (1890–1969) Communist trained Vietnamese leader; declared Vietnam independent of France's rule.

Hooker, Thomas (1586?–1647) Puritan minister; left the Massachusetts Bay Colony and founded Connecticut.

Hoover, Herbert Clark (1874–1964) thirty-first president of the United States (1929–1933); led the distribution of food and supplies to war-torn Europe during World War I; became a scapegoat for the depression after the stock market crash of 1929.

Hoover, J. Edgar (1895–1972) director of the Federal Bureau of Investigation from 1924–1972.

Houston, Samuel (1793–1863) commander of Texas volunteer army; first president of the Republic of Texas.

Hudson, Henry (d. 1611) English explorer who claimed the New York area for the Dutch.

Humphrey, Hubert (1911–1978) thirty-eighth vice president of the United States under President Johnson (1965–1969).

Hutchinson, Anne (1591–1643) resident of the Massachusetts Bay Colony who was forced to leave because of her dissenting religious views.

I

Ibn Battuta (1304–1369?) Arab geographer; traveled extensively in Africa in the 1330s.

J

Jackson, Andrew (1767–1845) seventh president of the United States; called the "common man's president" because of the wide increase in the franchise.

Jackson, Thomas (Stonewall) (1824–1863) Confederate army general; led the rout of Union forces at the First Battle of Bull Run in July 1861.

Jay, John (1745–1829) first chief justice of the U.S. Supreme Court (1789–1795); traveled to Britain at the request of George Washington to ratify Jay's Treaty, signed on November 19, 1794, which kept the U.S. out of war with Britain, and set the stage for the Pinckney Treaty signed the next year with Spain.

Jefferson, Thomas (1743–1826) third president of the United States; author of the Declaration of Independence.

Johnson, Andrew (1808–1875) vice president under President Lincoln; assumed the presidency upon Lincoln's death; seventeenth president of the United States (1865–1869); was impeached, then acquitted by one vote.

Johnson, Lyndon B. (1908–1973) thirty-sixth president of the United States.

Joseph (c. 1840–1904) Indian chief who led a band of Nez Percé Indians trying to escape to Canada.

K

Kennedy, John F. (1917–1963) thirty-fifth president of the United States (1961–1963); known for his firm handling of the Cuban missile crisis; assassinated in November 1963 in Dallas, Texas, by Lee Harvey Oswald.

Kennedy, Robert (1925–1968) brother of President John F. Kennedy; Attorney General (1961–1964).

Khomeini, Ayatollah (1900–1989) fundamentalist leader of the Iranian revolution against the Shah of Iran and religious leader of Iran from 1979–1989.

King, Martin Luther, Jr., Dr. (1929–1968) African American minister and civil rights leader; belief in nonviolence was patterned after Mohandas Gandhi.

L

L'Enfant, Pierre-Charles (1754–1825) original designer for the city of Washington, D.C., in 1801; due to his fierce temper, he was fired before his work was completed; Benjamin Banneker completed the work.

Lafayette, Marquis de (1757–1834) French aide to General Washington who helped to secure France's support for the Revolutionary War.

LaFollette, Robert (1855–1925) progressive governor of Wisconsin who turned Wisconsin into an experimental laboratory for progressive policies.

Las Casas, Bartolomé de (1474–1566) first priest ordained in America; fought against Indian enslavement.

Lee, Robert E. (1807–1870) Confederate army general and commander in chief of the Confederate army.

Lewis, John L. (1880–1969) head of the United Mine Workers; he was committed to organizing all workers within an industry into industrial unions.

Lewis, Meriwether (1774–1809) private secretary of President Jefferson; sent to map the Louisiana Purchase.

Lincoln, Abraham (1809–1865) sixteenth president of the United States (1861–1865); known for issuing the Emancipation Proclamation; assassinated in 1865 by John Wilkes Booth.

Lowell, Francis Cabot (1775–1817) Boston merchant; built the first complete textile mill in the U.S.

M

MacArthur, Douglas (1880–1964) American general; commanded allied troops in the Pacific during World War II; supervised the postwar occupation of Japan; led United Nations forces during the Korean War.

Madison, James (1751–1836) author of the Virginia Plan and called the "Father of the Constitution;" fourth president of the United States.

Mahan, Alfred Thayer (1840–1914) American naval officer and historian; stressed the important role of sea power in the world.

Malcolm X (1925–1965) a militant civil rights leader, a Black Muslim, and one of Elijah Muhammad's followers.

Mandela, Nelson (1918–) South African activist, statesman, and Nobel laureate; elected the first black president of South Africa in 1994.

Mao Zedong (1893–1976) leader of China's Communist forces.

Marshall, George C. (1880–1959) American military commander; secretary of state (1947–1949); played an important role in the postwar economic recovery of western Europe.

Marshall, John (1755–1835) Chief Justice of the Supreme Court from 1801–1835, exerted the power of judicial review in *Marbury v. Madison* (1803).

Marshall, Thurgood (1908–1993) first African American to be appointed to the Supreme Court.

Mather, Cotton (1663–1728) minister; contributed to the hysteria of the witchcraft trials; successfully inoculated his family against smallpox.

McCarthy, Eugene (1916–) American politician; opposed the Vietnam War; convinced President Johnson not to run for reelection.

McCarthy, Joseph (1908–1957) U.S. Republican senator who made unproven charges about Communists working in the U.S. State Department.

McClellan, George B. (1826–1885) Union general whose procrastination led to Union army defeats.

McKinley, William (1843–1901) twenty-fifth president of the United States (1897–1901); aided business; made the U.S. a world power through its victory in the Spanish-American War; opposed the unlimited coinage of silver; assassinated in 1901 in Buffalo, New York.

McNamara, Robert (1916–) former president of Ford Motor Company and secretary of defense from 1961–1968.

Metacomet (1639?–1676) chief of the Wampanoag tribe; called King Philip by the English.

Monroe, James (1758–1831) fifth president of the United States (1817–1825); one of the founders of the Jeffersonian Republican Party; co-negotiator of the Louisiana Purchase; author of the Monroe Doctrine.

Mott, Lucretia (1793–1880) early advocate of women's rights.

Muhammad (c. 570–632) prophet-founder of the religion of Islam.

Muhammad, Elijah (1897–1975) African American religious leader and founder of the Nation of Islam, a separatist movement also known as the Black Muslims.

N

Nader, Ralph (1934–) American lawyer and consumer protection advocate; achieved national attention in the 1960s, when he published *Unsafe at Any Speed*; brought about changes in many industrial practices and a number of consumer protection laws.

Nimitz, Chester (1885–1966) American admiral; leader of the U.S. troops in World War II during the battle of Midway.

Nixon, Richard M. (1913–1994) thirty-seventh president of the United States (1969–1974); brought an end to the Vietnam War and improved relations with the Soviet Union and China; participated in illegal activities in the Watergate scandal which prompted his resignation on August 8, 1974.

O

O'Connor, Sandra Day (1930–) Supreme Court justice appointed in 1981.

Oglethorpe, James (1696–1785) English general and trustee of Georgia; developed rules for the colonists to live by so they might become more self-sufficient.

Opechancanough (c. 1622) second leader of the Confederacy of the Indians of the Chesapeake area; organized an attack on the Jamestown Colony.

Oppenheimer, J. Robert (1904–1967) American physicist and government advisor, who directed the development of the first atomic bombs.

Osceola (c. 1800–1838) Seminole Indian chief; led his tribe in the Seminole War in Florida.

P

Paine, Thomas (1737–1809) author of *Common Sense,* an influential pamphlet giving reasons for independence.

Parks, Rosa (1913 –) African American seamstress, living in Mobile, Alabama; refusal to give up her seat on a city bus to a white person sparked the civil rights movement.

Peale, Charles Willson (1741–1827) American artist.

Penn, William (1644–1718) English founder of the Pennsylvania settlement as a colony for fellow Quakers and a haven for religious radicals.

Perkins, Frances (1882–1965) American social reformer, who became the first female member of the cabinet when President Franklin D. Roosevelt named her secretary of labor in 1933.

Perot, Ross (1930–) wealthy businessman and 1992 presidential election Independent candidate.

Perry, Oliver Hazard (1785–1819) U.S. Navy captain; leader of the American fleet that secured control of Lake Erie from the British in 1813.

Pierce, Franklin (1804–1869) Democrat elected to serve as the fourteenth president of the United States.

Polk, James K. (1795–1849) eleventh president of the United States; elected on an expansionist platform.

Pontiac (c. 1720–1769) chief of the Ottawa Indians who led a great uprising against the British.

Popé (c. 1630–1690) Pueblo Indian leader who coordinated an attack against Spanish settlers in 1680 and drove them from Santa Fe, New Mexico.

Powell, Colin (1937–) American general; chaired the Joint Chiefs of Staff; played a major role during the Persian Gulf War in 1991.

Powhatan (1550?–1618) Indian Confederacy leader; aided the Jamestown colonists until they raided Indian supplies.

Q

Quincy, Josiah, Jr. (1744–1775) American lawyer and upper-class colonist who recorded his resentment of British interference in colonial affairs.

R

Raleigh, Sir Walter (1554–1618) English adventurer who settled the region from South Carolina north to present-day New York City under a charter from Queen Elizabeth I of England.

Randolph, A. Philip (1889–1979) American labor leader; supporter of civil liberties; instrumental in persuading President Franklin D. Roosevelt to set up the Fair Employment Practices Committee.

Reagan, Ronald (1911–) fortieth president of the United States.

Rehnquist, William (1924–) Supreme Court justice appointed in 1986.

Riis, Jacob (1849–1914) American social reformer, photographer, and journalist.

Robinson, Jackie (1919–1972) American athlete and business executive; joined the Brooklyn Dodgers in 1946, and became the first black to play major league baseball; elected to the Baseball Hall of Fame in 1962.

Rockefeller, John D. (1839–1937) Oil magnate and philanthropist; founded Standard Oil Co. in 1870; through careful management, slashed the cost of refining petroleum.

Rockefeller, Nelson A. (1908–1979) American politician; vice president of the United States under President Ford (1974–1977); replaced President Ford as vice president when Nixon resigned in 1974; son of John D.

Rockefeller.

Rolfe, John (1585–1622) Jamestown Colony planter whose experiments developing tobacco types saved the colony from economic disaster.

Roosevelt, Eleanor (1884–1962) Franklin D. Roosevelt's wife and a major champion for civil rights and humanitarian issues.

Roosevelt, Franklin D. (1882–1945) Democratic governor of New York elected thirty-second president of the United States.

Roosevelt, Theodore (1858–1919) vice president under President McKinley; assumed the presidency after McKinley's death; twenty-sixth president of the United States (1901–1909); led the American people and Congress toward progressive reforms and a strong foreign policy.

Rosenberg, Ethel (1915–1953) and Julius (1918–1953) alleged American spies; tried and executed for treason in 1953. Their guilt is still debated.

S

Sacajawea (c.1786–1812) Shoshone woman who guided Lewis and Clark on their exploration of the Louisiana Purchase.

Sacco, Nicola (1891–1927) Italian immigrant and anarchist executed for the 1920 murders of a paymaster and a guard in a Massachusetts shoe factory; believed to be innocent by many.

Santa Anna, Antonio López de (1794–1876) Mexican general, revolutionary, and leader who sent forces to put down the Texas rebellion.

Scott, Dred (1795?–1858) American slave who brought suit in a state court on the grounds that residence in a free territory released him from slavery; lost the state case and a later appeal in the federal circuit court; the Dred Scott case was one of the causes of the American Civil War.

Sequoya (c. 1760–1843) developed an alphabet for his Cherokee language and helped most of his tribe become literate in their language.

Serra, Junípero (1713–1784) Spanish priest who set up a chain of missions from San Diego to San Francisco.

Sherman, William Tecumseh (1820–1891) United States General in the Civil War; his successful campaign in Georgia (1864) split the confederacy in two and made an important contribution to the Union victory.

Sitting Bull (c. 1831–1890) Sioux Indian chief who resisted government demands that his tribe leave the Black Hills of South Dakota and Montana.

Slater, Samuel (1768–1835) British machinist who helped build the first cotton yarn spinning mill in the United States.

Smith, John (c. 1580–1631) English captain and leader of the Jamestown Colony.

Smith, Joseph (1805–1844) founder of the Church of Jesus Christ of Latter-day Saints.

St. Jean de Crèvecoeur, J. Hector (1735–1813) French immigrant who reported on Europeans adopting Indian lifestyles.

Stalin, Joseph (1879–1953) leader of the Soviet Union during World War II.

Stanton, Elizabeth Cady (1815–1902) American social reformer; led the struggle for woman suffrage with Susan B. Anthony.

Stevens, Thaddeus (1792–1868) leader of the Radical Republicans in the House of Representatives who insisted that African Americans be given full citizenship rights.

Stowe, Harriet Beecher (1811–1896) author of *Uncle Tom's Cabin*.

Stuart, Gilbert (1755–1828) early American painter noted for his portraits of George Washington.

Sumner, Charles (1811–1874) American statesman and orator, known for his stand against slavery.

Swift, Gustavus (1839–1903) American meat packer; created a new marketing system for the meat-packing industry by using railroads to ship dressed meat.

T

Taft, Robert (1889–1953) midwestern Republican conservative senator opposed to foreign aid and to U.S. involvement in NATO and the United Nations.

Taft, William H. (1857–1930) Twenty-seventh president of the United States; elected in 1909.

Taney, Roger (1777–1864) American jurist and fifth chief justice of the U.S. Supreme Court; well known for his controversial decision in the Dred Scott case.

Taylor, Zachary (1784–1850) twelfth president of the United States; general who led American troops into the disputed Texas-Mexican zone.

Tecumseh (1768–1813) Shawnee chief; called for and led a united Indian resistance to white settlers moving west.

Tenskwatawa (c. 1775–1834) Shawnee Indian religious leader known as the Prophet.

Thomas, Clarence (1948–) American jurist; associate justice of the U.S. Supreme Court, replacing the retiring justice Thurgood Marshall; his confirmation hearings were jarred by allegations of sexual harassment brought against Thomas by Anita Hill.

Thoreau, Henry David (1817–1862) American writer, philosopher, and naturalist, whose work demonstrates how the abstract ideals of libertarianism and individualism can be effectively instilled in a person's life.

Tisquantum (c. 1580–1622) called Squanto by the Plymouth colonists; befriended the Pilgrims, taught them farming techniques, and helped them establish treaties with neighboring Indian tribes.

Toussaint-L'Ouverture (c. 1743–1803) Haitian leader of the slave revolt against France.

Truman, Harry S (1884–1972) vice president under President F. D. Roosevelt; assumed the presidency upon Roosevelt's death; thirty-third president of the United States (1945–1953); known for ordering the atomic bomb to be dropped on two cities in Japan at the close of World War II; signed the Marshall Plan to rebuild Europe after World War II.

Trumbull, John (1756–1843) painter of important historical events.

Truth, Sojourner (1797–1883) American abolitionist and women's rights advocate; born into slavery, she was freed when New York State emancipated slaves in 1828.

Tubman, Harriet (c. 1820–1913) former slave who worked as a spy and scout for the Union army; also worked secret missions with the underground railroad to bring slaves north to freedom before the Civil War.

Turner, Frederick Jackson (1861–1932) American historian; awarded the Pulitzer prize in 1933 for history; stated that American society had been shaped mainly by the western frontier rather than by European influence, and that the frontier had played a large part in the creation in American democracy.

Turner, Nat (1800–1831) Virginia slave who was executed for leading a small band of followers against white plantation owners in 1831.

Twain, Mark See Clemens, Samuel.

Tweed, William Marcy (1823–1878) leader of the New York City Tweed Ring of corrupt city officials.

Tyler, John (1790–1862) vice president of the United States under President Harrison; assumed the presidency after Harrison's death; tenth president of the United States.

V

Van Buren, Martin (1782–1862) eighth president of the United States; head of a New York Democratic political organization.

Vespucci, Amerigo (1454–1512) explorer for whom America was named because he realized the lands described by Columbus were a new continent.

W

Ward, Aaron Montgomery (1843–1913) created the first direct-mail retail company by using the railroads.

Warren, Earl (1891–1974) American jurist; chief justice of the U.S. Supreme Court (1953–1969); best known as the chief justice who led the U.S. Supreme Court in making sweeping changes in civil rights laws and in criminal procedures.

Warren, Mercy Otis (1728–1814) writer of political tracts, plays, and poems that dramatized the Patriot cause.

Washington, Booker T. (1868–1915) African American leader; president of the Tuskegee Institute of Alabama.

Washington, George (1732–1799) first president of the United States.

Webster, Noah (1758–1843) author, educator, and editor who developed a dictionary of American English.

Wheatley, Phyllis (1753?–1784) first notable black author in the colonies.

Wheelwright, John (c. 1638) a minister who, with his followers, set up a non-church-related government in Exeter, New Hampshire.

White, John (c. 1587) leader of the second attempt to create an English colony in Roanoke, Virginia.

Whitefield, George (1714–1770) notable traveling minister of the Great Awakening era.

Whitney, Eli (1765–1825) inventor of the cotton gin (1793).

Williams, Roger (1603?–1683) extreme Separatist minister who founded Providence, Rhode Island, after being banished from the Massachusetts Bay Colony.

Wilson, Woodrow (1856–1924) twenty-eighth president of the United States.

Y

Yeltsin, Boris (1931–   ) president of the Russian Republic; elected in popular elections in June 1991.

Young, Brigham (1801–1877) leader of the Mormon (Latter-day Saints) colony in Utah.

Z

Zenger, Peter (1697–1746) editor of New York newspaper; tried for criminal libel. His trial helped establish the concept of freedom of the press.

A

abolition in U.S. history, the ending of slavery. **260**

abstract art name given to style of art in which the painter distorts or rearranges forms and colors, rather than portraying them realistically. **600**

abstract expressionism art form in which artists seek to convey their innermost feelings without reference to physical objects or conventional shapes. **849**

Adams–Onis Treaty (1819) treaty by which the U.S. obtained Florida from Spain. **242**

Adena mound-building people who built their mounds in various animal and bird shapes. **17**

affirmative action laws and programs designed to provide women and minorities with greater opportunities in employment, business, and education. **1002**

agrarian relating to farmers, fields, and agriculture. **498**

agribusiness industry consisting of large, corporate-run farms. **831**

agricultural revolution the beginning of systematic planting of crops as a food source. **15**

Albany Plan of Union plan for the English colonies, authored by Benjamin Franklin, to develop a common defense; rejected by both the colonies and the Iroquois Indians. **113**

Alien and Sedition Acts (1789) acts designed to stop pro-France and antiwar activities and to maintain Federalist power. **212**

Allies name given to the U.S. and its allies during World War I and II. **616**

amendment change or addition to an existing document. **156**

American Federation of Labor (AFL) national federation of unions organized in 1886. **444**

American System economic measures fostered by Henry Clay to promote the growth of manufacturing. **242**

American system of manufacture system based on the principle of manufacturing items with interchangeable parts. **299**

amnesty official pardon for an offense. **377**

anarchist person who believes all governments should be abolished, usually by violent means. **492**

Anasazi Colorado society, known as the Ancient Ones, who were long-distance traders as well as farmers. **18**

ancestor worship belief in the power of one's ancestors to influence daily life through performing ritual ceremonies. **25**

animism religious belief in a chief god or creator, and a number of lesser gods or spirits who control animals, winds, rain, and fertility. **22**

annex bring into the Union. **281**

anthropologists scientists who study the physical, cultural, and social factors of human behavior. **13**

Anti-Federalists opponents of the ratification of the Constitution. **161**

anti-Semitism prejudice and discrimination against Jewish people. **468**

Antietam, Battle of (1862) bloodiest single day of fighting in the Civil War; a serious setback for the South. **372**

apartheid South African policy that legalized racial separation and discrimination. **1055**

appeasement British and French policy before World War II, attempting to satisfy Hitler by giving in to his demands. **721**

Appomattox Courthouse scene of General Robert E. Lee's surrender of the Confederate army to Ulysses S. Grant on April 19, 1865. **388**

arbitrate negotiate solutions with an impartial third party. **521**

archeologists scientists who study the material remains of past human life and activities. **13**

armistice mutual agreement between combatants to end hostilities. **527**

arms race peace-time buildup of weapons among major nations. **518**

Articles of Confederation first government of the United States, which took the form of a loose alliance of member states; its weaknesses led to the creation of the Constitution. **148**

assembly line arrangement of machines, equipment, and workers so that work passes from operation to operation in a direct line. **300**

astrolabe navigation instrument used to help determine latitude. **30**

Atlantic Charter (1941) agreement between President Franklin D. Roosevelt and Prime Minister Winston Churchill on the principles and national policies necessary to guarantee peace after World War II. **706**

attrition wearing down the enemy by inflicting as many casualties as possible. **905**

Australian ballot printed ballot that contains all the candidates' names, is distributed only at polling places, and is marked by voters in secret. **499**

Glossary

B

baby boom period from 1945 to 1960 that showed an astonishing increase in the birth rate. **831**

backlash negative reaction to a social or political movement demanding change. **924**

Bacon's rebellion (1676) civil conflict in Virginia; led to stronger local self-government. **94**

balance of power political situation in which no country is strong enough to conquer any other. **516**

balance of trade difference between the value of imports and exports. **1070**

banking panic situation caused when too many depositors withdrew savings from threatened banks. **681**

barrios Hispanic urban neighborhoods. **926**

Battle of New Orleans Andrew Jackson-led victory that occurred weeks after the War of 1812 had ended. **222**

Bay of Pigs (1961) site on Cuba's southern coast where a planned invasion of Cuba by Cuban exiles trained by U.S. advisors turned into a fiasco. **869**

belligerents nations at war with each other. **618**

Berlin blockade (1948) Soviet block of all overland rail links into the city of Berlin, East Germany. **783**

Berlin Wall structure built and policed by the Soviets between East Berlin and West Berlin. **873**

bicameral two-house legislature. **147**

Big Three U.S., Britain, and the USSR, the principal World War II allies. **741**

Bill of Rights first ten amendments to the Constitution; protects the liberties of the individual. **166**

bimetallic standard money backed by both gold and silver. **501**

Black Hawk War massacre of Sauk and Fox Indians trying to return to Illinois. **276**

Black Tuesday October 29, 1929; the worst day of the Great Stock Market Crash, when stock values plummeted. **679**

black codes laws enacted by southern legislatures restricting freedoms of African Americans. **396**

black power term coined at a 1966 civil rights rally; used by African Americans demanding economic and political rights. **924**

blue-collar workers industrial workers paid hourly or by the piece. **461**

Bolsheviks members of Lenin's radical Communist Party in Russia. **625**

Bonus Army of 1932 veterans of World War I who gathered in Washington, D.C., demanding payment of a war bonus not due until 1945. **690**

Boston Massacre (1770) incident in Boston when a street mob attacked British soldiers, resulting in the killing of several colonists by British soldiers. **124**

Boston Tea Party (1773) demonstration in which American Patriots threw British tea from ships in Boston Harbor to protest the Tea Act. **125**

braceros Mexican nationals recruited to work temporarily on farms during World War II. **926**

brinkmanship political strategy that involves pushing a dangerous situation to the edge of war. **814**

Bull Run, First Battle of (1861) first major battle of the Civil War near Manassas, Virginia, resulting in a Confederate victory. **369**

Bull Run, Second Battle of (1862) major Confederate victory in Virginia. **371**

Bunker Hill, Battle of (1775) first formal battle of the Revolution fought at Breed's Hill. **128**

Burgesses, House of Virginia assembly, established in 1619, that managed affairs until 1774. **94**

C

Cajuns descendants of exiles from the French colony of Acadia (Nova Scotia) who settled in Louisiana. **46**

Camp David Accords 1978 peace agreement negotiated by Jimmy Carter between Israel and Egypt. **1004**

capitalist person who supports an economic system based on private ownership and unrestricted, free-market competition. **492**

caravel ship developed by the Portuguese that made long ocean voyages possible. **31**

carpetbaggers northern Republicans who moved to the South after the Civil War to profit from Reconstruction efforts. **400**

Carter Doctrine (1980) statement that warned the Soviets that the U.S. would fight to protect its vital interests in the Persian Gulf region. **1004**

cash crop product grown as a source of income. **55**

cede grant by treaty. **242**

Central Powers name given to Germany and Austria-Hungary and their allies during World War I. **616**

checks and balances system to guarantee a balance of power among the three branches of government. **166**

chronology a sequence of events in order of their happening. **27**

circular letter statements or arguments written by one colonial assembly and shared with the other colonial assemblies. **122**

city-manager system practice of hiring professional managers to oversee city government. **563**

civic virtue   political and social characteristics such as conscientiousness, responsibility, and patriotism.   **145**

Civil Rights Act of 1866   bill that made it a federal offense for a state to violate civil rights.   **399**

Civil Rights Acts of 1964   legislation outlawing racial discrimination and segregation in many areas.   **894**

civil disobedience   intentional breaking of a law perceived to be unjust.   **813**

civil liberties   basic rights protected by the Constitution against powers of the government.   **168**

civil rights   those rights people have by virtue of being citizens.   **397**

civil service   employment system of selecting and hiring on the basis of competitive exams.   **481**

clemency   official pardon   **992**

Coercive Acts   a set of acts passed by Parliament intending to punish Massachusetts for its role in the Boston Tea Party and its challenge to British authority.   **126**

Cold War   label given to tense Soviet-American relations after World War II.   **774**

collaborators   supporters of the Nazi regimes in conquered countries during World War II.   **771**

collective bargaining   right of workers to join unions and as a group to negotiate hours, wages, and working conditions with their employers.   **714**

collective security   Woodrow Wilson's view that countries should form an international organization to ensure world peace.   **628**

Committee of Correspondence   group of Patriots organized before the American revolution to exchange information about British activities.   **125**

commonwealth   a community founded on laws that would benefit the common good.   **61**

compact   a solemn agreement.   **60**

Compromise of 1850   agreement between northern and southern states concerning slavery, presented as a set of four pairs of resolutions.   **339**

Confederate States of America   official name taken by the states that seceded from the Union.   **357**

conquistadores   Spanish explorers and soldiers; forced native American peoples to accept Spanish rule.   **34**

conscription (1862)   compulsory enlistment of people into the army.   **381**

consent decrees   agreements by corporations to follow government regulations to avoid prosecution.   **590**

conservation movement   practices and policies adopted to preserve the nation's natural resources.   **581**

conservative   political approach that favors little or gradual change rather than abrupt change.   **128**

Constitutional Convention (1787)   discussed revision of the Articles of Confederation; resulted in the creation of the Constitution.   **154**

consumer culture   valuing of material goods over thrift and saving.   **827**

consumer goods   goods that people use in their daily lives; used to measure the standard of living.   **647**

containment policy   Harry Truman's policy to contain the Soviet Union within its post-World War II boundaries.   **782**

contraband   illegal or prohibited goods.   **618**

contras   rebels in Nicaragua who received aid from the U.S. to fight the Marxist Sandinista government.   **1029**

cooperatives   workshops and stores owned collectively by workers.   **443**

Coral Sea, Battle of the (1942)   pivotal battle in the Pacific which blocked Japan's drive to Australia.   **759**

counterculture   group of people within a society who hold values that oppose mainstream values.   **935**

counterinsurgency tactics   special military tactics used against rebel forces.   **886**

crop lien   agreement that pledged part of a farmer's crop to a merchant who provided seeds and food.   **405**

Cuban Missile Crisis (1962)   tense confrontation between the Soviets and the U.S. as a result of Soviet-built missile sites in Cuba.   **874**

cubism   modern art form that emphasizes flat surfaces and geometric angles.   **666**

culture war   struggle among sociological groups over national identity and values.   **1097**

Currency Act (1765)   act that prohibited colonists from printing their own paper money.   **119**

D

Dawes Act of 1887   bill that divided Indian reservations into individual family farms in an attempt to integrate Indians into mainstream America.   **457**

Dawes Plan (1924)   U.S. plan to aid Germany by scaling down its World War I debt and arranging for loans from American banks.   **660**

de facto   in reality; as a matter of practice, not law.   **810**

de jure   according to the law.   **810**

Declaration of Independence (1776)   document authored by Thomas Jefferson declaring that the colonies had the right to be free and independent states.   **131**

Declaratory Act   act that clearly restated Parliament's right to legislate for and tax the colonies.   **120**

demobilization   reducing the size of the armed forces.   **777**

Glossary

demographers scientists who study human populations. **1081**

depression slowdown of economic activity, resulting in high unemployment and business failures. **502**

détente attempt to relax tensions between the U.S. and the Soviet Union. **972**

diplomatic alliance organization whose members work together to meet political goals. **46**

diplomatic mission foreign service office that conducts economic and political business with the host country. **513**

direct primary elections that enable voters, instead of party committees, to select party candidates. **567**

direct representation representation by agents elected by the eligible voters of that district. **119**

dissenters those who do not agree with commonly held views, especially political and religious views. **47**

doctrine of nullification argument that states had the power to refuse to enforce acts of Congress. **249**

doctrine of states' rights belief in the supremacy of the states over the federal government; the states could nullify acts of Congress. **213**

dollar diplomacy foreign policy that encouraged trade and investments overseas. **612**

domino theory term used to describe the chain reaction when communism takes root in one area and spreads to neighboring countries. **813**

doves people opposed to war on moral grounds. **909**

downsize reduce the number of employees, usually those in middle management. **1093**

dry farming methods of farming that conserve soil moisture by deep plowing, and by letting fields lie fallow in alternate years. **449**

due process steps that guarantee fair and reasonable treatment under the law. **152**

due process clause section of the Fourteenth Amendment stating that no state could deprive any person of life, liberty, or property without due process of law. **591**

E

economy of scale ability to produce goods at lower costs by buying in large quantities at lower costs. **1071**

egalitarian classless society where all people are considered equal. **23**

Eisenhower Doctrine (1958) policy approved by Congress giving the president blanket permission to use U.S. forces to assist other nations in their struggles against overt Communist aggressions. **820**

elastic clause provision that gives Congress the power to make "all laws which shall be necessary and proper;" also called the necessary and proper clause. **168**

electoral college body of electors, equal in number to the representatives and senators from each state; officially elect the president and vice president. **157**

emancipation in U.S. history, the freeing of enslaved African Americans. **260**

Emancipation Proclamation (1863) President Lincoln's proclamation on January 1, 1863, that slaves in Confederate-held territory were freed. **375**

Embargo Act of 1807 short-lived act signed by Jefferson; ended commerce with foreign nations. **218**

embassy diplomatic mission staffed with an official ambassador. **513**

Emergency Quota Law (1921) precedent-setting legislation that restricted the number of immigrants from Europe to a maximum of 350,000 per year. **669**

Enlightenment (Age of Reason) eighteenth century intellectual movement suggesting that the universe was orderly and governed by rational laws that could be understood by humans. **89**

escalation increased U.S. involvement in Vietnam. **895**

ethnohistorian scientist who uses the data from other specialists along with oral histories and written words to study human cultures. **13**

excise tax indirect tax on the manufacture, sale, or consumption of a product within a country. **205**

executive agreement similar to a treaty, but binding only during a specific president's term of office; does not require Senate approval. **610**

executive privilege right claimed by the president or his advisors not to testify before congressional committees or to surrender secret documents. **819**

expansionists those who believed the U.S. should extend across the entire North American continent. **289**

expressionism artistic style that portrays feelings and emotions associated with objects, rather than the objects themselves. **666**

F

factory system method of production that combined machines and workers in mills and factories. **297**

Fair Deal Harry Truman's domestic program aimed at recovery from World War II. **788**

fall line imaginary line connecting points where highlands meet a coastal plain, and rivers become navigable for transporting goods to coastal ports. **77**

fallow fields left unplanted or untilled. **449**

fascism a centralized, autocratic government led by a dictator merging the power of state and business. **720**

federal reserve banks twelve regional banks that ease or tighten credit by raising or lowering the interest rates charged to other banks for borrowing money. **588**

Federal Trade Commission federal agency created in 1914; regulates trade and business. **590**

federalism relationship of independent states that share power with a central government. **161**

Federalists supporters of the ratification of the Constitution and the newly formed federal government. **161**

Fifteenth Amendment (1870) forbids denying the right to vote on the basis of race, color, or previous condition of servitude. **402**

filibustering extremely long congressional speeches aimed at preventing a vote being taken. **788**

First Continental Congress (1774) gathering of delegates from all colonies (except Georgia) to discuss the response to Parliament's Coercive Acts. **126**

flapper liberated young woman of the 1920s. **651**

Fourteen Points Woodrow Wilson's plan for peace in Europe that proposed a world order based on collective security. **628**

Fredericksburg, Battle of (1862) One of the worst Union disasters of the Civil War, led by General Ambrose Burnside in Virginia. **382**

Freedmen's Bureau temporary agency created in 1865 to assist in the care of refugees in the South, especially for freed African Americans. **397**

freedom of contract right to enter into any contract one chooses. **567**

French and Indian War war between England and France that began in America (1754) but spread to Europe where it was known as the Seven Years' War. **113**

friend-of-the-court legal argument (brief) written by a third party supporting one side in court cases. **781**

frontier line line of settlement inhabited by fewer than two people per square mile. **449**

Fugitive Slave Act of 1850 law making it legal for slave owners to claim African Americans who had escaped to the North. **342**

Fundamental Orders of Connecticut first written constitution in America, signed in 1639. **64**

fundamentalists Christians who believe in a literal interpretation of the Bible. **672**

G

gag rule (1836) House resolution banning discussion of antislavery petitions submitted to Congress. **264**

genetic engineering discovering and using techniques to manufacture and to alter life forms. **1094**

Geneva Accords (1954) agreement among 19 nations to end fighting in Indochina, temporarily dividing Vietnam at the 17th parallel. **817**

geologists scientists who study the physical structure of the earth. **13**

gerrymandering redrawing of election district boundaries to favor a group or groups. **882**

ghetto distinct neighborhood within a city, isolated by social and economic discrimination. **572**

glasnost Soviet policy establishing greater openness within their society. **1026**

glass ceiling term for the problems that women encounter as they rise from lower managerial levels in the workplace. **1085**

global economy integrated, interdependent economy developed on an international scale. **1069**

Good Neighbor policy Franklin Roosevelt's foreign policy to respect the territorial integrity of other nations. **720**

Gramm-Rudman-Hollings Act (1985) law requiring major federal deficit reductions over a five-year period and automatic budget cuts if the president and Congress do not agree on a budget. **1021**

grandfather clause (1867) means of preventing African Americans from voting: stated that any man whose father or grandfather had the right to vote on January 1, 1867, was entitled to vote. **411**

Granger laws laws passed in the 1860s to regulate the railroads by prohibiting rate discrimination and rebates, and establishing maximum rates. **489**

grassroots political or social movement which starts and is fueled at a local level. **811**

Great Awakening (1730-1760) burst of religious enthusiasm that spread across the northern and middle colonies and Virginia. **91**

Great Compromise plan that broke the deadlock at the Constitutional Convention by proposing representation based on a two-house legislature. **156**

greenbacks paper currency issued by the Union government at the beginning of the Civil War. **366**

gridlock situation in which neither the president nor Congress has sufficient political clout to produce positive action. **1050**

gross national product (GNP) total value of domestic and international goods and services produced by a nation each year. **551**

Glossary

growth industry an industry whose rapid expansion contributes greatly to the economy. **647**

guerrilla warfare nontraditional military tactics, including surprise attacks and sabotage. **522**

Gulf of Tonkin Resolution (1964) Congressional measure granting Lyndon Johnson authority to "take all necessary measures to repel any armed attack against forces of the United States." **895**

Gullah language formed by slaves in South Carolina from a mixture of African languages and English. **80**

gunboats flat-bottomed steam-driven "floating forts" used to carry Union cannons and supplies up shallow southern rivers. **367**

H

Harlem Renaissance period in the early 1900s when Harlem, New York, blossomed as a cultural center. **666**

hate crimes illegal acts against an individual or a group because of race, religion, or ethnicity. **1092**

hawks supporters of the Vietnam War who saw it as part of a global struggle against communism. **909**

hierarchy originally, a ranking made up of priests and bishops; any social system with rankings of power. **49**

Ho Chi Minh Trail primary route by which North Vietnam supplied its allies in the South. **885**

Hohokam Indians of the Southwest, known as the Vanished Ones, who left many artifacts. **18**

holding company corporation created to hold stock in and to provide central management for several other companies. **488**

Holocaust Nazi program of systematic extermination of European Jews, resulting in the murder of 6 million, two-thirds, of Europe's Jews. **763**

Homestead Act of 1862 law granting 160 acres of land in the West to any settler who would stay on the land for five years. **381**

Hopewell early advanced culture whose people were particularly artistic and social. **18**

House Un-American Activities Committee (HUAC) established to search for Communist influences in the U.S. during the 1940s and 1950s. **788**

hundred days initial spurt of legislative activity during a president's administration. **703**

I

Immigration and Nationality Act of 1965 ended quotas that favored immigration from Northern Europe. **1077**

impeachment Constitutional power granted to Congress to remove a president from office. **401**

imperialism policy or practice of one nation gaining control of other peoples and territories, and building foreign empires for military and trade advantages. **516**

implied powers those powers considered necessary to carry out specified powers. **168**

impound refusal to release funds (authorized by Congress). **967**

impressment forcible seizure of men from American ships to serve in the British navy. **207**

incumbent current officeholder. **206**

indentured servants people, mainly from Northern Europe, who contracted service for a specified amount of time in exchange for passage to the colonies and sustenance. **74**

industrial union union that was open to all workers in an industry, whether skilled or unskilled. **495**

information superhighway term used to describe the many different aspects of electronic media. **1100**

information technology devices and machines that allow people to store, manipulate, and share large amounts of data. **1094**

initiative laws laws that allow voters to bypass state legislatures to propose legislation. **567**

injunction court order. **504**

installment buying system of purchasing expensive items by paying for them in monthly payments. **681**

interest-group democracy legislative provisions that give something to nearly every special interest group in the nation. **706**

Internet (Net) world's largest computer network. **1101**

internment camps closed compounds where Japanese Americans were confined during World War II. **753**

interstate commerce goods shipped from one state to another. **244**

Intolerable Acts see Coercive Acts. **126**

Iran-contra scandal funds received from an illegal exchange of arms sales to Iran that were used to support Nicaraguan contra forces. **1029**

Iron curtain term given by Winston Churchill to describe the barriers between Communist Eastern European nations and those in Western Europe. **774**

Iroquois League Indian religious and political organization formed in approximately 1370. **46**

Iwo Jima, Battle of (1945) month-long battle in the Pacific in which U.S. marine divisions overcame Japanese resistance. **765**

J

Jamestown colony first enduring colony of the London Company; named for King James I of England. **51**

Jim Crow laws laws that imposed white supremacy throughout the South by expanding segregation. **411**

joint-stock companies system by which many individuals purchased stock in a venture and shared both the profits and the risks of failure. **50**

judicial review power of the judicial branch to interpret and review articles of the Constitution. **169**

Judiciary Act of 1789 act that provided for a chief justice and five associate judges to serve on the Supreme Court. **202**

jurisdiction area of control. **148**

K

kamikaze attacks by Japanese pilots who deliberately crashed their bomb-laden planes onto American warships. **765**

Kansas-Nebraska Act (1854) law that divided Nebraska into two territories and provided that the issue of slavery would be decided by popular sovereignty. **347**

Kentucky and Virginia Resolutions documents that laid the basis for the doctrine of states' rights. **213**

King Philip's War conflict between Wampanoag tribe and English settlers that ended Indian resistance in New England. **83**

kivas round structures built mostly underground by the Anasazi people. **19**

Knights of Labor labor organization founded in 1869 for both skilled and unskilled workers, including women and African Americans. **443**

Korean War (1950-1952) U.S. involvement in Korea under United Nations auspices. **794**

L

laissez-faire policy of limited government interference. **256**

lame duck defeated office holder who has not yet left office. **696**

Land Ordinance of 1785 act that provided for the survey and orderly sale of lands in the Northwest Territory. **151**

land-grant railroads railroads built with congressional loans and grants of public lands that railroad companies sold to raise money. **430**

large policy early nineteenth-century foreign policy that saw imperialism and sea power as the key to national survival in international relationships. **519**

League of Nations now defunct international organization formed after World War I. **629**

Lecompton Constitution (1855) Kansas constitution drafted by proslavery legislators and rejected by Congress. **352**

legal precedent former court rulings on a specific matter. **594**

Lend-Lease Act (1941) allowed the president to "lend, lease, or otherwise dispose of" arms and supplies for any country whose security was vital to U.S. defense. **723**

Levittowns residential suburbs named for William Levitt, built using mass production methods. **836**

Leyte Gulf, Battle of (1944) largest naval battle in recorded history in which American naval forces crippled the Japanese fleet. **760**

life expectancy average number of years one is statistically expected to live. **1086**

limited liability corporate legal arrangement restricting stockholders' losses to the value of their stock. **487**

limited war war whose strategic goal is less than the total annihilation or defeat of the enemy. **795**

Little Big Horn, Battle of the (1876) unsuccessful U.S. cavalry raid on an Indian village on Big Horn Mountain in Montana. **454**

loose constructionists those who believe that the Constitution's elastic clause gives Congress the authority needed to carry out specified powers. **204**

Lost Generation name given by Gertrude Stein to disillusioned writers of the 1920s. **664**

Louisiana Purchase (1803) purchase by President Jefferson of French-owned territory that almost doubled the size of the United States. **214**

M

mandate an authorization from the people to act. **875**

manifest destiny belief that the U.S. was fated to reach from the Atlantic to the Pacific Ocean. **289**

Marshall Plan U.S.-financed program of European economic recovery after World War II. **783**

martial law temporary military rule. **366**

matrilineal society where descent is traced through the mother's family. **23**

matrilocal society where males move in with the wife's family after marriage. **23**

Mayflower Compact Pilgrim document for self-governance in the new colony at Plymouth. **60**

McCarthyism term named after Senator Joseph McCarthy to describe the process of accusing people without proving the charges. **791**

mechanization using machines to do work formerly done by humans or animals. **437**

melodramas popular theatrical fare at the end of the Civil War featuring villains, heroes, and heroines. **479**

mercantilism economic system in which countries gained wealth by acquiring colonies to provide markets and raw materials for the mother country. **96**

mercenaries soldiers for hire. **115**

metes and bounds system of surveying used in the South that resulted in irregular land patterns. **150**

Midway, Battle of (1942) vital victory for American forces in the Pacific that marked a turning point in World War II. **759**

military-industrial complex collaboration between the nation's armed forces and defense industries. **823**

minutemen military units formed by colonists to respond to emergencies at a "minute's notice." **126**

missile gap idea born during the Cold War that the Soviets had surged ahead of the U.S. in the production of long-range missiles. **865**

missionary diplomacy Woodrow Wilson's policy based on the belief that foreign relations should rest on morality and idealism, not power and force. **613**

Mississippian mound-building society located in what is now the U.S. Midwest whose artifacts indicate a highly sophisticated culture. **18**

Missouri Compromise (1820) amendment to the Missouri statehood bill attempting to settle the question of slavery in the Louisiana Territory by prohibiting slavery north of the 36° 30´ line. **247**

Modern Republicanism label used by Dwight Eisenhower to describe his domestic program that emphasized cutting taxes, reduced spending, and balancing the budget. **806**

Molasses Act of 1733 act passed to discourage colonial trade with the French West Indies. **118**

monopoly exclusive control over a particular commodity, service, or market for a given product or service. **125**

Monroe Doctrine (1823) landmark of American foreign policy stating U.S. opposition to any foreign power interfering in the Western Hemisphere. **243**

Montreal Protocol (1987) historic agreement of major industrial nations to limit the use of chlorofluorocarbons (CFCs). **1095**

moratorium temporary suspension during the Great Depression of debt payments owed to the U.S. **691**

mother culture a group of people whose way of life is adopted in part by other groups. **16**

Mound Builders people who constructed earthen mounds used for purposes such as burial grounds. **17**

muckrakers label given to progressive authors who exposed government and corporate corruption. **563**

multinational corporations businesses with operations in more than one country. **1070**

N

National Association for the Advancement of Colored People (NAACP) organization formed by African American leaders and white progressives in 1909 to fight racial prejudice and discrimination. **573**

National Labor Relations Act of 1935 (Wagner Act) law that guaranteed workers a union of their own choosing. **714**

National Organization for Women (NOW) organization formed in 1966 to promote full equality and equal opportunity for women. **939**

National Security Council Document 68 (NSC-68) findings of a review ordered by Harry Truman that resulted in greatly increased defense spending. **792**

nativist person prejudiced against immigrants. **307**

Navigation Act of 1651 law passed by the British Parliament to assure that profits accruing from the colonies would be retained by England. **97**

Nazi Party The National Socialist German Workers' Party led by Adolf Hitler. **721**

necessary and proper clause provision that gives Congress power to make laws they deem necessary; also known as the elastic clause. **168**

New Deal Franklin Roosevelt's plan to end the Great Depression through federal aid programs. **696**

New Federalism the process of returning power to states and local governments. **967**

New Freedom slate of reforms, including lower tariffs and overhaul of the banking system, proposed by Woodrow Wilson in the 1912 election. **587**

New Frontier legislative plan proposed by John F. Kennedy focusing on the economy, aid to the poor, and the space program. **865**

New Jersey Plan plan presented at the Constitutional Convention that called for simple amendments to the Articles of Confederation. **156**

New Nationalism Theodore Roosevelt's reform program in which he proposed strict regulation of corporations, conservation, and social reform. **585**

New Right movement begun by activists of the 1970s and 1980s whose goals included restoring "a traditional, moral order" to the U.S. **1012**

Glossary

Nineteenth Amendment (1920) Constitutional amendment granting the right to vote to all women. **597**

nonaggression pact (1939) Agreement between Germany and the Soviet Union not to invade each other's territory. **722**

North Atlantic Free Trade Agreement (NAFTA) regional agreement giving special trade advantages to the U.S., Canada, and Mexico. **1064**

North Atlantic Treaty Organization (NATO) mutual-defense treaty signed by 12 nations against the Soviet Union and its Eastern bloc. **784**

Northwest Ordinance of 1787 act that provided political control over the Northwest Territory. **151**

Nuclear Nonproliferation Treaty (1968) agreement signed by nuclear powers to stop the spread of nuclear weapons. **973**

Nuclear Test Ban Treaty (1963) treaty signed by Soviets and the United States limiting atomic testing in the atmosphere, under water, and in outer space. **874**

O

Okinawa, Battle of (1945) American victory over entrenched Japanese forces. **765**

oligopoly situation when a few firms control most of the market for particular items. **806**

Olive Branch Petition statement of loyalty to the king that blamed British ministers for colonial problems. **128**

Olmecs early indigenous Americans living along the Mexican Gulf shore. **16**

on margin buying stock with a small amount down and borrowing the rest from a stockbroker. **677**

Open Door Policy statement of U.S. intention to keep trade in China open to all nations. **532**

Organization of Petroleum Exporting Countries (OPEC) association of oil-producing countries that controls the price of imported oil and gas. **970**

P

Palestine Liberation Organization (PLO) Arab nationalist organization dedicated to regaining lands on the West Bank of the Jordan River which had been controlled by Israel. **1028**

Paris Peace Accords (1973) agreement ending U.S. involvement in Vietnam. **966**

partisan member of a political party. **242**

patroons Dutch settlers who owned large estates on the Hudson River. **46**

peaceful coexistence living in peace, while respecting one another's differences. **814**

Pennsylvania Dutch German immigrants to Pennsylvania; misnamed due to confusion of the name of the German language, Deutsche, with the word *Dutch*. **76**

peonage system by which debtors and their families are bound to their creditors due to the unfair conditions of the crop lien system. **405**

perestroika Soviet policy allowing more freedom in the Soviet economy, moving it toward a market economy. **1026**

picket line line, formed by striking workers outside a factory, that union members and sympathizers do not cross. **716**

planned obsolescence practice of manufacturing consumer goods so that they wear out quickly and need frequent replacing. **828**

pocket veto method for presidents to reject a bill during the final ten days of a Congressional session by refusing to sign the bill. **393**

political socialist person who hopes to do away with capitalism by way of the ballot. **492**

poll tax tax (now illegal) that had to be paid before a person voted. **411**

pooling agreement attempt to eliminate competition by price fixing, and by dividing up the market among controlling companies. **487**

popular sovereignty in U.S. history, principle that allows citizens to decide for themselves issues such as slavery. **345**

postindustrial economy economic changes of the mid-1900s when the job and economic focus changed from producing goods to providing services, such as health, education, accounting, and government. **830**

praying towns Indian settlements set up by Puritans for converting Indians to Christianity. **83**

precedent an established convention or rule that serves as a model for future rulings. **60**

presidios Spanish colonial period forts, usually connected with a mission. **42**

price leader company that sets a profitable price for a product or service that is adopted by the rest of the industry. **559**

prime interest rate interest rate at which a central bank lends money to other banks. **1001**

primogeniture right of oldest child, usually a son, to inherit the entire estate. **146**

privateers seamen sponsored by the English monarchy whose aim was to attack and seize Spanish ships. **49**

Proclamation of 1763   proclamation by King George III reserving all land west of the Appalachian Mountains for the American Indians.   **117**

Proclamation of Neutrality (1789)   declaration that the U.S. would pursue a course friendly and impartial to the belligerent powers (France and Great Britain).   **207**

productivity   rate of output of workers.   **649**

progressivism   wave of reform activity in the United States in the early twentieth century.   **561**

prohibition   outlawing the manufacture, sale, and use of alcoholic beverages.   **568**

propaganda   material deliberately designed to promote public support for or against a project or person.   **623**

proprietor   legal owner of a business or concern.   **55**

protocol   formal code of government etiquette.   **214**

pueblo   both a building of the Anasazi people and a settlement.   **19**

Pueblo Indians   indigenous Indians of New Mexico who initially resisted the Spanish settlers.   **43**

puppet regime   a government under the control of another, stronger power.   **744**

purge   arrest, removal, or execution of people suspected of disloyalty.   **783**

Puritans   Protestant group that wanted to purify and change the Church of England.   **57**

Q

quadrant   navigation instrument used to show direction.   **30**

Quartering Act (1765)   act that required colonists to provide barracks and supplies for British troops stationed in the colonies.   **119**

Quebec Act (1774)   act that dealt with the administration of defeated French subjects in Canada.   **126**

R

radical   person with an extreme point of view.   **65**

Radical Republicans   extreme element in the Republican party that demanded Union control over newly restored southern states.   **393**

ratification   official approval by a legal body.   **148**

rationing   method of ensuring fair distribution of scarce goods by issuing stamps that were later exchanged for these items.   **747**

reactionary   person who favors a former or outmoded political system; ultraconservative.   **898**

rebate   discount from a published rate demanded by large volume shippers on railroads.   **487**

recall   procedure to allow voters to remove an elected official from office.   **567**

Reconstruction   name given to the process of restoring states to the Union after the Civil War.   **391**

reconversion   changing the economy and military from wartime to peacetime operations.   **776**

Redemption   process of restoring power to native-born whites in the South.   **409**

referendum   special election for a measure passed or proposed by the state legislature or through popular initiative.   **352**

refugees   people fleeing intolerable political, social, or economic conditions of their home countries.   **522**

regulatory state   government regulated economy that ensures that businesses and corporations do not engage in practices that endanger the public.   **576**

Renaissance   period beginning in 1330s of rebirth of classical Greek and Roman knowledge.   **30**

rendezvous   meeting held at a designated time and place.   **286**

reparations   payments made by defeated nations to the victors for war damages.   **629**

republicanism   belief that sovereignty resides in a body of citizens entitled to vote and that such power is exercised by elected representatives.   **145**

reservations   lands set aside by the U.S. for American Indian tribes.   **276**

restraining order   method used by the Federal Trade Commission to stop unfair business practices.   **590**

revenue sharing   federal tax money given as grants to the states and local governments.   **967**

reverse discrimination   actions penalizing members of the majority in order to help minorities.   **1002**

revival   renewal of religious interest.   **257**

revival meetings   meetings held to reawaken religious fervor and devotion.   **91**

revolutionary socialist   person who supports use of violence to eliminate capitalism.   **492**

right-to-work law   state law that permits nonunion employees to work in a union-organized shop.   **779**

Roosevelt Corollary (1904)   addendum to the Monroe Doctrine stating that the U.S. alone had the right to intervene in domestic affairs of Latin America.   **609**

rugged individualism   idea that the route to national wealth was allowing individuals the freedom to operate with minimal government interference.   **691**

rule of reason   principle applied in trust cases to decide if a merger would result in a reasonable or unreasonable restraint of trade.   **651**

S

sachem head of an Iroquois tribe. **23**

salutary neglect period when the English Parliament enforced few laws that affected the colonies. **116**

sanctuary movement networks organized to aid those seeking asylum in the U.S. who were not granted refugee status by the government. **1079**

Saratoga, Battle of decisive battle of the War for Independence; convinced the French to support the Americans. **136**

scalawags white southerners who cooperated with the Radical Republicans. **400**

Scopes trial (1925) court case testing the Tennessee state law prohibiting teaching scientific theory of evolution in public schools. **672**

secession official withdrawal of states from the Union. **221**

Second Continental Congress (1779) delegates meeting in Philadelphia who assumed responsibility for conducting the American Revolutionary War. **128**

Second Great Awakening (Great Revival) new wave of religious fervor in the Northeast in the 1830s. **257**

Second New Deal Franklin Roosevelt's 1935 set of legislative proposals. **710**

secondary boycotts practice of one union assisting another by refusing to buy an employer's goods or services during a labor dispute. **779**

segregated separated by race. **376**

self-determination belief that ethnic groups of former colonies and conquered territories should be allowed to determine their own futures. **628**

Seneca Falls Convention (1848) meeting held at Seneca Falls, New York, marking the beginning of the women's rights movement in the U.S. **265**

separate-but-equal doctrine Supreme Court ruling that states could impose segregation as long as facilities were equal for both races; overturned in *Brown v. Board of Education of Topeka, Kansas* in 1954. **413**

Separatists also known as Pilgrims; Protestants who separated from the corrupt English church. **57**

settlement houses community centers opened in immigrant neighborhoods by young middle-class volunteers. **561**

sharecroppers farmers in the South who used land they did not own to raise crops, and gave the landowner a part of the harvested crops in exchange. **405**

Sharpsburg, Maryland town near the site of the Battle of Antietam. **372**

Shays's Rebellion (1786) demonstration march by Massachusetts farmers to stop the sale of farms for nonpayment of taxes and debts. **153**

Shiloh, Battle of (1862) Civil War battle near Pittsburgh Landing, Tennessee; a costly and bloody Union victory. **369**

sit-down strikes strategy used by striking workers who sit down at their jobs, and refuse to leave the plant until their demands are met. **715**

Social Darwinism application of Darwin's ideas about "survival of the fittest" to human society. **515**

Social Security Act of 1935 foundation for modern welfare system providing assistance to retired people, the unemployed, and the handicapped. **710**

social gospel practice of helping the unfortunate in the inner city as one aspect of social reform. **561**

socialist person who believes that sources of wealth should be owned by the producers or workers who create the wealth. **492**

Sons of Liberty Patriot groups throughout the colonies organized in opposition to the Stamp Act. **120**

Southeast Asia Treaty Organization (SEATO) organization whose original purpose was to defend this area from Communist aggression. **817**

sovereignty independent, political authority. **145**

Spanish Armada huge naval force sent by Spain in 1588 to destroy British shipping; it was destroyed instead. **50**

speakeasy illegal saloon that flourished during prohibition. **668**

specie gold and silver coin. **255**

Specie Circular executive order that demanded payment in silver and gold coin for public lands. **255**

spheres of influence practice of informally establishing and recognizing areas of control within a foreign territory or country where colonization is not practical. **517**

spirituals religious folk songs that developed from enslaved African American culture. **316**

spoils system policy of rewarding campaign workers and party supporters with government jobs. **251**

squatter's rights claim made by settlers on farms lacking a clear legal title. **77**

stagflation slow-growing, stagnant economy, coupled with high inflation. **968**

Stalingrad, Battle of turning point of World War II in Eastern Europe when Soviet forces stopped the Eastern advances of German troops. **744**

Stamp Act (1765) act that required a government

stamp on a wide variety of legal documents and printed matter. **119**

Stamp Act Congress meeting called by Massachusetts to discuss mutual problems of the colonies. **120**

stewardship belief in people's responsibility for the care of the environment. **22**

stock claim on a corporation's assets giving the holder a share of the corporation's ownership and profits. **487**

stock speculation financially risky cycle of investing money in corporate stocks to push prices up, especially when the increase does not represent real growth or increase in the value of the corporation. **677**

Stono Rebellion revolt by enslaved African Americans in South Carolina in 1739. **82**

strict constructionists those who believe that government is limited to those powers specifically mentioned in the Constitution. **204**

suburbia cultural aspects of suburban life. **840**

suburbs residential areas surrounding cities. **655**

suffrage right to vote. **248**

Sugar Act (1764) act that imposed duties on sugar and coffee, but reduced the duty on molasses. **118**

summit conference meeting between high-ranking officials **814**

sun belt the South and southwestern regions of the United States. **833**

supply-side economics theory that high taxes discourage work, investments, and productivity, while lower taxes give people more money to spend, resulting in rapid economic growth and increased tax revenues for the nation. **1015**

supremacy clause provision that ensures that the Constitution is the highest law of the land by giving priority to federal laws over state laws. **158**

T

Taft-Hartley Act (1947) legislation aimed at reducing union power and at stopping certain labor practices. **779**

Tammany Hall Democratic Party organization in New York City run by "Boss" Tweed. **468**

Tariff of Abominations name given by southern congressmen to the high Tariff of 1828. **249**

tariff tax on foreign-made (imported) goods. **242**

Tea Act of 1773 act that gave exclusive right to sell tea in North America to the East India Tea Company. **125**

Teapot Dome Scandal fraud committed during Warren Harding's administration, leasing U.S. government oil reserves in Teapot Dome, Wyoming, and Elk Hills, California, to private developers. **660**

telecommuting working at home or in remote locations using information technology to communicate. **1094**

temperance movement movement aimed at reducing or stopping the consumption of alcohol. **258**

tenant farming system of renting land for cash payments. **405**

terrorism violent acts aimed at civilians. **522**

Tet Offensive (1968) attack by North Vietnam that signified the beginning of the end of U.S. involvement in Vietnam. **911**

Thirteenth Amendment (1865) Constitutional amendment abolishing slavery. **394**

Three Mile Island, Pennsylvania site of a nuclear power plant that experienced a partial meltdown of its nuclear reactor core in 1979. **999**

Three-fifths Compromise agreement that determined a slave would be counted as three-fifths of a person for representation in the House of Representatives and for taxation. **157**

Tiananmen Square site in Beijing, China, where students protesting for greater democracy were massacred. **1055**

Toleration Act of 1649 issued by Lord Calvert of Maryland to guarantee freedom of religion to all Christians. **54**

town meetings meetings common in New England; eligible voters met to discuss issues and to instruct their representatives. **94**

Townshend Acts (1767) acts that included a new set of duties and gave custom officials authority to issue writs of assistance. **121**

township and range system of surveying used first in New England and the Midwest that resulted in regular land patterns. **150**

trade unions organizations of workers to improve wages and working conditions. **443**

Trail of Tears devastating forced march of Cherokee Indians to the West. **278**

Treaty of Ghent (1814) treaty that ended the War of 1812 with Britain. **220**

Treaty of Guadalupe Hidalgo (1848) treaty ending the war with Mexico. **292**

Treaty of Paris (1763) treaty that officially ended the Thirty Years' War. **115**

Treaty of Paris (1783) treaty that officially ended the Revolutionary War. **149**

Treaty of San Lorenzo (1795)   Also known as Pinckney's Treaty; this treaty with Spain opened up the Mississippi River to American shipping.   **208**

triangular trade   commercial network that involved trade among America, Africa, and Europe.   **72**

tribute   payment made for protection.   **16**

Truman Doctrine (1947)   document justifying the use of the military to contain communism.   **782**

trust   combination of companies that dominate an industry, control prices, and eliminate all, or most, of the competition.   **488**

trustees   those who acted for the king, supervising use of the land and the residents.   **56**

turnpikes   privately built toll roads   **269**

Twenty-second Amendment (1951)   Constitutional amendment limiting presidents to two elected terms.   **779**

U

underclass   people who lack necessary education and skills, and are trapped in poverty in urban ghettos.   **1088**

underground railroad   northern escape route for fugitive slaves.   **30**

urban renewal   rebuilding of inner cities.   **807**

utopia   ideal community, such as those described by Edward Bellamy in his book *Looking Backward*.   **492**

V

vaudeville   popular entertainment featuring variety shows, comedy, songs and dances, and other acts.   **479**

Vietcong   Vietnamese Communists.   **886**

Vietnamization   The steps taken by Richard Nixon to reduce U.S. responsibility for the war in Vietnam.   **961**

vigilance committees   groups of African Americans who watched for slave catchers and helped fugitives escape.   **343**

Virginia Plan   James Madison's plan for a new structure of government, providing for three branches, executive, legislative, and judicial.   **155**

virtual representation   system by which all members of Parliament represented all English citizens.   **119**

W

war hawks   congressmen who favored war with the British in 1812.   **218**

ward boss   local political party leader.   **467**

watershed   main channel of water that lesser streams enter and the drainage areas of those streams.   **36**

Whigs   Patriots who believed they were preserving principles of English constitutionalism; named for the English party claiming British ministers were corrupting Parliament and society.   **128**

Whiskey Rebellion (1794)   uprising of Pennsylvania farmers who refused to pay the excise tax on liquor; the government response confirmed its authority.   **205**

white-collar workers   people employed in offices who dressed for work in shirts and ties; generally clerical and professional workers.   **461**

wildcat strikes   strikes conducted without official union approval.   **748**

Wilmot Proviso (1846)   act prohibiting slavery in the newly acquired Mexican territory.   **335**

work relief   Depression-era, federally funded work programs to put unemployed people back to work.   **703**

writ of assistance   general warrant that gave British inspectors the right to search any warehouse or private home that might contain illegal goods.   **118**

X

XYZ Affair   scandal resulting from attempted bribery of an American commission by French agents.   **209**

Y

Yamasee Border War   attacks and counterattacks over a six-year period in North Carolina resulting in the destruction of the Tuscarora Indian tribe.   **85**

yellow journalism (yellow press)   sensationalized news reporting.   **522**

Z

Zimmermann telegram   wire that instructed the German ambassador to persuade Mexico to enter into an alliance against the U.S. in exchange for Texas, New Mexico, and Arizona.   **619**

Glossary

A

Index

Dylan, Bob, 937
Dynamic Sociology (Ward), 598–599

E

Eagleton, Thomas, 976
Early, Jubal, 389
early Americans. *See* Indians (Native American)
Earth Day, *p925*
East Berlin, 814. *See also* Berlin Wall
East Germany, 814, 973. *See also* Germany; West Germany
East River, 472
Eckford, Elizabeth, 808, *p808*
An Economic Interpretation of the Constitution (Beard), 599
Economic Opportunity Act, 895
Economic Recovery Tax Act, 1016
economy, of New England, 71–72; and mercantilism, 96–97; and Civil War, 378–379, 389; in post-Civil War South, 405–406; and railroads, 431; as political issue, 482–483; of 1920s, 647, 649; and productivity, 649; effect of New Deal on, *c718;* and World War II, 745–748; following World War II, 776–779; and Eisenhower administration, 806, 809; and laissez-faire policy, 809; prosperity in, 827–829; postindustrial, 830; and Kennedy administration, 876, 878; and the environment, 925; and stagflation, 968; and energy crisis, 968–970, *p969;* and Nixon administration, 968–970; and Ford administration, 986, 988; and American resources, 987; and Carter administration, 1001, 1018; and supply-side economics, 1015–1016; and Reagan administration, 1015–1019, 1021–1022; and Bush administration, 1058–1059; global, 1069–1071, 1073; of scale, 1071, 1087; and economic map, 1072; and families, 1083–1085; opportunities in, and race, 1088–1089. *See also* budget deficits; industry; inflation
economy of scale, 1071, 1087
Ederle, Gertrude, 663
Edison, Thomas Alva, 436, 438, *p438*, 553, 704
editorial cartoon, analysis of, 412, 815, 989; interpretation of, 697
education, in colonies, 87; and social reform movement, 258–259; during Reconstruction, 406, 407; and Chautauqua movement, 553–554; and Progressive Era, 599; and Great Society, 899–900; and Hispanic Americans, *c928;* and Bilingual Education Act of 1968, 930; and school prayer, 1014, 1022; and science, 1092
Education, Department of, 998, 1024
Edwards, Jonathan, 91–92, 93
EEOC (Equal Employment Opportunity Commission), 1024, 1050, 1051
egalitarian society, 23

Egypt, and World War II, 744; and Aswân High Dam, 818; and Suez War, 818; and threat to Lebanon, 820; and Yom Kippur War, 970, 975; and Six-Day War, 975; and peace settlement with Israel, 1004–1005; and anti-Soviet alliance, 1027
Ehrlichman, John, 960, 977, *p977,* 978, 979
Eighteenth Amendment, 596, 622, 668, 669
Eighth Amendment, *c167*
eight-hour day, 493–494, 552, 577
Einstein, Albert, 766, *p1078*
Eisenhower, Dwight D., *p800,* 800–825, 868, 878, 1012; and World War II, 744, 757, *p757,* 763, 801; and election of 1952, 800, 801–802, *p802,* 1021; and cabinet, 802–803, 867; and Korean War, 803–804; and McCarthyism, 804–806; and domestic policies, 804–807, 865; and Modern Republicanism, 806; and election of 1956, 807, 809, 1021; and civil rights issues, 808, 811, 881; and school desegregation, 808; and Earl Warren appointment, 810; foreign policy of, 813–818, 819–821, 823, 864, 865, 869, 885, 974; and Khrushchev, 814, 821, 823; and Eisenhower Doctrine, 820
Eisenhower Doctrine, 820
Eisenstadt v. Baird, 885
El Alamein, Egypt, 744
elastic clause, 168
elderly, and Medicare Act, 900, 1086; and population, 1085–1086; and life expectancy, 1086; and poverty, 1086; and Social Security, 1086
election(s), of 1792, 206; of 1800, 213, *m213,* 240, 248; of 1816, 241; of 1820, 241; of 1824, 247–248; of 1828, 249, 251; of 1832, 255; of 1840, 256–257, 264; of 1844, 290; of 1848, 337; of 1852, 347; of 1856, 347, 348–349; of 1860, 353, 355–357, *m357;* of 1864, 385–386; of 1868, 402; of 1876, 409–410, 481; of 1884, 480; of 1888, 482–483; of 1896, 486, 506–509, *m509,* 523, 689; of 1892, 499; primary, direct, 567–568; of 1900, 577; of 1904, 580; of 1908, 582; of 1912, 584, 585, *m585,* 587, 1061; of 1916, 590, 597; of 1918, 630; of 1920, 631, 657; of 1924, 658, 689; of 1928, 659, *m659;* of 1932, 694–696, 698–699; of 1940, 695, 723; of 1936, 710, 711; of 1944, 749; of 1948, 786–788, *m787,* 791, 877; of 1952, 800, 801–802; of 1956, 807, 809; of 1960, 823, 864, 865–867, *m867,* 875, 958; of 1964, 892, *m896,* 896–898, 899, 1061; of 1968, 913, 956, 957–959, *m959,* 976; of 1972, 975, 976–977; of 1976, 995–997, *m996, c1021;* of 1980, 1007, 1012, *c1021;* of 1984, *c1021;* of 1988, 1046, 1047, *m1047,* 1049, 1060; of 1992, 1058, 1060–1061, *m1061;* of 1994, 1065, 1067
electoral college, 157

electrical manufacturing industry, 487, 649, 828, 988
electricity, 436, 647
Elementary and Secondary Education Act, 899
Eliot, T. S., 664
Elizabeth I, Queen of England, 47, 49, 50
Elkins Act, 580
Ellington, Duke, 665
Ellis Island, 466
Ellison, Ralph, 849
Ellsberg, Daniel, 962, 963, 965, *p965*
El Salvador, 1030, 1055, 1079
Ely, Richard T., 599
emancipation, 260, 374
Emancipation Proclamation, 362, 374–375, 384, 393
Embargo Act, 218
embassy, 513
emerged from Northwest Territory, 151–152
Emergency and Relief Construction Act, 688, 690
Emergency Banking Act, 703, 707
Emergency Farm Mortgage Act, 706
Emergency Quota Law, 669
Emergency Railroad Transportation Act, 706
Emergency Relief Appropriation Act, 710
Emerson, Gloria, 993
Emerson, John, 351
Emerson, Ralph Waldo, 127
Employment Act, 777
Empress of China (ship), 513
energy, and Daylight Saving Time, 622; and crisis of 1973, 968–970, *p969;* American consumption and importation of, 987; and problems during Ford administration, 988; and crisis during Carter administration, 998–999; nuclear, 999. *See also* oil industry
Energy, Department of, 998
Energy Security Act, 999
England, colonists from, 40, 47–52, *p50,* 54–67, *m55;* and Spanish rivalry, 47, 49; defeat of Spanish Armada by, 50; American colonial imports from, *c121;* skilled workers from, 306; immigrants from, 466, 1078. *See also* Great Britain
Engle v. Vitale, 884–885
English Channel, 663
Enlightenment, 89–90
Enola Gay (plane), 765
environment, and DDT, 901; and Rachel Carson, 901, 925; and economy, 925; and pollution, 925, 970; and energy needs, 970; important legislation regarding, *c971;* and Nixon administration, 971; and Reagan administration, 1018; and North American Free Trade Agreement, 1064; and twenty-first century concerns, 1095–1096

Index

Text and Photo Acknowledgments

TEXT ACKNOWLEDGMENTS
Positions: L (left); **R** (right); **T** (top)

680 Ludlow Music, Inc., New York; **732** "War, Women, and Work", reprinted with permission of the Putnam Publishing Group from *The Homefront: America During World War II* by Mark Jonathan Harris, Franklin D. Mitchell and Steven J. Schechter. Copyright ©1984 by Mark Jonathan Harris, Franklin D. Mitchell and Steven J. Schechter; **734L** From *The Good War* by Studs Terkel. Copyright ©1984 by Studs Terkel. Reprinted by permission of Pantheon Books, a division of Random House, Inc.; **734RT** Reprinted from *Americans Remember the Home Front* by Roy Hoopes. Copyright ©1992 published by arrangement with The Berkley Publishing Group; **734–735** "An Indefensible Moral Position" Copyright 1945, Christian Century Foundation. Reprinted by permission from the August 29, 1945, issue of *The Christian Century;* **735** "Private Prosperity, Public Squalor" excerpts from *The Affluent Society* by John Kenneth Galbraith. Copyright ©1958 by John Kenneth Galbraith. Reprinted by permission of Houghton Mifflin Company. All rights reserved; **736L** "In The Cities, People Were Doing Things" Copyright ©1970 by The New York Times Company. Reprinted by permission; **736R** "A Vast Wasteland" reprinted with permission of Simon & Schuster from *Equal Time: The Private Broadcaster and The Public Interest* by Newton N. Minow. Copyright ©1964 by Newton N. Minow; **736–737** "I Am Waiting" by Lawrence Ferlinghetti, from *A Coney Island of The Mind.* Copyright ©1958 by Lawrence Ferlinghetti. Reprinted by permission of New Directions Publishing Corp.; **856** "Letter from Birmingham Jail" reprinted by arrangement with the Heirs to the Estate of Martin Luther King, Jr., c/o Writers House, Inc. as agent for the proprietor. Copyright 1963 by Martin Luther King, Jr., copyright renewed 1991 by Coretta Scott King; **856–857** "Kennedy Without Tears" Tom Wicker, *Esquire,* 61 (June 1964), The Hearst Corporation; **857L** "Johnson's Public Honeymoon" reprinted by permission of the Putnam Publishing Group from *Lyndon: An Oral History* by Merle Miller. Copyright ©1980 by Merle Miller; **857R** "Vice President Humphrey Urges Caution" Humphrey Family Advisory Committee; **859** "I Was Bound to Be Crucified" from *Excerpts from Lyndon Johnson and The American Dream* by Doris Kearns. Copyright 1976 by Doris Kearns. Reprinted by permission of HarperCollins Publishers, Inc.; **860** "Malcolm X Advocates Bolder Action" ©1965, 1989 by Betty Shabazz and Pathfinder Press; **861** "A Full Tribalizing Process" Copyright ©1970 by the New York Times Company. Reprinted by permission; **862** "The New American Revolution Has Begun" from *Without Marx or Jesus: the New American Revolution Has Begun* by Jean-Francois Revel, Bantam Doubleday Dell Publishing Group, Inc.; **949** "Nixon's Ideological War" reprinted with permission of Simon & Schuster from *Breach of Faith: The Fall of Richard Nixon* by Theodore White. Copyright ©1975 by Theodore White; **949–950** "Have We Overcome?" from *Have We Overcome? Race Relations Since Brown,* edited by Michael Namorato ©1979 University Press of Mississippi. Reprinted by permission of University Press of Mississippi; **950–951** Are Quotas Good for Blacks?" reprinted from *Commentary,* June 1978, by permission; all rights reserved; **951–952** "The Duke: More Than Just a Hero" Copyright ©1979 *The Washington Post.* Reprinted with permission; **952** "A New Right Activist Explains His Movement" Richard A. Viguerie, Conservative Spokesman and Direct Marketing Expert; **953** "The Zero-Sum Society" excerpts from *The Zero Sum Society* by Lester Thurow. Copyright ©1985 by Basic Books, Inc. Reprinted by permission of Basic Books, a division of HarperCollins

Publishers, Inc. **954** "The Landslide of 1984" Copyright ©1984 Time Inc. Reprinted by permission; **1039** "So What Do Polls Mean?" Copyright ©1995, *The Washington Post,* reprinted with permission. **1040** "The Third Wave" from *The Third Wave* by Alvin Toffler. Copyright ©1980 by Alvin Toffler. Used by permission of Bantam Books, a division of Bantam Doubleday Dell Publishing Group, Inc.; **1041RT** "Liberate Us From the Liberators" from *Women Who Do and Women Who Don't Join the Women's Movement* by Robyn Rowland, International Thomson Publishing Services, Routledge (RKP), 1984; **1041** "Betty Friedan Reflects on the Women's Movement" reprinted with the permission of Simon & Schuster from *The Second Stage* by Betty Friedan. Copyright ©1981, 1986 by Betty Friedan; **1041–1042** "Women's Generation Gap" from "When We Were Your Age" from *Making Sense* by Ellen Goodman. Copyright ©1989 by the Washington Post Company. Used by permission of Grove/Atlantic, Inc.; **1042–1043** "The Unending Dream" from *American Dreams: Lost and Found* by Studs Terkel. Copyright ©1980 by Studs Terkel. Reprinted by permission of Pantheon Books, a division of Random House, Inc.

PHOTO ACKNOWLEDGMENTS
Positions: L(left); **R**(right); **T**(top); **C**(center); **B**(bottom).
Key: AP/WW (AP/Wide World Photos); BB (Brown Brothers); CBA (Corbis-Bettmann Archive); CP (Culver Pictures, Inc.); FPG (FPG International); NW (North Wind Picture Archives); PR (Photo Researchers, Inc.); UPI/CB (UPI/Corbis-Bettmann).

Contents **vi-T** ©George Holton/PR; **vi-B** CP; **vii-T** ©David Doody/FPG; **vii-B** CBA; **viii-T** CBA; **viii-B** CP; **ix-T** The Ronald Reagan Presidential Library & Museum/The Telesis Foundation/ Courtesy of the Collection of Joshua M. Landish/©Don Milici; **ix-B** CBA; **x-T** NW; **x-B** Courtesy of the Museum of the American Numismatic Association; **xi-T** Scala/Art Resource, NY; **xi-B** Breton Littlehales/National Geographic Image Collection; **xii-T** National Archives; **xii-B** BB; **xiii-T** Collection of Delton Lee Johnson, Santa Paula, CA; **xiii-B** ©R. Foulds/ Washington Stock Photo, Inc.; **xiv-T** Staff Photographer/Dwight D. Eisenhower Library; **xiv-B** Barbie is a trademark of Mattel, Inc. Used with permission. ©1990 Mattel, Inc. All Rights Reserved; **xv** AP/WW; **xvi-T** Courtesy of Apple Computer, Inc.; **xvi-B** Photographed with the permission of the FIDM Museum & Library Foundation at the Fashion Institute of Design and Merchandising, Los Angeles, CA/©Don Milici; **xvii** ©Tony Stone Images/Ken Biggs.

Preface **xxv-LC** Photo ©Anne van der Vaeren/The Image Bank; **xxv-BL** ©1994 Gary Schultz/Alaska Stock Images; **xxv-RT** ©Tony Stone Images/Lori Adamski Peek; **xxv-RC** CB; **xxv-LB** CBA; **xxvi-LT** Courtesy of the American Numismatic Association; **xxvi-LC** NW; **xxvi-LB** ©F. Hibon/SYGMA; **xxvi-RT** CBA.

Unit Openers **2** Schalkwijk/Art Resource, NY; **102** CBA; **230** The Metropolitan Museum of Art, Bequest of Edward W.C. Arnold, The Edward W.C. Arnold Collection of New York Prints, Maps and Pictures, 1954. (54.90.870); **324T** Pennsylvania Capitol Preservation Committee; **324B** The Museum of the Confederacy, Richmond, Virginia, photography by Katherine Wetzel; **418** NW; **540** ©1995 Nawrocki Stock Photo, Inc.; **636** Mitchell Jamieson, *An Incident in Contemporary American Life*, 1941, The U. S. Department of the Interior, Washington, D.C., photographer David Allison; **730** Printed by permission of The Norman Rockwell Family Trust, Copyright ©1945 The Norman Rockwell Family Trust, photo courtesy of The Norman Rockwell Museum at Stockbridge; **854** Dallas Museum of Art, gift of the Art Museum League, Mr. and Mrs. George V. Charlton, Mr. and Mrs. James B. Francis, Dr. and Mrs. Ralph Greenlee Jr., Mr. and Mrs. James H.W. Jacks, Mr. and Mrs. Irvin L. Levy, Mrs. John W. O'Boyle, and Dr. Joanne Stroud in honor of Mrs. Eugene McDermott/©1995 Jasper Johns/Licensed by VAGA, New York, NY; **946** ©Peter Gridley/FPG; **1036** ©Jeffrey Dunn/Viesti Associates, Inc.

Unit Archives **4LB** Bridgeman/Art Resource, NY; **4RC** 1582(2) Photo by Logan, Courtesy Department of Library Services, American Museum of Natural History; **7** Ashmolean Museum, University of Oxford; **8** CBA; **10LC** Courtesy of the Simon Wiesenthal Center Beit HaShoah Museum of Tolerance Library/Archives, Los Angeles, CA; **10RB** Courtesy of The Newberry Library; **11** Collection of Perna L. White; **104** CBA; **106** NW; **108** Smithsonian Institution; **111** Bureau of Engraving; **235L** CBA; **235RC** Woolaroc Museum, Bartlesville, OK; **236** CBA; **238** Photographed with the permission of the FIDM Museum & Library Foundation at the Fashion Institute of Design and Merchandising, Los Angeles, CA/©Don Milici; **326** The Ronald Reagan Presidential Library & Museum/The Telesis Foundation/Putnam Museum of History and Natural Science, Davenport, Iowa/©Don Milici; **329** CBA; **330** CBA; **332** CBA; **421** Courtesy, U.S. Bicycling Hall of Fame, Somerville, NJ; **423** Archive Photos; **426** CP; **544** CBA; **545** Photographed with the permission of the FIDM Museum & Library Foundation at the Fashion Institute of Design and Merchandising, Los Angeles, CA/©Don Milici; **547** ©Charles Orrico/ SuperStock, Inc.; **638L** Archive Photos/Hirz; **638R** CP; **639** CBA; **641** Library of Congress; **732** CP; **733** BB; **737** CBA; **856** AP/WW; **858** UPI/CB; **859L** AP/WW; **859RB** ©Lawrence Schiller; PR; **860L** UPI/CB; **860R** AP/WW; **861** AP/WW; **948** ©John Neubauer/PhotoEdit; **950** Courtesy CDS Gallery, NY; **952** CBA; **954** Archive Photos; **1038** UPI/CB; **1039RB** AP/WW; **1040** ©Tony Stone Images/Lois & Bob Schlowsky **1041** ©David Young-Wolff/PhotoEdit; **1042** ©Tom Hollyman/Photo Researchers; **1043** UPI/CB; **1044** ©Tony Stone Images/Pete Saloutos.

Enduring Constitution (flag background): **88; 210; 250; 398; 490; 592; 670; 789; 883; 962; 1048** ©Michael Rutherford/SuperStock, Inc.

Chapter 1 **12** Peabody Museum of Art, Harvard University, Photograph by Hillel Burger; **15L** Erich Lessing/Art Resource, NY; **15R** Arizona State Museum, University of Arizona; **16** ©Nathaniel Tarn/PR; **17** Serpent Mound State Memorial Park, Ohio, U.S.A. Photo by: T. Linck/SuperStock, Inc.; **18L** National Park Service; **18R** Courtesy of Moundville Archaeological Park and the University of Alabama Museums; **19** ©David M. Grossman/PR; **20L** ©Tim Davis/PR; **20C** Peabody Museum of Art, Harvard University; **20R** Courtesy Ohio Historical Society; **22** Courtesy Winterthur Museum; **24** #1582(2) Photo by Logan, Courtesy Department of Library Services, American Museum of Natural History; **26LT&RB** ©George Holton/PR; **30** CBA; **33** CBA; **35RT** Scala/Art Resource, NY; **35B** Courtesy of The Newberry Library; **36** Biblioteca Medicea Laurenziana.

Chapter 2 **40** Autry Museum of Western Heritage, Los Angeles; **41** BB; **43** Arizona State Museum, University of Arizona; **44** Museum of Indian Arts and Culture/Laboratory of Anthropology, Santa Fe; **45** NW; **47** CBA; **48T** Bridgeman/Art Resource, NY; **48B** Copyright British Museum; **49** CBA; **50LT** CBA; **50RB** Bridgeman/Art Resource, NY; **51** CP; **52L** Ashmolean Museum, University of Oxford; **52R** CBA; **53** CP; **54** BB; **56** BB; **57** CBA; **58** ©Gail Shumay/FPG; **60L** ©1995 Nawrocki Stock Photo, Inc.; **60R** CBA; **61** CBA; **62** CP; **63** CBA; **64** CBA; **67** ©Francis G. Mayer/PR; **69** Mervyn Greenfield.

Chapter 3 **70** Abby Aldrich Rockefeller Folk Art Center, Williamsburg, VA; **71T** Stock Montage, Inc.; **71B** Courtesy of the Pilgrim Society, Plymouth, Massachusetts; **73** NW; **74** CP; **75** Abby Aldrich Rockefeller Folk Art Center, Williamsburg, VA; **77** CP; **78** Stock

Montage, Inc.; **79T** ©1995 Nawrocki Stock Photo, Inc.; **79B** ©1995 Nawrocki Stock Photo, Inc.; **80** The Gibbes Museum of Art/Carolina Art Association, *View of Mulberry Plantation (House and Street)* by Thomas Coram; **83** CP; **87** CBA; **88T** Rare Books and Manuscripts Division, The New York Public Library, Astor Lenox and Tilden Foundations; **88B** NW; **90L** CP; **90R** CBA; **91L** BB; **91R** Princeton University; **92T** Courtesy of the National Portrait Gallery, London; **92B** The Metropolitan Museum of Art, Rogers Fund, 1942 (42.95.20). ©1979 The Metropolitan Museum of Art; **94** NW; **95** Courtesy Peabody Essex Museum, Salem, MA, Acc. #1246/Photo by Mark Sexton; **97** NW.

Chapter 4 **112** Colonial Williamsburg Foundation; **115** NW; **117** CP; **119L** NW; **119R** ©1995 Nawrocki Stock Photo, Inc.; **120** The Historical Society of Pennsylvania; **122** Library of Congress; **124** CBA; **125** CBA; **126** ©David Doody/FPG; **127** Courtesy of the Concord Museum, Concord, MA; **129L** NW; **129R** CBA; **130** Bequest of Winslow Warren, Courtesy Museum of Fine Arts, Boston; **131L** ©1995 Nawrocki Stock Photo, Inc.; **131R** Smithsonian Institution; **132** Yale University Art Gallery; **134** CBA; **135T** Courtesy of The Mount Vernon Ladies' Association and The Founders Society; **135B** CBA; **136** Yale University Art Gallery; **137** Courtesy of The Valley Forge Historical Society; **139** Anne S.K. Brown Military collection, Brown University Library; **140** Yale University Art Gallery; **141** Courtesy, The Henry Francis du Pont Winterthur Museum; **143** CBA.

Chapter 5 **144** Independence National Historical Park; **146** CP; **148** CP; **152** CBA; **153LT,CT&RT** Courtesy of the Museum of the American Numismatic Association; **153B** CBA; **155T** Photo ©Anne van der Vaeren/The Image Bank; **155B** CBA; **156T** BB; **156B** CBA; **160** James T. Potter, AIA; **162** The Library of Congress; **163L** Library of Congress/Courtesy National Geographic Society; **163R** ©Jack Zehrt/FPG, National Portrait Gallery; **164L** National Portrait Gallery, Smithsonian Institution/Art Resource, NY; **164R** CP; **165** NW; **169** ©M. Win/Washington Stock Photo, Inc.

Constitution of the United States of America **173** ©Comstock; **175** ©Paul Conklin/PhotoEdit; **180** John F. Kennedy Library; **182** PR; **187** ©Don Milici; **189** CBA; **190** ©Joe Sohn/Chromosohm/Stock, Boston, Inc.; **191** Library of Congress; **192** ©Comstock; **193** CBA; **195** CBA; **197** ©Bob Daemmrich/Stock, Boston, Inc.; **199** ©Joseph Sohm/Stock, Boston, Inc.

Chapter 6 **200T&B** Courtesy of the Museum of the American Numismatic Association; **201** NW; **202T** Collection of The New-York Historical Society; **202B** Daniel Huntington (1816–1906), *The Republican Court* (1861), oil on canvas, 6167.6 x 277.0 (66 x 109), The Brooklyn Museum 39.536.1, Gift of the Crescent-Hamilton Athletic Club; **203** Collection of The New-York Historical Society; **205** NW; **207** CBA; **208** CBA; **209** Courtesy, Independence National Historical Park; **210** Engraving by Alonzo Chappell, Collection of the Supreme Court of the United States; **212** CBA; **215** CBA; **216** CBA; **217L** National Portrait Gallery, Smithsonian Institution/Art Resource, NY; **217R** National Museum of American Art, Washington, D.C./Art Resource, NY; **218** ©1995 Nawrocki Stock Photo, Inc.; **220T** CBA; **220B** CBA; **222** CBA; **223** ©M. Bognovitz/Washington Stock Photo, Inc.; **224L** CBA; **224R** CBA; **227** FPG.

Chapter 7 **240** FPG; **241** The Metropolitan Museum of Art, Bequest of Seth Low, 1929. (29.89); **242** CP; **249** ©1995 Nawrocki Stock Photo, Inc.; **250** Courtesy of the South Carolina Library, University of South Carolina; **251** CBA; **252** Courtesy of the Boston Art Commission, 1995; **254** Courtesy of the R. W. Norton Art Gallery, Shreveport, LA; **255** CBA; **256** CBA; **257** CBA; **258** CBA; **259T** CP; **259B** CBA; **261LT** BB; **261RT** Library of Congress; **261B** The Library of Congress/PR; **262** CBA; **263** Library of Congress; **264L&R** FPG; **265** CP.

Chapter 8 **268** Autry Museum of Western Heritage, Los Angeles; **269** Shelburne Museum, Shelburne, VT, photograph by Ken Burris; **270** CP; **271** CBA; **275** National Museum of American Art, Smithsonian Institution, gift of Mrs. Joseph Harrison Jr./Art Resource, NY; **276** CBA; **278** Woolaroc Museum, Bartlesville, OK; **280** CP; **281** Autry Museum of Western Heritage, Los Angeles; **282** CBA; **284T** The State Preservation Board, Austin, TX; **284B** NW; **285** CP; **286LB&RT** Courtesy, Museum of Church History and Art, Salt Lake City; **287** Denver Public Library, Western History Department; **288** CP; **290** CBA; **292** Collection of W.H.D. Koerner III, Photograph courtesy of Brandywine River Museum, ©The Curtis Publishing Company, W. H. D. Koerner (1878-1938); **293** CBA.

Chapter 9 **296** Museum of American Textile History; **297** CBA; **298** CBA; **299T** CP; **299B** CBA; **300** CBA; **303** CP; **304L** Photographed with the permission of the FIDM Museum & Library Foundation at the Fashion Institute of Design and Merchandising, Los Angeles, CA/©Don Milici; **304R** Courtesy of the Massachusetts Historical Society; **305LT** NW; **305RT** CBA; **306** CP; **308** CP; **309** CBA; **311** NW; **312** CBA; **313L** From *Slave Songs of the Georgia Sea Islands* by Lydia Parrish. Copyright ©1942 by Lydia Parrish and 1969 by Maxfield Parrish Jr. Reprinted by permission of the publisher, The University of Georgia Press, Athens; **313R** Re-created with permission from The Wren's Nest, Joel Chandler Harris Association; **314&315** *Slave Market, Richmond, Virginia*, 1862/The Collection of Jay P. Altmayer/ Photograph courtesy of Kennedy Galleries, Inc., NY; **317** CP; **318** NW; **319** CBA.

Chapter 10 **334** The Ronald Reagan Presidential Library & Museum/The Telesis Foundation/Putnam Museum of History and Natural Science, Davenport, Iowa/©Don Milici; **335** CP; **337** Courtesy of Millard Fillmore House, Studio Aurora/Eric Demme, 1995; **338** NW; **340T** NW; **340B** NW; **341L** CBA; **341C** Library of Congress; **341R** National Portrait Gallery, Smithsonian Institution/Art Resource, NY; **342T** NW; **342B** The Ronald Reagan Presidential Library & Museum/The Telesis Foundation/Putnam Museum of History and Natural Science, Davenport, Iowa/©Don Milici; **344** Library of Congress; **346** Harriet Beecher Stowe Center, Hartford, CT; **349LT** CBA; **349RT** CBA; **349RB** CBA; **350** CP; **351L** Collections of the Supreme Court; **351R** ©Tom McHugh/PR; **353** Courtesy of the Illinois State Historical Library; **354L** CBA; **354R** The Ronald Reagan Presidential Library & Museum/The Telesis Foundation/photo courtesy State Historical Society of Iowa, Iowa City/©Don Milici; **355** CBA; **356L** ©Sally Andersen-Bruce, The Museum of American Political Life, University of Hartford; **356R** CP; **359** CBA; **361** CP.

Chapter 11 **362L&R** The Ronald Reagan Presidential Library & Museum/The Telesis Foundation/Courtesy of the Collection of Joshua M. Landish/©Don Milici; **363** CBA; **364T** CBA; **364B** The Museum of the Confederacy, Richmond, Virginia/Photography by Katherine Wetzel; **365** CP; **366L&R** Courtesy of the American Numismatic Association; **367** CBA; **368RT** CBA; **368LB** The Ronald Reagan Presidential Library & Museum/The Telesis Foundation/Exhibit of Civil War sabers displayed at the Ronald Reagan Presidential Library, the private collection of Susan Bubnar, Port Hueneme, CA/©Don Milici; **369L** Library of Congress; **369R** The Ronald Reagan Presidential Library & Museum/The Telesis Foundation/Courtesy of the Illinois Historic Preservation Agency/©Don Milici; **370** The Ronald Reagan Presidential Library & Museum/The Telesis Foundation/Courtesy of John O. Franchi/©Don Milici; **371T** The Ronald Reagan Presidential Library & Museum/The Telesis Foundation/Courtesy of Dr. Gordon E. Dammann/©Don Milici; **371B** The Ronald Reagan Presidential Library & Museum/The Telesis Foundation/Courtesy of the Collection of Joshua M. Landish/©Don Milici; **372** CBA; **373** CBA; **375T** Harry T. Peters Collection, Museum of the City of New York;

375B The Ronald Reagan Presidential Library & Museum/The Telesis Foundation/Courtesy of The Manassas Museum, Manassas, VA/©Don Milici; **376** Division of Photographs and Prints, The Schomburg Center for Research in Black Culture, the NYUPL Astor, Lennox and Tilden Foundations; **377** Harry T. Peters Collection, Museum of the City of New York; **378** The Ronald Reagan Presidential Library & Museum/The Telesis Foundation/Courtesy of The American Red Cross/©Don Milici; **379** *The Gun Foundry* by John Ferguson Weir, Putnam County Historical Society, Cold Spring, NY; **380L** CBA; **380R** The Ronald Reagan Presidential Library & Museum/The Telesis Foundation/National Park Service, Clara Barton National Historic Site/©Don Milici; **381L** PR; **381R** The Ronald Reagan Presidential Library & Museum/The Telesis Foundation/Courtesy of the Collection of Joshua M. Landish/©Don Milici; **382** Library of Congress; **383T** CBA; **383B** CBA; **384RT** CP; **384LB** CP; **384RB** The Ronald Reagan Presidential Library & Museum/The Telesis Foundation/Courtesy of Dr. Gordon E. Dammann/©Don Milici; **385** The Ronald Reagan Presidential Library & Museum/The Telesis Foundation/National Archives/©Don Milici; **386L** Division of Rare and Manuscript Collections, Cornell University Library; **386R** CBA; **387** The Ronald Reagan Presidential Library & Museum/The Telesis Foundation/Courtesy of the Collection of Joshua M. Landish/©Don Milici; **388** CP; **389** CBA.

Chapter 12 **392** Joseph H. Bailey/©National Geographic Society; **394LT** ©T. Xavier/Washington Stock Photo, Inc.; **394R** CBA; **395L** CP; **395R** Boston Athenaeum; **398** CBA; **401L** CP; **401R** CBA; **402** CBA; **403** CP; **404** ©1995 Nawrocki Stock Photo, Inc.; **405** FPG; **406LB** CP; **406RT** Archive Photos; **407** CBA; **409** CBA; **410** CBA; **411** CP; **412** CP.

Chapter 13 **428** Autry Museum of Western Heritage, Los Angeles; **430** NW; **431** CP; **432** CP; **434L** Sears, Roebuck and Co.; **434R** CBA; **435** Smithsonian Institution; **436** Library of Congress; **438L,RT,RB** CBA; **439** Smithsonian Institution; **440L&R** CP; **442LT** CBA; **442RB** CP; **443** NW; **445T** NW; **445B** CBA; **446T** Autry Museum of Western Heritage, Los Angeles; **446B** Buffalo Bill Historical Center, Cody ,WY; **447** Courtesy of the Montana Historical Society, Mackay Collection; **448T&B** Autry Museum of Western Heritage, Los Angeles; **449** CBA; **450** Autry Museum of Western Heritage, Los Angeles; **452** CBA; **454L** Buffalo Bill Historical Center, Cody, WY; **454R** NW; **455T** U.S. Signal Corps photo no. 111-SC-89580 in the National Archives; **455B** Autry Museum of Western Heritage, Los Angeles; **457** Private Collection. Photograph courtesy James Graham & Sons, New York.

Chapter 14 **460** NW; **462** CP; **463T** CBA; **463B** Archive Photos; **464L** CP; **464R** The Jacob Riis Collection, #108, Museum of the City of New York; **465** CP; **466** CP; **468** NW; **470** Denver Public Library, Western History Department; **471** CBA; **472** CBA; **473T** NW; **473B** CBA; **474** PR/©The Harry T. Peters Collection, Museum of the City of New York; **475** NW; **476L** CBA; **476R** Courtesy, U.S. Bicycling Hall of Fame, Somerville, NJ; **477** Reprinted with permission of the U. S. Bicycling Hall of Fame, Somerville, NJ; **478** CP; **479L** CP; **479C** Autry Museum of Western Heritage, Los Angeles; **479R** CBA; **480** CBA; **481** CBA.

Chapter 15 **486** ©Sally Andersen-Bruce, The Museum of American Political Life, University of Hartford; **488L** Puck/Library of Congress; **488R** CP; **490** CBA; **492L** CBA; **492R** Archive Photos; **494L** CP; **494R** CBA; **494RB** CBA; **496** UPI/CB; **497** CBA; **498** Library of Congress; **499** ©Sally Andersen-Bruce, The Museum of American Political Life, University of Hartford; **500** CP; **501L,LC,RC,R** Courtesy of the Museum of the American Numismatic Association; **502** CP; **503** CP; **504** CBA; **505** CP; **506** Archive Photos; **507** CBA; **508L** NW; **508R** Archive Photos; **509LT** ©Sally Andersen-Bruce, The Museum of American Political Life, University of Hartford; **509R** CP.

Chapter 16 **512** Scala/Art Resource, NY; **513** ©1995 Nawrocki Stock Photo, Inc.; **515** ©1995 Nawrocki Stock Photo, Inc.; **516** Archive Photos; **518** CBA; **519** ©1995 Nawrocki Stock Photo, Inc.; **520L** CP; **520R** CBA; **521** CP; **523** CBA; **525** State Historical Society of Wisconsin; **526T** ©1995 Nawrocki Stock Photo, Inc.; **526B** Courtesy, Frederic Remington Art Museum, Ogdensburg, NY; **529L** BB; **529R** ©1995 Nawrocki Stock Photo, Inc.; **531** Naval Historical Foundation; **533** ©1995 Nawrocki Stock Photo Inc; **535** CP.

Chapter 17 **550** CBA; **551** CBA; **552T&B** National Baseball Library & Archive, Cooperstown, NY; **553T&B** CP; **556LT** CP; **556RB** The Museum of Modern Art, NY. Gift of Abby Aldrich Rockefeller. Photograph ©1995 The Museum of Modern Art, NY; **557&558** George Wesley Bellows (American 1882-1925) *Cliff Dwellers* , 1913. Oil on canvas. H: 39-1/2" x W:41-1/2" (100.3 x 105.3 cm). Los Angeles County Funds, Los Angeles County Museum of Art, ©1995 Museum Associates, Los Angeles County Museum of Art. All Rights Reserved. 16.4; **560** Archive Photos; **562L** Jane Addams Memorial Collection, Special Collections, The University Library, The University of Illinois at Chicago; **562R** CP; **564L&R** CP; **566** PR; **567** Archive Photos; **569L** (poker chips): Autry Museum of Western Heritage, Los Angeles; **569R** CP; **570T** (sailor suit & shoes): Photographed at and with the permission of The Fashion Institute of Design and Merchandising, Los Angeles, CA/©Don Milici; (Gibson dress & parasol): Photographed with the permission of the FIDM Museum & Library Foundation at the Fashion Institute of Design and Merchandising, Los Angeles, CA/©Don Milici; **570B** CBA; **571** CP; **572L&R** Archive Photos; **573** Archive Photos.

Chapter 18 **576** FPG; **578** CP; **579T** NW; **579B** CBA; **581LT** Breton Littlehales/National Geographic Image Collection; **581RB** NW; **583** FPG; **584L** ©Sally Andersen-Bruce, The Museum of American Political Life, University of Hartford; **584R** CP; **585** CP; **588** Archive Photos; **589** Portrait by Charles Sidney Hopkinson, Collection of the Supreme Court of the United States; **590** CBA; **592** FPG; **596LB** ©1995 Nawrocki Stock Photo, Inc.; **596CT** Archive Photos; **596RB** Photographed with the permission of the FIDM Museum & Library Foundation at the Fashion Institute of Design and Merchandising, Los Angeles, CA/©Don Milici; **598** ©Paul Thompson/FPG; **599LB** Archive Photos; **599RB** ©Paul Thompson/FPG; **600L** Philadelphia Museum of Art, Louise and Walter Arensberg Collection, ©1996 Artists Rights Society (ARS), NY/ADAGP Paris; **600R** Collection of The University of Arizona Museum of Art, Tucson, Gift of Oliver James. The Georgia O'Keeffe Foundation/Artists Rights Society (ARS), NY.

Chapter 19 **604** National Archives; **605** CP; **606** BB; **608** BB; **610** ©1995 Nawrocki Stock Photo, Inc.; **611L** CBA; **611R** BB; **613** Stock Montage, Inc.; **614** BB; **615** CP; **619T** Copyright ©1915 by The New York Times Company. Reprinted by permission; **619B** Stock Montage, Inc.; **620L** Archive Photos/Lambert; **620R** Archive Photos/American Stock; **622LT** BB; **622C** (costume): Photographed with the permission of the FIDM Museum & Library Foundation at the Fashion Institute of Design and Merchandising, Los Angeles, CA/©Don Milici; **622RB** CBA; **623** National Archives; **624** ©1995 Nawrocki Stock Photo, Inc.; **625** CBA; **629** CBA; **631L** Stock Montage, Inc.; **631R** ©1995 Nawrocki Stock Photo, Inc.

Chapter 20 **646** ©Tom Burnside/PR; **647** Courtesy of the Ford Archives, Henry Ford Museum, Dearborn, MI; **648** CP; **649** Caulfield and Shook Collectors, neg. #71790, University of Louisville Photographic Archives; **650L** (man's costume): Photographed at and with the permission of The Fashion Institute of Design and Merchandising, Los Angeles, CA/©Don Milici; **650C** (woman's costume): Photographed with the permission of the FIDM Museum & Library Foundation at the Fashion Institute of Design and Merchandising, Los Angeles,

CA/©Don Milici; **650R** Archive Photos/Hirz; **652** (dress,hat, & beads): Photographed at and with the permission of The Fashion Institute of Design and Merchandising, Los Angeles, CA/©Don Milici; **652C** CP; **653** Archive Photos; **654** The Phillips Collection, Washington, D.C./Courtesy of the artist and Francine Seders Gallery, Seattle, WA; **656** Library of Congress/FPG; **657** ©National Portrait Gallery/Tom McHugh/PR; **658L** CP; **658R** CBA; **659** Photo from European Picture Service/FPG; **661** CP; **662** ©1995 Nawrocki Stock Photo, Inc.; **663L** (hat & bat): National Baseball Library & Archive, Cooperstown, NY; **663RT** CP; **663RB** CBA; **664** CBA; **665T** CBA; **665B** From the Collection of the Louisiana State Museum; **666** Archive Photos; **668** National Portrait Gallery, Smithsonian Institution/Art Resource, NY; **669** Museum of City of New York, Permanent Deposit of the Public Works Project through the Whitney Museum/©1995 Estate of Ben Shahn/Licensed by VAGA, New York, NY; **670** ©Jerry Sieve/FPG; **672** CBA; **673** CBA.

Chapter 21 **676** New York Stock Exchange Archives; **677** Archive Photos; **678TR** BB; **678LB** CP; **682** Library of Congress; **683T** USIA/National Archives; **683B** CP; **684** BB; **685T** CBA; **685B** UPI/CB; **687L** Archive Photos; **687B** CBA; **688RT** CBA; **688LB** Library of Congress/PR; **689** BB; **690** Archive Photos/Hackett; **693RT** BB; **693LB** Archive Photos; **693BR** CP; **694** BB; **695T** UPI/CB; **695B** ©Sally Andersen-Bruce, The Museum of American Political Life, University of Hartford; **696&697** Franklin D. Roosevelt Library and Museum; **698** BB.

Chapter 22 **702** Collection of Delton Lee Johnson, Santa Paula, CA; **703** Archive Photos; **704LB** Collection of Delton Lee Johnson, Santa Paula, CA; **704RT** Archive Photos; **705** BB; **706** CP; **707** UPI/CB; **708L** BB; **708R** Archive Photos; **709** Ellis Herwig/Stock Boston; **710** Franklin D. Roosevelt Library and Museum; **711** National Portrait Gallery, Smithsonian Institution/Art Resource, NY; **712L&R** CP; **714** Archive Photos; **715T&B** BB; **716** UPI/CB; **717** Washington Post/Franklin D. Roosevelt Library and Museum; **720** Library of Congress; **721** CP; **722T** Herbert Hoover Presidential Library-Museum West Branch, IA; **722B** UPI/CBA.

Chapter 23 **740** Collection of John Nichols; **741T** UPI/CB; **741B** National Archives; **745T** CP; **745B** Stock Montage, Inc.; **746** CBA; **747** Collection of Bob Binsley; **750LT** Collection of John Nichols; **750RT** (uniform): Photographed with the permission of the FIDM Museum & Library Foundation at the Fashion Institute of Design and Merchandising, Los Angeles, CA/©Don Milici; **750BR** (flag): Collection of Delton Lee Johnson, Santa Paula, CA; **751LT** Collection of Craig Logsdon; **751LB** National Archives; **751RB** CP; **752** ©Al Gretz/FPG; **753L&R** UPI/CB; **754** BB; **756L** CP/Photo by U.S. Army Signal Corps; **756R** UPI/CB/U.S. Army Signal Corps Photo/ACME; **757** U.S. Army/Dwight D. Eisenhower Library; **761** ©1995 Nawrocki Stock Photo, Inc.; **762T** Collection of William Nash, Santa Paula, CA; **762B** UPI/CB; **763L** CP; **763R** Collection of Perna L. White; **764T** Courtesy of the Simon Wiesenthal Center Beit HaShoah Museum of Tolerance Library/Archives, Los Angeles, CA; **764C** Main Commission for the Investigation of Nazi War Crimes, courtesy of the United States Holocaust Memorial Museum; **764LB** UPI/CB; **764RB** (doll & uniform): Courtesy of the Simon Wiesenthal Center Beit HaShoah Museum of Tolerance Library/Archives, Los Angeles, CA; **765LB** ©J. McGuire/Washington Stock Photo, Inc.; **765RT** Collection of Maurice G. Ragner, Santa Paula, CA; **766LB** Archive Photos; **766RT** ©Scott Camazine/PR; **767** U.S. Army Photograph.

Chapter 24 **770** ©G. Petrov/Washington Stock Photo, Inc.; **772T&B** UPI/CB; **774&775** UPI/CB; **777L&R** UPI/CB; **778** UPI/CB; **780** UPI/CB; **782L** Richmond Times-Dispatch/Frederick O. Seibel Papers (#2531) Special Collections Department, University of Virginia;

782R ©R. Foulds/Washington Stock Photo, Inc.; 783 UPI/CB; 784 CBA; 787 UPI/CB; 788 UPI/CB; 790T UPI/CB; 790B Stock Montage, Inc.; 793 UPI/CB; 795L&R UPI/CB; 796 BB.

Chapter 25 800 Staff Photographer/Dwight D. Eisenhower Library; 802L UPI/CB; 802R George Silk/LIFE Magazine ©Time, Inc.; 803 UPI/CB; 805T "We have documentary evidence that his man is planning a trip to Moscow" from Herblock's Here and Now (Simon & Schuster, 1955); 805B UPI/CB; 807 UPI/CB; 808 UPI/CB; 810 Photo by Harris Ewing, Collection of the Supreme Court Society of the United States; 811 AP/WW; 812T UPI/CB; 812B ©Bruce Roberts/PR; 814R UPI/CB; 814L&815 "Don't be afraid—I can always pull you back" from Herblock's Special for Today (Simon & Schuster, 1958); 818 CBA; 820 UPI/CB; 822 UPI/CB.

Chapter 26 826 UPI/CB; 828T FPG; 828B CBA; 829T (costume): Photographed with the permission of the FIDM Museum & Library Foundation at the Fashion Institute of Design and Merchandising, Los Angeles, CA/©Don Milici; 829L&B Hula Hoop®, Courtesy Mattel Sports/Photo ©Tyler Roddick; 829C BB; 830 BB; 832T CBA/NY Daily Mirror Collection; 832RB UPI/CB; 834 ©1970 Elliott Erwitt/Magnum Photos, Inc.; 836 UPI/CB; 837 CBA; 839 UPI/CB; 840 Photograph courtesy of Tupperware U.S., Inc.; 841 FPG; 842 Tooker, George, The Subway, 1950, Egg Tempera on composition board, Sight: 18-1/8 x 36-1/8 in. (46 x 91.8 cm.), Collection of Whitney Museum of American Art. Purchase, with funds from the Juliana Force Purchase Award. 50.23. Copyright ©1995/Whitney Museum of American Art; 843L Archive Photos; 843CB Archive Photos/Camera Press; 843RT UPI/CB; 844 CBA; 846 FPG; 847T ©Sanford Roth/PR; 847BCP; 848 Number 1, 1950 (Lavendar Mist) by Jackson Pollock, Ailsa Mellon Bruce Fund, ©1995 Board of Trustees, National Gallery of Art, Washington, 1950. Oil, enamel, and aluminum on canvas, ©1996 Pollock-Krasner Foundation/Artists Rights Society (ARS) NY; 849 ©Bruce Roberts/PR.

Chapter 27 864 John F. Kennedy Library; 866LT John F. Kennedy Library; 866LB,CB&RB John F. Kennedy Library/CBS News Archives; 867 John F. Kennedy Library; 868LT John F. Kennedy Library; 868RT (costume): Photographed with the permission of the FIDM Museum & Library Foundation at the Fashion Institute of Design and Merchandising, Los Angeles, CA/©Don Milici; 868B UPI/CB; 869 AP/WW; 870 UPI/CB; 873 John F. Kennedy Library; 874 U.S. Navy/FPG; 876 UPI/CB; 879 NASA; 880 UPI/CB; 881T FPG; 881B AP/WW; 882 AP/WW; 884T CBA; 884B Photo by Robert S. Oakes, National Geographic Society, Collection of the Supreme Court of the United States; 887 AP/WW; 888RT CBA; 888 LB FPG; 889T CBA; 889B John F. Kennedy Library.

Chapter 28 892 Yoichi R. Okamoto/LBJ Library Collection; 893 ©Karl Hubenthal; 896 Yoichi R. Okamoto/LBJ Library Collection; 899 George Tames, NYT Pictures; 900 UPI/CB; 901 CBA; 902L AP/WW; 902R UPI/CB; 905 UPI/CB; 906T&B UPI/CB; 909 AP/WW; 910 UPI/CB; 913 AP/WW; 914 UPI/CB; 915L AP/WW; 915R Copyright ©1967 by The New York Times Company. Reprinted by permission.

Chapter 29 918 AP/WW; 919 "Help!" from The Herblock Gallery (Simon & Schuster, 1968); 920 UPI/CB; 921 ©Lawrence Schiller/PR; 922LT&RB UPI/CB; 923 UPI/CB; 925 ©Julian Wasser/Time Magazine; 929 ©PIX Publishing, 1977/FPG; 930 UPI/CB; 933L&R AP/WW; 935 AP/WW; 936T ©Bonnie Freer/PR; 936RB Archive Photos; 937L&C (costumes) Photographed with the permission of the

FIDM Museum & Library Foundation at the Fashion Institute of Design and Merchandising, Los Angeles, CA/©Don Milici; 937R ©C.J. Zimmerman, 1970/FPG; 938 ©Edward Lettau/PR; 940 AP/WW; 943 UPI/CB.

Chapter 30 956 AP/WW; 958T Archive Photos; 958B AP/WW; 959 Archive Photos; 963 Copyright ©1971 by the New York Times Company. Reprinted by permission; 964 CBA; 965 UPI/CB; 966 UPI/CB; 968L&R AP/WW; 969 UPI/CB; 971 Archive Photos; 973 Richard Nixon Library and Birthplace; 974 AP/WW; 976 Archive Photos; 977L Archive Photos; 977R Los Angeles Times Syndicate/©Conrad; 978 Archive Photos.

Chapter 31 984B ©Sally Andersen-Bruce, The Museum of American Political Life, University of Hartford; 986L Courtesy Gerald R. Ford Library; 986R Copyright ©1974 by The New York Times Company. Reprinted by permission; 987 ©1994 Gary Schultz/Alaska Stock Images; 988&989 Draper Hill, ©1975, The Commercial Appeal, Memphis, TN. Used with permission; 990 Archive Photos; 991 Courtesy Gerald R. Ford Library; 992 UPI/CB; 993 Universal/Shooting Star ©All Rights Reserved; 995 UPI/CB; 997 UPI/CB; 999 UPI/CB; 1000 Courtesy Jimmy Carter Library; 1001 Cartoon by Draper Hill, ©1977, Detroit News, Detroit, MI; 1002 AP/WW; 1006T AP/WW; 1006B UPI/CB.

Chapter 32 1010 UPI/CB; 1011 Archive Photos; 1012 UPI/CB; 1013 UPI/CB; 1014T UPI/CB; 1014RB Courtesy Ronald Reagan Library; 1015 AP/WW; 1016T ©Sebastiao Salgado/Magnum Photos, Inc.; 1016C ©1995 Len Boro/Rothco; 1018 CBA; 1019 (campaign button); ©Sally Andersen-Bruce, The Museum of American Political Life, University of Hartford; 1019RB Courtesy Ronald Reagan Library; 1020 Reuters/CB; 1022 ©Jim Borgman, reprinted with special permission of King Features Syndicate; 1025T ©1983 Time, Inc., reprinted by permission; 1025B NASA; 1026 Courtesy Ronald Reagan Library; 1028 AP/WW; 1029 UPI/CB; 1031 UPI/CB.

Chapter 33 1046 From the collection of the George Bush Presidential Library and Museum; 1049 UPI/CB; 1050 Cartoon by Draper Hill, ©1992 Detroit News, Detroit, MI; 1051L&R Reuters/CB; 1052 AP/WW; 1053 AP/WW; 1055LT&RB Reuters/CB; 1057 Reuters/CB; 1059 Draper Hill, ©1990 The Commercial Appeal, Memphis, TN. Used with permission; 1060 AP/WW; 1063T AP/WW; 1063B Reuters/CB; 1064 Photo by Richard Strauss, Smithsonian Institution, Collection of the Supreme Court of the United States; 1065 Reuters/CB; 1066 NASA; 1067 Archive Photos/Ron Sachs; 1068 Archive Photos/IMAPRESS; 1069 ©Rick Maiman/SYGMA; 1073 ©F. Hibon/SYGMA.

Chapter 34 1076 ©Tony Stone Images/Lori Adamski Peek; 1077 AP/WW; 1078 ©1996 Estate of Ben Shahn/Licensed by VAGA, New York, NY; 1082 CBA; 1086 ©Paul Conkling/PhotoEdit; 1087 ©Bill Aron/Photo Edit; 1088 ©Spencer Grant/PR; 1091RT UPI/CB; 1091LB The NAMES Project Foundation/photo ©David Alosi and Ron Vak; 1092 AP/WW; 1093 ©Tom Hollyman/PR; 1094 ©Tony Stone Images/Steven Peters; 1095 ©Tony Stone World Wide/Barry Bomzer; 1096 ©David Young-Wolff/Photo Edit; 1097 Reuters/CB; 1098 ©Miriam Schapiro, Presentation, 1982 acrylic and fabric on canvas, 90"x144". Private collection. Courtesy Steinbaum Krauss Gallery, NYC; 1099 Courtesy, Estate of Romare Bearden; 1101 SPL/PR; 1103 UPI/CB.

Presidents' Gallery 1128–1133 Bureau of Engraving.